Stephane Bressan Josef Küng
Roland Wagner (Eds.)

Database and Expert Systems Applications

17th International Conference, DEXA 2006
Kraków, Poland, September 4-8, 2006
Proceedings

Springer

Volume Editors

Stephane Bressan
National University of Singapore
School of Computing
3 Science Drive 2, Singapore 117543, Republic of Singapore
E-mail: steph@nus.edu.sg

Josef Küng
Roland Wagner
University of Linz
Institute for Applied Knowledge Processing (FAW)
Altenbergerstraße 69, 4040 Linz, Austria
E-mail:{jkueng,rrwagner}@faw.uni-linz.ac.at

Library of Congress Control Number: 2006931200

CR Subject Classification (1998): H.2, H.4, H.3, H.5, I.2, J.1

LNCS Sublibrary: SL 3 – Information Systems and Application, incl. Internet/Web and HCI

ISSN 0302-9743
ISBN-10 3-540-37871-5 Springer Berlin Heidelberg New York
ISBN-13 978-3-540-37871-6 Springer Berlin Heidelberg New York

Springer is a part of Springer Science+Business Media

springer.com

Typesetting: Camera-ready by author, data conversion by Scientific Publishing Services, Chennai, India
Printed on acid-free paper SPIN: 11827405 06/3142 5 4 3 2 1 0

Lecture Notes in Computer Science 4080

Preface

The annual international conference on Database and Expert Systems Applications (DEXA) is now well established as a reference scientific event. The reader will find in this volume a collection of scientific papers that represent the state of the art of research in the domain of data, information and knowledge management, intelligent systems, and their applications.

The 17th instance of the series of DEXA conferences was held at the Andrzej Frycz Modrzewski Cracow College in Kraków, Poland, during September 4–8, 2006.

Several collocated conferences and workshops covered specialized and complementary topics to the main conference topic. Four conferences – the 8th International Conference on Data Warehousing and Knowledge Discovery (DaWaK), the 7th International Conference on Electronic Commerce and Web Technologies (EC-Web), the 5th International Conference on Electronic Government (EGOV), and the Third International Conference on Trust, Privacy, and Security in Digital Business (TrustBus) – and 14 workshops were collocated with DEXA.

The whole forms a unique international event with a balanced depth and breadth of topics. Its much-appreciated conviviality fosters unmatched opportunities to meet, share the latest scientific results and discuss the latest technological advances in the area of information technologies with both young scientists and engineers and senior world-renown experts.

This volume contains the papers selected for presentation at the conference. Each submitted paper was reviewed by three or four reviewers, members of the Program Committee or external reviewers appointed by members of the Program Committee. Based on the reviews, the Program Committee accepted 90 of the 296 originally submitted papers.

The excellence brought to you in these proceedings would not have been possible without the efforts of numerous individuals and the support of several organizations.

First and foremost, we thank the authors for their hard work and for the quality of their submissions.

We also thank A Min Tjoa, Norman Revell, Gerald Quirchmayr, Gabriela Wagner, the members of the Program Committee, the reviewers, and the many others who assisted in the DEXA organization for their contribution to the success and high standard of DEXA 2006 and of these proceedings.

Finally we thank the DEXA Association, the Austrian Computer Society, the Research Institute for Applied Knowledge Processing (FAW), and The Andrzej Frycz Modrzewski Cracow College for making DEXA 2006 happen.

June 2006

Stéphane Bressan (National University of Singapore),
Josef Küng (FAW, University of Linz, Austria)
and Roland Wagner (FAW, University of Linz, Austria).

Organization

Program Committee

Conference Program Chairpersons
Stéphane Bressan, National University of Singapore, Singapore
Josef Küng, FAW, University of Linz, Austria

Workshop Chairpersons
A Min Tjoa, Technical University of Vienna, Austria
Roland R. Wagner, FAW, University of Linz, Austria

Publication Chairperson
Vladimir Marik, Czech Technical University, Czech Republic

Local Arrangement Chairperson
Janusz Wielki, Opole University of Technology, Poland

Program Committee
Witold Abramowicz, The Poznan University of Economics, Poland
Michel Adiba, IMAG - Laboratoire LSR, France
Hamideh Afsarmanesh, University of Amsterdam, The Netherlands
Ala Al-Zobaidie, University of Greenwich, UK
Walid G. Aref, Purdue University, USA
Ramazan S. Aygun, University of Alabama in Huntsville, USA
Leonard Barolli, Fukuoka Institute of Technology (FIT), Japan
Kurt Bauknecht, Universität Zürich, Switzerland
Bishwaranjan Bhattacharjee, IBM T.J. Watson Research Center, USA
Sourav S Bhowmick, Nanyang Technological University, Singapore
Omran Bukhres, Purdue University School of Science, USA
Luis Camarinah - Matos, New University of Lisbon, Portugal
Antonio Cammelli, ITTIG-CNR, Italy
Malu Castellanos, Hewlett-Packard Laboratories, USA
Barbara Catania, Universita' di Genova, Italy
Aaron Ceglar, Flinders University of South Australia, Australia
Wojciech Cellary, University of Economics at Poznan, Poland
Elizabeth Chang, Curtin University, Australia
Sudarshan S. Chawathe, University of Maryland, USA
Henning Christiansen, Roskilde University, Denmark
Rosine Cicchetti, IUT, University of Marseille, France
Frans Coenen, The University of Liverpool, UK
Carlo Combi, Università degli Studi di Verona, Italy
Tran Khanh Dang , HoChiMinh City University of Technology, Vietnam

John Debenham, University of Technology, Sydney, Australia
Misbah Deen, University of Keele, UK
Elisabetta Di Nitto, Politecnico di Milano, Italy
Gill Dobbie, University of Auckland, Australia
Johann Eder, University of Vienna, Austria
Amr El Abbadi, University of California, USA
Tomoya Enokido, Rissho University, Japan
Peter Fankhauser, Fraunhofer IPSI, Germany
Ling Feng, University of Twente, The Netherlands
Eduardo Fernandez, Florida Atlantic University, USA
Simon Field, Matching Systems Ltd., Switzerland
Mariagrazia Fugini, Politecnico di Milano, Italy
Antonio L. Furtado, Pontificia Universidade Catolica do R.J., Brazil
Manolo Garcia-Solaco, IS Consultant, USA
Georges Gardarin, University of Versailles, France
Alexander Gelbukh, Centro de Investigacion en Computacion (CIC), Instituto Politecnico Nacional (IPN), Mexico
Parke Godfrey, The College of William and Mary, Canada
Jan Goossenaerts, Eindhoven University of Technology, The Netherlands
William Grosky, University of Michigan, USA
Le Gruenwald, University of Oklahoma, USA
Abdelkader Hameurlain, University of Toulouse, France
Wook-Shin Han, Kyungpook National University, Korea
Igor T. Hawryszkiewycz, University of Technology, Sydney, Australia
Wynne Hsu, National University of Singapore, Singapore
Mohamed Ibrahim, University of Greenwich, UK
Dimitris Karagiannis, University of Vienna, Austria
Randi Karlsen, University of Tromsö, Norway
Rudolf Keller, Zühlke Engineering AG, Switzerland
Latifur Khan, University of Texas at Dallas, USA
Myoung Ho Kim, KAIST, Korea
Stephen Kimani, University of Rome "La Sapienza," Italy
Masaru Kitsuregawa, Tokyo University, Japan
Gary J. Koehler, University of Florida, USA
John Krogstie, SINTEF, Norway
Petr Kroha, Technische Universität Chemnitz-Zwickau, Germany
Lotfi Lakhal, University of Marseille, France
Christian Lang, IBM T.J. Watson Research Center, USA
Jiri Lazansky , Czech Technical University, Czech Republic
Mong Li Lee, National University of Singapore, Singapore
Thomas Lee, University of Pennsylvania, USA
Young-Koo Lee, Kyung Hee University, Korea
Michel Leonard, Université de Genève, Switzerland
Tok Wang Ling, National University of Singapore, Singapore
Volker Linnemann, University of Luebeck, Germany
Mengchi Liu, Carleton University, Canada
Peri Loucopoulos, UMIST, UK

Feng Luo, Clemson University, USA
Sanjai Kumar Madria, University of Missouri-Rolla, USA
Vladimir Marik, Czech Technical University, Czech Republic
Simone Marinai, University of Florence, Italy
Heinrich C. Mayr, University of Klagenfurt, Austria
Subhasish Mazumdar, New Mexico Tech, USA
Pietro Mazzoleni, Università di Milano, Italy
Dennis McLeod, University of Southern California, USA
Elisabeth Metais, CNAM, France
Mukesh Mohania, IBM-IRL, India
Yang-Sae Moon, Kangwon National University, Korea
Reagan Moore, San Diego Supercomputer Center, USA
Tadeusz Morzy, Poznan University of Technology, Poland
Noureddine Mouaddib, University of Nantes, France
Günter Müller, Universität Freiburg, Germany
Mario Nascimento, University of Alberta, Canada
Wilfred Ng, University of Science & Technology, Hong Kong
Matthias Nicola, IBM Silicon Valley Lab, USA
Gultekin Ozsoyoglu, University Case Western Research, USA
Georgios Pangalos, University of Thessaloniki, Greece
Stott Parker, University of Los Angeles (UCLA), USA
Oscar Pastor, Universidad Politecnica de Valencia, Spain
Verónika Peralta, Universidad de la Republica, Uruguay
Günter Pernul, University of Regensburg, Germany
Evaggelia Pitoura, University of Ioannina, Greece
Gerald Quirchmayr, Univ. of Vienna, Austria, Univ. of South Australia, Australia
Fausto Rabitti, CNUCE-CNR, Italy
Wenny Rahayu, La Trobe University, Australia
Isidro Ramos, Technical University of Valencia, Spain
P. Krishna Reddy, International Institute of Information Technology, India
Werner Retschitzegger, University of Linz, Austria
Norman Revell, Middlesex University, UK
Sally Rice, University of South Australia, Australia
John Roddick, Flinders University of South Australia, Australia
Colette Rolland, University Paris I, Sorbonne, France
Elke Rundensteiner, Worcester Polytechnic Institute, USA
Domenico Sacca, University of Calabria, Italy
Simonas Saltenis, Aalborg University, Denmark
Marinette Savonnet, Université de Bourgogne, France
Erich Schweighofer, University of Vienna, Austria
Ming-Chien Shan, Hewlett-Packard Laboratories, USA
Keng Siau, University of Nebraska-Lincoln, USA
Darunee Smavatkul, Chiangmai University, Thailand
Giovanni Soda, University of Florence, Italy
Uma Srinivasan, University of Western Sydney, Australia
Bala Srinivasan, Monash University, Australia
Olga Stepankova, Czech Technical University, Czech Repuplic

Zbigniew Struzik, The University of Tokyo, Japan
Makoto Takizawa , Tokyo Denki University, Japan
Katsumi Tanaka , Kyoto University, Japan
Yufei Tao, City University of Hong Kong, Hong Kong
Stephanie Teufel , University of Fribourg, Switzerland
Jukka Teuhola, University of Turku, Finland
Bernd Thalheim, University of Kiel, Germany
J.M. Thevenin, University of Toulouse, France
A Min Tjoa, Technical University of Vienna, Austria
Roland Traunmüller, University of Linz, Austria
Aphrodite Tsalgatidou, University of Athens, Greece
Genoveva Vargas-Solar, LSR-IMAG, France
Krishnamurthy Vidyasankar , Memorial Univ. of Newfoundland, Canada
Jesus Vilares Ferro, University of Coruña, Spain
Pavel Vogel, TU München, Germany
Roland Wagner, University of Linz, Austria
Vilas Wuwongse, Asian Institute of Technology, Thailand
Jeffrey Yu, The Chinese University of Hong Kong, Hong Kong
Gian Piero Zarri, CNRS, France
Arkady Zaslavsky, Monash University, Australia
Baihua Zheng, Singapore Management University, Singapore

External Reviewers

Alexander Bienemann
Hans-Joachim Klein
Peggy Schmidt
Gunar Fiedler
Alain Casali
Lotfi Lakhal
Noel Novelli
Cyril Pain-Barre
Nicolas Prcovic
Lipyeow Lim
Eugenio Cesario
Alfredo Cuzzocrea
Andrea Gualtieri
Riccardo Ortale
Andrea Pugliese
Massimo Ruffolo
Francesco Scarcello
Agustinus Borgy Waluyo
Franck Morvan
Sharifullah Khan
Christophe Bobineau
Cyril Labbe
Norbert Meckl
Jan Kolter
Jörg Gilberg
Ludwig Fuchs
Wolfgang Dobmeier
Rasmus Knappe
Davide Martinenghi
Kyoung Soo Bok
Beda Christoph Hammerschmidt
Dirk Kukulenz
Henrike Schuhart
Christian Koncilia
Marek Lehmann
Karl Wiggisser
Thomas Weishäupl
Miguel A. Alonso
Jose A. Gonzalez-Reboredo
Fco. Mario
Manuel Vilares
Francisco J. Ribadas
Victor M. Darriba
Michael Oakes

Hans-Joachim Klein
Peggy Schmidt
Gunar Fiedler
Victor Cuevas Vicenttin,
José Luis Zechinelli MartiniHéctor
Manuel Pérez Urbina
Alberto Portilla Flores
Hanh Tan,
Huagang Li
Ping Wu
Shyam Anthony
Stacy Patterson
Ahmed Metwally
Arsany Sawires
Nagender Bandi
Dawid Weiss
Witold Andrzejewski
Robert Wrembel
Krzysztof Krawiec
Christos Ilioudis
Jiaheng Lu
Wei Ni
Tian Yu
Christian Schläger
Rolf Schillinger
Björn Muschall
Victoria Torres
Marta Ruiz
Javier Muñoz
Sergiusz Strykowski
Jacek Chmielewski
Wojciech Wiza
Franck Ravat
Huang Zhiyong
Masato Oguchi
Botao Wang
Shingo Ohtsuka
Kazuo Goda
Zhenglu Yang
Anirban Mondal
Wee Hyong Tok
Artur Boronat
Nenifer Pérez
José H. Canós
Pepe Carsí
Silke Eckstein
Harumi Kuno
Jim Stinger
An Lu
James Cheng
Yiping Ke
Arne Ketil Eidsvik

Table of Contents

Data and Information II

XML III

Data and Information III

Datamining and Data Warehouses

Database Applications I

XML IV

Data and Information IV

XML V

Data and Information V

Datamining and Data Warehouses

Database Applications II

WWW I

Bioinformatics

WWW II

Process Automation and Workflow

Knowledge Management and Expert Systems

Database Theory I

Query Processing I

Database Theory II

Query Processing II

Database Theory III

Knowledge Management and Expert Systems

Database Theory IV

Privacy and Security

Database Theory V

Efficient Processing of Multiple XML Twig Queries

Huanzhang Liu, Tok Wang Ling, Tian Yu, and Ji Wu

School of Computing, National University of Singapore
{liuhuanz, lingtw, yutian, wuji}@comp.nus.edu.sg

Abstract. Finding all occurrences of a twig pattern in an XML document is a core operation for XML query processing. The emergence of XML as a common mark-up language for data interchange has spawned great interest in techniques for filtering and content-based routing of XML data. In this paper, we aim to use the state-of-art holistic twig join technique to address multiple twig queries in a large scale XML database. We propose a new twig query technique which is specially tailored to match documents with large numbers of twig pattern queries. We introduce the *super-twig* to represent multiple twig queries. Based on the *super-twig*, we design a holistic twig join algorithm, called *MTwigStack*, to find all matches for multiple twig queries by scanning an XML document only once.

1 Introduction

Recently, XML has emerged as a standard information exchange mechanism on the Internet. XML employs a tree-structured model to represent data. XML query languages, such as XQuery and XPath, typically specify patterns with selection predicates on multiple elements for matching XML documents. Twig pattern matching has been identified as a core operation in querying tree-structured XML data.

Many algorithms have been proposed to match XML twig pattern [3,7,8,11]. [3] decomposes the twig pattern into binary structural relationships, then matching the binary structural relationships and merging these matches. Bruno et al. [7] improved the methods by proposing a holistic twig join algorithm, called *TwigStack*. The algorithm can largely reduce the intermediate result comparing with the previous algorithms. Later on, Chen et al. [8] proposed a new *Tag+Level* labeling scheme and *iTwigJoin* algorithm to improve *TwigStack*. Lu et al. [11] designed a novel algorithm, called *TJFast*, which employed *extended Dewey* to match XML twig queries.

XML query processing also arises in the scenario of information dissemination, such as publish-subscribe (pub-sub) systems. In a typical pub-sub system, many user submitted profiles are presented by XPath expressions, and an XML document is presented as input. The goal is to identify the queries and their matches in the input XML document, and disseminate this information to the users who posed the queries [4,9].

S. Bressan, J. Küng, and R. Wagner (Eds.): DEXA 2006, LNCS 4080, pp. 1–11, 2006.

In a huge system, where many XML queries are issued towards an XML database, we expect to see that the queries have many similarities. In traditional database systems, there have been many studies on efficient processing of similar queries using batch-based processing. Since pattern matching is an expensive operation, it would save a lot in terms of both CPU cost and I/O cost if we can process multiple similar twig queries simultaneously and only scan the input data once to get all the results. [6] has proposed *Index-filter* to process multiple simple XPath queries (no branch) against an XML document and it aims to find all matches of multiple simple path queries in an XML document. To eliminate redundant processing, it identifies query commonalities and combines multiple queries into a single structure. But *Index-Filter* does not consider how to process multiple twig queries.

Motivated by the recent success in efficient processing multiple XML queries, we consider the scenario of matching multiple XML twig queries with high similarity against an XML document.

The contributions of this paper can be summarized as follows:

- We introduce a new concept, called *super-twig*, which combines multiple twig queries into just one twig pattern. We also give the algorithm of constructing *super-twig*.
- Based on *super-twig*, we develop a new multiple twig queries processing algorithm, namely *MTwigStack*. With the algorithm, we can find all matches of multiple twig queries by scanning input data only once.
- Our experimental results show that the effectiveness, scalability and efficiency of our algorithm for multiple twig queries processing.

The rest of this paper is organized as follows. Preliminaries are introduced in Section 2. The algorithm *MTwigStack* is described in Section 3. Section 4 is dedicated to our experimental results and we close this paper by conclusion and future work in Section 5.

2 Preliminaries

2.1 Data Model

We model XML documents as ordered trees, each node corresponding to an element or a value, and the edges representing element-subelement or element-value relationships. Each node is assigned a region code (*start*:*end*, *level*) based on its position in the data tree [3,6,7], *start* is the number in sequence assigned to an element when it is first encountered and *end* is equal to one plus the *end* of the last element visited, *level* is the level of a certain element in its data tree. Each text value is assigned a region code that has the same *start* and *end* values. Then structural relationships between tree nodes (elements or values), such as parent-child or ancestor-descendant, whose positions are labelled with region encoding can be determined easily. Figure 1 (a) shows an example XML data tree with region encoding.

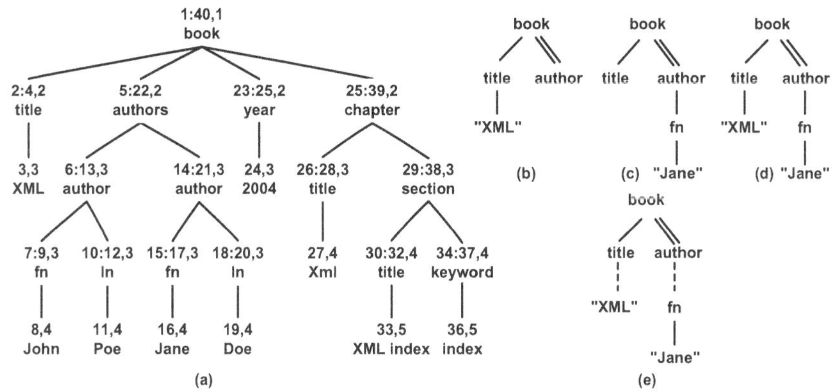

Fig. 1. An XML tree (a), three twig queries (b, c, d) and the super-twig query (e)

2.2 Super-Twig Query

When multiple twig queries are processed simultaneously, it is likely that significant commonalities between queries exist. To eliminate redundant processing while answering multiple queries, we identify query commonalities and combine multiple twig queries into a single twig pattern, which we call *super-twig*. *Super-twig* can significantly reduce the bookkeeping required to answer input queries, thus reducing the execution time of query processing. We will use q (and its variants such as q_i) to denote a node in the query or the subtree rooted at q when there is no ambiguity. We introduce the concepts *OptionalNode* and *OptonalLeafNode* to distinguish *super-twig* query from general twig queries.

In this paper, we only consider the tree patterns belonging to the fragment of XPath $XP^{\{/,//,[\,]\}}$ [5] and the scenario that commonalities only existing in the top parts of the twigs. Given a set of twig queries against an XML document, $Q = \{q_1, \ldots, q_k\}$ belonging to $XP^{\{/,//,[\,]\}}$, and assuming there is no repeated node in each query, we combine all the queries into a *super-twig* such that:

- The set of nodes in the super twig pattern equals the union of the sets of nodes of all individual twig queries;
- Each twig query is a subpattern (defined by [10]) of the super twig pattern;
- If the queries have different root nodes, we rewrite the queries whose root nodes are not the root of the XML document and add the document's root as the root node of the queries. Then the root node of the super twig pattern is same as the document's root;
- Suppose n is a query node which appears in q_i and q_j, P_i and P_j are the paths from the *root* to n in q_i and q_j respectively, P_i is same as P_j and m is the parent node of n in these two queries. If the relationship between m and n is Parent-Child (P-C) in q_i, Ancestor-Descendant (A-D) in q_j, then the relationship between m and n in *super-twig* is relaxed to A-D;
- Suppose n is a query node in one query q_i of Q, and m is the parent node of n in q_i. Let Q_n is the subset of twig queries of Q which contain node n, and Q_m is the subset of twig queries which contain node m (the path from its

root to m must be a prefix of the path from its root to n). If $Q_n \subset Q_m$, we call n an *OptionalNode*. And if all the relationships between m and n in Q_n are P-C relationships, then the relationship between m and n in the super twig pattern is P-C (called *optional parent-child* relationship and depicted by a single dotted line); otherwise, the relationship between m and n in the super twig is A-D (called *optional ancestor-descendant* relationship and depicted by double dotted lines);

- Following the same situations of the above item and assuming n is *OptionalNode*, let $Q_x = Q_m - Q_n$. If m is a leaf node in some queries of Q_x (so $Q_x \neq \emptyset$), then we call m an *OptionalLeafNode*.

Example 1. In Figure 1, (e) shows the *super-twig* query of three queries (b), (c) and (d). *"XML"* and *fn* are *OptionalNodes*, *title* and *author* are *OptionalLeafNodes*. The edge which connects *"XML"* to *title* represents *optional parent-child* relationship. It means that we can output path solution "book-title" whether or not the element *title* has a child whose content is *"XML"* in an XML document, or output path solution "book-title-'XML' " when the element *title* has a child whose content is *"XML"* in an XML document.

2.3 Super-Twig

To combine multiple twigs into a *super-twig*, we should normalize them first. It means to obtain a unique XPath query string from a tree pattern sorting the nodes lexicographically. We use the method proposed in [12], for example, the normal form of /a[q][p]/b[x[z]/y] is /a[p][q]/b[x[y][z]]. Then we design an algorithm according to the principles proposed in the last section, as shown in Algorithm 1. We input twig queries one by one and output the *super-twig* presented by XPath query.

Algorithm 1. *SuperTwig* (s, r, q)

input: s is the current *super-twig* and r is its root, q is a twig query

$q = NormalizeTwig(q)$
if $s = NULL$ **then** return q
rewrite q and s with the root of document
let s_k denote each children(r) in s for $k = 1, \ldots, n$ and $j = 1$
for each child q_i of the root r_q in q
  findmatchedNode = FALSE
  while $j \leq n$
    if $q_i = s_j$ **then**
      update the edge between r and s_j
      SuperTwig(subtree(s_j), subtree(q_i), s_j)
      let findmatchedNode = TRUE and break while
    else $j{+}{+}$
  if findmatchedNode = FALSE **then**
    if isLeaf(r) **then** r is marked as *OptionalLeafNode* in s
    append subtree(q_i) to s below r and assign edge between r and q_i
    q_i is marked as *OptionalNode* in s
return s

3 Multiple Twig Queries Matching

3.1 Data Structure and Notations

Let SQ denote the *super-twig* pattern, and *root* represent the root node of SQ. In our algorithm, each node q in SQ is associated with a list T_q of database elements, which are encoded with (*start*:*end*, *level*) and sorted in ascending order of the *start* field. We keep a cursor C_q for each query node q. The cursor C_q points to the current element in T_q. Initially, C_q points to the head of T_q. We can access the attribute values of C_q by $C_q.start$ and $C_q.end$.

In *MTwigStack* algorithm, we also associate each query node q in the *super-twig* query with a stack S_q. Each data node in the stack consists of a pair: (region encoding of a element from T_q, pointer to a element in $S_{parent(q)}$). Initially, all stacks are empty. During query processing, each stack S_q may cache some elements and each elements is a descendant of the element below it. In fact, cached elements in stacks represent the partial results that could be further contributed to final results as the algorithm goes on.

3.2 The MTwigStack Algorithm

Given the *super-twig* query SQ of $\{q_1, \ldots, q_n\}$ and an XML document D, a match of SQ in D is identified by a mapping from nodes in SQ to elements and content values in D, such that: (i) query node predicates are satisfied by the corresponding database elements or content values, and (ii) the structural relationships between any two query nodes are satisfied by the corresponding database elements or content values. The answer to the *super-twig* query SQ with n twig queries can be represented as a set $R = \{R_1, \ldots, R_n\}$ where each subset R_i consists of the twig patterns in D which match query q_i.

Algorithm *MTwigStack*, for the case when the lists contain nodes from a single XML document, is presented in Algorithm 2. We execute *MTwigStack(root)* to get all answers for the *super-twig* query rooted at *root*. *MTwigStack* operates in two phases. In the first phase, it repeatedly calls the *getNext*(q) function to get the next node for processing and outputs individual root-to-leaf and root-to-*OptionalLeafNode* path solutions. After executing the first phase, we can guarantee that either all elements after C_{root} in the list T_{root} will not contribute to final results or the list T_{root} is consumed entirely. Additionally, we guarantee that for all descendants q_i of *root* in the *super-twig*, every element in T_{q_i} with *start* value smaller than the *end* value of last element processed in T_{root} was already processed. In the second phase, the function *mergeAllPathSolutions*() merges the individual path solutions for respective original twig queries.

To get the next query node q to process, *MTwigStack* repeatedly calls function *getNext(root)* and the function will call itself recursively. If q is a leaf node of the *super-twig*, the function returns q without any operation because we need not check whether there exist its descendants matching the *super-twig*; otherwise, the function returns a query node q_x with two properties: (i) if $q_x = q$, then $C_q.start < C_{q_i}.start$ and $C_q.end > C_{q_{max}}.start$ for all $q_i \in children(q)$ and

Algorithm 2. `MTwigStack`(*root*)

1: **while** NOT end(*root*) **do**
2: q = getNext(*root*)
3: **if** NOT isRoot(q) cleanStack($S_{parent(q)}$, $C_q.start$)
4: cleanStack(S_q, $C_q.start$)
5: **if** isRoot(q) OR NOT empty($S_{parent(q)}$)
6: push(C_q, S_q)
7: **if** isLeaf(q) outputSolution(S_q), pop(S_q)
8: **else if** isOptionalLeafNode(q) outputSolution(S_q)
9: **else** advance(C_q)
10: **end while**
11: mergeAllPathSolutions()

Function getNext(q)

1: **if** isLeaf(q) return q
2: **for** $q_i \in$ children(q) **do**
3: n_i = getNext(q_i)
4: **if** $n_i \neq q_i$ return n_i
5: q_{min}= the node whose *start* is minimal *start* value of all $q_i \in$ children(q)
6: q_{max}= the node whose *start* is maximal *start* value of all $q_i \in$ children(q) which are not *OptionalNodes*
7: **while** $q_{max} \neq$ NULL and $C_q.end < C_{q_{max}}.start$ **do** advance(C_q)
8: **if** $C_q.start < C_{q_{min}}.start$ return q
9: **else** return q_{min}

Procedure cleanStack(S_p, $qStart$)

1: pop all elements e_i from S_p such that $e_i.end < qStart$

Procedure mergeAllPathSolutions()

1: **for** each $q_i \in Q$ **do**
2: read the path solution lists whose leaf node is a leaf node of q_i
3: merge the path solutions and check the relationships between any two nodes

q_i is not *OptionalNode* (lines 5-8 in Func. *getNext(q)*). In this case, q is an internal node in the *super-twig* and C_q will participate in a new potential match. If the maximal *start* value of C_q's children which are not *OptionalNodes* is greater than the *end* value of C_q, we can guarantee that no new match can exist for C_q, so we advance C_q to the next element in T_q (see Figure 2(a)); (ii) if $q_x \neq q$, then $C_{q_x}.start < C_{q_j}.start$, for all q_j is in siblings of q_x and $C_{q_x}.start < C_{parent(q_x)}.start$ (lines 9 in Func. *getNext(q)*). In this case, we always process the node with minimal *start* value for all $q_i \in children(q)$ even though q_i is *OptionalNode* (see Figure 2(b)). These properties guarantee the correctness in processing q.

Next, we will process q. Firstly, we discard the elements which will not contribute potential solutions in the stack of q's parent (see Figure 2(c)) and execute the same operation on q's stack. Secondly, we will check whether C_q can match the *super-twig* query. In the case that q is *root* or the stack of q's parent is not empty, we can guarantee C_q must have a solution which matches the subtree rooted at q. If q is a leaf node, then it means that we have found a root-to-leaf path which will contribute to the final results of some or all queries; hence, we can output possible path solutions from the node to *root*; especially, if q is an *OptionalLeafNode*, we can also output the path for some queries, but we do not pop up S_q because q is an internal node and maybe will contribute to other queries in which q is not a leaf node. Otherwise, C_q must not contribute any solutions and we just advance the pointer of q to the next element in T_q (see Figure 2(d)).

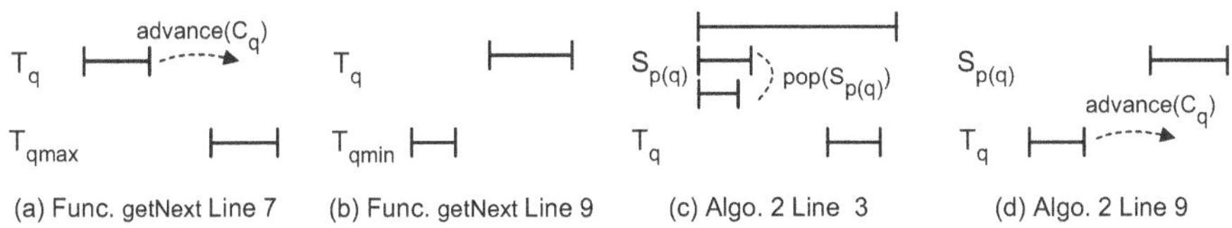

Fig. 2. Possible scenarios in the execution of *MTwigStack*

In [7], when *TwigStack* processes a leaf node, it outputs root-to-leaf solutions. However, for *super-twig*, there are leaf nodes and optional leaf nodes. Different from *TwigSack* in the first phase, *MTwigStack* will output path-to-leaf and path-to-*OptionalLeafNode* solutions if a node q of *super-twig* is leaf or *OptionalLeafNode* (it means q is a leaf node in some queries). Furthermore, in the function *getNext*(q), q_{max} is the node whose *start* is maximal *start* value of all q's children which are not *OptionalNodes*. This restriction guarantees that some nodes in T_q are not skipped mistakenly by *advance*(C_q) when some children of q are not necessary for all the twig queries.

After all possible path solutions are output, they are merged to compute matching twig instances for each twig query respectively. In this phase, we will not only join the intermediate path solutions for each query but also check whether P-C relationships of the queries are satisfied in these path solutions. Merging multiple lists of sorted path solutions is a simple practice of a multi-way merge join. In this paper, we do not explain the details for saving space.

MTwigStack is a modification of the *TwigStack* algorithm. The main diversification is to introduce the concept of *OptionalLeafNode*, which is treated as a leaf node when processing the *super-twig*. The algorithm will output intermediate matches when processing the *OptionalLeafNodes* as they are in fact leaf nodes of some twig queries. Hence, we can easily modify other algorithms such as *iTwigJoin* [8], *TJFast* [11], etc.

Example 2. In Figure 3, SQ is the *super-twig* of q_1, q_2, and q_3; in SQ, C is an *OptionalLeafNode*, D and E are *OptionalNodes*; *Doc*1 is an XML document. Initially, *getNext*(A) recursively calls *getNext*(B) and *getNext*(C). At the first loop, a_1 is skipped and C_A advances to a_2 because a_1 has no descendant node C. Then node B is returned and $q = B$. Now the stack (S_A) for parent of B is empty, hence, $b1$ is skipped and C_B points to $b2$. In the next loop, A is returned and $a2$ is pushed into S_A; next, B is returned and ($a2$, $b2$) is output; then A is returned again and $a3$ is pushed into S_A but $a2$ will be not popped; B is returned and $b3$ is pushed into S_B, ($a3$, $b3$) and ($a2$, $b3$) are output. At the sixth loop, C is returned and c_1 is pushed into S_C. C is an *OptionalLeafNode*, hence ($a3$, $c1$) and ($a2$, $c1$) are output but $c1$ is not popped. Next D is returned and $d1$ is pushed into S_D; Then F is returned, (a_3, c_1, d_1, f_1) and (a_2, c_1, d_1, f_1) are output. Next, $c2$ is processed, ($a3$, $c2$) and ($a2$, $c2$) are output. Finally, E is returned, then ($a3$, $c2$, $e1$), ($a3$, $c1$, $e1$), ($a2$, $c2$, $e1$) and ($a2$, $c1$, $e1$) are output. At the second phase, *mergeAllPathSolutions*() merges the path solutions of (A, B) and (A, C) for q_1, (A, B) and (A, C, D, F) for Q_2, and (A, B) and (A, C, E) for q_3. In this phase, we also check whether P-C relationships are satisfied.

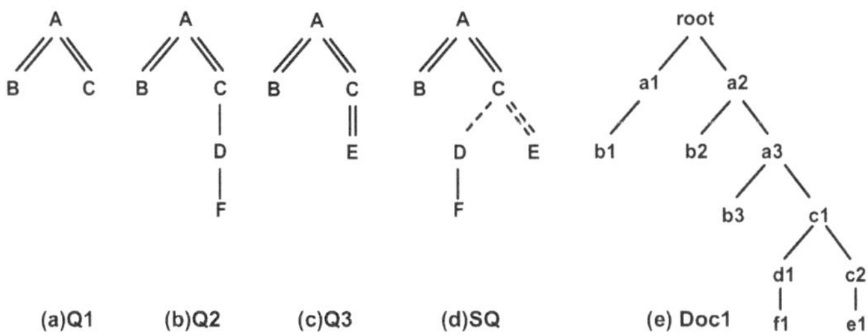

Fig. 3. Illustration to *MTwigStack*

4 Experimental Evaluation

4.1 Experimental Setup

We implemented *MTwigStack* algorithm in Java. All experiments were run on a 2.6 GHz Pentium IV processor with 1 GB of main memory, running windows XP system. We used the TreeBank [1] and XMark [2] data sets for our experiments. The file size of TreeBank is 82M bytes, and the file sizes of XMark are 128KB, 2MB, and 32MB respectively. We test our *MTwigStack* comparing with *TwigStack* [7] and *Index-Filter* [6] with different numbers of queries on these different data sets.

The set of queries consists of 1 to 10000 twig queries, with a random number of nodes between 10 to 20. The total number of distinct tags in these twig queries is less than 30% of total distinct tags (75 tags) for XMark data sets, and is less than 15% of total distinct tags (249 tags) for TreeBank data set.

4.2 Experimental Results

MTwigStack vs. TwigStack. Figure 4 (a) shows the execution time of *TwigStack* to the execution time of *MTwigStack* on the four data sets when processing different numbers of queries. We find that whatever the data size is, when there is only one query, these two methods consume the same time; with the number of queries increasing, the processing time increase of *MTwigStack* is far lower than the increase of *TwigStack* (e.g. the ratio is about 60 for 1000 queries on the TreeBank data set). This is explained by the fact that *MTwigStack* process all the multiple queries simultaneously, while *TwigStack* needs to match the queries one by one.

In table 1, we show the number of elements scanned by *MTwigStack* and *TwigStack* when processing different numbers of queries. Obviously, *MTwigStack* scans far less elements than *TwigStack* does. The reason is, for the nodes which appear in multiple queries, *MTwgStack* scans them only once. But extremely, *MTwigStack* and *TwigStack* will scan the same number of elements only when there is no node that appears in all the queries repeatedly, that is, all nodes in the multiple queries are distinct.

MTwigStack vs. Index-Filter. We implemented *Index-Filter* as follows: firstly, decomposing twig pattern into simple path queries for each twig query and combining these path queries into a *prefix tree*; next, executing the *Index-Filter* algorithm to get intermediate solutions for each path; finally, joining the path solutions which belong to the same query and eliminating useless solutions.

Figure 4 (b) shows the execution time of *Index-Filter* to the execution time of *MTwigStack*. With the increase of data size and number of queries, *Index-Filter* will run longer time even though it scans the same number of elements as *MTwigStack* does, as shown in Table 1. The reason is, *Index-Filter* decomposes a twig query into multiple simple paths during query processing and it will

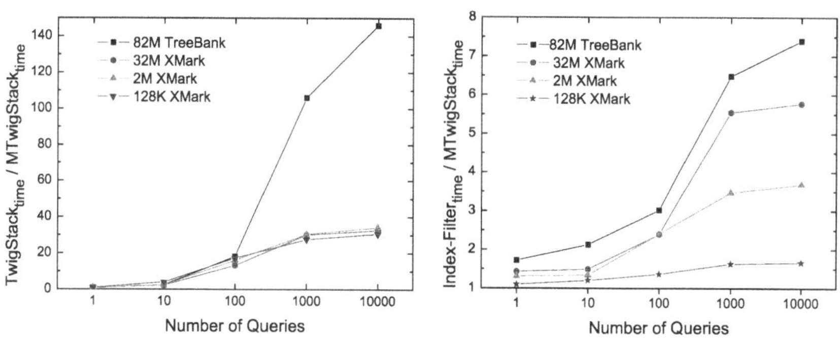

(a) MTwigStack vs. TwigStack (b) MTwigStack vs. Index-Filter

Fig. 4. Execution time ratio for different data sets

Table 1. The number of scanned elements

Data Set	128K XMark		2M XMark		32M XMark		82M TreeBank	
No. of Queries	10	100	10	100	10	100	10	100
MTwigStack	286	397	5027	6059	78167	96357	1278766	1465232
Index-Filter	286	397	5027	6059	78167	96357	1278766	1465232
TwigStack	2312	18455	40337	354260	635718	6005265	11685319	106760340

Table 2. The number of intermediate path solutions

Data Set	128K XMark		2M XMark		32M XMark		82M TreeBank	
No. of Queries	10	100	10	100	10	100	10	100
MTwigStack	29	33	349	459	5401	7386	646	678
Index-filter	134	157	2332	2827	37197	44797	496691	498688
TwigStack	127	1215	1237	10425	19897	172360	775	3965

produce many useless intermediate path solutions, as shown in Table 2. Merging more path solutions also need consume more time. Furthermore, *Index-Filter* also requires more space to keep intermediate results.

5 Conclusion and Future Work

In this paper, we proposed a new twig join algorithm, called *MTwigStack*, to process multiple twig queries with a high structural similarity. Although holistic twig join has been proposed to solve single twig pattern, applying it to multiple twig patterns matching is nontrivial. We developed a new concept *super-twig* with *OptionalNode* and *OptionalLeafNode* to determine whether an element is in the shared structure of the XML twig patterns. We also made the contribution by processing the shared structure in the *super-twig* only once. The experimental results showed that our algorithm is more effective and efficient than the applying *TwigStack* to each individual twig quires, or applying *Index-Filter* by decomposing twig queries into many simple path queries.

In the future, we will improve the algorithm based on the following two issues: one is to design an efficient index scheme to fasten the processing speed. Another issue is our method only supports a subset of XPath queries. Some queries, such as //A[B]/C and //D[B]/C, can not be processed efficiently. We will try to process more XPath queries.

References

1. Treebank. Available from http://www.cis.upenn.edu/treebank/.
2. The xml benchmark project. Available from http://www.xml-benchmark.org.
3. S. Al-Khalifa, H. Jagadish, N. Koudas, J. Patel, D. Srivastava, and Y. Wu. Structural joins: A primitive for efficient XML query pattern matching. In *Proceedings of ICDE*, 2002.
4. M. Altinel and M. Franklin. Efficient filtering of XML documents for selective dissemination of information. In *Proceedings of VLDB*, 2000.
5. S. Amer-Yahia, S. Cho, L. K. S. Lakshmanan, and D. Srivastava. Minimization of tree pattern queries. In *Proceedings of ACM SIGMOD*, 2001.
6. N. Bruno, L. Gravano, N. Koudas, and D. Srivastava. Navigation- vs. index-based XML multi-query processing. In *Proceedings of ICDE*, 2003.
7. N. Bruno, N. Koudas, and D. Srivastava. Holistic twig joins: Optimal XML pattern matching. In *Proceedings of ACM SIGMOD*, 2002.

8. T. Chen, J. Lu, and T. Ling. On boosting holism in XML twig pattern matching using structural indexing techniques. In *Proceedings of ACM SIGMOD*, 2005.
9. Y. Diao, M. Altinel, M. Franklin, H. Zhang, and P. Fischer. Path sharing and predicate evaluation for high-performance XML filtering. In *ACM Transactions on Database Systems (TODS)*, volume 28, pages 467–516, 2003.
10. S. Flesca, F. Furfaro, and E. Masciari. On the minimization of xpath queries. In *Proceedings of VLDB*, 2003.
11. J. Lu, T. Ling, C. Chan, and T. Chen. From region encoding to extended dewey: On efficient processing of XML twig pattern matching. In *Proceedings of VLDB*, 2005.
12. B. Mandhani and D. Suciu. Query caching and view selection for xml databases. In *Proceedings of VLDB*, 2005.

Effectively Scoring for XML IR Queries

Zhongming Han, Jiajin Le, and Beijin Shen

College of Information Science and Technology of Donghua University
1882 Yanan Road Shanghai P.R. China (200051)
hx_zm@mail.dhu.edu.cn, klein_beijin@mail.dhu.edu.cn

Abstract. This paper focuses on relevance scoring for XML IR queries. We propose a novel and effective algorithm for relevance scoring, which considers both structural information and semantic. Experiments show that the algorithm can effectively improve the Precision and Recall for XML information retrieval.

1 Introduction

Effectively finding the useful information from XML documents has became a challenging problem. For different xml retrieval systems, there is a very common and important problem: relevance scoring. In traditional information retrieval system, the score unit is the document, which is fixed. However, in XML retrieval system, the unit is the element included in one or more documents. Furthermore the element could not be defined when one retrieval query is proposed. During the query process, according to the relevance between the query fragment and the document, appropriate elements could be selected to return. So it is very important to utilize the document structure information in ranking not only in filtering. Furthermore, relevance score should be related to element semantic in XML documents, i.e. element names and element types. However, these factors are not considered yet in current XML IR system.

In this paper, we propose a novel and effective algorithm to compute the relevance score that considers both the frequency distribution of the terms, structural distribution of the terms and semantic of the elements. Our main contributions are as follows:

- A relevance scoring algorithm is presented, which considers both the term frequency, structural relevance and semantic of the element. The associated ranking function is proposed too.
- The comprehensive experiments are conducted to evaluate all the related technologies.

2 Preliminary

We assume that a single document D is a node labelled acyclic tree with the set V of nodes and the set E of edges, and labels are taken from the set L of

S. Bressan, J. Küng, and R. Wagner (Eds.): DEXA 2006, LNCS 4080, pp. 12–21, 2006.

strings. Furthermore, text values come from a set T of text strings and they can be attached to any type of nodes, not just leaf nodes. *root* is the root of the D. The following definitions introducc some fundamental notions used in the rest of the paper.

Definition 1. *Let n_1 and n_2 be two nodes in an XML document. If n_2 is a child node of n_1, i.e. $n_2 \in children(n_1)$, then local position of n_2, dcnotcd $lposition(n_2)$, is the position of node n_2 in $children(n_1)$ with respect to nodes that have the same label $label(n_2)$. The arity of node n_2, $arity(n_2)$, is the number of nodes with label $label(n_2)$ in the n_1's list of children.*

Definition 2. *Let n_1 and n_2 be two nodes in an XML document. If n_2 is a child node of n_1, i.e. $n_2 \in children(n_1)$, then sibling position of n_2, denoted $sposition(n_2)$, is the position of node n_2 in $children(n_1)$ with respect to nodes that are child nodes of $label(n_1)$.*

An XML document from Sigmod Record in XML is listed in Table 1.

Table 1. XML Document Example

```
<Papers>
  <Article>
    <Title='XML Information Retrieval'><\Title>
    <Authors='David Jon, John Tom'><\authors>
    <section>
      <title='Introduction'><\title>
      <text='...XML... information retrieval...'><\text>
    <\section>
  <\Article>
  <Article>
    <title='XML Data Query'><\Title>
    <Authors="David John"><\Authors>
    <section>
      <title='Basic Concepts'><\title>
      <text='...XML... retrieval...'><\text>
    <\section>
  <\Article>
<\papers>
```

As we all know, the structural information of XML documents is very important to both XML query and XML information retrieval. Thus, a summary tree is presented, which includes label paths for the XML document and is a node labelled acyclic tree with the set V of elements. Formally, we define summary tree as follows.

Definition 3. *A summary tree ST for an XML document D is a tree (V, root,children),where V is a finite set of element coming from the label set of D;*

root $\in V$ *is the root of D; children is a mapping from elements to a partially ordered sequence of child elements. This tree satisfies:*

- *For each path p in ST, there is a corresponding label path in D;*
- *For each label path in D, there is a corresponding path p in ST;*
- *For two nodes* N_1 *and* N_2 *with same parent node and different label in D,if* $sposition(N_1) < sposition(N_2)$, *then the element of* $label(N_1)$ *appear earlier than* $label(N_2)$.

Figure 1 shows the summary tree for the XML document listed in Table 1.

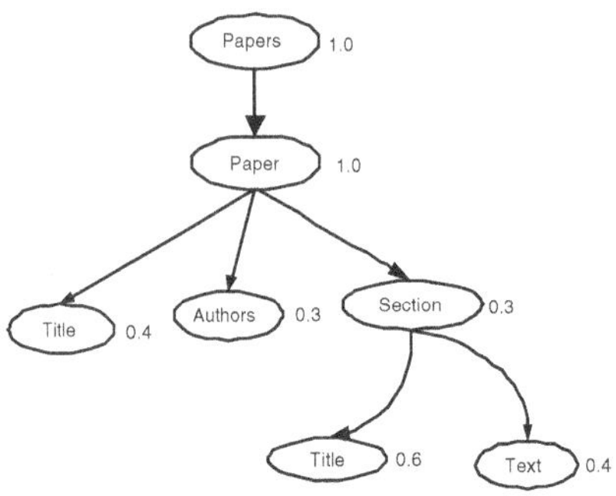

Fig. 1. The summary tree

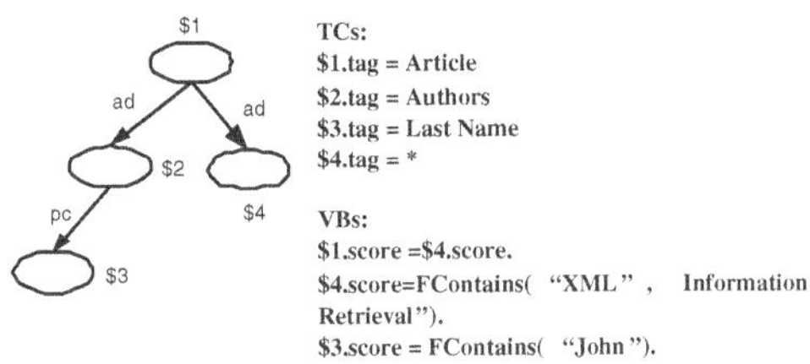

Fig. 2. Scored Pattern Tree

Usually, an XML data query can be represented by an XQuery expression. However even a simple XML IR style query cannot be easily transformed into an XQuery expression. the following is a simple example.

Example 1 *Find all document components in DBLP.xml that are part of an article written by an author with the last name 'John' and are about 'XML'. Relevance to 'Information Retrieval'.*

An XML IR style query can be viewed as a scored pattern tree. Like definition in [6], we can define scored pattern tree. However the differences are we distinguish the different constraints and '*' node can be applied.

Definition 4. *A scored pattern tree is a triple* $p = (T, F, S)$, *where* $t = (V, E)$ *is a rooted node-labelled and edge-labelled tree such that:*

- *Each node in V labelled by a distinct integer;*
- $E = E_c \bigcup E_d$ *consists of pc-edges(parent-child relationship) and ad-edges (ancestor-descendant relationship);*
- *F is a conjunction of predicates, including tag constraints (TCs), value-based constraints (VBs) and node constraints (NCs);*
- *S is a set of score and rank functions applied to nodes;*

For the XML IR style query, example 1, the terms 'XML' and 'Information Retrieval' are not explicitly applied to a node. Then we apply these term constraints to an extra node '*' in the scored pattern tree,which is shown in figure 2. Meanwhile, we add a score function to the parent node.

3 Relevance Scoring

For XML information retrieval system, TF need to be modified because the unit of XML IR is element not document. Formally, we denote $TF(te, e)$ for term frequency of term te in element e. It means the number of occurrences of term te in element e. For each unique term in the XML fragment of query answer, the inverse document frequency IDF is calculated as:

$$IDF(te) = \log \frac{N}{n(te)} \tag{1}$$

with N being the total number of unique terms, and $n(te)$ the number of text fragments in which term t occurs.

Using $TF(te, e)$ and IDF to evaluate the relevance for term te of element e is sufficient for term constraints explicitly applied to a node. So we use $TF(te, e) * IDF(te)$ for relevance score for terms belonging to an XML element explicitly.

In our intuition, the relevance score for the term constraints applied to a '*' node involves the following aspects:

- Term Frequency(TF)
- Structure Relevance. Different terms are possibly distributed over different elements. The shorter the distance between these different elements is, the higher the relevance score will be.
- Semantic Relevance. Since a term is possibly distributed over different elements. Thus, the term could have different meanings. This means that the semantic of the element could affect the relevance score of the term.

3.1 Structural Relevance

We propose a new concept, term distance, which can reflect the term structure distribution. The following is the formula by which the term distance can be computed.

$$TD(te_1, te_2) = \tag{2}$$

1. 1, if $pa(te_1) = pa(te_2)$
2. $|spos(pa(te_1)) - spos(pa(te_2))|$, if $pa(pa(te_1)) = pa(pa(te_2))$
3. $|lev(pa(te_1)) - lev(pa(te_2))|$, if $pa(te_1)//pa(te_2)$ or $pa(te_2)//pa(te_1)$
4. $|lev(pa(te_1)) - lev(te_c))| + |lev(pa(te_2)) - lev(te_c))|$, Otherwise.

Where $TD(te_1, te_2)$ means term distance between te_1 and te_2. Function $spos$ returns $sposition$ of the element. Function $pa(te_i)$ returns corresponding parent element of the term. And $pa(te_1)//pa(te_2)$ means that $pa(te_1)$ and $pa(te_2)$ have ancestor-descendant relationship. Function lev returns the level of the element. te_c is the common ancestor element for te_1 and te_2.

When te_1 and te_2 have the same parent,the term distance is the minimum according to the formula. When $pa(pa(te_1))$ and $pa(pa(te_2))$ are different and these two elements do not satisfy ancestor-descendant relationship, these terms should have less relevance. Based on term distance of two terms, term distance for more terms can be computed by the following formula.

$$TD(te_1, te_2, \cdots, te_n) = \sum_{i=1}^{n-1} TD(te_i, te_{i+1}) \tag{3}$$

Based on term distance, the structural relevance score for n terms in the '*' node can be computed by formula 4.

$$RS^t = \frac{1}{1 + TD(te_1, te_2, \cdots, te_n)} \times \sum_{i=1}^{n} TF(te_i, pa(te_i)) \tag{4}$$

Since the relevance is for a '*' node and the parent node has the same relevance function with the '*' node, the relevance of corresponding parent node also have been computed.

3.2 Semantic Relevance

The same term in a XML IR style query could occur on different elements, which have different semantics. Then for these terms, it should have different relevances. It is the intuition of considering semantic relevance.

Consider example 1 over the document fragment listed in Table 1. The term 'Information retrieval' occurred thrice in different elements. Then relevances should be different. For example, the relevance score for element 'title' should be higher than for element 'section'.

The first sub-question for computing semantic relevance is how to weigh semantic for elements. We denote semantic relevance weight for an element $sew(e_i)$. Basically, semantic relevance weights produced by any methods should satisfy two properties:

1. For any element e with child elements, $\sum sew(e_i) = 1$, $\forall e_i \in children(e)$.
2. For any element e, $0 \leq sew(e) \leq 1$.

From Property 1, we can know that the semantic weight is local weight. Obviously, the semantic of an element has affinity to the semantics of sub-elements. As for the descendent elements, there is less semantic affinity. Property 2 guarantees that each semantic weight is normalization.

The number labelled in each element in Figure 1 means the semantic weight for the element.

How to evaluate semantic relevance for terms of a '*' node based on the summary tree with semantic weights? Firstly, when a term te is found in the node with label e in the XML document, then the label path also has been knowing. By searching the path of the element in the summary tree, we can get a list of semantics from the summary tree. Thus, the semantic weight of this element can be computed by formula 5.

$$WS(e) = \prod_{e_i \in path(e)} sew(e_i) \tag{5}$$

where $path(e)$ is the path from $root(PT)$ to the element e, PT is the query pattern tree. And $sew(e_i)$ means the semantic weight of element e_i.

Thus, based on formula 5, the semantic relevance score of term te can be obtained by formula 6.

$$RS^s(te, e) = \sum_{e_i} TF(te, e_i) * WS(e_i) \tag{6}$$

Where e_i means that element that term te occupy. Formula 5 counts all the elements where the term te appears. Usually, a '*' node will possess more term constraints. Then, the semantic relevance for terms of a '*' node N_* of the IR style query can be computed by formula 7.

$$RS^s = \sum_{te_i \in term(N_*)}^{\oplus} RS^s(te_i, e_i) \tag{7}$$

where $term(N_*)$ is the set of terms that users assign to a '*' node. Formula 6 counts all the elements where these terms appear. The $\sum^{\oplus}$ represents boolean sum, which is discussed in the next subsection.

3.3 Integrated Relevance Score

To flexibly support boolean predicate connection, two boolean predicate 'and' and 'or' are implemented in our method. The boolean connectives in a query statesmen can be assigned a score based on the probabilistic interpretation of relevance score of the terms.

$RS(s_1 \text{and} s_2) = RS(s_1) \times RS(s_2)$
$RS(s_1 \text{or} s_2) = RS(s_1) + RS(s_2) - RS(s_1) \times RS(s_2)$

We can combine this interpretation to express more complex queries. In formula 7, the boolean sum is interpreted by this interpretation. The last step for computing complete relevance score for the '*' node is to integrate the structure relevance and semantic relevance. The simple method is weight sum.

$$RS(N_*) = \alpha * RS^t + (1 - \alpha) * RS^s \tag{8}$$

where $RS(N_*)$ means the relevance score of a '*' node of the XML IR style query. RS^t and RS^s are structure relevance score and semantic relevance score for the '*' node in the query respectively. α is a parameter can be selected by users or experts. The parameter α represents the preference of the users for structural relevance and semantic relevance. The optimum value of this parameter could be learned during experiments.

We denote $RS(Q)$ for integrated relevance score for an XML IR style query. The formula for computing is $RS(Q)$ listed as follows.

$$RS(Q) = \sum_{e_i \in G,} TF(te_i, e_i) + \sum_{N_{*_i} \in GS} RS(N_*) \tag{9}$$

where G is the set of nodes, to which some terms applied. And all paths of these nodes have not '*' node. GS is the set of '*' nodes. In an query pattern tree, it is possible that more than one '*' node appear in it.

4 Experiment

We choose SIGMOD Record in XML [22] and sample data collection for XQuery 1.0 and XPath 2.0 Full-Text Use Cases [20]. The first data collection consists of a collection of three books. For more competitive purposes, we extended this data collection to 100 books, which have the same structure with the origin elements. The extended Data collection have more than 10000 elements with total size of 40MB. Based on the XML database system [23] and HiD [24]index structure, we implement the query algorithm and score algorithm.

Table 2. Queries for Experiment

Query	Content
Q1	/books/book//subject[.ftcontains "usability"]
Q2	/books/*[.ftcontains "usability testing"]
Q3	/books/book[./* [.ftcontains "goal" & "obstacles" & "task"]]/title ftcontains "Software"
Q4	/books/book[./*[.ftcontains "usability testing"]]/Authors/*[.ftcontains "Software"]
Q5	/books/book[/metadata/*[."usability testing"]]//content/*[.ftcontains "Software"]
Q6	/IndexTermsPage//Author[.ftcontains "Han"]
Q7	/IndexTermsPage/*[.ftcontains "XML" | "Information Retrieval"]
Q8	/IndexTermsPage[/Author/*[.ftcontains "Wang"]]//abstract ftcontains "XML"

Table 2 list the queries. We use 'ftcontains' phrase to represent the full text retrieval, and use '&' and '|' to respectively represent the 'and' and 'or' relationship between two terms. Query 1 to query 5 ran over the data collection. Query 6 to query 8 ran over Sigmod Record in XML. For objectively evaluating the effectiveness of our algorithm, we investigated the Precision and Recall measure, which are often used to evaluate different algorithms of IR system. We tested our algorithm with two steps on each query with different parameter α. We mainly analyze results for average precision and average recall for different parameter α values.

The average precision values for different parameter are shown in fig.3(a), where V_Precsion_1 represent the average precision for queries running on SIGMOD Record in XML and V_Precsion_2 represent the average precision for queries running on data collection for Query 1.0 and XPath 2.0 Full-Text Use Cases. It is clear that the average precision reach its highest at about $\alpha = 0.64$ for SIGMOD Record and about $\alpha = 0.45$ for data collection for Query 1.0 and XPath 2.0 Full-Text Use Cases.

The average recall values for different parameter are shown in fig.3(b), where V_Recall_1 represent the average recall for queries running on SIGMOD Record in XML and V_Recall_2 represent the average recall for queries running on data collection for Query 1.0 and XPath 2.0 Full-Text Use Cases. The average recall

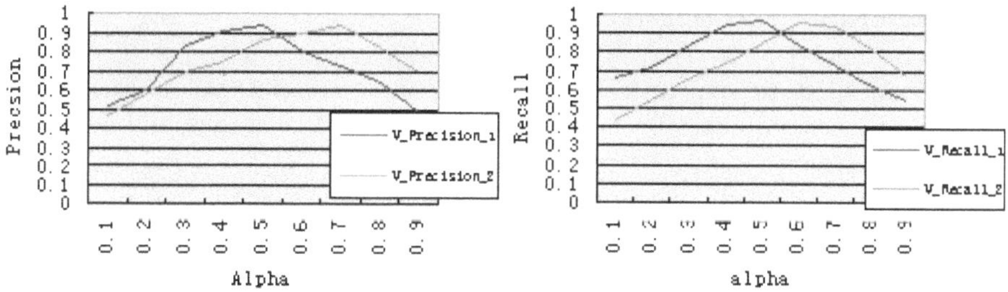

(a) Average Precision with Different Parameter (b) Average Recall with Different Parameter

Fig. 3. Experiment Results

reach its highest at about $\alpha = 0.65$ for SIGMOD Record and about $\alpha = 0.42$ for data collection for Query 1.0 and XPath 2.0 Full-Text Use Cases.

From these experiments, we can know that better relevance can be obtained under different optimize value for different XML document.

5 Related Work

XML query languages with full text search are presented in some papers, such as [2,6,7,11,16]. These languages have different features. In [2], a language XIRQL is presented, which integrates IR related features. However the language presented in this paper is based on XQL but not on XQuery [18] and XPath [19], so does the language presented in [11]. TeXQuery [6] is a powerful full-text search extension to XQuery, which provides a rich set of fully composable full text search primitives. TeXQuery satisfies the FTTF Requirements specified in [17].

Some XML retrieval systems which can handle XML full text query to some extent are presented in [1,3,4,5,6,8,9]. Timber system [1] is a system integrating information retrieval techniques into a XML database system. System [3] targets to support more specific user friendliness via a very simple fragment-based language. In [6], a bulk-algebra called TIX is presented. It can be used as a basis for integrating information retrieval techniques into a standard pipelined database query evaluation engine. The XRANK system [8] for ranked keyword search over XML documents is presented in this paper, which considers the hierarchical and hyperlinked structure of XML documents, and a two-dimensional notion of keyword proximity. In [9], FleXPath, a framework that integrates structure and full-text querying in XML is presented.

Vector space model is still used to evaluate relevance score by some researches [10,3]. Ranking approach [3]is assigning weights to individual contexts by extended vector space model. Main contribution of [10] is to dynamically derive the vector space that is appropriate for the scope of the query from underlying basic vector spaces. Researches [12,13,14,15] focus on how to query full text on XML documents. Most of these researches show that combining structure index and inverted list can have better performance for querying tasks.

6 Conclusion and Future Work

In this paper, we present an effective algorithm to compute relevance scoring for XML IR style query, which takes both structural relevance and semantic relevance into account.

The INEX document collection is an XML document,which is frequently used to test different system supported XML IR style query. However, we have not yet been able to access the collection by now. Next, we will have our algorithms run over this data collection. In traditional IR system, dictionary or thesaurus can be used to improve performance. In XML IR query system, effectively utilizing dictionary or thesaurus is also an ongoing research job.

References

1. Cong Yu, Hong Qi, H. V. Jagadish. Integration of IR into an XML Database. In First Annual Workshop of the Initiative for the Evaluation of XML Retrieval (INEX), 2002.
2. N. Fuhr and K. Grobjohann. XIRQL: A Query Language for Information Retrieval in XML Documents. In Proceedings of the 24th Annual ACM SIGIR Conference on Research and Development in Information Retrieval, 2001.
3. Y. Mass, M. Mandelbrod, E. Amitay, D. Carmel,Y. Maarek, and A. Soffer. JuruXML-an XML retrieval system at INEX'02.
4. ET. Grabs, H.-J. Schek. Flexible Information Retrieval from XML with PowerD-BXML. In INEX 2002.
5. T. Schlieder and H. Meuss. Result Ranking for Structured Queries against XML Documents. In DELOS Workshop on Information Seeking, Searching and Querying in Digital Libraries, 2000.
6. Shurug Al-Khalifa, Cong Yu, H. V. Jagadish. Querying Structured Text in an XML Database.In Sigmod 2003.
7. Sihem AmerYahia, Chavdar Botev, Jayavel. TeXQuery: A FullText Search Extension to XQuery. In WWW 2004.
8. L. L. Guo, F. Shao, C. Botev, J. Shanmugasundaram. XRANK: Ranked Keyword Search over XML Documents. In Sigmod 2003.
9. Sihem AmerYahia, Laks V.S. Lakshmanan, Shashank Pandit. FleXPath: Flexible Structure and FullText Querying for XML. In Sigmod 2004.
10. T. Grabs and H.-J. Schek. Generating Vector Spaces On-the-fly for Flexible XML Retrieval. In Proceedings of the ACM SIGIR Workshop on XML and Information Retrieval, 2002.
11. Daniela Florescu, Donald Kossmann, Ioana Manolescu. Integrating Keyword Search into XML Query Processing. In Proc. of the Intern. WWW Conference, Amsterdam, 2000.
12. R.Sacks-Davis, T.Dao, J.A. Thom, J.Zobel. Indexing Documents for Queries on Structure, Content and Attributes. Proc. of International Symposium on Digital Media Information Base (DMIB), Nara, 1997.
13. Jaap Kamps, Maarten de Rijke, Borkur Sigurbjornsson. Length. Normalization in XML Retrieval. In ACM SIGIR 2004.
14. Hugh E. Williams, Justin Zobel, Dirk Bahle. Fast Phrase Querying with Multiple Indexes. In ACM Transactions on Information Systems 22(4):573-594, 2004.

15. Raghav Kaushik, Rajasekar Krishnamurthy, Jeffrey F. Naughton,Raghu Ramakrishnan. On the Integration of Structure Indexes and Inverted Lists. In Sigmod 2004.
16. Taurai T. Chinenyanga, Nicholas Kushmerick. An expressive and efficient language for XML information retrieval.In J. American Society for Information Science & Technology 53(6):438-453 2002.
17. The World Wide Web Consortium. XQuery and XPath Full-Text Requirements.http://www.w3.org/TR/xmlquery-full-text-requirements/.
18. The World Wide Web Consortium. XQuery 1.0: An XML Query Language. http://www.w3.org/TR/xquery/.
19. The World Wide Web Consortium. XML Path Language (XPath) 2.0. http://www.w3.org/TR/xpath20/.
20. he World Wide Web Consortium. XQuery 1.0 and XPath 2.0 Full-Text Use Cases. http://www.w3.org/TR/xmlquery-full-text-use-cases/.
21. Initiative for the Evaluation of XML Retrieval. http://www.is.informatik.uni-duisburg.de/projects/inex03/.
22. Sigmod Record in XML. http://www.sigmod.org/sigmod/dblp/db/conf /xml/index.html.
23. Galax.http://www.galaxquery.com.
24. Zhongming Han, Congting Xi, Jiajin Le. Efficiently Coding and Indexing XML Document.In DASFAA 2005.

Selectively Storing XML Data in Relations

Wenfei Fan[1] and Lisha Ma[2]

[1] University of Edinburgh and Bell Laboratories
[2] Heriot-Watt University

Abstract. This paper presents a new framework for users to select relevant data from an XML document and store it in an existing relational database, as opposed to previous approaches that shred the entire XML document into a newly created database of a newly designed schema. The framework is based on a notion of XML2DB mappings. An XML2DB mapping extends a (*possibly recursive*) DTD by associating element types with semantic attributes and rules. It extracts either part or all of the data from an XML document, and generates SQL updates to increment an existing database using the XML data. We also provide an efficient technique to evaluate XML2DB mappings in parallel with SAX parsing. These yield a systematic method to store XML data selectively in an existing database.

1 Introduction

A number of approaches have been proposed for shredding XML data into relations [3,6,14,15], and some of these have found their way into commercial systems [10,7,13]. Most of these approaches map XML data to a newly created database of a "canonical" relational schema that is designed starting from scratch based on an XML DTD, rather than storing the data in an existing database. Furthermore, they often store the entire XML document in the database, rather than letting users select and store part of the XML data. While some commercial systems allow one to define schema-based mappings to store part of the XML data in relations, either their ability to handle recursive DTDs is limited [7,10] or they do not support storing the data in an existing database [13]. In practice, it is common that users want to specify what data they want in an XML document, and to increment an existing database with the selected data. Moreover, one often wants to define the mappings based on DTDs, which may be recursive as commonly found in practice (see [4] for a survey of real-life DTDs).

Example 1.1. Consider a *registrar* database specified by the relational schema R_0 shown in Fig. 1(a) (with keys underlined). The database maintains *student* data, *enroll*ment records, *course* data, and a relation *prereq*, which gives the prerequisite hierarchy of courses: a tuple *(c1, c2)* in *prereq* indicates that *c2* is a prerequisite of *c1*.

Now consider an XML DTD D_0 also shown in Fig. 1(a) (the definition of elements whose type is PCDATA is omitted). An XML document conforming to D_0 is depicted in Fig. 1(b). It consists of a list of *course* elements. Each *course* has a *cno* (course number), a course *title*, a *prere*quisite hierarchy, and all the *students* who have registered for the course. Note that the DTD is recursive: *course* is defined in terms of itself via *prereq*.

S. Bressan, J. Küng, and R. Wagner (Eds.): DEXA 2006, LNCS 4080, pp. 22–32, 2006.

```
Relational schema R0:
course(cno, title),
student(ssn, name),
enroll(ssn, cno),
prereq(cno1, cno2).

DTD D0:
<!ELEMENT db       (course*)>
<!ELEMENT course   (cno, title,
                    prereq, takenBy)>
<!ELEMENT prereq   (course*)>
<!ELEMENT takenBy  (student*)>
<!ELEMENT student  (ssn, name)>
```

(a) Relational schema R_0 and DTD D_0

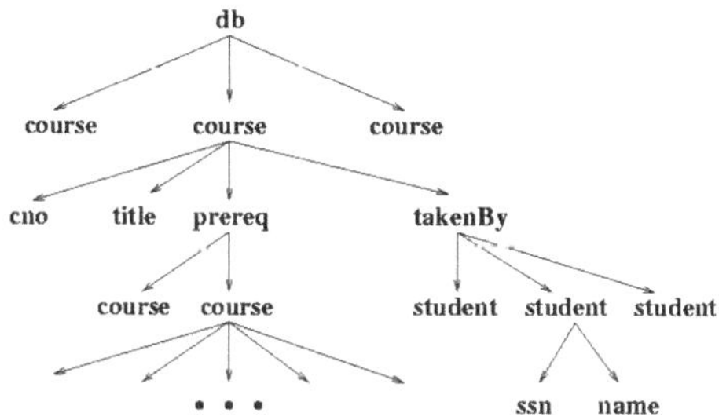

(b) An XML document of D_0

Fig. 1. Relational Schema R_0, DTD D_0 and an example XML document of D_0

We want to define a mapping σ_0 that, given an XML document T that conforms to D_0 and a relational database I of R_0, (a) extracts from T all the CS *courses*, along with their *prerequisites* hierarchies and *students* registered for these related courses, and (b) inserts the data into relations *course*, *student*, *enroll* and *prereq* of the relational database I, respectively. Observe the following. (a) We only want to store in relations a certain part of the data in T, instead of the entire T. (b) The selected XML data is to be stored in an existing database I of a predefined schema R_0 by means of SQL updates, rather than in a newly created database of a schema designed particularly for D_0. (c) The selected XML data may reside at arbitrary levels of T, whose depth cannot be determined at compile time due to the recursive nature of its DTD D_0. To our knowledge, no existing XML shredding systems are capable of supporting σ_0. □

Contributions. To overcome the limitations of existing XML shredding approaches, we propose a new framework for mapping XML to relations. The framework is based on (a) a notion of XML2DB *mappings* that extends (*possibly recursive*) DTDs and is capable of mapping either part of or an entire document to relations, and (b) a technique for efficiently evaluating XML2DB mappings.

XML2DB mappings are a novel extension of attribute grammars (see, *e.g.*, [5] for attribute grammars). In a nutshell, given a (*possibly recursive*) XML DTD D and a predefined relational schema R, one can define an XML2DB mapping $\sigma : D \to R$ to select data from an XML document of D, and generates SQL inserts to increment an existing relational database of R. More specifically, σ extends the DTD D by associating semantic attributes and rules with element types and their definitions in D. Given an XML document T of D, σ traverses T, selects data from T, and generates SQL inserts Δ by means of the semantic attributes and rules during the traversal. Upon the completion of the traversal, the SQL updates Δ are executed against an existing database I of R, such that the updated database $\Delta(I)$ includes the extracted XML data and is guaranteed to be an instance of the predefined schema R. For example, we shall express the mapping σ_0 described in Example 1.1 as an XML2DB mapping (Fig. 2(a)).

To evaluate efficiently an XML2DB mapping σ, we propose a technique that combines the evaluation with the parsing of XML data by leveraging existing SAX [9] parsers. This allows us to generate SQL updates Δ in a single traversal of the document without incurring extra cost. To verify the effectiveness and efficiency of our technique we provide a preliminary experimental study.

Taken together, the main contributions of the paper include the following:

- A notion of XML2DB mappings, which allow users to increment an existing relational database by using certain part or all of the data in an XML document, and are capable of dealing with *(possibly recursive)* XML DTDs in a uniform framework.
- An efficient technique that seamlessly integrates the evaluation of XML2DB mappings and SAX parsing, accomplishing both in a single pass of an XML document.
- An experimental study verifying the effectiveness of our techniques.

The novelty of our uniform framework consists in (a) the functionality to support mappings based on *(possibly recursive)* DTDs from XML to relations that, as opposed to previous XML shredding approaches, allows users to map *either part of or the entire* XML document to a relational database, rather than core-dumping the entire document; (b) the ability to extend an *existing* relational database of a *predefined* schema with XML data rather than creating a new database starting from scratch; (c) efficient evaluation techniques for XML2DB mappings via *a mild extension of* SAX *parsers* for XML.

Organization. Section 2 reviews DTDs and SAX. Section 3 defines XML2DB mappings. Section 4 presents the evaluation technique. A preliminary experimental study is presented in Section 5, followed by related work in Section 6 and conclusions in Section 7.

2 Background: DTDs and SAX

DTDs. Without loss of generality, we formalize a DTD D to be (E, P, r), where E is a finite set of *element types*; r is in E and is called the *root type*; P defines the element types: for each A in E, $P(A)$ is a regular expression α defined by PCDATA $\mid \epsilon \mid B_1, \ldots, B_n \mid B_1 + \ldots + B_n \mid B^*$, where ϵ is the empty word, B is a type in E (referred to as a *child type* of A), and '$+$', ',' and '$*$' denote disjunction, concatenation and the Kleene star, respectively (we use '$+$' instead of '$|$' to avoid confusion). We refer to $A \rightarrow P(A)$ as the *production* of A. A DTD is *recursive* it has an element type defined (directly or indirectly) in terms of itself.

Note that [2] all DTDs can be converted to this form in linear time by using new element types and performing a simple post-processing step to remove the introduced element types. To simplify the discussion we do not consider XML attributes, which can be easily incorporated. We also assume that the element types $B_1, \ldots, B_n$ in $B_1, \ldots, B_n$ (resp. $B_1 + \ldots + B_n$) are distinct, w.l.o.g. since we can always distinguish repeated occurrences of the same element type by referring to their positions in the production.

SAX Parsing. A SAX [9] parser reads an XML document T and generates a stream of SAX events of five types: startDocument(), startElement(A, eventNo), text(s), endElement(A), endDocument(), where A is an element type of T and s is a string (PCDATA). The semantics of these events is self-explanatory.

3 XML2DB Mappings: Syntax and Semantics

In this section we formally define XML2DB mappings.

Syntax. The idea of XML2DB mappings is to treat the XML DTD as a grammar and extend the grammar by associating semantic rules with its productions. This is in the same spirit of Oracle XML DB [13] and IBM DB2 XML Extender [7], which specify XML shredding by annotating schema for XML data. When the XML data is parsed *w.r.t.* the grammar, it recursively invokes semantic rules associated with the productions of the grammar to select relevant data and generate SQL updates.

We now define XML2DB mappings. Let $D = (E, P, r)$ be a DTD and R be a relational schema consisting of relation schemas $R_1, \ldots, R_n$. An XML2DB mapping $\sigma : D \rightarrow R$ takes as input an XML document T of D, and returns an SQL group of inserts Δ which, when executed on a database I of R, yields an incremented instance ΔI of schema R. The mapping extracts relevant data from T and uses the data to construct tuples to be inserted into I. More specifically, σ is specified as follows.

• For each relation schema R_i of R, σ defines a *relation variable* Δ_{R_i}, which is to hold the set of tuples to be inserted into an instance I_i of R_i. The set Δ_{R_i} is initially empty and is gradually incremented during the parsing of the XML document T.

• For each element type A in E, σ defines a semantic attribute $\$A$ whose value is either a relational tuple of a fixed arity and type, or a special value $\top$ (denoting $\$r$ at the root r) or $\bot$ (denoting undefined); intuitively, $\$A$ extracts and holds relevant data from the input XML document that is to be inserted into the relational database I of R. As will be seen shortly, $\$A$ is used to pass information top-down during the evaluation of σ.

• For each production $p = A \rightarrow \alpha$ in D, σ specifies a set of semantic rules, denoted by $rule(p)$. These rules specify two things: (a) how to compute the value of the semantic attribute $\$B$ of B children of an A element for each child type B in α, (b) how to increment the set in Δ_{R_i}; both $\$B$ and Δ_{R_i} are computed by using the semantic attribute $\$A$ and the PCDATA of text children of the A element (if any). More specifically, $rule(p)$ consists of a sequence of *assignment* and *conditional statements*:

$rule(p)$	:=	statements
statements	:=	ϵ | statement; statements
statement	:=	X := expression | if C then statements else statements

where ϵ denotes the empty sequence (*i.e.*, no semantic actions); and X is either a relation variable Δ_{R_i} or a semantic attribute $\$B$. The assignment statement has one of two forms. (a) $\$B := (x_1, \ldots, x_k)$, *i.e.*, tuple construction where x_i is either of the form $\$A.a$ (projection on the a field of the tuple-valued attribute $\$A$ of the A element), or val (B'), where B' is an element type in α such that it precedes B in α (*i.e.*, we enforce sideways information passing *from left to right*), B's production is of the form $B' \rightarrow$ PCDATA, and val (B') denotes the PCDATA (string) data of B' child. (b) $\Delta_{R_i} := \Delta_{R_i} \cup \{(x_1, \ldots, x_k)\}$, where $(x_1, \ldots, x_k)$ is a tuple as constructed above and in addition, it is required to have the same arity and type as specified by the schema R_i. The condition C is defined in terms of equality or string containment tests on atomic

Relational variables: $\Delta_{\text{course}}, \Delta_{\text{prereq}}, \Delta_{\text{student}}, \Delta_{\text{enroll}}$, with $\emptyset$ as their initial value.

Semantic rules:

db → course*
$course := ⊤;

course → cno, title, prereq, takenBy
if val (cno) contains 'CS' or ($course ≠ ⊥ and $course ≠ ⊤)
then $prereq := val (cno); $takenBy := val (cno);
$\Delta_{\text{course}} := \Delta_{\text{course}} \cup \{(\text{val (cno), val (title)})\}$;
if $course ≠ ⊤ and $course ≠ ⊥
then $\Delta_{\text{prereq}} := \Delta_{\text{prereq}} \cup \{(\text{\$course, val (cno)})\}$;
else $title := ⊥; $prereq := ⊥; $takenBy := ⊥;

prereq → course*
$course := $prereq;

takenBy → student*
$student := $takenBy;

student → ssn, name
if $student ≠ ⊥
then $\Delta_{\text{student}} := \Delta_{\text{student}} \cup \{(\text{val (ssn), val (name)})\}$;
$\Delta_{\text{enroll}} := \Delta_{\text{enroll}} \cup \{(\text{val (ssn), \$student})\}$;

(a) XML2DB mapping σ_0

Relational variables: $\Delta_{\text{course}}, \Delta_{\text{prereq}}, \Delta_{\text{student}}, \Delta_{\text{enroll}}$, with $\emptyset$ as their initial value.

Semantic rules:

db → course*
$course := ⊤;

course → cno, title, prereq, takenBy
$prereq := val (cno); $takenBy := val (cno);
$\Delta_{\text{course}} := \Delta_{\text{course}} \cup \{(\text{val (cno), val (title)})\}$;
if $course ≠ ⊤
then $\Delta_{\text{prereq}} := \Delta_{\text{prereq}} \cup \{(\text{\$course, val (cno)})\}$;

prereq → course*
$course := $prereq;

takenBy → student*
$student := $takenBy;

student → ssn, name
$\Delta_{\text{student}} := \Delta_{\text{student}} \cup \{(\text{val (ssn), val (name)})\}$;
$\Delta_{\text{enroll}} := \Delta_{\text{enroll}} \cup \{(\text{val (ssn), \$student})\}$;

(b) XML2DB mapping σ_1

Fig. 2. Example XML2DB mappings: storing part of (σ_0) and the entire (σ_1) the document

terms of the form val (B'), $\$A.a, \top, \bot$, and it is built by means of Boolean operators and, or and not, as in the standard definition of the selection conditions in relational algebra. The mapping σ is said to be *recursive* if the DTD D is recursive.

We assume that if p is of the form $A \to B^*$, $rule(p)$ includes a single rule $\$B := \$A$, while the rules for the B production select data in each B child. This does not lose generality as shown in the next example, in which a list of *student* data is selected.

Example 3.2. The mapping σ_0 described in Example 1.1 can be expressed as the XML2DB mapping $\sigma_0 : D_0 \to R_0$ in Fig. 2(a), which, given an XML document T of the DTD D_0 and a relational database I of the schema R_0, extracts all the CS courses, their prerequisites and their registered students from T, and inserts the data as tuples into I. That is, it generates $\Delta_{\text{course}}, \Delta_{\text{student}}, \Delta_{\text{enroll}}$ and Δ_{prereq}, from which SQL updates can be readily constructed. Note that a *course* element c is selected if either its *cno* contains 'CS' or an ancestor of c is selected; the latter is captured by the condition *($course ≠ ⊥* and *$course ≠ ⊤)*. The special value ⊥ indicates that the corresponding elements are not selected and do not need to be processed. Note that the rules for *takenBy* and *student* select the data of *all* student who registered for such courses. □

Semantics. We next give the operational semantics of an XML2DB mapping $\sigma : D \to R$ by presenting a conceptual evaluation strategy. This strategy aims just to illustrate the semantics; a more efficient evaluation algorithm will be given in the next section.

Given an input XML document (tree) T, $\sigma(T)$ is computed via a top-down depth-first traversal of T, starting from the root r of T. Initially, the semantic attribute $\$r$ of r is assigned the special value $\top$. For each element v encountered during the traversal, we do the following. (1) Identify the element type of v, say, A, and find the production $p = A \rightarrow P(A)$ from the DTD D and the associated semantic rules $rule(p)$ from the mapping σ. Suppose that the tuple value of the semantic attribute $\$A$ of v is t. (2) Execute the statements in $rule(p)$. This may involve extracting PCDATA value val (B') from some B' children, projecting on certain fields of the attribute t of v, and performing equality, string containment tests and Boolean operations, as well as constructing tuples and computing union of sets as specified in $rule(p)$. The execution of $rule(p)$ assigns a value to the semantic attribute $\$B$ of each B child of v if the assignment of $\$B$ is defined in $rule(p)$, and it may also increment the set Δ_{R_i}. In particular, if p is of the form $A \rightarrow B^*$, then each B child u of v is assigned the same value $\$B$. (3) We proceed to process each child u of v in the same way, by using the semantic attribute value of u. (4) The process continues until all the elements in T are processed. Upon the completion of the process, we return the values of relation variables $\Delta_{R_1}, \ldots, \Delta_{R_n}$ as output, each of which corresponds to an SQL insert. More specifically, for each Δ_i, we generate an SQL insert statement:

insert into R_i select * from Δ_{R_i}

That is, at most n SQL inserts are generated in total.

Example 3.3. Given an XML tree T as shown in Fig 1(b), the XML2DB mapping σ_0 of Example 3.2 is evaluated top-down as follows. (a) All the *course* children of the root of T are given $\top$ as the value of their semantic attribute \$*course*. (b) For each *course* element v encountered during the traversal, if either \$*course* contains 'CS' or it is neither $\perp$ nor $\top$, *i.e.*, v is either a CS course or a prerequisite of a CS course, the PCDATA of *cno* of v is extracted and assigned as the value of \$*title*, \$*prereq* and \$*takenBy*; moreover, the set Δ_{course} is extended by including a new tuple describing the course v. Furthermore, if \$*course* is neither $\top$ nor $\perp$, then Δ_{prereq} is incremented by adding a tuple constructed from \$*course* and val (*cno*), where \$*course* is the *cno* of c *inherited* in the top-down process. Otherwise the data in v is not to be selected and thus all the semantic attributes of its children are given the special value $\perp$. (c) For each *prereq* element u encountered, the semantic attributes of all the *course* children of u *inherit* the \$*prereq* value of u, which is in turn the *cno* of the *course* parent of u; similarly for *takenBy* elements. (d) For each *student* element s encountered, if \$*student* is not $\perp$, *i.e.*, s registered for either a CS course c or a prerequisite c of a CS course, the sets Δ_{student} and Δ_{enroll} are incremented by adding a tuple constructed from the PCDATA val (*ssn*), val (*name*) of s and the semantic attribute \$*student* of s; note that \$*student* is the *cno* of the course c. (e) After all the elements in T are processed, the sets Δ_{course}, Δ_{student}, Δ_{enroll} and Δ_{prereq} are returned as the output of $\sigma_0(T)$. □

Handling Recursion in a DTD. As shown by Examples 3.2 and 3.3 XML2DB mappings are capable of handling recursive DTDs. In general, XML2DB mappings handle recursion in a DTD following a data-driven semantics: the evaluation is determined by the input XML tree T at run-time, and it always *terminates* since T is finite.

Storing Part of an XML Document in Relations. As demonstrated in Fig. 2(a), users can specify in an XML2DB mapping what data they want from an XML document and store only the selected data in a relational database.

Shredding the Entire Document. XML2DB mappings also allow users to shred the entire input XML document into a relational database, as shown in Fig. 2(b). Indeed, for any XML document T of the DTD D_0 given in Example 1.1, the mapping σ_1 shreds the entire T into a database of the schema R_0 of Example 1.1.

Taken together, XML2DB mappings have several salient features. (a) They can be evaluated in a *single* traversal of the input XML tree T and it visits each node *only once*, even if the embedded DTD is recursive. (b) When the computation terminates it generates sets of tuples to be inserted into the relational database, from which SQL updates Δ can be readily produced. This allows users to update an existing relational database of a predefined schema. (c) The semantic attributes of children nodes *inherit* the semantic attribute of their parent; in other words, semantic attributes pass the information and control top-down during the evaluation. (d) XML2DB mappings are able to store either part of or the entire XML document in a relational database, in a *uniform framework*.

4 Evaluation of XML2DB Mappings

We next outline an algorithm for evaluating XML2DB mappings $\sigma : R \rightarrow D$ in parallel with SAX parsing, referred to as an *extended* SAX *parser*. Given an XML document T of the DTD D, the computation of $\sigma(T)$ is combined with the SAX parsing process of T.

The algorithm uses the following variables: (a) a relation variable Δ_{R_i} for each table R_i in the relational schema R; (b) a stack S, which is to hold a semantic attribute $\$A$ during the evaluation (parsing); and (c) variables X_j of string type, which are to hold PCDATA of text children of each element being processed, in order to construct tuples to be added to Δ_{R_i}. The number of these variables is bounded by the longest production in the DTD D, and the same string variables are repeatedly used when processing different elements. Recall the SAX events described in Section 2. The extended SAX parser incorporates the evaluation of σ into the processing of each SAX event, asbreakfollows.

• startDocument(). We push the special symbol $\top$ onto the stack S, as the value of the semantic attribute $\$r$ of the root r of the input XML document T.

• startElement(A, eventNo). When an A element v is being parsed, the semantic attribute $\$A$ of v is already at the top of the stack S. For each child u of v to be processed, we compute the semantic attribute $\$B$ of u based on the semantic rules for $\$B$ in $rule(p)$ associated with the production $p = A \rightarrow P(A)$; we push the value onto S, and proceed to process the children of u along with the SAX parsing process. If the production of the type B of u is $B \rightarrow$ PCDATA, the PCDATA of u is stored in a string variable X_j. Note that by the definition of XML2DB mappings, the last step is only needed when p is of the form $A \rightarrow B_1, \ldots, B_n$ or $A \rightarrow B_1 + \ldots + B_n$.

• endElement(A). A straightforward induction can show that when this event is encountered, the semantic attribute $\$A$ of the A element being processed is at the top of the stack S. The processing at this event consists of two steps. We first increment the set Δ_{R_i} by executing the rules for Δ_{R_i} in $rule(p)$, using the value $\$A$ and the PCDATA values stored in string variables. We then pop $\$A$ off the stack.

• text(s). We store PCDATA s in a string variable if necessary, as described above.

• endDocument(). At this event we return the relation variables Δ_{R_i} as the output of $\sigma(T)$, and pop the top of the stack off S. This is the last step of the evaluation of $\sigma(T)$.

Upon the completion of the extended SAX parsing process, we eliminate duplicates from relation variables Δ_{R_i}s, and convert Δ_{R_i} to SQL insert command Δ_is.

Example 4.4. We now revisit the evaluation of $\sigma_0(T)$ described in Example 3.3 using the extended SAX parser given above. (a) Initially, $\top$ is pushed onto the stack S as the semantic attribute \$*db* of the root *db* of the XML tree T; this is the action associated with the SAX event startDocument(). The extended SAX parser then processes the *course* children of *db*, pushing $\top$ onto S when each *course* child v is encountered, as the semantic attribute \$*course* of v. (b) When the parser starts to process a *course* element v, the SAX event startElement(course, eNo) is generated, and the semantic attribute \$*course* of v is at the top of the stack S. The parser next processes the *cno* child of v, extracting its PCDATA and storing it in a string variable X_j; similarly for *title*. It then processes the *prereq* child of u, computing \$*prereq* by means of the corresponding rule in $rule(course)$; similarly for the *takenBy* child of v. After all these children are processed and their semantic attributes popped off the stack, endElement(course) is generated, and at this moment the relation variables Δ_{course} and Δ_{prereq} are updated, by means of the corresponding rules in $rule(course)$ and by using \$*course* at the top of S as well as val (*cno*) and val (*title*) stored in string variables. After this step the semantic attribute \$*course* of v is popped off the stack. Similarly the SAX events for *prereq* and *takenBy* are processed. (c) When endDocument() is encountered, the sets Δ_{course}, Δ_{student}, Δ_{enroll} and Δ_{prereq} are returned as the output of $\sigma_0(T)$. □

Theorem 4.1. *Given an* XML *document* T *and an* XML2DB *mapping* $\sigma : D \to R$, *the extended* SAX *parser computes* $\sigma(T)$ *via a single traversal of* T *and in* $O(|T||\sigma|)$ *time, where* $|T|$ *and* $|\sigma|$ *are the sizes of* T *and* σ, *respectively.* □

5 Experimental Study

Our experimental study focuses on the scalability of our extended SAX parser, denoted by ESAX, which incorporates the XML2DB mapping evaluation. We conducted two sets of experiments: we ran ESAX and the original SAX parser (denoted by SAX) (a) on XML documents T of increasing sizes, and (b) on documents T with a fixed size but different shapes (depths or widths). Our experimental results showed (a) that ESAX is linearly scalable and has the same behavior as SAX, and (b) the performance of ESAX is only determined by $|T|$ rather than the shape of T. The experiments were conducted on a PC with a 1.40 Ghz Pentium M CPU and 512MB RAM, running Windows XP. Each experiment was repeated 5 times and the average is reported here; we do not show confidence interval since the variance is within 5%.

We built XML documents of the DTD of Fig. 1(a), using the Toxgene XML generator (http://www.cs.toronto.edu/tox/toxgene). We used two parameters, X_L and X_R, where X_L is the depth of the generated XML tree T, and X_R is the maximum number of children of any node in T. Together X_L and X_R determine the shape of T: the larger the X_L value, the deeper the tree; and the larger the X_R value, the wider the tree.

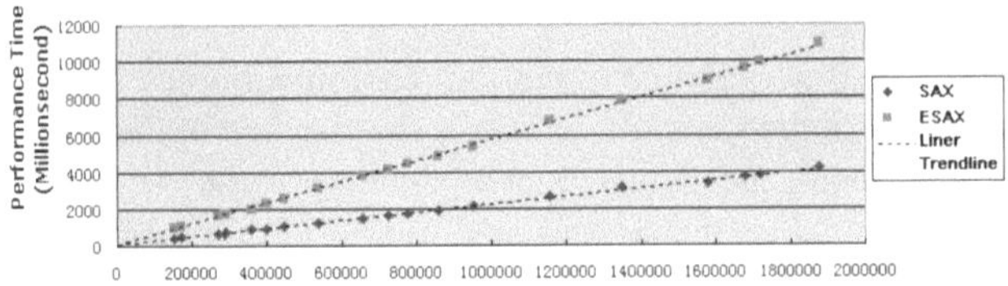

Fig. 3. Scalability with the size of XML document T: vary $|T|$

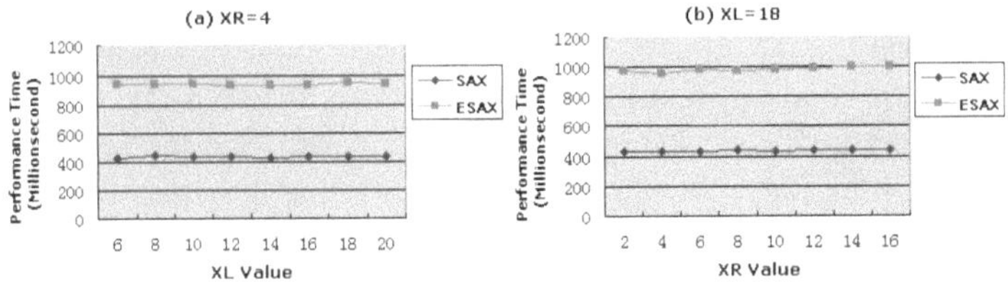

Fig. 4. Scalability with the shape of XML document T: vary X_L and X_R with a fixed $|T|$

Figure 3 shows the scalability of ESAX by increasing the XML dataset size from 153505 elements (3M) to 1875382 (39M). The time (in ms) reported for ESAX includes the parsing and evaluation time of XML2DB mapping. As shown in Fig. 3, ESAX is linearly scalable and behaves similarly to SAX, as expected. Furthermore, the evaluation of an XML2DB mapping does not incur a dramatic increase in processing time vs. SAX.

To demonstrate the impact of the shapes of XML documents on the performance of ESAX, we used XML documents T of a fixed size of 160,000 elements, while varying the height (X_L) and width (X_R) of T. Figure 4 (a) shows the elapsed time when varying X_L from 8 to 20 with $X_R = 4$, and Fig. 4(b) shows the processing time while varying X_R from 2 to 16 with $X_L = 12$. The results show that ESAX takes roughly the same amount of time on these documents. This verifies that the time-complexity of ESAX is solely determined by $|T|$ rather than the shape of T, as expected.

6 Related Work

Several approaches have been explored for using a relational database to store XML documents, either DTD-based [3,15,13,7] or schema-oblivious [6,14,10] (see [8] for a survey). As mentioned in section 1, except [10,7] these approaches map the entire XML document to a newly created database of a "canonical" relational schema, and are not capable of extending an existing database with part of the data from the document.

Microsoft SQL 2005 [10] supports four XML data-type methods QUERY(), VALUE(), EXIST() and NODES(), which take an XQuery expression as argument to retrieve parts of an XML instance. However, the same method is not able to shred the entire document into relations via a single pass of an XML document, in contrast to our uniform framework to store either the entire or part of an XML document. Furthermore, it does not support semantic-based tuple construction, *e.g.*, when constructing a tuple (a, b), it does not allow one to extract attribute b based on the extracted value of a, which is supported by XML2DB mappings via semantic-attribute passing. Both Oracle XML DB [13] and IBM DB2 XML Extender [7] use schema annotations to map either the entire or parts of XML instances to relations. While Oracle supports recursive DTDs, it cannot increment an existing database. Worse, when an element is selected, the entire element has to be stored. IBM employs user-defined *Document Access Definitions* (DADs) to map XML data to DB2 tables, but supports only fixed-length DTD recursion (see also [12] for upcoming XML support in DB2). Neither Oracle nor IBM supports semantic-based tuple construction, which is commonly needed in practice.

We now draw the analogy of XML2DB mappings to attribute grammars (see, *e.g.*, [5]). While the notion of XML2DB mappings was inspired by attribute grammars, it is quite different from attribute grammars and their previous database applications [11]. First, an attribute grammar uses semantic attributes and rules to constrain the parsing of strings, whereas an XML2DB mapping employs these to control the generation of database updates. Second, an attribute grammar outputs a parse tree of a string, whereas an XML2DB mapping produces SQL updates.

Closer to XML2DB mappings are the notion of AIGs [2] and that of structural schema [1], which are also nontrivial extensions of attribute grammars. AIGs are specifications for schema-directed XML integration. They differ from XML2DB mappings in that they generate XML trees by extracting data from relational sources. Furthermore, the evaluation of AIGs is far more involved than its XML2DB mapping counterpart. Structural schemas were developed for querying text files, by extending context-free grammars with semantic attributes. The evaluation of structural schemas is different from the SAX-parser extension of XML2DB mappings.

7 Conclusion

We have proposed a notion of XML2DB mappings that in a uniform framework, allows users to select either part of or an entire XML document and store it in an existing relational database of a predefined schema, as opposed to previous XML shredding approaches that typically shred the entire document into a newly created database of a new schema. Furthermore, XML2DB mappings are capable of supporting recursive DTDs and flexible tuple construction. We have also presented an efficient algorithm for evaluating XML2DB mappings based on a mild extension of SAX parsers. Our preliminary experimental results have verified the effectiveness and efficiency of our technique. This provides existing SAX parsers with immediate capability to support XML2DB mappings.

We are extending XML2DB mappings by incorporating (a) the support of SQL queries and (b) the checking of integrity constraints (*e.g.*, keys and foreign keys) on the underlying relational databases. We are also developing evaluation and optimization techniques to cope with and leverage SQL queries and constraints.

Acknowledgment. Wenfei Fan is supported in part by EPSRC GR/S63205/01, GR/T27433/01 and BBSRC BB/D006473/1. We thank Hamish Taylor for the helpful comments.

References

1. S. Abiteboul, S. Cluet, and T. Milo. Querying and updating the file. In *VLDB*, 1993.
2. M. Benedikt, C. Y. Chan, W. Fan, J. Freire, and R. Rastogi. Capturing both types and constraints in data integration. In *SIGMOD*, 2003.
3. P. Bohannon, J. Freire, J. Haritsa, M. Ramanath, P. Roy, and J. Siméon. Bridging the XML relational divide with LegoDB. In *ICDE*, 2003.
4. B. Choi. What are real DTDs like. In *WebDB*, 2002.
5. P. Deransart, M. Jourdan, and B. Lorho (eds). Attribute grammars. *LNCS*, 1988.
6. D. Florescu and D. Kossmann. Storing and querying XML data using an RDMBS. *IEEE Data Eng. Bull*, 1999.
7. IBM. DB2 XML Extender. *http://www-3.ibm.com/software/data/db2/extended/xmlext/.*
8. R. Krishnamurthy, R. Kaushik, and J. Naughton. XML-SQL query translation literature: The state of the art and open problems. In *Xsym*, 2003.
9. D. Megginson. SAX: A simple API for XML. *http://www.megginson.com/SAX/.*
10. Microsoft. XML support in Microsoft SQL server 2005, December 2005. *http://msdn.microsoft.com/library/en-us/dnsql90/html/sql2k5xml.asp/.*
11. F. Neven. Extensions of attribute grammars for structured document queries. In *DBPL*, 1999.
12. M. Nicola and B. Linden. Native XML support in DB2 universal database. In *VLDB*, 2005.
13. Oracle. Oracle database 10g release 2 XML DB technical whitepaper.
14. A. Schmidt, M. L. Kersten, M. Windhouwer, and F. Waas. Efficient relational storage and retrieval of XML documents. In *WebDB*, 2000.
15. J. Shanmugasundaram, K. Tufte, G. He, C. Zhang, D. DeWitt, and J. Naughton. Relational databases for querying XML documents: Limitations and opportunities. In *VLDB*, 1999.

A Context-Aware Preference Model for Database Querying in an Ambient Intelligent Environment

Arthur H. van Bunningen, Ling Feng, and Peter M.G. Apers

Centre for Telematics and Information Technology, University of Twente,
P.O. Box 217, 7500 AE Enschede, The Netherlands
{bunninge, ling, apers}@cs.utwente.nl

Abstract. Users' preferences have traditionally been exploited in query personalization to better serve their information needs. With the emerging ubiquitous computing technologies, users will be situated in an Ambient Intelligent (AmI) environment, where users' database access will not occur at a single location in a single context as in the traditional stationary desktop computing, but rather span a multitude of contexts like office, home, hotel, plane, etc. To deliver personalized query answering in this environment, the need for context-aware query preferences arises accordingly. In this paper, we propose a knowledge-based context-aware query preference model, which can cater for both *pull* and *push* queries. We analyze requirements and challenges that AmI poses upon such a model and discuss the interpretation of the model in the domain of relational databases. We implant the model on top of a traditional DBMS to demonstrate the applicability and feasibility of our approach.

1 Introduction

With the coming anytime/anywhere ubiquitous data access paradigm in an AmI environment, context plays an important role in information delivery and dissemination. Database and recommendation systems nowadays are more and more aware of the context while serving users' information needs. In this paper, we investigate user's query preferences in an AmI environment, taking their applicable contexts into account. Our design of the context-aware preference model is influenced and guided by the following AmI philosophies:

- *Smartness requirement.* The smartness requirement in an AmI environment implies reasoning and learning capabilities that the preference model must possess, calling for an inevitable knowledge ingredient. For example, a user may input a preference like *prefer a nearby restaurant when the weather is bad.* With the model, it should be able to infer the applicability of the preference no matter whether it rains or snows, since both are bad weather.
- *Proactiveness requirement.* Following the smartness requirement, the database systems in an AmI environment should proactively deliver anytime/anywhere useful information to their users. The designed context-aware query preference model should therefore provide sufficient flexibility and adaptiveness to the two access modes, namely *pull query* where users actively query databases to pull relevant information, and *push query* where the systems push proactively possibly relevant

S. Bressan, J. Küng, and R. Wagner (Eds.): DEXA 2006, LNCS 4080, pp. 33–43, 2006.

information to users (e.g., querying the background information about a person when s/he enters a room).

- *Closure requirement.* To support preference propagation and deduction, the model should preferably possess the closure property so that the output preference can serve as the input context of some other preferences. For instance, suppose a user has two preferences: "*prefer cheerful TV programs when having a bad mood*" and "*prefer channel 5 if looking for cheerful TV programs*" As a consequence, when this user has a bad mood, *cheerful TV programs on channel 5* will be the most preferable program alternatives for him/her.
- *Scalability requirement.* Performance is highly demanded at data management level to process real-time queries raised by different users anytime/anywhere in an AmI environment. The context-aware preference model must be easily interpreted and executed in a database world to achieve scalability.
- *Traceability requirement.* The behaviors of database querying systems in an AmI environment, and thus the preference model should be traceable by the users. In other words, it should be possible for a human to conveniently enter, view, and edit context-aware preferences in a way which is close to the world model of the users. An intuitive user-friendly interface for preference declaration is therefore needed.

In the following sections, we first review some closely related work in Section 2. We present our knowledge-based context modeling approach, followed by the context-aware query preference modeling using Description Logics in Section 3. We depict a framework for implanting this model on top of a traditional DBMS, and interpret the model in a relational database in Section 4. The implementation of the model in serving pushing queries is illustrated in Section 5. We conclude the paper in Section 6.

2 Related Work

The notion of preference query was first introduced to the database field in [1]. It extended the Domain Relational Calculus to express preferences for tuples satisfying certain logical conditions. Since its introduction, extensive investigation has been conducted, and two main lines of approaches have been formed in the literature to deal with users' preferences, namely, quantitative and qualitative [2]. The qualitative approach intends to directly specify preferences between the tuples in the query answer, typically using binary preference relations. An example preference relation is "*prefer one book tuple to another if and only if their ISBNs are the same and the price of the first is lower.*" These kinds of preference relations can be embedded into relational query languages through relational operators or special preference constructors, which select from their input the set of the most preferred tuples (e.g., winnow [2], PreferenceSQL BMO [3], and skyline [4]). The quantitative approach expresses preferences using scoring functions, which associate a numeric score with every tuple of the query. Then tuple t_1 is preferred to tuple t_2 if and only if the score of t_1 is higher than the score of t_2. A framework for expressing and combining such kinds of preference functions was provided in [5]. [6] presented a more rich preference model which can associate degrees of interest (like scores) with preferences over a database schema.

Recently, situated and context-aware preferences start to receive attentions due to the fact that user preferences do not always hold in general but may depend on underlying situations [7,8]. [7] used the ER model to model different situations. Each situation has an *id* and consists of one timestamp and one location. It can also have one or more influences (e.g., a personal and a surrounding influence). Such situations are linked with uniquely identified preferences through a m:n relation. An XML-based preference repository was developed to store and manage the situated preferences. [8] used a combination of context and non-context attribute-value pairs associated with a degree of interest to define a preference. The work reported in this paper distinguishes from these two studies in the following three aspects. First, our study targets at the Ambient Intelligent environment which has high demands on smartness, reasoning, proactiveness, traceability, etc. Driven by these requirements, we propose a knowledge-based context-aware preference model, where both contexts and preferences are treated in a uniform way using Description Logics. Second, we take both pull and push queries into consideration while designing our context-aware query preference model. Third, we interpret and implant this preference model upon a traditional DBMS.

3 A Knowledge-Based Context-Aware Query Preference Model

A context-aware query preference states, among a set of alternatives, a particular like or dislike for some of these alternatives under certain contexts, like "*prefer sporting TV programs when the user is dinning*", "*prefer TV programs of the human interest genre when the user is doing some free time activity with some friend(s) around*", etc. The term *context* here refers to the situation under which a database access happens. Our context-aware query preference model tightly couples a preference with its applicable contexts, and expresses both in a uniform way.

In the following, we describe our approach of modeling context, followed by the representation of context-aware query preferences.

3.1 Context Categorization and Modeling

We view context from two perspectives: *user-centric* and *environmental* [9]. Examples of user-centric contexts are: user's background (e.g., working area, friends, etc.), behavior (activity, intention, etc.), physiological state (temperature, heart rate, etc.), and emotional state (happy, sad, fear, etc.). Environmental contexts can be physical environment (e.g., location, time, humidity, etc.), social environment (e.g., traffic jam, surrounding people, etc.), and computational environment (e.g., surrounding devices, etc.).

In the literature, there exist several possibilities to model context. Most of them are surveyed in [10,11], where it is concluded that *ontology based languages* are preferable for context modeling. Driven by the reasoning/inference requirement as described in Section 1, we exploit a variant of Description Logics (DL) to represent context for several reasons. First, DL [12] is a (decidable) fragment of first order logic, and is especially suited for knowledge representation. It forms the basis of ontological languages such as OWL, which has been used to model context in [13]. Furthermore, there exist many tools for dealing with DL knowledge bases such as reasoners and editors. Finally, extensive research has been conducted to investigate the relationship between databases and DL, and map a DL knowledge base into database schemas [14].

As known, a DL knowledge base consists of a TBox and an ABox. The TBox (i.e., the vocabulary) contains assertions about *concepts* (e.g., Child, Female) and *roles* (e.g., hasRoom, hasActivity). The ABox contains assertions about *individuals* (e.g., ROOM3061). Concepts and roles can be either *atomic* or *constructed* using concept and role constructors *intersection* ($\sqcap$), *union* ($\sqcup$), and *complement* ($\neg$) (e.g., Child $\sqcap$ Female, hasRoom $\sqcap$ hasActivity). The *top concept* ($\top$) and *bottom concept* ($\bot$) denote respectively all individuals and no individuals. A role specific operator is the *role-inverse* which defines the inverse of a certain role (e.g., *roomOf* is the inverse of *hasRoom*, denoted as $hasRoom \equiv roomOf^{-1}$). Moreover, roles can have full and existential quantification (e.g., $\forall$ hasChild.Female denotes the individuals of whose children are all female, and $\exists$ hasChild.Female denotes the individuals having a female child). A *concept expression* contains a set of concepts and/or quantified roles which are connected via concept and role constructors. The basic inference on concept expressions in DL is *subsumption* $C \sqsubseteq D$, which is to check whether the concept denoted by D (the *subsumer*) is more general than the one denoted by C (the *subsumee*).

We use DL to describe a world model (i.e., ontology) upon which our context-aware query preferences can be founded. A small ontology example is given in Figure 1, where concepts are represented in CamelCase (e.g. *OfficeActivity*) , roles in lowerCamelCase (e.g. *hasRoom*), and individuals in all capital letters (e.g. *ROOM3061*).

We express diverse contexts of query preferences via DL concept expressions. For example, the DL concept expression $\{PETER\} \sqcap (\exists\, hasActivityType.FreeTimeActivity) \sqcap (\exists\, hasFriend(\exists\, hasRoom(\exists\, roomOf.\{PETER\})))$ describes such a context that user PETER is doing some free time activity with at least one friend in the same room.

$$
\begin{aligned}
Person &\sqsubseteq Thing \sqcap \forall\, hasRoom.Room \\
&\quad \sqcap \forall\, hasActivityType.ActivityType \\
&\quad \sqcap \forall\, hasFriend.Person \\
&\quad \sqcap \forall\, hasTvInterest.Genre \\
Room &\sqsubseteq Location \\
TVProgram &\sqsubseteq Thing \sqcap \exists\, hasGenre.Genre \\
hasRoom &\equiv roomOf^{-1}
\end{aligned}
\qquad
\begin{aligned}
ActivityType &\sqsubseteq Thing \\
FreeTimeActivity &\sqsubseteq ActivityType \\
Relaxing &\sqsubseteq FreeTimeActivity \\
Sporting &\sqsubseteq FreeTimeActivity \\
Location &\sqsubseteq Thing \\
Genre &\sqsubseteq Thing \\
hasTvInterest &\equiv tvInterestOf^{-1}
\end{aligned}
$$

Fig. 1. A simplified ontology example using DL

3.2 Context-Aware Query Preference Modeling

Beyond contexts, DL concept expressions also offer a natural way to convey information needs. For instance, the DL concept expression $TvProgram \sqcap (\exists\, hasGenre.\{HUMAN\text{-}INTEREST\})$ can be viewed as a query which selects all *TvProgram* individuals of the *HUMAN-INTEREST* genre. Therefore, in a similar fashion as context, we describe users' preferences through DL concept expressions. Formally, we define a **context-aware query preference** as a tuple of the form $(\mathcal{C}ontext, \mathcal{P}reference)$, where

$\mathcal{C}ontext$ and $\mathcal{P}reference$ are DL concept expressions. When a preference is applicable to any context, $\mathcal{C}ontext = \top$.

As an example, user PETER's context-aware query preference "*prefer TV programs of the human interest genre while doing some free time activity*" can be specified as:

$$Context : \{PETER\} \sqcap (\exists\, hasActivityType.FreeTimeActivity)$$
$$Preference : TvProgram \sqcap (\exists\, hasGenre.\{HUMAN\text{-}INTEREST\})$$

In comparison with this preference example, where the preferred genre (*HUMAN-INTEREST*) of TV programs is a constant, sometimes, a users preference varies with the concrete context. For instance, "*prefer TV programs of the common genre interests while with at least one friend in the same room*". In this case, the preferred genres of TV programs depend on whom the user is with at that moment. In this case, we use a variable v to denote it:

$$Context : \{PETER\} \sqcap (\exists\, hasFriend.((\exists\, hasRoom.(\exists\, roomOf.\{PETER\})) \sqcap v)$$
$$Preference : TvProgram \sqcap (\exists\, hasGenre.((\exists\, tvInterestOf.\{PETER\}) \sqcap (\exists\, tvInterestOf.v)))$$

We call this kind of preferences **variable context-aware query preference**, and the former **constant context-aware query preference**.

4 Implanting the Context-Aware Query Preference Model on Top of a DBMS

Context-aware query preferences can assist two kinds database accesses. 1) In the *pull* access mode, context-aware preferences can be used for query augmentation (e.g., enforcing the query constraint *genre="HUMAN-INTEREST"* to the user's query over TV programs when s/he is doing some free time activity with some friend(s) in the same room.) 2) In the *push* access mode, context-aware preferences can be used as query triggers (e.g., retrieving the background information about a person when s/he is nearby).

4.1 The Framework

Figure 2 shows the pull-push query execution framework equipped with the context-aware query preference model. It contains six major components. 1) The *context supplier* is responsible for supplying the current query context $Context_{cur}$. Some static contexts like user's background, friends, TV programs, etc. can be obtained from *context database*; while some dynamic contexts like user's location, emotion, traffic, surrounded people, etc. can be obtained from sensors or external service providers. 2) The *preference selector* selects from the *preference repository* relevant context-aware query preferences, if necessary by reasoning. A context-aware preference ($\mathcal{C}ontext$, $\mathcal{P}reference$) is related to a database access if ($Context_{cur} \sqsubseteq \mathcal{C}ontext$) and the preference $\mathcal{P}reference$ contains concepts which can be mapped to certain relations included in the user's query q_{user} (pull query) or included in the database (push query). 3) In the pull mode, the *query adaptor* augments user's query q_{user} with the relevant preference, and optimizes it further into q'_{user}. 4) In the push mode, the *query*

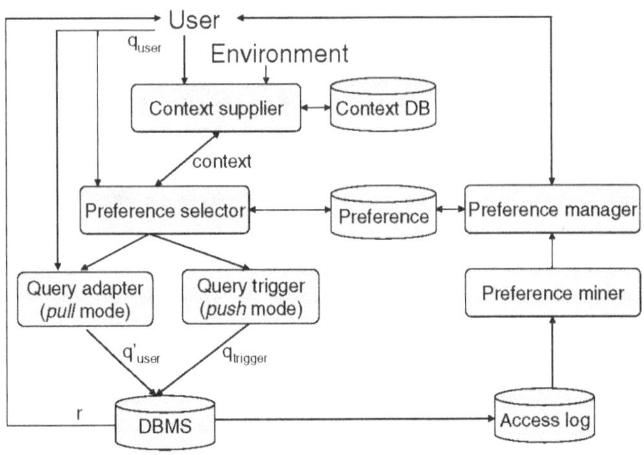

Fig. 2. The preference aware pull-push query framework

trigger proactively generates a query $q_{trigger}$ according to the preference, and sends it to the underlying DBMS for execution. 5) User-system interactions are recorded in the *access log*, from which the *preference miner* can discover users' context-aware preferences. Users can also directly input their preferences. 6) The *Preference manager* is responsible for storing, maintaining, and managing users' context-aware preferences.

4.2 Explicating the Context-Aware Query Preferences in a Database World

To integrate context-aware preferences with database queries, we need to provide a way which can explicate context-aware query preferences (including $\mathcal{C}ontext$ DL concept expression and $\mathcal{P}reference$ DL concept expression) in a database world[1].

Since the basic elements of DL are concepts and roles, we propose to view each concept as a table, which uses the concept name as the table name and has one *ID* attribute. The tuples of the table correspond to all the individuals of the concept. A virtual table *TOPTABLE* contains all the individuals in the domain. Similarly, we view each role as a table, with the role name as its table name and containing two attributes *SOURCE* and *DESTINATION*. For each tuple of the table, the role relates the *SOURCE* individual with the *DESTINATION* individual. Figure 3 gives examples of this method.

We adapt the approach of [15] to express DL concept expressions using SQL queries (Table 1, where C, D, E are DL concepts, R is a DL role, and a is a DL individual).

An important remark here is that we provide a uniform tabular view towards both static and dynamic contexts, despite the later (e.g., location, surrounding people, etc.) must be acquired real-time from external sources/services like sensor networks. This is in line with the efforts of the sensornet community which has embraced declarative

[1] We focus on the relational data model in this study.

Person

ID
ERIC
PETER
MAARTEN
...

Room

ID
ROOM3061
ROOM4061
...

TVProgram

ID
OPRAH
24
VOYAGER
...

Relaxing

ID
READING
SLEEPING
PLAYPIANO
...

hasActivityType

SOURCE	DESTINATION
ERIC	READING
PETER	SLEEPING
MAARTEN	PLAYPIANO
...	...

hasTvInterest

SOURCE	DESTINATION
ERIC	HUMANINTEREST
PETER	HUMANINTEREST
MAARTEN	SCIFI
...	...

hasFriend

SOURCE	DESTINATION
ERIC	PETER
PETER	ERIC
PETER	MAARTEN
...	...

hasRoom

SOURCE	DESTINATION
PETER	ROOM3061
ERIC	ROOM3061
MAARTEN	ROOM4061
...	...

hasGenre

SOURCE	DESTINATION
OPRAH	HUMANINTEREST
24	THRILLER
VOYAGER	SCIFI
...	...

Fig. 3. Role and concept tables

Table 1. Mapping DL concept expressions to SQL query expressions

DL	SQL
C	SELECT ID FROM C
a	VALUES ('a')
$\top$	(SELECT ID FROM TOPTABLE)
$\bot$	NULL
$\neg D$	(SELECT ID FROM TOPTABLE) EXCEPT (SELECT ID FROM D)
$D \sqcap E$	(SELECT ID FROM D) INTERSECT (SELECT ID FROM E)
$D \sqcup E$	(SELECT ID FROM D) UNION (SELECT ID FROM E)
$\exists R.D$	SELECT R.SOURCE FROM R WHERE R.DESTINATION IN (SELECT ID FROM D)
$\forall R.D$	(SELECT ID FROM TOPTABLE) EXCEPT (SELECT R.SOURCE FROM R WHERE DESTINATION IN ((SELECT ID FROM TOPTABLE) EXCEPT (SELECT ID FROM D)))

queries as a key programming paradigm for large sets of sensors [16]. Here, we take the SQL query language as a uniform interface to the contexts. Another reason for doing this is that AmI imposes the need for storing context histories, which can be explored later for analysis purpose to achieve smartness [17].

With the mapping mechanism in Table 1, we can construct an SQL query for the DL concept expression $\mathcal{C}ontext$ in ($\mathcal{C}ontext$, $\mathcal{P}reference$). A non-empty query result implies that the current context includes/complies with $\mathcal{C}ontext$. The associated $\mathcal{P}reference$ is then activated for either query adaptation (when a user's pull query contains table(s) which is/are specified in $\mathcal{P}reference$) or query trigger (where $\mathcal{P}reference$ is translated into SQL as a proactive push query).

As an example, suppose a user raises a pull query for TV programs.

```
SELECT ID FROM TvProgram
```

The context-aware preference

$$Context : \{PETER\} \sqcap (\exists hasFriend.(\exists hasRoom.(\exists roomOf.\{PETER\})))$$
$$Preference : TvProgram \sqcap (\exists hasGenre.\{HUMAN\text{-}INTEREST\})$$

contains a concept *TvProgram* which appears in the query. Its *Context* expression is translated straightforward into:

```
SELECT * FROM ((VALUES ('PETER'))
INTERSECT
  (SELECT hasFriend.SOURCE FROM hasFriend
   WHERE hasFriend.DESTINATION IN
      (SELECT hasRoom.SOURCE FROM hasRoom
       WHERE hasRoom.DESTINATION IN
         (SELECT roomOf.SOURCE FROM roomOf
          WHERE roomOf.DESTINATION IN (VALUES ('PETER')))
   ))) AS contexttable
```

which can then be optimized into:

```
SELECT *
FROM hasFriend, hasRoom, roomOf
WHERE hasFriend.SOURCE = 'PETER' AND
      hasFriend.DESTINATION = hasRoom.SOURCE AND
      hasRoom.DESTINATION = roomOf.SOURCE AND
      roomOf.DESTINATION = 'PETER'
```

Note that to execute the above query, some reasoning is needed based on the knowledge that *roomOf* is the inverse of *hasRoom*, and *FreeTimeActivity* embraces *Relaxing*, *Sporting*, etc.

When the query returns a non-empty result, the original pull query will be augmented with the additional constraint in the WHERE clause:

```
SELECT ID FROM TvProgram
WHERE ID IN
  (SELECT hasGenre.SOURCE FROM hasGenre WHERE hasGenre.DESTINATION IN
         (VALUES ('HUMAN INTEREST')))
```

5 Implementation

We implement the context-aware preference model by creating a plugin for Protégé [2] (a free open source ontology editor and knowledge-base framework) and apply the model to *push* queries on top of DB2 DBMS through DB2 triggers.

The plugin enables one to define the world model (ontology), including the context and preference notions. By combining both context and preference DL concept expressions, context-aware query preferences can then be constructed and further stored in an OWL-based knowledge base. This plugin can also facilitate the generation of the corresponding relational database schema based on the ontology and preferences. A screenshot of inputing a preference's applicable context DL expression is shown in Figure 4.

A context-aware query preference may trigger a push query proactively. For example, consider a preference "*retrieving the TV interest of the person when s/he enters room ROOM3061*"

$$\textit{Context}: \{v\} \sqcap \exists\, \textit{hasRoom}.\{\textit{ROOM}3061\}$$
$$\textit{Preference}: \exists\, \textit{tvInterestOf}.v$$

[2] http://protege.stanford.edu

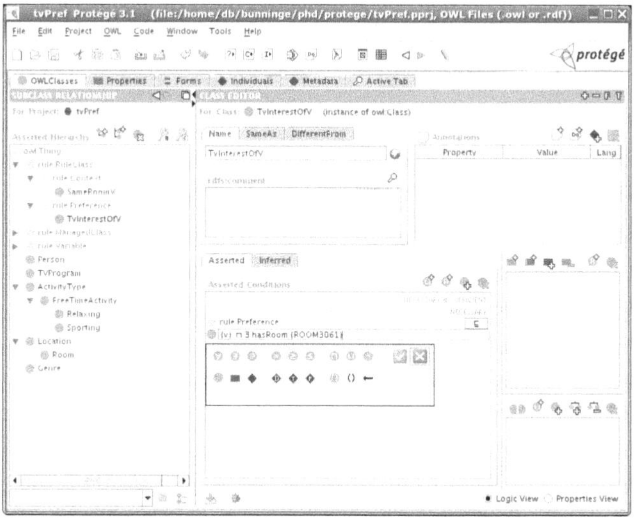

Fig. 4. Screenshot of inputting a preference's context expression

A DB2 query trigger can be created as follows (Figure 5):

```
CREATE TRIGGER queryTvInterest AFTER INSERT ON hasRoom
REFERENCING NEW AS n FOR EACH ROW
  WHEN (n.DESTINATION IN VALUES ('ROOM3061'))
    SELECT SOURCE
    FROM   tvInterestOf
    WHERE  DESTINATION = n.SOURCE
```

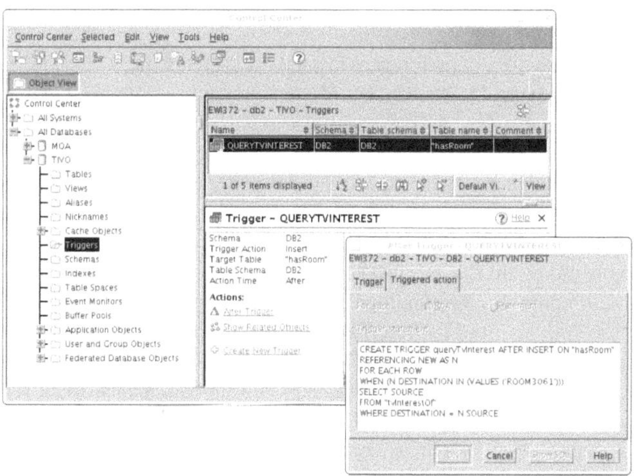

Fig. 5. The trigger in DB2

According to the example database schema in Figure 3, the query result will include *HUMAN-INTEREST*.

6 Conclusion

In this paper, we presented a context-aware query preference model for personalized information delivery and dissemination in an AmI environment. Revisiting the challenges raised by AmI, we adopted a knowledge-based approach to facilitate reasoning/inference (smartness requirement). The natural correspondence between DL concept expressions and data requests ensures the applicability of the model to both pull and push queries (proactiveness requirement). Preferences and associated applicable contexts are treated uniformly through DL concept expressions (closure requirement). Interpreting the knowledge-based preference model into a database world enables to address the scalability requirement. Through user-defined preferences, we can achieve the traceability requirement. We implanted the model on top of a DB2 DBMS and created a Protégé plugin was for defining, storing, and managing the context-aware preferences, and applying them to database queries.

Of course there remains much more to be done. Next to obvious directions, such as testing the scalability of the approach on realistic data sets and analyzing the expressive power of the model, we are currently investigating the uncertainty problem due to the imprecise context measurement and its impact on the context-aware query preference model.

References

1. Lacroix, M., Lavency, P.: Preferences; putting more knowledge into queries. In: VLDB '87. (1987) 217–225
2. Chomicki, J.: Preference formulas in relational queries. ACM Trans. Database Syst. **28**(4) (2003) 427–466
3. Kießling, W.: Foundations of preferences in database systems. In: VLDB '02. (2002) 311–322
4. Börzsönyi, S., Kossmann, D., Stocker, K.: The skyline operator. In: ICDE '01. (2001) 421–430
5. Agrawal, R., Wimmers, E.: A framework for expressing and combining preferences. In: SIGMOD '00. (2000) 297–306
6. Koutrika, G., Ioannidis, Y.: Personalized queries under a generalized preference model. In: ICDE '05. (2005) 841–852
7. Holland, S., Kießling, W.: Situated preferences and preference repositories for personalized database applications. In: ER '04. (2004) 511–523
8. Stefanidis, K., Pitoura, E., Vassiliadis, P.: On supporting context-aware preferences in relational database systems. In: First International Workshop on Managing Context Information in Mobile and Pervasive Environments (MCMP'2005). (2005)
9. Feng, L., Apers, P., Jonker, W.: Towards context-aware data management for ambient intelligence. In: DEXA '04. (2004) 422–431
10. Strang, T., Linnhoff–Popien, C.: A context modeling survey. In: Workshop on Advanced Context Modelling, Reasoning and Management. (2004)
11. van Bunningen, A.: Context aware querying - challenges for data management in ambient intelligence. Technical Report TR-CTIT-04-51, University of Twente, P.O. Box 217 (2004)

12. Baader, F., Calvanese, D., McGuinness, D., Nardi, D., Patel-Schneider, P., eds.: The Description Logic Handbook Cambridge University Press (2003)
13. Chen, H., Finin, T., Joshi, A.: The soupa ontology for pervasive computing. In: Ontologies for Agents: Theory and Experiences. Springer. (2005)
14. Borgida, A.: Description logics in data management. IEEE TKDE **7**(5) (1995) 671–682
15. Borgida, A., Brachman, R.: Loading data into description reasoners. In: SIGMOD '93. (1993) 217–226
16. Deshpande, A., Guestrin, C., Madden, S., Hellerstein, J., Hong, W.: Model-driven data acquisition in sensor networks. In: VLDB '04. (2004) 588–599
17. First international workshop on exploiting context histories in smart environments (ECHISE). (2005)

ANDROMEDA: Building e-Science Data Integration Tools

Víctor Cuevas-Vicenttín, José Luis Zechinelli-Martini, and Genoveva Vargas-Solar*

Research Center of Information and Automation Technologies, UDLAP
Ex-hacienda Sta. Catarina Mártir s/n, San Andrés Cholula, México
* National Council on Scientific Research (CNRS), LSR-IMAG,
BP 72 38402 Saint-Martin d'Hères, France
{joseluis.zechinelli, victor.cuevasv}@udlap.mx,
Genoveva.Vargas@imag.fr

Abstract. This paper presents ANDROMEDA (Astronomical Data Resources Mediation), an XML-based data mediation system that enables transparent access to astronomical data sources. Transparent access is achieved by a global view that expresses the requirements of a community of users (i.e., astronomers) and data integration mechanisms adapted to astronomical data characteristics. Instead of providing an ad hoc mediator, ANDROMEDA can be configured for giving access to different data sources according to user requirements (data types, content, data quality, and provenance). ANDROMEDA can be also adapted when new sources are added or new requirements are specified. Furthermore, in ANDROMEDA the data integration process is done in a distributed manner, taking advantage of the available computing resources and reducing data communication costs.

Keywords: data and information integration, XML query processing, distributed databases, data mediation.

1 Introduction

In recent years, there has been a prodigious increase in the quantity of available data for astronomical research. Extended surveys like 2dF, SDSS, 2MASS, VIRMOS, and DEEP2 are making available huge amounts of high quality data covering distinct wavelengths (x-ray, optical, infrared, radio). In the years to come, astronomers will be able to generate calibrated data far more rapidly than they can process and analyze them. Consequently, the need arises for tools and applications that will help them to deal with these vast amounts of valuable data.

The complexity associated with the large size and the wide wavelength coverage nature of these databases will be augmented by the existence of measurement errors, deviations and tendencies in the data. Still, the greatest difficulty is the absence of homologation between the different databases. Each one has its own set of parameters and its own access tools, which makes the cross match between them a significantly difficult task [12].

Virtual Observatory (VO) projects have emerged to develop solutions to the growing burden of the large amounts of data. The VO is an integrated facility that links the vast astronomical archives and databases around the world, together with analysis tools

S. Bressan, J. Küng, and R. Wagner (Eds.): DEXA 2006, LNCS 4080, pp. 44 – 53, 2006.

and computational services. Several VO projects are now funded through national and international programs, and many of them work together under the International Virtual Observatory Alliance (IVOA) to share expertise and develop common standards and infrastructures for data exchange and interoperability [4]. Thanks to VO projects, it will be possible to access online a detailed sky map or object class catalogue instead of relying on restricted and expensive observational facilities. Query engines will become more sophisticated, providing a uniform interface to all these datasets [9].

Driven by this vision, the objective of our work is to provide data integration mechanisms that can help astronomers to avoid the tedious task of manual data integration. Such mechanisms can be tuned for accessing specific collections of data sources according to different information requirements. Therefore, inspired in [1, 5, 7] we propose an approach for automatically generating mediation queries and applying the necessary transformations for integrating astronomical data. This paper presents our approach for integrating astronomical data and the design and implementation of ANDROMEDA (Astronomical Data Resources Mediation).

The remainder of this paper is organized as follows. Section 2 describes ANDROMEDA, its architecture, data sources, and implementation issues. Section 3 introduces our approach for integrating astronomical data. Section 4 presents an experimental validation that we conducted with real astronomical data. Section 5 compares related works with our solution. Finally, Section 6 concludes the paper and discusses future work.

2 ANDROMEDA

ANDROMEDA is an XML based astronomical distributed data mediation system for integrating astronomical data sources used in the Mexican Virtual Observatory at INAOE (National Institute of Astrophysics, Optics, and Electronics). Users specify their information needs through a mediation schema created with their expert knowledge through a multiple choice interface [3] which is then transformed into the XML Schema language. The mediation schema contains the data elements of interest that should be retrieved from one or several of the astronomical data sources. Currently, ANDROMEDA only supports spatial search queries expressed by specifying the right ascension and declination coordinates of the centre of a circular area in the celestial sphere, the radius of the circle, and the data sources of interest. The data corresponding to all the astronomical objects (i.e. stars or galaxies) found in such area are retrieved. The coordinates are given in decimal format according to the J2000 epoch convention and the radius in arc minutes, via a web interface. ANDROMEDA has been implemented in Java and relies on SAXON 8.0-B for executing XQuery expressions.

2.1 Architecture

Figure 1 illustrates the general architecture of ANDROMEDA. The system consists of a series of cooperating nodes of equal capabilities. In turn, each instance of ANDROMEDA deployed in a particular node follows the wrapper-mediator architecture [13]. In this architecture, a mediator provides a uniform interface to query integrated views of heterogeneous information sources while wrappers provide local views of data sources in a global data model [5].

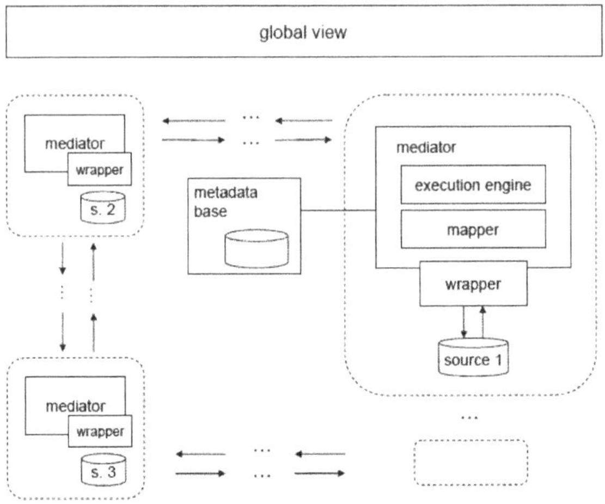

Fig. 1. ANDROMEDA general architecture

The current prototype version of ANDROMEDA enables access to three data sources: Sky Server photometric data [10], Two Micron All Sky Survey [11] photometric data, and Sky Server spectrographic data[1]. All of these are public databases that provide an HTML form in which the user can specify an area of the sky of interest; the results can be obtained in several formats such as HTML, text, and XML. Each of these databases is accessed via a specific wrapper that retrieves the results in XML and applies XSL transformations to them; in order to present a local view, referred to as exported schema, to the mediator.

The ANDROMEDA mediator adopts the semi-structured data model as pivot model, using XML and its related standards. It gives a global view of a set of data sources while making transparent their heterogeneity by automating data integration. The mediator receives a spatial search query ought to be responded in terms of the mediation schema. It dispatches the query to the local data sources, retrieves partial results and integrates them. The final result is in accordance to the given user requirements as expressed in the mediation schema.

ANDROMEDA is designed in such a way that different machines can have an instance of the mediator and cooperate in order to answer a query. This allows taking advantage of the locality of data sources to reduce communication costs as well as performing pipelined parallel execution, thereby achieving better QoS in terms of resource utilization and response time.

2.2 Query Execution

When a query is received on a particular node, an evaluation plan is generated to execute it. This plan consists of a tree of join nodes that successively perform a spatial

[1] Although both, the photometric and spectrographic data of the Sky Server [10] are accessible by a single interface, for validation purposes we considered them as separate data sources.

join procedure and structural transformations to integrate the data of its children in accordance to the mediation schema; as well as scan and mapping operators at the leaves that obtain the data from the sources. The root node represents the information desired by the user that contains the data from all of the data sources of interest.

The query plan is evaluated by an execution engine following the iterator model. Scan operators retrieve data from wrappers, and then mapping operators transform these data into their corresponding mapping schema. The mapping schema is an intermediate schema that presents the data of an exported schema in a structure that resembles as close as possible that of the mediation schema. The `Mapper` module creates the associated mapping schemata and mapping queries for each of the registered sources according to the mediation schema.

The data items manipulated by the iterators are DOM trees, each one representing an astronomical object. Using a technique described in the next section, the join nodes generate the identifiers necessary to perform a hash join on the data from different sources. The transformation of mapped data into the mediation schema also occurs at the join nodes, which rely on an algorithm [3] that manipulates the nodes to reorganize them to adhere to the mediation schema.

When ANDROMEDA is deployed on different machines, each of which contains a data source, the query plan can be evaluated in a distributed manner. In this case send and receive operators are added to the query plan and each operator is assigned a machine for its execution, communication is performed by sockets. The scheduling of the operators is driven by data locality, scans are assigned to the machines where the relevant data resides and joins are assigned to the machine of the larger input. This distributed evaluation strategy in conjunction with the iterator model, which enables pipelined parallelism, allows reducing computation time for intensive queries.

3 Astronomical Data Integration

The key aspect in ANDROMEDA is the automatic generation of mediation queries for integrating data (populating completely or partially de mediation schema) based on metadata relating the sources and the mediation schema. Such metadata are essential during the integration process. The automation of the integration process is especially beneficial as the number of data sources increases, relieving the user of the burden of performing manual integration. In our approach, astronomical data integration is executed in three phases:

- Identify for each data source which of its data elements are relevant, i.e., useful to populate the mediation schema. The relevant elements can be found provided it is established a priori which elements in the exported schemata correspond to elements in the mediation schema. The result of this first phase is a series of couples `<mapping schema, intentional specification>`. Each couple associates a mapping schema (expressed as a tree) with its intentional specification expressed as an XQuery statement, which allows transforming a document from the exported into the mapping schema.
- Apply matching operations to the mapped instances of the different sources to determine when they represent the same astronomical object, deriving groups of instances encompassing all of the desired data elements.

- Transform these instances encompassing the data from the various mapping schemata into entities that adhere to and populate the mediation schema. This can be done by generating a mediation query, expressed as an XQuery statement, which intentionally expresses the content of the mediation schema in terms of mapped sources.

3.1 Mapping Schemata and Queries Generation

The objective of this phase is to identify for each exported schema a *mapping schema* (i.e., the set of nodes that are relevant for populating the mediation schema) and to compute an XQuery expression that specifies how to transform data from the exported schema to the *mapping schema*. Data integration is possible as long as meta-information describing the semantic correspondences[2] between data sources and mediation schemas (attribute equivalence) is available. Then mediation query expressions can be applied in order to populate the mediation schema.

For example, consider the exported and mediation schemata presented in Figure 2. The tree on the top represents the mediation schema, while the exported schema corresponding to the Sky Server spectrographic data source is located at the bottom. The dashed lines represent semantic correspondences between elements.

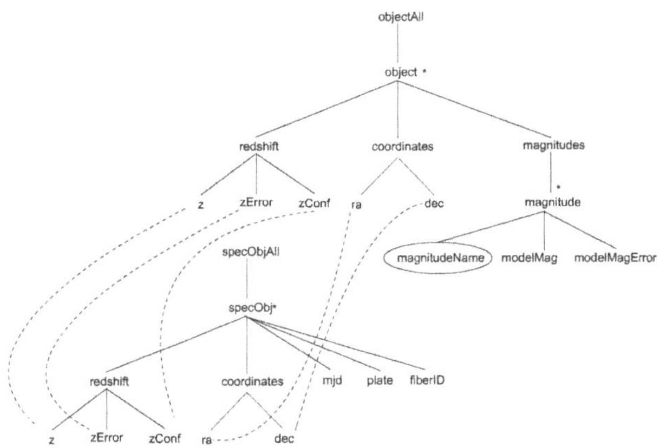

Fig. 2. Mediation and exported schemata

In order to find the relevant nodes in an exported schema we perform an algorithm consisting of two phases. First, the mediation schema tree is traversed in preorder to find all the nodes that have a semantic correspondence with a node in the exported schema or that are `no-text` nodes. These nodes are used to create a new tree with a structure resembling that of the mediation schema. Next, it is necessary to eliminate all the remaining `no-text` leaves of the tree that do not have semantic correspondences with nodes in the mediation schema. This is done by a procedure based on a postorder traversal of the new tree. Once completing its second phase the algorithm yields the schema tree presented in Figure 3.

[2] A semantic correspondence establishes a relationship between two elements that refer to the same object of the real world.

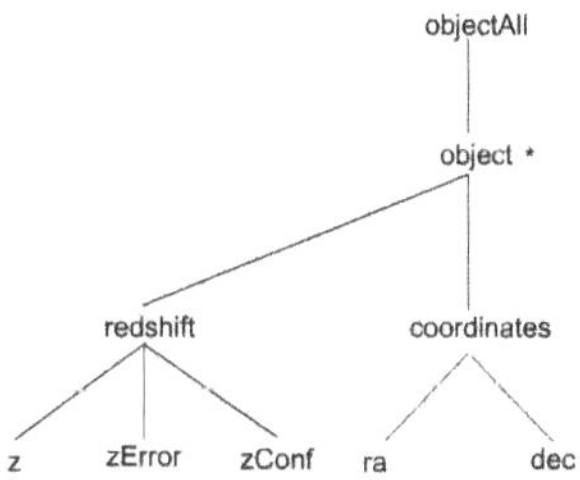


```
<objectAll>{
   for $var1 in doc("SkyServerSpectraData.xml")
   /specObjAll/specObj return
   <object>
      <redshift>
<zConf>{$var1/redshift/zConf/text()}</zConf>
         <zError>{$var1/redshift/zErr/text()}</zError>
            <z>{$var1/redshift/z/text()}</z>
      </redshift>
      <coordinates>
            <dec>{$var1/coordinates/dec/text()}</dec>
            <ra>{$var1/coordinates/ra/text()}</ra>
      </coordinates>
   </object>
}</objectAll>
```

Fig. 3. Final Sky Server spectrographic data mapping schema

Finally, this mapping schema tree is traversed for creating its intentional description as an XQuery expression. The algorithm used to generate this expression is presented in [3] along with the algorithm for obtaining the mapping schema tree. The derived mapping XQuery expression is shown in Figure 3.

3.2 Matching Operations

Having a mapping schema and its associated XQuery statement for each source, it is necessary to determine when the instances from different sources represent the same astronomical object in order to be able to integrate them. In the case of astronomical data sources, usually no universal identifiers are available for uniquely identifying a particular object (e.g. star or galaxy). So in our solution we consider a spatial join, in which entries of the same object are identified in different data sources based on their position (right ascension and declination coordinates).

Due to the variability on the position measured by each survey, which is worsened by the different error magnitudes of each survey, object positions are approximate and thus the same object can have different positions in different data sources. To overcome these discrepancies, the mediator performs a spatial join procedure based on the Hierarchical Triangular Mesh (HTM) [6].

Fig. 4. The Hierarchical Triangular Mesh subdivision scheme

The HTM (see Figure 4) is the indexing structure used in the SDSS Science Archive to partition the data by location on the celestial sphere. The HTM divides the surface of the unit sphere into spherical triangles in a hierarchical scheme in which the subdivisions have roughly equal areas. This recursive subdivision scheme allows generating ids for triangles of increasingly smaller areas that correspond to higher depths in the subdivision scheme. Given the coordinates of an object, its corresponding HTM id at a given depth can be efficiently computed and used as a foreign key with an acceptable precision degree. Thus the problem is reduced to a traditional join and any of the existing techniques can be applied for its evaluation.

3.3 Transformation of Mapped Instances into the Mediation Schema

The objective of this phase is to take the instances from the different mapped sources identified as representing the same physical object, and transform their structure to create a single entity in accordance with the mediation schema. The result of this phase is a collection of instances that populate the mediation schema. This is achieved by generating an XQuery expression that specifies the mediation schema intention. The complete transformation algorithm is presented in [3].

We should point out that when the data elements from the different mapped sources are integrated, not all of the elements should be handled the same way. The *coordinates* elements, for example, require special considerations; since the same astronomical object does not have exactly the same position in different data sources. In order to provide a global view over the data, each object needs to be associated with singular coordinate values. This is done by a simple transformation function which computes the average of the values of the object's position for all the involved sources. Furthermore, multi-valued nodes (e.g. *magnitude* elements) from different sources should be grouped together in order to respect the syntax of the mediation schema. The generated mediation XQuery expression for the integration of the exported schemata of the Sky Server photometric and Sky Server spectrographic data sources according to the mediation schema shown in Figure 2 follows:

```
<objectAll>{
for $var1 in
doc("SkyServerPhotoMappedData.xml")/objectAll/object
for $var2 in   doc("SkyServerSpectraMappedData.xml")/objectAll/object
where ( andromedaf:distance(
number($var1/coordinates/ra/text()),
number($var1/coordinates/dec/text()),
number($var2/coordinates/ra/text()),
number($var2/coordinates/dec/text()) ) < 0.08 )
return
   <object>
      <magnitudes>
         {for $var3 in $var1/magnitudes/magnitude
          return $var3}
      </magnitudes>
      <coordinates>
         <ra>{(number($var1/coordinates/ra/text()) +
            number($var2/coordinates/ra/text()) div 2}
         </ra>
         <dec>{(number($var1/coordinates/dec/text()) +
           number($var2/coordinates/dec/text())
           div 2}
         </dec>
      </coordinates>
      <redshift>
         <zConf>{$var2/redshift/zConf/text()}</zConf>
         <zError>
            {$var2/redshift/zError/text()}
         </zError>
         <z>{$var2/redshift/z/text()}</z>
      </redshift>
   </object>
}</objectAll>
```

The transformations performed by the previous XQuery expression can be alternatively achieved on a one by one basis by the means of operators that manipulate the data structures associated with the instances. The latest version of our system, described in Section 2, follows this approach. This provides advantages such as flexibility to evaluate the query in a distributed manner and using algorithms well suited for this particular scenario.

4 Experimentation

We validated ANDROMEDA with a realistic experiment that consists of a list of objects in the SDSS of particular relevance to the INAOE. The objective was to obtain the data for each of these objects available from both Sky Server and 2MASS. For the spatial join procedure, we used an HTM depth of 16 corresponding approximately to 0.0014 degrees (aprox. 5 seconds of arc) side length as was suggested. Since the positions of the objects in the SDSS were given, we only needed to give a radius similar to the spatial join tolerance itself. In this case we used a radius of 0.1 arc minutes. For the list containing 409 objects, matches were found for 322 of them, and within these 322 objects, multiple possible matches were found for 71 objects. The total execution time was approximately 20 minutes.

In addition, to determine the global query execution time of our solution we tried to integrate as much objects as possible from all three of the incorporated data sources by defining increasingly larger regions. The evaluation was done in a Dell Inspiron 8600, Intel Pentium M 1.50GHz, 512MB RAM (the same as for the previous experiment). The first observation is that execution time increases polynomially with respect to the number of objects to be integrated.

The statistics concerning this experiment are summarized in Figure 5. For a 2 arc minutes radius, results contain respectively 508 objects from Sky Server photometric (139,983 bytes), 22 objects from Two Mass (6,595 bytes) and 2 from Sky Server spectrographic (555 bytes). Both of these last two objects could be integrated (matches were found in the other surveys). The largest radius that could be processed under the specified conditions was 18 arc minutes, representing 60 integrated objects (96,570 bytes). Our execution time is reasonable even if it will be penalizing for

radius (arcmin)	time (msec)	time (sec)	retrieved objects				file sizes (bytes)			
			SkyServerPhoto	TwoMASS	SkyServerSpectra	Global	SkyServerPhoto	TwoMASS	SkyServerSpectra	Global
1	6599	6,599	143	10	2	2	139983	6595	555	3284
2	5598	5,598	508	22	2	2	496980	14439	555	3284
4	17655	17,66	1616	79	4	4	1580806	51678	1043	6502
6	40198	40,2	2755	144	10	8	2695023	94134	2506	12939
8	74888	74,89	3859	234	18	12	3775458	152957	4460	19367
10	131949	131,9	5173	332	27	19	5060981	216997	6647	30616
12	228839	228,8	6700	444	37	24	6554558	290199	9084	38663
14	394297	394,3	8538	594	49	37	8352454	388212	11989	59540
16	663905	663,9	10539	777	60	47	10309689	507790	14661	75632
18	1034667	1035	12746	961	74	60	12468276	628033	18059	96570

Fig. 5. Query results

large sky areas and it can remain interesting even if the number of sources increases. Additional statistics we recollected demonstrate that the time required for data integration and the communication between nodes does not exceed the time required to obtain the data from the Web and transform them into their mapping schemata.

Finally, it is important to note that providing transparent access to astronomical data sources and enabling data integration must also be evaluated under qualitative criteria. It is always a significant advantage to automate a process that is in general done manually.

5 Related Work

Several approaches have been proposed for astronomical data integration and the construction of the Virtual Observatory. SkyQuery [2] is probably the most representative prototype of a federated database application for this purpose. It is implemented using a set of interoperating Web services. In SkyQuery, a portal provides an entry point into a distributed query system relying on metadata and query services provided by a series of SkyNodes. The query system consists of individual databases representing a particular survey located at different sites along with their wrappers. SkyQuery receives queries expressed in a query language similar to SQL; it locates the referenced SkyNodes and submits the query to every SkyNode. The final result is computed by applying a probabilistic spatial join to partial results. SkyQuery differs from our system in that it does not provide a unified global view over the set of data sources, so the user needs to be familiar with the schema of each data source in order to build a query and interpret results. Especially when the number of sources increases, it is desirable that the user does not need to remember details about each source.

Other existing partially automated astronomical data integration approaches concern homogeneous relational data sources [8]. However, astronomical data integration is still mostly done manually especially when heterogeneous data are involved. The challenge we address is to provide an integrated view over a set of astronomical data sources, thus making transparent to the users the heterogeneity of these sources.

6 Conclusions and Future Work

The methodology and algorithms presented in this paper provide a feasible solution to the integration of distributed, heterogeneous and autonomous data sources in the domain of astronomy. In addition, the inclusion of new data sources can be achieved with relative ease. Our prototype implementation demonstrates that our approach provides a viable method for astronomical data integration. The system provides users a unified global view over the set of data sources, while it hides the specificities of each source. The particularities of astronomical data were addressed by adapting existing techniques specifically designed for this domain. The distributed execution strategy allows taking advantage of shared resources.

Distributed query evaluation opens the opportunity to introduce partitioned parallelism techniques in the future. Thus, this integration strategy makes the current version of ANDROMEDA more suitable for large databases. In the future we expect to deploy ANDROMEDA on several machines and evaluate the efficiency of our distributed execution strategy. To obtain more representative results we plan to compare the efficiency of our system with SkyQuery, under the consideration that we do not aim to provide the same capabilities. The query evaluation strategy can also be significantly improved by incorporating more sophisticated scheduling techniques. The overall performance of the system could also be improved by using alternative data structures for the manipulation of XML trees. There is also room for improvement in the spatial join procedure, by taking into consideration the specificities of each data source in order to lead to more reliable cross identification of objects among different surveys.

References

[1] Bouzeghoub, M., Farias-Lóscio, B., Kedad, Z., and Soukane, A. Heterogeneous Data Source Integration and Evolution. In *Proceedings of the 13th International Conference on Database and Expert Systems Applications DEXA '02.* Aix-en-Provence, France, 2002.

[2] Budavári, T., Malik, T., Szalay, A., and Thakar, A. SkyQuery – A Prototype Distributed Query Web Service for the Virtual Observatory. In Payne, H. E., Jedrzejewski, R. I., and Hook, R. N., eds. *Astronomical Data Analysis Software and Systems XII ASP Conference Series,* Vol. 295, 2003.

[3] Cuevas-Vicenttín, V., Zechinelli-Martini, J.L., Vargas-Solar, G., *ANDROMEDA: Astronomical Data Mediation for Virtual Observatories.* Research Report, RR n° 1082-I, LSR-IMAG, Grenoble, 2006.

[4] Hanisch, R. J., and Quinn, P. J. *The IVOA.* http://www.ivoa.net/pub/info/TheIVOA.pdf

[5] Kedad, Z., and Xue, X. Mapping generation for XML data sources: a general framework. In *Proceedings of WIRI 2005*, in conjuction with ICDE'05, 2005.

[6] Kunszt, P., Szalay, A., and Thakar, A. The Hierarchical Triangular Mesh. ESO Astrophysics Symposia, Vol. 6, 2001.

[7] Métais, E., Kedad, Z., Comyn-Wattiau, I., and Bouzeghoub, M. Using Linguistic Knowledge in View Integration: toward a third generation of tools. *International Journal of Data and Knowledge Engineering (DKE)*, 1 (23), North Holland, 1997.

[8] Nieto-Santisteban, M. A. When Database Systems Meet the Grid. Microsoft Technical Report, MSR-TR-2004-81, 2004.

[9] Szalay, A., Gray, J., Kunszt, P., and Thakar, A. Designing and Mining Multi-Terabyte Astronomy Archives: The Sloan Digital Sky Survey. In *Proceedings of ACM SIGMOD Conference*, 2000.

[10] Szalay, A., Kunszt, P., Thakar, A., Gray, J., and Slutz, D. The Sloan Digital Sky Survey and its Archive. In Manset, N., Veillet, C., and Crabtree, D., eds. *Astronomical Data Analysis Software and Systems IX ASP Conference Series*, Vol. 216, 2000.

[11] 2MASS Explanatory Supplement to the 2MASS All Sky Data Release. http://www.ipac.caltech.edu/2mass/releases/allsky/doc/explsup.html

[12] Terlevich, R., López-López, A., and Terlevich, E. El Grupo de Ciencia con Observatorios Virtuales del INAOE, 2003. http://haro.inaoep.mx/ov/archivos/ObservatorioVirtual.pdf.

[13] Wiederhold, G., Mediators in the architecture of future information systems. *Computer*, Vol. 25, 1992.

Improving Web Retrieval Precision Based on Semantic Relationships and Proximity of Query Keywords

Chi Tian[1], Taro Tezuka[2], Satoshi Oyama[2], Keishi Tajima[2], and Katsumi Tanaka[2]

[1] Informatics of the Faculty of Engineering, Kyoto University
Yoshida-honmachi, Sakyo-ku, Kyoto, 606-8501 Japan
tianchi@dl.kuis.kyoto-u.ac.jp

[2] Department of Social Informatics, Graduate School of Informatics, Kyoto University
Yoshida-honmachi, Sakyo-ku, Kyoto, 606-8501 Japan
{tezuka, oyama, tajima, tanaka}@dl.kuis.kyoto-u.ac.jp

Abstract. Based on recent studies, the most common queries in Web searches involve one or two keywords. While most Web search engines perform very well for a single-keyword query, their precisions is not as good for queries involving two or more keywords. Search results often contain a large number of pages that are only weakly relevant to either of the keywords. One solution is to focus on the proximity of keywords in the search results. Filtering keywords by semantic relationships could also be used. We developed a method to improve the precison of Web retrieval based on the semantic relationships between and proximity of keywords for two-keyword queries. We have implemented a system that re-ranks Web search results based on three measures: *first-appearance term distance*, *minimum term distance*, and *local appearance density*. Furthermore, the system enables the user to assign weights to the new rank and original ranks so that the result can be presented in order of the combined rank. We built a prototype user interface in which the user can dynamically change the weights on two different ranks. The result of the experiment showed that our method improves the precision of Web search results for two-keyword queries.

1 Introduction

Based on recent studies, queries involving one or two keywords are most common in Web searches [1][2]. While most Web search engines perform very well for a single-keyword query, their precisions is not as good for queries involing two or more keywords because the search results usually contain a large number of pages with weak relevance to the query keywords. The reasons for this are as follows:

1. Generally, a Web page consists of numerous parts describing different subjects. Such a page is not always an exact in the search results when the query keywords are included in different parts of the Web page, so the precision of the search is low.
2. Subject structure in a Web page is rarely considered in ranking algorithms of Web search engines. For example, Google's [3] ranking algorithm[1] is based on the number of cover links, while subject structure is not considered.

[1] Google ranking algorithm, PageRank.

S. Bressan, J. Küng, and R. Wagner (Eds.): DEXA 2006, LNCS 4080, pp. 54–63, 2006.

For example, when we used a two-keyword query "Shijo Street" and "Chinese food" for the search, we acquired not only Web pages about Chinese food restaurants on Shijo Street, but also those about restaurants other than Chinese on Shijo Street and Chinese food restaurants that are not on Shijo Street were included in the highly ranked results. This is caused by the keywords appearing in remote places on Web pages and the semantic relationship between them is weak. One method of removing such "noise" is to focus attention on the proximity of the query keywords. In addition, there is a technique of filtering based on semantic relationships between query keywords.

We developed a method to improve the precision of web retrieval by the semantic relationships between and proximity of query keywords for two-keyword queries. In our method, we first send query keywords to a Web search engine and acquire search results. We then perform morphological analysis on the results and analyze three measures for proximity. We defined *first-appearence term distance*, *minimum term distance*, and *local appearance density* as the measures, and re-ranked search results based on them. Furthermore, we assigned weights for the original rank from the Web search engine and the new rank and combined them. We developed a system with a user interface that enables a user to dynamically change the weight assigned to the original and new ranks. The system displays the results in order of the combined rank.

The rest of this paper is organized as follows. Section 2 is the related work. Section 3 explains the semantic relationships between query keywords. Section 4 discusses our method and the mechanism of the re-ranking algorithm. Section 5 describes the prototype user interface. Section 6 discusses the experiment. Section 7 outlines our conclusions and future work plans.

2 Related Work

2.1 Proximity of Query Keywords

The term distance between query keywords in a document is widely used in the field of information retrieval [4][5]. Callan showed that the precision of information retrieval was improved by performing the retrieval in a restricted domain rather than in the full text [6]. As a method of Web page retrieval based on the proximity of query keywords, Sadakane and Imai developed a high-speed algorithm to extract the Web page in which most keywords appear together [7]. In contrast, our method not only focuses attention on the proximity of, but also on the semantic relationships between query keywords to improve the precison of Web retrieval. Although a proximity operation is already performed in most full-text retrieval systems, it is rarely performed in Web information retrieval.

2.2 Density Distribution of Query Keywords

The technique of using density distribution of query keywords is widely used in the field of information retrieval. Kurohashi et al. developed a method for detecting important descriptions of a word based on its density distribution in text [8]. Sano et al. developed a method of scoring and extracting the inner structure of a Web page by the density distribution of query keywords [9]. Nakatani et al. developed a method to divide a Web page into meaningful units by the density distribution of query keywords [10]. We substituted local appearance density[2] for density distribution to improve the precision of Web retrieval.

2.3 Roles of Query Keywords

Usually, multiple query keywords has an asymmetrical relationship like a subject modifying type[3]. Oyama and Tanaka developed a method to improve the precision of Web retrieval based on the hierarchical structure of query keywords [11]. In contrast, we focused attention on the semantic relationships between keywords.

3 Semantic Relationships Between Query Keywords

In this section, we explain the semantic relationships between query keywords for two-keyword queries. Mainly, there are two semantic relationships between query keywords. A and B represent the query keywords.

3.1 Subject Modifying Type

In this case, one keyword represents a particular subject and the other modifies it. The two keywords are subordinating and can be joined in the form "B of A." For example, query keywords such as "Japan, History" belong to the subject modifying type.

This type of keywords is used when a user wants to do a search about a particular aspect of a subject.

3.2 Subject Juxtapoing Type

In this case, both keywords represent an individual subject. They belong to parallel structures and can be joined in the form "A and B" For example, keywords such as "Precision, Recall" belong to the subject juxtaposing type.

This type of keywords is used when a user wants to do a search about the relationship between two different subjects.

4 Our Method

4.1 Summary of Our Method

The flow of our method is shown in Figure 1.

(1) Input query keywords and assign weights for the original and new ranks, then do a search and acquire search results.
(2) Perform morphological analysis [12] on the search results and analyze them using measures for proximity.
(3) Re-rank the search results based on the measures for proximity, and calculate the new ranks.

---

[2] Local appearance density is defined in Section 4.

[3] Subject modifying type is explained in detail in Section 3.

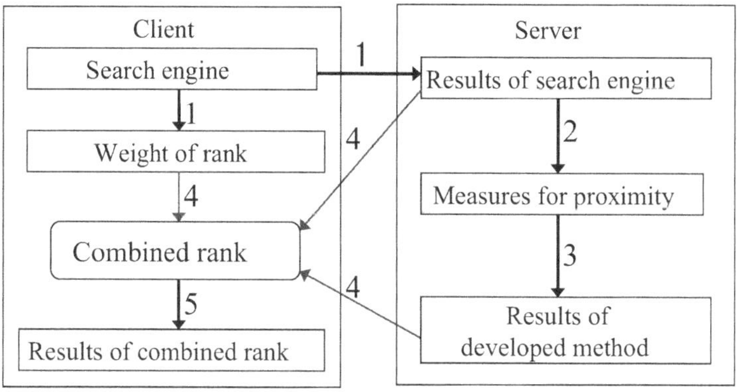

Fig. 1. Flow of our method

(4) Combine the ranks by the weight of the original and new ranks.
(5) Display the results in order of combined rank.

4.2 Measures for Proximity

A and B represent the query keywords. Functions that we will describe in this section are defined as follows:

- $TD(A, B)$: The term distance between A and B.
- $first(A)$: The first appearance of A in a Web page.
- $last(A)$: The last appearance of A in a Web page.
- $first(A, B)$: The first appearance of A and B.
- $last(A, B)$: The last appearance of A and B.
- $f_{\{M,N\}}(A, B)$: The sum of A and B appearing in the range of $\{M, N\}$.

(1) First-appearance Term Distance (FTD)

$$FTD(A, B) = TD(first(A), first(B)), \tag{1}$$

FTD means the term distance (TD) between the first appearances of A and B in a Web page. For example, the FTD of A and B is 4 in Figure 2. The reason for using

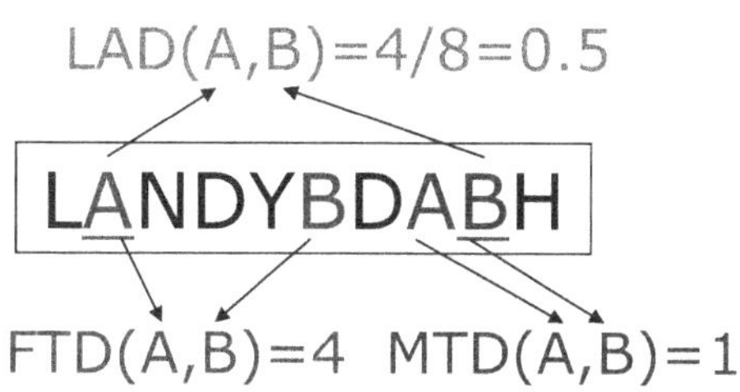

Fig. 2. FTD, MTD, and LAD

FTD is based on a hypothesis that important terms always appear in the forefront of a document. In other words, we suppose that both query keywords emerge at the top of a document when they are contained in the subject of the document.

(2) Minimum Term Distance (MTD)

$$MTD(A, B) = min(\{TD(A, B)\}), \tag{2}$$

MTD means the smallest of all term distances between A and B in a Web page. For example, the MTD of A and B is 1 in Figure 2. The reason for using MTD is based on a hypothesis that related terms appear in close proximity.

(3) Local Appearance Density (LAD)

$$LAD(A, B) = \frac{f_{\{first(first(A), first(B)), last(last(A), last(B))\}}(A, B)}{TD(first(first(A), first(B), last(last(A), last(B))) + 1}, \tag{3}$$

LAD is defined as a ratio of *the sum of two keywords (A and B)* to *the sum of all terms* appearing between the first and last appearance keywords. For example, the LAD of A and B in Figure 2 is 0.5. The reason for using LAD is based on a hypothesis that important terms appear repeatedly in a Web page.

4.3 Re-ranking Algorithm

(1) Re-ranking by FTD
In the FTD method, the original results of a Web search engine are re-ranked based on the FTD of the query keywords. We performed the sorting of the search results and ranked them in ascending order of FTD. The smaller the FTD, the higher the ranking of the results.

(2) Re-ranking by MTD
In the MTD method, the original results of a Web search engine are re-ranked based on the MTD of the query keywords. We performed the sorting of the search results and ranked them in ascending order of MTD. The smaller the MTD, the higher the ranking of the results.

(3) Re-ranking by LAD
In the LAD method, the original results of a Web search engine are re-ranked based on the LAD of the query keywords. We performed sorting of the search results and ranked them in descending order of LAD. The higher the LAD, the higher the ranking of the results.

4.4 Combining Results from Web Search Engine and Re-ranking Method

We developed a method to combine the results from a Web search engine and a re-ranking method by operating a user interface. The combination value (Z) is defined as follows:

$$Z = (1 - S)X + SY, \tag{4}$$

$$\Longrightarrow \begin{cases} S = 0 \Rightarrow Z = X, \\ S = 1 \Rightarrow Z = Y, \end{cases} \tag{5}$$

X represents the rank of the result from the Web search engine, Y represents the rank using our method. $S(S \in [0,1])$ represents the weight of Y and $(1 - S)$ represents the weight of X.

We combined the ranks of search results from the Web search engine and our method and re-ranked the combined rank based on the ascending order of Z. As shown in equation 5, the combined rank is equal to the rank from search engine when the value of S is 0, and the combined rank is equal to the rank in our re-ranking method when the value of S is 1. A user can set the value of S close to 0 if he or she wants to emphasize on the results of Web search engine. Also, the user can set the value of S close to 1 if he or she wants to emphasize on the results of the re-ranking method.

5 User Interface

5.1 User Interface Overview

We implemented a prototype system SSRP (Search by Semantic Relationship and Proximity) based on our method.

As shown in Figure 3, the prototype user interface consists of four areas as follows.

1. Input area
2. Summary area
3. Analysis area
4. Display area

A user inputs query keywords into the input area, sets the weight of the rank on scroll bar, and does a search with a Web search engine. The analysis results of each re-ranking method are output in the analysis area. In addition, snippets of search results and text contents are displayed in the summary area. The Web page including images is displayed in the display area.

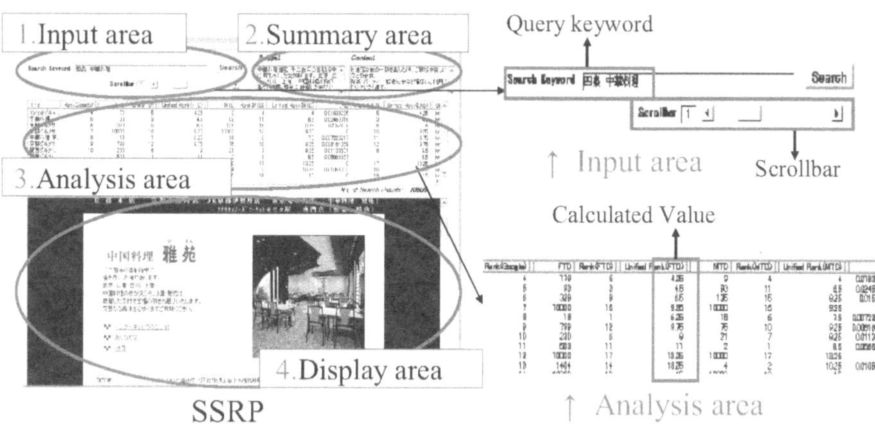

Fig. 3. User interface of SSRP

5.2 Senario Example

Figure 3 shows a sample image of our prototype system when searching with a two-keyword query "Chinese food, Shijo Street". First, we input the query keywords in the input area and set the value of scroll bar to 1. In this system, we prepared five levels of scrollbar values from 0 to 4. We calculated the combined rank based on the standards shown as follows.

- Level 0 (S= 0): Use only the ranking by a conventional search engine.
- Level 1 (S= 0.25): Put more weight on the ranking by a conventional search engine.
- Level 2 (S= 0.5): Put equal weight on the ranking by a conventional search engine and the ranking by our re-ranking method.
- Level 3 (S= 0.75): Put more weight on the ranking by our re-ranking method.
- Level 4 (S= 1): Use only the ranking by our re-ranking method.

Next, the system performs morphological analysis and outputs results in the analysis area, where not only the title, URL, snippet, and Web contents of search results, but also the first-appearance term distance, the minimum term distance, the local appearance density, and the rankings based on them are displayed.

6 Evaluation

6.1 Experiment Setup

We performed the experiment[4] with 20 pairs of subject modifying type and 10 pairs of subject juxtaposing type query keywords (Table 1). We set the number of search results acquired from Google as 20. In the experiment, we applied each re-ranking method to the top 20 search results acquired from Google. Then, we evaluated the three re-ranking methods and Google by comparing the precision[5] of the results.

6.2 Experimental Results

We compared the average precision in the FTD, MTD, and LAD methods with that obtained from Google using the query keywords in Table 1. Figure 4 shows the average precision of subject modifying type keywords. Figure 5 shows the average precision of subject juxtaposing type keywords. Table 2 shows the improvement point in average precision for each re-ranking method compared to Google for subject modifying type (SMT) keywords.Table 3 shows the improvement point in average precision for each re-ranking method compared to Google for subject juxtaposing type (SJT) keywords.

6.3 Discussion of Experimental Results

(1) Discussion of subject modifying type query keywords
As shown in Table 2, the MTD method is superior for subject modifying type query keywords. In the MTD method, improvements in average precision were 19.0, 11.0,

[4] The experiment was performed in Japanese.
[5] Precision is the ratio of conformity of documents in search results. [13]

Table 1. Query keywords used for experiment

Subject modifying type		
$Q1$	Kyoto	notable sights
$Q2$	Kyoto University	Information department
$Q3$	gravity	definition
$Q4$	Java	origin
$Q5$	Japan	history
$Q6$	robot	history
$Q7$	Shijo Street	Chinese food
$Q8$	Kiya Street	Japanese food
$Q9$	cake	recipe
$Q10$	PowerPoint	use
$Q10 - Q20$: abbreviated		

Subjcct juxtaposing type		
$Q1$	appetite	season
$Q2$	age	sleep
$Q3$	employment rate	economy
$Q4$	salary	academic background
$Q5$	height	longevity
$Q6$	precison	recall
$Q7$	calorie	diet
$Q8$	age of marriage	number of children
$Q9$	memory	age
$Q10$	character	blood type

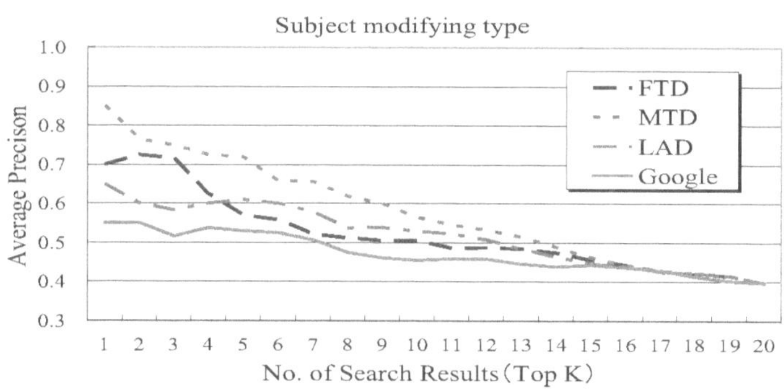

Fig. 4. Results of subject modifying type

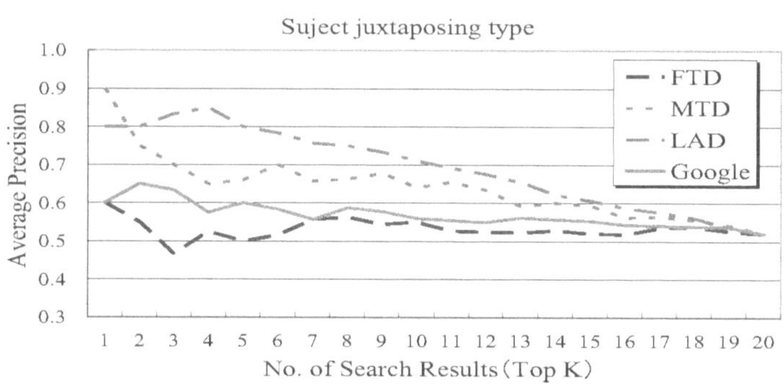

Fig. 5. Results of subject juxtaposing type

Table 2. Improvement in precison compared to Google (SMT)

SMT	Top5	Top10	Top15	Average
FTD	4.0	5.0	1.4	5.0
MTD	**19.0**	**11.0**	**2.0**	**10.7**
LAD	8.0	7.5	0.3	4.6

Table 3. Improvement in precison compared to Google (SJT)

SJT	Top5	Top10	Top15	Average
FTD	−10.0	−1.0	−3.3	−3.7
MTD	6.0	8.0	4.0	7.2
LAD	**20.0**	**15.0**	**5.3**	**12.3**

and 2.0 points for the top 5, 10, and 15 search results, respectively. In addition, the average improvement was 10.7 points. The improvement with the MTD method is more significant than that with either the FTD or LAD methods. The average improvement was 5.0 points with the FTD method and 4.6 points with the LAD method. Though the improvement is not significant, it appears to have a certain level of effect. For subject modifying type query keywords, the average precision was improved in all the three re-ranking methods. Particularly, the MTD method showed the most significant improvement.

(2) Discussion of subject juxtaposing type query keywords
As shown in Table 3, the LAD method is superior for subject juxtaposing type query keywords. In the LAD method, the improvements in average precision were 20.0, 15.0, and 5.3 points for the top 5, 10, and 15 results, respectively. In addition, the average improvement was 12.3 points. The improvement with the LAD method is more significant than that with either the FTD or MTD methods. In the MTD method, the average improvement was 7.2 points, and this is the most significant improvement next that with the LAD method. On the other hand, in the FTD method, the average improvement was -3.7 points, which means that the average precision in the FTD method is inferior to that for the results obtained using Google. For subject juxtaposing type query keywords, the average precision was improved in the LAD and MTD methods. Particularly, the LAD method showed the most significant improvement.

7 Conclusion

We developed a method to improve the precision of Web retrieval based on the semantic relationships between and proximity of keywords for two-keyword queries. We have implemented a system that re-ranks Web search results based on three measures: *first-appearance term distance*, *minimum term distance*, and *local appearance density*. Furthermore, the system enables the user to assign weights to the new and original ranks so that the result can be presented in order of the combined rank. We built a prototype user interface in which a user can dynamically change the weights on two different ranks. The evaluation experiment showed that for subject modifying type query keywords, the MTD method had the most remarkable effect on improving Web retrieval precision and for subject juxtaposing type query keywords, the LAD method had the most remarkable effect on improving Web retrieval precision.

Our future works will include a system for judging the semantic relationships between query keywords automatically and performing the most effective re-ranking method and developing a method for using more than three query keywords in a Web search.

Acknowledgements

This work was supported in part by the Japanese Ministry of Education, Culture, Sports, Science and Technology under the 21st Century COE (Center of Excellence) Program "Informatics Research Center for Development of Knowledge Society Infrastructure" (Leader: Katsumi Tanaka, 2002-2006), and Grant-in-Aid for Scientific Research on Priority Areas: "Cyber Infrastructure for the Information-explosion Era," Planning Research: "Contents Fusion and Seamless Search for Information Explosion" (Project Leader: Katsumi Tanaka, A01-00-02, Grant#: 18049041), and Grant-in-Aid for Young Scientists (B) "Trust Decision Assistance for Web Utilization based on Information Integration" (Leader: Taro Tezuka, Grant#: 18700086).

References

1. B. J. Jansen, A. Spink, J. Bateman and T. Saracevic: Real life information retrieval: A study of user queries on the Web. ACM SIGIR Forum, Vol. 32, No. 1, pp. 5-17, 1998.
2. Trellian, http://www.trellian.com/
3. Google, http://www.google.co.jp
4. T. Yamamoto, H. Hashizume, N. Kando, and M. Shimizu: Full-text search: Technology and applications, Maruzen Co., Ltd., 1998.
5. M. Saraki and Y. Nitta: Regular expression and text mining, Akashi Shoten Co.,Ltd, 2003.
6. J. Callan: Passage-level evidence in document retrieval. Proceedings of the 17th Annual International ACM SIGIR Conference, pp. 302-309, 1994.
7. K. Sadakane and H. Imai: On k-word Proximity Search. IPSJ SIG Notes 99-AL-68, 1999.
8. S. Kurohashi, N. Shiraki, and M. Nagao: A method for detecting important descriptions of a word based on its density distribution in text. IPSJ, Vol. 38, No. 04, pp.845-854, 1997.
9. R. Sano, T. Matsukura, K. Hatano, and K. Tanaka: Web document retrieval based on minimal matching subgraphs as units and word appearance density. IPSJ, Vol.99, No.61, pp.79-84, 1999.
10. K. Nakatani, Y. Suzuki, and K. Kawagoe: Personalized Web link generation method using Keywords and Document Similarities. DBSJ Letters, Vol. 4, No. 1, pp.89-92, 2005.
11. S. Oyama and K. Tanaka: Web search using hierarchical structuring of queries. DBSJ Letters, Vol.1, No.1, pp.63-66, October 2002
12. Japanese language morphological analysis system: Chasen, http://chasen.naist.jp/hiki/chasen
13. C. J. van Rijsbergen: Information Retrieval (Second Edition), Butterworths, 1979.

From Extreme Programming to Extreme Non-programming: Is It the Right Time for Model Transformation Technologies?

Óscar Pastor

Department of Information Systems and Computation
Valencia University of Technology
Camino de Vera s/n, 46071 Valencia, España
Phone: +34 96 387 7000; Fax: +34 96 3877359
opastor@dsic.upv.es

Abstract. Object-Oriented Methods, Formal Specification Languages, Component-Based Software Production... This is just a very short list of technologies proposed to solve a very old and, at the same time, very well-known problem: how to produce software of quality. Programming has been the key task during the last 40 years, and the results have not been successful yet. This work will explore the need of facing a sound software production process from a different perspective: the non-programming perspective, where by non-programming we mainly mean modeling. Instead of talking about Extreme Programming, we will introduce a Extreme Non-Programming (Extreme Modeling-Oriented) approach. We will base our ideas on the intensive work done during the last years, oriented to the objective of generating code from a higher-level system specification, normally represented as a Conceptual Schema. Nowadays, though, the hip around MDA has given a new push to these strategies. New methods propose sound model transformations which cover all the different steps of a sound software production process from an Information Systems Engineering point of view. This must include Organizational Modeling, Requirements Engineering, Conceptual Modeling and Model-Based Code Generation techniques. In this context, it seems that the time of Model Transformation Technologies is finally here…

1 Introduction

The main problem historically faced by the Software Engineering and Information Systems communities is how to obtain a software product of quality. What we mean by quality in this context is to have a final software product that lives up to the customer expectations, as they are gathered in the corresponding source Requirements Model. Going step by step from the Problem Space (conceptual level) to the Solution Space (software technology level) is supposed to be the task of a sound Software Process, intended to lead this Model Transformation Oriented set of activities.

Apparently, it is a simple task to state the quoted problem: how to provide an adequate Software Process that fulfills the goal of building software of quality. But the last forty years have made clear that this is a major problem. We need the right

S. Bressan, J. Küng, and R. Wagner (Eds.): DEXA 2006, LNCS 4080, pp. 64 – 72, 2006.

tools, but the reality is that they are not being provided. The ever-present software crisis problem is not being solved by just working on programming-based software-production processes. We should wonder why this happens, and how this could be solved. The main objective of this keynote is to answer these questions.

Section 2 states the problem and introduces some alternatives intended to overcome it. In section 3, an example of a Software Process that covers the relevant phases of Requirements Modeling, Conceptual Modeling, and Software Product generation will be presented. After that, some reflections around the more significant present and future trends related with how to put into practice Model Transformation Technologies will be discussed. Conclusions and references end up the work.

2 The Problem

During the last decades, software engineering courses around the world have extensively argued -using different formats- over how complicated to construct a software system is. Commonly, it is known that

- costs can be increased at any time,
- the final product is too frequently delivered out of time,
- the provided functionality is not the one required by the customers,
- it is not guaranteed that the system will work

It is also well-known and well-reported the cost of this low quality. For instance, in an study done by Giga Group, Gartner Group, Standish Group, CCTA and the Brunel University, and presented in [6], it is reported that at least $350 Billion are lost each year on Information Technology, due to abandoned projects, rectification of errors or consequential losses due to failures. Certainly, not all of this could have been saved by following a better process. Operational errors and changing business conditions are a source of unpredictable problems, even if a sound and complete Software Production Process is provided. In any case, the estimation of potential savings presented in the quoted report is at least $200 Billion per year, a huge amount of money lost due to the absence of the desired Software Process.

Summarizing, in terms of stating the problem, we face a problem that is at the same time simple to state and complicated to solve. The issue is that producing an Information System today is costly (because expensive resources have to be used over extended periods of time), much too slow for modern business conditions, very risky (in the sense that it is hard to control and with a high failure rate) and highly unsafe (because it introduces hidden failure points).

The main problem is that the development process has not changed much over the past 40 years; that is, the task of programming is still the "essential" task. Programming is the key activity associated with the fact of creating a software product. But considering the very bad results the programming-oriented techniques are historically obtaining, a simple question arises: is it worth looking for a better way of producing software?

We should ask ourselves why so many software systems historically fail to meet the needs of their customers. For decades, the "silver bullet" has apparently been provided to the community in the form of some new, advanced software technology, but always unsuccessfully. We have a large list of technologies that were intended to solve the problem: we could set down in this list Assembler, Third Generation Languages, Relational Databases, Declarative Programming, Methodologies and CASE tools (Structured Analysis and Design, Object-Oriented Modelling, UML-based), Component-based Programming, Aspect-based, Agent-Oriented, Extreme Programming, Agile Methods, Requirements Engineering, Organizational Modelling... But always, the same "phantom of the opera": the unsolved Crisis of Software notion.

Going back to this idea of "programming" as the key strategy for building a software product, the characteristics of the well-known Extreme Programming approach should be commented. Generally speaking, this approach is mainly based on the idea of having developers (programmers) that interpret the business descriptions providing by the Business Owner. Developers create and refine the source code that finally conforms the operational system by properly integrating all the corresponding software modules. In any case, not only programming, but programming at the extreme is the issue here. The key skill is programming, and the most important idea is that "the code is the model".

According to all the negative results commented above, just going one step further on programming does not seem to be the correct way. On the contrary, it seems that one could easily conclude that, with such an strategy, no solution will be provided for the problem of providing software of quality. But are there any alternatives?

2.1 Extreme Non-programming

Proposed initially in [6], there is a first challenging alternative, and it is centered on the idea that programming is not the way. Extreme Non-Programming (XNP) stresses the idea that the conceptual model is the key artifact of a Software Production Process. The model includes an structured business description, obtained through the interaction with the Business Owner, and the corresponding machine readable views (the programs) should be generated from the model following a model transformation process.

In this case, the key skill is modeling, and the main idea is that "the model is the code" (instead of "the code is the model"). Under this hypothesis, a sound Software Production Process should provide a precise set of models (representing the differents levels of abstraction of a system domain description), together with the corresponding transformations from a higher level of abstraction to the subsequent abstraction level. For instance, a Requirements Model should be properly transformed into its associated Conceptual Schema, and this Conceptual Schema should be converted into the corresponding Software Representation (final program).

Assuming that behind any programmer decision, there is always a concept, the problem to be properly faced by any Model Transformation Technology is the problem of accurately identifying those concepts, together with their associated software representations. A precise definition of the set of mappings between conceptual primitives or conceptual patterns and their corresponding software representations, provides a solid basis for building Conceptual Model Compilers.

2.2 Conceptual Schema-Centric Development (CSCD)

XNP is not the only alternative. In [1], Prof. Olivé presents his CSCD approach as a grand challenge for Information Systems Research. Close to the central ideas of XNP, CSCD is based on the assumption that, to develop an Information System (IS), it is necessary and sufficient to define its Conceptual Schema.

Being the advancement of science or engineering the primary purpose of the formulation and promulgation of a grand challenge, the proposal focuses on the advancement of IS engineering towards automation. Even if this is not at all a new, disruptive proposal (see how [10], dated at 1971, already argues on the importance of facing the automation of systems building to improve the software production process), the fact is that, forty years later, this goal of automated systems building has not been achieved. There has been a lot of progress, definitely yes, but still today the design, programming and testing activities require a substantial manual effort in most projects. In neither of the two most popular development approaches –Visual Studio or Eclipse- the automation of the system building plays a significant role. Again, programming is the central activity and most (if not all) tool improvements are directed to help with the complex task of writing a program, but not with the task of compiling a conceptual model to avoid the repetitive, tedious and complex task of programming.

At this point, is it necessary to think about why has this goal not been achieved. Is it probably unachievable? Is it perhaps worthless to continue trying? Of course, we don't think so. On the contrary, even accepting that a number of problems remain to be solved (especially technical problems, and problems related with the maturity of the field and the lack of standards), the situation is changing drastically, mainly from this last aspect of the absence of standards.

Recent progress on widely accepted and well-known standards as UML [4], MDA [3], XMI, MOF, J2EE, .NET, among others, are really providing an opportunity to revisit the automation goal. The MDA proposal is specially relevant, because it intends to provide Software Processes where Model Transformation is a natural consequence of this view of using models at different levels of abstraction, to represent the Computer-Independent Model (CIM) at the highest level, the Platform Independent Model (PIM) as the subsequent level of abstraction, and finally moving progressively to the solution space through the Platform Specific Model (PSM) and to the final code. The corresponding transformations between those models provide a kind of Software Process where all the previous ideas fit perfectly well. Industrial tools as OptimalJ [2] and ArcStyle [5] allows to experiment these approaches in practice with quite interesting reported results.

2.3 Model Transformation Technology Through Model Compilation

In the same line of argumentation, there is still a third alternative. The overall objective of Model Transformation Technology (MTT) is to improve software development productivity. This objective is pursued by contributing to the realisation of the vision of model-driven software development. Model Compilation plays a basic role in achieving this objective. Under the hypothesis that behind any programmer decision there is always a concept, the task of a sound MTT is to correctly get those concepts, to define the corresponding catalog of conceptual patterns, and to associate to each of them its corresponding software representation. This set of mappings constitutes the core of a Conceptual Model Compiler.

Assuming that the history of Software Engineering (SE) has been one of growing levels of abstraction, MTT technology is just one step further. From the programming languages point of view, SE first moved from Binary to Assembler code, then from Assembler to what we consider today to be "Source Code". Next logical step is to move from Source Code to Conceptual Schemas. This is the step taken by Conceptual Model Compilers.

From the industrial point of view, there are some industrial tools providing such a kind of full Model-Based Code Generation environments, e.g. OlivaNova Model Execution [7], what allow us to conclude that we are really entering the time of Model Compilation seen as an operational technology. More details on this potential type of solutions are given in the next section.

Finally, before closing this section we want to remark that these three approaches are not the only existing alternatives. We could add the works of S. Kent on Model Driven Engineering [11], or the proposal of K. Czarnecki around Generative Programming [12] Al these works are providing a context where we can talk about real solutions to the problems commented for the current software production processes.

3 The Solutions

In practical terms, what we mean by Extreme Non Programming is just a software production process, where Requirements Modeling and Conceptual Modeling are the key issues, and where the Conceptual Model becomes the program itself in the sense that it can be transformed into the final software product through a process of Model Compilation.

Any Software Process XNP-compliant will start by specifying a precise Requirements Model, where the organization structure and relevant components are properly described, and where the software system is not –yet- an active actor. This Requirements Model has to be transformed into a Conceptual Schema, where a particular solution for the Software System is considered, but still at a higher level of abstraction than the programming level. Model Execution tools will be the responsible of compiling the model and generating the final application. Working within a XNP strategy, the final product will be compliant to the business model that originates it, as the whole process is conceived to assure that.

The alternatives presented in the previous section are closely related when we talk about concrete solutions. In the rest of this section, we present what could be seen as an example of a complete software production process that combines functional requirements specification, conceptual modelling (including data, behaviour and user interaction design), and implementation. It is defined on the basis of OlivaNova Model Execution (ONME) [7], a model-based environment for software development that complies with the MDA paradigm by defining models of a different abstraction level. Figure 1 shows the parallelism between the models proposed by MDA and the models dealt with in OO-Method [8], the methodology underlying ONME.

At the most abstract level, a Computation-Independent Model (CIM) describes the information system without considering if it will be supported by any software application; in OO-Method, this description is called the *Requirements Model*. The Platform-Independent Model (PIM) describes the system in an abstract way, still disregarding the underpinning computer platform; this is called the *Conceptual Model* in OO-Method. ONME implements an automatic transformation of the Conceptual Model into the *source code* of the final user application. This is done by a *Model Compilation* process that has implicit knowledge about the target platform. This step is equivalent to the Platform Specific Model (PSM) defined by MDA.

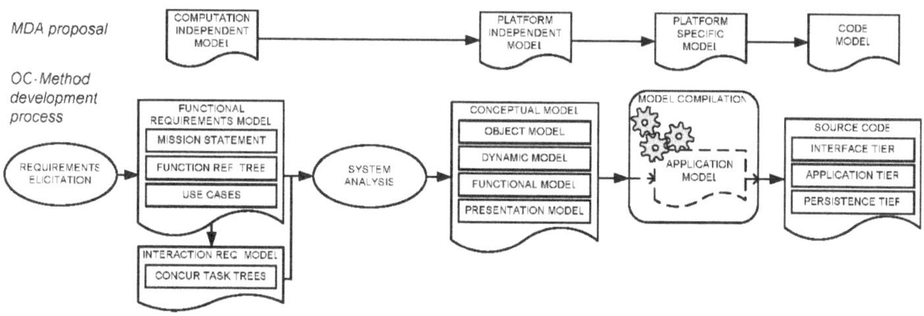

Fig. 1. An MDA-based development framework for Information Systems development

An important aspect to highlight is that data, function and user interaction modeling are the three basic components that must be present in every considered level of abstraction. The success of the final software product is only achieved when all these three basic modeling perspectives are properly integrated and managed.

The modeling strategies vary depending on the considered level of abstraction. For instance, at the requirements modeling level, either a functional, use-case oriented strategy or a goal-oriented modeling approach could be followed from a functional point of view. Concurrent Task Trees [9] could provide a sound basis for User Interface-oriented Requirements Gathering.

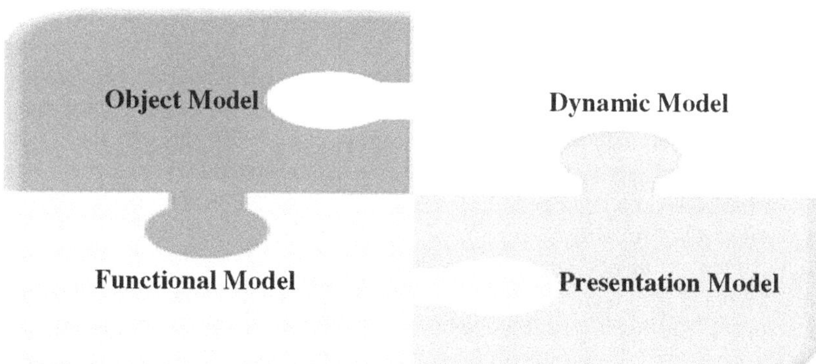

Fig. 2. A Conceptual Schema must integrate the four complementary views of object modeling, dynamic modeling, functional modeling and presentation modeling

At the Conceptual Modeling level, an Object Model, a Dynamic Model, a Functional Model and a Presentation Model (see Figure 2) are the correct projection of the Requirement Models, while a Model Compiler is the responsible of generating the fully-functional Software Product. This approach provides a rigorous Software Production Process, that makes true the statement "the Model is the Code", and where programming in the conventional, old-fashioned way is not anymore the essential task, but instead modeling is.

4 The Present and the Future…

We introduce in this section some final reflections. It seems to be clear that adoption of MTT requires tools. Why don't sound tools accompany these initiatives? Probably it is just a matter of time, and we are just now facing the right time. The usefulness of these tools is quite obvious considering the bad current situation. Usability should just be a logical consequence of adoption and usefulness.

We have discussed that we face a precise problem –how to produce software with the required quality-, we have seen a set of potential valid solutions (XNP, CSCD, MTT…). A relevant set of challenging proposal are on the table to do SE better, and for the first time, CASE tools could be perceived as a powerful help to solve the problem of obtaining a correct and complete software product. For too many years, CASE tools have been perceived as a "problem generator" more than a "code generator", because instead of providing a solution for having a better software production process, they were seen as a new problem –how to use the CASE tool properly- added to the main software production problem. To avoid this situation, the modelling effort must be strongly and clearly perceived as a basic effort for generating quality software. And to do that, it must be proved that the model can be the code of the application to be. As it has been said before, this is the real challenge to overcome, and it is successfully being faced.

But would this be accepted even if tools are available? Why do industry mainly ignore current tools that really implement MTT? The programming inertia is still too strong. In a world were programming is seen as the essential SE-oriented task, it is not easy to make programmers accept that the model compiler will do the greatest part of the conventional programming work.

On the other side, this is not a new situation. Assembler programmers were in the past very sceptical when they were told that a close-to-english programming language called COBOL would do the Assembler programming work through the associated Compiler, and even better than them. But nowadays no people are worried about the quality of the Assembler generated by Compilers, because they have reached by far the required level of reliability.

We will face the same situation with the Model Compilers. It is hard to accept by now that a Java program is just the result of a Conceptual Model Compilation process. But the truth is that this is possible, and that in fact there are already tools that provide this capability.

Another important question is to wonder about the role of Interaction / Presentation Modelling. It is curious to remark that, being user interface design and implementation, one of the most costly tasks related with software production, it is not normally present at modeling level. Everybody knows the Entity-Relationship or the UML Class Diagram Model as a representative of Data / Object Modeling resp. When we talk about Functional Modeling, Data Flow Diagrams, UML Interaction Diagrams, etc. are well-known techniques. But what about asking which is a well-known, widely accepted User Interaction Modelling Approach? There is no consensus on that matter.

Probably, the reason of this situation is that traditionally the SE community has been interested in defining methods and processes to develop software by specifying its data and behaviour disregarding user interaction. On the other hand, the Human-Computer Interaction community has defined techniques oriented to the modelling of the interaction between the user and the system, proposing a user-oriented software construction. Within a sound MTT-based technology, these two views have to be reconciled by integrating them in a whole software production process.

In any case, the lack of a precise User Interaction Modelling strategy, properly embedded in the conventional data and functional modelling tasks is one common problem of many MTT-based approaches. To overcome this problem, a User Interaction Model must be present in any software production process to deal with those aspects related with the user interface to be. This model must be integrated with the other systems views in the context of a unified system model, and this must be properly faced at all the relevant levels of abstraction (requirements, conceptual, code).

5 Conclusions

Even though we've been talking about the Crisis of Software for the last decades, producing an Information System today is still a costly process (expensive resources are used over extended periods), much too slow than required for modern business conditions, very risky (hard to control, and with a high failure rate) and highly unsafe (due to the many hidden failure points). Considering that the software development process has not changed much over the last forty years, and that it has been basically centered on the idea of programming, it is time to wonder if it is worth looking for a better way. The fact is that Programming by itself, or complemented with some initial modeling activity, has failed in providing a solution to the ever-present software crisis problem. A new perspective is needed to solve the problem of generating a correct and complete Software Product.

If Programming is not the answer, its most modern versions as Extreme Programming could just generate "extreme failures", and we could be talking about the Crisis of Software issue for many more years. Extreme Programming is just putting even more emphasis on the programming task, while the well-known problems associated to the software production process are still present, if not enlarged. What we propose is just avoiding programming at the traditional low-level, machine-oriented level of abstraction, and to accomplish a new non-programming-based process, centered on concepts which are closer to the user domain and the human way of conceptualizing reality. We called it Extreme Non Programming (XNP).

Accepting that this new perspective is really needed, in this paper we argue on a software production process based on the idea of Non-Programming. What we call Extreme Non-Programming (a term already introduced in [6]), is basically in the line of the modern approaches based on MDA, Model Transformation-based Technologies, Conceptual-Schema Centered Development and the like.

We have presented the fundamentals for providing those XNP methods (with their supporting tools) based on a different "motto": the idea that "the model is the code" instead of the conventional, programming-based where "the code is the model". According to that, Computer-Aided Software Development Environments intended to deal with Information Systems Development through the required process of successive Model Transformation, are strongly required.

In particular, precise Conceptual Schemas must be provided, and how to convert them into their corresponding software products, by defining the mappings between conceptual primitives and their software representation counterparts, should be the basis for a sound transformation process. These mappings are the core of a Model Compiler, intended to make real the following statement: "to develop an Information System, it is necessary and sufficient to define its Conceptual Schema". The automation of systems building becomes in this way an affordable dream, just looking for tools (some of them already existing as commented before) to justify its adoption in practice.

References

[1] A. Olivé, "Conceptual Schema-Centric Development: A Grand Challenge for Information Systems Research" Procs. Advanced Information Systems Engineering, 17th International Conference, CAiSE 2005, Porto, Portugal, June 13-17, 2005. Lecture Notes in Computer Science 3520 Springer 2005
[2] Compuware. www.compuware.com/products/optimalj/, last visited June 2006
[3] http://www.omg.org/mda, last visited June 2006
[4] http://www.uml.org , last visited June 2006
[5] Interactive Objects www.arcstyler.com/ , last visited June 2006
[6] Morgan,T. "Business Rules and Information Systems – Aligning IT with Business Goals", Addison-Wesley, 2002
[7] OlivaNova Model Execution System, CARE Technologies, http://www.care-t.com.
[8] Pastor O., Gomez J., Infrán E. and Pelechano V. "The OO-Method approach for information systems modeling: from object-oriented conceptual modeling to automated programming". In Information Systems 26(7), Elsevier, 2001, pp. 507-534.
[9] Paternò, F., "Model-Based Design and Evaluation of Interactive Applications", Springer-Verlag, Berlin, 2000.
[10] Teichroew,D.,Sayani,H. "Automation of System Building", Datamation, 1971
[11] Kent,S. "Model Driven Engineering. IFM'02. Proceeding of the Third International Conference on Integrated Formal Methods, Springer Verlag, 2002, 286-298.
[12] Czarnecki,K. Generative Programming. Principles and Techniques of Software Engineering Based on Automated Configuration and Fragment-Based Component Models. Department of Computer Science and Automation. Technical University of Ilmenau, 1998

Using an Oracle Repository to Accelerate XPath Queries*

Colm Noonan, Cian Durrigan, and Mark Roantree

Interoperable Systems Group, Dublin City University, Dublin 9, Ireland
{cnoonan, cdurrigan, mark}@Computing.DCU.ie

Abstract. One of the problems associated with XML databases is the poor performance of XPath queries. Although this has attracted much attention by the research community, solutions are either partial (not providing full XPath functionality) or unable to manage database updates. In this work, we exploit features of Oracle 10g in order to rapidly build indexes that improve the processing times of XML databases. Significantly, we can also support XML database updates as the rebuild time for entire indexes is reasonably fast and thus, provides for flexible update strategies. This paper discusses the process for building the index repository and describes a series of experiments that demonstrate our improved query response times.

1 Introduction

Native XML databases perform badly for many complex queries where the database size is large or the structure complex. Efforts to use an index are hampered by the fact that the reconstruction of these indexes (after update operations) is time-consuming.

In previous research [9], we devised an indexing method to improve the performance of XPath queries. In this work, we focused on the theoretical aspects of indexing and devised a method of providing fast access to XML nodes based on the principal axes used by XPath to generate query results. In our previous work we introduced the PreLevel indexing method and provided theoretical proofs of its ability to cover the full functionality of the XPath Query Language and presented optimised algorithms for XML tree traversals [9]. For each of the *primary* XPath axes, conjunctive range predicates were derived from the intrinsic properties of the *preorder* traversal ranks and *level* ranks. By recording both preorder and level rankings (together with appropriate element values) in the PreLevel index, we provided algorithms to facilitate optimised query response times.

The work presented in our current paper was carried out as part of the FAST project (Flexible indexing Algorithm using Semantic Tags). This research is funded by a *Proof of Concept* grant where theoretical ideas are deployed to provide state-of-the art solutions to current problems. The contribution of this

* Funded By Enterprise Ireland Grant PC/2005/0049.

S. Bressan, J. Küng, and R. Wagner (Eds.): DEXA 2006, LNCS 4080, pp. 73–82, 2006.

work is in the provision of a new XPath Query Interface that performs well against the current efforts in the area. Furthermore, we have extended the work in [9] by delivering a fast method of creating the Semantic Repository and also by introducing a multi-index system to fine-tune query performance.

The paper is structured as follows: in §2, we discuss similar research in XML querying; in §3, an outline of the FAST Repository is provided, together with the process used to construct it; in §4, we describe our process for semantic query routing; in §5, we provide experimental data in §6, we offer some conclusions.

2 Related Research

Our approach is to employ a native XML database and support the query processing effort with an indexing method deployed using traditional database techniques. In this section, we examine similar efforts in this area.

XML Enabled Databases. Many researchers including [5,13] have chosen to enable relational databases systems rather than employ a native XML database. In [13], they explore how XML enabled databases can support XML queries by:

1. Utilising two separate indexes on element and text values.
2. Incorporating the MPMGJN algorithm, that is different from the standard merge join algorithms found on commercial databases.
3. Converting XQuery expressions into SQL statements.

The results [13] suggest that the MPMGJN algorithm is more efficient at supporting XML queries than any of the join algorithms found in commercial XML enabled databases. By incorporating the MPMGJN algorithm into the query execution machinery of the RDBMS, they can become efficient in XML storage and processing. However, this approach requires that all XML queries be converted to SQL and in [7], they show that not all XQuery expressions can be translated into SQL, and in some cases, translate into inefficient SQL statements. A further disadvantage of enabled XML databases is their inefficiency at retrieving entire or subsets of an XML document, as it may require several costly joins to construct the required result [3].

Native XML Databases. Our PreLevel index structure is an extension of the *XPath Accelerator* [4], which uses an index structure designed to support the evaluation of XPath queries. This index is capable of supporting the evaluation of all XPath axes (including **ancestor**, **following**, **child**, etc) [2]. It employs a SAX processor to create pre and post order encoding of nodes that capture the structural and value-based semantics of an XML document. Furthermore, the ability to start traversals from arbitrary context nodes in an XML document allows the index to support XPath expressions that are embedded in XQuery expressions.

In [11], the experience of building Jungle, a secondary storage manager for Galax (an open source native XML database) is detailed. In order to optimise query processing, they used the *XPath Accelerator* and indexing structure. However, one major limitation they encountered was the evaluation of the **child** axis, which they found to be as expensive as evaluating the **descendant** axis. They deemed this limitation to be unacceptable and designed their own indexes to support the **child** axis. Although the XPath Accelerator's *pre/post* encoding scheme has since been updated in [5] to use *pre/level/size*, our PreLevel Structure as demonstrated in [9] supports highly efficient evaluations of not just children but also of descendants of any arbitrary node. The Jungle implementation experience also highlighted the significant overhead imposed at document loading time by a *postorder traversal*, which is not required by the PreLevel index structure.

3 The FAST Repository

The processing architecture illustrated in Fig. 1 has three levels: *document* level, *metadata* level and *storage* level. In this section, we begin by describing the role of the processors connecting the levels and at the end of the section, we present the comparative times for a range of XML databases. For reasons of clarity, we now present some of the terminology we use. The metadata extraction file (see *1* in Fig. 1) is a text document; the Oracle table identified as *2* in the same figure is called the Base Index Table (BIT); and the set of tables identified as *3* are called the Primary Index Tables (PIT).

3.1 Metadata Extraction

The *Metadata Extractor* processes the document set at level 1 to generate the metadata document set at level 2. A basic SAX parser has been enhanced with semantic rules that trigger events to extract the data required for the PreLevel indexing method. These events deliver the attributes stored in the metadata document and are described below:

- As each node is visited the `PreOrder` and `Level` events obtain the pre-order value of the node and the level at which it occurs in the XML document tree.
- For performance reasons, the `Position` event determines the position of each node as it occurs at each level in the hierarchy (left to right). This is used to optimise algorithms that operate across a single level.
- As each node is read, the `Parent` event returns the *preorder* value of the node's parent.
- The `Type` event is used to distinguish between elements and attributes.
- The `Name` and `Value` events record the name and value of the node.
- The `FullPath` event is used to record the entire XML path (from node to root).
- The DocID event is fired by the eXist database to provide its internal document identifier for the XML document.

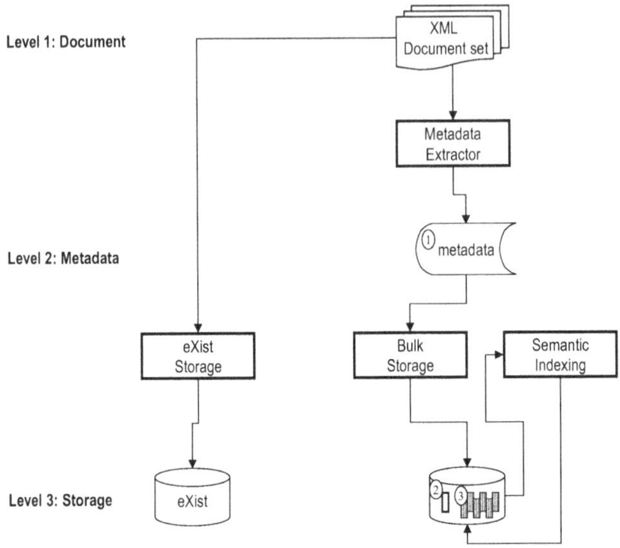

Fig. 1. Repository Processing Architecture

3.2 eXist Storage Processor

The eXist database [6] provides a schema-less storage of XML documents in hierarchical collections and can store a large amount of XML data. It also uses built-in methods to store XML documents in its document store with indexed paged files. The eXist Storage Processor stores an XML document in the form of collections (of sub-documents), in a hierarchical structure. There is a single *parent* collection that acts as the root and using this organisational structure, eXist ensures the speed of querying and information retrieval is significantly faster.

3.3 Bulk Storage Processor

One of the problems with constructing indexes for XML documents is that they tend to be very large with one or more tuples for each node. Thus, building the index can be time-consuming and makes the prospect of document updates difficult. While some form of incremental updating process can be used to address this problem, we sought to find a means of building entire indexes quickly. Using Oracle, it is possible to significantly reduce the time required for large amounts of information (in the case of DBLP, millions of rows) to be inserted, through a bulk loading process. Oracle's SQL*Loader provides a means of bypassing time consuming SQL INSERT commands by presenting the loader with a control file containing a metadata description of a large text file (generated by our Metadata Extraction processor).

The Oracle Storage Processor loads the text file generated by the Metadata Extractor and creates the control file required by the SQL*Loader. The output from this processor is the creation of the Base Index Table (BIT) in Oracle.

3.4 Semantic Indexing Processor

This processor is used to create a set of Primary Index Tables that can be used to improve times for different types of queries. At present, the semantic rules are quite simple. Initially, a Metadata Table is created containing useful statistics of the XML data and one set of statistics contains the total number of data elements in the document set (`EntireTotal`), each element name (`ElemName`), the number of element types (`ElemTypeCount`) and the number of occurrences of this element (`ElemTotal`). For each element that exceeds a threshold T_{ix}, the Semantic Index Processor generates a Primary Index Table. T_{ix} is calculated by multiplying the average number of elements (`ElemAvg = EntireTotal/ElemTypeCount`) by an `IndexFactor` that is currently set at 2, based on our empirical study of XML document content. Thus, an element whose value for `ElemTotal` $\geq T_{ix}$ will have a Primary Index Table created. We have found that this has performance advantages over the creation of multiple indexes on the Base Index Table.

3.5 Repository Build Times

In our experiments, we built the semantic repository for five XML databases on a Dell Optiplex GX620 (3.20GHz) workstation with 1GB RAM on a Windows platform. In Fig. 2 we provide the build times for five standard XML databases [12]. The role of the Bulk Storage Processor played a significant role as the time required to generate the Semantic Repository for DBLP using SQL INSERT commands was 8.13 hours and is now reduced to 258.9 seconds using the same workstation.

Name	Size	Rows	Elems.	Atts.	Levels	BIT	PIT	BIT+PIT
DBLP	127MB	3736407	3332130	404276	6	258.9s	299.0s	557.9s
Line Item	30MB	1022978	1022976	2	3	63.4s	3.7s	67.1s
UWM	2MB	66735	66729	6	5	3.8s	0.3s	4.1s
AT_meta	28MB	552987	492005	60982	9	59.4s	75.7s	135.1s
Mondial	1MB	69846	22423	47423	5	3.4s	1.6s	5.0s

Fig. 2. Repository Construction Times

4 Query Processing

The first role of the Query Router (QR) is to classify the query into one of the following three categories:

- **Index Query.** These queries are resolved at the index level and are regarded as text node queries (see §5).
- **Partial XPath Query.** These queries are processed and routed to more precise locations in the database. They then use the XQuery processor of the native XML database.

– **Full XPath Query.** These queries are resolved at the index level to generate a set of unique eXist identifiers. These identifiers allow direct access to the result documents in the database and do not require eXist's XQuery Interface.

For reasons of space, we concentrate on the *Partial XPath Query* category as this employs all features of the Semantic Repository and works with the native XML database to generate the query result set. The QR currently accepts only XPath queries as input but will convert these to XQuery FLWOR expressions on output.

4.1 Query Router

The Query Router breaks the *location path* of an XPath expression into its *location steps*. Each location step comprises an *axis*, a *node test* (specifies the node type and name) and zero or more *predicates*. The role of this processor is to modify the XPath axis to provide a more precise location using the algorithms described in [9] and the data stored in the Semantic Repository. In *example 1*, the XPath query retrieves the book titles for the named author.

Example 1. //book[author = 'Bertrand Meyer']/title

In Fig. 3(a), the location steps generated by the XPath parser are shown. The XPath axes, the appropriate nodes and the predicate for the *book* node are displayed. The main role of the Query Router is to provide a more precise location path and thus improve query performance. Using the descendant-or-self axis from the root, query processing involves the root node and all of its descendants until it finds the appropriate *book* node: our optimiser (using the PreLevel index) can quickly identify a precise path from the root to this *book* node. In this example, it requires a modified location step as displayed in Fig. 3(b).

The Base Index Table is the default index used to improve performance but before this takes place, a check is made to determine if one of the Primary Index Tables can be used. In the *node test* part of the XPath expression, the Query Router checks to see if one of the PIT set is sorted on that particular element and if so, can use that index.

Example 2. for $title in doc('/db/dblp/dblp.xml')/dblp/book[author ='Bertrand Meyer']/title return $title

Step	Axis	Node Test	Predicates
1	descendant-or-self	node()	
2	child	book	[author = 'Bertrand Meyer']
3	child	title	

(a)

Step	Axis	Node Test	Predicates
1	child	dblp	
2	child	book	[author = 'Bertrand Meyer']
3	child	title	

(b)

Fig. 3. Location Steps

The final part of this process is the construction of one or more XQuery FLWOR expressions by inserting the modified axis expressions into the `for` clause. This expression in example 2 is passed to the native XQuery processor to complete the result set.

5 Details of Query Performance

All experiments were run using a 3GHz Pentium IV machine with 1GB memory on a Windows XP platform. The Query Router runs using Eclipse 3.1 with Java virtual machine (JVM) version 1.5. The Repository was deployed using Oracle 10g (running a LINUX operating system, with a 2.8 GHz Pentium IV processor and 1GB of memory) and eXist (Windows platform with a 1.8 GHz Pentium IV processor and 512MB of memory) database servers. The default JVM machine settings of eXist were increased from -Xmx128000k to -Xmx256000k to maximise efficiency. The DBLP XML database was chosen (see Fig. 2 for details) for its size. For the purpose of this paper, we extracted a subset of the original query set [8], and extended a categorisation originally used in [1].

- *Empty queries* (Q5) are those that return zero matches.
- *Text node queries* (Q6) are queries that return text nodes i.e. XPath queries that end with the `text()` function.
- *Wildcard queries* (Q2) are queries that contain a wildcard character.
- *Punctual queries* (Q1, Q3, Q4) query only a small portion of the database and have a high selectivity, thus they return a small number of matches.
- *Low selectivity queries* (Q6, Q7) are queries that may return a large number of matches.

Table 1. DBLP Queries used in our experiments

Query	XPath Expression	Matches
Q1	//inproceedings[./title/text() = 'Semantic Analysis Patterns.']/author	2
Q2	//inproceedings[./*/text() = 'Semantic Analysis Patterns.']/author	2
Q3	//book[author = 'Bertrand Meyer']/title	13
Q4	//inproceedings[./author = 'Jim Gray'][./year = '1990']/@key	6
Q5	//site/people/person[@id = 'person']	0
Q6	//title/text()	328,859
Q7	/dblp/book/series	420

5.1 Queries and Performance Measures

In order to obtain contrasting results, we ran all queries under varying *support modes*:

1. **eXist**. The XPath query is executed using the eXist query processor only.
2. **eXist + BIT**. The XPath query pre-processed using the Base Index Table before being passed to the eXist query processor.

3. **eXist + PIT**. The XPath query pre-processed using a Primary Index Table before being passed to the eXist query processor.
4. **PreLevel**. The XPath query is processed at the PreLevel index without using the eXist query processor.

For each query, all the execution times are recorded in milliseconds (ms), together with the number of matches. The times were averaged (with the first run elimination) to ensure that all results are warm cache numbers.

Table 2 displays the execution times for each of the seven queries in each support mode. Some of the queries (Q2, Q6) in the eXist mode failed to return any results (R2, R6), as eXist continually returned an *out of memory* error. Although the eXist user guide suggests the alteration of JVM settings in order to address the problem, even with optimum JVM settings, these queries fail to generate a result.

Table 2. Query Execution Times

Result	eXist	eXist+BIT	eXist+PIT	PreLevel
R1	20,324.1	19,807.8	19,408.2	N/A
R2		19,864.4	19,412.9	N/A
R3	801.1	759.3	As eXist + BIT	N/A
R4	3,209	2,819.9	2,721.3	N/A
R5	178	6	As eXist + BIT	N/A
R6		102,641.2	100,083.4	16,648.2
R7	234.2	1,480	As eXist +BIT	N/A

5.2 Performance Analysis

Results R1, R3 and R4 show that the Query Router (QR) can make a significant difference to *punctual queries*. Furthermore, the results indicate that the PIT (where available) is more efficient than the BIT at routing XPath queries.

Result *R5* suggests that the QR can efficiently handle queries that return empty result sets. This is because the QR will always consult its Semantic Repository (SR) to ensure that a query has a positive number of matches before passing the query to eXist. The multi-index feature of the SR ensures that this type of query is identified quickly. As *text node queries* (Q6) require only the PreLevel index for processing, they run far more efficiently in the PreLevel mode.

Result R7 indicates that the QR will not improve the performance of *child queries*. This is not unexpected as eXist handles this form of query well. The QR performs less favourably because it must perform an index look-up in order to determine the respective document URI(s) which are required in each XQuery expression. However we believe that with the incorporation of a meta-metatable containing summarised data for each fullpath expression and their respective document URIs, the QR will be able to outperform eXist for even this form of query. This research forms part of ongoing research and initial results are positive [10].

The eXist processor cannot handle the upper scale of *low selectivity queries* such as Q6 that return a very large number of matches. However the QR can process the upper scale of *low selectivity* queries, by:

- Utilising our Semantic Repository to calculate the number of matches for a *low selectivity query*.
- If the number of matches is greater than a set threshold (50,000 in our current experiment setup), the QR will break the *low selectivity* query into a number (equal to (number of matches/threshold) + 1) of *child* queries.
- The resulting child queries are equivalent to the *low selectivity query*.

The eXist processor also fails to handle wildcards where the search range is high or the database is very large (Q2). If there is a wildcard character in the *node test* or *predicate* clauses, the QR removes the wildcard by processing the wildcard option at the PreLevel index. This aspect of the QR is not yet fully functional: it can only remove wildcards in certain queries.

6 Conclusions

In this paper, we presented our approach to improving the performance of XPath queries. In this context, we discussed the construction of the FAST Semantic Repository, which includes an indexing structure based upon our prior work on level based indexing for XPath performance. In our current work, we provide an extended indexing structure deployed using Oracle 10g and exploit some of Oracle's features to ensure a fast rebuilding of the index. Using our Query Router we can then exploit our indexing structures in one of two broad modes: using the indexing method to fully resolve the query; use either the Base or Primary Index Table together with the eXist XQuery processor to generate the result set. The Query Router accepts XPath expressions as input and creates XQuery expressions (where necessary) for the eXist database.

We also describe a series of experiments to support our claims that XPath expressions can be optimised using our indexing structures. Together with the fast rebuilding of the index, this method supports not only fast XPath queries, but also a strong basis for the provision of updates. The construction time for a large index is between 60 and 260 seconds, and this allows for rebuilding the index multiple times during the course of the day. This provides the basis for appending to updateable indexes with full rebuilds at set intervals. Thus, our current research focus is on managing update queries. We are also examining the cost of PIT builds against their increase in query performance as a fine-tuning measure for the index. Finally, our next version of the FAST prototype should include an interface for both XPath *and* XQuery expressions.

References

1. Barta A., Consens M. and Mendelzon A. Benefits of Path Summaries in an XML Query Optimizer Supporting Multiple Access Methods. In *Proceedings of the 31st VLDB Conference*, pp 133-144, Morgan Kaufmann, 2005.
2. Berglund A. et al. XML Path Language (XPath 2.0), *Technical Report W3C Working Draft*, WWW Consortium 2005. (`http://www.w3.org/TR/xpath20/`).

3. Beyer K. et al. System RX: One Part Relational, One Part XML. In *Proceedings of ACM SIGMOD Conference on Management of data*, pp 347-358, ACM Press, 2005.
4. Grust T. Accelerating XPath Location Steps. In *Proceedings of the 2002 ACM SIGMOND International Conference on the Management of Data*, volume 31, SIGMOND Record, pp 109-120, ACM Press, 2002.
5. Grust T., Sakr S. and Teuber J. XQuery on SQL Hosts. In *Proceedings of the 30th International Conference on Very Large Databases (VLDB)*, pp 252-263, Morgan Kaufmann, 2004.
6. Meier W. eXist: An Open Source Native XML Database. In *Web, Web-Services, and Database Systems*, LNCS 2593, pp 169-183, Springer, 2002.
7. Manolescu I., Florescu D., Kossmann D. Answering XML Queries on Heterogeneous Data Sources, In *Proceedings of the 27th International Conference on Very Large Databases (VLDB)*, pp 241-250, Morgan Kaufmann, 2001.
8. Noonan C. XPath Query Routing in the FAST Project. *Technical Report ISG-06-01*, `http://www.computing.dcu.ie/~isg`, 2006.
9. O'Connor M., Bellahsene Z. and Roantree M. An Extended Preorder Index for Optimising XPath Expressions. In *Proceedings of 3rd XML Database Symposium (XSym)*, LNCS Vol. 3671, pp 114-128, Springer, 2005.
10. Roantree M. The FAST Prototype: a Flexible indexing Algorithm using Semantic Tags. *Technical Report ISG-06-02*, `http://www.computing.dcu.ie/~isg`, 2006.
11. Vyas A., Fernández M. and Simèon J. The Simplest XML Storage Manager Ever., In *Proceedings of the First International Workshop on XQuery Implementation, Experience and Perspectives <XIME-P/>, in cooperation with ACM SIGMOD*, pp 27-42, 2004.
12. The XML Data Repository. `http://www.cs.washington.edu/research/xmldatasets/`, 2002.
13. Zhang C. et al. On Supporting Containment Queries in Relational Database Management Systems, In *Proceedings of the 2001 ACM SIGMOD International Conference on the Management of Data*, pp 425-436, ACM Press, 2001.

A Relational Nested Interval Encoding Scheme for XML Data*

Gap-Joo Na and Sang-Won Lee

Dept. of Computer Engineering, Sungkyunkwan University, Suwon-si, Kyunggi, 440-746
{factory, swlee}@skku.edu

Abstract. As XML is rapidly becoming the de-facto standard for data representation and exchange in the Internet age, there has been a lot of research on how to store and retrieve XML data in relational databases. However, even though the XML data is mostly tree-structured, the XML research community has shown little attention to the traditional RDBMS-based encoding scheme for tree data. In this paper, we investigate one of the encoding schemes, called Nested Interval, for the storage and retrieval of XML data. In particular, our approach is very robust in updating XML data, including insertion of new node. In fact, the existing RDBMS-based XML storage and indexing techniques work very poorly against XML data update because the XML data should be re-encoded from the scratch for virtually any update in XML data. In contract, Nested Interval scheme does not require re-encoding all nodes. In this respect, our approach is a viable option for storing and querying update-intensive XML application.

1 Introduction

As XML is rapidly becoming the de-facto standard for data representation and exchange in the Internet age, a lot of research has been done on how to store and retrieve XML data in DBMS(database management system). The existing work is mainly on how to store and retrieve XML data efficiently in native XML database management system, ORDBMS(object-relational database management system), or pure RDBMS(relational database management system).

Among these research, the pure RDBMS-based research on XML data is getting more popularity recently as the relational databases are more dominant for XML storage in market shares [1][2][3]. However, the existing RDBMS-based research has a common problem that we must re-index whole document when a new XML document insertion or a new element insertion. In order to attack this problem, we review one of the traditional RDBMS-based encoding scheme, called Nested Interval [6], and apply it for storage and retrieval of XML data. This technique can efficiently insert new XML data into the relational databases incrementally, which is impossible or very inefficient in the existing approach.

* This research was supported by the Ministry of Information and Communication, Korea under the Information Technology Research Center support program supervised by the Institute of Information Technology Assessment, IITA-2005-(C1090-0501-0019).

S. Bressan, J. Küng, and R. Wagner (Eds.): DEXA 2006, LNCS 4080, pp. 83 – 92, 2006.

The XML data is in general tree-structured. Traditionally, RDBMS is known to be inefficient in storing tree data. Recently, however, several RDBMS-based encoding schemes for tree data have been proposed, which are not intended for XML data [5,6,7,8,9]. In particular, Nested Interval tree encoding with continued fractions [8] is very smart tree encoding scheme in RDBMS. In this paper, we introduce this technique for storing and retrieving XML data, implement a Web-based XML storage system based on the technique, and show that this scheme is very efficient in managing the XML data, including the XML update.

The remainder of this paper is organized as follows. In Section 2, we examine related work how to store and query a tree-structured data in RDBMS and a recent well-known RDBMS-based XML encoding scheme, called XPath Accelerator. In Section 3, we present the nested interval tree encoding scheme with continued fractions. Section 4 describes an implementation of the nested interval encoding scheme with continued fractions. Finally, Section 5 concludes with some future work.

2 Related Work

This section briefly reviews the three representative techniques for representing tree-structured data in RDBMS [5] and also one of the well-known RDBMS-based XML encoding scheme, called XPath Accelerator.

2.1 Adjacency List Model

Adjacency List model[5] is the method to store a current node key and a parent node key to store tree-structured data. So, this storage model is easy to search a parent node from arbitrary node, but the main problem with this approach is that it is inefficient to find child node, ancestor node and descendant node.

2.2 Materialized Path Model

In this model, we can store each node with the whole path from root node. The path-value represents a node as an ordered position. For example, the root node is '1' and '1.1' is a first child node of the root node. The main advantage of this technique is that we can find a position of current node with only a path value.

2.3 Nested Set Model

In case of Nested Set model[5], each node is indexed using the left(denoted as lft) and right(denoted as rgt) columns and these columns are stored in a table. Using this indexing technique, we can know that total node number equals (root node's rgt)/2. In the nested set model, the difference between the (lft, rgt) values of leaf nodes is always 1, and the descendants of a node can be found by looking for the nodes whose (lft, rgt) numbers are between the (lft, rgt) values of their parent node. If a parent node has (p_lft, p_rgt) and a child node has (c_lft, c_rgt), their relation is the relation p_lft < c_lft, p_rgt > c_rgt. So we can get easily result as we query. Fig.1. shows an example of Nested Set Model. However, this indexing technique has the disadvantage that we should re-index the whole nodes when a new node is inserted, updated, or deleted.

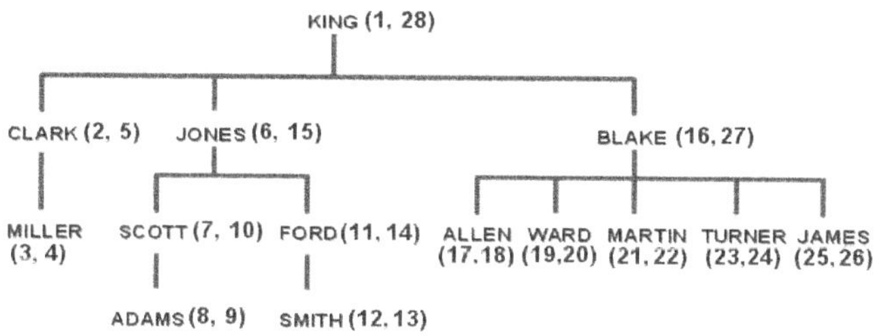

Fig. 1. Structure of Nested Set model

2.4 Xpath Accelerator

XPath Accelerator[4], an index model to store XML document in RDBMS, indexes a node to pre-ordered value and post-ordered value. Fig.2. shows how nodes can index to pre-ordered value and post-ordered value. Pre-ordered and post-ordered value stored in RDBMS as we shown Fig.2. Using this indexing model, we can find ancestor, following, preceding and descendant nodes in the pre/post plane as shown in Fig.2. However, this indexing technique has a serious disadvantage. When there is any change in stored XML data, we should re-index all nodes like Nested Set indexing model.

NODE	PRE	POST
a	0	7
b	1	5
c	7	6
d	2	0
e	3	4
f	4	1
g	5	3
h	6	2

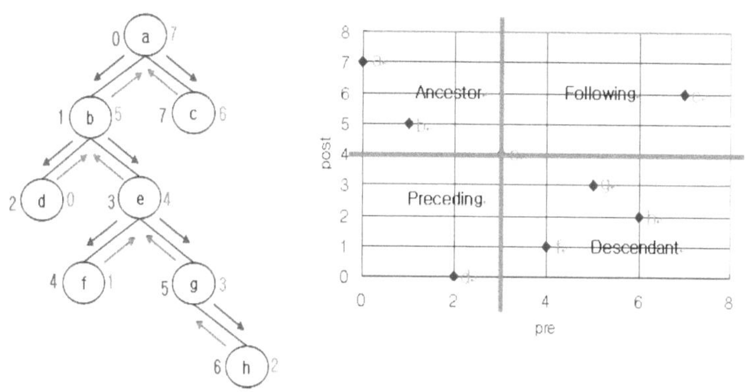

Fig. 2. Pre-order and post-order traverse

3 Nested Interval Tree Encoding with Continued Fractions

In this section, we review a recent relational approach, called continued fractions, to apply Nested Interval model [6] to store tree-structured data in RDBMS. This approach is proposed to support efficient updates in hierarchical data. The concept of Nested Interval generalizes the idea of Nested Set [5]. Thus, from Nested Interval encoding, we can easily calculate Materialized Path. Consequently, we can exploit the advantages of both models. However, Nested Interval model encodes each node with binary rational numbers and thus the size of binary encoding data grows exponentially, both in breadth and in depth.[6] So, in this paper, we adopt a new variant of the nested interval model, called Nested Interval Tree Encoding Scheme with continued fractions[8].

3.1 Basic Structure

A basic structure of the Nested Interval is similar to that of Nested Set, but the difference between Nested Interval and Nested Set is to represent a node by a rational numbers in Nested Interval. Like Nested Set, if a parent node has (p_lft, p_rgt) and a child node has (c_lft, c_rgt), their relation is plft <= clft and crgt >= prgt. So we can find easily the relationship of nodes.

Nested Interval model uses a rational number set because integer number set can not represent infinity number between lft and rgt value. One example of such a policy would be finding an unoccupied segment (lft1, rgt1) within a parent interval (plft, prgt) and inserting a child node ((2*lft1+rgt)/3, (lft1+2*rgt1)/3) as we shown Fig.3. After insertion, we still have two more unoccupied segments (lft1, (2*lft1+rgt)/3) and ((lft1+2*rgt1)/3), rgt1) to add more children to the parent node.

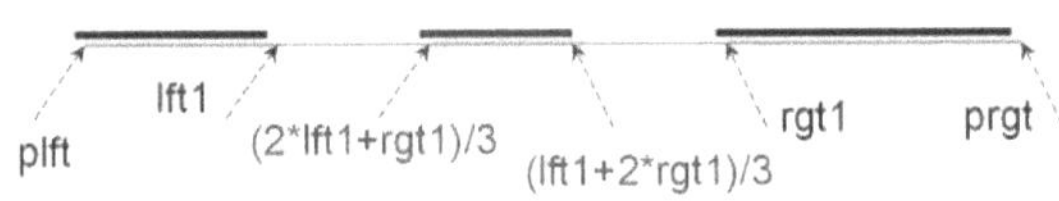

Fig. 3. Nested Interval

3.2 Nested Intervals Tree Encoding with Continued Fractions

In basic Nested Interval scheme [6], each node has a represent binary rational number. But this scheme has a serious problem that the size of binary encoding grows exponentially, both in breadth and in depth. More seriously, it can cause numeric overflow. To solve this problem, we use Nested Intervals Tree Encoding with continued fractions [8].

First, we describe how a node, which encodes a materialized path, can be converted into a rational number, which is unique to each node. Next, we describe how we can get relations of nodes with mathematical computation.

3.2.1 The Encoding

Nested Interval labels tree node with rational numbers a/b such that $a \geq b \geq 1$ and GCD(a,b)=1, where GCD is the abbreviation for Greatest Common Divisor. For example, node with a=181 and b=34 can be converted to Materialized Path '5.3.11' by using Euclidean Algorithm[8].

$$
\begin{aligned}
181 &= 34 * \mathit{5} + 11 \\
34 &= 11 * \mathit{3} + 1, \\
11 &= 1 * \mathit{11} + 0
\end{aligned}
$$

3.2.2 Continued Fractions

And then, the materialized path '5.3.11' can be converted to rational number by using simple continued fractions. The following is an example. (Materialized Path '5.3.11' => Rational Number '181/34')

$$5+\cfrac{1}{3+\cfrac{1}{11}}=\frac{181}{34}$$

3.2.3 Nested Intervals

In previous section, we could know that one node has a unique Rational Number value. But, for XML retrieval, we have to know the interval of each node. For this, we mapped every continued fraction into an interval in 2 steps. First, we associate a rational number with each continued fraction as follows:

$$5+\cfrac{1}{3+\cfrac{1}{11+\cfrac{1}{x}}}=\frac{181x+16}{34x+3}$$

Then, we assume $x \in [1, \infty)$. Substituting the boundary values for x into the Rational Function for Materialized Path '5.3.11', we can find that it ranges inside the (181/34, 197/37] semi-open interval. Moreover, we can find rational number of parent node in same time. In a nested interval (a/b, c/d), rational number of parent node is (a-c)/(b-d).

3.3 XPath Style Queries

To query XML data, we present the details of translating each step in an XPath style query to use our indexing model. The purpose of this paper is to present suitability for XML storage and retrieval. So, we describe how XPath style queries[4] can be computed easily with mathematics computation. In this section, we explain how to compute relationship of nodes mathematically.

3.3.1 Child Node and Parent Node

To get the parent node, first, we have to find the Materialized Path of a current node, and then we can get parent node value with the path. For example, if one node has a rational value '181/34', we can get Materialized Path '5.3.11' with using Euclidean Algorithm. Next, we represent path 5.3.11 as matrix product.

$$\begin{bmatrix}5 & 1\\1 & 0\end{bmatrix}\cdot\begin{bmatrix}3 & 1\\1 & 0\end{bmatrix}\cdot\begin{bmatrix}11 & 1\\1 & 0\end{bmatrix}=\begin{bmatrix}181 & 16\\34 & 3\end{bmatrix}$$

In the result matrix, (1,2) value / (2,2) value is a rational value of parent node. So the parent node of '181/34' is '16/3'. To get the child node, we can easily calculate node value with using matrix product. For more detail processing, refer the paper [8].

3.3.2 Ancestor Node and Descendant Node

We can find ancestor node and descendant node using Nested Interval. Relation between ancestor node (ax, ay) and descendant node (dx, dy) is ax < dx < dy < ax. So, we can get relation of two nodes.

3.3.3 Following Node and Preceding Node

Following node and preceding node can also get to use Nested Interval and using 3.3.1. First, we can get the nested interval of parent node (px, py), and then following node (fx, fy) is px<py<fx<fy. And we can get preceding nodes (prx, pry) to use reverse relation.

prx<pry<px<py

3.3.4 Following-Sibling and Preceding-Sibling

To get next sibling node (following node), we just add two nodes (current node, parent node). But, we must add two nodes separately about numerator, denominator.

For example, we can get next sibling node '5.3.12' of current node '5.3.11'. Current node is '181/34' and parent node of the node is '16/3', so, following sibling node '5.3.12' is '181+16 / 34+3'. In the same manner, preceding sibling node '5.3.10' is '181-16 / 34-3'.

4 Implementations

Now, we describe how to implement Nested Interval indexing model system in a commercial RDBMS. Even though our system uses a particular commercial RDBMS, it can be applied to any RDBMS products.

Our implementation uses 2.0GHz Pentium IV processor with 1GB of physical memory running Redhat AS3 Linux Server. We use an Apache 2.0 Web-Server compiled with PHP 4.1.12 and Oracle 10g database management system. Our XML data used [11] (The Plays of Shakespeare in XML).

4.1 System Architecture

Fig.4. shows the system architecture and it consists of two processes. One process is to store XML data as following step.

(1) Parsing XML document using JAVA SAX Parser[10] to Materialized Path.
(2) Encoding Materialized Path to Nested Interval Scheme using Java stored procedure.
(3) Storing XML data to RDBMS.

The other process is to query process. User must input pure SQL query to the system because our system can not support to XPath query. We will add an Xpath Parser(Xpath -> SQL) to the system later.

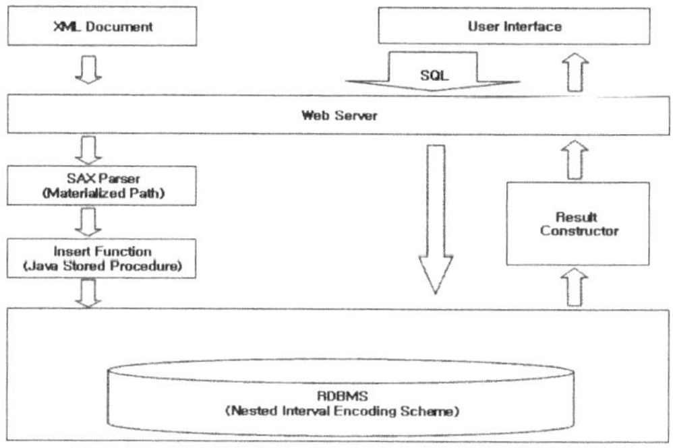

Fig. 4. System Architecture

4.2 Mapping Functions

We implement some functions that map Materialized Path into Nested Interval with an XML document to store RDBMS. Each function was coded using Java Class, and they are called from Oracle PL-SQL. Followings are functions of each group.

- *Storing function group* : x_numer, x_denom, y_numer, y_denom, …
- *Relation function group* : parent_numer, distance, child_numer, ...
- *Path function group* : path, path_numer, path_denom, sibling_number, …

4.3 Table Scheme and Data Inserting

We create a table for storing XML document in RDBMS and table scheme is following.

```
CREATE TABLE XML_DOCS(
    DOCID         INT    NOT NULL,
    NODEID        INT    NOT NULL,
    DOC_NAME      VARCHAR2(30)    NOT NULL,
    NODE_TYPE     INT    NOT NULL,
    NODE          VARCHAR2(100),
    CONTENT       VARCHAR2(2000),
    L_NUMER       INT    NOT NULL,
    L_DENOM       INT    NOT NULL,
    R_NUMER       INT    NOT NULL,
    R_DENOM       INT    NOT NULL,
    P_NUMER       INT,
    P_DENOM       INT,
    DEPTH         INT,
    CONSTRAIONT XML_PK PRIMARY KEY(DOCID, NODEID));
```

4.4 Inserting XML Document

When we insert each node into the table in RDBMS, we can use the previous scheme. And when we insert XML document for the first time, we can insert values calculated through the parsing stage with functions.

```
INSERT INTO XML (DOCID, NODEID, DOC_NAME, NODE_TYPE, NODE, CONTENT, L_NUM
ER, L_DENOM, R_NUMER, R_DENOM, P_NUMER, P_DENOM, DEPTH)
VALUES(8, 2, 'hamlet.xml', 1, 'TITLE', ' ', path_numer('2.2'), path_denom('2.2'), path_numer('2.2')+ pat
h_pnumer('2.2'), path_denom('2.2')+ path_pdenom('2.2'), path_pnumer('2.2'), path_pdenom('2.2'), depth
(path_numer('2.2'), path_denom('2.2')))
```

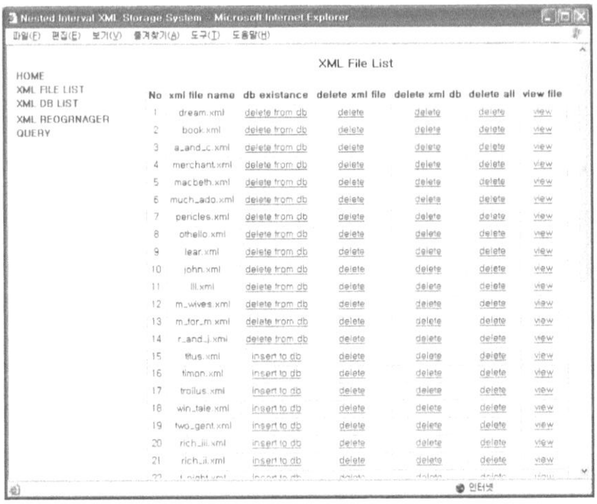

Fig. 5. XML File List

This insert step can be processed automatically like Fig.5., and it takes the constant time because our indexing technique has the advantage that it does not need to re-index whole document when we insert additional nodes into RDBMS. Table.1. shows a result that the total time increases linearly as we insert new nodes. For this experiment, first we deleted mid-nodes of an XML document in [10] and parsed it. And then, we stored XML document in RDBMS and inserted new nodes that had been deleted. So we could obtain the result that the inserting time per each node is increase linearly.

Table 1. Total elapsed time vs. Number of nodes

Number of node(add new nodes)	100	500	1000	2000	3000	4000	5000
Total Elapsed Time(ms)	96	510	997	1992	3013	4101	5078

4.5 Translating XPath Queries into SQL Queries

The following is an example that describes how XPath query translate into SQL query. In the system, we have to query using only SQL query. So user must convert an Xpath to SQL manually. The conversion can be decided performance of query process. So Xpath parser(Xpath to SQL) is very important and hard to develop. We will develop efficient XPath parser as soon as possible. So, currently we query to the system manually like Fig.6.

<Query for descendant node>
- //ACT/ descendant::TITLE

SELECT x1.doc_name, x1.node||'('||x1.l_numer||'/'||x1.l_denom||','|| x1.r_numer||'/'||x1.r_denom ||')', x2.node||'('||x2.l_numer||'/'||x2.l_denom||','|| x2.r_numer||'/'||x2.r_denom ||')' FROM xml x1, xml x2
WHERE x1.node='ACT' and x2.node='TITLE' AND x1.docid=x2.docid AND x1.l_numer/x1.l_denom < x2.l_numer/x2.l_denom AND x1.r_numer/x1.r_denom > x2.r_numer/x2.r_denom
[Elapsed: 00:00:00.10 Sec]

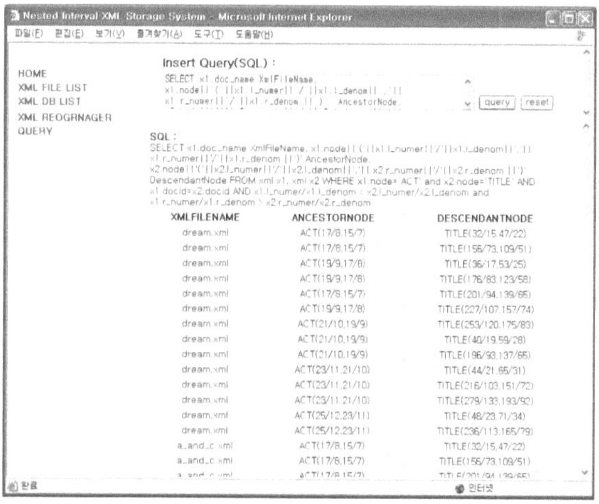

Fig. 6. XML Retrieval

In case of related research XPath Accelerator[3], in order to improve the performance in query processing, they try to narrow scanning range(from one value to infinity). But in our scheme Nested Interval, each node has fixed range, which is called Nested Interval. So, we can expect much better performancc to query large volume data.

5 Conclusions and Future Work

In this paper, we exploited the nested interval model for encoding tree data in RDBMS, and applied the technique for XML storage, in particular, in order to avoid re-indexing the whole data whenever an update occur in XML document. The Nested Interval model generalizes nested set so it provides the same advantages of both Nested Set and Materialized Path. The key advantage of Nested Interval is that we do not need to re-index whole document as additional nodes inserted in RDBMS. And we can find easily position values of each node by calling some functions which use mathematical computation. So we can find a position value of parent or child node without access RDBMS. In conclusion, Nested Interval model, which is proposed to store tree-structure data, can be used for XML storage as we have shown in section 4.

Our next work is to develop Xpath Parser, which translates XPath queries into SQL queries automatically. By using this parser, we can expect user convenience. And we must show the performance advantages of our scheme, through various benchmark tests. Lastly, we will apply this scheme to ORDBMS by using extensible index[12][13]. So, users can handle and index the XML data as easily as they do numeric or string data with B+ tree index.

References

1. D.Floresce, D.kossman, "Storing and Querying XML data Using a RDBMS", IEEE Data Engineering Bulletin, Vol.22, No 3, 1999
2. I. Tatarinov et al., "Storing and Querying Ordered XML Using a Relational Database System", Proc. ACM SIGMOD Int'l Conf. on Management of Data, 2002
3. Torsten Grust, "Accelerating XPath Location Steps", ACM SIGMOD, Madison, June, 2003
4. W3C, XML Path Language(XPath), Version 1.0, W3C Recommendation, November 1999
5. CELKO.J, "Joe Celko's Trees & Hierarchies in SQL for Smarties", Morgan Kaufmann, 2004
6. TROPASHKO, V. 2003a. Trees in SQL:Nested Sets and Materialized Path. http://www. dbazine.com/tropashko4.shtml
7. V. TROPASHKO "Nested Intervals with Farey Fractions.", http://arxiv.org/html/cs.DB/ 0401014
8. V. TROPASHKO "Nested Intervals Tree Encoding with Continued Fractions.", http:// arxiv.org/pdf/cs.DB/040251
9. V. TROPASHKO "Nested Intervals Tree Encoding in SQL.", SIGMOD 2005
10. http://www.saxproject.org/
11. The Plays of Shakespeare in XML. (http://www.xml.com/pub/r/396)
12. S. Sundara et al., "Developing an Indexing Scheme for XML Document Collections using the Oracle8i Extensibility Framework," Proceedings of VLDB 2001
13. Oracle Corp., "Data Cartridge Developer's Guide 10g Release1 (10.1)," http://download-west.oracle.com/docs/cd/B14117_01/appdev.101/b10800/toc.htm

A Prototype of a Schema-Based XPath Satisfiability Tester

Jinghua Groppe and Sven Groppe

University of Innsbruck, Technikerstrasse 21a, AT-6020 Innsbruck, Austria
{Jinghua.Groppe, Sven.Groppe}@uibk.ac.at

Abstract. The satisfiability test of queries can be used in query optimization for avoiding submission and computation of unsatisfiable queries. Thus, applying the satisfiability test before executing a query can save evaluation time and transportation costs in distributed scenarios. Therefore, we propose a schema-based approach to the satisfiability test of XPath queries, which checks whether or not an XPath query conforms to the constraints in a given schema. If an XPath query does not conform to the constraints given in the schema, the evaluation of the query will return an empty result for every XML document. Thus, the XPath query is unsatisfiable. We present a complexity analysis of our approach, which proves that our approach is efficient at typical cases. We present an experimental analysis of our developed prototype, which shows the optimization potential of avoiding the evaluation of unsatisfiable queries.

1 Introduction

XPath is a query language for XML data. A key determinant in XPath evaluation is the satisfiability problem of XPath queries. An XPath query Q is unsatisfiable, if the evaluation of Q on any XML document (which conforms to a schema) returns every time an empty answer. Therefore, the satisfiability test of XPath queries plays a critical role in query optimization. The application of the satisfiability test can avoid unnecessary submission and evaluation of unsatisfiable queries, thus saving processing time and query cost. Therefore, several contributions focus on the satisfiability test of XPath queries with or without respect to schemas [1][6][7][8].

We focus on the satisfiability test in the presence of XML Schemas, since the satisfiability test with schemas can detect more errors in XPath queries than without schemas. Our approach supports recursive and non-recursive schemas and all XPath axes.

Our approach evaluates XPath queries on XML Schema definitions rather than the instance documents of the schemas. Since the satisfiability test for the XPath subset supported by our approach in the presence of schemas is undecidable [1], we present an incomplete, but fast satisfiability tester, i.e. if our tester returns *unsatisfiable*, then we are sure that the XPath query is unsatisfiable, but if our tester returns *maybe satisfiable*, then the XPath query may be satisfiable or may be unsatisfiable. Note that we do not loose correctness in the proposed application scenarios of our satisfiability tester when using an incomplete tester.

Related Work. Many research efforts are dedicated into the satisfiability problem of XPath queries. [1] theoretically studies the complexity problem of XPath satisfiability

S. Bressan, J. Küng, and R. Wagner (Eds.): DEXA 2006, LNCS 4080, pp. 93 – 103, 2006.

in the presence of DTDs, and shows that the complexity of XPath satisfiability depends on the considered subsets of XPath queries and DTDs. We present a practical algorithm for testing the satisfiability of XPath queries. [6] investigates the problem of XPath satisfiability in the absence of schemas. [8] examines the test of satisfiability of tree pattern queries (i.e. reverse axes are not considered) with respect to non-recursive schemas. [7] suggests an algorithm to test the satisfiability of XPath queries, but allows only non-recursive DTDs and does not support all XPath axes. We support recursive schemas and all XPath axes. [5] filters the unsatisfiable XPath queries by a set of simplification rules while we use the constraints given by an XML Schema definition to check the satisfiability of XPath. [3] extends the applications of satisfiability test to optimizations for XML query reformulation and shows how to reduce the containment and intersection test of XPath expressions to the satisfiability test. We extend our contribution in [4] by a complexity analysis of our approach, which shows that our approach is efficient for typical cases, and a performance analysis, which proves the optimization potential of using our satisfiability tester in query optimization.

The rest of the paper is organized as follows: Section 2 describes the supported subsets of XPath and XML Schema. Section 3 describes a data model for XML Schema, which is used by our XPath satisfiability tester that is presented in Section 4. Section 4 also includes a complexity analysis of our XPath satisfiability tester. A comprehensive performance analysis is presented in Section 5. Finally, we end up with the summary and conclusions in Section 6.

2 XPath and XML Schema

In this paper, we consider the basic properties of the XPath language [13][14]. Let e be an XPath expression, q be a predicate expression of XPath and C be a literal, i.e. a string or a number. The abstract syntax of the supported XPath subset is defined in Extended Backus Naur Form (EBNF) as follows:

```
e::= ele | /e | e/e | e[q] | axis::nodetest.
q::= e | e=C | e=e | q and q | q or q | not(q) | (q) | true() | false().
axis::= child | attr | desc | self | following | preceding | parent | ances | DoS | AoS | FS | PS.
nodetest::= label | * | node() | text().
```

where we write DoS for descendant-or-self, AoS for ancestor-or-self, FS for following-sibling and PS for preceding-sibling. Furthermore, we use attr as short name for attribute, desc for descendant and ances for ancestor.

We support the subset of the XML Schema language [12], which contains the most important language constructs to express XML Schema definitions, where a given XML Schema definition must conform to the following rules defined in EBNF.

```
XSchema ::= <schema > (elemD|attrGD|groupD|compTD)* </schema>.
elemD ::= <element name='N' occurs? (type='T')?> <complexType (mixed='true')?
              (ref='N')?> complexType? </complexType> (attrR|attrD)* </element>.
groupD ::= <group name='N'> complexType? </group>.
compTD ::= <complexType name='N'> complexType </complexType>.
complexType ::= <all occurs?> complexType?</all> | <sequence occurs?> complexType?
                  </sequence> | (elems|groupR)*.
```

```
elems ::= (elemD | <element ref='N'  occurs? />)*.
groupR ::= <group ref='N'/>.
attrR ::= <attributeGroup ref='N'/>.
attrGD ::= <attributeGroup name='N'> (attrD)*  </attributeGroup>.
attrD ::= <attribute name='N' type='T' (use= 'required')?/>
occurs ::= minOccurs=num maxOccurs=(num|'unbounded').
```

where T is a simple type, N is a name and num is a number.

Example 1. Fig. 1 presents an example of an XML Schema definition web.xsd, which describes webpages.

```
(D1) <schema>
(D2)  <group name='pages'>
(D3)   <sequence>
(D4)    <element name='page'
          minOccurs='0' maxOccurs='1'>
(D5)     <complexType>
(D6)      <sequence>
(D7) <element name='title' minOccurs='0'
       maxOccurs='1' type='string'/>
(D8) <element name='link'
      minOccurs='0'>
(D9)  <complexType>
(D10)   <group ref='pages' minOccurs='0'
           maxOccurs='unbounded'/>
       </complexType> </element>
     </sequence> </complexType>
   </element> </sequence> </group>

(D11) <element name='web'>
(D12)  <complexType>
(D13)   <group ref='pages'
  minOccurs='0' maxOccurs='unbounded'/>
      </complexType> </element>
    </schema>
```

Fig. 1. An XML Schema definition web.xsd

3 Data Model for XML Schema Language

Based-on the data models for the XML language given by [11] and [9], we develop a data model for XML Schema for identifying the navigation paths of XPath queries on an XML Schema definition. The transitive closure f^+ and reflexive transitive closure f^* of a relationship function f: T→Set(T) are defined as follows:

$$f^n(x) = \{ z \mid y \in f^{n-1}(x) \wedge z \in f(y) \}, \text{ where } f^0(x) = \{x\},\ f^1(x) = f(x)$$
$$f^+(x) = \cup_{n=1}^{\infty} f^n(x) \text{ and } f^*(x) = \cup_{n=0}^{\infty} f^n(x)$$

An XML Schema definition is a set of nodes of type Node. There are four specific Node types in an XML Schema definition, which are associated with *instance nodes* of the XML Schema defintion: root, iElem, iAttr and iText. Accordingly, we define four functions of Node→Boolean to test the type of a node: isRoot, isiElem, isiAttr, and isiText, which return true if the type of the given node is a root node, is of type iElem, iAttr or iText respectively, otherwise false.

Definition 1 (*instance nodes*). The instance nodes of an XML Schema definition are

- <element name=N> (which is of type iElem),
- <attribute name=N> (which is of type iAttr),
- <complextType mixed= 'true'> (which is of type iText),
- <element type=T> (which is of type iText), where T is a simpleType.

Definition 2 (*succeeding nodes*). A node N2 in an XML Schema definition is a *succeeding node* of a node N1 in the XML Schema definition if

- N2 is a child node of N1, or
- N1=<element type=N> and N2=<complexType name=N> with the same N, or
- N1=<element ref=N> and N2=<element name=N> with the same N, or
- N1=<group ref=N> and N2=<group name=N> with the same N, or
- N1=<attributeGroup ref=N> and N2=<attributeGroup name=N> with the same N.

Definition 3 (*preceding nodes*). Node N1 in an XML Schema definition is a *preceding node* of a node N2 in the XML Schema definition if N2 is a *succeeding node* of N1.

Fig. 2 defines the relation functions of Node→Set(Node), which relate a schema node to other schema nodes. For instances, root(x) returns the root node of the document in which x occurs; iChild relates a node to its instance child nodes. For computing iChild(x), an auxiliary function S(x) is defined, which relates the node x to the self node and all the descendant nodes of x, which occur before the instance child nodes of x in the document order. iDesc relates a node to all its instance descendant nodes and is defined to be the transitive closure $iChild^+$. The relation function iSibling(x) relates the node x to its instance sibling nodes. iBranch(x) relates node x to all the instance element nodes excluding any ancestors and descendants of the node x. iPS(x) relates the node x to its instance sibling nodes that occur before node x in the document order, and iPreceding(x) relates node x to its instance branch nodes that occur before node x in the document order. We write y<<x to indicate that the node y occurs before the node x in the document order of an instance document. The document order is computed from an XML Schema definition in the following way: if a set of elements is declared as sequence with the attribute maxOccurs set to `1`, the document order of elements is the order in which they are defined; if it is declared as all or as sequence with the attribute maxOccurs set to a number greater than `1`, any element of this set of elements can occur before any other elements of this element set in an instance document.

$$root(x) = \{ y \mid isRoot(y)\}$$
$$succe(x) = \{ y \mid y \text{ is a } \textit{succeeding} \text{ node of } x \}$$
$$prece(x) = \{ y \mid y \text{ is } \textit{preceding} \text{ node of } x \}$$
$$S(x) = \cup_{i=0}^{\infty} S_i, \text{ where } S_0 = \{x\}, S_i = \{ z \mid y \in S_{i-1} \wedge z \in succe(y) \wedge \neg isiElem(z) \wedge \neg isiAttr(z) \}$$
$$P(x) = \cup_{i=0}^{\infty} P_i, \text{ where } P_0 = \{x\}, P_i = \{ z \mid y \in P_{i-1} \wedge z \in prece(y) \wedge \neg isiElem(z) \wedge \neg isiAttr(z) \}$$
$$iChild(x) = \{ z \mid y \in S(x) \wedge z \in succe(y) \wedge (isiElem(z) \vee isiText(z)) \}$$
$$iAttribute(x) = \{ z \mid y \in S(x) \wedge z \in succe(y) \wedge isiAttr(z) \}$$
$$iParent(x) = \{ z \mid y \in P(x) \wedge z \in prece(y) \wedge isiElem(z) \}$$
$$iSibling(x) = \{y \mid z \in iParent(x) \wedge y \in iChild(z)\}$$
$$iBranch(x) = \{y \mid y \in iChild^+(root(x)) \wedge y \notin iParent^*(x) \wedge y \notin iChild^+(x) \wedge \neg isiAttr(y)\}$$
$$iDesc(x) = \{z \mid z \in iChild^+(x)\}$$
$$iAnces(x) = \{z \mid z \in iParent^+(x)\}$$
$$iDoS(x) = \{z \mid z \in iChild^*(x)\}$$
$$iAoS(x) = \{z \mid z \in iParent^*(x)\}$$
$$iPS(x) = \{y \mid y \in iSibling(x) \wedge y << x\}$$
$$iFS(x) = \{y \mid y \in iSibling(x) \wedge x << y\}$$
$$iPreceding(x) = \{y \mid y \in iBranch(x) \wedge y << x \}$$
$$iFollowing(x) = \{y \mid y \in iBranch(x) \wedge x << y\}$$

Fig. 2. Used relation functions

Let NodeTest be the type of the node test of XPath. An auxiliary function attr(x, name) retrieves the value of the attribute name of the node x. The function NT: Node × NodeTest→Boolean, which tests a schema node against a node test of XPath, is defined as:

- NT(x, *) = isiElem(x) ∨ isiAttr(x)
- NT(x, **text()**) = isiText(x)
- NT(x, **node()**) = true
- NT(x, label) = (isiElem(x) ∧ (attr(x, name)=label)) ∨ (isiAttr(x) ∧ (attr(x, name)=label))

4 Satisfiability Tester for XPath Queries

Our proposed XPath satisfiability tester evaluates an XPath query on an XML Schema definition, and computes a set of *schema paths* to the possible nodes specified by the XPath query when the XPath query is evaluated by a common XPath evaluator on XML instance documents of the schema. If an XPath query cannot be evaluated completely, the schema paths for the XPath query are computed to an empty set of schema paths, i.e. the XPath query is unsatisfiable according to the schema.

Definition 4 (*Schema paths*). A schema path is a sequence of pointers to either the schema path records <XP', N, z, lp, f> or the schema path records <o, {f, ..., f}>, where

- XP' is an XPath expression,
- N is a node in an XML Schema definition,
- z is a set of pointers to schema path records,
- lp is a set of schema paths,
- f is a schema path list, or a predicate expression q', and q' ∈ {true(), false(), self::node()=C}, where C is a literal, i.e. a number or a string, and
- o is a keyword.

XP' is the part of a given XPath query, which has been evaluated; N is a resultant node of a schema whenever XP' is evaluated by our satisfiability tester on the schema definition; z is a set of pointers to the schema path records in which the schema node is the parent of the schema node of the current schema path record. Note whenever a schema path record is the first schema path record of a loop, the schema path record has more than one possible parent schema path record. lp represents loop schema paths; f represents either a schema path list computed from a predicate q that tests the node N, or the predicate expression q itself from which no schema paths can be computed like true() or false(), but also including self::node()=C. o represents operators like or, and and not.

4.1 Computing Schema Paths

We use the technique of the denotational semantics [10] to describe our XPath satisfiability tester, and define the following notations. Let z be a pointer in a schema path and d is a field of a schema path record, we write z.d to refer to the field d of the schema path record to which the pointer z points. We use the letter S to represent the size of a schema path p, thus p(S) to represent the last pointer, p(S-1) the pre-last pointer, and so on.

Fig. 3 defines the denotational semantics L of the XPath satisfiability tester. The function L takes an XPath expression and a schema path as argument and yields a set of new schema paths, and is defined recursively on the structure of XPath expressions. For evaluating each location step of an XPath expression, our XPath satisfiabiliy tester first computes the axis and the node test of the location step by iteratively taking the schema node p(S).N from each schema path p in the path set as the context node. The path set is computed from the part xp" of the XPath expression, which has been evaluated by the XPath satisfiability tester. For each resultant node r selected by the current location step xp_f, a new schema path is generated based on the old path p. The auxiliary function ϑ(r, g) generates a new schema path record e=<xp', r, g, -, ->, adds a pointer to e at the end of the given schema path p and returns a new schema path, where xp'=xp"/xp_f and g is a set of pointers to schema path records.

L: XPath expression × schema path → set(schema path)

- $L\lceil e_1|e_2\rfloor(p) = L\lceil e_1\rfloor(p) \cup L\lceil e_2\rfloor(p)$
- $L\lceil /e\rfloor(p) = L\lceil e\rfloor(p_1) \wedge p_1=(<\!/,/,\text{-},\text{-},\text{-}\!>)$
- $L\lceil e_1/e_2\rfloor(p) = \{ p_2 \mid p_2\in L\lceil e_2\rfloor(p_1) \wedge p_1\in L\lceil e_1\rfloor(p) \}$
- $L\lceil \text{self::n}\rfloor(p) = \{ \vartheta(p(S).N, p(S).z) \mid NT(p(S).N, n) \}$
- $L\lceil \text{child::n}\rfloor(p) = \{\vartheta(r, p(S)) \mid r\in iChild(p(S).N) \wedge NT(r,n)\}$
- $L'\lceil \text{self::n}\rfloor(p) = \{ p \mid NT(p(S).N, n) \}$
- $L\lceil \text{desc::n}\rfloor(p) = \{ p' \mid p'\in \cup_{i=1}^{\infty} L'\lceil \text{self::n}\rfloor(p_i) \wedge$
  $\forall k\in\{1, \ldots, S\text{-}1 \}: p_i(k).N\neq p_i(S).N \vee p_j(k).XP'\neq p_i(S).XP'$
  where $p_i\in L\lceil \text{child::}*\rfloor(p_{i-1}) \wedge p_1\in L\lceil \text{child::}*\rfloor(p)$, or
  $p'\in \cup_{i=1}^{\infty} L'\lceil \text{self::n}\rfloor(p_{i-1}) \wedge X(p_i(k), (p_i(k),..,p_i(S\text{-}1))) \wedge$
  $Z(p_i(k), p_i(S).z)) \wedge \exists k\in\{ 1,.., S\text{-}1 \}: p_i(k).N=p_i(S).N \wedge$
  $p_i(k).XP'=p_i(S).XP'$, where $p_i\in L\lceil \text{child::}*\rfloor(p_{i-1}) \wedge$
  $p_{i-1}\in L\lceil \text{child::}*\rfloor(p_{i-2}) \wedge p_1\in L\lceil \text{child::}*\rfloor(p)$.
- $L\lceil \text{parent::n}\rfloor(p) = \{ \vartheta(r, x) \mid r=Z1.N \wedge Z1\in p(S).z \wedge$
  $x=Z1.z \wedge NT(r,n) \}$
- $L\lceil \text{ances::n}\rfloor(p) = \{ p' \mid p'\in \cup_{i=1}^{\infty} L'\lceil \text{self::n}\rfloor(p_i) \wedge$
  $\forall k\in\{1,.., S\text{-}1\}: p_i(k).N\neq p_i(S).N \vee p_i(k).XP'\neq p_i(S).XP'$,
  where $p_j\in L\lceil \text{parent::}*\rfloor(p_{i-1}) \wedge p_1\in L\lceil \text{parent::}*\rfloor(p)$, or
  $p'\in \cup_{i=1}^{\infty} L'\lceil \text{self::n}\rfloor(p_{i-1}) \wedge X(p_i(k), (p_i(k),..,p_i(S\text{-}1))) \wedge$
  $Z(p_i(k), p_i(S).z)) \wedge \exists k\in\{1,.., S\text{-}1\}: p_i(k).N=p_i(S).N \wedge$
  $p_i(k).XP'=p_i(S).XP'$, where $p_i\in L\lceil \text{parent::}*\rfloor(p_{i-1}) \wedge$
  $p_{i-1}\in L\lceil \text{parent::}*\rfloor(p_{i-2}) \wedge p_1\in L\lceil \text{parent::}*\rfloor(p)$.
- $L\lceil \text{DoS::n}\rfloor(p)= L\lceil \text{self::n}\rfloor(p) \cup L\lceil \text{desc::n}\rfloor(p)$
- $L\lceil \text{AoS::n}\rfloor(p) = L\lceil \text{self::n}\rfloor(p) \cup L\lceil \text{ances::n}\rfloor(p)$
- $L\lceil \text{FS::n}\rfloor(p) = \{ \vartheta(r, p(S).z) \mid r\in iFS(p(S).N) \wedge NT(r,n) \}$
- $L\lceil \text{following::n}\rfloor(p) = L\lceil \text{AoS:: }*\text{/FS :: }*\text{/DoS::n}\rfloor(p)$
- $L\lceil \text{PS::n}\rfloor(p) = \{ \vartheta(r, p(S).z) \mid r\in iPS(p(S).N) \wedge NT(r,n) \}$
- $L\lceil \text{preceding::n}\rfloor(p) = L\lceil \text{AoS:: }*\text{/PS :: }*\text{/DoS ::n}\rfloor(p)$
- $L\lceil \text{attr::n}\rfloor(p) = \{ \vartheta(r, p(S)) \mid r\in iAttr(p(S).N) \wedge NT(r,n) \}$
- $L\lceil e[q]\rfloor(p) = A(\{L\lceil q\rfloor(p'+f)\}, S, p')$, where $f=\emptyset \wedge p'\in L\lceil e\rfloor(p)$
- $L\lceil e[q_1[q_2]]\rfloor(p) = A(\{L\lceil q_1[q_2]\rfloor(p'+f)\}, S, p')$,
  where $f=\emptyset \wedge p'\in L\lceil e\rfloor(p)$
- $L\lceil e[\text{self::node()=C}]\rfloor(p) = A(\{\text{'self::node()=C'}\}, S, p')$,
  where $p'\in L\lceil e\rfloor(p)$
- $L\lceil e[e_1 = C]\rfloor(p) = L\lceil e[e_1[\text{self::node()=C}]]\rfloor(p)$
- $L\lceil e[q_1][q_2]\rfloor(p) = A(\{A(\{L\lceil q_2\rfloor(p'+f_2), L\lceil q_1\rfloor(p'+f_1)\}, S, f)\},$
  $S, p')$, where $p'\in L\lceil e\rfloor(p) \wedge f=(<\text{'and'}, \text{-}>) \wedge f_1=\emptyset \wedge f_2=\emptyset$.
- $L\lceil e[q_1 \text{ and } q_2]\rfloor(p) = L\lceil e[q_1][q_2]\rfloor(p)$
- $L\lceil e[q_1 \text{ or } q_2]\rfloor(p) = A(\{A(\{L\lceil q_2\rfloor(p'+f_2), L\lceil q_1\rfloor(p'+f_1)\}, S, f)\},$
  $S, p')$, where $p'\in L\lceil e\rfloor(p) \wedge f=(<\text{'or'}, \text{-}>) \wedge f_1=\emptyset \wedge f_2=\emptyset$.
- $L\lceil e[q_1 = q_2]\rfloor(p) = A(\{A(\{L\lceil q_2\rfloor(p'+f_2), L\lceil q_1\rfloor(p'+f_1)\}, S, f)\},$
  $S, p')$, where $p'\in L\lceil e\rfloor(p) \wedge f=(<\text{'='}, \text{-}>) \wedge f_1=\emptyset \wedge f_2=\emptyset$.
- $L\lceil e[\text{not}(q)]\rfloor(p) = A(\{A(\{L\lceil q\rfloor(p'+f_1)\}, S, f)\} , S, p')$,
  where $f=(<\text{'not'}, \text{-}>) \wedge p'\in L\lceil e\rfloor(p) \wedge f_1=\emptyset$.

Fig. 3. Formulas for constructing schema paths

In the case of recursive schemas, it may occur that the XPath satisfiability tester revisits a node N of the XML Schema definition without any progress in the processing of the query. We call this a *loop*. A loop might occur when an XPath query contains the axis desc, ances, preceding or following, which are boiled down to the recursive evaluation of the axis child or parent respectively. We detect loops in the following way: Let r be a visited schema node when evaluating the part xp' of an XPath expression. If there exists a schema path record p(i) in p, such that p(i).N=r, and p(i).XP'=xp', a loop is detected and the loop path segment is lp = (p(i), ...,p(S)). lp will be attached to the schema node p(i).N where the loop occurs. For computing $L\lceil \text{desc::n}\rfloor(p)$, we first compute $p_i \mid p_i\in L\lceil \text{child::}*\rfloor(p_{i-1})$ where $p_1=L\lceil \text{child::}*\rfloor(p)$. If no loop is detected in the path p_i, i.e. $\forall k\in\{1, ..., S\text{-}1\}: p_i(k).N\neq p_i(S).N \vee p_i(k).XP'\neq p_i(S).XP'$, $L'\lceil \text{self::n}\rfloor(p_i)$ is then computed in order to construct a possible new path from p_i. If a loop is detected in the path p_i, i.e. $\exists k\in\{1,.., S\text{-}1\}: p_i(k).N=p_i(S).N \wedge p_i(k).XP'=p_i(S).XP'$, a loop path segment, i.e. $\{p_i(k), ..., p_i(S\text{-}1)\}$ is identified. The function X modifies the schema path record, which is the head of the loop, by adding the loop path into the schema path record, i.e. X(p_i(k), (p_i(k),..,p(S-1))), and returns true. Furthermore, although the schema nodes in two schema path records are the same, i.e. p_i(k).N=p_i(S).N, these two nodes have different parents, i.e, $p_i(k).z \neq p_i(S).z$. Therefore, the new parent p_i(S).z has to be recorded and this is done by the function Z, which adds a parent pointer into the schema path record p_i(k), i.e. Z(p_i(k), p_i(S).z), and returns true.

The schema paths of a predicate are attached to the context node of the predicate. The function A(F, i, p) writes F into the field p(i).f and returns the modified schema path p. The parameter F = {f_1,..,f_k} is computed from a set of predicates q_1,..q_k. f_i is either a schema path list computed from a predicate q_i, or is the predicate expression q_i itself when q_i does not contain location steps. The node p(i).N is the context node of these predicates. q_i is evaluated to false if q_i is computed to the empty schema paths with the exception of not(q_i), which is computed to true. For instance, L⟦e[q_1 and q_2]⟧(p) is computed to empty paths if q_1 or q_2 are evaluated to false. When computing the schema paths of a predicate, the XPath satisfiability tester initializes a schema path variable f with null, which is logically concatenated with the main path p, denoted by p+f, for the need of both finding the context node of the predicate and finding the nodes specified by reverse axes in the predicate, which occur before the context node of the predicate in the document order.

Example 2. Our XPath satisfiability tester evaluates XPath queries Q=//page[not(parent::web)]/title and Q'=//link/title[AoS::page] on the XML Schema definition in Fig. 1 and computes the schema paths (cf. Fig. 4) from Q. Fig. 5 is the graphical representation of Fig. 4, in which we only present the schema node item of schema path records. An empty set of schema paths is computed from Q', since the element title is not a child of the element link, thus Q' is unsatisfiable.

```
(R1) { (</,  /,  -,  -,  -> ,
(R2)    <Q1, D11, {R1}, -, ->,
(R3)    <Q1, D4, {R2, R4},
(R4)       {(<Q1, D8, {R3}, -, ->)},
(R5)       {(<'not',
(R6)            {(<q1, D11, {R1}, -, ->)})} >,
(R7)    <Q, D7, {R3}, -, -> )}
where Q1=//page[not(parent::web)]
        q1=parent::web
```

Fig. 4. Schema paths of the query Q

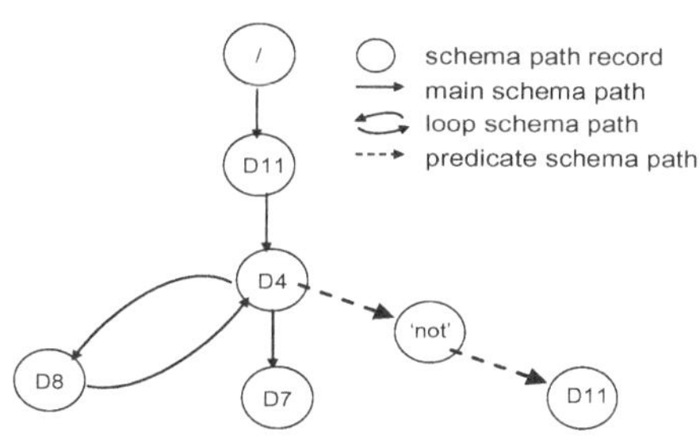

Fig. 5. Graphical representation of schema paths of Fig. 4

4.2 Satisfiability Test

Definition 5 (*Satisfiability of XPath queries*). A given XPath query Q is satisfiable according to a given XML Schema definition XSD, if there exists an XML document D, which is valid according to XSD, and the evaluation of Q on D returns a non-empty result. Otherwise Q is unsatisfiable according to XSD.

Proposition 1 (*Unsatisfiable XPath queries*). If the evaluation of an XPath query Q on a given XML Schema definition XSD by the XPath satisfiability tester generates an empty set of schema paths, then Q is unsatisfiable according to XSD.

Proof. The XPath satisfiability tester is constructed in such a way that the XPath satisfiability tester returns an empty set of schema paths, if the constraints given in Q and the constraints given in XSD exclude the constraints of the other. Thus, there does not exist a valid XML document according to XSD, where the application of Q returns a non-empty result.

If the XPa satisfiability tester computes a non-empty set of schema paths for an XPath query, the XPath query is only *maybe* satisfiable, since the satisfiability test of XPath queries formulated in the supported subset of XPath is undecidable[1].

4.3 Complexity Analysis

Let a be the number of location steps in query Q and let N be the number of *instance nodes* in an XML Schema definition. Each schema path contains at most a*N nodes, each of which can be the start node of at most $O(\Sigma_{i=1}^{N-1}(N!/(N-i)!))$ different schema paths of length 1 to N in the worst case of a preceding or a following axis until we recognize a loop. Thus, for each schema path of the result of the previous location step, we can detect at most $O(a*N*\Sigma_{i=1}^{N-1}(N!/(N-i)!))=O(a*N*N!)$ different schema paths as the result of the current location step. For all locations steps, we can detect at most $O((a*N*N!)^a)$ different schema paths, each of which contains at most $O(a*N)$ schema nodes, for Q. Therefore, the worst case complexity of both the run-time and the space is $O(a*N*(a*N*N!)^a)$.

We assume that the typical case is characterized as follows: Each instance schema node in an XML Schema definition has only a small number of successor nodes. Furthermore, we assume that the query Q specifies a small node set so that we only detect a small number, which is less than a constant k, of schema paths. Therefore, the complexity of both runtime and space is $O(k*a*N)$ for the typical case.

5 Performance Analysis

We have implemented a prototype of the XPath satisfiability tester in order to verify the correctness of our approach and to demonstrate the optimization potential for avoiding the evaluation of unsatisfiable XPath queries. The performance study focuses on the detection of unsatisfiable XPath queries by our XPath satisfiability tester and the evaluation of these unsatisfiable queries by common XPath evaluators.

The test system for all experiments is an Intel Pentium 4 processor 2.4 Gigahertz with 512 Megabytes RAM, Windows XP as operating system and Java VM build version 1.4.2. We use the XQuery evaluators Saxon version 8.0 (//saxon.sourceforge.net) and Qizx version 0.4pl (//www.xfra.net/quizxopen) in order to evaluate the XPath queries. We use the XPathMark benchmark [2] as the source of our experimental data, and transform the benchmark DTD benchmark.dtd into the XML Schema definition benchmark.xsd by using the tool Syntext Dtd2xs-2.0 (//freshmeat.net/projects/syntext_dtd2xs/). We generate data from 0.116 Megabytes to 11.597 Megabytes by using the data generator of [2], and modify the queries of [2] into unsatisfiable queries.

Fig. 7 presents the evaluation time of the used unsatisfiable XPath queries (see Fig. 6) on benchmark.xsd by our XPath satisfiability tester, which detects that these queries are unsatisfiable and avoids the unnecessary evaluation of these unsatisfiable queries. Fig. 8 and Fig. 9 present the evaluation time of these queries using the Saxon and the Qizx evaluator respectively when an empty result is returned. Fig. 10 and Fig. 11 present the speed-up factors by our approach over the Saxon evaluator and the Qizx evaluator respectively. The experimental results show that our approach can check the satisfiability of XPath queries effectively. Our approach is 26 times (4.2 times respectively) faster on average when evaluating the XPath queries with

Q1: /site/closed_auctions/closed_auction/
annotation/description/parlist/text/keyword
Q2: /site/regions/*/item[parent::america]
Q3: /open_auctions/open_auction[bidder
[people/attribute::person='person0']/
following-sibling::bidder]
Q4: /descendant::keyword[name]
Q5: /descendant::text[italic]
Q6: /descendant-or-self::persons/
person[name='WANG']
Q7: /descendant-or-self::item
[not(self::node()/mailbox)]
Q8: /descendant::person
[address and not(emailaddress)]

Fig. 6. Used unsatisfiable XPath queries

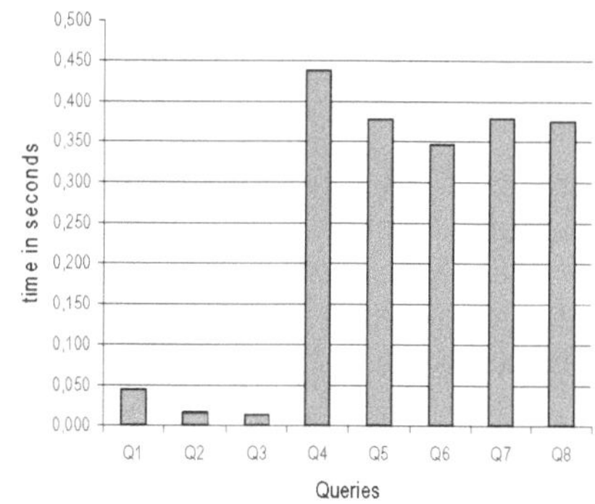

Fig. 7. Time of testing satisfiability with our prototype

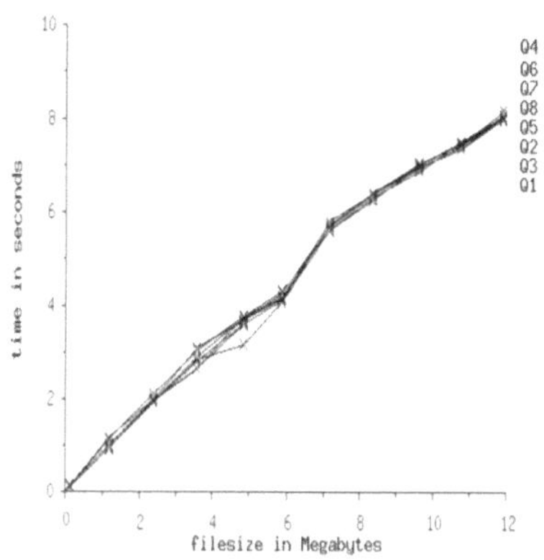

Fig. 8. Processing the queries in Fig.6 with Saxon Evalutor

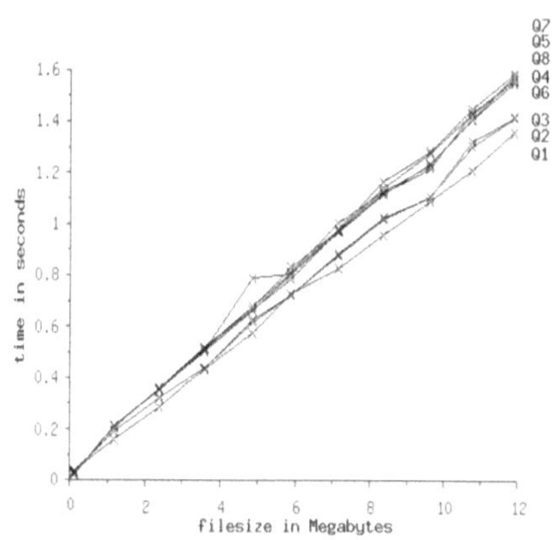

Fig. 9. Processing the queries on Fig. 6 with Qizx Evalutor

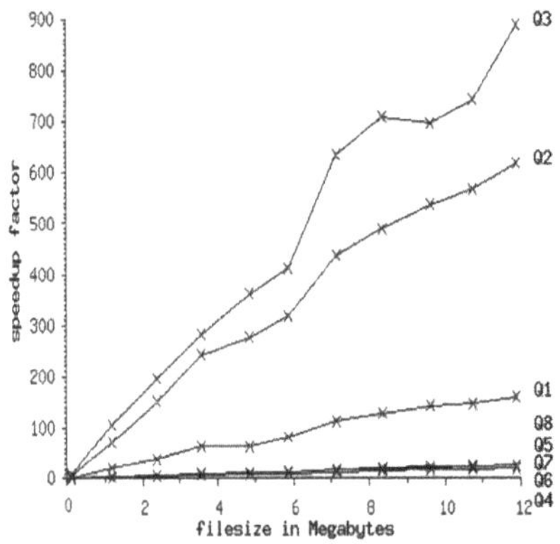

Fig. 10. Speedup factor by our prototype over Saxon

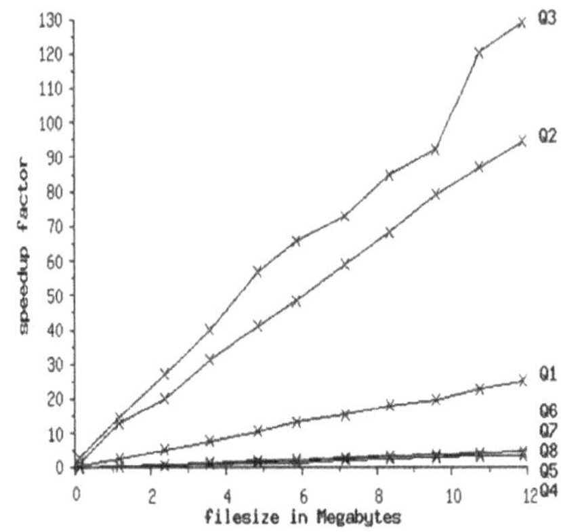

Fig. 11. Speedup factor by our prototype over Qizx

desc axis, and 546 times (87 times respectively) faster when evaluating the XPath queries without desc axis than Saxon (Qizx respectively) at 12 Megabytes in comparison with the evaluation of the unsatisfiable queries. Different queries have remarkably influence on the evaluation performance of our satisfiability tester, e.g. the queries with desc axis are 15 times slower than the queries without desc axis.

6 Summary and Conclusions

We have proposed a data model for XML Schema language, which identifies the navigation paths of XPath queries on XML Schema definitions. Based-on the data model, we have developed a satisfiability tester of XPath queries, which evaluates XPath queries on an XML Schema definition in order to check whether or not the queries conform to the constraints imposed by the schema definition. When an XPath query does not conform to the constraints in a given schema definition, our satisfiability tester computes an empty set of schema paths, i.e. the XPath query is unsatisfiable, otherwise the XPath query is only maybe satisfiable. Our approach supports all XPath axes and recursive as well as non-recursive schemas. The experimental results of our prototype show that application of our approach can significantly optimize the evaluation of XPath queries by filtering unsatisfiable XPath queries. A speed-up factor up to several magnitudes is possible.

References

1. M. Benedikt, W. Fan, F. Geerts: XPath Satisfiability in the presence of DTDs. In PODS 2005.
2. M. Franceschet: XPathMark – An XPath benchmark for XMark. Research report PP-2005-04, University of Amsterdam, the Netherlands, 2005.
3. S. Groppe: XML Query Reformulation for XPath, XSLT and XQuery. Sierke-Verlag, Göttingen, Germany, 2005. ISBN 3-933893-24-0.

4. J. Groppe, S. Groppe: Filtering Unsatisfiabile XPath Queries, ICEIS 2006, Paphos-Cyprus.
5. S. Groppe, S. Böttcher and J. Groppe: XPath Query Simplification with regard to the Elimination of Intersect and Except Operators. In XSDM'06 in association with ICDE'06.
6. J. Hidders: Satisfiability of XPath Expressions. DBPL 2003. LNCS 2921, pp. 21–36.
7. A. Kwong, M. Gertz: Schema-based optimization of XPath expressions. Techn. Report University of California, 2002.
8. L. Lakshmanan, G. Ramesh, H. Wang, Z. Zhao: On Testing Satisfiability of Tree Pattern Queries. In VLDB 2004.
9. D. Olteanu, H. Meuss, T. Furche, F. Bry : XPath: Looking Forward. XML-Based Data Management (XMLDM), EDBT Workshops, 2002.
10. D.A. Schmidt: The structure of Typed programming languages. MIT Press, Cambridge, MA, USA, 1994.
11. P. Wadler: Two semantics for XPath. Tech. Report, 2000.
12. W3C: XML Schema Part 1: Structures Second Edition. W3C Recommendation, www.w3.org/TR/xmlschema-1, 2004.
13. W3C: XPath Version 1.0, W3C Recommendation, www.w3.org/TR/xpath/, 1999.
14. W3C: XPath Version 2.0, W3C Working Draft, www.w3.org/TR/xpath20/, 2003.

Understanding and Enhancing the Folding-In Method in Latent Semantic Indexing

Xiang Wang and Xiaoming Jin

School of Software, Tsinghua University, Beijing 100084, China
xiang_w00@mails.tsinghua.edu.cn,
xmjin@tsinghua.edu.cn

Abstract. Latent Semantic Indexing(LSI) has been proved to be effective to capture the semantic structure of document collections. It is widely used in content-based text retrieval. However, in many real-world applications dealing with very large document collections, LSI suffers from its high computational complexity, which comes from the process of Singular Value Decomposition(SVD). As a result, in practice, the folding-in method is widely used as an approximation to the LSI method. However, in practice, the folding-in method is generally implemented "as is" and detailed analysis on its effectiveness and performance is left out. Consequentially, the performance of the folding-in method cannot be guaranteed. In this paper, we firstly illustrated the underlying principle of the folding-in method from a linear algebra point of view and analyzed some existing commonly used techniques. Based on the theoretical analysis, we proposed a novel algorithm to guide the implementation of the folding-in method. Our method was justified and evaluated by a series of experiments on various classical IR data sets. The results indicated that our method was effective and had consistent performance over different document collections.

1 Introduction

Latent Semantic Indexing(LSI), proposed by Deerwester et al.[1] in 1990s, is one of the most widely used and effective methods in content-based text retrieval. LSI is based on Vector Space Model(VSM) and uses a mathematical tool called Singular Value Decomposition(SVD) to explore the underlying semantic structure of the vector space built by VSM. In real-world applications, the most critical problem of LSI lies in its high computational complexity. It is difficult, if not impossible, to apply LSI on very large document collections directly.

Instead, the folding-in method, which was proposed together with LSI[1], is commonly used in practice. The folding-in method utilizes a subset of original document collection as the training set and performs SVD on the training set instead as an approximation. Consequentially, the most important issue about the folding-in method is the selection of training set. With proper selection, the performance of the folding-in method in practice would be satisfiable[2][3][4]. However, there is no comprehensive theoretical or empirical analysis of different selection strategies. For document collections with different semantic structures,

S. Bressan, J. Küng, and R. Wagner (Eds.): DEXA 2006, LNCS 4080, pp. 104–113, 2006.

or *distributions*, a given training set selection strategy may perform inconsistently. Therefore, it is desirable to design a principled training set selection strategy, which would have reliable performance over document collections with various distributions.

In this paper, we analyzed the underlying principle of the folding-in method in detail with a linear algebra approach. We theoretically illustrated that the essential of the folding-in method is a subspace tracking process with reduced information. In other words, when choosing the training set, it is expected that the subspace decided by the training set is a good approximation of the subspace decided by the original document collection. Therefore, the performance of the folding-in method mainly depends on the deterioration of the subspace derived by the training set from the actual one.

Based on our theoretical conclusion, various selection strategies were analyzed and a novel selection strategy was proposed. We showed that existing methods are effective only in some cases while not in other cases. Especially for dynamic document collections or document collections with varied distributions, the deterioration of existing methods could be large. To solve such problem, we proposed a new training set selection strategy, which is deterministic. It utilizes the linear algebra properties of document collection and selects document vectors that best approximate the target subspace as the training set. Thus it is effective on various document collections and outperforms existing methods in general.

A series of experiments were conducted to evaluate the retrieval performance of our method. Existing methods were also implemented as the baseline. It was clearly showed that our method consistently outperformed existing methods and was robust against different document collections.

The rest of the paper is organized as following: The folding-in method was analyzed theoretically in Sect. 2; Our novel training set selection strategy was proposed in Sect. 3; Experimental results were presented in Sect. 4; Related works were introduced in Sect. 5; In Sect. 6 we drew our conclusion.

2 Understanding the Folding-In Method

2.1 Background and Preliminaries

The motivation of Latent Semantic Indexing(LSI) is to decompose the vector space generated from a document collection under Vector Space Model(VSM) with Singular Value Decomposition(SVD), and then reduce the dimension of the vector space. By the dimension-reduction process, the influence of synonymy and polysemy, which is considered as *noise*, is removed[1].

Given a $m \times n$ term-document matrix A, which is generated by VSM, each matrix element a_{ij} is the weight of term i in document j. The n columns of A represent n documents in the document collection. In LSI, SVD is performed on A. It writes:

$$A = U\Sigma V^T, \tag{1}$$

where U, Σ, V are $m \times r$, $r \times r$, $n \times r$ matrices respectively. Here r is the rank of A and $\Sigma = diag(\sigma_1, \sigma_2, \ldots, \sigma_r)$ and $\sigma_1 \geq \sigma_2 \geq \cdots \geq \sigma_r > 0$ are the singular values of A. Also note that the columns of U and V are orthogonal, which means that $U^TU = I$ and $V^TV = I$, where I is the identity matrix[5].

The effectiveness of LSI comes from the dimension reduction process based on the result of SVD[6][7][8]. A rank-k approximation to A is created, where $k \leq r$. It writes:

$$A_k = U_k \Sigma_k V_k^T, \tag{2}$$

where U_k is a $m \times k$ matrix whose columns are the first k columns of U, V_k is a $n \times k$ matrix whose columns are the first k columns of V, and $\Sigma_k = diag(\sigma_1, \sigma_2, \ldots, \sigma_k)$. It is easy to see that the rank of A_k is k and A_k is called a rank-k approximation of A. In fact, it has been proved that A_k is the best rank-k approximation of A in terms of *Frobenius* norm[9].

For document i, $1 \leq i \leq n$, its original vector representation d_i is the ith column of A, where d_i is a $m \times 1$ vector. Now document i is indexed as:

$$\hat{d}_i = U_k^T d_i. \tag{3}$$

Here $\hat{d}_i$ is a $k \times 1$ vector, and is sometimes referred as the *pseudo-document* representation of document i. For a query q, where q is the $m \times 1$ vector representation of the query, we firstly compute its pseudo-document representation by $\hat{q} = U_k^T q$. Then the similarity between document i and query q is defined as the cosine value of the angle between $\hat{d}_i$ and $\hat{q}$[7], which writes $sim(d_i, q) = \frac{\hat{q}^T \cdot \hat{d}_i}{\|\hat{q}\|_2 \|\hat{d}_i\|_2}$.

Since the computational complexity of SVD is very high[6], in practice, the folding-in method is used as an approximation to LSI[1]. Instead of performing SVD on A, a subset of the columns of A is selected as the *training set*. Suppose A_1 is a $m \times n_1$ matrix, whose columns are a subset of the columns of A. The SVD process is performed on A_1, similarly we have $A_1 = U_1 \Sigma_1 V_1^T$. And then we also find the rank-k approximation of A_1, which writes $A_{1k} = U_{1k} \Sigma_{1k} V_{1k}^T$. Now all the documents in the document collection A are indexed as:

$$\hat{d}_i = U_{1k}^T d_i, \tag{4}$$

where $1 \leq i \leq n$.

2.2 Analyzing the Performance of the Folding-In Method

As an approximation to LSI, where does the deterioration of the folding-in method come from? In [6], it was mentioned that the orthogonality of V_k is corrupted by the folding-in step. In [7], it was claimed that for those documents not in A_1, if they are almost orthogonal to the columns of U_{1k}, their information is likely to be lost in the folding-in step. However, we illustrate the underlying principle under the folding-in method from an alternative point of view and analyze existing training set selection strategies theoretically.

We emphasize that the process of LSI substantially can be considered as a process of subspace tracking. Denote the range space of A to be S, i.e. $S = \{Ax | \forall x \in \mathbb{R}^n\}$, then UU^T is an orthogonal projection from $\mathbb{R}^m$ onto S. Similarly, denote the range spaces of A_k to be S_k, then UU_k^T is an orthogonal projection from $\mathbb{R}^m$ onto S_k. Furthermore we have $S = range(UU^T)$, and $S_k = range(U_k U_k^T)$[5]. Notice that S_k is a k-dimensional subspace of S. Consequentially, the essential of LSI can be considered as a process to capture an optimal k-dimensional subspace of S with respect to A, which is S_k, through the SVD process. We can see that S_k is decided by U_k, thus the most critical problem of LSI should be how to find U_k, or any matrix that can approximate U_k properly.

Recall the process the of the folding-in method, we will find that it is essentially trying to track the target subspace S_k by approximating U_k with U_{1k}. Denote the range space of A_1 to be S_1 and the range space of A_{1k} to be S_{1k}, then U_1 and U_{1k} are expected to approximate U and U_k respectively, and $S_{1k} = range(U_{1k} U_{1k}^T)$ is supposed to be an approximation to S_k. Thus the deterioration of the folding-in method is caused by the difference between S_{1k} and S_k. Having that S_{1k} is decided by U_{1k} and U_{1k} is decided by A_1, this is exactly how the selection of training set decides the performance of the folding-in method.

Based on above analysis, let us review some existing training set selection strategies to see why they are effective in some cases while not in other cases. Random sampling and its variations are among the most commonly used strategies. Their effectiveness relies on a statistical expectation that the sample could retain the structure of original vector space. With prior knowledge of a given document collection on its distribution, we can hopefully find a representative sample and then find the subspace S_{1k} that is close enough to S_k. The danger of sampling lies behind the fact that prior knowledge of any document collection is generally unavailable so that we do not know whether our sample is proper.

Similarly, sometimes clustering is used as a training set selection strategy. Normally the centroids of clusters are used as the training set and they are expected to retain the structure of original vector space. However, the proper selection of clustering techniques and parameter tuning also require prior knowledge of document collections, which would be unavailable in many cases.

3 A Novel Training Set Selection Strategy

3.1 Algorithm

As we have analyzed, the performance of a given training set is determined by the deterioration between the subspace decided by the training set and the target subspace, which is decided by the original document collection. Nevertheless, existing methods do not fully utilize the semantic structure of the document collection. Thus we proposed a method which utilizes the semantic properties of document collection so that an enhancement of the performance of the folding-in method can be guaranteed over various document collections. Our method focuses on the relationship between document vectors and target subspace. The vectors most close to the target subspace are selected to rebuild a new subspace as an approximation to the original one.

Now we introduce our training set selection strategy as below. Given a document collection and the corresponding $m \times n$ term-document matrix A, we would like to find a $m \times n_1$ matrix A_1 whose columns are a subset of the columns of A as the training set. In addition, it is assumed that the columns of A are all normalized, i.e. given d any column of A, we have $\|d\|_2 = 1$.

Following Eq. 1 and Eq. 2, we have $A_k = U_k \Sigma_k V_k^T$. For $1 \leq i \leq n$, we have $\hat{d}_i = U_k^T d_i$, where $\hat{d}_i$ is the pseudo-document representation of document d_i. As we have mentioned before, $U_k U_k^T$ is an orthogonal projection onto S_k, so $\|\hat{d}_i\|_2 = \|U_k^T d_i\|_2$ is the length of the projection of d_i on subspace S_k. Also note that $\|d_i\|_2 = 1$ for any $1 \leq i \leq n$, larger $\|\hat{d}_i\|_2$ implies smaller angle between vector d_i and subspace S_k. In other words, those documents with longer projection are more close to the subspace S_k. Intuitively, in sense of plane fitting, we should choose documents that are most close to S_k as the training set and consequentially the subspace S_{1k} decided by the training set will best approximate S_k. That is to say, we compute $w_i = \|U_k^T d_i\|_2$ for all $1 \leq i \leq n$, and the first n_1 documents with largest w_i are selected as the training set.

However, with further consideration, we notice that from Eq. 2, we have $U_k^T A_k = \Sigma_k V_k^T$, which is equivalent to that $\hat{d}_i = U_k^T d_i = \Sigma_k v_i^T$, where v_i is the ith row of V_k. It reminds us that the vector representation of a document includes two parts: global weight and local weight[7]. In the context of our problem, Σ_k contains the k largest singular values of A, i.e. Σ_k is decided by A. For $1 \leq i \leq k$, σ_k is only related to the k-th dimension of the subspace, which is a linear combination of original m dimensions[7]. The value of σ_k represents the significance of the k-th dimension, which is related to the statistical properties of the whole document collection. Thus it can be considered as *global* weight. On the other hand, v_i reflects the relation between elements within document d_i, which can be considered as *local* weight.

In practice, we usually have $n_1 \ll n$. Since Σ_{1k} is decided by A_1, it would be biased from Σ_k, which is decided by A. To avoid the influence of biased global weights, during the training set selection process, we ignore the global weights Σ_k and only take the local weights V_k^T into consideration. Our method TS is summarized as in Algorithm 1.

Algorithm 1. Training Set Selection Strategy TS

Input: A, k, n_1
Output: A_1
1. Find U_k for A.
2. Compute $w_i = \|v_i\|_2$ for all $1 \leq i \leq n$.
3. The first n_1 documents with largest w_i are selected as the columns A_1, which is the training set.

3.2 Implementation of Our Method

Notice that in Algorithm 1, our method is based on the result of the SVD on A. However, in practice, the folding-in method is used only when it is difficulty or impossible to compute SVD for A. That is to say, Algorithm 1 cannot be applied in real-world applications.

To solve the problems in real-world applications, such as large document archives or text streams, including news streams, emails and blog websites, our method can be implemented in an incremental and greedy style. Specifically, for very large document collection, we can divide it into several smaller block as subjected to our computational capability. We apply TS method to find the training set for each block. Then we merge the training sets into one as the final result, or we can also perform TS method further to find a new training set with smaller size. The performance of such implementation will be showed below in Sect. 4.

3.3 Remarks

In our method, the training set is derived from subspace S_k, which represents the semantic structure of the document collection. Therefore, the selection process actually becomes a process determined by the semantic structure of corresponding document collections. Such relation gives our method stable performance, in comparison with random sampling method whose performance is unexpectable. Moreover, as opposed to various clustering methods, our method is more deterministic and does not need extra ad hoc tunings except for the LSI factor k, as discussed below.

There are two parameters that influence the performance of TS method. The first one is n_1. It is obvious that bigger training set leads to better performance. The other important parameter is k. For different document collections, the optimal values of k are different[8][10]. Nevertheless, it is necessary to mention that in our TS method, as the global weights matrix Σ_k is ignored, all terms are equally weighted. As a result, in practice, the value of k should not be too large with respect to n_1. Otherwise the influence of some local semantic properties of the training set would defect the performance of our method.

4 Experiments

4.1 Methodology

To evaluate the performance of our method, experiments were conducted over several classical IR data sets[1], as listed in Table 1. We used TMG 2.0[2] to remove stop words, assign term weights, and normalize document vectors. In practice, various weighting strategies are used in order to enhance the retrieval performance. However, weighting strategy was not the focus of our work. Therefore we simply used term frequency only through our experiments.

Our method was evaluated in two ways. The first one was to compute $e_{fd} = \|A - U_{1k}U_{1k}^T A\|_F$ and compare it to $e_{lsi} = \|A - U_k U_k^T A\|_F$. Here e represents the

[1] ftp://ftp.cs.cornell.edu/pub/smart.

[2] http://scgroup.hpclab.ceid.upatras.gr/scgroup/Projects/TMG/

Table 1. Data sets used in experiments

Identifier	Description	Documents	Terms	Queries
MED	Medical abstracts	1033	5735	30
CISI	Information science abstracts	1460	5544	35
NPL	Large collection of very short documents	11429	7536	93

Table 2. Approximation error of different selection strategies

	LSI	TS	Rand-best	Rand-avg
MED	28.6173	29.5181	29.9066	30.0368
CISI	32.7119	34.2771	34.3745	34.5770

approximation error between A and A_k and e_{lsi} is the minimal error among all rank-k matrices A_k. We will show that the approximation error of our method is more close to e_{lsi} than other methods. The second metric used was the precision-recall metric with respect to LSI. That is to say, we firstly performed LSI on the document collection and took the first 10 most relevant documents suggested by LSI for each query as the referenced results. Then we performed our method to calculate recall and precision for each query. Here we used the result of LSI instead of the standard referenced revelent documents for each query because that we were mainly concerned with how close our method approximates LSI rather than its actual retrieval results.

To be compared with, we also performed folding-in method with a random sampling strategy. As far as we concern, there is no specific sampling method mentioned in the literature for the folding-in method. To be statistically reliable, we used 100 different randomly generated samples as the training set through all experiments and the average and highest performance were recorded as baseline.

4.2 Results and Analysis

Firstly, we performed the folding-in method on MED and CISI collection with TS and random sampling strategy respectively. The NPL collection was not used due to the limitation of the memory space of our computer. Then $\|A - U_{1k}U_{1k}^T A\|_F$ was computed and compared with $\|A - U_k U_k^T A\|_F$ from LSI, see Table 2. Here k was 25 and the size of training set n_1 was 100. We can see that the approximation error of our method was always smaller than random sampling method.

Then we performed retrieval task on MED and CISI with TS and random sampling strategy and evaluated them with respect to the results of LSI, as described above. Here still we had k to be 25 and n_1 to be 100. See Fig. 1. The average precision used here was the mean of average precision at recall level 20%, 50%, and 80%. We can see that the retrieval performance of TS method was better than the average performance random sampling strategy on MED and very close to the best performance of random sampling method. Here we address

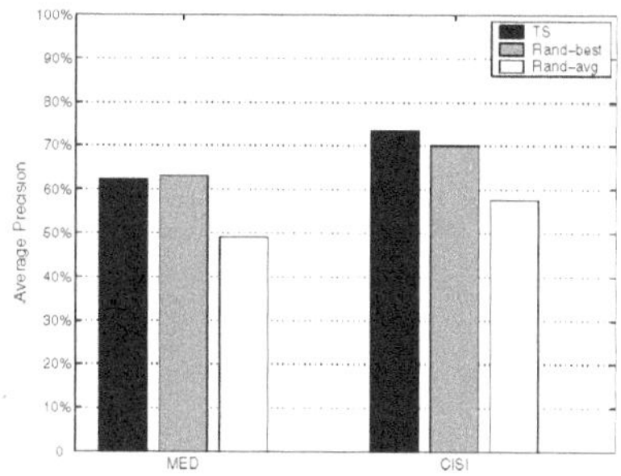

Fig. 1. Average precision with respect to LSI over MED and CISI collection

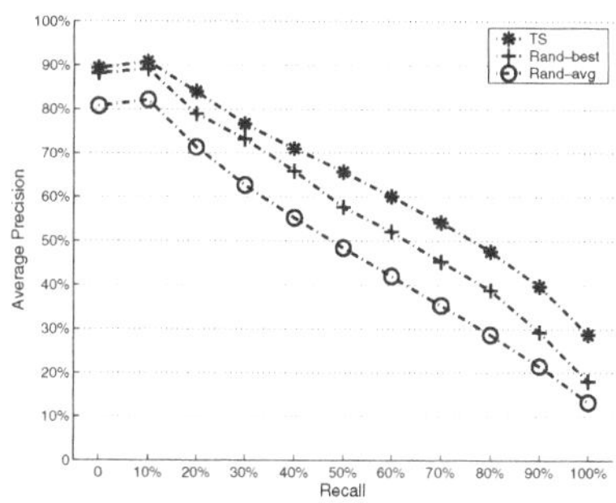

Fig. 2. Average precision with respect to LSI over NPL collection

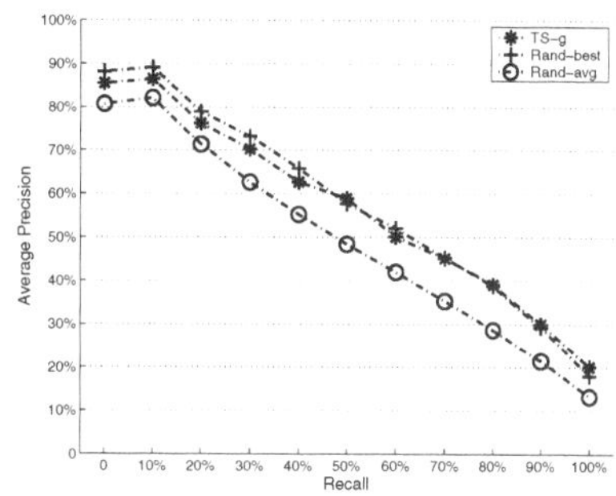

Fig. 3. Retrieval performance of incremental method over NPL collection

that due to the lack of guidance in sampling process, the best performance of randomly sampling is generally unexpectable. On CISI, the performance of TS method even outperformed the best performance of random sampling method. Similar experiment was conducted on the larger document collection NPL. Here we had k to be 50 and n_1 to be 200. The result was plotted in 11-pt precision-recall curve, see Fig. 2. We can see that at each recall level, the average precision of TS method was higher than the best performance of random sampling method.

Furthermore, we simulated the situation of dealing with very large document collection and applied our strategies in an incremental style . The first 10000 documents of NPL collection were used and divided into 5 groups. We firstly applied TS method on each group to find a training set with 200 documents for each group. Then the 5 training sets were merged into one and a new training set with 200 documents was selected out of them. The new training set was used as the training set for the whole NPL collection. Then retrieval task was performed on NPL collection and the result was in Fig. 3. Here we still had k to be 50. It was clearly showed that for large document collections, where our method was applied in an incremental way, the performance of TS method still outperformed the average performance of random sampling method and approached the best performance of random sampling method, which was unguaranteed though.

5 Related Work

LSI was proposed by Deerwester et al. in [1] and was later discussed more comprehensively in [6]. It was applied on text retrieval and proved to be effective [2][3][4][10]. LSI was analyzed from a linear algebra point of view by Berry et al. in [7].

The most essential process of LSI is SVD, which is costly to compute. The computational complexity of LSI and SVD was discussed in [6][11][12]. Due to the high computational complexity of LSI, in real-world application, the folding-in method, which was introduced together with LSI in [1], is widely used to handle very large document collections, e.g. in [13][14]. The performance of the folding-in method relies on the selection of training set. The deterioration of the folding-in method was mentioned in [6] and [7], very briefly and incomprehensively though.

In practice, as the folding-in method is widely implemented, there are several commonly used training set selection strategies. The most straightforward strategy is random sampling[2][3][4]. Random sampling may work well sometimes while its performance cannot be guaranteed over document collections with various distributions. Clustering is also used as a preprocessing subroutine[15]. Documents in the collection are firstly clustered and the centroids of all clusters are regarded as the training set of the document collection. However, the performance of such kind of methods heavily relies on the clustering method used. Without prior knowledge of the document collection, the performance of clustering could not be guaranteed either.

6 Conclusion

LSI has been accepted as an effective retrieval method, which can explore the latent semantic structure of document collections. In practice, the folding-in method is widely used as an approximation to LSI to deal with large document collections. The performance of the folding-in method is mainly decided by the selection of training set. However, the underlying principle of the folding-in method and the training set selection strategy had never been discussed in detail. As a result, the performance of the folding-in method had been unexpectable.

In this paper, the effectiveness and performance of the folding-in method was analyzed with a linear algebra approach. We suggested that the selection of training set is in fact a process of subspace tracking. Based on theoretical analysis, a novel training set selection method was proposed. It is easy to understand and implement. It can be applied on document collections with various distributions and needs no extra parameter tuning. Through a series of experiments, we showed that our method had superior performance on different data sets, where random sampling method was also implemented as the baseline. We also showed that the performance of our method when applied in an incremental style as in real-world application scenario was satisfiable.

Acknowledgements. This work was supported by the NSFC 60403021 and the National Key Fundamental Research Program of China 2004CB719400. The authors thank the anonymous reviewers for their helpful comments and advice.

References

1. Scott C. Deerwester, Susan T. Dumais, Thomas K. Landauer, George W. Furnas, and Richard A. Harshman. Indexing by latent semantic analysis. *Journal of the American Society of Information Science*, 41(6):391–407, 1990.
2. Susan T. Dumais. LSI meets TREC: A status report. In *The First Text REtrieval Conference(TREC1)*, pages 137–152, 1992.
3. Susan T. Dumais. Latent semantic indexing(LSI) and TREC-2. In *The Second Text REtrieval Conference(TREC2)*, pages 105–116, 1993.
4. Susan T. Dumais. Latent semantic indexing(LSI): TREC-3 report. In *The Third Text REtrieval Conference(TREC3)*, pages 105–115, 1994.
5. Gene H. Golub and Charles F. Van Loan. *Matrix Computations.* The Johns Hopkins University Press, Baltimore MD, 3rd edition, 1996.
6. Michael W. Berry, Susan T. Dumais, and Gavin W. O'Brien. Using linear algebra for intelligent information retrieval. *SIAM Rev.*, 37(4):573–595, 1995.
7. Michael W. Berry, Zlatko Drmač, and Elizabeth R. Jessup. Matrix, vector spaces, and information retrieval. *SIAM Rev.*, 41(2):335–362, 1999.
8. April Kontostathis and William M. Pottenger. A framework for understanding LSI performance. In *Proceedings of ACM SIGIR Workshop on Mathematical/Formal Methods in Information Retrieval (ACMSIGIRMF/IR '03)*, 2003.
9. C. Eckart and G. Young. The approximation of one matrix by another of lower rank. *Psychometrika*, 1:211–218, 1936.
10. Susan Dumais. Enhancing performance in latent semantic indexing (LSI) retrieval. Technical Report TM-ARH-017527, 1990.
11. Gavin W. O'Brien. Information management tools for updating an SVD-encoded indexing scheme. Master's thesis, The University of Knoxville, Tennessee, TN, 1994.
12. Ricardo D. Fierro and Eric P. Jiang. Lanczos and the Riemannian SVD in information retrieval applications. *Numer. Linear Algebra Appl.*, 12(4):355–372, 2005.
13. Chung-Min Chen, Ned Stoffel, Mike Post, Chumki Basu, Devasis Bassu, and Clifford Behrens. Telcordia LSI engine: Implementation and scalability issues. In *RIDE '01: Proceedings of the 11th International Workshop on research Issues in Data Engineering*, 2001.
14. Chunqiang Tang, Sandhya Dwarkadas, and Zhichen Xu. On scaling latent semantic indexing for large peer-to-peer systems. In *SIGIR '04: Proceedings of the 27th annual international ACM SIGIR conference on Research and development in information retrieval*, pages 112–121, 2004.
15. Devasis Bassu and Clifford Behrens. Distributed LSI: Scalable concept-based information retrieval with high semantic resolution. In *Proceedings of the 3rd SIAM International Conference on Data Mining (Text Mining Workshop)*, 2003.

DCF: An Efficient Data Stream Clustering Framework for Streaming Applications

Kyungmin Cho, Sungjae Jo, Hyukjae Jang, Su Myeon Kim, and Junehwa Song

Department of Electrical Engineering and Computer Science
Korea Advanced Institute of Science and Technology (KAIST)
{kmcho, sjjo, hjjang, smkim, junesong}@nclab.kaist.ac.kr

Abstract. Streaming applications, such as environment monitoring and vehicle location tracking require handling high volumes of continuously arriving data and sudden fluctuations in these volumes while efficiently supporting multi-dimensional historical queries. The use of the traditional database management systems is inappropriate because they require excessive number of disk I/O in continuously updating massive data streams. In this paper, we propose DCF (Data Stream Clustering Framework), a novel framework that supports efficient data stream archiving for streaming applications. DCF can reduce a great amount of disk I/O in the storage system by grouping incoming data into clusters and storing them instead of raw data elements. In addition, even when there is a temporary fluctuation in the amount of incoming data, it can stably support storing all incoming raw data by controlling the cluster size. Our experimental results show that our approach significantly reduces the number of disk accesses in terms of both inserting and retrieving data.

Keywords: Data Archiving, OLAP, Clustering, R-tree, Fast Insertion, Query Performance.

1 Introduction

Rapid and continued advances in sensor and wireless communication technologies have fueled a new type of application called streaming applications [16] such as habitat and environment monitoring, RFID-enabled supply chain networks, vehicle location tracking, and transaction log analysis. Such applications have different workload characteristics from traditional applications. Extremely high volumes of data are continuously generated from a lot of data sources. These data need to be stored in permanent storage systems in order to apply analysis tools such as online analytical processing (OLAP) and data mining. These analytical operations are complex and require quite high processing costs. Additionally, in some special situations such as a forest fire, the application monitoring those events must face a sudden rise in data updates.

In such streaming applications, the high costs of disk accesses overload the storage system. Processing a high volume of continuous data requires numerous disk accesses in the storage system in order to write new incoming data into disk and update the index structure. Processing retrieval queries also causes many disk accesses to look up the index structure and retrieve the corresponding data from disk. In the case of

S. Bressan, J. Küng, and R. Wagner (Eds.): DEXA 2006, LNCS 4080, pp. 114 – 122, 2006.

temporary load peaks, the situation would become much more severe. Considering these challenges, for streaming applications, exploiting traditional data management systems, which are designed to support applications over static data sets, is inappropriate.

In this paper, we propose DCF (Data Stream Clustering Framework), a novel framework that supports efficient data stream archiving for streaming applications. It can handle high rates of data insertion and adapt to sudden spikes in the input rate while not degrading retrieval performance. DCF can reduce a great amount of disk I/O for both index updates and look-ups. The key idea of DCF is adopting the scheme of *cluster indexing*, in which the storage system stores data in units of clusters and leaf nodes in the index structure point to clusters instead of individual data. In the case of an insertion, a set of data is grouped into a cluster based on a clustering policy and inserted the cluster via a single insertion operation. Hence, the total number of insertion operations, each of which causes multiple disk accesses, can be considerably reduced. In addition, DCF constructs the resulting index structure with fewer indexing nodes, thereby reducing the index lookup time. DCF also provides the ability to adapt to load fluctuations by monitoring the rate of incoming data and controlling cluster size.

The cluster indexing scheme could cause two additional overheads in retrieving data from disk, since the retrieval operation returns data in units of clusters, not as individual data items. Depending on the cluster size, a cluster could occupy more than one disk block and thus may require multiple disk block accesses to get a cluster from disk. Thus, although the larger cluster size yields the better insertion performance, the retrieval performance is decreased as the cluster size increases. However, typically retrieving a data item from disk requires at least one disk block access. A good compromise is confining the cluster size less than one block, thereby avoiding this overhead. There is another overhead in filtering out unwanted data from a retrieved cluster, but this computation cost of post-processing can be ignored. Typically, the dominant cost of processing a query is the time that it takes to bring a block from disk into main memory. Once we have fetched the block, the time to scan the entire block is negligible.

The rest of the paper is organized as follows. Section 2 describes the proposed DCF. In Section 3, we discuss the scheme of cluster indexing. Section 4 presents experimental results. Section 5 reviews related work. Finally, Section 6 concludes our work.

2 DCF Framework

This section details how our DCF framework is constructed and how it handles a large number of data streams and queries. As shown in Figure 1, DCF is composed of three components: the Clusterer, Load Monitor, and Query Handler. The back-end storage system is responsible for indexing, storing and retrieving stream clusters.

Our framework processes two types of queries: insertion and retrieval queries. For insertion requests, which are stream data elements, the Clusterer first receives and clusters them according to the clustering policy. The clustering policy is a system parameter set by the system administrator. Then, data elements are stored in the internal buffer and periodically sent to the back-end storage system.

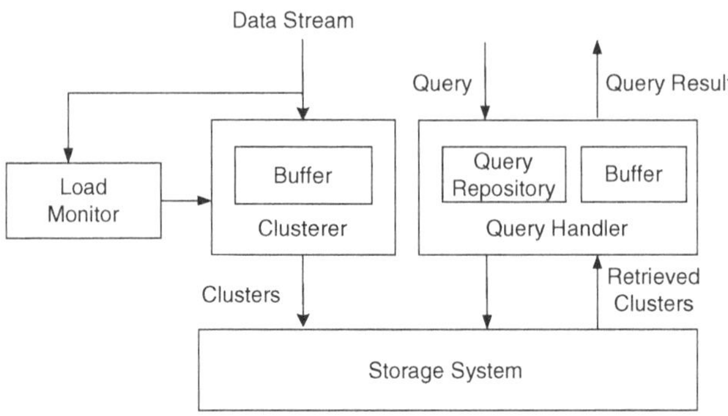

Fig. 1. Overall Architecture of DCF

In the case of a retrieval queries, the Query Handler (QH) temporarily stores the query information for post-processing, then forwards the query to the storage system. The QH has to delay the forwarding of the query until all the corresponding data are processed and stored in the storage system. Since the result is in the form of clusters, the QH needs to do post-processing on the result. Next, we will describe each component in detail.

Clusterer

The Clusterer receives data streams from data stream sources. Its primary role is making incoming data into a set of clusters. When receiving a data element, the Clusterer assigns it to the proper cluster, and then loads the data into the buffer. In order to prevent the storage system from being overloaded, the Clusterer should bound the total number of generated clusters to the maximum available update rate that the storage system can hold. The Clusterer receives the data arrival rate from the Load Monitor and uses this information for load adaptation. Depending on the data input rate, more data elements are included in one cluster. Also, note that the Clusterer could use multiple threads to manage multiple requests efficiently.

Load Monitor (LM)

The Load Monitor is in charge of monitoring the data input rate and notifying the Clusterer. Once the input rate of stream data reaches a threshold, the LM warns the Clusterer.

Query Handler (QH)

The Query Handler is mainly responsible for processing retrieval queries. Since the query result is a series of clusters, it could contain a set of data not matching the range of user's query. Thus, the QH unpacks the clusters and filters out unnecessary data elements in order to return the exact query results. For this filtering process, the QH stores and maintains a list of user queries, which are registered in the Query Repository when receiving them. In the context of streaming applications, it is common for a number of users to show similar interests. Thus, with the aid of more intelligent refinement or buffering scheme, the query processing could be further optimized by reusing the pre-fetched clusters.

3 Cluster Indexing

This section describes the difference between *cluster indexing* and *data indexing*, and several advantages of cluster indexing.

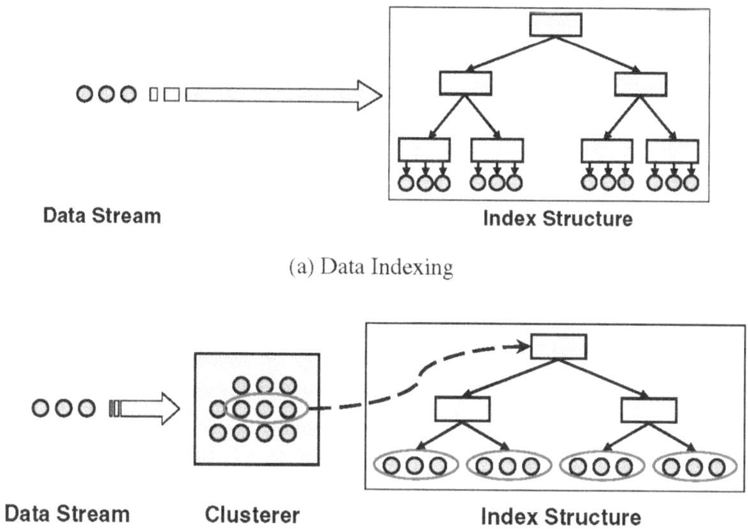

(b) Cluster Indexing

Fig. 2. Brief scheme of data indexing and cluster indexing

Figure 2-(a) shows data indexing, the existing indexing process where leaf nodes in the index structure point to individual data. On the other hand, Figure 2-(b) shows cluster indexing where the storage system stores data in units of clusters grouped by the Clusterer. Leaf nodes in the index structure point to clusters instead of individual data. Hence, cluster indexing leads to an index structure with fewer nodes as compared to data indexing and thus reduce the tree height of the index structure. Given N number of data and fanout f, the height of index structure can be described as $h = \left|\log_f N\right| - 1$. Since cluster indexing reduces the total number of indexed objects N to $N' = N/C$, where C is average cluster size, the height of resulting index structure is likely to be reduced.

Cluster indexing, which has the reduced number of the indexed objects, provides several advantages in both insertion and retrieval operations. It can reduce the number of disk I/O occurred in insertion operations by reducing the frequency of updating index structure. Due to the shortened height of the resulting index structure, the number of nodes visited by a retrieval query is decreased. Cluster indexing is also beneficial in supporting complex queries such as region query or k-nearest-neighbor query. As noted, cluster indexing groups individual data based on its proximity and stores them in one cluster. Thus, for collecting a number of data belonging to the queried area, cluster indexing only need to search a small number of clusters.

We use R-tree (an R-tree [1] or one of its variants) as an index structure for cluster indexing. We assume that the main purpose of data stream archiving is online analytical processing and data mining operations, so the most prevalent query type is the multi-attribute range query. R-tree is the most common index structure for such query type. Also, R-tree doesn't need to be modified for cluster indexing, since R-tree and our cluster indexing scheme use the same data representation type. Every object is abstracted as Minimum Bounding Rectangle (MBR) in R-tree and the Clusterer represent clusters as MBR.

4 Experiment

In this section, we demonstrate the performance benefit of DCF compared with the existing approach. For evaluation, we made DCF prototype in GNU C/C++ and we ran performance comparisons on the Linux platform. For rapid DCF prototyping, existing library package including the R-tree and the storage manager [15] was used for the storage system. The fill factor of the R-tree is set to 40% and the maximum number of entries each node can hold in the R-tree index structure is set to 100.

As an experimental scenario, we suppose that DCF is used for a taxi location tracking application. It receives and manages all the position data of taxis in a downtown area. Our experimental scenario is modeled with the following parameters: (1) the size of the area is 30Km x 30Km, (2) the total number of taxis varies from 1,000 to 8,000, (3) every taxi reports its new position – longitude, altitude, and time - every three seconds, (4) all the taxis move at an average speed of 60Km/h, (5) initially all vehicles are uniformly distributed over the whole area and continue to move to the top-right direction. According to the above scenario, we synthetically generate position data of vehicles using the *"Generate_Spatio_Temporal_Data"* (GSTD) [14], which is a well-known spatiotemporal data generator.

Clustering policies affect the retrieval performance of the index structure. To show this effect, we present three different clustering algorithms, which are a well-known K-means clustering algorithm, a 3D R-tree clustering algorithm which is used for spatiotemporal databases, and a Hash-based clustering algorithm.

The Hash-based clustering is the simplest way to group data streams into clusters. Each data consists of several attributes. Entire attributes' value ranges are divided into equal sized grids in the Hash algorithm. Incoming data stream's attribute values are hashed into a specific grid. Data in the same grid are periodically grouped into a cluster. In this scheme, there is no overlap between clusters.

The K-means clustering [17] is the most popular clustering algorithm. We give parameter values; the number of clusters k, the coarsening value C, and the refining value R, and the flush values $fmin$ and $fmax$. Initially, the first k data become a cluster of size one, and the next data elements are assigned to the closest cluster. After finishing the first assignment, the K-means algorithm repeats the calculation of the centroid for each cluster and reassigns all data to the closest cluster.

The 3D R-tree clustering periodically builds a small in-memory 3D R-tree [18] with incoming data stream. Data elements pointed to by the same leaf-node of the in-memory R-tree are grouped as one cluster. Because the tree algorithm is a one-pass algorithm, overlaps between clusters are much larger than other two clustering algorithms.

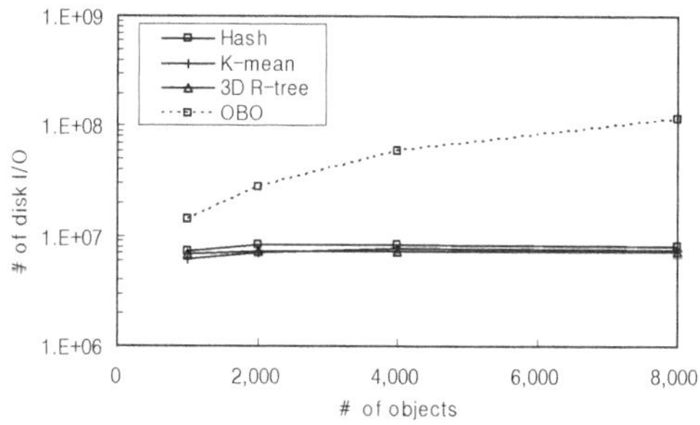

Fig. 3. Insertion performance with varying number of objects

In order to examine the insertion performance of DCF, we measure the total number of disk I/O for updating the index structure. The two hours of position data generated from 1,000, 2,000, 4,000, and 8,000 cars are inserted into the index structure. As shown in Figure 3, in the case of OBO insertion, the total number of disk I/O increases with the number of objects. However, in the case of the clustering schemes, the total number of disk I/O remains stable since our cluster indexing scheme generates equal or fewer clusters than the maximum number of data which can be handled by the storage system, which is assumed to be 200 insertions per second in our experiment.

The total number of nodes at each level after finishing the whole insertion process is shown in Table 1. We can see that DCF has a smaller space requirement than OBO insertion.

Table 1. Total number of nodes and height of the resulting R-tree index structure

# of objects	Hash-based		K-mean		3D R-tree		OBO	
	# of nodes	Height	# of nodes	Height	# of nodes	Height	# of nodes	Height
1,000	19,370	4	16,370	4	21,246	4	63,779	4
2,000	22,612	4	19,591	4	22,562	4	120,846	4
4,000	23,168	4	21,553	4	22,774	4	233,901	5
8,000	24,429	4	22,755	4	22,800	4	394,652	5

We also investigate the retrieval performance of our approach. The query type is the window query, which is "find all objects that exists in a certain area during a certain time range." The ranges of queries are 0.05%, 0.1%, 0.5%, and 1% of the total range with respect to each dimension. Each query set includes 1,000 queries. We measure the total number of disk I/O caused by index lookup operations to process each query set when the R-tree is populated with data generated from 1,000, 2,000, 4,000, and 8,000 objects.

As seen in Figure 4, DCF using the Hash-based and the K-mean clustering algorithms outperforms the existing OBO approach. However, DCF using the 3D R-tree clustering algorithm shows that its retrieval performance decreases more severely as the query range increases. From 0.1% of the query range, the 3D R-tree clustering algorithm generates a resulting R-tree having worse retrieval performance than OBO insertion. This indicates that DCF does not always provide better retrieval performance than OBO insertion. We measure the MBR overlap between clusters

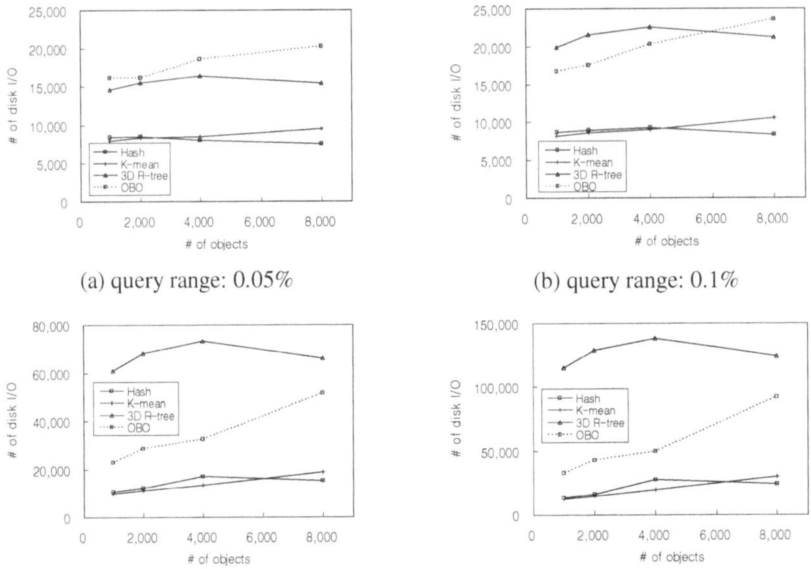

(a) query range: 0.05%
(b) query range: 0.1%
(c) query range: 0.5%
(d) query range: 1%

Fig. 4. Retrieval Performance with varying number of objects at different query ranges

Table 2. MBR overlap of clusters generated over the same period

# of objects	Hash-based	K-mean	3D R-tree
1,000	0.00E+00	3.88E-11	1.94E-10
2,000	0.00E+00	5.54E-10	1.23E-08
4,000	0.00E+00	5.56E-09	3.69E-07
8,000	0.00E+00	3.12E-08	1.27E-06

generated over the same period as shown in Table 2. The larger overlap increases the number of nodes to be traversed and results in an inefficient index structure. The clusters generated by the 3D R-tree clustering algorithm show the largest overlap between clusters such that its overlap is almost two orders of magnitude larger. Thus, although cluster indexing generates fewer objects to be indexed and allows the resulting R-tree to be more compact, a poor clustering algorithm like the 3D R-tree clustering algorithm results in an index structure with poor retrieval performance.

5 Related Work

Many researchers have studied indexing overhead reduction, since indexing is the most serious bottleneck in handling large amounts of data. [2][3] try to mitigate indexing overhead by dropping those updates which do not affect the current structure. They are very effective in handling position data of moving objects. However, they are not suitable for data archiving where every update should be recorded without any loss of data. a bottom-up R-tree [4] speeds up index updates by utilizing locality among incoming data.

Bulk loading approaches [5][6][7][8][9][10] have been proposed to efficiently build multidimensional index structures such as R-trees on massive amounts of data. In these approaches, input data are first sorted according to a certain criteria such as proximity. Then, a number of sorted data are grouped together and the index tree is built upon the data groups. The indexing overhead is reduced by about a factor of the average size of the groups. However, since all the data should be known before using bulk loading, this approach can not be used directly for streaming applications, where data are continuously coming from data sources.

Bulk updating, a.k.a. bulk insertion, [11][12][13] is an approach to efficiently load a bulk of data into an already existing index tree. [11] achieves this goal by creating new index trees on partitions of incoming data, then the index trees are merged with a pre-existing big tree. [12] further improves the performance of index merging by exploiting the characteristics of an existing index tree while constructing a new small index tree. However, there still remains the problem of how to efficiently build the small tree when updates occur very frequently. [13] reduces the frequency of index updates by delaying the propagation of insertions to other tree nodes until a threshold number of data are collected. But this approach requires too much main memory for buffering. Especially, this problem becomes very serious in historical data archiving since the indexing tree grows endlessly. In addition, bulk updating techniques do not address the problem of adapting to load fluctuations, which happens frequently when dealing with stream-based applications.

6 Conclusion

In this paper, we describe DCF, a novel framework that supports data stream archiving for streaming applications. High volumes of continuously arriving data cause a lot of disk I/O, overloading the storage system. The proposed framework, DCF can reduce a great amount of disk I/O in both updating and looking up index structure. The basic idea of DCF is indexing a group of data, namely a cluster, instead of individual data. Our experimental studies show that DCF is very effective in reducing disk I/O resulting from updating index structures, and it is beneficial in reducing the number of disk accesses required to process queries due to the compactness of the index structure.

Possible future works include thorough cost analysis in order to reveal influential factors to retrieval performance, exploration about standard criterion for developing a clustering algorithm, and an adaptive load management mechanism for DCF.

References

1. Antonin Guttman, R-Trees: A Dynamic Index Structure for Spatial Searching, In Proceedings of ACM SIGMOD, pages 47-57, 1984
2. Ouri Wolfson, A. Prasad Sistla, Sam Chamberlain, and Yelena Yesha, Updating and Querying Databases that Track Mobile Units, Special issue on mobile data management and applications of distributed and parallel databases, Vol. 7, Issue 3, July, 1999, pp 257-387

3. Dongseop Kwon, Sangjun Lee, and Sukho Lee, Indexing the Current Positions of Moving Objects Using the Lazy Update R-tree, Proceeding of the Third International Conference on Mobile Data Management, Singapore, January, 2002
4. Mong Li Lee, Wynne Hsu, Christian S. Jensen, Bin Cui, and Keng Lik Teo, Supporting Frequent Updates in R-Trees: A Bottom-Up Approach, In Proceedings of the 29th VLDB Conferences, Berlin, Germany, pages 608-619, 2003
5. Christos Faloutsos, M. Ranganathan, and Yannis Manolopoulos, Fast Subsequence Matching in Time-Series Databases, Proceeding of ACM SIGMOD Conference, Mineapolis, MN, 1994.
6. Ibrahim Kamel, and Christos Faloutsos, On Packing R–trees, Proceedings of the second international conference on Information and Knowledge Management, Washington D.C., US., pp 490-499, 1993
7. D. J. Dewitt, N. Kabra, J. Luo, J. M. Patel, and J.-B. Yu. Client-server Paradise, In Proceedings of the 20th International Conference on Very Large Data Base (VLDB '94), pages 558-569, Morgan Kaufmann, 1994
8. Kamel, M. Khalil, and V. Kouramajian, Bulk insertion in dynamic R-trees. In Proceedings of the 4th International Symposium on Spatial Data Handling (SDH '96), pages 3B.31-3B.42, 1996
9. S. T. Leutenegger, M.A. Lopez, and J. Edgington. STR: A simple and efficient algorithm for R-tree packing. Proceedings of the Thirteenth International Conference on Data Engineering, pages 497-506, 1997
10. N. Roussopoulos and D. Leifker, Direct spatial search on pictorial databases using packed R-trees, In Proceedings ACM-SIGMOD International Conference on Management of Data, SIGMOD Record, Vol 14.4, pages 17-31
11. Li Chen, Rupesh Choubey, and Elke A. Rundensteiner, Bulk-insertions into R-trees using the samll-tree-large-tree approach. In Proceedings of the sixth ACM international symposium on Advances in geographic information systems, pages 161-162, 1998.
12. Taewon Lee, Bongki Moon, and Sukho Lee, Bulk Insertion for R-tree by Seeded Clustering, Proceeding of the DEXA 2003, pp. 129-138
13. L. Arge, K. H. Hinrichs, J. Vahrenhold, and J. S. Vitter, Efficient Bulk Operations on Dynamic R-trees. Algorithmica, 33 (1), pages 104-128, 2002
14. Yannis Theodoridis, and Mario A. Nascimento, Generating Spatiotemporal Datasets on the WWW, SIGMOD Record, Vol 29., No 3., pp 39-43, 2000
15. http://www.cs.ucr.edu/~marioh/spatialindex/index.html
16. Lukasz Golab, M. Tamer Ozsu, Data Stream Management Issues – A Survey, Technical Report CS 2003-08, University of Waterloo, April 2003
17. M. R. Anderberg, Probability and Mathematical Statistics, Academic Press, New York, San Francisco, London, 1973
18. M. Vazirgiannis, Y. Theodoridis, and T. Sellis, Spatio-temporal composition and indexing for large multimedia applications, Multimedia Systems, 6(4):284-298, 1998

Analysis of BPEL and High-Level Web Service Orchestration: Bringing Benefits to the Problems of the Business

Adam Strickland[1], Dick Whittington[1], Phil Taylor[1], and Bing Wang[2]

[1] The Salamander Organization, York Science Park, York, United Kingdom
{Adam.Strickland, Dick.Whittington, Phil.Taylor}@tsorg.com
[2] University of Hull, Computer Science, Cottingham Road, Hull, United Kingdom
B.Wang@hull.ac.uk

Abstract. As a business evolves, the number of systems used to run the business increases. This can be either through continued development of the IT strategy, or acquisition of other companies with different systems. For any business there is a real requirement to link these systems. Web services and Web service orchestration offer a secure, accessible, scalable and future-proof mechanism for system communication. This linking of disparate systems within a company's IT strategy contributes towards a key SOA strategy. Generally, a company's IT strategy is arranged and organised by high-level business managers; not technical IT officers. Due to the fact that SOA implementations are generally a very technical implementation, business personnel are unable to get heavily involved in the process at the present time. This paper presents the concepts behind Service Oriented Architectures and Web service orchestration. A custom software tool for developing SOA strategies via BPEL and Web service orchestration is outlined towards the end of the paper. Based on an established modelling tool, the SOA add-in is capable of producing complex SOA strategies for a company's IT department. This tool is pitched at a sufficient level for semi-technical business managers to be able to utilise it in an efficient manner. This moves away from the traditional low-level design being carried out by highly skilled IT professionals. We also discuss potential future improvements to the BPEL standard.

Keywords: Web Service, BPEL, WSDL, SOA, model checking.

1 Introduction

The Web services framework exists to provide a standards-based implementation of the Service Oriented Architecture computing paradigm. Here, disparate IT systems built on differing technologies can communicate with each other in a distributed systems architecture. In order to operate in an SOA environment, services must declaratively define their functional and non-functional requirements and capabilities in an agreed, machine-readable format [1]. Based on declarative service descriptions, selection and binding are an integral part of an SOA environment. A consequence of this binding capability is a looser coupling model between applications.

S. Bressan, J. Küng, and R. Wagner (Eds.): DEXA 2006, LNCS 4080, pp. 123 – 137, 2006.

By collating services that can communicate with each other in a self-contained manner, new applications are created that can form a key role in an SOA strategy. Such an application could follow a composition pattern to achieve a business goal, solve a scientific problem, or provide new service functions in general.

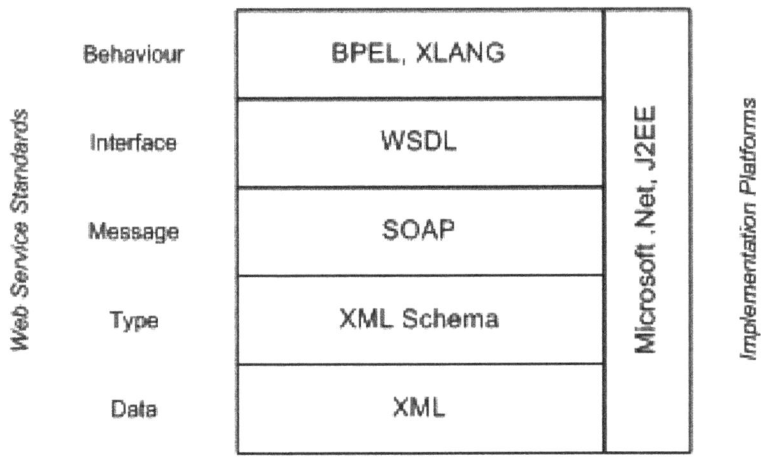

Fig. 1. Web Services Standards Stack

Fig 1 displays a stack of standards for Web services whereby XML [4] sits as the foundation. Since communicating Web services can be deployed at different locations using different implementation platforms, agreeing on a set of standards for data transmission and service descriptions is very important. XML messages form the basic standard for Web service communication. XML schema [5] forms the basis of the type system for Web service XML messages. The SOAP [6] communication protocol can then be used to transmit XML messages. Interfaces for Web services is described in WSDL [3] which, very importantly, describes the ports that other Web services can connect to in order to communicate with each other. Although a WSDL specification defines the public interface of a Web service, it does not provide any information regarding its behaviour. Behavioural descriptions of Web services can be defined using higher-level standards such as BPEL [2] or XLANG [7]. Web service orchestrations based on these standards is supported by different (and competing) implementation platforms such as Microsoft .Net [8] and J2EE [9]. Finally, Web service descriptions can be listed publicly on UDDI [10] servers. UDDI provides the basis of a 'Yellow Pages' listing functionality for Web services. From here, services can be searched for and utilised via their WSDL descriptions.

In order to move beyond the basic Web service framework into the behavioural nature of interacting services; service composition and quality of protocols are required. Several specifications have been proposed in these areas, most notably Business Process Execution Language for Web Services (BPEL4WS), Web Services Coordination (WS-Coordination) [11] and Web Services Transactions (WS-Transaction) [12] to support robust service interactions, Web Services Security (WS-Security), and Web Services reliable messaging (WS-ReliableMessaging). All of these aspects are critical elements of meaningful business interactions.

In this paper we focus on how the three specifications, BPEL4WS (or BPEL for short), WS-Coordination and WS-Transaction support creating robust service compositions. BPEL provides a mechanism for defining service compositions in the form of organised collections of Web services (sometimes called choreographies [1]). A choreography consists of the aggregation of services according to certain business rules. WS-Coordination and WS-Transaction complement BPEL to provide mechanisms for defining specific standard protocols for use by transaction processing systems, workflow engines, or other applications that need to coordinate multiple Web services. We briefly describe the key aspects of each specification and explain how the three fit together to provide a framework for composing and coordinating distributed Web services. Finally, we look at a software tool that can be used to create the aforementioned Web service choreographies (or orchestrations) that adhere to the BPEL specification.

2 Background Review

The development of Web service technology for integrating wide-spread legacy systems is not sufficient for multi-company applications. This is due to the fact that Web services themselves cannot describe their own behaviour. However, service orchestration paradigms are able to do this; this is illustrated in the Web Services Stack in Figure 1. Web service orchestrations address such behavioural needs. Modern day e-business transactions are a prime candidate for orchestrations and SOA-based technologies. Take the example of a travel booking through a website. hen we use a website for booking flights we are using a service provided by the flight provider and also services provided by individual airlines. We may even request the lowest quote from several different airlines during the transaction. Figure 2 shows a typical business activity model for a flight booking Web service orchestration. Clients register their interest in booking a flight by logging on to a travel agent's site. They fill in the

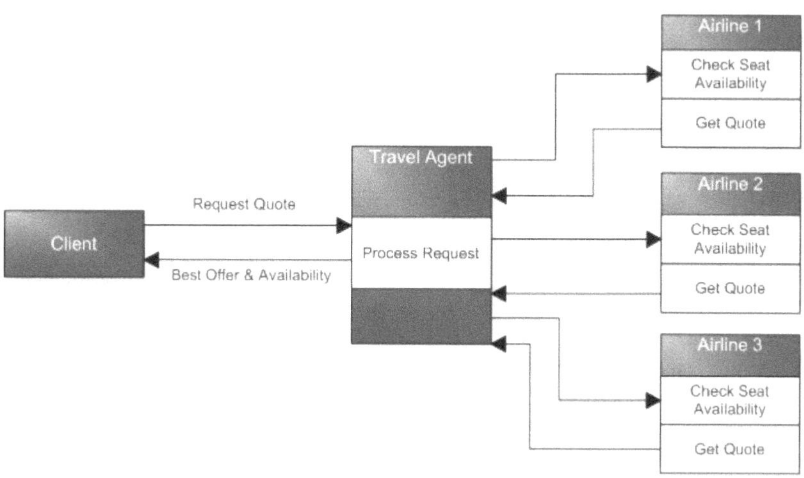

Fig. 2. A Flight Booking Orchestration Model

request for travel, specifying the origin, destination and preferred travel dates. The travel agent's service now passes this information to various airlines to obtain the availability of seats and their best quotes. The availability, along with the lowest fare is then communicated back to the calling clients.

This is one contemporary example of how today's e-business transactions are operated. However, this kind of application architecture can also be used by companies with disparate IT systems, possibly resulting from mergers or just general business growth. An example of Web service orchestration here may be the booking of employees onto training courses. Course registration could be handled by disparate systems that provide their own Web services. The client application would pass an employee's data to these services in order to retrieve a course availability date. Once this data is received the client application could go ahead and book the employee on a course. Here, we can see that the Web service framework is identical to that of an e-business implementation.

Service orchestration is a very powerful tool, although does still have a small number of drawbacks. Firstly, transactional processing is made very difficult in orchestrations due to the fact that processes can potentially be very long running. For example, an employee may be part-way through booking a training course when he/she decides to go to lunch leaving the process open. This makes transactional processing almost impossible. Also, orchestrations are stateless by nature meaning that no data can be stored in between individual Web service calls. This can be worked around however, by passing key data into services as parameters in the individual operation calls.

Web service orchestrations and SOA strategies provide companies with many benefits. The industry-standard orchestration paradigm (BPEL) is built on a foundation of XML. Like Web services themselves, which are also built on XML, this provides an extensible framework of technologies for pulling together disparate IT systems. BPEL also extends the basic WSDL functionality of Web services in order to provide self-contained units of logic which are essentially software systems in their own right. This makes for a powerful tool in a company's SOA armoury.

3 Orchestration Composition

BPEL is an XML-based specification language that specifies how to define a business process in terms of compositions of existing Web services. BPEL models the actual behaviour of a participant in a business interaction as well as the visible message exchange behaviour of all the parties involved in the orchestration.

3.1 Defining Orchestration Business Protocols

A BPEL orchestration is a container for the individual processes, activities and workflows within. Each orchestration is defined using the same WSDL XML schema language as the contained services; facilitating common-language components. This permits one BPEL orchestration to be contained within another as if it was an atomic service. Indeed they can be treated as Web Services due to the fact that they contain their very own WSDL definition in order to define their interface and port bindings. A process, like any Web service, supports a set of WSDL interfaces that enable it toexchange messages with its partners. The process interacts with them by invoking operations and passing their message types back and forth via the process service interface. Figure 3 illustrates such a set of interactions. Here, the external links (Partners) are external to the core process itself.

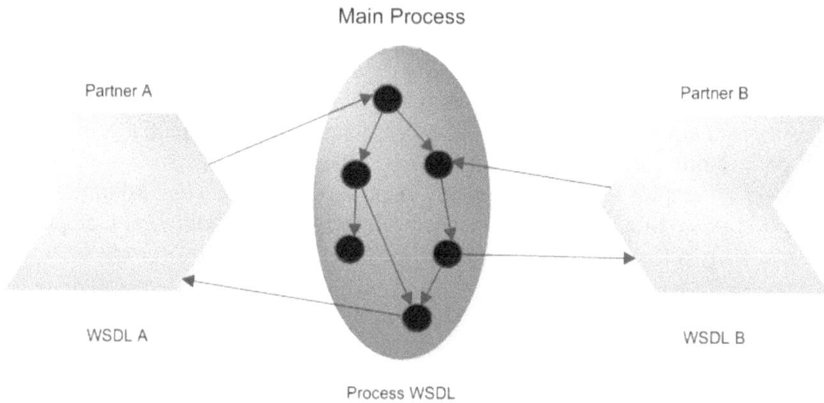

Fig. 3. A BPEL process interacting with two partners: black circles are activities, arrows are control links

The interaction between a BPEL orchestration and its partners is generally assumed to be a peer-to-peer conversational one, in which each party invokes operations. This is performed by sending messages to, or receiving messages from the other activities within the orchestration.

Only abstract interfaces are used in the partner definitions, which makes BPEL orchestrations platform and transport-independent. This means that the same BPEL process may be accessed over standard HTTP using SOAP messages, as well as, say, J2EE protocols such as IIOP and JMS [13].

3.2 Nature of BPEL Orchestrations

Once the partners for a process are defined, a set of primitive activities is used to define how messages are exchanged with each partner. These activities are similar to those used in modular programming languages and define the logic and workflow elements of the orchestration. A message is sent to a partner using an Invoke activity. The BPEL process can wait for a process operation to be invoked by an external client using the Receive activity. The response of an input/output operation is returned via the Reply activity. The BPEL specification also includes structural primitives that may be combined to form complex data-manipulation algorithms: Sequence defines an ordered set of steps; Switch implements Boolean conditional logic; While to define loops; Pick to execute one of several alternative paths provided by a set of events; and Flow to execute a set of steps in parallel. Additional primitives are provided to support abnormal process termination.

3.2.1 Fault Handling and Compensation

BPEL provides comprehensive support for dealing with errors through the use of Fault and Compensation handlers. Fault handlers provide a structured model in order to deal with unexpected errors within a process. This is very similar to the Try-Catch methodology in Java and .Net programming languages. Fault handling is closely related to the concept of Compensation. Compensation [18] is BPEL's answer to ACID transactions [19]. However, BPEL processes are potentially very long running processes meaning that the ACID transaction model would not suit the needs of most businesses running such processes. Therefore, Compensation effectively provides an 'undo' path in order to reverse the actions of a business process (such as cancelling a booking for an employee training course). A process designer would define the process that occurs when a compensation handler is triggered. The BPEL Compensation model is closely related to the protocols defined by the WS-Transaction specification.

3.2.2 WS-Coordination and WS-Transaction

WS-Coordination defines a framework that supports the concept of pluggable coordination models. The approach to implementing a specific coordination model is to extend the mechanisms provided by WS-Coordination. Specific coordination and transaction models are each represented as a coordination type supporting a set of coordination protocols. A coordination protocol is the set of well-defined messages that are exchanged between Web service participants. The correct execution of a set of distributed activities is taken care of via coordination protocols, such as completion protocols, synchronization protocols, or outcome notification protocols. The WS-Coordination framework defines three main elements commonly required by various coordination models:

- A Coordination Context – the shared, extensible context representing the coordination that is sent to the distributed participants.
- An Activation Service – the service used by clients to create a coordination context.
- A Registration Service – the service used by participants to register resources for inclusion in specific coordination protocols.

The Activation and Registration services are generic. Together with the set of services that represent the specific coordination protocols for a given coordination type, they make up a Coordination service (shortened to Coordinator).

In order to coordinate a set of Web services, the coordination client starts the coordination by sending a request message to the Activation service of a chosen coordinator. A CoordinationContext is then created by the Activation service. The CoordinationContext contains a global identifier, expiration information, the port reference for the Registration service, and can also be extended to include atomic transaction information. The port reference is a WSDL definition type that is used to identify a specific port. When the client initiates a Web service invocation, the CoordinationContext must be sent along with the application message. The service being invoked can then discover the Registration service's port reference to register for the coordination protocol that it wishes to participate in.

WS-Transaction supports WS-Coordination by defining two particular coordination types: "Atomic Transaction (AT)" and "Business Activity (BA)". ATs model short-running atomic transactions, whereas BAs model business transactions for long running processes.

ATs are analogous to traditional distributed transactions and map to the 'Atomicity' element of the ACID model. The AT coordination type supports this in an 'all or nothing' sense. It also includes the two-phase commit protocol.

The BA coordination type supports transactional coordination of long running processes. BAs do not require resources to be held, although they do require business logic to be applied in the event of exceptions. Participants in BAs are viewed as business tasks that are children of the BA for which they register. The participant list is dynamic and participants are loosely-coupled.

4 Orchestration Software Tools

Our work on gaining an understanding for the BPEL specification with regard to SOA strategies led us to look at methods for creating BPEL orchestrations themselves. A number of commercially available software tools that aid the process of creating BPEL orchestrations exist. Tools such as IBM WebSphere Studio Application Developer [15] allow for the creation of BPEL orchestrations via the in-built GUI. Orchestration processes can then be deployed and executed in a production environment using WebSphere Business Integration Server Foundation [16]. Oracle's BPEL Process Manager provides a similar GUI interface, although it is specifically designed for the generation of BPEL workflows and orchestrations. Similarly, the process can then be deployed onto the bundled Oracle server and run under a production environment.

The two tools mentioned here have one thing in common; that is that their target audience is predominantly the highly-skilled IT professional. This would pose little problem for the kind of company whose IT strategy was determined by these kinds of employees with a high level of technical expertise. However, we have found that larger companies wanting to adopt SOA IT strategies would ideally like to have their SOA models and processes designed by employees with a greater business knowledge than a technical one. For this reason we have developed a BPEL orchestration tool to specifically meet the needs of business-oriented users.

4.1 MooD® and Process Activation

The Salamander Organization Ltd, based in York, UK, has developed the MooD® Transformation Toolset to support large-scale business transformation programmes. The software is marketed to business managers and consultants, enabling them to discover and map organisational processes, systems, people, performance measures, and map them to real-world systems and applications through an award-winning patented process called Activation; the output is something Salamander calls a Knowledge Map and this can be published onto an intranet and in other document forms. Under the auspice of a two-year Knowledge Transfer Partnership programme the University of Hull and The Salamander Organization have collaborated to extend the visual and integration capabilities of MooD to include BPEL orchestrations within the business modelling context.

The MooD Transformation Toolset may be extended using an add-in mechanism. We used this to create the BPEL orchestration add-in called Process Activation, allowing users to construct and 'storyboard' business process models, using MooD Business Developer's familiar user interface. The Process Activation add-in extends MooD's process modeling capabilities in such a way that they be 'activated' in order to execute Web service operations. The difference between MooD Process Activation and other BPEL orchestration tools however, is that here we are only really interested in the general workflow of a particular process. We are not concerning ourselves with the more complex elements of orchestration construction, such as compensation and fault handling. The primary purpose of Process Activation is to 'storyboard' orchestrations before exporting them into a BPEL-compliant server tool of choice. Once in the production server tool the lower level operations can be 'filled-in' before being deployed and put into production.

4.2 Process Activation Features

Because Process Activation is aimed at business personnel rather than technical employees, the more complex BPEL constructs are either unavailable or abstracted from the user.

Before orchestrations can be created, Web services have to be imported into Process Activation. This can be done in one of three ways. We can import an individual service by locating its WSDL and importing it. This method is fine if we know where the service resides. However, if the location of the service is unknown, we can browse UDDI servers and search for services that reside there. Here, multiple services can be imported simultaneously. Finally, if a service that we require has not been created and deployed to a web server, we can create a pseudo service within Process Activation. This is known as Requirements generation. Here, if we know what the individual operation interfaces will look like, we can design the interface stubs of each operation within a service. Despite the fact that the process cannot actually be executed, it enables the 'storyboarding' of an orchestration to take place without necessarily having all required services available.

In terms of BPEL activities, Process Activation contains only the more basic ones. Process workflow logic is covered with the While and Choose activities, whilst Wait and Abort activities are also included to improve BPEL compliance. The Assign activity is included but only to transform the value of an available BPEL variable. The assigning of parameters to Web service operations is handled in a much simpler way and is abstracted from the user. This is described in the following section.

Process Activation also includes two other process types – the 'start node' and 'end node'. These can be placed on a model to show the start and end points of a process execution flow and are an integral part of the BPMN standards [17] for business process modelling.

4.3 Using Process Activation

Through its Business Developer user interface MooD is capable of holding complex models with detailed graphical content. MooD models are generally made up of a number of 'processes' that can be linked via relationships. For Web service orchestration these processes can be 'Process Activated' by dragging the name of an imported Web service operation onto the required process on the model. This forms the basis of a BPEL Invoke activity.

The available BPEL activities can be added to a model by selecting them from the custom Process Activation menu. Once added, they can be connected to the rest of the model through the use of specialist relationship links that are custom to Process Activation. Expressions for Choose and While activities are added to the orchestration via an easy-to-use expression builder that should provide all the functionality required to create powerful BPEL orchestrations.

Figure 4 shows an example BPEL orchestration that has been created within MooD Process Activation. We can see the flow control logic of the Choose operators; however, we are not concerned in inputting complex assign statements in order to manipulate variables before passing them into Web service invocations. Instead, we map data flows onto Web service parameters using a much higher level parameter mapping technique. This is done by simply pairing each link (the black lines in Figure 4) to the appropriate parameter required to invoke the Web service operation (the yellow ellipses). The user completes this mapping through a simple user interface, whereby the required parameters of an operation can be mapped to the available data flows. Compare this to the traditional BPEL engineering tools, in which complex BPEL Assign statements have to be written by hand in XPath.

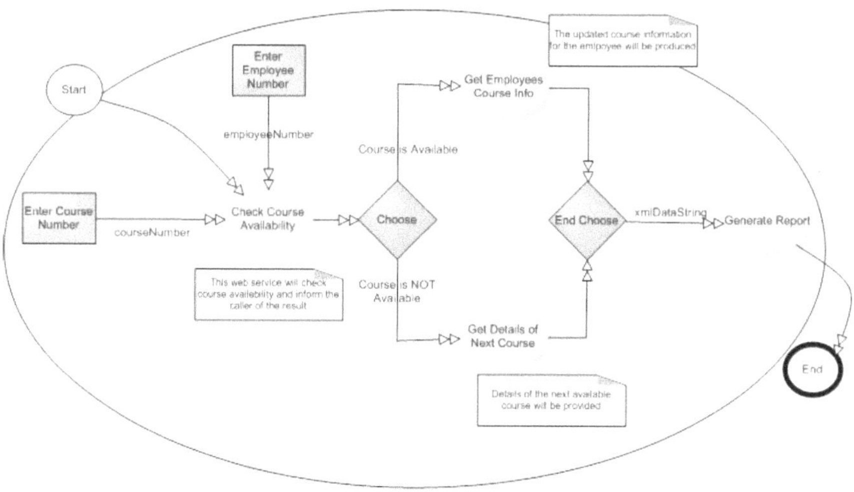

Fig. 4. An example orchestration from MooD Process Activation

As soon as an orchestration is created and the basic validation is passed it can be executed within the Process Activation environment. Here, we are executing our orchestration in a kind of 'debug' mode. This is where we concern ourselves with how the process would run under a full executable environment, i.e. we can check that our conditional workflow logic is operating correctly, that all Web services are being invoked with the correct parameters, and ultimately, that the expected value(s) are output at the end of the process. Note, that this execution is only possible if all of the services in the orchestration are bound and therefore can be executed. Any service operations that have been created using Process Activation's Requirements generation cannot be executed.

4.4 Process Activation to BPEL

Once we are confident that our orchestration contains the appropriate workflows and returns the correct data, it is ready to be placed in a production environment in order to form part of an SOA implementation. This is the ultimate aim of Process Activation; that an orchestration can be storyboarded and loosely constructed before being exported into a workflow engine of choice. Oracle BPEL Process Manager and IBM WebSphere are two such products.

The answer to server tool interoperability lies of course in BPEL. Due to the fact that BPEL is by nature an XML-based scripting language, it is inherently interoperable. Because Process Activation provides BPEL compliance, its orchestrations can be exported to the BPEL XML scripting language. Once the BPEL is generated, it can then be imported into the platform of choice.

The next section of the paper outlines a current shortcoming in the BPEL specification. The issue here is that each server tool interprets the tying together of collaborated Web services in a slightly different way. Whilst the BPEL specification is standard, the collaborative service definitions are not. For this reason Process Activation is able to target specific server and workflow tools. These are called Export Activators in Process Activation and currently target four workflow engines:

- Oracle BPEL Process Manager
- IBM WebSphere Business Integration Server Foundation
- BEA WebLogic
- Microsoft BizTalk

Due to the extensible nature of the Export Activator architecture, new server tools could be added with little extra effort.

Currently, Process Activation contains sufficient functionality for orchestrations to be storyboarded before being exported into a server tool of choice. Future functionality is set to include a corresponding BPEL import feature that will import some BPEL generated from a server tool. This may include more complex BPEL activities that have been 'filled in' whilst deployed on the BPEL server. This 'round-trip' capability will ensure both the business-level representation and IT implementation are synchronized and remain up-to-date.

We have seen here that Process Activation is simple to use. By omitting complex BPEL activities and abstracting programmatic logic away from the user, more business-oriented personnel are able to use the tool for their SOA requirements.

5 Process Activation Case Study

Now that we have seen how Process Activation and MooD can be used together, let us now look at a hypothetical real-world example of its use.

One type of company The Salamander Organization work with is large multinationals. One such example could be a media company who already use MooD software to map out processes for the generation of advertisements within newspapers. Due to the high-level nature of the process models, they would have always been created and maintained by business personnel, rather than the technical equivalent. Prior to the implementation of Process Activation, the company may use these models to produce training and technical documentation for their advertising employees to use in the production of newspaper advertisements.

The various tasks required in order to generate a successful advertisement in a newspaper may require a number of disparate IT systems to be utilized. For example, advertisement content is created and updated on one system, whereas approval and publication is carried out on another. Due to the fact that these systems are built on radically different technologies and that they are widespread, the media company would have had to undertake the task of advertisement creation manually. This would be a very painstaking and costly process. A well pitched SOA implementation would solve these problems.

The disparate IT systems used for advertisement generation could all be managed by the media company. Therefore, each system would be able to provide a Web service interface in order to expose their inherent functionality. As soon as these services were implemented and available for use, the final hurdle to overcome would be service collaboration. This is where the BPEL specification for Web service orchestration plays the key role in an SOA implementation.

The media company would need to implement a workflow BPEL-engine in order to realize their SOA implementation. For the purposes of this scenario the media company already have IBM WebSphere implemented in a production environment. Due to the fact that the company's advertisement creation processes would have already been defined within The Salamander Organization's MooD software, they would have already 'storyboarded' their orchestration. By using the Process Activation add-in for MooD, they could simply attach Web service operations to the existing MooD processes in order to create a fully-functional end-to-end process.

The advertisement creation process is illustrated in Figure 5. The individual tasks that make up the overall process are categorized by role (represented by the light blue and yellow swim lanes). The blue boxes on the model indicate individual subprocesses within the orchestration. The processes with Operation boxes above them are mapped onto Web service operations to form part of the BPEL orchestration. Notice that the model shown here is a purely linear one, i.e. there is no use of conditional logic or iterative looping functionality. However, future orchestrations designed by the company could contain such functionality.

Once the company is confident that their orchestration is operating correctly within Process Activation, it is time to deploy it to IBM WebSphere Business Integration Server Foundation Edition. In order to do this they would simply use the Process Activation BPEL Export Activator for IBM WebSphere. The exported orchestration would then be imported into IBM WebSphere. Here, lower-level functionality could be added to the orchestration, such as exception handling and concurrent processing via the BPEL Flow activity. As soon as the orchestration is configured to be executed within a production environment it can be deployed to the WebSphere Foundation Server where it is put into production. Once this has taken place the media company would see the immediate benefits of having an automated advertisement creation process. The manual invocation of disparate systems would no longer be necessary saving valuable time and cumulative effort in their daily business operations.

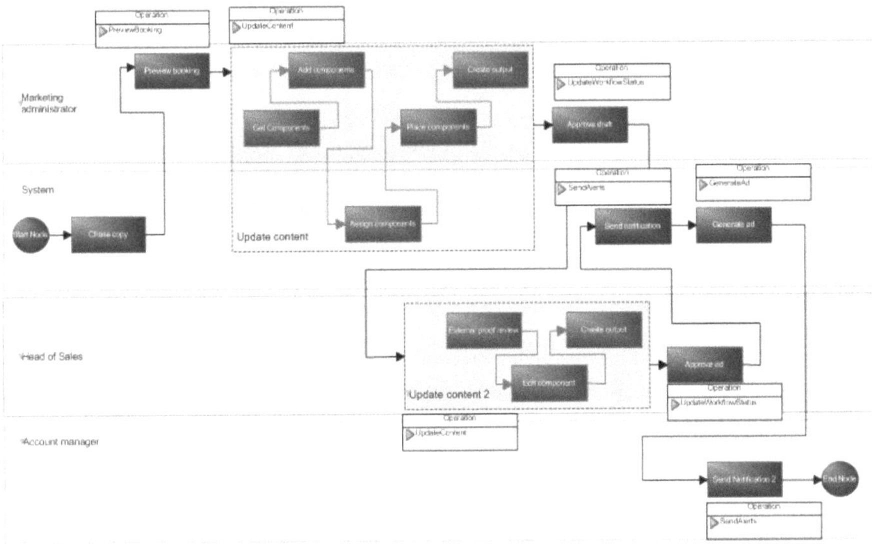

Fig. 5. The Advertisement Creation Process

6 BPEL Specification Improvements

As a standard for Web service orchestration, BPEL addresses the majority of requirements for a company to implement SOA. However, we have identified a portion of the specification that seems to be currently omitted.

In order to import a valid BPEL orchestration into a workflow engine, such as Oracle BPEL Process Manager, 3 separate files are required.

- An XML file containing the BPEL activities that make up the orchestration workflow of the process. This file acts as the BPEL process 'roadmap'.
- A WSDL file that contains the interface and binding data for the whole BPEL process. This ensures that the whole process can be treated as a Web service in its own right.
- A BPEL Suitcase file. This is an XML-based file that tells the BPEL engine where it can find the WSDL files that belong to the Web service partners used in the BPEL process.

Figure 6 shows an Oracle BPEL Process Manager BPEL Suitcase file that contains links to three separate WSDL files. The first is the 'client' WSDL; this is the WSDL for the BPEL process and defines the interface for the BPEL receive and reply activities. The remaining two 'partnerLinkBinding' elements exist to tell the Oracle

```
<?xml version = '1.0' encoding = 'UTF-8'?>
<BPELSuitcase>
  <BPELProcess id="CourseBooking" src="CourseBooking.bpel">
    <partnerLinkBindings>
      <partnerLinkBinding name="client">
        <property name="wsdlLocation">CourseBooking.wsdl</property>
      </partnerLinkBinding>
      <partnerLinkBinding name="CourseEnquiries">
        <property name="wsdlLocation">CourseEnquires.wsdl</property>
      </partnerLinkBinding>
      <partnerLinkBinding name="EmployeeEnquiries">
        <property name="wsdlLocation">EmployeeEnquiries.wsdl</property>
      </partnerLinkBinding>
    </partnerLinkBindings>
  </BPELProcess>
</BPELSuitcase>
```

Fig. 6. An Oracle BPEL Suitcase file

workflow engine where to find the WSDL files for the associated Web service partners in the BPEL process. Without this information the BPEL process would be unable to be executed in a production environment.

Similarly, IBM WebSphere has a requirement to know where the Web service partner WSDL files are located in order to execute the BPEL process. This is achieved through the use of an additional WSDL file for the BPEL process. As well as the WSDL to define the interface for the BPEL process, an additional one is used to define the location of each Web service partner. The principle here is very similar to that of the BPEL Suitcase used in Oracle BPEL Process Manager.

```
<partnerLinks>
  <partnerLink name="client" partnerLinkType="client:EmployeeCourseBooking"
    myRole="EmployeeCourseBookingProvider"/>
  <partnerLink name="CourseEnquiries" partnerLinkType="ns1:CourseEnquires"
    partnerRole="CourseEnquires_Role"/>
  <partnerLink name="EmployeeEnquiries" partnerLinkType="ns3:EmployeeEnquiries"
    partnerRole="EmployeeEnquiries_Role"/>
</partnerLinks>
```

Fig. 7. An example of Partner Link declarations in the existing BPEL specification

The issue with having Web service partner locations defined in a separate file is that each workflow tool vendor interprets this concept in a slightly different way. This means that in order to import BPEL orchestrations into workflow engines, extra files have to be created differently depending on which tool is being targeted. Essentially, this leads to a lack of interoperability within the BPEL specification. One of the advantages of specifications and standards is that interoperability is gained between similar software tools and engines. However, the BPEL specification loses some of this interoperability due to the fact that special measures have to be taken in order to inform the workflow engine where specific WSDL files are located.

Figure 7 shows an implementation of Partner Links in a BPEL file that adheres to the current specification. Very simply, the partner link has a name that is used to reference it in the document, a type that references a namespace, and a role that is referenced when the partner's services are invoked.

```
<partnerLinks>
  <partnerLink name="client" partnerLinkType="client:EmployeeCourseBooking"
    myRole="EmployeeCourseBookingProvider" location="http://www.example.com/EmployeeCourseBooking.wsdl"/>
  <partnerLink name="CourseEnquiries" partnerLinkType="ns1:CourseEnquires"
    partnerRole="CourseEnquires_Role" location="http://www.example.com/CourseEnquires.wsdl"/>
  <partnerLink name="EmployeeEnquiries" partnerLinkType="ns3:EmployeeEnquiries"
    partnerRole="EmployeeEnquiries_Role" location="http://www.example.com/EmployeeEnquiries.wsdl"/>
</partnerLinks>
```

Fig. 8. Our recommendation for the BPEL specification regarding Partner Links

We believe that the BPEL specification could be improved in order to state the locations of WSDL files that are associated to partner links. Figure 8 contains the same partner links declarations as those shown in Figure 7, with one significant difference. Here, we have added a 'location' element to each 'partnerLink' element. This element contains the physical location of the WSDL file associated with the partner link. By including this tool vendors would no longer have to implement bespoke methods for informing the BPEL engine of where to locate WSDL files for partner links. Therefore, BPEL would be a true standard and would place SOA in a stronger position within the IT community.

7 Conclusions

Due to their inherent technical nature, the design and storyboarding of BPEL orchestrations must be undertaken at a particularly low and technical level. We at the University of Hull, working in conjunction with The Salamander Organization have designed and implemented a BPEL design tool that can be used by business personnel rather than the more technically skilled IT employees of a company. This tool can deploy SOA technologies into the domain of the business person in order to achieve a common understanding across the high-level business layer and the lower-level technical IT layer of a business. We have shown that this can make SOA along with BPEL an even stronger proposition for companies wanting to undertake SOA implementations as part of a wider transformation programme.

The Web services framework is very much coming to the forefront of the IT community as we move ever-closer to an SOA-governed IT world. Over the last few years SOA has evolved into a technology stack based on XML standards. BPEL design tools and server-based engines such as IBM WebSphere and Oracle BPEL Process Manager have helped BPEL Web service orchestrations become a large part of a company's IT strategy.

Whilst the BPEL specification addresses many needs with regard to SOA and service orchestration, it is by no means perfected. In this paper, we have outlined issues regarding the location of partner link WSDL files within a BPEL process. This means that for a high level design tool like Process Activation certain server tools have to be specifically targeted for BPEL export. With the improvements to the BPEL specification suggested here, any compliant workflow engine could simply import and execute a single BPEL file, along with its associated WSDL.

Acknowledgements

Our thanks to the Knowledge Transfer Partnership (KTP) for facilitating the collaborative work between The University of Hull and The Salamander Organization Ltd. Extended thanks must go to The Salamander Organization Ltd and MooD International Ltd for the opportunity to develop the Process Activation BPEL add-in for their existing MooD® product.

References

1. Francisco Curbera, Rania Khalaf, Nimal Mukhi, Stefan Tai, Sanijiva Weerawarana. The next step in Web Services. October 2003.
2. Business Process Execution Language for Web Services (BPEL), Version 1.1 http://www.ibm.com/developerworks/library/ws-bpel May 2003.
3. Web Services Description Language (WSDL) 1.1. http://www.w3.org/TR/wsdl March 2001
4. Extensible Markup Language (XML). http://www.w3.org/XML
5. XML Schema. http://www.w3.org/XML/Schema
6. Simple Object Access Protocol (SOAP) 1.1. W3C http://www.w3.org/TR/SOAP
7. XLANG. Microsoft http://www.devx.com/enterprise/Link/7962
8. Joseph Williams. The Web services debate J2EE vs .Net. Communications of the ACM, 46(6):59-63, June 2003.
9. Gerry Miller. .Net vs J2EE. Communications of the ACM, 46(6):64-67, June 2003.
10. UDDI, Version 3.0.2 http://uddi.org/pubs/uddi_v3.htm October 2004
11. Web Services Coordination (WS-Coordination) 1.0 http://www-106.ibm.com/developerworks/library/ws-coor
12. Web Services Transaction (WS-Transaction) 1.0 http://www-106.ibm.com/developerworks/library/ws-transpec
13. Mukhi, n., Khalaf, R., and Fremantle, P. Multi-protocol Web services for enterprises and the grid. In Proceedings of EuroWeb '02 (Oxford, UK, December 2002).
14. Oracle BPEL Process Manager 10.1 http://www.oracle.com/technology/products/ias/bpel/
15. IBM WebSphere Studio Application Developer Integration Edition 5.1. http://www-306.ibm.com/software/awdtools/studioappdev/
16. IBM WebSphere Business Integration Server Foundation http://www-306.ibm.com/software/integration/wbisf/
17. Business Process Modeling Notation (BPMN) http://www.bpmn.org/Documents/BPMN%20V1-0%20May%203%202004.pdf
18. Van der Aalst, W. and van Hee, K. Workflow Management: Methods, Models and Systems. MIT Press, 2002.
19. Khaled Nagi. A Robust Approach for Scheduling Orders in a Competitive Just-In-Time Manufacturing Environment

Rewriting Queries for XML Integration Systems

Ling Li, Mong Li Lee, and Wynne Hsu

National University of Singapore, School of Computing
{lil, leeml, whsu}@comp.nus.edu.sg

Abstract. A data integration system typically creates a target XML schema to represent an application domain and source schemas are mapped to the target schema. A user poses a query over the target schema, and the system rewrites the query into a set of queries over the data sources. Existing algorithms generate a set of static rules based on the target schema and mappings, and rewrite the target query using these rules. We design a flexible and dynamic approach that rewrites XML queries directly based on the mappings between the target and source schemas. Theoretical analysis and experiments on both synthetic and real-world datasets indicate that the proposed approach is efficient and scalable.

1 Introduction

A data integration system is an important framework for supporting querying across multiple heterogeneous data sources in a uniform manner. A target schema is created to model a particular application domain and source schemas are mapped to the target schema. A user issues a query over the target schema and the data integration system reformulates the query into queries that can be executed over the data sources. In this way, a user can retrieve comparatively more information than querying each source individually.

In a dynamic environment like the Web, data sources may change their schemas, and new data sources may be added to an integration system. These changes will affect the mappings between the target and source schemas. [9] develop a framework for automatically adapting the mappings as schemas evolve. [5] describe an automatic solution called MAVERIC to detect broken mappings. [11] present a mapping composition approach to maintain the mappings between the target and source schemas as the source schemas change.

[10] examine how XML queries can be rewritten in a data integration system. Based on the mappings between the target and source schemas, their method generates a set of rules that specify the transformations needed to rewrite a target query into a set of queries over the source schemas. However, using a set of static rules to rewrite queries in a data integration system is not suitable in a dynamic environment since changes in the mappings will require the regeneration of invalidated rules.

Related Work. Query rewriting is an important task in query optimization and data integration, and has been well-studied in the context of relational databases

S. Bressan, J. Küng, and R. Wagner (Eds.): DEXA 2006, LNCS 4080, pp. 138–148, 2006.

[2,3,7,8]. Recent works [1,4,6,10] examine approaches to rewrite XML queries. [1,4] address the problem of rewriting XML queries for optimization.

[10] investigate the problem of rewriting target queries in XML data integration systems and develop a method to generate rewriting rules from the mappings between the target and source schemas. The method uses target constraints to specify how the retrieved data is merged. This approach is expensive for two reasons. First, changes in the mappings will require the regeneration of invalidated rules. Second, unnecessary substitutions are introduced when rewriting queries based on the rules, which increases the complexity of the process.

Contribution. We investigate how queries in a data integration system can be rewritten directly based on the mappings between target and source schemas. We develop a basic rewriting method to handle both simple path and branch XML queries. We give a theoretical analysis of the correctness and time complexity of the proposed method. Experiment results indicate that the proposed approach scales well with respect to mapping and query complexities.

2 Motivating Example

Consider the target schema T_{12} in Fig 1 and source schemas S_1 and S_2 in Fig 2 and Fig 3 respectively. T_{12} captures the textbook and lecturer information of a module, with *code* as the key. The mappings between S_1 and T_{12}, and S_2 and T_{12} are given by M_1 and M_2 respectively. These mappings map modules with 4 credits in the source schemas S_1 and S_2 to the target schema T_{12}.

Based on the target schema T_{12} and mapping M_1, [10] will generate two rewriting rules, one each for the non-leaf nodes *module* and *book* in T_{12}:

R_1: module = $\lambda()$.{
    for m1 in module1 where m1.credit = 4
    return [module = [code = m1.code, book = SK_0(m1.code),
        lecturer = m1.lecturer]]}
R_2: SK_0 = λ(l1).{
    for m1 in module1, b1 in m1.book where l1 = m1.code and m1.credit = 4
    return [book = [ISBN = b1.ISBN,title = b1.title,
        author = b1.author, price = b1.price]]}

```
Target schema T12:
  <!DOCTYPE module [
    <!ELEMENT module (book+, lecturer+)>
    <!ATTLIST module code ID #REQUIRED>
    <!ELEMENT book (title, author+, publisher+, price)>
      <!ATTLIST book ISBN ID #REQUIRED>
      <!ELEMENT title (#PCDATA)>
      <!ELEMENT author (#PCDATA)>
      <!ELEMENT publisher (#PCDATA)>
      <!ELEMENT price (#CDATA)>
    <!ELEMENT lecturer (#PCDATA)>
  ]>
```

Fig. 1. Target Schema T_{12}

Source schema S_1:

```
<!DOCTYPE module1 [
 <!ELEMENT module1 (credit, book+, lecturer+)>
 <!ATTLIST module1 code ID #REQUIRED>
 <!ELEMENT credit (#CDATA)>
 <!ELEMENT book (title, author+, price)>
  <!ATTLIST book ISBN ID #REQUIRED>
  <!ELEMENT title (#PCDATA)>
  <!ELEMENT author (#PCDATA)>
  <!ELEMENT price (#CDATA)>
 <!ELEMENT lecturer (#PCDATA)>
]>
```

Mapping M_1:

```
foreach m1 in module1, b1 in m1.book
where m1.credit = 4
exists m in module, b in m.book
with m.code = m1.code
 and b.ISBN = b1.ISBN
 and b.title = b1.title
 and b.author = b1.author
 and b.price = b1.price
 and m.lecturer = m1.lecturer
```

Fig. 2. Source Schema S_1 and the Corresponding Mapping

Source schema S_2:

```
<!DOCTYPE module2 [
 <!ELEMENT module2 (credit, book+, lecturer+)>
 <!ATTLIST module2 code ID #REQUIRED>
 <!ELEMENT credit (#CDATA)>
 <!ELEMENT book (title, publisher+, price)>
  <!ATTLIST book ISBN ID #REQUIRED>
  <!ELEMENT title (#PCDATA)>
  <!ELEMENT publisher (#PCDATA)>
  <!ELEMENT price (#CDATA)>
 <!ELEMENT lecturer (#PCDATA)>
]>
```

Mapping M_2:

```
foreach m2 in module2, b2 in m2.book
where m2.credit = 4
exists m in module, b in m.book
with m.code = m2.code
 and b.ISBN = b2.ISBN
 and b.title = b2.title
 and b.publisher = b2.publisher
 and b.price = b2.price
 and m.lecturer = m2.lecturer
```

Fig. 3. Source Schema S_2 and the Corresponding Mapping

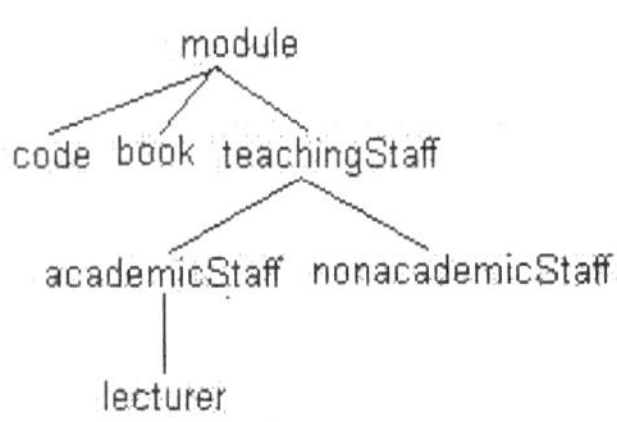

Fig. 4. Source Schema S_3

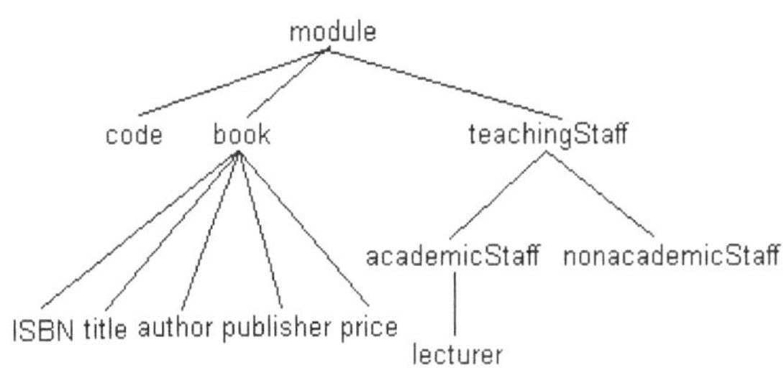

Fig. 5. Target Schema T'_{12}

Since a rewriting rule is created for each non-leaf node in the target schema, the time complexity for the rule generation step is $O((n_t - l_t) * f_t)$, where n_t is the number of nodes in the target schema, l_t is the number of leaf nodes, and f_t is the average fanout of a non-leaf node. This is significant because a target schema tends to be highly complex with many nodes.

Figure 4 shows a source schema S_3. If we integrate S_3 with S_1 and S_2, we will obtain a new target schema T'_{12} (see Figure 5). The evolution of the target schema from T_{12} to T'_{12} will change the mapping between S_1 and the target schema T'_{12} as follows (changes are highlighted in **bold**):

Mapping M_1':
foreach m1 in module1, b1 in m1.book where m1.credit = 4
exists m in module, b in m.book,**t in m.staff, a in t.acadStaff**
with m.code = m1.code and b.ISBN = b1.ISBN
and b.title = b1.title and b.author = b1.author
and b.price = b1.price and **a**.lecturer = m1.lecturer

With the addition of the non-leaf node *staff* and *acadStaff* in the target schema T_{12}', two new rewriting rules need to be generated, and the existing rule for $module(R_1)$ needs to be updated as follows:

R_1': module = $\lambda()$.{
for m1 in module1 where m1.credit = 4
return [module = [code = m1.code, book = SK_0(m1.code),
staff = SK_1**(m1.code)**]]}

The rewriting rule for $book(R_2)$ remains valid since there is no change in the child nodes of this element in the target schema. We also find that the rewriting rule approach tends to introduce unnecessary substitutions. Suppose we issue query Q_A on T_{12}':

Q_A: for m in module, t in m.staff, a in t.acadStaff
where a.lecturer = "John" return m.code

The QueryTranslate algorithm in [10] first applies rule R_1' to substitute the element *module* in query Q_A with the corresponding element *module1* in the source schema S_1. A new variable, say m1', is introduced to denote the element *module1*. The elements *m.code* in the *return* clause of Q_A is replaced with *m1'.code*. Next, the element *staff* in the *in* clause of Q_A is substituted with the right-hand side of the rule SK_1 as indicated in the *return* clause of R_1'. This substitution process continues until only source elements occur in the *in* clause of the query Q_A. We observe that some of the substitutions are not necessary, e.g., the substitutions for the elements *staff* and *acadStaff* when rewriting Q_A to a query over S_1 since these two elements are not modelled in S_1.

3 Rewriting Queries Dynamically

In this section, we describe the proposed method to rewrite target queries directly based on the mappings between the target and source schemas. Let us issue query Q_B on the target schema T_{12} to retrieve information about each module.

Q_B: for p in module, q in p.book return p.code, q.ISBN, q.title, p.lecturer

Step 1. Rewrite query variables.
We use the mappings between the target and source schemas to unify and replace each element variable that occurs in the target query with the corresponding element variable of the target schema in the mapping. The *for* and *in* clauses of the query will be emptied. This step facilitates the subsequent mapping of target elements to the source elements.

Algorithm 1. Basic_Rewrite

```
Input: Target schema T; Query Q; Mapping M between source schema S and T
Output: Q' - query on source schema S
   /* Step 1. Rewrite variables */
for each element E1 in in clause of query Q do
   find variable e1 that corresponds to E1 in M;
   replace all variables corresponding to E1 with e1 in all clauses except for clause in Q;
   empty for and in clauses in Q;
   /* Step 2. Map elements in query */
for each element E in Q do
   find corresponding element E' in with clause in M;
   replace E with E';
   /* Step 3. Add where clause */
for each where clause W in M after foreach clause do
   add W to where clause in Q;
   /* Step 4. Complete rewriting by adding variables */
for each variable V in Q do
   call addVariable(V);

FUNCTION addVariable(V)
   check if V already exists in for clause of Q;
   if V is a new variable then
      find same variable in foreach clause;
      add both variable and corresponding element in in clause I after foreach clause in M to for
      and in clauses in Q;
      for each variable V' that appears in I do
         call addVariable(V');
```

The variables p and q in query Q_B denote the elements *module* and *book* respectively. However, the mapping M_1 uses the variables m and b to denote the corresponding elements. Step 1 will replace all the p with m, and all the q with b. The resulting query on the source S_1 is:

Q_{1_1}: for in return m.code, b.ISBN, b.title, m.lecturer

Next, we use the mapping M_2 to rewrite Q_B to query Q_{2_1} on source S_2

Q_{2_1}: for in return m.code, b.ISBN, b.title, m.lecturer

Step 2. Map query elements.
We replace the elements in the query with the corresponding elements in the source schema according to the mapping between the target and source schemas. Any query elements that do not have the corresponding elements in the mapping are discarded since these elements will not be modeled in the source schema. The queries obtained after mapping the elements are:

Q_{1_2}: for in return m1.code, b1.ISBN, b1.title, m1.lecturer
Q_{2_2}: for in return m2.code, b2.ISBN, b2.title, m2.lecturer

Step 3. Add *where* clause.
We augment the query with the *where* clause in the mapping which specifies the conditions that materialize the source data to the target schema.

Q_{1_3}: for in where m1.credit = 4
return m1.code, b1.ISBN, b1.title, m1.lecturer
Q_{2_3}: for in where m2.credit = 4
return m2.code, b2.ISBN, b2.title, m2.lecturer

Step 4. Add paths of elements.
Finally, we specify the paths to the element variables in the query. The path information is found in the *foreach* and *in* clauses that corresponds to the source schema. The final queries issued on S_1 and S_2 are Q_{1_4} and Q_{2_4}:

Q_{1_4}: for m1 in module1, b1 in m1.book where m1.credit = 4
return m1.code, b1.ISBN, b1.title, m1.lecturer
Q_{2_4}: for m2 in module2, b2 in m2.book where m2.credit = 4
return m2.code, b2.ISBN, b2.title, m2.lecturer

4 Theoretical Analysis

4.1 Soundness and Completeness

Lemma 1: Let T be the target schema of source schemas $S_1, S_2, \ldots, S_N$, and DS_1, DS_2, ..., DS_N be the data sources of $S_1, S_2, \ldots, S_N$ respectively. Let M_i be the mapping between S_i and T, $1 \leq i \leq N$. A tuple t' is retrieved via T iff there exists some corresponding tuple t, $t \in DS_i$ such that t satisfies the conditions specified in M_i, $1 \leq i \leq N$.

Based on Lemma 1, we partition the set of tuples retrieved via T into N sets $W_1, W_2, \ldots, W_N$, where W_i is the set of tuples retrieved from data source DS_i.

Lemma 2: Let M_i be the mapping between a source schema S_i and target schema T. Suppose Q_{M_i} is the query generated from M_i, and $Q_{M_i}(DS_i)$ is the set of tuples retrieved by Q_{M_i} from the data source DS_i that corresponds to the source schema S_i. A tuple t $\in Q_{M_i}(DS_i)$ iff t $\in W_i$, where W_i is the set of tuples retrieved via T which originates from DS_i.

Theorem 1: Algorithm Basic_Rewrite is sound and complete.

Proof: Let T be a target schema and $S_1, S_2, \ldots, S_N$ be N source schemas that are mapped to T. Let DS_1, DS_2, ..., DS_N be the data sources of $S_1, S_2, \ldots, S_N$ respectively, and M_i be the mapping between S_i and T, $1 \leq i \leq N$. Let Q be a query issued over T. The first two steps in Basic_Rewrite uses M_i to rewrite Q to Q_i such that all the elements expressed in terms of T are mapped to the corresponding elements expressed in terms of S_i. Since these two steps do not add or change any constraints in the original query Q, the rewritten query Q_i will capture the same constraints as Q.

Step 3 in Basic_Rewrite combines the mapping conditions in M_i with the constraints in Q_i. This gives us the query $Q_i.Q_{M_i}$ where Q_{M_i} denotes the query that is generated from mapping M_i. Sine query constraints are commutative

$$Q_i.Q_{M_i}(DS_i) \equiv Q_i(Q_{M_i}(DS_i)) \tag{1}$$

Let W_i denote the set of tuples that is retrieved from DS_i via T. From Lemma 2, the set of tuples $Q_i(Q_{M_i}(DS_i))$ is equal to Q(W_i).

$$Q_i.Q_{M_i}(DS_i) \equiv \text{Q}(W_i) \tag{2}$$

Since Q can be answered by each source individually, we have

$$\bigcup_{i=1}^{N} Q(W_i) \equiv Q(\bigcup_{i=1}^{N} W_i) \equiv Q(W) \text{ where } W = \bigcup_{i=1}^{N} W_i \quad (3)$$

From (2) and (3), we have

$$\bigcup_{i=1}^{N}(Q_i.Q_{M_i}(DS_i)) \equiv Q(W) \quad (4)$$

Thus, Algorithm Basic_Rewrite is sound and complete. □

4.2 Time Complexity

Next, we examine the complexity of the proposed approach. In the worst case, a query on the target schema will contain the maximum possible number of elements in each clause. Let n_t be the total number of nodes in the target schema, and l_t be the number of leaf nodes. Then we have $(n_t - l_t)$ variables in the *for* and *in* clauses. Both the *where* and *return* clauses will have l_t elements. Let n_s be the total number of nodes in the source schema, and l_s be the number of leaf nodes. The mapping between the target and source schemas will have l_s number of elements in the *where* clause after the *foreach* clause.

Step 1 processes each element in the *in* clause of the query and looks for the corresponding variable in the mapping. These variables are used to replace the element variables in the *where* and *return* clauses of the query. This takes $O((n_t - l_t) * l_t)$ time. Step 2 maps and replaces each element in the query with the corresponding element in the mapping. This takes $O(l_t)$ time since the number of elements in the query is proportional to l_t. Step 3 adds the elements of the *where* clause in the mapping to the query. The time complexity is proportional to the number of elements in the *where* clause, i.e., $O(l_s)$. Step 4 finds the paths of all the element variables in the query. Since we have $(n_s - l_s)$ non-leaf nodes in the source schema, this step requires $O((n_s - l_s) * h_s)$, where h_s is the depth of the source schema. Thus, the total time complexity of *Basic_Rewrite* is $\mathbf{O}((n_t - l_t) * l_t + l_t + l_s + (n_s - l_s) * h_s)$.

5 Experiment Evaluation

We implement the algorithms Basic_Rewrite and QueryTranslate [10] in JAVA. The experiments are run on a 1.68 GHz Pentium 4 with 1 GB RAM, running WinXP. We repeat each experiment 8 times, and record the average time.

5.1 Mapping Complexity

Depth of Target Schema. We use the *chain* scenario in [10] (see Figure 6) to evaluate the performance when the depth of the target schema varies. The *chain* scenario simulates the situation where multiple inter-linked XML schemas (*component* schemas) of a source schema are mapped into an XML target schema with a large number of nesting levels. By varying the number of *component* schemas in each source schema, we can change the depth of the target schema. We issue two queries on the target schema in the *chain* scenario:

Q_{c1}: for t_1 in T_1, t_2 in $t_1.T_2$, t_3 in $t_2.T_3$ return $t_3.B_3$
Q_{c2}: for t_1 in T_1, t_2 in $t_1.T_2$, $\ldots$, t_n in $t_{n-1}.T_n$ return $t_n.B_n$

Query Q_{c1}, which is adapted from [10], tests whether a rewriting method is affected by the depth of the target schema. We design a second query Q_{c2} to evaluate the performance as the depth of the target schema increases.

Figure 8 shows that changing the depth of the target schema does not affect the time taken by algorithm Basic_Rewrite to rewrite Q_{c1} since the rewriting is carried out directly based on the mapping between the source and target schema. In contrast, the time to rewrite Q_{c2} grows linearly as the depth of the target schema grows. Increasing the depth of the target schema increases the number of elements in the *in* clause of Q_{c2}, while increasing the number of component schemas increases the number of elements in *where* clause in the mapping, which affects the last step in the Basic_Rewrite algorithm.

Figure 9 shows that Basic_Rewrite clearly outperforms QueryTranslate. QueryTranslate rewrites queries based on rewriting rules which requires element

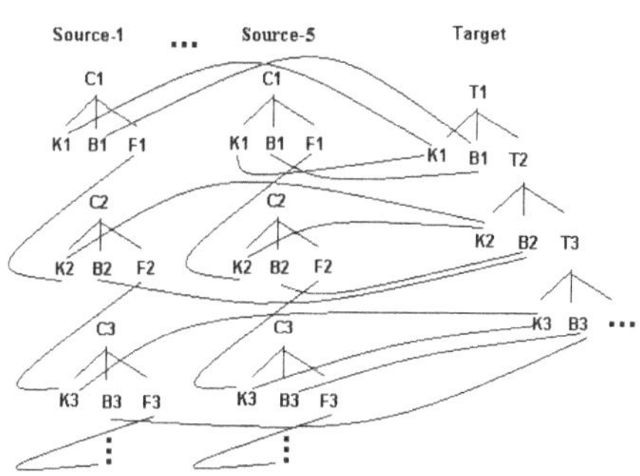

Fig. 6. Chain Scenario

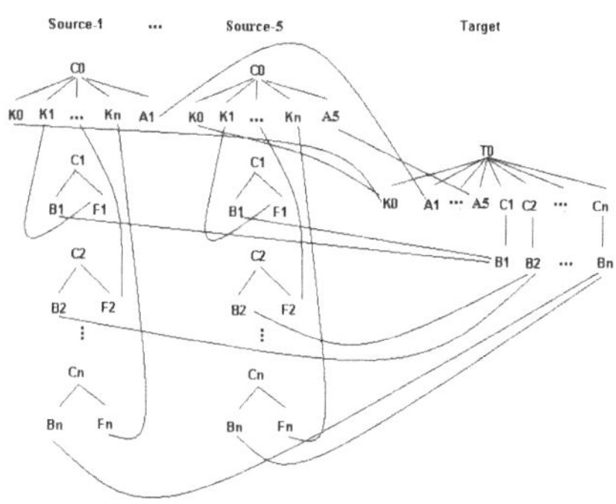

Fig. 7. Authority Scenario

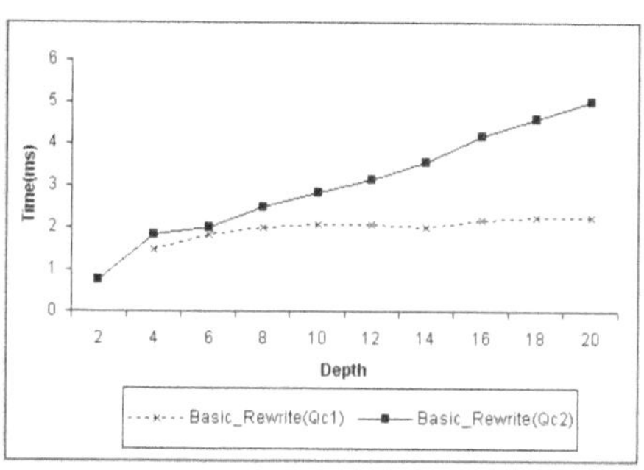

Fig. 8. Cost of Basic_Rewrite (NoSources = 5)

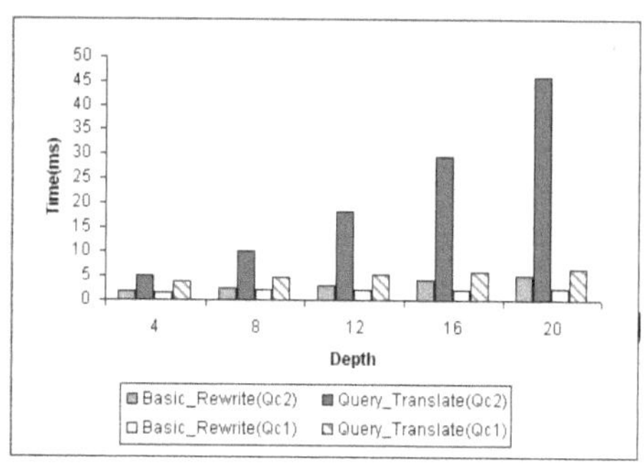

Fig. 9. Cost of Approaches as Depth of Target Schema Increases (NoSources = 5)

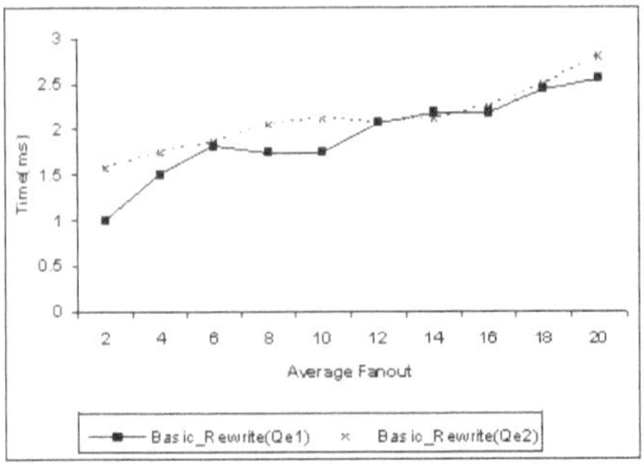

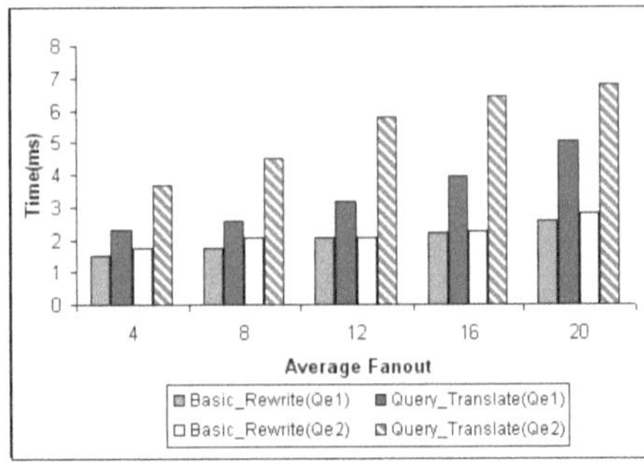

Fig. 10. Cost of Basic_Rewrite (NoSources = 5)

Fig. 11. Cost of Approaches as Fanout of Target Schema Increases (NoSources = 5)

variables in the query to be iteratively substituted by variables in the rewriting rules. Thus, renaming and resolution of the variables are needed, with redundant substitutions.

Fanout of Target Schema. We use the *authority* scenario in [10] (see Figure 7) to investigate how the two approaches are affected by the average fanout of the target schema. The average fanout of the target schema is varied by the number of *component* schemas in each source schema. We use the two target queries from [10].

Q_{e1}: <u>for</u> t_0 <u>in</u> T_0 <u>return</u> $t_0.A_1, \ldots, t_0.A_5$
Q_{e2}: <u>for</u> t_0 <u>in</u> T_0, c_1 <u>in</u> $t_0.C_1$, c_n <u>in</u> $t_0.C_n$ <u>return</u> $c_1.B_1$, $c_n.B_n$

Figure 10 shows the time taken by Basic_Rewrite increases linearly as the average fanout of the target schema increases. This is because of the linear increase in the number of the *component* schemas of a source schema. Figure 11 shows that algorithm Basic_Rewrite outperforms QueryTranslate [10] for the same reasons as given in the *chain* scenario.

5.2 Query Complexity

We investigate the performance of the proposed approach as the query complexity increases. We use a nested query which contains a single variable in the *for* and *return* clauses in each subquery. The query complexity is increased by increasing the number of levels (subqueries) in the query. Figure 12 shows that Basic_Rewrite scales well as the number of subqueries increases.

5.3 Real World Scenario

Finally, we demonstrate how the proposed approach handles a wide range of queries in a real world scenario efficiently. We use the real world *module* schema in *http://www.comp.nus.edu.sg/ lil/module/* as the target schema, and design 6 source schemas with varying depth (5 to 11) and average fanout (4 to 10). We issue the following queries on the target schema, and record the time taken by the algorithms Basic_Rewrite and QueryTranslate:

Q1. retrieve details of each module: id, level, credits, date
Q2. retrieve module id, lectures, tutorials, and total times
Q3. retrieve essential readings of each module
Q4. retrieve the elements *book1* and *book2* in each module
Q5. retrieve readings of each module
Q6. retrieve details of each lecturer

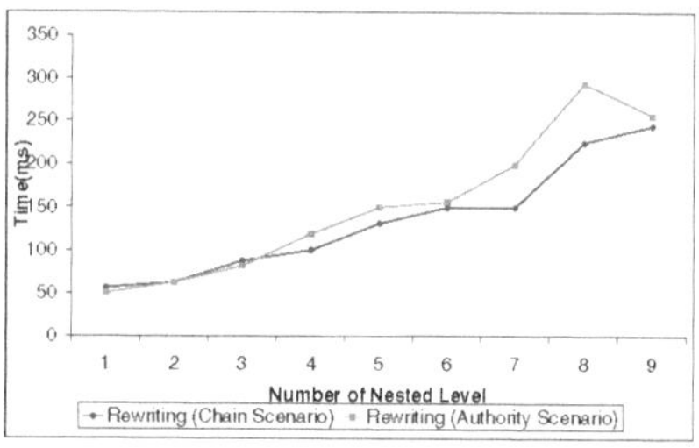

Fig. 12. Cost to Rewrite Nested Queries

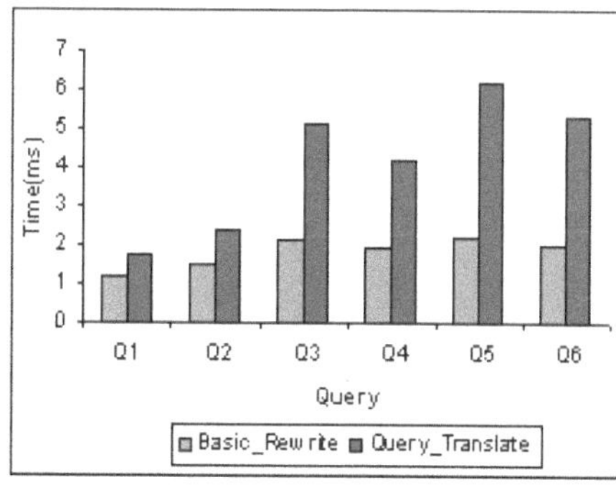

Fig. 13. Cost of Approaches in Real World Scenario (NoSources = 5)

Figure 13 clearly indicate that Basic_Rewrite outperforms QueryTranslate. Rewriting queries directly from the mappings is definitely more optimal compared to using pre-generated rewriting rules.

6 Conclusion

Motivated by the drawbacks of rewriting queries using pre-generated rules, we develop a method to rewrite queries directly based on the mappings between the target and source schemas. From the theoretical analysis and experimental results, we conclude that rewriting queries directly from the mappings between the target and source schemas is both efficient and scalable with respect to mapping and query complexities.

References

1. D. Calvanese, G. Giacomo, and M. Lenzerini. Rewriting of regular expressions and regular path queries. *Computer and System Sciences*, 64, 2002.
2. S. Chaudhuri. An overview of query optimization in relational systems. *ACM SIGMOD*, 1998.
3. D. Florescu, L. Raschid, and P. Valduriez. Using heterogeneous equivalences for query rewriting in multidatabase systems. *COOPIS*, 1995.
4. I. Manolescu, D. Florescu, and D. Kossmann. Answering xml queries over heterogeneous data sources. *VLDB*, 2001.

5. R. McCann, B. AlShebli, Q. Le, H. Nguyen, L. Vu, and A. Doan. Mapping maintenance for data integration systems. *VLDB*, 2005.
6. Y. Papakonstantinou and V. Vassalos. Query rewriting for semistructured data. *ACM SIGMOD*, 1999.
7. H. Pirahesh, J.M. Hellerstein, and W. Hasan. Extensible/rule based query rewrite optimization in starburst. *ACM SIGMOD*, 1992.
8. R. Pottinger and A. Levy. A scalable algorithm for answering queries using views. *VLDB*, 2000.
9. Y. Velegrakis, R.J. Miller, and L. Popa. Mapping adaptation under evolving schemas. *VLDB*, 2003.
10. C. Yu and L. Popa. Constraint-based xml query rewriting. *ACM SIGMOD*, 2004.
11. C. Yu and L. Popa. Semantic adaptation of schema mappings when schemas evolve. *VLDB*, 2005.

A Tale of Two Approaches: Query Performance Study of XML Storage Strategies in Relational Databases

Sandeep Prakash and Sourav S. Bhowmick

School of Computer Engineering,
Nanyang Technological University, Singapore
assourav@ntu.edu.sg

Abstract. Several recent papers have investigated a relational approach to store XML data and there is a growing evidence that *schema-conscious* approaches are a better option than *schema-oblivious* techniques as far as query performance is concerned. This paper studies three strategies for storing XML document including one representing schema-conscious approach (SHARED-INLINING) and two representing schema-oblivious approach (XParent and SUCXENT++). We implement and evaluate each approach using benchmark *non-recursive* XQueries. Our analysis shows an interesting fact that schema-conscious approaches are not always a better option than schema-oblivious approaches! In fact, it is possible for a schema-oblivious approach (SUCXENT++) to be faster than a schema-conscious approach (SHARED-INLINING) for 55% of the benchmark queries (the highest observed factor being 87.8 times). SUCXENT++ also outperforms XParent by up to 1700 times.

1 Introduction

Recently, there has been a substantial research effort in storing and processing XML data using relational backends. This approach either shred the XML documents into relational tables using some sort of encoding scheme [1,5,7,8,12,15,18,19] or use a BLOB column to store the XML document [6,20,21]. BLOB-based approaches use stored procedures to invoke an external XPath/XQuery processor. The main advantages of this approach are fast retrieval of full XML document and ability of storing any XML document irrespective of the availability of the schema. However, in this paper, we focus on shredding-based approaches as in the BLOB-based approaches, usually the entire XML document must be brought into memory before processing, severely limiting the size of the data and optimization possibilities.

The shredding-based approaches can be classified into two major categories: the *schema-oblivious* and the *schema-conscious* approaches. In brief, the *schema-oblivious* method consists of a fixed schema which is used to store XML documents. This approach does not require existence of an XML schema/DTD. Some examples of schema-oblivious approaches are Edge approach [7], XRel [18], XParent [8], SUCXENT++[12]. The *schema-conscious* method, on the other hand,

S. Bressan, J. Küng, and R. Wagner (Eds.): DEXA 2006, LNCS 4080, pp. 149–160, 2006.

derives a relational schema based on the DTD/XML schema of the XML documents. Examples of such approaches are SHARED-INLINING [15] and LegoDB [1]. Once XML data is stored using either schema-conscious or schema-oblivious approach, an XQuery/XPath is translated into SQL for evaluation. A comprehensive review of methods for XML-to-SQL query translation and their limitations is beyond the scope of this paper and can be found in [9].

In this paper, we study the performance of schema-conscious and schema-oblivious approaches and compare these alternatives. In particular, we compare the performance of one schema-conscious approach (SHARED-INLINING [15]) with two representative schema-oblivious approaches (XParent[8] and SUCXENT++[12]). At this point, one would question the justification of this work as a growing body of research suggests that schema-conscious approaches perform better than schema-oblivious approaches. After all, it has been demonstrated in [16] that schema-conscious approaches generally perform substantially better in terms of query processing and storage size. However, we believe that the superiority of schema-conscious approaches (such as SHARED-INLINING) as demonstrated in [16] may not hold anymore! This is primarily due to the following reasons.

The Edge approach[7] was used in [16] as the representative schema-oblivious approach for comparison. Although the Edge approach is a pioneering relational approach, we argue that it is not a good representation of the schema-oblivious approach as far as query processing is concerned. In fact, XParent [8] and XRel [18] have been shown to outperform the Edge approach by up to 20 times, with XParent outperforming XRel [8,11]. This does not necessarily mean that XParent outperforms schema-conscious approaches. However, it does raise the question whether there exists a schema-oblivious approach in the literature that can outperform XParent significantly and consequently outperform a schema-conscious approach? In [12], we provided answer to this question by presenting a novel schema-oblivious approach called SUCXENT++ (**S**chema **U**n**c**onscious **X**ML **En**abled Sys**t**em) that outperforms XParent by up to 15 times and a schema-conscious approach (Shared-Inlining) by up to 8 times for certain types of *recursive XML queries*. A recursive XML query is an XML query which contains the descendant axis (//) [10].

Although our effort in [12] asserts that it is indeed possible for a schema-oblivious approach to outperform the schema-conscious approach, it was demonstrated only for recursive XML queries. Naturally, we would like to know whether this result holds for *non-recursive* XML queries. Note that a non-recursive XML query does not contain any descendant axis. Such queries are prevalent in GUI-based XML query formulation framework in the presence of DTDs/XML schemas. *In other words, is it possible for* SUCXENT++ *to outperform XParent and* SHARED-INLINING *for non-recursive XML queries as well?* In this paper, we provide the answer to this question.

2 Related Work

One of the earliest work on performance evaluation of XML storage strategies was carried out by Tian *et al.* [16]. In this paper five strategies for storing XML documents were studied including one that stores documents in the file system, three that uses a relational database system (Edge and Attribute approaches [7], SHARED-INLINING [15]), and one that uses an object manager. Recently, Lu *et al.* [11] reported results on benchmarking six relational approaches on two commercial RDBMS and two native XML database systems using the XMark[14] and XMach[2] benchmarks. Both these efforts showed that schema-conscious approaches perform better than schema-oblivious approaches. Our study differs from the above efforts in the following ways. First, we consider a relatively more efficient schema-oblivious storage strategy (SUCXENT++) compared to the approaches used in [16,11] for our study. Second, we evaluate the performance of our representative systems on much larger data sets (1GB) having richer variety (data and text-centric single and multiple documents). Note that the maximum size of the data set was 140 MB and 150MB in [16] and [11], respectively. This gives us a better insight on the scalability of the representative approaches. Third, we experimented with wider and richer variety of XML queries. Finally, contrary to the insight gained by Tian *et al.* and Lu *et al.*, we show that it is indeed possible for a schema-oblivious approach to outperform a schema-conscious approach for certain types of non-recursive XML queries.

XMach-1 [2] is a multi-user benchmark that is based on a Web application and considers text documents and catalog data. The goal of the benchmark is to test how many queries per second a database can process at what cost. Additional measures include response times, bulk load times and database or index sizes. XMark [14] is a single-user benchmark. The database model is based on the Internet auction site and therefore, its database contains one large XML document with text and non-text data. XOO7 [3] was derived from OO7 [4], which was designed to test the efficiency of object-oriented DBMS. Besides mapping the original queries of OO7 into XML, XOO7 adds some specific XML queries. Workloads of the above benchmarks, cover different functionalities, but leave out a number of XQuery features [17]. XBench [17] was recently proposed to cover all of XQuery functionalities as captured by XML Query Use Cases. As our work is based on XBench data set and queries, we also cover all these functionalities. In summary, all of these are application benchmarks and measure the overall performance of a DBMS. That is, they compare the performance of different RDBMSs (e.g., IBM DB2, SQL Server in XBench) and native XML DBMS (e.g., X-Hive) for processing XML data. On the contrary, we focus on evaluating performance of schema-oblivious and schema-conscious approaches on a *specific* commercial RDBMS.

3 Background

In this section, we present the framework for our performance study. We begin by identifying the representative schema-oblivious and schema-conscious systems chosen for our performance study and justify their inclusion. Then, we present the experimental setup and data sets used for our study.

3.1 Representative Systems

We chose XParent[8], SUCXENT++[13], and SHARED-INLINING [15] as representative shredding-based approaches for performance study. The reasons are as follows.

First, we intend to ensure that the implementation of our selected storage scheme does not require modification of the relational engine. This is primarily because such approach enhances portability and ease of implementation of the storage approach on top of an off-the-shelf commercial RDBMS. Consequently, we did not choose the dynamic intervals approach [5] and the approach in [19] as these approaches enhance the relational engine with XML-specific primitives for efficient execution. Note that in the absence of such XML-specific primitives, the query processing cost can be expensive in these approaches. For instance, without the special relational operators defined in [5], the query performance is likely to be inferior even for simple path expressions [9].

Second, the selected approach must have good query performance. Jiang *et al.* [8] showed that XParent outperforms Edge [7] (up to 20 times) and XRel [18] approaches significantly. In [12], we have shown that SUCXENT++ outperforms XParent (up to 15 times) and SHARED-INLINING [15] (up to 8 times) for certain types of recursive XML queries. Moreover, XParent takes 2.5 times more storage space compared to the SUCXENT++ approach. Hence, XParent and SUCXENT++ are chosen as representatives of the schema-oblivious approach.

Finally, we chose SHARED-INLINING over LegoDB [1] as the representative of schema-conscious approaches for the following reasons. First, SHARED-INLINING is widely used in the literature as a representative of schema-conscious approaches. Second, unlike SHARED-INLINING , LegoDB is application and query workload-dependent. Third, despite our best efforts (including contacting the authors), we could not get the source code of LegoDB.

3.2 Experimental Setup

Prototypes for SUCXENT++, XParent and SHARED-INLINING were developed using Java JDK 1.5 and a commercial RDBMS[1]. The experiments were conducted on a P4 1.4GHz machine with 256MB of RAM and a 40GB (7200rpm) IDE hard disk. The operating system was Windows 2000 Professional.

The XBench [17] data set was used for comparison of storage size, insertion and extraction times, as it provides a comprehensive range of XML document types. We studied both data-centric and text-centric applications consisting of single as well as multiple XML documents. We also test for scalability (small (10MB), normal (100 MB) and large (1 GB) dataset) of the schema-conscious and schema-oblivious approaches. Figures 1(a) and 1(b) summarize the characteristics of the data sets used. In our experiments, we create separate database instances for all the scenarios. For example, we create three database instances for TC/SD, called TC/SD-small, TC/SD-normal, and TC/SD-large. A total of 22 queries as described in [17] were tested on this data set. The list of queries

[1] Our licensing agreement disallows us from naming the product.

	SD (Single Document)	MD (Multiple Document)
TC (Text-centric)	Online dictionaries	Digital libraries, news corpus
DC (Data-centric)	E-commerce catalogs	Transactional data

(a) Data set

Data set	No of Nodes		
	10MB	100MB	1GB
DC/MD	219,382	2,183,331	23,821,115
DC/SD	238,260	2,394,886	24,810,315
TC/MD	229,258	2,335,180	23,704,294
TC/SD	279,004	2,765,209	28,419,013

(b) Data set of XBench

Fig. 1. Data set of XBench

#	Query	Characteristics
1	for $order in input()/order[@id="1"] return $order/customer_id	- DCMD - Exact match
2	for $a in input()/order[@id="2"] return $a/order_lines/order_line[1]	- DCMD - Exact match, ordered access
3	for $a in input()/order[@id="4"] return $a//item_id	- DCMD - Exact match - One '//' axis
4	for $a in input()/order where $a/total gt 11000.0 order by $a/ship_type return <Output> {$a/@id}{$a/order_date}{$a/ship_type} </Output>	- DCMD - Sort - Return multiple elements
5	for $a in input()/order[@id="6"] return $a	- DCMD - Exact match - Document reconstruction
6	for $order in input()/order, $cust in input()/customers/customer where $order/customer_id = $cust/@id and $order/@id = "7" return <Output>{$order/@id}{$order/order_status}{$cust/first_name}{$cust/last_name}{$cust/phone_number}</Output>	- DCMD - Join - Multiple return elements
7	for $item in input()/catalog/item[@id="I1"] return $item	- DCSD - Exact match
8	for $item in input()/catalog/:item where every $add in $item/authors/author/contact_information/mailing_address satisfies $add/name_of_country = "Canada" return $item	- DCSD - Quantification
9	for $a in input()/catalog/item[@id="I6"] return <Output> {$a/authors/author[1]/contact_information/mailing_address} </Output>	- DCSD - Document construction
10	for $a in input()/catalog/:item where $a/date_of_release gt "1990-01-01" and $a/date_of_release lt "1991-01-01" and empty($a/publisher/contact_information/FAX_number) return <Output> {$a/publisher/name} </Output>	- DCSD - Data type casting - Irregular data

Fig. 2. XBench queries

and their characteristics is shown in Figures 2 and 3. *Observe that we focus on non-recursive XML queries.*

The queries were executed in the *reconstruct* mode where not only the internal nodes are selected, but also all descendants of that node. Several steps were taken to ensure the consistency of the test results. Prior to our experiments, we ensure that statistics had been collected, allowing well-informed plan selection. Each test query was executed 6 times while the performance results of the first run discarded. A 95% confidence interval was computed. In our experiments, the estimated error was small ($< 10\%$). The bufferpool of the DBMS was cleared before each run to ensure times reported are from cold runs. Also, appropriate indexes were constructed for all the three approaches through a careful analysis on the benchmark queries. Note that the RDBMS we have used can only create an index for *varchar*, which is less than 255. Hence, in schema-oblivious approaches, if a single text in the "value" attribute exceeds the limit, which is highly possible for text-centric XML documents, then we cannot create an index on this attribute to facilitate XML query processing. Similar to [11], we use a two-table approach to handle short/long data values separately.

#	Query	Characteristics
11	for $size in input()/catalog/:item/ attributes/size_of_book where $size/length*$size/width*$size/ height > 500000 return <Output> {$size/../../title} </Output>	- DCSD - Data type casting
12	for $prolog in input()/article/prolog where $prolog/authors/author/name="Ben Yang" return $prolog/title	- TCMD - Exact match
13	for $a in input()/article[@id="8"]/body/ section[@heading="introduction"] return <HeadingOfSection> {$a/@heading} </HeadingOfSection>	- TCMD - Two conditions
14	for $a in input()/article where some $b in $a/body/abstract/p satisfies (contains($b, "the") and contains($b, "hockey")) return $a/prolog/title	- TCMD -Quantification
15	for $a in input()/article[@id="5"] return <Output> {$a/prolog/title} {$a/prolog/authors/author/name} {$a/prolog/dateline/date} {$a/body/abstract} </Output>	- TCMD - Multiple return paths
16	for $a in input()/article/prolog/ authors/author where empty($a/contact/text()) return <NoContact> {$a/name} </NoContact>	- TCMD - Irregular data
17	for $a in input()/article where contains ($a//p, "the hockey") return <Output> {$a/prolog/title} {$a/body/abstract} </Output>	- TCMD - Text search - One '//' axis
18	for $ent in input()/dictionary/e where $ent/hwg/hw="the" return $ent	- TCSD - Exact match - Reconstruction
19	for $ent in input()/dictionary/e where $ent/*/hw = "and" return $ent/ss/s/qp/*/qt	- TCSD - Path expressions
20	for $a in input()/dictionary/e [hwg/hw="the"]/ss/s/qp/q order by $a/qd return <Output> {$a/a}{$a/qd} </Output>	- TCSD - Sorting
21	for $a in input()/dictionary/e where contains ($a, "hockey") Return $a/hwg/hw	- TCSD - Text search
22	for $ent in input()/dictionary/e where $ent/ss/s/qp/q/qd="1900" return $ent/hwg/hw	- TCSD - Exact match - Deep path

Fig. 3. XBench queries (contd.)

4 Data-Centric Query Processing

In this section we study the performance of the representative approaches (SHARED-INLINING , SUCXENT++, and XParent) for XML queries on data-centric XML documents. The reader may refer to [15], [12,13], and [8] for algorithmic details related to XML query translation and evaluation. Note that we do not discuss storage size, document insertion and extraction performance here as we have already presented this in [13]. In general, SUCXENT++ is 5.7 - 47 times faster than XParent and marginally better than SHARED-INLINING as far as insertion time is concerned. SUCXENT++ is also the most efficient among the three approaches as far as document extraction is concerned. On the other hand, SHARED-INLINING requires the least amount of storage. XParent takes 2.5 times more storage space compared to SUCXENT++.

We use the queries Q1 to Q11 in Figures 2 and 3 for our performance study. The results are shown in Figure 4. The maximum time we allowed a query to run for all experiments was 60 minutes; if the execution did not finish in that period, we do not show it in the figures. Note that we use the optimized version of SUCXENT++ for our performance study. In non-optimized SUCXENT++, the join between the **Path** and **PathValue** tables took a significant portion of the query processing time. The optimized version of SUCXENT++ reduces this overhead by altering the translated SQL queries. The join expression `v1.PathId = p1.Id and p1.PathExp =` ***path*** in a translated SQL query is replaced with `v1.PathId =` ***n*** where ***n*** is the `PathId` value corresponding to ***path*** in the table `Path`. Similarly, `v1.PathId = p1.Id and p1.PathExp LIKE` ***path%*** is replaced with `v1.PathId >= n and v1.PathId <= m`. For the second case `PathId`s are

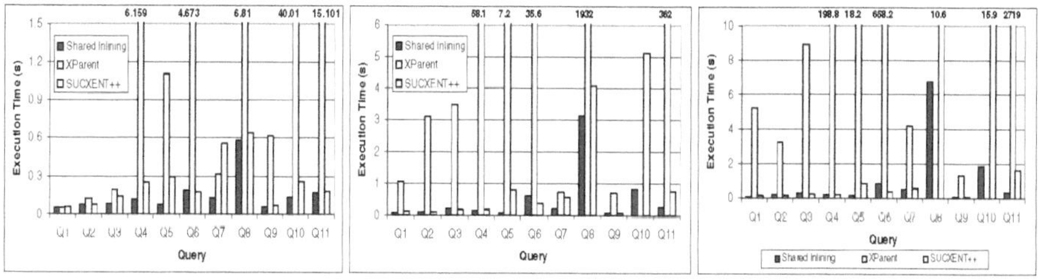

(a) 10 MB (b) 100 MB (c) 1 GB

Fig. 4. Query performance (data-centric)

assigned in lexicographic order and (n, m) correspond to the first and last occurrences of expressions that have the prefix *path*. Furthermore, the optimized version also incorporates strategies to optimize recursive path expressions. The reader may refer to [12,13] for further details. We now elaborate on the performance results.

Query Q1 [Exact match (DCMD)]: For all three data sizes SHARED-INLINING performs the best. This can be explained based on the relational schema generated for SHARED-INLINING and the SQL query corresponding to query Q1. The SHARED-INLINING version involves a single predicate on a single table. All other approaches involve several joins and predicates. Observe that XParent performs marginally better than SUCXENT++ for the 10MB data set. This is due to two reasons. First, SUCXENT++ involves θ-joins whereas XParent use equi-joins. Second, the data set has several small documents instead of one large document. The translations of both schema-oblivious approaches involve a join of the *DocId* attribute to filter nodes in the same document. This generates much smaller join sizes and the results are particularly obvious for equi-join based queries. However, for the 100MB and 1GB data sets SUCXENT++ performs better than XParent by up to 41.7 times. This is due to the following reasons. First, XParent incurs a greater number of joins on a much larger data set. Second, the optimization strategies in SUCXENT++ reduce the number of path joins significantly. This reduces the advantage of equi-joins to a great extent as the data size increases.

Queries Q2, Q3 [Exact match and ordered access (DCMD)]: SUCXENT++ outperforms both SHARED-INLINING and XParent for these queries as data size increases (see Figure 6 also). This is because for SHARED-INLINING as data size increases the cost of join operation to extract *order_line* and *item_id* (especially with descendant axis) from other tables increases. SUCXENT++ performs better than XParent due to its more optimal storage strategy (as discussed above).

Query Q4 [Sort and return multiple elements (DCMD)]: SHARED-INLINING performs better than the other two approaches. The main observation here is that SUCXENT++ significantly outperforms XParent (up to 970 times) with the increase in data size. This is because the number of joins in the translated SQL statement increases with the number of predicates or return clause elements in the XQuery query. Observe that this query has quite a few return elements (in addition to a sort operation). As a result, XParent requires a greater number of joins (and on larger data) than SUCXENT++.

Query Q5 [Document reconstruction (DCMD)]: SHARED-INLINING performs better as evaluation of `@id=6` is faster due to smaller (fragmented) tables. But the cost of join becomes higher with increasing data size and therefore the gap between SHARED-INLINING and SUCXENT++ decreases.

Query Q6 [Join and multiple return elements (DCMD)]: SUCXENT++ now performs better than both SHARED-INLINING and XParent (up to 1629 times better than XParent). This can be attributed to the fact that even SHARED-INLINING has to execute more joins for this query as it involves an XQuery join. XParent is outperformed significantly by other two approaches due to larger number of joins.

Query Q7 [Exact match (DCSD)]: SHARED-INLINING performs significantly better for smaller data size than the other two approaches. However, the gap between SUCXENT++ and SHARED-INLINING decreases with the increase in data size (reasons are similar to the above discussion). Observe that XParent outperforms SUCXENT++ for the small data set. However, SUCXENT++ performs better than XParent for the 100 MB and 1GB data sets. This is because, unlike the DCMD version of this query, the join on the *DocId* attribute no longer generates small join sizes and the advantages of equi-joins are negated by the large data size in XParent.

Query Q8 [Quantification (DCSD)]: This query is quite complex as it involves quantification in the form of the `every` clause. The SHARED-INLINING approach performs the best even though it has to execute quite a few joins as well. This is because the execution of the quantification clause is much better in the SHARED-INLINING approach. SUCXENT++ performs significantly better than XParent. In fact, XParent failed to return results in 60 minutes for the 1GB data set and are, therefore, not included in the figures.

Query Q9 [Document Construction (DCSD)]: SHARED-INLINING outperforms SUCXENT++ for 10MB and 100MB data sets. With its inherent greater data fragmentation one would expect SHARED-INLINING to perform the worst. However, the query involves a predicate and the construction is only for a small part of the document - with the entire part available in a single table. As a result SHARED-INLINING performs better. Particularly, for smaller data size the join cost to extract child elements is not significant enough for SHARED-INLINING . Cost of evaluating `@Id=I6` is lower for SHARED-INLINING due to smaller tables. However, as the data size increases the cost of the join increases. As a result, the overall performance difference is not as significant with the increase in data size. In fact, for 1GB data set SUCXENT++ marginally outperforms SHARED-INLINING . Note that the mapping strategies in [15] do not allow mapped documents to be faithfully reconstructed [9]. Hence, the resulting mapping may be lossy.

Query Q10 [Irregular Data (DCSD)]: For SHARED-INLINING , all the data required for this query could be found in just one table. Therefore, SHARED-INLINING performs the best. Also, the empty clause is quite easily implemented by using `= null` in the corresponding SQL statement. The translation for schema-oblivious approaches is quite complicated as there is no notion of `"null"` in these two approaches. Both approaches implement this query using the SQL `not in` clause. As a result the performance is much worse than that of SHARED-INLINING . SUCXENT++ as expected outperforms XParent. In fact, XParent failed to complete execution in 60 minutes for the 100 MB and 1 GB data sets.

Query Q11 [Datatype Casting (DCSD)]: SHARED-INLINING can implement datatype casting in a much cleaner fashion than schema-oblivious approaches. Schema-oblivious approaches (in this case at least) store all data as strings in a single column. SHARED-INLINING uses several different columns and each can be assigned a specific datatype. As a result, the query performance in SHARED-INLINING is much better. In the schema-oblivious approach, data has to be first filtered based on the path expression and only then can it be typecast. Note that this query has five path expressions. As a result the number of joins in XParent is significantly higher than in SUCXENT++. Therefore, SUCXENT++ significantly outperforms XParent by up to 1700 times.

5 Text-Centric Query Processing

Text search plays a very important role in XML document systems. In this section we study the performance of the representative approaches for XML queries on text-centric XML documents. We use the queries Q12 to Q22 in Figure 3 for our performance study. The results are shown in Figure 5. Note that for fair comparison we use the default text processing support of the RDBMS and do not build any additional full text indexes on the underlying RDBMS.

Query Q12 [Exact match (TCMD)]: The performance characteristics for this query are quite similar to those of Q1 except that the difference between

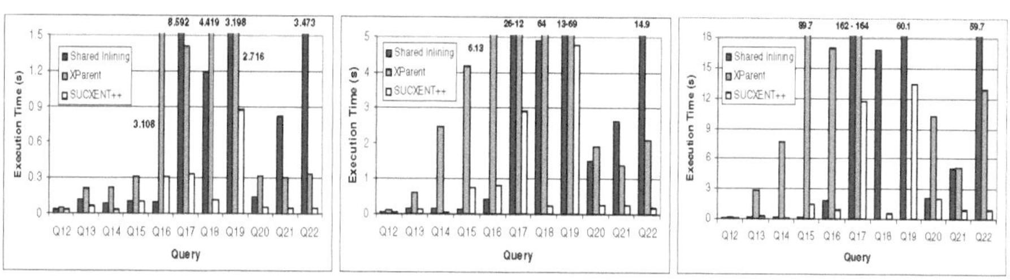

(a) 10 MB (b) 100 MB (c) 1 GB

Fig. 5. Query performance (text-centric)

SHARED-INLINING and the schema-oblivious approaches is not a significant as in the data-centric case (Q1 to Q3). This is because the query in the SHARED-INLINING approach requires two tables (compared to one in Q1).

Queries [Q13 to Q15 (TCMD)]: For Q13, the evaluation of `@heading="introduction"` is faster for SHARED-INLINING . The join operation to extract child elements is not very expensive for this query. For larger data sizes SHARED-INLINING outperforms SUCXENT++ mainly due to the smaller table that needs to be queried for evaluating `@heading="introduction"`. For SUCXENT++ the **PathValue** table becomes quite large for larger data sets and hence it takes longer time. Q14 has the `contains` clause which requires all child elements to be queried. This involves a large number of joins for SHARED-INLINING . Consequently, SUCXENT++ performs better. SHARED-INLINING performs better for Q15 for the same reasons as discussed for Q13.

Query Q16 [Irregular Data (TCMD):] Unlike Q10, this query has only two path expressions. The join cost for SHARED-INLINING increases significantly with the increase in data size (especially in the absence of an exact predicate) due to several steps in the path expressions. As a result, even though both the schema-oblivious approaches perform worse than SHARED-INLINING for smaller data size, SUCXENT++ performs better for 1GB data set.

Query Q17 [Text search (TCMD)]: SHARED-INLINING performs significantly worse than the schema-oblivious approaches. This is due to the recursive nature of the query. In SHARED-INLINING , the resolution of the path expression `/article//p` requires the use of the UNION operator on three sub-queries. In addition, one of the sub-queries requires a join across several tables. Due to reasons discussed earlier, SUCXENT++ performs better than XParent.

Query Q18 [Exact match/Reconstruction (TCSD)]: SUCXENT++ again performs the best. Unlike in Q9, SHARED-INLINING has to join four tables to reconstruct the element `e`.

Queries Q19, Q20 [Path expressions (TCSD)]: SUCXENT++ performs better than all the other approaches. XParent performs the worse due to the multiple path expressions in the query. SHARED-INLINING performs slightly worse due to multiple joins in the resulting SQL query - although the performance is still comparable to SUCXENT++. Specifically, SHARED-INLINING involves both join and the union operators due to the wild card path expressions `/dictionary/e/*/hw` and `/dictionary/e/ss/s/qp/*/qt`.

Query Q21 [Text search (TCSD)]: SUCXENT++ performs the best for this query again. The query for the SHARED-INLINING approach has several joins in small subqueries that are finally combined with a UNION clause. This is due to the `contains` clause in the XQuery query. In addition, SHARED-INLINING must execute multiple joins to reconstruct the `hw` element. However, with increasing size querying for `"hockey"` in the **PathValue** table becomes more and more

Query	Shared-Inlining / SUCXENT++			XParent / SUCXENT++		
	10MB	100MB	1GB	10MB	100MB	1GB
Q1	0.89	0.57	0.70	0.98	8.75	41.71
Q2	1.00	0.96	1.59	1.60	27.03	24.60
Q3	0.61	1.04	1.29	1.37	18.21	39.16
Q4	0.47	0.80	0.96	24.58	320.96	970.07
Q5	0.26	0.10	0.15	3.76	8.87	21.78
Q6	1.06	1.55	2.16	26.55	88.91	1629.09
Q7	0.23	0.33	0.92	0.57	1.26	7.06
Q8	0.91	0.77	0.64	10.62	472.97	DNF
Q9	0.76	0.93	1.07	8.29	9.48	16.62
Q10	0.52	0.16	0.12	153.33	DNF	DNF
Q11	0.95	0.33	0.22	84.84	475.41	1699.74

Query	Shared-Inlining / SUCXENT++			XParent / SUCXENT++		
	10MB	100MB	1GB	10MB	100MB	1GB
Q12	1.07	0.67	0.92	1.67	1.81	3.24
Q13	1.96	1.09	0.91	3.62	4.27	11.45
Q14	2.55	2.64	3.85	6.67	45.76	134.26
Q15	1.04	0.17	0.10	3.10	5.56	62.41
Q16	0.30	0.51	1.89	10.02	7.63	18.05
Q17	26.12	9.14	13.90	4.30	4.23	14.06
Q18	10.56	20.63	33.01	39.11	270.90	DNF
Q19	3.67	2.75	4.48	3.12	14.55	DNF
Q20	2.59	5.73	1.04	5.93	7.34	5.07
Q21	16.38	9.89	5.49	6.00	5.21	5.63
Q22	69.46	87.84	68.66	6.70	12.38	14.81

Fig. 6. Performance summary

expensive compared to searching for it in smaller tables in SHARED-INLINING . Therefore, the gap reduces with increasing data size.

Query Q22 [Exact match (TCSD)]: This query presents a "deep" path expression resulting in several joins for the SHARED-INLINING approach. As a result SUCXENT++ significantly outperforms SHARED-INLINING by up to 88 times.

6 Summary

In this paper, we compared the performance of one schema-conscious approach (SHARED-INLINING [15]) with two representative schema-oblivious approaches (XParent[8] and SUCXENT++[12]). We show that it is indeed possible for a schema-oblivious approach to outperform a schema-conscious approach for several types of *non-recursive* XML queries. Figure 6 provides summary of the performance results for the compared approaches with respect to SUCXENT++. These figures show the ratio of time taken for a given approach to the time taken in SUCXENT++. If a query fails to execute in 60 minutes then we show it as "DNF" in the corresponding column. Observe that SHARED-INLINING outperforms XParent for all queries except Q22. However, SUCXENT++ can be several times faster than the schema-conscious approach (SHARED-INLINING) for text-centric documents; the highest observed factor being 87.8. On the other hand, SHARED-INLINING fares better for large data-centric XML documents as it outperforms SUCXENT++ for 73% of the benchmark queries (Queries Q1 - Q11).

SUCXENT++ significantly outperforms XParent for all non-recursive queries that we have experimented with. In particular, SUCXENT++ is 7-1700 times (excluding "DNF" queries in XParent) faster than XParent for queries (Q1-Q11) on large data-centric XML documents (1GB). For large text-centric documents, it is still 3-134 times faster. Note that the optimization techniques in SUCXENT++ as described in [12] can also be applied to XParent. A preliminary study of the query plans generated by the RDBMS for XParent suggests that XParent can also benefit from these optimizations. However, a considerable performance difference shall still exists between SUCXENT++ and XParent, especially for large data set, primarily due to XParent's large storage requirements and consequently greater I/O-cost.

References

1. P. Bohannon, J. Freire, P. Roy, J. Simeon. From XML Schema to Relations: A Cost-based Approach to XML Storage. *In IEEE ICDE*, 2002.
2. T. Böhme, E. Rahm. XMach-1: A Benchmark for XML Data Management. *In German Database Conference*, 2001.
3. S. Bressan, M-L. Lee, Y. G. Li, Z. Lacroix, U. Nambiar. The XOO7 Benchmark.*In EEXTT*, 2002.
4. M. Carey, D. DeWitt, J. Naughton. The OO7 Benchmark. *In ACM SIGMOD*, 1993.
5. D. DeHaan, D. Toman, M. P. Consens, M. T. Ozsu. A Comprehensive XQuery to SQL Translation Using Dynamic Interval Coding. *In ACM SIGMOD*, 2003.
6. L. Ennser, C. Delporte, M. Oba, K. Sunil. Integrating XML and DB2 XML Extender and DB2 Text Extender. *IBM Redbooks*, 2001.
7. D. Florescu, D. Kossman. Storing and Querying XML Data using an RDBMS. *IEEE Data Engineering Bulletin.* 22(3), 1999.
8. H. Jiang, H. Lu, W. Wang and J. Xu Yu. Path Materialization Revisited: An Efficient Storage Model for XML Data. *13th Australasian Database Conference (ADC'02)* , 2002.
9. R. Krishnamurthy, R. Kaushik, J. F. Naughton. XML to SQL Query Translation Literature: The State of the Art and Open Problem.*In XSym*, 2003.
10. R. Krishnamurthy, V. T. Chakaravarthy, R. Kaushik, J. F. Naughton. Recursive XML Schemas, Recursive XML Queries, and Relational Storage: XML-to-SQL Query Translation.*In IEEE ICDE*, 2004.
11. H. Lu, H. Jiang, J. X. Xu, G. Yu et al. What Makes the Differences: Benchmarking XML Database Implementations. *In ACM Trans. on Internet Technology*, 5(1), 2005.
12. S. Prakash, S. S. Bhowmick, S. K. Madria. Efficient Recursive XML Query Processing Using Relational Databases. *In ER*, 2004.
13. S. Prakash, S. S. Bhowmick, S. K. Madria. Efficient Recursive XML Query Processing Using Relational Databases. *To appear in Data and Knowledge Engineering Journal*, Special Issue on Best Papers of ER 2004, Elsevier Science, 2006.
14. A. Schmidt, F. Waas, M. Kersten, M. J. Carey, I. Manolescu and R. Busse. XMark: A Benchmark for XML Data Management. *In VLDB*, 2002.
15. J. Shanmugasundaram, K. Tufte et al. Relational Databases for Querying XML Documents: Limitations and Opportunities. *In VLDB 1999.*
16. F. Tian, D. DeWitt, J. Chen and C. Zhang. The Design and Performance Evaluation of Alternative XML Storage Strategies. *ACM Sigmod Record, Vol. 31(1), 2002.*
17. B. Yao, M. Tamer Özsu, N. Khandelwal. XBench: Benchmark and Performance Testing of XML DBMSs. *In ICDE*, Boston, 2004.
18. M. Yoshikawa, T. Amagasa, T. Shimura, and S. Uemura. XRel: A Path-based Approach to Storage and Retrieval of XML Documents Using Relational Databases. *ACM TOIT* 1(1):110-141, 2001.
19. C. Zhang, J. Naughton, D. Dewitt, Q. Luo and G. Lohmann. On Supporting Containment Queries in Relational Database Systems. *In ACM SIGMOD*, 2001.
20. Microsoft SQL Server 2000 SDK Documentation, Microsoft 2000, `http://www.microsoft.com`.
21. Oracle XML DB. `http://www.oracle.com`.

Visual Specification and Optimization of XQuery Using VXQ

Ryan H. Choi, Raymond K. Wong, and Wei Wang

[1] National ICT Australia, Sydney, NSW 2052, Australia
[2] School of Computer Science and Engineering
The University of New South Wales, Sydney, NSW 2052, Australia
{ryanc, wong, weiw}@cse.unsw.edu.au

Abstract. As the popularity of XML increases, the need for querying collections of XML data from various systems becomes imperative. Proposed by W3C, XQuery is becoming a standard for querying such systems. However, the complexity of XQuery prevents its usage by broad audience. This paper proposes a visual XQuery specification language called VXQ to address this issue. By intuitive abstractions of XML and XQuery, the proposed system can generate XQueries for users that have little knowledge about the language. We show that our visual language is more expressive than previous proposals. Finally, we extend our proposed visual XQuery to support query rewriting and optimization for multiple XQuery systems.

1 Introduction

The extensive use of XML in today's applications requires a wide range of users to interact with and query XML documents to acquire the information they desire. However, expressing a request for the right information in a form of a query language can be a difficult task for those who do not have good XML and/or database backgrounds. XQuery is the *de facto* standard query language designed for retrieving XML data by W3C, which has recently gained attention among database communities and industry. Although the motivation behind XQuery is to better facilitate data exchange among various types of applications, especially over the Internet, the complexity of the query language has made itself not as successful as expected despite its rich expressive power. To make the language appealing to broader audiences, a user-friendly, visual design environment which generates XQuery expressions without being exposed to the complexity of the language can be very useful.

This paper describes a prototype for visual query specification called VXQ that enables users to easily generate efficient XQuery expressions. To enhance the user experience, users only need to draw graphs, diagrams and select available options without the need of remembering the complex syntax of XQuery language. The user interface of the system is heavily based on mouse movements, pop-up menus and dialog boxes, and keyboard input is limited to a minimum.

S. Bressan, J. Küng, and R. Wagner (Eds.): DEXA 2006, LNCS 4080, pp. 161–171, 2006.

In addition, users do not need to know the structure of the documents including the names of elements that they wish to query. This is because the system automatically generates the schema of XML documents involved in the query, and presents the schema with a list of relevant elements in the interface. It implicitly checks the correctness of the diagrams by limiting the options that users can select. These design choices can greatly reduce the chance of drawing queries that produce *empty* or *incorrect* results due to typing mistakes or misunderstanding of the underlying data schema.

Another distinct feature of our prototype is to automatically rewrite queries expressed by users to semantically equivalent queries which are more likely to be efficient. It is not uncommon that queries expressed by users are not always the most efficient form, in terms of their execution performance. Our system can rewrite the original user queries into semantically equivalent ones that are likely to have better runtime performance against the backend XML query processing system. Our experiments using several popular XQuery processing backends (e.g., Galax [1] and Saxon [2]) have shown that, in practice, even simple query rewriting often reduces the query execution times significantly even though many XQuery processors perform their own internal optimizations.

The goal of this paper is to make complex XML query languages, such as XQuery, easier for non-technical users without limiting the features provided by the languages. One interesting application will be an XQuery learning and designing tool that interacts with users visually. It guides the user to design a query, verifies the query, and even suggests equivalent queries expressed in a more efficient form.

The organization of this paper is as follows. Sec. 2 presents related work, and Sec. 3 overviews our prototype system. Sec. 4 demonstrates its expressive power by visually expressing some queries from the W3C XML Use Cases [3]. Sec. 5 demonstrates how a query can be optimized by automatic query rewriting to improve runtime performance. Finally, Sec. 6 concludes the paper.

2 Related Work

Visual or graphical query languages have been complementary approaches to formal query languages in database systems. In RDBMSs, QBE [4] is a typical example, which has been integrated into products like Microsoft Access. With QBE, queries are formulated by filling "examples" of the values to be queried in the templates of relations. Equivalent SQL queries can then be generated without loosing the ability to express the core queries in a user-friendly environment. It is expressive and supports advanced queries including grouping, aggregation, etc. A number of graphical languages had also been proposed for object-oriented databases, such as G [5], G+ [6], Graphlog [7].

With the wide adoption of XML and its query languages, there has been much interests in graphical query language for XML. Due to the increasing complexities in XML query languages (e.g., XQuery), graphical XML query languages play an important role in simplifying the query formulation for casual users and providing a means to verify the correctness of the query visually. Existing work can be classified into two categories—form-based approach influenced by PESTO [8], and the graph-based approach motivated by XML-GL [9]. Examples of form-based approaches include EquiX [10], QSByE [11], GXML-QL [12], XMLApe [13], BBQ [14], XQForms [15], Xing [16] and GXQL [17]. Examples of graph-based approaches include WC-Log [18], its descendant XML-GL [9] and XQBE [19].

Most of the previous approaches do not support all of the advanced constructs in XML Query Languages. In addition, the complexity of the graph layout on the screen could be rather high for moderate complex queries. In contrast, the VXQ proposed in this paper can visually express all `flwor` expressions and advanced features such as XPath predicates/axes, restructuring output, nested for loops and if-then. The complexity of large graphs is reduced by exploiting intuitive mouse movements such as drag-and-drops and automatically generated options/selections. A *unique* feature of our system is the ability to rewrite the query into an equivalent but more efficient one such that a good balance between usability and quality of the query in terms of the efficiency can be achieved. At our best knowledge, our prototype is the first implementation that addresses these issues.

3 System Overview

A snapshot of the query interface of our system is presented in Fig. 1. The interface contains two main parts, and they are separated by a vertical separator in the middle. The left side is called the *source pane* and the right is called the *query pane*. The purpose of the source pane is to represent the structures of the source XML documents and let the user explore the documents, and allow them to select part(s) of the documents to be queried and further processed. The query pane lets the user visualize the query, and its layout can be used to project the the structure of the query results. A rectangle denotes an element and an oval represents an attribute. There are other visual elements for XPath

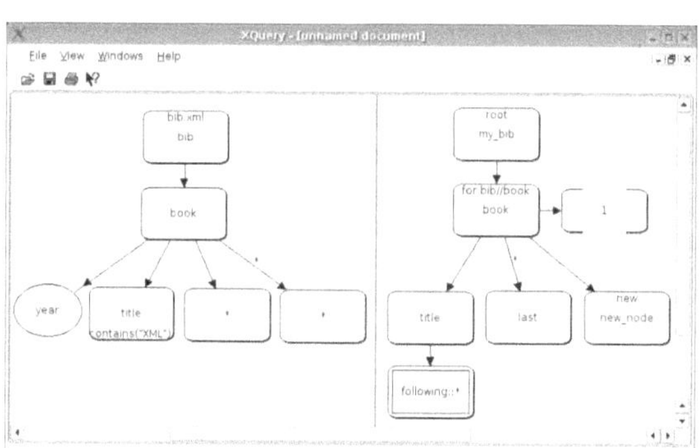

Fig. 1. The query interface of the system

predicates and axes that can be displayed on both panes. These are explained later in this section. We will call all graphical constructs of the system on either pane *nodes*.

Users can obtain the automatically generated XQuery by exploring the schema graph for the XML documents on the source pane first, and then specifying the output layout and constraints on the query pane. In the first step, users need to load an XML document that they wish to query into the source pane. To do this, they right click on the source pane and select the 'New Root Element' option using the pop-up menu. A dialog box appears and asks for a filename or url of the XML document to be loaded. After loading the specified document, a root node is displayed on the source pane. A *root node* on the source pane is a special node which conceptually represents the entire XML document as well as the root element of it. The name of the document is shown inside the node. In Fig. 1, `bib` is the name of the root element of `bib.xml`.

Users can navigate an XML document by "expanding" a node in the source pane. Right clicking on a node brings up a pop-up menu. It displays all the names of the descendant elements and attributes of the selected node. Choosing an element or an attribute creates a new node under the selected node. The name of the new node is determined by the name of the element in the XML document it represents. A special node `*`, called a *wildcard* node, is also supported. It is used to represent any elements at a particular level. For example, in Fig. 1, the `book` and the wildcard node on the source pane represent the path expression `book/*`. The parent-child relationship is represented by an arrow—it originates from a parent node and points to a child node. The arrow is drawn automatically every time a new child node is created. The arrow with `*` represents an ancestor-descendant relationship between two nodes. For example, the relationship between the `book` and `last` nodes on the query pane is `book//last`.

Expanding nodes can be repeated until the leaf nodes are reached. The source pane only allows creating new nodes by expanding parent nodes, except the creation of the root nodes as discussed above. Any node that is no longer needed during the construction of a query (e.g., users build a query by adding and deleting nodes in a trial and error fashion) can be deleted. Deleting a node simply removes itself and all of its descendant nodes.

The query pane on the right displays which parts of the source documents are to be retained and how the query results are structured. There are several ways of creating nodes on the query pane. One way is by dragging a node from the source pane and dropping it on the query pane. If a node is dropped *over* (i.e., on top of) another node, the dragged node will become a child node of the destination node on the query pane. This means all the elements represented by the dragged node will be nested inside the destination node. This is the primary method to retain the nodes of interest for output and therefore to include them in the query results. A node created in this way is later translated into either (nested) `for` or `let` clauses.

Users may add predicates that will be inserted to the `where` clause of query expressions. To do this, they right click on the node on the source pane to which they want to add predicates, and select the 'Add Predicate' option on the pop-up menu. They then type the predicates in the dialog box that appears. The predicates that the user supplied are displayed at the bottom part of the node. For example, in Fig. 1, only the `titles` that contain 'XML' are to be selected.

Users may insert XPath predicates and axes into an element to further qualify the final query results. A node that looks like a pair of "big square brackets" is called a *predicate node* and is used to represent a XPath predicate. It is typically placed next to the node which contains the predicate. A predicate node is added by right clicking on a node and selecting 'Add Predicate' option on the pop-up menu. Users then supply a predicate expression by selecting a XPath predicate from the list that appears automatically or by typing it in explicitly. The name of the predicate node is the same as the predicate which it represents. A node with double borders is called an *axis node*. It denotes an axis. Predicate and axis nodes can be combined and nested to any depth level.

4 Running Examples

This section presents two examples to illustrate the expressiveness of VXQ by visually specifying queries from the W3C XMP XQuery Use Cases [3]. Due to limited space, we present and group only a few queries from [3]. However, our implementation is expressive enough and works correctly for the use cases in [3].

4.1 Selection, Projection and Sort

Query 1. *For each book found in* ***bib.xml*** *and is published by Addison-Wesley after 1991, list the year, title, publisher, price and the last name of the authors of the book. In addition, present those books in alphabetical order by titles, publishers, prices and last name of authors. [Combined Q1, Q3 and Q7 in [3]].*

```
<bib>
{ for $a in doc("bib.xml")/bib/book
  where $a/@year > 1991 and
        $a/publisher = "Addison-Wesley"
  order by $a/author/last ascending,
           $a/title ascending,
           $a/publisher ascending,
           $a/price ascending
  return
    <book year="{$a/@year}">
       {$a/title}
       {$a/publisher}
       {$a/price}
       {$a/author/last}</book>
}
</bib>
```

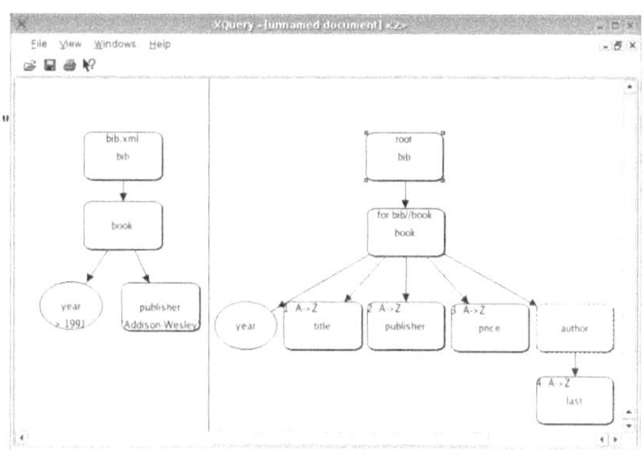

Fig. 2. Query 1

Query 1 is expressed as in Fig. 1. After loading `bib.xml`, we expand the `bib` node to display the `book`, and expand it again to display `year` and `publisher` nodes on the source pane. We then add the two predicates '> 1991' and 'Addison-Wesley' to them.

On the query pane, we create a new root node and name it as `bib`. The `book` node is drag-and-dropped over the root node, and is expanded similarly to the nodes on the source pane to create their child nodes. If any other nodes were to be renamed, we would type new names for them at this stage.

By default, a node on the query pane represents itself and all of its descendant nodes. If we did not expand the `author` node, all descendant elements such as `first` would be included in the query results. The `author` node is drawn in dashed lines to show that the `author` elements are not part of the result.

To specify a sorting order, we first invoke a sorting-order dialog box, and click on the nodes on the query pane in the order we wish to sort the query results. We can optionally specify how each element is sorted—in `ascending` (default, represented as `'A->Z'`) or `descending` (represented as `'Z->A'`) order. In this example, we simply click on the `title`, `publisher`, `price` and `last` nodes. If we wished to sort `price` in descending order, we would select `'descending'` option for `price`. The nodes on the query pane display their ordering if they are to be involved in the sorting criteria.

4.2 If-Then Statements

Query 2. *For each book that has at least one author, list the title and first two authors, and an empty "et-al" element if the book has additional authors [Q6 in [3]].*

Query 2 is expressed as in Fig. 3. This example has been modified such that it uses a XPath predicate (`[count(author)>0]`). The `book` node on the source pane is drag-and-dropped over onto the `bib` node on the query pane, and the `author` node on the source pane is drag-and-dropped over onto the `book` node which was

```
<bib>
{  for $b in doc("bib.xml")
      //book[count(author) > 0]
   return <book>
      { $b/title }
      { for $a in $b/author[position()<=2]
        return $a }
      { if (count($b/author) > 2)
        then <et-al/>
        else () }
   </book>
}
</bib>
```

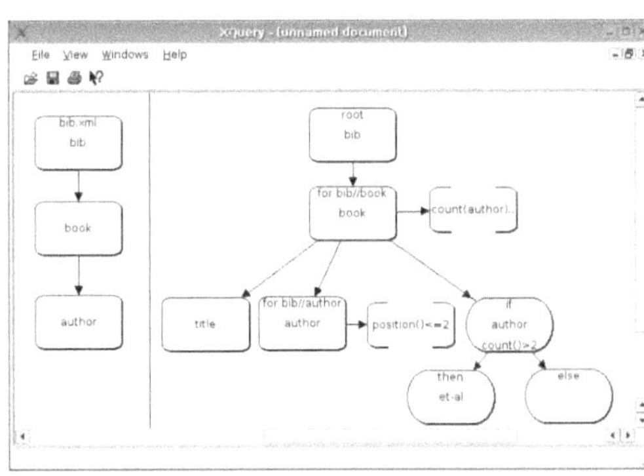

Fig. 3. Query 2

just created. Note that both the `book` and `author` elements are created by drag-and-drop processes and have the same root element. The two drag-and-dropped nodes are translated to nested `for` clauses.

We create a if-then statement as follows. We first expand the `book` node to display `author` node on the query pane. We then "convert" this `author` node to a "if" node by right clicking on it and selecting the 'if-then statement' option. The rectangular node is then changed to a rounded-edge rectangular node to indicate that the node now represents a if-then statement. We add predicates by right clicking on the `if` node similar to adding predicates to any other nodes. We now expand the `if` node twice to display `then` and `else` nodes on the query pane. We finally add "et-al" statement to the `then` node and we leave the `else` node as it is.

5 Query Rewriting

XML query optimization has become a popular topic in database research community. However, most of the popular XML query processors do not have sophisticated, in-built query optimization mechanisms. Even some XQuery processors have in-built query optimization modules, their performances on different queries are various due to their different optimization techniques. In this section, we present an example of how a graphical query expression drawn by user is rewritten to semantically equivalent but more efficient expression. VXQ can be integrated with multiple XQuery processors for visually specifying XQuery interactively. During the interaction with the underlying XQuery processors, the performance characteristics of each processor will be collected and used to determine the best set of rewriting rules for that processor. As a result, the visually specified XQuery will be rewritten to a more efficient form (i.e., optimized for a given XQuery processor) and displayed to the user for reference and further modification.

Many rewriting rules can be applied by our system before a query is executed by the backend XQuery processors. In our experiments, we used Galax [1] and open source version of Saxon [2] as the XQuery processors. All the experiments were conducted on a Pentium 4M 2GHz machine with 384Mb ram running Debian Linux without turning off their built-in query optimizations. The XML documents we used were generated by XMark [20]. All the queries were executed five times and the average times were taken.

Consider the Query in Fig. 4(a), which is expressed as in Fig. 5(a). The two binary predicates in the `where` clause can equally be expressed by using XPath predicates. The efficiency of the query is likely to be improved because by applying predicates at early stage, it may reduce the size of the elements to which each variable has to be bounded. It therefore reduces the number of iterations that have to be made resulting in increasing performance, although this method is highly implementation dependent.

We further improve the efficiency of the query by replacing '//' by a path containing only '/' whenever it is possible using the structure of the documents

```
<sellers>
{ for $i in doc("10m.xml")
     //open_auctions//open_auction
  for $j in doc("50m.xml")
     //open_auctions//open_auction
  where $i/seller/@person = $j/seller/@person and
        $i/seller/@person > "person1000" and
        $j/seller/@person < "person2000"
  return <s-happiness> {$i/seller}
             {$i/annotation/happiness}
             {$j/annotation/happiness}
          <s-happiness>
} <sellers>
```

(a) Initial query

```
<sellers>
{ for $i in doc("10m.xml")
    /site/open_auctions/open_auction}  <--
         [seller/@person>"person1000"] <--
  for $j in doc("50m.xml")
    /site/open_auctions/open_auction   <--
         [seller/@person<"person2000"] <--
  where $i/seller/@person = $j/seller/@person
  return <s-happiness> {$i/seller}
           {$i/annotation/happiness}
           {$j/annotation/happiness}
         </s-happiness>
} <sellers>
```

(b) Optimized query using rewriting rule 1 & 2 (<-- denotes changes)

Fig. 4. Query rewriting

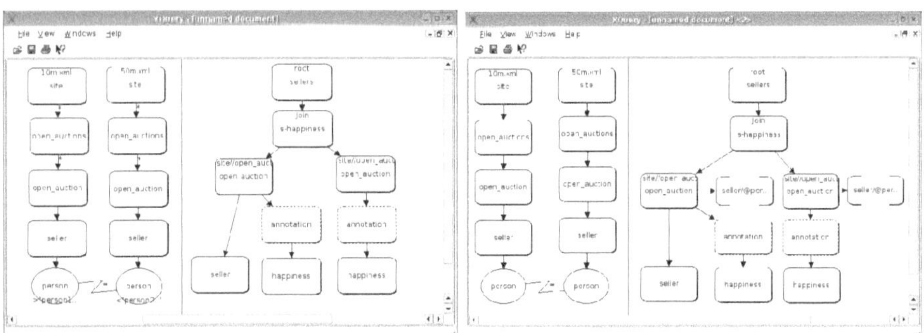

(a) Query drawn by user. (b) Rewritten query.

Fig. 5. VXQ query rewriting

obtained from our own XML schema which has already been generated. The modified query after the rewriting, denoted as the second rewriting rule, is shown in Fig. 4(b). Fig. 5(b) shows the graphical representation of the same query after applying both rewriting rules.

Other example rewriting rules supported by our system are listed as follows.

Rewriting |: Paths that contain common subexpressions separated by `|` such as `a/b/c | a/b/d` are rewritten as `a/b/(c|d)`. We find that it reduces query execution times by more than 10% when used with Galax for some sets of documents. Saxon does similar optimization internally so it is not affected.

Replacing count(): For example, count($x)>5 is rewritten as exists($x)[6] which is likely to be more efficient because only the first five elements are likely to be read.

Replacing count($x)=0: This special case of count() is replaced by empty($x) to avoid unnecessary counting of elements.

Removing duplicate predicates: Predicate such as `[@year>2000 and @year>1995]` is replaced by `[@year>2000]`.

Fig. 6 shows the execution times taken before and after applying our query rewriting. The experiment shows that our first rewriting rule reduces the query execution time by 38% for large document sets when queried by Saxon, although it does not have any effect on Galax. Our second rewriting rule reduces execution times for both Galax and Saxon by 13–59%.

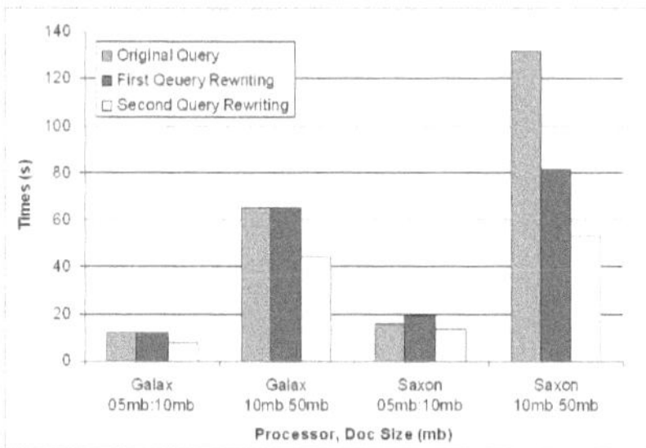

Fig. 6. Query execution times

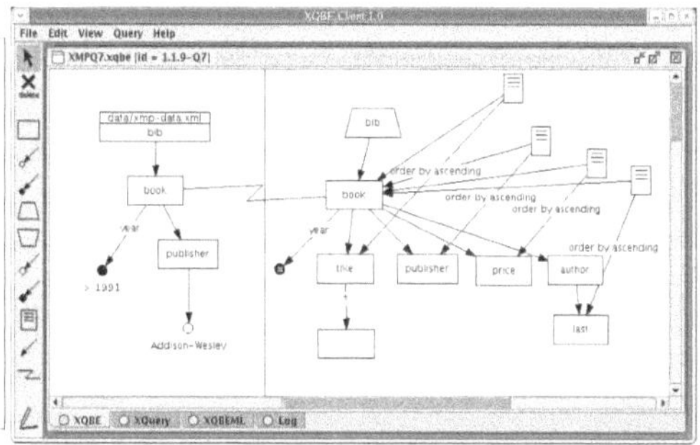

Fig. 7. The XQBE representation of Query 1

Our system is the first graphical query implementation which addresses the issue of query rewriting at the query design level. We showed that semantically equivalent queries but in different formats run with different runtime costs, and the performance of a query processor can be improved by rewriting some parts of a query. We also showed that even the processors that perform their own optimizations benefit from our query rewriting (e.g., Galax).

In a heterogeneous database environment, various backend systems or middleware may be involved in processing and answering a query. Hence, the goal of the query rewriting in this paper is to find the most efficient query expression for a particular XQuery processor involving a particular set of XML documents at query design phase. Our query rewriting techniques can be applied repeatedly for each underlying XQuery processor to find the efficient query expression, and display it graphically to the users.

6 Conclusion

We have presented a visual XQuery specification prototype called VXQ which generates executable XQuery expressions from their given visual specification. We showed that our visual language is more expressive than previous proposals, such as XQBE, by illustrating the visual specification of various W3C XQuery Use Cases. For example, XQBE is visually more complicated and less scalable than VXQ. Fig. 7 shows the XQBE equivalent of Query 1. In general, VXQ can express and generate many queries that cannot be visually specified and generated by previous graphical query languages such as XQBE and GXQL, for instance Q3–Q7 in the XQuery Use Cases. Finally, VXQ supports query rewriting to optimize queries for individual underlying XQuery processors and presents the rewritten queries for further editing.

The future research work includes extending VXQ to support advanced features of XQuery such as user defined functions and conducting detailed user evaluation. For users without extensive knowledge about XQuery, VXQ can be evaluated by how it helps users to learn XQuery and how well it interactively and intuitively generates XQueries. For users who have experience in XQueries, it can be evaluated by how well it generates efficient XQueries quickly on mobile devices such as PDAs.

References

1. Galax: (2005) `http://www.galaxquery.org/`.
2. Kay, M.H.: Saxon (2005) `http://saxon.sourceforge.net/`.
3. W3C: Xml query use cases (2003) `http://www.w3.org/TR/xquery-use-cases/`.
4. Zloof, M.M.: Query-by-example: A database language. IBM Systems Journal **16**(4) (1977) 324–343
5. Cruz, I.F., Mendelzon, A.O., Wood, P.T.: A graphical query language supporting recursion. In: SIGMOD '87: Proceedings of the 1987 ACM SIGMOD international conference on Management of data, New York, NY, USA, ACM Press (1987) 323–330
6. Cruz, I.F., Mendelzon, A.O., Wood, P.T.: G+: Recursive queries without recursion. 2nd Int. Conf. on Expert Database Systems (1988) 355–368
7. Consens, M.P., Mendelzon, A.O.: The graphlog visual query system (1990)
8. Carey, M., Haas, L., Maganty, V., Williams, J.: Pesto: An integrated query/browser for object databases. Proc. of the 22nd Int. Conf. on Very Large Databases (VLDB) (1996) 203–214
9. Ceri, S., Comai, S., Damiani, E., Fraternali, P., Paraboschi, S., Tanca, L.: XML-GL: A graphical language for querying and restructuring XML documents. In: Sistemi Evoluti per Basi di Dati. (1999) 151–165
10. Cohen, S., Kanza, Y., Logan, Y.A., Nutt, W., Sagiv, Y., Serebrenik, A.: Equix easy querying in xml databases. WebDB (Informal Proceedings) (1999) 43–48
11. Filha, I.M.R.E., Laender, A.H.F., da Silva, A.S.: Querying semistructured data by example: The qsbye interface (2002)
12. Gupta, A., Khan, Z.: Graphical xml query language (2000) College of Computing, Georgia Institute of Technology `http://www.cc.gatech.edu/computing/Database/faculty/xml/xmlql.html`.
13. Mark, L., et al: Xmlape (2002) College of Computing, Georgia Institue of Technology `http://www.cc.gatech.edu/projects/XMLApe/`.
14. Munroe, K.D., Papakonstantinou, Y.: BBQ: A visual interface for integrated browsing and querying of XML. In: VDB. (2000)
15. Petropoulos, M., Vassalos, V., Papakonstantinou, Y.: Xml query forms (xqforms): declarative specification of xml query interfaces. In: WWW '01: Proceedings of the 10th international conference on World Wide Web, New York, NY, USA, ACM Press (2001) 642–651
16. Erwig, M.: A visual language for xml. In: IEEE Symp. on Visual Languages. (2000) 47–54

17. Qin, Z., Yao, B.B., Liu, Y., McCool, M.: A graphical xquery language using nested windows (2004) School of Computer Science, University of Waterloo, Waterloo, Ontario, Canada N2L 3G1.
18. Comai, S., Damiani, E., Posenato, R., Tanca, L.: A schema based approach to modeling and querying www data. FQAS'98 (1998)
19. Braga, D., Campi, A.: A graphical environment to query xml data with xquery. In: Fourth International Conference on Web Information Systems Engineering, IEEE Computer Society (2003) 31–40
20. The XML Benchmark Project: (2001) `http://www.xml-benchmark.org/`.

MSXD: A Model and a Schema for Concurrent Structures Defined over the Same Textual Data

Emmanuel Bruno and Elisabeth Murisasco

Université du Sud Toulon-Var
LSIS - Equipe INCOD - UMR CNRS 6168
Avenue de l'Université, BP 20132
F-83957 La Garde cedex, France
{bruno, murisasco}@univ-tln.fr

Abstract. This work aims at defining a model and a schema for multistructured (noted MS) textual documents. Our objectives are (1) to describe several independent hierarchical structures over the same textual data (represented by several structured documents) (2) to consider annotations added by the user in each structured document and (3) to define weak constrains over the concurrent structures and annotations. Our proposal is based on the use of hedge (the foundation of RelaxNG). It is associated with an algebra defined on the structures and annotations of a document in order to specify constraints between them (by means of Allen's relations).

1 Motivation and Objectives

XML documents [1] are mainly hierarchical. The hierarchy, captured in a tree-like structure [2], corresponds to one level of analysis of the data contained into the document (e.g a logical analysis). But, some applications - especially in context of document - centric encoding - need to consider more than one hierarchy over the same text, which correspond to different analysis for different uses of that document. Since SGML [3], physical and logical structures of a document tend to be separated. The physical structure is generally automatically generated by transformation of the logical structure (DSSSL, XSLT). But the construction of a structure from another one is not the general case: the structures are generally independent and they are not conjointly used. This aspect has been already identified with the CONCUR feature of SGML.

Recently, works about concurrent markups have been published [4,5,6,7,8,9,10,11]. They propose solutions to describe multiple hierarchies (with overlapping) into a single document. Our work stands is this context.

We aim at defining a model called MSXD (MultiStructured XML Documents) and a schema for multistructured (MS) documents. Our work is based on the use of hedges [12] (the foundation of RelaxNG [14]).

Our objectives are:

– to propose several segmentations of the same text,
– to define a hierarchical structure for each of these segmentations (producing several structured documents over the same text). Each structure must exist

S. Bressan, J. Küng, and R. Wagner (Eds.): DEXA 2006, LNCS 4080, pp. 172–181, 2006.

independently from others and there is no main structure. They could be stored in separate XML documents (the text is then replicated),
- to insert user annotations into each structured document
- to define a MS schema in order to describe weak constraints over the concurrent structures and annotations (by means of Allen's relations).

Each structure is represented by an XML document with possible annotations, their schema is defined with RelaxNG. The MS document is never instantiated: we want to keep each structure safe (for its construction and manipulation).

To illustrate our work, we choose, as running example, an extract of the sonnet "Mon rêve familier", by the French poet Verlaine. The same text is fragmented and marked up in three ways: its physical structure $S1$ (see figure 1, the text is mainly tagged with `Stanza` and `Verse`), its linguistic structure $S2$ (see figure 2, `Sentences` are marked up), and its rhythmic structure $S3$ (see figure 3, the text is split with `R` while `Enj` and `Rej` mark up enjambments: a part of a text in a verse rejected in the next verse). Each structure is independent from the others. In $S3$, the user adds annotations (in italic font): each textual fragment tagged by `R` begins by an annotation tagged by `Syl` which indicates the number of syllables contained in the fragment. This number is a textual data added to the text of the poem and so missing in the other structures ($S1$ and $S2$).

Structures and annotations can be defined by means of a grammar like a DTD, an XML schema [13] or an relaxNG schema. Annotations are not used for structuring the text (contrary to structures), it is the reason why they are described with a separated vocabulary. Users could share both the schema of a structure and an instance of a document for personal annotations (They could also share the schema of an annotation).

```
<Sonnet>
  <Head>
    <Title>Mon rêve familier</Title><Author>Monsieur Paul Verlaine</Author>
 </Head>
  <Stanza>
    <Verse>Je fais souvent ce rêve étrange et pénétrant</Verse>
    <Verse>D'une femme inconnue, et que j'aime, et qui m'aime,</Verse>
    <Verse>Et qui n'est, chaque fois, ni tout à fait la même</Verse>
    <Verse>Ni tout à fait une autre, et m'aime et me comprend.</Verse>
  </Stanza>
 ...
</Sonnet>
```

Fig. 1. Physical structure $S1$

Notice that the relationship (eventually weak) between parts of these structures is not defined. It could be useful to use it during querying and to check consistency between structures. Here, `Sentence` (figure 2) are always contained in `Stanza` (figure 1), an enjambment, tagged by `Enj` in figure 3, always overlaps a group of two `Verses` (figure 1). The rejected fragment, tagged by `Rej` in figure 3, always begins a `Verse`.

This paper is organized as follows: section 2 presents the related works. The section 3 describes the MSXD model, section 4 proposes a schema enabling to express constraints between structures and annotations, section 5 concludes.

```
<Poem>
  <Text>Mon rêve familier</Text>
  <Text>Monsieur <Name>Paul Verlaine</Name></Text>
  <Sentence>Je fais souvent ce rêve étrange et pénétrant
    D'une femme inconnue, et que j'aime, et qui m'aime,
    Et qui n'est, chaque fois, ni tout à fait la même
    Ni tout à fait une autre, et m'aime et me comprend.</Sentence>
  ...
</Poem>
```

Fig. 2. Linguistic structure $S2$

```
<Poem title='Mon rêve familier' author='Monsieur Paul Verlaine'>
  <R><a:Syl>4</a:Syl>Je fais souvent</R>
  <Enj><R><a:Syl>4</a:Syl>ce rêve étrange</R>
       <R><a:Syl>4</a:Syl>et pénétrant</R>
       <Rej><R><a:Syl>6</a:Syl>D'une femme inconnue,</R></Rej>
  </Enj>
  <R><a:Syl>3</a:Syl>et que j'aime,</R>
  <R><a:Syl>3</a:Syl>et qui m'aime,</R>
  <R><a:Syl>3</a:Syl>Et qui n'est,</R>
  <R><a:Syl>3</a:Syl>chaque fois,</R>
  <R><a:Syl>6</a:Syl>ni tout à fait la même</R>
  <R><a:Syl>6</a:Syl>Ni tout à fait une autre,</R>
  <R><a:Syl>6</a:Syl>et m'aime et me comprend.</R>...
</Poem>
```

Fig. 3. Rhythmic structure $S3$

2 Related Works

If we look at available XML standards, it seems clear that the standard tree-like model [2] and namespaces [15] could be used to represent MS documents if each structure is hierarchical and can be merged with others. Nevertheless, this is not the case in general. In our example, some elements from the physical and linguistic structures can overlap (`Verse` and `Sentence`). The problem of overlapping is not recent (see [16] for a review).

Several works have studied multistructured documents in the context of XML for document-centric encoding. For example, a syntactic solution is proposed by TEI[1] to link different structures using a part of the document structure. It needs to choose either a flat representation of the MS document or a main (hierarchical) structure and to use references (ID/IDREF) in order to describe the other structures. Another solution is to propose a new markup language and model such as LMNL [6] to overcome the limitations of hierarchical markup in XML and to get an instance of a MS document. The model is not XML compatible even if it is able to import/export. Notice that this proposal considers user annotations. A very interesting framework is proposed in [10]. It is a new model based on Goddags data structure [4] which is a generalization of DOM trees for the representation of multi hierarchical XML documents. This proposal defines an XML compatible model and an extension of XPath (specific axis for concurrent querying such like overlapping) to navigate between different structures

[1] `http://www.tei-c.org/P4X/NH.html`

sharing the same textual data. We are close to this proposal. Indeed, we want to keep the hierarchical aspect of each structures, then classical XML tools remain available. Moreover, Goddag does not provide mechanisms to add annotations. Finally, none of these proposals describe relationships between structures.

Another proposal, the colored trees [17], deals with multiple hierarchies but in a data-centric context. It aims at sharing atomic data and it does not consider overlapping, it is out of our scope.

3 The MSXD Model

Definition 1. *A Multistructured document M is a triplet (T, V, S) where T is a textual value, V a set of segmentations of T and S a set of structures associated to segmentations from V.*

A MS document can be seen as a textual value augmented with different hierarchical structures defined over it. These structures share the same text but concern (in general) different strings extracted from that text.

Definition 2. *A segmentation of the textual value V of length l is a list X_V of strings such that $X_V = \{x_i | x_i = V[b_i..e_i]$ and $b_0 = 0$ and $e_i \geq b_i$ and $b_i = e_{i-1} + 1$ and $e_{|X_v|-1} = l - 1\}$. We define two functions for each $X_V[i]$, $start(X_V[i]) = b_i$ and $end(X_V[i]) = e_i$.*

We use two concepts to define *structures*: *fragments* to mark up a segmentation and *annotations* to represent values added by users to fragments. Fragments positions in the textual value are useful to compute their relative positions.

Definition 3. *A fragment f is defined over a segmentation X_V of the textual value V and an alphabet Σ_V:*

1. *$f = \epsilon$ (the empty fragment), $start(f) = end(f) = 0$ (by default)*
2. *$f = v_i$ with $v_i \in X_V$, $start(f) = start(X_V[i])$, $end(f) = end(X_V[i])$*
3. *$f = v < x >$ with $v \in \Sigma_V$ and x a fragment, $start(f) = start(x)$ $end(f) = end(x)$ (f is called a tree)*
4. *$f = xy$ with x and y two fragments and $start(y) = end(x) + 1$, $start(f) = start(x)$, $end(f) = end(y)$.*

Definition 4. *An annotation is defined over an alphabet Σ_A and a finite set of variables X_A:*

1. *ϵ (the empty annotation)*
2. *$a < v >$ ($a \in \Sigma_A$, $v \in X_A$)*
3. *$a < x >$ ($a \in \Sigma_A$, x an annotation)*
4. *xy (x and y two annotations)*

Notice that rule 4 in definitions 3 and 4 produces sequences of fragments or annotations. We do not make distinction between a fragment or an annotation and a singleton sequence containing that fragment or that annotation. Moreover, we do not consider nested sequences.

A fragment can be annotated. Let x be a fragment and a an annotation, an annotated fragment f has the following form: $f = x[a]$ with $start(f) = start(x)$, $end(f) = end(x)$ and $annotation(f) = a$ (the function $annotation(f)$ returns annotations associated to f). Several annotations added to the same fragment are cumulative and their order is not taken into account. If an annotation is added to a sequence of fragments, it is added to the last item of the sequence.

Definition 5. *A structure is a tree f (a labelled fragment) over a segmentation of the textual value V, $end(f) = |X_V| - 1$ and $start(f) = 0$.*

For our example, V is the text of the poem preceded of its title and the name of the poet. We define three segmentations X_V^1, X_V^2 and X_V^3, and three structures $S1$, $S2$ and $S3$ defined over them (and represented as XML documents, see figures 1, 2 and 3). Annotations have been added to $S3$.

For the physical analysis, $\Sigma_V^1 = \{Sonnet, Head, Title, Author, Stanza, Verse\}$, $X_V^1 = x_1 ... \cup ... x_6$, with in particular $x_1 =$ *"Mon rêve familier"* and $x_3 =$ *"Je fais souvent ce rêve étrange et pénétrant"*.

For the linguistic analysis, $\Sigma_V^2 = \{Poem, Text, Name, Sentence\}$, $X_V^2 = x_1 ... \cup ... x_4$, with in particular $x_1 =$ *"Mon rêve familier"*, and
$x_3 =$ *" Je fais souvent ce rêve étrange et pénétrant*
D'une femme inconnue, ..., et qui m'aime,
Et qui n'est, chaque fois, ni tout à fait la même
Ni tout à fait une autre, ... et me comprend.".

For the rhythmic analysis, $\Sigma_A = \{Syl\}$, $\Sigma_V^3 = \{Poem, Title, Author, R, Rej, Enj\}$, $X_A = \{3, 4, 6\}$ and $X_V^3 = x_1 ... \cup ... x_{13}$, with $x_1 =$ *"Mon rêve familier"* and $x_{13} =$*"et m'aime et me comprend."*.

We give now some examples of fragments respectively constructed over segmentations X_V^1 and X_V^3

- $f_1 = x_1$ with $x_1 =$*"Mon rêve familier"*, $start(f_1) = 1$ and $end(f_1) = 17$,
- $f_2 = Title < x_1 >$, $start(f_2) = start(f_1)$, $end(f_2) = end(f_1)$,
- $f_3 = x_2$ with $x_2 =$ *"Monsieur Paul Verlaine"*, $start(f_3) = 18$, $end(f_3) = 39$,
- $f_4 = Author < x_2 >$, $start(f_4) = start(f_3)$ and $end(f_4) = end(f_3)$,
- $f_5 = f_2 f_4$, $start(f_5) = start(f_2) = 1$ and $end(f_5) = end(f_4) = 39$

  The XML elements `<Title>Mon rêve familier</Title><Author> Monsieur Paul Verlaine</Author>` extracted from $S1$ can be represented in our model by `Title<"Mon rêve familier">Author<"Monsieur Paul Verlaine">`

- $f_1 = x_3$ with $x_4 =$ *"Je fais souvent"*, $start(f_1) = 31$, $end(f_1) = 45$
- $f_2 = R < x_4 >$, $start(f_2) = start(f_1)$, $end(f_2) = end(f_1)$
- $f_3 = f_2[a_1]$ with a_1 is an annotation, $a_1 = syll < 4 >$, $start(f_3) = start(f_2)$, $end(f_3) = end(f_2)$ (an annotation has the same position than the fragment to which it is linked), $annotation(f_3) = a_1$

  The XML element `<R><Syl>4</Syl>Je fais souvent</R>` extracted from $S3$, can be represented in our model by `R<"Je fais souvent">[Syl<"4">]`

Our model is designed so that Allen's relations [18] can be used on fragments in order to calculate their relative position inside a segmentation or between two segmentations. If f_1 and f_2 are defined on the same segmentation the predicates *meets* and *overlaps* are always false.

Definition 6. *Predicates on two fragments f_1 and f_2 are defined over one or two segmentations on the same textual value:*

$$\begin{array}{lll}
before(f_1, f_2) & \equiv finishes(f_2, f_1) & \equiv end(f_1) < start(f_2) \\
before(f_1, f_2, n) & \equiv finishes(f_2, f_1, n) & \equiv start(f_2) - end(f_1) = n \\
meets(f_1, f_2) & \equiv met\text{-}by(f_2, f_1) & \equiv end(f_1) = start(f_2) \\
during(f_1, f_2) & \equiv contains(f_2, f_1) & \\
 & \multicolumn{2}{l}{\equiv start(f_1) > start(f_2) \text{ and } end(f_1) < end(f_2)} \\
overlaps(f_1, f_2) & \equiv is\text{-}overlapped(f_2, f_1) & \\
 & \multicolumn{2}{l}{\equiv start(f_1) < start(f_2) \text{ and } end(f_1) > start(f_2)} \\
 & \multicolumn{2}{l}{\text{and } end(f_1) < end(f_2))} \\
starts(f_1, f_2) & \equiv started\text{-}by(f_2, f_1) & \\
 & \multicolumn{2}{l}{\equiv start(f_1) = start(f_2) \text{ and } end(f_1) < end(f_2)} \\
finishes(f_1, f_2) & \equiv finished\text{-}by(f_2, f_1) & \\
 & \multicolumn{2}{l}{\equiv end(f_1) = end(f_2) \quad \text{ and } start(f_1) > start(f_2)} \\
equals(f_1, f_2) & \multicolumn{2}{l}{\equiv start(f_1) = start(f_2) \text{ and } end(f_1) = end(f_2)}
\end{array}$$

Finally, we need to compute the level of a fragment in a structure. This level captures the parent/child relationship between two fragments of a structure.

Definition 7. *Let $F(s)$ (s is a structure) be the set of fragments f such that $f = s$ or $\exists x \in F(s), \exists a \in \Sigma_V | x = a < f >$. The function $level(s, f)$ returns the level of the fragment f in the structure s, it is calculated with the following algorithm:*

- $level(s, s) = 0$
- $level(s, y) = level(s, x) + 1$ *with* $x = a < y >$ *(x and $y \in F(s)$),*

Here are examples of predicates and level calculus for our poem:

- $f_i = enj < ... >$ (used in $S3$) and $f_j = verse < ... >$ (used in $S1$), $overlaps(f_i, f_j)$ is true.
- $f_i = sonnet < ... >$ (used in $S1$), $f_j = poem < ... >$ (used in $S2$) and $f_k = poem < ... >$ (used in $S3$), $equals(f_i, f_j)$ and $equals(f_j, f_k)$ are true.
- $level(S1, sonnet < ... >) = 0$, $level(S1, head < ... >) = 1$, $level(S1, title < ... >) = 2$, ..., $level(S1, stanza < ... >) = 1$.

4 A Schema for Multistructured Documents

We see that for a given MS document, each structure can be described using an XML syntax, thus its schema can be described using RelaxNG. We choose RelaxNG because our model is close to the use of hedges to model XML

Structure S1

```
default namespace =
  "http://sis.univ-tln.fr/msxd/
    poem/physical"
start =
  element Sonnet {
    element Head {
      element Title { text },
      element Author { text },
    },
    element Stanza {
      element Verse { text }+
    }+
  }
```

Structure S2

```
default namespace =
  "http://sis.univ-tln.fr/msxd/
    poem/linguistic"
start =
  element Poem {
    element Text {
      (text
       | element Name { text })+
    }+,
    element Sentence { text }+
  }
```

Structure S3

```
default namespace =
  "http://sis.univ-tln.fr/msxd/
    poem/rythmic"
start =
  element Poem {
    attribute author { text },
    attribute title { text },
    (R
     | element Enj {
        R+,
        element Rej { R }
       })+
  }
R = element R {text}
  }
```

Annotation A3

```
default namespace =
 "http://sis.univ-tln.fr/annot"
start = element Syl = {text}
```

Fig. 4. $S1$, $S2$, $S3$ and $A3$ grammars

```
<MsXml>
 <TextalValue uri="http://sis.univ-tln.fr/msxd/value/reve"/>
 <Structure   type="http://sis.univ-tln.fr/msxd/structure/poem/physical"
              uri="http://sis.univ-tln.fr/msxd/instance/S1.xml"
 <Structure   type="http://sis.univ-tln.fr/msxd/structure/poem/linguistic"
              uri="http://sis.univ-tln.fr/msxd/instance/S2.xml"
 <Structure   type="http://sis.univ-tln.fr/msxd/structure/poem/rythmic"
              uri="http://sis.univ-tln.fr/msxd/instance/S3.xml"
</MsXml>
```

Fig. 5. XML syntax for our running example

documents and the design of RelaxNG is based on this theory [12]. Figure 4 shows the grammars for the structures and annotation of our example.

We define an XML syntax for MS documents (see figure 5). Segmentations are implicit. We consider as annotations any information in a structure that is not defined into the grammar.

We define a schema for MS documents as a set of rules (*vs* a content model definition) because our structures are weakly coupled and the MS document is not hierarchical. Allen's relations enable to constrain both the relative position of fragments belonging to different structures and the position of annotations into a structure. The constrains are expressed using XPath based predicates, we suppose that an XPath expression applied to a structure returns a sequence of fragments or a sequence of annotations.

```
<MsXmlSchema xmlns:a='http://sis.univ-tln.fr/annot'>
 <!-- Identification of the structures and annotations -->
 <Structures>
  <Structure type="http://sis.univ-tln.fr/msxd/structure/poem/physical"
             alias="poem_physical" grammar="poem_physical.rnc"/>
  <Structure type="http://sis.univ-tln.fr/msxd/structure/poem/linguistic"
             alias="poem_linguistic" grammar="poem_linguistic.rnc"/>
  <Structure type="http://sis.univ-tln.fr/msxd/structure/poem/rythmic"
             alias="poem_rythm" grammar="poem_rythm.rnc"/>
 <Structures>
 <Annotations>
  <Annotation type="http://sis.univ-tln.fr/annot"
              alias="rythm_annot" grammar="rythm_annotation.rnc"/>
 <Annotations>
 <Constrains>
 <!-- RELATIVE CONSTRAINTS BETWEEN STRUCTURES -->
 <!-- Sonnet and poem are equals -->
  <Equal>
     <Fragments type="poem_physical" select="/Sonnet"/>
     <Fragments type="poem_linguistic" select="/Poem"/>
  </Equal>
  <Equal>
     <Fragments type="poem_linguistic" select="/Poem"/>
     <Fragments type="poem_rythm" select="/Poem"/>
  </Equal>
  <!-- Attributes or elements title and author are equals -->
  <Equal>
     <Fragments type="poem_physical" select="/Sonnet/Head/Title"/>
     <Fragments type="poem_rythm" select="/Poem/@title"/>
  </Equal>
  <Equal>
     <Fragments type="poem_physical" select="/Sonnet/Head/Author"/>
     <Fragments type="poem_rythm" select="/Poem/@author"/>
  </Equal>
  <!-- A reject begins a verse -->
  <Begins>
     <Fragments type="poem_rythm" select="Rej"/>
     <Fragments type="poem_physical" select="Verse"/>
  </Begins>
  <!-- A enjambment must overlap two verses -->
  <Overlaps>
     <Fragments type="poem_rythm" select="Enj"/>
     <Fragments type="poem_physical" select="Verse"/>
  </Overlaps>
  <!-- First Sentence begins just after (meets) Head -->
  <Meets>
     <Fragments type="poem_physical" select="Head"/>
     <Fragments type="poem_linguistic" select="Sentence[1]"/>
  </Meets>
  <!-- Each sentence append after the head of the sonnet -->
  <Succeeds>
     <Fragments type="poem_linguistic" select="Sentence"/>
     <Fragments type="poem_physical" select="Head"/>
  </Succeeds>
 <!-- Each sentence is contained in a stanza -->
  <During>
     <Fragments type="poem_linguistic" select="Sentence"/>
     <Fragments type="poem_physical" select="Stanza"/>
  </During>
 <!-- CONSTRAINTS ON THE POSITION OF ANNOTATIONS INSIDE STRUCTURES -->
 <!-- Each R must be begun an annotation Syl -->
  <Begun-by>
    <Fragments type="poem_rythm" select="R"/>
    <Fragments type="rythm_annot" select="a:Syl"/>
  </Begun-by>
 <!-- Each Syl must begin a R -->
  <Begin>
    <Fragments type="rythm_annot" select="a:Syl"/>
    <Fragments type="poem_rythm" select="R"/>
  </Begin>
 </Constrains>
</MsXmlSchema>
```

Fig. 6. A grammar for our MD document

Definition 8. *A Multistructured document schema is a triplet* (G_S, G_A, C) *where* G_S *and* G_A *are two sets of grammars defining respectively valid structures and annotations,* $C = \{c_i | c_i = c(p_1 \text{ in } s_1, p_2 \text{ in } s_2)\}$ *is a set of constrains, where c is the name of an allen's predicate and* p_1, p_2 *are XPath expressions applied to the structures* s_1 *and* s_2*. The constrain is true if for each fragment* f_1 *in* $val(p1)$*, it exists a fragment* f_2 *in* $val(p_2)$ *such that* $c(f_1, f_2)$ *is true. A document is valid according to the schema if and only if every constrains in C are true.*

The figure 6 (see comments in the figure) shows an XML syntax for MS documents schemas and illustrates some constrains between fragments (*overlaps*) or fragment and annotations (*begun-by*). Every constrain could be read in the same way, for example the first one: *every fragments matching* ***"/Sonnet"*** *in every documents valid according to the structure (whose alias is)* ***"poem_physical"*** *must be* **equal** *to at least one fragment matching* ***"/Poem"*** *in every document valid according to the structure (whose alias is)* ***"poem_linguistic"***.

5 Conclusion

In this paper, our intention was to define a model and a schema for MS documents. Our contributions are (1) keeping the hierarchical aspect of each structures for using XML tools (proposed by goddags but not by LMNL), (2) adding annotations (proposed by LMNL but not by goddags) (3) first step towards validation across multiple hierarchies [16]. Recall that a multistructured document is defined as a set of fragments (possibly annotated) defined on the same textual value and grouped in concurrent hierarchical structures. We showed how each structure and the corresponding annotations can be described in an XML document. The MS document is never instantiated. A schema is defined as a set of rules, Allen's relations are used to constrain the relative position of fragments in the structures and the position of annotations in a structure. We are developing a prototype to implement our model (see `http://sis.univ-tln.fr/msxd/`).

Our current work is to study the complexity of the validation and to propose an efficient algorithm. The main perspective is to integrate Allen's relations in XPath to be able to select fragments using their relative position with fragments from other structures or even their content model in other structure. So the expression of multistructured constrains would be possible. In a proposal, currently reviewed, we have defined an extension of XQuery. To illustrate this possible use of our model, we give here some simple XQueries:

Q1 - Children of the fragments ***Poem*** *in every structures (i.e.* ***Head, Stanza*** *(in S1),* ***Text, Sentence*** *(in S2),* ***R, Enj*** *(in S3),*
`msxd:doc("doc.msxd")/Poem/*`

Q2 - Verses containing rejects
`msxd:doc("doc.msxd")//Verse[descendant::Rej]`

Q3 - First ***Sentence*** *after* ***Head***
`msxd:doc("doc.msxd")/Poem/Head/following::Sentence[1]`

References

1. Bray, T., Paoli, J., Sperberg-McQueen, C.M.: Extensible Markup Language (XML) 1.0. Rec., W3C (1998)
2. Fernandez, M., Malhotra, A., Marsh, J., Nagy, M., Walsh, N.: XQuery 1.0 and XPath 2.0 Data Model. Draft, W3C (2003)
3. Goldfarb, C.F., Rubinsky, Y.: The SGML handbook. Clarendon Press, Oxford (1990)
4. Sperberg-McQueen, C.M., Huitfeldt, C.: Goddag: A data structure for overlapping hierarchies. In: DDEP/PODDP. (2000) 139–160
5. Sperberg-McQueen, C.M., Burnard, L.: Tei p4 guidelines for electronic text encoding and interchange (2001)
6. Tennison, J., Piez, W.: Layered markup and annotation language (lmnl). In: Extreme Markup Languages 2002. (2002)
7. Durusau, P., O'Donnell, M.B.: Concurrent markup for xml documents. In: Proceedings of XML Europe Atlanta 2002. (2002)
8. N. Chatti et al.: Vers un environnement de gestion de documents à structures multiple. In: Proceedings of BDA 2004, Montpellier, France (2004) 47–64
9. Witt, A.: Multiple hierarchies : news aspects of an old solution. In: Extreme markup language 2004 Conference Proceedings. (2004)
10. Dekhtyar, A., Iacob, I.E.: A framework for management of concurrent xml markup. Data and Knowledge Engineering **52**(2) (2005) 185–208
11. Hilbert, M., Schonefeld, O., Witt, A.: Making concur work. In: Extreme Markup Languages 2005. (2005)
12. Murata, M.: Hedge automata: a formal model for XML schemata. `http://www.xml.gr.jp/relax/hedge_nice.html` (2000)
13. Biron, P.V., Malhotra, A.: XML Schema Part 2: Datatypes. Rec., W3C (2001)
14. Clark, J., Murata, M.: RELAX NG Specification. Technical report, OASIS (2001)
15. Bray, T.: Namespaces in XML 1.1. Rec., W3C (2004)
16. DeRose, S.: Markup overlap : a review and a horse. In: Extreme markup language 2004 Conference Proceedings. (2004)
17. H. V. Jagadish et al.: Colorful XML: One Hierarchy Isn't Enough. In: SIGMOD Conference. (2004) 251–262
18. Allen, J.: Time and time again : The many ways to represent time. International Journal of Intelligent Systems **6(4)** (1991) 341–355

Estimating Aggregate Join Queries over Data Streams Using Discrete Cosine Transform

Zhewei Jiang[1], Cheng Luo[1], Wen-Chi Hou[1], Feng Yan[1], and Qiang Zhu[2]

[1] Department of Computer Science, Southern Illinois University
Carbondale, IL 62901, USA
{zjiang, cluo, hou}@cs.siu.edu
[2] Department of Computer and Information Science, University of Michigan
Dearborn, MI 48128, USA
qzhu@umich.edu

Abstract. Data stream processing is required to be an on-line, one-pass, and time and space efficient process. In this paper, we develop a framework for estimating equi-join query size based on the cosine transform. The discrete cosine transform (DCT) is able to provide concise and accurate representations of data distributions. It can also be updated easily in the presence of insertions and deletions. We have performed analyses and experiments to compare the DCT with sketch-based methods. The experimental results show that given the same amount of space, our method yields more accurate estimates than sketch methods most of the time. Experimental results have also confirmed that the cosine series can be updated quickly to cope with the rapid flow of data.

1 Introduction

Many applications, such as telephone fraud detection, network monitoring, telecommunications data management, etc., generate data in the form of a continuous stream rather than a persistent data set. Elements of data streams arrive continuously and there is no control over the order in which they arrive. Moreover, a data stream is usually unbounded and there is only one chance to look at it as it passes by.

The queries over data streams are typically referred to as continuous queries because they are issued once and then run continuously [4]. Continuous query processing generally requires queries to be executed in real-time using limited space, and thus it must be an on-line, one-pass, and time and space efficient process.

Approximate aggregate query processing has been an important research topic in traditional databases for more than a decade. Various techniques, such as sampling [1, 13], histogram [8, 9, 10], wavelet [5, 12], sketch [2, 3, 15], and discrete cosine transform [11, 14] etc., have been proposed. Although those methods provide the effective frameworks for the query processing over traditional data set, they suffer from some serious drags when they are adapted to the data stream. Details shall be discussed in section 2.

In this research, we shall focus on estimation of aggregate queries with equi-join operations over data streams. To the best of our knowledge, only Dobra et al. [6] addresses the same type of query as we do here – multi-equi-join query over continuous data stream. We develop a framework for estimating aggregate equi-join queries using

S. Bressan, J. Küng, and R. Wagner (Eds.): DEXA 2006, LNCS 4080, pp. 182 – 192, 2006.

the discrete cosine transform (DCT). DCT has a simple update scheme for dynamic data stream environments. We perform analysis on estimation errors and conduct experiments to compare the space requirement, estimation speed, accuracy, and updatability with the sketch methods. The experimental results show that DCT yields much better estimates, from several times up to hundreds of times better, in most cases than the sketch-based methods.

The rest of the paper is organized as follows. Section 2 is a brief survey of the techniques used in aggregate query processing. Section 3 introduces the background of the discrete cosine transform for estimating aggregate queries. Section 4 details our method on estimating aggregate query with equi-join operators. In section 5, we compare estimation accuracy, speed, space, and updatability of our approach with the sketch methods for single and multiple join queries. Section 6 concludes.

2 Related Work

In this section, we briefly review techniques used in approximate aggregate query processing and discuss their potentials in aggregate join queries over data streams. Here, a join mainly refers to an equi-join.

There is a long history of using sampling in aggregate query processing and selectivity estimation on traditional data [12,13]. While sampling may be very dynamic, the accuracy on join queries is far from satisfactory unless the sample size is very large [1]. Histogram provides a simple way to represent data distributions for selection queries [10] and join size estimation [8,9]. The storage space of histograms can increase dramatically when the number of dimensions increases. This situation is further exacerbated by usually large domains of attribute values in data stream applications. Wavelet Transform has been used to compress histograms into small numbers of coefficients. It has been used for range, point, and range-sum queries [5,12]. Unfortunately, as the number of dimensions increases, the accuracy also degrades drastically. The update of the wavelet coefficients also faces a severe challenge in data stream environment. Alon et al. [3] uses a set of independent randomized linear-projection variables, called atomic sketches, to estimate (self)join sizes. It has been shown that the expected value of the square of the atomic sketch X is the size of the self-join. Furthermore, Alon et al. [2,3] uses groups of such independent atomic sketches to estimate the join size. Here, we shall call Alon et al.'s sketch method [2,3] the basic sketch as it has become the basis of several other methods. To improve the accuracy, Dobra et al. partitions the underlying join attribute domains and estimates the join size of each sub-domain individually using sketches [6]. This approach however requires a priori knowledge of the data distributions and relies on the independence assumption of join attributes, which may not be feasible in data stream environment. Ganguly's skimmed sketch [15] skims (extracts) the dense frequencies that are greater than a certain threshold into another distribution. Better estimation results than the basic sketch [3] are reported. However, extra space, in the order of the attribute domain size, is needed to store the (extracted) dense frequencies. Discrete cosine transform (DCT) provides an elegant way to approximate data distributions [11,14]. Similar to the wavelet transform, DCT requires only a small amount of space to store approximated data distributions. Another advantage of the method is that its coefficients can be updated easily and dynamically. As compared to histogram based DCT, our DCT implementation can approximate attributes with large domains, which are often the case in data stream environments, more easily and accurately. Furthermore the performance of histogram based DCT is constrained by the underlying histograms, while ours does not.

3 DCT Approximation

3.1 Attribute Values and Normalization

In general, an attribute can either be numerical or categorical. By mapping each categorical value to a distinct number, we can here assume all attributes are numerical. Since join attributes generally have discrete domains, we shall assume each join attribute X_k has a domain $\{1, 2, \ldots, n_k\}$. To simplify the notations and implementation of the cosine transform, a normalization of the attribute values to the domain (0, 1) is performed first. Let $\max X_i$ and $\min X_i$ be the maximal and minimal values of attribute X_i of the data stream, respectively. Then, each value v of X_i is normalized as follows:

$$v^z = \frac{2(v - \min X_i) + 1}{2(\max X_i - \min X_i + 1)} \tag{3.1}$$

where v^z denotes the normalized value of v. The range (0, 1) is partitioned into $2n_k$ regions according to the grid points and $\{1, 2, \ldots, n_k\}$ is mapped to $\{1/2n_k, 3/2n_k, \ldots, (2n_k-1)/2n_k\}$. Note that we have tried not to map attribute values to the starting and ending values of the normalized domain (0, 1). The minimal and maximal values of an attribute can usually be determined based on knowledge of the data. For example, the minimal and maximal values of the attribute "Age" can be reasonably assumed to be 0 and 150, respectively. From now on, we shall assume all attributes are so normalized to a domain (0, 1), unless otherwise stated.

3.2 Discrete Cosine Transform (DCT)

To illustrate the applications of discrete cosine transform to attribute value distributions, we first consider a one-dimensional case. Let N be the total number of tuples seen so far in the data stream, and n be the number of distinct values in the attribute of concern. We define the basis functions: $\phi_k(x) = 1$ if $k = 0$; otherwise, $\phi_k(x) = \sqrt{2}\cos k\pi x$. The DCT coefficients, $\alpha_k, k \geq 0$, of frequency function of the attribute value are computed by

$$\alpha_k = \frac{1}{N}\sum_{i=1}^{N}\phi_k(v_i) = \frac{1}{N}Count_{v_i} \cdot \phi_k(v_i) \tag{3.2}$$

where v_i is the ith value (i.e., $v_i = (2i-1)/2n$) of the attribute, and $Count_{v_i}$ is the number of tuples in the data stream with the value v_i.

The DCT is known to have an excellent engergy compaction property, where most of the signal information tends to be concentrated in a few low-frequency components of the transform [16]. Therefore, the distribution, in common practice, is approximated by the first m coefficient terms, where m is a number that is much smaller than the domain size n. To apply the transform to the d-dimensional case, the distribution is approximated by its m^d coefficients, $\alpha_{k_1,\ldots,k_d}$ $0 \le k_1,\ldots,k_d \le m-1$:

$$\alpha_{k_1,\ldots,k_d} = \frac{1}{N}\sum_{i=1}^{N}[\prod_{j=1}^{d}\phi_{k_j}(t_{ij})], \tag{3.3}$$

where $\phi_{k_j}(t_{ij}) = \sqrt{2}\cos k_j \pi t_{ij}$ with $\phi_0(t_{ij}) = 1$, and t_{ij} is the jth attribute of the ith tuple t_i.

As observed from Eq. (3.3), each coefficient $\alpha_{k_1,\ldots,k_d}$ of the transform is just the average of the sum of the products of the basis functions (i.e., ϕ) on the tuples. Therefore, for insertion or deletion of a tuple, we just compute the "contribution" of that tuple to the transform separately and then combine it with the old coefficients. That is, for the arrival of a new tuple $t = (t_1, t_2, \ldots, t_d)$ in the data stream which has already had N tuples, $\alpha_{k_1,\ldots,k_d}$ is updated as

$$\alpha'_{k_1,\ldots,k_d} = \frac{N}{N+1}\alpha_{k_1,\ldots,k_{d1}} + \frac{1}{N+1}\prod_{j=1}^{d}\phi_{k_j}(t_j) \tag{3.4}$$

Here, $\alpha'_{k_1,\ldots,k_d}$ represents the updated coefficient. Similarly, to delete a tuple $t = (t_1, t_2,\ldots, t_d)$, the coefficient is updated as

$$\alpha'_{k_1,\ldots,k_d} = \frac{N}{N-1}\alpha_{k_{11},\ldots,k_{d1}} - \frac{1}{N-1}\prod_{j=1}^{d}\phi_{k_j}(t_j) \tag{3.5}$$

As observed, coefficients can be updated easily. Note that the set of coefficients derived by the above incremental update scheme (using Eq. (3.4)) is exactly the same as if we had derived it in a batch fashion using Eq. (3.3). This property implies that the DCT is suitable for ordinary relations as well as data streams. The updates of the coefficients can be performed on-line as well as in batch.

4 Estimating Join Size

A typical equi-join query may look like "Select Count(*) from R_1, R_2, …., R_n where $R_i.A = R_j.B$ and $R_k.C=R_l.D$ and …". Without loss of generality, we assume that each pair of attributes in a join operation (predicate), e.g., $R_i.A$ and $R_j.B$ or $R_k.C$ and $R_l.D$, have the same domains and are normalized to (0, 1).

4.1 Join Size Estimation

Consider a query with a single equi-join predicate, say, $R_1.A = R_2.B$. Let n be the domain size for both attributes A and B, and $\{a_k\}$ and $\{b_k\}$ be the DCT coefficients of $R_1.A$ and $R_2.B$, respectively. By Parseval's identity [16]

$$\sum_{k=0}^{n-1}\frac{Count_{A_{v_i}}}{N_1}\cdot\frac{Count_{B_{v_i}}}{N_{21}} = \sum_{k=0}^{n-1}\frac{a_k}{\sqrt{n}}\cdot\frac{b_k}{\sqrt{n}} \tag{4.1}$$

Here, $Count_{A_{v_i}}$ and $Count_{B_{v_i}}$ denote the number of tuples whose values are v_i in R_1.A and R_2.B, respectively. On the other hand, the join size, denoted as J, is computed as:

$$J = \sum_{k=0}^{n-1} Count_{A_{v_i}} Count_{B_{v_i}} . \tag{4.2}$$

By using only the first m coefficients, J is estimated by:

$$Est = \frac{N_1 N_2}{n} \sum_{k=0}^{m-1} a_k b_k \tag{4.3}$$

As shown by Eq. (4.3), the join size estimate can be easily derived by adding up the products of corresponding coefficients. Discussions on queries with multiple equi-join should follow directly.

4.2 Error Analysis

In this section, we give a brief discussion on the number of coefficients needed to guarantee the relative error to be smaller than a threshold e.

We assume both relations have the same size N, for simplicity. Let n be the size of join attribute domains. As shown in Eq. (4.3), the join size estimate *Est* of the two relations is calculated as

$$Est = \frac{N^2}{n} \sum_{k=0}^{m-1} a_k b_k = \frac{N^2}{n} + \frac{N^2}{n} \sum_{k=1}^{m-1} a_k b_k . \tag{4.4}$$

As shown in Eq (4.2), we only need the first n terms to compute the actual join size J. That is,

$$J = \frac{N^2}{n} \sum_{k=0}^{n-1} a_k b_k = \frac{N^2}{n} + \frac{N^2}{n} \sum_{k=1}^{n-1} a_k b_k . \tag{4.5}$$

We know that $a_0 = 1$, and from Eq. (3.2), $a_k = \frac{1}{N} \sum_{i=1}^{n} count_{v_i} \sqrt{2} \cos k\pi v_i , k \geq 1$.

Since $-1 \leq \cos k\pi v_i \leq 1$, we derive $-\sqrt{2} \leq a_k \leq \sqrt{2}$. similarly, $b_0 = 1$ and $-\sqrt{2} \leq b_k \leq \sqrt{2}$. Using the bounds $-\sqrt{2} \leq a_k , b_k \leq \sqrt{2}$, we obtain

$$| J - Est | = | \frac{N^2}{n} \sum_{k=m}^{n-1} a_k b_k | \leq \frac{2N^2(n-m)}{n} . \tag{4.6}$$

The relative error is defined as

$$relative\_error = \frac{| J - Est |}{J} \leq \frac{2N^2(n-m)}{Jn} \tag{4.7}$$

by assuming J > 0. To guarantee the relative error to be smaller than or equal to a given number *e*, from Eq. (4.7), we derive $n - \frac{eJn}{2N^2} \leq m$. Consequently, the space requirement to guarantee an error *e* is:

$$m = n - \left\lfloor \frac{eJn}{2N^2} \right\rfloor \tag{4.8}$$

As a simple comparison, the basic sketch [3] has a best case space bound $\Omega(N^2/J)$ and worst case bound $O(N^4/J^2)$[17]. By boosting the basic sketch's worst case bound to $O(N^2/J)$,the skimmed sketch [15] has a space bound of $\Theta(N^2/J)$. However, this bound is valid only when the join size is greater than a sanity bound of $N^{3/2}$ or NlogN [3]. When the join size is small, the required space could be much greater than the bounds given above. Moreover, the skimmed sketch uses extra space to store extracted frequencies; this extra space is in the order of n (i.e., O(n)). In general, it is very difficult or impossible to derive tighter bounds for our approach as well as other approaches because of the diversities of the frequency functions, which are further complicated by the join operations. However, there are some interesting properties that may shed some light on the comparisons. That is, the best and worst cases of our approach happen to be the worst and best cases of the sketches'. We shall discuss these situations in the following.

4.2.1 Best/Worst Case Error

The cosine transform approximates smooth distributions better. Therefore, the best case, in terms of estimation accuracy, happens when the join attribute values are uniformly distributed, regardless of the range of the attribute values n is. The cosine coefficients $a_0=1$ and $b_0=1$. As for a_k and b_k, $1 \le k \le m$, they can be derived as:

$$a_k = \frac{1}{N}\sum_{i=1}^{n} count_{V_i} \cdot \sqrt{2} \cdot \cos k\pi_{V_i} = \frac{\sqrt{2}}{n}\sum_{i=1}^{n} \cos\frac{k\pi(2i-1)}{2n} = 0 \tag{4.9}$$

Similarly, $b_k = 0$. Thus, the join size estimate *Est* is:

$$Est = \frac{N^2}{n}\sum_{k=0}^{m-1} a_k b_k = \frac{N^2}{n} \cdot a_0^2 \cdot b_0^2 = \frac{N^2}{n} = J \tag{4.10}$$

That is, using only the first term of the transforms, i.e., $a_0=b_0=1$, is already enough to represent the uniform distributions and gives no-error join size estimation.

On the other hand, both sketch methods could have a problem for the uniform distribution. They require at least $O(\frac{N^2}{J}) = O(\frac{N^2}{N^2/n}) = O(n)$ space, which makes them not better than the brute-force method. As a result, for uniform distributions, the atomic sketches are very small, which result in the join size estimate of (close to) 0 as compared to the actual join size N^2/n, no matter how large a space is used. Note that our approach requires only 1 coefficient for uniform distributions.

The worst case happens when all the tuples in a data stream have the same and sole join attribute value. Let v_{j_1} and v_{j_2} be the sole join attribute values in the two data streams, respectively. Due to space limitation, we shall consider only the case where $v_{j_1} = v_{j_2}$ Since $J=N^2$ in this case, by Eq. (4.8), the number of coefficients needed to guarantee the relative error is smaller than or equal to e is $m = n - \left\lfloor \frac{en}{2} \right\rfloor$. On the other hand, the sketch methods can obtain the exact join size ($J=N^2$) because there is only one value in the attributes. The sketch methods have their lower bound O(1) space here.

From the discussion above, we derive that $\Omega(1)$ and $O(n - \lfloor \frac{en}{2} \rfloor)$ are our lower and upper space bounds, respectively.

As observed each method has its strengths and weaknesses. No single method is best for all distributions. Therefore, in the next section we shall perform extensive experiments to see how they react to different types of data and which method is likely to cope with more types of data, especially real-life (like) data.

5 Experimental Results

We shall compare our method with Alon's basic sketch [3] and Ganguly's skimmed sketch [15] as none of these requires a priori knowledge of data distributions and an independence assumption of join attributes as does Dobra's [6].

5.1 Data Sets and Performance Measure

Experiments are performed on synthetic data sets as well as real-life data sets. We generate two types of synthetic data. The first type possesses several distinct characteristics; it is used to explore the strengths and weaknesses of these estimation methods. The second type of data consists of several real-life like datasets; they are generated by the data generator proposed in [6,12]. The data generated are correlated and sparsely clustered, which are believed to be similar to the real-life data. The data sets are used to assess the potentials of the methods in real world applications. For the real-life data sets, we chose the Current Population Survey data as [6]. The results are omitted for the space limitation, Readers can find it in [17].

We compare the accuracies of the methods by using the same number of coefficients (for our methods) or atomic sketches (for others). The commonly used average relative error is adopted as the accuracy measure. The relative error is defined as |Act(ual) − Est(imate)| / Act(ual). Each result is the average of 200 queries. Note that skimmed sketch uses additional O(n) space to store extracted dense frequencies. The additional space used, from thousands to 10^5, is not reported in the figures presented here and is generally much larger than the largest number of coefficients or atomic sketches used in other methods.

5.2 Experiments on Synthetic Data

5.2.1 Synthetic Data Type I

Two relations, R_1 and R_2, are generated, each with 10^7 (N) tuples. Each relation has an attribute with a domain size of 10^5 (n). These figures are the same as the experimental setting in related papers [6,12,15]. The frequencies of the attribute values in the relations follow the Zipfian distributions. A zipf value of 0.5, 1, or 1.5 roughly represents a slightly skewed, skewed, or a highly skewed distribution, respectively. Besides skew, correlations and smoothness are also instilled in the join attribute values by using different mappings from the frequencies to attribute values in two relations. Here, positively correlated attributes, say, A and B, refer to the cases where if the frequency of a value x in A is greater than the frequency of another value y in A, then the frequency of x in B is also greater than y in B. Smoothness is introduced by orderly mapping frequencies to attribute values.

Figures 1 to 4 show how these methods perform with different types of data. As observed in Figure 1, sketches perform better than the cosine method. Actually, the positively correlated case is a generalization of the self-join case for which the sketch was shown to be most suitable [3]. However, as the positive correlations weaken, their performance degrades and our approach performs better as shown in Figures 2, 3 and 4. For example, with 500 coefficients (or atomic sketches), the relative errors of the skimmed and basic sketches are 2.7 and 8.3 times greater than the cosine method in the weak positively correlated case (Figure 2), 9.3 and 33.4 times in the independent case (Figure 3) and 3.0 and 8.9 times in the negatively correlated case (Figure 4).

The data set used in Figure 2 is obtained by permuting only 10% of the frequencies of R_2 in Figure 1. The permutation introduces some randomness and weakens the positive correlations.

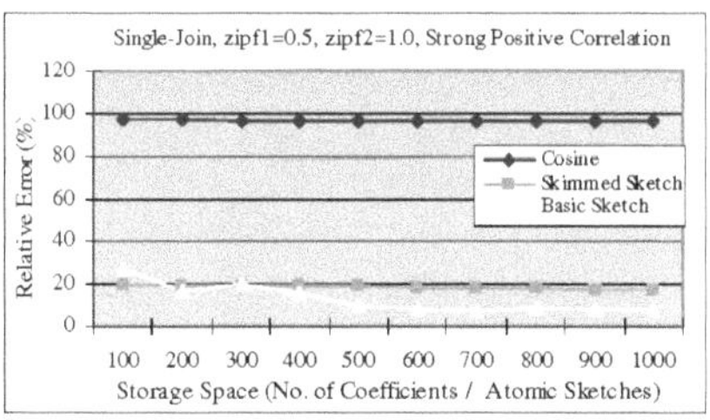

Fig. 1. Strong Positively Correlated Attributes

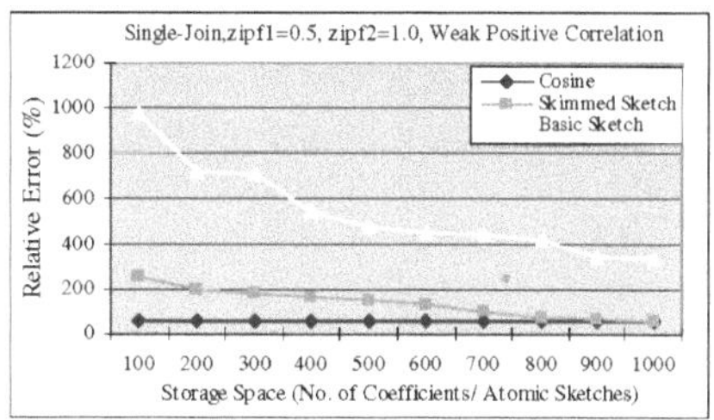

Fig. 2. Weak Positively Correlated Attributes

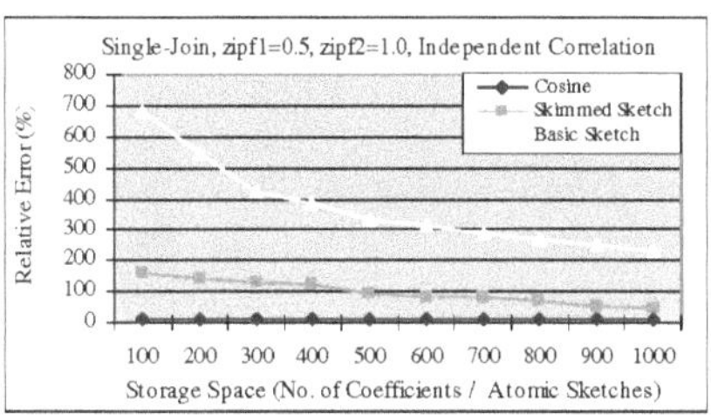

Fig. 3. Independent Join Attributes

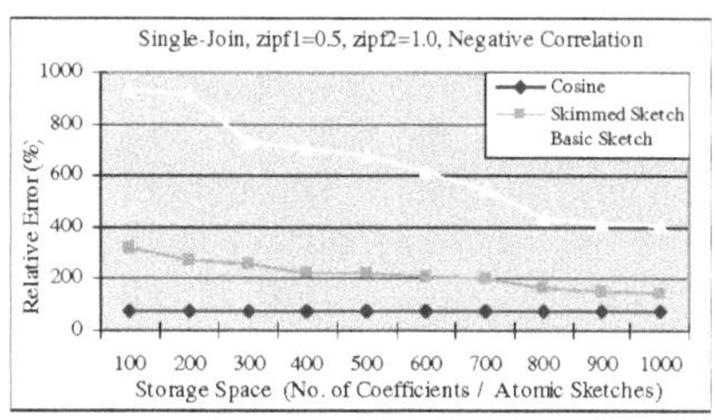

Fig. 4. Negatively Correlated Attributes

Let us now examine the impact of the smoothness of distribution functions on the performance by comparing Figures 1 and 5. The data used in these two figures are basically identical, except that the frequency functions of R_1 and R_2 in Figure 1 are rugged (due to the random mapping between frequencies and attribute values) while they are smooth in Figure 5 (due to the orderly mapping between frequencies and attribute values). The two relations are positively correlated just like in Figure 1. As observed, smoothness plays in favor of the cosine method. The cosine method has improved its performance a lot here, as compared to Figure 1, on this strongly correlated dataset due to the smoothness. For example, with 500 coefficients, the cosine method yields an average error of 56.24% in Figure 4, down from 96.58% in Figure 1. As expected, smoothness has no effect on sketches since as they do not approximate distributions.

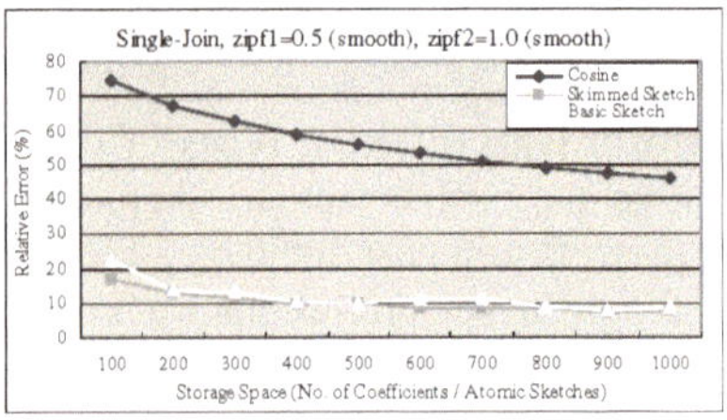

Fig. 5. Strong Positively Correlated Attributes with Smooth Distributions

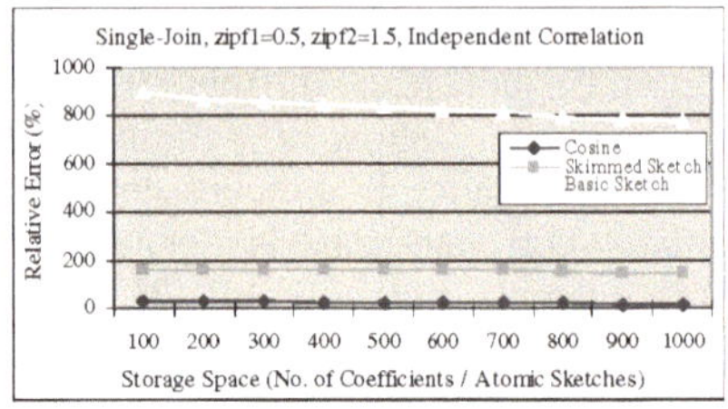

Fig. 6. Independent Join Attributes with Skewer distributions

Let us now examine the effects of skew by comparing Figures 3 and 6. When the distributions become skewer, all methods suffer from performance degradation. For example, with 500 coefficients, the relative errors of the cosine, skimmed sketch, and basic sketch increase from 9.98%, 92.40%, and 333.09% (in Figure 3) to 24.21%, 158.76%, and 837.85% (in Figure 6), respectively. The skew does not seem to play particularly in favor of any method. But still the errors of skimmed and basic sketches are several times up to tens of times greater than ours, respectively.

As a short summary of this qualitative study, we observe that the sketch methods are suitable for strong positively correlated data, while our approach is more suitable for from weak positively correlated, random, to negatively correlated data. In addition, our approach can also benefit from the smoothness of distributions functions, which often exhibits in the real-life data, such as the distributions of ages and salaries of employees.

5.2.2 Synthetic Data Type II

The purpose of this experiment is to assess the potentials of these methods in real-life applications. We implemented the data generator proposed by Vitter, et al.[12] and extended by Dobra, et al. [6] to generate real-life like data. The data are clustered and positively correlated. The datasets are generated by distributing tuples across and within the randomly picked rectangular regions (clusters) in the multi-dimensional attribute space of a relation. We also choose the same parameter setting as in [6]: skew across regions (z_{inter}) =1.0 and skew within each region (z_{intra}) =0.0-0.5; number of regions=10 and 50 (the later is in addition to Dobra's [6]); size of each domain=1024; size of each relation=10^7, volume of each region =1,000 – 2,000 and perturbation parameter p=0.5 - 1.0.

Figure 7 and 8 show the results of single-join queries with different numbers of clusters. Again, the cosine method outperforms the sketch methods. For example, with 500 coefficients in Figure 7, our method generates an average error of 0.60% while the errors of skimmed sketch and basic sketch method are 7.98% and 8.24%, respectively, which are 13.2 and 13.6 times greater than ours. Figure 8 shows a similar result as the number of clusters increases to 50. The superiority of our method in these experiments is mainly due to the not so strong positive correlations (as compared to that in Figure 1) in the data although the clusters are still positively correlated. Randomness sets in when the centers of the clusters are selected randomly within their respective shrunk regions in the correlated relations. Clustered data could also make the distribution curves a little smoother than a completely random distribution.Similar results are observed in the two-join query cases, the results are presented in [17] and are omitted here for reasons of space.

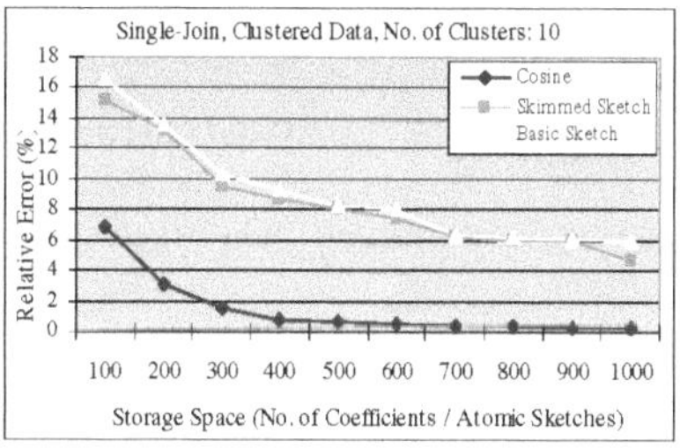

Fig. 7. Single-Join Query, Cluster Data, No. of Clusters: 10

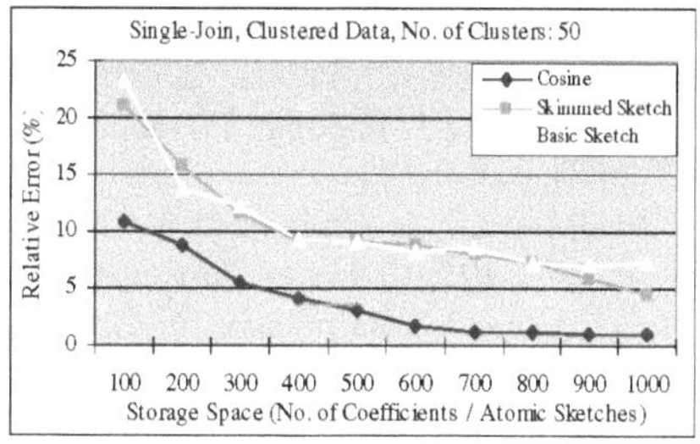

Fig. 8. Single-Join Query, Cluster Data, No. of Clusters: 50

5.3 Computation Speed

When a tuple arrives, we immediately update the coefficients, following Eq. (3.4). On the average, it takes 0.32 μs to update one coefficient. So, even for the case with 10,000 coefficients, it takes only 3.2 ms to do the job. To estimate join sizes, we follow Eq. (4.3). On the average, it takes about 0.4 ms to derive an estimate from 10,000 coefficients. As for the sketch methods, to update 10,000 atomic sketches, it takes about 1.0 ms, which is faster than ours; this is due to simpler computations involved in updating atomic sketches. But to derive an estimate from 10,000 atomic sketches, it would take 1.6 ms, as compared to our 0.4 ms, because they need to find the median of a large number of group means. Nevertheless, all these approaches have demonstrated their abilities to cope with the on-line one-pass dynamic properties of data stream processing.

6 Conclusions and Future Work

In this paper, we discuss equi-join query size estimation over data streams with limited storage space. We use cosine series to approximate distributions of data streams and then use them to estimate equi-join queries. Experimental results have shown that our approach produces faster and more accurate estimates than sketches in most of the situations. We have also demonstrated that our approach can be updated dynamically and quickly. The proposed method is well suited for approximate equi-join queries over continuous data streams. Our method can also be directly applied to non-equal-joins, range, and point queries.

References

[1] S. Acharya, P. Gibbons, V. Poosala, and S. Ramaswamy. "Join synopses for approximate query answering", In *SIGMOD. ACM Press*, 1999, pp275-28

[2] N. Alon, Y. Matias and M.Szegedy. "The Space Complexity of Approximation the Frequency Moments", In *Proc of 28th Annual ACM STOC*, May 1996, pp 20-29

[3] N. Alon, P.B Gibbons, Y. Matias and M.Szegedy. "Tracking Join and Self-join Sizes in Limited Storage", In *proc of the 18th ACM PODS* May 1999, pp.10-20
[4] S. Babu and J. Widom. "Continuous queries over data streams". *SIGMOD Record*, 2001, 30(3): pp109-120.
[5] A. Bulut and A. K. Singh. "SWAT: Hierarchical stream summarization in large networks". In *IEEE 19th ICDE*, Mar 2003 pp303-314
[6] A. Dobra, M. Garofalakis, J. Gehrke, and R. Rastogi. "Processing complex aggregate queries over data stream", In *ACM-SIGMOD,* June 2002, pp61-72.
[7] A. C. Gilbert and Y. Kotidis and S. Muthukr- ishnan and M. J. Strauss, "Surfing Wavelets on Streams: One-pass Summaries for Approximate Aggregate Queries", In *Proc. of VLDB*, 2001, Sep, 2001 , pp79-88
[8] Y. Ioannidis and S. Christodoulakis. "Optimal Histograms for Limiting Worst-Case Error Propagation in the Size of Join Results". *ACM TODS,* Dec1993, Vol. 18, No. 4, 709-748.
[9] Y. E. Ioannidis and V. Poosala. "Balancing Histogram Optimality and Practicality for Query Result Size Estimation". In *ACM SIGMOD*, 1995, pp233-244.
[10] N. Koudas, S. Muthukrishnan and D. Srivastava. "Optimal Histograms for Hierarchical Range Queries (Extended Abstract) (2000)", In *PODS,* 2000, pp196 - 204
[11] J-H. Lee, D-H. Kim and C-W Chung, "Multi-dimensional Selectivity Estimation Using Compressed Histogram Information", *SIGMOD 1999*, pp205-214.
[12] J.S. Vitter and M. Wang. "Approximate Computation of Multidimensional Aggregates of Sparse Data Using Wavelets." *SIGMOD*, 1999, pp193- 204
[13] Y-L Wu, D. Agrawal and A. E. Abbadi, "Applying the Golden Rule of Sampling for Query Estimation", *ACM SIGMOD 2001,* May 2001, pp 449- 460
[14] F. Yan, W-C. Hou, Q. Zhu, "Selectivity Estimation Using Orthogonal Series", *8th DASFAA,* March, 2003, pp 157-164.
[15] S. Ganguly, M. Garofalakis, R. Rastogi, "Processing Data-Stream Join Aggregates Using Skimmed Sketches", *Proc of EDBT*, March 2004, pp. 569-586
[16] W. L. Briggs and V. E. Henson, *DFT : an owner's manual for the discrete Fourier transform*, Philadelphia : Society for Industrial and Applied Mathematics Published, 1995.
[17] Z. Jiang, W. Hou, Y. Feng, Q. Zhu, "Estimating Aggregate Join Queries Over Data Streams Using Cosine Series", www.cs.siu.edu/~zjiang

Evaluation of a Probabilistic Approach to Classify Incomplete Objects Using Decision Trees

Lamis Hawarah, Ana Simonet, and Michel Simonet

TIMC-IMAG
Institut d'Ingenierie et de l'Information de Santé
Faculté de Médecine
38700 LA Tronche
{Lamis.Hawarah, Ana.Simonet, Michel.Simonet}@imag.fr
http://www-timc.imag.fr

Abstract. We describe an approach to fill missing values in decision trees during classification. This approach is derived from the ordered attribute trees method, proposed by Lobo and Numao in 2000, which builds a decision tree for each attribute and uses these trees to fill the missing attribute values. Both our approach and theirs are based on the Mutual Information between the attributes and the class. Our method takes the dependence between attributes into account by using the Mutual Information. The result of the classification process is a probability distribution instead of a single class. In this paper, we present tests performed on some real databases using our approach and Quinlan's method. We analyse the classification results of some instances in test data and finally we discuss some perspectives.

1 Introduction

Decision Trees are one of the most popular classification algorithms currently in use in Data Mining and Machine Learning. Decision Trees belong to supervised classification methods and are built from a training data set, according to the divide-and-conquer approach [18]. Once built, decision trees are used to classify new cases. A case is classified by starting at the root node of the tree, testing the attribute specified by this node, then moving through the tree until a leaf is encountered; the case is classified by the class associated with the leaf. It may happen that some objects do not have any value for some attributes. This problem, known as the problem of missing values, may occur during the building phase of the decision tree. It may also occur during the classification phase: when classifying an object, if the value of a particular attribute which was branched on in the tree is missing, it is not possible to decide which branch to take in order to classify this object, and the classification process cannot be completed. Our objective is to classify an object with missing values. There are

S. Bressan, J. Küng, and R. Wagner (Eds.): DEXA 2006, LNCS 4080, pp. 193–202, 2006.

several methods to deal with missing values using decision trees [20], [15]. The simplest one is to ignore instances containing missing values [15]. The methods in [7] and [15] consist in replacing an attribute's missing values with its most probable value. Quinlan's method [18] replaces missing values with a distribution of probability. The CART method [5], which constructs binary decision trees, consists in using a *surrogate split* when an unknown value is found in the attribute originally selected. Other methods include *the lazy decision tree* method [8], Shapiro's method [16] and the *Ordered Attribute Trees method* [12], [13], [14]. Our work is situated in the framework of probabilistic decision trees [5], [17], [18]. We use a probabilistic decision tree, instead of a classic decision tree, by keeping on each leaf in a decision tree all the class values with their probabilities. Replacing an unknown attribute by only one value eliminates some other possible values; therefore, giving a probability distribution for each unknown attribute instead of a single value seems to us closer to reality. We aim at using the dependencies between attributes to predict missing attribute values; when we estimate the values of an unknown attribute from its dependent attributes, we use the maximum amount of information contained in the object in order to fill the missing values of this attribute. In our work, we are interested in the type of approaches which use decision trees to fill in missing values [12], [16], because if a decision tree is able to determine the class of an instance thanks to the values of its attributes, then it can be used to determine the value of an unknown attribute from its dependent attributes. Decision trees are suitable to represent relations among the most important attributes when determining the value of a target attribute [12]. In our work, we extend the *Ordered Attribute Trees* method *(OAT)*, proposed by Lobo and Numao [12]; it uses decision trees to deal with missing values in training data and test data [13], [14]. In this paper, we first present Lobo's approach *(OAT)*. We then describe our method to estimate missing values, that uses the dependencies between attributes and gives a probabilistic result; we test our approach on real data bases and we compare our results with Quinlan's results. We also measure the quality of our classification results by comparing each instance in the test data with all the instances in the training data using a Distance Function. Finally, we present some perspectives.

1.1 Ordered Attribute Trees Method

Ordered Attribute Trees (OAT) is a supervised learning method to fill missing values in categorical data. It uses decision trees as models for estimating unknown values. This method constructs a decision tree for each attribute, using a training subset that contains instances with known values for the attribute. These cases in the training subset, for a target attribute, are described only by the attributes whose relation with the class has lower strength than the strength of the relation between the target attribute and the class. The resulting decision tree is called an *attribute tree*. This method uses *Mutual Information* [19] as a measure of the strength of relations between the attributes and the class[1]. There is an order for the construction of the attribute trees. This order is guided by the *Mutual Information* between the attributes and the class. The method orders the attributes from those with low mutual information to those with high mutual information. It constructs attribute trees according to this order. These trees are used to determine unknown values for each attribute. The first attribute tree constructed is a one-node tree with the most frequent value among the values of the attribute. An attribute tree is constructed for an attribute A_i using a training subset which contains instances with known values for the attribute A_i, and the attributes whose missing values have already been filled before. Then, the attributes A_k for which $MI(A_i, C) < MI(A_k, C)$ are excluded [12]. During the calculation of $MI(A_i, C)$, instances which have missing values for the attribute A_i are ignored [14]. This method is not general enough to be applicable to every domain [14]. The domains in which there are strong relations between the attributes appear to be the most suitable to apply the *OAT* method. In this method, the idea to start by dealing with the attribute which is the less dependent on the class [12], [13], [14] is interesting, because it is the attribute which has the least influence on the class.

2 Probabilistic Approach

We present in this section our work that estimates missing values during classification using a decision tree to predict the value of an unknown attribute from its dependent attributes [9]. This value is represented by a probability distribution. We have two proposals. The first one simply extends *Lobo's OATs* with probabilistic data; the second uses the dependence between attributes and also gives a probabilistic result [9], [10].

2.1 Probabilistic Ordered Attribute Trees (POATs)

For each attribute we propose to construct an *attribute tree* using Lobo's *OAT* approach, enriched with probabilistic information. We call these trees *Probabilistic Ordered Attribute Trees (POAT)* [9]. The *POAT* method extends *OATs* on two points: 1) each leaf in such an *attribute tree* is associated with a probability distribution for the possible attribute values instead of its most probable value;

---

1 Mutual Information (MI) between two categorical random variables X and Y is the average reduction in uncertainty about X that results from learning the value of Y:

$$MI(X,Y) = -\sum_{x \in D_x} P(x) log_2 P(x) + \sum_{y \in D_y} P(y) \sum_{x \in D_x} P(x|y) log_2 P(x|y) \qquad (1)$$

D_x and D_y are the domains of the categorical random variables X and Y. $P(x)$ and $P(y)$ are the probability of occurrence of $x \in D_x$ and $y \in D_y$, respectively. $P(x|y)$ is the conditional probability of X having the value x once Y is known to have the value y.

2) attributes used to build a *POAT* for an attribute A_i are those whose missing values have already been filled before and are dependent on A_i. The result of classifying an object with missing values using *POAT* is a class distribution instead of a single class. These trees give a probabilistic result which is more refined than Lobo's initial *OATs*. However, they do not take into account all the dependencies between attributes, because they are built in an ordered manner. Therefore, we suggest another approach *(Probabilistic Attribute Trees)* which is based on the dependencies between attributes.

2.2 Probabilistic Attribute Trees (PATs)

To take into account the dependencies, we calculate the *Mutual Information* between each pair of attributes in order to determine for each attribute its dependent attributes. Then, a *Probabilistic Attribute Tree (PAT)* is constructed for each attribute, using all the attributes depending on it. A *PAT* is a decision tree whose leaves are associated with distributions of probability for the attribute values. For an attribute A_i we first determine its set of dependent attributes: $Dep(A_i) = \{A_j \mid MI(A_i, A_j) > threshold\ ^2\}$. Then we construct for A_i a *Probabilistic Attribute Tree (PAT)* according to its A_j.

3 Experimentation

In this section, we will test our approach on several databases and compare our results with those generated by Quinlan's method [18]. Each database is tested on several thresholds. To choose a threshold, we calculate the average of the Mutual Information calculated between each attribute and the class, we then choose some thresholds that are closer to this average [11]. Because *Mutual Information*, between an attribute and the class, tends to be high when the number of this attribute values is high [6], we use *Normalized Mutual Information* as proposed by Lobo and Numao [14] instead of *Mutual Information. Normalized Mutual Information* used is defined as:

$$MI_N(X,Y) \equiv \frac{2MI(X,Y)}{\log ||D_x|| + \log ||D_y||} \tag{2}$$

3.1 Testing and Comparison with C4.5 Method

First, we have tested our approach on the *vote* database [4]. A training data, which has 232 instances with 16 discrete attributes (all are Boolean and take the values: y or n), is used to construct our *POATs* and *PATs*. The class in this database can take two values (*Democrat* and *Republican*). This training data does not have any missing values. However, we used a test data which contains 240 objects with missing values. The missing values rates in the test data are shown in Table 1. The average of Normalized Mutual Information is 0.26. Therefore,

[2] A threshold will be fixed.

Table 1. The missing values rates

ID	Attributes	Missing values rates
1	handicapped-infants	05,00 %
2	water-project-cost-sharing	24,58%
3	adoption-of-the-budget-resolution	04,58%
4	**physician-fee-freeze**	48,33%
5	**el-salvador-aide**	08,75%
6	religious-groups-in-schools	04,58%
7	anti-satellite-test-ban	07,50%
8	aid-to-nicaraguan-contras	07,08%
9	mx-missile	10,41%
10	immigration	02,50%
11	synfuels-corporation-cutback	11,25%
12	**education-spending**	17,08%
13	superfund-right-to-sue	13,75%
14	crime	08,33%
15	duty-free-exports	14,58%
16	export-administration-act-south-africa	50,20%

we have tested our approach on several thresholds: 0.2, 0.3, 0.4 and 0.5. The result of the tests is shown in Table 2. The column 50% in Table 2 contains the percentage of objects having probability 0.5 for each value of class.

Generally, when we decrease the threshold, we increase the degree of dependence between attributes, and consequently we use more attributes to construct our trees. In this case, we decrease the number of instances on each leaf in each tree. In Table 2, we note that when we decrease the threshold, our results improve and the best results are obtained by PATs for 0.2 threshold.

The only attribute used to construct the decision tree using C4.5 method is *physician-fee-freeze* which has the greatest influence on the decision. However, if this attribute is unknown, C4.5 calculates its frequency in all the training data without taking into account the other attributes which depend on it. Consequently, in the test data each object which has a missing value for *physician-fee-freeze* is classified *Democrat* with probability 0.53 and *Republican* with probability 0.47. Contrary to C4.5, each object in which the attribute *physician-fee-freeze* is unknown is classified according to attributes depending on *physician-fee-freeze.*

For the threshold 0.5, our *probabilistic decision tree* corresponding to the training data is also constructed using only the attribute *physician-fee-freeze.* The *physician-fee-freeze's PAT* is constructed using the attribute *el-salvador-aid.* Consequently, when *physician-fee-freeze* is unknown, we calculate his probability according to *el-salvador-aid.*

For the threshold 0.4, our *probabilistic decision tree* corresponding to the training data is constructed using the attributes *physician-fee-freeze, el-salvador-aid* and *education-spending.* The *PAT* for *physician-fee-freeze* is constructed using

Table 2. Result of testing *PAT* and *C4.5* on *vote* database

Vote database	Threshold	Good classification	Bad classification	50%
	0.2	**91.25%**	**08.33%**	**0.41%**
	0.3	90%	09.16%	0.83%
PAT	0.4	88.33%	11.66%	
	0.5	87.08%	12.91%	
C4.5		**83.75%**	**16.25%**	

Table 3. Result of testing *C4.5* and *PAT* with threshold 0.4 *Vote* database

physician-fee	el-salvador	education-spend	crime	PAT results	C4.5 results
?	y	y	y	**(11%, 89%)** [1]	(53%, 47%)
?	?	n	n	**(99%, 01%)**	(53%, 47%)
?	y	n	n	**(85%, 15%)**	(53%, 47%)

[1](11%, 89%)means classification's result is 11% for Democrat and 89% for Republican

Table 4. Result of testing *PAT* and *C4.5* on *Breast-cancer* database

Breast-cancer database	Threshold	Good classifi	Bad classifi	50%
	0.02	**76.08%**	**19.56%**	**4.34%**
PAT	0.03	70.65%	23.91%	5.43 %
	0.04	71.73%	28.26%	
C4.5		**70.65%**	**29.34%**	

el-salvador-aid, *education-spending* and *crime*. Consequently, when *physician-fee-freeze* is unknown, we calculate its probability according to its dependent attributes, and so on. For example, in Table 3, we notice that the probability distribution of each object depends on the other attributes values. However, with C4.5, this distribution depends only on *physician-fee-freeze*'s frequency. In our work, when two attributes are dependent and unknown at the same time[3], we deal first with the attribute which is less dependent on the class by using its *POAT* constructed according to the first proposal. Then, for the other attribute, we use its *PAT* constructed according to the second proposition.

We now present tests performed on the *Breast-cancer* database [4]. We have constructed our *PATs* and *POATs* using a training data that has 277 objects without missing values. Each object contains 9 discrete attributes whereof the attribute *breast-quad* has 5 values, *age* has 9 values, *tumor-size* has 12 values, *inv-nodes* has 13 values, and each of the attributes *menopause* and *deg-malig* has 3 values; the class can take two values (*no-recurrence-events, recurrence-events*). Therefore, using *Normalized Mutual Information* is important here because some attributes values's number are more than two. We also use a test data that has

[3] Cycle problem.

92 objects. The missing values rates in test data are: 60.86% for the attribute *node-caps*, 39.13% for the attribute *deg-malig*, 16.30% for *irradiat* and 3.23% for *tumor-size*. The result of classification of all objects in test-data is shown in Table 4. We notice that for all the thresholds, our result is equal or better than that given by C4.5.

3.2 Analysis of Classification Result

Our approach is based on the dependence between attributes. We aim at measuring the quality of our classification results to improve the performance of our approach. For this purpose, we are interested in an algorithm [3] called *Relief Algorithm*[4] which has been shown to be very efficient in estimating attributes.

RELIEF. The key idea of Relief is to estimate attributes according to how well their values distinguish among instances that are near each other. For that purpose, given a randomly selected instance R from m instances, RELIEF [2] searches for its two nearest neighbors: one H from the same class and the other M from different class. It uses a function *diff* that calculates the difference between the values of attribute for two instances. For a discrete attribute this difference is either 1 when the values are different or 0 when the values are equal. Estimating the quality *W[A]* of attribute A is defined as shown below:

$$W[A] = W[A] - \mathit{diff}(A, R, H)/m + \mathit{diff}(A, R, M)/m \quad (3)$$

The original *Relief* can deal with discrete and continuous attributes. However, it cannot deal with incomplete data and is limited to two-class problem. Its extension which solves these and some other problems is called *ReliefF* [1], [2]. *ReliefF* is able to deal with incomplete and noisy data and can be used for evaluating the attribute quality in multi-class problem. *ReliefF* also generalizes function *diff(A,* $Instance_1$*,* $Instance_2$*)* to deal with missing values. This function becomes for a discrete attribute A:

$$diff(A, I_1, I_2) = \begin{cases} 0 \ \texttt{if} & V^{(A,I_1)} = V^{(A,I_2)} \\ 1 \ \texttt{if} & V^{(A,I_1)} \neq V^{(A,I_2)} \\ 1 - P(V^{(A,I_2)}|Class_{I_1}) \ \texttt{if} & \texttt{A is unknown in } I_1 \end{cases} \quad (4)$$

Where:

- $V^{(A,I_j)}$ is the value of A in the instance I_j
- $Class_{I_1}$ is the value of class in the instance I_1
- $1 - P(V^{(A,I_2)}/Class_{I_1})$ is the probability that two instances I_1 and I_2 have different value of the given attribute A when one of instances (I_1 here) has unknown value of A .

We notice that this function calculates also the probability that two instances I_1 and I_2 have different value of the given attribute A when both instances have unknown attribute values, but we do not explain it in equation 4. However, we can find it in [1], [2].

[4] The algorithm relies entirely on statistical analysis and employs few heuristics.

Calculating the Distance Between Instances. *Relief* and *ReliefF* inspired us to calculate the distance between two instances using function in equation 4. The first instance is from the test data with missing values, the other one is from the training data without unknown attributes. The total distance is simply the sum of difference over all the attributes [2]. The Distance function is shown in equation 5 below:

$$Distance(I_1, I_2) = \sum_{j=1}^{j=n} diff(A_j, I_1, I_2)^5 \tag{5}$$

For example, if the distance between two instances is 5, it means that there are 5 attributes whose values are different in the two instances.

In our experimentation, to measure the quality of our classification results, we compare each instance in the test data with all the instances in the training data by calculating the distance between them using the function in equation 5. Then for each test instance, we calculate the frequency of its nearest instances from each class. This frequency, which is a statistical result, will be compared with the classification result obtained by the *PAT* approach for the same test instance. For this purpose, we propose an algorithm which is presented below.

Instance Analysis Algorithm

```
Input: test instance Inst,  n training instances I;
Output: for Inst: frequency of nearest instances from the same class
        and frequency of nearest instances from the different class;
Function Instance-Analysis(Inst:test instance,
                 I:array[1..n] of instances):Pc:array[1..2] of real;
Const
  near=5,
var
 nbSCL, nbDCL, k, near: integer;
                   dis: real;
 begin
  nbSCL=0, nbDCL=0;
  For k:=1  to n  do
      begin
       dis= Distance(Inst,I[k])
       If dis < near   {the two instances are nearest neighbor}
       then
         If (two instances Inst and I[k] are from the same Class)
           then nbSCL++
           else nbDCL++;
      end; (*for k*)
 Pc1= P(nearest instances from the same class)= nbSCL/(nbDCL+nbSCL)
 Pc2= P(nearest instances from the different class)= nbDCL/(nbDCL+nbSCL)
 end;
return(Pc);
```

[5] n is the number of attributes.

Table 5. Result of testing *Instance Analysis Algorithm* on *Vote* database

physician-fee	el-salvador	education	crime	near=8	near=10	near=12
?	y	y	y	(16%, 83%)	(29%, 70%)	(38%, 61%)
?	?	n	n	(91%, 08%)	(84%, 15%)	(70%, 29%)
?	y	n	n	(92%, 07%)	(75%, 24%)	(57%, 42%)

In the algorithm given above, we present only the treatment of two-class problems. However, in our experimentation, we also deal with the mutli-class problem. The constant *near* is fixed by the user. We consider that two instances are nearest if the distance between them is lower than *near*. For a test instance, this algorithm tells us statistically about the proportion of its nearest instances from each class. We then compare this frequency with the classification result obtained by the *PAT* approach for the same test instance.

Results: To illustrate our experience using the *Instance Analysis Algorithm* proposed above, we present only the result of testing this algorithm on the same examples as presented in Table 3 from the *vote* database. The *vote* database has 16 attributes, so the constant *near* may be 8, 9, 10, 11, or 12. Table 5 contains the results of testing this algorithm only when *near* is 8, 10 and 12. By comparing Table 3 which contains *PAT's* results and C4.5's results with Table 5 which contains statistical results according to *Analysis-Instance* algorithm for the same examples, we remark that *PAT's* results in Table 3 are closer to the statistical results in Table 5 when *near* is 8. Therefore, they are better than the C4.5's results when *near* is 8, 10 or 12. Therefore, our results are closer to reality.

4 Conclusion and Perspectives

In this paper, we have introduced a probabilistic approach to fill missing values in decision trees during classification. We proposed replacing an unknown attribute with a probability distribution and taking into account the dependence between attributes. We tested our approach on some real databases and we compared our results with those given by C4.5 for the same databases. We are also inspired by *Relief* and its extensions to calculate the distance between two instances with missing values. For each instance in the test data, our *Analysis-Instance* algorithm tells us statistically the proportion of its nearest instances from each class. We compared the results obtained by *Analysis-Instance* algorithm with *PAT's* results and C4.5's results. Moreover, we observed that our classification results are closer to reality and better than those given by C4.5. We note that a recursive algorithm, which is not presented in this paper, is proposed in our approach *(PAOTs and PATs)* to classify an instance with missing values. This algorithm is more complex. In future work, we are currently calculating the complexity of this algorithm and testing our approach on more databases.

References

1. Robnik-Sikonja M., Kononenko I.: Attribute Dependencies, Understandability and Split Selection in Tree Based Models. In: Bratko, I. and Dzeroski, S., (eds.), Machine Learning: Proceedings of the Sixteenth International Conference ICML99), pages 344–353. Morgan Kaufmann Publishers (1999)
2. Kononenko, I.: Estimating attributes: Analysis and extensions of RELIEF. In Proceedings of the 1994 European Conference on Machine Learning (1994) 171–182.
3. Kira, K. and Rendell, L.A.: A Practical Approach to Feature Selection In Sleeman, D. and Edwards, J. (eds.) Proceedings of International Conference on Machine Learning, pages 249-256, Morgan Kaufmann, (1992)
4. Blake C.L. and Merz C.J.: UCI Repository of machine learning databases [http://www.ics.uci.edu/ mlearn/MLRepository.html]. Irvine, CA: University of California, Department of Information and Computer Science (1998)
5. Breiman L., Friedman J.H., Olshen R.A. and Stone C.J.: Classification and Regression Trees, Wadsworth and Brooks (1984)
6. Crémilleux B.: Induction automatique: aspects théoriques, le systéme ARBRE, Applications en médecine. Thése de doctorat, Université Joseph Fourier(1991)
7. Kononenko I., Bratko I. and Roskar E.: Experiments in Automatic Learning of Medical Diagnostic Rules, Technical Report, Jozef Stefan Institute, Ljubljana, Yugoslavia (1984)
8. Friedman J.H., Kohavi R. and Yun Y.: Lazy Decision Trees, AAAI (1996)
9. Hawarah L., Simonet A. and Simonet M.: A probabilistic approach to classify incomplete objects using decision trees, Spain, DEXA. LNCS 3180 pp. 549-558, (2004)
10. Hawarah L., Simonet A. and Simonet M.: Classement d'objets incomplets dans un arbre de dcision probabiliste, Deuxime atelier sur la "Fouille de donnes complexes dans un processus d'extraction des connaissances", Paris, EGC (2005)
11. Hawarah L., Simonet A. and Simonet M.: Evaluation d'une approche probabiliste pour le classement d'objets incompltement connus dans un arbre de dcision, Troisime atelier sur la "Fouille de donnes complexes dans un processus d'extraction des connaissances", Lille, EGC (2006)
12. Lobo O.O. and Numao M.: Ordered estimation of missing values, Pacific-Asia Conference on Knowledge Discovery and Data Mining(1999)
13. Lobo O.O. and Numao M.: Ordered estimation of missing values for propositional learning, Japanese Society for Artificial Intelligence, JSAI, vol.15, no.1(2000)
14. Lobo O.O. and Numao M.: Suitable Domains for Using Ordered Attribute Trees to Impute Missing Values. IEICE TRANS. INF. and SYST., Vol.E84-D, NO.2 (2001)
15. Quinlan J.R.: Unknown attribute values in induction. Proc. Sixth International Machine Learning Workshop, Morgan Kaufmann (1989)
16. Quinlan J.R.: Induction of decision trees. Machine Learning, 1, pp.81–106 (1986)
17. Quinlan J.R.: Probabilistic decision trees, in Machine Learning: an Artificial Intelligence Approach, ed.Y.Kodratoff, vol.3, Morgan Kaufmann, San Mateo, pp.140-152 (1990)
18. Quinlan. J.R: C4.5 Programs for Machine Learning, Morgan Kaufmann(1993)
19. Shannon C.E., Weaver W.: Théorie Mathématique de la communication, les classiques des sciences humaines (1949)
20. White A.P. Liu W.Z., Thompson S.G. and Bramer M.A.: Techniques for Dealing with Missing Values in Classification. LNCS 1280, pp. 527-536 (1997)

Multiway Pruning for Efficient Iceberg Cubing

Xiuzhen Zhang and Pauline Lienhua Chou

School of CS & IT, RMIT University, Melbourne, VIC 3001, Australia
{zhang, lchou}@cs.rmit.edu.au

Abstract. Effective pruning is essential for efficient iceberg cube computation. Previous studies have focused on exclusive pruning: regions of a search space that do not satisfy some condition are excluded from computation. In this paper we propose inclusive and anti-pruning. With inclusive pruning, necessary conditions that solutions must satisfy are identified and regions that can not be reached by such conditions are pruned from computation. With anti-pruning, regions of solutions are identified and pruning is not applied. We propose the multiway pruning strategy combining exclusive, inclusive and anti-pruning with bounding aggregate functions in iceberg cube computation. Preliminary experiments demonstrate that the multiway-pruning strategy improves the efficiency of iceberg cubing algorithms with only exclusive pruning.

1 Introduction

Since the introduction of the CUBE operator [6], the computation of data cubes has attracted much research [3,7,10]. Data cubes consist of aggregates for partitions produced by group-by's of all subsets of a given set of grouping attributes called dimensions. Given an aggregation constraint, aggregates in a data cube that satisfy the constraint form an iceberg cube [3]. Pruning is critical to the efficiency of iceberg cube computation, as the cube size grows exponentially with the number of dimensions. With traditional pruning strategies [1,3,4,7,9,10] regions of the search space that do not satisfy a constraint are identified and then pruned from computation.

In this paper, we propose two new pruning techniques. (1) Inclusive pruning identifies conditions that the solutions must meet, and units under search that do not meet any of these conditions can not be solutions and thus are pruned. (2) Anti-pruning identifies regions where all units in the regions are solutions and testing for pruning is saved. We also propose inclusive and anti-pruning strategies with bounding aggregate functions for efficient iceberg cubing. Our initial experiments confirm that multiway-pruning improves the efficiency of cubing.

With traditional pruning, conditions are identified that warrant non-solutions. In this sense, it is termed *exclusive pruning*. With traditional exclusive pruning, the larger the solution set, the more tests for the pruning condition result in fruitless effort and become extra unnecessary cost. To the contrary of exclusive pruning, the cost for inclusive pruning does not increase and anti-pruning becomes better with larger solution set. Exclusive, inclusive and anti-pruning are

S. Bressan, J. Küng, and R. Wagner (Eds.): DEXA 2006, LNCS 4080, pp. 203–212, 2006.

collectively called the *multiway pruning* strategy. Without inclusive pruning and anti-pruning, traditional exclusive pruning still compute the complete solutions and prunes correctly. However, it incurs extra cost. Inclusive and anti-pruning can not replace exclusive pruning, but complement exclusive pruning and in many cases greatly reduce the cost for pruning.

1.1 Related Work

Studies in the iceberg cubing literature have all focused on exclusive pruning strategies in iceberg cube computation [3,7,10,12].

Another related area is constraint data mining. Several types of constraints have been proposed and their properties are used for pruning [1,8,9]. All these work focus on exclusive pruning, expect in Reference [8]. The succinct constraints in Reference [8] are conceptually similar to inclusive pruning, however they are constraints orthogonal to the constraints for exclusive pruning. Our inclusive pruning does not rely on extra constraints and it is used to enhance exclusive pruning.

The term *inclusive pruning* was coined by Webb [11] in the area of machine learning. Specific pruning rules were developed for classification learning. We introduce inclusive pruning into iceberg cube mining and develop inclusive pruning strategies for aggregation constraints based on bounding.

The concept of border was used in data mining to represent large spaces [2,5]. Rather than computing borders, we focus on using borders for more effective pruning and to compute all solutions in the space represented by borders.

2 Preliminaries on Data Cubes

Dimensional datasets are defined by *dimensions* and *measures*. In Table 1, there are 4 dimensions Month, Product, SalesMan (Man) and City, and Sale (aggregated as Sum(Sale)) is the measure. Throughout this paper we use upper-case letters to denote dimensions and lower-case letters to denote dimension-values. For example $(\mathtt{A}, \mathtt{B}, \mathtt{C})$ denotes a group-by and $(\mathtt{a}, \mathtt{b}, \mathtt{c})$ denotes a partition of tuples from the $(\mathtt{A}, \mathtt{B}, \mathtt{C})$ group-by, and is called a *group*. We also use an upper case letter for a measure attribute to represent the set of values for the measure.

The group-bys in a data cube form a lattice structure called the *cube lattice*. Fig. 1 shows an example 4-dimensional cube lattice, where each node denotes a group-by list. The empty group-by that aggregates all tuples in a dataset is at the bottom of the lattice and the group-by with all dimensions is at the top of the lattice. Group-bys form subset/superset relationships. Groups from different group-bys also form super-group/sub-group relationships.

A special value "*" is assumed in the domain of all dimensions, which can match any value of the dimension. With the Sales dataset, the $(\mathtt{Jan}, *, *, *)$ group denotes the partition of tuples with $\mathtt{Month} = \mathtt{January}$ and no restriction on values for the other dimensions. For simplicity, $(\mathtt{Jan}, *, *, *)$ is also written as $(\mathtt{Jan})$. The 3-dimensional group $(\mathtt{Jan}, \mathtt{TV}, \mathtt{Perth})$ is a sub-group of the 2-dimensional groups $(\mathtt{Jan}, \mathtt{TV})$, $(\mathtt{Jan}, \mathtt{Perth})$ and $(\mathtt{TV}, \mathtt{Perth})$.

Table 1. A sales dataset, partially aggregated

Month	Prod	Man	City	Cnt(*)	Sum(Sale)
Jan	Toy	John	Perth	5	200
Mar	TV	Peter	Perth	40	100
Mar	TV	John	Perth	20	100
Mar	TV	John	Syd	10	100
Apr	TV	Peter	Perth	8	100
Apr	Toy	Peter	Syd	5	100

Table 2. The bounds of some aggregate functions ($\{X_i \| i = 1..n\}$ are MSPs)

F	upper bound; lower bound
Cnt	$\text{Sum}_i\ \text{Cnt}(X_i)$; $\text{Min}_i\ \text{Cnt}(X_i)$
Max	$\text{Max}_i\ \text{Max}(X_i)$; $\text{Min}_i\ \text{Max}(X_i)$
Min	$\text{Max}_i\ \text{Min}(X_i)$; $\text{Min}_i\ \text{Min}(X_i)$
Avg	$\text{Max}_i\ \text{Avg}(X_i)$; $\text{Min}_i\ \text{Avg}(X_i)$
Sum	if there exists $\text{Sum}(X_i) > 0$, $\text{Sum}_{\text{Sum}(X_i)>0}\ \text{Sum}(X_i)$, otherwise $\text{Max}_i\ \text{Sum}(X_i)$; if there exists $\text{Sum}(X_i) < 0$, $\text{Sum}_{\text{Sum}(X_i)<0}\ \text{Sum}(X_i)$, otherwise $\text{Min}_i\ \text{Sum}(X_i)$

Given a dataset S of n dimensions A_1, ..., A_n with the measure X, the data cube of applying F on S can be expressed in two ways: (1) Cube($A_1, ..., A_n$) can be viewed as the set of possible group-bys, or the set of possible groups for all group-bys. (2) $\text{Cube}(X) = \{X_i = \{t[X] \mid t \in g_i\} \mid g_i \text{ is a partition of the cube}\}$; that is, a data cube is expressed as partitions of multi-set of measure values following the grouping of tuples.

3 Bounding Aggregate Functions

Bounding was proposed as a technique to prune for complex aggregation constraints [12]. The idea of bounding is to estimate the upper and lower bounds for data cubes from the most specific partitions (MSPs) of data. The Sales dataset comprises 6 MSPs, as shown in Table 1. Each MSPs has been aggregated with functions Count(*) (denoted as Cnt(*)) and Sum(Sale).

We generalize the original definition of data cubes [6]. Fig. 1 shows Cube(ABCD), and it can be decomposed into two lattice structures: The nodes in the right polygon form Cube(BCD). For each partition of data with $a_i \in$ domain(A), the nodes in the left polygon form a data cube on dimensions {B, C, D} conditioned on $a_i \in$ domain(A). In later discussions we use the term data cube to refer to both unconditional data cubes and conditional data cubes.

The concept of data cube core was coined by Gray et al. [6] it was generalized to conditional data cubes. Given Cube($A_1, ..., A_n$) over measure X, all n-dimensional partitions $\{(a_1, ..., a_n) | a_i \neq *, a_i \in \text{domain}(A_i), 1 \leq i \leq n\}$ comprise the *core* of the data cube and each partition g in the core is a *Most Specific Partition* (MSP). The multi-set of measure values for tuples in an MSP g, namely $\{t[X] | t \in g_i\}$, is an MSP of the measure. All aggregates in a data cube can be computed from its MSPs. In Fig. 1, any group in Cube(BCD)$|a_1$ can be computed from some (a_1, b_i, c_j, d_k) groups and any group in Cube(BCD) can be computed

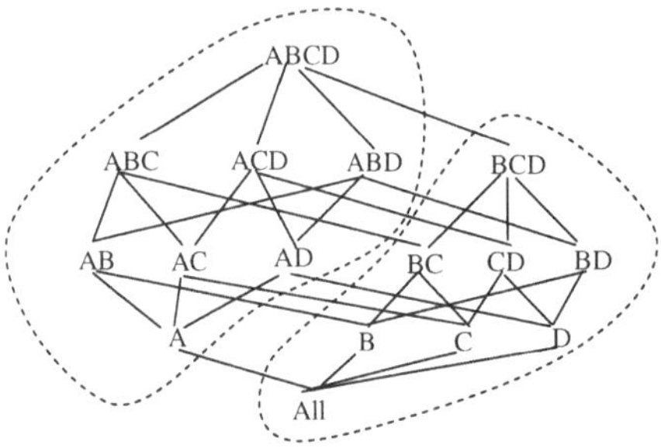

Fig. 1. Cube(ABCD) decomposition

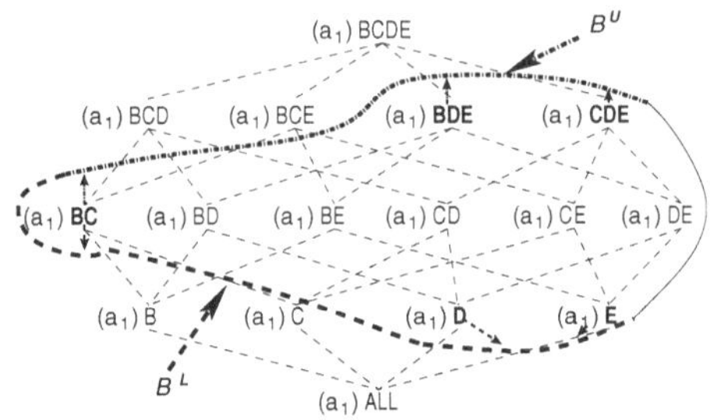

Fig. 2. *An anti-pruning border on the lattice conditioned on (a_1)*

from some $(\mathtt{b_i}, \mathtt{c_j}, \mathtt{d_k})$ groups, where i, j and k iterates over values in the domain of B, C and D respectively.

Given an aggregate function F, and a multi-dimensional dataset with measure X, the upper (lower) bound for a data cube is a real number such that for any partition $X_i \in \text{Cube}(X)$, $F(X_i)$ is no larger (smaller) than the upper (lower) bound. An aggregate function F is boundable for a data cube if the upper and lower bounds for the data cube can be determined with a single scan of the local aggregate values of the MSPs. The bounds for some commonly seen aggregate functions are listed in Table 2. We use Count(*) as an example to explain. The Count(*) for any group in a data cube is no larger than $\text{Sum}_i\,\text{Cnt}(X_i)$, the sum of Count(*) all MSPs. The Count(*) for any group in a data cube is no smaller than $\text{Min}_i\,\text{Cnt}(X_i)$, the smallest Count(*) among all MSPs. Moreover, these bounds are the tightest bounds for Count(*). Indeed arithmetic expressions of base functions Sum, Count, Min, and Max are boundable. Details of bounding algorithms are discussed in Reference [12].

4 Inclusive Pruning with Bounding

Inclusive pruning is applied before computing the bounds of data cubes for exclusive pruning. Dimension values that solutions in a lattice must have are called *inclusive dimension values.* Groups that are defined by only non-inclusive dimension-values are definitely not solutions and should be pruned.

Definition 1. *Given a data cube to be computed with some constraint, the inclusive dimension values are those that define groups that are solutions.*

From this definition, dimension values that do not involve any solutions are non-inclusive dimension values.

Theorem 1 (Inclusive pruning). *Given a cube lattice $\mathcal{L}$, an aggregation constraint, and a set of inclusive dimension values, groups in $\mathcal{L}$ that are defined by only non-inclusive dimension values are not solutions and can be pruned.*

Proof. All solution groups in $\mathcal{L}$ must be grouped by at least one inclusive dimension value. A group in $\mathcal{L}$ whose grouping dimension values are solely defined by non-inclusive dimensions can not be a solution and so can be pruned.

The question to answer now is how to identify the inclusive dimension values in a cube lattice before it is computed. As will be seen in Section 6, the inclusive dimension values for a cube are decided in the previous computation of its super-cubes: all dimensions-values whose bounds have non-empty intersection with the interval defined by thresholds of the given constraint are inclusive dimension values for the cube. Importantly these bounds can be computed by a single traversal of the MSPs. As a result we have the benefit of pruning with little extra cost. Inclusive pruning is achieved by removing branches that contain only non-inclusive dimension-values. Note that these branches are pruned from all sub-trees that are to be computed.

5 Anti-pruning with Bounding

When the selectivity of an aggregation constraint is high, a large number of groups are qualified as iceberg groups. When the data is skewed, the iceberg groups reside in a few regions of the cube. In both cases, examining the pruning conditions on these groups does not result in any pruning. We introduce the notion of the *Anti-pruning border* to mark regions where all groups are solutions.

Definition 1. (Anti-pruning region) *In iceberg-cubing, given a lattice $\mathcal{L}$ an anti-pruning region is a convex space of groups that are all solutions. An anti-pruning region $\mathcal{B}$ can be denoted as $\langle \mathcal{B}^L, \mathcal{B}^U \rangle$: $\mathcal{B}^L$ is the lower border where none of their supergroups are in $\mathcal{B}$. $\mathcal{B}^U$ is the upper border consisting of groups in $\mathcal{B}$ where none of their subgroups are in $\mathcal{B}$.*

Example 1. *An example anti-pruning border on the lattice of* B, C, D, *and* E *conditioned on (a_1) is shown in Fig. 2. The upper border consists of the $(a_1\mathsf{BC})$, $(a_1\mathsf{BDE})$, and $(a_1\mathsf{CDE})$ group-bys and the lower border consists of the $(a_1\mathsf{BC})$, $(a_1\mathsf{D})$, and $(a_1\mathsf{E})$ group-bys. The anti-pruning region contains groups that are supergroups of some group in the $(a_1\mathsf{BC})$, $(a_1\mathsf{BDE})$, and $(a_1\mathsf{CDE})$ group-bys as well as subgroups of some group in the $(a_1\mathsf{BC})$, $(a_1\mathsf{D})$, and $(a_1\mathsf{E})$ group-bys.*

An anti-pruning region is a maximum region in a group-lattice where pruning is unnecessary. The groups within the region covered by the anti-pruning borders are definitely solutions. We aim to compute anti-pruning regions that are lattices with little extra cost. We observe that lattices are convex spaces: Given a lattice conditioned on a group g, the lattice is a convex space where all groups are subgroups of g and supergroups of some MSPs. We make use of bounding to detect anti-pruning regions that are lattices, as shown in the observation below.

Observation 1. *Given a lattice conditioned on a group g, if both bounds satisfy a given constraint, the MSPs are the upper anti-pruning border $\mathcal{B}^U$, and g is the lower anti-pruning border $\mathcal{B}^L$; the lattice of g is an anti-pruning region. All groups in the lattice satisfy the constraint.*

For iceberg cubes with complex aggregation constraints, the cost of checking for the pruning conditions is high. Detecting a group-lattice that is an anti-pruning region supposedly improves the efficiency of cubing algorithms.

6 Multiway Bound-Prune Cubing on G-Trees

The Group tree (G-tree) is our data structure for cubing. The G-tree for an n-dimensional dataset is of depth n, where each level represents a dimension. A common path starting from the root collapses the tuples with common dimension-values. Each tree node keeps the local aggregates necessary to compute the iceberg cube for a given aggregate function. A G-tree is constructed by one scan of the input data.

The G-tree in Fig. 3 represents the Sales dataset. To compute the data cube with aggregate function Average, the local aggregates in each node are Sum(`Sale`) and Cnt($*$). On the leftmost path node (`March`) shows that there are 70 tuples with Sum(`Sale`) $= 300$ in the (`March`, $*, *, *$) group, whereas the node (`Peter`) shows that there are 40 tuples with Sum(`Sale`) $= 100$ in the (`March`, `TV`, `Peter`, $*$) group.

6.1 Top-Down Aggregation on G-Trees

Top-down aggregation on G-trees is based on the following observation: Construction of an n-dimensional G-tree has computed n group-bys, namely the group-bys whose dimensions are prefixes of the given list of dimensions. With the G-tree in Fig. 3, the root node has the aggregate for the group $(*, *, *, *)$ with Cnt$(*)$ $= 88$ and Sum(`Sale`) $= 700$; The nodes at level one compute the aggregates for groups in (`Month`, $*, *, *$), which are (`March`, $*, *, *, 70, 300$), (`January`, $*, *, *, 5, 200$), and (`April`, $*, *, *, 13, 200$). The nodes at the next 3 levels compute the aggregates for (`Month`, `Product`), (`Month`, `Product`, `Man`), and (`Month`, `Product`, `Man`, `City`) respectively.

Let A, B, C and D denote the four dimensions of the Sales dataset. The group-bys that are not represented on the G-tree in Fig. 3 are computed by collapsing one dimension at a time to construct sub-G-trees. In Fig. 4, each node represents a G-tree and all group-bys that are simultaneously computed on the G-tree. The `ABCD`-tree representing the tree of Fig. 3 is at the top. The group-bys `(A,B,C,D)`, `(A,B,C)`, `(A,B)`, `(A)` and `()` are computed on the `(A,B,C,D)`-tree. The sub-trees of the `ABCD`-tree, (−`A`)`BCD`, `A`(−`B`)`CD`, and `AB`(−`C`)`D`, are formed by collapsing on dimensions A, B, and C respectively.

6.2 Multiway Pruning on G-Trees

In Fig. 3, the leaf nodes of the G-tree are the MSPs for Cube (`Mon`, `Prod`, `Man`, `City`). The dimensions after "/" in each node of Fig. 4 denote prefix dimensions for the tree at the node and all its sub-trees. `A` is the prefix dimension for the `ACD`-tree and its sub-trees. All group-bys that are computed on the `ACD`-tree and its sub-trees form data cubes conditioned on some A-value, Cube(`CD`)$|a_i$, where i iterates over

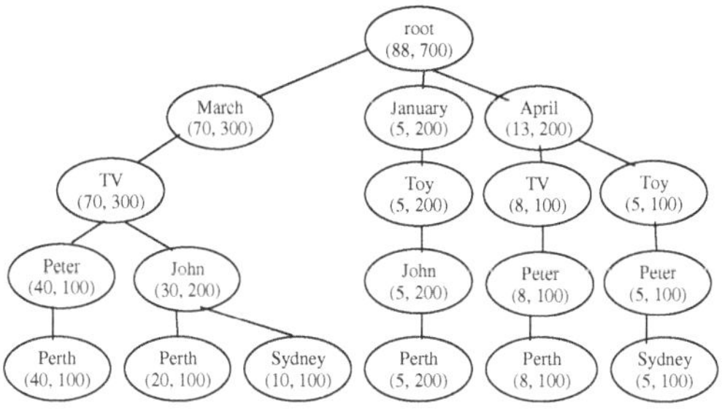

Fig. 3. A sample G-tree

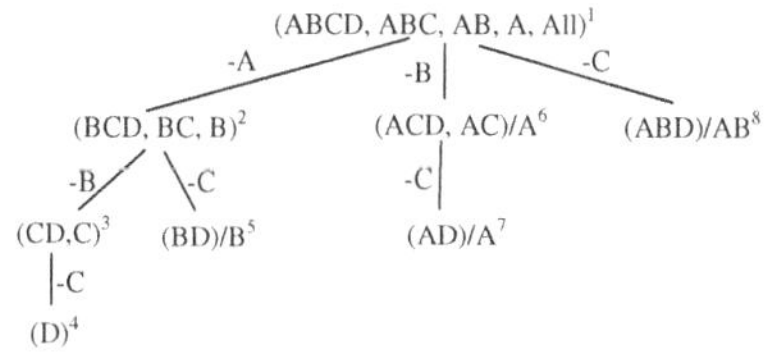

Fig. 4. Top-down cubing of a 4 dimensional data cube with shared dimensions

the values of A. The leaf nodes originated from a_i are the MSPs for Cube(CD)|$\texttt{a}_\texttt{i}$. The bounds for Cube(ACDE)|$\texttt{a}_\texttt{i}$ are obtained by a traversal of the leaf nodes originated from $\texttt{a}_\texttt{i}$. With the G-tree over dimensions Month, Product, Man, and City in Fig. 3, before collapsing on Product, we calculate the bounds for the cube lattices conditioned on each dimension value. Following Fig. 2, the bounds for Cube (Product, Man, City)|March are computed from the three leaf nodes originated from (March) of G:

$$\overline{\text{Avg}(\text{Cube}\,(\texttt{Man}, \texttt{City})|\texttt{Mar})} = \text{Max}(\{100/40, 100/20, 100/10\}) = 10;$$
$$\underline{\text{Avg}(\text{Cube}\,(\texttt{Man}, \texttt{City})|\texttt{Mar})} = \text{Min}(\{100/40, 100/20, 100/10\}) = 2.5.$$

Inclusive pruning is achieved by identifying $\mathcal{I}$, the set of inclusive dimension-values for a cube lattice before its aggregates are computed. Given a G-tree G on dimensions $A_1, ..., A_n$, the bounds for Cube$(A_{k+1}, ..., A_n)|a_1, ..., a_{k-1}, 1 < k < n$, are computed from the leaf nodes originated from the node a_k. If the bound interval does not violate the given constraint, a_k should be added to $\mathcal{I}$. After $\mathcal{I}$ is obtained, the G-tree is traversed again in depth-first order for inclusive pruning. At each node, if its dimension-value is from $\mathcal{I}$, the traversal to its children is terminated because the branch is not to be trimmed. If the traversal reaches a leaf node, the branch is trimmed. From the leaf upwards, the nodes on the branch that have no children are deleted.

Observation 2 (Inclusive pruning). *Consider computing an iceberg cube with the constraint "$F(X)$ in $[\delta_1, \delta_2]$". Given a G-tree with n dimensions A_1, ..., A_n, Suppose $[b_1, b_2]$ are the bounds for* Cube$(A_{k+1}, ..., A_n)|a_1, ..., a_{k-1}$, *the sub-cube by collapsing a_k $(1 < k < n)$, inclusive dimension-values are those a_k such that $[b_1, b_2] \cap [\delta_1, \delta_2] \neq \phi$. Branches defined by only non-inclusive dimension-values are pruned from computation.*

After inclusive pruning branches on a G-tree that can not contain solutions have been pruned from computation. With the bounds computed for each cube lattice, exclusive- and anti-pruning are then applied.

Observation 3 (Exclusive- and anti-pruning). *Consider computing an iceberg cube with the constraint "$F(X)$ in $[\delta_1, \delta_2]$". Given a G-tree for dimensions $A_1, ..., A_n$, let $[b_1, b_2]$ be the bounds for* $\text{Cube}(A_{k+1}, ..., A_n)|a_1, ..., a_{k-1}$*, the cube by collapsing A_k $(1 < k < n)$. If $[b_1, b_2] \cap [\delta_1, \delta_2] = \phi$, the branches originated from the node $(a_1, ..., a_{k-1})$ can be pruned; otherwise if $[b_1, b_2] \cap [\delta_1, \delta_2] = [b_1, b_2]$, all groups in* $\text{Cube}(A_{k+1}, ..., A_n)$ *are qualified groups.*

6.3 The MBPC Algorithm

We present the Multiway Bound-Prune Cubing (MBPC) algorithm for computing iceberg cubes, with inclusive- exclusive and anti-pruning strategies. The algorithm is shown as Algorithm 1.

Algorithm 1. The MBPC Algorithm

// Assume that an n-dimensional G-tree T with aggregate function F is constructed.
// The iceberg cube is computed by calling MBPC($T(A_1, ..., A_n)$, ϕ).
Input: a) T is a G-tree with conditional base B.
    b) Aggregate constraint " $F(X)$ in $[\delta_1, \delta_2]$" is assumed global.
Output: The iceberg groups in the iceberg cube.
MBPC($T(B_1, ..., B_m)$, B)
(1) **for each** dimension $i = 1..m-1$ **do**
(2)   **for each** node b_i of dimension B_i on T
(3)   Output the group g conditioned on B if F(g) in $[\delta_1, \delta_2]$;
(4)   Compute the bounds $[b_1, b_2]$ and $\mathcal{I}$ for $Cube(B_{i+1}, ..., B_m)|B \cup \{b_i\}$;
      // inclusive pruning
(5)   Prune branches formed by only dimension-values from $\neg\mathcal{I}$;
(6)   **if** ($[b_1, b_2] \cap [\delta_1, \delta_2] = \phi$)
(7)   break; *// exclusive pruning*
(8)   **else if** ($[b_1, b_2] \cap [\delta_1, \delta_2] = [b_1, b_2]$)
(9)   compute all groups in $\text{Cube}(B_{i+1}, ..., B_m)|B \cup \{b_i\}$;
(10)   break; *//anti-pruning*
(11)   for $j = i + 1..m$ do
(12)   Construct the sub-tree T_s by collapsing B_j;
(13)   **MBPC**($T_s, B \cup \{b_i\}$);

A G-tree is built by one scan of the input dataset and is the input for MBPC. MBPC is a recursive procedure where with each recursion, an additional dimension-value is accumulated in g, the group to be computed. For the ease of presentation, one group g is processed a time in Algorithm 1. Indeed with top-down cubing on the G-tree, multiple groups are simultaneously processed. The steps involved in each group are the same.

At line 3 of the algorithm, the groups that are computed on an G-tree are conditioned on the conditional base B of the tree. Initially the conditional base is empty. The prefix dimension-value before the collapsing dimension is accumulated into the conditional base B within each recursion. The bounds are obtained

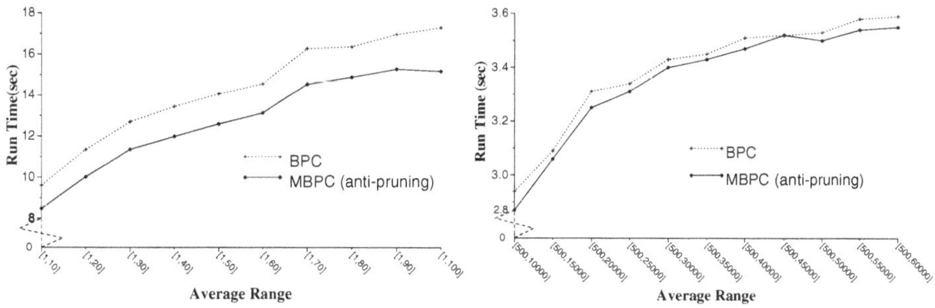

(a) Weather (100,000 tuples, 9 dimensions) (b) Census (88,443 tuples, 12 dimensions)

Fig. 5. Performance comparison of MBPC (anti-pruning) and BPC

when the branches under the prefix groups are amalgamated. No extra scan of the tree is required.

Inclusive pruning (line 5) is applied before further aggregation of subgroups. For the top-down iceberg cubing on the G-tree, a list $\mathcal{I}$ is created when the G-tree is built. The list consists of dimension-values of the G-tree, each is associated with a bit-vector. When the G-tree is traversed in depth-first order to obtain the bounds for the nodes on the G-tree, the bounds for the dimension-values in the the list are also obtained; they determine which branches can be trimmed.

The test for anti-pruning (line 8) can be combined with that for exclusive pruning (line 6) as a single test, where the intersection of the two ranges is performed only once. Anti-pruning (line 9) is applied by aggregation of groups without any bounding or bounding test being performed.

7 Experiments

We conducted preliminary experiments to examine the performance of MBPC. We implemented MBPC with anti-pruning and compared its performance with that of BPC, that uses only exclusive bound pruning. Experiments were conducted on a PC with i686 processor running GNU/Linux.

Two datasets were used in our experiments. The weather dataset[1] is the weather reports collected at various weather stations globally in 1985. Nine of the attributes such as `station-id`, `longitude`, and `latitude` are used as dimensions and the cardinalities range from 2 to 6505. Numbers between 1 and 100 were randomly generated as the measure. The US census dataset[2] was collected from surveys about various aspects of individuals in the households in US in 1990. The original dataset has 61 different attributes such as `hrswork1`(hours worked last week) and `valueh`(value of the house). We selected 12 discrete

[1] http://cdiac.ornl.gov/ftp/ndp026b/SEP85L.DAT.Z

[2] ftp://ftp.ipums.org/ipums/data/ip19001.Z

attributes as dimensions and a numeric attribute as the measure. Census is dense and skewed and Weather is very sparse.

The results of computing iceberg cubes with the constraint "Avg(X) in $[\delta_1, \delta_2]$" are shown in Fig. 5. The time reported does not include time for output. Generally anti-pruning further improves the efficiency of the BPC algorithm. Moreover, as δ_2 get larger and the iceberg cube to compute get larger, more pronounced improvement can be observed. MBPC shows significant improvement in run time over BPC on Weather. MBPC outperforms BPC consistently by about 13% for different aggregation constraint thresholds. MBPC shows modest improvement over BPC on the Census dataset.

8 Conclusions

We have proposed multiway pruning strategies in iceberg cubing: exclusive, inclusive and anti-pruning. We have also presented an iceberg cubing algorithm with the multiway pruning strategy with bounding. Our initial experiments with anti-pruning has shown that the multiway pruning strategy can significantly improve efficiency of cubing algorithms, especially on computing large cubes. More extensive experiments are underway to examine the effectiveness of inclusive pruning and the multiway pruning strategy with respect to general data characteristics.

References

1. R. Agrawal and R. Srikant. Fast algorithms for mining association rules. In *Proc. of VLDB'94*, pages 487–499, Santiago, Chile.
2. R. J. Bayardo. Efficiently mining long patterns from databases. In *Proc. of SIGMOD'98*, pages 85–93.
3. K Beyer and R Ramakrishnan. Bottom-up computation of sparse and iceberg cubes. In *Proc. of SIGMOD'99*.
4. L. Chou and X. Zhang. Computing complex iceberg cubes by multiway aggregation and bounding. In *Proc. of DaWak'04 (LNCS 3181)*, Zaragoza Spain.
5. G. Dong and J. Li. Efficient mining of emerging patterns: Discovering trends and differences. In *Proc. of KDD'99*, pages 15–18, San Diego, USA.
6. J Gray et al. Data cube: a relational aggregation operator generalizing group-by, cross-tab, and sub-totals. *Data Mining and Knowledge Discovery*, 1(1), 1997.
7. J Han, J Pei, G Dong, and K Wang. Efficient computation of iceberg cubes with complex measures. In *Proc. of SIGMOD'01*.
8. R. Ng, L. V. S. Lakshmanan, J. Han, and A. Pang. Exploratory mining and pruning optimizations of constrained associations rules. In *Proc. of SIGMOD'98*.
9. J. Pei, J. Han, and L. V. S. Lakshmanan. Mining frequent itemsets with convertible constraints. In *Proc. of ICDE'01*.
10. K. Wang et al. Divide-and-approximate: A novel constraint push strategy for iceberg cube mining. *IEEE TKDE*, 17(3):354–368, March 2005.
11. G. I. Webb. Inclusive pruning: a new class of pruning rules for unordered search and its application to classification learning. In *Proc. of ACSC'96*.
12. X. Zhang, L. Chou and G. Dong. Efficient computation of iceberg cubes by bounding aggregate functions. *IEEE TKDE*, In submission.

Mining and Visualizing Local Experiences from Blog Entries

Takeshi Kurashima*, Taro Tezuka, and Katsumi Tanaka

Department of Social Informatics,Graduate School of Informatics,
Kyoto University,
Yoshida-Honmachi, Sakyo-ku, Kyoto 606-8501, Japan
{ktakeshi, tezuka, tanaka}@dl.kuis.kyoto-u.ac.jp
http://www.dl.kuis.kyoto-u.ac.jp/

Abstract. We describe a way to extract visitors' experiences from Weblogs (blogs) and also a way to mine and visualize activities of visitors at sightseeing spots. A system using our proposed method mines association rules between locations, time periods, and types of experiences out of blog entries. Association rules between experiences are also extracted. We constructed a local information search system that enables the user to specify a location, a time period, or a type of experience in a search query and find relevant Web content. Results of experiments showed that three proposed refinement algorithms applied to a conventional text mining method raises the precision and recall of the extracted rules.

1 Introduction

An important characteristic of Weblogs (blogs) is that they contain many descriptions of people's experiences in the real world, including experiences specific to certain time periods and geographic regions. Until recently, people gathered local information mainly from tour guides, magazine articles, local portal sites, and other commercial sources. Unfortunately, these sources contain only a small amount of information about the experiences and impressions of people who actually visited the various places. In contrast, blog entries contain a vast amount of this type of information. Actual experiences, unlike commercially prepared tourist guides or media reports, are of particular importance to potential visitors and market analysts tracking local trends. Indeed, experiences expressed on blogs are feedback from people who received local advertisements.

In this paper, we propose a way to extract tourists' experiences from blogs and also a way to mine and visualize the activities of tourists at sightseeing spots. The system obtains association rules between locations, time periods, and types of experiences based on blog entries. By combining extractions of geographic keywords with the entry time stamps, the system extracts rules among

* Kurashima is currently with NTT Cyber Solutions Laboratories, NTT Corporation, 1-1 Hikarinooka, Yokosuka-shi, Kanagawa 239-0847, Japan.

S. Bressan, J. Küng, and R. Wagner (Eds.): DEXA 2006, LNCS 4080, pp. 213–222, 2006.

these three attributes. It also extracts rules between experiences to examine the behaviors of visitors.

As an application of our proposed method, we constructed a local information search system that enables the user to specify a location, a time period, and a type of experience in a search query. The system returns candidates for the unspecified attributes. The user can choose from these candidates and move to relevant Web content. Since the extracted rules are based on activities described by a large number of blog authors, they should reflect the common preferences of visitors.

2 Related Work

Kumar et al. discussed blog link structures and proposed using *time graphs* and *time-dense community tracking* to represent the growth of blog communities and to track changes within communities [1][2]. Bar-Ilan examined links between blogs and their postings and obtained statistics [3]. Nakajima et al. also analyzed blog link structures and identified bloggers who played important roles in the blog community [4]. Fujimura et al. developed the EigenRumor algorithm for calculating a "hub score" and "authority score" after consolidating link in each blogger [5]. These analyses focused only on the relationships between blogs; they did not target the content of blog entries.

There has been a variety of research into aggregating blog entries. Okumura et al. proposed a system that collects blog entries and presents aggregated results [6][7]. The *blogWatcher* extracts hot topics that are attracting a lot of attention based on the *burst* extraction method proposed by Kleinberg [8]. Avesani et al. proposed a system that aggregates blog entries on specified topics [9]. Unlike our system, they are generic extraction systems that do not perform spatial aggregation.

There are various services that unify geographic information with blogs. DC Metro Blogmap and nyc bloggers link personal blogs to metro maps. Users of these services can find bloggers related to specific areas in a city [10][11]. World-Kit is a toolkit for creating map-based applications on the Web; it has also been applied to a blog mapping service [12]. These services require manual registration and do not support the automatic extraction of knowledge from blog entries.

In our previous papers, we suggested a method for experience extraction [13][14]. However, there were several remaining problems. One was that the precisions of extracted experiences were relatively low. Another was that the visualization method for browsing experiences was not described at full length. In this paper, we first indicate the method of experience extraction improved by considering dependency between the terms and analyzing Fillmore's case grammer. We then go into the detail of visualization method of experiences, and indicate the implemented map interface. As a new type of rules, we also mined rules between experiences. At the evaluation section, we present rules extracted by this type of mining.

3 Experience Mining Method

Our proposed experience mining method consists of three steps.

1. Collect blogs
2. Extract experiences
3. Mine association rules

Before the association rules are extracted, transaction sets are extracted from the blog entries. A transaction is a tuple consisting of a location, a point in time, an action, and an object of action. To obtain rules for actual experiences, we extract sentences that refer to actions. In text mining, the target data are documents that are not structured, so it is important to index the documents because the accuracy of the extracted rules greatly depends on it.

A simple sentence that describes a visitor's experience consists of an action and its object. In our approach, we first extract pairs of verb, noun, and particle from blog entries and enter them into the database. The system then applies three refinement algorithms based on the case of the object and on the verb meaning. The system can then spatially and temporally extract specific association rules from the blog entries because visitors' real-life experiences most likely have limited spatial and temporal extensions. The time attribute of each transaction is extracted from the RSS metadata of the corresponding blog entry, and the location attribute is extracted from the place name in the entry. Visitors often describe where they visited and the actions they performed in the same blog entry. Therefore, a co-occurrence between an action and a place name is likely to be found. Furthermore, the system extracts association rules between experiences. The following subsections describe each of these steps in more detail.

3.1 Blog Collection

Blog entries are collected using generic blog search engines provided by blog hosting services. The system first sends location name as query to generic blog search engine, and retrieve search results in RSS metadata format. The system then extract titles, contents, links, and dates from search results. The results are stored in blog database.

3.2 Experience Extraction

Analyze Dependencies. From the collected entries, transaction sets are extracted. The scheme for a transaction is

$$T = (DID, Time, Location, verb_1, ..., verb_m, noun_1, ..., noun_n, particle_1, ..., particle_o)$$

DID: document id
$Time$: date of blog entry containing the sentence
$Location$: location name (query)

The system first morphologically analyzes the $verb_i$, $noun_i$, $particle_i$ tuples extracted from each document and obtains a set of verbs for each blog entry. It then analyzes the dependencies between terms using dependency parsers. Each of the obtained verbs, phrasal units depend on the verb are extracted. Phrasal units consist of a noun and a particle.

Refinement 1: Extract Fillmore's Objective. To extract only the rules related to experiences, the transaction database must be refined. The system does this using Fillmore's case grammar, in which each phrase has a case meaning indicating its role in modifying the sentence predicate. Fillmore categorized case meaning into nine types, including agentive, instrumental, and objective. We extract sentences containing Fillmore's objective from the transactions because an experience consists of an action and its object. In Japanese, case meanings are expressed using case particles. According to a survey, the object is generally marked by "wo" or "ni" [15]. We extract sentences containing these particles.

Refinement 2: Extract Verbs Referring to Actions. In general, sentences are categorized into three groups based on their verbs.

1. "Do" statements (ex. *I saw autumn leaves.*)
2. "Become" statements (ex. *The autumn leaves turned yellow.*)
3. "Be" statements (ex. *Autumn leaves are beautiful.*)

Experiences are most closely related with the "do" statements because they indicate user action. For each of the transactions, the system eliminates any verbs not used in a do statement as well as any nouns and particles dependent on them.

Refinement 3: Eliminate Verbs Indicating Movements. Actions that do not take place in a specified location are eliminated. For example, verbs such as "go" and "come" do not indicate actions that take place at a specified location. They indicate movement toward a location. For each of the transactions, the system eliminates these verbs as well as any nouns and particles dependent on them.

3.3 Association Rule Mining

Spatially and Temporary Specific Experiences. The first target of our association rule mining is spatially and temporary specific experiences. We assume there is a strong correlation between a time, a location, a verb, and its object in the description of visitors' activities. When a visitor writes about his or her experiences on a blog, he or she generally describes where he or she visited and what he or she did, so there is usually a correlation between a location and an activity. Three types of rules are extracted.

- **Type 1:** [Location, (Time)] $\Rightarrow$ [Verb, Noun]
  The Type 1 rule is useful to visitors wanting to know about typical activities taking place at a specific place and in a certain time period.
- **Type 2:** [Location, Verb, (Time)] $\Rightarrow$ [Noun]
  The Type 2 rule is useful to visitors wanting to know about the object of a specified activity taking place at a specific place and time.

- **Type 3:** [Verb, Noun, (Time)] $\Rightarrow$ [Location]
  The Type 3 rule is useful to visitors wanting to know about the location of a specified activity and object.

Between Experiences. The second target is association rules between experiences. A typical application of association rule mining is a "market-basket analysis," which is used to specify groups of products that are likely to be purchased together. The results are useful to retails planning a marketing strategy. In the same way, the extracted rules between experiences are also useful to travel agents and potential tourists planning a trip. Therefore, the following type of rules is also extracted.

- **Type 4:** [Verb, Noun] $\Rightarrow$ [Verb, Noun]

These association rules are extracted using the APRIORI algorithm [16]. Other rules, such as those between nouns, are eliminated because they do not match our purpose.

4 Application

A system implementing our proposed method presents rules extracted from blogs and supports the user in finding local information. The user specifies a location, a time period, or a type of experience in a search query. The system returns candidates for the unspecified attributes and visualizes them on a map interface. The user chooses from among the candidates to reach relevant Web content. Since the rules are based on information provided by a large number of blog authors and the ratio of commercial blogs is still small, the rules reflect common visitor preferences.

4.1 Visualization of Experiences

The visualization module uses Type 1 rules and visualizes their consequents, which consist of a verb-noun pair on a map interface. A visual interface is shown in Figure 1. The user chooses a location name from a set of candidates, and by selecting an experience associated with the location name, the user can reach Web content of his or her interest.

The user can also specify the time attribute by a pull-down menu. By specifying an action in the text input field, the user can search for objects associated with it. For example, if the user inputs "eat" in the text input field, popular foods such as "yudouhu (boiled tohu)," "yatsuhashi (traditional cinnamon cookie)," and "matcha (green powdered tea)" are presented, together with a map indicating their associated locations. The user can then choose a destination based on his or her preference. In this instance, the system presents Type 2 rules.

4.2 Ranking of Location Names

The system ranks location names based on the extracted association rules. The user can search for Web pages of sightseeing spots using an experience query.

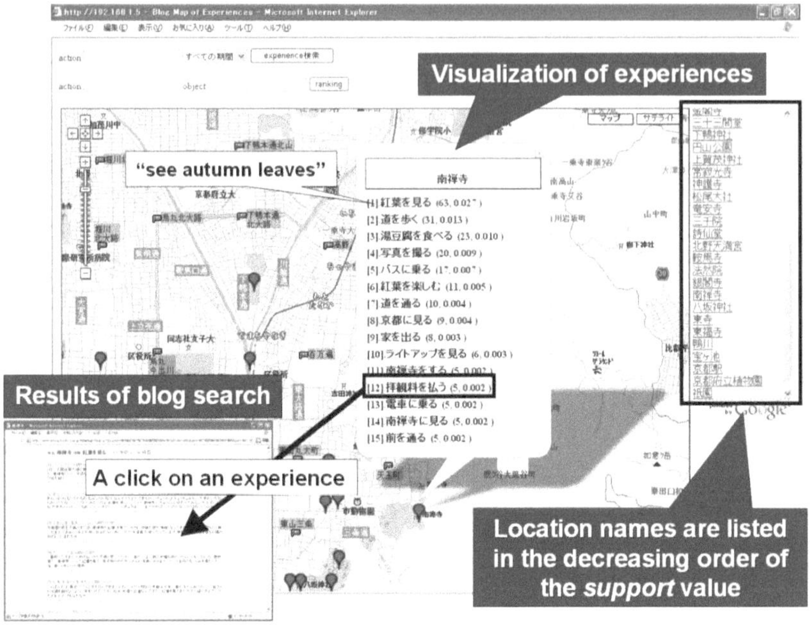

Fig. 1. Visual user interface for browsing experiences

This is useful when the wants to find the locations for a specified activity and object. The ranking results reflect their actual popularity among the bloggers. The rankings often differ greatly from the biased information in advertisements. They are calculated from the Type 3 rules. The ranking results are presented in the list box.

4.3 Blog Search

By clicking on an experience presented on the map interface, a user can refer to blog entries that contain the term. In other words, the experiences are used as a query index for the blog search engine. A user can obtain information specific to an experience of interest. Impressions based on a real-life experience are often found in blogs containing a description of an experience. A series of these user manipulations correspond to asking someone who actually experienced it what they think about it. This approach is a popular and efficient method of gathering information in the real world as well.

5 Evaluation

5.1 Prototype System

We evaluated our proposed method using a prototype system based on the implementation described in the previous section. The system configuration is shown

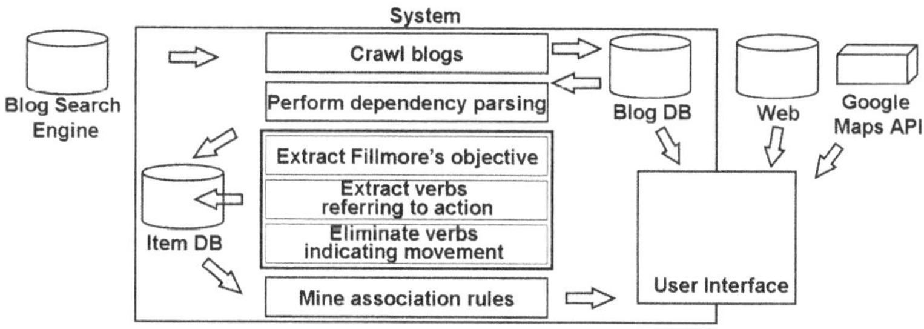

Fig. 2. System configuration

in Figure 2. It collects blog entries from two popular blog hosting services in Japan: "Bulkfeeds" [17] and "goo blog " [18]. The blog entries were morphologically analyzed using the Chasen morphological analyzer [19]. Chasen divides sentences into words and estimates their parts of speech. Dependency parsing between words was performed using the CaboCha, which is based on support vector machines [20]. The dependency between words was analyzed using the Chasen results. A collection of verbs referring to actions was obtained from the lexical database of the Japanese Vocabulary System [21], which categorizes verbs into a tree structure and groups verbs referring to actions into one top-level category. We manually selected verbs indicating movement, e.g., "go," "come," and their synonyms. The interface was implemented using the Google Maps API [22].

5.2 Evaluation of Refinement Algorithms

Association rules were mined from the data after each of the three refinement algorithms was applied. We then calculated the recall and precision for different numbers of the extracted rules and observed whether each algorithm improved the recall and precision. The blog data used for this evaluation was as follows.

- Target locations: 30 popular sightseeing spots in Kyoto City, Japan
- Number of blog entries: 62,396
- Period covered by blog entries: August 15-December 15, 2005

We first extracted the Type 1 rules from each transaction set. The top i rules were obtained in decreasing order of the *support* value. We then evaluated the extracted verb-noun pairs to see whether they described experiences specific to location and time. Table 1 is the average precision and recall. As shown in Figure 3, application of each refinement algorithm improved the precision of the rule set, and the final rule set had the highest precision.

In our previous work, Type 1 rules contained too much noise, and the precisions of these rules were around 10 percent [13][14]. The precisions of the rules extracted after applying refinement methods described in this paper were around 60 percent (for top 5 rules).

Table 1. Average precision and recall after application of refinement algorithms

	top i rules	Unrefined	Refinement 1	Refinement 1 and 2	Refinement 1,2, and 3
Precision	5	0.093	0.133	0.200	0.580
	10	0.077	0.140	0.270	0.427
	15	0.089	0.151	0.253	0.356
Recall	5	0.090	0.128	0.208	0.575
	10	0.149	0.256	0.525	0.752
	15	0.260	0.433	0.676	0.872

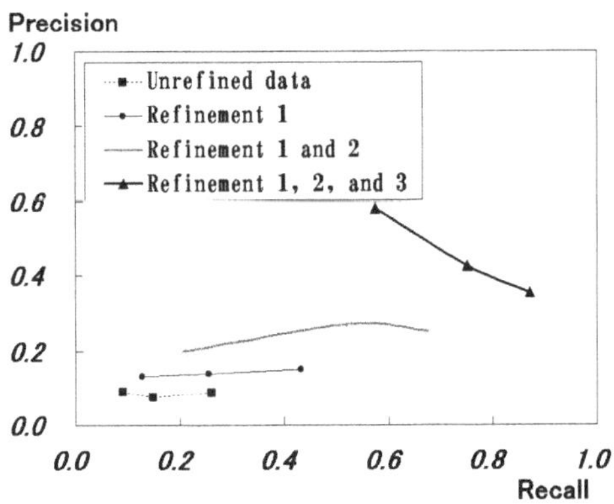

Fig. 3. Precision-recall curves after application of refinement algorithms

5.3 Results of Extraction of Association Rules Between Experiences

In the implementation described in Section 4, the extraction of association rules between experiences and the visualization of such rules were not implemented. They were implemented in our evaluation prototype. The blog entries used for the evaluation were as follows.

- Target locations: 139 popular temples in Japan
- Number of blog entries: 20,593
- Period covered by blog entries: January 1-15, 2006

The value of the minimum *support* value is 5, and the minimum *confidence* value is 0.30. We extracted 15 rules, and their average *confidence* is 0.50. The visualization of the extracted rules is shown in Figure 4. The *support* of each rule is represented by the width of its arc, and the number on each arc indicates the *confidence* value. The rules, their *antecedent* has a number of items, are expressed by using the box-shaped areas as points of union. For example, discovering association rule *buy an amulet* $\Rightarrow$ *consult an oracle* enable market analysts to formulate marketing strategy that selling space of amulet is located close to the place where an oracle is consulted. The result is also useful to visitors planning a new year's visit to a shrine.

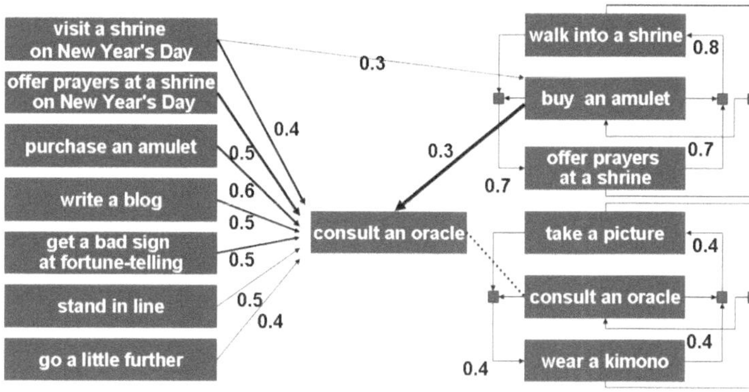

Fig. 4. Visualization of association rules between experiences

6 Conclusion

In this paper, we described a system for extracting geographically specific activities by applying text mining and association rule mining to blog content. We implemented a novel local information system that enables the user to find relevant Web content by specifying a location, a time period, or a type of experience, based on the extracted data from blog entries. We also proposed a method of extracting association rules between different activities at a specific geographic location. The result of the experiment showed that the system can extract relevant activities for various sightseeing spots at relatively high precisions. Our future work includes experiments with a larger number of blog entries, and further evaluation with a larger group of subjects.

Acknowledgments

This work was supported in part by the Japanese Ministry of Education,Culture, Sports, Science and Technology under the 21st Century COE (Center of Excellence) Program "Informatics Research Center for Development of Knowledge Society Infrastructure" (Leader: Katsumi Tanaka, 2002-2006), and Grant-in-Aid for "Development of Fundamental Software Technologies for Digital Archives," Software Technologies for Search and Integration across Heterogeneous-Media Archives (Project Leader: Katsumi Tanaka), and Grant-in-Aid for Young Scientists (B) "Trust Decision Assistance for Web Utilization based on Information Integration" (Leader: Taro Tezuka, Grant#: 18700086).

References

1. R. Kumar, J. Novak, P. Raghavan and A. Tomkins, On the bursty evolution of blogspace, Proceedings of the 12th International World Wide Web Conference, pp. 568-576, 2003
2. R. Kumar, J. Novak, P. Raghavan and A. Tomkins, Structure and evolution of blogspace, Communications of the ACM, 47(12) pp. 35-39, 2004

3. J. Bar-Ilan, An outsider's view on 'topic-oriented' blogging, Proceedings of the Alternate Papers Track of the 13th International World Wide Web Conference, pp. 28-34, 2004
4. S. Nakajima, Identifying Agitators as Important Blogger based on Analyzing Blog Threads, The Eighth Asia-Pacific Web Conference (APWeb2006), LNCS 3841, pp. 285-296, 2006
5. K. Fujimura, T. Inoue, and M. Sugisaki, The Eigen Algorithm for Ranking Blogs, In Proceedings of the WWW2005 2nd Annual Workshop on the Weblogging Ecosystem: Aggregation, Analysis and Dynamics, 2005
6. M. Okumura, T. Nanno, T. Fujiki and Y. Suzuki, Text mining based on automatic collection and monitoring of Japanese weblogs, The 6th Web and Ontology Workshop, The Japanese Society for Artificial Intelligence, 2004
7. T. Fujiki, T. Nanno, Y. Suzuki and M. Okumura, Identification of bursts in a document stream, First International Workshop on Knowledge Discovery in Data Streams (in conjunction with ECML/PKDD 2004), pp. 55-64, 2004
8. J. Kleinberg, Bursty and hierarchical structure in streams, Proceedings of the 8th ACM SIGKDD International Conference on Knowledge Discovery and Data Mining, pp. 91-101, 2002
9. P. Avesani, M. Cova, C. Hayes and P. Massa, Proceedings of the WWW2005 2nd Annual Workshop on the Weblogging Ecosystem: Aggregation, Analysis and Dynamics, Chiba, Japan, 2005
10. DC Metro Blogmap, http://www.reenhead.com/map/metroblogmap.html
11. nyc bloggers, http://www.nycbloggers.com/
12. worldKit, http://www.brainoff.com/worldkit/index.php
13. T. Kurashima, T. Tezuka, and K. Tanaka, Blog Map of Experiences: Extracting and Geographically Mapping Visitor Experiences from City Blogs, WISE2005, pp. 496-503, Springer-Verlag, 2005
14. T. Tezuka, T. Kurashima, and K. Tanaka, Toward Tighter Integration of Web Search with a Geographic Information System, Proceedings of the Fifteenth World Wide Web Conference (WWW2006), Edinburgh, Scotland, 2006
15. The National Language Research Institute, Cases and Japanese Postpositions, The National Language Research Institute, 1997
16. R. Agrawal and R. Srikant, Fast algorithms for mining association rules in large databases, Proceedings of the 20th International Conference on Very Large Data Bases, pp. 487-499, 1994
17. Bulkfeeds, http://bulkfeeds.net/
18. goo blog, http://blog.goo.ne.jp
19. Chasen, http://chasen.aist-nara.ac.jp/index.html
20. CaboCha, http://chasen.org/ taku/software/cabocha/
21. Japanese Vocabulary System, http://www.ntt-tec.jp/technology/C404.html
22. Google Maps API http://www.google.com/apis/maps/

Mining RDF Metadata for Generalized Association Rules

Tao Jiang and Ah-Hwee Tan

School of Computer Engineering
Nanyang Technological University, Nanyang Avenue, Singapore 639798
{jian0006, asahtan}@ntu.edu.sg

Abstract. In this paper, we present a novel frequent generalized pattern mining algorithm, called *GP-Close*, for mining generalized associations from RDF metadata. To solve the *over-generalization* problem encountered by existing methods, GP-Close employs the notion of *generalization closure* for systematic *over-generalization reduction*. Empirical experiments conducted on real world *RDF* data sets show that our method can substantially reduce pattern redundancy and perform much better than the original generalized association rule mining algorithm *Cumulate* in term of time efficiency.

1 Introduction

Resource Description Framework (RDF)[1] is a specification proposed by the World Wide Web Consortium (W3C) for describing and interchanging semantic metadata on the Semantic Web [1]. Due to the continual popularity of the Semantic Web, in a foreseeable future, there will be a sizeable amount of RDF-based content available on the web, offering tremendous opportunities in discovering useful knowledge from large RDF databases.

The basic element of RDF is RDF statements, each consisting of a subject, a predicate, and an object. For simplicity, we use a triplet of the form <subject, predicate, object> to express a RDF statement. Based on RDF, RDF Schema[2] (RDFS) is further proposed for defining vocabulary definitions. A RDF vocabulary defines a set of types (RDFS classes) and predicates (RDF properties) for describing web resources. Taxonomic relations between classes (properties) can also be defined. Given a set of RDF vocabularies that defines a set of taxonomies of RDFS classes, generalized association rule mining can be applied to RDF documents for discovering generalized associations between RDF statements. The discovered associations may have applications including optimizing RDF storage and query processing, enhancing information source recommendation in Semantic Web, and association-based classification or clustering of web resources.

Generalized association rule mining (GARM) [2] extends association rule mining [3] by exploiting item taxonomies in the mining task. Given a set of items $\mathcal{I}$

[1] http://www.w3.org/RDF/
[2] http://www.w3.org/TR/rdf-schema/

S. Bressan, J. Küng, and R. Wagner (Eds.): DEXA 2006, LNCS 4080, pp. 223–233, 2006.

and a large database of transactions $\mathcal{D}$, where each transaction is a set of items $T \subseteq \mathcal{I}$ with a unique identifier *tid*, an association rule is an implication of the form $X \Rightarrow Y$, where $X, Y \subseteq \mathcal{I}$ (called itemsets or patterns) and $X \cap Y = \emptyset$. A taxonomy $\mathcal{T}$ is defined as an acyclic directed graph on the set of all items $\mathcal{I}$. An edge in $\mathcal{T}$ from i_1 to i_2 represents an "*is-a*" relationship. GARM aims to discover rules spanning items across different levels of taxonomies.

The unique characteristics of RDF data sets lie in the large sizes of RDF documents and the complex structures of the RDF statement hierarchies wherein a RDF statement can be generalized in many ways, by generalizing its subject, object, predicate, or their combinations (see Figure 1(b) in subsection 3.2). In GARM, *frequent pattern mining* (FPM) is usually the most time-consuming part. For RDF data sets, existing GARM algorithms extracting all possible frequent generalized patterns do not work efficiently due to the fact that a large portion of the frequent generalized patterns is *over-generalized*. Processing over-generalized patterns can seriously increase the computation cost and degrade the performance of the mining algorithms. In this paper, we present a novel algorithm, called *GP-Close* (Closed Generalized Pattern Mining), for mining frequent generalized patterns from RDF metadata with *full over-generalization reduction*. We employ the notion of *generalization closure* to formulate over-generalization reduction as a *closed pattern mining* problem [4] [5].

The rest of the paper is organized as follows. Section 2 introduces the related work. Section 3 formalized the problem of mining frequent generalized patterns from RDF metadata and highlights the over-generalization problem. Section 4 presents the GP-Close algorithm. Section 5 reports our experiments based on two real world RDF data sets. Concluding remarks are given in the final section.

2 Related Work

Generalized association rule mining was first proposed in [2], where a family of algorithms, namely *Basic*, *Cumulate*, *Stratify*, *Estimate* and *EstMerge*, was reported. *Basic* is almost a direct application of Apriori algorithm [6] to the extended transaction databases. *Cumulate* extends Basic by employing three optimization strategies: filtering the useless ancestors in transactions, pre-computing items' ancestors, and pruning itemsets containing an item and its ancestors. Based on Cumulate, further optimizations are involved in *Stratify*, *Estimate*, and *EstMerge*. However, they only perform marginally better than Cumulate.

In [7], *Prutax* algorithm makes use of tidset-intersection for support counting to avoid multiple database scans. It adopts a right-most and depth-first search (DFS) strategy for itemset enumeration. Prutax further guarantees that the generalized itemsets are always generated before their specialized itemsets. The downward closure property and taxonomy information are also used for candidate pruning. More recently, an algorithm, *SET* [8], adopted a *tax-based* and *join-based* strategy for itemset enumeration. Nevertheless, this strategy may cause problems when the taxonomies used in the mining process are not tree-structured. In such cases, duplicated patterns may be generated.

A common limitation of the above algorithms is that they generate all the frequent patterns including over-generalized ones. On RDF data sets, most of the extracted patterns may be over-generalized. Calculation of over-generalized patterns can seriously increase computation cost. Over-generalization problem is first identified in [9] when mining generalized substructure in connected graphs. Though [9] adopted a pruning strategy to remove some over-generalized patterns, it did not provide a solution for full over-generalization reduction.

3 Mining Frequent Generalized Patterns from RDF Data

3.1 Problem Statement

We define the frequent generalized pattern mining task based on a simplified view of RDF model as follows.

Definition 1. *Let* $\mathcal{V} = \{\mathcal{E}, \mathcal{P}, \mathcal{H}, domain, range\}$ *defines an* **RDF vocabulary**, *where* $\mathcal{E} = \{e_1, e_2, \ldots, e_m\}$ *is a set of entity identifiers;* $\mathcal{P} = \{p_1, p_2, \ldots, p_n\}$ *is a set of predicate identifiers; and* $\mathcal{H}$ *is a directed acyclic graph. An edge in* $\mathcal{H}$ *represents an* **is-a** *relationship between two entities(See Figure 1(a)). If there is an edge from* e_1 *to* e_2*, we say* e_1 *is a parent of* e_2 *and* e_2 *is a child of* e_1*. We call* $\hat{e}$ *an* **ancestor** *of* e*, if there is a path from* $\hat{e}$ *to* e*. The function,* domain: $\mathcal{P} \rightarrow 2^{\mathcal{E}}$*, relates a predicate to a set of entities that can be its subject. The function,* range: $\mathcal{P} \rightarrow 2^{\mathcal{E}}$*, relates a predicate to a set of entities that can be its object.*

The above definition simplifies the RDF model in two aspects:

- We treat instances and RDF classes both as entities. Correspondingly, we treat "rdf:type" and "rdfs: subClassOf" predicates as "is-a" relation without discrimination. By this way, we can integrate instances and RDF classes into one taxonomy so that the mining task can be simplified.
- We do not consider the hierarchy of RDF properties (predicate hierarchy) at the current stage. However, the predicate hierarchy can be easily incorporated into the generalized association mining framework.

Definition 2. *Given a RDF vocabulary* $\mathcal{V} = \{\mathcal{E}, \mathcal{P}, \mathcal{H}, domain, range\}$*, we define a* **relation** *(RDF statement)* r *on* $\mathcal{V}$ *as a triplet* $<x, p, y>$*, where* $x, y \in \mathcal{E}$*,* $p \in \mathcal{P}$*,* $x \in domain(p)$*, and* $y \in range(p)$*. We call* x*,* p*, and* y *the* **subject**, *the* **predicate**, *and the* **object** *of* r*. A relation* $\hat{r} = <x_1, p_1, y_1>$ *is called a* **generalized relation** (**ancestor**) *of another relation* $r = <x_2, p_2, y_2>$*, if and only if: (1)* $\hat{r} \neq r$*, (2)* $p_1 = p_2$*, (3)* x_1 *is an ancestor of* x_2 *or* $x_1 = x_2$ *and (4)* y_1 *is an ancestor of* y_2 *or* $y_1 = y_2$*. We use* $\mathcal{R}^{\mathcal{V}}$ *to denote the set of all relations on* $\mathcal{V}$*. Relations in* $\mathcal{R}^{\mathcal{V}}$ *and their generalization/specialization relationships form a* **relation hierarchy**, $H_r^{\mathcal{V}}$ *(see Figure 1(b)).*

Definition 3. *A* **relationset** (**pattern**) *is a set of relations* $X \subseteq \mathcal{R}^{\mathcal{V}}$ *(*X *does not contain both a relation and its ancestor). We call* X *a* **generalized relationset** *of another relationset* Y *and* Y *a* **specialized relationset** *of* X*, if and*

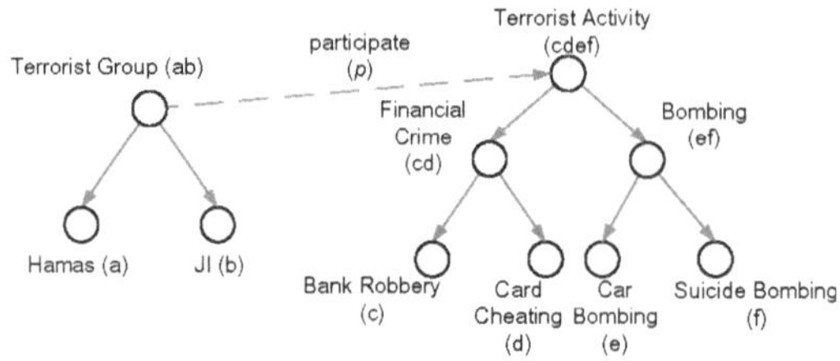

(a) A sample RDF vocabulary.

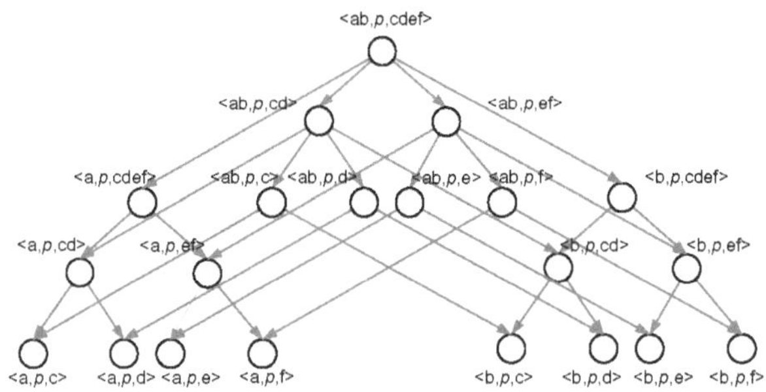

(b) Generalized relation hierarchy.

Pattern ***X***:
{<Terrorist Group, *participate*, Financial Crime>, <Terrorist Group, *participate*, Car Bombing>}
Generalization Closure of ***X***:
{<Terrorist Group, *participate*, Financial Crime>, <Terrorist Group, *participate*, Car Bombing>, <Terrorist Group, *participate*, Bombing>, <Terrorist Group, *participate*, Terrorist Activity>}

(c) An illustration of generalization closure.

Fig. 1. Elements of RDF data sets

only if: (1)$X \neq Y$, (2)$\forall r \in X, \exists r^* \in Y$ such that $r = r^*$ or r is an ancestor of r^* and (3) $\forall r^* \in Y, \exists r \in X$ such that $r = r^*$ or r is an ancestor of r^*. Given a set of RDF documents $\mathcal{D}$, where each document consists of a set of relations, the **support** *of a relationset X ($supp(X)$) is defined as the proportion of RDF documents containing X or a specialized relationset of X.*

Based on the above definitions, given a set of RDF documents, our task of mining frequent generalized patterns is to extract *frequent* relationsets (patterns) whose supports are larger than a predefined *minimum support* (*minsup*).

3.2 Over-Generalization and Mining Closed Generalization Closures

We explain the over-generalization problem using an example. Figure 1(a) shows a RDF vocabulary $\mathcal{V} = \{\mathcal{E}, \mathcal{P}, \mathcal{H}, domain, range\}$, where $\mathcal{E} = \{a, b, c, d, e, f, ab, cd, ef, cdef\}$, $\mathcal{P} = \{p\}$, $dom(p) = \{a, b, ab\}$, and $range(p) = \{c, d, e, f, cd, ef, cdef\}$. Figure 1(b) shows the relation hierarchy containing all relations in $\mathcal{R}^{\mathcal{V}}$. A sample RDF database $\mathcal{D}$ on $\mathcal{V}$ is shown in Table 1. Given $minsup = 50\%$, all frequent

Table 1. A sample RDF database

ID	RDF Documents
1	<a, *p*, d> <a, *p*, e>
2	<b, *p*, c> <b, *p*, e>
3	<a, *p*, f>
4	<b, *p*, f>

Table 2. Frequent generalized relationsets in sample RDF database

Support	Frequent Generalized Relationsets (*minsup*=50%)
50%	{<a, *p*, ef>} {<a, *p*, cdef>} {<ab,*p*,cd>} {<ab, *p*, e>} {<ab, *p*, f>} {<b, *p*, ef>} {<b, *p*, cdef>} {<a, *p*, cdef> <ab, *p*, ef>} {<ab, *p*, cd> <ab, *p*, e>} {<ab, *p*, cd> <ab, *p*, ef>} {<ab, *p*, ef> <b, *p*, cdef>}
100%	{<ab, *p*, ef>} {<ab, *p*, cdef>}

generalized relationsets are listed in Table 2. Note that some patterns look quite similar, e.g. {<ab, *p*, cd>, <ab, *p*, e>} and {<ab, *p*, cd>, <ab, *p*, ef>}. In fact, the second pattern is a generalization of the first one and they have the same support (50%). Intuitively, with the same support, a specialized pattern should be more interesting than its generalizations as the information conveyed by the specialized pattern is more precise. Therefore, the second pattern is redundant. Based on this observation, we define over-generalization as follows:

Definition 4. *A frequent relationset X is* **over-generalized** *if there exists a specialized relationset Y of X with $supp(X) = supp(Y)$.*

In Table 2, six (46%) frequent patterns (underlined) are *over-generalized.* In real-world RDF data sets, the proportion of over-generalized patterns may be much higher than this. For reducing redundant over-generalized patterns, we propose an innovative approach based on the notion of generalization closures.

Definition 5. *Given a RDF vocabulary $\mathcal{V} = \{\mathcal{E}, \mathcal{P}, \mathcal{H}, domain, range\}$ and $\mathcal{R}^{\mathcal{V}}$ on $\mathcal{V}$, we define a function φ_{gc} on $2^{\mathcal{R}^{\mathcal{V}}}$: $\varphi_{gc}X = \bigcup_{r \in X} \mathcal{G}(r)$, where $X \subset \mathcal{R}^{\mathcal{V}}$ and $\mathcal{G}(r)$ is a set of relations that contains r and all its generalized relations. φ_{gc} is a* closure operator *[10], called* **generalization closure operator**. *And $\varphi_{gc}X$ is called the* **generalization closure** *of X.*

A sample generalization closure of a pattern X is shown in Figure 1(c). We can prove that φ_{gc} is a *closure operator* and all generalization closures form a *closure system* [10] with the three properties: $X \subseteq Y \Rightarrow \varphi_{gc}X \subseteq \varphi_{gc}Y$ (monotony), $X \subseteq \varphi_{gc}X$ (extensity), and $\varphi_{gc}\varphi_{gc}X = \varphi_{gc}X$ (idempotency).

Five useful lemmas related to generalization closures are listed below. The first three lemmas are intuitive. For the space limitation, we only give the proofs of Lemma 4 and 5.

Lemma 1. *Given a relationset X and a RDF database $\mathcal{D}$, $supp(X) = supp(\varphi_{gc}X)$.*

Lemma 2. *Given X is a generalized relationset of Y, $\varphi_{gc}X \subset \varphi_{gc}Y$ holds.*

Lemma 3. *Given two generalization closures $\varphi_{gc}X$ and $\varphi_{gc}Y$ ($X, Y \subseteq \mathcal{R}^{\mathcal{V}}$), $\varphi_{gc}X \cup \varphi_{gc}Y$ is also a generalization closure ($\varphi_{gc}(X \cup Y)$).*

Lemma 4. *Given a frequent relationset X, if $\varphi_{gc}X$ is closed (i.e. there is not a $\varphi_{gc}Y \supset \varphi_{gc}X$ where $supp(\varphi_{gc}X) = supp(\varphi_{gc}Y)$), X is not over-generalized.*

Proof. Suppose X is over-generalized. It follows that there is a specialized pattern Y of X, where $supp(Y) = supp(X)$. According to Lemma 1 and 2, easy to see that $\varphi_{gc}(X) \subset \varphi_{gc}(Y)$ and $supp(\varphi_{gc}(X)) = supp(\varphi_{gc}(Y))$, i.e. $\varphi_{gc}(X)$ is not closed. This is contradictory to the statement that $\varphi_{gc}(X)$ is closed.

Lemma 5. *The support of all frequent relationsets can be derived from the set of all frequent closed generalization closures.*

Proof. As each relationset X has a generalization closure $\varphi_{gc}(X)$ with the same support, the support of X can be derived from $\varphi_{gc}(X)$ by the following ways:

1. If $\varphi_{gc}(X)$ is a closed closure, $supp(X) = supp(\varphi_{gc}(X))$.
2. Otherwise, there exists a closed closure $\varphi_{gc}(Y) \supset \varphi_{gc}(X)$ and does not exist a closed closure $\varphi_{gc}(Z)$ with $\varphi_{gc}(X) \subset \varphi_{gc}(Z) \subset \varphi_{gc}(Y)$. It follows that $supp(X) = supp(\varphi_{gc}(X)) = supp(\varphi_{gc}(Y))$.

Lemma 4 and 5 motivate us to discover all *closed generalization closures* for over-generalization reduction.

4 GP-Close Algorithm

Based on Lemma 4 and 5, we propose an algorithm, called GP-Close (Closed Generalized Pattern Mining), for discovering all closed generalization closures. Comparing with existing GARM algorithms, such as Cumulate, our algorithm discover closed generalization closures but not frequent generalized patterns. However, Lemma 5 shows that all frequent generalized patterns can be easily derived from the output of the GP-Close algorithm.

4.1 Closure Enumeration and Sorting

Lemma 3 guarantees that we can gradually generate larger closures by merging smaller ones. Based on this, GP-Close adopts a depth-first closure enumeration method using an enumeration tree. The pseudo-code of GP-Close algorithm is presented in Algorithm 1 and 2. GP-Close first calculates all 1-frequent relationsets. Then, the generalization closures of the 1-frequent relationsets are created and sorted (see Algorithm 1). A *support-increasing and length-decreasing* strategy is adopted for closure sorting. This implies that the specialized closures will be enumerated first. Later in this section, we will discuss this in more details.

Figure 2 shows the closure enumeration process based on the RDF database in Table 1. Initially, the enumeration tree contains only the root closure, i.e. the

Algorithm 1. GP-Close

Input:
RDF database: $\mathcal{D}$
Generalized relation lookup table: GRT
Support Threshold: $minsup$
Output:
The set of all closed frequent generalization closures: $\mathcal{C}$

$ce\_tree.root = \emptyset$ //initialize closure enumeration tree
$ce\_tree.root.supp = 1$
$ce\_tree.gc\_list = \{\varphi_{gc}\{r\} | r \in \mathcal{R}^{\mathcal{V}} \wedge supp(r) \geqslant minsup\}$ ////Constructing child closure set of $ce\_tree.root$ from 1-frequent RDF statements by looking up GRT
Sort($ce\_tree.gc\_list$) //sort closures (length-decreasing/support-increasing)
Closure-Enumeration(ce_tree, $\mathcal{C} = \emptyset$)
return $\mathcal{C}$

empty set with the support of 100%, and a set of closures of 1-frequent relationsets as children of the root (see Algorithm 1). Then, for each child of the root closure, we can expand it by merging it with other child closures. For example, in Figure 2, the closure $\{<ab, p, f>, <ab, p, ef>, <ab, p, cdef>\}$ is combined with the closure $\{<ab, p, cd>, <ab, p, cdef>\}$ to generate a larger closure $\{<ab, p, f>, <ab, p, ef>, <ab, p, cd>, <ab, p, cdef>\}$. Using this child closure as the root and the newly generated closures as its children, a sub closure enumeration tree is constructed (Algorithm 2 line 7 - 22). We can see that all descendants of a (sub) enumeration tree are expansions of the tree root. If a (sub) tree root can be subsumed by a discovered closed closure, i.e. it is not closed, traversing this (sub) tree cannot generate new closed generalization closures. Therefore, the (sub) tree can be pruned (Algorithm 2 line 1). For example, in Figure 2, the closure $\{<ab, p, cd>, <ab, p, cdef>\}$ is subsumed by the closed closure $\{<ab, p, f>, <ab, p, ef>, <ab, p, cd>, <ab, p, cdef>\}$. As a result, the corresponding sub closure enumeration tree is pruned. The following are three cases in which one closure can subsume another:

1. A *specialized closure* can subsume a generalized closure.
2. A closure can be subsumed by one of its *super relationsets* (*closures*).
3. A closure can be subsumed by a *super set of its specialized closures.*

Our specialization-first sorting strategy increases the occurrences of subsumption cases (1) and (3), i.e. there is a larger probability that a later constructed enumeration tree can be pruned.

The function *Prune* (Algorithm 2 line 2) performs two tasks. One is removing infrequent closures. Another is checking the subsumption among children of the current enumeration tree root and eliminating the closures that can be subsumed. In Figure 2, $\{<b, p, cdef>, <ab, p, cdef>\}$ can be subsumed by $\{<b, p, ef>, <b, p, cdef>, <ab, p, ef>, <ab, p, cdef>\}$. Thus it can be pruned.

The function *Closed-Closure* (Algorithm 2 line 3) generates the closed generalization closure. It finds all child closures that have the same support as the

Algorithm 2. Closure-Enumeration

Input:
Closure enumeration tree: *ce_tree*
A set of discovered closed frequent generalization closures: $\mathcal{C}$
Output:
The expanded set of closed frequent generalization closures: $\mathcal{C}$

1: If $\exists c^* \in \mathcal{C}$ where c^* subsumes n, return $\mathcal{C}$. //Subtree Pruning
2: Prune($ce\_tree.gc\_list$)
3: c = Closed-Closure(ce_tree)
4: $\mathcal{C} = \mathcal{C} \cup \{c\}$ //if c is not subsumed by another closed closure $c^* \in \mathcal{C}$
5: $candidates = \emptyset$
6: **for** each closure $gc_i \in ce\_tree.gc\_list$ **do**
7: $ce\_tree^*.root = gc_i$; $ce\_tree^*.gc\_list = \emptyset$ //initialize a sub enumeration tree
8: **for** each $gc_j \in ce\_tree.gc\_list$, with $i < j$ **do**
9: $gc^* = gc_i \cup gc_j$
10: **if** $gc_i.tidset \neq null$ and $gc_j.tidset \neq null$ **then**
11: $tidset = gc_i.tidset \cap gc_j.tidset$
12: **if** tidset-buffer is not overflow **then**
13: $gc^*.tidset = tidset$; $gc^*.supp = |tidset|$
14: **else**
15: $gc^*.supp = |tidset|$
16: **end if**
17: **else**
18: $candidates = candidates \cup \{gc^*\}$
19: **end if**
20: $ce\_tree^*.gc\_list = ce\_tree^*.gc\_list \cup \{gc^*\}$
21: **end for**
22: If $candidates \neq \emptyset$, perform *hash-counting*($candidates$).
23: Closure-Enumeration(ce_tree^*, $\mathcal{C}$)
24: **end for**
25: return $\mathcal{C}$

root of current closure enumeration tree. We call such child closures ***support-undescending expansions*** of the root closure (or simply *undescending expansions*). Then, these undescending expansions are merged to form a closed closure. In Figure 2, there exist two undescending expansions $\{<ab, p, ef>, <ab, p, cdef>\}$ and $\{<ab, p, cdef>\}$ of root closure $\{\}$, so that $\{<ab, p, ef>, <ab, p, cdef>\}$ is extracted as a closed closure. If there is no such undescending expansion, the root will be extracted as a closed closure.

4.2 Hybrid Support Counting

Some existing association rule mining algorithms propose to use the *transaction ID set* (*tidset*) for itemset support counting [5]. However, in real life applications, tidsets may not be able to fit into the physical memory. A hybrid counting strategy is thus designed in GP-Close for handling data sets under different circumstances. It allows users to define a tidset buffer with a maximum buffer size. The support counting is initially performed by scanning databases (DB). During DB scans, the algorithm tries to build tidsets for candidate closures if these tidsets can fit into the pre-located buffer. The constructed tidsets are then used for subsequent tidset based support counting (Algorithm 2 line 10-17).

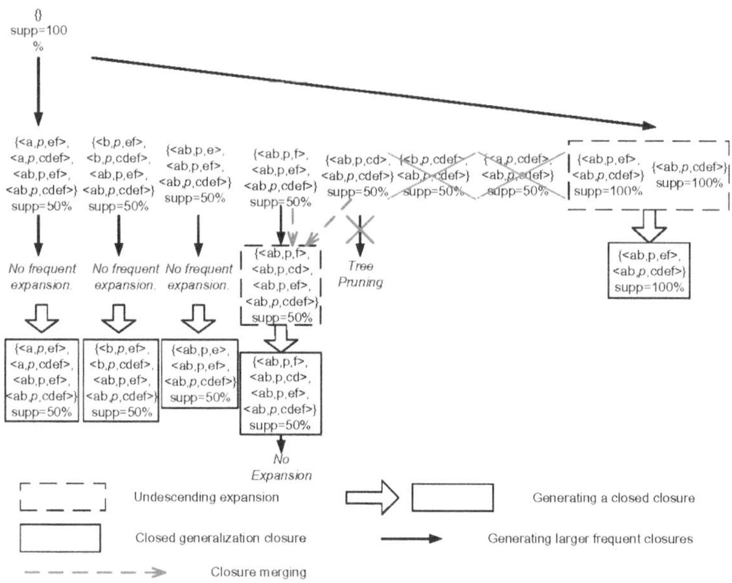

Fig. 2. Closure Enumeration

5 Experiments

The GP-Close algorithm was implemented using Java (JDK 1.4.2). GP-Close with different sizes of tidset buffer were used in our experiments, namely GP-Close-*0*, GP-Close-*500*, and GP-Close-*50000*, with a tidset buffer of 0 KB, 500 KB, and 50,000 KB respectively. We also implemented the Cumulate algorithm [2] as a reference of performance comparison.

5.1 Data Sets

Our experiments are conducted on two real world RDF data sets, namely the foafPub data set provided by the UMBC eBiquity Research Group and the ICT-CB data set extracted from an online database of International Policy Institute for Counter-Terrorism. foafPub is a set of RDF files that describes peoples and their relationships with the use of the FOAF vocabulary[3]. ICT-CB documents are descriptions of car bombing events. The statistics of the RDF vocabularies and RDF documents in the two data sets are summarized in Table 3.

5.2 Performance Study

Figure 3(a) and 3(d) show the computation time of the algorithms with respect to minimum support. We find that Cumulate can work properly only with high *minsup*. When the *minsup* is high, the performance of the algorithms are comparable. The GP-Close-*0* is slightly slower than other versions of GP-Close due

[3] http://xmlns.com/foaf/0.1/

Table 3. Statistics of the foafPub and ICT-CB Data Sets. N_d - number of RDF documents, N_r - number of RDF relations, N_r^* - number of distinct RDF relations, N_{gr} - number of distinct generalized relations.

RDF Data set	RDF property	RDF class	Instance	Avg. Fanout	N_d	N_r	N_r^*	N_{gr}	Min len.	Max len.	Avg. len.
foafPub	36	6801	66613	13	6170	85778	83759	207119	1	3188	14
ICT-CB	53	1806	2546	3	127	2224	1814	175020	1	104	17

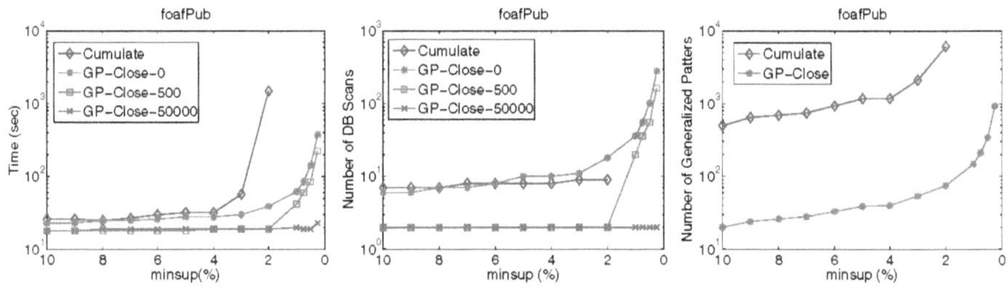

(a) Exec time on foafPub (b) DB scans on foafPub (c) Patterns from foafPub

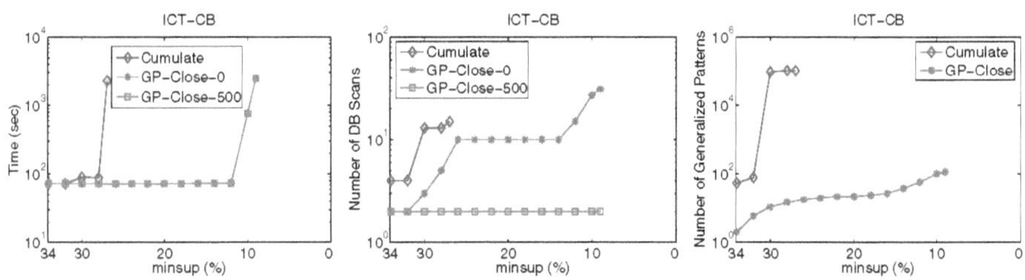

(d) Exec time on ICT-CB (e) DB scans on ICT-CB (f) Patterns from ICT-CB

Fig. 3. Performance of GP-Close compared with Cumulate

to the fact that it involves more IO accesses. When the *minsup* is low, all three versions of GP-Close algorithm perform more than an order of magnitude faster than Cumulate. This is because the CPU computation becomes the bottleneck of the algorithms as the number of frequent patterns increases.

Figure 3(b) and 3(e) show the number of DB scans performed by the algorithms. The overall trend is that the number of DB scans increases when *minsup* decreases. For GP-Close-*50000*, the tidsets can always fit in the tidset buffer after two DB scans. The number of DB scans performed by GP-Close-*0* increases rapidly as more branches of the enumeration tree are constructed when *minsup* decreases. However, for low *minsup*, though GP-Close-*0* and GP-Close-*500* scan for many more times than Cumulate, the performance of the two algorithms is still more than one order of magnitude better than Cumulate. This further reflects the fact that when *minsup* is low, the bottleneck of the algorithms lies in CPU computation instead of IO access.

Figure 3(c) and 3(f) show that the number of closed generalization closures is almost one to two orders of magnitude smaller than the number of all frequent relationsets discovered by Cumulate. This is despite the fact that all frequent relationsets can be derived from the set of closed generalization closures. Note that a scale is used in Figure 3(c). Therefore, the stable margin between the two curves actually implies an exponential growth in the difference between the number of frequent generalized patterns and the number of closed closures.

6 Conclusion

This paper has presented an innovative approach for mining frequent generalized patterns from RDF metadata with *over-generalization reduction*. We presented the GP-Close algorithm which efficiently discovers a small set of closed frequent generalization closures from which all frequent generalized patterns can be derived. Extensive experiments show that our proposed method can substantially reduce the pattern redundancy and perform much better than the original GARM algorithm *Cumulate* in term of time efficiency.

References

1. Berners-Lee, T., Hendler, J., Lassila, O.: Semantic web. Scientific American **284**(5) (2001) 35–43
2. Srikant, R., Agrawal, R.: Mining generalized association rules. In: VLDB '95, San Francisco (1995) 407–419
3. Agrawal, R., Imielinski, T., Swami, A.N.: Mining association rules between sets of items in large databases. In: SIGMOD Conference. (1993) 207–216
4. Bastide, Y., Taouil, R., Pasquier, N., Stumme, G., Lakhal, L.: Mining frequent patterns with counting inference. SIGKDD Explorations **2**(2) (2000) 66–75
5. Zaki, M.J., Hsiao, C.J.: Charm: An efficient algorithm for closed itemset mining. In: SDM. (2002)
6. Agrawal, R., Srikant, R.: Fast algorithms for mining association rules in large databases. In: Proceedings of VLDB'94, Santiago de Chile. (1994) 487–499
7. Hipp, J., Myka, A., Wirth, R., Güntzer, U.: A new algorithm for faster mining of generalized association rules. In: PKDD. (1998) 74–82
8. Sriphaew, K., Theeramunkong, T.: A new method for finding generalized frequent itemsets in generalized association rule mining. In: ISCC. (2002) 1040–1045
9. Inokuchi, A.: Mining generalized substructures from a set of labeled graphs. In: ICDM. (2004) 415–418
10. Ganter, B., Wille, R.: Formal Concept Analysis: Mathematical Foundations. Springer-Verlag New York, Inc., Secaucus, NJ, USA (1997)

Analysing Social Networks Within Bibliographical Data

Stefan Klink[1],
Patrick Reuther[2], Alexander Weber[2], Bernd Walter[2], and Michael Ley[2]

[1] Institute of Applied Informatics and Formal Description Methods,
Universität Karlsruhe (TH), Germany
Stefan.Klink@aifb.uni-karlsruhe.de
[2] Department for Databases and Information Systems,
University of Trier, Germany
{reuther, aweber, walter, ley}@uni-trier.de

Abstract. Finding relationships between authors and thematic similar publications is getting harder and harder due to the mass of information and the rapid growth of the number of scientific workers. The **io-port.net** portal and the **DBLP** Computer Science Bibliography including more than 2,000,000 and 750,000 publications, respectively, from more than 450,000 authors are major services used by thousands of computer scientists which provides fundamental support for scientists searching for publications or other scientists in similar communities.

In this paper, we describe a user–friendly interface which plays the central role in searching authors and publications and analysing social networks on the basis of bibliographical data.

After introducing the concept of multi-mode social networks, the *DBL–Browser* itself and various methods for multi-layered browsing through social networks are described.

1 Introduction

Nowadays, searching for relevant publications, similar authors, and interesting conferences is more crucial than ever. But the modern information society faces the severe dilemma that more and more information is available but exploring relevant information for satisfying the users' information need is still a very challenging task. Most traditional retrieval systems are strictly document oriented.

In contrast to common web information systems like Yahoo, Lycos, or Google (Scholar), bibliographical data bases like the DBLP [14] or io-port.net [9] offer much more information which can not be directly retrieved by querying. The latter provide abundant information, i. e., about author relationships, conferences, and the evolvement of scientific communities. Although basic information, i. e., the author/coauthor relationship is given directly in the bibliographical entity relations beyond documents are not detected by traditional systems and are not accessible by the user.

With the *DBL–Browser* we have attempted to work against this problem by providing an efficient way for browsing a given bibliographical data base.

S. Bressan, J. Küng, and R. Wagner (Eds.): DEXA 2006, LNCS 4080, pp. 234–243, 2006.

By combining both textual and visual browsing functionality we established a browsing–based retrieval and visualisation system which enables users to better understand their search domain and consequently offers the opportunity to expand their original query. As already indicated by [4] users like both the graphical nature of information organisation and multi–level browsing systems. Both mentioned features are central parts in our browser.

For the digital library domain we developed a combination of the query–based and browsing–based approach which in comparison with the mentioned practices is superior for solving the vocabulary problem [10]. Starting from an unspecific query or using hyperlinks to browse from the 'homepage' users can browse through the bibliographical data. During the browsing process all data is visualised by appropriate graphical techniques which help users to understand their search domain, helps them find relevant authors or publications and above all provides information about further researchers or related conferences/journals.

2 Multi-mode Social Networks

The theoretical background of this paper is based on the theory of social networks [17]. Due to the fact that bibliographical data contains not only authors but also single publications, conferences, journals, etc. common one-mode diadic author networks are not sufficient to represent the given network structure. In our case, we need so called multi-mode social networks described in the following paragraphs.

2.1 Basics of Social Networks

A social network can be seen as a graph $G = (V, E)$ in which the vertices V represent the actors, the edges E a tie between these actors. Clustering describes the situation that if one actor has a tie (of arbitrary origin) to two other actors then it is likely that these two individuals will start a tie as well. This can easily be seen while looking at friends one has and then at the friends they have. It is likely, as Watts points out that there will be a certain overlap between these two sets of people [18]. If the clustering is advanced and the characteristic path length in a social network satisfies certain conditions, then the observed social network is a specific subtype of network, a so called small world network.

Such a small world network is the basis of the new algorithm for similarity measurement. The network considered is the co-author network constructed from the DBLP database. The actors are the authors listed in the dataset. A tie between two authors is inserted into the graph if the actors collaborated one a single publication. The usage of co-author networks or co-author relationships in general is not new in order to find synonyms [12], [8], [6], [7], [3]. However the manner of how the information is used is innovative.

2.2 Multi-mode Social Networks

For representing additional information multi-mode networks are needed. In contrast to common one-mode networks with authors as actors and coauthorship as relation, multi-mode networks are capable to represent relationships of and to affiliations, single publications, conferences, journals, etc. These kinds of networks are also known as *affiliation or membership networks* where one set of actors (here: authors) and multiple sets of events (here: publications, affiliations, conferences, journals, etc.) are present [17, Chapter 8]. Relationships within bibliographical data can be listed as a hierarchy with increasing indirection:

- authors within the same publication (i. e., coauthors),
- coauthors of coauthors (i. e., friend-of-a-friend),
- authors of the same conference (journal issue) (i. e., DEXA'06),
- authors of the same conference stream (journal) (i. e., VLDB),
- authors within similar conferences (journal),
- authors with similar publications.

Coauthors. Needless to say that the elementary form of a relationship is the coauthor relationship of authors which have written the same publication. Of cause they are thematically connected and do know each other.

Coauthors of Coauthors. But thinking one step further, regarding coauthors of coauthors, then it is possible that these scientists do not know each other but nevertheless they are thematically connected and possible publishing in a similar area. This idea is also the basis of classical social networks environments in the business area, i. e., FOAF [16] or openBC [15].

Clustering in the context of coauthor networks describes that it is likely for two initially not collaborating authors to get to know each other if they have a common coauthor. In this case these three authors are each connected by a tie and form a triangle in the network. Formally a triangle $\triangle = (V_\triangle, E_\triangle)$ can be described as a subgraph of G consisting of three vertices with $V_\triangle = \{A_1, A_2, A_3\} \subset V$ and $E_\triangle = \{e_{A_1,A_2}, e_{A_2,A_3}, e_{A_3,A_1}\} \subset E$. However if there exists no tie between the two not collaborating authors not a triangle but using the terminology of Watts a Connected Triple between these three authors occurs in the graph. A Connected Triple $\wedge = \{V_\wedge, E_\wedge\}$ can be described as a subgraph of G consisting of three vertices with $V_\wedge = \{A_1, A_2, A_3\} \subset V$ and $E_\wedge = \{e_{A_1,A_2}, e_{A_1,A_3}\} \subset E$. The actor connecting the two not connected actors is called *center* of the connected triple.

Authors Within the Same Conference/Workshop or Journal Issue. Another level of relationship is the one of authors within the same Conference/ Workshop or Journal issue. Indeed, they are all working within the same thematically area – otherwise they wouldn't have been published there – but especially on huge international conferences it is unlikely, that all authors know each other. Nevertheless, the thematically relationship between these authors is interesting for social analysis. With the help of this information it is possible to get further information about relevant topics for own research areas.

Authors Within the Same Conference/Workshop or Journal Stream. Analogue to the paragraph above but more weakly is the relationship of authors within the same Conference/Workshop or Journal stream. The relationship is weaker because during time research interests of authors could change or the topics presented and discussed in conferences or journals could shift to more 'modern' themes. But regarding social networks authors which have changed research interests are of interest because their knowledge on this field might be present even now.

Authors Within Similar Conferences/Workshops or Journal Streams. In most cases authors are publishing not only in one conference, i. e., VLDB, but also in other conferences which are thematically similar to each other. Or, even more, they are related to each other in the case that they are alternating, i. e., ICDAR and DAS, MKWI and WI, or that they are local or international, respectively, i. e., ECML and ICML. However, it is very likely, that an author of the ECML is researching in the same area than an author of the ICML, namely machine learning.

For calculating this kind of relationship, the definition of a similarity of conferences/workshop or journal stream, respectively, is crucial. Such a similarity can be calculated in different ways. First the similarity can be calculated on the basis of all the authors that published in the journals. The bigger the overlap between the scientists publishing in two streams is, the higher the similarity of the the streams is. A second approach is to consider the topics of the journals. This can be obtained by making use of title, abstract and fulltext if available in order to calculate a similarity. As a last approach one could combine the author and the topic based approach.

Similar Authors. The most general and most complex relationship is the similarity criterium on author level. For that, an appropriate similarity measurement between two authors must be defined, which regards as much information as possible to use every hint which authors might be similar to each other, despite the fact that they never heard of each other.

One example building a similarity measurement on the basis of bibliographical data is using the upper mentioned Connected Triples.

In order to calculate the similarity between two authors the amount of connected triples they both are member of, but in which neither of them is a center is used as a simple similarity function.

$$Sim(i,j)_{ConnectedTriple_{Basic}} = \frac{|C_{\wedge_{ij}}|}{max_{k=0\ldots m,l=0\ldots m}|(C_{\wedge_{kl}})|} \quad (1)$$

Fig. 1 shows recall precision curves calculated on basis of the DBLP-SUB02-03 collections in which the performance of standard Jaro-Winkler distance, ConnectedTriple$_{Basic}$ and a combination of the previous mentioned criteria is illustrated. Using only ConnectedTriple$_{Basic}$ and not considering any syntactical characteristics is, although not very effective, a possibility to identify synonyms. Syntactical approaches like the Jaro-Winkler exceed the semantical based ConnectedTriple$_{Basic}$ distance. However, the best result can be achieved by combining syntactical and semantical similarity measures.

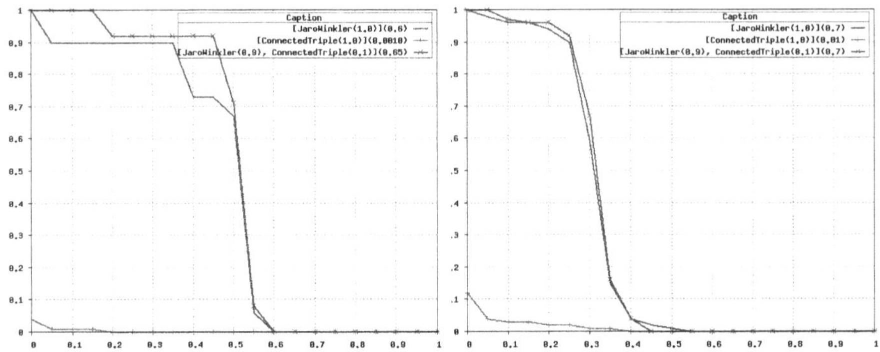

Fig. 1. Recall/Precision curves for DBLP-SUB02 and DBLP-SUB03 showing Connected Triple_{Basic}

This simple form of similarity function relying on the amount of Connected Triples can be systematically improved by considering different other aspects on how the triples emerged and which characteristics they have. Such enhancements are for example to consider the amount of publications which lead to the number of Connected Triples. It is possible that two publications lead to n Connected Triples for two authors, if in these two publications once n authors collaborated with author A_1 and in the other publications the same n authors published with A_2 but not with A_1. Besides making use of topical and time aspects can improve the performance of the Connected Triple Approach.

More comprehensive similarity measurements are taking into account in which conference/workshop streams or journals the authors are publishing. Furthermore, if abstracts or full-text is available, then text-based similarity measurements known from information retrieval are additionally used to calculate the similarity of authors [1], [2], [10]. Extracting and comparing affiliation data could be also valuable to a certain amount, if it is correct. But one difficulty is, that nowadays affiliations can change very rapidly and due to the grow of companies and departments diverse themes are researched within one company.

3 Multi-layered Browsing

In this section we will show how the theoretical aspects of social networks described above can be applied with the help of our *DBL–Browser*.

3.1 Introducing the Bibliographical Data

The DBLP (*Digital Bibliography & Library Project*) [14] indexes more than 750,000 publications published by more than 450,000 authors and is accessed more than two million times a month on the main site maintained at our department (June 2006). The bibliographical database is focused on a high quality which is restricted to the main bibliographical data. Very limited resources prevent us to produce detailed meta-data or abstracts of a substantial number. For each attribute of the meta-data the degree of consistency makes the difference: By crawling the web it is easy to produce a huge number of bibliographic records without duplicate detection, standardization of journal names, conference names, person names, etc. But as soon as you try to guarantee that an entity (journal, conference, person, ...) is always represented by exactly the same character string and no entities share the same representation, data maintenance becomes very expensive. As a result the underlying data for analysing social networks is of remarkable quality.

The information portal *ioport.net* [9] contains a more comprehensive bibliographical database where separate databases like CompuScience, DBLP, LEABIB and The Collection of Computer Science Bibliographies (CCSB) are integrated within one common portal. With the help of thematically focused internet crawlers based on ontologies the portal provides more than two million publications in various fields of computer science with the ability to access the abstracts and full-texts via third-party providers like TIBORDER or via direct links to the publisher like SpringerLink, etc.

3.2 Browsing Bibliographical Data

To browse large bibliographic data sets we developed a specialised tool, that helps the user to navigate through the complex data: The Digital Bibliographic Library Browser (*DBL–Browser*). The main idea is to have always a textual and at least a graphic representation of the current visible data. There are several things, that make the *DBL–Browser* an easy–to–use everyday application: One of the main aspects is it's straightforward user interface. Anybody using a common web–browser is able to use the *DBL–Browser*. All essential features are at hand – like searching and filtering the data. The search system has all typically functions, with additional features such as combined searches or vague searches, based on the Levenshtein distance [13].

In addition to the classic navigation, the user interface offers the concept of *Tabs*, thus the user is able to put different stages of a search session into different tabs. These tabs can be visually aligned to show more than one part of information at one time or giving different visualisations of the same information – so you can have a histogram view of an author as well as a view showing authors that are related to the current author. We call this *multi–layered* browsing, because the user is always able to get different views (layers) to the same data. For example, they can switch between a chronological text representation of all publications from a given author to a graphical histogram, showing the same data in a different representation.

The other main feature of the browser is the additional navigation provided by the *everything–is–clickable* concept. Every piece of information shown by the browser provides a link to more associated information, i. e., a search or a Table of Contents (TOC) page.

3.3 Analysing Social Networks

With it's searching and browsing capability the *DBL–Browser* is predestined for analysing social networks. As described in section 2.2, we are regarding not only plain networks but also multi-mode networks with various hierarchy levels. The *DBL–Browser* is capable of supporting all levels of the hierarchy listed the section above.

Coauthors. After searching for an author or a specific publication, the bibliographical data can be visualised in a textual manner in form of a tabular. Every coauthor is listed in the original occurrence of the publication (see Fig. 2). Due to the proofed quality, the names are normalised and surname as well as the lastname is written out, i. e., "Ian Witten" or "James L. Peterson".

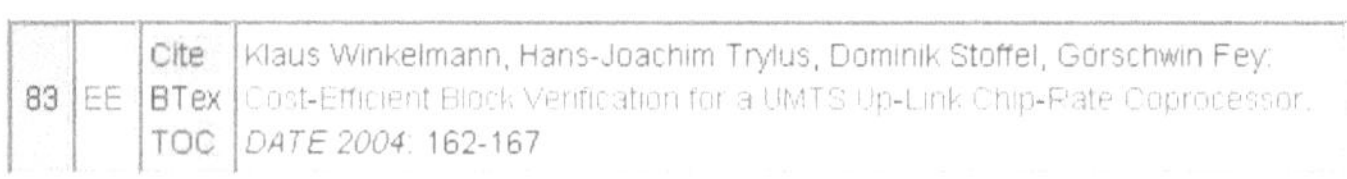

83	EE	Cite BTex TOC	Klaus Winkelmann, Hans-Joachim Trylus, Dominik Stoffel, Görschwin Fey: Cost-Efficient Block Verification for a UMTS Up-Link Chip-Rate Coprocessor. *DATE 2004*: 162-167

Fig. 2. Textual visualization in tabular form

Coauthors of Coauthors. Due to our *everything–is–clickable* concept, the user of the *DBL–Browser* is just one click away from further coauthors. The only thing to do is to click on any authors' name in the first line. Then all publications of that author is visualised again in the same form. Though the *DBL–Browser* gives an easy support for browsing from one author to coauthors to their coauthors to their coauthors etc. to get a quick overview of the coauthorship network.

Authors Within the Same Conference/Workshop or Journal Issue. More on the meta-level is the relationship of authors within the same conference/ workshop or of one Journal issue. These authors do not have a direct connection and maybe they do not know each other – except well established Professors researching since a long time within this community. And even these, rarely have a direct coauthorship relationship but they are publishing since years within the same community and same theme. For this case a relationship on conference level is needed for analysing the social network. The *DBL–Browser* provides a visualisation for each Conference/Workshop and Journal on issue level as a Table Of Content (TOC) page (see Fig. 3).

Authors Within the Same Conference/Workshop or Journal Stream. As illustrated in Fig. 3 on the top left side, all conferences of all years are listed and can be accessed with one single click. Again, for each conference the table of content is generated and all publications from all authors are visualised in a tabular form. Thus, social network analysis within a conference or journal stream is just a matter of some clicks and getting an overview of the key-players is very easy and comfortable.

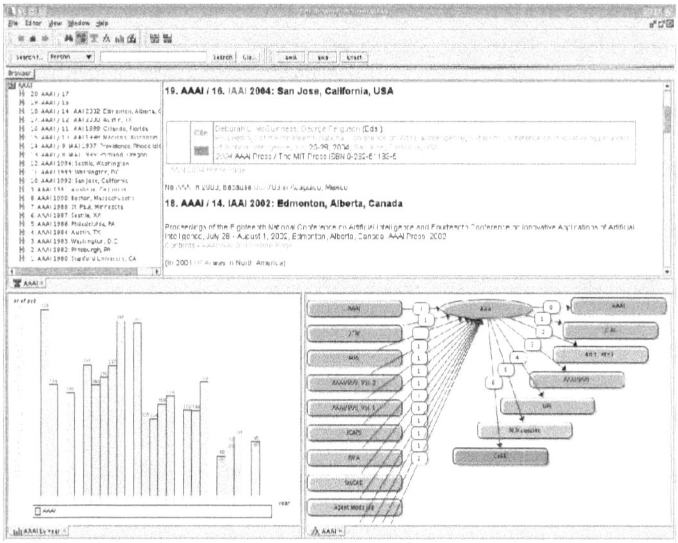

Fig. 3. TOC of the AAAI in the DBL-Browser with histogram and similarity

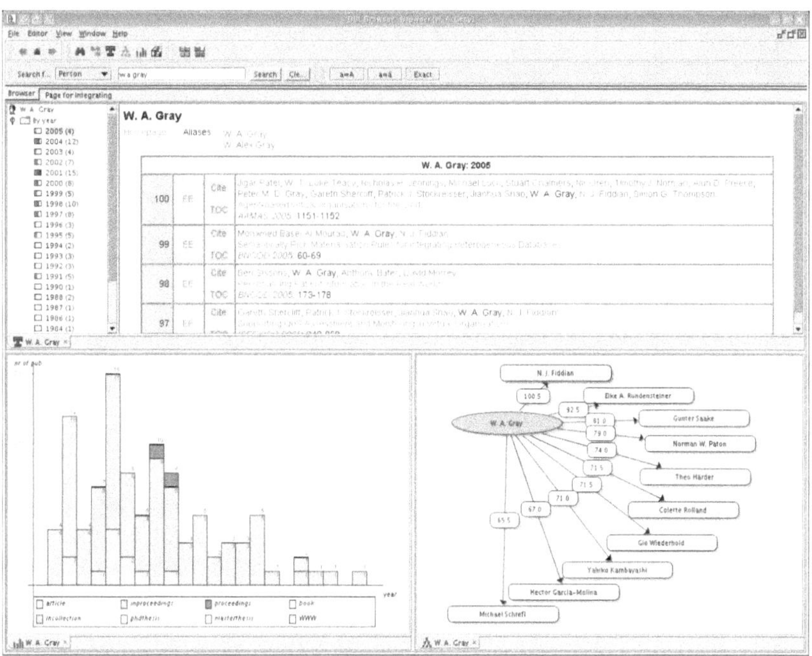

Fig. 4. Textual an graphics visualization of an author

Authors Within Similar Conferences/Workshops or Journal Streams. As mentioned above, finding authors of similar conferences or similar journal streams is not trivial and heavy depending on the appropriate similarity. The *DBL–Browser* provides a visualisation for similar conferences or journal streams (see Fig. 3) which makes it easy to see the relation between them and to get a quick overview of similar conferences or journals, respectively.

Similar Authors. Finding similar authors is even more complex and getting the right ones out of the hundreds of thousands of authors within the database is a nearly inextricable task by using a web search engine. But using the *DBL–Browser*, similar authors are visualised sorted by their similarity (see Fig. 4). Furthermore, darker colors indicate that these authors are coauthors.

Encouragement

Main parts of this work was supported by the German Ministry for Education and Research (bmb+f) in the SemIPort and FIS-I project [11], [5].

Our intention is to provide the *DBL–Browser* as a framework for experiments. Due to its modularisation, it is an easy challenge for anyone interested to integrate his or her ideas and algorithms. The XML and compressed version of the DBLP data and the source code of the browser are available on our web server (http://dbis.uni-trier.de/DBL-Browser/). Feedback and further ideas are also very welcome.

Unfortunately it is far beyond our resources to include all publications we are asked to consider but we hope to find more sponsors ...

References

1. R. Baeza-Yates and B. Ribeiro-Neto. *Modern Information Retrieval.* Addison-Wesley Publishing Company, 1999. `http://citeseer.nj.nec.com/433337.html`.
2. N. J. Belkin and W. B. Croft. Retrieval techniques. *Annual Review of Information Science and Technology*, 22:109–145, 1987.
3. I. Bhattacharya and L. Getoor. Iterative record linkage for cleaning and integration. In *Proceedings of the 9th ACM SIGMOD Workshop on Research Issues in Data Mining and Knowledge Discovery, DMKD 2004, Paris, France, June 13, 2004*, pages 11–18. ACM, 2004.
4. Y. Ding, G. G. Chowdhury, S. Foo, and W. Qian. Bibliometric information retrieval system (BIRS): A web search interface utilizing bibliometric research results. *Journal of the American Society for Information Science*, 51(13):1190–1204, 2000.
5. P. Fankhauser et al. Fachinformationssystem Informatik (FIS-I) und Semantische Technologien für Informationsportale (SemIPort). In A. B. Cremers et al., editors, *GI Jahrestagung (2)*, volume 68 of *LNI*, pages 698–712. GI, 2005.
6. H. Han et al. Two supervised learning approaches for name disambiguation in author citations. In H. Chen et al., editors, *ACM/IEEE Joint Conference on Digital Libraries, JCDL 2004*, pages 296–305, Tuscon, AZ, USA, 2004. ACM.
7. H. Han, C. L. Giles, and H. Zha. A model-based k-means algorithm for name disambiguation. In *Proceedings of the Second International Semantic Web Conference (ISWC-03) Workshop on Semantic Web Technologies for Searching and Retrieving Scientific Data*, 2003.

8. H. Han, H. Zha, and C. L. Giles. Name disambiguation in author citations using a k-way spectral clustering method. In M. Marlino, T. Sumner, and F. M. S. III, editors, *Proceedings of the ACM/IEEE Joint Conference on Digital Libraries, JCDL 2005*, pages 334–343. ACM, 2005.
9. Informatics online. `http://www.io-port.net/`, 2006.
10. S. Klink. *Improving Document Transformation Techniques with Collaborative Learned Term-based Concepts*, volume 2956 of *Lecture Notes in Computer Science*, pages 281–305. Springer-Verlag, Berlin, Heidelberg, New York, April 2004.
11. S. Klink, M. Ley, E. Rabbidge, P. Reuther, B. Walter, and A. Weber. Visualising and mining digital bibliographic data. In P. Dadam and M. Reichert, editors, *INFORMATIK 2004 - Informatik verbindet, Band 2, Beiträge der 34. Jahrestagung der Gesellschaft für Informatik e.V. (GI)*, volume 51 of *LNI*, pages 193–197. GI, 2004.
12. M.-L. Lee, W. Hsu, and V. Kothari. Cleaning the spurious links in data. 19(2):28–33, 2004.
13. V. I. Levenshtein. Binary codes capable of correcting spurious insertions and deletions of ones (original in Russian). *Russian Problemy Peredachi Informatsii*, 1:12–25, 1965.
14. M. Ley. The DBLP Computer Science Bibliography: Evolution, Research Issues, Perspectives. In A. H. F. Laender and A. L. Oliveira, editors, *SPIRE*, volume 2476 of *Lecture Notes in Computer Science*, pages 1–10. Springer, 2002.
15. Open business club. `http://www.openBC.com/`, 2006.
16. Friend of a Friend project. `http://www.foaf-project.org/`, 2006.
17. S. Wasserman and K. Faust. *Social Network Analysis: Methods and Applications*, volume 8 of *Structural Analysis in the Social Sciences*. Cambridge University Press, New York, 1994.
18. D. J. Watts. *Six Degrees: The Science of a Connected Age*. W. W. Norton & Company, New York, 2004.

Automating the Choice of Decision Support System Architecture

Estella Annoni, Franck Ravat, Olivier Teste, and Gilles Zurfluh

IRIT-SIG (UMR 5505)Institute
University of Paul Sabatier
118 Route de Narbonne
F-31062 Toulouse Cedex 9
{annoni, ravat, teste, zurfluh}@irit.fr

Abstract. Due to the wide-spread use of decision support systems (DSS), methods are required by software companies. Several concepts and methods have been suggested for decision-making. The development of DSS is still complex due to the variety of architectures, the number and the type of modules which compose them.

Therefore, This paper present our method of DSS development, which is based on an architecture of 1 to 4 levels, focusing on the choice of an adapted architecture (composed of data warehouses and data marts). Our method is based on a mixed approach integrating the assessment of existing sources and user requirements. These are taken into account from the early step of DSS engineering, e.g. from the analysis step, so DSS architecture choice integrates them.

1 Introduction

1.1 Context

The development of decision support systems (DSS) is widespread in companies. However, increasing the use of such systems follows an anarchical development due to inappropriate development methods. For example the design methods of information systems (IS) used by designers turn out to be inadequate [1]. The standard representation model (E-R) rarely matches multidimensional concepts of the DSS [2].

The DSS development is a very complex task [3] due to multiple architectures. Current approaches tend to develop architectures with several levels. Each level is composed of modules [4] and [5]. A collaboration with the I-D6 company[1] allows us to identify a DSS architecture based on four modules (see figure 1):

- the Decision Gateway (DG) is an interface for accessing directly to data sources,
- the Operational Data Store (ODS) is an intermediate storage area which allows the copy, the cleaning, the consolidation and the preparation of data upstream in order to transform them in to an homogeneous format. So, it offers an external and homogeneous view of the existing data sources which are varied, distributed and independent. This system is often based on relational schemas without the management of historicization,

[1] I-D6 is the Software Company collaborator of the CIFRE PhD led by one of the authors.

S. Bressan, J. Küng, and R. Wagner (Eds.): DEXA 2006, LNCS 4080, pp. 244–253, 2006.

- the Data Warehouse (DW) is a centralized storage space where enterprise data are integrated into aggregated levels and eventually with an history of the different refreshments. Data warehouses are based on traditional data models which are generally relational or object models. They ensure historicization and aggregation.
- the Data Mart (DM) is a consistent set of data which fulfill a specific user class requirements. This data organization must make easy decision-making activities. The multidimensional model is a reference because it improves the analysis of an interest item for the enterprise, called fact. This analysis is done by axis which represent the context of analysis, called dimensions. The most used representation is the well-known star schema [6].

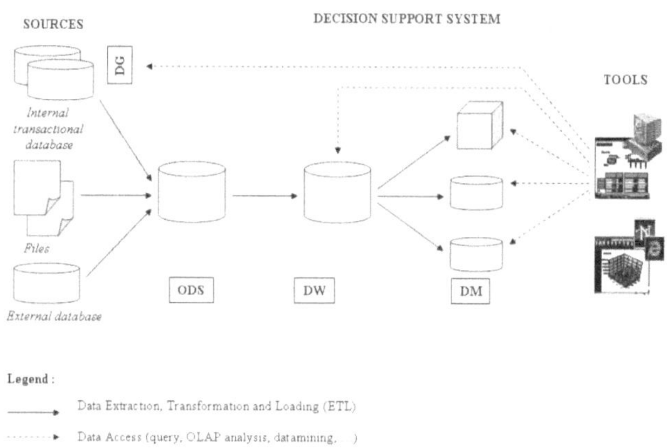

Fig. 1. DSS architectural modules

Basically, DSS architectures are a combination of one or several DSS architectural modules. This architecture enables us to manage separately the functional problems of loading, storage and presentation [3]. All these challenges mandate specific design methods for DSS, adapted to user requirements and which integrate the multiple architectures. Regarding the complexity and the time required for DSS development, it would be interesting to define an automatic process. Thus, we define a process which guides the DSS architecture definition task [3].

1.2 Related Work

Several methods have been suggested : top-down, bottom-up and mixed methods.

The top-down approach defines DSS from the analysis of the operational database model. In [7] and [8] the authors provide to build a data mart from the E-R sources. They find out respectively the "Multidimensional Model" and the "Dimensional Fact Model" which represent the subject and the axis of the analysis. This approach is very heavy when the number and the complexity of existing data sources are hight. Moreover, the user requirements are not taken into account.

The bottom-up approach defines the DSS from the user requirement analysis. In [9], the authors define a multidimensional database lifecycle based on a "Bus Matrix Architecture". The drawback of this approach is schemas which could end up impossible to implement due to a lack of data and/or heavy costs of data retrieval and integration. In [10], the authors offer a first solution by integrating existing sources, but only at a physical level. They do so after the transformation of the user requirements into a "Unified Multidimensional Schema".

Due to the drawbacks of these two approaches, a third has been put forward, mixing the two previous ones. It has been the object of numerous important propositions [1], [4] and [11]. The authors generate an ideal multidimensional schema from user requirements and confront the latter to several candidate schemas defined by the analysis of sources. The more complete method, suggested by [4], is based on an iterative and incremental lifecycle. However, as the previous works, these do not guide the designer for the DSS architecture choice. Furthermore, the assessment of the data sources is realized later, during a third step named the "confrontation step".

This paper is organized in 5 sections. Section 2 describes the approach of our method, e.g. DSS Trident approach. Afterwards, we focus on the automation of the choice of an adequate architecture in section 3. We present an example in section 4 . We conclude by summarizing the properties of our proposition and present some outlines to future work in section 5.

2 Our Approach: DSS Trident

2.1 DSS Trident Specificities

The tasks and processes that we define are based on requirements formulated by groups of DSS actors. Therefore, before presenting our approach, we will define the groups of actors and their requirements. Like the authors [12], we distinguish three groups which have different roles : users, business and system. In remainder of this paper, the word "users" will refer to end-users, and the word "actors" will refer to all DSS actors (users, business, system).

The "DSSRequirements" are requirements formulated by all actors. Therefore we can find, the "UsersRequirements", the "SystemRequirements" and the "BusinessRequirements". The "UsersRequirements" are both functional and non-functional requirements. The "SystemRequirements" are related to technical aspects like existing data sources and DSS modules. The "BusinessRequirements" put specific roles in DSS projects. They solve problems about project management, technical requirement like security, performance and strategic plan. Therefore, we provide the DSS Trident approach which is an extension of the Y process provided by [13].

The Y diagram, also called "Two Track Unified Process" (2TUP), is the UML process of development based on four steps : Initialization, Elaboration, Construction and Transition. We extend it with the Business track (see figure 2). Thus, it integrates strategic and technical aspects of DSS business group. The Trident is composed of three tracks corresponding to requirements classification [14]. They represent respectively (from left to right in figure 2) "UsersRequirements" analysis, "BusinessRequirements"

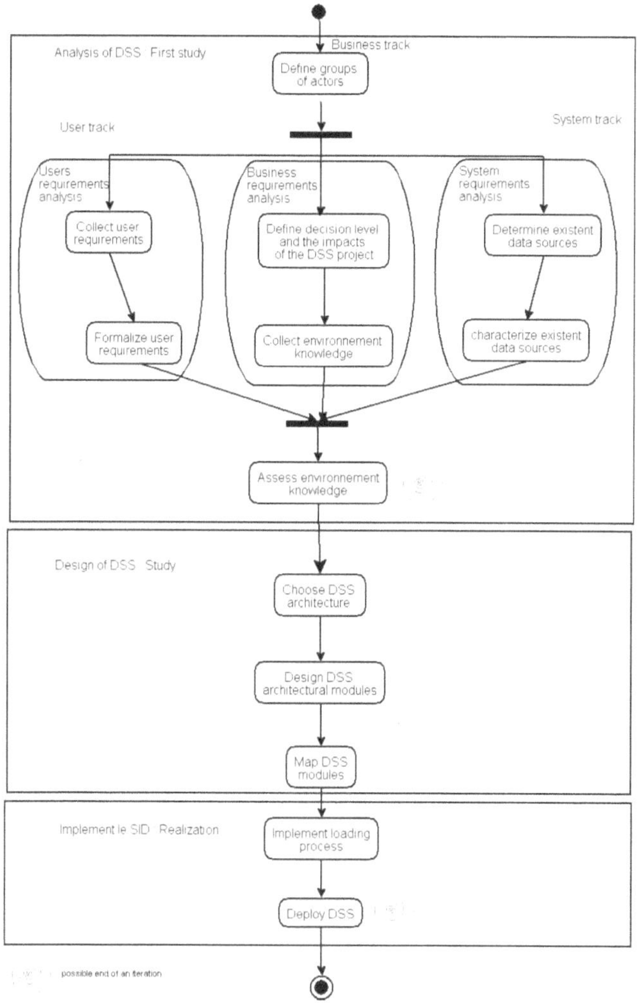

Fig. 2. Activity diagram of DSS Trident

analysis and "SystemRequirements" analysis. The Trident allows parallel treatment of these tracks. They are related to the first step of our approach: the "First study" of the DSS.

2.2 DSS Trident Steps

This first step begins by defining groups of actors, more precisely the definition of the three groups, roles and members properties. It finishes by the task "Assess environment knowledge". It determines whether the data required by DSS requirements are presented on existing sources and if not, it allows designers to count the missing data.

The second step, called "Study", consists in the designing of the DSS engineering. It follows three stages, starting with the choice of architecture and finishing with the definition of mapping schemas from a module to another or from the sources to a module via the conceptual design of modules. The choice of an architecture which is relevant regarding requirements is monitored by DSS Trident approach.

The third step is the DSS implementation, called "Realization". It starts with the implementation of the modules and their treatments. It finishes with the deployment of a prototype or the final system, according to iterations of the lifecycle (the spiral picture in figure 2). The DSS Trident is an iterative and incremental process based on two main iterations. The first iteration allows the assessment of the added value brought to the company. Thus, it is possible to determine the feasibility and to generate a prototype in order to verify the suitability of the system regarding the DSS requirements. The three analysis, upstream of the design process, determine the adapted architecture and the required treatments on the data sources. The end of the first iteration corresponds to the deployment of a prototype, with the actors feedbacks about DSS adequacy after testings. Unlike the 2TUP, our first iteration does not cover all the four steps. But, it covers only the first two steps "Initialization" and "Elaboration" in order to avoid design of schemas which could end up impossible to implement.

Note that without adequacy between DSS requirements and existing sources, the end of the "First-study" step occurs after the task "Assess environment knowledge". The next iteration must start by integrating these feedbacks. In this instance, the project lasts for three iterations. Actually, each time the evaluation of knowledge highlights problems, an iteration is added to the project lifecycle. Consequently, a project with n (n integer) tasks of assessing environment knowledge will last n+1 iterations. The final iteration (the n+1 th) allows designers to fulfill the goals related to the two latter steps of a project based on 2TUP process : "Construction" and "Transition". During this iteration, the DSS is implemented and evaluated in the production environment, after which it will go into maintenance step.

According to the classification of the approaches, our method of DSS development is based on a mixed approach monitored by DSS requirements [14]. Contrary to the existing mixed approaches, we integrate data sources earlier, more precisely at the conceptual level to design adequate schemas and to select an adapted architecture.

3 Choice of the DSS Architecture

3.1 Heterogeneous Architectures Typology

As we mentioned in section 1.1, a particularity of DSS compared to IS is the number of modules which can be combined to build an architecture. For this reason, we present the possible and valid combinations in our architectural context which attempts exhaustiveness.

DSS architecture are composed of the four modules which compose the set E={DG, ODS, DW, DM}. The number of possibilities are the combination of 1, 2, 3 and 4 modules of E, therefore 15. But some combinations of modules are invalid, so we provide the DSS architecture typology, commonly used by the I-D6 company.

Table 1. Valid combinations of DSS heterogeneous architecture

	Number of type of modules			
	1	2	3	4
Architecture	$\{DG^{1..N}\}$	$\{DG^{1..N}, DM^{1..N}\}$	$\{DG^{1..N}, ODS^{1..N}, ODS^{1..N}, DM^{1..N}\}$	$\{DG^{1..N}, DM^{1..N}, DW\}$
	$\{DW\}$	$\{DG^{1..N}, DW\}$	$\{DG^{1..N}, ODS^{1..N}, DW\}$	
		$\{ODS^{1..N}, DM^{1..N}\}$	$\{DG^{1..N}, DM^{1..N}, DW\}$	
		$\{ODS^{1..N}, DW\}$	$\{ODS^{1..N}, DM^{1..N}, DW\}$	
		$\{DM^{1..N}, DW\}$		

The definition of the DSS architecture must satisfy some coherence rules as follows:

- all the modules must be reachable by the actor queries, to have access at detailled levels of data,
- an ODS is an intermediate module in which the data are not kept. So, DSS cannot only be composed of {ODS} or {ODS, DG}. So, these two combinations are not valid,
- a DSS architecture composed of more than one data mart must contain a data warehouse in order to integrate the data,
- a DSS architecture can be composed of several modules of the same type, without several data warehouse module in order to keep the data in a unique data storage and to simplify the requests.

3.2 Automation of the DSS Architecture Choice

In our approach the choice is entirely driven by the analysis of the three user groups requirements. The “First study” step let us know the production context of the next DSS. This context is defined by the 5-tuple LDT, LDE, LEE, LSC, LCD. We define these 5 measurable criteria to qualify the requirements. More precisely, we define

- LCD: the task of assessing environment knowledge determine the cover level of the requirements,
- LDT: the user group assesses the level of data transformation,
- LEE: the system group assesses the level of existing equipment,
- LSC: the level of sources complexity evaluated by system group,
- LDE: the business group assesses the level of decision design expected.

With these five levels, the definition of the DSS architecture is automatic. This process is implemented by the function “architecture_choice” which has the following interface:

TCover X TTransformation X TArchitecture X TComplexity X TDecision -> TArchitecture.

This function has five input parameters and one output which is the adapted architecture defined according to the activity diagrams shown in figure 3 and figure 4. The datatypes mean:

- TCover expresses whether the concerned data sources are "vertical" or "transverse",
- TTransform expresses the type of transformation: "little transformed" or "transformed"
- TArchitecture expresses the combination of types and number of modules. The function does not calculate the number of data mart, which can be calculated with the number of existing data marts and gateways in the company C_{old} and the number of different user classes of the next DSS C_{new}. Thus, the number of data marts or the number of different classes of users (new and old) of the system C_{DSS} is calculated as follows:

$$\begin{aligned} &\text{if } C_{old} \cap C_{new} = \oslash \\ &\qquad \text{then } C_{DSS} = C_{old} + C_{new} \\ &\text{if } C_{old} \cap C_{new} \neq \oslash \\ &\qquad \text{then } C_{DSS} = C_{old} + C_{new} - C_{old \cap new} \end{aligned}$$

- TComplexity expresses the degree of data sources complexity: "little complex" or "complex",
- TDecision expresses the decision design expected: "not complete" or "complete".

For performance reasons we implement our architecture_choice function, with an array of five dimensions corresponding to the input parameters. Results coming from analysis of the three types of requirements are independent, and the number of possible values of

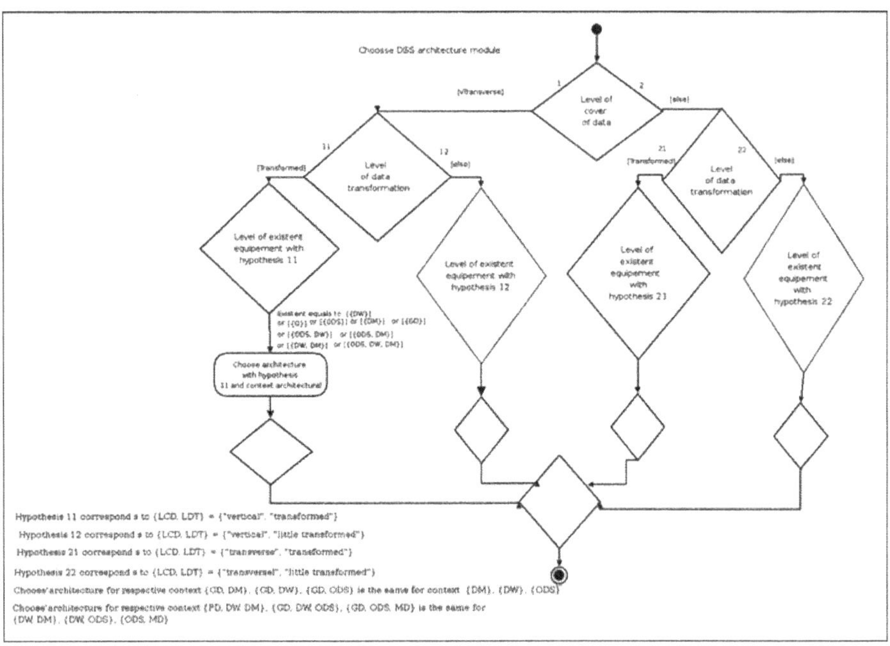

Fig. 3. Activity diagram of the DSS architecture choice

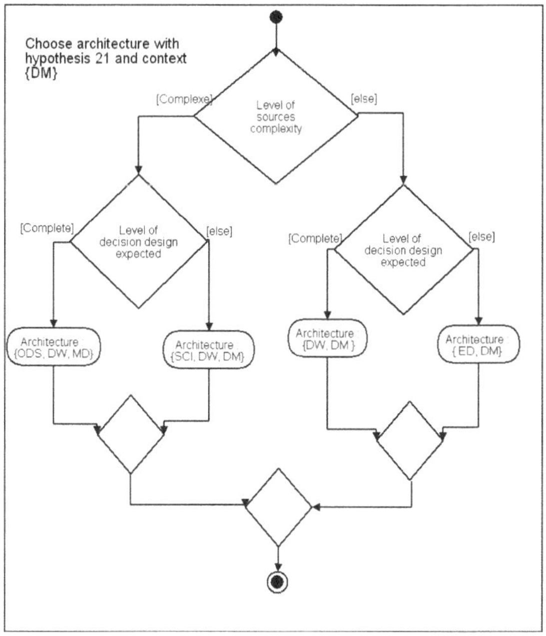

Fig. 4. Activity diagram of the DSS architecture choice with the subcontext {"transverse", "transformed",{DM}}

levels LDT, LDE, LEE, LSC, LCD are respectively 2, 2, 12, 2, 2. Therefore number of contexts is 2*2*12*2*2 equals to 184. Each dimension of the array has respectively 2, 2, 12, 2, 2 possible values. The array has 184 cells which contains the DSS architecture adapted to the 184 contexts.

4 Application

We consider a project with a company which expect a complete DSS. Before, the designers of this company managed their sales with several distant and heterogeneous data sources which are distributed. However, they have already a data mart for planing management. We assume that the "First study" is finished. Thus, the production context {LDT, LDE, LEE, LSC, LCD} is defined by the 5-tuple {"transverse", "transformed", {DM}, "complex", "complete"}. The cover level of DSS requirements (LDT) is transversal because this project takes into account several classes of users which are these of sales. The level of data transformation (LDE) is transformed because the users need consolidated data from several data sources which are not in the same currency. The existing architectural module is a DM, then level of existing equipment (LEE) is a set composed of this only element. The level of sources complexity is complex because the data sources are heterogeneous and distributed. Moreover, they are distant thus it is necessary to gather them in a same storage space. The business group require a DSS architecture complete regarding DSS requirements, hence the level of decision design expected is complete.

From these five values, we can define an adapted architecture. Hence, we execute the function architecture_choice with the parameters as follows architecture_choice ("transverse", "transformed", {DM}, "complex", "complete"). The process of the architecture choice assesses the following adapted architecture : {ODS, DW, 2 DM}. This architecture has been chosen according to the following criteria:

- sources are distributed and complex. They are managed by the ODS,
- the company has already a data mart related to the planning. The users of the existing data mart are not the same of this project users. Hence, there are two different user classes : sales and planning,
- as there are two data marts, the architecture is composed of a data warehouse.

Now, the designers can define the multidimensional conceptual schema of our project which is composed of each architectural module schema.

5 Conclusion

This paper provides our automatic choice of decision support system (DSS) architecture. This task takes place in a mixed approach of DSS development called DSS Trident. Our DSS design method includes the earliest confrontation of these three groups of actors (users, business, system) requirements which drives the DSS architectural modules choice. One of the contributions is the five measurable criteria to assess DSS environment about user requirements, data sources and strategic plans. With these five criteria, DSS architecture choice is monitored according to a proposed activity diagram.

This proposition must also satisfy the I-D6 requirements about DSS architecture choice automation for an easy maintenance system. Thus, we will continue by integrating the reuse concepts in our design method to capitalize the recurrent points of design methods used on several projects. In this perspective, we plan to provide reusable components in order to achieve the quickening of the DSS development and the reliability of DSS.

References

1. Bonifati, A., Cattaneo, F., Ceri, S., Fuggetta, A., Paraboschi, S.: Designing data marts for data warehouses. ACM Trans. Softw. Eng. Methodol. **10**(4) (2001) 452–483
2. Trujillo, J., Palomar, M., Gomez, J., Song, I.Y.: Designing data warehouses with OO conceptual models. Computer **34**(12) (2001) 66–75
3. Sen, A., Sinha, A.P.: A comparison of data warehousing methodologies. Commun. ACM **48**(3) (2005) 79–84
4. Luján-Mora, S., Trujillo, J.: A comprehensive method for data warehouse design. In: DMDW. (2003)
5. Golfarelli, M., Rizzi, S., Saltarelli, E.: Wand: A case tool for workload-based design of a data mart. In: SEBD. (2002) 422–426
6. Kimball, R.: The data warehouse toolkit: practical techniques for building dimensional data warehouses. John Wiley & Sons, Inc., New York, NY, USA (1996)

7. Cabibbo, L., Torlone, R.: A logical approach to multidimensional databases. Lecture Notes in Computer Science **1377** (1998) 155–162
8. Golfarelli, M., Rizzi, S.: Methodological framework for data warehouse design. In: DOLAP '98, ACM First International Workshop on Data Warehousing and OLAP, November 7, 1998, Bethesda, Maryland, USA, Proceedings, ACM (1998) 3–9
9. Kimball, R., Reeves, L., Thornthwaite, W., Ross, M., Thornwaite, W.: The Data Warehouse Lifecycle Toolkit: Expert Methods for Designing. John Wiley & Sons, Inc., New York, NY, USA (1998)
10. Akoka, J., Comyn-Wattiau, I., Prat, N.: From uml to rolap multidimensional databases using a pivot model. Technical report (2001)
11. Cavero, J.M., Costilla, C., Marcos, E., Piattini, M.G., Sánchez, A.: A multidimensional data warehouse development methodology. (2003) 188–201
12. Bruckner, R., List, B., Schiefer, J.: Developping requirements for data warehouse systems with use cases, AMCIS (1999)
13. Roques, P.: UML in Practice - The Art of Modeling Software Systems Demonstrated Through Worked Examples and Solutions. John Wiley & Sons, Inc., New York, NY, USA (2003)
14. Annoni, E., Ravat, F., Teste, O., Zurfluh, G.: Les systèmes d'informations décisionnels : une approche d'analyse et de conception à base de patrons. revue RSTI srie ISI, Méthodes Avancées de Développement des SI **10**(6) (2005)

Dynamic Range Query in Spatial Network Environments

Fuyu Liu, Tai T. Do, and Kien A. Hua

School of Electrical Engineering and Computer Science
University of Central Florida, Orlando, FL, USA
{fliu, tdo, kienhua}@cs.ucf.edu

Abstract. Moving range queries over mobile objects are important in many location management applications. There have been quite a few research works in this area. However, all existing solutions assume an open space environment, which are either not applicable to spatial network environment or require non-trivial extensions. In this paper, we consider a new class of query called *Dynamic Range Query*. A dynamic range query is a moving range query in a network environment, which retrieves the moving objects within a specified network distance of the moving query point. As this query point moves in the network, the footprint (or shape) of the query range changes accordingly to reflect the new relevant query area. Our execution strategy leverages computing power of the moving objects to reduce server load and communication costs. This scheme is particularly desirable for many practical applications such as vehicles in a street environment, where mobile energy is not an issue. We describe the design details and present our simulation study. The performance results indicate that our solution is almost two magnitudes better than a query index method in terms of server load, and requires similar number of messages when compared to a query-blind optimal scheme.

1 Introduction

With the advance in wireless communication technology and advanced positioning systems, there have been many research efforts in query processing for mobile objects. One important query type is monitoring query which, unlike traditional queries, requires real-time processing and has a relatively long lifetime. Moreover, object mobility entails frequent location updates during query execution.

A typical mobile data management system has one or more central servers and a large number of moving objects. Two scalability issues for such a system are server side computation cost and wireless communication cost. Most existing solutions take a centralized approach where moving objects need to report their locations to a central server periodically [2, 4, 6, 7, 9, 10, 12, 16, 17]. The focus of these solutions is to efficiently compute query results without worrying about location updates. More recently, some distributed approaches have been proposed [8, 1, 3, 15]. In this environment, moving objects utilize their own computing power to help process queries in order to reduce server load and avoid frequent location update.

In terms of the spatial database, most existing solutions assume an open space environment, in which moving objects can move freely without any restriction on their movement. In this paper, we focus on processing moving range queries over a spatial network, in which objects move over a set of connecting network segments.

S. Bressan, J. Küng, and R. Wagner (Eds.): DEXA 2006, LNCS 4080, pp. 254–265, 2006.

This environment models manmade transportation networks (airways, seaways, roadways, and railroads) more realistically. A moving range query is issued by a moving object to monitor neighboring moving objects within a defined network distance (range) of the querying object. As the querying object moves, the footprint (shape) of the query region also changes; hence, we name this class of queries *Dynamic Range Query* (DRQ) in this paper. This name also clearly distinguishes the studied query from the traditional rectangular-shaped range queries [1]. Many practical applications can benefit from an efficient processing of DRQ. As an example, a truck carrying sensitive material from location A to location B may want to continuously monitor the surrounding traffic. This monitoring task can be accomplished by issuing a DRQ, in which the querying object is the truck and the range is whatever deemed safe for that truck.

In this paper, we propose an efficient solution for processing DRQ. In our technique, the road network is partitioned into road segments, and moving objects need only update their location when they move into a new segment. Upon a location update, the server informs the moving object the queries overlapping its current road segment. The moving object then monitors these relevant queries, and contacts the server to update the affected query results as it moves in or out of the corresponding queries. The contributions of this paper are as follows:

- To the best of our knowledge, we are the first to consider a new class of queries with the footprint of the query area changes dynamically with query mobility.
- We propose a scalable distributed solution for processing the DRQ that leads to reduced server load and substantial savings in wireless communication costs. Besides the distributed query processing model, the solution also contains another notable technical contribution, in which we introduce a novel concept called *Edge Distance* to speed up network distance computation on mobile objects.

The remainder of this paper is organized as follows. Related work is discussed in Section 2. In Section 3, we give formal definitions and present background information. The proposed solution is introduced in Section 4. We evaluate our solution with simulation in Section 5. Finally, we conclude this paper in Section 6.

2 Related Work

Q-index [8] is the first to address the problem of static range query monitoring over moving objects. In Q-index, queries are indexed by an R-tree and mobile objects probe the R-tree to determine if they are included by the queries. Q-index avoids periodical updates from moving objects by introducing a concept called *safe region*. Each moving object is assigned a safe region. As long as a moving object is moving in its safe region, it does not need to report to the server with its location update. In [1], Cai and Hua proposed a Monitoring Query Management (MQM) technique that also addresses the same problem. In their technique, each moving object is assigned a *resident domain*. A moving object needs to monitor all queries whose regions intersect with its assigned resident domain and reports to the server when it enters or exits any of these queries' regions. Gedik and Liu introduced a MobiEyes system [3], which is capable of answering moving queries over moving objects. In MobiEyes, the underlying open space is divided into grid cells. Each moving query has a *monitoring region* which is defined as a union of cells that can be potentially intersected by the query region, provided that the query's focal object moves within its current cell. The moving object only needs to monitor queries whose monitoring regions intersect with its current cell. Recently, Hu et al. proposed a framework in [15] to answer monitoring queries over moving objects, where mobile clients use safe regions to help reduce communication cost. All these solutions mentioned above assume an open space as the underlying network. As pointed out in Section 1, traditional query models used in an open space are not applicable in a spatial network environment.

Query processing in a spatial network environment has been studied in the literature. Tao et al. [11] proposed algorithms on how to compute static range queries and nearest neighbor queries in a spatial network. A network Voronoi diagram-based algorithm [5] is proposed by Kolahdouzan for k nearest neighbor search. Cho et al. [13] introduced a novel method to answer continuous k nearest neighbor in a road network. A system demonstrated by Huang et al. [14] can answer k nearest neighbor queries effectively. However, all these works are trying to answer either snapshot queries or moving nearest neighbor queries on static objects, and none of them are applicable to answer moving range queries on moving objects.

3 Preliminaries

In this section, we first define the underlying spatial network. We then give definitions for moving objects, dynamic range queries and monitoring regions.

Definition 1 (Network). A network is an undirected graph $G = (N, E)$, where N is a set of nodes, and E is a set of edges. Distance between two nodes n_i and n_j is denoted by $d(n_i, n_j)$. If two nodes are directly connected by an edge, $d(n_i, n_j)$ is equal to the length of the edge. If the two nodes are not directly connected, $d(n_i, n_j)$ denotes the shortest network distance from n_i to n_j.

Definition 2 (Edge). An edge is expressed as $<n_i, n_j>$, where n_i and n_j are two nodes. We assume that there is a universal labeling for nodes, and we express an edge in a way such that $n_i < n_j$ to avoid ambiguity. We refer to n_i and n_j as the *start* node and the *end* node of an edge, respectively. In this paper, we use road segment and edge interchangeably whenever there is no confusion.

The next definition introduces a new concept, edge distance, which is not typical in conventional graph theory. Edge distance will be utilized by mobile objects to compute network distances efficiently in Section 4.5.

Definition 3 (Edge Distance). The distance between any two different edges e_i and e_j can be classified into the following four types: *SS, SE, ES, EE*, depending on the types of nodes connecting the two edges. If both nodes are *start* (*S*) nodes, then the distance type is *SS*. If one node is a *start* node and the other one is an *end* (*E*) node, then the distance type is *SE*. Similarly, there are distance types *ES* and *EE*. Formally, given $e_i = <n_{is}, n_{ie}>$ and $e_j = <n_{js}, n_{je}>$, $d_{xy}(e_i, e_j) = d(n_{ix}, n_{jy})$, where $x, y \in \{S, E\}$. When the two edges are the same, we define an extra distance type called *SAME* (*SM*) and the distance is zero. Formally, if $i = j$, $d_{SM}(e_i, e_j) = 0$, otherwise, $d_{SM}(e_i, e_j) = \infty$.

Consequently, the shortest distance between any two edges can be expressed as $d(e_i, e_j) = min_{type \in \{SM, SS, SE, ES, EE\}}\{d_{type}(e_i, e_j)\}$

Definition 4 (Moving Object). A moving object is represented by a moving point in the road network. At any one time, an object o can be described as $<e, pos, direction, velocity, reportTime, hasQuery>$, where e is the edge that o is moving on and pos is the distance from o to the *start* node of e. Formally, if $e = <n_i, n_j>$, then $d(o, n_i) = pos$ and $d(o, n_j) = d(n_i, n_j) - pos$. If o is moving from the *start* node of e to the *end* node of e, the *direction* is set to 1; otherwise, the *direction* is set to -1. *reportTime* records the time when the *pos* is reported. *hasQuery* is a boolean variable which indicates whether o has issued a DRQ or not. In the rest of this paper, we refer to moving objects that have issued monitoring queries as *query objects*, and moving objects that have not issued monitoring queries as *data objects*. Distance between any two objects o_i and o_j, denoted as $d(o_i, o_j)$, is the shortest network distance from o_i to o_j. It can be calculated by using Property 1 below.

Property 1. Assume the positions of objects o_i and o_j are denoted as $<e_i, pos_i>$ and $<e_j, pos_j>$, where $e_i = <n_a, n_b>$ and $e_j = <n_c, n_d>$. The distance between o_i and o_j can be calculated as follows: if $e_i = e_j$, then $d(o_i, o_j) = |pos_i - pos_j|$; otherwise, $d(o_i, o_j) = min_{x\in\{a,b\},\, y\in\{c,d\}}\{d(o_i, n_x) + d(n_x,n_y) + d(n_y, o_j)\}$

Property 2. For a moving object, with *pos*, *direction*, *velocity*, and *reportTime* all known, and provided that the moving object still moves on the same edge, the new position of the moving object at current time *currentTime* can be calculated as $(currentTime - reportTime) \times velocity \times direction + pos$

Definition 5 (Dynamic Range Query). A DRQ q can be denoted as $<o, length>$, where o is the object issuing the query, and *length* is the range of the query. Assume the set of all moving objects as O, $q.results = \{o_i \mid o_i \in O, d(o, o_i) \leq length\}$

Definition 6 (Monitoring Region). A monitoring region of a DRQ is a set of edges that can be reached by the query's range while the query object moves within its current edge. Formally, for a query $q = <o, length>$ where o moves on edge e, its monitoring region $r = \{e_i \mid e_i \in E, d(e, e_i) < length\}$. If an edge is included in a query's monitoring region, we say that this edge *intersects* with the query's monitoring region.

In order to handle long road segments, such as highways, we set a maximum road length allowed in the system. Any road segments longer than that maximum will be cut into multiple shorter road segments. At each position where the road segment is cut, a virtual node is created and the resultant shorter road segments become virtual edges. In our system, virtual nodes and virtual edges are treated just like real nodes and real edges.

4 Proposed Solution

In this section, we give assumptions for our system first and discuss the designs for the server and moving objects in detail.

4.1 System Assumption

1. Every moving object is equipped with some kind of positioning devices.
2. Every moving object can determine its current road segment ID and its relative position on the road segment by communicating with the server. Moving objects

only needs to communicate with the server each time they enter a new road segment. (A moving object knows that it has entered a new segment if its relative position on the previous segment is less than zero or greater than the length of that segment.)

3. Every moving object has some computing power to perform data processing.

4.2 Server Data Structure

On the server, the road network is stored with an adjacency matrix. Information about query objects and monitoring queries are also stored on the server. Besides, for each road segment, all queries whose monitoring regions *intersect* with it are stored. We use the following three tables in our system: a query object table to store query objects in the format of <*oid, eid, pos, direction, velocity, reportTime*>, a query table to store monitoring queries in the following format: <*qid, oid, eid, length, monitoringRegion, results*>, and a segment-query table to store monitoring queries for each road segment in the format of <*eid, list of queries*>.

4.3 Server Side Message Processing

Our system treats data object and query object differently in message processing. We start the discussion with the data object.

In the initialization phase, a data object sends to the server a message containing its location and where it is heading. The server first finds the segment that the data object is on, and then determines the data object's relative position on that segment and the object's moving direction (either -1 or 1) using Definition 4 given in Section 3. The server expects the following kinds of messages from a data object.

- When a data object exits its current segment and enters a new segment, it will provide the server with its new location and request a new set of queries to be monitored. The server will first remove the data object from the current query results (if the data object is covered by any query), and send the data object a new set of queries, the length of the new segment, the data object's relative position on the new segment, and its new moving direction.
- When a data object finds out that it enters or exits a query's region (the detail will be discussed in Section 4.5), it will notify the server. The server will update the query result accordingly.

Apart from playing the role of a data object for other queries, a query object needs to do some extra steps. In the initialization phase, queries are submitted to the server by query objects. After the server receives the request from a query object, the server first saves the information about the query object and the query, and calculates the monitoring region for the query using the algorithm mentioned in Procedure 1. After finding the monitoring region, the server will update the segment-query table and notify moving objects on all segments of that monitoring region about this DRQ using broadcast. How moving objects respond to the broadcast message will be discussed in Section 4.5. There are three kinds of messages expected from a query object.

- When a query object moves to a new road segment, it needs to report to the server. The server will take the following four steps. In step one, the server will look up in the monitoring query table and retrieve the query's current monitoring region, and then notify all data objects in the monitoring region to stop monitoring the query. In step two, the server will update the information for the query object and the query. In step three, the server will find a new monitoring region for the query with the updated location. In the last step, the server will update the segment-query table and broadcast a message to notify all data objects in the new monitoring region to add this query for monitoring.

- When a query object changes its velocity, it will notify the server. The server will update the query object table and broadcast the updated information.
- When a query object requests a different query range, the system treats it as the query object is moving to a new road segment.

Given a query q_i = <o_i, *qlength*>, and o_i moving on edge e_i = <n_s, n_e>, the server determines the monitoring region of the query by calling Procedure 1 and Procedure 2. The pseudocodes for Procedure 1 and Procedure 2 are provided below. Procedure 2 utilizes a depth-first search to retrieve all edges included in the monitoring region starting from the input node. The outputs of these two procedures are a set of tuples with format <*e, type, dist*>, where *e* is the edge included in the monitoring region, *type* is the type of the edge distance from *e* to e_i defined by Definition 3 in Section 3, and *dist* is the actual distance.

```
Procedure 1: CalculateMonitoringRegion
Input: queryEdge e_i = <n_s, n_e>, queryLength qLength
Output: {<e, type, dist> | e ∈ E,type ∈ {SM, SS, SE, ES, EE}, dist = d_type(e, e_i) < qLength }
    r = {<e_i, SM, 0>}
    Find the start and end nodes of e_i
    r = r ∪ FindEdge(n_s, e_i , 0, start, qLength)
    r = r ∪ FindEdge(n_e, e_i , 0, end, qLength)
    Sort entries in r, remove duplicates. For entries
with same e and type,keep the one with the shortest dist.
    Return r

Procedure 2: FindEdge
Input: startNode n, startEdge se, startDist dist, queryNodeType t, queryLength len
Output: {<e, type, dist >}
    r = ∅ // initialization
    For each adjacent edge e of node n and e ≠ se
      If(n is the start node of edge e)
        If(t = start)r = r ∪ <e, SS, dist>
        Elseif(t = end)r = r ∪ <e, SE, dist>
      Else // n is the end node of edge e
        If(t = start)r = r ∪ <e, ES, dist>
        Elseif(t = end)r = r ∪ <e, EE, dist>
      If((dist + e.length) < len)
        Find the other node of edge e as n'
        r = r ∪ FindEdge(n', e,(dist+e.length), t,len)
    Return r
```

Here we show an example using the above algorithms. Assume a simple road network as drawn in Fig. 1, a query object A is moving on edge n_1n_6, where n_1 is the *start* node and n_6 is the *end* node, and the query's range is 5. Then in the first line of Procedure 1, we include the current edge into the result set as <n_1n_6, *SM, 0*>. Next, in line 3 of Procedure 1, we call Procedure 2 and add the following entries into the result set: <n_1n_2, *SS, 0*>. Because the length of edge n_1n_2 is less than the query's range (line 11 through line 13 in Procedure 2), Procedure 2 is called again. This time, <n_2n_3, *SS, 3*> is added. Next, <n_2n_{10}, *SS, 3*> is added. Similarly, <n_1n_8, *SS, 0*>, <n_1n_9, *SS, 0*> are added. After executing line 4 and line 5 in Procedure 1, we get the final result set as {<n_1n_2, *SS, 0*>, <n_1n_2, *EE, 4*>, <n_1n_6, *SM, 0*>, <n_1n_8, *SS, 0*>, <n_1n_9, *SS, 0*>, <n_2n_3, *EE, 2*>, <n_2n_3, *SS, 3*>, <n_2n_{10}, *SS, 3*>, <n_2n_{10}, *SE, 4*>, <n_3n_4, *SE, 2*>, <n_3n_6, *EE, 0*>, <n_5n_6, *EE, 0*>, <n_6n_7, *SE, 0*>}. In Fig. 1, all thick edges are included in the monitoring region.

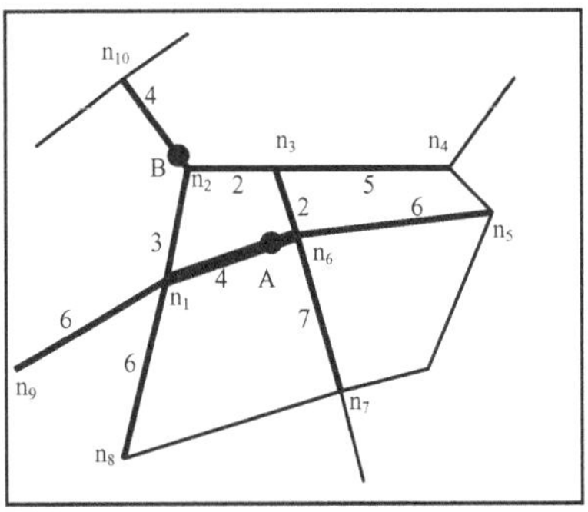

Fig. 1. An example of calculating monitoring region

4.4 Moving Object Data Structure

On a moving object, a table is used to store all queries whose monitoring regions intersect with the edge that the object is on. An entry in the table has the following format: <*qid, oid, qLength, eLength*, {<*type, dist*>}>, where *qid* is the query id, *oid* is the corresponding query object id, *qLength* is the query's range, *eLength* is the length of the road segment that the query object is on, and {<*type, dist*>} stores a set of tuples, where each tuple specifies the edge distance type and the actual distance from the query object's segment to the moving object's segment. For each stored query, the corresponding query object's information is also stored.

4.5 Moving Object Message Processing

While a moving object is moving on a road segment, it needs to listen to broadcast messages from the server. If its road segment is covered by a new query's monitoring region, the moving object needs to add that query into its monitoring query list. If the message is for update of an existing query, the moving object will update that query in its monitoring query list.

A moving object needs to periodically check queries in its monitoring query list with the algorithm discussed in Procedure 3. If it enters a query region or exits a query region, it will notify the server, and the server will update the query result accordingly. Besides, a moving object also needs to periodically check if it is still in its current road segment. If it enters a new road segment, it will first remove all old queries from its current monitoring query list and send a message to the server with its new location. After receiving a new set of queries and the new segment information, the moving object will save these data and start the periodic checking steps again.

```
Procedure 3: CalculateDistanceToQueryObject
Input: objectPosition oPos, objectEdgeLength oeLength,
monitoring queries: {<qid, oid, qLength, eLength,
{<type, dist>}>}
Output: {<qid>}
1. r = ∅ // initialization
2. For each query q in the monitoring query list
2.     d = ∞, minDist = ∞ // initialization
3.     Estimate query object's current position as qPos
4.     For each <type, dist> tuple in query q
5.       If(type=SM) d = |oPos - qPos|
6.       Elseif(type=SS) d = oPos + qPos + dist
7.       Elseif(type=SE) d = oPos+(eLength-qPos)+dist
8.       Elseif(type=ES) d = (oeLength-oPos)+qPos+dist
9.       Else d = (oeLength-oPos)+(eLength-qPos)+dist
10.      If (d < minDist) minDist = d
11.    If(minDist ≤ qLength) r = r ∪ {qid}
12. Return r
```

Procedure 3 takes inputs as the data structures stored in the moving object as described in section 4.4, and outputs the list of monitoring queries still containing the moving object in their results. Specifically, in step 3, we apply Property 2 in Section 3 to estimate the current position of the query object, given that necessary information about the query object is available. Then with the pre-calculated edge distances {<*type, dist*>} between two edges in which the data object and query object are currently moving on, step 4-10 uses Property 1 in Section 3 to compute the shortest distance between the data object and the query object. Finally, step 12 returns all monitoring queries that contain the data object in their results. The interesting point of the algorithm is the utilization of pre-calculated edge distances. By using the server to carry out the computationally expensive computation of edge distances, we gain the following advantages: 1) there is no need to transfer the network map from the server to mobile objects for shortest network distance computation, and 2) we avoid the expensive shortest path computation on mobile objects. Even in the case in which each mobile object possesses a network map, pre-calculated edge distances can still be useful in realizing the second advantage.

We still use the example given in Section 4.3 to illustrate the idea. In Fig. 1, assume the query object A is at location 3.6 on edge n_1n_6, and there is a data object B at location 0.5 on edge n_2n_{10}. From the discussion of Section 4.3, we know that the data object B has two entries for the query issued by the query object A stored as {<*SS, 3*>, <*SE, 4*>}. Using the first entry will yield a distance as 7.1, which is out of the query's range (the range is 5). With the second entry, the distance will be 4.9, and the data object B should be included into the query's result.

5 Performance Study

A simulator is implemented to evaluate the performance of our technique. The performance metrics we use include:

- **Server side work load**. The work load can be characterized by I/O time and CPU time, of which I/O time is more dominant. Therefore, server side work load is measured as the total number of road segments accessed in order to answer queries.
- **Server side communication cost**. This is measured by counting the total number of received messages and sent messages to reflect bandwidth consumption.
- **Moving object side communication cost**. We count both received messages and sent messages to measure energy consumption. However, since sending message is more costly than receiving message in a wireless environment, we set the cost for uplink twice as the cost for downlink (i.e. two received messages are counted as one message).

As mentioned in Section 2, all existing distributed approaches are not applicable to a spatial network environment or extensions are non-trivial; therefore, we compare our technique with centralized approaches.

For the server side work load, we compare our technique with one popular centralized solution: query index [8]. The query index scheme is adapted for the spatial network environment, where queries are indexed by a segment-query table that is similar to the table used in our technique. In this segment-query table, for each segment, all queries whose ranges (note: not monitoring regions) intersect with that segment are saved. Each time when a moving object updates its location, the system first retrieves the segment that the object is on, then compare the object's new location with all queries stored in that segment to determine if this moving object is included by some queries. Every time when a query object updates its location or requests a different query range, first the system will treat it as a data object and find out which queries cover this object, then the system will update the segment-query table accordingly.

We also compare communication cost against a centralized approach, where moving objects send messages to the server whenever they change velocities or move to new road segments. When a moving object moves to a new road segment, the server will send the moving object a message containing information about the new road segment to help the moving object determine when it moves out of the new road segment. At each time unit, the server will estimate every moving object's new location, and answer all queries with the newly estimated locations. This solution is optimal on communication cost if we assume that moving objects have no information about queries, in other words, this is a query-blind optimal solution. Other than this approach, we also include a naïve approach which serves as a basis for comparison. In the naïve approach, all moving objects report their locations to the server at every time step. Consequently, the server does not need to send any message back to moving objects.

5.1 Simulation Setup

The area of interest in our simulation is a square shaped region of 10,000 square miles. A synthetic road network is generated by first placing nodes randomly on the region, then connecting nodes randomly to form road segments. In our setup, there are 2000 nodes and 4000 edges. The longest road segment allowed in our simulation is 20 miles. Moving objects are randomly placed on road segments with initial velocities and directions. The velocities of these moving objects follow a Zipf distribution with a deviation of 0.7, and the values are between 0.5 and 1 mile per time unit. The direction is set as either 1 or -1. When a moving object approaches a road intersection, it will move to a new randomly selected road segment. At each time unit, one tenth of the moving objects will change their velocities.

Query objects are selected randomly from the moving objects. In our simulation, there are 100,000 moving objects in total and we vary the number of queries from 10 to 1000 to test the scalability of the system. Query's range is also specified randomly where the maximum range length allowed is 2 miles. We run simulation for 10 times and take the average as the final output. Each simulation lasts for 200 time units. The simulation was run on a Pentium 4 2.6GHz desktop pc with 2GB memory.

5.2 Simulation Results

Fig. 2.a shows the server loads for our technique and the query index method when the number of queries increases from 10 to 1000. Please note that the y-axis is in logarithmic scale. It is observed that our technique provides almost two magnitudes of improvement on server load. This is mainly because computations carried out on moving objects can reduce a lot of work load on the server.

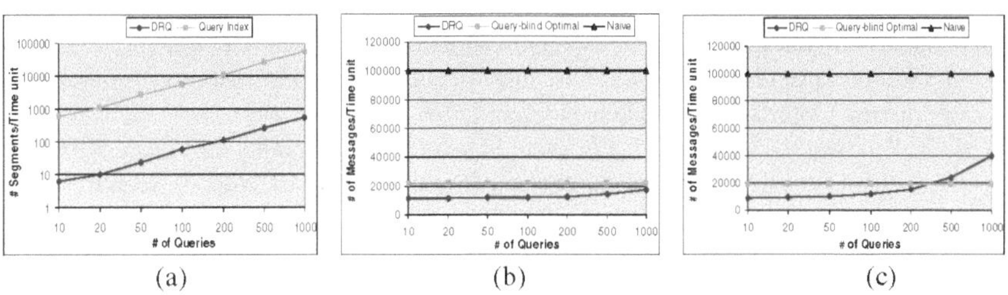

Fig. 2. Effect of # of queries on (a) Server side work load, (b) Server side communication, (c) Moving object side communication

Fig. 2.b and 2.c study communication cost on server side and moving object side by varying the number of queries. The number of messages per time unit is plotted as a function of the number of queries. As shown by the figures, in our technique, the number of messages increases as the number of queries increases, simply because more queries require more communication. However, in the query-blind optimal method, the number of messages is not affected. The reason is that the majority of communication cost is from the moving objects changing segment or speed, as long as the total number of moving objects stay the same, the communication cost will not vary significantly. On the server side, our technique is always better than the query-blind optimal method even when there are 1000 concurrent queries. On the moving object side, when the number of queries is small, our technique performs better than the query-blind optimal method. When there are too many queries involved, our technique has a higher communication cost than the query-blind optimal method. But the cost is still acceptable considering that the huge gain obtained in server load. In these two figures, we also include the naïve method for comparison, which has a much higher communication cost.

6 Conclusions and Future Work

In this paper, we propose a distributed solution to answer dynamic range query over moving objects in spatial network environments. Our solution uses road segments as building blocks for monitoring regions of moving queries. Moving objects utilize their own computing power to help reduce server load and save wireless bandwidth. The simulation results show that our method is almost two magnitudes better than the query index method in terms of server load and has lower communication cost when there are light or medium amount of queries when compared to the query-blind optimal scheme. Future work of this study will be extending our technique to answer more complicated moving monitoring queries.

References

[1] Y. Cai and K. A. Hua. An adaptive query management technique for efficient real-time monitoring of spatial regions in mobile database systems. In *IEEE IPCCC*, 2002
[2] K. Mouratidis, M. Hadjieleftheriou, D. Papadias, Conceptual Partitioning: An Efficient Method for Continuous Nearest Neighbor Monitoring. In *SIGMOD* 2005
[3] B. Gedik and L. Liu, MobiEyes: Distributed Processing of Continuously Moving Queries on Moving Objects in a Mobile System, in *EDBT* 2004
[4] P. K. Agarwal, L. Arge, and J. Erickson. Indexing moving points. In *PODS*, 2000
[5] M. R. Kolahdouzan, C. Shahabi: Voronoi-Based K Nearest Neighbor Search for Spatial Network Databases. In *VLDB* 2004: 840-851
[6] G. Kollios, D. Gunopulos, and V. J. Tsotras. On indexing mobile objects. In *PODS*, 1999
[7] X. Xiong, M. Mokbel, W. Aref, SINA: Scalable Incremental Processing of Continuous Queries in Spatio-temporal Databases. In *SIGMOD*, 2004
[8] S. Prabhakar, Y. Xia, D. V. Kalashnikov, W. G. Aref, and S. E. Hambrusch. Query indexing and velocity constrained indexing: Scalable techniques for continuous queries on moving objects. *IEEE Transactions on Computers*, 51(10), 2002
[9] S. Saltenis, C. S. Jensen, S. T. Leutenegger, and M. A. Lopez. Indexing the positions of continuously moving objects. In *SIGMOD*, 2000
[10] Y. Tao and D. Papadias. Time-parameterized queries in spatio-temporal databases. In *SIGMOD*, 2002

[11] D. Papadias, J. Zhang, N. Mamoulis, Y. Tao: Query Processing in Spatial Network Databases. In *VLDB* 2003: 802-813
[12] Y. Xia, S. Prabhakar, S. Lei, R. Cheng, R. Shah: Indexing continuously changing data with mean-variance tree. *SAC* 2005: 1125-1132
[13] H. Cho, C. Chung: An Efficient and Scalable Approach to CNN Queries in a Road Network. In *VLDB* 2005: 865-876
[14] B. Huang, Z. Huang, D. Lin, H. Lu, Y. Song, H. Li: ITQS: An Integrated Transport Query System. In *SIGMOD* 2004: 951-952
[15] H. Hu, J. Xu, D. L. Lee: A Generic Framework for Monitoring Continuous Spatial Queries over Moving Objects. In *SIGMOD* 2005
[16] X. Yu, K. Q. Pu, and N. Koudas. Monitoring k-nearest neighbor queries over moving objects. In *IEEE ICDE*, 2005.
[17] X. Xiong, M. Mokbel, W. Aref, SEA-CNN:Scalable Processing of Continuous K-Nearest Neighbor Queries in Spatio-temporal Databases. In *IEEE ICDE* 2005.

Context and Semantic Composition of Web Services

Michael Mrissa[1], Chirine Ghedira[1], Djamal Benslimane[1], and Zakaria Maamar[2]

[1] Claude Bernard Lyon 1 University, Lyon, France
firstname.lastname@liris.cnrs.fr
[2] Zayed University, Dubai, U.A.E
zakaria.maamar@zu.ac.ae

Abstract. Composition of Web services is a cornerstone step in the development of interoperable systems. However, Web services still face data-heterogeneity challenges, although several attempts of using semantics. In addition, the context in which Web services evolve is still somehow "ignored", hampering their adaptability to changes in composition situations. In this paper, we argue how context permits to determine the semantics of interfaces that Web services expose to third parties. We show the need for a context- and semantic-based approach for Web services composition.

Keywords: Web service, semantics, context, composition, mediation.

1 Introduction

Web services are now accepted as standards for bridging heterogeneous applications. Web services possess the capability of deploying high-level processes referred to as composite Web services. Composition addresses the situation in which a user request cannot be satisfied by a single Web service, whereas a composite Web service consisting of a combination of Web services (either simple or composite) could satisfy this request [2]. A composition is always associated with a specification that describes amongst others the list of component Web services, their execution chronology, and the corrective strategies in case of exceptions.

Current approaches only achieve Web services composition at the level of message interactions [6]. The standard Web services protocol stack (SOAP, WSDL, UDDI) was not initially built with meeting the requirements of semantic exchange. Composition needs, too, to be conducted at the semantic level. Ignoring or poorly assessing semantics are obstacles to composition since Web services have to be initially checked whether they can effectively work together [8].

Despite multiple attempts, the smooth automation of Web services semantic reconciliation remains a challenge. First, description techniques of the semantic functionalities of Web services are still in their "infancy" stage, despite the tremendous growth in semantic description languages like OWL-S [7]. Second, the context in which Web services evolve is to a certain extent "ignored", which hampers their adaptability to changes in composition situations.

S. Bressan, J. Küng, and R. Wagner (Eds.): DEXA 2006, LNCS 4080, pp. 266–275, 2006.

In this paper we aim at *investigating how context drives the semantic reconciliation of Web services.* The rationale of this reconciliation is backed by Maamar et al., who argue that Web services composition is subject to satisfying two conditions [5]. The first condition is that Web services must agree on the meaning of the exchanged data. And the second condition is that semantic-data conflicts must be automatically resolved using the information that context caters. In this paper we focus on data heterogeneities that arise when Web services from different origins take part in a composition. We propose a language for enhancing Web services descriptions with data semantics. This language is integrated into a *semantic-mediation architecture* that solves information heterogeneities using semantic values and Web services' context.

The role of context in data conflicts of type value is not properly handled in other semantic composition systems. Our proposed solution is built upon Sciore et al.'s work who suggest using the concept of *semantic value* to solve such conflicts [11]. A semantic value is a basic value (i.e., type instance such as like "5" is an "integer" instance), which has a semantic information for facilitating its contextual understanding, e.g., "5(currency=euro)" describes "5" units of currency of type euros. This semantic information will be anchored to the *semantic context* of the Web service.

Section 2 overviews related work on context awareness and semantics of Web services. Section 3 motivates the need for semantics in Web service description and details how WSDL is extended into $\mathcal{SVE}$-WSDL (standing for $\mathcal{S}$emantic-$\mathcal{V}$alue $\mathcal{E}$nhanced-WSDL). Section 4 explains the semantic-based mediation architecture for Web services engaged in composition. The implementation of this architecture is also given in this section. Finally, Section 5 draws our conclusions and overviews different aspects of future work.

2 Related Work

2.1 Semantics and Web Services

Semantic Web services constitute an active domain of research. There are several ways of inserting semantics into Web Services. One way consists of using description languages like OWL-S [7], and another way consists of extending syntactic standards like WSDL with semantic features [10,13].

The first way consists of developing languages to semantically describe Web services: OWL-S and WSMO (Web Service Modeling Ontology) [1] currently are the leading languages towards semantic description of Web services. OWL-S is based on the OWL description language and was intended to be combined with syntactic description languages like WSDL. WSMO uses F-Logic to describe the features of Web services. Based on OWL-S, several research projects have been developed for example ODESWS [3] and METEOR-S (LSDIS) [10]. In these systems, ontologies are used to annotate Web services [12], which is useful during discovery, selection, and composition.

Martin et al. introduced the OWL-S language to describe a Web service along a profile, a model, and a grounding [7]. The service profile answers "what does the service do?". The service model answers "how does the service work?". And the service grounding answers "how to access the service?". Spencer et al. propose a rule-based approach to semantically match outputs and inputs of Web services [14]. An inference engine analyzes OWL-S descriptions and generates multiple data transformation rules using a description-logic reasoning system.

The second way of inserting semantics into Web Services enriches WSDL with the semantics of a domain expressed in an ontology The WSDL-S language [10] from the LSDIS laboratory, extends the WSDL format by adding an "LSDIS-Concept" element to the "part" tag of the WSDL input/output message. This additional element does not itself contain the semantic information, but it rather refers to an element described in an OWL ontology. With the help of the extensibility support of WSDL, files can be extended with semantic information [13].

2.2 Context and Web Services

In the area of Web services, context has been recently investigated in many research projects. The main objective of these projects is to facilitate the development and deployment of context-aware and adaptable Web services. Standard Web services descriptions are augmented with context information (e.g., location, time, user profile) and new frameworks are developed to support this. The approach proposed in [9] is intended to provide an enhancement of WSDL language with context aware features. The proposed Context-based Web Service Description Language (CWSDL) adds to WSDL a new part called Context Function which is used to select the best Web service. This function represents the sensitivity of the Web service to the context. Another interesting approach was proposed in [4] to deal with context in Web services. The approach consists of two parts: a context infrastructure and a context type set. The context infrastructure allows context information to be transmitted as a SOAP header-block within the SOAP messages.

3 Semantics and Context for Web Services Composition

3.1 A Motivating Example

The following simple yet-realistic example discusses why semantic mediation is a key step for Web services composition. Let us assume planning a trip to Japan. The airport of our destination city offers free-of-charge access to the Internet. Promotion fliers distributed to passengers contain some recommended hotels with their HTTP addresses. A hotel, which has attractive rates, provides a Web service interface[1] for booking price estimation (implementation technology transparent to passengers). To check if this hotel is affordable for an European passenger, the following composition of Web services occurs: *HotelBooking* for estimate charges in Yens based on a number of booking nights, and *PersonalEuroBanking* for payment management.

[1] A WSDL interface is the set of functions with their input and output parameters.

This example highlights the importance of semantic reconciliation between both Web services. The semantics of their interfaces needs to be explicitly described for a free-of-conflict composition. Indeed each Web service manages a different currency, so there are two heterogeneous semantic contexts in this example: the first Web service in a "Japanese" semantic context delivers figures in Yens, whereas the second one in an "European" semantic context expects figures in Euros. The composition is not sensitive if the data from the first Web service is directly submitted to the second one without any extra-processing. This results in managing figures (e.g., 100 Yens, 250 Euros) without a real understanding of their appropriateness. This calls for adapting data between services. In this example, currency from *HotelBooking* service needs to be converted so that it matches the currency used by *PersonalEuroBanking* service.

3.2 The Core Idea of the Proposed Approach

In a simple composition (Figure 1-(a)), Web services' interfaces are described using WSDL. During Web services interactions, any data conflict of type value is resolved in ad-hoc way at the level of the receiver Web-service. For example, upon reception of a value V in Yens from WS_1, WS_2 explicitly converts it into V' in local currency.

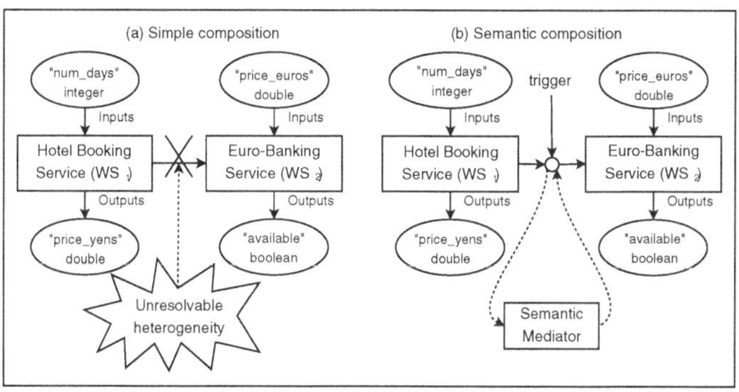

Fig. 1. Simple *vs.* semantic composition

To conduct semantic composition that includes the context of the exchanged data (Figure 1-(b)), the context that defines these data's role must be provided. This context is any metadata that explicitly describes the meaning of the data to be exchanged between Web services. When Web services' inputs and outputs are described using metadata, they can automatically be transformed from one context to another one during Web services execution. By automatically, we mean that conversion function is not embedded into the body of any Web service. This function is loosely-attached to Web services (i.e., independent), and becomes, thus, an active component that intervenes during Web services composition and execution. A possible solution to achieve a semantic composition of Web services is built upon the semantic-value concept.

3.3 Semantic Value Concept

Sciore et al. introduce the notion of semantic value to describe a value (i.e., type instance) with additional semantic information (its context) [11]. Formally, a semantic value A is defined as follows: $A = a(p_1 = a_1, ...p_i = a_i, ..., p_n = a_n)$ where a is a simple value, p_i a property, and a_i a simple or a semantic value.

While a simple value is simply defined as an instance of a type (e.g., 5 as integer), a semantic value associates a value with a context in which its interpretation happens. For example, 5(context=(currency, euro)) is a semantic value that defines 5 as a currency in euros. Recursive descriptions is also possible since the value of a property can also have its own context, e.g. 5(currency, euro (context=(scalefactor,1000))) is a recursive description of the semantic value 5.

It is important to note that the values "5" and "50" can be considered as different with each other if considered as simple values. However, they can be considered as equivalent if they are interpreted as semantic values with different contexts, e.g., 5(currency, euro) = 50(currency, yen) when 1 euro worths 10 yens.

Then, the main purpose of enabling semantic mediation between Web services consists of associating context to web services and using conversion functions to convert a semantic value from the context of a Web service to another. The semantic value 5(currency, euro) can be converted into another semantic value 50(currency, yen). Depending on the conversion to adopt, a conversion function can be lossless or lossy (like for compression/decompression), total or non-total (for example city to country is not reversible), and order preserving or not (if a $<$ b then cvt(a) $>$ cvt(b) where cvt is a function).

3.4 From WSDL to $\mathcal{SVE}$-WSDL

To develop an enriched semantic description of a Web service, we investigated how the representation of some WSDL elements could be extended. Each representation would be associated with some specific information that depends for example on the ontology that the Web service binds to. To add more semantics to Web services' descriptions, we proposed $\mathcal{SVE}$-WSDL as an extension of WSDL. This extension adds the concept of semantic value to a WSDL description.

To keep the paper self-contained, we overview the main structure of a WSDL document: `<type>` element defines data types exchanged in messages. `<message>` element describes the data elements of an operation. Each message consists of one or more parts. Each part has a `<name>` element, a `<type>` element, and may consist of additional `<element>` elements. These three constructs define the names and types of the parameters that are used by the Web service in the message. For platform independence requirement, WSDL uses XML syntax to define data types. Some message parts may be of type complex, and may contain a structure of several XML Schema elements. `<portType>` element provides an abstract description of the Web service. It defines the operations (using one or more `<operation>` elements) that can be performed over a Web service, and the messages involved. Each operation may contain one `<input>`, one `<output>`, and one `<fault>` sections. Each section contains a `<message>` element that specifies what the Web service receives (input

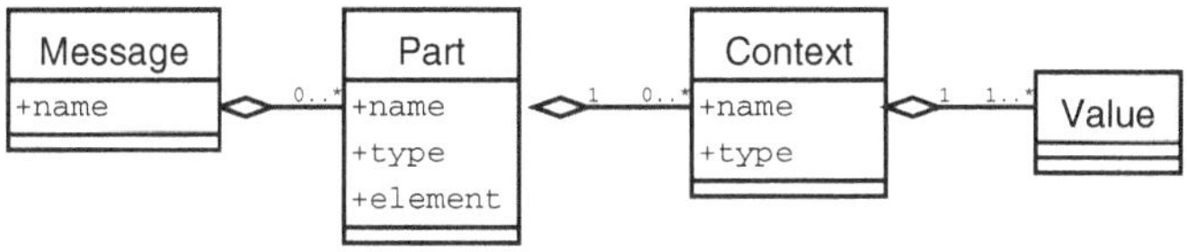

Fig. 2. Proposed extension of the WSDL metamodel

message) and sends when its execution fails (fault message) or succeeds (output message). Finally, `<binding>` element defines the message format and protocol details for each port. Several protocols may be used such as SOAP over HTTP.

Our proposal for $\mathcal{SVE}$-WSDL is to bind a semantic value description to the inputs and outputs of a Web service. The extension of the WSDL metamodel is partially shown in Figure 2. It is now enhanced with context meta-class associated with part meta-class. Input and output elements contain a single message, that consists of one or several parts. In fact, we aim at extending each part of a message with an additional element to be referred to as "context". Compared to the concept of semantic values of Sciore et al. [11], `<part>` tag describes the simple value and `<context>` structure represents the semantics associated with this value. As a result, we define a structure to describe the context to be associated with the values described in `<part>` elements of a Web service's messages. This structure consists of: (i) a `<name>` element that labels the semantic information; (ii) a `<type>` element that indicates the type of the semantic information; (iii) a `<value>` element that contains the information itself; and an optional `<context>` element providing additional context information to the `<value>` element, thus enabling recursive descriptions. Listing 1.1 illustrates a part of a $\mathcal{SVE}$-WSDL description of a Web service.

```
<?xml version="1.0" encoding="UTF-8"?>
<definitions name="HotelService" tns="http://example.HotelService/" ...>
    <message name="HotelServiceEndpoint-Booking">
        <part name="Num-Days" type="xsd:integer">
            <context name="time" type="xsd:string" value="time-unit">
                <context name="duration" type="xsd:string" value="day"/>
            </context>
        </part>
    </message>
    <message name="HotelServiceEndpoint-BookingResponse">
        <part name="price" type="xsd:int">
            <context name="currency" type="xsd:string" value="yen"/>
            <context name="scalefactor" type="xsd:string" value="1"/>
        </part>
    </message>
    <portType name="HotelServiceEndpoint">
        <operation name="Booking" parameterOrder="Num-Days">
            <input message="tns:HotelServiceEndpoint-Booking"/>
            <output message="tns:HotelServiceEndpoint-BookingResponse"/>
        </operation>
    </portType>
...
</definitions>
```

Listing 1.1. $\mathcal{SVE}$-WSDL description of a Web service

4 Semantic-Based Mediation for Web Services

4.1 Components of the Architecture

Figure 3 presents the architecture for context- and semantic-based mediation of Web services composition. It consists of six components:

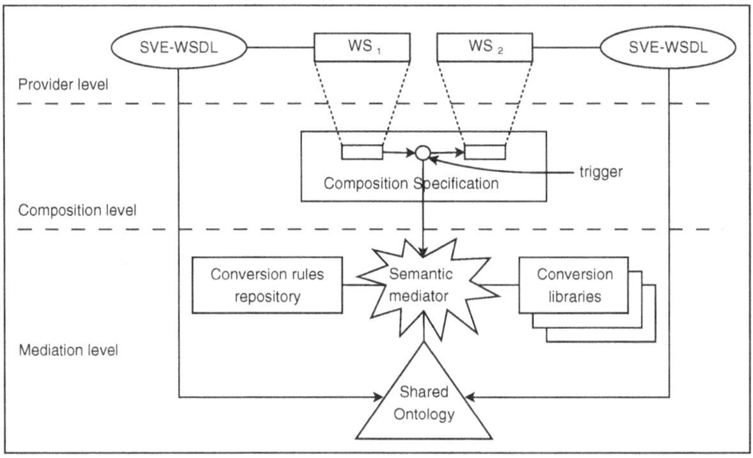

Fig. 3. $\mathcal{SVE}$-WSDL mediation architecture

$\mathcal{SVE}$-WSDL Annotations. They extend WSDL descriptions of Web services by using semantics. Web services can now "understand" the values they exchange. Interesting to note that Web services still exchange simple values during the execution, so that the interactions with Web services during invocation remain unchanged. These values are more understandable since their semantics in terms of meta-data can be extracted from $\mathcal{SVE}$-WSDL descriptions. The Web service's provider does not have to undertake any changes, except of adhering their WSDL description to the $\mathcal{SVE}$-WSDL format.

Value Triggers. The data flow during composition needs to be intercepted at some points between component Web services. To keep Figure 3 clear, triggers are not represented. A trigger intervenes between Web services, extracts data from SOAP messages, and sends a conversion request to the semantic mediator. Then the trigger waits for an answer from the mediator and, depending on the answer it receives (or a timeout), either forwards converted data to the next Web service(s), or throws an exception. Still remains the question about where to physically place the triggers. For scalability reasons, we recommended that triggers should be along with the specification execution program, most of the times on the client side. An example of implementation is to use the BPELJ language for specifying the composition, and to integrate the triggers under the form of code snippets that are located between composed Web services. Indeed, as shown (Figure 1-(b)), the trigger intercepts the values exchanged during composition and passes them on to the mediator where data heterogeneities remain unresolved in a simple composition. Thus, triggers do not have to know that they are part of an architecture that deals with semantic values. This separation between the actual mediation process and the composition specification allows a better scalability and adaptability of the architecture to future modifications.

Semantic Mediator. It works in close collaboration with the triggers by receiving their outputs. The semantic mediator is a service (either local service or Web service). It acts as a listener that gets a semantic value from a source context and returns, if possible, the conversion of this value to a target context. To this end, the semantic mediator is supported in its work with a conversion rules repository while searching for the appropriate conversion functions. The mediator delivers the resulting basic value to the trigger that sent out the request, or returns an exception in case of non semantic comparability (i.e. the conversion is not meaningful). The semantic comparability of two semantic values is detailed in Sciore's work [11].

Conversion Rules Repository. It contains the mappings between terms used in various semantic contexts and lists as well the conversion opportunities between these terms. It is expected that the repository can refer to several conversion libraries including remote ones. New conversion libraries can be added upon request, i.e., each time a composition requires new conversion functions for a new application domain.

Conversion Libraries. Conversion functions are stored in libraries and permit converting semantic values from one context into another.

Application Domain Ontologies. The mediator refers back to these ontologies to check whether or not it is possible to clearly identify a semantic value. We do not discuss here the mechanisms that could help the mediator identify a term in an ontology, as we focus on the enhancement of the process of mediation with semantic values. This point is to be considered in future work. For the moment, let us consider that the identification of the terms is performed by a simple pattern-matching technique. For instance, in the domain of currencies, providers may differently name the same concept (devise, currency, moneyUnit, etc.) and its instances (USD, Dollar, USDollars, etc.). The ontologies help the mediator find out what similarities and inconsistencies are between semantic value descriptions.

4.2 Architecture Operation Through the Prototype

A prototype that supports the proposed architecture is fully operational. We use Java^{TM} NetBeans environment. Figure 4 is the GUI to read/write *context* annotations from/to WSDL files.

As part of our implementation efforts, we developed the context-aware mediation architecture for Web services. This consists of reading context annotation

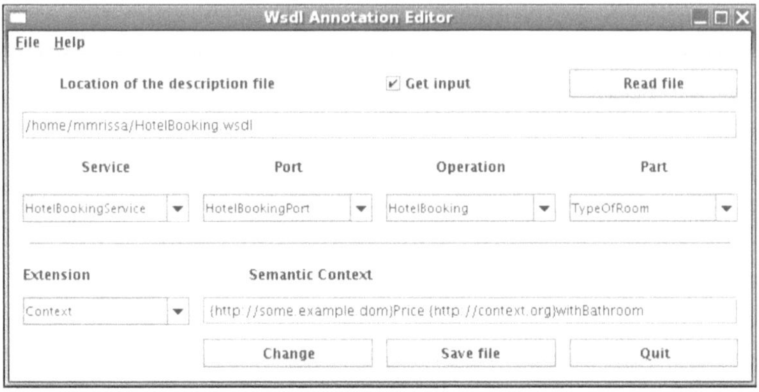

Fig. 4. Screenshot of the WSDL extension editor

from WSDL files and converting data received from a source context to a target context. This mediation is part of the example given in Section 3.1. We deployed the "HotelBooking", "Mediation" and "PersonalEuroBanking" Web services on an Apache Axis server and composed them using BPEL. The implementation shows that dynamic and accurate interpretation of context enable a meaningful composition to be performed. With the context-aware mediation Web service and annotated WSDL files, not only the "price" semantic types match, but data is transformed at the execution stage, to comply with the different scale factors, heterogeneous date formats (that allow getting up-to-date conversion rates between currencies), and different VAT rates (that also are not always included in the price) that form the *context* of data.

5 Conclusion

In this paper we presented an approach that supports semantic interoperability among individual Web services engaged in composition. To this end we enhanced WSDL descriptions of Web services with semantic metadata for capturing contextual information. We also proposed an architecture that exploits these ontological annotations for adapting data on the fly when they are transferred from Web service to another constitutive one. The heart of our architecture is the context mediator; which adapts exchanged data so as to be compliant with the receiver's requirements.

Our future work revolves around different aspects. First, the use of context should be considered, so that applications can become aware of their environment. Second, different local ontologies can be used when providers develop Web services, so there is a need to generate contextual mappings between ontologies in an automatic way.

References

1. S. Arroyo and M. Stollberg. WSMO Primer. WSMO Deliverable D3.1, DERI Working DRAFT. Technical report, WSMO, 2004. http://www.wsmo.org/2004/d3/d3.1/.
2. J. Bézivin, S. Hammoudi, D. Lopes, and F. Jouault. Applying MDA Approach for Web Service Platform. In *Proceedings of The IEEE Enterprise Distributed Object Computing Conference (EDOC'2004)*, Monterey, California, 2004.
3. Ó. Corcho, A. Gómez-Pérez, M. Fernández-López, and M. Lama. ODE-SWS: A Semantic Web Service Development Environment. In *Proceedings of The first International Workshop on Semantic Web and Databases (SWDB'2003)*, Berlin, Germany, 2003.
4. M. Keidl and A. Kemper. A framework for context-aware adaptable web services. In *Proceedings of The 9th International Conference on Extending Database Technology (EDBT'2004)*, Heraklion, Greece, 2004.
5. Z. Maamar, D. Benslimane, and N. C. Narendra. What Can Context do for Web Services? *Communications of the ACM*, 2006 (forthcoming).
6. Z. Maamar, N. C. Narendra, and S. Sattanathan. Towards an Ontology-based Approach for Specifying and Securing Web Services. *Journal of Information & Software Technology, Elsevier Science Publisher*, 2006 (forthcoming).
7. D. L. Martin, M. Paolucci, S. A. McIlraith, M. H. Burstein, D. V. McDermott, D. L. McGuinness, B. Parsia, T. R. Payne, M. abou, M. Solanki, N. Srinivasan, and K. P. Sycara. Bringing Semantics to Web Services: The OWL-S Approach. In *Proceedings of The First International Workshop on Semantic Web Services and Web Process Composition (SWSWPC'2004)*, San Diego, California, USA, 2004.
8. B. Medjahed, A. Rezgui, A. Bouguettaya, and M. Ouzzani. Infrastructure for E-Government Web Services. *IEEE Internet Computing*, 7(1), 2003.
9. Soraya Kouadri Mostéfaoui and Béat Hirsbrunner. Towards a context-based service composition framework. In Liang-Jie Zhang, editor, *ICWS*, pages 42–45, Las Vegas, Nevada, USA, 2003.
10. P. Rajasekaran, J. A. Miller, K. Verma, and A. P. Sheth. Enhancing Web Services Description and Discovery to Facilitate Composition. In *Proceedings of The First International Workshop on Semantic Web Services and Web Process Composition (SWSWPC'2004)*, San Diego, California, USA, 2004.
11. E. Sciore, M. Siegel, and A. Rosenthal. Using semantic values to facilitate interoperability among heterogeneous information systems. *ACM Transactions on Database Systems*, 19(2), 1994.
12. A. P. Sheth and C. Ramakrishnan. Semantic (Web) Technology In Action: Ontology Driven Information Systems for Search, Integration and Analysis. *IEEE Data Engineering Bulletin*, 26(4), 2003.
13. K. Sivashanmugam, K. Verma, A. P. Sheth, and J. A. Miller. Adding Semantics to Web Services Standards. In *Proceedings of The International Conference on Web Services (ICWS'2003)*, Las Vegas, Nevada, USA, 2003.
14. B. Spencer and S. Liu. Inferring Data Transformation Rules to Integrate Semantic Web Services. In *Proceedings of The International Semantic Web Conference (ISWC'2004)*, Hiroshima, Japan, 2004.

An Efficient Yet Secure XML Access Control Enforcement by Safe and Correct Query Modification

Changwoo Byun and Seog Park

Department of Computer Science, Sogang University,
Seoul, 121-742, South Korea
{chang, spark}@dblab.sogang.ac.kr

Abstract. This work is a proposal for an efficient yet secure XML access control enforcement which has been specifically designed to support fine-grained security policy. Based on metadata in the DTD, we propose the SQ-Filter which is a pre-processing method that checks on necessary access control rules, and rewrites a user's query by extending/eliminating query tree nodes, and by injecting operators that combine a set of nodes from the user's query point of view. The scheme has several advantages over other suggested schemes. These include small execution time overhead, and safe and correct query modification. The experimental results clearly demonstrate the efficiency of the approach.

1 Introduction

As various users and applications require the distribution and sharing of information in Extensible Markup Language (XML) documents [1], the need for an efficient yet secure access of XML data has become very important. Despite this, relatively little work has been done to enforce access controls particularly for XML databases in the case of query access. Developing an efficient mechanism for XML databases to control query-based access is therefore the central theme of this paper.

We focused our attention on two problems: the abstraction of access control rules that correspond to a user's query, and the generation of a safe query.

The abstraction of access rules means the development of an effective and efficient choosing mechanism that abstracts only necessary access control rules based on a user's query. Meanwhile, the generation of a safe query is the development of an efficient query rewriting mechanism that transforms an unsafe query into a safe yet a correct one that keeps the user's access control policies.

We implemented the Secure Query Filter system (SQ-Filter), and came up with detailed performance analyses of its implementation.

The rest of the paper is organized as follows. Section 2 briefly reviews related works and describes their weaknesses. Section 3 gives the metadata of the Document Type Definition (DTD) and the basic notations for the SQ-Filter system. In Section 4, we present an overview of the SQ-Filter system and the

S. Bressan, J. Küng, and R. Wagner (Eds.): DEXA 2006, LNCS 4080, pp. 276–285, 2006.

construction algorithms used. Section 5 presents the results of our experiments, which reveal the effective performance of the SQ-Filter system as compared to the QFilter [10]. Finally, Section 6 summarizes our work.

2 Related Works

Authorizations for XML documents should be associated with protection objects at different granularity levels. To enforce the fine-level granularity requirement, the specification of the object uses XPath expressions.

In the studies of E. Damiani textitet al. [3], E. Bertino textitet al. [4,5] and Gabilon and Bruno [6], the object part of access control rule is associated with each XML document/DTD. It provides a useful algorithm for computing the view using tree labeling. However, aside from its high cost and maintenance requirement, this algorithm is also not scalable for a large number of users.

M. Murata textitet al. [9] simply focused on filtering out queries that do not satisfy access control policies. B. Luo textitet al. [10] took extra steps to rewrite queries in combination with related access control policies before passing these revised queries to the underlying XML query system for processing. However, the shared Nondeterministic Finite Automata (NFA) of access control rules is not made by a user's query but by a user (or a user's role) itself. Thus, the shared NFA involves many unnecessary access control rules from the user's query point of view. Although the proposed NFA-based algorithm is useful for rewriting queries with path expressions starting from the root, this approach is very inefficient for rewriting queries with the descendant-or-self axis("//") due to the exhaustive navigation of NFA which results in performance degradation and the generation of unsafe queries as described in Section 4.5.

3 Preliminary

3.1 Basic Notations

It is important that the search mechanism returns safe answers, which means they do not contain any data that violate access control policies.

Definition 1. [Safe Query] If a query is assured to retrieve only safe answers, it is called a safe query; otherwise, it is an unsafe query.

Generally speaking, an XPath expression [2] declares the query requirement by identifying the node of interest via the path from the root of the document to the elements which serve as the root of the subtrees to be returned [11]. QFilter [10] defines these semantics as 'answer-as-subtrees'. We call the root of sub-trees to be returned as ***target nodes***. For example, the target node of an XPath, */site/people/person* is a *person* node.

In this paper, we focus on the 'answer-as-subtrees' model to define a new concept of the access control rule (ACR).

Definition 2. [Three Integrity Rules of ACR]

1. It is impossible for any node to have both a negative and a positive ACR. If a conflict occurs between positive and negative ACRs, the negative ACR takes precedence.
2. We also assume "denial downward consistency"[1] [9].
3. It is impossible for any node which is not in the scope of positive ACRs to have negative ACRs.

Meanwhile, XPath 2.0 [2] supports operators (i.e., UNION, INTERSECT, and EXCEPT) that combine two sets of node. They are invariably used in conjunction with path expressions, so they are useful in transforming unsafe queries into safe queries. We confirm these operators by using XML spy 2006 version[2].

3.2 PRE/POST Structure

Figure 1(a) shows that the nodes of the DTD[3] tree are assigned with PRE(order) and POST(order) ranks, as seen when parsing the DTD tree sequentially.

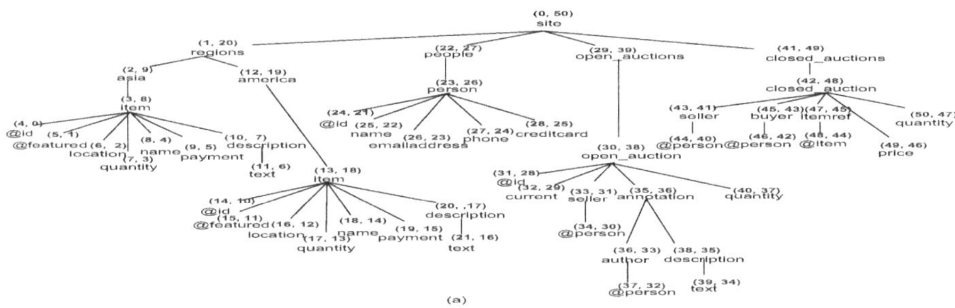

Tag-Name	Pre	size	level	post	Parent
site	0	50	0	50	
regions	1	20	1	20	site
asia	2	9	2	9	regions
item	3	8	3	8	asia
@id	4	0	4	0	item
@featured	5	0	4	1	item
location	6	0	4	2	item
quantity	7	0	4	3	item
name	8	0	4	4	item
payment	9	0	4	5	iem
description	10	1	4	7	item
text	11	0	5	6	description
...	...	...	...	...	...
people	22	6	1	27	site
person	23	5	2	26	people
@id	24	0	3	21	person
name	25	0	3	22	person
emailaddress	26	0	3	23	person
phone	27	0	3	24	person
creditcard	28	0	3	25	person

Tag-Name	Pre	size	level	post	Parent
open_auctions	29	11	1	39	site
open_auction	30	10	2	38	open_auctions
@id	31	0	3	28	open_auction
current	32	0	3	29	open_auction
seller	33	1	3	31	open_auction
@person	34	0	4	30	seller
annotation	35	4	3	36	open_auction
author	36	1	4	33	annotation
@person	37	0	5	32	author
description	38	1	4	35	annotation
text	39	0	5	34	description
quantity	40	0	3	37	open_auction
closed_auctions	41	9	1	49	site
closed_auction	42	8	2	48	closed_auctions
seller	43	1	3	41	closed_auction
@person	44	0	4	40	seller
buyer	45	1	3	43	closed_auction
...	...	...	...	...	...
quantity	50	0	3	47	closed_auction

(b)

Fig. 1. (a) DTD PRE/POST Structure of auction.dtd, (b) Relational Storage of (a)

[1] The combination of a negative authorization with positive authorizations allows the definition of positive authorizations as exceptions to a negative authorization at a higher level in granularity hierarchy.

[2] http://www.altova.com

[3] It is a portion of an auction.dtd source extracted from the XMark [12], which we consider as a running example in our paper.

Figure 1(b) shows the actual relational DTD representation. LEVEL refers to a DTD tree level, and SIZE is the sub-tree size of any node. This PRE/SIZE/LEVEL encoding is equivalent to PRE/POST since $POST = PRE + SIZE - LEVEL$ [7,8].

4 Overview of the SQ-Filter System

4.1 The Architecture of the SQ-Filter System

The architecture of the SQ-Filter system is shown in Figure 2. The primary input is a user's query. If an input query is accepted, the output may be the original input query or a rewritten query which has filtered out conflicting or redundant parts from the original query. Otherwise, the output may be the result of rejecting the query. This concept is similar to that of the QFilter [10].

The SQ-Filter system is divided into two parts. At compile time, the SQ-Filter system constructs the actual relational DTD representation (in Section 3.2). It also constructs *ACRs* and *PREDICATES* databases. At run time, the SQ-Filter system runs three components, namely, *QUERY ANALYZER*, *ACR-FINDER*,

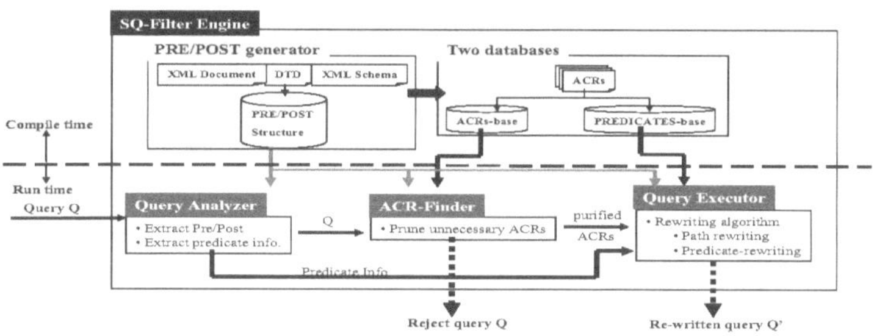

Fig. 2. The Architecture of the SQ-Filter System

Positive ACRs

(R1): /site/regions/*/item[location="LA"]
(R2): /site/people/person[name = "chang"]
(R3): /site/open_auctions/open_auction
(R4): //open_auction[quantity]/seller

Negative ACRs

(R5): /site/regions/*/item/payment
(R6): /site/people/person/creditcard
(R7): /site/*/open_auction[@id>50]/seller[@person="chang"]

(a)

ACR+-base

rule	path	Pre	Post	P_link
R1	/site/regions/*/item	3, 13	8, 18	P1
R2	/site/people/person	23	26	P2
R3	/site/open_auctions/open_auction	30	38	
R4	//open_auction[quantity]/seller	33	31	p3

ACR−-base

rule	path	Pre	Post	P_link
R5	/site/regions/*/item/payment	9, 19	5, 15	
R6	/site/people/person/creditcard	28	25	
R7	/site/*/open_auction[@id>50]/seller[@person="chang"]	33	31	p4, p5

PREDICATES-base

P-id	Parent-PRE	property	operator	value
P1	3, 13	location	=	LA
P2	23	name	=	chang
P3	30	quantity		
P4	30	@id	>	50
p5	33	@person	=	chang

(b)

Fig. 3. (a) Sample positive/negative ACRs, (b) Sample *ACRs* and *PREDICATES* databases and *QUERY EXECUTOR*. We describe them in detail in the following sections. Meanwhile, in this section, we describe the two databases.

After a security officer determines the ACRs of which each object part uses an XPath expression in Figure 3(a), each ACR information is stored into *ACRs* and *PREDICATES* databases in Figure 3(b). Note that the entity of PRE and POST columns may be more than two. For example, the target node of *R1* is *item*. The (PRE, POST) value set of the *item* is (3, 8) and (13, 18). This value set is stored into the PRE and POST columns, respectively. Moreover, *R1* has one predicate ([location="xxxx"]). The parent element of the predicate is *item*. The entity of Parent-PRE column is (3, 13), and the entities of property, operator, and value columns are 'location', '=', and 'xxxx', respectively. Finally, P1 as Predicate ID is stored into the P_link column in the *ACRs* database. In a similar way, other ACRs are stored into the *ACRs* and *PREDICATES* databases.

4.2 QUERY ANALYZER Component

The objective of the *QUERY ANALYZER* (QA) is to acquire information from a user's query. Given a query *Q1*, the target node of *Q1* is *phone* node.

Q1: */site/people/person[name="chang"]/phone/*

First, the QA looks up the Figure 1(b) and gets the (27, 24) value of the target node *phone*. It also obtains the predicate information of *Q1*. Note that there may also be more than two (PRE, POST) pairs. However, all (PRE, POST) pairs may not be the (PRE, POST) pairs of the user's query. Let a user's query be footnotesize*/site/regions/america/item*. The target node of the user's query is the *item* node. Although the (PRE, POST) pairs of the *item* are (3, 8) and (13, 18), (3, 8) is not a suitable (PRE, POST) pair of the given query. Its main idea is that the preorder (postorder) value of each node of a user's query is less (greater) than that of the target node of the user's query. Figure 4 shows the pruning algorithm that eliminates the unsuitable (PRE, POST) pairs of a user's query.

```
Input : a user's query
Output : suitable (PRE, POST) values of the target node of the query

BEGIN
for each (PRE_tn, POST_tn) value of projection node of the query
{    for (PRE_step, POST_step) value of each step of the query
         If (!(PRE_step < PRE_tn and POST_step > POST_tn))
               break;
     suitable_(PRE, POST) set := (PRE_tn, PRE_tn)
}
END
```

Fig. 4. The Prune-TNs Algorithm

4.3 ACR-FINDER Component

The objective of *ACR-FINDER* (ACR-F) component is to extract the necessary ACRs out of the *ACRs* database. Recall *Q1* as shown in Section 4.2. By the QA, the (PRE, POST) value of the target node *phone* is (27, 24). As shown in Figure 5(a), namely, the PRE/POST plane of ACRs, only *R2* is necessary for *Q1* because the target node of *R2* has an ancestor relation to that of *Q1*. *R1* and *R5* (*R3*, *R4*, *R6*, and *R7*) are a preceding (following) relation of the query. They are

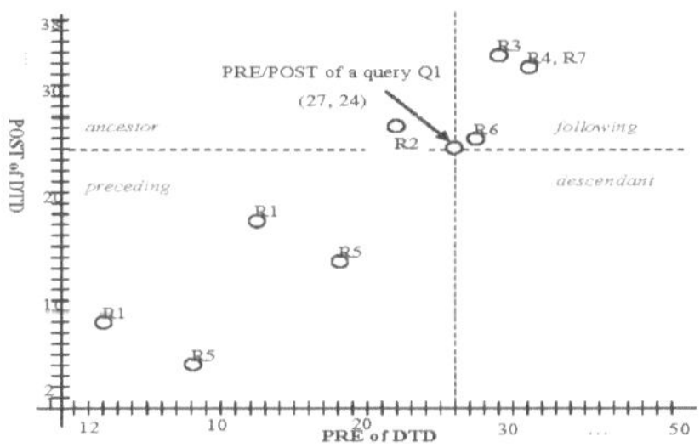

(a)

```
Input: (Pr_Q, Po_Q) := QA(query), ACRs
Output: suitable ACRs'
BEGIN
for each rule R1 in ACRs
if ((Pr_Q ≥ Pr_R1 and Po_Q ≤ Po_R1) or // ACENSTOR
(Pr_Q ≤ Pr_R1 and Po_Q ≥ Po_R1))    // DESCENDANT
ACRs':= R1;
END
```

(b)

Fig. 5. (a) Semantics of PRE/POST Plane of Positive ACRs, (b) The ACR-FINDER Algorithm

identified as unnecessary ACRs for *Q1*. Figure 5(b) shows the *ACR-FINDER* algorithm which finds descendant-or-self (or ancestor-or-self) ACRs that correspond to a user's query.

4.4 QUERY EXECUTOR Component

The goal of the *QUERY EXECUTOR* (QE) is to make a safe query by extending/eliminating query tree nodes and combining a set of nodes by the operators. Before describing our method in detail, we give sample queries as follows:

(*Q2*): */site/people/person/creditcard/*

(*Q3*): *//open_auction[@id<100]*

A user's query passed by the ACR-F may be classified into three relations as compared to an ACR: *SELF*, *ANCESTOR*, and *DESCENDANT*.

Before describing the process of the QE, we introduce two functions: the *REFINE* and *PREDICATE* functions. The *REFINE* function focuses on replacing a wild card "*" with an actual node name (element tag) and removing superfluous "//" axes.

For example, the *REFINE* function gets the XPath expression: */site/regions/*/item*.

Since the (PRE, POST) value set of the target node (*item*) of the XPath is (3, 8) and (13, 18), the *REFINE* function begins first (3, 8). In the reverse order, once the *REFINE* function meets the "*" node, it obtains *item* before the node. The (PRE, POST) value of *item* is (3, 8). The *REFINE* function gets the parent node (*asia*) of the *item* as shown in Figure 1(b). Finally, the *REFINE* function gives the output */site/regions/asia/item*. In the case of (13, 8) value, the *REFINE* function results in */site/regions/america/item*.

Another example is */site/people//name*. Although the (PRE, POST) value set of the target node (*name*) of the XPath is (8, 4), (18, 14) and (25, 22), only (25, 22) is selected by the Prune_TNs alogorthm. Once the *REFINE* function meets the "//" node, it obtains *name* before the node and the next node (*people*). As shown in Figure 1(b), each LEVEL of *name* and *people* is 3 and 1, respectively. $LEVEL_{name} - LEVEL_{people} = 2$. In this case, it is the same as *people/*/name*. Finally, the *REFINE* function results in */site/people/person/name*.

In addition, we introduce the *PREDICATE* function. From the query rewriting point of view, it is desirable to keep the predicate's position of a user's query or ACRs in the process of refining the user query. At compile time, each predicate content and position information of the ACRs is stored in the *PREDICATES* database as shown in Figure 3(b). When the QE prompts the *REFINE* function, the latter subsequently prompts the *PREDICATE* function which adds predicates of ACRs into the user's query. The *PREDICATE* function also considers some optimizations in Figure 6. We think that the optimization between a query and a negative ACR is the same with the negative ACR. In the future, we will consider some other optimizations.

Predicate of a query	Predicate of a positive ACR	Predicate of a negative ACR	Optimization
[@id = "1"]	[@id = "1"]		[@id = "1"]
[@id = "1"]	[@id = "3"]		reject
[@id > "1"]	[@id > "3"]		[@id > "3"]
[@id > "1"]	[@id < "3"]		[@id > "1" and @id < "3"]
[@id = "1"]		[@id = "1"]	[@id = "1"]
[@id = "1"]		[@id = "3"]	[@id = "3"]
[@id > "1"]		[@id > "3"]	[@id > "3"]
[@id > "1"]		[@id < "3"]	[@id < "3"]

Fig. 6. Examples of the Optimizations of Predicates

We omit the algorithms of the *REFINE* function and the *PREDICATE* function for brevity's sake.

Step 1. (Handling negative ACRs)

- **Case 1.1 (SELF)**. SELF means that the (PRE, POST) pair of a user's query is equal to that of an ACR. If a user's query is SELF related to a negative ACR, the output of the QE is that the query is rejected. The (PRE, POST) pair of *Q2* is (28, 25). As shown in Figure 3(b), *R6* (in the negative *ACRs* database) has a value of (28, 25). In this case, the QE rejects *Q2*. However, when predicates exist in negative *ACRs*, the output range part of the user's query is disallowed to access. As a result, the QE transforms the query except the region of the negative ACR.
- **Case 1.2(DESCENDANT)**. DESCENDANT means that the preorder (postorder) value of a user's XPath query is greater (less) than that of an ACR, respectively. As a result, it is similar to Case 1.1.
- **Case 1.3 (ANCESTOR)**. ANCESTOR means that the preorder (postorder) value of a user's query is less (greater) than that of an ACR, respectively. If a user's query is ANCESTOR related to a negative ACR, the QE rewrites the query except the region of the negative ACR. For example, *Q3* (30, 38) is ANCESTOR related to *R7* (33, 31) by the *ACR-FINDER* algorithm. Thus, the QE prompts the *REFINE* function, then *Q3* is transformed as follows:
  Q3': *Q3* EXCEPT
  (*/site/open_auactions/open_auction[@id>50]/seller[@person="chang"]*).
  Then *R4* (go to Step 2) should be taken for granted.

- **Case 1.4** (**Null**). If any negative ACR does not exist against a user's query, the QE proceeds to Step 2.

Step 2. (Handling positive ACRs)

- **Case 2.1** (**SELF**). If a user's query is SELF related to a positive ACR, the QE prompts the *REFINE* function.
- **Case 2.2** (**DESCENDANT**). It is similar to Case 2.1.
- **Case 2.3** (**ANCESTOR**). If a user's query is ANCESTOR related to some positive ACRs, the user's query may contain the unsafe parts of an XML document. Thus, the user's query should be transformed into a safe query. *Q3* (30, 38) is also ANCESTOR related to *R4* (33, 31). First, the QE prompts the *REFINE* function whose output is
  /site/open_auctions/open_auction[quantity][@id< 100]/seller.
  Second, the QE combines the refined query of positive ACRs with that of negative ACRs as shown in Case 1.3 of Step1 by injecting the EXCEPT operator between them:
  (*/site/open_auctions/open_auction[quantity][@id< 100]/seller*)
  EXCEPT
  (*/site/open_auactions/open_auction[@id> 50]/seller[@person= "chang"]*)

4.5 Comparison with QFilter

In this section, we point out the QFilter's mistake from the query rewriting point of view. After checking the DTD as shown in Figure 1(a), we found that the rewritten query of Q3 generated by the QFilter is wrong. Without any metadata support from the DTD (*i.e.*, order information among elements), if a user's query contains //-child and a shared NFA does not contain /-child or //-child state, the navigation of the shared NFA runs to each final state. If answer model is "answer-as-nodes", the query is rejected. However, if answer model is "answer-as-subtrees", the QFilter appends //-child to each final state. As a result, the output may be an incorrectly rewritten query as follows:

((*/site/regions/*/item[@location= "LA"]//open_auction[@id< 100]*) UNION
(*/site/people/person[name= "chang"]//open_auction[@id< 100]*)UNION
(*/site/open_auctions/open_auction[@id< 100]*) UNION
(*//open_auction[quantity][@id< 100]/seller*))
EXCEPT
((*/site/regions/*/item/payment//open_auction[@id< 100]*)UNION
(*/site/people/person/creditcard//open_auction[@id< 100]*) UNION
(*/site/*/open_auction[@id< 100 and @id> 50]*))

5 Experiments

We compared the performance of our SQ-Filter with QFilter [10] according to syntactic data sets generated by the publicly available XMark [12]. We present two experiments[4] based on this implementation. To estimate the effectiveness and efficiency of the SQ-Filter system, we generated 26 ACRs (8 positive and 18 negative) for each experiment.

We implemented the QFilter, SQ-Filter, and SQ-NFA(combining SQ-Filter with the NFA technique) in the Java programming language using the Eclipse v.3.1.1 development tool.

First, using random 100 XPath queries for each query type, we measured the number of rejecting query. A rejection query refers to a user's query which is always denied. The result is shown in Figure 7(a). From this, we can observe that the QFilter's rejection rate of queries with the "//" axis is not 100%. In particular, the QFilter's rejection rate of queries starting with the "//" axis is 0%.

Second, we measured each average processing time for the output (rejection, rewritten query) per 30, 50, 100, 200, 300, and 500 random queries, accordingly. By the ACR-F in Section 4.3, the SQ-Filter and the SQ-NFA use ACRs less than the QFilter. In addition, The SQ-Filter and the SQ-NFA can rewrite queries faster with the "*" wildcard and the "//" axis. The result is shown in Figure 7(b). From this, we can also see that the SQ-Filter and the SQ-NFA can better degrade the processing time than the QFilter.

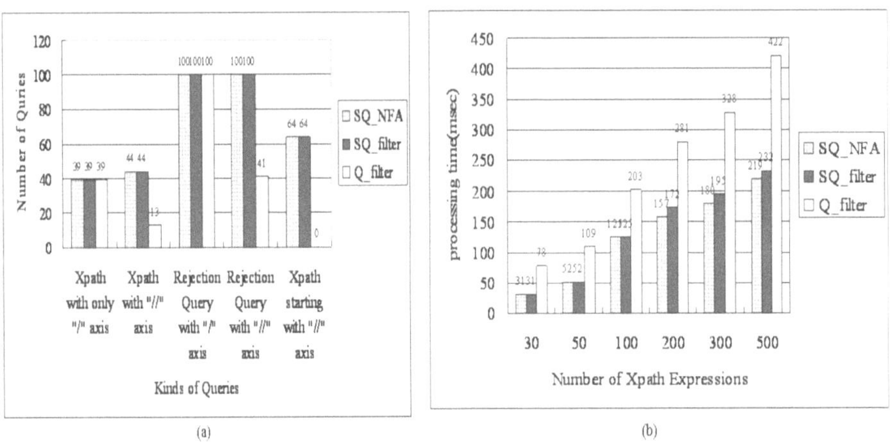

Fig. 7. (a) The number of rejecting prohibited queries corresponding to various query types, (b) Processing time of the security check on XPath queries

6 Conclusion

The SQ-Filter system for XML access control enforcement described in this paper exploits the tree properties encoded in the PRE/POST plane to eliminate unnecessary access control rules for a user's query, and to reject unauthorized queries

[4] The experiments were performed on a Pentium IV 2.66GHz platform, with an MS-Windows XP OS and 1 GB of main memory.

ahead of rewriting. In addition, the SQ-Filter system exploits the simple hash tree of a DTD to find a parent node of a node with the descendant-or-self axis ("//"), and to rewrite an unsafe query into a safe one by receiving help from operators combining the two sets of node. We note that our work is the very first to explore this important area of secure yet efficient access of XML data using only the necessary access control rules of a user in an XML document.

In the future, we will plan to add update operations in the SQ-Filter system.

Acknowledgements

This work was supported by grant No. (R01-2006-000-10609-0) from the Basic Research Program of the Korea Science and Engineering Foundation.

References

1. T. Bray, J. Paoli, C. M. Sperberg-McQueen, E. Maler, F. Yergeau. Extensible Markup Language (XML) 1.0, World Wide Web Consortium (W3C), 2004. (http://www.w3.org/TR/REC-xml)
2. A. Berglund, S. Boag, D. Chamberlin, M. F. Fernández, M. Kay, J. Robie, and J. Siméon. XPath 2.0, World Wide Web Consortium (W3C), 2005. (http://www.w3.org/TR/xpath20/)
3. E. Damiani, S. Vimercati, S. Paraboachk and P.Samarati, "A Fine-grained Access Control System for XML Documents", ACM Trans. Information and System Sec., Vol.5, No.2, May 2002.
4. E. Bertino, S. Castano, E. Ferrari, M. Mesiti, "Specifying and Enforcing Access Control Policies for XML Document Sources", WWW Journal, Baltzer Science Publishers, Vol.3, N.3, 2000.
5. E. Bertino, S. Castano, E. Ferrai, "Securing XML documents with Author-x", IEEE Internet Comput-ing, May.June, pp.21-31, 2001.
6. A. Gabillon and E. Bruno, "Regulating Access to XML Documents", *In Proc. IFIP WG11.3 Working Conference on Database Security*, 2001.
7. T. Grust, "Accelerating XPath Location Steps", *In Proc. of the 21st Int'l ACM SIGMOD Conf. on Management of Data*, pages 109-120, Madison, Wisconsin, USA, June 2002.
8. T. Grust, M. van Keulen, and J. Teubner, "Staircase Join: Teach a Relational DBMS to Watch its Axis Steps", *Proc. of the 29th VLDB Conference*, Berlin, Germany, September 2003.
9. M. Murata, A. Tozawa, and M. Kudo, "XML Access Control using Static Analysis", *In ACM CCS*, Washington D.C., 2003.
10. B. Luo, D. W. Lee, W. C. Lee, P. Liu, "Qfilter: Fine-grained Run-Time XML Access Control via NFA-based Query Rewriting", *In Proc. of the Thirteenth ACM Conference on Information and Knowledge Management 2004* (CIKM'04), November 8, 2004, Washington, USA.
11. S. Mohan, A. Sengupta, Y. Wu, J. Klinginsmith, "Access Control for XML- A Dynamic Query Rewriting Approach", *Proc. of the 31st VLDB Conference*, Trondheim, Norway, 2005.
12. A. R. Schmidt, F. Waas, M. L. Kersten, D. Florescu, I. Manolescu, M. J. Carey, and R. Busse. The XML Benchmark Project. Technical Report INS-R0103, CWI, April 2001.

Detecting Information Leakage in Updating XML Documents of Fine-Grained Access Control

Somchai Chatvichienchai[1] and Mizuho Iwaihara[2]

[1] Dept. of InfoMedia, Siebold University of Nagasaki, Nagasaki, Japan
somchaic@sun.ac.jp
[2] Dept. of Social Informatics, Graduate School of Informatics, Kyoto University, Kyoto, Japan
iwaihara@i.kyoto-u.ac.jp

Abstract. To provide fine-grained access control to data in an XML document, XML access control policy is defined based on the contents and structure of the document. In this paper, we discuss confidential information leakage problem caused by unsecure-update that modifies contents or structures of the document referred by the access control policy. In order to solve this problem, we propose an algorithm that computes update constraints of a user on some data in the document under access control policy of the user. We also propose an algorithm that decides whether a given update request of a user against an XML document is an unsecure-update under the user's access control policy.

1 Introduction

XML [11] is rapidly gaining popularity as a mechanism for sharing and delivering information among businesses, organizations, and users on the Internet. The need of protecting confidential data in XML documents is becoming more and more important. A number of XML access control models are proposed in the literature [1, 4, 7]. Recently XACML [8] has been approved by OASIS as a standard access control markup language for XML documents. To provide fine-grained access control to data in XML document, these models use path expressions of XPath [12] for locating sensitive nodes in XML documents. The identification of a sensitive node is no longer restricted to the value of the node itself but depends on the context, the form of the path (from the root node to that node) and the children/descendants of that node. Hence definition of *access authorization rules* (authorization rules, for short) is strongly related to the node values and the structural relationship between nodes of XML documents. Updating XML data is still a research issue [10, 2]. In [10], a set of basic update operations for both ordered and unordered XML data is proposed. The authors describe extensions to the proposed standard XML query language, XQuery [13], to incorporate the update operations. In [2], the authors have proposed an infrastructure for managing secure update operations on XML data. Each subject in the collaborative group only receives the symmetric key(s) for the portion(s) he/she is enabled to see and/or modify. Additionally, attached to the encrypted document, a subject receives some control information, with the purpose of making him/her able to locally verify the correctness of the updates performed so far on the document, without the need of interacting with the document server.

S. Bressan, J. Küng, and R. Wagner (Eds.): DEXA 2006, LNCS 4080, pp. 286 – 296, 2006.

Motivating Scenarios: Consider the sample XML document of Fig.1(a) that is stored at a database server. Suppose that Jane is allowed to maintain information of members of sales teams which take care of zones whose area codes are less than 20. Jane is not allowed to access wage information of a member whose position is chief. Based on this security requirement, the security manager defines authorization rules shown in Fig.1(b) for Jane. *R1* states that Jane is allowed to read/write data of the subtree rooted by *sales_teams* node of *sales_teams.xml*. *R2* states that Jane is not allowed to read/write wage data of the team members whose positions are 'chief'. Based on the authorization rules of Fig.1(b), the view over *sales_teams.xml* for Jane is shown at Fig.2(b).

Information Leakage Problem by Update Operation: Jane can read Sara's wage to which she is not allowed to access by issuing an update request modifying position value of Sara from "chief" to "salesperson" and requesting the server to send her the view over the updated *sales_teams.xml*.

Information Leakage Problem by Append Operation: Jane can read information of Jack to which she is not allowed to access by issuing an update request that appends another area node of value "10" after the area node of value "20" and requesting the server to send her the view over the updated *sales_teams.xml*.

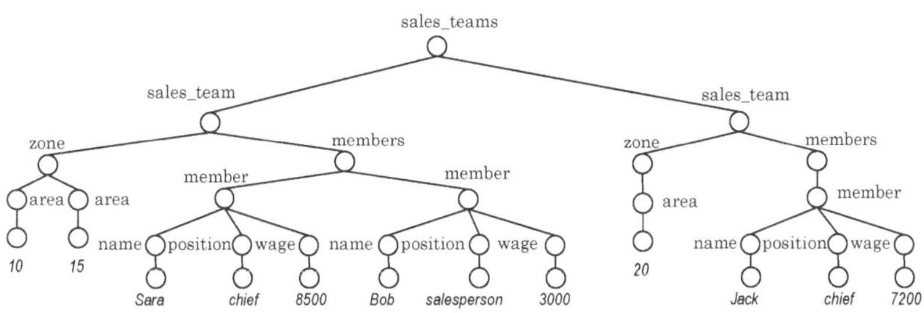

(a) An example of an XML document (*sales_teams.xml*).

R1: <*Jane, sales_team.xml, /sales_team, rw, +* >
R2: <*Jane, sales_team.xml, //member[position= 'chief']/wage, rw, –* >
R3: <*Jane, sales_team.xml, /sales_team[zone/area≥ '20']/members, rw, –* >
R4: <*Jane, sales_team.xml, /sales_team[zone/area< '20']//member, rw, +* >

(b) Authorization rules of *Jane*.

Fig. 1. An example of a sample XML document and sample authorization rules

In aspect of security control, data update of users should not result in these confidential information leakage problems. These problems arise because there is no authorization rule denying Jane to modify/append the data referred by the predicates of path expression of authorization rules. To the best of our knowledge, there is no previous work discussing this problem. The objective of this paper is to propose a technique that decides whether a given update request against an XML document will not cause the information leakage problem. In order to simplify our solution, the inference problem [14] is not in the scope of this paper.

The contribution of this paper is summarized as follows:

1. We define properties of secure remove, append, and change operations that will not cause the information leakage problem.
2. Given an XML document tree and access control policy of a subject, we show a polynomial-time algorithm that computes security labels enforcing sufficient update constraints to prevent the information leakage problem.
3. Given an XML document tree with security labels, access control policy of a subject and an update request on the document tree, we show a polynomial-time algorithm that decides whether an update request of the subject can be permitted under the access control policy and will not cause the information leakage problem.

The rest of the paper is organized as follows. In Section 2, we give formal definitions of XML tree, tree patterns, tree embedding, authorization rules and update requests. Section 3 presents a formal definition of the problem. In Section 4, we present an algorithm that computes security labels that impose update constraints in depth. An algorithm deciding whether a given update request is not unsecure-update is also presented. Finally, the last section concludes this paper.

2 Basic Concepts and Definitions

2.1 Trees, Tree Patterns and Tree Embedding

We view an XML document as an unordered tree. Each node in the tree corresponds to an element, attribute or value. The edges in the tree represent immediate element-subelement or element-value relationships. Attribute nodes and text values can be handled similarly to element nodes.

Definition 2.1 (XML Trees): An XML tree is a tree $t = <V_t, E_t, r_t>$ over an infinite alphabet Σ, where V_t is the node set and E_t is the edge set; $r_t \in V_t$ is the root of t; and each node v in V_t has a label (denoted as $label_t(v)$) from Σ. ▮

We assume that each text node is labeled with its textual value. In this paper, we discuss a fragment of XPath, called *Simple XPath*, which can be generated by the following grammar ('ε' is the empty path, 'l' is a label for element or attribute name, and 'c' is a string constant):

$$(Simple\ xpath)\ p ::= \varepsilon \mid l \mid /p \mid //p \mid p_1/p_2 \mid p_1//p_2 \mid p[q]$$
$$(Qualifier)\ q ::= p \mid p\ \theta\, c$$
$$(Comparison\ \text{operator})\ \theta ::= \ < \mid \leq \mid = \mid \geq \mid >$$

The above simple XPatoh expressions can be represented by the following tree patterns.

Definition 2.2 (Tree Patterns): A tree pattern p is a tree $<V_p, E_p, r_p, o_p, c_p>$ over Σ, where V_p is the node set and E_p is the edge set. Each node v in V_p has a label from Σ, denoted as $label_p(v)$. $r_p, o_p \in V_p$ are the root and output node of p respectively. c_p is a labelling function assigning a symbol from {'<', '≤', '=', '≥', '>'} to a text node. ▮

We present a child edge with a single line and present a descendant edge with a double line. For example, an XPath query *members[//name="Sara"]//position* is represented as a tree pattern shown in Fig. 2(a), where the double circle node denotes the output node. In order to compute XPath expressions without knowledge of DTD of the XML tree, we assume that tree patterns of XPath expressions of authorization rules have the following properties: For the leaf node whose type is an element or attribute, the edge between the leaf node and its parent nodes is a child-edge. For the leaf node whose type is a text node, the edge between its parent node v and the parent of v is a child-edge.

If an XML tree has nodes that are satisfied by a tree pattern, all nodes of the tree pattern must have a corresponding matching node in the XML tree, and each predecessor-successor relationship of nodes in the tree pattern should be guaranteed by those in the XML tree. This is also known as the tree embedding. The following definition of tree embedding is inspired by the unordered path inclusion defined in [6].

(a) The tree pattern p of *members[//name="Sara"]//position.*

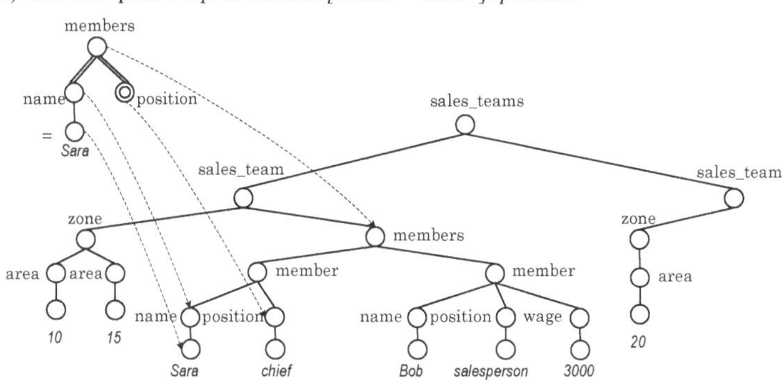

(b) The view v of Jane over *sales_teams.xml.*

Fig. 2. Embedding of the tree pattern p on the view v

Definition 2.3 (Tree Embedding): Given an XML tree $t = <V_t, E_t, r_t>$ and a tree pattern $p = <V_p, E_p, r_p, o_p, c_p>$, an embedding from p to t is a function *emb*: $V_p \rightarrow V_t$, with the following properties for every $x, y \in V_p$:

- Label-preserving: $\forall x \in V_p$, $label_p(x) = label_t(emb(x))$;
- Structure-preserving: $\forall e = (x, y) \in E_p$, if $label_p(e)$ = '/', $emb(y)$ is a child of $emb(x)$ in t ; otherwise, $emb(y)$ is a descendent of $emb(x)$ in t; and
- Value-matching: $\forall x \in V_p$ where $emb(x) \in V_t$ is a text node, the Boolean expression: $label_t(emb(x))\ c_p(x)\ label_p(x)$ is true. ∎

Let $t = <V_t, E_t, r_t>$ be an XML tree, $p = <V_p, E_p, r_p, o_p>$ be a tree pattern, *emb*: $V_p \rightarrow V_t$ be an embedding from p to t. We denote by $\eta(t, p, emb) = \{v_i \in V_t \mid emb(v_j) = v_i$ and $v_j \in V_p\}$ the set of nodes of t mapped from p by *emb*. We also denote by $\tau(t, p) = \{v_i \in V_t \mid \exists v_k \in p(t)\ (v_i = emb(v_k)$ or v_i is a descendant of $emb(v_k))\}$ the node set of the subtrees rooted by $p(t)$. Furthermore, we define that the result of evaluating an empty pattern ε over any XML tree is an empty tree. Figure 2 depicts the embedding of p over XML tree t.

2.2 Authorization Rules

We use the term *access control policy* for a set of *authorization rules*. Each authorization rule has the following format: <*subject*, *doc-id*, *path*, *priv*, *sign*>, where *subject* is a user name, a user group, or a role[9]; *doc-id* denotes an XML document identifier; *path* denotes a path expression of XPath identifying nodes within the XML document; *priv* is either read denoted by r or read/write denoted by rw; and $sign \in \{\text{'+'}, \text{'–'}\}$, where '+' denotes grant and '–' denotes denial. Authorization specified on a node is propagated to its all descendant nodes. The possibility of specifying authorization with different sign introduces potential conflicts among authorization rules. Here, the conflict resolution of the model is based on the following policies:

- *Descendant-take-precedence:* An authorization rule specified at a given level in the document hierarchy prevails over the authorization rules specified at higher levels; and
- *Denial-take-precedence:* In case conflicts are not solved by *descendant-take-precedence* policy, the authorization rule with negative sign takes precedence.

Table 1. Necessary privileges for executing an update request

op	*content*	**Necessary privilege**
The *remove* operation allows the subtrees rooted by the selected context nodes to be removed.		The *read/write* privileges on the selected context nodes and all of their descendant nodes.
The *append* operation appends a new node as a child of the context node.	Element name, attribute name, or textual value of the new node.	The *read* privilege on the selected context node. The *read/*write privilege on the new node.
The *change* operation allows the text node of the selected context node to be changed.	The new textual value.	The *read/write* privileges for removing the selected context node. The *read/write* privilege on the new node.

2.3 Update Requests

We give a definition of an update request as follows: <*subject*, *op*, *doc-id*, *path*, *content*>, where *subject* is a user name, a user group or a role; *op* is *remove*, *append*, or *change* operation; *doc-id* is an XML document identifier; *path* denotes a path expression of XPath identifying the context nodes within the XML tree; and *content* denotes either (*i*) name of an element / attribute, or (*ii*) textual value of the node to be written. Table 1 explains details of the *op* argument of an update request and necessary privileges of a subject for executing the operation. In this paper, for simplicity we assume that the documents before and after update hold the same *doc-id*.

3 Problem Formulation

In order to solve the information leakage problem, we need to impose update constraints on the nodes and structural relationship between nodes that are referred by path expressions of negative authorization rules. Therefore, we need to compute an authorization type (positive or negative) of the subject on nodes of the XML tree. Read and write privileges of the subject on node $v \in V_t$ under an access control policy A, denoted by $read_A(v)$ and $write_A(v)$, respectively; where values of $read_A(v)$ and $write_A(v)$ are '+' or '–'. In Section 4, we will explain how to compute $read_A(v)$ and $write_A(v)$. We define tree-mapping used to denote how a node of an XML tree before update is mapped to that of XML tree after update as follows.

Definition 3.1 (Tree Mapping): Let t be an XML tree before update and t' be the XML tree after executing update u. Let N_t be the node set of t, and $N_{t'}$ be the node set of t'. $tmap_u$: $N_t \rightarrow N_{t'}$ is a mapping from N_t to $N_{t'}$.

Definition 3.2 (Unsecure-Update Request): Let N_t be the node set of XML tree t before update, and $N_{t'}$ be the node set of XML tree t' after executing update u of subject s, and $tmap_u$: $N_t \rightarrow N_{t'}$ is a mapping from N_t to $N_{t'}$ by u. u is an *unsecure-update request* under access control policy A of subject s if there exist $v \in N_t$ and $v' \in N_{t'}$ such that $v' = imap_u(v)$ and $read_A(v)$ = '–' and $read_A(v')$ = '+'. ∎

For example, *information leakage* by update request u: <*Jane*, *change*, *sales_teams.xml*, *//member[name="Sara"]/position*, *"salesperson"*> occurs under access control policy A = {*R1*, *R2*, *R3*, *R4*} because wage of Sara which is confidential information becomes readable by Jane after executing u.

We use the following notations for defining properties of remove, append and change requests which are secure update requests.

Definition 3.3 (Relevant Node Set): Let t be an XML tree, $Path = \{p_1, p_2, .., p_m\}$ be a set of path expressions of authorization rules of access control policy A, and emb_i be an embedding from p_i to t. *Relevant node set* of t under *Path*, denoted by *RelNode(t, Path)*, is defined as follows:

$$RelNode(t, Path) = \{v \mid v \in \eta(t, p_i, emb_i), p_i \in Path, i=1,..,m\}, \text{ where}$$
$\eta(t, p_i, emb_i)$ is the set of nodes of t mapped from p_i by emb_i. ∎

Lemma 1 (Secure Remove Request): Let t be an XML tree, A be an access control policy of subject s on t. Let $Path^-$ be the set of path expressions of authorization rules with negative sign, and $RelNode(t, Path^-)$ be the relevant node set of t under $Path^-$. <s, "remove", t, p, > is a secure update request under A if the following conditions hold:

- $\forall v \in \tau(t, p)$ $write_A(v)$ = '+', where $\tau(t, p)$ is the node set of the subtrees rooted by $p(t)$; and
- $p(t) \cap RelNode(t, Path^-) = \varnothing$. ∎

Due to space limitation, all proofs are presented at [3].

Definition 3.4 (Relevant Paths): Let t = <V_t, E_t, r_t> be an XML tree, and <s, "append", t, p, *content*> be an append request. Let $Path = \{p_1, p_2, .., p_m\}$ be a set of path expressions of authorization rules of access control policy A. *Relevant paths* of p for appending *content* under A, denoted by *RelPath(p, content, A)*, is the subset Q of *Path* where each $q \in Q$ holds one of the following properties:

(i) q has a text node v s.t. the Boolean expression: $label_t(v)\ c_q(v)$ *content* (where $c_q(v) \in$ {'<', '≤', '=', '≥', '>'}) is true and the parent node of v has the same label as that of the parent of the output node of p, or
(ii) q has a leaf node v of element or attribute type s.t. $label_t(v)$ = *content* and the parent node of v has the same label as that of the parent of the output node of p

We denote *SubRelPath(p, content, A)* the set of path expressions computed from path expressions of *RelPath(p, content, A)* by deleting node v of the above property. ∎

Lemma 2 (Secure Append Request): Let $t = <V_t, E_t, r_t>$ be an XML tree, A be an access control policy of subject s. Let A^- and A^+ be the set of authorization rules with negative sign and positive sign, respectively, where $A^- \cup A^+ = A$. <s, "append", t, p, *content*> is a secure append request under A if the following conditions hold:

(1) $\forall v \in p(t)\ read_A(v)$ = '+' ;
(2) One of the following conditions hold:
  2.1 $\forall v \in p(t)$, $write_A(v)$ = '+' ; or
  2.2 $\exists q^+ \in SubRelPath(p, content, A^+)$ s.t. $q^+(t) \supseteq p(t)$;
(3) $\neg \exists q^- \in SubRelPath(p, content, A^-)$ s.t. $q^-(t) \cap p(t) \neq \emptyset$; and
(4) $p(t) \cap RelNode(t, SubRelPath(p, content, A^+)) = \emptyset$. ∎

Lemma 3 (Secured Change Request): Let t be an XML tree, A be access control policy of subject s. Let A^- and A^+ be the set of authorization rules of subject s with negative sign and positive sign, respectively, where $A^- \cup A^+ = A$, and $RelNode(t, A^-)$ be the relevant node set of t under A^-. <s, "change", t, p, *content*> is a secure update request under A if the following conditions hold:

(1) $\forall v \in p(t)\ write_A(v)$ = '+';
(2) $\exists q^+ \in SubRelPath(p, content, A^+)$ s.t. $q^+(t) \supseteq p(t)$;
(3) $\neg \exists q^- \in SubRelPath(p, content, A^-)$ s.t. $q^-(t) \cap p(t) \neq \emptyset$; and
(4) $p(t) \cap RelNode(t, SubRelPath(p, content, A^+)) = \emptyset$. ∎

4 An Approach to Detecting the Information Leakage Problem

We now present the *LabelTree* algorithm which computes necessary security labels of nodes of a given XML tree $t = <V_t, E_t, r_t>$ under a given access control policy A of a subject. There are two types of security labels: *read label* and *write label*. Read label of node v under A, denoted by $rlbl(v)$, has one of the following values: '+R', '-R', and ϕ where '+R' denotes permitting read on the subtree rooted by v, '-R' denotes denying read on the subtree rooted by v, and ϕ denotes no label. The write label set of node v under A, denoted by $wlbl(v)$, has the following values: '+W', '-W', '-w' and ϕ, where '+W' denotes permitting write on the subtree rooted by v, '-W' denotes denying write on the subtree rooted by v, and '-w' denotes denying write on v.

4.1 Security Label Computing Algorithm

As shown in Fig. 3, for each authorization rule R_i of A, Step4 through Step11 of *LabelTree* assign read and write labels to the nodes addressed by $path_i$ of R_i. If sign of the authorization rule is negative, Step13 through Step16 of *LabelTree* also assign '-w' to the nodes of t mapped from nodes of tree pattern of $path_i$ in order to prevent the confidential information leakage problem. As depicted in Fig. 4, *LabelTree* generates write label '-*w*' for the nodes that are mapped from tree pattern p depicted in Fig. 2(b) by tree embedding so that Jane is not allowed to modify names/values of these nodes and structural relationship among these nodes. For simplicity, ϕ which denotes no label is not shown in Fig.4.

Algorithm *LabelTree* (t, A)
Input: 1. XML tree $t = <V_t, E_t, r_t>$, and
2. Access control policy $A = \{R_1, R_2, .., R_m\}$ of subject s on t.
Output: XML tree t with security labels.
Method:
Step1: Initialize read and write labels of each $v \in V_t$ with ϕ.
Step2: **For** each $R_i = <s, doc\text{-}id_i, path_i, priv_i, sign_i> \in A$, where $1 \leq i \leq m$ **do** {
Step3: Let p be the tree pattern of $path_i$. Compute $p(t)$.
Step4: **For** each $u_k \in p(t)$ **do** {
Step5: **If** ($priv_i$ = 'r' or $priv_i$ = 'rw') **then**
Step6: **If** ($sign_i$ = '+') and ($rlbl(u_k) = \phi$) **then** $rlbl(u_k)$ = '+R'
Step7: **Else If** $sign_i$ = '-' **then** $rlbl(u_k)$ = '-R' /* *denial-take-precedence* */
Step8: **If** ($priv_i$ = 'w' or $priv_i$ = 'rw') **then**
Step9: **If** ($sign_i$ = '+') and ($wlbl(u_k) = \phi$) **then** $wlbl(u_k)$ = '+W'
Step10: **Else If** $sign_i$ = '-' **then** $wlbl(u_k)$ = '-W' /* *denial-take-precedence* */
Step11: **Else If** $sign_i$ = '+' and '-W' $\notin wlbl(u_k)$ **then** $wlbl(u_k) = wlbl(u_k) \cup$ '+W'
Step12: **If** $sign_i$ = '-' **then** {
Step13: Let emb_k be the embedding from $p = <V_p, E_p, r_p, o_p>$ to t, where $u_k = emb_k(o_p)$.
Step14: **For** each $v \in V_p$ and $v \neq o_p$ **do**
Step15: /* update constraint for preventing information leak of u_k */
Step16: **If** '-W' $\notin wlbl(u_k)$ **then** $wlbl(emb_k(v)) = wlbl(emb_k(v)) \cup$ '-w'
}
}
}
Step17: **return** t.

Fig. 3. The *LabelTree* Algorithm

Theorem 1: Given an XML tree $t = <V_t, E_t, r_t>$, an access control policy $A = \{R_1, R_2, .., R_n\}$ for subject s, where $R_i = <s, doc\text{-}id_i, p_i, priv_i, sign_i>$, *LabelTree* computes security labels for document nodes of t in $O(|t|^2 \bullet |A|)$ where $|t|$ is the size of t and $|A|$ is the number of authorization rules of A.

Proof: Gottlob et al. [5] have proposed the linear-time algorithms for XPath processing by using a form of dynamic programming. Based on this, computation of the node set satisfied by the XPatterns [5], which covers our simple XPath expression, is processed in time $O(|t| \bullet |p|)$, where $|t|$ denotes the size of the XML document tree and $|p|$ is the size of the query. The complexity of step3 is $O(|t|\bullet|p|\bullet|A|)$. The complexity of step4 thru step16 is $O(|p|\bullet|p(t)|\bullet|A|)$. Since $|p|$ and $|p(t)|$ can be as big as $|t|$, the complexity of *LabelTree* is bounded by $O(|t|^2\bullet|A|)$. ∎

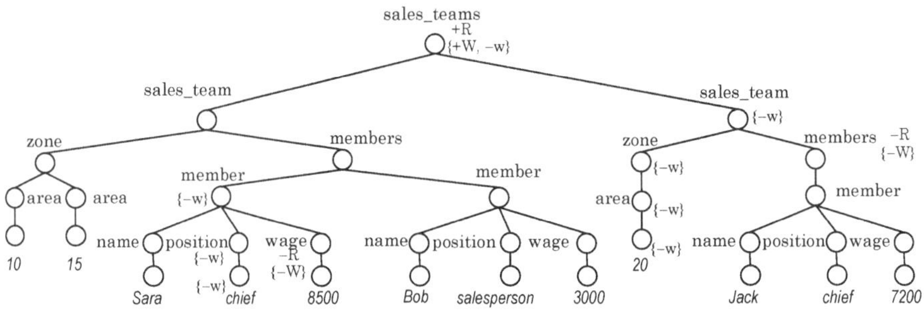

Fig. 4. The XML tree after labeling read/write security labels by the *LabelTree* algorithm

Now we explain how to compute $read_A(v)$ and $write_A(v)$ of subject s on document node v of XML tree t from the read and write labels of t. $read_A(v)$ is determined by the following criteria.

- In case $rlbl(v) \neq \phi$, $read_A(v)$ is the sign of $rlbl(v)$.
- In case $rlbl(v) = \phi$, $read_A(v)$ is the sign of '+R' or '-R' of the nearest ancestor node of v.

$write_A(v)$ is determined by the following criteria.

- In case '-w'$\in wlbl(v)$ or '-W'$\in wlbl(v)$, $write_A(v)$ is equal to '-'
- In case $wlbl(v) = \{$'+W'$\}$, $write_A(v)$ is equal to '+'.
- In case $wlbl(v) = \phi$, $write_A(v)$ is the sign of '+W' or '-W' of the nearest ancestor node of v.

For example, write privilege of Jane on text node (whose value is "*Sara*") is '+' which is determined by the sign of '+W' of sales_teams node.

Based on the read labels computed from access control policy A, the view for subject s on XML tree t can be computed by the following criteria. Node v of t can be pruned out from t if one of the following conditions holds.

- v is a leaf node and $read_A(v)$ = '-'; or
- v is not a leaf node and each node v' of the subtree rooted by v has $read_A(v')$ = '-'.

By the above criteria, we need not to rewrite an XPath query of the subject on the view to match the original structure of the underlying document tree.

4.2 Update Request Checking Algorithm

Given an access control policy A of a subject s, and XML tree t with security labels computed by *LabelTree* and an update request *updreq* of s on t, we propose the algorithm *UpdReqCheck* (see Fig. 5) that decides whether *updreq* on t can be permitted under A without the confidential information leakage problem. The main idea is that *UpdReqCheck* first checks if all data used to evaluate $p(t)$ of the update request is in the view of subject s. By checking the properties of the update request, *UpdReqCheck* decides whether subject s has privilege to execute *updreq* and *updreq* is not an unsecure update request.

Algorithm *UpdReqCheck* (t, A, *updreq*, *Permit*)
Input:
1. XML tree $t = <V_t, E_t, r_t>$ with read and write labels,
2. Access control policy A of subject s on t, and
3. Update request *updreq* of s on t, where *updreq* = <*s*, *op*, *doc-id*, *p*, *content*>.

Output:
Permit = *TRUE* if the update request should be permitted, *FALSE* otherwise.
Method:
Step1: Let A^- and A^+ be the sets of authorization rules with negative sign and positive sign, respectively, where $A^- \cup A^+ = A$. $Path^-$ and $Path^+$ be the sets of path expressions of A^- and A^+, respectively. *Permit* = FALSE.
Step2: Compute $p(t)$.
Step3: **For** each $v_i \in p(t)$ **do** {
Step4: /* Check if all document nodes mapped from p by embedding is in the view of subject s */
Step5: Let emb_i be the embedding from p to t such that v_i is mapped to the output node of p.
If ($\forall v \in \eta(t, p, emb_i)$, $read_A(v)$ = '+') **then** {
Step6: **If** *op* = 'remove' or *op* = 'change' **then**
Step7: /* Check properties of remove/change request */
If ($\exists v \in \tau(t, p)$ $write_A(v)$ = '–') or
($v_i \in RelNode(t, Path^-)$) **then return** *Permit*.
Step8: **If** *op* = 'append' or *op* = 'change' **then** {
/* Check properties of append/change request */
Step9: **If** $read_A(v_i)$ = '–' or $write_A(v_i)$ = '–' or
$\neg\exists q^+ \in SubRelPath(p, content, A^+)$ s.t. $v_i \in q^+(t)$) or
$\exists q^- \in SubRelPath(p, content, A^-)$ s.t. $v_i \in q^-(t)$ or
$v_i \in RelNode(t, SubRelPath(p, content, A^+))$ **then return** *Permit*.
}
}
}
Step10: *Permit* = TRUE.
Step11: **return** *Permit*.

Fig. 5. The *UpdReqCheck* algorithm

Theorem 2: Given an XML tree $t = <V_t, E_t, r_t>$ with security labels, access control policy A of s on XML tree t, and an update request *updreq* <*s*, *op*, *doc-id*, *p*, *content*>, *UpdReqCheck* decides whether *updreq* is not an unsecure update request under A in $O(|t|^2 \cdot |p| \cdot |A|)$, where $|t|$ is the size of t, $|p|$ is the size of query of *updreq*, $|A|$ is the number of authorization rules of A.

Proof: Computation of $p(t)$ at Step2 can be done in $O(|t| \cdot |p|)$. Step3 is processed $|p(t)|$ times. Time complexity of processing Step3 and Step9 is bounded by $O(|t| \cdot |p| \cdot |A| \cdot |p(t)|)$. As total time complexity of step2 thru step9 is $O(|t| \cdot |p| + |t| \cdot |p| \cdot |A| \cdot |p(t)|)$ and $|p(t)|$ can be as big as $|t|$, time complexity of *UpdReqCheck* is bounded by $O(|t|^2 \cdot |p| \cdot |A|)$. ∎

5 Conclusion and Future Work

In this paper, we have presented confidential information leakage problem when modifying XML documents with fine-grained access control. The problem may occur when the system allows a user modifying the values or the structural relationship between document nodes referred by path expressions of the authorization rules. We have discussed properties of secure append, remove and change operations for XML documents. Given an XML document tree, access control policy of a subject, we have proposed the polynomial-time algorithm that decides whether a given update request against the labeled XML tree is permitted under the subject's access control policy and will not cause the information leakage problem. We are going to investigate the possibility of utilizing DTDs or schemas of XML documents to reduce the complexity of computing security labels for XML tree and the complexity of deciding whether a given update request is unsecure.

References

1. E. Bertino, S. Castano, E. Ferrari, M. Mesiti, "Specifying and Enforcing Access Control Policies for XML Document Sources," WWW Journal, vol.3, n.3, 2000.
2. E. Bertino, G. Mella, G. Correndo, E. Ferrari. "An infrastructure for managing secure update operations on XML data," In Proc. of 8th ACM Symposium on Access Control Models and Technologies (SACMAT03), pp.110-122, 2003.
3. S. Chatvichienchai, "Detecting Confidential Data Disclosure in Updating XML Documents", Technical Report No.2006-01, Siebold University of Nagasaki, 2006.
4. E. Damiani, S. De Capitani di Vimercati, S. Paraboschi, P. Samarati, "A Fine-Grained Access Control System for XML Documents," ACM TISSEC, vol. 5, no. 2, 2002.
5. G. Gottlob, C. Koch, and R. Pichler, "XPath Query Evaluation: Improving Time and Space Efficiency". In Proc. 19th IEEE International Conference on Data Engineering (ICDE'03), 379-390, 2003.
6. P. Kilpelainen and H. Mannila. "Ordered and unordered tree inclusion" Siam Journal on Computing, pp.340-356, 1995.
7. M. Kudo and S. Hada, "XML Document Security based on Provisional Authorization," Proc.7th ACM Conf. Computer and Communications Security, pp. 87-96, 2000.
8. OASIS XACML Technical Committee, "eXtensible Access Control Markup Language (XACML) Version 2.0," http://www.oasis-open.org/specs/index.php#xacmlv2.0 (Feb 2005).
9. R. Sandhu, E. Coyne, H. Feinstein, and C. Youman, "Role-Based Access Control Models," IEEE Computer, 29(2), pp.38-47, 1996.
10. I. Tatarinov, G.Z. Yves, A.Y. Halevy, D.S. Weld. "Updating XML". In ACM SIGMOD 2001, Santa Barbara, California, USA (May 2001).
11. W3C (2000). Extensible Markup Language (XML) 1.0 (Second Edition). Available at http://www.w3c.org/TR/ REC-xml (Oct 2000).
12. W3C (1999). XML Path Language (XPath) Version 1.0. Available at http://www.w3c.org/TR/xpath (Nov 1999).
13. W3C (2005). XML Query Language (XQuery) Version 1.0. Available at http://www.w3.org/TR/xquery/. (Nov 2005).
14. X. Yang, C. Li: Secure XML Publishing without Information Leakage in the Presence of Data Inference. VLDB 2004: pp.96-107, Toronto, Canada (Aug 2004).

Faster Twig Pattern Matching Using Extended Dewey ID*

Chung Keung Poon and Leo Yuen

Department of Computer Science
City University of Hong Kong
{ckpoon, leo}@cs.cityu.edu.hk

Abstract. Finding all the occurrences of a twig pattern in an XML database is a core operation for efficient evaluation of XML queries. Recently, Lu *et al.* [7] proposed the TJFast algorithm that uses the *extended Dewey* labelling scheme and reported better performance compared with other *state-of-the-art* holistic twig join algorithms, both in terms of number of elements scanned and stored during the computation. In this paper, we designed an enhancement to further exploit the power of the *extended Dewey ID*. This reduces the CPU cost and also favors indexed inputs. Our algorithm can be shown analytically as efficient as TJFast in terms of worst case I/O, and experimentally performs significantly better.

1 Introduction

An XML document can be naturally modelled as a tree in which nodes represent XML elements while edges represent nesting between elements. A query in many important XML query languages such as XPath and XQuery can also be modelled as a tree in which nodes represent node tests in location steps while edges represent the structural relationships between nodes connected by the edges. Finding all the occurrences of such tree pattern (a.k.a twig pattern) in an XML document is a core operation for efficient evaluation of XML queries.

An early approach for the problem proceeds by breaking down the twig pattern into edges representing the required binary structural relationships (*e.g.*, parent-child, ancestor-descendant), then applying structural joins to match the binary relationships against the XML document and finally stitching together these basic matches. With clever labelling schemes (*e.g.* region or prefix coding) for the XML documents, the structural relationships between two nodes can be determined using only their labels without actually traversing the document tree. However, the problem of such approach is that the intermediate results can become very large, independent of the input and output sizes.

Other algorithms such as ViST [10] and PRIX [8] work by serializing the twig pattern and the XML document into strings and then finding common subsequences. However, time-consuming postprocessing is needed to remove false hits and false dismissals from the subsequence matchings.

* This research was fully supported by a grant from the Research Grants Council of the Hong Kong SAR, China [Project No. 9040906 (RGC Ref. No. CityU 1164/04E)].

S. Bressan, J. Küng, and R. Wagner (Eds.): DEXA 2006, LNCS 4080, pp. 297–306, 2006.

Another line of development started by Bruno *et al.* [1] is to recursively build up the matchings following the structure of the twig pattern. Their algorithm, TwigStack, is provably optimal for twig queries with only ancestor-descendant relationship under their specific I/O model. Jiang *et al.* [4] modified and enhanced TwigStack to TSGeneric^+ to favor indexed input data stream and to reduce the query time by avoiding certain useless recursive calls. Other algorithms along this line includes the GTwigMerge algorithm of Jiang *et al.* [3] that deals with twig pattern with OR-predicates and the TwigStackList algorithm of Lu *et al.* [6] which is a look-ahead approach to better handle query twigs with parent-child edge. It is proved in [2] that no algorithm for twig queries can read the input stream only once under the model of Bruno *et al.* when the twig contains parent-child edges.

All these stack-based algorithms rely on a labelling scheme called *region encoding* which allows for checking of ancestor-descendant relationship using the labels of two nodes only. Recently, Lu *et al.* [7] proposed the *extended Dewey* labelling scheme in which one can derive the names of all the elements on the path from the root to an element given the *extended Dewey ID* of this element. This unique feature is essential to their algorithm, TJFast, that requires scanning, by far, the least number of input elements and storing the smallest amount of intermediate results among all holistic twig join algorithms under the same I/O model.

In this paper, we observe that TJFast has not yet fully utilized the power of the *extended Dewey* labelling. By a small twist to TJFast, we obtain an improved algorithm which we called TJFaster. Compared with TJFast, our algorithm is more effective in skipping elements and hence avoids more useless recursive calls. It also replaces certain root-leaf path matchings by simpler label comparisons. Further, it fits well on indexed input. We perform a comprehensive experiment to demonstrate the benefits of our algorithm over the previous one.

The rest of the paper is organized as follow. After stating the problem, model and some notations in the next section, the *extended Dewey ID* is given in the section 3. This is followed by details of our enhancement and the experimental evaluation in section 4 and 5 respectively. The paper is then concluded in section 6.

2 Problem Statement, Model and Notations

In the rest of this paper, "node" refers to a tree node in the query twig pattern while "element" refers to an element in the XML document. For any node v in the query tree, we let P_v be the path from the root to v; and Q_v be the query subtree rooted at v *together* with P_v. The path P_e for element e in the document tree is similarly defined.

We say that Q_v has a *matching* if there is a mapping of Q_v to the document tree that preserves the node types and structural relations of edges in Q_v. A node v *matches* an element e if Q_v has a matching in which node v is mapped to e. Let v_{tb} be the *top branching node* in the query tree, *i.e.*, the branching node that is an ancestor of all branching nodes in the query tree. Thus, our problem is to find all the matchings of $Q_{v_{tb}}$.

A matching of Q with n nodes $(v_1, \cdots, v_n)$ can be represented as an n-tuple $(d_1, \cdots, d_n)$ where for $1 \leq i \leq n$, node v_i is mapped to element d_i in the XML document in the matching.

Following the model employed in Ref. [1,7], we assume that each leaf f in the query tree is associated with a stream T_f of all the elements that match the node type of f, sorted in ascending lexicographical order of their labels. A stream T supports the get(T) function that reads the "current" element of the stream, the advance(T) function that moves the stream cursor to the next element and the eof(T) function that tells if T reaches its end. Initially, the stream cursor points to the first element of T.

To describe our algorithms, we assume the following functions (whose implementations are straightforward): isLeaf(v) and isBranching(v) determine if a query node v is a leaf or a branching node respectively, leafNodes(v) returns the set of leaf nodes in the twig rooted at v; and dbl(v) (for *direct branching or leaf node*) returns the set of all branching nodes b and leaf nodes f in the twig rooted at v such that there is no branching nodes along the path from v to b or f, excluding v, b or f. We will also refer to the (conceptual) functions $anc(e)$ and $desc(e)$ which denote the set of all ancestors and descendants of an element e in the document respectively.

3 Extended Dewey ID and Some Intuition

Tatarinov *et al.* [9] proposed the *Dewey ID* labelling scheme to represent the position of an element occurrence in an XML document. By labelling the root as an empty string ε, each non-root element u is labelled as $label(s).x$ where u is the x-th child of s. From now on, writing "$a < b$" means that element a has a smaller label than that of b.

The *extended Dewey ID* [7] encodes not only the positions but also the element names along the path from the root to the element. To overcome the problem of large label size, Lu *et al.* made use of schema constraints such as DTD or XML schema. They embedded such constraints in a *finite state transducer* so that given the *extended Dewey ID* of an element, all the element names along the path from the root to that element can be decoded efficiently. Due to this *ancestor name vision* property, determining if there is a matching between a simple query path (*i.e.* without twig) and a document path is now straightforward (taking time linear to the sum of lengths of the two paths). The remaining problem is to determine which root-leaf path matchings can be combined to form a matching for the whole query tree.

To give some intuition of our algorithm, consider the following problem that pops up again and again, namely, that of finding a matching for Q_v where v is a branching node with dbls $v_1, \ldots, v_d$. Suppose for each i, some matchings of Q_{v_i} have been found and S_{v_i} stores a set of elements with which v_i matches. Furthermore, assume that all the elements in each S_{v_i} lie on the same path (in the document tree). Now we want to combine the matchings of the Q_{v_i}'s to form matchings of Q_v.

Let e_i be the maximum element in S_{v_i}, *i.e.*, the element with the largest depth since all elements in S_{v_i} lie on the same path. Define $\mathsf{MB}(v_i,v)$ as the set of all ancestors, a, of e_i such that a can match node v in the path solution of e_i to P_{v_i}. Observe that if there is an element a present in all the $\mathsf{MB}(v_i,v)$'s, then for each i, there is a matching of Q_{v_i} such that the path P_v is mapped in the same way for different i's (in particular, node v is mapped to element a) while the subtree rooted at v_i is mapped to the document subtree rooted at e_i. This forms a matching for Q_v. In fact, other matchings may be possible by mapping the subtree rooted at v_i to elements in S_{v_i} higher than e_i but below a.

To detect if such an element a exists, it suffices to check for the intersection of $\mathsf{MB}(v_{max}, v) \cap \mathsf{MB}(v_{min}, v)$ where v_{max} and v_{min} are the children with the maximum and minimum e_i respectively. Any element in the intersection must also be present in every other $\mathsf{MB}(v_i,v)$ and hence qualifies for such an a. Also, note that all the elements in $\mathsf{MB}(v_{max}, v) \cap \mathsf{MB}(v_{min}, v)$ must lie on the same path from the root to the lowest common ancestor of e_{max} and e_{min} in the document tree. Hence we can set S_v to be $\mathsf{MB}(v_{max}, v) \cap \mathsf{MB}(v_{min}, v)$.

Thus we can associate with each node b in the query twig a set S_b and build up the matchings from the leaves towards the top branching node v_{tb} using the above idea. This gives us a recursive approach for the problem.

4 Details of Our Design

Our algorithm has the same high level structure as TJFast (shown in Algorithm 1). Like other holistic twig join algorithms, it operates in two phases. In the first phase (line 1-7), some solutions to individual root-leaf path patterns are computed. In the second phase (line 8), these solutions are merged to form the answers to the query twig pattern. To allow for efficient merging of root-leaf path into output during the second phase, a *blocking* technique is used in outputSolutions(line 5) so that the path solutions are in sorted order, irrespective of the root-leaf path provided. It is commonly employed in previous works [1,2,3,4,6,7], and its details are omitted due to space limitation. From now on, we focus on the task of outputting all and only those individual root-leaf paths that can be merged in the second phase, without duplication.

Algorithm 1. TJFaster

1: **for all** f $\in$leafNodes(root) **do**
2:    locateMatchedLabel(f)
3: **while** $\exists f \in$ leafNodes(root) : $\neg$ eof(T_f) **do**
4:    f_{act} =getNext(v_{tb})
5:    outputSolutions(f_{act})
6:    advance($T_{f_{act}}$)
7:    locateMatchedLabel(f_{act})
8: mergeAllPathSolutions()

The procedure locateMatchedLabel(f) locates the first element e in T_f such that P_e matches P_f. This is done by repeatedly matching get(T_f) with P_f and calling advance(T_f) until a match is found. It is called in the initialization step (line 1-2) and whenever a stream has just been advanced (line 6-7).

Function getNext(v) is the core function in the algorithm. Our getNext function is very similar to that of TJFast (shown in Algorithm 2). Later, we will point out the inefficiency in the function and the changes we made. Taking a query node v as parameter, the function updates the set S_v and returns a query leaf node $f \in$ leafNodes(v) whose stream is "safe to advance". Roughly speaking, S_v will be updated to contain the set of elements to which v maps, in the same matching of Q_v when get(T_f) is matched to f unless there is no such matching. Note that this set of elements will lie on the same (document) path.

By using the top branching node v_{tb} as parameter, TJFaster calls getNext repeatedly to identify the next stream f_{act} to advance among all the input streams. Before advancing $T_{f_{act}}$, those path matching solutions are output (in outputSolutions) if all the elements along the path of get(T_f) that match a branching node b can be found in the corresponding set S_b.

The main weakness of TJFast is that the leaf streams are only advanced in line 6 and 7 after an expensive call to getNext(v_{tb}) in the main loop. We will show here

Algorithm 2. getNext(v)

```
if isLeaf(v) then
    return v
else
    skipElement(v) {newly introduced in TJFaster}
    for all v_i ∈dbl(v) do
        f_i = getNext(v_i)
        if isBranching(v_i) ∧ empty(S_{v_i}) then
            return f_i
        e_i = max{p|p ∈MB(v_i, v)}
    min = minarg_i{e_i}
    max = maxarg_i{e_i}
    for all v_i ∈dbl(v) do
        if ∀e ∈MB(v_i,v):e ∉ anc(e_max) then
            return f_i
    for all e ∈MB(v_min, v) do
        if e ∈ anc(e_max) then
            S_v = ((desc(e) ∪ anc(e)) ∩ S_v) ∪ {e}
    return f_min
```

Function MB(v, b)

```
if isBranching(v) then
    Let e = max{p|p ∈ S_v}
else
    Let e =get(T_v)
return the set of ancestors, a, of e such that b can be mapped to a in some mapping
    of P_v to P_e.
```

that there are other elements that will surely not contribute to any matchings and that we can identify them while performing a call to getNext. The immediate benefit is the saving of more useless recursive getNext calls. Moreover, we can filter elements by checking only their lexicographic order. This way, path pattern matchings need not be done on all input elements. Furthermore, in addition to the existing advance method, if the input stream T is indexed and supports an efficient method to forward the cursor to the first element such that get(T)$> e$ for any given element e, the I/O access can also be saved.

To achieve the above improvement, all we need is to add the function call SkipElement(v) (see Algorithm 3) in line 4 of getNext(v) (Algorithm 2).

Algorithm 3. skipElement(v)

Let f_{max} be leaf f $\in$LeafNodes(v) with the maximum get(T_f)
$a =$ the highest ancestor of get($T_{f_{max}}$) such that P_v matchable to P_a
for all f in leafNodes(v) **do**
    if empty(S_v) or $\forall e \in S_v$: get(T_f) $\notin desc(e)$ **then**
        while get(T_f) $< a$ **do**
            advance(T_f)
        locateMatchedLabel(f)

Given a query node v as a parameter, SkipElement skips those elements in the leaf streams in the twig rooted at v that cannot contribute to any output solution. Clearly, Q_v has a matching only if an element in each stream in leafNodes(v) is found to share at least one common ancestor a such that v matches a. In particular, P_v has to match P_a. The following lemma is also obvious:

Lemma 1. *Consider two elements, a and b in the document tree. If $a < b$, then either a precedes b (i.e., b follows a), or a is an ancestor of b (i.e., b is a descendant of a).*

We now argue that SkipElement(v) will only advance a stream T_f if get(T_f) cannot participate in any matching of Q_v. Note that we need only consider the possibility of get(T_f) forming a matching of Q_v with other get($T_{f'}$) or elements following them for all f' $\in$leafNodes(v). The other matchings involving elements of a stream $T_{f'}$ preceding get($T_{f'}$), if any, should have been processed already by the construction of getNext(v).

We first consider the case when S_v is empty. So there has not been any matching of Q_v. Consider two arbitrary leaves f and f' in leafNodes(v) and let a be the highest ancestor of get(T_f) such that P_v matches P_a. Suppose get($T_{f'}$) has a smaller label than that of a. Then get($T_{f'}$) precedes a (by Lemma 1) and by definition of a, get($T_{f'}$) cannot participate in any matching of Q_v involving get(T_f). Furthermore, get($T_{f'}$) precedes get(T_f) as well (since a <get(T_f)). Hence, get($T_{f'}$) cannot participate in any matching involving elements of T_f following get(T_f). In other words, get($T_{f'}$) is not useful in generating any new matching of Q_v. Hence it is safe to advance $T_{f'}$.

Note that the above argument holds for any f. Picking the stream f with the largest a will result in skipping the largest number of elements. In SkipElement(v), we therefore choose $f = f_{max}$ that maximizes get(T_f) (Line 1-2). This will give the largest corresponding ancestor a among all streams $f \in$leafNodes(v).

For the case when S_v is not empty, S_w is also nonempty for any descendant w of v. Moreover, some of the elements in the S_w's may form a matching of Q_v, possibly with some get(T_f) for some f in leafNodes(v). If a get(T_f) is involved, it can be proved that get(T_f) must be a descendant of some element in S_v. Hence we have the following lemma which is important in proving our algorithm correctness.

Lemma 2. *Let v, a and f be as defined in Algorithm 3. If S_v is empty, or* get(T_f) *is not a descendant of some element in S_v, then T_f can be advanced until* get(T_f) $> a$ *without missing any matching of Q_v.*

Theorem 1. *Given a twig query Q and an XML database D, algorithm* TJFaster *correctly returns all the answers for Q on D.*

Now we analyse the complexities of our algorithm. Note that our algorithm uses no more space than that of TJFast. As for the query time, note that the stream cursors never go back during the execution of the algorithm. Therefore, the worst-case I/O time is $O(n)$ for any index method used, where n is the total number of input elements. Morever, any element scanned by TJFaster is also scanned by TJFast (which reads every input element in each stream once). Therefore, our algorithm is asymptotically no worse than TJFast in terms of the I/O cost. The next section will show that in practice, our algorithm is much faster than TJFast.

5 Experimental Evaluation

In this section, we present our experimental evaluation on the effectiveness of our enhancement. All experiments were conducted on a 2.6GHz Pentium 4 processor with 1GB main memory running Windows XP. We implemented TJFast and TJFaster in JDK 1.4 using PostgreSQL. TJFaster uses the identical program code with TJFast except for the additonal SkipElement function. We tested the algorithms with the following well-known datasets:

XMark : A synthetic benchmark dataset generated by the XML Generator, containing information about auctions.
Shakespeare plays : Shakespeare's plays in XML format.
TreeBank : A file with deep recursive structure.

We are interested in the following three performance measures: (1) the number of elements skipped, (2) the number of getNext calls, and (3) the elapsed time (which counts only the CPU cost). We measure the elapsed time by fetching the whole input streams into main memory before executing the algorithms. The number of elements skipped will indicate the effectiveness of the SkipElement

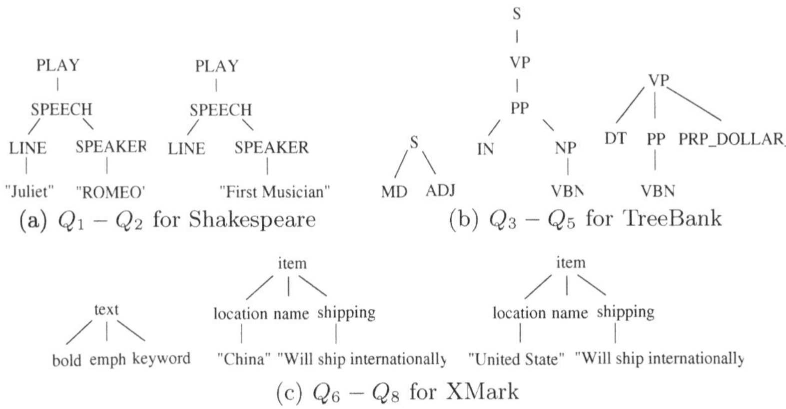

Fig. 1. Twig Queries Tested

function and hence the reduction in the CPU cost of algorithm. If the input streams are indexed so that the cursors can be advanced directly to the desired element (without going through the uncessary elements), we expect that the I/O cost will also be proportional to the CPU cost.

We tested two twig queries in Shakespeare play "The Tragedy of Romeo and Juliet", three twig queries in TreeBank and three twig queries in XMark (Figure 1). We included some nodes that select text value (indicated by the double quotation marks) to control the selectivity. These queries represent some useful queries with semantic. Queries without text value are adopted from experiments in other earlier papers. All edges in the experimental queries are ancestor-descendant edges because TJFast deals with parent-child edges much in the same way as ancestor-descendant edges, though without guaranteeing optimality.

The major results are shown in Table 1 and Figure 2. The input size is counted as the total number of elements in all the input streams while the output size is the number of output elements in the leaf streams before the merging in phase 2.

Table 1. Major results

Query	Input Size	Output Size	# of elts. skipped in TJFaster	# of getNext calls TJFast	# of getNext calls TJFaster	Elapsed Time (in ms) TJFast	Elapsed Time (in ms) TJFaster	% of elts. skipped	Useless Recursion Avoided
Q_1	167	0	149	495	48	47	1	89.2%	90.3%
Q_2	3102	18	2641	9306	1383	313	78	85.1%	85.1%
Q_3	13670	18	12434	40710	3654	1562	172	91.0%	91.0%
Q_4	168536	15732	126000	298890	47520	15235	4860	74.8%	84.1%
Q_5	155886	3349	128693	375664	30456	16375	2703	82.6%	91.9%
Q_6	21156	10276	9403	84624	47012	3047	2219	44.4%	44.4%
Q_7	5360	0	4400	10824	36	375	31	95.1%	99.7%
Q_8	7919	1173	2944	17264	5488	578	297	37.2%	68.2%

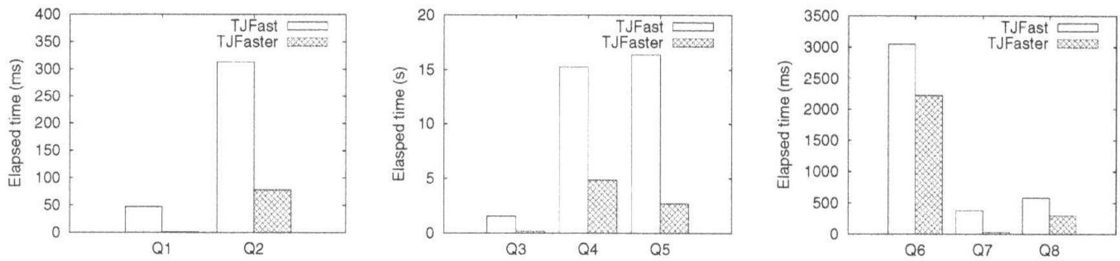

Fig. 2. Experimental results on computational time

The results show that the elapsed time is highly correlated to the number of getNext calls and the number of elements skipped. Moreover, the enhanced performance can now reflect the output size better rather than depending heavily on the input size as TJFast does. (For example, compare the elapsed time of Q_4 and Q_5 for the two algorithms.) We conclude that this optimization improves the previous design significantly, especially if the query is selective (i.e., produce small outputs).

6 Conclusions and Future Work

XML twig pattern matching is a key issue for XML query processing. In this paper, we have proposed TJFaster as an efficient algorithm to address this problem using some unexplored feature of *extended Dewey ID*. Our design improves the performance of the TJFast significantly when the selectivity is high. If an index of the input stream can efficiently support the finding of the successor of a given label, the new algorithm can avoid accessing elements that do not contribute to final results to save I/O access. Even without index support, the optimization saves the processing time in doing useless recursive calls and root-leaf pattern matchings.

For future work, we would like to apply the principle to *region encoding*, making use of RI-Tree[5], a relational data structure for selecting all intervals enclosing a given query point. Yuen and Poon [11] showed that an RI-tree can be used to support the ancestor axis efficiently in XPath when we regard each element as an interval, using *region encoding*. This may be used to substitute the *ancestor name vision property* when *extended Dewey ID* cannot be used.

References

1. Nicolas Bruno, Nick Koudas, and Divesh Srivastava. Holistic twig joins: optimal XML pattern matching. In *Proceedings of the 2002ACM SIGMOD Conference on the Management of Data*, pages 310–321, 2002.
2. Byron Choi, Malika Mahoui, and Derick Wood. On the optimality of holistic algorithms for twig queries. In *DEXA*, pages 28–37, 2003.

3. Haifeng Jiang, Hongjun Lu, and Wei Wang. Efficient processing of XML twig queries with or-predicates. In *SIGMOD '04: Proceedings of the 2004 ACM SIGMOD international conference on Management of data*, pages 59–70, New York, NY, USA, 2004. ACM Press.
4. Haifeng Jiang, Wei Wang, Hongjun Lu, and Jeffrey Xu Yu. Holistic twig joins in indexed XML documents. In *Proceedings of the 30th International Conference on Very Large Data Bases*, 2003.
5. Hans-Peter Kriegel, Marco Potke, and Thomas Seidl. Managing intervals efficiently in object-relational databases. In *Proceedings of the 26th International Conference on Very Large Data Bases*, pages 407–418, 2000.
6. Jiaheng Lu, Ting Chen, and Tok Wang Ling. Efficient processing of XML twig patterns with parent child edges: a look-ahead approach. In *CIKM '04: Proceedings of the thirteenth ACM conference on Information and knowledge management*, pages 533–542, New York, NY, USA, 2004. ACM Press.
7. Jiaheng Lu, Tok Wang Ling, Chee-Yong Chan, and Ting Chen. From region encoding to extended dewey: on efficient processing of XML twig pattern matching. In *VLDB '05: Proceedings of the 31st international conference on Very large data bases*, pages 193–204. VLDB Endowment, 2005.
8. Praveen Rao and Bongki Moon. PRIX: indexing and query XML using Prüfer sequences. In *20th International Conference on Data Engineering*, pages 288–300, 2004.
9. Igor Tatarinov, Stratis D. Viglas, Kevin Beyer, Jayavel Shanmugasundaram, Eugene Shekita, and Chun Zhang. Storing and querying ordered XML using a relational database system. In *Proceedings of the 2002ACM SIGMOD Conference on the Management of Data*, pages 204–215, 2002.
10. H. Wang, S. Park, W. Fan, and P. Yu. Vist: A dynamic index method for querying XML data by tree structures, 2003.
11. Leo Yuen and Chung Keung Poon. Relational index support for XPath axes. In *XSym*, pages 84–98, 2005.

A Vector Space Model for Semantic Similarity Calculation and OWL Ontology Alignment

Rubén Tous and Jaime Delgado

Distributed Multimedia Applications Group (DMAG)
Universitat Politècnica de Catalunya (UPC), Dpt. d'Arquitectura de Computadors
Universitat Pompeu Fabra (UPF), Dpt. de Tecnologia
rtous@ac.upc.edu, jaime.delgado@upf.edu

Abstract. Ontology alignment (or matching) is the operation that takes two ontologies and produces a set of semantic correspondences (usually semantic similarities) between some elements of one of them and some elements of the other. A rigorous, efficient and scalable similarity measure is a pre-requisite of an ontology alignment process. This paper presents a semantic similarity measure based on a matrix represention of nodes from an RDF labelled directed graph. An entity is described with respect to how it relates to other entities using N-dimensional vectors, being N the number of selected external predicates. We adapt a known graph matching algorithm when applying this idea to the alignment of two ontologies. We have successfully tested the model with the public testcases of the Ontology Alignment Evaluation Initiative 2005.

1 Introduction

1.1 Motivation

For many knowledge domains (biology, music, web directories, digital rights management, etc.) several overlapping ontologies (middle ontologies) are being engineered. Each one is a different abstraction and representation of the same or similar concepts. There are proliferating also a myriad of problem-specific ontologies (lower ontologies) for many applications, metadata repositories, personal information systems and peer-to-peer networks.

To enable collaboration within and across information domains, software agents require the semantic alignment (mapping) of the different formalisms. The alignment process will identify the equivalences between some entities (e.g. classes and properties) of the participating ontologies, and the different levels of confidence. These mappings are required before the querying of semantic data from autonomous sources can take place.

1.2 Ontology Alignment Formal Definition

Ontology alignment (or matching) is the operation that takes two ontologies and produces a set of semantic correspondences (usually semantic similarities) between some elements of one of them and some elements of the other. Several

S. Bressan, J. Küng, and R. Wagner (Eds.): DEXA 2006, LNCS 4080, pp. 307–316, 2006.

ontology alignment algorithms have been provided like GLUE [2], OLA [7] or FOAM [4]. A more formal definition, borrowed from [3], can be given:

Definition 1. Given two ontologies $\mathcal{O}$ and $\mathcal{O}'$, an *alignment* between $\mathcal{O}$ and $\mathcal{O}'$ is a set of correspondences (i.e., 4-uples): $< e, e', r, n >$ with $e \in \mathcal{O}$ and $e' \in \mathcal{O}'$ being the two matched entities, r being a relationship holding between e and e', and n expressing the level of confidence [0..1] in this correspondence.

It is typically assumed that the two ontologies are described within the same knowledge representation language (e.g. OWL [12]). Here we will focus on automatic and autonomous alignment, but other semi-automatic and interactive approaches exist.

1.3 Semantic Similarity Measures

The ontology alignment problem has an important background work in discrete mathematics for matching graphs [8][13], in databases for mapping schemas [14] and in machine learning for clustering structured objects [1]. Most part of ontology alignment algorithms are just focused on finding close entities (the "=" relationship), and rely on some *semantic similarity* measure.

A semantic similarity measure tries to find clues to deduce that two different data items correspond to the same information. Data items can be ontology classes and properties, but also instances or any other information representation entities. Semantic similarity between ontology entities (within the same ontology or between two different ones) may be defined in many different ways. The recently held Ontology Alignment Evaluation Initiative 2005 [11] has shown that the best alignment algorithms combine different similarity measures. [7] provides a classification (updating [14]) inherited from the study of similarity in relational schemas. This classification can be simplified to four categories when being applied to ontologies: Lexical, Topological, Extensional and Model-based.

1.4 Our Approach

The work presented in this paper takes a topological or structure-based semantic similarity approach. As ontologies and knowledge-representation languages evolve, more sophisticated structure-based similarity measures are required. In RDF (Resource Description Framework [15]) graphs, relationships are labeled with predicate names, and trivial distance-based strategies cannot be applied. Some works like [6] explore similarity measures based on structure for RDF equivalent bipartite graphs.

Our work focus also in RDF, but faces directly the natural RDF labelled directed graphs. The approach can be outlined in the following two points:

1. To compute the semantic similarity of two entities we have taken the common RDF and OWL predicates as a semantic reference. Objects are described and compared depending on how they relate to other objects in terms of these predicates. We have modeled this idea as a simple vector space.

2. To efficiently apply our similarity measure to the ontology alignment problem we have adapted it to the graph matching algorithm of [5].

2 Representing RDF Labelled Directed Graphs with a Vector Space Model (VSM)

In linear algebra a *vector space* is a set V of *vectors* together with the operations of addition and scalar multiplication (and also with some natural constraints such as closure, associativity, and so on). A vector space model (VSM) is an algebraic model introduced a long time ago by Salton [16] in the information retrieval field. In a more general sense, a VSM allows to describe and compare objects using N-dimensional vectors. Each dimension corresponds to an orthogonal feature of the object (e.g. weight of certain term in a document).

In an OWL ontology, we will compare entities taking into consideration their relationships with all the other entities present in the ontology - First we will focus on similarity within the same ontology, next we will study its application to the alignment of two ontologies -. Because relationships can be of different nature we will model them with a vector space. For this vector space, we will take as dimensions any OWL, RDF Schema, or other external predicate (not ontology specific) e.g. *rdfs:subClassOf*, *rdfs:range* or *foaf:name*. We can formally define the relationship of two nodes in the model:

Definition 2. Given any pair of nodes n_1 and n_2 of a directed labelled RDF graph $\mathcal{G}_{\mathcal{O}}$ representing the OWL ontology $\mathcal{O}$, the relationship between them, $rel(n_1, n_2)$, is defined by the vector $\{arc(n_1, n_2, p_1), ..., arc(n_1, n_2, p_N)\}$, where arc is a function that returns 1 if there is an arc labelled with the predicate p_i from n_1 to n_2 or 0 otherwise. p_i is a predicate from the set of external predicates $\mathcal{P}$ (e.g. {*rdfs:subClassOf*, *foaf:name*}).

$$\begin{aligned} rel(n_1, n_2) = &\{arc(n_1, n_2, p_1), ..., arc(n_1, n_2, p_N)\} \mid \\ & n_1, n_2 \in \mathcal{G}_{\mathcal{O}} \;\wedge\; \forall i \in [0; N], p_i \in \mathcal{P} \end{aligned}$$

$$arc(n_1, n_2, p_i) = \begin{cases} 1 & \text{if there is an arc labelled with } p_i \text{ from } n_1 \text{ to } n_2; \\ 0 & \text{otherwise.} \end{cases}$$

Example 1. Let us see a simple example. Take the following graph $\mathcal{G}_{\mathcal{A}}$ representing an ontology $\mathcal{O}_{\mathcal{A}}$. Imagine a trivial two-dimensional vector space to model the relationships between nodes. External predicates *rdfs:domain* and *rdfs:range* have been chosen for dimensions 0 and 1 respectively.

The relationship between the property *directs* and the class *director* will be described by $\{1, 0\}$. The relationship between the property *actsIn* and the class *movie* will be described by $\{0, 1\}$, and so on.

Now, the full description of an entity can be achieved with a vector containing the relationships between it and all the other entities in the ontology. Putting all

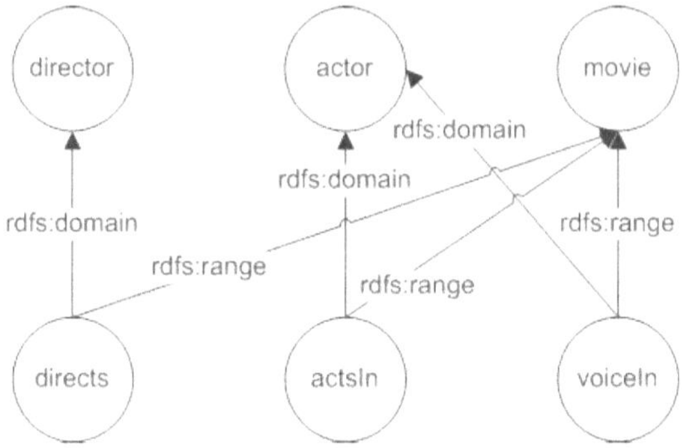

Fig. 1. $\mathcal{G}_{\mathcal{A}}$

the vectors together we obtain a three-dimensional matrix $\mathcal{A}$ representation of the labelled directed graph $\mathcal{G}_{\mathcal{A}}$ (row order: *director*, *actor*, *movie*, *directs*, *actsIn*, *voiceIn*):

$$\mathcal{A} = \begin{pmatrix} (0,0) & (0,0) & (0,0) & (0,0) & (0,0) & (0,0) \\ (0,0) & (0,0) & (0,0) & (0,0) & (0,0) & (0,0) \\ (0,0) & (0,0) & (0,0) & (0,0) & (0,0) & (0,0) \\ (1,0) & (0,0) & (0,1) & (0,0) & (0,0) & (0,0) \\ (0,0) & (1,0) & (0,1) & (0,0) & (0,0) & (0,0) \\ (0,0) & (1,0) & (0,1) & (0,0) & (0,0) & (0,0) \end{pmatrix}$$

3 Similarity of Entities Within the Same Ontology

In the general case, the correlation between two vectors x and y in an N-dimensional vector space can be calculated using the scalar product. We can normalize it by dividing this product by the product of the vector modules, obtaining the cosine distance, a traditional similarity measure. In our case, vectors describing entities in terms of other entities are composed by relationship vectors (so they are matrices). We can calculate the scalar product of two of such vectors of vectors V and W using also the scalar product to compute $V_i W_i$:

$$V \cdot W = \sum_{i=1}^{N} \sum_{j=1}^{M} V_{ij} W_{ij}$$

Applying this equation to the above example we can see that the scalar product of e.g. the vector describing *directs* and the vector describing *actsIn* is $directs \cdot actsIn = 1$. The scalar product of *actsIn* and *voiceIn* is $actsIn \cdot voiceIn = 2$, and so on. Normalizing these values (to keep them between 0 and 1) would allow to obtain a trivial similarity matrix of the ontology entities. However, we aim to propagate the structural similarities iteratively, and also to apply this idea to the alignment of two different ontologies. In the following sections we will describe how to do it by adapting the ideas described in [5].

4 Applying the Model to an Ontology Alignment Process

To calculate the alignment of two ontologies represented with our vector space model we have adapted the graph matching algorithm of [5]. This adapted algorithm calculates entity similarities in an RDF labelled directed graph by iteratively using the following updating equation [1] :

Definition 3. $S_{k+1} = BS_kA^T + B^TS_kA, k = 0, 1, ...$
where S_k is the $N_B * N_A$ similarity matrix of entries s_{ij} at iteration k, and A and B are the $N_B * N_B * N_P$ and $N_A * N_A * N_P$ three-dimensional matrices representing $\mathcal{G_A}$ and $\mathcal{G_B}$ respectively. N_A and N_B are the number of rows of A and B, and P is the number of predicates selected as dimensions of the VSM.

Note that, as it is done in [5], initially the similarity matrix S_0 is set to 1 (assuming for the first iteration that all entities from $\mathcal{G_A}$ are equal to all entities in $\mathcal{G_B}$). If we start the process already knowing the similarity values of some pair of entities, we can modify this matrix accordingly, and keep the known values between iterations.

Example 2. Let's see a simple example. Take the following graphs $\mathcal{G_A}$ and $\mathcal{G_B}$. Figure 2 shows their corresponding RDF labelled directed graphs.

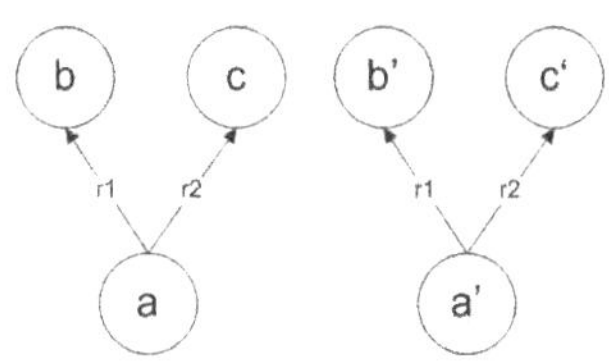

Fig. 2. $\mathcal{G_A}$ (left) and $\mathcal{G_B}$ (right)

$$A = \begin{pmatrix} (0,0) & (1,0) & (0,1) \\ (0,0) & (0,0) & (0,0) \\ (0,0) & (0,0) & (0,0) \end{pmatrix} B = \begin{pmatrix} (0,0) & (1,0) & (0,1) \\ (0,0) & (0,0) & (0,0) \\ (0,0) & (0,0) & (0,0) \end{pmatrix} S_0 = \begin{pmatrix} 1 & 1 & 1 \\ 1 & 1 & 1 \\ 1 & 1 & 1 \end{pmatrix}$$

$$S_1 = BS_0A^T + B^TS_0A = \begin{pmatrix} 2 & 0 & 0 \\ 0 & 1 & 0 \\ 0 & 0 & 1 \end{pmatrix}$$

[1] The graph matching algorithm from [5] is exactly the same as the algorithm shown here, but using simple matrices of 1's and 0's instead of matrices of vectors. We omit more details to avoid redundancies and because the paper remains self-contained.

To normalize the similarity matrix (to keep its values between 0 and 1) [5] divides all its elements by the Frobenius norm of the matrix, defined as the square root of the sum of the absolute squares of its elements.

$$S_1 = S_1/frobeniusNorm(S_1) = \begin{pmatrix} 0,816 & 0 & 0 \\ 0 & 0,408 & 0 \\ 0 & 0 & 0,408 \end{pmatrix}$$

Iterating the algorithm 4 times it converges to the following result:

$$S_4 = \begin{pmatrix} 0,577 & 0 & 0 \\ 0 & 0,577 & 0 \\ 0 & 0 & 0,577 \end{pmatrix}$$

So, as expected the entities a', b' and c' (rows) are similar to a, b and c (columns) respectively.

4.1 Computational Cost and Optimization

Because the number of selected external predicates $p_i \in \mathcal{P}$ can be small and it is independent of the size of the ontologies, operations involving relationships vectors can be considered of constant cost, and the general algorithm of order $O(N^2)$. Because the number of nodes can be considerably high, some optimizations are required to constraint the processing time. Inspired in [6], we have classified nodes into five types: Properties (p), Classes (c), Instances (i), External Classes (c') and External Instances (i'). Because nodes from one type cannot be similar to nodes of another type, the matrices can be rewritten (rows and columns correspond to types previously mentioned and in the same order):

$$A = \begin{pmatrix} A_{p-p} & A_{p-c} & A_{p-i} & A_{p-c'} & A_{p-i'} \\ A_{c-p} & A_{c-c} & A_{c-i} & A_{c-c'} & A_{c-i'} \\ A_{i-p} & A_{i-c} & A_{i-i} & A_{i-c'} & A_{i-i'} \\ A_{c'-p} & A_{c'-c} & A_{c'-i} & A_{c'-c'} & A_{c'-i'} \\ A_{i'-p} & A_{i'-c} & A_{i'-i} & A_{i'-c'} & A_{i'-i'} \end{pmatrix}$$

$$S_k = \begin{pmatrix} S_p & 0 & 0 & 0 & 0 \\ 0 & S_c & 0 & 0 & 0 \\ 0 & 0 & S_i & 0 & 0 \\ 0 & 0 & 0 & S_{c'} & 0 \\ 0 & 0 & 0 & 0 & S_{i'} \end{pmatrix}$$

Definition 4. The S_{k+1} equation can be decomposed into three formulas:

$$\mathbf{S_{p_{k+1}}} = B_{p-p}S_{p_k}A^T_{p-p} + B_{p-c}S_{c_k}A^T_{p-c} + B_{p-i}S_{i_k}A^T_{p-i} + B_{p-c'}S_{c'_k}A^T_{p-c'} + B_{p-i'}S_{i'_k}A^T_{p-i'} + B^T_{p-p}S_{p_k}A_{p-p} + B^T_{c-p}S_{c_k}A_{c-p} + B^T_{i-p}S_{i_k}A_{i-p} + B^T_{c'-p}S_{c'_k}A_{c'-p} + B^T_{i'-p}S_{i'_k}A_{i'-p}$$

$$\mathbf{S_{c_{k+1}}} = B_{c-p}S_{p_k}A_{c-p}^T + B_{c-c}S_{c_k}A_{c-c}^T + B_{c-i}S_{i_k}A_{c-i}^T + B_{c-c'}S_{c'_k}A_{c-c'}^T + B_{c-i'}S_{i'_k}A_{c-i'}^T + B_{p-c}^T S_{p_k}A_{p-c} + B_{c-c}^T S_{c_k}A_{c-c} + B_{i-c}^T S_{i_k}A_{i-c} + B_{c'-c}^T S_{c'_k}A_{c'-c} + B_{i'-c}^T S_{i'_k}A_{i'-c}$$

$$\mathbf{S_{i_{k+1}}} = B_{i-p}S_{p_k}A_{i-p}^T + B_{i-c}S_{c_k}A_{i-c}^T + B_{i-i}S_{i_k}A_{i-i}^T + B_{i-c'}S_{c'_k}A_{i-c'}^T + B_{i-i'}S_{i'_k}A_{i-i'}^T + B_{p-i}^T S_{p_k}A_{p-i} + B_{c-i}^T S_{c_k}A_{c-i} + B_{i-i}^T S_{i_k}A_{i-i} + B_{c'-i}^T S_{c'_k}A_{c'-i} + B_{i'-i}^T S_{i'_k}A_{i'-i}$$

$S_{c'_{k+1}}$ and $S_{i'_{k+1}}$ are diagonal matrices passed as input parameters. They are kept unchanged between iterations.

4.2 Comparison Against Algorithms Based on Bipartite Graphs

The use of an algorithm to measure similarity between directed graphs could lead to think that it would be better to directly apply it over the ontologies equivalent bipartite graphs (like it is done in [6]), instead of adapting it to RDF labelled directed graphs. However, our approach has some advantages; on one hand we reduce critically the number of nodes and the computational cost. On the other hand, in bipartite graphs the core predicates of OWL are treated as all the other nodes, while in our model they become the semantic reference to describe and compare entities. Figure 3 shows the equivalent bipartite version of the previous example with two graphs of three nodes.

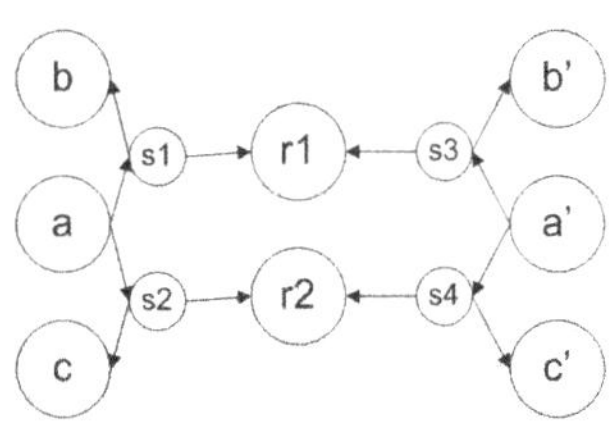

Fig. 3. $\mathcal{G_A}$ (left) and $\mathcal{G_B}$ (right)

Appying the alignment algorithm for bipartite graphs described in [6] we obtain the following similarity matrix between a', b', c' and a, b, c:

$$X_{22} = \begin{pmatrix} 0,405 & 0 & 0 \\ 0 & 0,153 & 0,05 \\ 0 & 0,05 & 0,153 \end{pmatrix}$$

As can be seen, the inclusion of statement nodes adds some symmetries not present in the original graphs, resulting in less precise results. Some similarities between nodes b' and c (and vice-versa) appear.

5 Results

To test our approach we have used the Ontology Alignment Evaluation Initiative 2005 testsuite [11]. The evaluation organizers provide a systematic benchmark test suite with pairs of ontologies to align as well as expected (human-based) results. The ontologies are described in OWL-DL and serialized in the RDF/XML format. The expected alignments are provided in a standard format expressed in RDF/XML and described in [11]. Because our model does not deal with lexical similarity, we have integrated our algorithm inside another hybrid aligner, Falcon [6] (replacing its structure similarity module by ours). This constraints the interest of the obtained results, but otherwise it hadn't been possible a comparative evaluation. Because most part of the tests include more lexical similarity than structural similarity challenges, our aligner and Falcon[2] obtain very similar results (the same for tests 101-104 and 301-304). The differences fall between tests 201-266, that we show in table 1.

Table 1. OAEI 2005 tests where our approach (vsm) obtains a different result than [6]

	vsm		falcon		foam		ola	
test	prec.	rec.	prec.	rec.	prec.	rec.	prec.	rec.
205	0.90	0.89	0.88	0.87	0.89	0.73	0.43	0.42
209	0.88	0.87	0.86	0.86	0.78	0.58	0.43	0.42
230	0.97	0.96	0.94	1.0	0.94	1.0	0.95	0.97
248	0.83	0.80	0.84	0.82	0.89	0.51	0.59	0.46
252	0.64	0.64	0.67	0.67	0.67	0.35	0.59	0.52
257	0.66	0.66	0.70	0.64	1.0	0.64	0.25	0.21
260	0.44	0.42	0.52	0.48	0.75	0.31	0.26	0.17
261	0.45	0.42	0.50	0.48	0.63	0.30	0.14	0.09
262	1.0	0.27	0.89	0.24	0.78	0.21	0.20	0.06
265	0.44	0.42	0.48	0.45	0.75	0.31	0.22	0.14
266	0.45	0.42	0.50	0.48	0.67	0.36	0.14	0.09

Rows correspond to test numbers, while columns correspond to the obtained values of precision (the number of correct alignments found divided by the total number of alignments found) and recall (the number of correct alignments found divided by the total of expected alignments).

From 50 tests our results just differ in 11 with respect to the aligner in which we have embedded our algorithm. We improve the results of Falcon in tests 205 and 206 (where labels have been replaced by synonyms), test 230 (where classes have been flattened) and test 262 (where everything except classes have been omitted). In test 257 (where names, comments and specialization hierarchy have been omitted) we just improve the recall value. In the other five tests our results are below the Falcon ones. We still cannot claim to outperform the original

[2] A description of all the tests can be obtained from [11]. Our results for tests not present in the table are the same as those of Falcon, and can be obtained in [6].

structural similarity algorithm of [6], but we can show that similar results (pretty good with respect to the other aligners) can be obtained by directly working over the RDF labelled directed graph, instead of working over the equivalent bipartite graph, that is bigger and can introduce symmetries not present in the original structure.

6 Related Work

The initial work around structure-based semantic similarity just focused on is-a constructs (taxonomies). Previous works like [10] measure the distance between the different nodes. The shorter the path from one node to another, the more similar they are. Given multiple paths, one takes the length of the shortest one. [17] finds the path length to the root node from the least common subsumer (LCS) of the two entities, which is the most specific entity they share as an ancestor. This value is scaled by the sum of the path lengths from the individual entities to the root. [9] finds the shortest path between two entities, and scales that value by the maximum path length in the is–a hierarchy in which they occur.

Recently, new works like [5] define more sophisticated topological similarity measures, based on graph matching from discrete mathematics. These new graph-based measures suit the particularities of the new ontologies, built with more expressive languages like OWL [12]. Our work is based on the previous work in [5], and also in its adaptation to OWL-DL ontologies alignment in [6]. This last work describes a structural similarity strategy called GMO (Graph Matching for Ontologies). Differently from our work, GMO operates over RDF bipartite graphs. It allows a more direct application of graph matching algorithms, but also increases the number of nodes and reduces scalability.

7 Conclusions

We have presented here an approach to structure-based semantic similarity measurement that can be directly applied to OWL ontologies modelled as RDF labelled directed graphs. The work is based on the intuitive idea that similarity of two entities can be defined in terms of how these two entities relate to the world they share (e.g. two red objects are similar with respect to the colour dimension, but their similarity cannot be determined in a general way). We describe and compare ontological objects in terms of how they relate to other objects. We model these relationships with a vector space of N dimensions being N the number of selected external predicates (e.g. *rdfs:subClassOf*, *rdfs:range* or *foaf:name*). We have adapted the graph matching algorithm of [5] to these idea to iteratively compute the similarities between two OWL ontologies. We have presented also an optimization of the algorithm to critically reduce its computational cost. The good results obtained in the tests performed over the Ontology Alignment Evaluation Initiative 2005 testsuite has proven the value of the approach in situations in which structural similarities exist.

Acknowledgements

This work has been partly supported by the Spanish administration (DRM-MM project, TSI 2005-05277).

References

1. M. Bisson. Learning in fol with a similarity measure. In *Proceedings of the 10th American Association for Artificial Intelligence conference, San-Jose (CA US), pages 8287*, 1992.
2. A. Doan, J. Madhavan, P. Domingos, and A. Halevy. Learning to map between ontologies on the semantic web, 2002. citeseer.ist.psu.edu/doan02learning.html.
3. M. Ehrig and J. Euzenat. Relaxed precision and recall for ontology matching. http://km.aifb.uni-karlsruhe.de/ws/intont2005/intontproceedings.pdf.
4. M. Ehrig and S. Staab. Qom - quick ontology mapping. citeseer.ist.psu.edu/727796.html.
5. Vincent D. Blondel et al. A measure of similarity between graph vertices: Applications to synonym extraction and web searching. *SIAM Rev.*, 46(4):647–666, 2004.
6. Wei Hu et al. Gmo: A graph matching for ontologies. In *Integrating Ontologies*, 2005.
7. J. Euzenat and P. Valtchev. Similarity-based ontology alignment in owl-lite. In *Proc. of ECAI 2004, pages 333–337, Valencia, Spain, August 2004*, 2004.
8. J. E. Hopcroft and R.M. Karp. An $\mathcal{O}(n^{5/2})$ algorithm for maximum matching in bipartite graphs. *SIAM J. Comput.*, 4:225–231, 1973.
9. C. Leacock and M. Chodorow. Combining local context and wordnet similarity for word sense identification. *WordNet: An Electronic Lexical Database*, 49(2):265–283, 1998.
10. J. H. Lee, M. H. Kim, and Y. J. Lee. Information retrieval based on conceptual distance in is-a hierarchies. *Journal of Documentation*, 49(2):188–207, 1993.
11. Ontology alignment evaluation initiative, 2005. http://oaei.inrialpes.fr/2005/.
12. Owl web ontology language overview. w3c recommendation 10 february 2004. See http://www.w3.org/TR/owl-features/.
13. C. H. Papadimitriou and K. Steiglitz. *Combinatorial optimization: algorithms and complexity*. Prentice-Hall, Inc., Upper Saddle River, NJ, USA, 1982.
14. E. Rahm and P. A. Bernstein. A survey of approaches to automatic schema matching. *VLDB Journal: Very Large Data Bases*, 10(4):334–350, 2001. citeseer.ist.psu.edu/rahm01survey.html.
15. Resource description framework. See http://www.w3.org/RDF/.
16. G. Salton. The smart retrieval system. *Experiments in Automatic Document Processing*, 1971.
17. Z. Wu and M. Palmer. Verbs semantics and lexical selection. In *Proceedings of the 32nd annual meeting on Association for Computational Linguistics*, pages 133–138, Morristown, NJ, USA, 1994. Association for Computational Linguistics.

Scalable Automated Service Composition Using a Compact Directory Digest

Walter Binder, Ion Constantinescu, and Boi Faltings

Ecole Polytechnique Fédérale de Lausanne (EPFL)
Artificial Intelligence Laboratory
CH–1015 Lausanne, Switzerland
firstname.lastname@epfl.ch

Abstract. The composition of services that are indexed in a large-scale service directory often involves many complex queries issued by the service composition algorithm to the directory. These queries may cause considerable processing effort within the directory, thus limiting scalability. In this paper we present a novel approach to increase scalability: The directory offers a compact digest that service composition clients download to solve the hard part of a composition problem locally. In this paper we compare two different digest representations, a sparse matrix and a Zero-Suppressed Reduced Ordered Binary Decision Diagram (ZDD). Our evaluation confirms that both representations are compact and shows that the ZDD enables more efficient service composition.[1]

Keywords: Web services, service composition, service directories, ZDDs.

1 Introduction

Service-oriented computing enables the construction of distributed applications by integrating services that are available over the web [9]. The building blocks of such applications are web services[2] that are accessed using standard protocols.

Service discovery is the process of locating providers advertising services that can satisfy a given service request. Automated service composition addresses the problem of assembling individual services based on their functional specifications in order to create a value-added, composite service that fulfills a service request. Most approaches to automated service composition are based on AI planning techniques [11,4,10,13]. They assume that all relevant service advertisements are initially loaded into a reasoning engine.

However, due to the large number of service advertisements and to the loose coupling between service providers and consumers, services are indexed in service directories. As loading a large directory of service advertisements into a reasoning engine is not practical, planning algorithms have been modified in order to dynamically retrieve relevant service advertisements from a service directory during composition [2,1].

[1] This work was supported by the Swiss National Funding Agency OFES as part of the European project KnowledgeWeb (FP6-507482).

[2] In this paper, *service* stands for *web service*.

S. Bressan, J. Küng, and R. Wagner (Eds.): DEXA 2006, LNCS 4080, pp. 317–326, 2006.

In such an approach, a single service composition may involve several complex directory queries, and each query may have to process a significant part of the directory. E.g., in the case of service composition algorithms using forward chaining, a single directory query may require the processing of up to 20% of the directory data, even though the directory uses an optimized index structure [1].[3] As the service directory is a shared resource, it is likely to become a performance bottleneck. Massive replication of the service directory is needed for scalability, which is expensive due to the large number of needed directory servers.

In this paper we present a novel approach to service composition, which avoids complex directory queries. In our approach, the directory offers a compact digest that summarizes the input/output behaviour of advertised services. The service composition clients download the digest and use it to solve the hard part of the composition problem locally. Only simple directory queries are issued to obtain the final result.

We compare two different representations of the directory digest, a sparse matrix and a Zero-Suppressed Reduced Ordered Binary Decision Diagram (ZDD). Both of them are compact, but the ZDD-based digest enables more efficient service composition algorithms.

The original contributions of this paper are: (1) a new approach of integrating service composition with large-scale service directories, (2) the introduction of a directory digest, (3) an evaluation of the digest size using different data structures, and (4) an evaluation of the performance of service composition algorithms leveraging the digest.

This paper is structured as follows: Section 2 introduces a simplified service description formalism and our definition of service composition. Section 3 gives an overview of service composition exploiting a directory digest. Section 4 evaluates the size of different digest representations. Section 5 evaluates the performance and scalability of service composition algorithms operating on the digest. Finally, Section 6 concludes this paper.

2 Definitions and Basic Service Composition Algorithm

Service descriptions are a key element for service discovery and service composition, as they enable automated interactions between applications. We distinguish between an invokable *service instance* (including service grounding) and its *service signature*. A service signature specifies the input/output behaviour of one or more service instances.

We describe a service signature S by two parameter sets – the *required input parameters* $in(S)$ and the *generated output parameters* $out(S)$. Each parameter is identified by a unique name in its set. We assume that the parameter name defines the semantics of the parameter. Despite its simplicity, our formalism is consistent with existing service description formalisms, such as WSDL [12] and OWL-S [7]. Part of the input/output specification of services described in WSDL or OWL-S can be mapped to our simplified formalism.

A *service directory* stores *service advertisements*, describing features of service instances available over the web. Each service advertisement includes the service signature of the advertised service instance.

[3] A naive directory implementation may have to process the whole directory contents in order to discover all relevant service advertisements.

A *service request* R is a query for a particular service functionality. R consists of a set of *provided input parameters* $in(R)$ and a set of *required output parameters* $out(R)$.

Service discovery involves the submission of a service request R to a service directory and the retrieval of service advertisements with a service signature S that matches R. In the literature, different matching relations between R and S have been studied [14,8,3]. One particularly useful matching relation is the *plugin match*, which requires that $in(S) \subseteq in(R)$ and $out(S) \supseteq out(R)$. I.e., given the provided input parameters $in(R)$, a service instance with service signature S can be invoked, which generates all required output parameters $out(R)$.

Even if there is no single service advertisement to fulfill a given service request R, it may be still possible to *compose* multiple services in such a way that the composite service (which can be represented as a workflow) meets R. E.g., assume there are service advertisements with the following signatures S_1 and S_2: $in(S_1) = \{A, B\}$, $out(S_1) = \{C\}$, $in(S_2) = \{B, C\}$, $out(S_2) = \{D\}$ Neither S_1 nor S_2 matches the service request R, where $in(R) = \{A, B\}$ and $out(R) = \{C, D\}$. However, a service instance with signature S_1 can be invoked with the provided input parameters $\{A, B\}$, which generates the output parameter C. Now the parameters $\{A, B, C\}$ are available, enabling an invocation of a service instance with signature S_2, which generates the required output parameter D.

Algorithm 1 shows a simple service composition algorithm using forward chaining. It takes a set of service signatures Dir and a service request R as inputs and returns $success$ resp. $failure$, depending on whether R can be fulfilled. For the sake of simplicity, we show only a decision algorithm; an extension to keep track of the applied services is trivial.

Algorithm 1. Simple decision algorithm based on forward-chaining to determine whether a service request R can be fulfilled by a set of service signatures Dir.

```
Compose(Dir, R) :
    services ← Dir ;
    availableInputs ← in(R) ;
    requiredOutputs ← out(R) ;
    while requiredOutputs ⊈ availableInputs do
        applicableServices ← {s ∈ services | in(s) ⊆ availableInputs} ;
        if applicableServices = ∅ then
            return failure ;
        newAvailableInputs ← ⋃_{s∈applicableServices} out(s) ;
        availableInputs ← availableInputs ∪ newAvailableInputs ;
        services ← services \ applicableServices ;
    return success ;
```

The algorithm iteratively extends the set $availableInputs$. In each iteration of the loop, it selects those service signatures for which all required input parameters are available and adds the output parameters of the selected service signatures to the set $availableInputs$. The algorithm terminates if all required output parameters are available or no further service signatures can be selected. In order to avoid the repeated selection of the same service signature, the set $services$ is updated to include only those service signatures that have not been selected yet.

3 Service Composition with Directory Digest

In previous work [1], we used complex directory queries in order to dynamically retrieve relevant service advertisements from a large-scale service directory during service composition. This approach caused very high workload within the service directory and consequently also slowed down the service composition algorithm because of expensive remote interactions with the service directory.

The approach presented here increases scalability by avoiding complex directory queries during composition. The service directory offers a compact digest that summarizes the service signatures of all service advertisements stored in the directory. Service composition clients download the digest, which contains sufficient information to perform service composition locally on the client side. The service composition client interacts with the service directory as follows:

1. Download Digest. The client periodically downloads the most recent version of the digest. As service advertisements usually remain valid for a longer period of time, the clients do not have to reload their copy of the digest for every service request. Typical refresh rates would be once per day, once per week, etc.
2. Transform Service Request R. As the digest is a compressed representation of the service signatures in the directory, full parameter names are not available in the digest. Hence, the composition client sends R to the directory and receives R^T. The directory maps each parameter of $in(R)$ (resp. $out(R)$) to the corresponding digest parameter of $in(R^T)$ (resp. $out(R^T)$). This translation is a simple mapping and can be processed in linear time with the number of parameters in R.
3. Compute Composition. Using the digest and R^T, the client locally computes a service composition, without any queries to the service directory. If the composition fails, the client may update its local copy of the digest and retry (the new version of the digest may include additional service signatures of recently added service advertisements).
4. Transform Composition Result. If the service request has been successfully solved in the step before, the client knows the signatures of the selected services that are part of the composition workflow. It asks the directory to provide service advertisements that match the selected service signatures. The resulting directory query looks only for *exact matches*, which can be processed very efficiently by the directory. E.g., the directory may simply use the service signature to compute a hash key and look up matching service advertisements in a hash table. If the desired service signature is not found in the directory (i.e., services have been removed recently), the client has to download an up-to-date digest and re-run the composition algorithm.

4 Directory Digest Representation

The digest representation should meet the following requirements:

- Incremental Update. The addition or removal of a service signature shall not require to rebuild the digest from scratch.
- Incremental Addition of Service Parameters. The addition of a new service parameter shall not require restructuring the digest.
- Compact Network Transfer Format. The (serialized) digest shall be as small as possible in order to reduce network bandwidth.
- Compact in-memory Representation. Also the in-memory representation of the digest shall be compact in order to allow clients with limited computing resources to keep a copy of the digest in memory.
- Enabling Efficient Service Composition. The digest representation shall enable efficient service composition algorithms.

In the following we consider different ways to represent the directory digest. In Section 4.1 we discuss simple matrix representations, whereas in Section 4.2 we argue for an efficient representation as a combination set.

4.1 Matrix Representation

The directory digest can be regarded as a bit matrix, where each column corresponds to a certain parameter and each row describes a service signature. Assume there are n different parameters used in service signatures in the directory, which are identified by their index i ($0 \leq i < n$). The column position $2i$ corresponds to the ith parameter used as input, while the position $2i+1$ corresponds to the ith parameter used as output. This representation is extensible, i.e., a new parameter can be included by adding 2 columns.

As an example, assume we have the parameters A (index 0), B (index 1), C (index 2), D (index 3) and the two example service signatures S_1 and S_2 of Section 2: $in(S_1) = \{A, B\}$, $out(S_1) = \{C\}$, $in(S_2) = \{B, C\}$, $out(S_2) = \{D\}$ This can be represented by the following bit matrix:

Column index Column meaning	0 A_{in}	1 A_{out}	2 B_{in}	3 B_{out}	4 C_{in}	5 C_{out}	6 D_{in}	7 D_{out}	Corresponding service
	1	0	1	0	0	1	0	0	S_1
	0	0	1	0	1	0	0	1	S_2

For a large number of parameters and a large number of different service signatures, the matrix may become quite large. For instance, assume we have 1000 different parameters and 10^6 different service signatures. The resulting matrix has $2 * 10^9$ bits, i.e., about 238MB.

However, in practice, the matrix is sparse, i.e., each row has only a few bits set, because the number of parameters per service signature is limited. Hence, a more compact representation can be obtained by listing the column indices of only those parameters that are present. If there are 1000 different parameters, the column indices range from 0 to 1999, which can be represented by 11 bits. As row delimiter, either an otherwise unused index (e.g., $2^{11} - 1$) may be defined or we add one extra bit to mark the end of a row. If we assume that on average each service has 3 input and 3 output parameters and we use an extra bit to mark the end of rows, the matrix can be represented by $(3 + 3) * 12 * 10^6$ bits, which is less than 9MB. Further reductions of the network transfer format could be obtained e.g. by applying standard compression algorithms. Concerning the in-memory representation, typically 16 bits would be used for a column index (byte alignment). I.e., a client keeping the matrix in memory would consume $(3 + 3) * 16 * 10^6$ bits, less than 12MB.

While the sparse matrix representation is compact and can be updated incrementally, it is not the best data structure for efficient service composition. In order to discover applicable service signatures, the whole matrix has to be processed repeatedly. Each iteration of the service composition algorithm causes processing effort that is proportional to the size of the matrix.

4.2 Combination Set Representation

If we consider a service signature a combination of parameters, the directory digest can be seen as a combination set. E.g., the example service signatures S_1 and S_2 shown before can be represented by the following combination set: $\{\langle A_{in}, B_{in}, C_{out}\rangle, \langle B_{in}, C_{in}, D_{out}\rangle\}$

Zero-suppressed Reduced Ordered Binary Decision Diagrams (ZDD) are known as an efficient representation of sparse combination sets [5]. ZDDs efficiently support set operations, such as union, intersection, and difference. Moreover, many specialized ZDD operations have been developed for particular use cases, such as e.g. the restriction and exclusion operations in the context of constraint satisfaction [6].

We adopted ZDDs, because they allow a compact digest representation and enable the implementation of efficient service composition algorithms exploiting ZDD operations. Below we discuss some experimental results concerning the size of the ZDD representation. In Section 5 we present performance measurements for a service composition algorithm that leverages ZDD operations.

In order to measure the size of ZDDs for different settings, we created service directories with an increasing number of randomly generated, distinct service signatures (0–10^6). Each service signature S has 3 input and 3 output parameters, randomly chosen from a set of 1000 different parameters with the constraint $in(S) \cap out(S) = \emptyset$. In practice, services often have parameters only from a single, domain-specific ontology (e.g., travel domain, financial domain, sports domain, etc.). Hence, we partitioned the 1000 parameters into an increasing number of domains (1–100) and required the input parameters (resp. the output parameters) of each service signature to come from the same domain (the input parameters' domain can be different from the output parameters' domain).

Fig. 1 shows the size of a ZDD representing a directory digest depending on the number of different service signatures and the number of domains. As ZDDs are graphs, we use the number of nodes in the graph as metric. Not surprisingly, the ZDD size increases with the number of distinct service signatures. A small number of domains results in larger ZDDs than a high number of domains. In the worst case (10^6 service signatures, 1 domain), the ZDD has about $2.9 * 10^6$ nodes. For 100 domains (each consisting of 10 parameters), 10^6 service signatures require only about 10^6 nodes. The reason for the smaller ZDD size is that the number of possible parameter combinations is reduced.

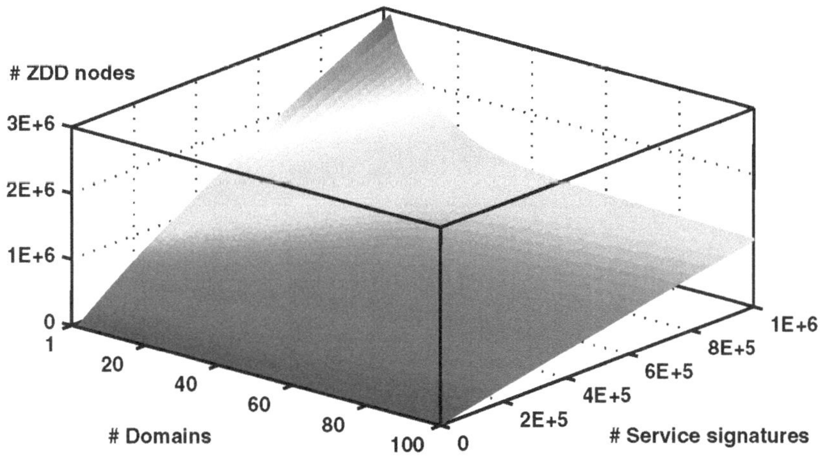

Fig. 1. Number of nodes in a ZDD representing a directory digest as a function of the number of service signatures in the digest and the number of domains

Our directory digest implementation is based on the JDD library[4], which is programmed in pure Java. Concerning the in-memory representation, JDD stores the ZDD nodes in an array of 32 bit integers. Each node uses 3 entries in the array: One entry stores a variable[5] and the other two entries store indices to other nodes. In total, a node consumes 12 bytes in memory. For the network transfer of the directory digest, the ZDD can be serialized more compactly: 11 bits are enough to store a parameter index and 24 bits suffice to index other nodes, i.e., 59 bits per node are sufficient. Further compression of the bitstream using standard compression techniques would be possible as well.

Fig. 2 compares the size of different directory digest representations. The sparse matrix is more compact, although in a setting with 20 domains, the ZDD representation is not much larger. As we will see in the next Section, the ZDD representation enables more efficient service composition algorithms.

5 Service Composition Performance

In this Section we present experimental results concerning the performance of service composition algorithms operating on a sparse matrix resp. on a ZDD representation of the directory digest. The algorithms are specialized implementations of the generic structure of Algorithm 1 introduced in Section 2.

As in-memory representation of the sparse matrix we chose an array of service signatures (matrix rows), where each service signature is an array of parameter indices (matrix columns). Moreover, we use a boolean array to indicate for each service signature whether it has been applied. The algorithm iterates through the array of service

[4] `http://javaddlib.sourceforge.net/`

[5] We map parameters to ZDD variables. We encode each parameter P as two different ZDD variables P_{in} and P_{out}. E.g., in our experimental setting we have 2000 ZDD variables.

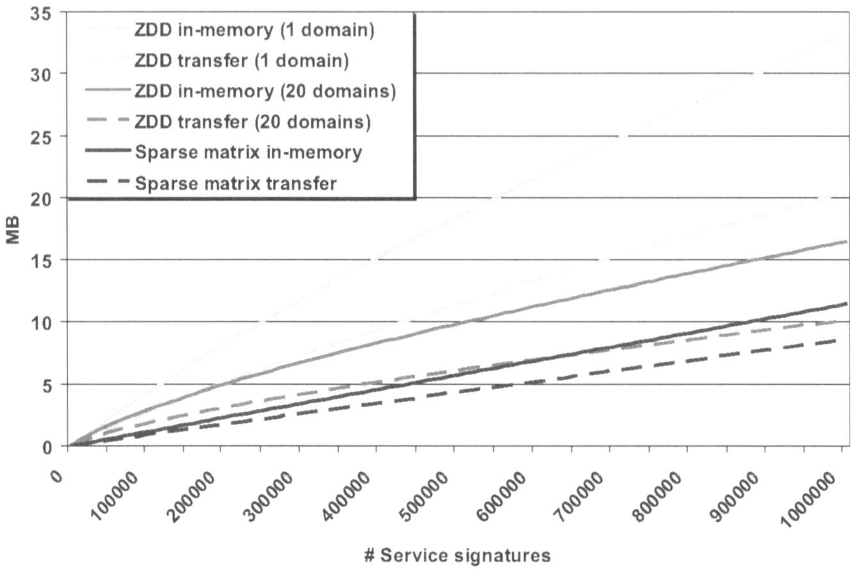

Fig. 2. Directory digest size (in megabytes) of in-memory and network transfer representations based on a sparse matrix resp. on a ZDD

signatures in a cyclic way, selecting and applying those signatures for which all required input parameters are available (and which have not been applied before).

Our ZDD-based service composition algorithm relies on the repeated application of the $subset0()$ primitive [5] in order to filter out those service signatures that require a parameter which is not available. The remaining service signatures are selected. Then the algorithm leverages the $subset1()$ primitive to test for each missing parameter, whether a selected service generates it as output. If at least one missing parameter becomes available, the whole process is iterated.

Fig. 3 compares the performance of the two service composition algorithms for different digest size (0–10^6) and distinct number of domains (1 and 20). As before, we assume 1000 possible parameters and service signatures with 3 input and 3 output parameters. Each measurement represents the total execution time for processing a set of 2000 random service requests. We chose service requests that are particularly hard to process, providing only 3 input parameters and requiring all 1000 output parameters. As we kept the set of 2000 service requests unchanged throughout all experiments, the percentage of solvable service requests is increasing with the number of service signatures in the digest. Both algorithms operate on the same digest contents and on the same set of service requests. For a fair comparison, we disabled all caches in the JDD library. As execution platform we chose a typical client system: Pentium 4, 2.4GHz clockrate, 512MB RAM, Windows XP, Sun JDK 1.5.0 Hotspot Server VM. In order to obtain reproducible measurements, we disabled background processes as much as possible. Each measurement represents the median of 15 executions on identical data.

As expected, the algorithm based on the sparse matrix digest representation performs linear with the number of service signatures in the digest. The number of domains does

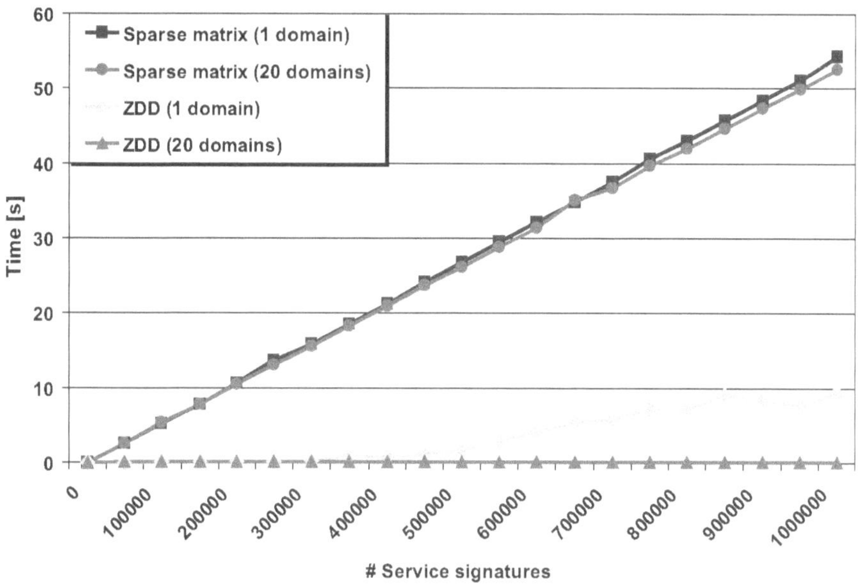

Fig. 3. Elapsed processing time [s] for 2000 random service requests

not have much impact on the performance (the matrix size is not affected by the number of domains). The algorithm based on the ZDD representation performs significantly better. In the case of a single domain (i.e., larger digest), the ZDD algorithm is 5–100 times faster than the matrix algorithm; in the case of 20 domains (i.e., smaller digest), the ZDD algorithm is 40–500 times faster. In the latter setting, the performance of the ZDD algorithm does not degrade with an increasing number of service signatures.

6 Conclusion

Service composition algorithms that dynamically retrieve relevant service advertisements from a large-scale service directory tend to issue a large number of complex directory queries, causing high workload within the directory. As such an approach does not scale well, we introduce a compact directory digest that is downloaded by service composition clients and allows to solve the hard part of a composition problem locally without expensive remote interactions with the directory. Directory queries are only needed to translate the initial composition problem and to obtain the final result. These queries are very simple and require only a lookup in a table, significantly reducing the workload in the directory and boosting scalability.

We compared two different representations of the directory digest – sparse matrix versus ZDD. Both representations result in a compact digest. However, a service composition algorithm based on the ZDD representation performs and scales significantly better than an algorithm operating on the matrix representation.

References

1. I. Constantinescu, W. Binder, and B. Faltings. Flexible and efficient matchmaking and ranking in service directories. In *2005 IEEE International Conference on Web Services (ICWS-2005)*, pages 5–12, Florida, July 2005.
2. I. Constantinescu, B. Faltings, and W. Binder. Large scale, type-compatible service composition. In *IEEE International Conference on Web Services (ICWS-2004)*, pages 506–513, San Diego, CA, USA, July 2004.
3. L. Li and I. Horrocks. A software framework for matchmaking based on semantic web technology. In *Proceedings of the 12th International Conference on the World Wide Web*, pages 331–339, 2003.
4. S. A. McIlraith and T. C. Son. Adapting Golog for composition of semantic web services. In D. Fensel, F. Giunchiglia, D. McGuinness, and M.-A. Williams, editors, *Proceedings of the 8th International Conference on Principles and Knowledge Representation and Reasoning (KR-02)*, pages 482–496, San Francisco, CA, Apr. 2002. Morgan Kaufmann Publishers.
5. S. Minato. Zero-suppressed BDDs for set manipulation in combinatorial problems. In *Proceedings of the 30th ACM/IEEE Design Automation Conference*, pages 272–277, Dallas, TX, June 1993. ACM Press.
6. H. G. Okuno, S. ichi Minato, and H. Isozaki. On the properties of combination set operations. *Information Processing Letters*, 66(4):195–199, May 1998.
7. OWL-S. DAML Services, `http://www.daml.org/services/owl-s/`.
8. M. Paolucci, T. Kawamura, T. R. Payne, and K. Sycara. Semantic matching of web services capabilities. In *Proceedings of the 1st International Semantic Web Conference*, pages 333–347, 2002.
9. M. P. Papazoglou and D. Georgakopoulos. Introduction: Service-oriented computing. *Communications of the ACM*, 46(10):24–28, Oct. 2003.
10. S. R. Ponnekanti and A. Fox. Sword: A developer toolkit for web service composition. In *11th World Wide Web Conference (Web Engineering Track)*, 2002.
11. S. Thakkar, C. A. Knoblock, J. L. Ambite, and C. Shahabi. Dynamically composing web services from on-line sources. In *Proceeding of the AAAI-2002 Workshop on Intelligent Service Integration*, pages 1–7, Edmonton, Alberta, Canada, July 2002.
12. W3C. Web services description language (WSDL) version 1.2, `http://www.w3.org/TR/wsdl12`
13. D. Wu, B. Parsia, E. Sirin, J. Hendler, and D. Nau. Automating DAML-S web services composition using SHOP2. In *Proceedings of 2nd International Semantic Web Conference (ISWC-2003)*, pages 195–210, 2003.
14. A. M. Zaremski and J. M. Wing. Specification matching of software components. *ACM Transactions on Software Engineering and Methodology*, 6(4):333–369, 1997.

Topic Structure Mining for Document Sets Using Graph-Based Analysis

Hiroyuki Toda[1,2], Ryoji Kataoka[1], and Hiroyuki Kitagawa[2,3]

[1] NTT Cyber Solutions Laboratories, NTT Corporation,
1-1 Hikarinooka Yokosuka-shi, Kanagawa 239-0847, Japan
[2] Graduate School of Systems and Information Engineering,
[3] Center for Computational Sciences,
University of Tsukuba, Tennoudai, Tsukuba-shi, Ibaraki 305-8573, Japan
toda.hiroyuki@lab.ntt.co.jp

Abstract. This paper proposes a novel text mining method for a document set based on graph-based analysis. Graph-based analysis first identifies the similarity links in the document set and then determines core documents, those that have the highest level of centrality. Each core document represents a different topic. Next, the centrality scores are used together with the graph structure to identify those documents that are associated with the core documents. This process results in a predetermined number of topics. For each topic the user is presented with a set of documents in three-layer structure: core document, supplemental documents (those that are strongly associated with the core document), and subtopic documents (those that are only slightly associated with the core document and supplemental documents). The user can select any the topics and browse the documents related to that topic. Furthermore, the user can select documents according to the level; for example, subtopic documents are assumed to contain information that differs from the topic indicated and so might be interesting. In analyses of a set of newspaper articles, we evaluate "accuracy of topic identification" and "accuracy of document collecting related to the topics". Furthermore, we show an example of document set visualization based on graph structure and centrality score; the results indicate the method's usefulness for browsing and analyzing document sets.

1 Introduction

Recently, the amount of information that can be accessed has vastly increased. Users now want to be able to find the desired documents from a document set, for example, search engine results, and latest news articles collected by RSS Reader. We assume that the user has two main goals.

- get an outline of the document set
- access the documents of specified topics present in the document set

The first goal is equivalent to browsing and summarizing with the user receiving a list of the main topics in the document set. The second goal is set by the

S. Bressan, J. Küng, and R. Wagner (Eds.): DEXA 2006, LNCS 4080, pp. 327–337, 2006.

user who has clear information needs; for this we must collect the documents related to the main topics and providing an understanding of how closely each document is related to the core document. Documents that are strongly related to the core document (supplemental documents) add depth and more details about the topic. Subtopic documents are only weakly associated with the core document and so are expected to provide unexpected or new information.

One solution to achive this goal is to apply clustering algorithms[5][4][9]. They are intended to output document clusters that assist the user in understanding the outline of the document set. Unfortunately, existing algorithms assume that all documents in the set have equal importance, and that it should be possible to put each document into some cluster. Real data sets, however, contain documents which are not related to any other document, do not have any clear cluster number, and so on. Another solution is to regard the clustering task as the task of extracting salient keywords [13][14][3][11]. Methods based on this approach present a salient keyword list together with the search result. One characteristic of these methods is that the cluster labels are clear. However, clustering is based on a simple rule, whether the document includes the keyword or not, so it is not likely to yield good clusters. Namely, clustering can yield several labels for one topic; some labels may be related to more than one topic.

This paper proposes a graph-based method that uses the level of similarity between documents to identify core documents, those that have the highest level of connection density. Each core document is taken to represent a different topic. The centrality scores of the documents is, together with the graph structure, used to segregate the documents so that we form sets of documents; one set equals one topic. Documents that are only weakly associated with the grouped documents are treated as outliers. Next, for each topic, the documents other than the core document are ranked as either supplemental documents, those that are strongly associated with the core document, and the subtopic documents, those that slightly associated with either of the other two types. To extract this information from the original document set, we create a graph structure based on the similarity of documents in the document set and determine node centrality for this graph. Though the metric of centrality was originally used for search result ranking[1][7] , this metric has been recently used for extracting sentences for document summarization, and the usefulness of this metric in extracting representative sentences that well represent the document has been reported[10][2].

However, we cannot develop good document segregation, according to topic, only using this score. Our proposal is to use both the centrality scores and the graph structure. Namely, we assign the graph structure to a 2-D plane and plot the centrality scores as the 3rd dimension. This allows us to extract mountains of nodes, each of which is founded on a core document. Experiments confirm the ability of our proposal to realize "main topic extraction" and "extraction of documents related to each main topic, with inner relationships". Moreover, we show that visualization of the document set using the structure promotes easier overviewing and browsing the document set.

In this paper, one "document" corresponds to one "node". When we explain the graph structure, we mainly use the word "node".

The paper is organized as follows. The next section introduces related works. In Section 3, we detail the proposed method. Section 4 evaluate the proposed method. Section 5 demonstrates the effectiveness of visualization. Finally we conclude the paper in Section 6.

2 Related Works

There is an increase in the use of techniques based on graphs to extract the implicit relationships between documents or other linguistic items. More recently, some research has used the centrality of graphs to rank linguistic items and extract some items from sets of linguistic items. Mihalcea et al.[10] experimentally proved that PageRank[1] is effective for achieving these goals if the edges of the graph have weight or do not have direction. They also report that the method is useful for the tasks of text summarization and keyword extraction. Erkan[2] also proposed a graph-based method for text summarization and reported that the method yields much higher precision than any other method. Furthermore, Kurland et al.[8] proposed a graph based on a language model for calculating PageRank and used it to rerank search results. Our method also uses the centrality score of graphs generated by the implicit relationships between documents. Though ordinary methods simply use the centrality score for ranking items or selecting top ranked items, we use both centrality score and graph structure for segregating items into topics.

3 Proposed Method

The method proposed in this paper first identifies the similarity links between all documents in the set, and then determines core documents, those that have the highest level of centrality. Each core document represents a different topic. Next, the centrality scores are used together with the graph structure to identify those documents that are most strongly associated with the core documents. Section 3.1 describes how the graph structure is generated. Section 3.2 explains the calculation of the centrality score of each node in the graph structure. The meaning of the centrality score of each node in the graph structure is elucidated in Section 3.3, along with information extraction based on node meaning.

3.1 Generation of Graph Structure

We construct a graph structure, where each node represents one document and each edge represents the relationship between a pair of documents. This graph structure is based on the "Interested Reader model" proposed by Kamvar[6]. This model is similar to the "Random Surfer model" of PageRank. It assumes that the document collection consists of documents covering several topics, and that the reader starts to read some document in the collection and go on to read other documents. The reader's next choice is strongly related to his current document. These transition probabilities define a Markov chain among the documents in the collection. If many documents are strongly related, the transition probability among the documents is high while the transition probability to other documents is low. Furthermore, this model assumes the following. The self transition probability is high, when all documents are dissimilar. On the other hand, when there are many similar documents, the self transition probability is low. According to the assumption, the matrix is calculated by following equation.

$$N = (A + d_{max}E - D)/d_{max} \tag{1}$$

Here, N is the matrix based on the "interested reader model". E is a unit matrix. D is a diagonal matrix whose elements $D_{ii} = \sum_j A_{ij}$, where d_{max} is the largest element of D. A is an adjacent matrix that indicates the similarity between nodes; it is defined in this paper as follows.

$$A_{i,j} = \begin{cases} sim(i,j) & if \;\; j \in TopSim_p(i) \\ 0 & otherwise \end{cases} \tag{2}$$

Here, $TopSim_p(i)$ means the set of documents that have top p ranked similarity with document i. Our reason for using only documents with highest similarity to generate the outlinks, is that accuracy is degraded when all similarity values are used[6][8]. $sim(i,j)$ is calculated by cosine measure of log tf-idf weighted document vectors.

We note that Kamvar[6] did not apply random jumping, which is a key characteristic of the "random surfer model". However, we use random jumping when calculating the centrality scores. Details are shown in the next subsection.

3.2 Calculating Centrality of the Graph

In this subsection, we explain how to calculate the centrality scores. We consider here PageRank since it is one of the most representative methods of calculating centrality. The definition is as follows.

$$S(V_i) = (1-d) \times \sum_{V_j \in IN(V_i)} \left(\frac{1}{|OUT(V_j)|} \times S(V_j)\right) + d \tag{3}$$

Here, $S(V_i)$ is the centrality score of node V_i. $IN(V_i)$ is the set of nodes linked to V_i. $OUT(V_i)$ is the set of nodes linked by V_i. d is a damping factor which represents the probability of random jumping. This random jumping helps the random walker move from periodic node or unconnected nodes to any node in the graph. In our method, we use PageRank to calculate the centrality and we also use random jumping. We differ from PageRank with regard to edge weighting; we use the following equation to calculate node centrality.

$$S(V_i) = (1-d) \times \sum_{\forall j} (N_{j,i} \times S(V_j)) + d \tag{4}$$

3.3 Data Mining Using Centrality Scores and the Graph Structure

Our proposal is to assign the graph structure to a plane and plot the node centrality scores in the 3rd dimension. A typical image is shown in Fig 1. The nodes named "ax"("bx") indicate the documents related to topic "a"("b").

The method of [8] simply uses the centrality scores to rank the documents. However, our purpose is to segregate items by extracting topics. We cannot extract items separately if only the centrality score is used. Namely, if we order the nodes in Fig. 1 according to their centrality score, we get the order "a1,a2,a3,b1,b2,a4,..." and the topics "a" and "b" are mixed together.

To realize the segregating, we use the mountain-like structure generated by the graph structure and centrality scores to uncover the topics and permit information extraction based on node meaning.

First, we consider the relationship between graph structure and centrality score. According to the definition of the centrality score, areas that have many edges have high scores. Such an area also has high transition probability between the nodes in the area and the similarity between each node in this area is high. That is to say, the documents in this area cover the same topic. Accordingly, each mountain-like area in Fig.1 is considered to correspond to a different topic. Next, we assign each node to one of 4 categories.

The 1st type are the top nodes ("a1" and "b1" in Fig.1) of the mountain-like areas (one top node per area). This kind of node has the highest transition probability from surrounding nodes and is the most representative of the topic. That is to say, the document of a top node specifies the main topic in the area. We call this "core document(node)".

The 2nd category are neighbor nodes ("a2", "a3", "a4" and "b2", "b3" in Fig.1). These nodes are reached from the top node only via two-way links either directly with the top node or via another neighbor node. A two-way link is bidirectional and has high connectivity. These nodes have high transition probability with the top node and their contents are similar to that of the top node. If the

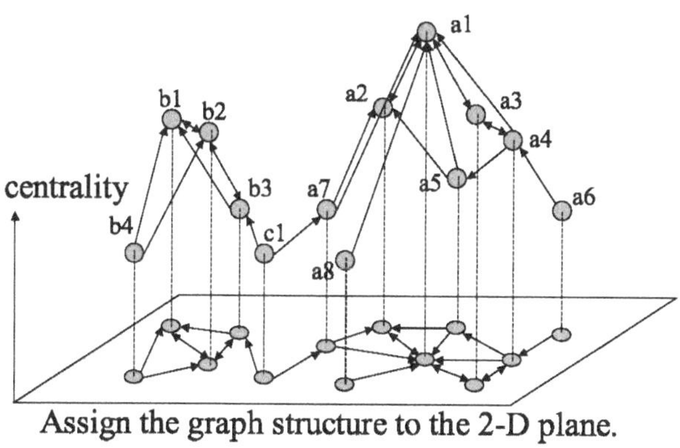

Fig. 1. Document set structure using graph structure and centrality score of each node in the graph

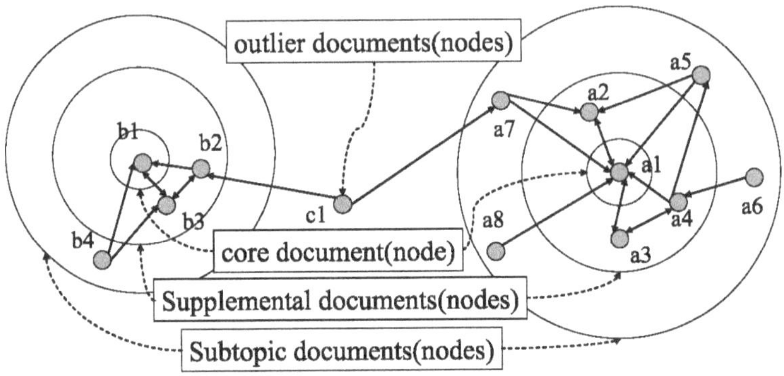

Fig. 2. Concept of our document set structuring

top node is quite close to one or more neighbors nodes, the topic may need to be identified from several nodes; this situation must be considered in subsequent research. We call these "supplemental documents(nodes)".

The 3rd category covers nodes that are linked to the top node or neighbor nodes; examples are "a5", "a6", "a7", "a8" and "b4" in Fig. 1. This type of node, which has higher transition probability to the top or top neighbor node than to outside nodes or self-transition, are documents that are strongly related to the topic. This kind of document provides somewhat unexpected information. We call these "subtopic documents(nodes)".

The last category is for nodes that are not strongly associated with any topic. "c1" of Fig.1 is an example of this type. This node does not have any other similar node and its self-transition probability is high. We call these "outlier documents(nodes)".

The 4 node categories are shown in Fig.2. The node set related to a topic is hierarchically sited around the top node.

To use this structure, the user can access the documents related to a particular topic. Furthermore, the user can select documents within one topic; for example, the document that is most representative of the topic or a document that many provide unexpected information. Furthermore, the relationship of two topics can be discerned through their sharing of supplemental nodes and subtopic nodes. Topics that sharing only outlier nodes are not related.

In Section 4.2, the result of topic identification by identifying the top nodes is shown. Section 4.3 shows the effectiveness of collecting documents according to their topic. In Section 5, we show an example of visualization using graph structure and centrality scores. It confirms that the proposed method is useful for browsing and overviewing document sets.

4 Evaluation

4.1 Evaluation Resource

In this evaluation, we used search results of a Japanese newspaper collection. The collection covers 2 years(1994 and 1995) and holds about 2000,000 articles.

Two data sets were created by submitting the queries "scandal or bribery or corruption" and "murder", and recording the top 200 search results. We called these sets "scandal" and "murder", respectively.

The documents in the sets were are manually labeled after being read. Each label reflects the dominant topic in the document. We created two main topic lists by selecting the topics with at least 2 or at least 3 documents. The documents were grouped according the main topic lists. Details are shown in Table 1.

Table 1. Specification of the corpora for evaluation

name of copora	scandal	murder
# of docs.	200	200
# of label(topics are described in 2 or more documents)	22	26
# of labeled docs.(topics are described in 2 or more documents)	170	98
# of label(topics are described in 3 or more documents)	19	13
# of labeled docs.(topics are described in 3 or more documents)	164	72

4.2 Main Topic Identification

Here, we show the performance of topic identification using the core document.

We used recall, precision, and F-Measure to evaluate the performance of topic identification. These scores are calculated by following equations, respectively.

$$\text{Recall} = \frac{\text{\# of identified relevant topics}}{\text{\# of relevant topics}} \tag{5}$$

$$\text{Precision} = \frac{\text{\# of identified relevant topics}}{\text{\# of identified topics}} \tag{6}$$

$$\text{F-Measure} = \frac{2 \times \text{Recall} \times \text{Precision}}{\text{Recall} + \text{Precision}} \tag{7}$$

In this evaluation, we use $p = 3, 5$ (p is the permissible number of outlinks in each node). The evaluation results are shown in Table 2[1]. When we use $p = 5$, the precision is very high for both sets but recall is very low. The reason is considered that some top nodes were connected to other top nodes. On the other hand, when we set $p = 3$, the precision falls but the recall rises significantly which increases the F-Measure. The improvement in recall is due to the reduction in link number. Namely, links between several pairs of top nodes disappear when ($p = 3$), top nodes are extracted as nodes that clearly identify different topics. This tendency was observed in both sets. We note that in some sets reducing p does not ensure that all top node links are broken. Further work is needed to address this problem with the goal of raising the recall performance.

[1] Precision(m), Recall(m),and F-Measure(m) are the results when we regard topics, which is descibed in m or more documents, as main topics.

Table 2. Evaluation result of topic identification

corpus	scandal	scandal	murder	murder
# of outlink(p)	3	5	3	5
Precision(2)	0.8095	1	0.8	0.6667
Precision(3)	0.8095	1	0.7333	0.6667
Recall(2)	0.7727	0.4545	0.4615	0.1538
Recall(3)	0.8947	0.5263	0.8462	0.3077
F-Measure(2)	0.7907	0.625	0.5854	0.25
F-Measure(3)	0.85	0.6897	0.7857	0.4211

When we regard main topics as the topics that are given in three or more documents, the F-Measure value is high (about 0.8) in both sets. However, the topics, which are given in just two documents, are not extracted in either set. This is because the top node is unclear when the related node number is 2. Therefore, we can say that topics can be extracted by this method if there are at least 3 representative nodes.

The above discussion shows that we can detect the top nodes, which represent main topics, using graph structure and the centrality scores of the nodes in the graph. However, there is room for improving accuracy and we anticipate a more advanced top node extraction method.

4.3 Document Collecting

We also evaluated the accuracy of document collection according to their topic. Document collection involves only "core document", "supplementary documents", and "subtopic documents".

We used F-score to evaluate the selected document set. F-score is an evaluation method of clustering. F-score represents the weighted average of accuracy of the clusters, which are most similar to the clusters in the correct cluster data. The detail of F-Score is shown in [15]. For evaluation, we used following two correct cluster data sets.

- Document sets of all topics described in 3 or more documents
- Document sets of all topics specified by the proposed method

The evaluation using the first correct cluster data set evaluates the proposed method in terms of topic identification and document selection. The second correct cluster data set, on the other hand, evaluate its document collection performance.

In this evaluation, we use $p = 3$ for topic identification because this value yields the highest accuracy as shown in Section 4.2. According to a preliminary experiment on collecting sub topic nodes, some nodes can be related to the topic, even if the transition probability to the top or neighbor nodes is slightly under 0.5(This value comes from subtopic node definition in Section 3.3). According, we also considered another value, 0.3, as threshold(t) in this experiment.

Table 3. Evaluation result of document collecting

corpus	scandal	scandal	murder	murder
threshold(t)	0.3	0.5	0.3	0.5
result when we use 1st correct cluster data	0.8185	0.7712	0.7847	0.7158
result when we use 2nd correct cluster data	0.8580	0.8073	0.8737	0.8230

The result is shown in Table 3. When $t = 0.5$, the F-score is lower than is true with $t = 0.3$. This tendency is same in every combination of corpora and correct cluster data. This is because it tends to select only high accuracy nodes in this setting ($t = 0.5$). We find that the coverage is narrow and the F-score is low.

When we use second correct cluster data set, the F-score value is high, greater than 0.8. This indicates that the proposed method can collect documents very accurately. This indicates that if the accuracy of topic identification is raised, the proposed method will become more useful.

The above evaluation results show that the proposed method can collect documents according to their topic with high accuracy. Setting $t = 0.3$ yields better accuracy than $t = 0.5$.

5 Visualization

In this section, we show an example of document set visualization based on the graph structure and centrality scores. We use some of the nodes described in Section 3.3. Furthermore, we provide an example of relation mining for two topics.

Fig. 3 and 4 shows a visualization of the "murder" set. In this visualization, the graph structure was generated by the Yamada's method[12] and the centrality scores are plotted on the 3rd dimension. The white spheres are nodes(documents) and lines between them are links. The direction of the link is represented by the

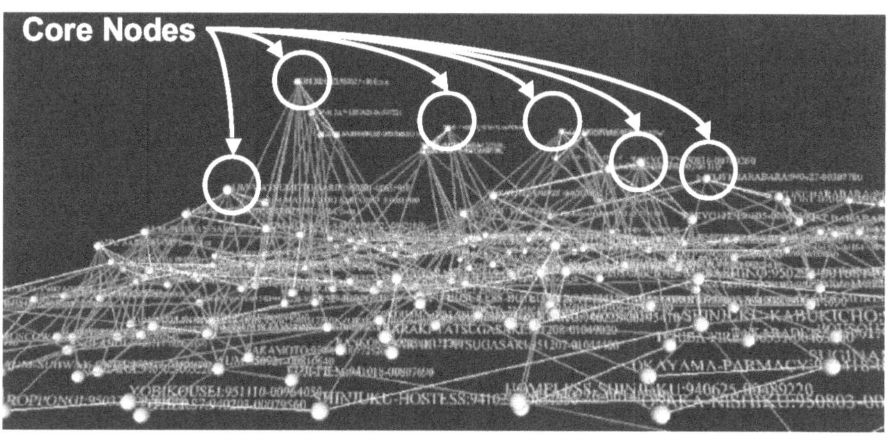

Fig. 3. Visualization example of corpus "murder"

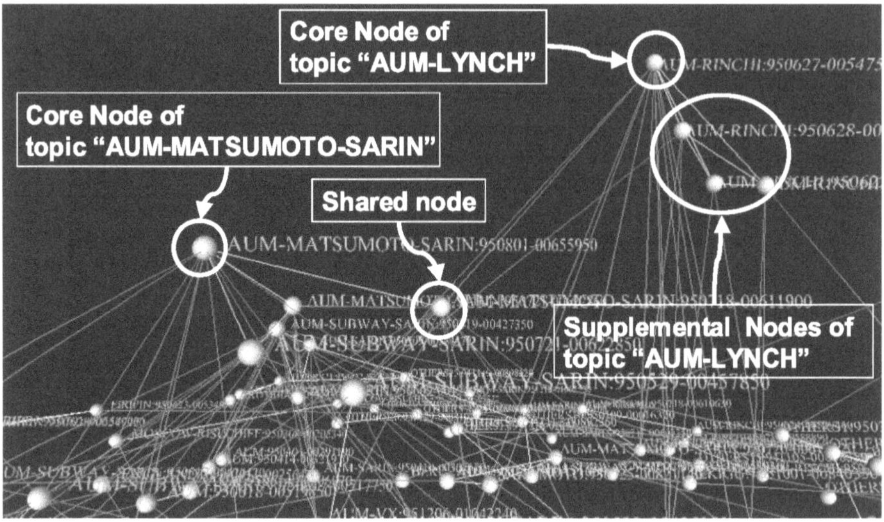

Fig. 4. Visualization example of corpus "murder"(zooming version)

gradation: the "from" side is light and the "to" side is dark. Two-way links are white. Though we show the label and document id of each node (the light colored characters), we could display the document titles instead of their labels.

In Fig. 3, there are several mountains, each mountain represents one topic and the top node is the "core document(node)". The positioning of the supplementary and subtopic documents makes it easy to find documents related to particular topics as well as understanding the relationships between topics.

Fig. 4 shows the two topics that share a high level node. This suggests that the two topics are strongly related. In fact, these topics involve murder by the same religious community.

It is clear that this visualization will provide new browsing methods and enhance the knowledge discovery process. The results indicate the method's usefulness for browsing and analyzing document sets.

6 Conclusion

This paper proposes a novel text mining method for document sets. The method uses graph structure and the centrality of nodes in the graph. The proposed method has three main benefits.

- Main topic identification of a document set
- Extraction of documents related to each main topic, with inner relationships
- Visualization of document set for browsing and mining

We conducted an evaluation using a newspaper article corpus. The results indicated that the method offers high accuracy. Furthermore, we showed an example of document set visualization based on graph structure and centrality score; the results indicate the method's usefulness for browsing and analyzing document sets.

Our future works include a comparison between proposed method and other state-of-the-art methods and refinement of the proposed method.

Acknowledgements

We would like to thank Dr. Kazumi Saito for providing us the graph visualization tool, and Dr. Ko Fujimura for a helpful discussion.

References

1. Brin, S. and Page, L.: "The anatomy of a large-scale hypertextual web search engine." *Proceedings of WWW7, pp.107-117,* 1998.
2. Erkan, G. and Radev, D. R.: "LexRank: Graph-based Lexical Centrality as Salience in Text Summarization." *Journal of Artificial Intelligence Research, Vo. 22, pp.457-479,* 2004.
3. Ferragina, P. and Gulli, A.: "The Anatomy of a Hierarchical Clustering Engine for Web-page, News and Book Snippets." *Proceedings of ICDM'04, pp.395-398,* 2004.
4. He, X., Ding, C. H. Q., Zha, H. and Simon, H. D.: "Automatic Topic Identification Using Webpage Clustering." *Proc. of ICDM'01, pp.195-202,* 2001.
5. Hearst, M., and Pedersen, J.: "Reexamining the cluster hypothesis: scatter/gather on retrieval results." *Proc. of SIGIR'96, pp.76-84,* 1996.
6. Kamvar, S. D., Klein, D. and Manning, C. D.: "Spectral Learning." *Proc. of IJ-CAI'03, pp.561-566,* 2003.
7. Kleinberg, J.: "Authoritative source in a hyperlinked environment." *Journal of the ACM, Vol. 46, pp.604-632,* 1999.
8. Kurland, O. and Lee, L.: "PageRank without hyperlinks: Structural re-ranking using links induced by language models." *Proc. of SIGIR'05, pp.306-313,* 2005.
9. Leuski, A.: "Evaluating document clustering for interactive information retrieval." *Proc. of CIKM'01, pp.33-40,* 2001.
10. Mihalcea, R. and Tarau, P.: "TextRank: Bringing Order into Texts." *Proc. of EMNLP'04, pp.404-411,* 2004.
11. Toda, H. and Kataoka, R.: "A search result clustering method using informatively named entities." *Proc. of WIDM'05, pp.81-86,* 2005.
12. Yamada, T., Saito, K. and Ueda, N.: "Cross-Entropy Directed Embedding of Network Data." *Proc. of ICML'03, pp.832-839,* 2003.
13. Zamir, O., and Etzioni, O.: "Grouper: A Dynamic Clustering Interface to Web Search Results." *Proc. of WWW8, pp.1361-1374,* 1999.
14. Zeng, H. J., He, Q. C., Chen, Z., Ma, W. Y. and Ma, J.: "Learning to Cluster Web Search Results." *Proc. of SIGIR'04, pp.210-217,* 2004.
15. Zhao, Y. and Karypis, G.: "Evaluation of Hierarchical Clustering Algorithms for Document Datasets" *Proc. of CIKM'02, pp.515-524,* 2002.

An Approach for XML Inference Control Based on RDF

Li Zhuan and Wang Yuanzhen

School of computer science and technology,
Huazhong University of science and technology,
Wuhan, Hubei, P.R. China
Zhuan.L@gmail.com, wangyz2005@163.com

Abstract. In this paper, we present a new approach for XML inference control, which is on the foundation of some improvements of an access control model that based on RDF. By using some concepts that derived from XML, such as XML type, XML object etc, we encapsulate the nodes of an XML document to represent the semantic relations among them. We also represent a method about document combination based on XML keys, which can maintain the structural consistency and content consistency between history files and original documents. Since the range of inference control is enlarged and the granularity of authorized objects is expanded, our approach can provide higher security and flexibility for XML documents.

1 Introduction

The widespread adoption of XML has made the security of XML documents to be a primary concern and one of the most important research points. Early researches [1], [2], [3] concern about the trust transmission of XML data. In those works, encryption and digital signature contributed to security by keeping information private and authenticating senders' identities. A number of recent researches [6], [7], [8] have considered access control models for XML data. Access control request that any user who wants to read or write any data must be proper authorized before he does such an access. Thus, it can prevent adversary from directly obtaining sensitive information.

However, indirectly disclosure cannot be avoided yet. For example, Figure 1 shows a segment of an XML document about hospital data [4]. Patient Alice's disease is sensitive and should not be released. Access control model can easily realize such a secure requirement by a proper authorization policy. However, an authorized user can easily infer out the truth by knowledge, "patients in the same ward have the same disease". Intuitively, inference is a potential threaten to the security of a system and needs to be researched in a new way as secure inference control.

Recent researches [4], [9] on XML inference control only consider some simple constraints between the nodes of a document, such as function dependency, etc., and abundant of other semantic information couldn't be effectively expressed yet. Gowadia and Farkas [5] have studied association sensitivity in XML access control. By using RXACL, they present an access control framework that provides flexible security granularity for XML documents. They adopt RDF statements to encapsulate XML nodes to represent security objects and the security policy. The idea in this paper is just derived from them. By the semantic representation ability of RDF, we can depict the relations between XML nodes conveniently.

S. Bressan, J. Küng, and R. Wagner (Eds.): DEXA 2006, LNCS 4080, pp. 338 – 347, 2006.

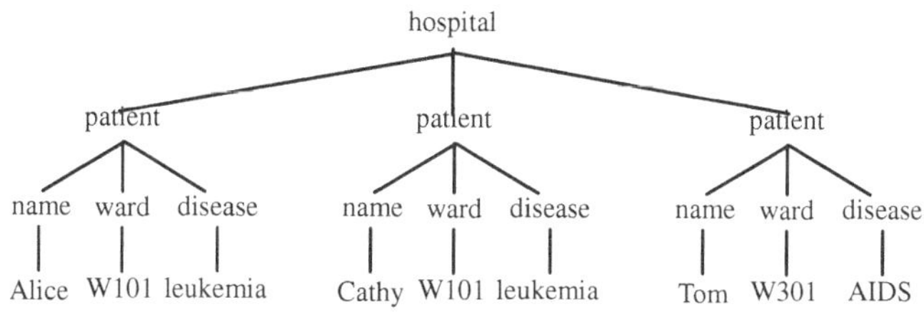

Fig. 1. A segment of an XML document about hospital data

Another significant problem is the query history. If a query is rejected because of security violation, adversary may decompose it into several valid sub-queries and submit each of them at an interval of any time. The combination of results may still cause the leakage of sensitive information. Hence, maintaining history files for every user is crucial for high secure of XML documents. A premise to realize such purpose is XML documents' combination. We also use RDF to redefine XML Key to conduct the combination of user's current query and his history file.

The outline of the rest paper is as follows. Section 2 gives us some preliminary concepts. The content in section 3 is our inference control architecture. In section 4, we improve the access model and adapt it for the inference control. Some main algorithms and procedure in the process of inference control are stated in section 5. Finally in section 6, we give our conclusion.

2 Preliminaries

2.1 XML Document Tree and Path Expression

An XML document is a semi-structured document that is consisted of a list of nested elements and values [10]. The structure of an XML document is described by DTD (Document Type Definition) that can be modeled a labeled tree.

Definition 1 (XML Document Tree). *An XML document tree is a 3-tuple of the following form: (V, E, r), where V is the node set of the tree and E denotes the arc set, r is the root of the tree. All nodes in V can be divided into two types: inner-node and leaf-node, corresponding to an element and a value in the document respectively. Each arc in E presents a parent-child relation between the nodes in V. Given two document tree* t_1 *and* t_2*, we say that* $t_1=t_2$ *if the V, E and r of one tree are all the same with the other tree's;* t_1 *has same structure with* t_2 *if both of them are valid in a same DTD specification.*

Using path-expression can exactly identify a node or a sub-tree in an XML document. We just use a simple but effectual subset of XPath, and redefine path-expression as *p*: $l_1/l_2/\ldots/l_n$, where "/" denote a parent-child relation.

Given a path-expression *p* of a document *t*, the nodes identified by *p* in *t* is the last node whose name is l_n after traversing *t* along with the sequence $l_1, l_2, \ldots, l_n$; the sub-trees identified by *p* is the tree whose root is l_n. We use *p*(*t*) to denote such sub-trees.

Definition 2 (Path Containment). *Given an XML document t and a path-expression p: $l_1/l_2/.../l_n$, we say that p is path contained in t if: (1) $l_1 \in t$ when n=1; and (2) p': $l_2/.../l_n$ is also path contained and l_1/l_2 is satisfied in t when n>1.*

Let *p.s* denote the start node in a path-expression and *p.e* is the end one, say *p* is an *absolute path-expression* of *t* if *p.s* is the root of *t*; otherwise, *p* is a *relative path-expression*. We use p^a and p^r denote them respectively. If two path-expression p_1 and p_2 which contained in document *t* satisfied $p_1.e/p_2.s$, then p_2 is a *sub-expression* of p_1 in *t*. Assume *P* is a path-expression set of *t*, for any $p' \in P$, if *p'* is contained in *p*(*t*), we say that *p.e* is the associate root of *P*, using *asscroot* denote. Obviously, the root of a document tree is the *asscroot* to any path-expression subset of it.

2.2 Resource Description Framework

The main limitation of XML is that it only provides syntax, notations and the hierarchies for data. RDF (Resource Description Framework) [11], which based on the idea of identifying resources by using URI, supplements this by providing semantic information in a standardized way.

Definition 3 (RDF Statement). *An RDF statement is a 3-tuple of the following form: (subject, predicate, object), where subject is used to identify resources; predicate describes different properties of the resources; object is the value corresponding to each property. Every Object might be a literals or another resource.*

Describing a resource in detail may need a few of statements. RDF models such statements as nodes and arcs in a graph. Every statement that belongs to a same resource has different arc and object node, but sharing one subject node. In the rest paper, we just use a single tuple to describe some objects and their relations, which derived from an XML document, instead of the graph.

3 Architecture

Being as a major supplement for information system's security, inference control is always built on access control system. The architecture of our XML inference control system is showed in Figure 2, which including two phases. In secure designing phase (I~II in the figure), administrators create an RDF repository, including RDF types, objects and semantic relations among them; specify the sensitive object for secure requirements; and finally establish a security policy for all the documents.

In secure running phase (1~9 in the figure), query engine will creates an answer for every request that submitted by users. The system will first check authorization for direct disclosure validations, according to the security policy. The query will be rejected if there are violations detected. Otherwise, the system will then check inference disclosure, which may appear in the result of the combination and inference extension of the answer and the user's history file. If there is no violation occurred, the history file will be updated before the answer's returning. Otherwise, history file will be maintained the same and the query is rejected.[1]

[1] For every user of the system, a separate XML document is created to record his query history. More secure method is to create one history file for all users in a same group, thus the common collusion among them would be avoided.

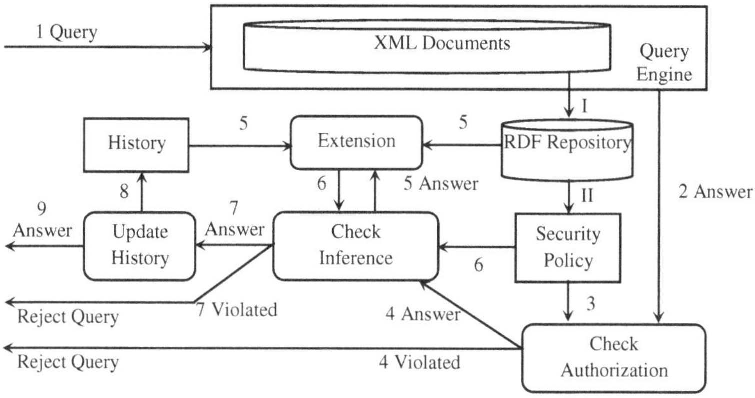

Fig. 2. XML inference control architecture based on RDF

4 Improvement of Access Control

4.1 Sensitive Objects and Their Authorization

Instead of using URI to identify resources and their semantic relations in the Web, we just use object id (OID) to distinguish different XML objects.

Definition 4 (XML Object). *Given an XML document, a simple XML object is a subtree, which is located by a path-expression of the document and is only once encapsulated by RDF statements; an associated XML object, which is also located by a path-expression, is a composition of simple objects and/or other associated objects.*

Not the same with simple objects, the path-expression in an associated object is used to identify the asscroot of its sub-objects.

Example 1. *Some XML objects of the document showed in Figure 1 are listed as:*

Simple objects: SO01 (locate: name/Alice, type: SIMPLE-OBJECT); SO02 (locate: disease/leukemia, type: SIMPLE-OBJECT); SO03 (locate: disease/AIDS, type: SIMPLE-OBJECT)

Associated object: AO01 (asscroot: hospital/patient, component: {SO01, SO02}, type: ASSC-OBJECT)

In the example, literals "SO01" etc., which represents a subject, is the identifier OID; predicate "type" represents the type of the object; predicate "locate" locates the object in the document; predicate "component" indicates the components of an associated object; the literals, which follows a colon, represents the object of a predicate that followed by that colon.

All privileges that a user obtained from authorized objects, are equated to what he can obtain directly from nodes. The sensitive designation on XML objects can be naturally transferred to the nodes; and also the secure requirements can be represented by object instead of node.

Definition 5 (XML Authorization). *An XML authorization is an RDF statement that describes the subject, type and object of it, where type can be divided into positive authorization and negative authorization, using "+" and "-" represent respectively. The granularity of authorization object is RDF object and (1) simple object has the same authorization type with the nodes encapsulated by it; and (2) sub-objects' authorization is positive if their parent object is positive authorized; and (3) sub-objects can have a different authorization from their negative authorized parent.*

Example 2. *An XML authorization that satisfied a security requirement: "Disease AIDS is sensitive to user US01".*

XML authorization: AU01 (user: US01, access-type: -, object: SO03, type: AUTHORIZATION)

Example 3. *An XML authorization that satisfied a security requirement: "Alice's disease is sensitive to user US01".*

XML authorization: AU02 (user: US01, access-type: -, object: AO01, type: AUTHORIZATION)

In these examples, predicates "user", "access-type" and "object" represent the subject, type and object of an authorization respectively.

Since XML object is the minimum granularity of authorization and is transparent to user, we assume that (1) a sensitive node's disclosure is equal to the whole simple object's, which encapsulate it; and (2) only all sub-objects have been disclosed will the parent object be disclosed.

4.2 Improvement

The above object-oriented model can simplify the specification of sensitive information and resolve the association sensitive problem opposite to node-oriented authorization. However, when the security requirement in Example 3 is expanded to all patients, a mass of redundancy will again appear in the security policy. If we could abstract XML type from XML objects that have same structures, then such situation will be ultimately avoid. In addition, XML type is also a foundation to describe semantic relations in a document.

Definition 6 (XML Type). *A simple XML type is similar to a simple XML object, but not include its leaf-nodes; an associated XML type is consisted of simple types and/or other associated types. XML types use TID to identify each other.*

Example 4. *Some XML types of the document showed in Figure 1 are listed as follows.*

Simple types: ST01 (locate: name, type: SIMPLE-TYPE); ST02 (locate: disease, type: SIMPLE-TYPE)

Associated type: AT01 (asscroot: hospital/patient, component: {ST01, ST02}, type: ASSC-TYPE)

XML object is an instance of its type and can automatically obtain the authorization specifications of it. Authorization on object can be changed and such operation will not affect other instance of the same type.

Example 5. *An XML authorization that satisfied a security requirement: "All patients' disease is sensitive to user US02".*

XML authorization: AU03 (user: US02, access-type: -, object: AT01, type: AUTHORIZATION)

There are always some conflicts included in a security policy. Existed conflict resolutions [6, 7] can be addressed in several standard ways such as general versus specific, negative versus positive, etc. These conflicted authorizations are related to a single authorized object. However, conflicts may also exist among different authorized objects, especially the ones that are semantic related. They are the origin of inference disclosure, and their resolution is the essence of the whole inference control.

After the nodes' objectifying and objects' typifying, we can conveniently use RDF to describe semantic relations in a document.

Example 6. *An XML relation of the document showed in Figure 1 is listed as follows.*

Simple types: ST04 (locate: ward, type: SIMPLE-TYPE)[2]

XML relation: RE01 (asscroot: hospital/patient, premise: ST04, conclusion: ST02, type: FD)

In the example, predicates "premise" and "conclusion" represents the two parties of the relation "RE01" respectively. How to use such a relation in the inference control procedure is indicated by the literals "FD", which will be described in detail by using RDF in a period of the system's realization.

A relation is called *I-relation* when one part of it will directly cause the other's disclosure, e.g. special prescription always determines a same disease. A relation is called *II-relation*, if there must be some conditions only in which a disclosure will take place. Relation *RE01* is just an example; adversary must need to find another patient, who is in the same ward with Alice, and her disease before using *RE01*. Our purpose of classifying XML relations is to take different expanding strategies in document extending period of inference control.

5 Secure Inference Control

5.1 Assumption of Inference Control

Not all inference activities should be controlled. Referring to "Closed world Assumption" in researches of relational database security [12], we present some similar assumptions to restrict the range of the resolution of inference control.

Assumption 1. *Inference is dependent on the nodes and their relations in an XML document. Otherwise, such an inference can't be controlled.*

Assumption 2. *The result of inference must exist in the document. Only the inference that causes the leakage of sensitive information in the document need to be controlled.*

---

[2] Other kind of relations may have different RDF representation and document- expanding strategy. Administrator can easily add them to the RDF repository.

In a closed access control strategy, all authorizations of some user generate a division of objects: *permit-set*, *explicit-refuse-set* and *implicit-refuse-set*. We assume that: all the objects in some query result are passed through security validation by access control mechanism; inference control mechanism should make sure that objects in *explicit-refuse-set* cannot be inferred from the result; objects in *implicit-refuse-set* needn't to be controlled even if they could be inferred out. That is, only the objects in *explicit-refuse-set* are considered as sensitive information under these assumptions.

5.2 Document's Security Validation

Both the direct disclosure control and inference disclosure control need to check the result to make sure whether the security policy is violated or not. Given a document, what we need to do is to finding whether there is a sensitive object to some user that is contained in the document. We give a validation procedure as follows.

```
Procedure 1. XML document's security check for some
user
Input: XML document t, Sensitive objects O of some user
Output: TRUE if the security is violated, otherwise
FALSE
Method:
1. For any object o in O:
(a) If o is a single object, then return TRUE if
o.locate is path contained in t.
(b) If o is an associated object, then return TRUE if
there exist a sub-tree identified by o.asscroot(t) that
contains all the sub-objects of o.
2. Return FALSE
```

5.3 Combination of Documents

Every query result is always a sub-tree with different structure, simple combination will cause a confusing and useless forest. To maintain *structural-consistency* between history file and original document, we use some non-existent *dummy* nodes, which will never returned to any user, to supplement every query result before merging it to history file.

Another problem is the node's *more* designation in a document's schema definition, which will inevitably cause same sub-trees to be simultaneously appeared in the result of a combination. Hence, it is also important to keep *content-consistency* between combination result and original document. We use XML keys as a main approach to eliminate such redundancy.

Definition 7 (XML Key). *An XML key is represented as* $(p^a, \{p_1^r, p_2^r, \ldots, p_n^r\})$, *where* p^a *indicates the root of a sub-tree to which the key belonged;* $p_1^r, p_2^r, \ldots,$ *and* p_n^r *indicate items of the key respectively, and all of them are the sub-express of* p^a *in t. An XML key* $(p^a, \{p_1^r, p_2^r, \ldots, p_n^r\})$ *is used to ensure that there not exist two different sub-tree* t_1 *and* t_2 *in t, whose roots are both* $p^a.e$ *and* $p_i^r(t_1) = p_i^r(t_2) (1 \le i \le n)$.

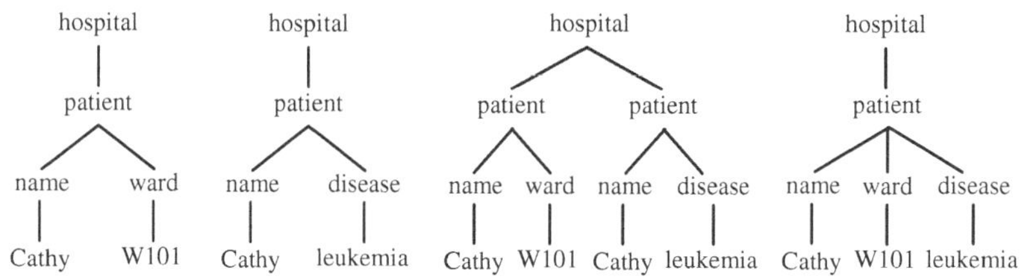

(a) Document t_1 (b) Document t_2 (c) Result of none key used (d) Result by using a key

Fig. 3. A comparison of the combination of XML documents

The approach of using XML keys in document combination is showed in algorithm 1.

Algorithm 1. Merging the documents of same structure
Input: XML document t and t', XML key set K of an original document that t and t' have same structure with
Output: result of the combination
Method:
1. Let n be the root of t'
2. If n is not a leaf-node, for each sub-node n' of n:
(a) If n' is not contained in t, or it is defined to be repeatable, then copy the sub-tree that root of it to t at a corresponding position;
(b) Otherwise, $n = n'$, goto 2 for a recursion
3. For each $k = (p^a, \{p_1^r, p_2^r, ..., p_n^r\})$ in K, if k is contained in t, let T be the sub-tree set of $p^a(t)$, and if T is not empty:
(a) Let t_1 be a sub-tree in T, $T = T - \{t_1\}$;
(b) For each t_2 in T, if $p_i^r(t_1) = p_i^r(t_2) (1 \leq i \leq n)$, then prune t_2 and merge it to t_1 in t recursively, $T = T - \{t_2\}$;
(c) If T is still not empty, repeat to execute (a)
4. Return the result t

Figure 3 is a comparison of document combination by using XML key *KY01* and none. It shows that in (c), there are two patients whose name are both *Cathy* and the result is not content consistency with original document in Figure 1; in (d) on the contrary, such a problem has been solved effectively by using the above algorithm with the key *KY01*.

5.4 Document Extension

A promise of inference disclosure detection is to obtain a maximum document tree from the combination result of all sub-trees that a user received. If there isn't any inf- erence disclosure in the maximum tree, then intuitively, the sub-tree is secure too. A successful inference in a given sub-tree is a repeated process; new incoming for the sub-tree will activate other relations to a further inference. Hence, the order of using relations for an expanding will impact the efficiency of inference control. It is necessary to compute and preserve all dependency chains among the relations beforehand.

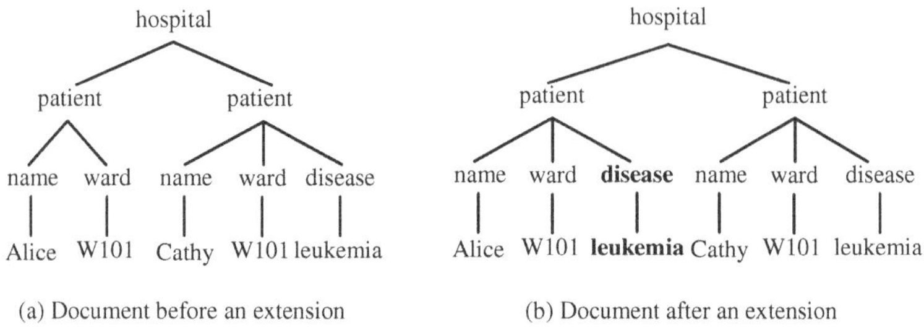

Fig. 4. An extension of XML document by using an II-relation

As mentioned in section 4.2, different kinds of relation has a different expanding strategy in document's extending. For I-relation, only its premise is contained in a tree will its conclusion can be used for an extension; and for II-relation, a sub-tree that only contains its premise will be expanded if there exist another sub-tree that contains both the premise and conclusion. Here, we give an algorithm of document's extension that forced by only one relation as below.

Algorithm 2. Document extending forced by a functional dependency relation
Input: XML document *t*, functional dependency relation *r*
Output: Result of the extension
Method:
1. Let *p* be the *asscroot* of *r*
2. If *r* is an I-relation, then expand *r.conclusion* to the sub-trees that are identified by *p*(*t*) and contain *r.premise*
3. If *r* is an II-relation, then let T_1 be a sub-tree set whose item is identified by *p*(*t*) and contains *r*, let T_2 be another sub-tree set whose item is also identified by *p*(*t*) but not contains *r*:
(a) If T_1 or T_2 is empty, then return *t*.
(b) Take a sub-tree *t'* out of T_1. For each sub-tree *t"* in T_2, if *r.premise* in *t'* and *t"* are the same, then expand *r.conclusion* in *t'* to the sub-tree, which *t"* corresponds in *t*, and remove *t"* from T_2;
(c) Repeat to execute (a).

Figure 4 is an example of document extension by using the II-relation *RE01* given in Example 6. The nodes with bold font are the new incoming for the document after extending.

When all the relations have been used and no other new node is inferred out, the result is the maximum tree. The following we need to do is to validate its security. If the maximum tree is secure, then the query result can be returned to the current user and the corresponding history will be updated too.

6 Conclusion

In this paper, we present a new approach of inference control, which is on the foundation of some improvements of an access control model that based on RDF. By using some concepts that derived from XML, such as XML type, XML object etc, we encapsulate the nodes of an XML document to represent the semantic relations among them. Thus the capability of inference description is improved. By studying the effect of query history in inference control, we represent a method about document combination based on XML keys, and develop some algorithms for such a combination and the extension after it. Since the range of inference control is enlarged and the granularity of authorized objects is expanded, our approach can provide higher security and flexibility for XML documents.

References

1. A. Kwong, M. Gertz. Authentic Publication of XML Document Data. In Proceedings of the 2nd International Conference on Web Information Systems Engineering, pages 331-340, 2001.
2. P. Devanbu, M. Gertz, C. Martel, and S. Stubblebine. Authentic Third-Party Data Publication. DBSec, 18: 101-112, 2000.
3. E. Bertino, B. Carminati, E. Ferrari, B. Thuraisingham, and A. Gupta. Selective and Authentic Third-Party Distribution of XML Documents. IEEE Transaction on Knowledge and Data Engineering, 16(10): 1263-1278, 2004.
4. Yang XC, Li C. Secure XML Publishing without Information Leakage in the Presence of Data Inference. In Proceedings of the 30th VLDB Conference, pages 96-107, 2004.
5. Vaibhav Gowadia, Csilla Farkas. RDF metadata for XML access control. In Proceedings of the 2003 ACM workshop on XML security, pages 39-48, 2003.
6. Damiani E, Vimercati SDC, Paraboschi S, Samarati P. A fine-grained access control system for XML documents. ACM TISSEC, 5(2): 169-202, 2002.
7. L. Bouganim, F. Dang Ngoc, P. Pucheral. Client-Based Access Control Management for XML documents. In Proceeding of the 30th VLDB Conference, pages 84-95, 2004.
8. Wenfei Fan, Chee-Yong Chan, Minos Garofalakis. Secure XML Querying with Security Views. In Proceedings of the 2004 ACM SIGMOD international conference on Management of data, pages 587-598, 2004.
9. C. Farkas, A. Stoica. Correlated data inference in ontology guided XML security engine. In Proceedings of 17th WG 11.3 working conference on Data and Application Security, 2003.
10. 10.W.W.W.Consortium. Extensible Markup Language 1.0 specification. W3C Recommendation, retrieved from http://www.w3.org/TR/2000/REC-xml-20001006, 2000.
11. 11.W.W.W.Consortium. RDF Primer. W3C Recommendation, retrieved from http://www.w3.org/TR/2004/REC-rdf-primer-20040210, 2004.
12. 12.D. E. Denning. A Preliminary Note on the Inference Problem in Multilevel Database Management Systems. In Proceedings of the National Computer Security Center Invitational Workshop on Database Security, 1986.

Recursive SQL Query Optimization with k-Iteration Lookahead

Ahmad Ghazal, Alain Crolotte, and Dawit Seid

NCR Corporation, Teradata Division
100 N. Sepulveda Blvd. El Segundo, CA, 90245
{ahmad.ghazal, alain.crolotte, dawit.seid}@ncr.com

Abstract. Relational implementation of recursive queries is part of the ANSI SQL99 and was implemented in Teradata V2R6. Recursive queries allow processing of hierarchical data like air flight schedules, bill-of-materials, data cube dimension hierarchies, and ancestor-descendant information (e.g. XML data stored in relations). The initial Teradata recursive query implementation is based on a static (fixed) execution plan for all recursive iterations. This may not be optimal since the intermediate results from recursive iterations vary in size. To address this problem, this paper proposes dynamic re-optimization techniques to produce execution plans that are optimal for all recursive iterations. The approach employs a mix of multi-iteration pre-planning and dynamic feedback techniques that are generally applicable to any recursive query implementation in an RDBMS. We validate our proposed techniques by conducting experiments on a prototype implementation using airline flights data.

1 Introduction and Problem Definition

For over two decades recursive queries were handled in deductive databases until the adoption of a recursive query standard in SQL99 allowed its implementation in commercial relational DBMS products. The motivation behind the implementation of recursive queries is to allow relational DBMS users to easily query hierarchical and directed graph data. The *recursive view* definition below shows an example of how recursion is specified in SQL99. This view is based on a table called `Flights` that contains a simplified airline roster. The `Flights` table consists of departure city, arrival city, departure time, arrival time and cost (one way trip fare).

```
CREATE RECURSIVE VIEW
all_trips (source, destination, src_time, dest_time, cost, depth, path) AS
SELECT  dep_city, arr_city, dep_daytime,  arr_daytime, cost, 0 as depth,
            cast(source||' '||destination as varchar(100))
FROM  Flights
UNION ALL
SELECT results_before.source,  next_leg.arr_city,  results_before.src_time,
    next_leg.arr_daytime,results_before.cost + next_leg.cost,  results_before.depth + 1,
    results_before.path||' '||next_leg.arr_city
FROM  all_trips results_before
        INNER JOIN  Flights next_leg ON results_before.destination = next_leg.dep_city
WHERE results_before.path not like '%'||next_leg.arr_city||'%';
```

The *all_trips* recursive view captures all multi-leg flights with no cycles (enforced by checking if the new arrival city is not part of the flight path). This view, like other

S. Bressan, J. Küng, and R. Wagner (Eds.): DEXA 2006, LNCS 4080, pp. 348 – 357, 2006.

recursive views, can be broken down into a *seed* part and a *recursive* part. The seed in the *all_trips* view is the first SELECT (simple select from Flights) which represents all direct flights. The second SELECT is the recursive part of the view where the `Flights` table is joined with *all_trips*. In general, both the seed and recursive part could be a UNION of *numerous* SELECT statements. A statement belongs to the seed if it does not reference the recursive view. All other statements (SELECTs that have self references) comprise the recursive part of the view.

To further illustrate the semantics of recursive queries, we describe the execution logic of recursive queries using the *all_trips* view as an example. The following procedure, which we will also use later to illustrate our new optimization techniques, describes the execution of query "`select * from all_trips`".

Procedure ***ExecuteAllTrips***
Begin

1. *Retrieve from Flights into Spool 1 and Spool 2.*
2. *Join Flights with Spool 2.*
3. *If join result is empty go to step 7.*
4. *Empty Spool 2.*
5. *Send join result to Spool 1 and Spool 2.*
6. *Go to step 2.*
7. *Return the contents of Spool 1 to the user as the final result of the query.*

End

The above steps are generated by the optimizer and executed by what is called the *execution engine*. The first step corresponds to performing the seed part (first SELECT). It produces the initial result and feeds into the recursion. The recursive steps are steps 2 - 6. Spool 2 is used to hold the running seed (recursive result in each iteration) which then becomes part of the cumulative result (held in spool 1). The final result is basically the UNION of the initial seed and the result of all recursive iteration. Notice that while in this simple example Spool 2 is joined only with the Flights table, in a complex query Spool 2 may be joined with many other tables in Step 2 (either in a multi-way join or as part of multiple unioned SELECT statements). Spool 2 may also be involved in an outer join or joined with subqueries.

The optimizer finds the best way to perform the seed and recursive steps based on cost estimates. For example, the optimizer may find an index access to Flights in step 1 above. The optimizer also finds the best join method to join Flights with Spool 2 in step 2 above. For complex queries, the join plan for Step 2 becomes more complex.

The initial Teradata implementation uses a *static* plan in step 2 based on the estimated demographics of Spool 2 computed once when it is first created. These demographics are basically the outcome of the seed steps. Hence, the plan is optimal for the first iteration of the recursive execution but may not be for subsequent iterations. The reason is that Spool 2's demographics may change during the recursive execution rendering the initial plan non-optimal. For example, as the cardinality of Spool 2 changes from iteration *i* to iteration *i*+1, it is possible that hash join is the optimal way to join Flights to Spool 2 in *i*-th iteration but merge join is the optimal way to do the same for the *i*+1th iteration.

We are aware of only a few solutions proposed to address the shortcomings of static plans for recursive queries. In the context of a deductive database system, [4] adopted a *feedback mechanism* to generate iteration specific plans when needed. This paper compared two alternatives: *The Never Strategy* (that never re-optimizes the initial plan) and *The Change Strategy* (that re-optimizes when cardinalities change). Since re-optimization is considered to be costly, [4] tried to avoid re-optimization for every iteration by using some rules to decide when to re-optimize and when to continue using the same plan for the next iteration. Specifically, three options were considered: (1) re-optimize if there is *any* change in cardinality, (2) re-optimize if cardinality increased/decreased by x percent for a given x, and (3) during the first iteration, rank relations by cardinality and re-optimize if the rank of any relation changes.

We also address the same problem but propose a different solution. Our solution is based on the observation that, in most cases, there are costs in re-optimizing at every step in addition to the optimization cost itself. Indeed, in order to collect feedback after a given iteration, the recursive result of that iteration needs to be written to disk (assuming this intermediate result is not small enough to fit in memory). After a plan is generated for the next iteration, the current iteration result is read again from disk to execute the iteration. In contrast, if no feedback/re-planning is needed, the execution engine can directly feed the join result of the i-th iteration to the (i+1)th iteration. As we explain in detail in 2.1, this leads to more efficient query execution including creating opportunities for inter-operator ("vertical") parallelism via pipelining.

The new technique we propose generates plans for the different iterations upfront to allow pipelining. Specifically, the optimizer tries to estimate the join cost of subsequent iterations based on predicted demographics at each of these iterations. Since most of the time the number of recursive iterations is not known, the optimizer generates plans for a fixed number k of iterations. This means, the query optimizer has access to plans for the subsequent k iterations (which can be different for different iterations) thereby allowing it to exploit pipelining. After k iterations (if applicable) the execution engine provides feedback (actual cardinality of the last recursive iteration) to the optimizer. The optimizer then generates the next k plans and so on.

By making the k plans available, our k-iteration lookahead planning also allows the optimizer to consider further optimization using global (multi-query) optimization techniques [13,14,15]. This optimization tries to identify common subexpressions and scans that can be shared among the k query plans.

In addition to using database demographics for estimating join cardinalities of the next k-iterations, we also investigate sampling based techniques to gain such estimates (currently only for queries whose recursive part involves a single table). Our sampling methods are inspired by sampling based techniques developed for estimating the cardinality of a relation's transitive closure [6,7,8]. [6,7] gave an algorithm that uses adaptive sampling for selecting starting nodes and uses breadth-first traversals to compute the size of these nodes' reachability set. An improvement of this method is presented in [8].

In general, although recursive queries have been supported in deductive databases, these systems do not normally use cost-based optimizations. Instead they use heuristics to select an order of execution based on a set of precedence rules for applicable techniques [5]. The work in [12] considers cost-based optimization of recursive queries in a parallel database. However, this paper did not address dynamic re-optimization. Ordonez [9] also deals with recursive query optimization in the Teradata RDBMS. The discussion in that paper was limited to selection pushdown, duplicate row elimination and using indexes on the base table and the result table.

There has been a significant amount of work on dynamic re-optimization of plans in a relational optimizer [1,2,3,10,11]. However, these studies did not consider recursive queries. Indeed this body of work can be viewed as complementary to ours in that it deals with changing a plan for a single iteration of a recursive plan while we deal with adaptive re-optimization of repetitive execution of joins.

The paper is organized as follows. Section 2 covers dynamic re-optimization techniques including our proposed k-iteration lookahead planning approach. Section 3 provides experimental results quantifying the benefits of our proposed method. We conclude in section 4 with a summary of results and future work.

2 Dynamic Optimization Techniques

As mentioned above, previous results on dynamic optimizations are based on the tradeoffs between producing more optimal plans and the overhead cost of re-optimization. However, in real-life decision support queries running on commercial database systems like Teradata, optimization time is a very small fraction of the total execution time. This may suggest that the problems of static plans can be simply solved by re-optimizing the plan at every recursive iteration based on the actual demographics produced in the previous iteration. In section 2.1 we discuss the demerits of such an approach, which we refer to as *Full-Feedback based dynamic optimization*. Then in section 2.2 we describe the *k*-iteration lookahead and sampling based planning techniques.

2.1 Full Feedback Based Optimization

In the Full-Feedback Planning (FFB) technique, the optimizer produces and sends a plan to the execution engine at every iteration, and the execution engine executes the plan and feeds back[1] the demographic information of the result to the optimizer. In general, the demographic information relevant to join planning includes cardinality, average, maximum and minimum number of rows per unique value, most frequent values and their frequency, field correlation information, and so on. Among these the two most critical values that can also be gathered cheaply are relation *cardinality* and *number of unique values*. The demographics sent by the execution engine are just the cardinality of the recursive iteration result which it produces for free. We can then use unique value demographics from the base table (e.g. Flights) and the seed as well as the current recursive result's cardinality to estimate the number of unique values.

Below we show the application of FFB to the execution of the *all_trips* recursive view described previously:

---

[1] It should be noted that there are many scenarios where feedback is not possible altogether. That happens when an SQL expression should be pre-compiled and the execution plan is stored. Examples are stored procedures and cached plans.

Procedure ***ExecAllTrips-FFB***
Begin

1. *i = 0*
2. *Retrieve from Flights into Spool 1 and Spool 2.*
3. *Optimizer finds plan for i-th iteration(0-th iteration is the initial seed)*
4. *Optimizer sends i-th iteration plan (steps) to execution engine.*
5. *Execution engine executes the plan*
6. *If i-th iteration result is empty go to step 10.*
7. *Send current join result to Spool 1 and Spool 2*
8. *Collect available demographics and send it back to the optimizer.*
9. *Increment i by one and go to step 3.*
10. *Return the contents of Spool 1 as the final result of the query.*

End

Pipelining. FFB generates the execution plan for each recursive iteration in isolation. As a result, the optimizer can not exploit pipelining to achieve cross-execution-step optimizations. Cross-execution-step optimization (aka vertical parallelism) allows a consumer operator to start before the producer finished execution. Pipelining is defined in different ways in the database literature and therefore we first define this term in the context of this paper. In an execution plan of some database query or queries, step X *pipelines* to step Y if

- the output of step X is used as input in step Y and
- The input of Step Y requires some preprocessing like sorting or relocation of data (*redistribution* or *duplication* in a distributed database system).
- Step X performs the preprocessing needed by step Y.

In *ExecAllTrips* shown in section 1, Steps 1 or Step 5 could pipeline into step 2 if the join step between Flights and Spool 2 requires first sorting of Spool 2 on the `destination` field. Specifically, the sort can be done along with the read steps of step 1 or step 5 rather than writing the result to disk and performing a separate sort step.

The optimizer finds out if a certain step X can pipeline into another step Y and includes the preparation processing in step X. That can *only* be done if both steps are seen by the optimizer, which is not possible for FFB. For example, in *ExecAllTrips-FFB*, the optimizer can not apply pipelining from step 7 in the *i*-th iteration into step 5 of the *i*+1th iteration since it produces the plan of only one iteration at a time.

Global Query Optimization (GQO). Another limitation of FFB is that it cannot take advantage of GQO. GQO finds an optimal plan for a set of queries. One important aspect of GQO is finding and leveraging common sub-expressions across multiple queries submitted as a batch. Since each iteration can be considered a "query", execution of a recursive query is equivalent to execution of a set of queries. And, since these queries have generally a lot in common, the chances of benefiting from GQO are high. Notice also that GQO is complementary to pipelining in that, once a shared expression is identified, its result is pipelined to its consumers in all iterations. Again, since it processes one iteration at a time, the FFB technique can not take advantage of GQO.

Finally, note that *ExecuteAllTrips*, the static planning approach, does not require feedback and can take advantage of pipelining and GQO since the execution steps for all iterations are known in advance. But, as mentioned before, *ExecuteAllTrips* has its own limitations due to its use of a fixed plan for all iterations.

2.2 Planning with k-Iteration Lookahead

Next we describe our new approach that avoids the limitations of both static planning and FFB. The approach, called *k-iteration lookahead planning* (KLP), is based on generating plans of multiple iterations before execution. One possible realization of KLP is to generate a plan every k iteration and use that same plan for the next k iterations. Another approach, which we pursue here, is to generate a possibly varying plan for each of the k iterations. The optimizer starts by finding the optimal plan for the first iteration the same way as exemplified in *ExecuteAllTrips*. A by-product of the plan of the first iteration is a size estimate of the result produced in that iteration. The optimizer uses that estimate to set the demographics of the input to the second iteration and proceeds with generating the second iteration plan. This process continues until a fixed k number of iterations are planned. Section 2.2.1 will discuss how the value of k is determined. In cases where k is less than the total number of iterations (TNI), the execution engine feeds back to the optimizer after k iterations. The optimizer then applies KLP for the next k iterations. This process continues for $\lceil TNI/k \rceil$ times.

Notice here that KLP essentially leverages the database demographics traditionally used for one-step join planning to generate multi-iteration join plans. Also note that the Full-feedback technique is indeed a version of KLP where $k = 1$. Hence, the estimates used by KLP for $k > 1$ can be less accurate than FFB. However, as our experiments will show, when k is set appropriately, the impact of lost accuracy is outstripped by gains from pipelining, GQO and saved cost of feedback/re-optimization. Also, as will be discussed below, confidence in the estimates can be considered in the determination of k for KLP.

2.2.1 Computing the Value of *k*

The value of k in KLP is determined by the optimizer for each query. The value of TNI is an upper bound on the value of k but in general it is difficult to find the exact value of TNI. However, there are common cases where an upper bound on the value of TNI can be found. One way to do this is by considering the number of distinct values (NDV) of the join fields involved in the recursion. For example, in the view *all_trips*, it is reasonable to assume that TNI ≤ *maximum(NDV(source), NDV(destination))*. This is true since the recursion in *all_trips* is not cyclic and is guaranteed to terminate. Cyclic recursion is not considered in this paper since it is either handled by a compilation error (by the optimizer) or a run-time error (by the execution engine).

Also, some recursive queries have an explicit condition to cap the recursion depth. For example, *all_trips* could have an explicit condition (or a condition pushed into the recursive part by query re-write) like "depth <= *V*" in the WHERE clause of the recursive part (second SELECT). It is not hard for the optimizer to find the limit value *V*. In fact some commercial databases require such a limit in any valid recursive query. If both NDV and depth limit are available, the value of TNI is set to the minimum of these values. Hence, the value of k can be chosen by the optimizer to be ≤ TNI.

Various issues can be considered in choosing the exact value of k. The key is the tradeoff between maximizing pipelining and GQO and producing good plans. Also, the CPU and I/O cost of gathering feedback and generating k plans (relative to data size) needs to be considered. The Teradata optimizer provides levels of confidence for the join plans and spool cardinality estimates. In this case, KLP can terminate generating plans when it determines that it has no confidence in the estimate of the join result. It can also stop generating new plans altogether if it finds that the optimization time of the i-th iteration is more (or above a certain threshold) than its estimated execution time. In our current prototype, the value of k is based on the confidence and parsing times as just described.

2.2.2 Sampling Based Demographics Estimation

Depending on the connectivity distribution the recursive table's underlying graph and the value of k, some of the plans produced by KLP may be inefficient if the estimates are significantly affected by the propagation of errors across the k iterations. Notice that misleading estimates caused by quick propagation of errors in size estimation is also a problem for base-table joins if the query expression involves several joins [16]. Since estimates feed into each other, KLP can be affected by this problem more severely. Here, we briefly discuss a sampling based approach to mitigate this problem in a particular class of queries. Our sampling technique is currently applicable only for queries whose *recursive part includes only the self-join* and whose *seed part does not join the recursive table with another table* (except in a semi-join like EXISTS, IN, NOT IN, etc.). For recursive queries that include joins of recursive results with other tables, in addition to the self-join, the result of each iteration is also affected by the joins with the other tables and our sampling technique does not currently factor in the impact of these joins. In queries where the recursive table is joined with another table in the seed part, the size of the seed may grow to be bigger than the recursive table itself or the distribution of values of source and/or sink fields may be completely different from the recursive table. Since our sampling only depends on the recursive table, it can not be used for cardinality estimation in such cases.

As we mentioned in the introduction, [6,7] have given an adaptive sampling based algorithm, henceforth called the *LN-algorithm*, for estimating the cardinality of the generalized transitive closure of a relation. Note that the transitive closure estimate produced by the LN-algorithm is essentially a cardinality estimate of a recursive query that uses the entire table as a seed. Hence, the global estimate found in this manner can be combined with selectivity estimates of a particular query's seed (produced by the optimizer) to estimate the recursive result cardinality of that query. However, instead of the transitive closure size, for join planning we need cardinality estimates at each iteration. We get these estimates by capturing per-iteration estimates as part of the LN-algorithm as described below.

Computing iteration estimates: As part of the general demographics collection in the database, we collect *recursive cardinality demographics* (RCD) for a given recursive table. Like any demographics collection, this incurs a one-time cost (updating this statistics during table update is beyond the scope of this paper). Below, again using the flights example, we give the algorithm which essentially extends the

LN-algorithm with a strategy to capture per-iteration statistics. As such, this algorithm inherits all the tight accuracy and confidence intervals of the LN-algorithm.

Procedure **CollectRCD**

```
    IterationEstimates [] /* array storing per-iteration cardinality */
    sampleClosure = 0;   noOfSamples = 0;
    while (sampleClosure >= αN)
          randomly choose  a source s from Flights;
             /* do breadth first search  */
          add s to ReachableSet;
          for i = 1 to TNI
                      copy ReachableSet to IterationReachableSet  and empty ReachableSet;
                      for each row r  in IterationReachableSet
                                ReachableSet = neighbors of r; /* can use index scan for this*/;
                                IterationEstimates[i] = IterationEstimates[i] + |ReachableSet|;
                                sampleClosure = sampleClosure + max (1, |ReachableSet|);
                                increment noOfSamples by 1;
End
```

In CollectRCD, N is the number of unique values of source and α is a function of the confidence interval within which we wish to estimate the size of the transitive closure. Specifically, α is set to $d(d+1)/(1-\sqrt{p})$, where $0 < p \leq 1$ is the confidence and d>0 is a fixed value[7]. Note that depending on availability of histograms on the source field, the random sampling can also be directed by the distribution in the histogram to get more representative samples.

Using RCD for dynamic planning. At the completion of CollectRSD, *IterationEstimates* will capture the sample-based cardinality at each iteration. As in the LN-algorithm, the size of the transitive closure can be estimated by *N* sampleClosure/ noOfSamples*. In a similar manner, we can estimate global size at iteration *i* as *N* IterationEstimates[i]/ noOfSamples*. When given a cardinality of any seed, $n < N$, we can replace *N* with *n* in the above to estimate its cardinality at iteration *i*. We can use these demographics to estimate join cardinality of an iteration in the execution of a given query in both non-feedback based and feedback-based way. In a non-feedback based approach, we generate all the *TNI* plans upfront based entirely on demographics from *IterationEstimates*. In a feedback-based approach like KLP, the current result size, *n*, is gathered as a feedback at every *k* iteration.

3 Experimental Results

In order to assess the performance of the KLP algorithm we built a real-life example on a 2-node NCR 5200 with 2 disk array modules. This configuration is fairly old but well-suited for this comparison task because it is balanced with respect to CPU and I/Os (the system does not favor a CPU-bound workload nor an I/O bound workload). On a set of 16 cities in the USA with two major hubs and graph topology such that the maximum path length (without loops) is 9 legs, we generated a database with 3,000 rows representing all flights for a week. The distances between cities were actual distances and the cost of flights was based on the actual between-city distances and a random factor. Arrival times were based on the number of miles between the departure city and the arrival city with a random element. To be able to get to the next leg, the passenger had to arrive no later than 45 minutes before the departure of the next flight and passengers would not get into a flight departing more than 12 hours after the arrival of the first flight. We used a view similar to *all_trips* depicted in section 1 with two addition al conditions to reflect the two constraints on departure and arrival times.

Two sets of experiments were conducted. The first set dealt with the simple case of two tables (one table joined recursively to itself) as in *all_trips* while the second set of experiments dealt with a more complex case with four tables (we added a table containing meals data and another for available seats). In each case the test consisted of selecting all rows from the recursive view. The first test was run with the current released Teradata implementation that employs static planning (this could be considered as the k=0 case). The other experiments were run on a prototype implementing the KLP algorithm with k=1, i.e. FFB, and k=3, i.e. KLP. Two KLP experiments were run: onc using optimizer estimates (OE) and another using sample-based estimates (SE). SE was run only for the simpler case of two tables with the algorithm described in section 2. The results obtained are summarized in Table 1 below. We show total time for 9 iterations. Due to lack of space, we do not show per-iteration times.

Table 1. Total runtime for two classes of queries (in seconds)

	static	k=1	k=3, KLP-OE	k=3, KLP-SE
simple	2496	2064	1795	1846
complex	2217	1983	1822	N/A

Overall, static planning had the worst performance. FFB performed better than static planning which suggests that although FFB's plans did not benefit from pipelining and GQO, still its gains due to better plans allowed to make up for this deficiency. As shown in table 1, the situation improves further with k-lookahead plans as better plans are obtained while at the same time benefiting from pipelining and GQO. The time shown for KLP-SE includes the sampling-based demographics collection also. For the simple SQL, in case of KLP-SE, we obtained the same plans as in KLP-OE. The runtime of KLP-OE is higher since we incurred the sampled statistics collection cost while the optimizer estimates are provided at no cost. Finally, note that although for both query types KLP provided an improvement over static and FFB, the percentage of improvement was higher for the simple SQL case than for the complex SQL case. This was expected due to the lower quality of the optimizer estimates in the more complex SQL case.

4 Conclusions and Future Work

In this paper, we identified several query optimization issues with the relational database implementation of recursive queries that were not addressed in prior research. We presented the KLP approach which avoids the problems of the static and the full feedback approaches and described how sampling and join cardinality estimates are exploited in this approach. In the future, we plan to explore ways to extend the use of sampling to more complex cases of recursive queries. In addition, we plan to devise a comprehensive framework of cost-based recursive query optimization that systematically considers all the relevant aspects of pipelining, GQO, parsing time, cost of sampling and the optimal value of k.

References

1. Chen, C. M and Roussopoulos, N., "Adaptive Selectivity Estimation Using Query Feedback", ACM SIGMOD Record", Vol. 23, No. 2, June 1994, 161-172
2. Brueining, D., Garnett, T, and Amarasinghe, S. "An Infrastructure for Adaptive Dynamic Optimization", Int. Symp. on Code Generation and Optimization, 265-275,2003.
3. Kabra, N. and DeWitt, D. J. "Efficient Mid-Query Re-Optimization of Sub-Optimal Query Execution Plans", Proceedings of the 1998 ACM SIGMOD International Conference on Management of Data, Seattle, 1998, pp. 106-117.
4. Derr, M. "Adaptive Query Optimization in a Deductive Database System", Proc. of the 2nd Int. Conf. on Information and Knowledge Management, 1993, pp. 206-215.
5. Zaniolo, Carlo, et al. Advanced Database Systems. Morgan Kauffman, 1997.
6. Lipton, R. J and Naughton, J. F. Estimating the size of generalized transitive closures. VLDB, 1989, pp: 315-326.
7. Lipton, R. J. "Query size estimation by adaptive sampling", J. of Computer and System Sciences, 51(1), 18 – 25, 1995.
8. Cohen, E. Size-estimation framework with applications to transitive closure and reachability, J. of Computer and System Sciences, 55 (3), 441 – 453, 1997.
9. Ordonez, C. "Optimizing recursive queries in SQL", SIGMOD 2005, pp: 834 – 839.
10. Markl, V. et al, "Robust query processing through progressive optimization", SIGMOD 2004, pp: 659 – 670.
11. Babu, S., Bizarro, P. and DeWitt, D., "Proactive re-optimization", SIGMOD 2005, pp: 107 – 118.
12. Zurek, T. and Thanisch, P. , "Optimization Strategies for Parallel Linear Recursive Query Processing", CSG Technical Report ECS-CSG-16-95, July 1995.
13. Sellis, T., "Multiple Query Optimization", ACM Transactions on Database Systems, pp: 23-52, 1988.
14. Roy, P., Seshadri, S., Sudarshan, S., Bhobhe, S., "Efficient and extensible algorithms for multi-query optimization", SIGMOD, 249–260, 2000.
15. Dalvi, N. N., et al. "Pipelining in multi-query optimization", PODS, 59 - 70, 2001.
16. Y. Ionnidis and S. Christodoulakis. "Optimal histograms for limiting worst-case error propagation in the size of join results". ACM TODS, 18(4), 709 – 748, 1993.

An Effective, Efficient XML Data Broadcasting Method in a Mobile Wireless Network*

Sang-Hyun Park, Jae-Ho Choi, and SangKeun Lee**

Department of Computer Science and Engineering,
Korea University, Seoul, South Korea
{newtypus, redcolor25, yalphy}@korea.ac.kr

Abstract. With the rapidly increasing popularity of XML, an effective method to transmit XML data over wireless broadcasting environments is urgently required. In this paper, a novel XML data streaming method for wireless broadcasting environments, is proposed. An XML stream is organized to enable a selective access scheme for simple XPath queries, by borrowing the path summary technique, which was originally devised for indexing semi-structured data. In order to utilize structure information as an XML stream index, the structure information and text values of an XML document are separated. In experimental results, the proposed method demonstrates superior performance over previous approaches with regard to both access and tuning time.

1 Introduction

In the future, propelled by the growth of mobile devices and wireless technologies, more services will be delivered in wireless broadcasting environments [12]. These services may include traffic conditions, weather reports, and financial information. The eXtensible Markup Language (XML) [2] has become a standard information exchange language on the Internet and an increasing amount of information is available in XML formats.

The research area of XML is currently expanding into wireless environments [13][15]. In particular, wireless data broadcasting can reduce bandwidth, since a large number of users requesting data items can be served at no additional cost [5]. Using an auxiliary index in a wireless broadcast, a client does not require access to all objects in a broadcast cycle to retrieve the desired data [10]. When initially accessing the broadcast index, the mobile client is able to predict the arrival time of desired data. Thus, it can stay in power saving mode most of the time and tune into the broadcast channel only when the requested data arrives.

The XML document consists of hierarchically nested elements, which can either be atomic, such as raw character data, or composite, such as a sequence of nested sub-elements. Tags stored with the elements describe the semantics of

* This work was supported by grant No. R01-2006-000-10510-0 from the Basic Research Program of the Korea Science & Engineering Foundation.

** Corresponding author.

S. Bressan, J. Küng, and R. Wagner (Eds.): DEXA 2006, LNCS 4080, pp. 358–367, 2006.

the data, i.e., data stored in XML is hierarchically structured and self-describing. Observed from this, structure information of XML documents might be used as a stream index to transfer XML documents from the server to clients via a broadcast channel. This observation is the basic idea of our work.

In this paper, with the benefit of wireless broadcasting, an XML streaming method for wireless broadcast as a way of disseminating information to a massive number of mobile clients equipped with battery powered palmtops, is considered. The contributions of this paper include the following.

- XML stream structure suitable for wireless broadcasting environments,
- Utilization of a path summary of an XML document as a stream index,
- Query processing technique over wireless XML stream, and
- Experimental results to demonstrate the effectiveness and the efficiency of the proposed method.

The paper is organized as follows. Section 2 presents related work. In Section 3, the XML streaming method is introduced and the query processing technique is presented. Section 4 presents experimental results and Section 5 provides concluding remarks.

2 Related Work

Some recent research has considered XML transmission through wireless networks. Xstream [15] provides middleware which can be used to stream XML documents over wireless environments and proposes fragmentation and packetizing strategies, based on the semantic and structural characteristics of a given XML document in wireless environments. However, the interest is not in the energy efficient transmission of an XML document, and the method does not provide a selective access scheme for client side streaming data. In addition, the work [13] presents a wireless streaming method for XML data, supporting energy efficient processing of queries in mobile clients over a stream. S-Node structure is defined as a streaming unit for XML data. The objective of this work is similar to that of our current work. However, S-Node still has redundancy of label paths in stream data, this causes access time latency.

Independently of this direction, the path summary technique [8] was introduced for efficient indexing of semi-structured data. Interestingly, we borrow the path summary technique and utilize it as a stream index in wireless broadcasting environments. With this idea, we could remove the redundancy of label paths of an XML document. Stream data can therefore be optimized for wireless broadcast environments, and a client is able to receive required XML data from broadcast channel, based on simple XPath queries.

3 Proposed XML Streaming Method

In this section, the XML data model and path summary is presented, and the XML streaming method for wireless broadcasting is introduced.

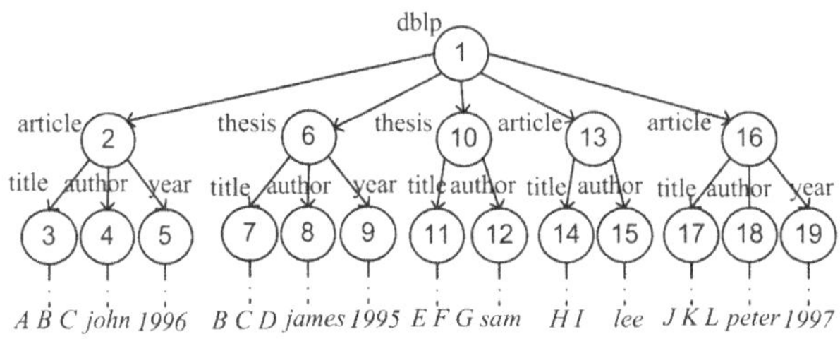

Fig. 1. An example of XML data tree

3.1 XML Data Model

An XML document consists of data and related structure information. An XML document can be formally defined as follows [7].

Definition 1. An XML document D is a tuple $d = (N_d, E_d, f_d, r_d)$, where:

- $N_d = N_d^e \cup N_d^a$ are finite nonempty *nodes* representing elements and attributes. Each element node $n \in N_d^e$ has an associated element identifier and each attribute node $n \in N_d^a$ has an associated value.
- $E_d = E_d^e \cup E_d^a$ is a set of edges representing an element-element relationship or a link (E_d^e) and an element-attribute relationship (E_d^a). E_d is a finite set of edges.
- f_d is a partial function $N_d \times E_d \rightarrow Str$, where Str is a finite set of element tags and attributes names.
- $r_d \in N_d$ is the *root* node of an XML document.

According to Definition 1, an XML document can be seen as an ordered labeled tree, where nodes represent elements and attributes, and edges represent relationships between them.

An XML document can be divided into two parts. The first part consists of element tags and attribute names. The second consists of text and attribute values. The attribute names and attribute values can be replaced by element tags and text values respectively. For simplicity, attributes and attribute values in an XML document are processed as element tags and text values. A node representing an element contains the element identifier and its associated text value. The first part may be regarded as structure information of an XML document.

For example, Figure 1 demonstrates a sample XML data tree with an element identifier in the circles and element name beside the circles. The element and text value relationship is represented by a dotted line.

Definitions of label path and equivalent nodes are now given, as in [16], which are useful for describing a path summary and data model of an XML stream.

Definition 2. A *label path* of a node n in an XML document D, is a sequence of dot-separated labels of the nodes on the path from the r_d to n.

In Figure 1, node 5 can be reached from the root node 1 through the path : 1→2→5. Therefore the label path of node 5 is *dblp.article.year*.

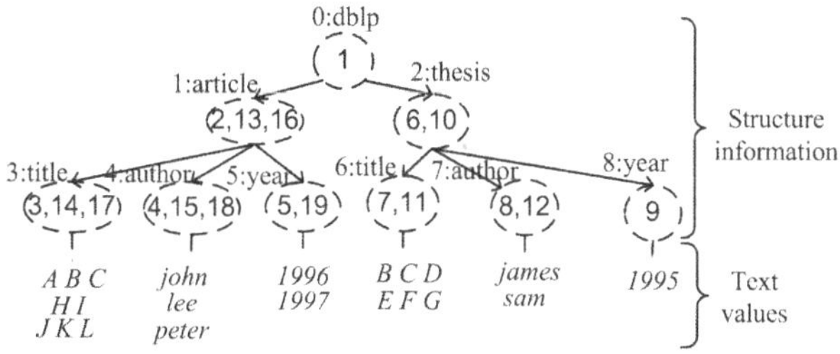

Fig. 2. A path summary of XML data tree

Definition 3. Nodes in an XML data tree D are equivalent if they have the same label path.

In Figure 1, nodes 5 and 19 are equivalent since label paths are the same *dblp.article.year*.

3.2 Path Summary

In an effort to improve the performance of query processing for the semi-structured data, the path summary has received a lot of attention [8]. For data tree D, a path summary sharing label path l for equivalent label paths is built. The set of nodes having the same label path can be merged into a group. The equivalent nodes in every group are sorted by their pre-order identifiers.

Figure 2 presents a path summary for the XML data tree presented in Figure 1. Each dotted circle represents a group and the number in the circle is the identifier of equivalent nodes. Each group has a label and an identifier listed above the group. In Figure 2, data nodes 4, 15, 18 are in group 4, since their label paths are the same *dblp.article.author*.

The order of group identifiers is made in a breadth-first manner, which is used to generate stream data for wireless broadcasting. In order to obtain the answers of a simple XPath query for duplicated label paths in an XML data tree, an XML tree should be traversed multiple times. A path summary provides efficient query facility for evaluating a simple XPath query. With the path summary in Figure 2, for instance, if a sample query Q_1 is */dblp/article/title* (i.e., if we want to know all titles of article in dblp), the answers will be text values of node 3, 14, and 17. Since path summary enables clients to minimize the node access frequency for simple XPath queries, this characteristic contributes to the XML data broadcasting method by reducing time and resource consuming.

3.3 The Structure of an XML Stream

Based on path summary of an XML document, an XML stream which has two kinds of groups, is organized. The first group contains structure information of an XML document, which takes the role of an index, whereas the second group contains text values. Each group is arranged according to the breadth-first order of a path summary.

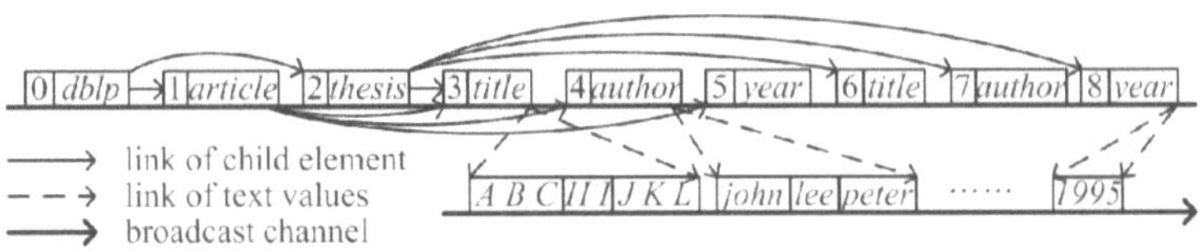

Fig. 3. The structure of XML stream

An index is transmitted prior to text values, through the broadcast channel. An index of an XML stream consists of a path summary of the XML document. In order to maintain the parent-child relationship of a path summary, each node in an index contains the distance of the next child nodes, meaning the time interval between two nodes. The order for text values is made consistent with the order of group identifiers in an index. Figure 3 presents the structure of an XML stream. Gray boxes represent the index of an XML stream and white boxes represent text values. An XML stream is defined as follows:

Definition 4. An XML stream XS is a data stream of D constructed from a path summary. XS consists of two kinds of group, g_{index} and g_{text}. Both g_{index} and g_{text} contain the following information.

- $g_{index}.id$: current node id. Identifiers are made according to the breadth-first manner from the path summary.
- $g_{index}.name$: current node name.
- $g_{index}.cname[\,]$: array of child nodes.
- $g_{index}.cname[k]$.address : distance to the kth child of current node.
- $g_{index}.text.address$: distance to the text values of current node.
- g_{text} : sequence of text values which arranged according to the order of $g_{index}.id$.

Note that, maintenance of all distances to the text values of the current node is not required. This is because simple XPath queries can be served from the index part, g_{index}, of an XML stream. For example, in Figure 3, each node in g_{index} only maintains the distance to the start and end position of text values.

Algorithm 1 presents the pseudo code used to construct an XML stream. First, a path summary is created, and all label paths of an XML data tree are removed. In order to separate structure information and text values in path summary, temporary storage, denoted as $list$, is used. If an intermediate node in a path summary has text values, they are stored in $list$. Whenever a new node is added to XS, the algorithm checks whether the current node has child elements or text values. If child elements exist, they are added to XS and distances from current node to each child node are recorded. When all element nodes are written to XS, text values in list and distance are added to XS. For example, the specific XML stream shown in Figure 3 is constructed from the path summary in Figure 2, which was derived from the XML data tree in Figure 1. Each node in the stream index has distance to its child elements and text values.

Algorithm 1. An algorithm to build XML stream XS

```
Function buildXMLStream( )
Input XML data tree D
Output XML Stream XS
begin
01: create a path summary P for D
02: for each node in P do /* trace nodes with breadth-first manner */
03:   if current node is a element node then
04:     write current node to XS;
05:     if current node has child elements then
06:       write child elements to XS;
07:       write distances from current node to each child element in XS
08:     else current node has text values then
09:       add the text values to list;
10:     end if
11:   else current node is text values
12:     add the text values to list;
13:   end if
14: end for
15: write text values of list to XS;
16: write distance from each element node to it's text values in XS;
17: return XS
end
```

3.4 Query Processing over an XML Stream

XPath [4] is a standard language for an XML data model. Mobile users can obtain parts of an XML document by describing an XPath expression. In this section, a selective access method for an XML stream is provided on the client side. Algorithm 2 presents the pseudo code to obtain results of user queries from the XML stream.

All nodes in an index maintain the array of child nodes and the distance to the each child node. If the root node of an XML stream is identified as the first label of a simple XPath query, the mobile client can obtain subsequent labels of a simple XPath query from the XML stream. All descendant nodes being irrelevant to the query, can be skipped using the child address in the XML stream, as demonstrated in line 06 and line 13. Thus, the client device can stay in power saving mode until the next child nodes are available in the broadcast channel. In Figure 3, for instance, if a clients query Q_2 is $/dblp/thesis/title/$, the client can identify the distance to the *thesis* node from the *dblp* node. Similarly, the client can identify the distance to the *title* node. From the *title* node, the client can know that the start and the end position of text values of the *title* node.

Algorithm 2. An algorithm to search XML Stream XS

Function readXMLStream( )
Input An XML Stream XS and a simple XPath query Q
Output An answers of query $\mathcal{A}$ satisfy Q
begin
  get the root node xs_{root} from XS;
  if the first node q of Q is same with xs_{root} then
    read xs_{root} from XS and write to $\mathcal{A}$;
    identify distance to the child node of q from xs_{root};
    delete q from Q;
    skip to the next child node;
    while (XS is not the end of stream and Q is not NULL)
      if the first node q of Q same with a current node xs in XS
        read xs from XS and write to $\mathcal{A}$;
        if (child node of q is not NULL) **then**
          identify distance to the child node of q from xs;
          delete q from Q;
          skip to the next child node;
        end if
      end if
    end while
  end if
end

4 Performance Evaluation

The XML streaming method algorithm was evaluated using four real-life XML data sets: XMARK [14], DBLP [11], Shakespeare [6] and SigmodRecord [3]. The data sets were stored on a local disk. The experiments were performed on Pentium III-2.8Ghz platform with MS-Windows XP Professional and 768Mbytes of main memory.

Generally, two kinds of criteria are used for evaluating the performance of wireless broadcasting [5][9]. Access time is the period of time elapsed from the moment a mobile client issuing a query, to the moment when the requested data is received by the client. Tuning time is the period of time spent by a mobile client staying active in order to obtain the requested data. The tuning time is frequently used to estimate the power consumption of a mobile client, since receiving data is power dominant in mobile environments. In this paper, we adopt both access and tuning time to evaluate the proposed scheme.

Our model consists of a single server, which serves multiple clients, one broadcast channel. In our simulation model, We assume broadcast bandwidth is fully utilized for broadcasting. To measure the access/tuning time, we just observe one client, because, in this simulation environment, the activity of a client does not affect the performance of other clients.

The algorithms were implemented to build and search an XML stream in Java programming language. The Apache Xerces parser [1] was used to parse XML data. As in [13], XML data are transmitted and accessed in the unit of buckets whose size is 64KB and the experiment for various simple XPath queries was performed. An answer of each query has redundant label paths in original XML document.

The XML data set and queries are listed in Table 1. The performance metrics are the stream size and the access/tuning time ratio of XML stream relative to the original XML data tree which are same with S-Node. The access and tuning time was measured by the number of buckets. These are defined as follows:

$$Time\ ratio = \frac{Number\ of\ buckets\ to\ read\ XML\ stream}{Number\ of\ buckets\ to\ read\ original\ XML\ data} \tag{1}$$

$$Size\ ratio = \frac{Size\ of\ the\ XML\ stream}{Size\ of\ original\ XML\ data} \tag{2}$$

Table 1. XML Data Set and XPath Queries

XML data	Size(MB)	The queries
XMARK	4.54	Q_1:/site/open_auctions/open_auction/bidder/increase/ Q_2:/site/open_auctions/open_auction/reserves/
DBLP	2.95	Q_3:/dblp/article/author/ Q_4:/dblp/www/editor/
Shakespeare	1.03	Q_5:/plays/play/act/scene/title/ Q_6:/plays/play/act/scene/speech/speaker/
SigmodRecord	0.48	Q_7:/SigmodRecord/issue/articles/article/title/ Q_8:/SigmodRecord/issue/articles/article/authors/author/

Figure 4(a) presents the size ratio of the XML stream to the different XML data sets. On average, the size of XML streams is reduced to 73% of the XML data tree. Since the redundancy of label paths in the XML data tree is removed, the size of an XML document which has a number of equivalent label paths (i.e., SigmodRecord) is reduced more than others. According to the properties of a query and/or a document, the performance of access and tuning time changes. In Figure 4(b), Q_7 and Q_8 require relatively more text values than other queries. If the results of a query are located at the end of an XML stream, access time becomes longer, such as Q_6. However, even in the worst case scenario, tuning time does not exceed access time, as presented in Q_3. The average tuning/access time ratio of an XML stream is 10% and 24% respectively. The performance of the proposed method is compared with S-Node [13] in terms of size ratio and access/tuning time ratio. The same XML data set and XPath queries are used in the S-Node, as presented in Table 2. Since the SwissProt data presents higher regularity in the structure, part of the original SwissProt data is used. The ratio of text values to tags are the same as with the original data.

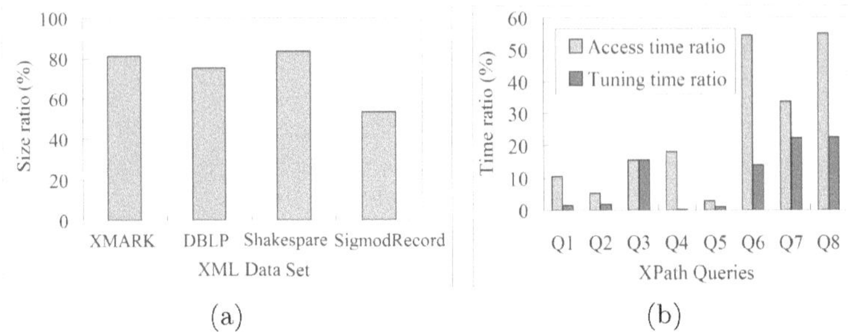

Fig. 4. Performance of proposed method

Table 2. XML Data Set and XPath Queries

XML data	Size(MB)	The queries
Mondial	1.7	Q_9:/mondial/country/province/ Q_{10}:/mondial/country/province/city/name/
SwissProt	9.93	Q_{11}:/root/entry/org/ Q_{12}:/root/entry/features/chain/

As expected, the proposed method is superior to that of S-Node. Since Mondial and SwissProt have high redundancy in terms of the label path, and the size of the XML stream is smaller than that of S-Node. In Figure 5(b), the performance of the access time ratio in Q_9 and Q_{12} significantly outperforms the S-Node. This can be explained as follows: the results of Q_9 and Q_{12} do not contain text values. Therefore, in the proposed method, each label only needs to be read once from the XML stream index. However, the S-Node should skip irrelevant nodes from the streaming data. Thus, the waiting time for receiving each label is longer than the proposed method.

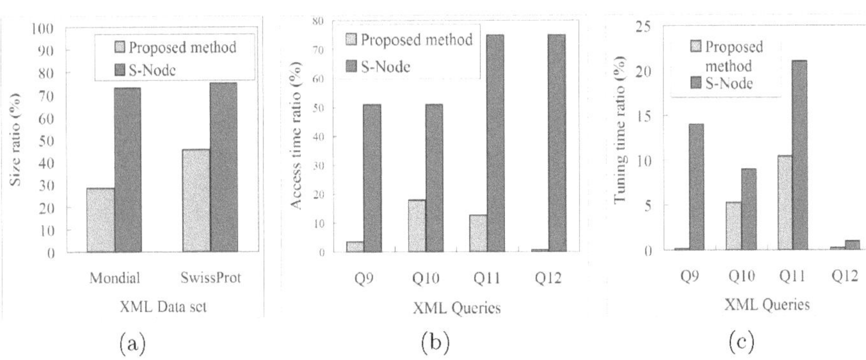

Fig. 5. Performance comparison of proposed method with S-Node

5 Conclusion

In this paper, a novel XML streaming method for wireless broadcasting environments has been proposed. Using the path summary of an XML data tree as an index of an XML stream, mobile clients can retrieve the desired parts of an XML stream through the broadcast channel. Algorithms to build and search the XML stream for simple XPath queries have been provided. The experimental results demonstrate that the proposed algorithms provide superior performance over previous work, with regard to access and tuning time. In the future, the XML data broadcasting method will be extended to support both complex XPath queries. Also, caching techniques in mobile computing will be considered.

References

1. Apache xml project. http://xml.apache.org/.
2. Extensible markup language. http://www.w3.org/XML.
3. Xml data repository. http://www.cs.washington.edu/research/xmldataset/.
4. Xml path language. http://www.w3.org/TR/XPath.
5. S. Acharya, R. Alonso, M. Franklin, and S. Zdonik. Broadcast disks: Data management for asymmetric communication. In *Proceedings of ACM SIGMOD Conference on Management of Data*, pages 199–210, 1995.
6. R. Cover. The xml cover pages. http://www.oasis-open.org/cover/xml.html.
7. E. F. Elisa Bertino. Secure and selective dissemination of xml documents. *ACM Transactions on Information and System Security*, 9(3):290–331, 2002.
8. R. Goldman and J. Widom. Dataguides: Enabling query formulation and optimization in semistructured databases. In *Proceedings of International Conference on Very Large Data Bases*, pages 436–445, 1997.
9. Q. Hu and W.-C. Lee. Hybrid index technique for power efficient data broadcast. *Distributed and Parallel Databases*, 9(2):151–177, 2001.
10. T. Imielinski, S. Viswanathan, and B. Badrinath. Data on air: Organization and access. *IEEE Transactions on Knowledge and Data Engineering*, 9(3):353–372, 1997.
11. M. Ley. Dblp xml records. http://www.informatik.uni-trier.de/~ley/db/.
12. F. J. O. Martinez, J. S. Gonzalez, and I. Stojmenovic. A parallel hill climbing algorithm for pushing dependent data in clients-providers-servers systems. *ACM/Baltzer Journal on Special Topics in Mobile Networks and Applications*, 9(4):257–264, 2004.
13. C.-S. Park, C. S. Kim, and Y. D. Chung. Efficient stream organization for wireless broadcasting of xml data. In *Proceedings of Asian Computing Science Conference*, pages 223–235, 2005.
14. A. Schmidt, F. Waas, M. L. Kersten, M. J. Carey, I. Manolescu, and R. Busse. Xmark: A benchmark for xml data management. In *Proceedings of the International Conference on Very Large Data Bases*, pages 974–985, 2002.
15. E. Y. Wong, A. T. Chan, and H. V. Leong. Xstream: A middleware for streaming xml contents over wireless environments. *IEEE Transactions on Software Engineering*, 30(12):918–935, 2004.
16. Q. Zou, S. Liu, and W. W. Chu. Ctree: A compact tree for indexing xml data. In *Proceedings of ACM International Workshop on Web Information and Data Management*, pages 39–46, 2005.

Formalizing Mappings for OWL Spatiotemporal Ontologies

Nacéra Bennacer

Supélec, Ecole Supérieure d'électricité
F-91192 Gif-Sur-Yvette Cedex, France
Nacera.Bennacer@supelec.fr

Abstract. Ontology mappings provide a common layer which allows distributed applications to share and to exchange semantic information. Providing mechanized ways for mapping ontologies is a challenging issue and main problems to be faced are related to structural and semantic heterogeneity. The complexity of these problems increases in the presence of spatiotemporal information such as geometry and topological intrinsic characteristics. Our proposal is intended for spatiotemporal ontologies and focuses on providing an integrated access to information sources using local ontologies. Our approach is set to build a system that guides users to derive meaningful mappings and to reason about them. To achieve this we use a description logic extended to spatiotemporal concrete domain. The ontology of each source is normalized in a common extended Ontology Web Language (OWL) which enables a natural correspondence with the spatiotemporal description logic formalism.

1 Introduction

Ontologies are today a crucial element for exchange information and sharing knowledge. Ontology mapping provides a common layer for applications to access to them and to exchange information in semantic manner. Ontology mapping is defined as a process relating the concepts of different ontologies sharing the same domain of discourse. It is required to enable a fragment of a more ambitious and complex task. For example in ontology integration, mappings enable to answer queries over a mediated ontology. For ontology alignment, mappings are defined to establish links between ontologies to reuse information from one another. For the migration of ontology instances, mappings enable to populate a target ontology given the extensions of the ontology sources. In ontology merging where the purpose is to build a single merged ontology, mappings are used to answer all the queries that are handled by each ontology source. Ontology mapping is considered by many researchers as similar to mapping conventional databases [1]. Indeed, techniques proposed in the literature for database schema mapping might be of interest to ontology mapping researchers but there are differences which should be considered [2, 3]. A variety of works originating from diverse communities focus on establishing such mappings and investigate various issues of ontology mapping, such as automation of mapping discovery task and mapping representation entailing fields ranging from machine learning, databases

S. Bressan, J. Küng, and R. Wagner (Eds.): DEXA 2006, LNCS 4080, pp. 368 – 378, 2006.

and linguistics (see Section 4). Central to the approaches claiming the automation is the use of heuristics identifying structural, syntactic features and linguistic naming similarities in input ontologies. The absence of structural and naming similarities between ontologies or the lack of common instances makes the automation of matching task difficult and generally based on strong and not realistic hypothesis. Main problems to be faced are related to semantic heterogeneity which is introduced when different modeling constructs and different terminologies are used to represent the same piece of information in different contexts related to information use of the involved ontology sources. This problem is not easy to solve and its complexity increases in the presence of spatiotemporal information as we have to deal with problems such as the granularity used for the representation of spatiotemporal objects. Moreover these objects possess various and complex intrinsic characteristics and are related by topological relations and by hierarchy and aggregation relations. Specifying mappings for those objects requires an appropriate knowledge-representation language preserving their semantics and allowing well-defined semantics for mapping between them. Our proposal focuses on providing an integrated access to spatiotemporal information sources using local ontologies where each one is provided adopting a common language OWL (Ontology Web Language) extended to spatiotemporal features. Our approach relies on a formal representation equipped by a powerful modeling constructs and reasoning capabilities to guide user to capture meaningful and consistent mappings and to reason about them. In particular, we use a description logic extended to spatiotemporal concrete domain $\mathcal{ALCRP}$(**D**) [4].

This paper is structured as follows. Section 2 presents an overview about spatiotemporal description logics. Section 3 presents our approach framework which relies on two formalisms OWL and $\mathcal{ALCRP}$(**D**). We focus in this section on specifying mapping phase and we illustrate it using an example dedicated to the tourism domain. Section 4 presents the related work. In Section 5 we conclude and summarize our work.

2 Spatiotemporal Description Logic Overview

Description Logics (DL) are terminological formalism family equipped with formal logic semantics and designed for representing knowledge and reasoning about it [5]. Elementary descriptions in a DL are atomic concepts, atomic roles, universal concept $\top$ and bottom concept $\bot$. Complex concepts and roles can be built from atomic ones using the considered DL constructors. Standard description logic $\mathcal{ALC}$ provides the following concept constructors: ¬C (negation), C⊓D (conjunction),. ∀R.C (value restriction) and ∃R.C (exists restriction) where C and D are concepts and R is an atomic role. For example a contemporary museum can be defined, using $\mathcal{ALC}$, as a museum which exposes contemporary paintings as follows:

Museum ⊑ TouristSite
ContemporaryMuseum ≡ Museum ⊓ ∃ expose.ContemporaryPainting

Where *TouristSite*, *Museum*, *ContemporaryPainting* are abstracts concepts and *expose* is an abstract role.

The expressiveness of $\mathcal{ALC}$ is insufficient to describe spatiotemporal objects. For representing and reasoning about these objects, spatial DLs are proposed in the

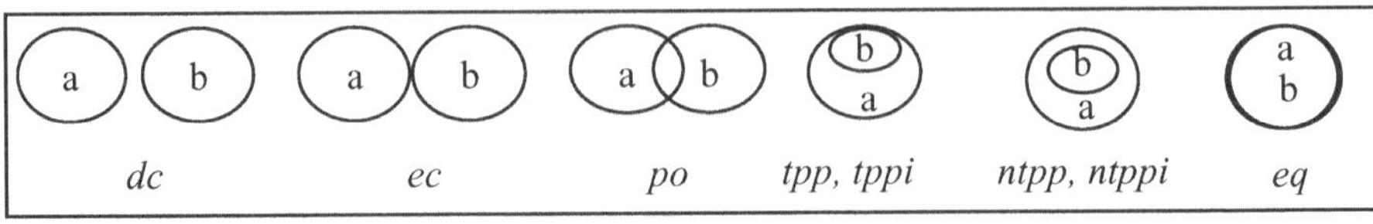

Fig. 1. Topological relationships RCC_8

literature and use qualitative spatial reasoning based on the well-known RCC_8 relations [6]. RCC_8 relations consist of eight exhaustive and mutually exclusive relations describing the relationships between any two regular closed regions in a topological space: *eq* (equal), *dc* (disconnect), *ec* (externally connected), *po* (partial overlap), *tpp* (tangential proper part), *ntpp* (non-tangential proper part) and their respective inverses *tppi* and *ntppi* (see Fig. 1). Using qualitative spatial reasoning derived from the RCC composition tables we can say that two objects are overlapping, disjoint from each other, that one is contained within the other, etc. Extending DLs with concrete domains allows for dealing with data types such as numbers, strings and in particular with specific dimensions of objects such as spatial or temporal features. The DL $\mathcal{ALC}(\mathbf{D})$ [7] divides the set of objects into two disjoint sets, the abstract and the concrete objects. Abstract objects can be related to abstract objects via abstract roles and to concrete objects via concrete roles. The relationships between concrete objects are described with a set of specific domain predicates. The pair consisting of a set of concrete objects and a set of predicates is a concrete domain. Thus, $\mathcal{ALC}(\mathbf{D})$ extends $\mathcal{ALC}$ operators by adding a new concept-forming predicate operator. The $\mathcal{ALCRP}(\mathbf{D})$ DL proposed in [4, 8] extends $\mathcal{ALC}(\mathbf{D})$ to build complex roles based on the role-forming predicate operator. In particular, an appropriate concrete domain $\mathbf{S_2}$ is defined for polygons using RCC_8 relations as basic predicates of concrete domain. Using $\mathcal{ALCRP}(\mathbf{S_2})$ we can define a monument that contains a museum as follows:

area ≡ ∃hasArea.isRegion and Monument ⊑ area
MonumentMuseum1 ≡ Monument ⊓ ∃contains.Museum
contains ≡ ∃ (hasArea)(hasArea).tpp-ntpp

Where the spatial role *contains* is defined using role constructor where *hasArea* is a concrete role in $\mathbf{S_2}$, *isRegion* is a $\mathbf{S_2}$ domain predicate and *tpp-ntpp* is a disjunction of *tpp* and *ntpp* $\mathbf{S_2}$ domain predicates.

For temporal aspect, the concrete domain **T** is a set of time intervals and the 13 Allen relations (*before*, *after*, *meets*, *met-by*, *overlaps*, *overlapped-by*, *during*, *contains*, *starts*, *started-by*, *finishes*, *finished-by*, *equal*) are used as basic predicates describing the relationships between intervals. The combination of $\mathbf{S_2}$ and **T**, $\mathbf{S_2}\oplus\mathbf{T}$, defines a spatiotemporal concrete domain. Thus, we can define using $\mathcal{ALCRP}(\mathbf{S_2} \oplus \mathbf{T})$ a museum that is spatially connected with a monument and their open times are overlapped as follows:

interval ≡ ∃hasDuration.isInterval and Museum ⊑ area ⊓ interval
MonumentMuseum2 ≡ Museum ⊓ ∃ connectOverlap.Monument
connectOverlap≡ ∃(hasArea, hasDuration)(hasArea, hasDuration).connected-overlaps
connected ≡ ∃ (hasArea)(hasArea).ec-po-tpp-tppi-ntpp-ntppi-eq

Where *hasDuration* is a concrete role in **T**, *isInterval* is a **T** domain predicate and connected-overlaps is a $\mathbf{S_2} \oplus \mathbf{T}$ domain predicate.

These descriptions combine not only abstract and concrete objects but also the spatial and temporal concrete domains. This aspect ensures that a reasoning system can be achieved according to the intended semantics of spatiotemporal objects. For our purpose we exploit $\mathcal{ALCRP}$ ($\mathbf{S_2} \oplus \mathbf{T}$) power expressiveness and reasoning services to describe ontology sources and matching between them.

3 Our Approach Framework

Figure 2 illustrates the components of our approach architecture. It is based on OWL domain ontology community which is constituted of a set of different domain ontology sources. The semantics of these ones are normalized to a uniform Ontology Web Language (OWL). The mediated agent encapsulates all necessary information to retrieve instances from different sources corresponding to a query. It provides an integrated access to information sources using semantic mappings between local ontologies and their semantic descriptions. OWL formalism is based on description logics and consequently the transformation into DL preserves naturally the mapping semantics. In particular, to fully describe spatiotemporal aspects, we extend OWL by preserving its natural transformation into $\mathcal{ALCRP}$ ($\mathbf{S_2} \oplus \mathbf{T}$) DL. Once the formalization in $\mathcal{ALCRP}$ ($\mathbf{S_2} \oplus \mathbf{T}$) description logic is provided for each spatiotemporal OWL source ontology representation, the inter-model mappings are established to completely characterize the set of instances of one concept in a model in terms of the set of instances of a concept in another model. This task is distinguished to be incremental, i.e. assertions can be further added to enrich the existing set of mapping assertions. Reasoning component is based on description logic reasoning mechanisms to derive the implicit information and to validate the source ontology descriptions and the mapping assertions between them. In the following we detail our approach using an example dedicated to tourism domain.

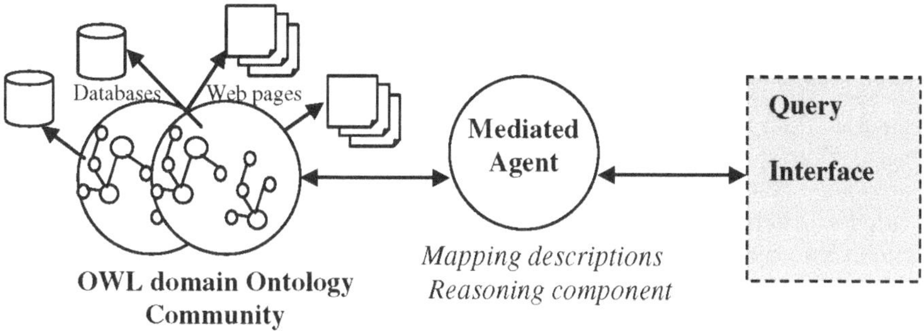

Fig. 2. Our approach architecture

3.1 OWL Formalism Extended to Spatiotemporal Objects

Ontology Web Language (OWL) is an ontology language for the semantic Web; developed by the W3C and layered on top of RDF Schema language. It extends RDFS's capabilities with richer modeling primitives. OWL is based on DLs [5] which offer

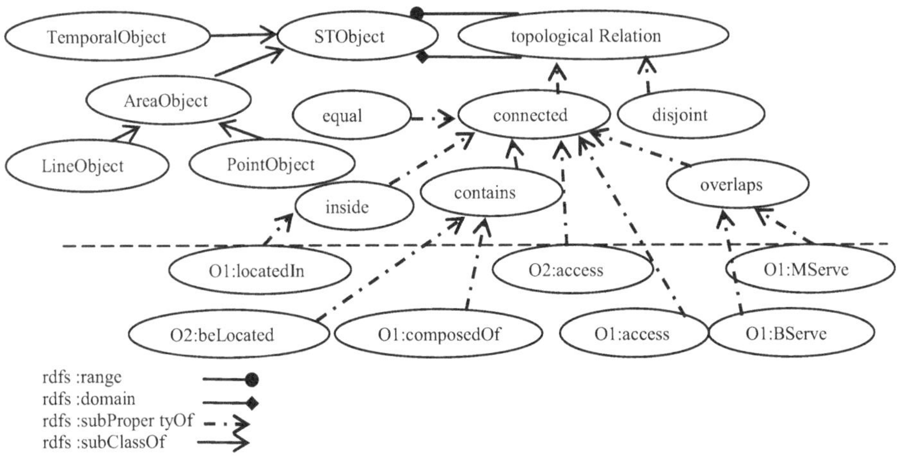

Fig. 3. OWL Extended to Spatiotemporal Objects

formal foundations to define the language semantics, to understand properties such as the complexity of inference problems and to use reasoning algorithms. In the following to illustrate OWL examples, we use RDF graph representation which is more readable than official OWL exchange syntax RDF/XML.

To describe spatiotemporal objects, *TemporalObject* and *AreaObject* classes are defined as subclasses of *STObject* class and *LineObject* and *PointObject* are defined as subclasses of *AreaObject*. These classes are type of *owl:class*. To describe topological relationships, *topologicalRelation* property is defined as type of *owl:ObjectProperty* that links *AreaObject* objects. The topological relations are categorized into two types using *connected* and *disjoint* subproperties. *equal*, *inside*, *contains* and *overlaps* properties are defined as subproperties of *connected* property and hold RCC_8 relation semantics (see Fig. 3). In the same way, temporal relationships based on Allen relations can be defined. Using these owl definitions, complex objects of domain of interest can be represented. For instance in Fig.4, a part of tourism ontology O1 is described; in particular spatiality (polygon, line or point) and temporality (an interval) features may be associated at the class or property definition levels. *TouristySite* concept has both spatiality (subclass of *AreaObject*) and temporality (subclass of *TemporalObject*) characteristics. The topological relation *locatedIn* is defined as a subproperty of *inside* property (see Fig. 3 and 4) to relate *TouristySite* objects (domain of property) to *District* objects (range of property).

3.2 Local Ontology Semantics in $\mathcal{ALCRP}(\mathbf{S_2} \oplus \mathbf{T})$ DL Formalism

In the following we consider the ontologies O1 and O2 depicted respectively in Figures 4 and 5 and we translate them in $\mathcal{ALCRP}(\mathbf{S_2} \oplus \mathbf{T})$ DL. The point and line geometries are considered as a polygon. The new roles *equal*, *contains*, *inside*, *overlaps* and *connected* are defined using role-forming constructor as follows:

equal $\equiv \exists$ (hasArea)(hasArea).*eq*
contains $\equiv \exists$ (hasArea)(hasArea).*tpp-ntpp*

inside ≡ ∃ (hasArea)(hasArea).*tppi-ntppi*
overlaps ≡ ∃ (hasArea)(hasArea).*ec-po*
connected ≡ ∃ (hasArea)(hasArea).*ec-po-tpp-tppi-ntpp-ntppi-eq*

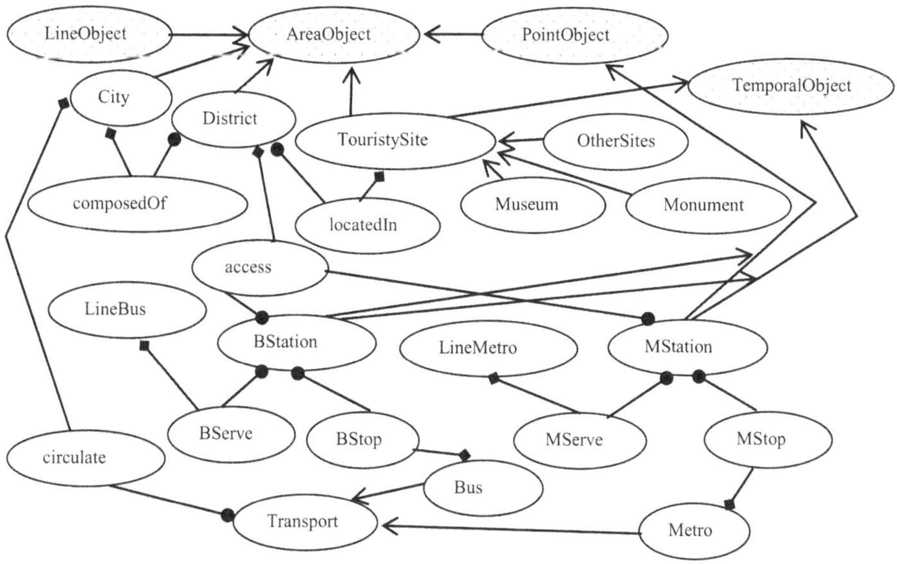

Fig. 4. Part of Ontology 1 in OWL

The formalization in $\mathcal{ALCRP}$ ($\mathbf{S_2} \oplus \mathbf{T}$) defined below focuses on spatiotemporal features. The four first assertions state that the *TouristySite* concept defined in O1 is an area characterized by an interval and covering *Museum*, *Monument* and *OtherSites* concepts which are mutually disjoint and subsumed by *TouristySite* concept. The *city* concept is an area spatially related (*contains*) to *District* concept and related to *Transport* concept by *circulate* role. In the same manner, District concept is an area spatially related to *TouristySite*, *BStation* and *MStation* concepts which are spatially related (*connected*) respectively to *LineBus* and *LineMetro* concepts.

O1:TouristySite ⊑ area ⊓ interval ⊓ (O1:Museum ⊔ O1:Monument ⊔ O1:OtherSites)
O1:Museum ⊑ O1:TouristySite ⊓ ¬ O1:Monument ⊓ ¬ O1:OtherSites
O1:Monument ⊑ O1:TouristySite ⊓ ¬ O1:Museum ⊓ ¬ O1:OtherSites
O1:OtherSites ⊑ O1:TouristySite ⊓ ¬ O1:Monument ⊓ ¬ O1:Museum
O1:City ⊑ area ⊓ ∃contains.O1:District ⊓ ∃ O1:circulate.O1:Transport
O1:District ⊑ area ⊓ ∃contains.O1:TouristySite ⊓ ∃connected.O1:BStation ⊓ ∃connected.O1:MStation
O1:Transport ⊑ O1:Bus ⊔ O1:Metro
O1:Bus ⊑ O1:Transport ⊓ ¬ O1:Metro ⊓ ∃Bstop.O1:BStation
O1:Metro ⊑ O1:Transport ⊓ ¬ O1:Bus ⊓ ∃Mstop.O1:MStation
O1:MStation ⊑ area ⊓ interval ⊓ ∃overlaps.O1:LineMetro
O1:BStation ⊑ area ⊓ interval ⊓ ∃overlaps.O1:LineBus

O1:LineMetro ⊑ area
O1:LineBus ⊑ area
O2:TouristPlace ⊑ area ⊓ interval ⊓ (O2:HistoryCulture ⊔ O2:Shopping ⊔ O2:ParkGarden)
O2:HistoireCulture ⊑ O2:TouristPlace ⊓ ¬ O2:Shopping ⊓ ¬ O2:ParkGarden
O2:ParkGarden ⊑ O2:TouristPlace ⊓ ¬ O2:HistoryCulture ⊓ ¬ O2:Shopping
O2:Shopping ⊑ O2:TouristPlace ⊓ ¬ O2:HistoryCulture ⊓ ¬ O2:ParkGarden
O2:District ⊑ area ⊓ ∃contains.O2:TouristPlace
O2:Center ⊑ area ⊓ ∃connected.O2:District ⊓ ∃connected.O2:TransportStation
O2:TransportStation ⊑ area ⊓ interval

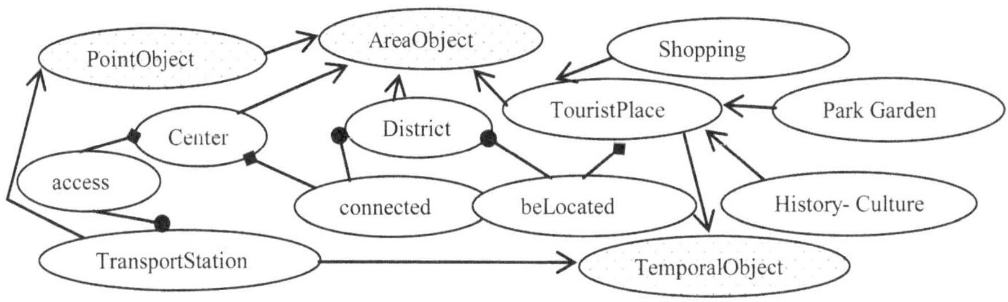

Fig. 5. Part of Ontology 2 in OWL

3.3 Mapping Semantic Specification

Given the two above ontology examples, the user has to define semantic mappings between their respective semantic descriptions. His task consists of firstly establishing similarity relations that exist between selected concepts. This selection may be proposed by the system from syntactic similarities between concept names and the concepts structurally related to them or from common instances of local ontologies. There are mainly three elementary mapping relations:

- Equivalence mapping relations state that two concepts are equivalent or not. Two concepts C1 and C2 are equivalent if the instances described by C1 can be described by C2 and inversely. In DL we test if C1 ≡ C2 assertion is true.
- Subsumption mapping relations state that a concept is subsumed by another concept. The concept C1 subsumes the concept C2 if the instances described by C1 can be described by C2 and the inverse is false. In DL we test if C1 ⊑ C2 assertion is true.
- Overlapping and Disjoint mapping relations state respectively that two concepts C1 and C2 have or not a subset of instances that can be described both by C1 and C2.

In the case of the ontologies O1 and O2, the user states the following subsumption mapping relations:

O2:District ⊑ O1:District
O2:ParkGarden ⊑ O1:OtherSites
O2:Shopping ⊑ O1:OtherSites

The first mapping relation concerns two concepts which have similar names; the user establishes that *District* concept of O2 subsumes *District* concept of O1 by querying the corresponding instances and by using their semantics. In fact, *District* concept is related to *Center* concept in O2 whereas *District* concept is related to *City* concept in O1. The two following relations concern concepts that are sub-concepts of *Tourist-Place* in O2 and *TouristySite* in O1 concepts which have similar names and are related to concepts for which a mapping is defined (*District* in O2 and *District* in O1). The user establishes these relations by querying the corresponding instances and by using their name semantics.

These elementary mapping relations describe only relations between two defined concepts and are insufficient to state the mapping relations between different ontologies describing similar concepts with different degree of detail. For example, the ontology O1 describes the tourist sites and transport means of the city whereas the ontology O2 focuses on describing the tourist sites and the transport located in the center of the city but categorizes more generally than O1 the different sites of tourism.

To describe the intersection between ontologies mapping relations should be defined involving new concepts and properties to relate and to constrain existent concepts and their properties and to enhance the expressive power of such assertions. In the following we emphasize the elementary and complex topological mapping relations. Elementary ones state that two spatial concepts C1 and C2 are related with topological relations. For example, the user can state that the concept *City* defined in O1 is related to the concept *Center* defined in O2 by *contains* topological relation. These two concepts can be selected by the system because they are related to concepts for which a mapping is defined (*District* in O2 and *District* in O1).

$\text{O1:City} \sqsubseteq \exists \text{contains.O2:Center}$

Complex topological mapping relations are needed to refine the above similarity relations to completely characterize and to enrich the relationships between different concept ontology sources. For example, the user can state that metro and bus station described in O1 and located in the center are also described by *TranportStation* concept defined in O2.

$\text{TransportStationCenter} \equiv (\text{O1:BStation} \sqcup \text{O1:MStation}) \sqcap \exists \text{inside.O2:Center}$
$\text{TransportStationCenter} \sqsubseteq \text{O2:TransportStation}$

We can also define museums and monuments located in the center as subconcepts of *HistoryCulture* concept defined in O2.

$\text{O1:Museum} \sqcap \exists \text{inside.O2:Center} \sqsubseteq \text{O2:HistoryCulture}$
$\text{O1:Monument} \sqcap \exists \text{inside.O2:Center} \sqsubseteq \text{O2:HistoryCulture}$

The typical kinds of reasoning services needed in order to support the designer in applying the mapping process is to check the consistency of the mappings and with the ontology sources For example, the reasoning system detect immediately that these assertions are inconsistent:
$\text{O1: Museum} \sqsubseteq \text{O2:HistoryCulture}$
$\text{O1: Monument} \sqsubseteq \text{O2:HistoryCulture}$

Indeed, the concepts *Museum* and *Monumen* of O1 describe respectively museums and monuments of the city while the concept *HistoryCulture* of O2 describes (among others) only those connected spatially to the center.

This specification is incremental the user defines elementary mappings for concepts found by the system by exploiting naming similarities between concepts and concepts related to them or from common instances between concepts found by querying local ontology instances. Typically queries allow the definition of new concepts relating source concepts to establish complex mappings. For example, T*ransportStationCenter* concept defined above is the result of query responding to metro and bus stations located in the center. Thus the user refines and enriches the mappings using complex topological relations. The reasoning component validates or invalidates the added mapping assertions regarding semantic descriptions of ontologies.

4 Related Work

Several works developed for constructing mappings are based on heuristics that identify structural and naming similarities using intentional or extensional descriptions of ontologies. PROMPT and PROMPTDIFF system presented in [9, 10] are based on linguistic similarity for matching concepts. ONION system presented in [11] is based on graph-based technique to define rules for mapping using algebra ontology operators. Its linguistic matcher looks at all pairs of terms from the two ontologies and assigns them a similarity score taking into account that nodes have many attributes in common, classes with common parents, and so on. GLUE system presented in [12] employs machine learning techniques to find mappings. It finds the most similar concepts using probabilistic measures and multiple learners exploiting information in concept instances and taxonomic structure of ontologies. FCA-Merge method defined in [13] for merging ontologies relies on the fact that the source ontologies should have a set of shared instances of the domain and annotated with concepts from source ontologies. Once the instances are extracted, FCA-Merge uses mathematical and natural processing techniques to derive a lattice of concepts relating the concepts from source ontologies. This construction is semi-automatic as it requires background knowledge about the domain. In the MAFRA framework [14], ontologies are described in RDFS representation and a Semantic Bridge Ontology (SBO) component establishes similarities between the source and target ontology entities. Other works are focused on the need of an appropriate formal representation language for well-defined mapping semantics. Mena and *al* [15] developed OBSERVER which helps the users by looking for synonyms, hyponyms and hypernyms defined between terms in source ontologies. Users pose then queries in DL terms using their own ontology then OBSERVER employs mappings to pose queries to source ontologies. In [16] a formal framework to merge a global ontology is defined. Ontology sources are expressed in DL, and mappings between them are expressed through suitable mechanisms based on queries. Two approaches are proposed, in the first one, the concepts of the global ontology are mapped into queries over the local ones. In contrast, the second approach requires reformulation of the concepts of the local ontologies in terms of the queries to the global ontology. In [17] a framework is defined for specifying mappings and their associated semantics. It enables mapping between models in different representation languages such as DAML+OIL, RDF and relational models without translating the models into a common language using a helper model.

5 Conclusion

Specifying mapping assertions is a crucial and difficult task all the more so that we have to deal not only with syntactic, structural and semantic heterogeneity but also with the inherent complexity of spatiotemporal objects. Our approach aims at providing an integrated access to spatiotemporal information sources using local ontologies where each one is provided adopting a common language OWL (Ontology Web Language) extended to spatiotemporal features. It exploits $\mathcal{ALCRP}(\mathbf{S_2} \oplus \mathbf{T})$ power expressiveness for mapping and reasoning services to detect both inconsistencies and implicit information in ontology mappings. It provides a support to reduce the effort required by a user to inspect the input ontologies, to understand the associated semantics, to capture and to establish incrementally meaningful mappings between ontology sources. The user defines elementary mappings found by the system using naming concept similarities or from common instances between concepts found by queries. Thus he refines and enriches the mappings. The reasoning component validates or invalidates the added mapping assertions regarding semantic descriptions of ontologies. Our approach carries a great flexibility and ensures a preservation of spatiotemporal semantics.

References

1. Rahm, A. and Bernstein, A., 2001. A survey of approaches to automatic schema matching. *The Very Large Database Journal*. 10(4) 334-350.
2. Kalfoglou, Y. and Schorlemmer, M., 2003. Ontology mapping: the state of the art. *The Knowledge Engineering Review*. 18(1) 1-31. Cambridge University Press.
3. Noy, NF. and Klein, M., 2002. Ontology evolution: not the same as schema evolution. *Knowledge and Information Systems*.
4. Haarslev, V., Lutz, C., Möller, R., 1999. A Description Logic with Concrete Domains and a Role-forming Predicate Operator. *Journal of Logic and Computation*. 9(3).
5. Baader, F., Horrocks, I., Sattler, U., 2003. Description logics as ontology languages for the semantic web. *Lecture Notes in Artificial Intelligence*. Springer.
6. Cohn, A.G., Hazarika, S. M., 2001. Qualitative Spatial Representation and Reasoning: an Overview. *Fundamenta Informaticae*, 46(1-2), 1-29.
7. Baader, F., Hanschke, P., 1991. A scheme for integrating concrete domains into concept languages. I*n proceedings of the Twelfth International Joint Conference on Artificial Intelligence (IJCAI)*. 452-457.
8. Lutz, C., 2003. Description Logics with Concrete Domains - A Survey. *In Advances in Modal Logics.*,4. King's College Publications.
9. Noy, N. and Musen, M., 2000. PROMPT: algorithm and tool for automated ontology merging and alignment. *Proceedings of the 17th National Conference on Artificial Intelligence (AAAI)*.
10. Noy, NF. and Musen, M., 2002. PROMPTDIFF: a fixed-point algorithm for comparing ontology versions. *Proceedings of the 18th National Conference on Artificial Intelligence (AAAI)*.
11. Mitra, P. and Wiederhold, G., 2002. Resolving terminological heterogeneity in ontologies. *Proceedings of the ECAI workshop on Ontologies and Semantic Interoperability*.
12. Doan, A., Madhavan, J., Domingos, P. and Halevy, A., 2002. Learning to map between ontologies on the semantic web. *Proceedings of the 11th International World Wide Web Conference (WWW)*.

13. Stumme, G., and Maedche, A., 2001. Ontology merging for federated ontologies on the semantic web. *Proceedings of the International Workshop for Foundations of Models for Information Integration (FMII).*
14. Maedche, A., Motik, B., Silva, N., Volz, R., 2002. MAFRA - A Mapping Framework for Distributed Ontologies. *Proceedings of the European Conference on Knowledge Acquisition and Management (EKAW).* Springer.
15. Mena, E., Kashyap,V., Illarramendi, A. and Sheth, A., 1998. Domain Specific Ontologies for Semantic Information Brokering on the Global Information Infrastructure. *Proceedings of the 1st International Conference on Formal Ontology in Information Systems(FOIS'98).*
16. Calvanese D., De Giacomo G., and Lenzerini M. "A Framework for Ontology Integration" In proceedings of International Semantic Web Working Symposium (SWWS 2001), pages 301-316, 2001.
17. Madhavan, J, Bernstein, PA, Domingos, P and Halevy, A, 2002, "Representing and reasoning about mappings between domain models" Proceedings of the 18th National Conference on Artificial Intelligence (AAAI'02).

Multi-term Web Query Expansion Using WordNet

Zhiguo Gong, Chan Wa Cheang, and Leong Hou U

Faculty of Science and Technology
University of Macau
Macao, PRC
{zggong, ma36600, ma36575}@umac.mo

Abstract. In this paper, we propose a method for multi-term query expansions based on WordNet. In our approach, *Hypernym/Hyponymy* and *Synonym* relations in WordNet is used as the basic expansion rules. Then we use WordNet Lexical Chains and WordNet semantic similarity to assign terms in the same query into different groups with respect to their semantic similarities. For each group, we expand the highest terms in the WordNet hierarchies with *Hypernym* and *Synonym*, the lowest terms with Hyponym and Synonym, and all other terms with only Synonym. Furthermore, we use collection related term semantic network to remove the low-frequency and unusual words in the expansions. And our experiment reveals that our solution for query expansion can improve the query performance dramatically.

1 Introduction

One challenging issue, among others, in information retrieval is the problem caused by word mismatch. That is, the query words may not rightly be contained in the document even though their semantics are highly relevant to the user's need. Evidently, if the word mismatch problem is not appropriately addressed by information retrieval systems, it could degrade their retrieval performance greatly. To deal with this problem, query expansion is one of the promising approaches. Typical methods include *Lexical-Based* [13, 14, 15], *Statistical-Based* [16,17,18], *Query-Log-Based* [19], and *Web Link-Based* [20].

Lexical-Based method utilizes some manually created lexical thesaurus for the expansion. For any term in the query, a list of semantic relevant terms is selected from the thesaurus and then used for the expansion. In such method, the thesaurus used is often collection independent, thus may not catch the dynamic change of the vocabulary used in the collection. Therefore, the effectiveness of such method is often not as expected in practice.

Statistical-Based solutions, on the other hand, describe word relations using their co-occurrences in the collection. Actually, term co-occurrences can be globally extracted in the scope of whole collection (Global Expansion) or locally obtained from the results of initial query (Local Expansion). With these methods, a term is selected for expansion if it has higher degree of co-occurrences with the query terms. The effectiveness of such kind of methods is dependant on the collection. If the size of collection is not huge enough, it may not well capture the relations between terms.

S. Bressan, J. Küng, and R. Wagner (Eds.): DEXA 2006, LNCS 4080, pp. 379 – 388, 2006.

Another problem lies in the fact that term relations captured are only pair based, without a semantic architecture among all the expanded terms. Therefore, it is hard to control the mutual impairing caused by multiple terms in the query.

Query-Log-Based expansion methodologies describe term-term relations by introducing users' click-though activities. In other words, term t_2 can be used to expand query term t_1 if, historically, many users, who query term t_1, have clicked documents which contain t_2 in the results. In general, users' click-through activities are captured in the system logs. As a matter of the fact, users click-though information can only be considered as implicit indicators for the term relations. That is, a user may click a result document just because he is motivated by any other reasons than relevant. As the result, it may provide poor performance if less people previously query the words. This is common especially when the system is just created.

Web Link-Based solutions expand Web queries with a thesaurus which is constructed by using links of the Web. To create the thesaurus, Web pages as the training set are selected manually. And the semantic of a target Web page of a link is represented as the words or concepts appearing in the anchor texts in the source page of the link. Then the semantic relations among the words or concepts are derived using the links.

The method in this paper belongs to the first type. However, we have two important improvements in the expansion: (1) clustering all terms of a query into different groups by their semantic similarities, then expanding each group by taking into account their positions in WordNet [6]; (2) reducing noise terms in the expansion by term co-occurrences supported by the collection.

In our approach, *Hypernym/Hyponymy* and *Synonym* relations in WordNet is used as the basic expansion rules. Then we use WordNet Lexical Chains and WordNet semantic similarity to assign terms in the same query into different groups with respect to their semantic similarities. For each group, we expand the highest terms in the WordNet hierarchies with *Hypernym* and *Synonym*, the lowest terms with Hyponym and Synonym, and all other terms with only Synonym. In this way, contradictory caused by full expansion can be well controlled. Furthermore, we use collection related term semantic network to remove the low-frequency and unusual words in the expansions. And our experiment reveals that our solution for query expansion can improve the query performance dramatically.

In reminder of this paper, section 2 provides our detail methodologies for query expansion with WordNet::Similarity and reduction using *TSN*. The experiment results are illustrated and discussed in section 3. Finally, we conclude our work in section 4.

2 Expansion Method

In this section, after a brief introduction of our previous work for single word query expansions, we address our multi-term query expansion methodologies in detail.

2.1 Single Term Query Expansion

In [7], we have addressed our solutions for single word query expansions using WordNet and TSN (Term Semantic Network). WordNet organizes words or concepts lexically into hierarchies. Figure 1 is a typical example in which term 'Software' can be semantically expanded along three chains, say, Hypernym (i.e. 'code'), Hyponym (i.e. 'program', 'freeware', 'shareware', 'upgrade', 'groupware') and Synonym (i.e. 'software system', 'software package', 'package'). Actually, Hypernym is the abstractive concepts of the term while Hyponym, reversely, includes specific concepts of the terms. And Synonym contains all the synonyms of the term. However, their impacts for the expansion are different in letter of retrieval performance.

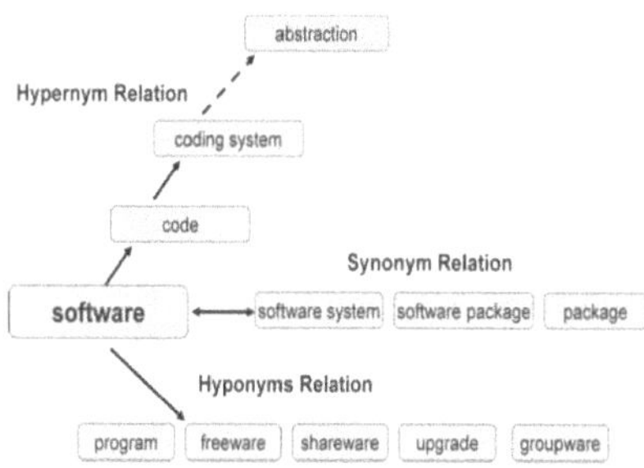

Fig. 1. An Example for WordNet

According to our experiments in previous research, WordNet may bring many noises for the expansion because of its collection independent characteristic. And it may not catch current state of words and their relationships since the explosive increase of the Web. To overcome those problems, collection-related *TSN* (Term Semantic Network) is created with respect to word co-occurrence in the collection. We use *TSN* both as a filter and a supplement for WordNet.

For any term t, let $Hyper_t$, $Hypo_t$, Syn_t and TSN_t stand for the concept sets of its Hypernym, Hyponym, Synonym, and Top-k of TSN respectively. Let $R(p|q)$ be the rank of Web page p with respect to query q. Ranking model *tf* or *tf*idf* is popularly employed in the information retrieval world because of its robustness and simplicity [8]. And in our Web image search system, we modify model *tf* into model *ttf* by incorporating term t's locations in p with respect to the corresponding Web image [5, 11]. For any single word query t, we define its expanded rank function $ER(p|t)$ as

$$ER(p\mid t)=R(p\mid t)+\alpha\cdot\sum_{z\in Hyper_t}R(p\mid z)+\beta\cdot\sum_{z\in Hypo_t}R(p\mid z)+\gamma\cdot\sum_{z\in Syn_t}R(p\mid z)+\delta\cdot\sum_{z\in TSN_t}R(p\mid z) \quad (1)$$

where α, β, γ and δ are factors used to indicate different effects from different expansion directions. In our work, we suppose the expansion along each dimension is independent. And we use Average Precision (*AP*) of the retrieval as the objective function in determining the optimal values of those factors which can maximize *AP* value. Table 1 shows the optimal factor values with their corresponding *AP* values in our Web image retrieval system [7].

Table 1. Factor Values and Average Precision

Factor	*Values*	*Average Precision*
α (Hypernyms)	0.47	0.2406
β (Hyponyms)	0.84	0.3888
γ (Synonyms)	0.70	0.3404
δ (Top-k of TSN)	0.94	0.3559

In Web image retrieval system [7], we combined the query expansions along each semantic dimension as our overall solution. Our experiments reveal that the combined expansion can provide a satisfied result for the Web query performance. However, previous method ignored the mutual affections among the terms in the same query.

2.2 Multi-term Query Expansion

Even though most of Web users search the Web with only one word, we still find many queries with multiple terms. For example, a user uses a pair words (computer, speaker) as one query to search Web images. Our previous expansion method will automatically expand these two words with three semantic relations independently. As a result, the expanded query will contain too many words which may include many noise words, thus, reduce the precision of the query results. For example, a Web user may use *q*=(software, groupware) as the query. With single word expansions, query *q* will be expanded to include all the words or concepts from both 'software' and 'groupware's WordNet expansions. However, as in figure 1, 'groupware' is in the Hyponym of 'software'. The user, who uses 'groupware' to combine 'software', implicitly wants to exclude other words in the Hyponym of 'software' for the query. Therefore, the overall expansions of these two words may bring many words which contradict to the user's query intention.

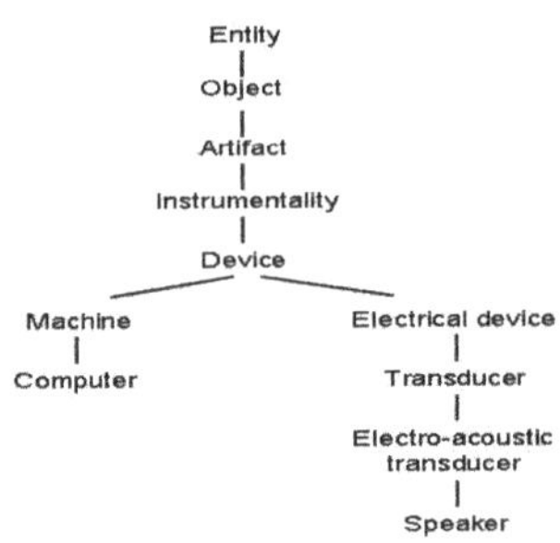

Fig. 2. Group Terms in the WordNet

Figure 2 shows another situation, in which "computer" and "speaker" have the closest super-ordinate class "device" along the WordNet chains. Even though 'speaker' is not in the direct Hyponym of 'computer', it is sill located in the lower level with respect to 'computer' in the WordNet hierarchies. Therefore, we also suppose 'speaker' is a restraint for 'computer' in Hyponym expansions of 'computer'. Reversely, 'computer' is taken as the constraint of 'speaker's Hypernym expansions.

In this work, we use Jian-Conrath [4] to measure the distances of two words in WordNet. In fact, this measure method combines WordNet lexical taxonomy structure with corpus statistical information such that the semantic distances between nodes in the semantic space constructed by the taxonomy can be better quantified with the computational evidence derived from a distributional analysis of corpus data.

Jian-Conrath approach uses the notion of information content, but in the form of the conditional probability of encountering an instance of a child-synset given an instance of a parent-synset. Thus the information content of the two nodes, as well as that of their most specific subsumer, is taken into account in the measure calculations. Notice that this formula measures semantic distance in the inverse of similarity as:

$$Dist(c_1, c_2) = 2\log(p(lso(c_1, c_2))) - (\log(p(c_1)) + \log(p(c_2)) \qquad (2)$$

where c_1 and c_2 are synsets, $p(c)$ is the probability of encountering an instance of a synset c in some specific corpus, $lso(c_1, c_2)$ is the similarity between two concepts lexicalized in WordNet to be the information content of their lowest super-ordinate (most specific common subsumer). Therefore, we could use this approach to measure the semantic strength between tow words.

The larger the $Dist(t_1, t_2)$ is, the farer term t_1 to term t_2 is in the WordNet hierarchies. In case $t_1 > t_2$ (t_1 is located in a higher level than t_2 in WordNet), we do not expand Hyponym for t_1 and Hypernym for t_2 as the reason we discussed previously. Going back for our last example, we only expand "computer" with Hypernym and Synonym relations, and "speaker" with Hyponym and Synonym relations. In fact, we will assign terms in the same query q into groups. Within each group, terms are clustered with respect to $Dist(t1,t2)$, and we expand Synonym for all terms and Hypernym only for the words on the highest level in the WordNet hierarchies, and Hyponym only for the words on the lowest level of WordNet hierarchies. Figure 3 provide our detail expansion algorithm.

STEP 1: Trace the corresponding super-ordinate concept C in WordNet Lexical Chain of original query terms Q: $\{t_1, t_2 \ldots t_n\}$
If t_i have identical concept C then put the t_i in expand group EG
Else expand t_i with WordNet three semantic relations and add in our expand query Q_E

STEP 2: Find the distance D_i between t_i and concept C

STEP 3: Calculate the similarity measure S_{ij} between terms t_i and t_j with Jian-Conrath method
If S_{ij} is less than similarity factor S_f then
    If check that terms t_i exist that S_{ik} greater than S_f then go to step 4
    Else remove t_i in EG and expand it with three semantic relations and add in Q_E
    If check that terms t_j exist that S_{jk} greater than S_f then go to step 4
    Else remove t_j in EG and expand it with three semantic relations and add in Q_E
Else go to step 4

STEP 4: Get the terms t_i has the lowest D_i, then expand it hypernym and synonym relations
Get the terms t_j has the highest D_j, then expand it hyponym and synonym relations
Other terms in EG expand it with synonym relation in WordNet
Join all these expand words in Q_E

STEP 5: Use Q_E as the new search query

Fig. 3. Algorithm of our expand method

Below we use some examples as illustrations for the algorithm. Let q=('Macau', 'camera', 'photo') be a three-term query. Our expansion algorithm divides them into two groups by checking their similarities. One group contains the word "Macau", another one contains "camera" and "photo". According to the similarity measure, "Macau" does not have similarity relation with other two words. Therefore, in this example, we expand 'Macau' via three WordNet chains. In the second group, "camera" and "photo" have a high degree in similarity and they are under the same concept in WordNet hierarchies, with 'camera' > 'photo'. So the system expands "camera" through hypernym and synonym relations and "photo" through hyponym and synonym relations (Figure 4).

Figure 5 provides another example, where query q=('movie', 'camera', 'character'). By tracing them in WordNet, these three words are under the same concept and with close similarity values mutually. Thus, our algorithm keeps them in one group, with WordNet hierarchal levels like 'movie'>'camera'> 'character'. In this case, the algorithm only expands "movie" with hypernym and synonym relations because of its highest WordNet hierarchical level within the group, and "character" is expanded in hyponym and synonym relations due to its lowest level within the group. The word "camera" is only expanded in synonym relation because its location in WordNet is between "movie" and "character".

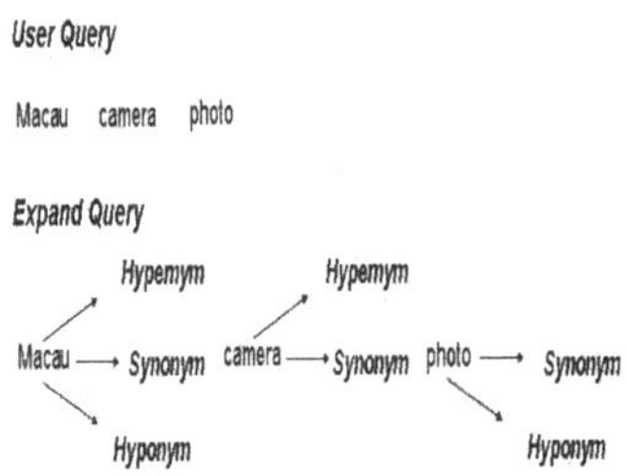

Fig. 4. Query expansion with two relative terms

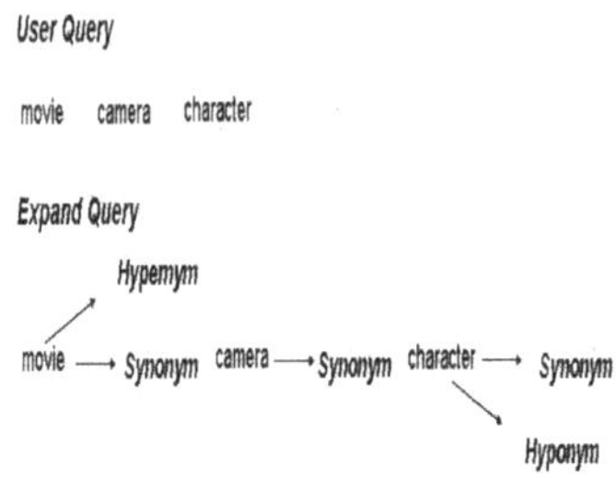

Fig. 5. Query expansion with three relative terms

2.3 Similarity Threshold for Grouping Words

As in our discussions of last section, term grouping in a multi-term query is a critical step in our expansion algorithm. In this section, we are going to determine the optimal similarity threshold for grouping terms in the query.

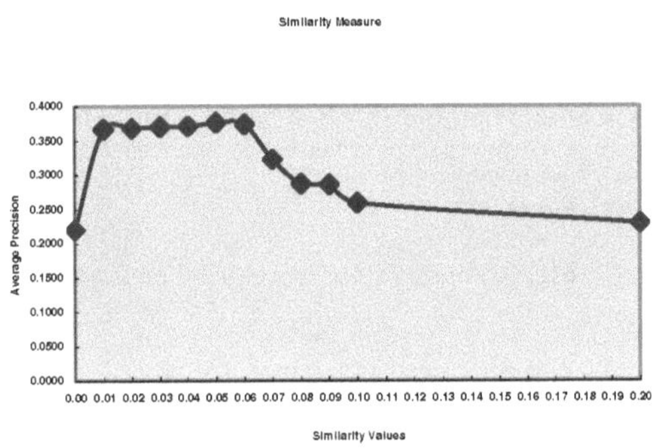

Fig. 6. Average precision versus Similarity Values

To determine the threshold value for term grouping, we select *AP* (average precision) as the objective function [8,9]. In other words, the optimal value for the similarity threshold should maximize *AP* values of retrievals. In this work, we use 40 single-word queries, 40 two-word queries, 20 three-word queries, 10 four-word queries and 10 five-words as our sample queries. And we select about 60% of them as our training set for the threshold determination. In the same query, if the similarity of two terms is over the threshold (*UD*) we assign them in the same group. Figure 6 is the performance of average precision via similarity threshold (*UD*). From this figures, it is obvious that the retrieval performance reaches its maximum when threshold *UD* is at 0.05. As a matter of the fact, in our sample data there are no pair of words whose similarity is greater than 0.2, so we ignore the figure plot when similarity range are between 0.2 to 1. Furthermore, we could find the retrieval performance drops down dramatically when the value is over 0.05.

2.4 Query Reduction

In general, query expansion using a thesaurus may be expanded to include too many words. And some of them are low-frequency and unusual words in the collection. Those unusual words may bring in some noise and decrease retrieval performances. Therefore, it is important to exclude noise words during query expanding. In our system, a term semantic network (*TSN*) is extracted from the collection. Actually, *TSN* is a direct graph with words as its nodes and the associations as the edges between two words.

To extract TSN from the collection, we use a popular association mining algorithm – Apriori [12] — to mine out the association rules between words. Here, we only consider one-to-one term relationship. Two functions—*confidence* and *support*— are used in describing word relations. We define *confidence* (*conf*) and *support* (*sup*) of term association $t_i \rightarrow t_j$ as follows, let

$$D(t_i, t_j) = D(t_i) \cap D(t_j) \tag{3}$$

where $D(t_i)$ and $D(t_j)$ stand for the documents including term t_i and t_i respectively. Therefore, $D(t_i) \cap D(t_j)$ is the set of documents that include both t_i and t_j. We define

$$Conf_{ti->tj} = \frac{\| D(t_i, t_j) \|}{\| D(t_i) \|} \tag{4}$$

where $\| D(t_i, t_j) \|$ stands for the total number of documents that include both term t_i, and t_j; and $\| D(t_i) \|$ stands for the total number of documents that include t_i ,

$$Sup_{ti->tj} = \frac{\| D(t_i, t_j) \|}{\|D\|} \tag{5}$$

where $\|D\|$ stands for the number of document in the database.

Fig. 7. Keyword filtering process of word "robot"

In this paper, we only remain the expanded words which have minimum confidence over 0.1 and support over 0.01 with the original query keyword into our query expansion. As the keyword "robot" in Fig 7, we filter out the words "golem, humanoid, mechanical man".

3 Evaluation

The crawler of our system gathered about 150,000 Web pages with a given set of seeds which are randomly selected from dot-com, dot-edu and dot-gov domains. After the noise images (icons, banners, logos, and any image with size less than 5k) removed by the image extractor, about 12,000 web images embedded in the Web pages are left. In order to calculate the precision/recall value, our system needs domain experts to annotate the sample Web images with their semantics. Our system provides a user-friendly interface, to let the experts define the corresponded meanings for each image easily by using the mouse [5]. Then the human experts are assigned to define the subjects of the Web images manually. And sometimes, more than one subject is defined for the same images. For example, concepts 'Laptop', 'Notebook' and 'Computer' may be annotated to the same Web image.

As in Figure 9, we have used different expansion method in our experiment in order to compare their performances. In the evaluation, we use the remaining 40% of the sample queries as the testing queries. Below are the descriptions for different expansion models:

No Expand – use original queries in the testing, without any expansion.
All Expand – use WordNet three semantic relations (Hypernym, Hyponyms, Synonym) to expand original queries fully, without word grouping.
UD_Expand – we treat all terms in the same query as one group without concerning their similarities, and only expand the highest level terms with hypernym and synonym relations and the lowest level terms with hyponym and synonym relations. Other terms only expand its synonym relation.
UD~0.05 – Group terms with the similarity threshold as 0.05 in the same query. In each group, we expand the highest terms with hypernym and synonym and lowest terms with hyponym and synonym, all others with only synonyms.
Reduction – This model is UD~*0.05* + *Term Reduction*. We use *UD~0.05* for term expansion, and remove noise words using *TSN*.

As revealed in Figure 8, even though *ALL_EXPAND* can improve recalls of queries a little bit, however, its retrieval precision is the lowest among all the models. The reason is due to the fact that, besides the noise words, there are too many words included in the expansion, and some of them are contradictory with each other. *UD_EXPAND* model has improved both precision and recall comparing with *NO_EXPAND* model. It impose some constraint on the expansion scope, thus reduce some contradictories among words in contrast to *ALL_EXPAND* method. *UD~0.05* model produce a quite good performance comparing with both *ALL_EXPAND* and *UD_EXPAND* models. That means grouping terms with similarity threshold UD=0.05 is both critical and necessary in improving the retrieval performances. This model can effectively reduce the contradictories among words when expanding the queries. This model overcomes the weaknesses of two extremes *–ALL_EXPAND* and *UD_EXPAND*. Finally, *REDUCTION* model is the best in term of retrieval performances among all those models. As we know, it enhances *UD~0.05* by further removing words which have lower associations with the words in the original query which may disturb the searching.

Through our discussions above, we can conclude that query expansions with WordNet yield significant increases in the number of correct documents retrieved and in the number of answerable queries, and query expansions followed by reduction makes even more substantial improvements.

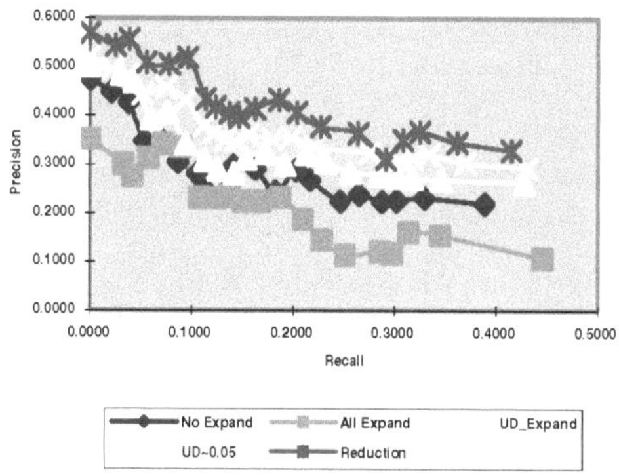

Fig. 8. Performance of Multi-term Query Expansion method

4 Conclusions

In this paper, we propose a method for multi-term query expansions. We use WordNet noun hypernym/hyponymy and synonym relations between words as the base expansion dimensions. In our approach, we divide terms in the same query into groups with respect to semantic similarities between terms. Within each group, the terms are closely related in semantics. We determine expansion dimensions for each word in the same group by their relative positions in the WordNet hicrarchies. We only expand the top words with Hypernym and Synonym, the bottom words with Hyponym and Synonym, all other words with only Synonyms. By this way, the contradictories among words in the expansions can be well controlled, thus retrieval performances can be improved. Furthermore, in order to avoid noise words in the expansions, we apply term co-occurrence information further to remove unusual words during query expansion processing.

References

1. Ted Pedersem, Siddharth Patwardhan and Jason Michelizzi, *WordNet::Similarity – Measuring the Relatedness of Concept*, In Proc. of Fifth Annual Meeting of the North American Chapter of the ACL (NACCL-04), Boston, MA, 2004.
2. WordNet::Similarity, http://search.cpan.org/dist/WordNet-Similarity/
3. Alexander Budanitsky and Graeme Hirst, *Semantic distance in WordNet: An experimental, application-oriented evaluation of five measures*, In NAACL Workshop on WordNet and Other Lexical Resources, 2001.
4. Jay J. Jiang and David W. Conrath, *Semantic Similarity Based on Corpus Statistics and Lexical Taxonomy*, In the Proceedings of ROCLING X, Taiwan, 1997

5. Zhiguo Gong, Chan Wa Cheang, Leong Hou U, *Web Query Expansion by WordNet*, DEXA 2005
6. Miller, G. A., Beckwith, R., Felbaum, C., Gross, D., and Miller, K., *Introduction to WordNet: An On-line Lexicala Database,* Revised Version 1993.
7. Zhiguo Gong, Leong Hou U and Chan Wa Cheang, *An Implementation of Web Image Search Engine*, Digital Libraries: International Collaboration and Cross-Fertilization: 7th International Conference on Asian Digital Libraries, ICADL 2004, Shanghai, China, December 13-17, 2004. Proceedings Pages:355 – 367
8. R. Baeza-Yates and B. Ribeiro-Neto, *Modern Information Retrieval,* Addison Wesley, 1999
9. R. K. Sriari, Z. Zhang and A. Rao, *Intelligent indexing and semantic retrieval of multimodal documents*, Information Retrieval 2(2), Kluwer Academic Publishers, 2000, pp. 1-37.
10. Hang Cui, Ji-Rong Wen, Jian-Yun Nie, Wei-Ying Ma, *Query Expansion by Mining User Logs*, IEEE Transactions on Knowledge and Data Engineering, Vol. 15, No. 4, July/August 2003, pp. 829-839
11. Zhiguo Gong, Leong Hou U and Chan Wa Cheang, Text-Based Semantic Extractions of Web Images, To appear in Knowledge and Information Systems: An International Journal, Springer.
12. R. Agrawaland R. Srikant, "Fast Algorithms for Mining Association Rules," *Proc. 20th Int'l Conf. Very Large Data Bases, (VLDB)*, Sept. 1994.
13. E. M. Voorhees, Query Expansion using Lexical-Semantic Relations. In Proceedings of the 17th ACM-SIGIR Conference, pp. 61-69, 1994.
14. A.F. Smeaton and C. Berrut. Thresholding postings lists, query expansion by word-worddistance and POS tagging of Spanish text. In Proceedings of the 4th Text Retrieval Conference, 1996.
15. Oh-Woog Kwon, Myoung-Cheol Kim, Key-Sun Choi. Query Expansion Using Domain-Adapted Thesaurus in an Extended Boolean Model. In Proceedings of ACM CIKM'94. pp. 140-146.
16. Yonggang Qiu and H.P. Frei. Concept Based Query Expansion. In Proceedings of ACM-SIGIR'93. pp. 160-169.
17. Jinxi Xu and W. B Croft. Improving the Effectiveness of Information Retrieval with Local Context Analysis. ACM Transactions on Information Systems, Vol. 18, No. 1, January 2000, pp. 79-112.
18. Jing Bai, Dawei Song, Peter Bruza, Jian-yun Nie, and Guihong Cao. Query Expansion Using Term Relationships in Language Models for Information Retrieval. In Proceedings of ACM CIKM'05, pp. 688-695.
19. B. Billerbeck, F. Scholer, H.E. Williams, and J. Zobel. Query Expansion Using Associated Queries. In Proceedings of ACM CIKM'03, pp. 2-9.
20. Z. Chen, S. Liu, W. Liu, A. Pu, and W. Ma. Building a Web Thesaurus from Web Link Structure. In Proceedings of ACM SIGIR'03, pp. 48-55.

Fast Computation of Database Operations Using Content-Addressable Memories

Nagender Bandi, Divyakant Agrawal, and Amr El Abbadi

Computer Science
University of California at Santa Barbara
{nagender, agrawal, amr}@cs.ucsb.edu

Abstract. Research efforts on conventional CPU architectures over the past decade have focused primarily on performance enhancement. In contrast, the NPU (Network Processing Unit) architectures have evolved significantly in terms of functionality. The memory hierarchy of a typical network router features a Content-Addressable Memory (CAM) which provides very fast constant-time lookups over large amounts of data and facilitates a wide range of novel high-speed networking solutions such as Packet Classification, Intrusion Detection and Pattern Matching. While these networking applications span an entirely different domain than the database applications, they share a common operation of searching for a particular data entry among huge amounts of data. In this paper, we investigate how CAM-based technology can help in addressing the existing memory hierarchy bottlenecks in database operations. We present several high-speed CAM-based solutions for computationally intensive database operations. In particular, we discuss an efficient linear-time complexity CAM-based sorting algorithm and apply it to develop a fast solution for complex join operations widely used in database applications.

1 Introduction

CPU speed has been increasing at a much faster pace than memory access speed over the past decades. Therefore, memory access has become a performance bottleneck for many applications. To overcome this bottleneck, fast memories called caches have been integrated into the memory hierarchy between the CPU and main memory. Recent research on DBMS performance [1,2], however, demonstrates that typical database applications suffer from poor cache performance. Caches exploit the principle of temporal and spatial locality by caching data that has recently been accessed and by prefetching blocks of data. Since many database applications have poor data locality, prefetching often pollutes precious cache space with irrelevant data. As a consequence, changes in data layout [3] and cache-conscious algorithms [2,4] have been proposed. Experimental results show that cache performance can be improved by applying these techniques. However, the gap between CPU speed and memory access speed continues to widen every year. Therefore we postulate a change at the hardware level in addition to the existing software techniques.

S. Bressan, J. Küng, and R. Wagner (Eds.): DEXA 2006, LNCS 4080, pp. 389–398, 2006.

While the memory hierarchy architecture of a conventional CPU has not changed significantly over the past decade, the changes are very evident in the case of network router architectures. Network Processing Units (NPUs), which form the core of a network router, now interface with a Ternary Content Addressable Memory (TCAM or just a CAM) in a similar fashion as a conventional processor interfaces with a DRAM. TCAMs are a new family of memories that, in addition to Read and Write, offer constant-time lookups (or searches) over large amounts of data. TCAMs have been successfully deployed in sophisticated routers primarily for their very fast lookup speeds with the leading solutions providing speeds as high as 133 Million lookups per second. Research efforts in the networking arena show TCAMs being increasingly used to provide a wide range of high speed networking solutions such as packet classification[5], intrusion detection[6]. Although networking and database applications span different domains, the very core of both these applications involves "looking-up" for a particular data entry among a huge data collection. In this context, we started exploring whether Content Addressable Memories can alleviate the memory-access latency problems which persist in the database systems.

As is the case in many research endeavors in computer science, it is worth noting that the notion of integrating associative search in the context of databases using specialize hardware is not a new idea. In fact, database pioneers in the 1970s proposed using associative memories for accelerating database performance [7]. However, these novel ideas were not widely accepted because such integration would have required significant investment in developing highly specialized hardware technology. Thus the notion of integrating associative search in databases perhaps was before its time. As silicon became cheaper and with the increasing demand from the network industry, TCAMs have become a commodity hardware. In particular, industry standard TCAMs can now have a capacity of a few megabytes at nominal costs. Thus, we believe the time is ripe to evaluate fine-grained hardware integration of TCAMs with conventional DBMSs.

We have been involved with the market leader in TCAM technology for the past few years in bringing this idea to fruition. Only recently we were able to create an integrated prototype which integrates TCAM with a conventional CPU. In [8], we described a novel architecture called *CAM-Cache*, which integrates a TCAM into the memory hierarchy of a general purpose processor. We also developed a software framework for building TCAM-based algorithms and integrating them into a commercial database. Building up on this frame-work, we develop new techniques and report the findings in this paper. The main contributions of this paper are:

- We present a fast linear-complexity sorting algorithm based on *CAM-Cache*. Although a theoretical analysis of a sorting algorithm using TCAMs was reported earlier [9], to the best of our knowledge, we are the first to report an evaluation of implementation of sorting on TCAM hardware. Using special features provided by a TCAM, we present an efficient variant of the TCAM-based sorting technique which requires 40% lesser number of TCAM searches as compared to the original sorting technique [9].

- We propose a novel non-equi join technique which is based on the high-speed sorting and range-matching capabilities of a TCAM. Experimental evaluation against efficient software-based techniques on a popular commercial database show significant performance improvement of this hardware-based technique over its software-based counterparts.

2 CAM-Cache

In this section, we briefly summarize the details of our CAM-Cache architecture [8] which extends the typical memory hierarchy (disk, memory and caches) and provides read, write and fast constant-time search functionality to a software application (e.g. database).

2.1 TCAM Primer

A TCAM provides read/write/constant-time search operations over a large array of data. The TCAM basically stores an array of words and given a query word, it compares the query word with each of the data entries in the array in parallel in a SIMD fashion and the first word from the top of the array which matches the query word is reported. Upon a successful match, the TCAM drives the matching address on its output lines. If there is more than one match for a given query word, a special flag inside the TCAM, the multi_hit flag, is set by the hardware.

2.2 CAM-Cache Architecture

The CAM-Cache architecture, which integrates the TCAMs into the memory hierarchy of CPU, consists of three hardware sub-units: A simple *FPGA*[1] also called a bridge processor, an array of *search engine* chips and an array of SRAM chips which store associative data. The bridge processor acts as a bridge between the CPU on one side and a search engine and SRAM on the other. In an ideal setup, the CPU would directly communicate with the TCAMs over the system bus in the same way as an NPU communicates with the TCAMs. As CPU architectural restrictions only allow new devices to be integrated through a set of standard interfaces (e.g., PCI) and not directly through the system bus, we need a device such as the bridge processor which understands this standard interface and interacts with TCAMs. A more detailed description of the architecture, the supported data model and the prototype can be seen in [8].

3 Database Functionality on CAM-Cache

In this section we discuss integrating database functionality on top of hardware functions provided by the TCAM. In our preliminary evaluation [8], we proposed a hardware-based database equi-join technique over CAM-Cache and

[1] Field Programmable Gate Array.

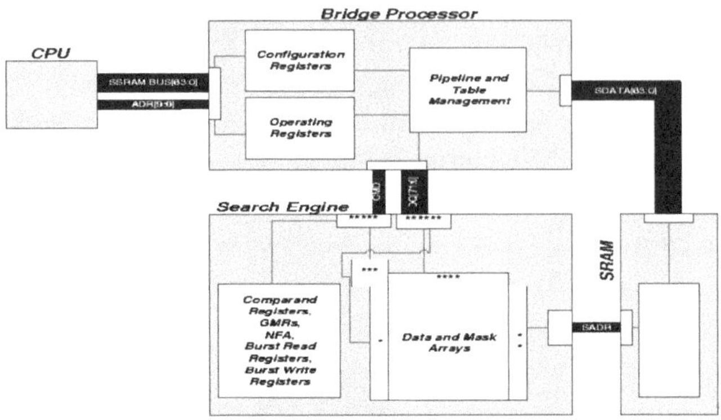

Fig. 1. CAM-Cache architecture

presented a feasibility analysis of our approach by comparing the performance against leading software-based equi-join solutions. Although datbase equi-joins, where two database relations are joined with a conditional of "=" over the join predicates, are the most commonly used joins, other forms of conditional joins (with conditionals of $\leq, \geq, inbetween, <>$), which we refer to as non-equi joins, are equally important. While equi-joins have very efficient hashing, sorting and index-based implementations, non-equi joins are typically implemented using nested loop joins or expensive sorting-based implementations. They do not have efficient hashing based solution because hashing does not preserve ranges. In this section, we develop a TCAM-based algorithm which efficiently solves the Non-equi joins. This technique is based on the capability to use the TCAM as an efficient linear-complexity sorting device.

3.1 Sorting Using CAM-Cache

Sorting using TCAM has already been described in the context of networks [9]. Panigrahy et al. [9] presented a TCAM-based sorting algorithm which has linear time complexity in the size of the input set. In this section, we describe the sorting algorithm described in [9] and using the special features provided by the TCAM, we implement an optimized variant of the original technique which decreases the number of TCAM accesses required by the sorting technique.

Searching Algorithm - Range Matching. The idea behind the TCAM-based sorting is primarily based on the ability to store and lookup for ranges (range-matching) in TCAMs using the masking feature of the TCAMs. The problem of range-matching can be described as follows. Given a set of disjoint ranges $\{(a_1, b_1), (a_2, b_2), ..., (a_k, b_k)\}$, searching for a value c returns the range (a_i, b_i) such that $a_i \leq c \leq b_i$.

Extended Longest Common Prefix (ELCP). In [9], Panigrahy et al. proposed the concept of Extended Longest Common Prefixes (ELCPs) for efficient range-matching. For any range (a, b), the Longest Common Prefix (LCP) range is a binary range with the prefix string representing the prefix shared by both ends of the range. A binary range is a range of numbers represented by a binary string (string of 0's and 1's) with a suffix of the string masked out. The authors of [9] show that simply storing the LCP for representing a range inside the TCAM does not suffice for range-matching. They proposed a variant of LCPs, called the Extended LCPs and show that ELCPs are sufficient for providing range-matching with efficient TCAM space usage. There are two ELCPs for every range. The 0-ELCP (similarly 1-ELCP) is basically the LCP of the range with the LCP extended by a bit value of 0 (1).

The authors [9] prove that for any value c in the range (a, b), the value c definitely matches either the 0-ELCP or the 1-ELCP. They divide the TCAMs into 2 logical spaces : one for storing the 0-ELCPs and the other for storing the 1-ELCPs. The range-matching problem degenerates to finding the longest prefix match inside both classes. However, TCAMs currently do not provide the longest prefix match support at the hardware level. In order to find a longest prefix match, a binary-search using different prefix lengths is performed.

Multi-hit Based Optimization. We observe that the binary search algorithm for finding an ELCP, as described in [9], can be made more efficient by utilizing the multi-match feature of the TCAM. In the original description, even if there is a single match inside the TCAM, the binary search continues for log(b) searches. For example, if there is only one prefix of length 17 and the data are 32-bit, the algorithm searches for prefixes of length 17-32, 17-24, 17-20, 17-18 and 17-17 while all the search results point to the same TCAM location because it is the only match for the given search key. This can be avoided using the multi-hit feature of the TCAM. As described in Section 2.1, the multi-hit bit is set as a result of a search command if there are more than 2 matches for the given search. In the case when the search result shows that the multi-hit is 0 and there is a match inside the TCAM, this implies that the current match location is the only possible match. Using this feature, a modified version of the original binary search [9] can be implemented which avoids multiple searches in the case of a single match. We refer to this **multi-hit** based implementation of the **binary search** as **MHBS** and discuss the performance improvement resulting from this optimization in the experimental section.

Sorting Algorithm (Tsort). The TCAM-based sorting algorithm is logically similar to the software-based insertion sort technique. An insertion sort over an input set of n numbers runs for n-*1* iterations. At the beginning of the ith iteration, the set of all the inputs read till that iteration are already sorted and the ith input is inserted into its proper position in the already sorted list of numbers. At the end of the nth iteration, the input set is sorted. The inner loop of the insertion sort has a linear complexity in the size of the input set thus resulting in an overall complexity of $O(n^2)$.

The TCAM-based insertion sort [9], which we refer to as Tsort, replaces the expensive O(n)-complexity inner loop of the insertion sort with a constant time

TCAM operation. This is achieved by exploiting the ability to store ranges and the constant time look-up capability of the TCAM. At any stage in the execution of Tsort, the set of input numbers which are already processed are sorted and stored inside the TCAM. The processed data is stored inside TCAM as a set of ranges. For each new input, the range which the input value falls into is split to create two new ranges. Once the insertion of the inputs into the TCAM is done, the sorted list needs to be retrieved from the TCAM. This can be easily done by storing pointer information along with each range to the next range. For example, if we suppose that before every insert, the pointer information from the lowest range to highest range can be traversed using pointer information, then we maintain this sorted order while inserting the new value. This is explained in the pseudo-code of the TSort algorithm given in Algorithm 1. For each TCAM entry, the associatedData basically stores the index of the particular entry in the actual sorted output. This data structure is used in the Non-equi join algorithm described later .For each input, an old range is deleted and two new ranges are inserted. Since each range requires two TCAM entries, the algorithm requires two free TCAM entries for each input which implies an overall space complexity of O(n). Further for each input, the algorithm requires finding the 0-ELCP or the 1-ELCP, this incurs $O(\log b)$ search complexity. Therefore the overall search complexity is $O(n \log b)$. Although in practice, the $\log b$ complexity typically results in 1 or 2 binary searches when the MHBS optimization is used, thereby resulting in linear complexity for the Tsort.

Algorithm 1. Tsort (set S of numbers)

```
for each input x in the input set S do
  match = searchForMatchingRange(input[i]);
  /* Now split this range say (x-y) into two new ranges. First insert (x -
  input[i]) replacing the original range of (x, y) at match. */
  InsertNewRange (@match, [x, input[i]], nextFreeTcamSpace);
  /* Insert the new range (input [i], y) into the next free tcam address. */
  InsertNewRange (@nextFreeTcamSpace, [input[i], y], nextInfo);
end for
/* Retrieval Phase */
nextPointer = searchForMatchingRange ( 0 );
counter = 0
while counter != n do
  associatedData [nextPointer] = counter
  sortData [counter++] = higherBoundOfRangeAt (nextPointer));
  nextPointer = searchForMatchingRange (nextPointer);
end while
```

3.2 Non-equi Joins (NTjoin)

We now describe an efficient run-time CAM-based non-equi join technique based on the Tsort technique describe above. The TCAM based non-equi join, which we refer to as the NTjoin, is logically similar to the indexing-based nested loop join which we refer to as NIJoin. In the case of NIJoin, an index is constructed over the inner relation and the outer relation iterates over this index to return the tuples which satisfy the given condition.

Algorithm 2. NTjoin (inner relation R, outer relation S)

```
Tsort (R) in blocks that fit into TCAM
for each block of R do
  for each tuple s in S do
    matchAddress = searchForMatchingRange (x);
    /* Now get the index of the matched range in the sorted list */
    index = associatedData [matchAddres];
    /* Depending on the conditional and using this index, perform a linear
    traversal of the sorted array generated during the Tsort */
  end for
end for
```

The NTjoin (described in Algorithm 2) consists of two phases : the *indexing* phase and the *join* phase. In the *indexing* phase, the inner relation of the non-equi join is sorted and indexed inside the TCAM. The Tsort technique described in the previous section is used to build a sorted version of the inner relation inside the TCAM. If the inner relation does not fit into the TCAM, it can be partitioned into blocks that can fit into the TCAM and the outer relation loops in a nested loop fashion for each block. During the retrieval stage of the Tsort, when the sorted data is retrieved and stored inside the main memory, we associate with each TCAM entry its corresponding index in the sorted list. Now when a new entry is looked up in the TCAM, it not only finds the matching range but also the index of the look-up key in the sorted list.

In the join phase, we loop through the outer relation in a nested loop fashion, issuing the search queries on the index of the inner relation which is built in the indexing phase. For example when the conditional is $\leq$, all the entries from the beginning of the sorted list till the index returned by the TCAM-lookupfor the predicate key in the outer relation can be returned. Similarly for the *in-between* queries, lookups for both ends of the *in-between* range can be executed to return the indexes of both the ends in the sorted list and thereby the result tuples. Thus the TCAM functions as both an efficient linear-time *sorter* but also as a high speed *index* for retrieving the index of any key in the sorted list. In the *join* phase of the algorithm, the outer relation of the non-equi join is iterated in a nested loop fashion over the TCAM-based index of the inner relation to return the result tuples. At this point we would like to point out that the NTjoin solution can be used to address the problem of multi-matches in the case of equi-join.

We now discuss the complexity analysis of the NTjoin technique. In the indexing phase, the algorithm uses Tsort which implies a cost of $O(n \log b)$ for building the sorted list inside the TCAM. During the join phase, each iteration accounts for a TCAM range-match followed by a retrieval of all matching tuples. This implies that the cost of the join phase is $O(n \log b)$. This is the cost in addition to the unavoidable cost of retrieving all the tuples. A detailed experimental evaluation of this technique is given in the next section.

4 Performance Evaluation

In this section, we present an evaluation of the TCAM-based database join operations. We conducted the experiments on a single CPU Intel Pentium IV 2.4GHz PC. The system bus speed is 533MHz. The CAM-Cache prototype interfaces with the CPU through a 32-bit 33MHz PCI interface. The PC has a 16-KB L1-I and a 16-KB L1-D cache (both are non-blocking). For the purpose of accessing the CAM-Cache prototype, drivers were developed on the Linux platform. All the techniques (the Tsort, the CJ and the NTjoins) are implemented in C and compiled using the GNU C compiler. The experiments are evaluated on the prototype described in Section 2. In all the cases, the actual performance as returned by the current prototype is reported. In order to evaluate the performance of the NTjoin algorithm against its software-based counterpart, we integrated them into a commercial database [8] which enables comparing the performance of our techniques against very efficient software-based approaches such as buffer-based Nested Loop, Nested Index, and Sort-Merge techniques. We first evaluate the performance of the Tsort technique with and without the multi-hit optimization followed by the evaluation of NTjoin.

The data sets used in all the experiments are randomly generated in the following manner: Each record consists of a join attribute (1 word) and (record-width−1) words of random data to simulate cache pollution. The join attribute is a uniformly distributed random number in a range that determines the join selectivity, i.e. how many tuples on the average have the same value. All experiments are performed over two tables that have the same number of entries.

4.1 Tsort

We now present the evaluation of the Tsort algorithm with and without the multi-hit based binary search optimization (MHBS) as described in the Section 3.1. Figure 2 shows the number of TCAM searches executed by both these techniques for datasets of sizes ranging from 1000 to 100000. The dotted curve in Figure 2 shows the results for the Tsort as described by Panigrahy et al [9]. It shows a linear increase in the number of searches with the size of the dataset which supports the expected O(n) behavior of the algorithm. The difference in the total number of TCAM searches for both techniques shows that the MHBS optimization reduces the total number of TCAM searches required by Tsort by as much as 40% in most cases.

4.2 NTjoin

We now present an evaluation of the NTjoin using the CAM-Cache architecture. We compare the performance of the NTjoin with the Nested Loop, Nested Index

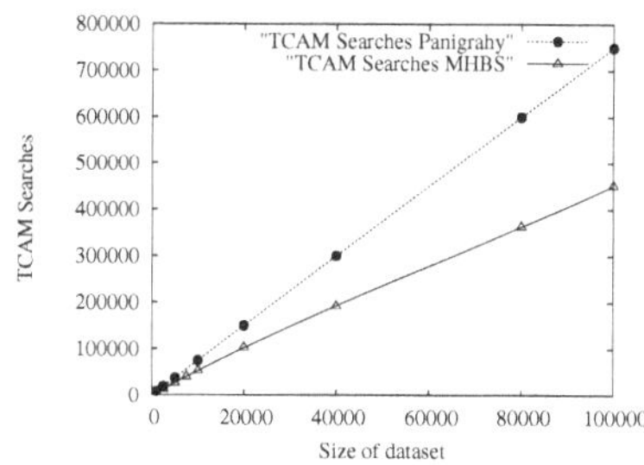

Fig. 2. Number of TCAM searches

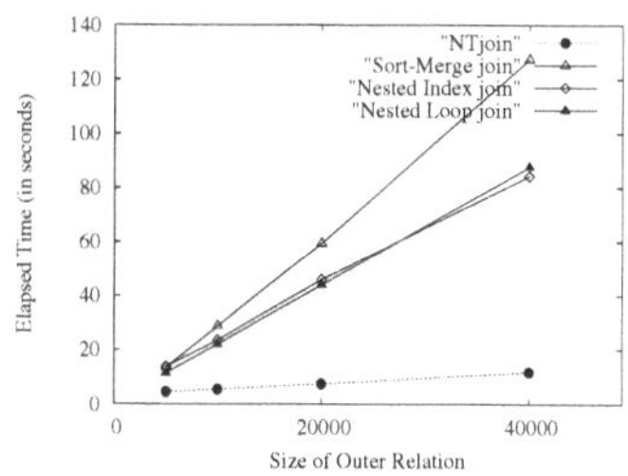

Fig. 3. NTjoin with Query set size = 10000

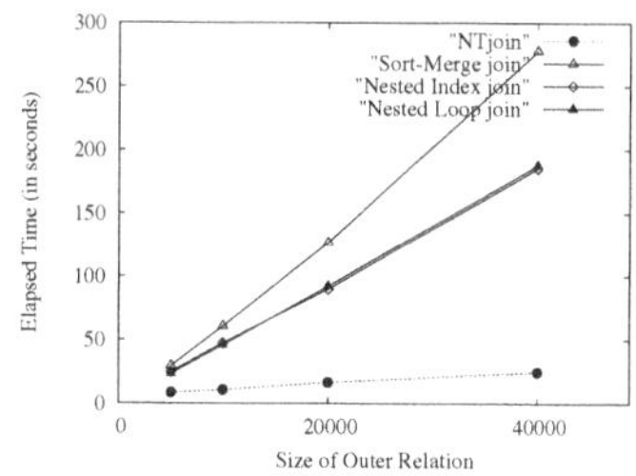

Fig. 4. NTjoin with Query set size = 20000

and the Sort-Merge join techniques. In the first set of experiments, we present the evaluation of the NTjoin with a non-equi join condition of "$\leq$". We then present an evaluation of how this technique performs in comparison with equi-join techniques at higher join factors.

Figures 3 and 4 shows the results of all the above join techniques for a non-equi join with "$\leq$" as the join condition. In the first experiment (Figure 3), a dataset of 10000 tuples is joined with datasets of sizes varying from 5000 to 40000 while in the second experiment, a dataset of 20000 tuples is used as the joining dataset (Figure 4). The results show that all the techniques exhibit an expected linear increase in the elapsed time with the size of the outer relation. It can be seen that the Nested Loop join performs as well as any other technique. This is because, when the size of the result set is large which is usually the case for non-equi joins, the pointer-based retrieval phase of the Nested Index join and the merging phase of the sort-merge joins, which generate the query result, become inefficient when compared to the simple block-based comparison technique invloved in the simple Nested Loop join. These results show that the TCAM-based NTjoin outperforms all the software-based techniques by a significant margin (average of 10 times) in all the cases. More importantly, it should be noted that the elapsed time of the NTjoin is the actual time required by the current prototype and does not exclude the PCI overhead incurred. This signifies the potential of a TCAM for functioning not only as a sorter but also as a very efficient range-matching engine which together form the core of the NTjoin.

5 Conclusion and Future Work

In this paper, we continue our endeavor to address the problem of "Where does the time go in a DBMS?" [1] by proposing changes at both hardware and software levels. We propose to exploit the TCAM technology, used widely in network router architectures, in order to alleviate the bottlenecks in current processor architectures. Building upon our proposed CAM-Cache architecture, which integrates a TCAM into the caching hierarchy of a conventional processor, we presented several techniques such as an efficient linear-complexity sorting technique and a fast non-equi database join. Through our performance analysis, we showed that despite the various overheads of the current prototype, this architecture has the potential for providing efficient alternative solutions for existing problems. Especially promising is the fact that TCAM-based algorithms provide a very-efficient mechanism for conditional joins, which represent a major challenge for software-based solutions.

References

1. A.G.Ailamaki, D.J.DeWitt, M.D.Hill, D.A.Wood: DBMSs On a Modern Processor: Where Does Time Go? In: VLDB. (1999) 266–277
2. P.Boncz, S.Manegold, M.L.Kersten: Database Architecture Optimized for the New Bottleneck: Memory Access. In: VLDB. (1999) 266–277
3. Shatdal, A., Kant, C., Naughton, J.: Cache Conscious Algorithms for Relational Query Processing. In: VLDB. (1994) 510–512
4. Chen, S., Ailamaki, A., Gibbons, P.B., Mowry, T.C.: Improving Hash Join Performance through Prefetching. In: ICDE. (2004)
5. Narlikar, G.J., Basu, A., Zane, F.: Coolcams: Power-efficient tcams for forwarding engines. In: INFOCOM. (2003)
6. Fang Yu, R.H.K.: Efficient Multi-Match Packet Classification with TCAM. In: IEEE Hot Interconnects 2004. (2004)
7. DeFiore.C.F, Berra.P.B.: 'A Data Management System Utilizing an Associative Memory'. In: AFIPS NCC Vol. 42. (1973)
8. Bandi, N., Schneider, S., Agrawal, D., Abbadi, A.E.: Hardware Acceleration of Database Operations using Content Addressable Memories. In: ACM, Data Management on New Hardware (DaMoN). (2005)
9. Panigrahy, R., Sharma, S.: Sorting and Searching using Ternary CAMs. In: IEEE Micro. (2003)

CLEAR: An Efficient Context and Location-Based Dynamic Replication Scheme for Mobile-P2P Networks

Anirban Mondal[1], Sanjay Kumar Madria[2], and Masaru Kitsuregawa[1]

[1] Institute of Industrial Science,University of Tokyo, Japan
{anirban, kitsure}@tkl.iis.u-tokyo.ac.jp
[2] Department of Computer Science, University of Missouri-Rolla, USA
madrias@umr.edu

Abstract. We propose CLEAR (Context and Location-based Efficient Allocation of Replicas), a dynamic replica allocation scheme for improving data availability in mobile ad-hoc peer-to-peer (M-P2P) networks. To manage replica allocation efficiently, CLEAR exploits user mobility patterns and deploys a super-peer architecture, which avoids both broadcast storm during replica allocation as well as broadcast-based querying. CLEAR considers different levels of replica consistency and load as replica allocation criteria. Our performance study indicates CLEAR's overall effectiveness in improving data availability in M-P2P networks.

1 Introduction

In a mobile ad-hoc peer-to-peer (M-P2P) network, mobile hosts (MHs) interact with each other in a peer-to-peer (P2P) fashion. Rapid advances in wireless communication technology coupled with the ever-increasing popularity of mobile devices (e.g., laptops, PDAs, mobile phones) motivate M-P2P network applications. However, data availability in M-P2P networks is lower than in traditional stationary networks because of frequent network partitioning due to user movement and/or users switching 'on' or 'off' their mobile devices. Notably, data availability is less than 20% even in a wired environment [16]. Hence, dynamic replica allocation becomes a necessity to support M-P2P network applications such as disaster-recovery and sales applications. Suppose a group of doctors, each of whom has a schedule, are moving in an earthquake-devastated region, where communication infrastructures (e.g., base stations) do not exist. They need to share data (e.g., number of injured people, number of empty stretchers, number of fatalities) with each other on-the-fly using mobile devices. Similarly, moving salespersons, who generally have a schedule, need to share total sales profits by means of mobile devices. Incidentally, absolute consistency is not a requirement in such applications [13]. For simplicity, this work considers only numerical data.

Traditional mobile replication techniques[12,18], which assume *stationary networks*, do not address frequent network partitioning issues. P2P replication services are not 'mobile-ready' [5,15] as current P2P systems have mostly ignored

S. Bressan, J. Küng, and R. Wagner (Eds.): DEXA 2006, LNCS 4080, pp. 399–408, 2006.

data transformation, relationships and network characteristics. Understandably, changes in data with location and time create new research problems [3]. Replication in M-P2P networks requires fundamentally different solutions [1,9] than in [10,12,14] due to free movement of MHs and wireless constraints. Interestingly, the techniques in [6,7,8] consider frequent network partitioning w.r.t. replication in mobile ad-hoc networks (MANETs), but they do not exploit MH mobility patterns for replication. Hence, they may unnecessarily replicate at MHs which would soon leave the region, while being unable to exploit MHs that would soon enter the region. In [6,7,8], since none of the MHs has a global view, the reallocation period needs to be determined in an ad-hoc manner, hence reallocation period may not match MH mobility patterns, thereby decreasing data availability. Moreover, the techniques in [6,7,8] incur high traffic due to possible broadcast storm as MHs exchange replica allocation-related messages with each other.

We propose CLEAR (Context and Location-based Efficient Allocation of Replicas), a dynamic replica allocation scheme for improving data availability in M-P2P networks. CLEAR deploys a super-peer architecture, the *super-peer* (**SP**) being an MH, which generally does not move outside the region and which has maximum remaining battery power and processing capacity. Since the M-P2P network covers a relatively small area, the total number of MHs can be expected to be low, thereby avoiding scalability problems. As we shall see later, this architecture avoids broadcast storm during replica allocation, eliminates broadcast-based querying since each MH knows about data and replicas stored at other MHs, and preserves P2P autonomy as queries need not pass via SP.

SP knows the *schedule* of every MH comprising the MH's mobility pattern and the data items that the MH is likely to access at different times. This makes it possible for CLEAR to replicate at MHs that would soon enter the region, while avoiding replication at MHs that would soon leave the region, thereby facilitating better resource utilization, likely better query response times and increased data availability. SP is able to determine a near-optimal reallocation period based on *global* information of MH schedules, hence it can better manage replica allocation. Finally, unlike existing works [6,7,8], CLEAR considers load, different levels of replica consistency and unequal-sized data items. Our performance study indicates that CLEAR indeed improves data availability in M-P2P networks with significant reduction in query response times and communication traffic as compared to some recent existing schemes.

2 Related Work

The work in [10] proposes a suite of replication protocols for maintaining data consistency and transactional semantics of centralized systems. The protocols in [9] exploit the rich semantics of group communication primitives and the relaxed isolation guarantees provided by most databases. The work in [4] discusses replication issues in MANETs. The proposal in [12] discusses replication in distributed environments, where connectivity is partial, weak, and variant as in mobile information systems. Existing systems in this area include ROAM [14],

Clique [15] and Rumor [5], while a scalable P2P framework for distributed data management applications and query routing has been presented in [11]. An update strategy, based on a hybrid push/pull Rumor spreading algorithm, for truly decentralized and self-organizing systems (e.g., pure P2P systems) has been examined in [3], the aim being to provide probabilistic guarantees as opposed to strict consistency. The work in [1] investigates replication strategies for designing highly available storage systems on highly unavailable P2P hosts.

The proposals in [6,7,8] present three replica allocation methods with periodic and aperiodic updates, which consider limited memory space in MHs for storing replicas, data item access frequencies and network topology, to improve data accessibility in MANETs. Among these, E-DCG+ [8] is the most influential replica allocation approach. E-DCG+ creates groups of MHs that are biconnected components in a network, and shares replicas in larger groups of MHs to provide high stability. In E-DCG+, the summation of RWR (read-write ratio) values of each data item in each group is calculated. In the order of the RWR values of the group, replicas of data items are allocated until memory space of all MHs in that group becomes full. Each replica is allocated at an MH whose RWR value for the data item is the highest among MHs that have free memory space. However, the architecture considered in [6,7,8] does not consider user mobility patterns, load sharing and tolerance to weaker consistency for data replication.

3 Context of the Problem

In CLEAR's super-peer architecture, each MH maintains recent read-write logs (including timestamps) of the data items that it owns, for hotspot detection purposes. Each data item d is owned by only *one* MH, which can update d *autonomously* anytime; other MHs cannot update d. To delete infrequently accessed replicas, each MH keeps track of replicas stored at itself. Memory space at each MH, bandwidth and data item sizes may vary. We assume location-dependent data access [17] i.e., an MH in region X will access data only from MHs in X. SP backs up information using the Internet as an interface to handle failures and we assume that some of the MHs have access to the Internet for backup purposes. If SP fails or network partitioning occurs, these MHs can connect to the Internet to obtain information, thereby enabling them to act as SP.

In practice, MH owners do not move randomly since they have some *schedule*. An MH M's schedule contains information concerning M's location during any given time period T and the data items required by M during T. Each MH owner initially sends his schedule to SP and if later on, his schedule changes significantly, he will keep SP updated about these changes by piggybacking such information onto replica allocation-related messages to SP. Thus, SP is able to exploit MH schedules for replica allocation purposes.

We define the **load** L_M of an MH M as follows:

$$L_M = \sum_{i=1}^{N_d} (n_{d_i} / s_{d_i}) / \eta_i \qquad (1)$$

where N_d is the total number of data items in M's job queue, n_{d_i} is data item d_i's recent access frequency and s_{d_i} denotes d_i's size. We use η_i to normalize load w.r.t. bandwidth. We compute η_i as $(B_{M_i} \div B_{min})$, where B_{M_i} is M's bandwidth. A straightforward way of determining B_{min} is to select a low bandwidth as B_{min} e.g., we have used 28 Kbps as the value of B_{min}.

To estimate the *effect* of updates on the ease of maintaining replica consistency for any data item d, we compute a measure **NQDC** for each replica of d as follows:

$$\begin{aligned} NQDC &= NQ \times C \quad if \; C \geq DC \\ &= 0 \quad otherwise \end{aligned} \tag{2}$$

where NQ indicates the number of queries recently answered by the replica, **DC** represents the value of **desired consistency** and C is the consistency with which queries were answered by the replica. We use three different levels of replica consistency, namely *high*, *medium* and *low*. SP maintains a table $T_{\epsilon,C}$, which contains the following entries: (x%, high), (y%, medium), (z%, low), where x, y, z are error-bounds, whose values are application-dependent and pre-specified by the system at design time. We assign the values of C for high, medium and low consistency as 1, 0.5 and 0.25 respectively. Similarly, the value of DC can be *high*, *medium* or *low* i.e., 1, 0.5 and 0.25 respectively, depending upon the application under consideration.

4 CLEAR: A Context and Location-Based Dynamic Replica Allocation Scheme for M-P2P Networks

This section discusses the CLEAR scheme. *Periodically* every TP time units, each MH sends a message containing the read-write log D_MH (including timestamps) of its own data items, the read log R_MH with timestamps for replicas residing at itself for the previous period, its available memory and load status to SP. SP combines the information in all these D_MHs and R_MHs to create D_SP and R_SP (both sorted in descending order of access frequency) respectively. Then SP executes the replica allocation algorithm depicted in Figure 1.

In Line 1 of Figure 1, $\psi = T_{Acc} \;/\; T_{num}$, where T_{Acc} is the sum of access frequencies of all data items in D_SP and T_{num} is the total number of data items in D_SP. In Line 2, SP computes the total NQDC value for any data item d by using the table $T_{\epsilon,C}$ and R_MH to compute the NQDC value for each of d's replicas and then summing up all these NQDC values. Any data item d with low total NQDC value is not considered for replica allocation because low NQDC value implies that d is frequently updated, which makes it more difficult to maintain replica consistency. Line 3 indicates that CLEAR performs replica allocation on-the-fly only when necessary and not during every TP time units.

As Lines 5-7 of Figure 1 indicate, CLEAR tries to replicate a data item d at the MH MH_{max}, which had the highest access frequency for d, or at one of MH_{max}'s k-hop neighbours. (A preliminary performance study revealed that

k=3 provides good performance for CLEAR.) Even though MH_{max} accesses d the maximum number of times, a number of other MHs in the vicinity of MH_{max} may also be interested in accessing d. Moreover, MH_{max} may be overloaded or it may not have adequate memory space for storing d's replica. Hence, SP checks the schedules of all the MHs, and considers MH_{max} and the MHs that would be in the close vicinity of MH_{max} in the near future as constituting the potential candidate set $DEST$ of MHs, where d may be replicated. In Line 10 of Figure 1, Dec_d is 'TRUE' if ($B_d - C_d \geq TH$), where B_d is benefit, C_d is cost and TH is a pre-defined application-dependent threshold parameter. SP consults its D_SP to find out n_d and t_d, where n_d is the number of times d was accessed during the last period and t_d is the time taken for each of those accesses. Then SP computes B_d as $(t_d \times n_d)$. C_d involves transmitting d from source MH *src* (i.e., d's owner) to destination MH *dest* (which will store d's replica) and is computed as $(\sum_{k=1}^{n_{hop}} (s_d/B_k))$, where s_d is d's size and B_k refers to transfer rates of connections between *src* and *dest* that d must 'hop' through to reach *dest* and n_{hop} is the number of hops required by d to reach *dest*. Finally, observe how CLEAR considers MH load and memory space, while allocating replicas.

Algorithm *CLEAR_REPLICA_ALLOCATION*
D_SP: Sorted list maintained by SP concerning access information of data items of all MHs

1) Select from D_SP data items, whose access frequency exceeds threshold ψ, into list *Rep*
2) Traverse *Rep* once to delete data items with low total NQDC values
3) if *Rep* is non-empty
4)   for each data item d in *Rep*
5)   Determine from D_SP the MH MH_{max} which made maximum number of accesses to d
6)   Check MH schedules to create a list of MH_{max}'s k-hop neighbours
7)   Create a set $DEST$ consisting of MH_{max} and its k-hop neighbours
8)   Delete MHs with low available memory space from $DEST$
9)   Delete MHs, which have low load difference with d's owner, from $DEST$
10)   for each MH M in $DEST$ { if (Dec_d != 'TRUE') Delete M from $DEST$ }
11)   Select the least loaded MH from $DEST$ as destination MH for storing d's replica

end

Fig. 1. Algorithm for CLEAR replica allocation scheme executed by SP

After performing replica allocation, SP sends a message to each MH informing them about replicas that have been allocated, data items and replicas at each MH, NQDC values of replicas at each MH and load of each MH. When an MH misses SP's message (e.g., due to it having been switched 'off' or due to it newly joining the network), it contacts its neighbours to obtain the latest information of SP. When a query Q arrives at any MH M, M answers Q if it stores the queried data item d or its replica. Otherwise, M identifies the set $DirQ$ of MHs, which store d's replica. M deletes (from $DirQ$) overloaded MHs, whose load exceeds the average system load since our aim is to replicate *only* at underloaded MHs. M sorts the remaining MHs in $DirQ$ to select the least loaded MH m into a set S. MHs, whose load difference with m is low, are also added to set S. From S, M selects the MH, which had the highest NQDC value for d's replica during the last period, for redirecting Q, any ties being resolved arbitrarily. Observe the inherent P2P autonomy in CLEAR's architecture in that queries need not pass via SP since any MH has adequate information to redirect queries. Given a total of N MHs, our approach incurs during a given period at most O(N) messages (1 message from each MH to SP and 1 message from SP to each MH if SP decides to perform replica allocation). In contrast, for a distributed architecture without an SP, each MH would have to broadcast its list of data items and replicas to every MH periodically to avoid flooding broadcast-based query retrieval, thereby resulting in O(N^2) messages for a given period.

5 Performance Evaluation

The MHs move according to the *Random waypoint model* [2] with speeds varying from 1 metre/s to 10 metres/s within a 1000 metre ×1000 metre area. Communication range of MHs (except SP) is a circle of 100 metre radius. MH memory space varies from 1 MB to 1.5 MB and each MH owns 4 data items, whose sizes vary from 50 Kb to 350 Kb. Each query requests one data item. Bandwidth between MHs varies from 28 Kbps to 100 Kbps, while probability of availability of an MH varies from 50% to 85%. Message header size is 220 bytes. Network topology does *not* change significantly during replica allocation since it requires only a few seconds [8]. 10 queries are issued in the network every second, the number of queries to be directed to each MH being determined by the Zipf distribution. TH is set to 10 seconds.

Table 1. Parameters used in Performance Study

Parameter	Significance	Default value	Variations
N_{MH}	Number of MHs	50	10, 20, 30, 40
δ	MH deviation (%) from expected mobility pattern	10	
ZF	Zipf factor	0.9	0.1, 0.3, 0.5, 0.7
TP	Time interval (10^2 s) at which each MH sends message to SP	1	
WP	Write probability (%)	20	10,30,40
DC	Desired consistency level	medium	low, high

Performance metrics are *average response time* (**ART**) of a query, *percentage success ratio* (**SR**) and **traffic** (i.e., total hop-count) during replica allocation. ART is $(\sum_{i=1}^{N_Q}(t_c - t_a))/N_Q$, where t_c is query completion time, t_a is query arrival time and N_Q is the total number of queries. SR is (Q_{DC}/Q_T)*100, where Q_{DC} and Q_T denote number of queries answered with the desired consistency level and total number of queries respectively. As reference, we adapt the **E-DCG+** approach [8] discussed in Section 2 to our scenario. As a baseline, we also compare CLEAR with an approach **NoRep**, which does not perform replication. Table 1 summarizes our performance study parameters. In Table 1, δ represents the percentage of time for which an MH fails to adhere to its expected mobility

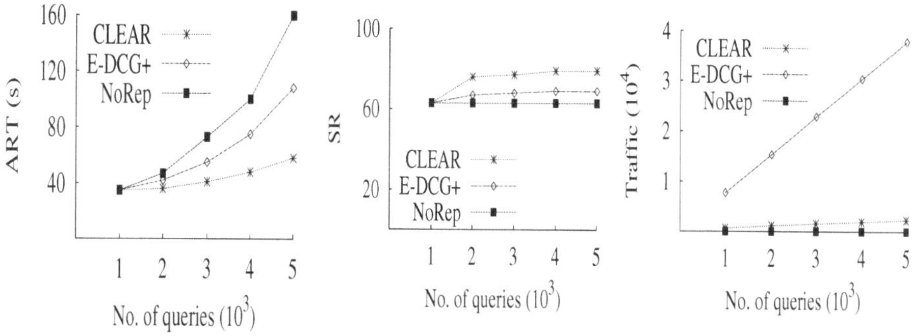

(a) ART (b) SR (c) Allocation Traffic

Fig. 2. Performance of CLEAR

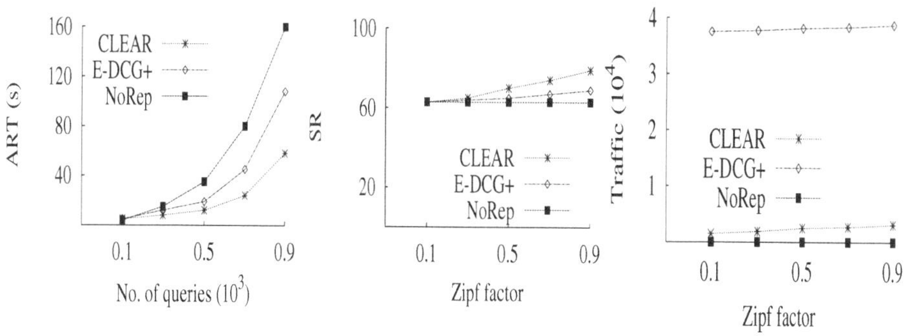

(a) ART (b) SR (c) Traffic

Fig. 3. Effect of variations in the workload skew

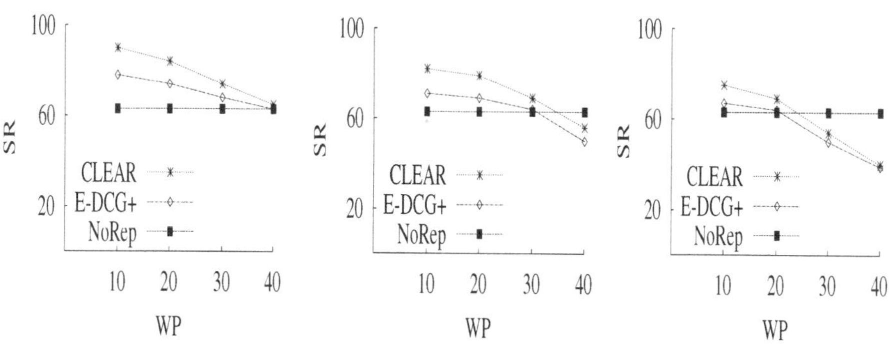

(a) DC=Low (b) DC=Medium (c) DC=High

Fig. 4. Effect of variations in write probability

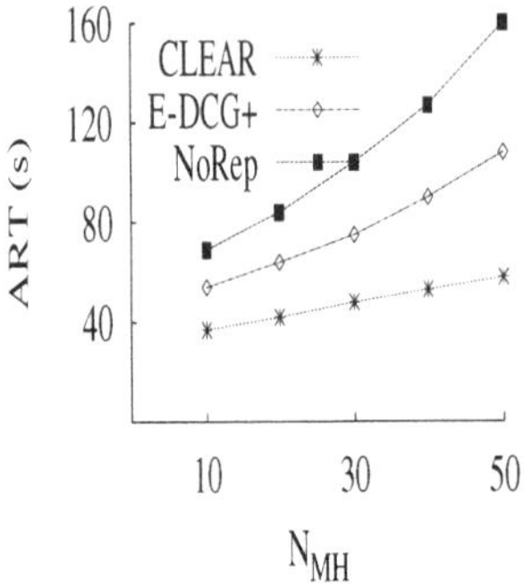

(a) ART

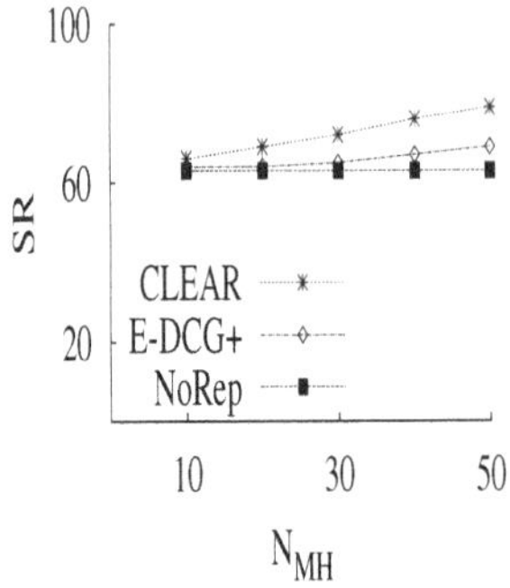

(b) SR

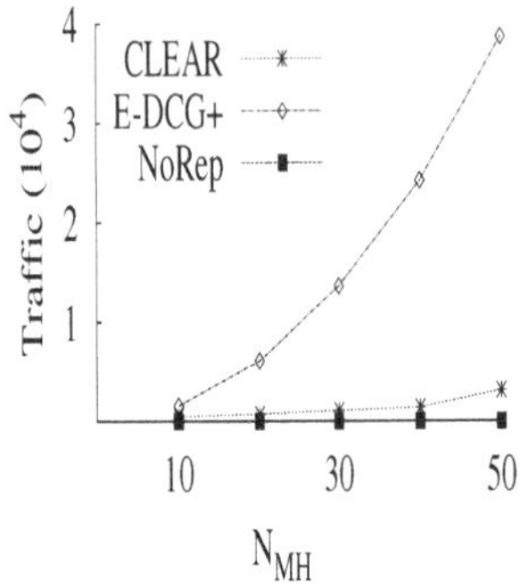

(c) Traffic

Fig. 5. Effect of variations in the number of MHs

pattern (e.g., due to the MH owner running late or due to unexpected circumstances). Furthermore, recall from Section 4 that TP is the time interval at which each MH sends its information to SP, based on which SP decides whether to allocate replicas, hence *TP* is *not* necessarily CLEAR's reallocation period. However, TP is E-DCG+'s reallocation period.

Performance of CLEAR

Figure 2 depicts the ART for a given number of queries for default values of the parameters in Table 1. As replica allocation is done every 100 seconds (i.e., after every 1000 queries since 10 queries are issued per second), Figure 2a indicates comparable ART for all three approaches for the first 1000 queries. Subsequently, the difference in ART between CLEAR and E-DCG+ keeps on increasing due to two reasons. First, unlike E-DCG+, CLEAR considers MH mobility patterns, hence it is capable of allocating replicas at MHs that would soon enter the region, while avoiding MHs which would soon depart from the region. Second, CLEAR allocates replicas to relatively underloaded MHs and redirects queries to replicas stored at underloaded MHs. However, since E-DCG+ does not consider load, it may allocate replicas to overloaded MHs, thereby incurring higher ART due to large job queues. Since NoRep does not perform replication, load imbalance is even more pronounced in case of NoRep than for E-DCG+. Experimental log files revealed that CLEAR outperformed E-DCG+ and NoRep by upto 46% and 64% respectively in terms of ART.

In Figure 2b, CLEAR provides higher SR than E-DCG+ due to two reasons. First, unlike E-DCG+, CLEAR considers consistency issues while directing a query (since it uses NQDC values). Second, updates to replicas are likely to be faster for CLEAR than for E-DCG+ since CLEAR allocates replicas to underloaded MHs, while E-DCG+ may allocate replicas to overloaded MHs with large job queues. For both CLEAR and E-DCG+, SR changes only very slightly after the first replica allocation period because most of the required replica allocations had already been performed in the first period. For NoRep, SR remains relatively constant since it depends only upon the probability of availability of the MHs. Both CLEAR and E-DCG+ provide better SR than NoRep because they perform replication, which increases data availability. Incidentally, during replica allocation, E-DCG+ requires every MH to broadcast its RWR values to every MH, thereby incurring $O(N_{MH}^2)$ messages, while CLEAR requires each MH to send only one message to SP and SP to send a message to each MH, thus incurring $O(N_{MH})$ messages, which explains the results in Figure 2c.

Effect of Variations in the Workload Skew

Figure 3 depicts the results when the zipf factor (ZF) is varied. For high ZF values (e.g., 0.9) involving high skew, CLEAR outperforms E-DCG+ in terms of ART and SR due to the reasons explained for Figure 2. As skew decreases, CLEAR's load-based replica allocation becomes less pronounced, hence performance gap between CLEAR and E-DCG+ decreases. Figure 3c's explanation is same as that of Figure 2c.

Effect of Variations in Percentage Write Probability (WP)

We varied WP to examine the impact on SR. Figure 4 depicts the results. In Figure 4a, as WP increases, SR decreases for both CLEAR and E-DCG+ primarily due to more replicas becoming inconsistent with increasing WP. But, CLEAR and E-DCG+ did not provide lower SR than NoRep due to DC being 'low'. As DC increases to 'medium' and 'high', stricter replica consistency is required, hence as WP increases, larger number of replicas become inconsistent. This explains why CLEAR and E-DCG+ provided lower SR than NoRep in the results in Figures 4b and 4c. However, we believe that this is a small price to pay as compared to the large ART gains achieved by CLEAR.

Effect of Variations in the Number of MHs

To test CLEAR's scalability within our application scenario, we varied the number N_{MH} of MHs, keeping the number of queries proportional to N_{MH}. The number of possible replica allocation periods was set at 5 for each case. Figure 5 depicts the results. At high values of N_{MH}, CLEAR outperforms E-DCG+ in terms of ART and SR, the explanation being same as that of Figure 2. However, as N_{MH} decreases, performance gap between the approaches keeps decreasing due to limited opportunities for replica allocation. Replica allocation traffic for E-DCG+ dramatically decreases with decreasing N_{MH} due to reduced broadcast traffic.

6 Conclusion

We have proposed the CLEAR dynamic replica allocation scheme for improving data availability in M-P2P networks. CLEAR exploits user mobility patterns and deploys a super-peer architecture that facilitates replica allocation, while maintaining P2P autonomy. CLEAR avoids both broadcast storm during replica allocation as well as broadcast-based querying. CLEAR considers different levels of replica consistency and load as replica allocation criteria. Our performance study indicates that CLEAR indeed improves M-P2P data availability.

References

1. R. Bhagwan, D. Moore, S. Savage, and G. M. Voelker. Replication strategies for highly available peer-to-peer storage. *Proc. Future Directions in Distributed Computing*, 2003.
2. J. Broch, D.A. Maltz, D.B. Johnson, Y.C. Hu, and J. Jetcheva. A performance comparison of multi-hop wireless ad hoc network routing protocol. *Proc. MOBI-COM*, pages 159–164, 1998.
3. A. Datta, M. Hauswirth, and K. Aberer. Updates in highly unreliable replicated peer-to-peer systems. *Proc. ICDCS*, 2003.
4. L.D. Fife and L. Gruenwald. Research issues for data communication in mobile ad-hoc network database systems. *Proc. SIGMOD Record*, 32(2):22–47, 2003.
5. R. Guy, P. Reiher, D. Ratner, M. Gunter, W. Ma, and G. Popek. Rumor: Mobile data access through optimistic peer-to-peer replication. *Proc. ER Workshops*, 1998.
6. T. Hara. Effective replica allocation in ad hoc networks for improving data accessibility. *Proc. IEEE INFOCOM*, 2001.
7. T. Hara. Replica allocation in ad hoc networks with periodic data update. *Proc. MDM*, 2002.
8. T. Hara and S. K. Madria. Dynamic data replication using aperiodic updates in mobile ad-hoc networks. *Proc. DASFAA*, 2004.
9. B. Kemme. Implementing database replication based on group communication. *Proc. Future Directions in Distributed Computing*, 2002.
10. B. Kemme and G. Alonso. A new approach to developing and implementing eager database replication protocols. *Proc. ACM TODS*, 25(3), 2000.
11. V. Papadimos, D. Maier, and K. Tufte. Distributed query processing and catalogs for peer-to-peer systems. *Proc. CIDR*, 2003.
12. E. Pitoura. A replication scheme to support weak connectivity in mobile information systems. *Proc. DEXA*, 1996.
13. E. Pitoura and B. Bhargava. Maintaining consistency of data in mobile distributed environments. *Proc. ICDCS*, 1995.
14. D. Ratner, P.L. Reiher, G.J. Popek, and G.H. Kuenning. Replication requirements in mobile environments. *Proc. Mobile Networks and Applications*, 6(6), 2001.
15. B. Richard, D. Nioclais, and D. Chalon. Clique: A transparent, peer-to-peer replicated file system. *Proc. MDM*, 2003.
16. S. Saroiu, P.K. Gummadi, and S.D. Gribbler. A measurement study of peer-to-peer file sharing systems. *Proc. MMCN*, 2002.
17. G. Tsuchida, T. Okino, T. Mizuno, and S. Ishihara. Evaluation of a replication method for data associated with location in mobile ad hoc networks. *Proc. ICMU*, 2005.
18. O. Wolfson, S. Jajodia, and Y. Huang. An adaptive data replication algorithm. *Proc. ACM TODS*, 22(4):255–314, June 1997.

Lossless Reduction of Datacubes

Alain Casali, Rosine Cicchetti, Lotfi Lakhal, and Noël Novelli

Laboratoire d'Informatique Fondamentale de Marseille (LIF),
CNRS UMR 6166, Université de la Méditerranée
Case 901, 163 Avenue de Luminy, 13288 Marseille Cedex 9, France
lastname@lif.univ-mrs.fr

Abstract. Datacubes are specially useful for answering efficiently queries on data warehouses. Nevertheless the amount of generated aggregated data is incomparably more voluminous than the initial data which is itself very large. Recently, research work has addressed the issue of a concise representation of datacubes in order to reduce their size. The approach presented in this paper fits in a similar trend. We propose a concise representation, called Partition Cube, based on the concept of partition and define an algorithm to compute it. Various experiments are performed in order to compare our approach with methods fitting in the same trend. This comparison relates to the efficiency of algorithms computing the representations, the main memory requirements, and the storage space which is necessary.

1 Introduction and Motivations

In order to efficiently answer OLAP queries [3], a widely adopted solution is to compute and materialize datacubes [6,15,1,8]. Due to the large amounts of processed data, such a computation needs costly execution time and large main memory space. Furthermore, it yields huge volume of results, and their storage requires enormous space on disk.

The approaches addressing the issues of datacube computation and storage attempt to reduce one of the quoted drawbacks. For instance the algorithms BUC [1] and HCUBING [8] argue that OLAP users are interested in general trends. Therefore they enforce anti-monotone constraints and partially compute datacubes (iceberg cubes). Other methods take benefit of the statistic structure of data for computing density distributions and answering OLAP queries in an approximate way [17,16,5]. "Information lossless" approaches aim to find the best compromise between OLAP query efficiency and storage requirements without discarding any possible query (even unfrequent). Their main idea is to pre-compute and store aggregates frequently used while preserving all the data (possibly at various aggregation levels) necessary to compute on line the result of a not foreseen query. Research work on view materialization exemplifies this kind of approaches [9,7]. Finally, also fitting in the information lossless trend, three methods[1]: the Condensed Cube [18], the Quotient Cube [10] and the Closed

[1] Apart from approaches based on physical techniques.

S. Bressan, J. Küng, and R. Wagner (Eds.): DEXA 2006, LNCS 4080, pp. 409–419, 2006.

Cube [2] favour the optimization of storage space while preserving the capability to answer what ever query. The two latter compute the two smallest representations of a datacube and thus are the most efficient for both saving storage space and answering queries like "Is this behavior frequent or not?". Moreover, the two proposed representations make it possible to compute the exact data of a whole datacube. But such a computation is performed on line and results in an additional and significant response time for decision makers.

In this paper we investigate another way of tackling the problem: we propose a new representation which fully and exactly captures all the information enclosed in a datacube. Thus any query can be answered without additional execution time. Moreover, our representation provides a simple mechanism which reduce significantly the size of aggregates to be stored. More precisely, our contributions are the following:

(*i*) we propose a concise representation of datacubes: the Partition Cube, based on simple concepts extending the partitional model [11]. The concept of concise representation has been firstly introduced in [13] for frequent itemsets and it is used in this paper as a lossless representation of datacubes;

(*ii*) we introduce a depth-first search algorithm called PCUBE in order to built up the Partition Cube. It enumerates the aggregates to be computed according to the lectic order [4]. The reason behind such a choice is to minimize main memory requirements (and avoid swaps);

(*iii*) finally, though various experiments, we compare our approach with the representations by Quotient Cube and Closed Cube. The comparison concerns two points: on one hand the efficiency of computation algorithms and main memory requirements, and on the other hand the necessary storage space. Our representation provides an important reduction of storage when compared to the datacube. But, as expected, the Quotient Cube and the Closed Cube are smaller than the Partition Cube (even if, in theory and for extreme cases, the two latter can require the double of or be equal to the size of datacube itself which is never the case for the Partition Cube). Concerning the efficiency of the concise representation computations, our algorithm is the most efficient and not main memory greedy. Finally, let us underline that, once the Partition Cube is stored, any query can be answered on line with no additional computation time.

The remainder of the article is as follows. Our proposal is detailed in section 2. We define the concepts of our representation, the algorithm PCUBE and a relational implementation of our representation. We also relate results of experiments in section 3. In conclusion, we resume the strengths of our contribution.

2 Partition Cubes

The approach proposed in this paper proposes a concise representation of datacubes: the Partition Cube. Firstly, we present the concepts of our approach, then an algorithm intended to compute such a representation is defined. We also proposed a relational implementation in order to represent our solution in the environment presently the most used for managing data warehouses.

2.1 Basis Concepts

In this section, we introduce a new characterization of datacube which is based on simple concepts. Inspired from the notions of the partitional model [11], we introduce the fundamental concepts of our approach.

Definition 1 **[DM-Classe]**. Let r be a categorical database relation and X a set of dimension attributes. The dimension-measure class, called DM-Classe for simplicity, of a tuple t according to X, denoted by $[t]_X$, is constituted by the set of couples (identifier(u), measure(u)) of all the tuples u which are agree with t [13,12] according to a set of attribute X (*i.e.* the set of tuples u having the same values than t for X). Thus, we have: $[t]_X = \{(u[RowId], u[\mathcal{M}]) \mid u[X] = t[X], \forall u \in r\}$.

Example 1. Let us consider the relation TRAVEL (*cf.* table 1) which contains the attributes Continent (C_1), Country (C_2), City (C_3) and Number (N) yielding the number of travels sold for a given destination.

Table 1. Relation TRAVEL

RowId	Continent	Country	City	Number
1	Europe	France	Marseille	1
2	Europe	Italia	Torino	3
3	America	France	Pointe-à-Pitre	15
4	America	Brazil	Rio de Janeiro	12

The DM-Class associated to the first tuple according to the attribute C_2 (Country) groups all the couples (identifier, measure) of tuples related to the country 'France': $[t_1]_{C_2} = \{(1,1), (3,15)\}$.

All the DM-Classes for an attribute set X are gathered within a single set: the Dimension-Measure Partition [2].

Definition 2 **[DM-Partition]**. Let r be a categorical database relation and X a set of dimension attributes, the DM-Partition of r according to X, denoted by $\Pi_X(r)$, is defined as follows: $\Pi_X(r) = \{[t]_X, \forall\, t \in r\}$.

Example 2. In our examples, for a better readability, the DM-Classes are delimited by $<$ and $>$ when writing the DM-Partitions. With our example, the DM-Partition associated to the attribute C_2 is: $\Pi_{C_2}(r) = \{< (1,1), (3,15) >, < (2,3) >, < (4,12) >\}$.

[2] DM-Partition in short.

Let us consider two DM-Partitions computed according to the attribute sets X and Y. Their product yields the DM-Partition according to $X \cup Y$. Such a product is performed by intersecting DM-classes of the two DM-Partitions and preserving only non empty classes (cardinality greater than or equal to 1).

Lemma 2 **(Product of DM-Partitions).** Let r be a categorical database relation, X and Y two sets of dimension attributes, $\Pi_X(r)$ and $\Pi_Y(r)$ their respective DM-Partition. The product of the DM-partitions $\Pi_X(r)$ and $\Pi_Y(r)$, noted by $\Pi_X(r) \bullet_p \Pi_Y(r)$, returns the DM-Partition over $X \cup Y$ and is obtained as follows: $\Pi_X(r) \bullet_p \Pi_Y(r) = \Pi_{X \cup Y}(r) = \{[t]_Z = [t]_X \cap [t]_Y : [t]_Z \neq \emptyset,\ [t]_X \in \Pi_X(r)$ and $[t]_Y \in \Pi_Y(r)\}$.

Example 3. With our relation, the DM-Partitions related to the attributes C_1 (Continent) and C_2 are the following: $\Pi_{C_1}(r) = \{< (1,1),\ (2,3) >, < (3,15),\ (4,12) >\}$ and $\Pi_{C_2}(r) = \{< (1,1),\ (3,15) >, < (2,3) >, < (4,12) >\}$. Thus $\Pi_{C_1C_2}(r) = \Pi_{C_1}(r) \bullet_p \Pi_{C_2}(r) = \{< (1,1) >, < (2,3) >, < (3,15) >, < (4,12) > \}$.

Once the DM-Partitions are computed, the cuboids of the datacube can be easily obtained. Any DM-Class originates a tuple of a cuboid and the measure value is achieved by applying the aggregative function on the set of measure values of the DM-Class.

Example 4. As a consequence, we have $\Pi_{C_1C_2}(r) = \{ < (1,1) > , < (2,3) > , < (3,15) >, < (4,12) >\}$, thus the cuboid according to C_1C_2 is composed of four tuples: (E, F, ALL), (E, I, ALL), (A, F, ALL) and (A, B, ALL). Moreover, we have $\Pi_{C_1}(r) = \{< (1,1),\ (2,3) >, < (3,15),\ (4,12) >\}$, thus the cuboid according to C_1 encompasses two tuples: $(E, \text{ALL}, \text{ALL})$ and $(A, \text{ALL}, \text{ALL})$. For the latter cuboid, the value of the aggregative function SUM, applied on each DM-Class, is 4 (1+3) and 27 (15+12) respectively.

Each DM-Class is represented by a couple of numbers: the former is one of the identifiers of the original tuples gathered within the considered class, and the latter is the computed measure. All the so built couples are grouped within a set: the Partition Cuboid.

Definition 3 **[Partition Cuboid]**. Let $\Pi_X(r)$ be a DM-Partition of r and f an aggregative fonction. For each DM-Classe, $[t]_X.\mathcal{M}$ is the value of the measure attribute. The Partition Cuboid according to the attribute set X, denoted by $Cuboid_X(r)$, is defined as follows: $Cuboid_X(r) = \{(t[RowId], f([t]_X.\mathcal{M})), \forall\ [t]_X \in \Pi_X(r)\}$.

Example 5. As a consequence, the cuboid according to C_1 is the following:

Table 2. Cuboid according to Continent for the aggregative function SUM

C_1	C_2	C_3	SUM(V)
E	ALL	ALL	4
A	ALL	ALL	27

Our representation of the datacube can be defined as the whole set of Partition Cuboids according to any dimension combination.

Definition 4 **[Partition Cube]**. Let r be a categorical database relation. The Partition Cube associated to r, denoted Partition_Cube(r), is specified as follows: Partition_Cube(r) = $\{Cuboid_X(r), \forall\ X \in \mathcal{P}(\mathcal{D})\}$, where $\mathcal{P}$ stands for the powerset lattice.

Example 6. The Partition Cube for the aggregative function SUM is given in table 3. It encompasses $2^3 = 8$ cuboids (because there are 3 dimensions), each of which corresponding to a dimension combination (used as an index to identify cuboids).

Table 3. Partition Cube for the aggregative function SUM

$Cuboid_\emptyset =$	$\{(1,31)\}$
$Cuboid_{C_1} =$	$\{(1,4),(3,27)\}$
$Cuboid_{C_2} =$	$\{(1,16),(2,3),(4,12)\}$
$Cuboid_{C_3} =$	$\{(1,1),(2,3),(3,15),(4,12)\}$
$Cuboid_{C_1C_2} =$	$\{(1,1),(2,3),(3,15),(4,12)\}$
$Cuboid_{C_1C_3} =$	$\{(1,1),(2,3),(3,15),(4,12)\}$
$Cuboid_{C_2C_3} =$	$\{(1,1),(2,3),(3,15),(4,12)\}$
$Cuboid_{C_1C_2C_3} =$	$\{(1,1),(2,3),(3,15),(4,12)\}$

2.2 The PCUBE Algorithm

In this section, we describe the principles of our algorithmic solution. In a first time, we recall the definition of the lectic order (inverse lexicographical order) [4] which is a strict linear order over the set of all subsets of a set. Then, we propose a new recursive algorithm for enumerating, according to the the lectic order, the subsets of $\mathcal{P}(\mathcal{D})$.

Definition 5 **[Lectic Order]**. Let $(\mathcal{D}, <_\mathcal{D})$ be a finite set totally ordered. We assume, by simplicity, that $\mathcal{D}$ can be defined as follows: $\mathcal{D} = \{A_1, A_2, \ldots A_n\}$. $\mathcal{D}$ is provided with the following operator:

$$\begin{aligned} Max : \mathcal{P}(\mathcal{D}) &\rightarrow \mathcal{D} \\ X &\mapsto \text{the last element of } X \text{ according to } <_\mathcal{D}. \end{aligned}$$

The lectic order, denoted by $<_l$, is defined as follows: $\forall\ X, Y \in \mathcal{P}(\mathcal{D})$, $X <_l Y \Leftrightarrow Max(X\setminus Y) < Max(Y\setminus X)$.

Proposition 1 *[4].* $\forall\ X, Y \in \mathcal{P}(\mathcal{D})$, $X \subset Y \Rightarrow X <_l Y$.

Recursive algorithmic schema for enumerating the subsets in lectic order

The new algorithm Ls (Lectic Subsets) gives the general algorithmic schema used by PCUBE. It is provided with two dimensional attribute subsets X and Y. The algorithm is based on a twofold recursion and the recursive calls form a binary balanced tree in which each execution branch returns a dimensional subset. The general strategy for enumerating dimensional attribute combinations consists in considering firstly all the subsets not encompassing a dimensional attribute, and then all the subsets which encompass it. More precisely, the maximal attribute, according to the lectic order, is discarded from Y and appended to X in the variable Z. The algorithm is recursively applied with (i) X and a new subset Y (from which the maximal attribute is pruned), then (ii) Z and Y. The first call of Ls is provided with two parameters $X = \emptyset$ and $Y = \mathcal{D}$.

Algorithm 1. Algorithm Ls

Input: X and Y two sets of dimensions
Output: $\mathcal{P}(Y)$

if $Y = \emptyset$ **then Return** X
$A := max(Y)$
$Y := Y\setminus\{A\}$
$LS(X, Y)$
$Z := X \cup \{A\}$
$LS(Z, Y)$

Lemma 5. The correctness of the algorithm Ls is based on proposition 1 and because of the distributive property of the lattice of the dimension attributes, we have: $\forall\ A \in \mathcal{D}, \forall\ X \subseteq \mathcal{D}, \mathcal{P}(X \cup A) \cap \mathcal{P}(\mathcal{D}\setminus(X \cup A)) = \emptyset$. Thus, each subset of dimension attributes is enumerated exactly once.

We propose an algorithm, called PCUBE, for computing datacubes. It fits in the theoretical framework previously presented. A pre-processing step in required in order to build DM-Partitions according to each single attribute from the input relation. While performing this initial step, the computation of the cuboid according to the empty set is operated and its result is yielded. If the original partitions $(\cup_{A\in\mathcal{D}}\Pi_A(r))$ cannot fit in main memory, then the fragmentation strategy proposed in [15] and used in [1] is applied. It divides the input relation in fragments according to an attribute until the original associated DM-partitions can be loaded. PCUBE adopts the general algorithm schema of Ls but it is intended to compute all desired aggregates and thus it yields the condensed representation of all possible cuboids. PCUBE deals with DM-partitions and enforces product of DM-partitions. Like Ls, its input parameters are the subsets X and Y. The DM-Partition associated to Z is computed by applying the product over the two partitions in memory: $\Pi_X(r)$ and $\Pi_A(r)$. The second recursive call is performed only if the DM-Partition according to Z is not empty. The pseudo-code of the algorithm PCUBE is given below.

Algorithm 2. Algorithm PCUBE

Input: Set of DM-Partitions $\{\Pi_A,\ A \in \mathcal{D}\}$, X and Y two set of dimension attributes
Output: Partition Cube

```
1: if Y = ∅ then
2:    WRITE_CUBOID(X)
3: else
4:    Y := Y \ max_{<D}(Y)
5:    PCUBE(r, X, Y)
6:    Z := X ∪ max_{<D}(Y)
7:    Π_Z(r) := Π_X(r) •_p Π_{max_{<D}(Y)}(r)
8:    if Π_Z(r) ≠ ∅ then PCUBE(r, Z, Y) End If
9: end if
```

2.3 Relational Representation

When the OLAP application is managed by a relational system, the Partition Cube can be stored through a relation (called Cube) in which each tuple describes a DM-Class of a cuboid according to X. More precisely, for each DM-Class, are known the identifier of its representing element, the measure value and the dimension combinaison (*DimId*). Like in the other approaches computing cubes, real values of dimensions are encoded with integers [15,1,8]. We propose the following schema for managing our representation:

$$r(\underline{RowId}, \mathcal{D}, \mathcal{M})$$
$$Dimension(\underline{DimId}, \mathcal{D})$$
$$Cube(\underline{RowId, DimId}, f(\mathcal{M}))$$

The relation *Dimension* is intended for storing all the dimension combinations. Its values are binary and for any attribute A, A has the value 0 if it does not belong to the considered combination, else its value is 1. Finally the original relation makes it possible to retrieve the real values of dimensions for various representing elements of the DM-Classes.

3 Experimental Evaluations

We choose to compare our approach with the two most concise representations not loosing information. Through these experiments, our aim is to compare the representation computation times, the underlying main memory requirements and the size of the datacube to be stored. In order to compute the Quotient Cube and Closed Cube, we use the algorithm CLOSE [14], proved to be very efficient for mining frequent closed patterns, because we have its sources. The computer has a Pentium 4 to 3 GHz with 1 Gb of RAM and runs under Windows XP. Implementations are performed in C++ and compiled with c++ (GCC) 3.3.3 (cygwin).

Table 4 gives the datasets used for experiments. In the last column, the size in bytes of the dataset is reported (each dimension or attribute is encoded as an integer requiring 4 bytes for any value). Remark: The two datasets `Mushroom` and `Joint_Objects_Tombs` require too much main memory (> 4Go) when computing the Quotient Cube and the Closed Cube with a minimum threshold equal to 1 (all the possible patterns), thus we have to state a minimum threshold to 5% and 1%.

Table 4. Datasets

Tables	# Attributes	# Tuples	Size
mushroom	23	8 124	747 408
death	5	389	7 780
TombNecropolis	7	1 846	51 688
TombObjects	12	8 278	397 344
Joint_Objects_Tombs	17	7 643	519 724

Table 5. Results of CLOSE executions

	CLOSE	
Tables	Time (s)	Max Memory (Mb)
mushroom 5%	110 (1m50s)	354,1
death	2,9	8,1
TombNecropolis	8,7	12,8
TombObjects	508,3 (8m30s)	721,0
Joint_Objects_Tombs 1%	24,5	36,3

Table 6. Results of PCUBE executions

	PCUBE	
Tables	Time (s)	Max Memory (Mb)
mushroom	4 173 (1h9m33s)	4,8
mushroom 5%	786 (13m6s)	4,7
death	<1ms	2,5
TombNecropolis	0,16	2,6
TombObjects	2,60	3,7
Joint_Objects_Tombs	83 (1m23s)	4,1
Joint_Objects_Tombs 1%	12,8	4,0

Tables 5 and 6 present the results obtained for the algorithms CLOSE and PCUBE for the various datasets. The column `Time` indicates in seconds the execution times and the column `Max Memory` shows in Mb the maximal used memory.

PCUBE is specially efficient and its memory requirements are incomparably lower than the ones of CLOSE. Concerning the size of datacube representations, the best results are obtained for the Closed Cube and then the Quotient Cube. Although more voluminous, the Partition Cube reduces significantly the size of stored data. For instance, the Partition Cube computed for the dataset `Mushroom` only needs 12% of the space necessary to store the datacube. In the worst case (few attributes) the gain is about 50%.

The counterpart of storage saving for the Quotient and Closed Cubes is an efficiency deterioration when evaluating OLAP queries. Actually, with these two representations, only a cover of a datacube is preserved and additional computations are necessary to answer OLAP queries.

- PCUBE computes a concise representation of the data cube which is based on its characterization (DM-Classes, DM-Partitions and their product). In such a representation, a row of the cube encompasses three elements: $RowId$, $DimId$ and $f(\mathcal{M})$. Moreover, $DimId$ can be encoded as a bit field to avoid the join operation with the relation Dimension when evaluating OLAP queries. In a similar way, the link with the original relation (through $RowId$) does not require a join operation but a direct index. When the number of dimensions is less than 32, each attribute value needs 4 bytes and thus each row 12 bytes. The representation includes the original relation. Thus its size is equal to: $NbRows \times 12 + RelationSize$.
- For the Quotient and the Closed Cubes, the size of any row is obtained by the product of the number of dimensions and the measure in the original relation by 4 bytes (dimensions are encoded as integers). The obtained size is: $NbRows \times (|Dim| + 1) \times 4$.

Table 7 illustrates the size of the three studied representations for the various datasets.

Table 7. Size of the datacubes

	Size of the datacube (byte)			
	"Classical"	Partition	Closed	Quotient
TombNecropolis	3 639 072	1 416 340	189 728	543 232
TombObjects	903 611 124	208 922 988	8 032 648	25 806 404
Joint_Objects_Tombs (1%)	58 848 264	10 327 768	4 485 168	9 720 576
Death	220 152	117 856	24 984	73 656
Mushroom (5%)	436 823 808	55 350 384	1 233 984	3 265 344

4 Conclusion

When addressing the issue of datacube computation and storage, we are interested in the two approaches proposing the most concise representations: the

Quotient Cube and Closed Cube. We propose an alternative method also providing a storage reduction but less important. Nevertheless, since all the data is stored, OLAP queries can be answered very efficiently (simple selections in a table) while other approaches require additional computations for yielding results. Let us underline that in the worst cases, when data is very sparse, the size of the Quotient Cube can be double of the datacube size and the Closed Cube can be as voluminous as the datacube. In contrast, when there are more than two dimensions, the Partition Cube is always smaller than the data cube. So our approach is a compromise between datacube storage reduction and efficient execution of OLAP queries.

References

1. K. Beyer and R. Ramakrishnan. Bottom-Up Computation of Sparse and Iceberg CUBEs. In *Proceedings of the International Conference on Management of Data, SIGMOD*, pages 359–370, 1999.
2. A. Casali, R. Cicchetti, and L. Lakhal. Extracting semantics from datacubes using cube transversals and closures. In *Proc. of the 9th ACM SIGKDD International Conference on Knowledge Discovery and Data Mining, KDD*, pages 69–78, 2003.
3. S. Chaudhuri and U. Dayal. An Overview of Data Warehousing and OLAP Technology. In *SIGMOD Record*, volume 26(1), pages 65–74, 1997.
4. B. Ganter and R. Wille. *Formal Concept Analysis: Mathematical Foundations*. Springer, 1999.
5. A. Gilbert, Y. Kotidis, S. Muthukrishnan, and M. Strauss. Surfing Wavelets on Streams : One-Pass Summaries for Approximate Queries. In *Proceedings of 27th International Conference on Very Large Data Bases, VLDB*, pages 79–88, 2001.
6. J. Gray, S. Chaudhuri, A. Bosworth, A. Layman, D. Reichart, M. Venkatrao, F. Pellow, and H. Pirahesh. Data cube: A relational aggregation operator generalizing group-by, cross-tab, and sub-totals. In *Data Mining and Knowledge Discovery*, volume 1(1), pages 29–53, 1997.
7. H. Gupta and I. Mumick. Selection of Views to Materialize in a Data Warehouse. In *IEEE Transactions on Knowledge and Data Engineering, TKDE*, volume 17 (1/2005), pages 24–43, 2005.
8. J. Han, J. Pei, G. Dong, and K. Wang. Efficient Computation of Iceberg Cubes with Complex Measures. In *Proceedings of the International Conference on Management of Data, SIGMOD*, pages 441–448, 2001.
9. V. Harinarayan, A. Rajaraman, and J. Ullman. Implementing data cubes efficiently. In *Proceedings of the International Conference on Management of Data, SIGMOD*, pages 205–216, 1996.
10. L. Lakshmanan, J. Pei, and J. Han. Quotient cube: How to summarize the semantics of a data cube. In *Proceedings of the 28th International Conference on Very Large Databases, VLDB*, pages 778–789, 2002.
11. D. Laurent and N. Spyratos. Partition semantics for incomplete information in relational databases. In *Proceedings of the International Conference on Management of Data, SIGMOD*, pages 66–73, 1988.
12. S. Lopes, J. M. Petit, and L. Lakhal. Functional and Approximate Dependency Mining: Databases and FCA points of View. In *Experimental and Theoretical Artificial Intelligence (JETAI): Special Issue on Concept Lattice-based theory, methods and tools for Knowledge Discovery in Databases*, volume 14(2-3), pages 93–114, 2002.

13. H. Mannila and H. Toivonen. Multiple Uses of Frequent Sets and Condensed Representations: Extended Abstract. In *Proceedings of the 2nd International Conference on Knowledge Discovery and Data Mining, KDD*, pages 189–194, 1996.
14. N. Pasquier, Y. Bastide, R. Taouil, and L. Lakhal. Discovering frequent closed itemsets for association rules. In *Proceedings of the 7th International Conference on Database Theory, ICDT*, pages 398–416, 1999.
15. K. Ross and D. Srivastava. Fast Computation of Sparse Datacubes. In *Proceedings of the 23rd International Conference on Very Large Databases, VLDB*, pages 116–125, 1997.
16. J. Shanmugasundaram, U. Fayyad, and P. Bradley. Compressed Data Cubes for OLAP Aggregate Query Approximation on Continuous Dimensions. In *Proceedings of the 5th ACM SIGKDD International Conference on Knowledge Discovery and Data Mining, KDD*, pages 223–232, 1999.
17. J. Vitter and M. Wang. Approximate Computation of Multidimensional Aggregates of Sparse Data Using Wavelets . In *Proceedings ACM SIGMOD International Conference on Management of Data, SIGMOD*, pages 193–204, 1999.
18. W. Wang, H. Lu, J. Feng, and J. Yu. Condensed Cube: An Effective Approach to Reducing Data Cube Size. In *Proceedings of the 18th International Conference on Data Engineering, ICDE*, pages 213–222, 2002.

Multivariate Stream Data Classification Using Simple Text Classifiers

Sungbo Seo[1,*], Jaewoo Kang[2,3], Dongwon Lee[4], and Keun Ho Ryu[1]

[1] Dept. of Computer Science, Chungbuk National University, Chungbuk, Korea
{sbseo, khryu}@dblab.chungbuk.ac.kr
[2] Dept. of Computer Science and Engineering, Korea University, Seoul, Korea
[3] Dept. of Computer Science, North Carolina State University, Raleigh, NC, USA
kang@csc.ncsu.edu
[4] College of Information Sciences and Technology, Penn State University, PA, USA
dongwon@psu.edu

Abstract. We introduce a classification framework for continuous multivariate stream data. The proposed approach works in two steps. In the preprocessing step, it takes as input a sliding window of multivariate stream data and discretizes the data in the window into a string of symbols that characterize the signal changes. In the classification step, it uses a simple text classification algorithm to classify the discretized data in the window. We evaluated both supervised and unsupervised classification algorithms. For supervised, we tested Naïve Bayes Model and SVM, and for unsupervised, we tested Jaccard, TFIDF, Jaro and JaroWinkler. In our experiments, SVM and TFIDF outperformed the other classification methods. In particular, we observed that classification accuracy is improved when the correlation of attributes is also considered along with the n-gram tokens of symbols.

1 Introduction

Different sensor network applications generate different types of data and have different requirements for data processing (e.g., long term monitoring of sea level change vs. real-time intrusion detection). Different data processing strategies need to be considered for the different types of applications. Even in the same application, the characteristics of data generated in the network sometimes changes over time. For example, in a network monitoring application, users may want to receive only 5% samples of original data when network operates normally, while they might want to receive full data for further analysis when an interesting pattern (e.g., similar to a predefined intrusion pattern) is detected. The ability of handling sensor data adaptively by detecting changing characteristics of data becomes important in many data-centric sensor applications.

In order to address this problem, we propose a scalable framework for multivariate stream data classification that allows using simple, well-understood text classifiers to classify multivariate streams, instead of building custom classification algorithms for

* Work performed while the author visited North Carolina State University.

S. Bressan, J. Küng, and R. Wagner (Eds.): DEXA 2006, LNCS 4080, pp. 420–429, 2006.

different sensor applications. The proposed method works in two steps as follows. It first discretizes the stream data into a string of symbols that characterize the signal changes, and then applies classification algorithms to classify the transformed data. This transformation simplifies the classification task significantly.

The classification model is learned from a user-labeled data. Users assign a descriptive label to each window in the training set. For example, if the sensor data in a window contains an intrusion pattern, the user labels the window as "intrusion". Similarly, if a window contains normal signals, it can be labeled as "normal". Once the classification model is built, the classifier can start taking new windows of data and predict the labels for the windows. For the classification step, we evaluated both supervised and unsupervised methods. For supervised, we tested Naïve Bayes Model and SVM, and for unsupervised, we tested Jaccard, TFIDF, Jaro and JaroWinkler.

We identify the contributions of our work as follows:

1. In order for fast pattern matching, we discretized the continuous sensor streams into a string of symbols characterizing signal changes. In order to allow partial matches and to retain temporal locality of patterns, we chunked the symbol strings into various lengths of n-grams. This representation gives rise to a large number of widely used string and vector-space classifiers.
2. The proposed framework and the classification model can be utilized for the sensor network querying and monitoring in general. It enables the real-time monitoring of continuous sensor data. Moreover, it can also be used for the analysis of historical data accumulated in a server. Using the method, we can serve ad-hoc queries such as finding windows that have similar data to the input pattern.

The rest of the paper is organized as follows. Section 2 introduces related work. Section 3 describes our multivariate stream data classification methods. Section 4 presents experimental results and Section 5 presents concluding remarks.

2 Related Work

In our problem context, sensor data is an unbounded multivariate time series data. Multivariate time series data classification methods were studied in [4, 5, 6, 7, 8], including On-demand Classifier [4], HMM (Hidden Markov Models) [5], RNN (Recurrent Neural Network), Dynamic Time Warping [5], weighted ensemble classifier [6] and SAX [7]. These methods involve large numbers of parameters and complex preprocessing step that need to be tuned. Due to the dynamic nature of sensor network environment and the diverse types of applications, the applicability and effectiveness of these specialized solutions is not immediately clear for the sensor network applications.

On the other hand, there exist many popular general purpose classifiers that work for string and vector-space models, including Bayesian classifiers [11], Support Vector Machines (SVM) [12] and string-distance based methods [14]. In our proposed approach, we discretize the multivariate continuous time series data into a series of symbols. This transformation allows sensor data to be viewed as a sequence of words consisting of the symbols, giving rise to such general purpose classifiers.

3 Multivariate Stream Data Classification

3.1 Problem Definition

In a hierarchically organized sensor network as shown in Fig. 1, a sensor node represents a collection of heterogeneous sensors collocated in the same geographical location. Each of these sensors monitors or detects different target objects or events. The sensor data generated from such a sensor node collectively forms a multivariate data stream. Each sensor node temporarily accumulates the sensor data and periodically sends it to the parent node in the upper layer. The parent node then collects data transmitted from children nodes and either relays it up to the chain (e.g., from sensor node to base station), or stores them in the repository or feeds them to the application for further processing (server node).

The problem we attempt to address in this paper can be formulated as follows. As illustrated in Fig.1, let $t_i = [s_{1i}, s_{2i}, \ldots, s_{mi}]$ be an m-dimensional tuple, representing sensor readings from *m* different sensors (s_1 to s_m) at time point *i*. Let $W_j = [t_{j*p+1}, t_{j*p+2}, \ldots, t_{(j+1)*p}]$ be a *j*-th window of size *p*, containing *p* tuples from t_{j*p+1} to $t_{(j+1)*p}$. Finally, let $T = [W_1, W_2, \ldots, W_\infty]$ be an unbounded stream of windows. Suppose the

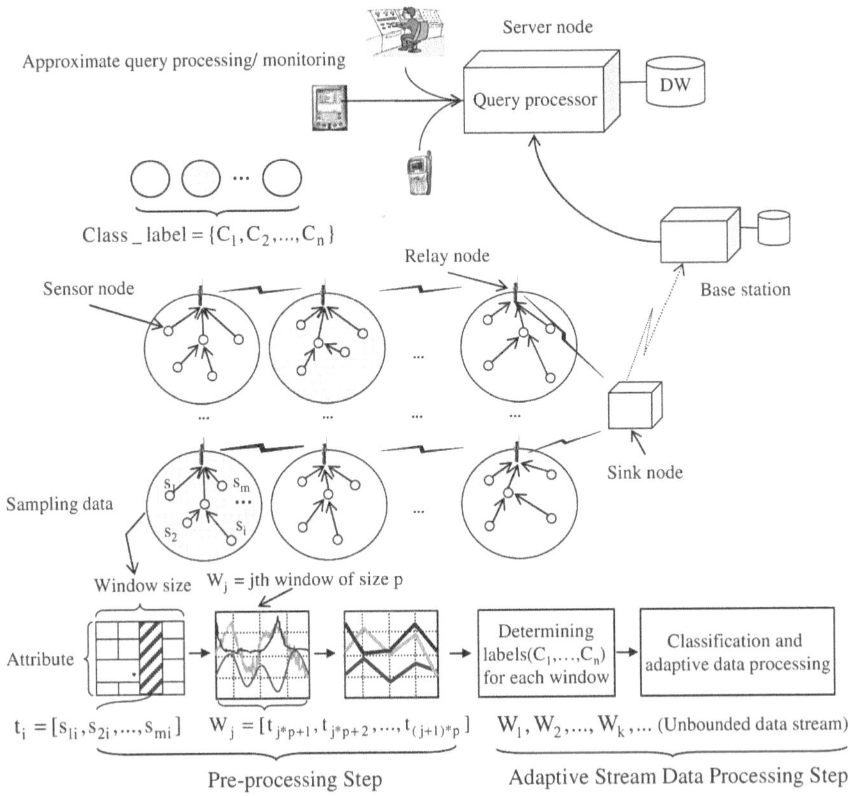

Fig. 1. Overview of real-time data analysis in wireless sensor networks

first k windows (W_1 to W_k) are pre-labeled by the user. Each user labeled window has a class label chosen from n labels, C_1 to C_n. Then, the problem is to build a classifier to predict the labels for all subsequent windows (W_{k+1} to W_∞) based on the labeled windows.

3.2 Preprocessing Step

Fig. 2 shows the preprocessing step for our approach. In this step, the continuous sensor stream is transformed into the combinations of discrete symbols which represent signal changes in each sensor stream, such as upward (*U* for steep inclination and *u* for moderate inclination), downward (*D* for deep and *d* for moderate) or stable (*S*) for a given time interval [t_i, t_{i+k}] where k being a constant between 1 and the window size p. This transformation greatly reduces the complexity of the raw data while retaining the structure of the time series data. For fast trend analysis and pattern matching, we use a hierarchical piecewise linear representation [9] and n-gram model [11] which together can represent various different types of multivariate stream data. In this paper, we used the five symbols (*U, u, D, d,* and *S*) as shown in Fig. 2(a). All the attributes in a window can be represented as in Fig. 2(b) using this representation.

We extended the original hierarchical piecewise linear representation, which splits the original patterns into a set of disjoint sub-patterns, with n-gram based pattern chunking in order to support partial matches and to preserve the orderings between the

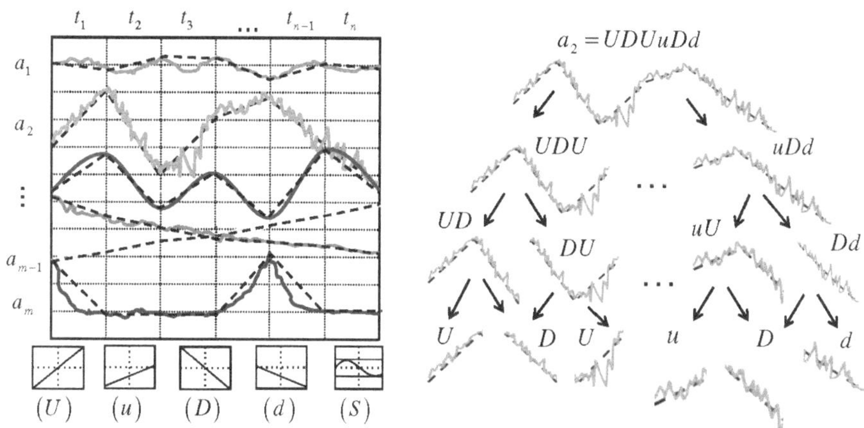

(a) Unit of sensing data

(b) Hierarchical piecewise linear representation

1-gram	*U, u, D, d, S*
2-gram	*UU, Uu, UD, … ,DS, dS, SS*
3-gram	*UUU, UuD , … , UuD,DSD*
4-gram	*UUUU, UuDd, …, DuUs*
5-gram	*UUUUU, UuDds, …, DuUds*
Correlation	a_1a_2 , a_1a_3 , … , $a_{m-1}a_m$

(c) List of n-gram and correlation

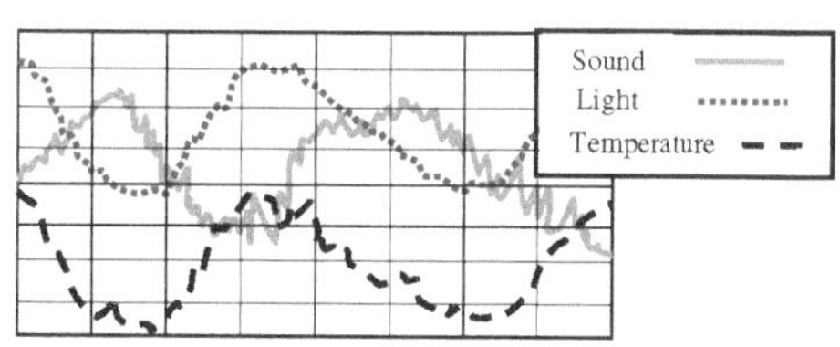

(d) Correlation of multivariate attributes

Fig. 2. The preprocessing step in multivariate data classification sub-patterns. Fig. 2(c) shows an example of n-gram based chunking. Moreover, in order to improve the classification accuracy, we exploit the inter-dependency structure that exists among the sensors (e.g., light and temperature), as illustrated in Fig 2(d).

We added the symbols representing the pairings of sensors that have a strong correlation (we used 0.6 as a threshold) into the list of original n-gram symbols as shown in the last row of Fig. 2(c). For example, if sensor a_1 and a_2 are correlated, we add a word, "a_1a_2", to the list. Once the data is transformed, we can simply treat them as a string of words and apply simple text classification algorithms to classify the data. In what follows, we will describe the details of the classification algorithms that we considered in our framework.

3.3 Supervised Methods

NBM (Naïve Bayes Model)**:** Bayesian classifiers are statistical classifiers and have exhibited high accuracy and speed when applied to a large database [11]. This technique chooses the highest posterior probability class using the prior probability computed from the training data set. For example, in the training phase, it learns the prior probability distribution such as, $P(uD|class{=}intrusion)$ and $P(a_1a_2|class{=}normal)$, from the training data. In the test step, for each unlabeled window, a posterior probability is evaluated for each class C_i, as shown in (1). The test data is then assigned to class C_i for which $P(C_i|X)$ is the maximum.

$$P(C_i \mid X) = \frac{P(X \mid C_i)P(C_i)}{P(X)}, \text{ where } P(X \mid C_i) = \prod_{k=1}^{n} P(x_k \mid C_i) \text{ for } 1 \le i, j \le m,\ i \ne j \qquad (1)$$

SVM (Support Vector Machine)**:** This method is one of the most popular supervised classification methods. SVM is basically two-class classifier and can be extended for the multi-class classification (e.g., combining multiple one-versus-the-rest two-class classifiers). In our model, each window is mapped to a point in a high dimensional space, each dimension of which corresponds to an n-gram word or a correlation pair. For example, if a sliding window, W_i is {uD=2, UUd=10, $UDDD$=5, a_ia_{i+1}=0.8}, feature vector lists are {uD, UUd, $UDDD$, a_ia_{i+1}} and values according to the frequency factor are {0.2, 0.8, 0.6, 0.8}. The coordinates of the point are the frequencies of the n-gram words or coefficients of the correlation pairs in the corresponding dimensions. SVM learns, in the training step, the maximum-margin hyper-planes separating each class.

In testing step, it classifies a new window by mapping it to a point in the same high-dimensional space divided by the hyper-plane learned in the training step. For experiments, we used the Radial Basis Function (RBF) kernel [12], $K(x_i, y_i) = e^{-\gamma\|x_i - y_i\|^2}, (\gamma > 0)$. The soft margin allows errors during training. We set 0.1 for the two-norm soft margin value.

3.4 Unsupervised Methods

String-based Distance: This scheme measures the distance between two strings in order to measure the similarity. We can obtain the best matching class by comparing the feature vectors (standard vector space representations of documents) of each known class with that of input data. Among many possible distance measures, we used two token-based string distance (Jaccard and TFIDF) and two edit-distance-based metrics (Jaro and Jaro-Winkler) that were reported to give a good performance for the general name matching problem in [14]. We briefly describe the metrics below. For details of each metric, refer to [13]. Using the terms of Table 1, the four metrics (2-5) can be defined as follows.

Table 1. Terms for string-based distance

Name	Descriptions	Name	Descriptions
x , y	n-grams and correlations for each sensor attribute.	$CC_{x,y}$	All characters in x common with y
C_x	All characters of x .	T_x	All n-gram and correlation terms for x .
$X_{x,y}$	# of transpositions of char in x relative to y		

$$\text{Jaccard}(x, y) = \frac{|T_x \cap T_y|}{|T_x \cup T_y|} \tag{2}$$

$$\text{TFIDF}(x, y) = \sum_{w \in T_x \cap T_y} V(w, T_x) \times V(w, T_y), \text{ where}$$

$$V(w,T_x) = log\left(TF_{w,T_y} + 1\right) \times \frac{log\left(IDF_w\right)}{\sqrt{\sum_{w}\left(log\left(TF_{w,T_y}+1\right) \times log\left(IDF_w\right)\right)}} \text{ (symmetrical for } V(w,T_y)\text{)}, \tag{3}$$

TF_{w,T_x} is the frequency of w in T_x , and IDF_w is the inverse of the fraction of names in a corpus containing w .

$$\text{Jaro}(x, y) = \frac{1}{3} \times \left(\frac{|CC_{x,y}|}{C_x} + \frac{|CC_{y,x}|}{C_y} + \frac{|CC_{x,y}| - X_{CC_{x,y},CC_{y,x}}}{2|CC_{x,y}|} \right) \tag{4}$$

$$\text{Jaro-Winkler}(x, y) = Jaro(x,y) + \frac{max(|L|,4)}{10} \times (1 - Jaro(x,y)), \text{ where } L \text{ is the longest common prefix of } x \text{ and } y \tag{5}$$

Vector-based Cosine Distance: This approach uses vector based distances to measure the similarity of the symbols. We model the n-gram symbols and correlation lists as vectors in the vector space. Each dimension of a vector corresponds to a unique term (i.e., an n-gram or an attribute pair for correlation) whose value consists of either a frequency of the term in the given window (if an n-gram) or the correlation coefficient of the two attributes (if an attribute pair). In order to measure the similarity of two vectors, we use a cosine distance, which is an angle between the two vectors, defined as: $Cos\theta = \frac{W_1 \bullet W_2}{\|W_1\| \bullet \|W_2\|}$ [11].

4 Experimental Results

In our experiment, we used two types of multivariate time series data obtained from [16]. Fig. 3(a) shows an example of the first data set containing six different classes of control patterns (Normal (a), Cyclic (b), Increasing trend (c), Decreasing trend (d), Upward shift (e), Downward shift (f)). Fig. 3(b) shows a fragment of the second data set which is robot traces containing force and torque measurements on a robot moving an object from one location to another. Each movement is characterized by 15 force/torque samples collected at regular time intervals starting immediately after failure detection. The trace data consists of 5 datasets, each of them defining a different learning problem labeled from LP1 to LP5 [16]. For experiments, we prepared a training data set that includes six different classes of control patterns and robot behavior classes such as normal, collision, and obstruction.

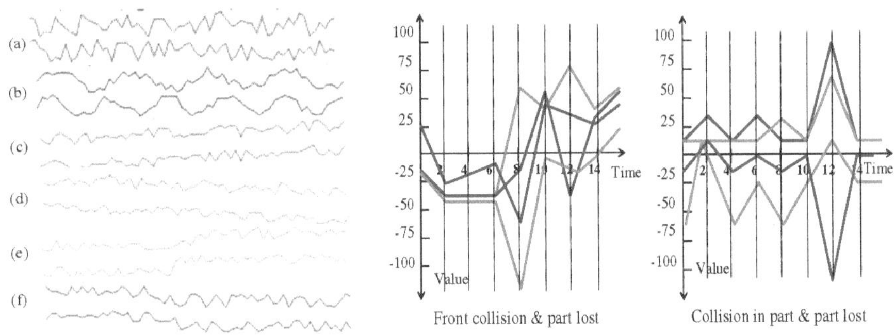

(a) Six different time series data

(b) Examples of typical robot traces

Fig. 3. Data set: SCCTS and robot execution data

We performed k-fold cross-validation in order to evaluate the accuracy of each classification method. For the k-fold cross-validation, an input data set (S) is randomly partitioned into k mutually exclusive subsets ($S = \{S_1, S_2, \ldots, S_k\}$) of equal size. Training and testing is performed k times. In iteration i, the subset S_i is reserved as the test set, and the remaining subsets are collectively used to train the classifier. The accuracy of the classifier is then the overall number of correct classifications from the k iterations, divided by the total number of trials.

The result of experiments is shown in Fig 4. Fig 4(a) shows the accuracy of the six classifiers discussed in Section 3 using only the n-gram tokens and not considering the correlation tokens (see Fig 2(c).) Fig 4(b) shows the result using the both types of tokens. Different lengths of n-gram tokens are compared. For example, "3-gram" in the x-axis represents the classifications using only tokens up to length three (i.e., 1-3 grams).

As expected, the accuracy was gradually improved as longer tokens were taken into consideration. The longer tokens are likely to capture more temporal locality of patterns. The accuracy was generally higher when the correlation tokens were used along with the n-gram tokens. Noticeable improvements were observed in 3 and 4-gram experiments as shown in Fig. 4.

As expected, supervised methods (NBM and SVM) were more accurate than unsupervised methods. SVM showed the best performance among the tested methods. Among the unsupervised methods, classifiers using token-based string distance metrics were more accurate than the ones using edit-distance metrics. For this experiment, we used the classification library and package obtained from [17, 18].

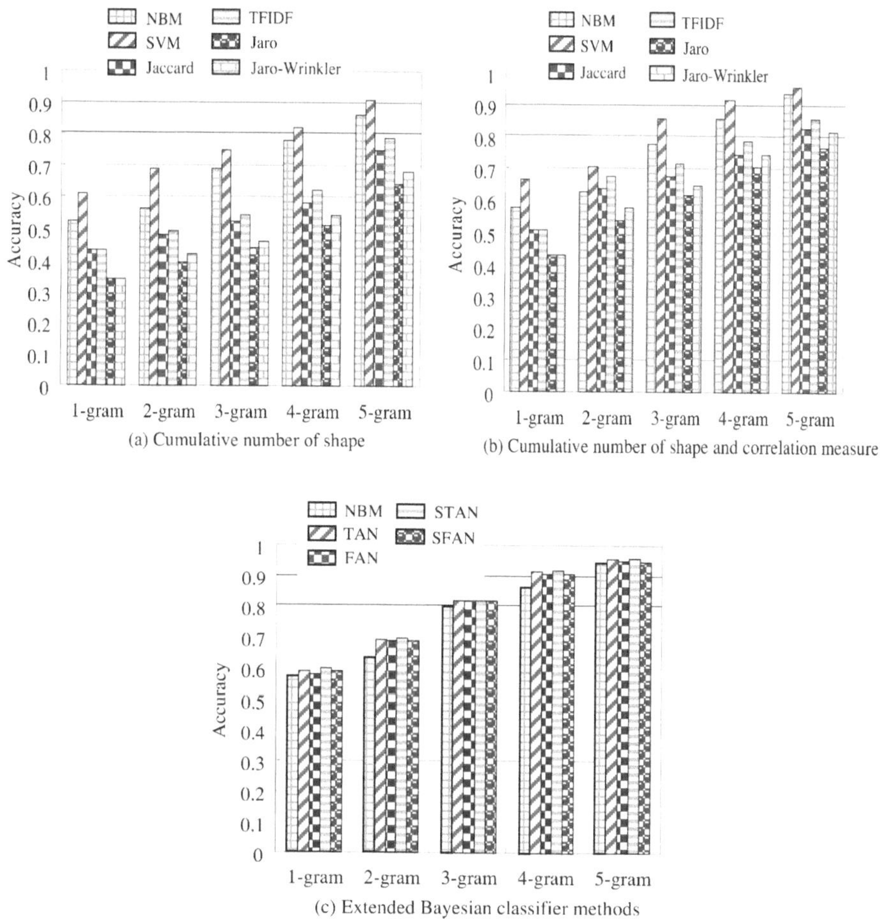

Fig. 4. Accuracy comparison (number of shapes and correlations between attributes)

Naïve Bayesian classifier in Fig. 4(a) assumes that the effect of an attribute on a given class is independent of the values of the other attributes. This assumption is called class conditional independence. However, attribute values of multivariate stream data collected from WSN may not be entirely independent from each others. For example, it is likely that the sensor readings of light and temperature would be correlated. In order to address this problem, in our experiment, we considered a set of extended Bayesian classifiers known to work well with correlated data, including TAN (Tree Augmented Naïve Bayes), FAN (Forest Augmented Naïve Bayes), STAN(Selective

Tree Augmented Naïve Bayes), and SFAN(Selective Tree Augmented Naïve Bayes) [15, 19]. Experimental results show that TAN and STAN method are better than the other methods as shown in Fig. 4(c). The result shows that the dependencies among attributes affect the classification accuracy for multivariate stream data.

5 Conclusion

In this paper, we proposed a scalable framework for multivariate stream data classification for continuous stream data. For classification, we employed the hierarchical piecewise linear representation to transform the continuous sensor streams into a discrete symbolic representation, which allows us to choose a classifier from a large pool of well-studied classification methods. We considered supervised methods including Naïve or extended Bayesian Model and SVM, and unsupervised methods including Jaccard, TFIDF, Jaro and Jaro-Winkler. In experimental results, SVM and TFIDF outperformed the other classification methods, and classification accuracy is higher when the correlations of attributes are also considered along with the n-gram token list.

Acknowledgement. This work was partially supported by the RRC Program of MOCIE and ITEP, and by ETRI (Telematics & USN Research Division) in Korea.

References

1. A. Mainwaring and J. Polastre, et al.: Wireless Sensor Networks for habitat monitoring. In WSNA (2002), pp.88-97
2. B. Xu and O. Wolfson.: Time-Series Prediction with Applications to Traffic and Moving Objects Databases. In MobiDE (2003), pp.56-60
3. R. C. Oliver and K. Smettem, et al.: Field Testing a Wireless Sensor Network for Reactive Environmental Monitoring. In ISSNIP (2004), pp.7-12
4. C. C. Aggrawal, J. Han, and P. S. Yu.: On Demand Classification of Data Streams. In KDD (2004), pp.503-508
5. M. W. Kadous and C. Sammut.: Classification of multivariate time series and structured data using constructive induction. Machine Learning Journal (2005), pp.176-216
6. H. Wang, W. Fan, P. S. Yu, and J. Han.: Mining Concept-Drifting Data Streams Using Ensemble Classifiers. In SIGKDD (2003), pp.226-235
7. J. Lin, E. Keogh, S. Lonardi, and B. Chiu.: A Symbolic Representation of Time Series with Implications for Streaming Algorithms. In DMKD (2003), pp.2-11
8. P. Geurts.: Pattern Extraction for Time Series Classification. PKDD (2001), pp.115-127
9. G. Xianping.: Pattern Matching in Financial Time Series Data. In Final Project Report for ICS 278 UC Irvine (1998)
10. R. Agrawal, G. Psaila, E. L. Wimmers, and Mohamed Zait.: Querying Shapes of Histories. In VLBD (1995), pp.502-514
11. J. Han and M. Kamber.: Data Mining Concepts and Techniques. Morgan Kaufmann Publishers (2000)
12. N. Cristianini and J. Shawe-Taylor.: An Introduction to Support Vector Machines. Cambridge University Press (2000)
13. W. W.Cohen, P. Ravikumar, and S. Fienberg.: A Comparison of String Distance Metrics for Naming-matching tasks. In IIWEB (2003)

14. B.W. On, D.W. Lee, J. W. Kang, and P. Mitra.: Comparative Study of Name Disambiguation Problem using a Scalable Blocking-based Framework. In JCDL (2005), pp.344-353
15. J. Chen and R. Greiner.: Comparing Bayesian Network Classifiers. In Proc. of UAI-99(1999), pp.101-108
16. S. Hettich and S. D. Bay.: The UCI KDD Archive [http://kdd.ics.uci.edu]. Irvine, CA: University of California, Department of Information and Computer Science
17. A Library for Support Vector Machines. http://www.csie.ntu.edu.tw/~cjlin/libsvm
18. SecondString (Jave-based Package of Approximate String-Matching): http://secondstring.sourceforge.net
19. Java Bayesian Network Classifier Toolkit: http://jbnc.sourceforge.net.

Location-Based Service with Context Data for a Restaurant Recommendation

Bae-Hee Lee[1], Heung-Nam Kim[1], Jin-Guk Jung[1], and Geun-Sik Jo[2]

[1] Intelligent E-Commerce Systems Laboratory,
Department of Computer Science & Information Engineering, Inha University
{coinone, nami, gj4024}@eslab.inha.ac.kr
[2] School of Computer Science & Engineering, Inha University,
253 Yonghyun-dong, Incheon, Korea 402-751
gsjo@inha.ac.kr

Abstract. Utilizing Global Positioning System (GPS) technology, it is possible to find and recommend restaurants for users operating mobile devices. For recommending restaurants, Personal Digital Assistants or cellular phones only consider the location of restaurants. However, a user's background and environment information is assumed to be directly related to recommendation quality. In this paper, therefore, a recommender system using context information and a decision tree model for efficient recommendation is presented. This system considers location context, personal context, environment context, and user preference. Restaurant lists are obtained from location context, personal context, and environment context using the decision tree model. In addition, a weight value is used for reflecting user preferences. Finally, the system recommends appropriate restaurants to the mobile user. For this experiment, performance was verified using measurements such as *k*-fold cross-validation and Mean Absolute Error. As a result, the proposed system obtained an improvement in recommendation performance.

1 Introduction

Using modern techniques, movement route and time in terms of destination can be tracked by mobile devices such as the PDA or cellular phone. In addition, mobile devices recommend restaurants in any area. Using GPS technology, these recommender systems display restaurants lists ordered by distance [6]. However, the user generally desires restaurants, which correlate with personal background information [5] or utilize both physical location and current environment information [4]. In other words, the recommender system is required to collect user information and consider user preferences in advance [1].

In this paper, a recommender system using context information and decision tree model for efficient recommendation is proposed. This system collects three types of context information, location, personal, and environment context, and also considers a weight in terms of user preferences. Location context represents the current user location using GPS technology, and displays restaurants according to distance from the current location. Personal context such as age, sex, and salary can be gathered and

S. Bressan, J. Küng, and R. Wagner (Eds.): DEXA 2006, LNCS 4080, pp. 430 – 438, 2006.

stored in the mobile device user profile. The decision tree model is used to analyze relationships with these demographical variables [5] and restaurant choices. In environment context information, season, weather, temperature and time are obtained, when accessing a web site, and user feelings are collected by analyzing mobile device input. Prior to a user recommendation request, environment context and personal context are required for analysis using the C4.5 algorithm with training data. As a result, a weight value in location context, personal context and environment context is used for reflecting user preferences. The outline of the paper is as follows. Section 2 concentrates on research, the recommendation system theory, and the context and data mining method. Section 3 describes a recommender system using context information and a decision tree model. Section 4 presents the experimental result. In Section 5, this study is concluded and future work is discussed.

2 Background and Related Work

Traditional recommendation system has used user profile to analysis and find similar user. The systems recommend restaurants to users from result of analysis [5]. However, these systems are lack of consideration of user mobility and environment. Other recommendation system provides service finding restaurant and providing information of restaurant by web site [1]. This system is closed to search system but not recommendation system. Recently research relating with context information is using user location to serve advertise, sale, and event information. This system analysis user preference though user profile and find restaurant satisfying user preference and closing user location [4]. In the rest of this part recent recommendation system theory, context and data mining technique are discussed.

2.1 Recommender System

Recommender systems, regarded as a component of personalization technology, are used mainly in personal information systems and E-Commerce to recommend appropriate products to customers. The trends in existing studies of recommending techniques can be generally divided into Demographic-based Recommendation, Content-based Recommendation and Collaborative Filtering. Demographic-based Recommendation uses demographic factors such as a user's sex, age, occupation, and so on, these factors are used to analyze the user's characteristic patterns and recommend products [7]. This system, one of the traditional recommending techniques, is widely used in strategic target marketing, using simple methods of information filtering. Content-based Recommendation is a method of filtering a user's request, including using entire product information or textual product information [8]. The advantages of these methods make it easy to reflect previous purchases and recommended results through a user's profile. The Collaborative Filtering method is based on user's product appraisal and other user's ratings, similar in terms of taste [9]. The process of recommending a product is divided into measuring similarity between users and predicting user preferences.

2.2 Context

Context can be defined as a description of aspects of a situation. In this way, context can seem similar to cases in case-base reasoning. Context as an internal representation in the computer should be a structure for information units and data. It is also natural to refer to context that is more or less similar to others contexts. Context information can be used to facilitate communication in human-computer interaction. The use of context is becoming important in interactive computing. Recently, there has been much discussion about the meaning and definition of context and context-awareness [15]. The concept of context has often been interwoven and used in many different fields. When information has to be conveyed from one element to another, the receiving element is required to know the reference of discussion. Dey and Abowd defined it as a piece of information that can be used to characterize the situation of a participant in an interaction [13]. Similarly, Chen and Kotz define context as the set of environmental states and rules that either determine application behavior or describe where the event occurs [14].

2.3 Decision Tree Algorithm

A decision tree is a flowchart-like structure in which each node denotes a test on an attribute. Each branch represents an outcome of the test and the leaf nodes represent classes or class distributions. Unknown samples can be classified by testing attributes against the tree. The path traced from root to leaf holds the class prediction for that sample. The basic algorithm for inducing a decision tree from the learning or training sample set is as follows [10]:

- Initially the decision tree is a single node representing the entire training set.
- If all samples are in the same class, this node becomes a leaf and is labeled with that class label.
- Otherwise, an entropy-based measure, *information gain*, is used as a heuristic for selecting the attribute that will best separate the samples into individual classes (the "decision" attribute).
- A branch is created for each value of the test attribute and samples are partitioned accordingly.
- The algorithm advances recursively to form the decision tree for the sub-sample set at each partition. Once an attribute has been used, it is not considered in descendent nodes.
- The algorithm stops when all samples for a given node belong to the same class or when there are no remaining attributes (or some other stopping condition).

The attribute selected at each decision tree level is the one with the highest *information gain*.

3 Location-Based Services with Context Data

The recommender system proposed in this paper for restaurant recommendation consists of two steps. First step, Context-based Data Mining, is to find relationship rules between restaurant choice and context information such as location context, personal context, and environment context. The system analyzes training data sets using a decision tree model. Next step, context factors, collects user's context information when a user requests a recommendation. In the third step the system generates three recommendation lists by analyzing user's context information with a decision tree model and, then recommendation lists integrates these lists giving proper weight values to each list reflecting user preference. The recommender system model based on context data mining is depicted in Fig. 1.

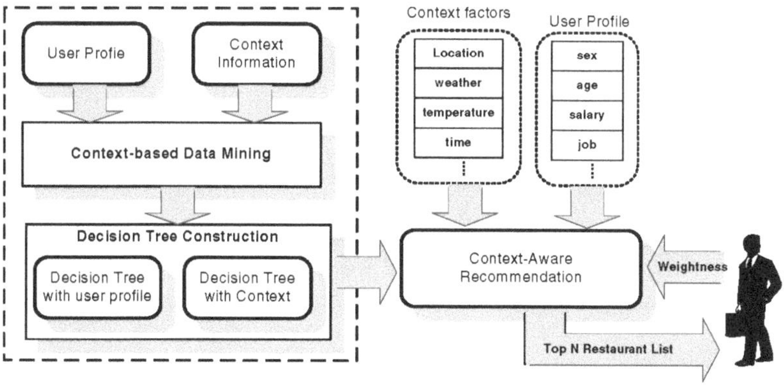

Fig. 1. System Overview for Location-based Mobile Services with Context data

In this paper, user context data is divided into three parts: location, personal, and environment context. These important factors are necessary for efficient recommendation. The recommender system is able to obtain current user location context using a GPS service. In addition, the distance between the user and particular restaurants is measured. User personal context is recorded in the user profile. The system also obtains preference factors that represent user interests. The weather information service of the Meteorological Agency serves current environment context to the recommender system. User feeling information, one of environment context, is found in the user profile.

3.1 Context-Based Data Mining

Let S be a set consisting of s data samples. Suppose the class label attribute has m distinct values defining m distinct classes, C_i (for i=1, …, m). Let s_i be the number of samples of S in class C_i. The expected information required to classify a given sample is given by

$$I(s_1, s_2, \ldots, s_m) = -\sum_{i=1}^{m} p_i \log_2(p_i) \tag{1}$$

where p_i is the probability that an arbitrary sample belongs to class C_i and is estimated by s_i/s.

Let attribute A contain v distinct values, $\{a_1, a_2, \ldots, a_v\}$. Attribute A can be used to partition S into v subsets, $\{S_1, S_2, \ldots, S_v\}$, where S_j contains those samples in S that have value a_j of A. Let s_{ij} be the number of samples of class C_i in a subset S_j. The *entropy*, or expected information based on the partitioning into subsets by A, is given by

$$E(A) = \sum_{j=1}^{v} \frac{s_{1j} + \ldots + s_{mj}}{s} I(s_{1j}, \ldots, s_{mj}) \tag{2}$$

The lower the *entropy* value, the greater the purity of the subset partitions. Note that for a given subset S_j,

$$I(s_{1j}, s_{2j}, \ldots, s_{mj}) = -\sum_{i=1}^{m} p_{ij} \log_2(p_{ij}) \tag{3}$$

where $p_{ij} = s_{ij}/|S_j|$, representing the probability that a sample in S_j belongs to class C_i.

The encoding information that would be gained by branching on A is

$$Gain(A) = I(s_1, s_2, \ldots, s_m) - E(A) \tag{4}$$

In other words, *Gain(A)* is the expected reduction in entropy caused by knowing the value of attribute A. The attribute having the largest *Information Gain* creates root node [10].

Five demographic factors such as age, sex, salary, marital status, and occupation are considered for analyzing the relationship between personal context and restaurant selection. The decision tree model using the C4.5 algorithm represents an analysis result as shown in Fig. 2. Environment context such as season, weather, temperature, time and user feeling are analyzed in order to find relationships for effective restaurant choice generation. The decision tree model identical to personal context analysis presents relationship rules as shown in Fig. 3.

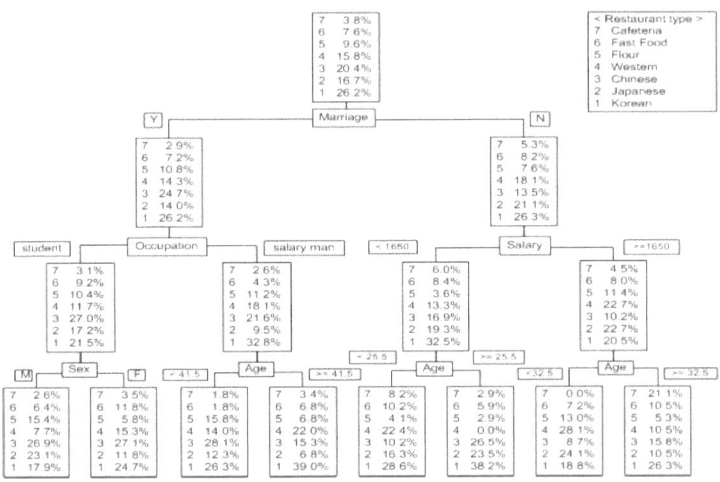

Fig. 2. Decision Tree with Personal Context

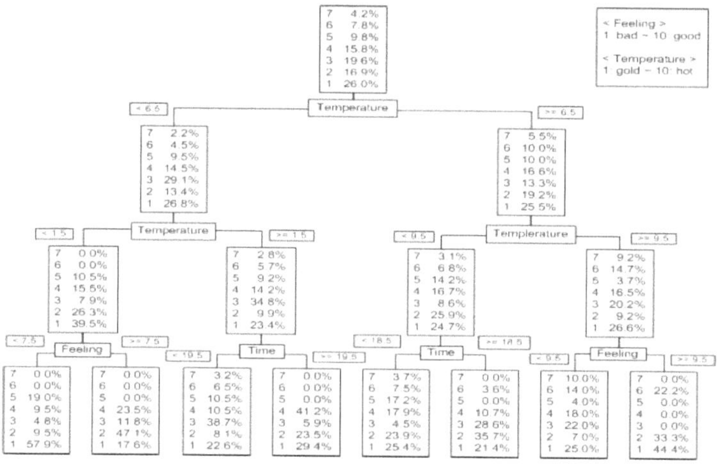

Fig. 3. Decision Tree with Environment Context

3.2 Recommendation with Feedback of User Preference

First of all, the recommender system generates three kinds of restaurant recommendation lists. Restaurant lists based on distance, personal context, and environment context with data mining are created by the system. Restaurants of each list obtain point values as a result of data mining. The three lists obtain weight values for reflecting user preference. Finally a recommender system presents an optimal restaurant list to the user.

Table 1. An example for Context factors

Initial List			Point for each factor		
Num	**Restaurant**	**Distance**	**Location context**	**Personal context**	**Environment context**
1	McDonald	2 km	7	2	3
2	Sushi	5 km	6	6	7
3	Bulgogi	7 km	5	5	5
4	Dim Sum	8 km	4	7	6
5	Kimbob	12 km	3	4	2
6	Sandwich	14 km	2	1	1
7	Outback	15 km	1	3	4

Table 2. An example for recommender system

Recommendation List			Point for weight
Num	**Restaurant**	**Distance**	
1	Sushi	5 km	6 + 6*2 + 7 = 25
2	Dim Sum	8 km	4 + 7*2 + 6 = 24
3	Bulgogi	7 km	5 + 5*2 + 5 = 20
4	McDonald	2 km	7 + 2*2 + 3 = 14
5	Kimbob	12 km	3 + 4*2 + 2 = 13
6	Outback	15 km	1 + 3*2 + 4 = 11
7	Sandwich	14 km	2 + 1*2 + 1 = 5

For example, if a user (age=28, sex=male, salary=2000$, marriage status=yes, occupation=student, season=summer, weather=fine, temperature=8, time=7pm, feeling=5, preference factor=personal context) issues a request to the restaurant recommendation service, the system will make recommendation list based on distance as shown in table 1. Restaurants obtain points in accordance with the data mining result described in Fig. 2, and Fig. 3. Three lists obtain weight values as user preferences and the system presents optimal restaurant list for the requestor as shown in table 2.

4 Experiment

In this section, performance of the recommender system is analyzed using "k-fold cross-validation," and Mean Absolute Error (MAE). Accuracy of the recommender system is calculated considering location, personal, and environment context. Then, the proposed system is compared with a general system using only location context and other systems. Experiments were carried out on a Pentium 2.8 GHz with 512MB RAM, running MS-Windows XP. The recommender system is implemented using JBuilder 9.0 and IIS 5.0. In the experiment 500 survey data sets were used for suggesting recommendations. The data sets contain personal and environment context. User preference and feeling can be extracted using personal context. Location context is gathered using GPS technology in the mobile device PDA.

4.1 Performance Measure

For performance measurement k-fold cross-validation is employed widely in estimating classifier accuracy. In k-fold cross-validation, the initial information is randomly partitioned into k mutually exclusive subsets or folds, S_1, S_2, ..., S_k, each of approximately equal size. Training and testing is performed k times. In the iteration i, the subset S_i is reserved as the test set, and the remaining subsets are used collectively to train a decision tree [10].

Statistical recommendation accuracy measures the closeness between the numerical recommendations provided by the system and the numerical ratings entered by the user for the same items. MAE is a measure of the deviation of recommendations from their true user-specified values. If $\{ r_1, r_2, ..., r_n \}$ are all the real values in the target set, and $\{ p_1, p_2, ..., p_n \}$ are the predicted values for the same ratings, and $E = \{ e_1, e_2, ..., e_n \} = \{ p_1 - r_1, ..., p_n - r_n \}$ are the errors, then the mean absolute error is

$$\overline{|E|} = \frac{\sum_{i=1}^{N} |e_i|}{N} \qquad (5)$$

The lower the MAE, the more accurately the recommendation engine predicts user ratings [11].

4.2 Experimental Results

"k-fold cross-validation" and "MAE" are used in the experiment for validating the performance of the recommender system.

Table 3. Recommender system models

Model	Remark
LS	System considering Location
LPS	System considering Location + Personal Context
LES	System considering Location + Environment Context
LPES	System considering Location + Personal + Environment Context

Table 4. Comparison of Mean Absolute Error

Model	LS	LPS	LES	LPES
MAE	0.923	0.887	0.875	0.826

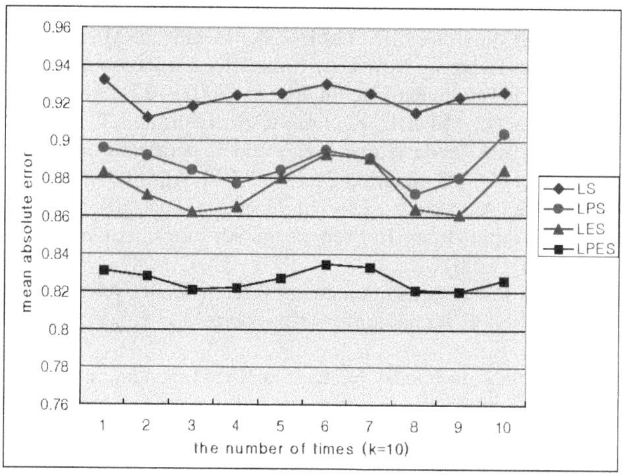

Fig. 4. Mean absolute error comparison (k=10)

In k-fold cross-validation, the experiment was repeated 10 times, with k set to 10. System considering Location + Personal + Environment Context (LPES) is compared to various recommender systems such as LS, LPS, and LES in Table 3 and Fig.4. The results demonstrate the superiority of the recommender system over a general system, based on location context and other systems. Table 4 shows a small, but statistically significant improvement in accuracy.

5 Conclusion and Future Work

Taking into account demands continuously growing environments, the personalized recommender system for Location-based mobile services is proposed. The proposed system presents two major improvements. First, user personal context and environment context is considered. These assist users in making more effective decisions. Second, user preference is reflected which lead different recommendation results. An experimental result confirms the effectiveness of use of context factor in personalized recommendation due to the proposed system obtained an improvement in recommendation performance.

Directions for future research include not only the factors considered in this paper, but also other factors related to the recommendations. For example, the driving direction of a user would also affect restaurant choice. Therefore, we will future study the impact of using other factors to form an optimal solution for context-aware mobile services.

Acknowledgement

This research was supported by the MIC(Ministry of Information and Communication), Korea, under the ITRC(Information Technology Research Center) support program supervised by the IITA(Institute of Information Technology Assessment).

References

1. Rashid, A. M., Albert, I., Cosley, D., Lam, S. K., McNee, S. M., Konstan, J. A., Riedl, J.: Getting to Know you: Learning New User Preferences in Recommender Systems. In Proc. of the 7th Int. Conf. on Intelligent User Interfaces (2002) 127–134
2. Cheverst, K., Davies, N., Mitchell, K., Friday, A., Efstratiou, C.: Developing a Context-aware Electronic Tourist Guide: Some Issues and Experiences. In Proc. of the CHI 2000 Conf. on Human Factors in Computing System, ACM, April (2000)17-24
3. Schopp, B., Ropnack, A., Markus, G.: The Need for Topological Time and Location in Mobile E-Business Applications. In Proc. of the 9th Euromicro Workshop on Parallel and Distributed Processing (2001)
4. Tang, H., Soo, V.: A Personalized Restaurant Recommender Agent for Mobile E-Service. In Proc. of the Conf. on E-Technology, E-Commerce and E-Service, IEEE, March (2004) 259 – 262
5. Park, K., Lee, H.: Study on Family Restaurant Recommendation for Customers based on Benefit Sought and Demographical Variables. In Proc. on The Korea Academic Society of Tourism and Leisure (2003)
6. Van Diggelen., F.: Indoor GPS Theory and Implementation. IEEE Position, Location & Navigation Symposium (2002)
7. Pazzani, M. J.: A Framework for Collaborative, Content-Based and Demographic Filtering. Artificial Intelligent Review (1999)
8. Claypool, M., Gokhale, A., Miranda, T., Murnikov, P., Netes, D., Sarti, M.: Combining Contents-Based and Collaborative Filters in an Online Newspaper. ACM SIGIR Workshop on Recommender Systems, Berkeley, CA (1999)
9. Sarwar, B., Karypis, G., Konstan, J., Riedl, J.: Item-based Collaborative Filtering Recommendation Algorithms. In Proc. of the Tenth International World Wide Web Conference on World Wide Web (2001)
10. Han, J., Kamber, M.: Data Mining: Concepts and Techniques. Morgan Kaufman (2001)
11. Good, N., Schafer, B., Konstan, J., Borchers, A. Sarwar, B., Herlocker, J., Riedle, J.: Combining Collaborative Filtering with Personal Agents for Better Recommendation. In Proc. of the AAAI conference (1999) 439-446
12. Shardanand, U., Maes., P.: Social Information Filtering: Algorithms for Automating "Word of Mouth" In Proc. of the SIGCHI Conf. on Human Factors in Computing Systems (1995)
13. Dey, A.K., Abowd, G.D.: Towards a better understanding of Context and Context-Awareness. GVU Technical Report GITGVU-99-22, College of Computing, Georgia Institute of Technolgy. 2, 2-14 (1999).
14. Chen, G., Kotz, D.: A Survey of Context-Aware Mobile Computing Research. Dartmouth Computer Science Technical Report TR2000-381 (2000).
15. Sachin S., Pravin V., Yugyung L.: Context-aware Data Mining using Ontologies. LNCS 2813, 405–418 (2003).

Cascaded Star: A Hyper-Dimensional Model for a Data Warehouse*

Songmei Yu, Vijayalakshmi Atluri, and Nabil Adam

MSIS Department and CIMIC
Rutgers University, NJ, USA
{songmei, atluri, adam}@cimic.rutgers.edu

Abstract. A data warehouse is defined as subject-oriented, integrated, time-variant and nonvolatile collection of data. Often, the data representing different subjects is multi-dimensional in nature, where each dimension of each subject could again be multi-dimensional. We refer to this as hyper-dimensional nature of data. Traditional multi-dimensional data models (e.g., the star schema) cannot adequately model these data. This is because, a star schema models one single multi-dimensional subject, hence a complex query crossing different subjects at different dimensional levels has to be specified as multiple queries and the results of each query must be composed together manually. In this paper, we present a novel data model, called the cascaded star model, to model hyper-dimensional data, and propose the cascaded OLAP (COLAP) operations that enable ad-hoc specification of queries that encompass multiple stars. Specifically, our COALP operations include cascaded-roll-up, cascaded-drill-down, cascaded-slice, cascaded-dice and MCUBE. We show that COLAP can be represented by the relational algebra to demonstrate that the cascaded star can be built on top of the traditional star schema framework.

1 Introduction

Data modelling is a fundamental research issue in a data warehouse. A traditional data warehouse normally uses one of the multidimensional data models such as the star schema, fact constellation schema or snowflake schema. This simple multidimensional data model is adequate to represent data pertaining to a single subject, and the associated OLAP operations can be executed along the dimension hierarchies accordingly.

However, in a decision-making process, we often encounter a situation where a subject is multidimensional and each dimension of this subject could be multidimensional by itself again. We refer to this as *hyper-dimensional* nature of data. Consider an example of a company manufacturing several brands of cars. The data warehouse stores the product portfolios to compare the performance of sales by time, by dealers, by car brands, in order to fine-tune the production and sales strategies and to conduct an analysis of customer buying patterns and their financial conditions. In this case, the central subject "Sales"

* The work is supported in part by the New Jersey Meadowlands Commission under the project Meadowlands Environmental Research Institute.

S. Bressan, J. Küng, and R. Wagner (Eds.): DEXA 2006, LNCS 4080, pp. 439–448, 2006.

has several attributes that have considerable influence on it, including "Time", "Dealer", "Brands" and "Customer". For each dimension, there could be other sub-dimensions associated with it. For example, within the dimension Customer, we believe that the customer's buying pattern is affected by several other factors such as the customer's salary, payment method and the home location, so the dimension again has three sub-dimensions. When a dimension becomes an attribute that has no sub-dimensions, we call it a single dimension. Since Sales has multiple dimensions and each of its dimensions in turn are multi-dimensional, the dimension Sales is hyper-dimensional, thus the data warehouse comprising of these dimensions is a *hyper-dimensional data warehouse* (HDW).

HDW poses challenging requirements with respect to the design of the data model, as well as specification of queries. The existing multidimensional data models are not adequate to model it because firstly, a single multidimensional data model by definition is only pertained to one subject with associated dimensions as single dimensions, which cannot model the multidimensional nature of each dimension and their inter-related relationships. Sccondly, the queries posed to this data warehouse are more complex than traditional ones, which usually cross several dimensions at different sub-dimension levels. Traditional OLAP operations on traditional data warehouse models are not capable to allow such complex queries.

For instance, it is intuitive to build a star model for each dimension in the earlier mentioned example. However, consider a more complex query: find out the average salary of male customers with down-payment is 0, and bought HONDAPLX4WD Plate XYZ with the red color, through Manager ABC in dealer DEF. In order to answer this query, we need to issue the following sub-queries:

- Sub-query 1: Retrieve the customers who bought the specified auto model through Manager ABC and Dealer DEF from the datase in figure 1(a).
- Sub-query 2: Retrieve the average salary of customers who are males and whose the down payments are 0, and bought the specified auto model from the dataset in figure 1(b).
- Sub-query 3: Retrieve the dealers who sell the specified auto model in Red from the dataset in figure (1(c).
- Sub-query 4: Join sub-query 1 and sub-query 2 to get result R, and then join R with sub-query 3 to get the final answer.

Obviously, a user has to write several queries separately to perform Selection-Projection-Join (SPJ) operations, first within each single star, and then compose the results of each query to obtain the final result. This is time consuming, labor intensive, and moreover, cannot support ad-hoc queries. The entire process again has to be done manually. Moreover, there could be no way to join results from each single star if there are no primary-foreign key restrictions. Our goal is to have a more effective data model that allows users to issue one single query, and to automatically execute the query more efficiently without users' intervention.

This paper is organized as follows. We present the cascaded star cube in section 2. In section 3, we introduce the cascaded OLAP (COLAP) operations

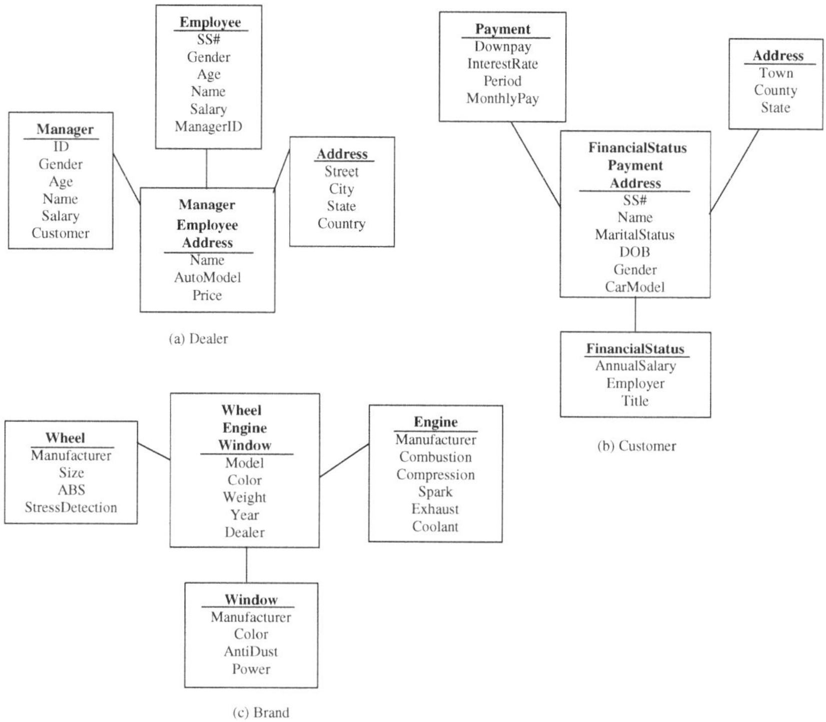

Fig. 1. Using a star model for a data warehouse

built for a cascaded star model. We present the related work in section 4. This paper is summarized in section 5.

2 A Cascaded Star Cube

Before we introduce the cascaded star model, we first define a single star cube that serves as the fundamentals for the star model.

Definition 1. *Single Star Cube. A single star cube $S^1 = (D, T)$, where:*

1. *D is the set of dimension tables where each dimension table $D_i \in D$ is $[A_i, PK_i]$ such that A_i is the set of attributes of D_i and PK_i is the primary key of D_i, and*
2. *$T = [V, PK_D]$ is the fact table such that V is the set of measures and $PK_D = \{PK_i\}$ where PK_i the primary key of $\{D_i \mid D_i \in D\}$.*

More specifically, a single star cube, is composed of central measures and several related dimensions. The central measures are represented in a central fact table T. The dimensions are represented in dimension tables, a set D, each of which consists of a primary key and several pre-defined attributes. Now we define a cascaded star cube by extending the single star cube. Figure 2 depicts an example, where a is a single dimension where each attribute within this dimension is a simple value, b, c, d, e and f represent different dimensions of A, and g represents one dimension of d. We refer to that b, c, d, e and f as sub-stars of A and A as a parent-star of b, c, d, e and f. Different from a single star cube, the primary key of a sub-star within a cascaded star cube is not derived directly by composing the primary keys of its sub-dimensions, but is the *star key*.

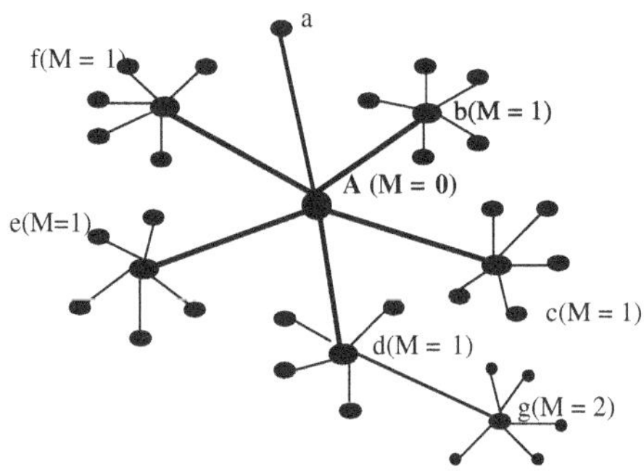

Fig. 2. A cascaded star model

A star key is essentially a primary key of a data cube that either serves as one dimension of its parent star, or has one or more sub-stars as its dimensions. It can be automatically generated by concatenating the primary keys from its sub-stars/dimensions so that the key is unique. A star key is necessary since it guarantees the simplicity and efficiency of join operation, especially when a star has multiple sub-stars and serves as a dimension as its parent-star. There is no need to propagate all the primary keys from the sub-stars to the parent-star.

Definition 2. *Star Key. A star key SK_i of a star S_i, is defined as $SK_i = g(PK_D)$ serving as the primary key of S_i, where:*

1. $PK_D = \{PK_1, \ldots, PK_n\}$ *is the set of primary keys for the sub-stars* $\{S_1$, ..., $S_k\}$ *and single dimensions of* S_i, *and*
2. g *is a concatenation function to generate* SK_i *from* PK_D *such that* SK_i *is unique.*

Definition 3. *Cascaded Star Cube. A cascaded star cube $S^C = (SS, D^C, T^C)$, where:*

1. SS *is the set of star cubes such that each* $S_i \in SS$ *is either a single star cube* S^1 *or a cascaded star cube* S^C, *and*
2. D^c *is the set of dimension tables of* S^C, *where each dimension table* $D_i \in D^C$ *is* $[A_i, PK_i]$ *such that* A_i *is the set of attributes of* D_i *and* PK_i *is the primary key of* D_i, *and*

3. $T^C = [V, SK_D, PK_D]$ *is the cascaded fact table such that* V *is the set of central measures,* $SK_D = \{SK_i\}$ *is the star key of* $\{S_i \mid S_i \in SS\}$*, and* $PK_D = \{PK_i\}$ *is the primary key of* $\{D_i \mid D_i \in D^C\}$*.*

Given a cascaded star cube $S^C = (SS, D^C, T^C)$, we refer to each $S_i \in SS$ as a sub-star of S^C. Each sub-star S_i consists of a star key SK_i as its primary key, a set of primary keys from its sub-dimensions, and its own measures V_i. By recursively defining the sub-stars, we reach the lowest level of dimensions that are single stars (S^1). We note that a single star cube is a special case of a cascaded star cube by set the value of SS to null.

Furthermore, given a cascaded star cube S^C, we refer to each $S_i \in SS$ as a sub-star of S^C at distance 1. Let $S^{central}$ be the central star cube. We use M, the value of the *star level*, to indicate the distance of a sub-star from the central star. In particular, we denote the star level of an S^C by $M(S^C)$ as the distance of S^C from $S^{central}$. Therefore, $M(S^{central}) = 0$. In addition, we use $m(S^C)$ to denote the *maximum star level* of a cascaded star S^C. In other words, $m(S^C)$ indicates the star level of the farthest sub-star of S^C.

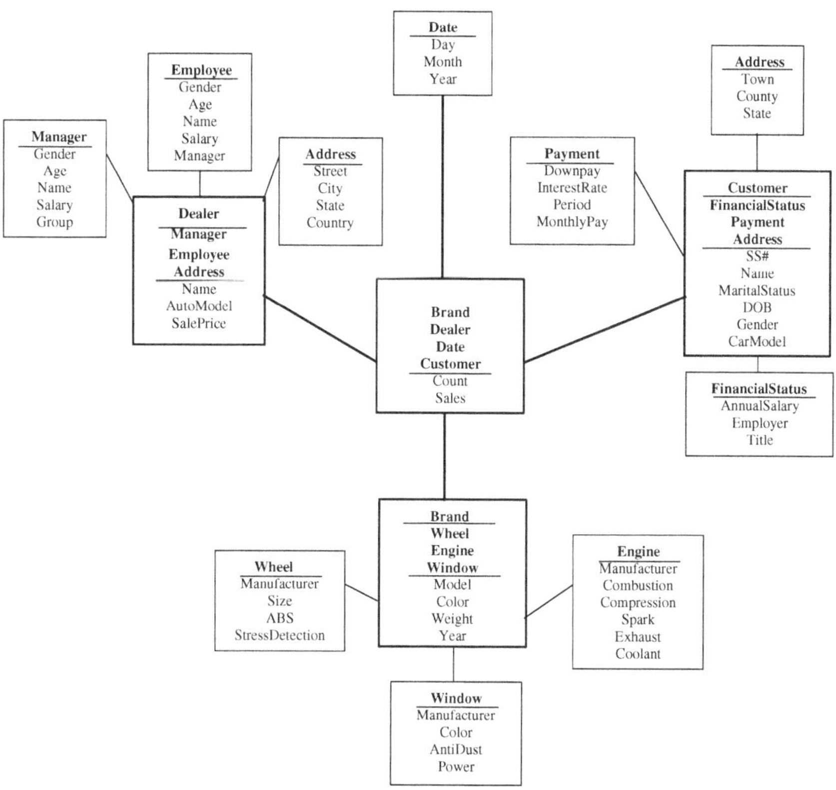

Fig. 3. A cascaded star model for an HDW

Now we revise the motivation example in figure 3. Then the query posed to figure 1 can be expressed in one single SQL-like statement and executed more efficiently by the system automatically as follows: "select avg(F.AnnualSalary) from Customer C, Dealer D, Manager M, Brand B, FinancialStatus F, Payment P, Sales S where C.Gender = Male and C.CarModel = HONDAPLX4WD Plate XYZ and P.downpay = 0 and D.Name = DEF and D.M.Name = ABC and B.color =Red and C.Customer = S.Customer and B.Brand = S.Brand and D.Dealer = S.Dealer and M.Manager = D.Manager and C.FinancialStatus = F.FiancialStatus".

3 Cascaded OLAP Operations

Typical OLAP operations include *roll-up, drill-down, slice, dice, pivot* and *CUBE* [1]. Since the OLAP operations constitute the basic and frequently used operations, we extend them in this paper so that they are applicable to an HDW and work on the cascaded star model. Specifically, our proposed *cascaded OLAP* (COLAP) operations include cascaded-roll-up, cascaded-drill-down, cascaded-slice, cascaded-dice and MCUBE. As pivot does not really involve aggregation and computation of measures, we will not discuss it further in this paper.

3.1 COLAP Operations

We first propose three new primitive COLAP operators, *traverse, decompose* and *jump*, which help us subsequently define the COLAP operations. Note here that the result from each primitive operator is also a relation by executing the relational algebra operators. Due to space limit, we will not give examples for each operator, which can be found in [2].

(1)Traverse. allows basic OLAP operations on single dimensions within an S^1 at some star level $M = k$ with $k > 0$ (for example, sub-stars b, c, g, e and f in figure 2, but not A and d since they have sub-stars as their dimensions). Generally, it consists of the relational operations (SPJ operations) on simple attributes within an S^1, where the operation process can be performed on the interested measures by rolling-up, drilling-down, slice or dice on the simple dimension hierarchies. The result is another smaller single star cube sliced and diced from S^1. This process can be expressed in the relational algebra as: $traverse(S) = \pi_{R_S}(\sigma_{(d=C)}(S \bowtie D))$, where S is a single star cube S^1, D is a set of single dimension tables with d is the set of attributes within D, C is a set of selection conditions need to be satisfied, R_S is a set of attributes being projected within S.

(2)Decompose. treats a sub-star as a dimension for operations on measures of a parent-star. For example, in figure 2, we can either traverse star g to perform operations on d, or traverse stars b, c, e and f to perform operations on A. The challenging issue is that one of the dimensions being traversed in S^C is a sub-star S^1 by itself. We cannot build a concept hierarchy on a star S^1 directly since it is not feasible to build a dimension hierarchy on a composite dimension. In such a case, we need to perform decomposition on the cascaded star until a single star with the highest M value is reached where all sub-dimensions are single dimensions. This process can be expressed in the relational algebra as: $decompose(P, Q) = \pi_{R_p}(\sigma_{d=C}(P \bowtie traverse(Q))$, where Q is a S^1 serving as one dimension of P which is a cascaded star S^C, d is the set of dimensions of Q, C is the set of selection conditions need to be satisfied, R_p is a set of attributes being projected within P.

(3)Jump. is to perform operations on source and destination stars with different M values. For example, in figure 2, one can request a jump from star b to star c, or from star c to star g. When a jump is requested, a join is made between the source star and the destination star. These two stars need not necessarily be on the same star level. In other words, these two stars may form sub-stars of their own parent-stars. However, we do not consider a jump from a sub-star to its parent-star since this can be accomplished by decompose. Note here that decompose is not a special case of jump because decompose only works on the parent-star and sub-star and jump does not request this kind of relationship. This process can be expressed in the relational algebra as: $jump(S_i, S_j) = \pi_{R_{i,j}}(traverse(S_i) \bowtie traverse(S_j))$, where S_i and S_j are the source and destination stars, and $R_{i,j}$ is the set of attributes of relations being projected from S_i or S_j.

Now we introduce cascaded-roll-up, cascaded-drill-down, cascaded-slice and cascaded-dice based on the primitive operators we developed above.

(a) Cascaded-roll-up. involves traversing by going to the lower star level of one or more than one sub-stars, or removing one or more than one sub-stars, and performing operations on the corresponding measures of parent-stars. We first do basic traverse on an S^1 with $M = k$. Then we reach its parent sub-star at $M = (k-1)$, which itself is an S^c. A decomposition is needed here, which could be iterated until we reach $M = 0$. The algebra expression is as follows: cascaded-roll-up(S^1, S^C) = decompose(S^C, traverse(S^1)).

(b)Cascaded-drill-down. is the opposite of cascaded-roll-up, where we start from an S^c at $M = k$ then drill down along one of its sub-star dimensions until reach the desired cascaded level at $M = n$, where $n > k$. Cascaded-drill-down allows navigation from less detailed to more detailed information by either stepping down the star levels or introducing additional sub-stars or dimensions. We do decomposition until we reach a single sub-star with $M = n$ and perform the basic traverse process accordingly. The algebra expression is as follows: cascaded-drill-down(S^C, S^1) = traverse(decompose(S^C, S^1).

(b)Cascaded-slice and Cascaded-dice. operations generate a sub-cube by specifying certain criteria on one (in case of cascaded-slice) or more than one (in case of cascaded-dice) sub-stars, resulting in a cascaded sub-star cube. Cascaded-slice first traverses a single star cube at $M = k$ to meet a certain selection requirement, then moves up one level to perform decomposition at that level. Basically, it is a two level operation, a parent-star and a sub-star, where we compute the interested measurements in the parent-star by specifying a selection criterion at the sub-star. A cascaded-dice operation is more complicated than cascaded-slice because it makes selections on more than one sub-star, and hence a jump operation is needed. This is also a two level operation. Note that here we assume a selection is made on only two sub-stars and it is easy to extend it to multiple sub-stars. The algebra expressions are as follows: cascaded-slice(S^C, S_1) = decompose(S^C, S_1), where $S_1(M = k)$ is a sub-star of $S^C(M = k - 1)$; cascaded-dice(S^C, S_1, S_2) = decompose(S^C, jump(S_1, S_2)), where S_1 and $S_2(M = k)$ are sub-stars of $S^C(M = k - 1)$.

3.2 MCUBE

To perform a CUBE computation on a cascaded star model, one needs to compute the cube by considering all the multiple levels. Evidently, the traditional CUBE operation is not adequate to serve the multi-dimensional queries because CUBE works only with a single star and cannot handle operations across multiple dimensions as sub-stars of a cascaded star S^C.

Definition of MCUBE. MCUBE, stands for *multiple cubes*, computes multiple CUBE operations on relations such as base tables and materialized views. We represent MCUBE in the algebra expression as follows: MCUBE(S^C) = *op*(V, cascaded-roll-up(S_i, S^C)), where *op* is a relational aggregate operator such as *sum*, V is the set of central measures of S^C, S_i is a set of sub-stars of S^C which can be either S^C or S^1. This expression indicates that MCUBE is essentially the aggregation process from multiple cascaded-roll-ups, hence cascaded-roll-up provides the basis for computing MCUBE.

The traditional CUBE function can be typically computed using the 2^N-*algorithm*[1], which has been implemented in the Microsoft SQL Server. We can extend it for the cascaded star cube (the extension is omitted for the space limit).

Steps in Processing MCUBE. Essentially, we first issue the SQL-like query using MCUBE. This query adopts the standard SQL format with MCUBE included. The query is processed by decomposing it and starting from the $m = 0$ level, and performing aggregate operations at each level.

Step 1: Aggregation on a single star cube. When $m = 0$, we are at a single star cube. MCUBE represents CUBE operations at this level, and the computation basically generates the power set of the aggregation columns. Basically, (1) it first aggregates over all $\langle$ select list $\rangle$ attributes in the CUBE clause as in a standard Group By. (2) Then it performs aggregate computation on the result from the sub-star by substituting ALL for the aggregation columns. If the cardinality of the N attributes are $C_1, \ldots, C_N$, then the cardinality of the resulting cube relation is $\prod(C_i + 1)(C_1 \times \ldots, C_N)$. The extra value in each domain is ALL. (3)If we only want a roll-up or drill-down, then the full CUBE is not necessary. Generally, performing CUBE on a single star involves computing views of an aggregation of interest on the relations.

Step 2: Aggregation on a cascaded star cube. When $m \geq 1$, we require aggregation on a star S^c with one or more of dimensions as sub-stars. This is where the MCUBE computation differs from that of the cube. For example, in figure 3, after performing MCUBE ($m = 0$) on Customer, we can aggregate the sales generated from step 1 on central star in order to view the total sales amount.

4 Related Work

Significant research in the area of data model of a data warehouses is due to [3,4,5,6,7,8,9]. For example, Jensen et al. in [6] construct multidimensional data model for location based services, where each dimension has partial containment relationship and can be transformed into simple dimension hierarchies accordingly. Timko et al. in [9] propose a data model to capture the complexities of location-based data in the static and dynamic contents. Generally, all of the above work addresses issues in data warehouses based on the star model. Specifically, they use the star schema to represent only one category of interested measures. Since they do not support the cascaded dimensions in their warehouses, the hyper-dimensional nature of data cannot be modelled, and users can only query on the limited measures within one subject domain and cannot effectively analyze the inter-relationships by submitting a single query.

Therefore, our work is to build a comprehensive data warehouse that is capable of storing different subject information where each of which is recorded for different purposes but all serve as the major dimensions to monitor the central subject, and hence is multi-dimensional in itself. The preliminary concepts of the cascaded star model are presented in [10], and additional challenges involved in processing the queries on an HDW have been identified in [11]. In this paper, we formalize the notions of the cascaded star model, which serve as the basis for cascaded OLAP operations that enable specification of complex analysis queries on this model. Based on the best of our knowledge, our proposed model and methods are currently the only work for the hyper-dimensional data warehouses, which analyze the inter-relationships among multiple subjects and generate associated OLAP results in an efficient way.

5 Conclusions and Future Research

In this paper we propose a new data modeling framework, cascaded star model, for a data warehouse by considering hyper-dimensional nature of data and the complexity of queries crossing different dimensions. First we showed a motivation example, which demands for a new data model to organize the data in a more effective way and answer complex queries more efficiently. Then we define the cascaded star cube. We revised the motivation example to show that a cascaded star model is better suited for complex query analysis for a data warehouse than a simple multidimensional data model. We then introduce the cascaded OLAP operations that enable data analysis on a cascaded star model.

Basically we made two important contributions in this paper. The first one is to extend a single star schema to a cascaded star schema by combining several stars, one of which could be a cascaded star by itself. Then we develop cascaded OLAP operators, including cascaded-roll-up, cascaded-drill-down, cascaded-slice cascaded-dice and MCUBE, to address complex operations on a cascaded star. Our future work will focus on incorporating COLAP into data mining functions such as classification and prediction to enhance interactive mining of knowledge at multiple levels of abstraction for Web Logs (Blogs) data.

References

1. Gray, J., Chaudhuri, S.: Data cube: A relational aggregation operator generating group-by, cross-tab, and sub-totals. Data Mining and Knowledge Discovery **1** (1997)
2. Yu, S., Atluri, V., Adam, N.: Cascaded star and cascaded olap for spatial data warehouses. Technical Report (2005)
3. Gupta, H., Mumick, I.: Selection of views to materialize in a data warehouse. Transactions of Knowledge and Data Engineering (TKDE) **17** (2005) 24–43
4. Han, J., Kamber, M. In: Data Mining: Concepts and Techniques. 1 edn. Morgan Kaufman Publishers (2001)
5. Han, J., Stefanovic, N., Koperski, K.: Selective materialization: An efficient method for spatial data cube construction. In: Proc. of 1998 Pacific-Asia Conf. on Knowledge Discovery and Data Mining. Lecture Notes in Computer Science, Springer (1998)
6. Jensen, C., Kligys, A., Pedersen, T., Timko, I.: Multidimensional data modeling for location-based services. Very Large Data Base Journal **13** (2004) 1–21
7. Shekhar, S., Lu, C., Tan, X., Chawla, S.: Map Cube: A Visualization Tool for Spatial Data Warehouses. In: Geographic Data Mining and Knowledge Discovery. 1 edn. Taylor and Francis (2001) 74–110
8. Stefanovic, N., Jan, J., Koperski, K.: Object-based selective materialization for efficient implementation of spatial data cubes. IEEE Transactions on Knowledge and Data Engineering(TKDE) **12** (2000) 938–958
9. Timoko, I., Pedersen, T.: Capturing complex multidimensional data in location-based warehouses. In: Proc. of ACM GIS. Lecture Notes in Computer Science, Springer (2004)
10. Adam, N., Atluri, V., Yu, S., Yesha, Y.: Efficient storage and management of environmental information. In Kobler, B., Hariharan, P., eds.: Proc. of the 19th IEEE Symposium on Mass Storage Systems, NASA (2002) 165–181
11. Adam, N., Atluri, V., Guo, D., Yu, S.: Chapter 18: Challenges in Environmental Data Warehousing and Mining. In: Data Mining: Next Generation Challenges and Future Directions. 1 edn. AAAI Press (2004) 315–335

Using JDOSecure to Introduce Role-Based Permissions to Java Data Objects-Based Applications

Matthias Merz and Markus Aleksy

University of Mannheim
Department of Information Systems III
L 5,5, D-68131 Mannheim, Germany
{merz, aleksy}@uni-mannheim.de

Abstract. The Java Data Objects specification is designed as lightweight persistence approach. Thus, JDO neither supports user authentication nor role-based authorization. Consequently, users are able to query the entire data store as well as to delete persistent objects without any restriction. The novel security approach JDOSecure was developed at the University of Mannheim to prevent unauthorized access to the data store while using the JDO API. Based on the dynamic proxy approach, JDOSecure introduces role-based permissions to JDO-based applications. In this paper we focuses on how JDOSecure enables Java Data Objects-based applications to deal with role-based permissions.

1 The Java Data Objects Specification

The Java Data Objects (JDO) industry standard appears to provide a promising framework for persisting Java objects in an efficient way. It was developed by an initiative of Sun Microsystems under the auspices of the Java Community Process [Jav04]. JDO enables application developers to deal with persistent objects in a transparent fashion and, in addition, enables the use of various data store types from different vendors. It also provides a Java oriented query language *JDO Query Language* (JDOQL), that acquires access to persistent instances from different data store types (e.g. relational or objectoriented databases).

To provide application programmers a common, transparent, and Java-centric data access technique on the one hand, and to achieve data store independency on the other, the JDO specification defines two types of interfaces. First, the JDO Application Programming Interface (API), which is of primary interest to application developers and allows to access and manage the JDO instance life cycle. And second, the JDO Service Providers Interface (SPI), which is of primary interest to container providers and JDO vendors. The JDO SPI specifies the contracts between suppliers of persistence-capable classes and the runtime environment [Jav04].

Every instance that should be managed by a JDO implementation has to implement the `PersistenceCapable` interface. As part of the JDO SPI, this interface has not to be implemented explicitly by an application developer.

S. Bressan, J. Küng, and R. Wagner (Eds.): DEXA 2006, LNCS 4080, pp. 449–458, 2006.

Instead, the JDO specification prefers a post-processor tool (*JDO-Enhancer*) that automatically implements the `PersistenceCapable` interface. It transforms regular Java classes into persistent classes by adding the code to handle persistence. A XML-based *persistence descriptor* has to be configured previously. The JDO-Enhancer evaluates this information and modifies the Java bytecode of these classes adequately. The JDO specification assures the compatibility of the generated bytecode for the use within different JDO implementations.

The interfaces and classes of the JDO API are located in the package `javax.jdo`. The construction of a `PersistenceManagerFactory` instance is usually done by calling the static `getPersistenceManagerFactory(Properties props)` method of the `JDOHelper` class. Using this method enables an later replacement of the currently preferred JDO implementation without source code modification. The `PersistenceManager` serves as primary application interface and provides methods to control the life cycle of persistent objects.

Although JDO provides a standardized, transparent and data store independent persistence solution including tremendous benefits to Java application developers, the JDO specification has been discussed critically in the Java community. For example, the substantial overlaps between Enterprise JavaBeans [Jav03] and JDO has been discussed in [KM03]. Beside of technical details like the JDO enhancement process [The03], the conceptual design as a lightweight persistence approach has been criticized sometimes. Some experts even suggest, to shift JDO to a more comprehensive approach including distributed access functions to the persistent objects and multi-address-space communication [The01]. As a result of it's lightweight nature, JDO does not provide a role-based security architecture, e.g. to restrict the access of individual users to the data store. With aid of a `PersistenceManager` instance, every user is able to query the entire data store as well as to delete any persistent object without further restriction.

To understand the benefits of JDOSecure and it's architecture in detail, the next section recalls the design of the Java 2 Security Architecture.

2 The Java 2 Security Architecture

The Java security architecture is based on three components: Bytecode verifier, class loader and security manager (cf. [Sun05] and [Gon02]). The bytecode verifier checks the correctness of the bytecode and prevents stack overflows. The class loader locates and loads classes into the Java Virtual Machine (JVM) and defines a unique namespace for each class. The security manager or, more accurately, the `AccessController` instance checks the invocation of security relevant operations e.g. local file system access, the setup of system properties or the use of network sockets.

The *code-centric authorization* architecture in Java 1.x allows to restrict the access to system resources depending on the source and the author/signer of the bytecode. It was intended to ensure that a malicious Java program could not damage the user's system. With introduction of the Java Authentication and Authorization Service (JAAS) in Java 1.4 it gets also possible to restrict the access to resources depending on the currently logged on user (*user-centric authorization*). During the authentication process a user is identified by the system e.g. with the help of user identification and password (cf. figure 1).

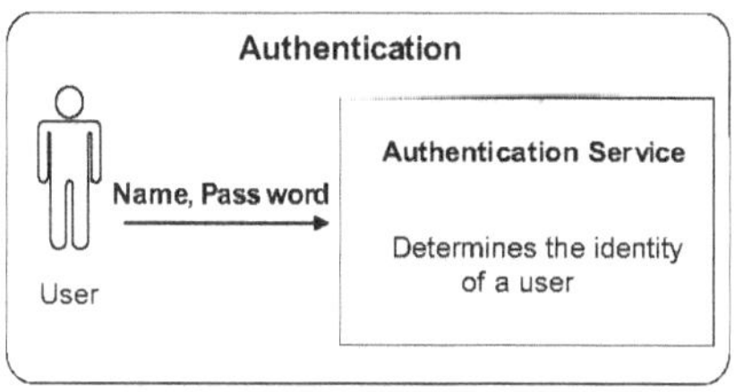

Fig. 1. Authentication Service

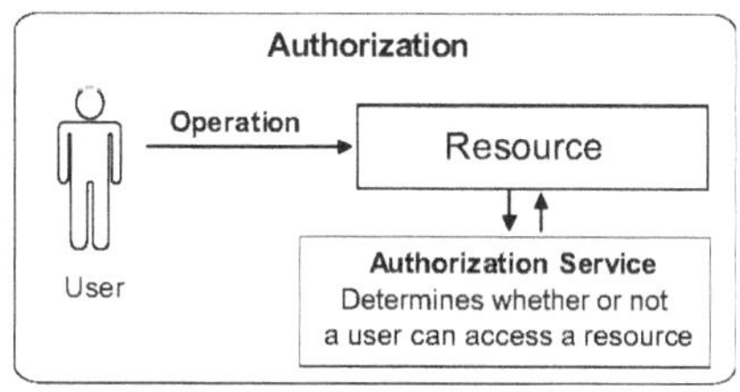

Fig. 2. Authorization Service

If the user identity is authenticated successfully, the system is able to validate the user permissions before granting access to security relevant resources (see figure 2). In Java this mechanism is implemented by the `SecurityManager` which delegates access-requests to the `AccessController`. This instance validates the permissions and allows or disallows the access to the resources.

3 Security Deficits of the JDO Specification

As already outlined in section 1, the JDO architecture is designed as a lightweight persistence approach without role-based security. Consequently, the JDO persistence layer does not provide any methods for user authentication or authorization. Every user has full access privileges to store, query, update, and delete persistent objects without further restriction. For example using the `getObjectById()` method allows to receive any persistent object whereas the `deletePersistent()` method enables a user to delete every object from the data store. Only the metadata access to `PersistenceCapable` instances is restricted by `JDOPermissions`.

At first glance, a slight improvement could be achieved by setting up individual user identifications at the level of the data store. This would allow the construction of different and user dependent `PersistenceManagerFactory` instances. If, however, all users should have access to a common database, individual user identifications and appropriate permissions have to be defined inside the data store. However, configuring user permissions to restrict the access to certain objects is quite complex. For example, when using a relational database, the permissions would have to be configured based on the object-relational mapping scheme and the structure of the tables. Thus, it leads to the disadvantage of causing a strong dependency between the user application on the one hand and the specific data store on the other. In addition, a later replacement of the currently preferred data store leads to a time consuming and expensive migration. It is obvious that the strong binding of security permissions to a specific data store would contradict the intention of JDO, which is to provide application programmers a data store independent persistence abstraction layer.

As outlined in the next section, JDOSecure considers an alternative approach and introduces data store independent and user specific permissions to JDO.

4 The Novel Security Approach JDOSecure

JDOSecure allows to control the access to store, query, update and delete persistent objects when using the JDO API. It introduces a fine grained access control mechanism to the JDO persistence layer and allows the definition of role-based permissions. Based on the dynamic proxy approach, JDOSecure is able to collaborate with any JDO implementation without source code modification or recompilation [Mer06].

4.1 Design Goals

Before we present the JDOSecure system architecture, the basic design goals will be outlined. As already mentioned, we did not aim at a complete redesign of JDO, but instead, we tried to provide the existing specification with additional functionality. Therefore, we put emphasis on the following aspects:

- Standard Compliance
  Introducing role-based access control functionality to JDO applications had to be realized without the need to modify or extend the JDO specification. The main reason for this design goal was to be able to keep standard compliance and portability of existing applications, so that they can be continued to operate. The functional enhancements were developed on the basis of "add-ons" of the standard in a way that they can be used comfortably by newly developed clients.
- Portability
  This is an important criterion, because JDOSecure-based applications should be able to run on a multitude of different JDO implementations. As a consequence, in order to guarantee portability, we have to refrain from using JDO implementation and data store specific features.
- Use of Existing Java Specifications
  By using existing Java specifications the developers can remain in the "Java world." This decision might shorten initial period and development time and thus can reduce development costs. Furthermore this aspect helps to improve the portability.

4.2 JDOSecure Authentication

As described in section 1, a `PersistenceManagerFactory` instance can be received by calling the static `getPersistenceManagerFactory(Properties props)` method of the `JDOHelper` class. In contrast to JDO vendor specific classes, using `JDOHelper` ensures an later replacement of the currently preferred JDO implementation without source code modification.

JDOSecure extends this concept in order to facilitate the collaboration between JDOSecure and any JDO implementation. Hence, JDOSecure provides a

JDOSecureHelper class which is derived from JDOHelper and serves as entry-point for JDO applications. The JDOSecureHelper class overrides the getPersistenceManagerFactory(Properties props) method.

The Properties object passed to the JDOHelper class contains amongst others user identification and password to access a JDO resource. As mentioned in section 3, the JDO architecture does not distinguish between different users and shifts this burden to the JDO resource. The JDOSecureHelper class is designed to close this gap. It analyzes the passed Properties object to authenticate a user at the JDO persistence layer when invoking the getPersistenceManagerFactory (Properties props) method.

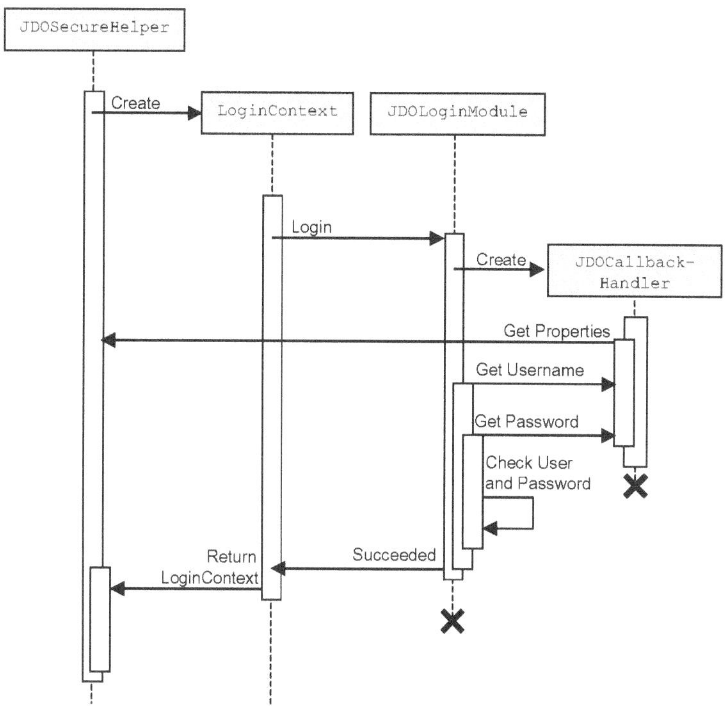

Fig. 3. UML Sequence Diagram to Outline the Authentication Process

As illustrated in Figure 3, the JDOSecureHelper class constructs a LoginContext instance. This instance forwards the authentication-request to the JDOLoginModule. A JDOCallbackHandler will be created and requests the Properties object that was previously be passed to the JDOSecureHelper instance. The JDOLoginModule gets the ConnectionUserName and the ConnectionPassword from the JDOCallbackHandler to authenticate the user. If this process is completed without throwing a FailedLoginException the LoginContext will returned to the JDOSecureHelper instance.

Once, a user has authenticated successfully, the `JDOSecureHelper` class constructs a new `PersistenceManagerFactory` instance (or more accurately a proxy object of this instance, cf. section 4.3). The basic idea in this context is to replace username and password in the `Properties` object, before the `JDOSecureHelper` class invokes the `getPersistenceManagerFactory(Properties props)` method of the original `JDOHelper` class. The intention of this replacement is to prevent a direct connection between user and JDO resource by using the `JDOHelper` class instead of the `JDOSecureHelper` class as a "workaround". The replaced password is unknown to the user and has to be configured by a security-administrator for the JDOSecure implementation and the JDO resource previously.

4.3 The JDOSecure Architecture

In an attempt to meet the JDOSecure design goals (cf. 4.1), the JDOSecure architecture implements the *dynamic proxy* pattern [Blo00]. A proxy instance implements the interfaces of a specific object and allows to control the access to it [GHJV95]. Whereas a static proxy has to be defined at compile time, the dynamic proxy concept allows the construction of a proxy instance at runtime [Blo00]. An dynamic proxy instance is always associated with an `InvocationHandler`. Any method invocation directed to proxy instance will be redirected to the `InvocationHandler.invoke()` method. The `invoke()` method allows to intercept method calls before they are forwarded to the original object.

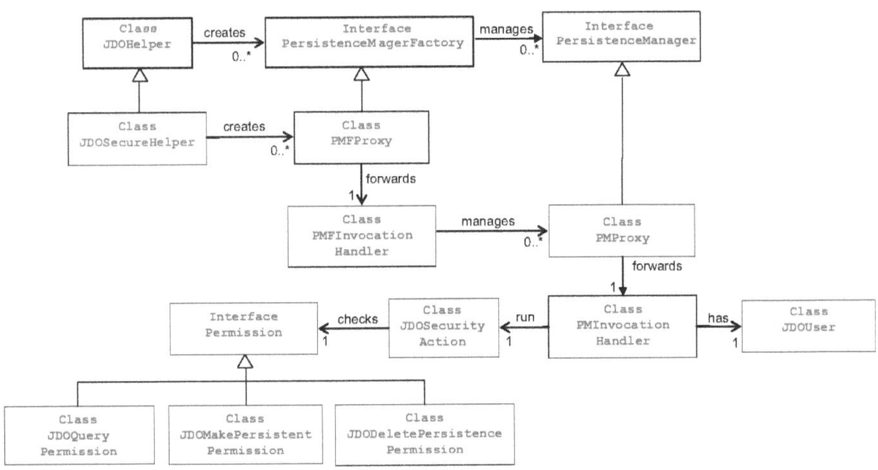

Fig. 4. Context between JAAS-Authorization and JDOSecure

The JDOSecure architecture implements the dynamic proxy concept as shown in figure 4. The basic idea is to interpose a proxy between `PersistenceManager` and a JDO-based application. This would allow to validate specific user permissions at the `PMInvocationHandler` instance, before a method call is forwarded to the `PersistenceManager`. If for example a user does not have the sufficient privilege to delete a `PersistenceCapable` object (`JDODeletePermission`, see section 4.4), a Java `AccessControlException` is thrown when invoking the `deletePersistent()` method and the forwarding to the `PersistenceManager` is avoided.

As mentioned above, the JDOSecure architecture avoids a direct user interaction with the original `PersistenceManagerFactory`-instance. This allows to manipulate method calls which are directed to the `PersistenceManagerFactory`. Invoking the `getPersistenceManager()` method, the `PMFInvocationHandler` does not return a `PersistenceManager` instance but another proxy object (`PMProxy`). JDOSecure uses the associated `InvocationHandler` instance (`PMInvocationHandler`) to manipulate method calls directed to the `PersistenceManager`. Thus, the `PMInvocationHandler` represents the entry-point to implement the authorization function and allows to determine whether or not a user is allowed to invoke a `PersistenceManager` method.

4.4 JDOSecure Authorization

JDOSecure enables the set-up of user specific permissions to allow or disallow the invocation of `PersistenceManager` methods. After completing the authentication phase and by invoking the `getPersistenceManager()` method, the user receives a proxy of a `PersistenceManager` instance (`PMProxy`). Thus, JDOSecure is able to use the assigned `PMInvocationHandler` to validate, if an already authenticated `JDOUser` has the permission to make a specific method invocation.

The permissions are located in a separate policy-file and can be defined individually for any user. In the recent version, JDOSecure distinguishes between different permissions as represented in Table 1. JDOSecure enables also the limitation of user permissions to a certain package or a specific class.

Table 1. JDOSecure Permissions

Methods of a `PersistenceManager`, that require specific permissions to be executed in the context of JDOSecure:	Necessary permission to invoke the according method for a specific class or package:
`makePersistent()` `makePersistentAll()`	`JDOMakePersistent-` `Permission` $< \mathit{Class} >$
`deletePersistent()` `deletePersistentAll()`	`JDODeletePersistent-` `Permission` $< \mathit{Class} >$
`getExtent()` `Query.execute()`	`JDOQueryPermission` $< \mathit{Class} >$
–	`JDOUpdatePermission` $< \mathit{Class} >$

With regard to the user permission defined in the policy-file the `PMInvocationHandler` is able to validate if a specific `PersistenceManager` method invocation is allowed. Thus, a `JDOSecurityAction` instance will be constructed and passed to the static `doAs(subject, action)` method of the `Subject` class. Consequently, the validation of the permissions is delegated to the `AccessController` as part of the Java 2 Security Architecture. If a user has the permission to make a method call with regard to a particular `PersistentCapable` object, the method call is forwarded to the original `PersistenceManager` instance. In the other case, a Java `AccessControlException` is thrown.

It becomes apparent that the presented approach is quite complex. Even worse, many details like the mechanism to control the update of object attributes by interposing a further proxy between a `StateManager` and a `PersistenceCapable` instance are disregarded in this context because of space limitations (for a more technical exposition on JDOSecure, we refer to [Mer06]). Nevertheless, JDOSecure is enable to restrict updates of object attributes, even though JDO does not provide a specific update-method as a result of JDO's *transparent persistence* concept.

5 Using JDOSecure in Context of a JDO Based Application

Having illustrated the basic architecture of JDOSecure in the last section, we are now focussing on how to use JDOSecure in context of a JDO-based application and present some interesting Java code snippets.

Initially, JDOSecure needs to be configured by setting up different user accounts and passwords. Therefore, JDOSecure provides two user configuration files. The users which are generally allowed to access the persistent instances of the data store by using JDO and JDOSecure have to be defined in the `JDOSecure-user-accounts.properties` file. When invoking the `getPersistenceManagerFactory(Properties props)` method of the `JDOSecureHelper` class, JDOSecure uses the information of this configuration file to authenticate a user. As mentioned in section 4.2, after a successful authentication, the username and password will be replaced before the `JDOSecureHelper` class invokes the `getPersistenceManagerFactory(Properties props)` method of the original `JDOHelper` class. Therefore, JDOSecure needs to know the user account and password to access the underlying database. This information has to be set up in the `JDOSecure.properties` file.

Beside the information to authenticate a user and enable JDOSecure to access the data store, a security-administrator has also to configure authorization settings. The set-up of user/role permissions have to be configured in the JAAS policy-file.

In a scenario where a "guest" should be allowed to query all instances of a package `sample`, the permission can be defined for this principal in a JAAS policy-file as follows. In this context, the security-administrator has the choice to treat the guest as a single user (`JDOUser`) or a general role (`JDORole`).

```
grant Principal JDOUser ''guest"{
  permission JDOQueryPermission ''sample.*";
}
```

As JDOSecure is based on JAAS, the Java SecurityManager has to activated to participate of the security benefits. One possibility is to use Java Virtual Machine command-line switches when invoking the JDO-based application, like outlined in the following code snippet:

```
-Djava.security.manager
-Djava.security.policy=JDOAccessControl.policy
-Djava.security.auth.login.config=JDOSecure_jaas.config
```

The first switch is responsible to activate the Java SecurityManager. The second line defines the source, where the user permissions are located, e.g. including a JDOQueryPermission for a principal guest as described above. And finally, the last line refers to a config file, which defines the JDOLoginModule to authenticate a user:

```
JDOAccessControl{
    JDOLoginModule required debug=false;
};
```

To interpose JDOSecure between a JDO-based application and a JDO implementation, only one modification in the Java source code has to be made. The JDOSecureHelper class has to be used instead of the JDOHelper to receive an instance of a PersistenceManagerFactory. Beside this slight modification only user account and password to access JDOSecure has to be configured adequately. However, an application should be extended by adding try and catch(AccessControlException ace) blocks to handle possible security exceptions at run-time.

It becomes apparent, that a user does not even be aware of the interception. Moreover, within these slight modifications it gets possible to introduce role-based permissions in every JDO-based application.

6 Conclusion and Further Work

In this article the novel security approach JDOSecure is introduced and the main advantages are highlighted. JDOSecure introduces a fine grained access control mechanism to the JDO persistence layer and allows the definition of role-based permissions. In the current version the permissions can be defined individually for every user/role with regards to certain operations (create, delete, update or query) and a specific class/package. Based on the dynamic proxy approach, JDOSecure is able to collaborate with any JDO implementation without source code modification or recompilation.

However, as it turns out in the last section, defining appropriate permissions in simple text-files becomes more and more complex with an increasing number of different users and roles. To simplify the process of introduce role-based permissions to Java Data Objects-based applications, we will develop a users, roles, and permissions management system for the use within an upcoming version of JDOSecure. This management system will allow to store the necessary authentication and authorization information in any arbitrary JDO resource. Furthermore, a Java-based administration utility with a graphical user interface will simplifies the maintenance of security privileges and permissions.

References

[Blo00] Jeremy Blosser. Explore the Dynamic Proxy API. http://java.sun.com/developer/ technicalArticles/DataTypes/proxy/, 2000.

[GHJV95] Erich Gamma, Richard Helm, Ralph Johnson, and John Vlissides. *Design Patterns, Elements of Reusable Object-Oriented Software*. Addison-Wesley Longman Publishing Co., Inc., Boston, MA, USA, 1st edition, 1995.

[Gon02] Li Gong. Java 2 Platform Security Architecture. http://java.sun.com/j2se/1.4.2/docs/guide/security/spec/security-spec.doc.html, 2002.

[Jav03] Java Community Process. JSR-153: Enterprise JavaBeans 2.1, 2003.

[Jav04] Java Community Process. JSR-012: Java Data Objects (JDO) Specification, Maintenance Draft Review, 2004.

[KM03] Axel Korthaus and Matthias Merz. A Critical Analysis of JDO in the Context of J2EE. In Al-Ani Ban, H. R. Arabnia, and Mun Youngsong, editors, *Proceedings of the 2003 International Conference on Software Engineering Research and Practice (SERP '03)*, volume I, pages p. 34–40. CSREA Press, 2003.

[Mer06] Matthias Merz. Using the Dynamic Proxy Approach to Introduce Role-Based Security to Java Data Objects. Eighteenth International Conference on Software Engineering and Knowledge Engineering (SEKE'06), San Francisco, USA, 5-7. July, 2006.

[Sun05] Sun Microsystems. *The Java Language Specification*. Addison-Wesley Professional, 3rd edition, 2005.

[The01] TheServerSide.COM. Craig Russell Responds to Roger Sessions' Critique of JDO. http://www.theserverside.com/articles/article.tss?l= Russelvs-Sessions, 2001.

[The03] TheServerSide.COM. A Criticism of Java Data Objects (JDO). http://www.theserverside.com/news/thread.tss?thread_id=8571, 2003.

A Forced Transplant Algorithm for Dynamic R-tree Implementation

Mingbo Zhang[1,2], Feng Lu[1], and Changxiu Cheng[1]

[1] State Key Laboratory of Resources and Environmental Information System, Institute of Geographic Sciences and Natural Resources Research, Chinese Academy of Sciences, Beijing, 100101, P.R. China
[2] Department of Architecture Engineering, Shandong University of Technology, Zibo, 255049, P.R. China
{zhangmb, luf, chengcx}@lreis.ac.cn

Abstract. Spatial access methods play a crucial role in spatial database management and manipulation. The R-tree and its variations have been widely accepted as some of the most efficient spatial indexing structures in recent years. However, neither considers storage utilization and the global optimization of a R-tree structure. Presented in this paper is a new optimization technique named forced transplant algorithm, which can improve the node storage utilization and optimize the R-tree overall structures at the same time. Our experiments show that the R-tree with our new optimization technique achieves almost 100% storage utilization and excellent query performance for all types of data.

1 Introduction

In order to handle spatial data in a large database efficiently, numerous spatial indexing structures have been proposed, such as grid file, buddy tree, K-D-B tree, hB tree and LSD tree for point dataset, R-tree, cell-tree and linear quad-tree for line, and polygon datasets (Gaede & Gunther, 1998). Among them, R-tree (Guttman, 1984) and its variations have been widely used in many spatial database related applications. A R-tree is a height-balanced tree and a natural extension of B-tree in k-dimensions space. Implemented with a heuristic optimization, the optimization parameters of R-tree include coverage, margin, dead-area, overlap, storage utilization, and distribution among other parameters (Theodoridis & Sellis, 1994). The known optimization parameters affect each other in such a complex way that it becomes impossible to get one without influencing the others, which may cause the deterioration of R-tree performance. Most R-tree variations, such as R+-tree (Sellis et al., 1987), R*-tree (Beckmann et al., 1990) and Hilbert R-tree (Kamel & Faloutsos, 1994), improved search performance with different optimization techniques.

However, none of the current R-tree implementation techniques considers both storage utilization and the global optimization of R-tree structure. In this paper, a new technique named forced transplant algorithm is proposed, which can improve the node storage utilization and optimize the R-tree overall structures simultaneously.

S. Bressan, J. Küng, and R. Wagner (Eds.): DEXA 2006, LNCS 4080, pp. 459 – 466, 2006.

The remainder of this paper is organized as follows. Section 2 reviews and analyzes the available optimization techniques of R-tree. Section 3 presents the forced transplant technique. Several experiments are conducted with real data sets, and the results are discussed and analyzed in section 4. Finally, a conclusion is drawn in section 5.

2 Optimization Techniques for R-tree

When different heuristic optimization approaches are adopted, various R-trees with differing structures can be constructed for the same datasets. In the course of construction, although no periodic reorganization is required, the directory rectangle formed by early data records will no longer be appropriate and the search performance of R-tree would deteriorate gradually along with the insertion of new data records. The traditional 1-to-2 node splitting algorithms with local dynamic reorganization have almost no effect on the optimization of global R-tree structures. Consequently, some optimization techniques for R-tree have been proposed to promote the reasonable flow of data records between index nodes, to optimize the overall structure of R-tree and to improve the node storage utilization.

The forced reinsertion was proposed by Beckmann. For an overflowed node, splitting is not executed at once, but first a set number of records are deleted from the overflowed node and then they are reinserted into the tree using the algorithm of 'ChooseLeaf' so that records have a chance of being reallocated into different nodes. The forced reinsertion significantly improves the search performance due to the reduction of overlapping between nodes and the decrease in the occurrence of node splitting. However, the forced reinsertion is time-consuming because all records in the overflowed node must be sorted first by distances between their centers and the center of the overflowed node, plus frequent calls to the insertion algorithm.

SHIFT insert algorithm (Garcia, et al., 1998), similar to the forced insertion, permits the early inserted records to choose more appropriate nodes so as to improve the data reorganization between sibling nodes and to optimize the global R-tree structure. Unlike forced reinsertion, SHIFT algorithm only creates a new node if no siblings can be found to absorb one of the subsets created by a split. So, SHIFT can improve storage utilization at the expense of additional node splitting and insert costs.

Node restructuring algorithm (Garcia, et al., 1999) performs post-optimization for existing R-trees. This algorithm calls recursions in the tree branches that need restructuring from bottom to the root. All of the overlapped sibling nodes must first be allocated to the node needing restructuring, and then split if the node becomes overflowed. The disadvantage of node restructuring algorithm is that no rules are used to decide the sequence of the overlapped nodes that would influence the global tree structure after restructuring.

Schreck & Chen (2000) proposed a branch grafting method aimed at getting more desirable results and reducing the number of nodes created in R-trees. The redistribution of entries is limited to the sibling nodes overlapped with the overflowed node, which makes the branch grafting method weak in the global optimization of R-trees.

The compact R-tree presented by Huang et al. (2001) mainly optimizes storage utilization. In this method, an entry may be removed from the overflowed node into an under-full sibling node. Splitting occurs only when all sibling nodes are full, so almost 100% storage utilization is achieved and the occurrence of the splitting is decreased. However, no efficient control is considered on the overall R-tree structure between sibling nodes that makes the search performance only at the same level of the R-tree generated by the quadratic splitting method.

As stated above, traditional 1-to-2 node splitting is essentially a type of local optimization algorithm since it does not consider other nodes when a split occurs, while the forced reinsertion, SHIFT, node restructuring and branch grafting method that can optimize the global tree structures belong to global optimization techniques. However, none of these algorithms can control node storage utilization effectively while optimizing the global structure of R-tree.

3 Forced Transplant Algorithm

Node storage utilization plays the same important role in R-tree structures as in global structure optimization. Therefore, we quantitatively control the node storage utilization according to static R-tree standard while optimizing the global structure of R-tree. Presented here is our optimization technique named forced transplant algorithm. It can be regarded as an improvement of storage utilization under global optimization, or global structure optimization upon a compact R-tree.

3.1 Basic Idea

The basic idea of forced transplant algorithm is shown in figure 1. If entry *e* is inserted into the full node *A* (the node capacity M=4), node *A* will overflow. Using the forced transplant, entry *A4* will be moved into sibling node *B*. Then, if node *B* is also full entry *B4* will be moved into sibling node *C*. Now, if node *C* is under-full the insertion finishes and node splitting is avoided. The final situation of nodes is shown in figure 2.

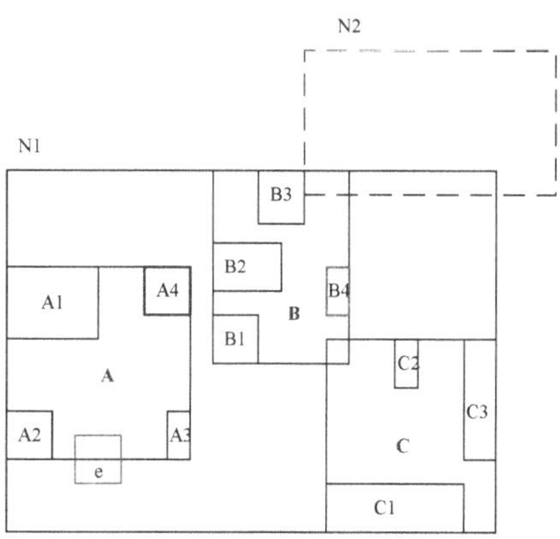

Fig. 1. Example of forced transplant

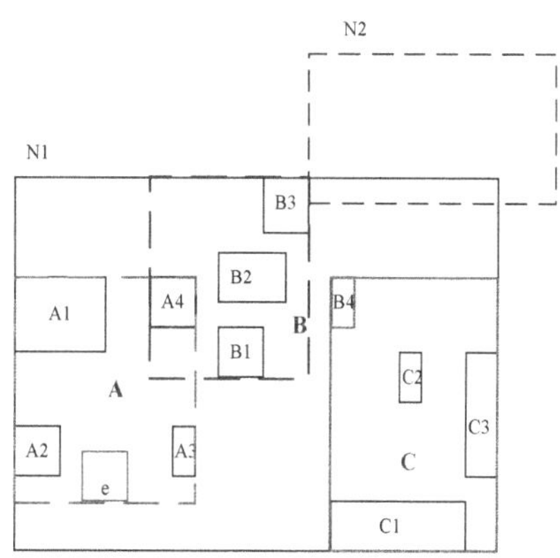

Fig. 2. Result of forced transplant

3.2 Algorithm Implementation

In the course of node insertion, if node *N* with M+1 entries overflows, an entry in node *N* will be moved into the most appropriate sibling node *Es* according to the criteria of least enlargement of MBR. The insertion will finish once node *Es* has available space, otherwise, the same operation will be applied to the overflowed node *Es*. If all siblings have been tried and node overflow still occurs, the final overflowed node will split and a new node will be created, and such splits will propagate up the tree. Therefore, splitting only occurs when all siblings have no available space so that high storage utilization can be achieved while keeping global structure optimization of R-tree.

The detailed procedure is as follows:

```
TransPlant(node N, entry E)
//Insert entry E into the full node N
{
    IF  N is root
        split(node N, entry E), return
    ENDIF
    mark N as dirty
    WHILE
    {
        IF all siblings of node N are dirty
            split(node N, entry E), return
        ELSE
            call FindSibling(node N, entry E),find a
            clean sibling Ns and an entry En in node N
            IF  Ns has available space
               insert entry En, return
            ELSE
               Ns overflows, mark Ns as dirty, let
               N=Ns, E=En
            ENDIF
        ENDIF
    } //end of WHILE
} //end of TransPlant

Algorithm FindSibling(node N, entry E)
FS1:For each entry En in node N
      find a clean sibling Ns, and let
      (area(N'∪Ns') - area(N∪Ns)) = Min.
      N' and Ns'are corresponding nodes after entry
      En is transferred into node Ns
FS2:For all pairs (Ns, En)
      select the pair with the minimum area enlargement
```

In the algorithm FindSibling, the CPU costs of finding the most appropriate pair of entry and sibling node are quadratic in the number of node capacity M, because for each entry the area enlargement with all siblings of the node has to be calculated. However, in order to reduce the CPU costs, we can reduce the number of entries and siblings for which the calculation is done. Thus, two improvement methods are proposed as follows:

- For overflowed node *N*, only p1 entries farthest to the centre of node *N* are selected
- For overflowed node *N*, only p2 siblings nearest to the centre of node *N* are selected

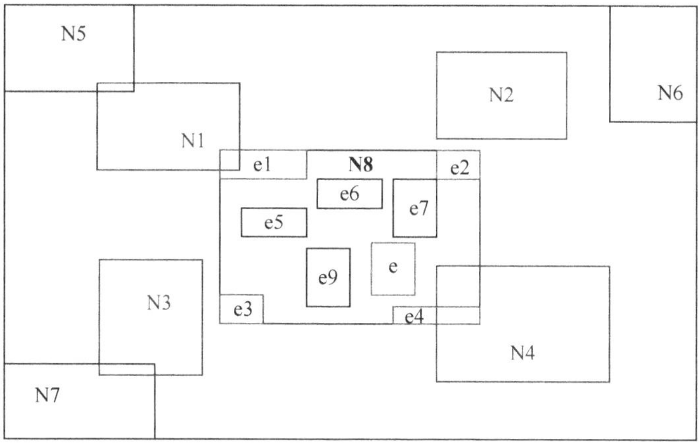

Fig. 3. Improvement of forced transplant procedure

In Figure 3, according to the improved procedure, only the farthest entries such as *e1, e2, e3 and e4* and the nearest nodes such as *N1*, *N2*, *N3* and *N4* to the center of node *N8* are selected to find the pair of entry and node that has the minimum area enlargement.

3.3 Comparison with Other Optimization Methods

Compared with other global optimization methods such as forced reinsertion, SHIFT, node restructuring and branch grafting, forced transplant algorithm can achieve almost 100% storage utilization. Compared with the compact R-tree, forced transplant algorithm can obtain an R-tree with global optimization.

In the example shown in figure 1, when using global optimization such as branch grafting, the full node *A* will split because no overlapped sibling nodes with node *A* can be found, which results in low storage utilization. When using the compact R-tree, the entry *A3* will be moved into sibling node *C*, which results in larger overlapping area.

4 Experiments

The forced transplant algorithm can be integrated with any R-tree splitting algorithm. Since R*-tree is widely regarded as one of the best variations of R-tree, we implemented an R-tree variant called Trans R*-tree with the integration of forced transplant algorithm and R*-tree. A large number of experiments were conducted with Trans R*-tree, R*-tree, NLS R-tree implemented with the new linear split algorithm (Ang & Tan, 2001), and the built-in GIST R-tree in PostgreSQL DBMS, to compare their performances on storage utilization and query performance. The experiment environment is as follows:

Hardware: a PC with one Intel Pentium 4 CPU, 2.0 GHz and 256M memory
Software: Redhat 7.4 Linux, PostgreSQL 7.4.2 DBMS (with PostGIS 0.8.2)
Datasets:

- *Tpoint.* Point data, 643582 records, skewed
- *Tline.* Line data, 899072 records, mildly skewed
- *Tpoly.* Polygon data, 122522 records, uniformly distributed

4.1 Storage Utilization

Figure 4 shows that the Trans R*-tree achieves almost 100% storage utilization for all of the three real data sets, while the other three R-trees only achieve 65% or less. The high performance of Trans R*-tree is due to the improved condition of node splitting in Trans R*-tree that makes records flow between the sibling nodes to avoid node splitting.

4.2 Query Performance

It is a common practice to compare spatial access methods in terms of page access (Disk I/O) for range queries. Figures 5, 6 and 7 show the number of disk access for various range query sizes on the three data sets. These figures clearly reflect that the Trans R*-tree outperforms the other three R-tree variants, especially for large extent querying.

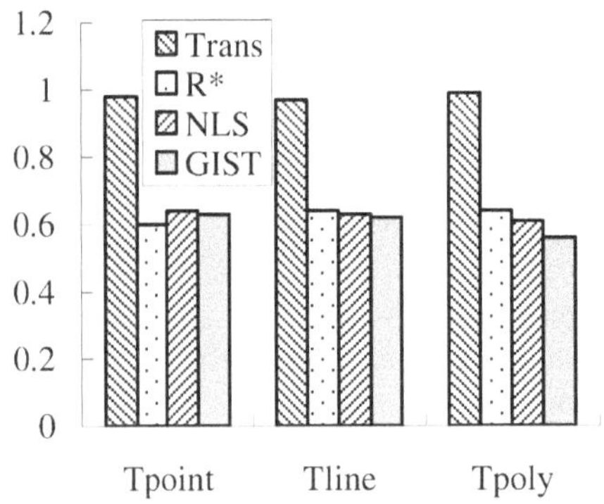

Fig. 4. Storage utilization for different R-trees

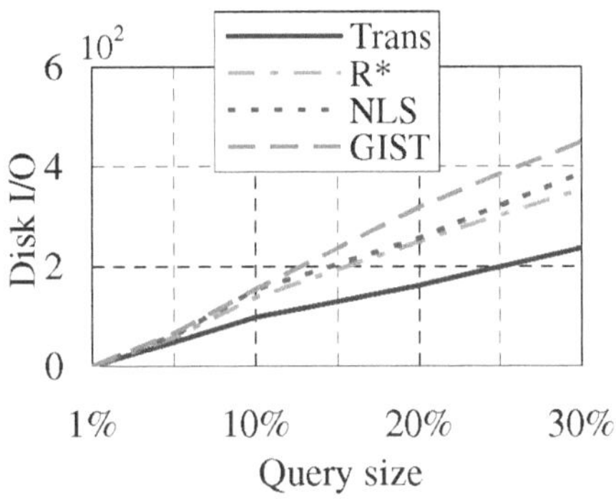

Fig. 5. Range query on Polygon dataset

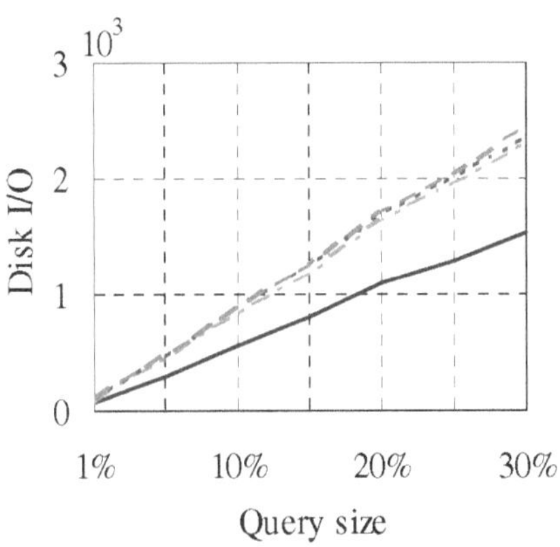

Fig. 6. Range query on Line dataset

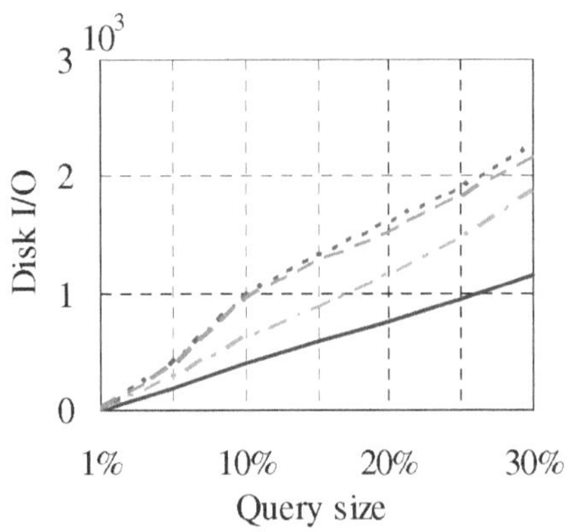

Fig. 7. Range query on Point dataset

5 Conclusion

This study presents a new optimization technique, named forced transplant algorithm, that is implemented on a PostgreSQL DBMS platform. The main merit of forced transplant algorithm is that it considers both R-tree global structure optimization and storage utilization optimization. Our experimental results clearly indicate that the Trans R*-tree, implemented with the integration of forced transplant algorithm and R*-tree, achieves almost 100% storage utilization and a better range search performance for all types of data than the other R-tree variations.

Our Trans R*-tree can be incorporated with some packed R-tree such as Hilbert packed R-tree (Kamel & Faloutsos, 1993), STR R-tree (Leutenegger *et al.*, 1997) and TGS R-tree (Garcia *et al.*, 1998) to manage massive spatial data more efficiently. Packed R-tree can be used to load data quickly and the Trans R*-tree can be used to maintain the global tree structure dynamically so as to guarantee that the query performance of R-tree will not degrade gradually during constant dynamic data updating.

Acknowledgments

This research was supported by the National Natural Science Foundation of China under grant No. 40401047 and Knowledge Innovation Project of CAS under grant No. CXIOG-D04-02.

References

1. Ang, C. H., Tan, T. C. New Linear Node Splitting Algorithm for R-trees. In: Proceedings of 5th SSD, Berlin, Germany, 1997, 339-349
2. Beckmann, N., Kriegel, H. P., Schneider, R., Seeger, B. The R*-Tree: An Efficient and Robust Access Method for Points and Rectangles. In: Proceedings of SIGMOD, Atlantic City, New Jersey, 1990, 322-331
3. Gaede, V., Gunther, O. Multidimensional Access Methods. ACM Computing Surveys. 1998, 30(2): 170-231
4. Garcia, Y., Lopez, M., Leutenegger, S. A Greedy Algorithm for Bulk Loading R-trees. In: Proceedings of 6th ACM-GIS, Washington, DC, 1998, 163-164
5. Garcia, Y., Lopez, M., Leutenegger, S. On Optimal Node Splitting for R-trees. In: Proceedings of 24th VLDB, New York, NY, 1998, 334-344
6. Garcia, Y., Lopez, M., Leutenegger, S. Post-optimization and Incremental Refinement of R-trees. In: Proceedings of ACM GIS'99, Kansas City, USA, 1999, 91-96
7. Guttman, A. R-trees: A Dynamic Index Structure for Spatial Searching. In: Proceedings of ACM SIGMOD, Boston, MA, 1984, 47-57
8. Huang, P.W., Lin, P.L., Lin, H.Y. Optimizing Storage Utilization in R-tree Dynamic Index Structure for Spatial Databases. Journal of Systems and Software, 2001, 55:291-299
9. Kamel, I., Faloutsos, C. Hilbert R-tree: an Improved R-tree Using Fractals. In: Proceedings of 20th VLDB, Santiago, Chile, 1994, 500-509
10. Kamel, I., Faloutsos, C. On Packing R-trees. In: Proceedings of CIKM, Washington, DC, USA 1993, 490-499
11. Leutenegger, S., Edgington, J. M., Lopez, M. A. STR: a Simple and Efficient Algorithm for R-tree Packing. In: Proceedings of 13th IEEE ICDE, Birmingham, England, 1997, 497-506

12. Schreck, T., Chen, Z. Branch Grafting Method for R-tree Implementation. Journal of Systems and Software, 2000, 53: 83-93
13. Sellis, T., Roussopoulos, N., Faloutsos, C. The R+-Tree: A Dynamic Index for Multi-Dimensional Objects. In: Proceedings of 13th VLDB, Brighton, England, 1987, 507-518
14. Theodoridis, Y., Sellis, T. Optimization Issues in R-tree Construction. In: Proceedings of IGIS. 1994, 270-273

An Approach for a Personal Information Management System for Photos of a Lifetime by Exploiting Semantics

Khalid Latif, Khabib Mustofa, and A. Min Tjoa

Institute of Software Technology & Interactive Systems
Vienna University of Technology,
Favoritenstrasse 9-11/188,
A-1040 Vienna, Austria
{klatif, khabib, amin}@ifs.tuwien.ac.at

Abstract. Photo collections are one of the promising sources to tell story of life in this digital era. In this paper we present our work on organizing photos of a lifetime by exploiting semantic annotations. The complexity in using semantic technology is managed by introducing an annotation template corresponding to who, when, where, and what. Semantics of each dimension are semi-automatically annotated following the ontology for personal information. The story telling is done by exploiting these semantics to form trails of the photos. The notion of landmarks is used for this purpose which also ensures effective navigation in the lifetime photo-space.

1 Introduction

The size of personal photo collections has grown a great deal with the increasing use of digital cameras. On the other hand ever increasing storage capacity inspires the vision to accumulate information without the need to delete old photos. Organizing such a large number of photo collections requires effective use of the photo metadata. This metadata can be separated into two categories: the general photo characteristics and the photo contents. The later, although can be automated for low level feature description, is manually annotated to lower the "semantic gap" [4] [13]. Currently available personal photo management tools mostly exploit first type of metadata with support for free text comments [7] [15]. In contrast the semantic photo annotation tools are mostly developed for annotating digital photo archives such as for artwork [9]. There remains a need to bring together both worlds without flooding the user with the complexity of underlying semantic technology.

The primary goal of this research is to build a personal information management system for photos of a lifetime by exploiting their semantics. This is done through semi-automatically annotating photos about persons (who), time (when) or event, location (where), and other objects and actions of persons (what) using already available ontologies. Additionally user preferred photos

S. Bressan, J. Küng, and R. Wagner (Eds.): DEXA 2006, LNCS 4080, pp. 467–477, 2006.

are declared landmarks, which serves two purposes. Firstly, while viewing an individual photo the landmarks being near to the photo in context are suggested as related photos. Secondly, the landmark photos are magnified when viewing whole photo collections. Thus the user is guided in navigating large photo space.

First we will briefly discuss existing approaches for personal photo management and semantic photo annotations. In the subsequent sections we will discuss the proposed annotation model, the use of landmarks for navigating lifetime photo collections and the user interaction for photo annotations. Finally we summarize the status of our work and an outlook of open issues.

2 Related Work

Photo collections, as one of promising sources to tell story of life in this digital era, has attracted many researchers to spend time for exploring its usage and proving its usefulness. Some solutions focus on personal photo organization while others bring together semantic annotations to photo collections in general. Due to the varying intentions of these tools we present them in different sections below:

2.1 Semantic Photo Annotation

Flickr[1] is an online application which allows to creating collections by dragging and dropping photos from timeline display. Annotations in Flickr are supported by tags. We have extended such tagging with ontologies and by connecting these tags with appropriate predicates from the ontology such as Person *playing* Football.

PhotoStuff [8] allows manual semantic annotation to images either on the web or local. It allows loading RDF-based ontologies for later annotating images with it. The taxonomy browser in SemanticLIFE is similar to their ontology tree view. Instead of exposing arbitrary property-value forms for encoding RDF annoations, our approach is based on the annotation template. The template based annoations gurantee sufficient metadata for describing images and the eas-of-use. Additionally instead of first drawing a region and then looking for the appropriate concept from the ontology for annotations we allow the user to select a concept and then draw a region for it.

Developed by Mindswap, SMORE [10] focuses more on semantic mark-up and ontology editing. It offers an extension for annotating text and images. Using these tools user can create metadata based on the loaded ontology. Furthermore, user can also define new concepts (class or property), to be added in the ontology.

Another promising multimedia annotation tool is M-Ontomat-Annotizer [4]. It supports metadata creation for an image or its selected region by associating it with a concept in the ontology.

---

[1] http://www.flickr.com

2.2 Personal Photo Organization

Among large number of other commercial photo management tools, Picassa[2] provides very good visualizations. It supports photo labelling and the photos having same label are considered one collection. Creation date is also used to automatically classify photos. Picassa provides good visualization for the timeline view of all collections. Similar to other commercial tools slideshow for collection is also supported.

PhotoFinder [11] supports visualization of collections in several ways. Drag-n-Drop is supported throughout the application for different tasks. It also supports limited annotation for persons. We have extended their annotation strategy in two dimensions: (1) using image region for annotation and labelling and (2) annotating events and other photo contents using semantic web technologies. In addition the person information is reused and linked to the existing personal address book and contacts. This allows more semantic queries to be fulfilled from the photo collections such as searching for "photos of all friends in Salzburg".

Girgensohn and colleagues investigated the performance issues in organizing large photo collections [7]. The tool support practically is not much different from the other commercial tools but comes with improved performance. Worth mentioning is a calendar view supported in their tool. In our prototype implementation we provide sorting and filtering based on time and date both for a particular collection and in lifetime view. We also provide sorting and filtering based on the concept taxonomy.

A different approach is presented in [3] for organizing large photo collections. It combines information from map data (GPS) with metadata of photos, by which a story of a trip will be more meaningfully constructed. Later on photos can be viewed on the location map and also based on the timeline. Additionally MyLifeBits provides an integrated view of the lifelong information items ranging from photos, documents, phone calls, emails, to web pages [6]. Our approach potentially differs from MyLifeBits as we exploit ontologies for managing semantics of these information items.

3 SemanticLIFE

The SemanticLIFE project is an attempt to realize the Vannevar Bush's vision of the **Memex** "*a device in which an individual stores all his books, records, and communications... an enlarged intimate supplement to his memory*"; and **associations of thoughts** "*The human mind... operates by associations. With one item in its grasp, it snaps instantly to the next that is suggested by the association of thoughts, in accordance with some intricate web of trails.*" [5] The architecture of SemanticLIFE system is presented elsewhere [1]. The range of data sources starts from communication data (emails, phone calls, and chat sessions) to personal documents, photos, web-browsing sessions and calendar

[2] http://picasa.google.com

data. SemanticLIFE realizes the associations of items in personal digital diary by annotating contents of these information items with ontologies. In this paper we specifically focus on organizing and annotating photo collections by exploiting their semantics.

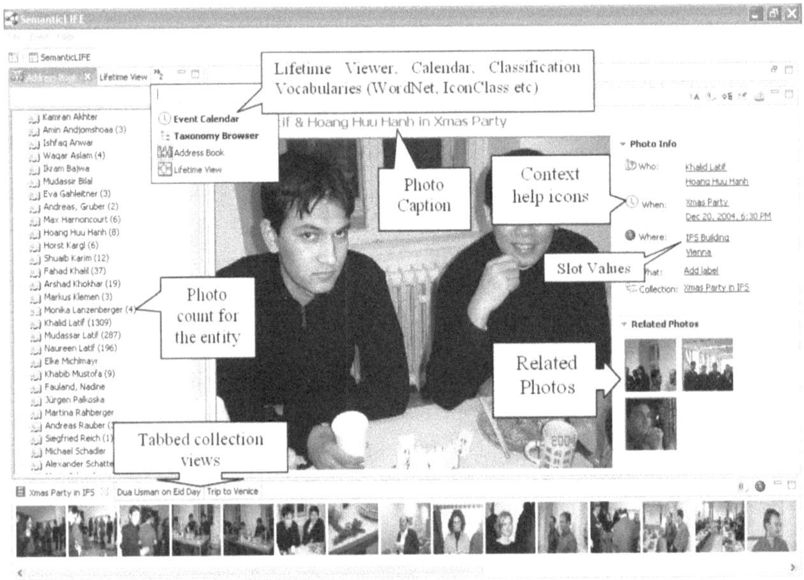

Fig. 1. Overview of photo annotation in SemanticLIFE

4 Annotation Model

The information of the photos can be separated into two categories: the general photo characteristics and the photo contents. The first category provides information about photo resolution, format, size, etc. Such information is present in the EXIF header of digital photos and is easily extracted. The second category describes what is depicted by the photo. The contents of personal digital photo vary largely, and may include a wide range of domains such as sports, entertainment, and sightseeing.

Utility of semantic annotations for describing such diverse photo contents is well established [4] [13]. But, comprehensability in such an annotated lifetime photo space and usability of Semantic Web technologies from the user interaction point of view is still an open issue. Common users mostly want easy access to their photo collections for viewing, using in their homepage, creating presentations, or sharing with other people. It is difficult to provide a unified way for annotating personal photos with arbitrary RDF. Even simple and otherwise trivial annotations are complex and hard to grasp for non-experts, regardless of any simplification in the visualization. On the other hand a simplified annotation model can lead to pragmatic interfaces.

In our recent work [12] we presented a study of the LATCH[3] model for organizing personal information items. The proposed annotation model corresponds to who, when, where, and what. The hypothesis is that such a structuring of annotation template on one hand provides adequate semantics to organize personal photo collections and on the other hand is easily comprehended by the user. The values for slots in the template are filled by creating semantic labels based on concepts in existing ontologies. Compared to keyword search such semantic annotations allow concept searching where users can specialize or generalize a query based on the concept hierarchy. The detail of the model is presented below:

Who: This axis describes the persons and other agents/actors depicted in the photo. For annotating persons the already available address book is presented to the user. Person names are also extracted from recently visited web pages and other user documents. The user is also suggested with these names during annotations. The detail of how we determine if a name should be suggested for a specific picture is explained in section 6.1. Digital photos are categorized as personal, professional photos, and art work [13]. Personal photo collections may include a photo of an art object. Such photos have a special actor, the *creator*, annotated as the original author of the object depicted in the photo. One such example is a painting depicted in a photo being annoated with its *artist* (where artist *isa* creator).

When & Where: These dimensions describe the time and location of the photos and the collections. Locations include concepts such as country, city, a region, and street address. For individual photos the time value describes the time the photo is taken which is extracted from the photo metadata in EXIF header. These dimensions can also be annotated with the scheduled events from existing calendar management applications like MS Outlook. An example case is explained in section 6.1. The time value is represented as an interval.

What: This axis has two dimensions: (1) *what actions* agents are doing such as a person eating sushi, playing football, and (2) what objects (other than agents described in *who*) are depicted in the photo such as palm tree, or a painting. The later can also be annotated in turn with context metadata, such as a painting within a photo maybe be annotated with the artist (who) information.

5 Photos as Landmarks

Humans make use of variety of practices for recollection. Use of *mnemonics* is one example of such practices. Originated with the ancient Greeks the idea is to associate parts of the information to well-known landmarks. In hypertext systems the opening web page is considered a landmark and every other web page in that

[3] LATCH originally stands for ***L**ocation*, ***A**lphabets*, ***T**ime*, ***C**ategory*, and ***H**ierarchy* [17]. We suggested replacing *Alphabets* with *Agent/Actor* for using it as organizing principle instead of ordering principle [12].

particular web application is linked with it [16]. Use of landmark events is also investigated for personal information space [14]. Traditionally personal photos are sorted into family album (the preferred ones) and "shoe-boxes". We argue that, while keeping the distinction, the connection of the photos in family album with those in shoe-boxes could be established in digital archives. This is done by declaring important photos as landmarks within a collection. All other photos in the same collection are automatically associated with the landmark photos. Some personal photo management applications make use of ranking, such as a count from zero to ten in PhotoFinder, to weight importance of a photo. While declaring a photo as important is one aspect, more important is to associate other relevant photos with it and suggesting them to the user. Thus retrieval of photos is made efficient by forming trails of associations and the user is guided in exploring the large photo-space.

For declaring a photo a landmark users assign a numeric weight ($10 \geq w > 0$) to the photo. This weight is later used in determining the size of thumbnail in collection view and also in search results view. The landmark weight also contributes in determining the nearness of one landmark with the other. We have implemented different set of rules based on the weights using Semantic Web Rule Language (SWRL). For example a landmark photo LP_x having weight x will be considered near a photo P_0 if any of the following holds:

- o LP_x and P_0 are in the same photo collection
- o LP_x and P_0 are directly connected (through manual linking)
- o Both LP_x and P_0 are annotated with the same concept C from the ontology.
- o LP_x has an annotation of concept type C_1; P_0 has an annotation of concept type C_2, and $SemanticDistance(C_1, C_2) < x$. The semantic distance is computed in several ways such as the manual associations, property-entity associations [2], topic similarity, and hierarchical concept distance. More detail of calculating semantic distance in nearness discovery of landmarks is presented in our prior work [12].

The photo viewer uses these rules to find landmark photos near the currently selected photo. User can set a threshold value (default to 4) for the number of relevant photos to show in the photo viewer. The priority is given to the photos with higher landmark weight. While viewing one photo from a collection the user is provided with photos which are semantically near the photo in context. Thus the whole photo collection turned out to be a web of trails.

6 User Interaction

Other than the taxonomy browser (classification view) which is an integral part of SemanticLIFE, three views are provided to the user for navigation and annotation of photos: (1) lifetime photos view, (2) collection view, and (3) the photo view. In the lifetime view representative thumbnails of all categories are displayed along with their titles and event information. The thumbnails are generated from combination of the landmark photos in the collection similar to "My Photos"

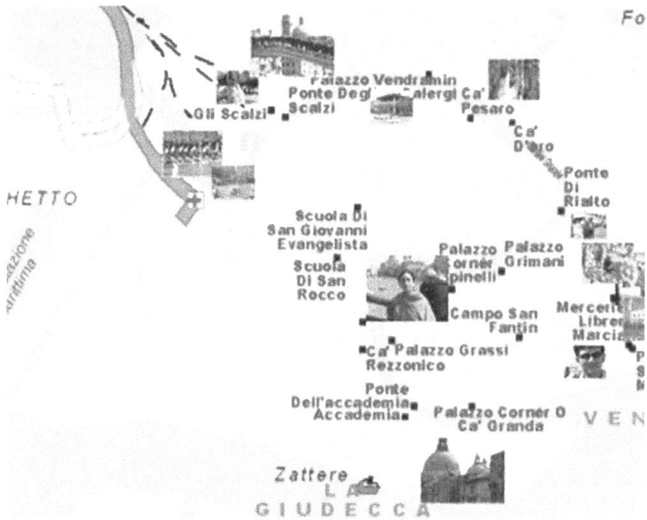

Fig. 2. Photos arranged on a map by the user. Magnification of a photo thumbnail depends on its landmark weight.

view in Windows XP in which first four photos are used to generate thumbnail of a folder. The collections in this view are sorted based on the timeline.

The collection view by default uses date/time for sorting the photos. Photos can also be sorted and filtered based on the concepts in the taxonomy hierarchy. A scattered plot mode with a background location map is also supported (see figure 2). Users can freely place the photos on a background map. The settings are preserved and could be seen anytime by selecting the location map mode in the collection view toolbar. Lastly the application is developed as an Eclipse rich client platform (RCP) which allows the user to arrange the views at the position of their choice.

6.1 Connecting Life Items

SemanticLIFE's repository is fed with different desktop information such as calendar entries/appointments, web browsing cache, emails, and address book. The photo annotation is an integral part of the system, so it utilizes and reuses the existing information by far. Most of the personal photos come from planned events, such as birthday party or a conference. Information about such events (if present) is fed by Outlook and Sunbird adaptors, and is stored in the repository after appropriate transformation to RDF (c.f. figure 3 showing scheduled event in Sunbird, the event website as visited by the user, and photo taken in that event.) Such existing items are an added help to the user in photo annotations. Items in the same date/time range are suggested to the user for their possible reuse during photo annotation. We also apply ANNIE[4] to the recently

[4] http://www.gate.ac.uk/annie/

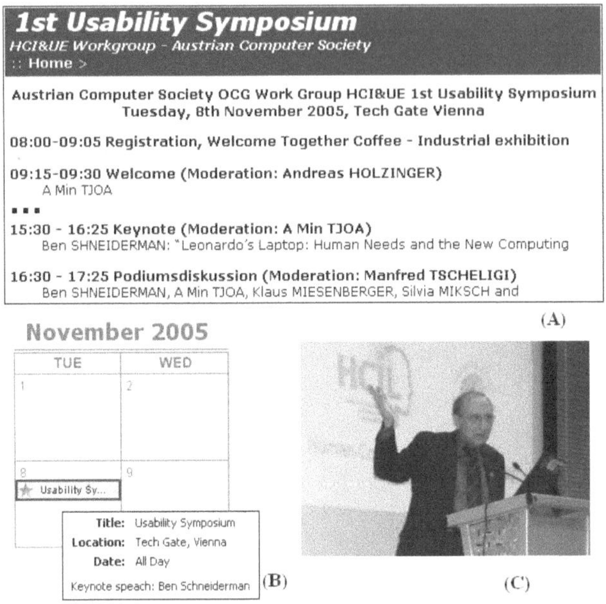

Fig. 3. (A) Part of the website showing program of the event, (B) scheduled event in Mozilla Sunbird, and (C) a picture taken in that event

fed life-items (such as web pages, emails, and documents) for extracting named-entitites such as person names. Clicking the *context help icon* in photo view (c.f. figure 1) displays a list of relevant entities being extracted by ANNIE. Any of these items/entities could be dragged and dropped on the photo or whole collection. Depending on the item type and its meta-data the appropriate slot is filled, thus users do not have to re-type.

6.2 Annotation of Individual Photo

Other than entering the metadata by hand, we support two strategies for photos annotations: (1) Existing information items such as persons in address book, event entries in calendar, and ontology contents from a vocabulary are dragged and dropped on the photo. This associates the prevalent concept to the whole photo. (2) A specific region of the photo could be annotated by first selecting the target concept from existing vocabulary (such as *Gondola* taken from WordNet). The taxonomy browser loads the ontology vocabularies in a tree structure for this purpose. The annotation marker on the photo view tool bar is then selected and a rectangle is drawn on the photo. This annotates the image region with currently selected concept in classification view. An RDF listing of the annoation is presented in figure 5. The rectangular region is hidden in the photo view unless the target concept is selected from the photo information which highlights the region (cf. figure 4).

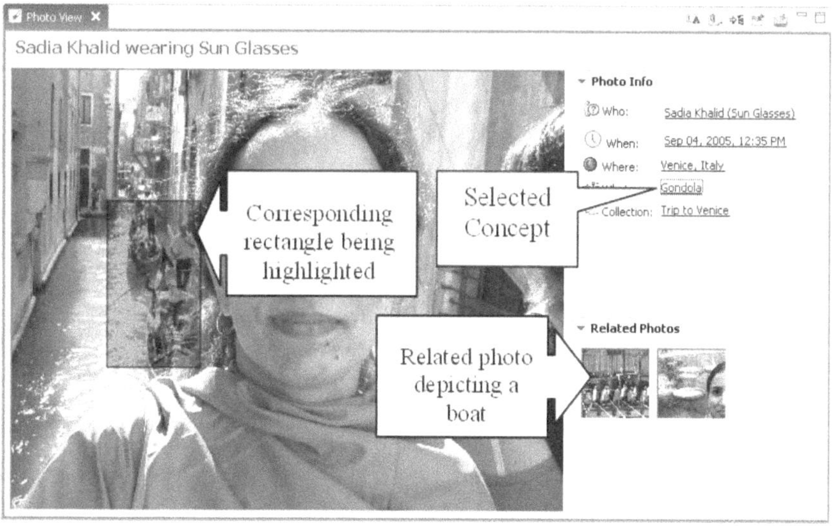

Fig. 4. The photo viewer with concept and region highlighting support. The selection of concept *Gondola* has highlighted the associated region.

```
<rdf:RDF xml:base="http://www.ifs.tuwien.ac.at/slife-core.owl"
  xmlns:foaf="http://xmlns.com/foaf/0.1/"
  xmlns:owl="http://www.w3.org/2002/07/owl#"
  xmlns:rdfs="http://www.w3.org/2000/01/rdf-schema#"
  xmlns:rdf="http://www.w3.org/1999/02/22-rdf-syntax-ns#"
  xmlns:reg="http://www.w3.org/2004/02/image-regions#">

    <foaf:Image rdf:ID="slph_1004285">
      <reg:hasRegion>
        <reg:Rectangle rdf:ID="slph_1004285_r01">
          <reg:coords>...</imreg:coords>
          <reg:regionDepicts rdf:resource=".../wordnet/1.6/Gondola-1"/>
        </reg:Rectangle>
      <reg:hasRegion>
    </foaf:Image>
</rdf:RDF>
```

Fig. 5. Abridged RDF listing of an annotation showing a rectangle within a photo which depicts a concept Gondola from WordNet

6.3 Annotating Collections

Collections can be created either (1) manually by dragging and dropping the selecting photos or (2) suggested by the system for un-sorted photos. The later task examines the EXIF header for possible match in date/time and other available characteristics. Similar to photo annotations, whole collections can also be tagged with ontology concepts or linked to other personal information items such as an event from the calendar data. Associating the metadata with the collection replicates the semantics to all member photos. Moreover a collection can become a part of another collection.

7 Conclusion and Future Work

We have presented our work on managing personal photo collections using semantic annotations. The proposed annotation model and use of landmarks have made the large photo collections a web of connected photos in which user can navigate from one collection to photos belonging to specific concepts and then to other semantically related photos. This way we tried to close the gaps in bringing together semantic photo annotations and personal photo management.

In near future we intend to extend our work for semantic relation discovery by exploiting more the semantics of the ontology concepts compared to the syntactical concept distance. Additionally we are working on semi-automatically developing a unified view of the concept hierarchies which otherwise belong to different domain ontologies. In DynamOnt project we are investigating an approach for dynamically building ontologies by reusing existing concept hierarchies through their mapping with the foundational ontology. We hope to enhance the work presented in this paper by benefiting from the findings of that project.

Acknowledgement

This work as part of the SemanticLIFE project is generously supported by ASEA-UNINET (ASEAN-EU Academic University Network) and HEC (Higher Education Commission of Pakistan). This research is also supported by the DynamOnt project which is funded by the Austrian Governments FIT-IT Research Initiative on Semantic Web.

References

1. Ahmad, M., Hoang, H.H., Karim, S., Khusro, S., Lanzenberger, M., Latif, K., Michlmayr, E., Mustofa, K., Nguyen, H.T., Rauber, A., Schatten, A., Tho, M.N., Tjoa, A.M.: Semanticlife - a framework for managing information of a human lifetime. In: Proceedings of 6th International Conference on Information Integration and Web-based Applications & Services, Jakarta, Indonesia, OCG Press (2004)
2. Aleman-Meza, B., Halaschek-Wiener, C., Arpinar, B., Ramakrishnan, C., Sheth, A.: Ranking complex relationships on the semantic web. IEEE Internet Computing **9**(3) (2005) 37–44
3. Aris, A., Gemmell, J., , Lueder, R.: Exploiting location and time for photo search and storytelling in mylifebits. Technical Report MSR-TR-2004-102, Microsoft Research (2004)
4. Bloehdorn, S., Petridis, K., Saathoff, C., Simou, N., Tzouvaras, V., Avrithis, Y., Handschuh, S., Kompatsiaris, Y., Staab, S., Strintzis, M.: Semantic annotation of images and videos for multimedia analysis. In: Proceedings of 2nd European Semantic Web Conference, Heraklion, Greece, Springer Verlag (2005)

5. Bush, V.: As we may think. The Atlantic Monthly (1945)
6. Gemmell, J., Bell, G., Lueder, R., Drucker, S., Wong, C.: Mylifebits: Fulfilling the memex vision. In: Proceedings of ACM Multimedia. (2002)
7. Girgensohn, A., Adcock, J., Cooper, M., Foote, J., Wilcox, L.: Simplifying the management of large photo collections. In: Proceedings of Human-Computer Interaction, IOS Press (2003)
8. Halaschek-Wiener, C., Schain, A., Golbeck, J., Grove, M., Parsia, B., Hendler, J.: A flexible approach for managing digital images on the semantic web. In: Proceedings of 5th International Workshop on Knowledge Markup and Semantic Annotation, Galway, Ireland (2005)
9. Hollink, L., Schreiber, G., Wielemaker, J., Wielinga, B.: Semantic annotation of image collections. In: Proceedings of Workshop on Knowledge Markup and Semantic Annotation. (2003)
10. Kalyanpur, A., Hendler, J., Parsia, B., Golbeck, J.: (Smore semantic markup, ontology, and rdf editor) http://citeseer.ist.psu.edu/555327.html.
11. Kang, H., Shneiderman, B.: Visualization methods for personal photo collections: Browsing and searching in the photofinder. In: Proceedings of IEEE International Conference on Multimedia and Expo. (2000) 1539–1542
12. Latif, K., Tjoa, A.M.: Combining context ontology and landmarks for personal information management. In: Proceedings of IEEE International Conference on Computing & Informatics, Kuala Lumpur, Malaysia (2006)
13. van Ossenbruggen, J., Troncy, R., Stamou, G., Pan, J.: Image annotation on the semantic web. Technical report, W3C Semantic Web Best Practices Working Group (2006) http://www.w3.org/2001/sw/BestPractices/MM/image_annotation.html.
14. Ringel, M., Cutrell, E., Dumais, S., Horvitz, E.: Milestones in time: The value of landmarks in retrieving information from personal stores. In: Proceedings of 9th International Conference on Human-Computer Interaction, Zurich (2003)
15. Schneiderman, B., Kang, H.: Direct annotation: A drag-and-drop strategy for labeling photos. In: Proceedings International Conference on Information Visualisation, London, England (2000)
16. Sorrows, M.E.: Recall of Landmarks in Information Space. Phd dissertation, School of Information Sciences, University of Pittsburgh (2004)
17. Wurman, R.S., Sume, D., Leifer, L.: Information Anxiety 2. Que (2000)

Topic Distillation in Desktop Search

Alex Penev, Matthew Gebski, and Raymond K. Wong

[1] National ICT Australia, Sydney, NSW 2052, Australia
[2] School of Computer Science and Engineering
The University of New South Wales, Sydney, NSW 2052, Australia
{alexpenev, francg, wong}@cse.unsw.edu.au

Abstract. Desktop Search, the search across local storage such as a personal computer, is a common practice among computer users. There has been much activity in Web-related Information Retrieval, but Desktop Search has only recently increased in popularity. As the structure and accessibility of data in a local environment is different to the Web, new algorithmic possibilities arise for Desktop Search.

We apply a connectivity analysis approach to the local environment—a filesystem. We describe how it can be used in parallel with existing tools to provide "more useful" ranked results. Our evaluation reveals that such an approach has promise, and we conclude that exploiting the organization of a filesystem is beneficial for Desktop Search.

1 Introduction

Desktop Search (DS) refers to searching of local, contained data stores, as opposed to searching a foreign and overwhelming repository such as the Internet. There are often many (and unfamiliar) documents that satisfy an Internet query, but users generally seek specific (and familiar) files on a desktop.

DS tools place emphasis on using an inverted file to facilitate near-real-time retrieval, by indexing the content and metadata of various known filetypes. One of the first such tools, Lotus Magellan (late 1980s), created a master index of different filetypes and allowed searching and viewing of files without the need to launch the associated viewer application. Such functionality is emulated by today's DS tools.

The field received more research attention following the prototype work of [1]. AskJeeves, Google, Microsoft and Yahoo have all since released DS tools, and there are currently more than twenty available[1]. By applying the inverted file index to local data, DS tools produce sub-second searches.

Inverted files substantially improve conventional disk-scanning methods, but only address the problem of speed. Discerning the relevance of results requires analyzing their content. Fortunately, simple content analysis is inexpensive when inverted files are involved, and the recent wave of DS tools has been welcomed by many. The tools mainly differ in their presentation, index size overhead, extent of filetype coverage, and brand power.

[1] http://www.goebelgroup.com/desktopmatrix.htm, visited Dec 2005.

S. Bressan, J. Küng, and R. Wagner (Eds.): DEXA 2006, LNCS 4080, pp. 478–488, 2006.

"Topic distillation" refers to educing high-quality documents that are most-representative of a given query topic[2]. Our motivation for this work lies in distilling such high-quality files to improve ranked DS results. For this, we adopt and adapt a connectivity analysis approach.

The remainder of this paper is organized as follows: §2 provides background on DS and connectivity analysis. §3 explains our approach and methodology, while §4 details our evaluation and observations. §5 highlights related work, and we draw conclusions in §6.

2 Background

2.1 Ranking in Desktop Search

Today's DS tools provide options to sort the results by metadata, such as lexically, chronologically, by filesize, or clustered by format. One problem with searching for local data is that the result set can still be large. Without knowing the metadata, sorting by these attributes is unlikely to be useful; the user will need to sequentially scan the result list ($\frac{n}{2}$ inspections on average).

We believe that a ranked list is useful to the user, as they may not always remember metadata (or even know it in the first place, if looking through files not authored by them). A choice to sort by relevance or by metadata will allow the user to pick a strategy they think will result in the fewest inspections. Several of today's DS tools provide such a choice, which supports our view.

Our goal is to improve ranked lists, by placing files that are most-representative of the query topic on top. On the assumption that the user's query adequately specifies their target, finding such representative files is coaxial to the problem of topic distillation. Originating in bibliometrics, connectivity analysis approaches have proven useful in solving this problem for Web IR[3,4].

2.2 Content and Connectivity Analyses

Content Analysis measures how well-representative a document is of a query. Approaches such as the Vector Space Model are popular.

Connectivity Analysis measures how well-connected a node is in a graph. The World Wide Web, a large directed graph, is regularly subjected to such analysis to elicit the popular pages. Two celebrated algorithms in Web-IR are *PageRank* and *Hypertext-Induced Topic Selection* (HITS).

PageRank[3] calculates the probability distribution of random walks, using the random surfer model on a query-independent global graph. Using the in-degree, PageRank deems a page as popular if it has many in-links (and even *more* popular, if the links come from already-popular pages).

HITS[5] argues that every document serves two purposes: to be an authority or to be a hub. An authority is a page with topic-relevant content, while a hub simply links to authorities (its content may be irrelevant). Like PageRank, HITS uses in-links for calculating authoritativeness. But it uses out-links for hubness. Depending on the situation, hubs can be more-useful search results.

Both of these algorithms are iterative, and "shake" the graph to distribute weight along the hyperlink-edges until an equilibrium is reached.

We chose to adopt HITS due to its classification of nodes as authorities and/or hubs, which maps intuitively to a filesystem (§3.1). PageRank lacks this classification, considering nodes as equals. Moreover, HITS uses a query-specific subgraph for its root set and subsequent calculations, allowing us to easily build on top of the retrieved results of an existing DS tool (§4.2).

2.3 HITS

HITS[5] gathers documents from the Web and nominates the best hubs and authorities among them. [6] notes that "a large amount of latent human judgment is encoded within hyperlinks, with links to another page offering some measure of conferred authority". This conferral of authority is used to distill reputable documents. Hubs and authorities exhibit a mutually-reinforcing, bipartite relationship, whereby a good hub should link to good authorities, and a good authority should be linked to by good hubs.

The algorithm begins by retrieving a small *root set* of pages via a search engine, i.e. a query-specific subgraph. Nodes in this set may be highly disconnected, and a *base set* is formed by augmenting the immediate neighborhood of documents that are 1 hop away. The augmented documents add structure to the graph, and may also include relevant pages that did not match the keywords but were frequently cited in the root set[2].

The base set induces a directed graph $G = (V, E)$, with vertices V and edges E representing pages and hyperlinks, respectively. All $v \in V$ are assigned both a hub and authority score, and HITS updates the new scores from the old using two alternating summations until the scores converge:

`HITS`. *in*: link-graph vertices V, directed edges E. *out*: hub/auth score vectors h/a.
1. $\forall v \in V$, initialize $h_0[v]$ and $a_0[v]$ to 1.
2. **for** iteration k **until** convergence:
3. $\quad \forall v \in V,\ \ h_k[v] := \sum_{o:(v \to o) \in E} a_{k-1}[o]$
4. $\quad \forall v \in V,\ \ a_k[v] := \sum_{i:(i \to v) \in E} h_{k-1}[i]$
5. $\quad$ normalize h_k and a_k.
6. **return** h and a

Algebraically, HITS computes the dominant eigenvectors of the $M^T M$ co-citation and MM^T coupling matrices, where M is the $|V| \times |V|$ non-negative adjacency matrix of the focused subgraph. The algorithm, as well as positively-weighted versions of it, has been shown to converge[5,7] under Perron-Frobenius.

Because HITS considers only the structure (in- and out-links), it is occasionally prone to undesirable behaviors, such as *mutually reinforcing relationships between hosts* (alleviated by reducing the weight of in-links from the same host[7]), and *topic drift* (alleviated by using content analysis to maintain focus on the query[7,8,5]).

[2] A classic example is that search engines are linked to by pages talking about "search engines", but rarely include those two keywords on their page.

3 Approach

While parts of HITS can be adopted to suit a filesystem, other parts need to be adapted. The most important is the concept of connectivity.

3.1 Filesystem Connectivity

On the Web or in research literature, connections/links are created by human judgment. It is evident that Web authors arrange information into directed graphs that link related content together. Unfortunately, a filesystem lacks this concept of *conferral of authority*. In a filesystem, the organization hierarchy involves human judgment, but the implicit links between files/dirs are not created on an individual basis. However, it has been noted[9] that users generally:

- organize files into subdirectories
- group related files together
- group related directories nearby

Therefore, while we lack the luxury of conferred links, we can exploit the organization of the filesystem hierarchy to determine "relevant neighborhoods" that contain relevant directories. We will retrieve *relevant files* (in a content analysis sense), but would prefer relevant files found in *relevant directories*. Since links are largely artificial[3], our notion of a *relevant directory* is not only one that contains relevant files, but also one that resides in a *relevant neighborhood*. The remainder of this section outlines the ways in which we construe HITS to suit this goal.

The concept of *hubs* and *authorities* conveniently map to *directories* and *files*, and by applying the mutually-reinforcing, bipartite relationship that they exhibit on the Web, we draw the analogy that a good directory should contain good files, and a good file should be contained in a good directory. The hub and authority scores tell us exactly this.

3.2 Root and Base Sets

The root set, the query-specific subgraph, can be built using the indexing and searching functionality of a current DS tool. We retrieve the top 250 results using Lucene[10]. To expand this set F of results into the base set, we use the filesystem hierarchy to add the missing structure into our graph: we create a directory set D that forms a spanning tree on F. No new files are added, but the simple injection[4] of directories—which dually serve as hubs—provide paths. Our base set, $D \cup F$, induces a strongly-connected link graph, where every node has a route to every other. We refer to the length of the (shortest) path between two nodes as their **degree-of-separation**, or δ.

This δ is the equivalent of Marchiori's "how many clicks"[11] an end-user needs to perform to get from one page to another, by using only atomic actions.

[3] Placing a new directory anywhere in the filesystem automatically causes unintentional paths (of some length) to many other node in the hierarchy.

[4] E.g. `/home/me/a.txt` will have `a.txt` in F, and `/home/me`, `/home` and the filesystem root `/` in D.

The δ for two directories α and β can be directly calculated from their paths, by finding their lowest common ancestor-or-self directory λ: $\delta(\alpha, \beta) = (|\alpha| - |\lambda|) + (|\beta| - |\lambda|)$, where $|n|$ is depth of n. For files, the immediate parent directory is used. Therefore, by construction, δ is 0 between a directory and itself, a file and itself, or a file and its immediate parent directory.

Similar to [11,12], we use δ as a fading factor to decay the influence of nodes upon each other as they get farther apart. We fade proportional to $\frac{1}{\delta^2}$, a non-linear penalizing curve that is harsh on distance but lenient on proximity. Other functions may be used[5].

3.3 Algorithm

Our `hitsFS` algorithm adapts HITS to our filesystem reinterpretation of what constitutes a link and a relevant hub.

`hitsFS`. *in*: dirs D, files F. *out*: hub scores h for D, authority scores a for F.

1. $\forall d \in D$ and $\forall f \in F$, initialize $h_0[d]$ and $a_0[f]$ to 1.
2. **for** iteration k **from** 1 **to** K:
3. $\quad \forall d \in D, \; h_k[d] \; := \sum_{f \in F : \delta(d,f)=0} a_{k-1}[f] \; + \sum_{d' \in D} \frac{h_{k-1}[d']}{(1+\delta(d,d'))^2}$
4. $\quad \forall f \in F, \; a_k[f] \; := \; ca(f) \times \sum_{d \in D} \frac{h_{k-1}[d]}{(1+\delta(d,f))^2}$
5. $\quad$ normalize h_k and a_k.
6. **return** h and a.

Intermediate results for the output vectors h and a during the k-th iteration are labeled as h_k and a_k. Line 3 updates the hub score for each d, by summing the weights of base set files that are in d. We then augment the surrounding neighborhood influence from other hubs (decayed by distance). Line 4 updates the authority scores, whereby a file f is influenced by its content analysis score ($ca(f)$, in [0,1] as returned by Lucene). HITS models an authority's score as the sum of hubs that point to it, which we achieve by summing the influence of other hubs on f (decayed by distance).

In our experiments, we set the number of iterations, K, to 20. We have noticed, however, that about 10 iterations are enough to stabilize the top-most scores—an observation supported by the literature.

4 Evaluation

4.1 Corpus

Unfortunately, existing work uses unsuitable corpora for our task. Link analysts have often focused on the Web, downloading large portions of online domains.

---

[5] Experimental results were remarkably similar with $2^{-\delta}$; however, we prefer the inverse-square-law, as it has physical interpretations, describing many natural force-distance relationships.

Such corpora are non-static and difficult to procure. As we are only interested in hierarchy and content (not hyperlinks), we used the JDK 1.5.0, a familiar corpus[6] that is widely variant in structure.

This corpus contains Java library code, which we tokenize[7] to remove syntax problems. In the modified corpus, there are 9267 files in 674 directories. There is an average of 13.8 files per dir (max 321, median 5), and 927 tokens per file (max 37812, median 463). The mean directory depth is 4.52 (max 9, median 4).

We index this modified corpus with several DS tools, described in the next section. Although Java classes generally reference other Java classes, we do not use these connections as "links" in any way.

4.2 Competition

We test our prototypes against three of the best[13] DS tools: Copernic Desktop Search, Google Desktop Search v2, and Microsoft's Windows Desktop Search[8]. We refer to these as *CDS*, *GDS*, and *MDS*. Our prototype, DirH, retrieves the top 250 results from Lucene v1.9 [10], and applies `hitsFS`.

We chose Lucene since it reports content analysis scores (VSM) that `hitsFS` needs, although any listing of documents with their similarity score suffices. As `hitsFS` seeks a single numerical representation for the top documents, the underlying metric may be a black-box.

We provide two versions of our prototype—**DirH0** and **DirH1**—which have Lucene and a modified-Lucene as backend. We include both Lucenes in our evaluation (*Luc*, *Lucmod*). The modifications are:

- stemming is enabled.
- document length norm is changed to 1 ($nwords^{-0.5}$ often penalizes longer files on length more than shorter files are penalized for lower TF).
- keywords-matched ratio is squared. Disjunctive matching and stemming significantly increase the number of matches, yet we still only use the top 250 as root set. We wish to doubly-penalize files that match only a few keywords, to promote better hubs by having more files represent them in the top 250.

These tools are summarized in Table 1.

4.3 Queries

Our experiment focused on ranking highly-representative file(s) at the top, for a given query topic. To promote objectivity in our results, the queries and their

[6] http://java.sun.com; specifically, the j2se/src/share/classes tree, without compiling natives.

[7] We delete non-java files, and use javadoc to generate documentation. This step removes the code/implementation, but semantic meaning is retained since comments account for much of the generated documentation. We then remove javadoc-introduced package/tree navigation pages. The extant files are API documentation versions of the original classes, which we strip clean of markup (html2text), tokenize and case-fold to plain-text.

[8] http://www.copernic.com, http://desktop.google.com, http://desktop.msn.com

target answers (Table 2) were taken from reputable Java FAQs[14,15]. However, since users tend to search using 3 terms or less[16,17], we have condensed the queries to at most 3 terms.

Table 1. Summary of DS tools trialled. Our prototypes are in bold.

DS Tool	Ranking?	Stemming?	Grouping?	Stopwords?	Path match?
CDS	No	Weak	AND	Index	Yes
GDS	Yes	No	AND	Index	Yes
MDS	Yes	Weak	AND	Index	Yes
Luc	Yes	No	OR	Ignore	No
DirH0	Yes	No	OR	Ignore	No
Lucmod	Yes	Porter	OR	Ignore	No
DirH1	Yes	Porter	OR	Ignore	No

Table 2. DS tools were subjected to the above queries

Id	Query	Targets
q1	connect remote server	java.net.{Socket, URLConnection}
q2	select file	javax.swing.JFileChooser
q3	call garbage collector	java.lang.System
q4	execute external program	java.lang.Runtime
q5	schedule thread	java.util.{Timer, TimerTask}
q6	make beep sound	java.awt.Toolkit
q7	linked list	java.util.{LinkedList, Vector, ArrayList}
q8	convert strings numbers	java.lang.{Integer, Double, Long, Short, Byte, Float}
q9	write object stream	java.io.Serializable
q10	play sound	java.applet.AudioClip
q11	list supported fonts	java.awt.Toolkit
q12	read data file	java.io.{FileInputStream, FileReader, BufferedReader, DataInputStream}
q13	write data file	java.io.{FileOutputStream, PrintWriter, PrintStream}
q14	append data file	java.io.{FileOutputStream, RandomAccessFile, DataOutputStream}
q15	format numbers	java.text.{NumberFormat, DecimalFormat}
q16	convert ip address	java.net.InetAddress
q17	generate random integer	java.util.Random
q18	display image	javax.swing.ImageIcon, java.awt.Image

4.4 Results

Each tool answered each query, but only the top 50 results were acknowledged. We report two metrics (Table 3): MRR and a Mean *normalized* Reciprocal Rank.

Since very few results are accepted as correct, a hit-and-miss tool can still be moderately competitive under MRR's steep $\frac{1}{r}$ curve[9]. In Fig. 1, we provide

[9] Softer curves (e.g. $\frac{1}{\sqrt{r}}$, $\frac{1}{1+\log r}$ or $\frac{n+1-r}{n}$) place DirH1 in the lead for both metrics.

Table 3. MRR and Mean normalized Reciprocal Rank results

Score	CDS	DirH0	DirH1	GDS	Luc	Lucmod	MDS	Avg.
MRR	0.089	**0.440**	0.416	0.224	0.358	0.305	0.314	0.307
MnormRR	0.087	0.323	**0.425**	0.224	0.272	0.292	0.254	0.268

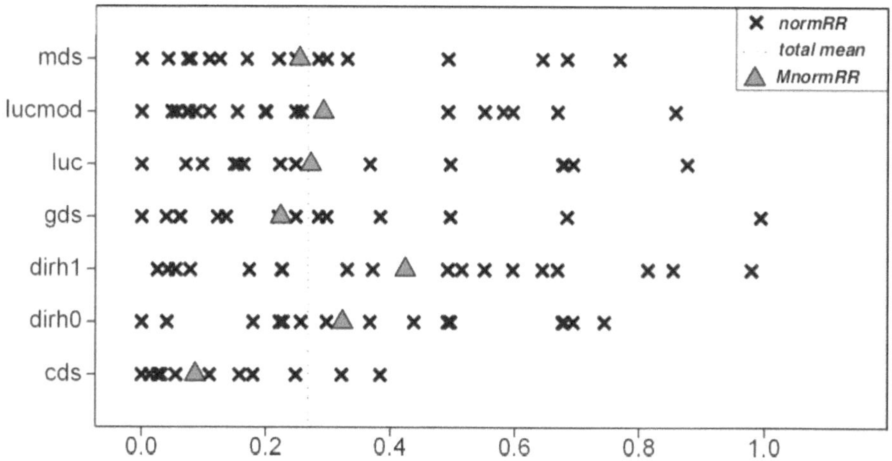

Fig. 1. Mean normalized Reciprocal Rank observations for Table 2 queries. MnormRR vector-normalizes the per-query RR scores to share the weight according to a tool's *relative performance* to the others. This graph shows that most tools are roughly equal and close to the mean, but both of our prototypes performed better on average.

a normalized RR metric, which shares the scores relative to the performance of the other tools. The interpretation of the graph is that our approach *generally ranks a target higher* than its competitors, when using the top 50 results.

The behavior for some queries was not unexpected. Luc often penalized targets on length, so Lucmod ranked them higher. DirH1 used Lucmod's higher content analysis placement to maintain a good ranking for the target.

Q6 was the only query which conjunctive tools failed on, since no file matched all words. Luc matched one term, ranking the target at 183rd. Lucmod matched a second term via stemming, and since it had no length penalty, placed the target in 3rd. DirH1 pushed it down to 5th, since its hub was only ranked 8th.

Several queries had very common terms. DirH1 deemed java.lang the best hub for q8, reporting all but one target (despite 92% of the corpus being matched). DirH0 listed 4 (15% match due to no stemming). Other tools did not report a target in their top 50. Stemming was unnecessary for q9, and all disjunctive tools matched 93% of the corpus. The "noise" from the numerous content-relevant files resulted in only GDS, DirH1 and MDS reporting the target.

DirH1 suffered from polysemy in some queries. It reported all targets for q7, but its top 25 positions were dominated by the sun.tools.doclets.formats.html package (classes refer to *link* and *list* in an HTML context). With stemming off, DirH0 avoided this problem.

For q7 and q10, the existence of better hubs caused our approach to lower the rank of Luc/Lucmod's content analysis suggested positions of the target. But for the other queries where either tool reported a target in the top 50, our approach placed a target in an equal or better rank.

In terms of performance, total processing time averaged to 2.01s on a 3.2MHz P4 with standard load. Most of this time was used for disk IO in the building of auxiliary data structures, which would normally be bootstrapped only once by a background-process DS tool. Computation of 20 iterations under `hitsFS` averaged to 0.064s, which does not grow with the size of the result set since we use a maximum root set size of 250.

5 Related Work

PageRank and HITS (§2.2, [3,5]) are popular connectivity analysis algorithms, and have had many suggested improvements (for a more-extensive survey, we refer to [6]). Our work builds on HITS by adapting the concepts of what constitutes a hub, an authority, a link, and relevance in a filesystem environment.

ARC[18] used a distance-2 HITS to compile authority lists comparable to human-powered taxonomies. A key idea was inspecting the small text-window surrounding anchors to judge the weight of a link, but this does not map to a filesystem. However, we do consider paths longer than HITS's distance-1.

[7,8] suggested pure connectivity analysis adjustments to improve HITS' accuracy by over 45%. However, ideas focused on treatment of nodes with skewed in/out-degree ratios, which lack an intuitive interpretation in a filesystem. But [8] defends our use of Lucene's VSM, by empirically arguing that there is little difference between VSM, CDR, TLS and Okapi.

[19] use HITS for companion and co-citation identification of related pages, improving on Netscape's "What's related" service. A key idea was to exploit the order of links on the page, but a filesystem's listing order of paths is determined by the operating system (e.g. ascii sort), and not human judgment.

[20] suggested using paths of arbitrary length to abate rare counter-intuitive results of HITS in weakly-connected graphs. We also consider arbitrary path lengths, but our strongly-connected graph has weighted path-lengths which we construct without their expensive matrix exponentiation method.

Using feedback to bias weights [21,20] merits further investigation for a filesystem, where more recently (or frequently) accessed (or modified) nodes could be given artificial boosts, since they appear to interest the user.

The methodology of our work is similar to [22,12], both of which modify PageRank and apply it to a new domain (labeled graph databases, and hyperlinked XML; their semantic links came from schemas and idrefs/xlinks). Our work differs in its applied environment, algorithm and interpretations.

6 Conclusion

We have adopted and adapted a connectivity analysis approach to improve ranked lists in local filesystem search. In a DS context, we hypothesized that favoring relevant files in relevant directories could yield better results.

We provided anecdotal evidence that this may be the case, using a real-world hierarchical corpus with real-world queries. Under MRR, we recognized Lucene as having better ranked results than the other commercial tools. Yet, our two prototypes—running on top of Lucene and a modified-Lucene—improved the MRR of their respective backend by 23% and 36%. Under a per-query normalized metric that shared scores according to relative performance, our prototypes improved the Mean normalized RR of their backends by 19% and 46%.

We conclude that traditional content analysis combined with some connectivity analysis is useful for relevance-ranked results in Desktop Search.

References

1. Dumais, S., Cutrell, E., Cadiz, J., Jancke, G., Sarin, R., Robbins, D.: Stuff I've Seen: a system for personal information retrieval and re-use. In: SIGIR. (2003)
2. Chakrabarti, S., Dom, B., Kumar, S.R., Raghavan, P., Rajagopalan, S., Tomkins, A.: Experiments in topic distillation. SIGIR workshop on Hypertext IR (1998)
3. Page, L., Brin, S., Motwani, R., Winograd, T.: The PageRank Citation Ranking: Bringing Order to the Web. Stanford Digital Library Technologies Project (1998)
4. Brin, S., Page, L.: The anatomy of a large-scale hypertextual Web search engine. Computer Networks and ISDN Systems **30**(1–7) (1998)
5. Kleinberg, J.: Authoritative sources in a hyperlinked environment. JACM **46**(5) (1999)
6. Marendy, P.: A review of world wide web searching techniques focusing on HITS and related algorithms that utilize the link topology of the world wide web to provide the basis for a structure based search technology (2001)
7. Bharat, K., Henzinger, M.R.: Improved algorithms for topic distillation in a hyperlinked environment. In: SIGIR. (1998)
8. Li, L., Shang, Y., Zhang, W.: Improvement of HITS-based algorithms on web documents. In: WWW. (2002)
9. Ravasio, P., Schär, S.G., Krueger, H.: In Pursuit of Desktop Evolution: User Problems and Practices With Modern Desktop Systems. TOCHI **11**(2) (2004)
10. The Apache Lucene Project: (2006) http://lucene.apache.org.
11. Marchiori, M.: The quest for correct information on the Web: Hyper search engines. Computer Networks and ISDN Systems **29**(8–13) (1997)
12. Guo, L., Shao, F., Botev, C., Shanmugasundaram, J.: XRANK: Ranked keyword search over XML documents. In: SIGMOD. (2003)
13. Noda, T., Helwig, S.: Benchmark Study of Desktop Search Tools. University of Wisconsin-Madison E-Business Consortium (2005)
14. The Java Tutorial: (1995–2005) http://java.sun.com/docs/books/tutorial.
15. Harold, E.: The comp.lang.java FAQ List (1995–1997) http://www.ibiblio.org/java/javafaq.html.
16. Anick, P.: Adapting a full-text information retrieval system to the computer troubleshooting domain. In: SIGIR. (1994)

17. Jansen, B., Spink, A., Bateman, J., Saracevic, T.: Real life information retrieval: a study of user queries on the Web. SIGIR Forum (1998)
18. Chakrabarti, S., Dom, B., Gibson, D., Kleinberg, J., Raghavan, P., Rajagopalan, S.: Automatic resource list compilation by analyzing hyperlink structure and associated text. In: WWW. (1998)
19. Dean, J., Henzinger, M.R.: Finding related pages in the world wide web. Computer Networks **31**(11–16) (1999)
20. Miller, J., Rae, G., Schaefer, F., Ward, L., LoFaro, T., Farahat, A.: Modifications of Kleinberg's HITS algorithm using matrix exponentiation and web log records. In: SIGIR. (2001)
21. Chang, H., Cohn, D., McCallum, A.: Creating Customized Authority Lists. In: ICML. (2000)
22. Balmin, A., Hristidis, V., Papakonstantinou, Y.: ObjectRank: Authority-based keyword search in databases. In: VLDB. (2004)

Interactions Between Document Representation and Feature Selection in Text Categorization*

Miloš Radovanović and Mirjana Ivanović

University of Novi Sad
Faculty of Science, Department of Mathematics and Informatics
Trg D. Obradovića 4, 21000 Novi Sad
Serbia and Montenegro
{radacha, mira}@im.ns.ac.yu

Abstract. Many studies in automated Text Categorization focus on the performance of classifiers, with or without considering feature selection methods, but almost as a rule taking into account just one document representation. Only relatively recently did detailed studies on the impact of various document representations step into the spotlight, showing that there may be statistically significant differences in classifier performance even among variations of the classical bag-of-words model. This paper examines the relationship between the idf transform and several widely used feature selection methods, in the context of Naïve Bayes and Support Vector Machines classifiers, on datasets extracted from the dmoz ontology of Web-page descriptions. The described experimental study shows that the idf transform considerably effects the distribution of classification performance over feature selection reduction rates, and offers an evaluation method which permits the discovery of relationships between different document representations and feature selection methods which is independent of absolute differences in classification performance.

1 Introduction

Automated Text Categorization (TC) differentiated as an independent field during the 1990s, and has since then provided a benchmark for practically every known Machine Learning technique [1]. Its applicability has also been widely acknowledged by Data Mining (ie. Text and Web Mining), Semantic Web, Digital Libraries, Information Retrieval and Natural Language Processing communities. The biggest appeal of TC, from a researcher's point of view, is in the high number of features of textual data (high dimensionality), even when documents are represented as a simple bag-of-words. For these reasons, the majority of Text Categorization research was concentrated at comparing how various Machine Learning techniques fare in such conditions, and devising methods for reducing the number of features without compromising classification performance, using feature selection or extraction.

Recently, several detailed studies appeared which investigate the impact of document representations – variations of the bag-of-words model – on classification performance. Leopold and Kindermann [2] experimented with the Support Vector Machines

* This work was supported by project *Abstract Methods and Applications in Computer Science* (no. 144017A), of the Serbian Ministry of Science and Environmental Protection.

S. Bressan, J. Küng, and R. Wagner (Eds.): DEXA 2006, LNCS 4080, pp. 489–498, 2006.

(SVM) classifier using different kernels, term frequency transformations and lemmatization of German. They found that lemmatization usually degraded classification performance, and had the additional downside of great computational complexity, making SVM capable of avoiding it altogether. Similar results were reported for Neural Networks on French [3]. Another study on the impact of document representation on one-class SVM [4] showed that, with a careful choice of representation, classification performance can reach 95% of the performance of SVM trained on both positive and negative examples. Kibriya et al. [5] compared the performance of SVM and a variant of the Naïve Bayes classifier called Complement Naïve Bayes (CNB) [6], emphasizing the importance of term frequency (tf) and inverse document frequency (idf) transformations for CNB. Debole and Sebastiani [7] investigated supervised learning of feature weights, and found that their replacement of the idf transform can in some cases lead to significant improvement of classification performance.

Our own study [8] demonstrated that there can be statistically significant differences between document representations for every considered classifier[1] with at least one of the standard performance measures: accuracy, precision, recall, F_1 and F_2 (see Section 2). The emphasis of the study was on determining the *relationships* between different transformations of the bag-of-words representation, including stemming, normalization of weights, tf, idf and logtf (the logarithm of $1+\mathrm{tf}$), ie. on determining their behavior when used in meaningful combinations. Performance of each classifier with different document representations was measured, and *representations* were compared, counting the number of statistically significant wins and losses of every representation for each classifier. In this scheme, the subtracted value of wins–losses expresses the "strength" of a particular representation when compared to others, in the context of a particular classifier. Figure 1, reproduced from [8], depicts the experimentally measured effect of the idf transform, when included in the document representation. The charts were obtained by adding up the wins–losses values of representations which include idf, and subtracting from that the wins–losses values of all representations not containing the idf transform. All values were additionally summed up over 11 datasets extracted from the dmoz Open Directory taxonomy of Web-page descriptions.

Figure 1a depicts the wins–losses differences without any kind of dimensionality reduction, while Fig. 1b[2] shows the values when only around 1000 most frequent features are retained (from a total of 3500–4500, depending on the dataset). There is a clear discrepancy between the effects of idf on CNB and SMO: while it degrades the performance of CNB and improves SMO without dimensionality reduction, with dimensionality reduction the result was completely opposite! This struck us as counterintuitive – discarding least frequent features meant discarding features with a high idf score, which should either have improved or degraded classification performance, but not both. Improvement would have happened in case the less frequent features were not discriminative (correlated with the class feature) and idf was giving them

[1] CNB, Platt's Sequential Minimal Optimization (SMO) method for SVM training, the Voted-Perceptron by Freund and Schapire, Aha, Kibler and Albert's Instance-Based variant of k-Nearest Neighbor, and revision 8 of Quinlan's C4.5, all implemented in WEKA.

[2] The IBk classifier is missing from the chart because it was completely broken by dimensionality reduction, for reasons similar to the breakdown of RF in Section 3.

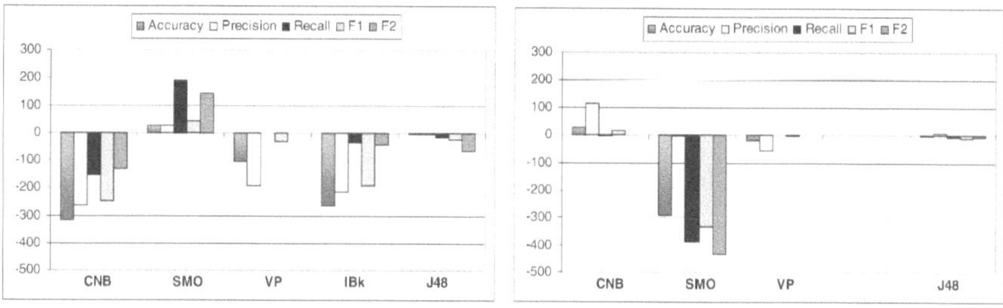

(a) (b)

Fig. 1. Effects of idf applied to tf before (a) and after dimensionality reduction (b)

unrealistically high weight, while degradation would have taken place if such features were highly discriminative (this depending on the actual datasets). Thus an interesting question was raised: do CNB and SMO function at such different levels that they were able to capture completely different notions of feature frequencies and weights?

Motivated by the above dilemma, this paper presents a follow-up experimental study which concentrates on the effect that the idf transform exhibits on several commonly used feature selection (FS) methods, and considers a wider array of reduction rates. Since the datasets used in our previous study were rather small in order to *avoid* issues of dimensionality reduction, this study uses bigger, more realistic datasets also extracted from the dmoz taxonomy.

The reason for using dmoz instead of some other more commonly employed TC corpora (like Reuters and OHSUMED) lies in the initial motivation for determining the best combination of document representation, FS method and classifier for building CatS [9]: a meta-search engine which sorts search results by automatically classifying them into topics derived from the dmoz taxonomy. CatS is currently available at http://stribog.im.ns.ac.yu/cats/.

The rest of the paper is organized as follows. The next section introduces the experimental setup: used datasets, document representations, feature selection methods and classifiers. Section 3 describes the most interesting findings about the interactions between document representations, feature selection methods, and reduction rates. The last section gives some concluding remarks and guidelines for possible future work.

2 The Experimental Setup

The WEKA Machine Learning environment [10] was used as the platform for performing all experiments described in this paper. Classification performance was measured by the standard metrics, which may be described in terms of possible outcomes of binary classification summarized in Table 1. *Accuracy* is the ratio of correctly classified examples into both classes: $(TP + TN)/(TP + TN + FP + FN)$; *precision* expresses the ratio of truly positive examples among all examples classified into the positive class: $TP/(TP + FP)$; *recall* describes the coverage of truly positive examples by the set of all examples classified into the positive class: $TP/(TP + FN)$; F_1 is the harmonic mean of precision and recall: $2 \cdot pr \cdot re/(pr + re)$; and F_2 is a mean which favors recall over precision: $5 \cdot pr \cdot re \,/(4 \cdot pr + re)$. For the sake of brevity only F_1 will be reported, since, on one hand, it is the most widely used evaluation measure in TC literature and, on the other, it is sufficient to illustrate all main points of the study.

Table 1. Outcomes of binary classification

		Predicted class	
		yes	no
Actual	yes	True Positive	True Negative
class	no	False Positive	False Negative

Datasets. The dmoz Open Directory is a large human-annotated collection of Web-page descriptions available at http://dmoz.org, and also used by Google. Its contents can be downloaded in RDF format, and are constantly evolving; the version from July 2, 2005 was used in our research. It has found its way into much Text and Web Mining applications [11,12,13,9], being the only freely available resource of its kind.

Initially, we restricted the domain of experimentation to 11 top level categories of dmoz which were considered suitable for the task of sorting search results [8,9], namely *Arts, Business, Computers, Games, Health, Home, Recreation, Science, Shopping, Society* and *Sports*. For the purposes of this study, six two-class datasets, summarized in Table 2, were extracted from the dmoz data. The table shows the number of features (not including the class feature) of each dataset, the total number of examples (documents), and the number of positive and negative ones. Every dataset corresponds to one dmoz topic from which positive examples are taken, while the negative ones are chosen in a stratified fashion from all other topics at the same level of the hierarchy, within a common parent topic. Thus, for each of the chosen first-level categories (*Arts, Computers, Sports*) the negative examples are extracted from all leftover dmoz data, while for the second-level topics (*Music, Roleplaying, Physics*) negative examples are restricted to their first-level parents (*Arts, Games,* and *Science*, respectively). All texts were preprocessed by eliminating stopwords using the standard stopword list from [14]. Since best document representations that were determined in [8] all included stemming, the Porter stemmer [15] was applied to every dataset.

Table 2. Extracted datasets

Dataset	Features	Examples		
		Total	Pos.	Neg.
Arts	14144	6261	3002	3259
Computers	15152	7064	3390	3674
Sports	14784	7694	3881	3813
Arts/Music	13968	8038	4069	3969
Games/Roleplaying	12530	8948	4574	4374
Science/Physics	10558	4973	2519	2454

Document Representations. Let W be the *dictionary* – the set of all terms (or features, in this case words) that occur at least once in a set of documents D. The bag-of-words representation of document d_j is a vector of weights $\boldsymbol{w}_j = (w_{1j}, \ldots, w_{|W|j})$. If w_{ij} is taken to be the frequency of the ith term in the jth document, the representation is referred to as the *term frequency* (tf) representation. *Normalization* can be employed to scale the term frequencies to values between 0 and 1, accounting for differences in the lengths of documents. The logtf transform can be applied to term frequencies, replacing the weights with $\log(1 + w_{ij})$. The *inverse document frequency* (idf) transform is expressed as: $\log(|D|/\mathrm{docfreq}(D, i))$, where $\mathrm{docfreq}(D, i)$ is the number of documents from D the ith term occurs in. It can be used by itself, or be multiplied with term frequency to yield the popular tfidf representation.

For each dataset, two different variations of the bag-of-words representation were generated, one just with term frequencies (tf), and the other using the tfidf representation. Normalization with regards to document length was performed in both cases, since it was shown in [8] to be beneficial to performance of the classifiers that will be considered in this paper.

Feature Selection. The examined feature selection methods are more-less well known and widely used in TC: chi-square (CHI), information gain (IG), gain ratio (GR), ReliefF (RF) and symmetrical uncertainty (SU) [16,17,18,10]. All these methods assign a score to every text feature based on its correlation with the class feature. CHI achieves this using the well known χ^2 measure from Statistics, while IG, GR and SU all come from the same stream of equations originating in the notion of *entropy* from Information Theory. RF is essentially different from all methods described above. It functions at a more algorithmical level, by taking a random example from the dataset and using its nearest neighbors (with regards to some vector distance metric) from each class to update the relevance of every feature.

In our experiments, the performance of classification was measured on datasets consisting of the top 100, 500, 1000, 3000, 5000, 7000 and 10000 features selected by each method, and on datasets with all features. The simple feature selection method from our previous study [8], which discards least frequent features, was not used. The reason was simple – it was difficult to follow the same reduction rates on different datasets without randomly discarding features with same frequencies of appearance, which would have compromised the validity of any reached conclusion.

Classifiers. The two classifiers implemented in WEKA that were used in the study are ComplementNaiveBayes (CNB) – a variant of the classic Naïve Bayes algorithm optimized for applications on text [6,5], and SMO – an implementation of Platt's Sequential Minimal Optimization method for training Support Vector Machines [19]. Both classifiers were employed using their default parameters (with the exception of turning off SMO's option for normalization of data, since it was done beforehand), meaning that SMO was used with the linear kernel, which is known to perform well on text [2].

Experiments were carried out on each dataset with a particular document representation, FS method and number of features, and classifier, in five runs of 4-fold cross-validation. Values of evaluation measures were compared using the corrected resampled t-test provided by WEKA, at $p = 0.05$, and averaged over runs and folds for further reporting.

The experiments in [8] showed that tf was the best document representation for CNB, but logtf was the winner for SMO. Despite that fact, this study uses tf as the baseline representation for both classifiers, in order to accurately capture the relationships between feature selection and the idf transform, and enable a more exact comparison of the behavior of the two classifiers.

3 Results

Figure 2 depicts the performance of CNB measured by F_1 for all considered feature selection algorithms and reduction rates, averaged over the six datasets, with the tf representation (a) and tfidf (b). It can be seen that CHI, IG and SU feature selection methods behave practically the same, which is somewhat surprising since CHI is based on rather different theoretical grounds. GR closely follows the three down to more radical reduction rates of 500 and 100, where its performance drops. RF proved to be a complete failure, in all probability not because of any shortcoming as a feature selection algorithm, or unsuitability for use in textual domains. It was a consequence of WEKA's implementation using the Euclidian measure when calculating document vector distances for determining nearest neighbors. Not until the late phases of experimentation did we realize that the Euclidian measure tends to deform with high numbers of features [20]. Therefore, the bad performance of RF may be treated as an experimental verification of this fact in the context of feature selection.

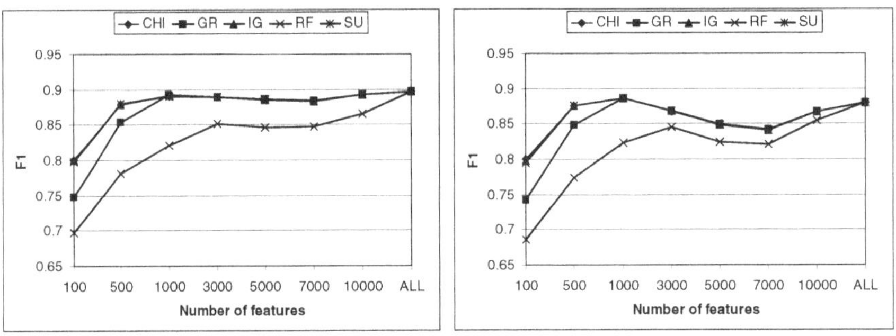

(a) (b)

Fig. 2. Performance of CNB measured by F_1, with tf (a) and tfidf representation (b)

The described trends in the performance of FS methods were consistent over all evaluation measures with both classifiers (except for GR exhibiting a boost in recall for CNB at low number of features), so the following comments will generally refer to the CHI–IG–SU trio.

Noticeable differences in the behavior of CNB in the two charts of Fig. 2 are the more obvious dent between 3000 and 10000 features for tfidf, and the fact that CNB performance with tfidf is scaled down several percent from tf. But, when instead looking at the summed-up statistically significant wins–losses values, shown in Fig. 3, the differences between reduction rates become more obvious[3]. What these charts depict is independent of absolute classifier performance at given reduction rates – they rather express how FS methods and reduction rates fare against one another within the realms of a particular classifier and document representation. Peaks at 1000 selected features and no feature selection are more clearly pronounced than in Fig. 2, as well as the dents between 3000 and 10000.

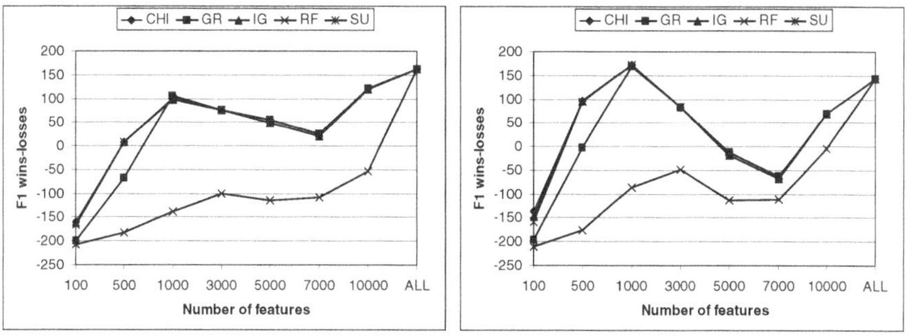

(a) (b)

Fig. 3. Summed up wins–losses for F_1 and CNB, with tf (a) and tfidf representation (b)

In order to express how the idf transform effects the behavior of the CNB classifier in conjunction with feature selection, the chart in Fig. 4a shows the wins–losses for tf (Fig. 3a) subtracted from the wins-losses for the tfidf representation (Fig. 3b). It can be seen that idf degrades the performance of CNB at higher numbers of features, while improving it in the 100–3000 range. Note that this is *relative* improvement/degradation – the performance of a FS method at a particular reduction rate is expressed only through comparison with its peers within the same document representation and classifier. Therefore, the 100–3000 range can only be viewed as the place to *expect* improvement when introducing the idf transform to the document representation. Whether improvement will actually take place is up to the datasets and classifiers – in our studies the tfidf representation proved inferior almost as a rule, but that may not always be the case [5,2]. Using wins–losses instead of values of performance measures effectively avoided the issue of scale when comparing feature selection methods on different document representations, sacrificing information about absolute performance to express the relationships between document representations and feature selection.

Figure 4b shows the corresponding graph of wins–losses differences introduced by idf for the SMO classifier. Contrary to the the chart for CNB, this chart points to *two* possible areas of idf performance improvement: one at higher numbers of features, approximately above the 8000 mark, and one in the lower feature counts below 800. This shows that the idf transform effects the two classifiers differently regarding FS reduction rates, and explains the discrepancy noticed in Section 1. With no feature selection

[3] The wins–losses axes ranges from -210 to 210: this is six datasets times 35 – the maximum number of wins (and losses) for a FS method at a particular number of features, out of a total of 5 methods $\cdot$ 7 reduction rates $+ 1 = 36$.

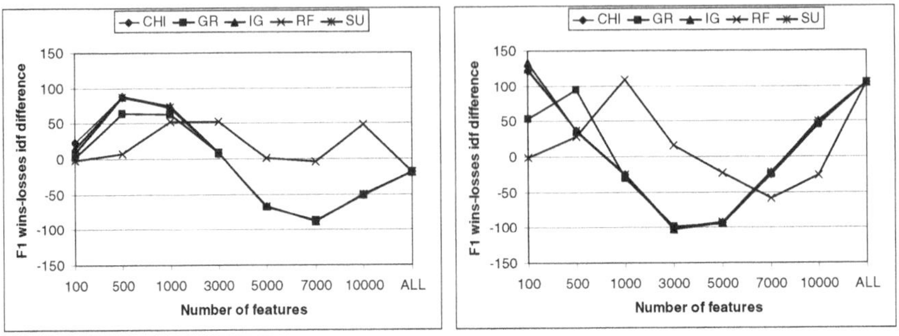

(a) (b)

Fig. 4. Effect of idf on F_1 wins–losses for CNB (a) and SMO (b)

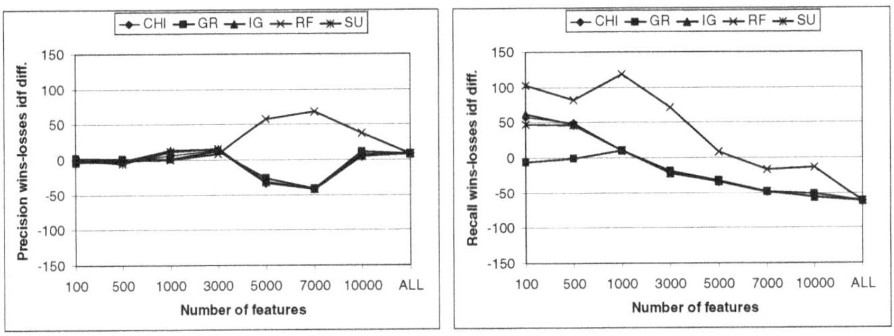

(a) (b)

Fig. 5. The effect of idf on precision (a) and recall wins–losses (b) for CNB

idf degrades CNB and improves SMO, while at 2000–3000 selected features[4] the effect is opposite. What makes the correspondence with our previous study [8] even more remarkable is the fact that different datasets, and even feature selection methods were used, thus supporting the validity of the approach.

However, the general shape of the curves for CNB and SMO in Fig. 4 (regarding the CHI–IG–SU trio) is quite similar, except for the drop of the CNB curve below the 500 feature mark. This may as well be followed by a corresponding drop for SMO at a lower number of features which was not measured. These observations indicate that the CNB and SMO classifiers may not behave in such opposing fashion with regards to the idf transform as was suggested, since the curves are not exactly contrary to one another.

As a side observation, we were struck by the fact that the wins–losses differences charts for the F_1 measure (Fig. 4) and accuracy (figure not shown) are practically identical. Accuracy is an old measure for evaluating Machine Learning techniques which is considered to be very sound, but is seldom used in textual domains since it does not

[4] This roughly corresponds to 1000 features from the previous batch of experiments since those datasets had a considerably lower number of features.

behave well in situations with highly imbalanced class distributions. On the other hand, F_1 is known to handle imbalanced class distributions well, *and* it has shown behavior practically identical to that of accuracy on our datasets which do not exhibit class imbalance. To appreciate the correlation between accuracy and F_1 better, consider the wins–losses differences charts for precision and recall (the two measures which comprise F_1) on CNB in Fig. 5, and the CNB chart for F_1, in Fig. 4a.

4 Conclusion

The intuition introduced in Section 1, that there may be significant interactions between the idf transform in the bag-of-words document representation, and feature selection, has been verified by the presented experimental study. The study concentrated on describing the interaction in the context of two commonly used classifiers for text: Naïve Bayes and Support Vector Machines. By examining wins–losses and their differences, instead of absolute values given by the F_1 evaluation measure, the experiments were able to quantify this interaction, making comparisons between the behaviors of classifiers with regard to the interaction possible. Thus the study concluded that the two examined classifiers behaved in different, but not entirely opposing ways.

Another possibility opened by the quantification of interaction between document representation and feature selection is the comparison of the behavior of *datasets*. One interesting direction of future work would certainly be to extend the experiments to corpora more commonly used in TC research, like Reuters, OHSUMED, WebKB, 20Newsgroups and the like, which would enable drawing some additional parallels with existing experimental and theoretical results.

Other basic bag-of-words transforms beside idf, like stemming, normalization and logtf, could also benefit from similar experimental treatment, although they appear not to be so strongly correlated with feature selection as idf (according to the evidence from [8]). But, it would be interesting to examine the behavior of supervised feature weighing schemes introduced by Debole and Sebastiani [7], which, unlike idf, do attempt to weigh text features in correspondence to the class feature. Intuitively, such transforms should generate wins–losses difference charts that are much more placid and closer to 0 than the ones in Fig. 4. Finally, the proposed method can be used in the context of more advanced document representation schemes, including n-grams [17], information derived from hyperlinks, and elements of document structure [11].

With the rapid expanse of research and applications of classification algorithms in the 1990s, the field of document representations was left somewhat under-studied. Recent papers focusing on issues of document representation [2,3,4,5,7,8] showed that some of the "old truths" (e.g. "tfidf is the best variant of the bag-of-words representation") may not always hold for new and improved algorithms. Further understanding of the relationships between document representation, feature selection, and classification algorithms can provide useful insights to both researchers and practitioners, assisting them in choosing the right tools and methods for their classification-related tasks.

References

1. Sebastiani, F.: Text categorization. In Zanasi, A., ed.: Text Mining and its Applications. WIT Press, Southampton, UK (2005)
2. Leopold, E., Kindermann, J.: Text categorization with Support Vector Machines. How to represent texts in input space? Machine Learning **46** (2002) 423–444
3. Stricker, M., Vichot, F., Dreyfus, G., Wolinski, F.: Vers la conception automatique de filtres d'informations efficaces. In: Proceedings of RFIA2000, Reconnaissance des Formes et Intelligence Artificielle. (2000) 129–137
4. Wu, X., Srihari, R., Zheng, Z.: Document representation for one-class SVM. In: Proceedings of ECML04, 15th European Conference on Machine Learning. LNAI 3201, Pisa, Italy (2004)
5. Kibriya, A.M., Frank, E., Pfahringer, B., Holmes, G.: Multinomial naive bayes for text categorization revisited. In: Proceedings of AI2004, 17th Australian Joint Conference on Artificial Intelligence. LNAI 3339, Cairns, Australia (2004) 488–499
6. Rennie, J.D.M., Shih, L., Teevan, J., Karger, D.R.: Tackling the poor assumptions of naive Bayes text classifiers. In: Proceedings of ICML03, 20th International Conference on Machine Learning. (2003)
7. Debole, F., Sebastiani, F.: Supervised term weighting for automated text categorization. In Sirmakessis, S., ed.: Text Mining and its Applications. Studies in Fuzziness and Soft Computing 138. Physica-Verlag, Heidelberg, Germany (2004) 81–98
8. Radovanović, M., Ivanović, M.: Document representations for classification of short Web-page descriptions. In: Proceedings of DaWaK06, 8th International Conference on Data Warehousing and Knowledge Discovery. LNCS 4081, Krakow, Poland (2006)
9. Radovanović, M., Ivanović, M.: CatS: A classification-powered meta-search engine. In: Advances in Web Intelligence and Data Mining. Studies in Computational Intelligence 23, Springer-Verlag (2006)
10. Witten, I.H., Frank, E.: Data Mining: Practical Machine Learning Tools and Techniques. 2nd edn. Morgan Kaufmann Publishers (2005)
11. Chakrabarti, S.: Mining the Web: Discovering Knowledge from Hypertext Data. Morgan Kaufmann Publishers (2003)
12. Gabrilovich, E., Markovitch, S.: Text categorization with many redundant features: Using aggressive feature selection to make SVMs competitive with C4.5. In: Proceedings of ICML04, 21st International Conference on Machine Learning, Baniff, Canada (2004)
13. Ferragina, P., Gulli, A.: A personalized search engine based on Web-snippet hierarchical clustering. In: Proceedings of WWW05, 14th International World Wide Web Conference, Chiba, Japan (2005) 801–810
14. Salton, G., ed.: The SMART Retrieval System: Experiments in Automatic Document Processing. Prentice-Hall (1971)
15. Porter, M.F.: An algorithm for suffix stripping. Program **14**(3) (1980) 130–137
16. Sebastiani, F.: Machine learning in automated text categorization. ACM Computing Surveys **34**(1) (2002) 1–47
17. Mladenić, D.: Machine Learning on non-homogenous, distributed text data. PhD thesis, University of Ljubljana, Slovenia (1998)
18. Kononenko, I.: Estimating attributes: Analysis and extensions of RELIEF. In: Proceedings of ECML97, 7th European Conference on Machine Learning. LNCS 1224, Prague, Czech Republic (1997) 412–420
19. Platt, J.: Fast training of Support Vector Machines using Sequential Minimal Optimization. In: Advances in Kernel Methods – Support Vector Learning. MIT Press (1999)
20. Aggarwal, C.C., Hinneburg, A., Keim, D.A.: On the surprising behavior of distance metrics in high dimensional spaces. In: Proceedings of ICDT01, 8th International Conference on Database Theory. LNCS 1973, London, UK (2001)

WebDriving: Web Browsing Based on a Driving Metaphor for Improved Children's e-Learning

Mika Nakaoka, Taro Tezuka, and Katsumi Tanaka

Graduate School of Informatics, Kyoto University
Yoshida-Honmachi, Sakyo, Kyoto, 606-8501, Japan
{nakaoka, tezuka, tanaka}@dl.kuis.kyoto-u.ac.jp
http://www.dl.kuis.kyoto-u.ac.jp

Abstract. A novel approach to Web browsing called "WebDriving" is described that automatically extracts information from the Web and places it in a 3D space, enabling children to easily view the information while "driving through the 3D world". The user can visualize not only the target Web page, but also the "peripheral information" (that is, linked and other related pages) in the same 3D world. This makes the user aware of other relevant Web pages while browsing the target Web page. Our WebDriving browser is well suited for theme-based "investigative learning", which is now being promoted at many elementary schools in Japan.

1 Introduction

Until recently, elementary schools in Japan have put so much weight on cram education that nurturing the ability of students to learn proactively has been severely neglected. Today, many elementary schools are starting to teach students to use the World Wide Web to gather information and to use it to make their own judgments. This is problematic with conventional Web information retrieval systems because they require entry of carefully chosen keywords to retrieve useful information. Children in particular have trouble identifying appropriate keywords due to their undeveloped ability to generalize concepts and to clearly specify for what they would like to search. They thus tend to receive a large number of irrelevant entries in their search results.

Today's technologies are changing the way children learn, and researchers working on new technologies for them must strive to understand their unique needs. Our research goal is to develop an easier way for children to access the World Wide Web and retrieve information. This will make the theme-based "investigative learning" approach currently being promoted at many Japanese elementary schools more effective. We have thus developed a Web browsing system that enables the user to visualize the information on a Web page in a way that fits the way a child seeks information; i.e. they are curious and look around restlessly.

In this paper, we first describe the current state of Web retrieval for children and the problems from the viewpoint of developmental psychology. Our proposed "WebDriving" browser is described in Section 3, and its usage for investigative learning is explained in Section 4. Product requirements are explained in Section 5. We discuss related work in Section 6 and end the paper with a short summary and a look at future work.

S. Bressan, J. Küng, and R. Wagner (Eds.): DEXA 2006, LNCS 4080, pp. 499 – 508, 2006.

2 Current State of Web Retrieval for Children and Problems from Viewpoint of Developmental psychology

2.1 Current State of Web Retrieval for Children

Our research goal is to develop an innovative tool to help elementary school students search for Web page. In particular, we focused on searching Web pages with images, since images are attractive content even for children who are haven't learned to read yet. We began by investigating how children today retrieve images from the Web.

With the help of their parents, children often begin by retrieving information from digital picture books. A search engine is not used. Using a digital picture book, a child starts at a high level and traces down to a target object and retrieves information about it. For example, to gather information about "dog", the child might enter "mammal" as the query, instead of "dog" or "doggie" or "puppy dog", as he or she normally would. Thus, the child has to know some abstracted vocabulary. However, elementary school children (12 years old and under) generally have poor abstraction and generalization abilities.

Many elementary schools in Japan are promoting the use of Web information retrieval systems that support theme-based "investigative learning". Rather than passively learning by simply listening to the teacher, students are being encouraged to actively learn by searching for and collecting information related to their own purposes, such as making presentation materials or exchanging opinions. A very popular site is "Yahoo! Kids Japan". By using this search engine, students can obtain information not yet included in their textbooks. This type of learning is effective because the information retrieved is from the wide-ranging Web, even though the student may have entered a query based on his or her prior experience of using a digital picture book. Needless to say, a wealth of information can thereby be obtained more actively, meaning that the search engine is useful for "investigative learning".

However, children cannot effectively use a directory-type search engine like Yahoo! Kids Japan, before acquiring enough amount of vocabulary. In addition, when children use a crawler type search engine, they can input only the words they commonly use as the query. Therefore, a large part of the retrieval results is of no value, and the child is often unable to judge whether a retrieved result is useful or not. To retrieve information more effectively, the user must be able to enter not only name of the target object but also abstract or specific keywords that are related to the object.

2.2 Problems from Viewpoint of Developmental Psychology

From the viewpoint of developmental or educational psychology, in Jean Piaget's stage theory, man's knowledge acquisition starts with the intuitive thinking period (the period when things are intuitively classified by appearance) and continues through the pre-operation period (the period when things are understood by specific operation) along with the skills to handle abstract concepts [1][2]. If children follow this process, their initial information retrieval can be described as "We know what we want, but we don't know how to express it like an adult". As they develop, their ability to express what they want improves.

In conventional Web information retrieval, appropriate keywords are needed to retrieve the target information, and the abilities to express the target both abstractly and specifically are needed. It is, however, too difficult for most children to identify appropriate keywords due to their lack of ability to generalize or specify concepts describing the information for which they want to search. Therefore, when performing information retrieval, children often encounter two problems in particular.

- A child can usually think of only one or two keywords, even if there are many potential keywords.
- A child often has difficulty in filtering relevant information from a large number of Web pages returned by a conventional Web search engine.

In addition, we should consider information retrieval by children in terms of the digital divide. A significant correlation has been found between the development of a child's intelligence and the environment he or she was brought up in [3]. This does not simply mean that a roomy house is necessary for a child's intelligence to develop. More important are a child's daily experiences.

In short, a new method is needed to support browsing and retrieval, one that improves the effectiveness of theme-based "investigative learning".

3 WebDriving

3.1 "Peripheral Information Space"

Browsing in a Web space includes movement between Web pages. When a user moves in the real world, he or she can acquire information from around the periphery of his or her present location by looking around. We call this "recognizing the peripheral space of the present location". In contrast, when visiting a Web space, a user can view only the visited page; information beyond the page is out of view. One way to solve this problem is let the user view other Web pages in addition to the visited one. We call such a space the "peripheral information space" of the visited Web page.

Our proposed Web navigation and browsing system enables the user to visualize the peripheral information space. This space is a collection of Web contents that are related in some way to the current target Web page; i.e. the target page has links to them and/or their contents are similar to those of the target page. The Web navigation and browsing is performed using two or more Web pages, which increases the likelihood of finding interesting pages.

In many cases, retrieving information using a conventional Web browser is ineffective when only a small number of keywords are specified, since the size of the Web is so large. Users will not have much luck using single- or double-word queries. The problem is that a child has only a small set of vocabulary, and it is often difficult for them to add more keywords to the query in order to get more specific results.

With our proposed browser, a single-word query is enhanced in an imperceptible manner by using the peripheral information space. In this paper, the peripheral information space includes all of the linked and other related pages, which extend around the current target page like a net.

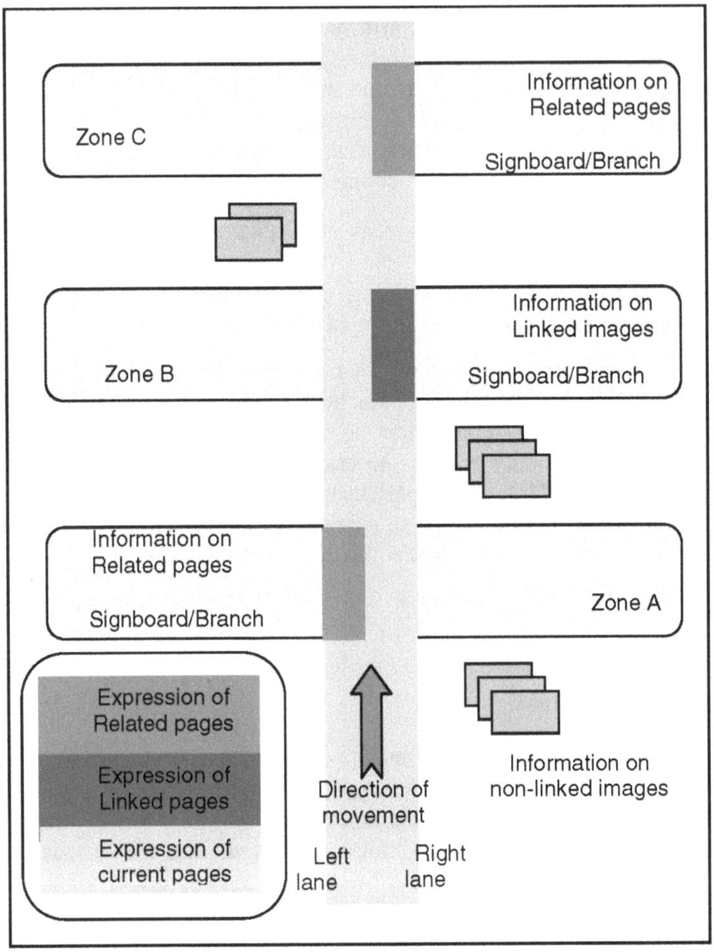

Fig. 1. Example of a driving course created by WebDriving

3.2 Features

Enabling the user to visualize the peripheral information space supports a beginner, i.e. a child, browsing Web pages. WebDriving has several useful features in particular.

- **"Driving game" browsing**: Searching the Web for information using a general search engine entails high initial costs: constructing an effective query and selecting the most relevant page from the search result. WebDriving makes the act of searching like a driving game, so only light motivation is necessary for children to start using it. Because it works like a driving game, its operation is easy and intuitive.
- **Peripheral information space visualization**: Most Web browsers uses Mosaic type approach; that is, only one page is displayed at a time. Presentation of peripheral information is very thin. WebDriving shows related pages in addition to

the current page, all in the same view. WebDriving enables the user to navigate through the Web space by presenting relevant and linked pages to the current page.

- **Browsing and attentive viewing of Web pages**: In WebDriving, the user can first skim through many Web pages, and then view interesting pages more attentively. These two phases are performed in a seamless manner. The driving interface is used for browsing, while a conventional Mosaic-type browser is used for attentive viewing.
- **Extracting significant parts independent from the author's intention**: An author of a Web page uses HTML tags to emphasize certain parts of the page that he or she thinks to be important. However, these parts do not always match with the parts that interest the viewers. WebDriving selects images and texts in a Web page based on criteria independent from the original emphasis by HTML tags placed by the author.

3.3 Semantics of WebDriving

WebDriving renders the linked and other related pages in the same 3D space as the target page. The system performs it by representing the current page as the main road and the images on the page as signboards along the road. WebDriving reads from the top to the bottom of the page in terms of HTML, and if a linked or other related page is found, it draws it as a branch road. Based on an analysis, the system draws the images in the linked and other related pages as signboards either on the right or left side of the road, each branch with corresponding green or orange blinking markers. An example of a constructed course is shown in Fig.1.

4 Use of WebDriving for Investigative Learning

4.1 Operation

Our proposed Web browsing system, WebDriving, works in the following steps:

1. The user selects a starting point, which is a bookmarked URL chosen beforehand by the teacher. This page is used as an original current page.
2. When the user stops the car, the current page is displayed on a conventional Mosaic-type Web browser.
3. Some of the images contained in the current page are presented as the surrounding terrain.
4. While the user drives the car, the system presents branching roads to linked pages and similar pages.
5. The system searches hyperlinks within the current page. Images contained within the anchor tags are presented as signboards appearing with a branch.
6. The system searches similar pages using Google's "related:" operator. Images contained in the similar pages are presented as signboards appearing with a branch.
7. When the user turns on a branch, the page indicated by the branch becomes the current page. The process then returns to step 2.

4.3 Driving Scene

The driving course generated for the current page is displayed, and the user browses the page contents as if driving a car. The page contents are displayed one after the other as signboards (see Fig. 2).

Fig. 2. Images in anchor tags are presented as signboards

The character string at the current location comes from the HTML title tag. The signboards and surrounding terrain are acquired from the images on the page. There is a side road ahead, next to the signboard with a triangular marker (see Fig. 3). The linked pages are displayed with orange markers, and the other related pages are displayed with green markers.

Fig. 3. A branch of the road indicated by signboards and markers

4.4 Mosaic-type View

When the user stops the car, the current page is displayed on a conventional Mosaic type Web browser (see Fig. 4). When the user presses the accelerator button, it returns to the driving mode. A similar and linked pages appear from the side as signboards.

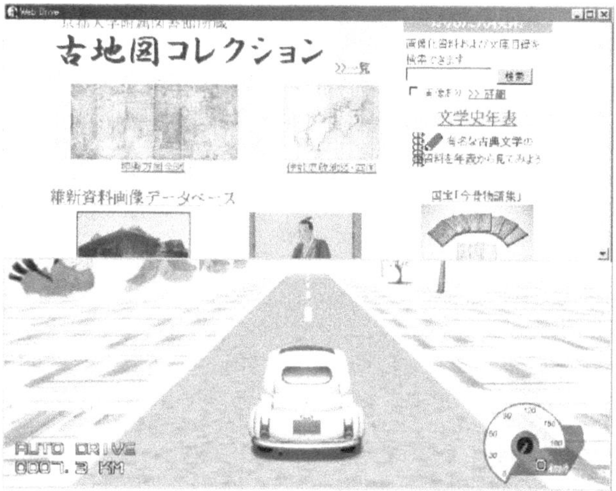

Fig. 4. The current page displayed on a conventional Mosaic-type Web browser

4.5 Branching of the Road

Branches from the main road are generated based on hyperlinks contained in the current Web page, and also by searching similar Web pages using Google Web API.

5 Product Requirements

Product requirements are as follows:

- Hardware requirements:
  - PC: OpenGL (has the practically performance)
  - Video Card: 3D Accelerator
    OpenGL Driver
- Software requirements:
  - Operating system : Windows XP
  - Runtime Environment: Java Runtime Environment 1.4.2
  - Programming Language: Java 2 Standard Edition 1.4.2

6 Related Work

There is a limit to how much information a user can understand at one time. Therefore, when presenting a huge amount of search results from the Web, its understanding can be facilitated by showing only part of it at a time and letting the user decide which further information is to be viewed sequentially. This is especially true in case of children performing Web search.

In the 'Fisheye view' technique [4][5][6], only information about an object that will promote the user's grasp of it is expanded and displayed. This information is overlapped and displayed concisely; the peripheral information of the object, when a user selects the one from what graphs etc. of sets of key words, in one window without the loss of the position.

In the 'Overview + detail / Focus + context' technique [7], the peripheral information is shown around the object and the window where detailed information on the object is shown. The position of the object is recorded in the overview, enabling the user to better understand the location of the object in the total context.

Janecek and Pu added a function for semantic searching (opportunistic searching) to the interface. A fisheye view that presents the image while interactively guiding information that was the most much meaning relation to the object at which the user was gazing, and implemented the system which proposes information the purpose is not clear [8][9][10].

In the field of Web information retrieval, many methods for using contents in the periphery have been proposed for supplementing the attributes of the target page. Because the key words are related to the Web contents, the links ahead tend to appear around the link anchor [11], by using the text in the link anchor environment [12] and by using the peripheral text around the document structure [13][14]. This has improved the accuracy of Web page retrieval by keyword searching.

Moreover, in not only Web page retrieval but also in image retrieval, metadata is extracted from the text of the image in the periphery to retrieve the images used on the Web page [15], and a method of doing the retrieval result image in the ranking based on the concept similar to the link approval rating has been proposed [16].

These approaches make it possible to use the contents in the periphery as contents on the target page.

7 Conclusion

Our proposed "WebDriving" browser automatically extracts information from the World Wide Web and places it in a 3D space, enabling children to easily view the information while "drive through a 3D world". The user not only can visualize a target Web page, but also its "peripheral information" (that is, similar Web pages and link destination pages) in the same 3D world. By using this novel tool, children can become aware, with only light motivation, of other relevant Web pages while browsing a target Web page. One shortcoming of this approach is that children sometimes focus too much on the act of driving and they sometimes forget their purpose of obtaining information.

We plan to enhance WebDriving by constructing an interface that will enable teachers to easily collect Web pages beforehand, thus enabling them to screen out inappropriate Web pages. To facilitate investigative learning, we will add a function for sharing collected information with others when searching for information related to school events, i.e. a class trip.

Acknowledgements

This work was supported in part by NEXT The 21st Century COE (Center of Excellence) Program "Informatics Research Center for Development of Knowledge Society Infrastructure" (Leader: Katsumi Tanaka, 2002-2006), NEXT Grant for "Development of Fundamental Software Technologies for Digital Archives", Software Technologies for Search and Integration across Heterogeneous-Media Archives (Project Leader: Katsumi Tanaka), NEXT Grant-in-Aid for Scientific Research on Priority Areas: "Cyber Infrastructure for the Information-explosion Era", Planning Research: "Contents Fusion and Seamless Search for Information Explosion" (Project Leader: Katsumi Tanaka, A01-00-02, Grant#: 18049041).

References

1. Linton, M: Transformations of memory in everyday life, in U. Neisser (Ed), Memory observed: Remembering in natural contexts. San Francisco: W.H. Freeman (1982).
2. Piaget, J.: The Child's Conception of the World (J. Tomlinson & A. Tomlinson, trans.). Savage, MD: Littlefield Adams Quality Paperbacks (1951: Originally published in 1929).
3. Japanese sentence pattern education society: First Japanese dictionary, Hayashishirou supervision, and Nippon Hoso Kyokai (NHK) Books (1995).
4. Utting, K. and Yankelovich, N.: Context and orientation in hypermedia networks, ACM Transactions on Information Systems, Vol. 7, No. 1, pp. 58–84 (1989).
5. Sarkar, M. and Brown, M.: Graphical fisheye views, Comm. of the ACM, Vol. 37, No. 12, pp. 73–83 (1994).
6. Furnas, G. W.: Generalized Fisheye View, Proceedings of ACM SIGCHI '86 Conference on Human Factors in Computing Systems, pp. 16–32 (1986).
7. Lamping, J., Rao, R. and Pirolli, P.: A Focus + Context Technique based on Hyperbolic Geometry for Visualizing Large Hierarchies, Proceedings if ACM SIGCHI '95 Conference on Human Factors in Computing Systems, pp. 401–408 (1995).
8. Janecek, P. and Pu, P.: Visual Interfaces for Opportunistic Information Seeking, in Proceedings of the 10th International Conference on Human-Computer Interaction (HCII'03), pp. 1131–1135, Crete, Greece (2003).
9. Janecek, P. and Pu, P.: An Evaluation of Semantic Fisheye Views for Opportunistic Search in an Annotated Image Collection, Int. Journal of Digital Libraries, Vol. 4, No. 4, Special Issue on "Information Visualization Interfaces for Retrieval and Analysis" (2004).
10. Janecek, P. and Pu, P.: Opportunistic Search with Semantic Fisheye Views, Proceedings of the 5th International Conference on Web Information Systems Engineering (WISE2004), Brisbane, Australia (2004).
11. Chakrabarti, S., Dom, B., Gibson, D., Kleinberg, J., Raghavan, P., Rajagopalan, S.: Automatic resource list compilation by analyzing hyperlink structure and associated text, Proceedings of the 7th International World Wide Web Conference (1998).
12. Glover, E. J., Tsioutsiouliklis, K., Lawrence, S., Pennock, D. M. and Flake, G. W.: Using Web Structure for Classifying and Describing Web Pages, Proceedings of the 11th International World Wide Web Conference, pp. 562–569 (2002).
13. Attardi, G., Gullì, A. and Sebastiani, F.: Automatic Web Page Categorization by Link and Context Analysis, Proceedings of THAI-99, European Symposium on Telematics, Hypermedia and Artificial Intelligence (Hutchison, C. and Lanzarone, G. (eds.)), Varese, IT, pp. 105–119 (1999).

14. Pant, G.: Deriving link-context from HTML tag tree, Proceedings of the 8th ACM SIGMOD workshop on Research issues in data mining and knowledge discovery, ACM Press, pp. 49–55 (2003).
15. Harmandas, V., Sanderson, M. and Dunlop, M. D.: Image retrieval by hypertext links, Proceedings of the ACM SIGIR '97 Conference on Research and Development in Information Retrieval, pp. 296–303 (1997).
16. Lempel, R. and Soffer, A.: PicASHOW: pictorial authority search by hyperlinks on the Web, Proceedings of the 10th International World Wide Web Conference, pp. 438–448 (2001).

Semantic Wikis for Personal Knowledge Management*

Eyal Oren[1], Max Völkel[2], John G. Breslin[1], and Stefan Decker[1]

[1] DERI Galway, Ireland
firstname.lastname@deri.org
[2] Forschungzentrum Informatik, Karlsruhe, Germany
voelkel@fzi.de

Abstract. Wikis are becoming popular knowledge management tools. Analysing knowledge management requirements, we observe that wikis do not fully support structured search and knowledge reuse. We show how Semantic wikis address the requirements and present a general architecture. We introduce our SemperWiki prototype which offers advanced information access and knowledge reuse.

1 Introduction

Wikis are collaborative hypertext environments, focused on open access, ease-of-use, and modification [8]. Wiki syntax is simple and allows creation of links and textual markup of lists and headings. Wikis commonly support binary data attachments, versioning and change management, change notification, full-text search, and access control.

Wikis are successful tools for collaborative information collection, as observed in the relatively high quality of the Wikipedia encyclopedia [4]. Lately, wikis are becoming popular for personal and organisational knowledge management as well. Knowledge workers use them individually, organisations deploy them internally, and project organisations collaborate through restricted-access wikis[1].

Since managing and enabling knowledge is "key to success in our economy and society" [16, p. 6], we analyse the requirements for knowledge management and how wikis support these requirements. Because knowledge is fundamentally created by individuals [9, p. 59], it is crucial to support these individuals in their personal knowledge management. Considering the knowledge creation spiral [9, p. 62–73], knowledge workers require support in:

1. **authoring:** codifying knowledge into information, enabling sharing
2. **finding and reminding:** finding and reminding of existing knowledge [17]
3. **knowledge reuse:** combining an existing body of knowledge [7]
4. **collaboration:** developing ideas through social interactions

* This material is based upon works supported by the Science Foundation Ireland under Grants No. SFI/02/CE1/I131 and SFI/04/BR/CS0694 and by the European Commission under the Nepomuk project FP6-027705.

[1] Our institutes use wikis for managing projects, clusters, and external collaborations; see http://twiki.org/cgi-bin/view/Main/TWikiStories for more anecdotes.

S. Bressan, J. Küng, and R. Wagner (Eds.): DEXA 2006, LNCS 4080, pp. 509–518, 2006.

1.1 Personal Knowledge Management Tools

Current tools for personal knowledge management have limitations: analog approaches are not automated and cannot be searched, traditional digital approaches are restrictive and do not support ad hoc structures.

Traditional tools such as todo lists or paper piles are very common [6] and are suitable for authoring, but they do not support finding, reminding, knowledge reuse, or collaboration. *Hierarchical filing* (of emails and files) allows browsing and (full-text) searching, but does not support authoring, knowledge reuse, reminding, and collaboration. *Personal information management* tools (e.g. MS Outlook) manage email, calendar, and tasks and support finding and reminding, but they do not support authoring, knowledge reuse, and collaboration.

1.2 Wikis for Knowledge Management

Wikis support authoring and collaboration to a high extent and are popular due to their simplicity and easy collaborative access [2]. On the other hand, wikis do not enable knowledge reuse and have only limited support for finding and reminding.

These limitations result from a lack of structure in the wiki content: almost all information is written in natural language, and has little machine-understandable semantics. For example, a page about the author John Grisham could contain a link to the page about his novel "The Pelican Brief". The English text would say that John Grisham wrote the Pelican Brief, but that information is not machine-understandable, and can therefore not be used for querying, navigating, translating, or aggregating any information.

More specifically, wikis do not allow structured access to data and do not facilitate consistent knowledge reuse:

Structured Access. A wiki does not offer structured access for browsing or searching information. One cannot currently **query** wiki systems, because the information is unstructured. For example, users looking for *"How old is John Grisham?"*, *"Who wrote the Pelican Brief?"*, or *"Which European authors have won the Nobel price for literature?"* cannot ask these questions directly. Instead, they have to navigate to the page that contains this information and read it themselves. For more complicated queries that require some background knowledge users need to manually combine the knowledge from several sources.

Another example of structured access to information can be found in page **navigation**: wikis allow users to easily make links from one page to other pages, and these links can then be used to navigate to related pages. But these explicit links are actually the only means of navigation[2]. If no explicit connection is made between two related pages, e.g. between two authors that have the same publishing company, then no navigation will be possible between those pages.

Knowledge Reuse. Reusing information through **reference and aggregation** is common in the real world. Consider for example that books are generally

[2] Except for back-references that appear on a page and show pages that reference it.

written by an author and published by the author's publisher. The books authored by John Grisham (on his page) should therefore also automatically appear as books published by Random House (on their page). But creating such a view is currently not possible in a wiki, and instead the information has to be copied and maintained manually.

In current wikis it is either assumed that people will speak a common language (usually English) or that **translations** to other languages will be provided. But manually translating pages is a maintenance burden, since the wiki system does not recognise the structured information inside the page text. For example, a page about John Grisham contains structured information such as his birth date, the books he authored, and his publisher. Updates to this information have to be migrated manually to the translated versions of this page.

2 Semantic Wikis

A Semantic wiki allows users to make formal descriptions of resources by annotating the pages that represent those resources. Where a regular wiki enables users to describe resources in natural language, a Semantic wiki enables users to additionally describe resources in a formal language. The authoring effort is relatively low: the semantic annotations are very similar to the layout or structural directives that are already in widespread use in ordinary wikis.

Using the formal annotations of resources, Semantic wikis offer additional features over regular wikis. Users can query the annotations directly ("show me all authors") or create views from such queries. Also users can navigate the wiki using the annotated relations ("go to other books by John Grisham"), and users can introduce background knowledge to the system ("all poets are authors; show me all authors").

In designing a Semantic wiki system several architectural decisions need to be taken. In this section, we explain the basic architecture and outline the design choices and their consequences.

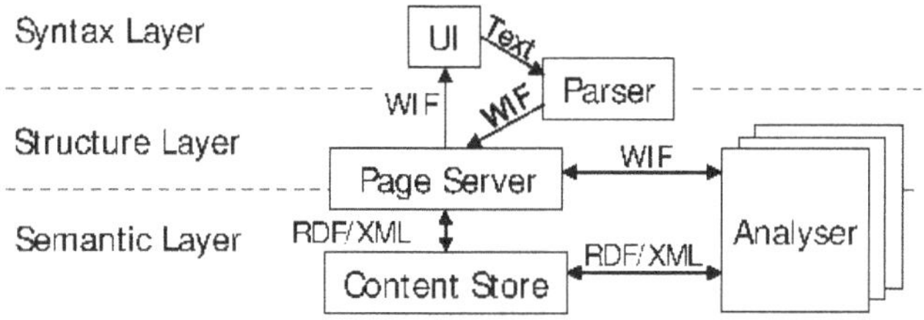

Fig. 1. Architecture of a Semantic wiki

2.1 Architecture Overview

A Semantic wiki consists (at least) of the following components: a user interface, a parser, a page server, a data analyser, and a data store, as shown in Fig. 1.

First we introduce each component, then we discuss the information access, the annotation language, and the ontological representation of the wiki.

overview: The *page server* encapsulates the business logic of the wiki and exposes its data in the neutral wiki interchange format WIF [15]. The *user interface* lets the user browse and query the wiki pages. When a page is edited, the WIF is converted to wiki syntax and the changed wiki syntax is *parsed* back to WIF. The *content store* stores all data as RDF, allowing querying with standard RDF query languages. The *analyser* interacts with the page server and the content store and augments pages and RDF with inferred relations; different types of analysers fit into the architecture, e. g. based on formal reasoning or on statistics.

user interface: responsible for all user interaction. If the wiki is web-based (the classical model), then the user interface is a web server. A desktop application can also act as the user interface component. In this case, collaboration is achieved by using a shared content store.
The user interface allows users to type text and annotations in a freely intermixed fashion. The user interface shows terms from shared *ontologies*, enabling users to browse for an appropriate term[3].

page server: includes standard wiki functionality such as version management, binary attachments, and access control.

parser: converts the text written by the user into objects: it parses the text for semantic annotations, layout directives, and links. This is transmitted in the wiki interchange format WIF.

content store: is responsible for storing and retrieving the semantic annotations, and for exchanging data with other information systems (such as other semantic wikis). An an off-the shelve RDF triple store can be used.

data analyser: is responsible for computing a set of related resources from a given page. In a regular wiki, this means finding all back-references, i.e. pages that link to the current one. In a Semantic wiki the relations between resources are much richer: the data analyser can use the annotations about the current and other pages to search for relevant relations in the content store (such as "other books by current author" or "other people with these parents").

2.2 Annotation Language

For the user of a Semantic wiki, the most visible change compared to conventional wikis is the modified annotation language. For Semantic wikis the annotation language is not only responsible for change in text style and for creating links, but also for the semantic annotation of wiki pages and for writing embedded queries in a page.

[3] Descriptions can be shared and understood if written in a common terminology, and browsing ontologies helps finding an appropriate common term.

Annotation Primitives. As in conventional wikis, internal links are written in CamelCase or by enclosing them in brackets; external links are written as full absolute URIs, or are abbreviated using namespace abbreviations.

Table 1. Annotation syntax

syntax	meaning
`rdf:type foaf:Person`	page has rdf:type foaf:Person
`dc:topic [http://google.com]`	page has dc:topic http://google.com
`dc:topic TodoItem`	page has dc:topic http://wikinamespace/TodoItem
`dc:topic ''todo''`	page has dc:topic "todo"
`?s dc:topic ?o`	embedded query for all pages and their topics
`?s dc:topic TodoItem`	embedded query for all todo items

The additional syntax for semantic annotations is shown in table 1: annotations are written on a separate line, and consist of a predicate followed by an object. Predicates can only be resources (identifiable things), objects can be either resources or literals. An example page is displayed in figure 2. It describes John Grisham, an author published by Random House.

JohnGrisham
`John Grisham is an author and retired lawyer.`
`rdf:type foaf:Person`
`dc:publisher RandomHouse`

Fig. 2. Example page

Subject of Annotations. Wiki pages often refer to real-world resources. Annotations can refer to a wiki page but also to the resource described on that page. For example, the triple "W3C created-on 2006-01-01" can refer to the creation date of the organisation or to the creation date of the wiki page about that organisation.

The question "what do URIs exactly identify" (of which the annotation subject is a subclass) is an intricate open issue on the Semantic Web[4]: a URI can for example identify an object, a concept, or a web-document.

Our approach is to explicitly distinguish the "document" and the "real-world concept" that it describes. Since we expect more annotations of the real-world concepts than annotations of the page itself, we attribute annotations by default to the real-world concept, and allow annotations about the page (such as its creation date, version, or author) to be made by prepending annotations with an exclamation mark.

For example, figure 3a shows a page that describes the World Wide Web consortium. The page explains the W3C and the annotations state that the

[4] See `http://www.w3.org/DesignIssues/HTTP-URI.html`.

```
W3C
The World Wide Web Consortium (W3C) develops interoperable
technologies (specifications, guidelines, software, and
tools) to lead the Web to its full potential

semper:about urn://w3.org
rdf:type wordnet:Organization
swrc:head http://www.w3.org/People/Berners-Lee/card#i

Now we have an annotation about the page itself:
!dc:date "2006/01/01"
```

(a) example page

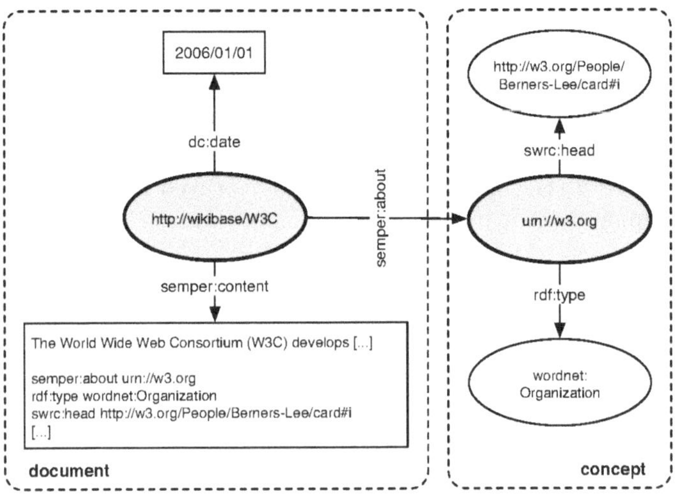

(b) RDF representation

Fig. 3. RDF representation of an example page

organisation is directed by Tim Berners-Lee. The last annotation, prepended with an exclamation mark, refers to the page (document) instead of to the W3C organisation: it states that the page was created on 2006-01-01. We use the "semper:about" predicate to relate the page to the concept that it describes.

Embedded Queries. Users can embed queries on any wiki page. These embedded queries are executed when a page is visited, and their results are included in the displayed page[5]. They could for example show aggregations (such as all the books written by John Grisham); embedding queries in page allows knowledge reuse by persistently combining pieces from different sources.

[5] Views resulting from embedded queries could be read-only or editable. Editable views cause some maintenance issues (should the change be recorded in the version history of the result page or of the page affected by the edit) similar to the view-update problem in databases.

As shown earlier in Table 1, embedded queries are written using triple patterns, sequences of subject, predicate, object, that can contain variables (names that start with a question mark). A triple pattern is interpreted as a query: triples matching the pattern are returned. Patterns can be combined to form joins. Fig. 4 shows the earlier example page about John Grisham, including an embedded query at the bottom of the page. The query returns all books written by JohnGrisham; it creates a view on the data that is displayed below the page text.

JohnGrisham

```
John Grisham is an author and retired lawyer.

rdf:type foaf:Person
dc:publisher RandomHouse

this query shows all his books:
?book dc:creator JohnGrisham
```

```
TheFirm dc:creator JohnGrisham
TheJury dc:creator JohnGrisham
ThePelicanBrief dc:creator JohnGrisham
```

Fig. 4. Page showing embedded query

2.3 Information Access

Information can be accessed by structured navigation and querying facilities.

Navigation. Navigation in ordinary wikis is limited to explicit links entered by users; it is not possible to navigate the information based on structural relations. A Semantic wiki provides the metadata necessary to navigate the information in a structured way. For example, knowing that John Grisham is an author, we can show all other authors in the system, and offer navigation to them.

Our approach for structural navigation is based on faceted meta-data browsing [18]. In faceted browsing, the information space is partitioned using orthogonal conceptual dimensions (facets) of the data, which can be used to constrain the relevant elements in the information space. For example, a collection of art works can consists of facets such as type of work, time periods, artist names, geographical locations, etc.

Common faceted browsing approaches construct the facets manually for a specific data collection. But since in a Semantic wiki users are free to add arbitrary metadata, manual facet generation does not suffice; instead, we have developed a technique to automatically generate facets for arbitrary data [11].

Querying. We distinguish three kinds of querying functionality: *keyword search*, *queries*, and *views*:

1. A *keyword-based full-text* search is useful for simple information retrieval, and supported by all conventional wiki systems.

2. *Structured queries* use the annotations to allow more advanced information retrieval. The user can query the wiki for pages (or resources) that satisfy certain properties. To retrieve for example all authors one can query for "?x type author". Triple patterns can be combined to form database-like joins: "?x type author and ?x has-publisher ?y" retrieves all authors and their publishing companies.
3. As discussed earlier, users can create persistent searches by *embedding queries* in pages. A query included on a page is executed each time the page is visited and continuously shows up-to-date query results.

3 Implementation

SemperWiki[6] is our prototype implementation of a Semantic wiki. We give only a brief overview of the implementation, see [10] for details. Figure 5 shows a screenshot from the desktop version, displaying a page about Armin Haller. The page freely intermixes natural language and simple semantic annotations stating that he is a male person. On the right hand side related items are shown based on the semantic annotations. Users are offered more intelligent navigation based on the metadata, in addition to the explicit links between pages. On the bottom of the page we see an embedded query, that shows a continuously up-to-date view of all pages created by Eyal Oren.

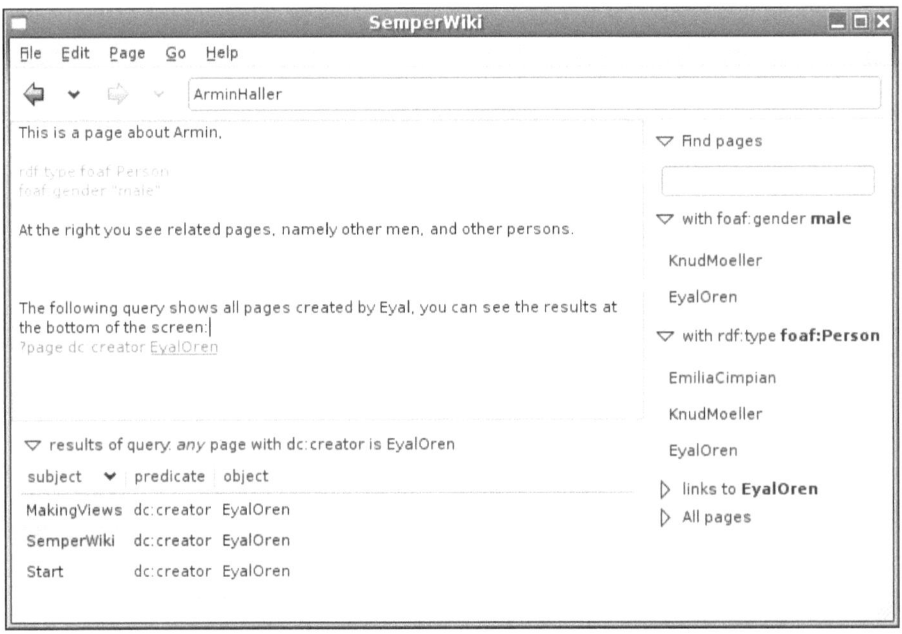

Fig. 5. Navigating and Information reuse

[6] `http://semperwiki.org/`

SemperWiki addresses the noted limitations of ordinary wikis. Concerning **structured access**, users can find related information through associative browsing: the wiki analyses the semantic relations in the data and provides navigational links to related information. Users can search for information using *structured queries*, in addition to simple full-text search.

Concerning **information reuse**, the semantic annotations allow better translation and maintenance; the annotations are language independent[7] and can be understood and reused without barriers. Users can also write *embedded queries*, creating saved searches (database views). These views can be revisited and reused, and provide a consistent picture of structured information. Furthermore all information is represented in RDF using standard Semantic Web terminologies which allows information exchange.

4 Related Work

Several efforts consider using Wikis as collaborative ontology editors, such as OntoWiki [5] or DynamOnt [3]. These efforts focus on ontology engineering rather than improving Wiki systems; they for instance do not follow the free-text editing model of Wikis.

Souzis [12] describes an architecture for Semantic wikis but focuses on annotating and representing page structure while we are concerned with page content, and discusses specific implementation decisions rather than generic architecture choices. Platypus [13] is a wiki with semantic annotations, but adding and using annotations requires significantly more effort than normal text. Both WikSAR [1] and Semantic Wikipedia [14] offer easy-to-use annotations, but neither allow reuse of existing Semantic Web terminologies, and both only allow simple annotations of the current page (thereby excluding blank nodes). Furthermore, none of the above consider the representation distinction between documents and pages.

5 Conclusion

Wikis are successful for information collection, but do not fully satisfy the requirements of personal knowledge management. We have shown how Semantic wikis augment ordinary wikis: using metadata annotations they offer improved information access (through structured navigation such as faceted browsing and structured queries) and improved knowledge reuse (through embedded queries and information exchange). We have implemented our architecture in a first prototype and plan to validate its usability in a future user study.

References

1. D. Aumueller and S. Aurer. Towards a semantic wiki experience - desktop integration and interactivity in WikSAR. In *Semantic Desktop (ISWC)*. 2005.
2. A. L. Burrow. Negotiating access within wiki: a system to construct and maintain a taxonomy of access rules. In *HyperText '04*, pp. 77–86. 2004.

[7] If ontologies contain translations of concept and property labels.

3. E. Gahleitner, W. Behrendt, J. Palkoska, and E. Weippl. On cooperatively creating dynamic ontologies. In *HyperText*, pp. 208–210. 2005.
4. J. Giles. Internet encyclopaedias go head to head. *Nature*, 438:900–901, 2005.
5. M. Hepp, D. Bachlechner, and K. Siorpaes. Ontowiki: Community-driven ontology engineering and ontology usage based on wiki. In *WikiSym*. 2005.
6. S. R. Jones and P. J. Thomas. Empirical assessment of individuals' 'personal information management systems'. *Beh. & Inf. Techn.*, 16(3):158–160, 1997.
7. A. Kidd. The marks are on the knowledge worker. In *CHI*, pp. 186–191. 1994.
8. B. Leuf and W. Cunningham. *The Wiki Way: Collaboration and Sharing on the Internet*. Addison-Wesley, 2001.
9. I. Nonaka and H. Takeuchi. *The Knowledge-Creating Company*. Oxford University Press, New York, 1995.
10. E. Oren. SemperWiki: a semantic personal Wiki. In *Semantic Desktop (ISWC)*. Nov. 2005.
11. E. Oren, *et al.* Annotation and navigation in semantic wikis. In *SemWiki (ESWC)*. Jun. 2006.
12. A. Souzis. Building a semantic wiki. *IEEE Intelligent Systems*, pp. 87–91, Sep. 2005.
13. R. Tazzoli, P. Castagna, and S. E. Campanini. Towards a semantic wiki wiki web. In *ISWC*. 2004.
14. M. Völkel, M. Krötzsch, D. Vrandecic, and H. Haller. Semantic wikipedia. In *WWW*. 2006.
15. M. Völkel and E. Oren. Towards a Wiki Interchange Format (WIF) – opening semantic wiki content and metadata. In *SemWiki (ESWC)*. Jun. 2006.
16. E. Wenger, R. McDermott, and W. M. Snyder. *Cultivating Communities of Practice*. Harvard Business School Press, 2002.
17. S. Whittaker and C. Sidner. Email overload: exploring personal information management of email. In *CHI*, pp. 276–283. 1996.
18. K.-P. Yee, K. Swearingen, K. Li, and M. Hearst. Faceted metadata for image search and browsing. In *CHI*, pp. 401–408. 2003.

Integration of Protein Data Sources Through PO

Amandeep S. Sidhu[1], Tharam S. Dillon[1], and Elizabeth Chang[2]

[1] Faculty of Information Technology, University of Technology, Sydney, Australia
{asidhu, tharam}@it.uts.edu.au
[2] School of Information Systems, Curtin University of Technical University, Perth, Australia
Elizabeth.Chang@cbs.curtin.edu.au

Abstract. Resolving heterogeneity among various protein data sources is a crucial problem if we want to gain more information about proteomics process. Information from multiple protein databases like PDB, SCOP, and UniProt need to integrated to answer user queries. Issues of Semantic Heterogeneity haven't been addressed so far in Protein Informatics. This paper outlines protein data source composition approach based on our existing work of Protein Ontology (PO). The proposed approach enables semi-automatic interoperation among heterogeneous protein data sources. The establishment of semantic interoperation over conceptual framework of PO enables us to get a better insight on how information can be integrated systematically and how queries can be composed. The semantic interoperation between protein data sources is based on semantic relationships between concepts of PO. No other such generalized semantic protein data interoperation framework has been considered so far.

1 Introduction

In accelerating quest for disease biomarkers, the use of high-throughput technologies, such as DNA microarrays and proteomics experiments, has produced vast datasets identifying thousands of genes whose expression patterns differ in diseased versus normal samples. Although many of these differences may reach statistical significance, they are not biologically meaningful. For example, reports of mRNA or protein changes of as little as two-fold are not uncommon, and although some changes of this magnitude turn out to be important, most are attributes to disease-independent differences between the samples. Evidence gleaned from other studies linking genes to disease is helpful, but with such large datasets, a manual literature review is often not practical. The power of these emerging technologies – the ability to quickly generate large sets of data – has challenged current means of evaluating and validating these data. Thus, one important example of a data rich but knowledge poor area is biological sequence mining. In this area, there exist massive quantities of data generated by the data acquisition technologies. The bioinformatics solutions addressing these data are a major current challenge. However, domain specific ontologies such as Gene Ontology [1], MeSH [2] and Protein Ontology (PO) [3, 4, 5, and 6] exist to provide context to this complex real world data.

S. Bressan, J. Küng, and R. Wagner (Eds.): DEXA 2006, LNCS 4080, pp. 519 – 527, 2006.

2 Protein Ontology Conceptual Framework

Advances in technology and the growth of life sciences are generating ever increasing amounts of data. High-throughput techniques are regularly used to capture thousands of data points in an experiment. The results of these experiments normally end up in scientific databases and publications. Although there have been concerted efforts to capture more scientific data in specialist databases, it is generally acknowledged that only 20 per cent of biological knowledge and data is available in a structured format. The remaining 80 per cent of biological information is hidden in the unstructured scientific results and texts. Protein Ontology (PO) [3, 4, 5, and 6] provides a common structured vocabulary for this structured and unstructured information and provides researchers a medium to share knowledge in proteomics domain. It consists of concepts, which are data descriptors for proteomics data and the relations among these concepts. Protein Ontology has (1) a hierarchical classification of concepts represented as classes, from general to specific; (2) a list of attributes related to each concept, for each class; and (3) a set of relations between classes to link concepts in ontology in more complicated ways then implied by the hierarchy, to promote reuse of concepts in the ontology. Protein Ontology provides description for protein domains that can be used to describe proteins in any organism. Protein Ontology Framework describes: (1) Protein Sequence and Structure Information, (2) Protein Folding Process, (3) Cellular Functions of Proteins, (4) Molecular Bindings internal and external to Proteins and (5) Constraints affecting the Final Protein Conformation. Protein Ontology uses all relevant protein data sources of information. The structure of PO provides the concepts necessary to describe individual proteins, but does not contain individual protein themselves. A database based on PO acts as instance store for the PO. PO uses data sources include new proteome information resources like PDB, SCOP, and RESID as well as classical sources of information where information is maintained in a knowledge base of scientific text files like OMIM and from various published scientific literature in various journals. PO Database is represented using XML. PO Database at the moment contains data instances of following protein families: (1) Prion Proteins, (2) B.Subtilis, (3) CLIC and (4) PTEN. More protein data instances will be added as PO is more developed. The Complete Class Hierarchy of Protein Ontology (PO) is shown in **Figure 1**. More details about PO is available at the website: **http://www.proteinontology.info/**

Semantics in protein data is normally not interpreted by annotating systems, since they are not aware of the specific structural, chemical and cellular interactions of protein complexes. Protein Ontology Framework provides specific set of rules to cover these application specific semantics. The rules use only the relationships whose semantics are predefined to establish correspondence among terms in PO. The set of relationships with predefined semantics is: {SubClassOf, PartOf, AttributeOf, InstanceOf, and ValueOf}.

The PO conceptual modeling encourages the use of strictly typed relations with precisely defined semantics. Some of these relationships (like SubClassOf, InstanceOf) are somewhat similar to those in RDF Schema but the set of relationships that have defined semantics in our conceptual PO model is small so as to maintain simplicity of the system. The following is a description of the set of pre-defined semantic relationships in our common PO conceptual model.

- *ProteinOntology*
  - *AtomicBind*
  - *Atoms*
  - *Bind*
  - *Chains*
  - *Family*
  - *ProteinComplex*
    - *ChemicalBonds*
      - *CISPeptide*
      - *DisulphideBond*
      - *HydrogenBond*
      - *ResidueLink*
      - *SaltBridge*
    - *Constraints*
      - *GeneticDefects*
      - *Hydrophobicity*
      - *ModifiedResidue*
    - *Entry*
      - *Description*
      - *Molecule*
      - *Reference*
    - *FunctionalDomains*
      - *ActiveBindingSites*
      - *BiologicalFunction*
        - *PathologicalFunctions*
        - *PhysiologicalFunctions*
      - *SourceCell*
    - *StructuralDomains*
      - *Helices*
        - *Helix*
          - *HelixStructure*
      - *OtherFolds*
        - *Turn*
          - *TurnStructure*
      - *Sheets*
        - *Sheet*
          - *Strands*
    - *Structure*
      - *ATOMSequence*
      - *UnitCell*
  - *Residues*
  - *SiteGroup*

Fig. 1. Class Hierarchy of Protein Ontology

SubClassOf: The relationship is used to indicate that one concept is a subclass of another concept, for instance: SourceCell SubClassOf FunctionalDomains. That is any instance of SouceCell class is also instance of FunctionalDomains class. All attributes of FunctionalDomains class (_FuncDomain_Family, _FuncDomain_Super-Family) are also the attributes of SourceCell class. The relationship SubClassOf is transitive.

AttrributeOf: This relationship indicates that a concept is an attribute of another concept, for instance: _FuncDomain_Family AttributeOf Family. This relationship also referred as PropertyOf, has same semantics as in object-relational databases.

PartOf: This relationship indicates that a concept is a part of another concept, for instance: Chain PartOf ATOMSequence indicates that Chain describing various residue sequences in a protein is a part of definition of ATOMSequence for that protein.

InstanceOf: This relationship indicates that an object is an instance of the class, for instance: ATOMSequenceInstance_10 InstanceOf ATOMSequence indicates that ATOMSequenceInstance_10 is an instance of class ATOMSequence.

ValueOf: This relationship is used to indicate the value of an attribute of an object, for instance: "Homo Sapiens" ValueOf OrganismScientific. The second concept, in turn has an edge, OrganismScientific AttributeOf Molecule, from the object it describes.

3 Comparing GO and PO

Gene Ontology (GO) [1] defines a structured controlled vocabulary in the domain of biological functionality. GO initially consisted of a few thousand terms describing the genetic workings of three organisms and was constructed for the express purpose of database interoperability; it has since grown to a terminology of nearly 16,000 terms and is becoming a de facto standard for describing functional aspects of biological entities in all types of organisms. Furthermore, in addition to (and because of) its wide use as a terminological source for database-entry annotation, GO has been used in a wide variety of biomedical research, including analyses of experimental data [1] and predictions of experimental results [7]. Characteristics of GO that we believe are most responsible for its success: community involvement; clear goals; limited scope; simple, intuitive structure; continuous evolution; active curation; and early use.

It is clear that organisms across the spectrum of life, to varying degrees, possess large numbers of gene products with similar sequences and roles. Knowledge about a given gene product (i.e., a biologically active molecule that is the deciphered end product of the code stored in a gene) can often be determined experimentally or inferred from its similarity to gene products in other organisms. Research into different biological systems uses different organisms that are chosen because they are amenable to advancing these investigations. For example, the rat is a good model for the study of human heart disease, and the fly is a good model to study cellular differentiation. For each of these model systems, there is a database employing curators who collect and store the body of biological knowledge for that organism. This enormous amount of data can potentially add insight to related molecules found in other organisms. A reliable wet-lab biological experiment performed in one organism can be used to deduce attributes of an analogous (or related) gene product in another organism, thereby reducing the need to reproduce experiments in each individual organism (which would be expensive, time-consuming, and, in many organisms, technically impossible). Mining of Scientific Text and Literature is done to generate list of keywords that is used as GO terms. However, querying heterogeneous, independent databases in order to draw these inferences is difficult: The different database projects may use different terms to refer to the same concept and the same terms to refer to different concepts. Furthermore, these terms are typically not formally linked with each other in any way. GO seeks to reveal these underlying biological functionalities by providing a structured controlled vocabulary that can be used to describe gene products, and shared between biological databases. This facilitates querying for gene products that share biologically meaningful attributes, whether from separate databases or within the same database.

Challenges faced while developing GO from unstructured and structured data sources are addressed while developing PO. Protein Ontology is a conceptual model that aim to support consistent and unambiguous knowledge sharing and that provide a framework for protein data and knowledge integration. PO links concepts to their interpretation, i.e. specifications of their meanings including concept definitions and relationships to other concepts. Apart from semantic relationships defined in Section 2, PO also model relationships like Sequences. By itself semantic relationships described in Section 2, does not impose order among the children of the node. In applications using Protein Sequences, the ability of expressing the order is paramount. Generally Protein Sequences are a collection of chains of sequence of residues, and that is the format Protein Sequences have been represented unit now using various data representations and data mining techniques for bioinformatics. When we are defining sequences for semantic heterogeneity of protein data sources using PO we are not only considering traditional representation of protein sequences but also link Protein Sequences to Protein Structure, by linking chains of residue sequences to atoms defining three-dimensional structure. In this section we will describe how we used a special semantic relationship like *Sequence(s)* in Protein Ontology to describe complex concepts defining Structure, Structural Folds and Domains and Chemical Bonds describing Protein Complexes. PO defines these complex concepts as *Sequences* of simpler generic concepts defined in PO. These simple concepts are *Sequences* of object and data type properties defining them. A typical example of *Sequence* is as follows. PO defines a complex concept of *ATOMSequence* describing three dimensional structure of protein complex as a combination of simple concepts of *Chains*, *Residues*, and *Atoms* as: *ATOMSequence Sequence (Chains Sequence (Residues Sequence (Atoms)))*. Simple concepts defining ATOMSequence are defined as: *Chains Sequence (ChainID, ChainName, ChainProperty)*; *Residues Sequence (ResidueID, ResidueName, ResidueProperty)*; and *Atoms Sequence (AtomID, Atom, ATOMResSeqNum, X, Y, Z, Occupancy, TempratureFactor, Element)*. Semantic Interoperability Framework used in PO is depicted **Figure 2**.

Therefore, PO reflects the structure and relationships of Protein Data Sources. PO removes the constraints of potential interpretations of terms in various data sources and provides a structured vocabulary that unifies and integrates all data and knowledge sources for proteomics domain (**Figure 3**). There are seven subclasses of Protein Ontology (PO), called Generic Classes that are used to define complex concepts in other PO Classes: Residues, Chains, Atoms, Family, AtomicBind, Bind,

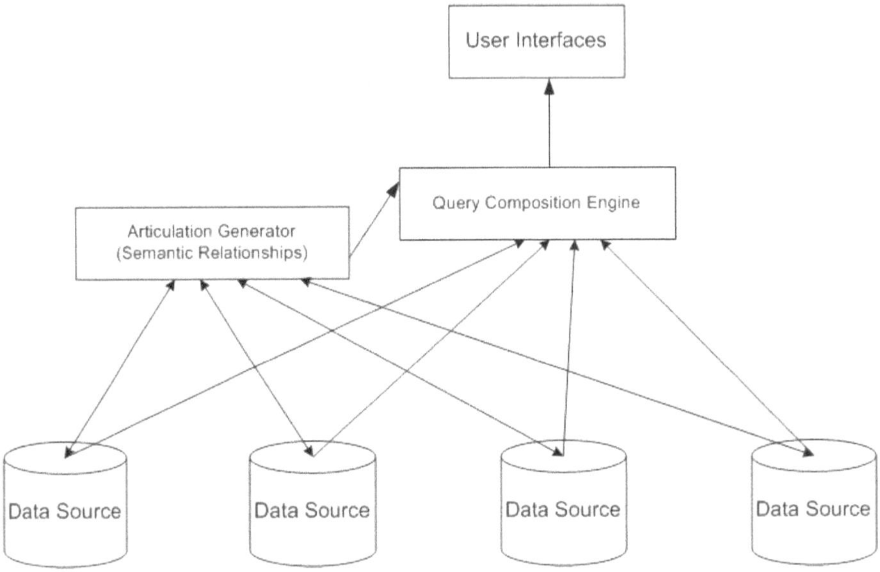

Fig. 2. Semantic Interoperability Framework for PO

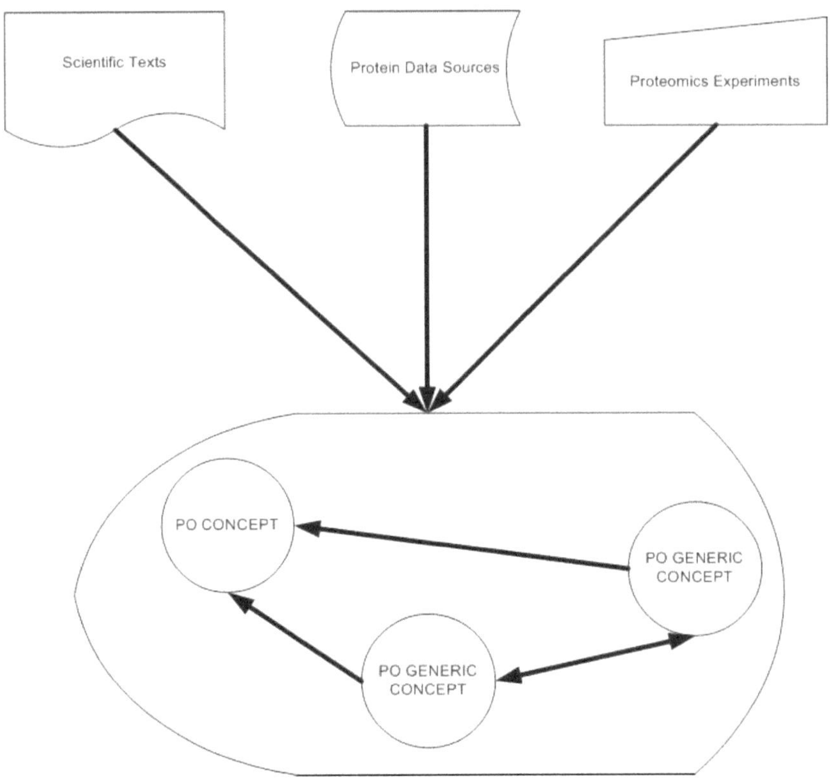

Fig. 3. Unification of Protein Data and Knowledge

and SiteGroup. Concepts from these generic classes are reused in various other PO Classes for definition of Class Specific Concepts. Details and Properties of Residues in a Protein Sequence are defined by instances of Residues Class. Instances of Chains of Residues are defined in Chains Class. All the Three Dimensional Structure Data of Protein Atoms is represented as instances of Atoms Class. Defining Chains, Residues and Atoms as individual classes has the benefit that any special properties or changes affecting a particular chain, residue and atom can be easily added. Protein Family class represents Protein Super Family and Family Details of Proteins. Data about binding atoms in Chemical Bonds like Hydrogen Bond, Residue Links, and Salt Bridges is entered into ontology as an instance of AtomicBind Class. Similarly the data about binding residues in Chemical Bonds like Disulphide Bonds and CIS Peptides is entered into ontology as an instance of Bind Class. All data related to site groups of the active binding sites of Proteins is defined as instances of SiteGroup Class. In PO the notions classification, reasoning, and consistency are applied by defining new concepts or classes from defined generic concepts or classes. The concepts derived from generic concepts are placed precisely into class hierarchy of Protein Ontology to completely represent information defining a protein complex.

As such PO can be used to support automatic semantic interpretation of data and knowledge sources, thus providing a basis for sophisticated mining of information.

4 Mining Facilitated by Protein Ontology

The Protein Ontology Database is created as an instance store for various protein data using the PO format. PO provides technical and scientific infrastructure to allow evidence based description and analysis of relationships between proteins. PO uses data sources like PDB, SCOP, OMIM and various published scientific literature to gather protein data. PO Database is represented using XML. PO Database at the moment contains data instances of following protein families: (1) Prion Proteins, (2) B.Subtilis, (3) CLIC and (4) PTEN. More protein data instances will be added as PO is more developed. The PO instance store at moment covers various species of proteins from bacterial and plant proteins to human proteins. Such a generic representation using PO shows the strength of PO format representation.

We used some standard hierarchical and tree mining algorithms [8] on the PO Database. We compared MB3-Miner (MB3), X3-Miner (X3), VTreeMiner (VTM) and PatternMatcher (PM) for mining embedded subtrees and IMB3-Miner (IMB3), FREQT (FT) for mining induced subtrees of PO Data. In these experiments we are mining Prion Proteins dataset described using Protein Ontology Framework, represented in XML. For this dataset we map the XML tags to integer indexes. The maximum height is 1. In this case all candidate subtrees generated by all algorithms would be induced subtrees. **Figure 4** shows the time performance of different algorithms. Our original MB3 has the best time performance for this data.

Quite interestingly, with Prion dataset of PO the number of frequent candidate subtrees generated is identical for all algorithms **(Figure 5)**. Another observation is that when support is less than 10, PM aborts and VTM performs poorly. The rationale for this could be because the utilized join approach enumerates additional invalid subtrees. Note that original MB3 is faster than IMB3 due to additional checks performed to restrict the level of embedding.

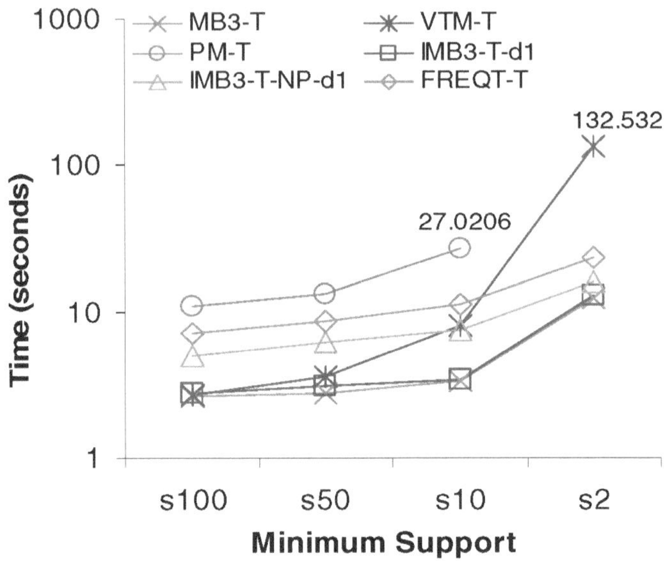

Fig. 4. Time Performance for Prion dataset of PO Data

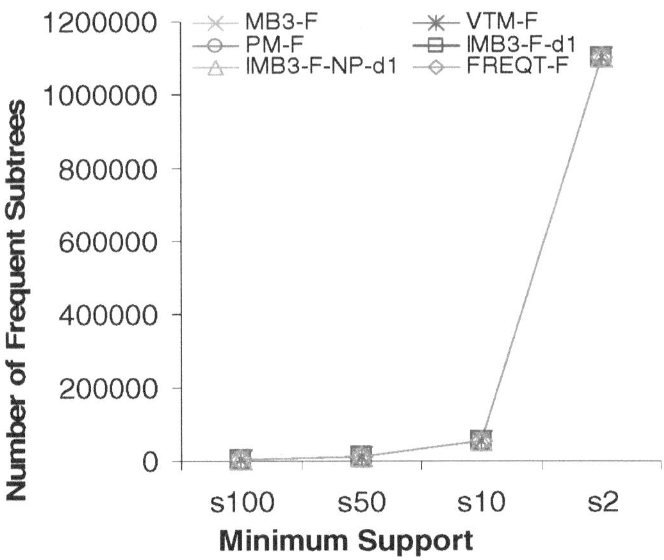

Fig. 5. Number of Frequent Subtrees for Prion dataset of PO Data

5 Conclusion

Protein Ontology (PO) provides a unified vocabulary for capturing declarative knowledge about protein domain and to classify that knowledge to allow reasoning.

Information captured by PO is classified in a rich hierarchy of concepts and their inter-relationships. PO is compositional and dynamic, relying on notions of classification, reasoning, consistency, retrieval and querying. In PO the notions classification, reasoning, and consistency are applied by defining new concepts or classes from defined generic concepts or classes. The concepts derived from generic concepts are placed precisely into class hierarchy of Protein Ontology to completely represent information defining a protein complex. As the Web Ontology Language (OWL) representation used in Protein Ontology is an XML-Abbrev based (Abbreviated XML Notation), it can be easily transformed to the corresponding RDF and XML formats without much effort using the available converters. Our Protein Ontology (PO) is the first ever work to integrate protein data based on data semantics describing various phases of protein structure. PO helps to understand structure, cellular function and the constraints that affect protein in a cellular environment. The attribute values in the PO are not defined as text strings or as set of keywords. Most of the Values are entered as instances of Concepts defined in Generic Classes. PO Database at the moment contains data instances of following protein families: (1) Prion Proteins, (2) B.Subtilis, (3) CLIC and (4) PTEN. More protein data instances will be added as PO is more developed. The PO instance store at moment covers various species of proteins from bacterial and plant proteins to human proteins. Such a generic representation using PO shows the strength of PO format representation.

References

[1] GO Consortium (2001). "Creating the Gene Ontology Resource: Design and Implementation." Genome Research 11: 1425-1433.
[2] Nelson, Stuart J.; Schopen, Michael; et al. (2004).The MeSH Translation Maintenance System: Structure, Interface Design, and Implementation. In: Fieschi, M. et al., editors. Proceedings of the 11th World Congress on Medical Informatics; 2004 Sep 7-11; San Francisco, CA. Amsterdam: IOS Press; pp. 67-69.
[3] Sidhu, A. S., T. S. Dillon, et al. (2006). Ontology for Data Integration in Protein Informatics. In: Database Modeling in Biology: Practices and Challenges. Z. Ma and J. Y. Chen. New York, NY, Springer Science, Inc.: In Press.
[4] Sidhu, A. S., T. S. Dillon, et al. (2006). Protein Ontology Project: 2006 Updates (Invited Paper). Data Mining and Information Engineering 2006. A. Zanasi, C. A. Brebbia and N. F. F. Ebecken. Prague, Czech Republic, WIT Press.
[5] Sidhu, A. S., T. S. Dillon, et al. (2005). Ontological Foundation for Protein Data Models. First IFIP WG 2.12 & WG 12.4 International Workshop on Web Semantics (SWWS 2005). In conjunction with On The Move Federated Conferences (OTM 2005). Agia Napa, Cyprus, Springer-Verlag. Lecture Notes in Computer Science (LNCS).
[6] Sidhu, A. S., T. S. Dillon, et al. (2005). Protein Ontology: Vocabulary for Protein Data. 3rd IEEE International Conference on Information Technology and Applications (IEEE ICITA 2005). Sydney, IEEE CS Press. Volume 1: 465-469.
[7] GO Consortium and S. E. Lewis (2004). "Gene Ontology: looking backwards and forwards." Genome Biology 6(1): 103.1-103.4.
[8] Tan, H., T.S. Dillon, et. al. (2006). IMB3-Miner: Mining Induced/Embedded Subtrees by Constraining the Level of Embedding. Accepted for Proceedings of PAKDD 2006.

3D Protein Structure Matching by Patch Signatures

Zi Huang[1,2], Xiaofang Zhou[1,2], Heng Tao Shen[1], and Dawei Song[3]

[1] School of ITEE, The University of Queensland, Australia
{huang, zxf, shenht}@itee.uq.edu.au
[2] Australian Research Council Centre in Bioinformatics, Australia
[3] Knowledge Media Institute & Centre for Research in Computing
The Open University, United Kingdom
d.song@open.ac.uk

Abstract. For determining functionality dependencies between two proteins, both represented as 3D structures, it is an essential condition that they have one or more matching structural regions called patches. As 3D structures for proteins are large, complex and constantly evolving, it is computationally expensive and very time-consuming to identify possible locations and sizes of patches for a given protein against a large protein database. In this paper, we address a vector space based representation for protein structures, where a patch is formed by the vectors within the region. Based on our previews work, a compact representation of the patch named *patch signature* is applied here. A similarity measure of two patches is then derived based on their signatures. To achieve fast patch matching in large protein databases, a match-and-expand strategy is proposed. Given a query patch, a set of small k-sized matching patches, called candidate patches, is generated in *match* stage. The candidate patches are further filtered by enlarging k in *expand* stage. Our extensive experimental results demonstrate encouraging performances with respect to this biologically critical but previously computationally prohibitive problem.

1 Introduction

The structure of a protein can be represented as a collection of points (atoms) or vectors (from one atom to another) in a three dimensional space. Certain structural regions of a protein often perform some specific functions. Analyzing the three-dimensional structure of a protein therefore provides a basis for understanding its biological functionality. Having one or more matching (similar) regions in structures has been considered as an essential condition for the existence of potential interaction between two proteins (e.g., for a designed drug to be effective on a protein). As 3D structures for proteins are large, complex and constantly evolving, it is very time-consuming to identify possible locations and sizes of such matching structural regions for a given protein against a large protein database.

S. Bressan, J. Küng, and R. Wagner (Eds.): DEXA 2006, LNCS 4080, pp. 528–537, 2006.

This problem has been studied in computational geometry. Geometric techniques have been used in many structure comparison methods. The most popular one is geometric hashing [6], which was developed in computer vision and now used in protein structure comparison. Geometric hashing defines a set of reference frames for a structure. The coordinates of all points in the structure are re-calculated in a reference frame, forming a reference frame system. Geometric features of the structure are calculated based on the reference frame systems and stored in a hash table. For any two structures, a model and a query, all possible reference frame systems will be generated respectively. Given a model reference frame system and a query one, the approach is to 'place the query on top of the model' and consider how many points coincide. Unfortunately, it is a fully comparison method for finding maximal coincidence points set between two structures. Thus, the computational cost is pretty expensive. The algorithm finds the best congruence between two 2D structures with m points each under translation and rotation invariance in $O(m^8)$ time[5]. The cost should be even higher for 3D case.

To alleviate this problem, solutions to the following issues are must: 1) compact representations of structural regions and 2) fast searching on the compact representations. The first issue enables efficient similarity matching which has been discussed in our previews work[3]. On the other hand, the second issue avoids redundant comparisons on non-similar regions. The most commonly used structure representation is the inter-atom distance matrix [4]. As the complexity of this representation is quadratic to the number of atoms, it is very expensive for processing a large number of proteins.

In this paper, we address a vector space based representation for protein structures, where a structural region is defined as a patch formed by the vectors within the region. We use a compact representation model called patch signature which we developed in the preview work[3]. Given a k-sized patch, patch signature characterizes the spatial relationship among the vectors via $(7k-10)$ inter-atom distances. patch signature is compact and linear to the number of atoms. The similarity between two patches can then be measured by comparing their patch signatures efficiently. The significance of patch signature lies in its linear complexity and results in fast similarity measure.

To search similar patches among a large database, a match-and-expand strategy is proposed to operationalize a scalable model. In the *match* stage, the matching sub-patches in a smaller size k are identified. A filter-and-refine approach is used to quickly prune away unmatched results in this stage. The expand stage extends the k-sized matches to larger sizes. The motivation is that if any pair of k sized sub-patches can not match, then the patches containing them can not match either. Our initial experimental results demonstrate an promising performance which proves the novelty and effectiveness of our methods.

The rest of the paper is organized as follows. Section 2 gives a brief introduction to 3D protein structure representations and its similarity measure. Patch database generation is introduced in Section 3, followed by detailed match-and-expand strategy in Section 4. Section 5 reports the experimental results and Section 6 concludes the paper.

2 Preliminaries

This paper essentially deals with the identification of matching structural regions, called "patches", between two proteins. Since proteins can be represented as geometric objects, the structure of the geometric space has a direct influence on the patch matching problem. In this section, a vector representation of proteins is introduced. The structural representation model called patch signature is then presented, followed by its similarity measure.

2.1 Protein, Bowtie and Patches

A protein (or more precisely, a snapshot of a protein, as the shape of a protein can change over time) can be defined as a set P of three dimensional vectors:

$$P = \{v_i | 1 \leq i \leq n | n = |P|\} \tag{1}$$

Each v_i denotes a vector of $\overrightarrow{C_\alpha C_\beta}$ for residue i. The number of vectors in a protein can vary between 10 to 10,000. The length of a vector (i.e., the distance between its α-end and β-end) is fixed at 1.5 Å (angstrom).

Any pair of vectors of a protein construct a *bowtie* (Fig.1(a)). A *patch* is defined as a spherical region of protein P, whose diameter is ε (ie. a distance cut-off) (Fig.1)(b). More formally, $M = \{v_1, v_2, ..., v_m\} \subseteq P$ $(m > 2)$ is a patch if and only if $(\forall v_i, v_j \in M, d_{\alpha\alpha}^{i,j} \leq \varepsilon) \wedge (\forall v_k \in M, \forall v_l \notin M, d_{\alpha\alpha}^{k,l} > \varepsilon)$.

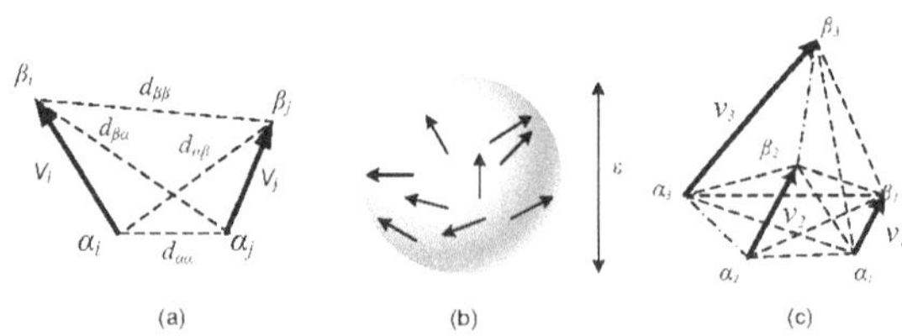

Fig. 1. (a)Spatial relationship between two vectors. Four internal distances are denoted as $d_{\alpha\alpha}$, $d_{\beta\beta}$, $d_{\alpha\beta}$, and $d_{\beta\alpha}$. (b) An example of patch. Each vector represents an amino acid. The diameter is ε. (c) A patch signature.

2.2 Patches Signature Based Similarity Measure

Given a patch M, any subset of M is called a sub-patch, which is extendable in size to $|M|$. A k-sized sub-patch is an *unordered* collection of k vectors and it has $k!$ representations. Ordering the vectors is necessary for generating a unique representation of the sub-patch.

To generate an ordering of the vectors, a *basevector* v_{i_b} needs to be selected as a starting point, based on which an ordering function $\phi_{i_b} : q \to q' | q, q' = 1..k$ is defined. An detailed ordering algorithm will be given later in Section 3. Now consider an ordered k-sized sub-patches, $S_\lhd = (v_{i_1}, v_{i_2}, ..., v_{i_k})$. According to [3], $S_\lhd$ can be represented by $7k - 10$ distances: $< d_{\alpha\alpha}^{i_1,i_2}, d_{\alpha\alpha}^{i_1,i_3}, ..., d_{\alpha\alpha}^{i_1,i_k}, d_{\alpha\alpha}^{i_2,i_3}, ..., d_{\alpha\alpha}^{i_2,i_k}, d_{\beta\beta}^{i_1,i_2}, , ..., d_{\beta\beta}^{i_1,i_k}, d_{\beta\beta}^{i_2,i_3}, ..., d_{\beta\beta}^{i_2,i_k}, d_{\alpha\beta}^{i_1,i_2}, d_{\alpha\beta}^{i_1,i_3}, ..., d_{\alpha\beta}^{i_1,i_k}, d_{\beta\alpha}^{i_1,i_2}, d_{\beta\alpha}^{i_1,i_3}, ..., d_{\beta\alpha}^{i_1,i_k} >$

Definition 1 (Matching Function ψ). *Given two ordered k-sized sub-patches, $S_{\triangleleft} = (v_{i_1}, v_{i_2}, ..., v_{i_k})$ and $S'_{\triangleleft} = (u_{i_1}, u_{i_2}, ..., u_{i_k})$. They are similar (denoted as $S_{\triangleleft} \approx_{\delta} S'_{\triangleleft}$ or in short $S_{\triangleleft} \approx S'_{\triangleleft}$) if there exists a one-to-one matching function from $S_{\triangleleft}$ onto $S'_{\triangleleft}$ (i.e. $\psi : S_{\triangleleft} \rightarrow S'_{\triangleleft}$) such that $\forall i_p, i_q = 1..k$, $\forall \rho, \varrho = \alpha, \beta$: $v_{i_p}, v_{i_q} \in S_{\triangleleft}, u_{\psi(i_p)}, u_{\psi(i_q)} \in S'_{\triangleleft} | d_{\rho\varrho}^{i_p,i_q} \approx d_{\rho\varrho}^{\psi(i_p),\psi(i_q)}$*

To compare two k-sized sub-patches $S = (v_{i_1}, v_{i_2}, ..., v_{i_k})$ and $S' = (u_{i_1}, u_{i_2}, ..., u_{i_k})$, we can first obtain an ordered k-sized sub-patch $S_{\triangleleft}$ by fixing a base vector. Each ordered k-sized sub-patch $S'_{\triangleleft} \in S'$ should be be compared with $S_{\triangleleft}$. $S \approx S'$ if $\exists S'_{\triangleleft} \in S'$ such that $S_{\triangleleft} \approx S'_{\triangleleft}$.

Two patches M and M′ are similar (denoted as $M \approx_{\delta,\gamma} M'$ or in short $M \approx M'$) if there exist sub-patch $S \subseteq M$, sub-patch $S' \subseteq M'$ and S is similar to S' under condition of $|S'| = |S'| \geq \gamma$. γ is a parameter determining the minimum size of sub-patches. Normally it is set to be within the range of 5-20.

3 Seed-Patch Database Generation

In this section we will investigate the generation of seed-patches, based on which a match-and-expand strategy is introduced for patch matching (i.e., finding maximal matching sub-patches) in the next section. First let us look at how an *unordered* sub-patch can be ordered.

Definition 2 (Ordering Function). *Given a k-sized sub-patch $S = \{v_{i_1}, v_{i_2}, ..., v_{i_k}\}$. For any basevector v_{i_b}, $b = 1..k$, an ordering function is defined as $\phi_{i_b} : q \rightarrow q' | q, q' = 1..k$ such that:*

1.$\phi_{i_b}(i_b) = 1$
2.if $\phi_{i_b}(i_p) < \phi_{i_b}(i_q)$, then $d_{\alpha\alpha}^{i_b,i_p} < d_{\alpha\alpha}^{i_b,i_q}$ $(p, q = 1..k)$

Definition 3 (Distance Sequence). *A distance sequence $D_S^{i_b}$ is defined as:*
$$D_S^{i_b} =< d_{\alpha\alpha}^{i_b,i_b}, d_{\alpha\alpha}^{i_b,\phi_{i_b}^{-1}(2)}, ..., d_{\alpha\alpha}^{i_b,\phi_{i_b}^{-1}(k)} >.$$
We use the notation $D_S^{i_b}[p]$ for the pth element of $D_S^{i_b}$ which is $d_{\alpha\alpha}^{i_b,\phi_{i_b}^{-1}(p)}$. The ordered k-sized sub-patch based on ϕ_{i_b} are denoted as $S_{\triangleleft}^{i_b} = (v_{\phi_{i_b}^{-1}(1)}, ..., v_{\phi_{i_b}^{-1}(k)})$.

Definition 4 (Basebowtie). *Given a k-sized sub-patch $S = \{v_{i_1}, v_{i_2}, ..., v_{i_k}\}$, $B_{v_{i_m},v_{i_n}}$ is the basebowtie of S, if the following conditions hold:*

1.if $B_{v_{i_p},v_{i_q}} \neq B_{v_{i_m},v_{i_n}}$, then $d_{\alpha\alpha}^{v_{i_m},v_{i_n}} \leq d_{\alpha\alpha}^{v_{i_p},v_{i_q}}$
2.if $B_{v_{i_p},v_{i_q}} \neq B_{v_{i_m},v_{i_n}}$ and $d_{\alpha\alpha}^{v_{i_m},v_{i_n}} = d_{\alpha\alpha}^{v_{i_p},v_{i_q}}$, then $i_m < i_p$ $(p, q = 1..k)$

Given a k-sized sub-patch $S = \{v_{i_1}, v_{i_2}, ..., v_{i_k}\}$. Suppose the basebowtie of S is $B_{v_{i_b},v_{i_j}}$, then $S_{\triangleleft}^{i_b} = (v_{\phi_{i_b}^{-1}(1)}, ..., v_{\phi_{i_b}^{-1}(k)})$ is called a seed-patch. A set of k-sized seed-patches is denoted as $SEED^k$.

Algorithm 1 [To determine the k-sized seed-patch of k-sized sub-patch $S = \{v_{i_1}, v_{i_2}, ..., v_{i_k}\}$.]

/* find the basebowtie and the basevector v_b */
min$d_{\alpha\alpha}$ = maxinum;
min$d_{\alpha\beta}$ = maxinum;
for (p = 1; p <= k; p++)
  for (q = 1; q <= k; q++){
    if (p$\neq$q) {
      if $d_{\alpha\alpha}^{i_p,i_q}$<min$d_{\alpha\alpha}${
        min$d_{\alpha\alpha}$ = $d_{\alpha\alpha}^{i_p,i_q}$; v_b = i_p;
        min$d_{\alpha\beta}$ = $d_{\alpha\beta}^{i_p,i_q}$; }
      elseif ($d_{\alpha\alpha}^{i_p,i_q}$==min$d_{\alpha\alpha}$) and
          ($i_p < v_b$){
        min$d_{\alpha\alpha}$ = $d_{\alpha\alpha}^{i_p,i_q}$; v_b = i_p;
        min$d_{\alpha\beta}$ = $d_{\alpha\beta}^{i_p,i_q}$; }}}
/* re-order the vectors */
for (p = 1; p <= k; p++) $\phi^{-1}(p)$ = i_p
for (p = 1; p < k; p++)
  for(q = p+1; q <= k; q++){
    if $d_{\alpha\alpha}^{i_b,i_p}$>$d_{\alpha\alpha}^{i_b,i_q}${
      swap($d_{\alpha\alpha}^{i_b,i_p}$,$d_{\alpha\alpha}^{i_b,i_q}$);
      swap($\phi^{-1}(p)$,$\phi^{-1}(q)$);}}
Output(ϕ);

Fig. 2. Algorithm1: Seed-patch creation

The seed-patch can be generated by Algorithm 1 (in Figure 2). Each seed-patch is described by its patch signature. Each seed-patch in $SEED^k$ will then be inserted into seed-patch database with protein entry, ordered vector ids and patch signature.

After a seed patch database has been built, next we present an efficient query processing strategy for a scalable solution for large patch databases.

4 The Match-and-Expand Strategy

In this section, we introduce a match-and-expand strategy for fast protein structure matching.

If two patches M and M' have a maximal matching sub-patch of K vectors, they must also have matching sub-patches of 1, 2, $\cdots$, $K-1$ vectors. The match-and-expand strategy, similar to philosophy of BLAST [2], matches the sub-patches of same size, then expand the size of matched sub-patch to further reduce the number of candidates. A set of all patches of size $k (k \leq K)$ is pre-computed for all proteins in the database. In order to check if M and M' have a matching sub-patch (of size no smaller than K), the k-sized sub-patches of M and M' are checked first. If no k-sized matching sub-patches are found, M and M' will not have any matching sub-patches. Otherwise, M and M' will be further checked, starting from their matching k-sized sub-patch, until finding maximal sized matching sub-patches. The k-sized sub-patches thus serve as **seeds**, from which larger sized patches can be generated and compared with much lower computational cost.

The choice of k is important. If it is too small, then the filter step may generate too many false hits; if it is too large, then the cost of materializing all k-sized patches can be very high. The experimental result of choosing k will be discussed later in Section 6.

Therefore, we can first transform a protein P of n vectors into a group $SEED^k$ of k-sized seeds. Note that $|SEED^k| << C_n^k$ as a sub-patch in $SEED^k$ is not an arbitrary combination of k vectors in P. Instead, the C_α-C_α distances between any two vectors in the patch must be within a distance cutoff $\varepsilon = 8\AA$. Nonetheless, $|SEED^k|$ can still be a very large number when n is large.

Given a query protein Q containing a set of patches $\mathbb{M}$. Each patch M in $\mathbb{M}$ can be split into $C_{|M|}^k$ k-sized sub-patches.

For each k-sized query sub-patch, $S_q = \{v_{i_1}, ..., v_{i_k}\}$, a set of ordered query sub-patches is defined as $S_{\triangleleft q} = \{S_{\triangleleft}^{i_q} | q = 1..k\}$. All these ordered sub-patches are used to search the seed-patches in the database.

To find all maximal matching patches between proteins P and Q. The match-and-expand strategy using k-sized seed patches consists of the following two stages:

1. *Match stage*: to find a set of matching k-sized sub-patches $C = \{(S, S') | S \in SEED^k, S' \in S_{\triangleleft q}, S \approx S'\}$.
2. *Expand stage*: for each $(S, S') \in C$, check if there exist $S^K \subseteq P$ and $S'^K \subseteq Q$, such that $S \subseteq S^K$, $S' \subseteq S'^K$, $S^K \approx S'^K$ for $K > k$.

Operationally the expand stage can be accomplished by incrementally expanding k-sized sub-patches S and S' by one vector each time until maximum matching patches are reached.

As illustrated in section 2.2, matching two sub-patches is too time consuming. When they are two ordered sub-patches, however, we can solve the problem in a heuristic way via a match-and-expand approach.

4.1 Match

In the match stage, we apply the filter-and-refine approach to speed up the matching processing for initial sized patches. Filter step derives a set of candidate matchings by applying heuristic rules, based on the orders on C_α-C_α distances. And refine step performs matching based on all the (7k-10) distances.

Filter. Several rules will be introduced in this section to derive the candidate matching functions $\psi_c : v_{i_p} \rightarrow u_{j_q}$ on two ordered sub-patches $S_\triangleleft = (v_{i_1}, ..., v_{i_k})$ and $S'_\triangleleft = (u_{j_1}, ..., u_{j_k})$ in a heuristic way. Note that v_{i_1} and u_{j_1} are basevectors of these two ordered sub-patches respectively. Candidate deriving can be considered as a filtering strategy of sub-patch matching.

Proposition 1. *Given two k-sized ordered sub-patches* $S_{\triangleleft}^{i_1} = (v_{i_1}, ..., v_{i_k})$ *and* $S'^{j_1}_{\triangleleft} = (u_{j_1}, ..., u_{j_k})$. *If* $S_{\triangleleft}^{i_1} \approx S'^{j_1}_{\triangleleft}$ *and* $\psi(v_{i_1}) = u_{j_1}$, *then* $D_S[p] \approx D_{S'}[p]$ *(i.e.* $d_{\alpha\alpha}^{i_1,i_p} \approx d'^{j_1,j_p}_{\alpha\alpha}$*), for any* $p = 2..k$

We can know from Proposition 1 that given two k-sized ordered sub-patches $S_{\triangleleft}^{i_1}$ and $S'^{j_1}_{\triangleleft}$, for any $p = 1..k$, if $D_S[p] \not\approx D_{S'}[p]$, then there does not exist a matching function ψ with $\psi(v_{i_1}) = u_{j_1}$ to make $S_{\triangleleft}^{i_1} \approx S'^{j_1}_{\triangleleft}$. It can be used to prune a large number of unnecessary comparisons. The matching function ψ can be derived from following rules.

Rule 1. $\psi(v_{i_p}) = u_{j_p}$, *if* $D_S[p] \approx D_{S'}[p]$, $\forall p = 1..k$

Rule 1 conducts a linear comparison between $D_S[p]$ and $D_{S'}[p]$. However, it does not consider possible cross-position mappings between v_{i_p} and u_{i_q} for $p \neq q$. The next rules address this problem.

Rule 2. *A new candidate matching function* ψ' *can be obtained from* ψ *by partial modification:* $\psi(v_{i_f}) = u_{j_g}$, $\psi(v_{i_g}) = u_{j_f}$, *if* $D_S[p] \approx D_{S'}[p]$, $D_S[f] \approx D_{S'}[g]$ *and* $D_S[g] \approx D_{S'}[f]$, $f, g, p = 2..k$

Proposition 2. *Given two k-sized ordered sub-patches* $S_{\triangleleft}^{i_1} = (v_{i_1}, ..., v_{i_k})$ *and* $S'^{j_1}_{\triangleleft} = (u_{j_1}, ..., u_{j_k})$ *satisfying* $D_S[p] \approx D_{S'}[p] | p = 2..k$. *If there exist* $2 \leq f, g \leq k, f \neq g$ *such that* $D_S[f] \approx D_{S'}[g]$ *and* $D_S[g] \approx D_{S'}[f]$, *then* $|D_{S'}[f] - D_{S'}[g]| \leq 2\delta$

Rule 3. *A new candidate matching function* ψ' *can be obtained from* ψ *by partial modification:* $\psi(v_{i_f}) = u_{j_g}$, $\psi(v_{i_g}) = u_{j_f}$, *if* $D_S[p] \approx D_{S'}[p]$, *and* $|D_{S'}[f] - D_{S'}[g]| < 2\delta$, $2 \leq f, g \leq k, \forall p = 2..k$

Due to the space limitation, the proofs of the propositions and rules are omitted. Rule 3 is derived from Proposition 2 and Rule 2, as a generalization of Rule 2. The resultant set of candidate matching functions from Rule 3 is a superset of that of Rule 2. As a consequence, Rule 3 may result in more false hits. When searching a database of n sub-patches against a query sub-patch, on the other hand, Rule 3 requires less computations than Rule 2. $C_k^2 \times n$ inter sub-patch cross-position comparisons for $D_S[g] \approx D_{S'}[f]$ are needed in Rule 2, while Rule 3 requires only C_k^2 internal cross-position comparisons once for $D_{S'}[g] \approx D_{S'}[f]$. Therefore, we use Rule 3 in our experiments instead of Rule 2.

Refine. A collection of candidate k-sized matching functions is then generated through the filter stage. They are further pruned by comparing all corresponding (7k-10) distances between two sub-patches. After the refine process, a collection of correct k-sized matching functions is obtained.

4.2 Expand

Given two patches $M = \{v_1, ..., v_m\}$ and $M' = \{u_1, ..., u_{m'}\}$, and two matching k-sized sub-patches $S_{\triangleleft} = (v_{i_1}, ..., v_{i_k}) \subseteq M$ and $S'_{\triangleleft} = (u_{j_1}, ..., u_{j_k}) \subseteq M'$ determined by a matching function $\psi : i_q \rightarrow j_q | q = 1..k$, a collection of $(k+1)$-sized matching sub-patches are derived by involving a new proper vector. The matching expansion continues until the maximal sized sub-patch is reached. Due to space limitation, the detailed algorithm is omitted here.

5 Experiments

In this section, we set up the experiments and report the results of an extensive performance study conducted to evaluate the proposed representation model and the match-and-expand strategy on protein data.

5.1 Experimental Setup

Test Data. A total number of 881 sample proteins are selected for our initial experiments according to the PDB_LIST_20040601 (R-factor<0.2 and Resolution<1.9) in the WHATIF relational database. The PDB structures stored in the WHAT IF relational database are a representative set of sequence-unique (a sequence identity percentage cutoff of 30%) structures generated from the X-ray protein PDB files available at a certain moment[1]. After pre-processing, 254,491 patches are generated from a total number of 881 proteins.

We also investigate the number of different sized sub-patches for the test data. It can be observed that the number of sub-patches reaches the peak when k is increased to 3 and then falls down as k increases. As a result, we mainly test the effect of k for values of 3 to 6 in the experiment.

Ten different sized proteins are selected as queries. All the experimental results reported later will be averaged over the 10 query proteins. The average number of vectors per query is 81.

Parameter Settings. There are several parameters need to be set for our model and search method, two of which are fixed in our experiments: distance cutoff ε is $8\mathring{A}$ and minimal size of sub-patches to output γ is 5. Two other parameters are variables. We will test how the different settings of them affect the performance.

- Similarity tolerance δ: $0.1\mathring{A}$, $0.3\mathring{A}$, $0.5\mathring{A}$, $0.7\mathring{A}$ and $1\mathring{A}$
- Size of seed patches k: 4, 5, 6

Performance Indicators. Our programs are written in C++ and running on Pentium 4 CPU (2.8GHZ) with 1G RAM. The major performance indicator we used is the CPU time to complete a query.

The complexities of the structure representation in existing works, such as distance matrix [4], are *quadratic* to the number of atoms in the protein. However, the number of distances in our patch signature model is *linear* to the number of vectors. Different level of complexities in representation leads to different level of computational cost. Obviously, existing works are not expected to be comparable with the patch signature approach. To choose a baseline for comparison with our match-and-expand method, we perform pairwise comparison of all distances between two patches for matching. Its performance is listed in Table 3(a). δ has no effect on the CPU time. Because the number of sub-patches becomes less and less as k changes from 4 to 6, its time plunges as k increases.

5.2 Experimental Results

Here we present the performance of the match-and-expand method. In match stage, different candidate deriving rules are combined and compared.

Effectiveness of Match Stage. For Rule 1 and Rule 1+Rule 3, their CPU time used for k-sized sub-patch matching are summarized in Fig.4 respectively, with respect to different k and δ. As we can see from Fig.4(a), for the same k, the CPU time goes up as δ increases since more sub-patches are compared. On the contrary, for the same δ, the CPU time drops as k increases since less sub-patches are larger sized. When Rule 3 is also considered, the constraint is relaxed and more sub-patches are compared so that all correctly matching sub-patches are returned. As shown in Fig.4(b), the performance of Rule 1+Rule 3, which returns correct results, is worse than that of Rule 1 only. Since Rule 1 does not guarantee to include all matching results, its recall, which is defined as the percentage of correctly matching sub-patches being returned as candidates, should be measured. Table 1 indicates its recall for different k and δ. As observed,

size\ δ	$\delta = 0.1$	$\delta = 0.3$	$\delta = 0.5$	$\delta = 0.7$	$\delta = 1$
k=4	15800	15800	15800	15800	15800
k=5	3960	3960	3960	3960	3960
k=6	121	121	121	121	121

(a) pairwise comparison

size\ δ	$\delta = 0.1$	$\delta = 0.3$	$\delta = 0.5$	$\delta = 0.7$	$\delta = 1$
k=4	12	37	95	170	310
k=5	<1	<1	<1	2	5
k=6	<1	<1	<1	3	7

(b) matching larger sized sub-patches

Fig. 3. CPU time(seconds) for computing matching k-sized sub-patches using pairwise comparison / matching larger sized sub-patches

size\ δ	$\delta = 0.1$	$\delta = 0.3$	$\delta = 0.5$	$\delta = 0.7$	$\delta = 1$
k=4	188	296	520	744	1040
k=5	24	25	65	73	75
k=6	<1	<1	<1	<1	<1

(a) Rule 1

size\ δ	$\delta = 0.1$	$\delta = 0.3$	$\delta = 0.5$	$\delta = 0.7$	$\delta = 1$
k=4	363	671	984	1411	9123
k=5	25	106	186	376	811
k=6	<1	3	4	17	53

(b) Rule 1+Rule 3

Fig. 4. CPU time(seconds) for computing matching k-sized sub-patches using Rule 1 / Rule 1+Rule 3

Table 1. Recall of Rule 1

size\ δ	$\delta = 0.1$	$\delta = 0.3$	$\delta = 0.5$	$\delta = 0.7$	$\delta = 1$
k=4	0.7	0.72	0.76	0.79	0.82
k=5	0.73	0.75	0.79	0.82	0.86
k=6	0.78	0.79	0.8	0.83	0.88

Rule 1 achieves best performance with satisfactory recall of about 80%. So it is a good choice when CPU time is a critical requirement.

Effectiveness of Expand Stage. Next, we test the expanding time based on the candidates returned from matching stage by Rule 1 and Rule 3. Fig.3(b) shows the average CPU time for expanding k-sized sub-patches to find maximal matching sub-patches. We can observe that the expansion process is accomplished much more quickly than the matching stage as shown in Fig.4(b). This is because the number of candidate sub-patches are much small after the match stage. However, re-look at Fig.3(a), we can see that our match-and-expand method outperforms baseline by more than an order of magnitude.

6 Conclusions and Future Work

In this paper, a match-and-expand strategy is proposed to achieve fast retrieval for matching patches based on their signatures. A rule-based heuristic algorithm, functioning as the filter-and-refine approach, is developed in match stage to derive a very small portion of patch signatures for comparison. The resultant set is further reduced in expand stage. Our extensive experiment results prove the significance of our model. We plan to design effective indexing methods for the compact patch signature representation to further improve the performance of patch matching in out future work.

Acknowledgements

The work reported in this paper has been funded in part by the Australian Research Council (Grant No. DP0663272) and the Co-operative Centre for Enterprise Distributed Systems Technology (DSTC) through the Australian Federal Government's CRC Programme (Department of Education, Science and Training).

References

1. Whatif relational database. http://www.cmbi.kun.nl/gv/whatif/select/.
2. S.F. Altschul, W Gish, W Miller, E.W. Myers, and D.J. Lipman. Basic local alignment search tool. *J Mol Biol*, 215(3):403–10, 1990.
3. Z. Huang, X. Zhou, D. Song, and P. Bruza. Dimensionality reduction in patch-signature based protein structure matching. In *Seventeenth Australiasian Database Conference*, pages 89–98, 2006.
4. I.N. Shindyalov and Bourne P.E. Protein structure alignment by incremental combinatorial extension (ce) of the optimal path. *Protein Engineering*, 11:739–47, 1998.
5. Hans-Peter Kriegel Stefan Berchtold, Daniel A. Keim. Using extended feature objects for partial similarity retrieval. *The VLDB Journal*, 6:333–348, 1997.
6. H. Wolfson. Geometric hashing: an overview. *IEEE Comp. Science and Eng.*, October-December:10–21, 1997.

Segmented Document Classification: Problem and Solution

Hang Guo and Lizhu Zhou

Computer Science & Technology Department
100084, Tsinghua University, Beijing, China
guohang@mails.tsinghua.edu.cn,
dcszlz@mail.tsinghua.edu.cn

Abstract. In recent years, structured text documents like XML files are playing an important role in the Web-based applications. Among them, there are some documents that are segmented into different sections like "title","body", etc. We call them "segmented documents". To classify segmented documents, we can treat them as bags of words and use well-developed text classification models. However different sections in a segmented document may have different impact on the classification result. It is better to treat them differently in the classification process. Following this idea, two algorithms: IN_MIX and OUT_MIX are designed to label segmented documents by a trained classifier. We perform our algorithms using four frequently used models: SVM, NaiveBayes, Regression and Instance-based Classifiers. According to the experiment on Reuters-21578, the performance of different classification models is improved comparing to the conventional bag of words method.

1 Introduction

Text Categorization problem is one of the most important problems in AI. In recent years, Machine Learning technologies have been well developed and are widely used to solve this problem[1]. Many automatic classifiers, such as NaiveBayes[2], Decision Tree, Rule-Based classifier, Instance-based classifier[3], Support Vector Machines[6][4], etc., have been proved to be effective on plain text documents. All of these classifiers treat a document as a bag of words.

As a result of the booming Internet resources, structured documents, like XML files, are playing a very important role on WWW. Among them, many documents only have simple structure that can help to segment documents into sections. For example, a document about a paper can be segmented into *Title, Abstract, Introduction* and *Body.* The content of each segment is a plain text. In this paper, we call this kind of documents *segmented documents.* Segmented documents are widely used in many web sites as the descriptive metadata of on-line resources like news, services, products, books, etc. For example, RSS[1] format is the standard of news exchange for many news sites. And we have the

[1] http://www.xml.com/pub/a/2002/12/18/dive-into-xml.html

S. Bressan, J. Küng, and R. Wagner (Eds.): DEXA 2006, LNCS 4080, pp. 538–548, 2006.

on-line *segmented documents* for all papers on CiteSeer[2]. Like CiteSeer, many websites have pre-defined templates for their resources. Their *segmented documents* are generated according to these templates. For many other websites, they do not provide on-line *segmented documents*. But their webpages are automatically generated. In this case, we can use data extraction technique to automatically generate *segmented documents*[5].

Though *segmented documents* are XML files, their structure is quite simple. Usually all the documents on one website are of the same structure. So XML-based tree miners like XRules[8], TreeMiner[9] are not applicable to classify *segmented documents*.

We can treat *segmented documents* as plain texts and use conventional models to classify them by ignoring their structural information on segmentation. But the method does not consider the important fact that in a document some text should have more weight on classification. For example, in most cases the text in the title of a paper are more important. Sometimes one skilled expert can categorize a paper only by its title. Therefore such structural information can be used to improve the performance of the classifier.

Since the plain text classification models have been well designed to deal with text categorization problem, we use these models as components to design new algorithms for *segmented documents categorization*. Our basic strategy is divide-and-conquer. It is easy to divide one *segmented document* into different parts since it is already segmented. The problem is how to emphasize the more important part. Our idea is that we can re-evaluate each segment as follows:

Solution 1. Before being classified, we put more weight on the words in the more important segments and then generate a new text document. It stands for the whole *segmented documents* in classification process.

Solution 2. We classify each segment first and then put more weight on the results of more important segments. The final result will be the combination of these partial predications.

Additionally, we don't want to train the classifiers on *segmented documents*. Usually human experts label the training set. And it might be expensive to label a new training set especially on *segmented documents*. Moreover if the resource holders don't have too much resources, there will not be enough *segmented documents* to train a classifier. Therefore a better alternative is to label the *segmented documents* by a trained text classifier. This classifier may be an encapsulated commercial product or be trained by labeled plain texts.

Generally speaking, in this paper we want to solve the problem: how to make good use of the structural information of *segmented documents* to increase the classification precision and recall without additional effort on training a new classifier. To accomplish that task, two important problems should be solved:

Problem 1. For *Solution 1*, how to generate a new document on different segments? The basic idea is to "emphasize" the words in more important

[2] http://citeseer.ist.psu.edu/oai.html

segments, like *title*. The documents should be indexed as vectors before being labeled. We can merge those vectors in the indexing phrase.

Problem 2. For *Solution 2*, how to make a final decision based on partial classification predications? The basic idea is to use the voting mechanism. Each segment votes on which category it belongs to. If a category gets over half of the "tickets", it will be associated to the whole document. Statistically, if the false rate of each predication is less than 1/2, the false rate of the final decision will be lower than any predications. [10] illustrates this problem.

We have designed two algorithms called IN_MIX and OUT_MIX. The former is based on the idea of *Solution 1* and the latter is based on *Solution 2*. The two algorithms are tested on four frequently used models: SVM, NaiveBayes, Instance-based classifier and Regression. Both have been proved to be effective on at least two models. The time cost of the former is almost the same as the plain text classification algorithm. For OUT_MIX, the upper bound of time cost is n times of the plain text classification algorithm, here n represents the number of segments used in classification.

This paper is organized as follows: In Section 2 we formally define the *structural text categorization* problem and introduce our *algorithms*. We discuss our experiments in Section 3. Section 4 glances at the related work. Finally, the paper will be concluded in Section 5.

2 Our Approach

2.1 Problem Description

A *segmented document set* $\mathcal{D}$ is associated with a predefined template $\mathcal{S}$, which is composed of named attributes $s_1, s_2, \ldots, s_n$. Suppose $\mathcal{T}$ is the set of texts, there is a value function $\theta : \mathcal{D} \times \mathcal{S} \rightarrow \mathcal{T}$. If $\theta(d, s_i) = t_i, d \in \mathcal{D}$, it means the value of attribute s_i of document d is t_i. t_i is one of the *segments* of d. The "importance" of different attributes is measured by attribute weight function WET: $\mathcal{S} \rightarrow [0, 1]$. Usually $\mathcal{S}$ is defined by the content provider. And WET is an empirical function, which can be modified according to different $\mathcal{S}$. However, in our experiment the value of WET slightly affects the classification results. It is discussed in section 3.3.

Given the set of categories $\mathcal{C}$, the task of *segmented text categorization(STC)* is to approximate the unknown target function $\Phi : \mathcal{D} \times \mathcal{C} \rightarrow \{T, F\}$. Here T stands for *true* and F stands for *false*. For plain text categorization problem, the target function is $\phi : \mathcal{T} \times \mathcal{C} \rightarrow \{T, F\}$. Before the training and the testing phrase, a document is usually indexed as a feature vector. The index function σ is defined as $\mathcal{T} \rightarrow \mathcal{V}$, $\mathcal{V}$ is set of feature vectors. The classification function λ is defined as $\mathcal{V} \times \mathcal{C} \rightarrow \{T, F\}$. Here we define $\phi = \sigma \bullet \lambda$.

The primary difference between STC and TC is the definition of document set. We assume that:

- segment t_i is a plain text. In other words, documents with nested structure are not considered in this paper.

- t_i has certain impact on the classification result. Because for most structured text documents on the Internet there are usually some unused attributes in classification. For example, suppose we have a paper defined as (*Title, Abstract, Author, Body, Publisher, Reference*), only *Title, Abstract and Body* are useful. Other attributes should be removed before classification.
- if $(i \neq j)$ then t_i and t_j are semantically different segments. That means the impact of t_i and t_j should be different.

2.2 Our Approach

In this section we will introduce our solutions on how to classify *segmented documents* by given plain text classifiers. We have designed two algorithms: IN_MIX and OUT_MIX. The inputs of the algorithms are:

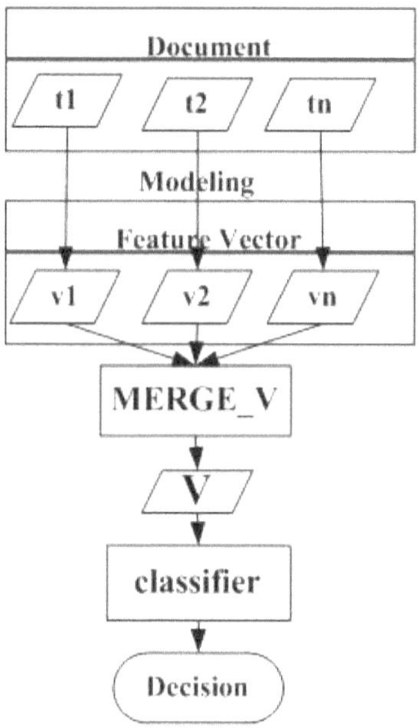

Fig. 1. IN_MIX

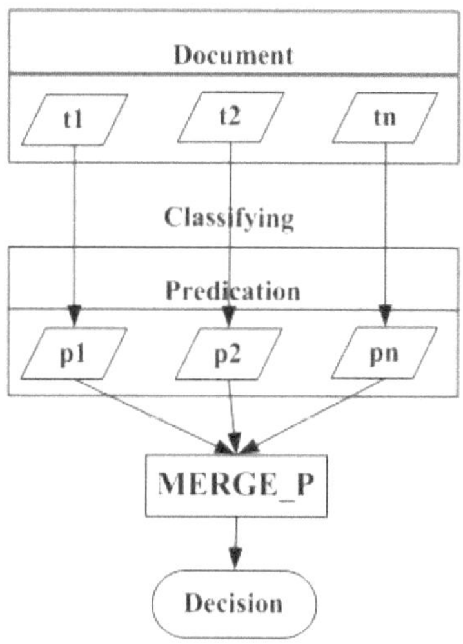

Fig. 2. OUT_MIX

- *segmented document set* $\mathcal{D}$, the associated template $\mathcal{S}$, the attribute weight function WET, and the value function θ.
- document feature vector V. In this paper we use the term vector with TFIDF.
- a trained plain text classifier. The output of the classifier is vector $P = (p_1, p_2, \ldots, p_{|\mathcal{C}|})$. Here $p_i \in [0, 1]$ is the "possibility" of document d in category $\mathcal{C}_i$. If inputs of the classifier are term vectors, function CLS_λ stands for the classification process. And if the input are texts, we use the function CLS_ϕ.

The outputs of the algorithms are the classification predications of each *segmented document.*

IN_MIX. As shown in Fig 1, the idea is to merge the attribute values as the input of the classifier. Intuitively we can "repeat" the important words. But the problem is they can only be "repeated" integral number of times. Therefore we merge the term vectors instead.

First, the TFIDF vectors for all t_i are calculated. Then we initialize the attribute weight function WET. The basic rule is that if s_i is more important than s_j, $WET(s_i) > WET(s_j)$. We have tried different functions in our experiment. And the influence of WET on the performance is shown on Table 4. After this, we merge the TFIDF vectors according to WET. The algorithm used is called MERGE_V:

```
Input: (s_1, v_1), (s_2, v_2), ..., (s_|S|, v_|S|); WET: S → [0, 1]; S      /*the size of v_i is the
same as that of document feature vector V*/
Output: v: vector of float number /* TFIDF vector*/
BEGIN
FOR all s_i in S
        IF (min_value> WET(s_i))            /* find the least important attribute*/
                min=i
                min_value=WET(s_i)
        END IF
END FOR
FOR all v_i
        v_i = v_i × (WET(S_i)/WET(S_min))            /* re-evaluate the TFIDF vector*/
        v=v+v_i            /* v and v_i are of the same size, v(j) = v(j) + v_i(j)*/
END FOR
output v
END
```

The output of MERGE_V is used as the term vector for a *segmented document*. It is labeled by a trained plain text classifier.

Comparing to the conventional classification algorithm, the additional cost is MERGE_V. Its time complexity is $O(|\mathcal{S}|)$. For most popular classification algorithms, the complexity is at least $O(|V| * |\mathcal{C}|)$. Here V is the document feature vector, in most cases it is much larger than $\mathcal{S}$. So the cost of MERGE_V can be ignored. It means the cost of IN_MIX is almost the same as the conventional classification algorithm. Our experiment result in Table 5 has proved that.

OUT_MIX. As shown in Fig 2, the idea is to merge the classification predications of different attributes. The advantage is that it only uses the output of the plain text classifier and cares nothing about the document indexing and dimensionality reduction process. Therefore it can be used on the "encapsulated" classifiers. We design an algorithm MERGE_P to unite the partial classification predications. The basic idea of MERGE_P is voting. If a segment of the document is classified into a category, this category will get one "ticket". If one category get over half of the tickets, the whole document will be associated with that category. If we cannot make the decision yet we will calculate the "confidence" of each prediction and then choose the highest one. Here the "confidence" is measured by the product of :

– the quotient of A and 1-A. Here A stands for the possibility of the document associate with this category. The higher this quotient is, the more believable this prediction would be.
– the weight of this attribute.

MERGE_P is described as follows:

```
Input: (S_1, P_1), (S_2, P_2), ..., (S_|S|, P_|S|); WET: S → [0, 1]
Output: P vector of float number; /* |P| = |P_i| = |C|, here |P| means the size of P*/
BEGIN
VAR other,max: vector of float number; isI=0, notI=0, index=0: int;
VAR P :vector of float number;
FOR all i < |P|
        FOR all P_j
                IF P_j(i) is the largest one in P_j
                        isI=isI+1              /* attribute j vote for category i */
                ELSE
                        notI=notI+1              /* attribute j do not vote for category i */
                END IF
        IF isI > notI
                P(i)=1            /* category i is associated with the whole document*/
        ELSE
                FOR all P_j
                        weight=P_j(i)/(1 − P_j(i)) × WET(s_i) /*compute the confidence*/
                        IF weight>max
                                max=weight
                                index=j
                        END IF
                P(i)=P_index(i)
                END FOR
        END IF
        END FOR
END FOR
normalize(P)          /* P(i) = P(i) / Σ_{k=1}^{|P|} P(k) */
output P
END
```

In terms of time cost, OUT_MIX exceeds IN_MIX. Because for one *segmented document* it has $|\mathcal{S}|$ segments to be labeled independently. Though each segment is shorter than the whole document, the overall cost is much higher. The complexity of MERGE_P is $O(|\mathcal{S}| * |\mathcal{C}|)$. Like MERGE_V, the cost of MERGE_P can be ignored comparing to the classification cost. The upper bound of the cost of OUT_MIX is $|\mathcal{S}|$ times that of classifying the whole document by a plain text classifier. Our results in Table 5 have proved that.

3 Experiment

3.1 Test Environment and Database

We select Reuters-21578[3] as our training and testing set. It is one of the most widely used news collection. Every document has two attributes: *Title* and *Body*. We use ModApte Split to determine the training set and testing set. Since we

[3] http://kdd.ics.uci.edu/databases/reuters21578/reuters21578.html

need both *Title* and *Body*, the documents missing *Titles* are abandoned. That makes our collection smaller than the standard ModApte Split.

Like many other studies, we are more interested in the top 10 most common categories. These categories are listed in Table 1. In our experiment, 5449 training documents and 2145 testing documents in these categories are used. We perform the experiment on a 1.5GHz workstation with 512M memory.

We choose four text categorization models to test both algorithms. They are all frequently used models. As shown in Table 2, one implementation is chosen for each model. These classifiers are implemented by **weka**[4] and **judge**[5]. They are both open source classification toolkits written in Java.

A small portion of documents in Reuters-21578 is associated with multiple categories. Therefore we train one classifier for each category to determine whether the document is associated with this category or not.

3.2 Experiment Process

For all the documents in the training set, we concatenate their titles and bodies as the training documents of the classifiers. Then the input texts are indexed as TFIDF doc-term matrix. We use the information gain algorithm (implemented by **weka**) to select 2500 keywords from *Body* and *Title*. After that, we have the feature vector $\mathcal{V}$ and TFIDF matrix. The former is the input of IN_MIX and the latter is the input of the classifier.

Firstly, we classify each document only by its title or body. The result is used as the input of OUT_MIX. Then the title and body are concatenated and labeled by the classifier for comparison. We choose F1 value to evaluate the performance of the classifiers since it is easier to calculate. Suppose π stands for precision and ρ for recall, $F1 = 2 * \pi * \rho / (\pi + \rho)$. The result is shown in Table 3. To evaluate the influence of the attribute weight function WET, nine WET functions are used in IN_MIX and OUT_MIX. The result is listed in Table 4. The time cost of IN_MIX and OUT_MIX is shown in Table 5.

3.3 Result Analysis and Discussion

Table 3 shows that IN_MIX performs well in SMO and IBk, while OUT_MIX is good for NaiveBayes Multinomial and Logistic. A possible reason is that NaiveBayes and Logistic are both based on statistics. The slight fluctuation of the input will not significantly affect the output. In OUT_MIX we can use the voting mechanism to increase the precision statistically. SMO and IBk are good for high-dimensional classification[4] but texts in the *Title* are too short to be properly labeled. That makes the predication based on *Title* really bad. So OUT_MIX works badly for them. SMO has achieved the best performance in this collection and IN_MIX can slightly increase its precision and recall in most categories. When choosing from these two algorithms for other classification models, we can use both of them and select the better one.

[4] http://www.cs.waikato.ac.nz/ml/weka/

[5] http://www3.dfki.uni-kl.de/judge/

Table 1. The Largest 10 Categories in Reuters-21578 ModApte

Category Name	Testing	Training	Total
earn	1044	2709	3753
acq	643	1488	2131
money-fx	141	460	601
crude	161	389	550
grain	134	349	483
trade	113	337	450
interest	100	289	389
ship	85	191	276
wheat	66	198	264
corn	48	160	208

Table 2. Classifiers Used

Classifier Type	Classifier Name
SVM	SMO [6]
NaiveBayes	Multinomial [2]
Regression	Logistic [7]
Instance Based	IBk [3]

Table 3. Results For Top 10 Categories

Performance Measured by F1 for Top 10 Categories

classifiers		earn	acq	money-fx	crude	grain	trade	interest	ship	wheat	corn	Total
SVM	All*	.8924	.7849	.5403	.6795	**.6980**	.6554	.6977	.6486	.5957	**.4898**	.7953
	IN	**.8961**	**.7862**	**.5411**	**.7109**	.6797	**.6629**	**.7011**	**.6575**	**.6136**	.4800	**.8005**
	OUT	.7496	.4411	.3333	.4044	.3404	.3048	.5588	.0732	.2667	.4888	.6177
Naive Bayes	All	**.8504**	**.8798**	.6879	.6593	.6262	.5469	**.7753**	.6207	.5286	.3167	.7674
	IN	.8120	.8606	.6620	.6493	.6027	.4940	.6017	.6182	.4713	.2667	.7370
	OUT	.8488	.8746	**.7287**	**.7278**	**.7186**	**.6026**	.6700	**.7310**	**.5882**	**.3902**	**.7974**
Regression	All	.8640	.5797	.2928	.3520	.4754	.5728	.2749	.5654	.1986	.1463	.5964
	IN	.8647	.5809	.2685	.3431	.4677	.5728	**.2764**	.5455	.1972	.1401	.5952
	OUT	**.8652**	**.5824**	**.3238**	**.3976**	**.5116**	**.6525**	.2727	**.6357**	**.1992**	**.2909**	**.6345**
Instance based	All	.7507	.5601	.3111	.2360	.2892	.1379	.4640	.1647	.1379	.0909	.6292
	IN	**.7831**	**.6125**	**.3436**	**.3676**	**.4404**	**.2316**	**.4932**	**.2222**	**.4638**	**.3333**	**.6590**
	OUT	.7373	.3575	.1849	.2065	.3182	.1149	.2963	.2174	.2667	0	.5777

*Here All means labeling Title+Body with plain text classifiers, IN stands for IN_MIX and OUT stands for OUT_MIX. The bold numbers are the best results.
**In this table, WET(Title)=0.6667, WET(Body)=0.3333

As shown in Table 4, the function WET might slightly affect the result. The possible reasons are: In IN_MIX, the words in *Title* is much less than those in *Body*. If the weight of *Title* is too high, they may be removed as noise. In OUT_MIX, $P_j(i)/(1 - P_j(i))$ is usually much bigger or smaller than WET(i). The final predication is largely dependent on $P_j(i)/(1 - P_j(i))$. Thus in our experiments, the value of WET is too small to affect the result evidently.

In terms of the time cost, Table 5 shows that the cost of IN_MIX is almost the same as conventional algorithms. The cost of OUT_MIX is higher because the document is labeled twice. Despite this, the total cost of OUT_MIX is less than twice the cost of conventional classifiers. It is because we only use part of a document each time.

Table 4. The Influence of WET Function on F1

	WET(Title)/WET(Body)	5	4	3	2	1*	1/2	1/3	1/4	1/5
OUT_	NaiveBayes	**.7995**	.7992	.7982	.7973	.7940	.7218	.7219	7219	.7219
MIX	Regression	.6352	.6350	**.6353**	.6345	.6318	.5519	.5519	.5519	.5519
IN_	Instance based	.6573	.6590	.6642	.6590	.6592	**.6612**	.6523	.6484	.6480
MIX	SVM	.8000	.8000	**.8005**	**.8005**	.7953	.7935	.7923	.7925	.7919

* This means that "Title" and "Body" are treated the same. In other words, it is the result of categorizing Title+Body.

Table 5. The total time cost of label 10 categories

Total Classification Time Cost of IN_MIX and OUT_MIX in Millisecond

CLassifiers	IN_MIX	OUT_MIX	Title+Body	IN_MIX / (Title + Body)	OUT_MIX / (Title + Body)
Logistic	156527	296577	153094	1.022	1.937
IBk	940051	1557070	934286	1.006	1.668
NaiveBayes	105658	201930	103330	1.022	1.954
SMO	112751	218104	112503	1.002	1.939

The documents in Reuters-21578 only contain two attributes and the text in *Title* segment is quite short. It might affect the result. We will test the algorithms on new datasets with more attributes and longer texts.

4 Related Work

Conventional automated documents categorization models can be divided into two classes: content-based models and structure-based models.

The former utilizes the textual information of the documents. So they are used for plain text categorization. [1] has introduced many frequently used models[2][6][4][3]. We can use ensemble methods to enhance the performance by combining the results of different classifiers [10]. The condition for the ensemble of classifiers to be more accurate than any of its individual members is studied in [13]. [11][12] compare the performance of different ensemble methods.

The latter focuses on the structure of the documents. They are applicable to more complicated documents like XML files. The first step of structure-based classification is structure pattern recognition. Many algorithms are designed to find frequent subtrees in XML collections[9][14][15]. Those subtrees are associated with certain categories in the training phrase. In the testing phrase this information can be used to label the documents according to the subtrees they have. [16] uses an associate based classifier on XML data. [8] introduces a rule-based classifier using the tree mining algorithm in [15].

As described in Section 1, these models are not applicable to *segmented documents* classification. That is because the plain text classifiers only treat the document as a bag of words. And we cannot use the XML classifiers to associate subtrees with the categories for all the *segmented documents* have the same structure.

5 Conclusion and Future Work

This paper introduces a kind of widely used document — *segmented document* and its classification problem. Current classification models are not applicable to these documents. We design two algorithms, IN_MIX and OUT_MIX, by which we can label *segmented documents* with a trained plain text classifier. These algorithms have been tested on Reuters-21578 and they can improve the performance of SVM, Instance Based classifier, NaiveBayes and Logistic.

Now we are trying to enhance the performance of IN_MIX and OUT_MIX and use them on other models and datasets. We are also interested in exploring the question of "optimal segment size".

Acknowledgement. This work is supported by National Nature Science Foundation of China under Grant No.60520130299.

References

[1] Fabrizio.S.:Machine Learing in Automated Text Categorization. ACM Computing Surveys, Vol34,(2002).
[2] Andrew M., Kamal N.:A Comparison of Event Models for Naive Bayes Text Classification, AAAI-98 Workshop on Learning for Text Categorization(1998).
[3] H Brighton, C Mellish: Advances in Instance Selection for Instance-Based Learning Algorithms, Conference on Data Mining and Knowledge Discovery, (2002)
[4] Joachims, T.: Text Categorization with Support Vector Machines: Learning with Many Relevant Features.10th European Conference on Machine Learning.(1998)
[5] Qi G., Zhiqiang Z., Lizhu Z., Jianhua F.: A Highly Adaptable Web Information Extractor Using Graph Data Model. The Forth Asia Pacific Web Conference (APWeb'02).Springer(2002).
[6] S.S. Keerthi, S.K. Shevade, C. Bhattacharyya, K.R.K. Murthy, :Improvements to Platt's SMO Algorithm for SVM Classifier Design. Neural Computation, 13(3), pp 637-649, (2001).
[7] le Cessie, S. and van Houwelingen, J.C: Ridge Estimators in Logistic Regression. Applied Statistics, Vol. 41, No. 1, pp. 191-201.(1992)
[8] Mohammed J.,Charu C.:XRules: An Effective Structural Classifier for XML Data. SIGKDD'03.(2003).
[9] Mohammed J.:Efficiently Mining Frequent Trees in a Forest : Algorithms and Applications. vol 17. (2005)
[10] TG Dietterich.:Ensemble Metholds in Machine Learnging. First International Workshop on Multiple Classifier Systems, Lecture Notes in Computer Science (pp. 1-15). New York: Springer Verlag.(2000)
[11] Bauner E.,Kohavi.R: A empirical comparison of voting classificaiton algorithms: Bagging, boosting, and variants. Machine Learning,36,105-139.(1999)
[12] Dietterich,T.G: An experimental comparison of three method for constructing ensembles of decision trees: Bagging, Boosting, Radomization. Machine Learing. (2000)

[13] Hansen L., Salamon P. Neural network ensembles. IEEE trans. Pattern Analysis and Machine Volume 12,Issue 10,Oct. 1990 Page(s):993 - 1001.(1990)
[14] Wang K., Liu H.: Discover Structural Association of Semistructured Data. Intell.12,993-1001(1999)
[15] T.Asai,et al.Efficient subtree discovery from large semi-structured data. International Conference on Data Mining (ICDM'02).Springer(2002)
[16] B.Liu, W. Hsu, Y.Ma. Integrating Classification and Association Rule Mining. SIGKDD'98.(1998)

User Preference Modeling Based on Interest and Impressions for News Portal Site Systems

Yukiko Kawai[1], Tadahiko Kumamoto[2], and Katsumi Tanaka[3]

[1] Undergraduate School of Science, Kyoto Sangyo University
Motoyama, Kamigamo, Kita-Ku, Kyoto-City 603-8555 Japan
Tel.: +81-75-705-2958; Fax: +81-75-705-1495
kawai@cc.kyoto-su.ac.jp
[2] National Institute of Information and Communications Technology
3-5 Hikaridai, Seika-cho, Soraku-gun, Kyoto, 619-0289 Japan
Tel.: +81-774-98-6876; Fax: +81-774-98-6990
kuma@nict.go.jp
[3] Graduate School of Informatics, Kyoto University
Yoshida-Honmachi, Sakyo-ku, Kyoto, 606-8501 Japan
Tel.: +81-75-753-5969; Fax: +81-75-753-4957
ktanaka@i.kyoto-u.ac.jp

Abstract. We have developed an application called My Portal Viewer (MPV)[1] that effectively integrates many articles collected from multiple news sites and presents these integrations through a familiar interface such as a page the user has often visited. MPV dynamically determines keywords of interest that a user might potentially be interested in based on the history of the articles the user has read and creates categories based on these interest words. MPV and many other similar integration systems, however, cause problems where users cannot find only their interest articles in each category because they are only ranked by frequency and the cooccurrence of keywords. We propose a new method of selecting further articles from each category using a user's impressions of articles. The improved MPV, called MPV Plus, selects and recommends more desirable articles using the method we propose. This paper presents the design concept and process flow of MPV Plus and reports on its effectiveness as evaluated in experiments.

1 Introduction

As the amount of Web content continues to increase, demand by users for applications that provide better quality content is becoming more urgent. In particular, applications that select and integrate information from the Web based on user preferences are needed to efficiently retrieve content. There is also need for a system that can effectively integrate high-quality content gathered from the Web according to a user's requirements. In news articles, how the articles are categorized in terms of integration is important. There are two basic criteria for article classification, the first is the frequency at which terms occur in each article[1][2], and the second is the structure of links and directories between pages[3][4]. Both

S. Bressan, J. Küng, and R. Wagner (Eds.): DEXA 2006, LNCS 4080, pp. 549–559, 2006.

criteria involve various algorithms and systems. Frequency, as a general trend, is defined as the rate of term occurrence in all collected or selected article pages.

We have developed an application called My Portal Viewer (MPV) that integrates a newspaper by gathering numerous articles from news sites based on user's preferences [1][5]. MPV collects and stores articles by crawling through Web sites and provides an MPV page that integrates the stored pages. This involves two concepts. The first is the user's access history based on his or her interests and knowledge, and the second is the "look and feel" of the MPV page that simulates his or her favorite news page. The MPV layout utilizes the users' favorite news page, with parts of the original content from the favorite page being replaced by the integrated content. Using the layout for the user's favorite news page enables him or her to easily locate the information they want from the content gathered. Replaced content such as categories, top news, and the articles in each category, on the other hand, is created by the frequency of term occurrence based on the history of articles that the user has read up to that time. Category names are identified by keywords, called "interest keywords", that a user is potentially interested in based on the history of articles that he or she has read. For instance, categories such as "Iraq", "Koizumi" and "Matsui" will have been named based on the user's history of operations. By using interest keywords as category names, the user can easily understand the content of articles in each category. The categories, however, cannot always classify and recommend favorite articles using only the occurrence frequency of terms such as interest keywords. For instance, if the category name is "Iraq", the previous MPV offers the possibility of different content articles such as "suicide bombing in Iraq" or "released hostage in Iraq".

We will now introduce a novel algorithm for "article impression" and a model that reflects the user's interests and impressions of articles. The improved MPV developed with the proposed model is called "MPV Plus" and it recommends articles that the user may have a greater affinity for.

2 Overview of MPV Plus

MPV Plus is an improved MPV with a method of selection based on a user's impressions of and interest in articles. The previous MPV has three unique technologies.

- The gathered articles are categorized by interest keywords and cooccurrence keywords that are extracted from the user's browsing history.
- The extracted interest keywords are category names.
- The layout for the original news portal page, which is specified by the user, is used for the interface of the integrated portal page, and only part of the content is replaced by gathered and categorized content, i.e. category names are replaced by interest keywords.

MPV Plus retains these techniques and introduces a new technique of selecting articles using user impressions of the articles. With the new technology, MPV

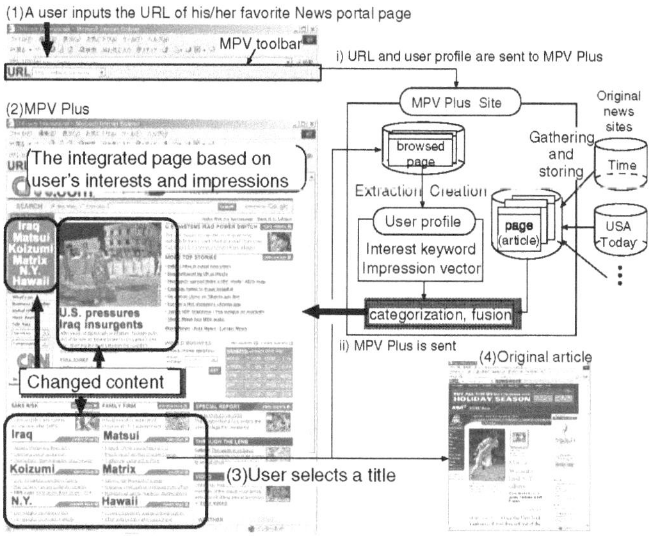

Fig. 1. Concept behind MPV Plus system

Plus can model a user's preferences, and the constructed preference model can adapt to other applications such as recommendation systems.

The unique characteristic of the modeling method is that it detects fluctuations in impressions of articles browsed by the user in each category. If there are small fluctuations in some impressions of an interest keyword, which is the category name, that means the user is interested in those impressions, however if there are large fluctuations the user is uninterested. In this paper, impressions are defined by an impression vector that has four elements, which are the value of impressions measure[1] such as "happy ⇔ unhappy", "acceptance ⇔ rejection", "relaxation ⇔ strain" and "fear ⇔ anger". Each element in the vector is a real number from 0 to 1. For instance, if the value of the vector's element such as "bright ⇔ dark" of an article about a topic is 0.1, the user's impression of the article was strongly bright. MPV Plus detects the vector for each article in each category, extracting each element of each vector. It then calculates an average value and a standard deviation using the extracted elements. The calculated four standard deviations for each element are fluctuations in the user's interest in the keyword. If the standard deviation of an element is above a certain threshold, MPV Plus assumes that the user is not interested in the interest keyword based on that impression, and the value of the vector's element is defined as a "*don't care*-term". If the standard deviation of an element is smaller than the threshold, the value of the vector's element is the average value. As described above, the impression vector of the interest keyword has four elements which have a "*don't care*-term" or "average value", and each element is determined by the standard

[1] This measure is based the concept of Plutchik[6] which has 8 impressions such as joy, acceptance, fear, surprise, sadness, disgust, anger, anticipation.

deviation. The impression vector detected by the interest keyword and the keyword itself are defined as the user's preferences. MPV Plus categorizes articles by interest keyword, and selects and recommends articles in each category using this impression vector.

An overview of MPV Plus is shown in Fig.1. The user specifies his or her favorite news portal page as the integration interface, and MPV Plus downloads the HTML document, detects the category names, and replaces these names with interest keywords on user preferences based on his or her browsing history. The articles gathered from various news sites are categorized using the interest keywords and the selected articles in each category are ranked by cooccurrence keywords and the cosine similarity of the impression vector. When a user reads an article, this changes his or her browsing history prompting the system to update his or her preferences. Preferences are updated as interest keywords and impression vectors are re-calculated. Furthermore, if different categories have articles that are the same, MPV Plus integrates those categories. When categories are integrated, the vectors are retained and calculated based on interest keywords.

3 User's Preferences for News Articles

3.1 Extracting Interest Keywords

The following process is used to extract interest keywords.

1. MPV Plus extracts and stores meta-data such as title, description, and URL after it downloads pages $P_1 \sim P_n$ from different news sites.
2. The description and title are analyzed with morphological analysis processing, which extracts proper and general nouns.
3. The weight of each word is calculated using the term frequency and weight of the three parts of speech as in the following equation: $w_{ij} = tf \cdot idf = (log(F_j + 1)/log(F_{all}))\ (cdotlog(N/N_j))$, where F_j is the frequency of the appearance of word j in page P_i, and F_j is the frequency of appearance of all words in P_i. N is the number of all pages gathered, and N_j is the number of pages with appearance of a word j.
4. When a user reads articles on pages M, the weight W_j of the word j in pages M is the summation of w_{ij}, using the next equation: $W_j = \sum_{i=1}^{M} w_{ij}$.
5. If the value of W_j is larger than a certain threshold, word j is detected as an interest keyword.

The interest keywords detected by weight W_j are replaced with the original category names. MPV Plus does not replace all detected interest keywords because the number of categories on the original news portal page are limited. Interest keywords that were not replaced with the original category are stored in a category called "other" after the "other" category has been created and replaced. The user selects the "other" category and obtains the remaining interest keywords from the other created page.

Table 1. Impression scales designed for MPV Plus

Impression Scale	Impression Words
1. Bright – Dark	Akarui (bright, encouraging), Ureshii (glad), Tanoshii (happy)
	Kurai (dark), Kanashii (sad), Kurushii (painful)
2. Acceptance – Rejection	Shonin (approval), Shonin-suru (approve), Aikou (love), Aikou-suru (love), Suki-da (like), Kyohi (rejection), Kyohi-suru (reject)
	Ken'o (aversion), Ken'o-suru (take an aversion), Kirai-da, (dislike)
3. Easing – Tension	Yuttari (comfortable), Yuttari-suru (feel easy), Nonbiri (peaceful) Nonbiri-suru (feel relieved), Yukkuri (slowly), Yukkuri-suru (take one's time)
	Kincho (tension), Kincho-suru (become tense), Kinkyuu (emergency)
4. Anger – Fear	Okoru (get angry), Dogou (roar), Osoreru (dread), Kowai (scary), Kyofu (fear)

Table 2. Examples of entries in impression dictionary

Entry word	No. 1	No. 2	No. 3	No. 4	Entry word	No. 1	No. 2	No. 3	No. 4
Sosei (revival)	0.91	0.521	0.429	0.000	Shototsu-suru (collide)	0.344	0.353	0.315	0.529
	0.464	0.582	0.732	0.328		1.004	1.016	1.099	0.948
Shukkoku	0.596	0.209	0.762	0.201	Kenen-suru (worry)	0.373	0.319	0.246	0.293
(departure from a country)	0.975	1.049	1.065	0.701		1.447	1.440	1.521	1.275
Shibou (death)	0.28	0.358	0.260	0.364	Hofu-da (rich)	0.597	0.676	0.761	0.466
	1.132	1.272	1.306	1.112		1.416	1.352	1.299	1.109
Dassen (derailment)	0.31	0.546	0.403	0.291	Saiteki-da (optimum)	0.622	0.671	0.743	0.192
	0.514	0.603	0.737	0.549		1.185	1.164	1.145	0.899
Dekakeru (go out)	0.639	0.754	0.887	0.590	Konnan-da (difficult)	0.318	0.305	0.307	0.317
	1.430	1.394	1.304	1.114		1.451	1.526	1.528	1.274
Chosen-suru (challenge)	0.618	0.687	0.752	0.500	Fumei-da (unknown)	0.359	0.367	0.336	0.359
	1.399	1.330	1.251	1.090		1.241	1.337	1.364	1.18

3.2 Generating Impression Vectors from News Articles

An impression vector is generated by the following procedure.

1. Words classified as action nouns, adjectives, or verbs are extracted from the information obtained from the Web page P_i in procedure 1 for interest word extraction.
2. Scale value S_{je} and weight M_{je} in impression scale $e(e = 1, \cdots, 4)$ of each word j are obtained by consulting our impression dictionary as described below.
3. Scale value O_{ie} in impression scale e of P_i is calculated by

$$O = \sum^{j} S_{je} \times |2S_{je} - 1| \times M_{je} \bigg/ \sum^{j} |2S_{je} - 1| \times M_{je} \qquad (1)$$

   where the $|2S - 1|$ term denotes an inclined distribution depending on scale value S. When scale value S is 0.5, the $|2S - 1|$ term is 0. When scale value S is 0 or 1, the $|2S - 1|$ term is 1. Many of the words that appear in the articles seem to be independent of the impressions of the articles. The inclined distribution described here was been introduced to remove the adverse effect that such general words cause in calculations.
4. An impression vector of P_i is generated in the form of "$(O_{i1}, O_{i2}, O_{i3}, O_{i4})$".

The impression dictionary used in procedure 2 was automatically constructed by analyzing the Nikkei Newspaper Full Text Database[2] [7] using an extended version of the method mentioned in Ref. [8]. The original method created an impression scale from a pair of impression words, but our extended version created an impression scale from multiple impression words. That is, we calculated which of two groups of impression words composing an impression scale of the words extracted from an input article would co-occur more frequently.

The groups of impression words used in constructing our impression dictionary are listed in Table 1, and part of the impression dictionary is in Table 2. The upper lines of each entry denote scale values, and the lower lines denote the weights in Table 2.

3.3 Impression Vector for Interest Keywords

In this section, we explain the method of detecting the impression vector for each interest keyword. The impression vector for each article has already been calculated using the method described above. The impression vector for each interest keyword is calculated using those article's vectors. The interest impression vectors are detected based on the articles read by a user and are modified based on a user's browsing history. If the user has bright impressions of articles on a topic he or she often reads about, the impression vector of the interest of the topic has a high value of e1 element. The following process shows how the detection of the impression vector of an interest keyword is detected.

1. $R_1, R_2, \cdots, R_m$ are article pages read by the user, and these pages have interest keyword j.
2. The impression vector for article page R_i is defined by $v_i = (v_{i1}, v_{i2}, v_{i3}, v_{i4})$.
3. μ_{je} is the average for each element $e (e = 1, 2, 3, 4)$ of the vector and σ_{je} is the standard deviation for each element of the vector.

$$\mu_{je} = \sum_{i=1}^{m} v_{ie} \Big/ m, \quad \sigma_{je} = \sqrt{\sum_{i=1}^{m} (v_{ie} - \mu_{je})^2 \Big/ (m-1)} \tag{2}$$

4. When the σ_{je} is less than the threshold, the fluctuations in the element of the vector are small, and the value for that element for interest keyword j is defined as μ_{je}. When σ_{je} is more than the threshold, the fluctuations in the element of the vector are large, and the value of that element of j's vector is defined by a "*don't-care*-term".

4 Selection and Ranking Based on User Preferences

MPV Plus selects articles from pages gathered using interest keywords and ranks the selected articles using cooccurrence keywords and impression vectors of the interest keyword.

[2] This database has over 2 million articles accumulated over the 12-year period from 1990 to 2001. Each edition consists of about 170,000 articles (200 MB).

1. Cooccurrence keyword k is extracted from the pages that have interest keyword j.
2. Value c_{jk} of cooccurrence is calculated by $c_{jk} = \{($ *the number of cooccurrence of* j *and* $k) + 1\}/\{($ *the frequency of* $j) + ($*the frequency of* $k)\}$
3. Article page P_i, which includes the interest keyword j, is selected from accessed articles m by the user.
4. Cosine similarity is detected by the distance between P_i and c_{jk} based on interest keyword j.
5. If the P_i is more than the threshold, the P_i is selected
6. The cosine similarity of impression D_i is detected by the distance between vector $v_i = (v_i1, v_i2, v_i3, v_i4)$ of P_i and the $v_j = (v_j1, v_j2, v_j3, v_j4)$ vector of interest keyword j, which was calculated in Section 3.3, and equation D_i is calculated as

$$D_i = \sum_{e=1}^{4}(v_{ie} \times v_{je}) \Big/ \sqrt{\sum_{e=1}^{4} v_{ie}^2 \times \sum_{e=1}^{4} v_{je}^2} \tag{3}$$

   However, if v_{je} is over the threshold, the calculation of v_{je} is excluded because v_{je} is a "*don't care* term".
7. P_i is displayed if D_i is bigger.

5 Integration of Categories

The categories for interest keywords are integrated by MPV Plus if different categories have many of the same articles. Each article is compared by the system based on whether other categories have the same article or not, and a new categories are created by merging categories with high rates of article overlap.

1. Product set $I \cap K$ and the union of sets $I \cup K$ are detected by the article set I of interest keyword i and the article set K of interest keyword k.
2. The number of elements is extracted by 1, and $|I \cap K|$ and $|I \cup K|$ are defined by the number that are extracted.
3. If $|I \cap K|/|I \cup K|$ is more than the threshold, categories i and k are integrated, and a new category is created. If $|I \cap K|/|I \cup K|$ is less than the threshold, the created category is separated as i and k.

The name of the new category combines the original category names. For instance, if the original category names are i and k, the new category's name is "i/k". The user can easily surmise the content of the new category after integration, because of the appearance of the original interest keywords.

6 Experimentation and Evaluation

We developed a prototype MPV Plus on Windows OS. The MPV Plus server has been constructed on a laptop PC that had a processor Pentium M 1.7 GB and a main memory of 2 GB, and developed by Perl and Microsoft Visual Studio .Net C#, and the morphological analysis was Mecab[9]. This section presents the experimental results obtained with the prototype system and discusses impression vector changes in interest keywords utilizing the user's browsing history. The system collected and stored meta-data on article pages from six news sites. The articles were collected on April 28, 2005 between 9:00-9:30 am and there was a total of 255 articles with meta-data. The MPV site categorized and integrated the meta-data based on the user preferences. The extraction threshold for keywords of interest was established as 0.06 because at least an interest keyword must be extracted from each article, and the extraction threshold for words such as proper nouns and general nouns in each article was established as 0.1 because at least 11 words must be extracted from each article.

6.1 Category Integration

Figure 2 shows another MPV Plus page created using the top page of another news site when the same user specified that page after he or she read the article. The original top page is on the left, and the MPV Plus page on the right. The content of the three areas of this Plus page has changed because the user's preferences have been modified by his or her browsing. First, the original category keyword area was mapped onto the user's interest keywords, and then the top news article with an image was selected based on interest keywords and displayed as an unread title. Then, the titles of each article in each category were replaced with articles containing interest keywords and higher impression vectors.

Figure 3 shows the integrated categories. The left side shows the original category such as "society", "sports", "business" etc., and the right side shows the category as replaced by our system. For example, "society " was replaced with "China". Furthermore, some replaced categories are integrated based on the ratio of the same articles they contain. For example, the categories named "Ichiro (baseball player)" and "Rangers (baseball team)" were integrated because many articles were shared by those categories.

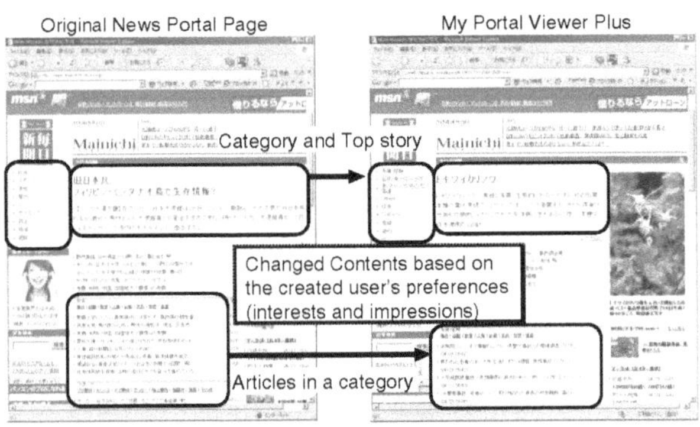

Fig. 2. MPV Plus page showing results

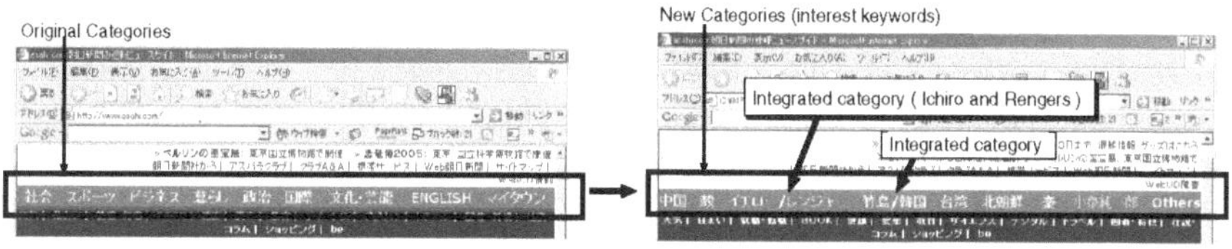

Fig. 3. Each category is integrated by MPV Plus

From those results, the user can easily access interesting news articles based on his or her preferences such as interests and impressions and does not need to access different news sites to look for target articles from various categories defined by the original news sites.

6.2 Impression Vector

To evaluate the article selection method based on impressions we have to consider three user browsing situations: (1) the user continuously selects a specific topic such as Iraq, (2) the user selects specific randomly repeated topics such as Iraq, Matsui, or Bush, and (3) the user selects topics that are not repeated. The impression vector can only be evaluated in situation (1) because each impression vector is calculated by each topic. We measured the average and standard deviation values of the impression vectors in situation (1) and considered how each value is changed by the user's browsing history.

Figure 4 shows the changes in the average and standard deviation values. Both graphs have values from *e1* to *e4*, and each value represents four elements of impression vectors. In this case, a user selects an article about "*topic of acountry*" which expresses an opinion the user agrees with or opposes. The user first selected the article at random and then gradually selected an article expressing an opinion he or she disagreed with. The standard deviation value

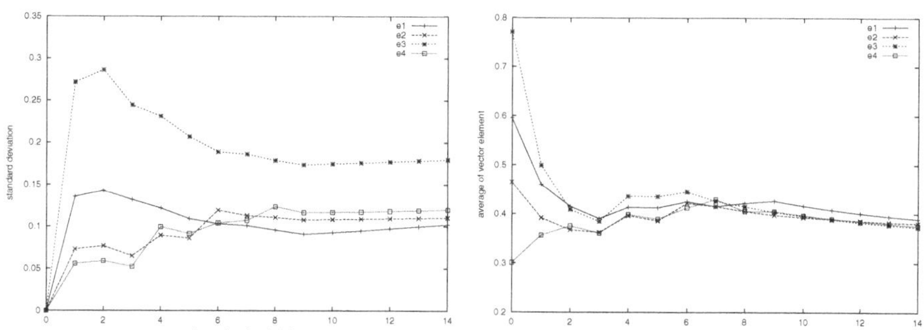

Fig. 4. Changes in average and standard deviation of impression vector based on user's browsing history (keyword of interest is a country name): Changes in standard deviation value (left), Changes in average value (right)

about *e1* of "happy ⇔ unhappy" and *e3* of "relaxation ⇔ strain" was a little high in the start (Fig.4 (left)). However, that value of *e1* and *e3* gradually decreased because the user's selection because he or she often selected articles expressing opinions in opposition to his or her own. So, the average value of *e1* was smaller than 0.5 (Fig.4 (right)), and this value shows that articles with unhappy impressions were selected by the user, and the impression is modeled correctly. Other average values of *e2*, *e3* and *e4* also showed that the selected articles had impressions of "rejection, strain, and anger". As in the above, we showed that MPV Plus can select and recommend articles to users based not only on interests but also on impressions.

7 Related Work

There has been considerable investigation of portal site technology for gathering, categorizing, personalizing, and integrating information.

MSN NewsPot[2] uses not only collection and classification technology but also personalization technology. A user's preferred articles are selected using personalized information based on his browsing history. However, the method of article selection is not good enough because the system only adapts to user interest, and the selected articles are not categorized.

Methods of extracting information about writers from movie reviews, book reviews, and production evaluation questionnaires also have been studied. Turney [10] proposed a method of classifying various genres of reviews into "recommended" or "not recommended". His method extracts specific patterns of phrases from input text, calculates mutual information, and takes the difference, where the two reference words were heuristically determined by him. However, using this method it is difficult to satisfy multiple impressions because the two reference words were designed only for a specific impression scale; "recommended – not recommended". We hit on the idea of classifying input documents into two or more impression classifications using a text classification method.

Many researchers have previously tackled the problem of creating more accurate classifiers using less accurate answer data [11,12]. However, they were not successful because their methods required a large amount of correct answer data. Our method, by contrast, can classify documents using only a little correct data, which can be reused as correct answer data, and which may contribute to the creation of classifiers that are sufficiently accurate.

8 Conclusions

We have proposed an algorithm of "interests and impressions of articles" and a modeling method of user preferences for the articles. The algorithm dynamically determines interest keywords and impression vectors which a user might potentially prefer based on a history of the articles that the user has read up to that time. Using the proposed modeling, we have developed a novel application called

"MPV Plus", which effectively integrates many articles collected from multiple news sites and recommends articles the user may have more affinity for.

We have developed a prototype that showed that users could easily access and read news articles of interest and with particular impressions from the collected articles. Based on this experimentation, which evaluated changes such as average and standard deviation value of impression vectors, we showed that MPV Plus can select and recommend articles for users using their interests and impressions. In the future, we plan to evaluate MPV Plus by monitoring many people, and will adapt the technology of user preference modeling to other types of Web sites such as shopping sites.

References

1. Yukiko Kawai, Daisuke Kanjo, and Katsumi Tanaka. My portal viewer: Integration system based on user preferences for news web sites. In *16th International Conference on Database and Expert Systems Applications (DEXA2005)*, pp. 156–165, August 2005.
2. Newsbot. http://uk.newsbot.msn.com.
3. GoogleNews. http://news.google.co.jp.
4. Deng Cai, Shipeng Yu, Ji-Rong Wen, and Wei-Ying Ma. Extracting content structure for web pages based on visual representation. In *APWeb*, Vol. 2642, pp. 406–417, Xian, China, 2003. Springer, Lecture Notes in Computer Science.
5. Yukiko Kawai, Daisuke Kanjo, and Katsumi Tanaka. Personal viewer for news content integration based on user's behavior. In *IPSJ Transactions on Databases*, June 2005.
6. Robert Plutchik and Henry Kellerman (eds). *Emotion: Theory, Research, and Experience*, Vol. 1 of *Academic Press Inc.*, pp. 3–33. 1980.
7. Inc. Nihon Keizai Shimbun. Nikkei newspaper full text database dvd-rom, 1990 to 1995 editions, 1996 to 2000 editions, 2001 edition.
8. Tadahiko Kumamoto and Katsumi Tanaka. Proposal of impression mining from news articles. In *Proceedings of International Conference on Knowledge-Based Intelligent & Engineering Systems, Melbourne, Australia (2005)*, 2005.
9. MeCab (2004). http://chasen.org/ taku/software/mecab/.
10. Peter D. Turney. Thumbs up or thumbs down? semantic orientation applied to unsupervised classification of reviews. In *Proc. Conference on Association for Computational Linguistics*, 2002.
11. Nagata M and Taira H. Text classification — Trade fair of learning theories. In *IPSJ Magazine, series 42*, 2001.
12. Tsukamoto K and Sassano M. Text categorization using active learning with AdaBoost. In *IPSJ SIG Notes, NL126-13*, 2001.

Cleaning Web Pages for Effective Web Content Mining*

Jing Li and C.I. Ezeife

School of Computer Science, University of Windsor,
Windsor, Ontario, Canada N9B 3P4
cezeife@uwindsor.ca
http://www.cs.uwindsor.ca/~cezeife

Abstract. Classifying and mining noise-free web pages will improve on accuracy of search results as well as search speed, and may benefit webpage organization applications (e.g., keyword-based search engines and taxonomic web page categorization applications). Noise on web pages are irrelevant to the main content on the web pages being mined, and include advertisements, navigation bar, and copyright notices. The few existing work on web page cleaning detect noise blocks with exact matching contents but are weak at detecting near duplicate blocks, characterized by items like navigation bars.

This paper proposes a system, WebPageCleaner, for eliminating noise blocks from web pages for purposes of improving the accuracy and efficiency of web content mining. A vision-based technique is employed for extracting blocks from web pages. Then, relevant web page blocks are identified as those with high importance level by analyzing such physical features of the blocks as the block location, percentage of web links on the block, and level of similarity of block contents to other blocks. Important blocks are exported to be used for web content mining using Naive Bayes text classification. Experiments show that WebPageCleaner leads to a more accurate and efficient web page classification results than comparable existing approaches.

Keywords: Web Page Cleaning, Noise Block, Web Content Mining, Classification, Near-Duplicate, Text Similarity.

1 Introduction

This paper states that noise on web pages have negative impact on web mining results, and should be cleaned before applying mining tasks to web pages. This paper proposes a preprocessing system, WebPageCleaner, which cleans web pages before mining their contents, for more effective and accurate mining results. Looking at a web page, it can be observed that it consists of many blocks.

* This research was supported by the Natural Science and Engineering Research Council (NSERC) of Canada under an Operating grant (OGP-0194134) and a University of Windsor grant.

S. Bressan, J. Küng, and R. Wagner (Eds.): DEXA 2006, LNCS 4080, pp. 560–571, 2006.

A block is a semantic part of a web page, which has its own text content, style and functionality. A web page usually contains main content blocks and noise blocks. Only the main content blocks represent the informative part that most users are interested in. Although other blocks are helpful in enriching functionality and guiding browsing, they negatively affect such web mining tasks as web page clustering and classification by reducing the accuracy of mined results as well as speed of processing. Thus, these blocks are called noise blocks in this context. For example, a CNN web page, has in the center of the page a sports news report, which is the main content of this page. In addition, there are advertisements, navigation bars, and others, positioned around the main content, which are regarded as noise blocks. Noise blocks negatively affect web content mining results because contents contained in noise blocks are irrelevant to the main content of the web page. As one of the approaches in web content mining, web page classification [Shen et al., 2004] is used to demonstrate the negative impact of noise blocks during web page mining. Web page classification is an application that is commonly seen in taxonomic web page categories used in web search, such as Yahoo directory (http://dir.yahoo.com). Thus, cleaning web pages before text classification techniques are applied to web pages during classification leads to more accurate results and is beneficial.

The basic idea of the web page cleaning system being proposed, WebPageCleaner, is first to segment web pages into a set of blocks using a vision-based page segmentation (VIPS) algorithm [Cai et al., 2003]. The VIPs algorithm segments web pages using Document object model (DOM) tree with a combination of human visual cues like tag cue, color cue, size cue etc. Then, WebPageCleaner identifies noise blocks using the following four features of noise blocks as observed on web pages: (1) the collection of web pages belonging to an enterprise web site share common contents and look and feel; (2) each of the site's web pages contains some noisy blocks that contain re-occurring common contents; (3) these noise blocks are usually located at the edges of the web page; and (4) noise blocks usually contain many links in their contents.

This paper contributes to the web page cleaning problem by applying an efficient web segmentation technique to web cleaning using appropriate parameters so as to improve on results of web content mining. Section 2 presents related work. The proposed WebPageCleaner system is illustrated with an example cleaning of a set of web pages in section 3. In section 4, the experimental results are shown, section 5 presents conclusions and future work.

2 Related Work

In [Lin & Ho, 2002], a system, InfoDiscoverer, is proposed to discover informative content blocks from web documents. It first partitions a web page into several content blocks according to HTML tag <TABLE>. A limitation of this work is that it is restricted to tabular (with <TABLE> tags) web pages. A style tree structure is proposed in [Yi, Liu & Li, 2003] to capture the layout and contents of pages in a given web site. Bar-Yossef et al. [Bar-Yossef & Rajagopalan, 2002] propose a template detection algorithm. Based on the number of links an HTML element has, it partitions each web page into several pagelets, which are units with well defined topic or functionality. Templates are then detected by identifying duplicate pagelets, but it does not work well when detecting near duplicate pagelets. A VIsion-based Page Segmentation (VIPS) algorithm is proposed in [Cai et al., 2003], that segments web pages using DOM tree with a combination of human visual cues, including tag cue, color cue, size cue, and others. The VIPS algorithm has been applied to information retrieval, information extraction, and learning block importance on a single page [Song et al., 2004]. It has not been used on web page cleaning on a set of web pages for the purposes of web page classification. This work is also related to approaches in data cleaning for data warehousing [Ezeife & Ohanekwu, 2005], [Hernandez & Stolfo, 1995] but applies to web page cleaning, for detecting noise blocks in web pages.

3 The Proposed WebPageCleaner System

The goal of WebPageCleaner is to improve web content mining (e.g., web page classification) results. The target sets of web pages are those belonging to organizations because the presentation style in one enterprise web site is similar and easy to capture across its numerous web pages. Then, cleaned files from each individual web site consisting of record descriptions of highly important blocks of the web sites, can simply be merged into a big dataset for mining.

Algorithm 1. *(WebPageCleaner:Eliminates Noise Blocks from Web Pages)*

Algorithm WebPageCleaner()
Input: a set of web pages (W) from a given web site, maximum number of blocks for outputting in each web page (N).
Output: a set of plain text documents with noisy items removed from input web pages.
begin
(1) Apply VIPS algorithm to segment set of web pages, W into blocks, and extract block features and store as database records (Section 3.1).
(2) Compute block importance based on the level of block content similarity, block position, and linkage percentage (Section 3.1).
(3) Generate cleaned files records by selecting N blocks with high importance from each web page.
end

Fig. 1. The Main WebPageCleaner Algorithm

3.1 Steps in WebPageCleaner System

Given a set of web pages from a web site, the whole cleaning system follows the three steps below in cleaning. Step 1: Block Extraction module first segments each web page into blocks, and extracts the contents and other features of blocks as database records. Step 2: Block Importance Retrieval module computes each block importance based on the similarity of the block contents, its position in the web page, and percentage of contained link texts; Step 3: Cleaned Files Generation module for grouping block records with high importance degrees in each web page into files for web content mining. Each module is described next. Algorithm for the main steps in the system is summarized in Figure 1.

Step 1: Block Extraction

Given a web page, WebPageCleaner, first extracts blocks using the VIPS page partition algorithm [Cai et al., 2003], which represents a web page as a semantic content tree by combining web page DOM tree and its visual cues (e.g., background color, font size, block location, etc) and presented as an XML file. Then, each block in the leaf nodes, and their features including ids, contents, positions, and percentage of linkages are extracted from the tree. A set of features for every block is stored in database relationships as: Blocks(PageID, BlockID, BlockText, Fingerprint, PosLevel, LinkPer, SimilarLevel, ImLevel), in which PageID denotes the web page being processed. BlockID represents the distinct block extracted from that page. BlockText is the text content in the block with punctuations removed and capitalization ignored. By doing this, the contents consist of a sequence of words separated by white spaces. Fingerprints are short tags for identifying large objects. In this paper, they are integer values for identifying long text documents calculated with Rabin's fingerprint formula [Rabin, 1981]. Fingerprint is used for quickly identifying duplicate blocks in the database. PosLevel indicates the location of block on the web page and the closer the PosLevel is to 1, the less important the block is. To compute the PosLevel, we first extract four features from the VIPS content tree, including PageRectWidth, PageRectHeight, ObjectRectLeft, and ObjectRectTop. PageRectWidth and PageRectHeight denote the width and the height of the web page respectively. ObjectRectLeft denotes the distance from blocks left edge to pages left edge. ObjectRectTop is the distance between blocks top edge and pages top edge. Based on these features, block's horizontal (P_x) and vertical (P_y) positions in the whole page using the top left corner as the origin are captured.

$$P_x = \frac{ObjectRectLeft}{PageRectWidth} \quad ; \quad P_y = \frac{ObjectRectTop}{PageRectHeight}$$

P_x and P_y range from 0 to 1. The closer they are either to 0 or 1, the closer the block is to the edge of the page, and higher the likelihood of the block being a noise block. To make position value consistent with other level metrics, which the closer it is to 0, the less important a block is, we introduce $PosLevel_x$ and $PosLevel_y$ as follows:

$$PosLevel_x = \begin{cases} 2P_x & \text{if } 0 \le P_x \le 0.5 \\ 2(1-P_x) & \text{if } 0.5 < P_x \le 1 \end{cases} \tag{1}$$

$PosLevel_y$ is defined in a similar way by substituting P_y for P_x. We further introduce PosLevel, which combines $PosLevel_x$ and $PosLevel_y$ to represent the position importance using a single parameter:

$$PosLevel = 1 - \frac{PosLevel_x + PosLevel_y}{2} \quad (0 \le PosLevel \le 1) \qquad (2)$$

According to formulars (1) and (2), we can get the PosLevel directly from P_x and P_y as follows:

$$PosLevel = \begin{cases} 1 - P_x - P_y & \text{if } 0 \le P_x \le 0.5 \text{ and } 0 \le P_y \le 0.5 \\ P_y - P_x & \text{if } 0 \le P_x \le 0.5 \text{ and } 0.5 < P_y \le 1 \\ P_x - P_y & \text{if } 0.5 < P_x \le 1 \text{ and } 0 \le P_y \le 0.5 \\ P_x + P_y - 1 & \text{if } 0.5 < P_x \le 1 \text{ and } 0.5 < P_y \le 1 \end{cases}$$

This way, a single position measurement PosLevel of a block is obtained, and closer the PosLevel is to 1, the less important a block is. LinkPer denotes the percentage of links in a block, which is obtained by dividing the length of link texts (in terms of number of characters) by the length of all texts in a block: $LinkPer = LinkTextLen/TextLen$, where LinkTextLen and TextLen can be extracted from the VIPS content tree. If the LinkPer is close to 1, a large percentage of contents are links in this block, then, it is more likely a noise block. SimilarLevel denotes how similar two block contents are. The initial value is set to 0 (indicating not similar). ImLevel denotes the overall importance of a block. The initial value of ImLevel is set to 1 (indicating important). After extracting block features from VIPs content tree, the similarity and importance levels of the blocks are not yet known, but each block at this stage is assumed unique and important. Both SimilarLevel and ImLevel are assigned new values in the second module after comparison with other block records. The result of this first stage of cleaning is a collection of blocks described with attributes of database table, Blocks.

Example Block Extraction from Sample Web Pages

Figure 2 shows fragments of two web pages P_1 and P_2 grabbed from Future Shop (http://www.futureshop.ca) web site. To segment these web pages into blocks, entails applying the VIPS [Cai et al., 2003] algorithm to P_1 and P_2 with Predefined Degree of Coherence value (PDoC) set to 6. PDoC is normally between 1 and 10, where higher PDoC (of around 10) partitions a web page into more blocks than lower PDoC (of around 1) does. The partition results are shown in Figure 2 (enclosed within rectangles). For page P_1, page features are obtained from the content tree, where for example, $PageRectWidth = 780$, $PageRectHeight = 2001$. After extracting each block in the leaf nodes of the content tree, three blocks are extracted from each web page. The BlockText is then processed by transforming all letters to lower case and removing punctuations. BlockText is obtained as "entire site advance search". Fingerprint is then calculated for this text, assume the value is 12178. Similarly, all of these attributes are computed for every block and the same process applied to page P_2. A Blocks table (the first six columns) as shown in Table 1 is the result of this phase of cleaning since initially SimilarLevel is set to 0 and ImLevel set to 1 for all records and their actual values determined in the second phase for final noisy block record elimination. Noisy blocks have relatively larger PosLevel and LinkPer values and also share same or similar contents as shown in the next section.

Fig. 2. Fragments of Two Web Pages with Their VIPS Partition Results

Table 1. Blocks Table after Block Extraction and Block Importance Retrieval

Page ID	Block ID	BlockText	Fingerprint	PosLevel	LinkPer	Similar Level	ImLevel
1	1	entire site advance search	12178	0.944	0.556	0	out
1	2-1	home tv video 40 and projection television more 40 and projection televisions	34098	0.724	0.903	0.2	0.478
1	2-2	toshiba 52hm84 52 digital widescreen dlp tv	18902	0.706	0	0	0.882
2	1	entire site advance search	12178	0.93	0.556	0.2	out
2	2-1	home computcr dcsktop computer more desktop computer	23412	0.71	0.859	0.2	0.481
2	2-2	hp pavilion a810 athlon 64 3300 2.4ghz computer	27681	0.696	0	0	0.884

Step 2: Block Importance Retrieval

Three phenomena for the block content exist: exactly same, approximately same, and different. Examples of exactly same contents include the heading of the web site, copyright notice, etc. They are noise blocks that should be removed first. The challenge is on how to recognize blocks with approximately same contents. Once we figure this out, the rest of the blocks with different contents are the distinguishable parts of a page that will be viewed as outputs in our problem or clean content. To delete blocks with same contents, WebPageCleaner, first goes through the Blocks table to delete all blocks with the same fingerprint values (same contents). Then, it calculates SimilarLevel for the rest of the blocks. SimilarLevel is defined as the number of common tokens over the number of all unique tokens in two blocks. It is obtained by sorting the Blocks table in ascending order according to BlockText attribute. This brings similar contents closely. Then, it calculates for each pair of neighboring blocks the similarity level as SimilarLevel. For example, after sorting Table 1 according to BlockText attribute, block 2–1 of page 2 is neighbor to block 2–1 of page 1. By counting the number of same and total unique words, SimilarLevel value of the two records is $2/10 = 0.2$. SimilarLevel value is set for both records being compared. As we slide down the window to compare new records, we probably get a new SimilarLevel for newly compared blocks. The rule is that if the new SimilarLevel is greater than the old SimilarLevel, then update the SimilarLevel value with the new one, otherwise, keep the old one. Thus, each block gets SimilarLevel with the most similar block that is neighboring to it. Finally, the block importance level ImLevel is obtained after getting values of PosLevel, LinkPer, and SimilarLevel for each block. ImLevel is defined as: $ImLevel = 1 - (1/2\ SimilarLevel + 1/3\ LinkPer + 1/6\ PosLevel)$, where $0 \leq ImLevel \leq 1$. In this formula, we take the SimilarLevel as the most important measurement, then, LinkPer and PosLevel. The reason is that the content is the most distinct feature that differentiates one block from the other. The percentage of links and block positions can be used as auxiliary measurements for deciding the block importance. The closer the ImLevel is to 1, the more important a block is. By applying block importance retrieval module to Table 1, the result is shown in the last two columns of Table 1 where records already removed due to Fingerprints are marked as 'out' and the SimilarLevel and ImLevel are now used for final record elimination.

Step 3: Cleaned Files Generation
In this module, up to N block records with the highest ImLevel value in each web page are exported to be integrated into cleaned records for mining. N typically represents the average number of informative blocks in each web page (e.g., although the example web page has 3 blocks, only one is informative) and N information can be obtained by observing VIPs partitioning results of various web pages, or from experience or fixed at a reasonable level of 3 as done by other techniques. For example, if we define N equal to 1 for this example, the output of Table 1 will be blocks 2-2 of page 1 and 2. Contents in BlockText attribute that belong to one web page are extracted to generate a plain text document, which contains the most relevant information of this web page. Mapping this result to the original web pages in Figure 2, we can see that the bottom right blocks of each page are final output blocks. After processing web pages with the above three modules, the problem of web page classification is transformed to a pure text classification problem without losing any representative information of the page.

4 Experiments and Performance Analysis

Experiments contain two parts: web page cleaning and classification on cleaning results of records. For experiments on web page cleaning, the execution speed between template detection method [Bar-Yossef & Rajagopalan, 2002] (TPL) and WebPageCleaner (WPC) is compared. Naive Bayes text classification has shown very good performance in many approaches [McCallum & Nigam, 1998]. By training a set of pre-labeled documents, the Naive Bayes classifier achieves the probability of words in given classes. The training models are then applied on testing documents to get the probability of classes given a document. For experiments on classification, Naive Bayes text classification is performed on (1) non-cleaned web pages with HTML tags removed(NC), (2) web pages cleaned using template detection method [Bar-Yossef & Rajagopalan, 2002] (TPL), and (3) web pages cleaned using the proposed WebPageCleaner (WPC), respectively. The classification accuracy and speed are compared for these three methods. Experiments on web page cleaning are performed on a PC with 2.39 GHz AMD CPU, 1.00 GB of RAM, running on Windows XP Operating System. Naive Bayes text classification is performed using the statistical text processing package, Rainbow toolkit [McCallum, 1996]. Classification accuracy is measured by the percentage of the number of correctly labeled documents divided by the total number of testing documents. $Accuracy = total\ number\ of\ correct\ classifications/total\ number\ of\ classifications \times 100\%$. Standard Error (SE) measures the variance that occurs between the sample means when a number of different samples are drawn from the same population to build the classifier for several trials. The smaller the standard error is, the more stable the classification done for each trial. $SE = \sqrt{\partial_1^2 + \partial_2^2 + \cdots + \partial_n^2/n}$ Efficiency is measured by the number of unique words in Naive Bayes classifier and the running speed (in seconds) of classification. Since word is the basic unit for generating Naive Bayes model and doing classification, using documents that have fewer number of words can result in better efficient classification.

Experiments on Web Page Cleaning. We downloaded 2500 web pages from 4 commercial product web sites, including Future Shop (http://www.futureshop.ca), Best Buy (http://www.bestbuy.com), CNet (http://www.cnet.com), and Amazon (http://www.amazon.com). These web pages contain products from 5 categories, including computer, TV, phone, software, and MP3. Details of distributions of pages are shown in Table 2. Execution time is compared between template detection method (TPL) with partition granularity, k of 3 and WebPageCleaner (WPC) with PDoC of 6. While the k and PDoc values used for the separate algorithms are not directly comparable, they are both selected through experience running the algorithms on a test data with varying values and selecting the k and PDoC values provide the best semantic grouping of page contents and best mining results. The number of cleaned blocks to select, N value is set to 3, which outputs up to three blocks with the highest importance level, the execution times achieved by algorithms TPL and WPC are shown in Table 3.

Table 2. Distribution of Experimental Web Pages in Their Web Site and Categories

	Web Sites	Computer	MP3	Phone	Software	TV	Total in Site
S1	Future Shop	173	62	140	243	134	752
S2	Best Buy	134	87	157	111	96	585
S3	CNet	161	107	197	74	299	838
S4	Amazon	70	98	47	18	92	325

Table 3. Execution times for TPL and WPC cleaning methods

Web Sites	Number of Pages	Execution Time (Second)	
		TPL	WPC
Best Buy	585	107	61
CNet	838	230	150
Future Shop	752	143	92
Amazon	325	100	54

4.1 Experiments on Web Page Classification

In this experiment, Naive Bayes text classification is applied on the three different data sets, cleaned using the three approaches of not cleaned (NC), Template (TPL) and WebPageCleaner (WPC). Classification accuracy and efficiency are compared on these three datasets. To run Naive Bayes text classification on the dataset, all experimental documents are divided into training data and testing data. Documents in training set have known their class labels, and are used for training classifiers. Testing documents are used to test the accuracy of the trained classifiers. To investigate the way that noisy contents affect classification results, we set two cases for experiments based on whether training data are selected evenly from each class of each web site or not. **Case 1:** training data is selected automatically and evenly. In experimental case 1, a small number of documents (less than 20%) are used for training. Six sub cases are set which use 25, 50, 75, 100, 250, 500 documents automatically selected from the whole data sets for training, and use the remaining documents for testing, respectively. The average percentage accuracy and standard error are shown in Table 4. The efficiency of classification on datasets obtained with different methods in experiment shown in Table 4 are measured with number of unique words and the running times from the three datasets as NC (58994 unique words, 10.06 sec time), TPL (53417, 4.56 sec) and WPC (32434, 3.35 sec). Running times present the average speed of classification on 10 trials of six sub cases for each dataset. **Case 2:** training data is selected unevenly. In this experiment, the dataset with 2500 documents is divided into four folds, which are 625 documents in each fold. To balance the effect by unevenly selected training sets, a four-fold cross validation is implemented on this experimental case. Four sub cases are set by using three folds for training, and one fold for testing each time. The classification accuracy and efficiency on each case of four-fold cross validation are shown in Table 5.

Table 4. Average accuracy on 10 trials with different number of training documents

Case	Train	Test	Methods	Average Accuracy (%)	Standard Error
1-1	25 (5 per class)	2475	NC	79.41	2.13
			TPL	88.63	1.41
			WPC	**91.10**	0.69
1-2	50 (10 per class)	2450	NC	90.52	1.01
			TPL	92.42	0.96
			WPC	**95.44**	0.40
1-3	75 (15 per class)	2425	NC	95.44	0.42
			TPL	94.19	0.70
			WPC	**97.05**	0.22
1-4	100 (20 per class)	2400	NC	94.89	0.43
			TPL	94.45	0.33
			WPC	**97.11**	0.20
1-5	250 (50 per class)	2250	NC	97.40	0.37
			TPL	97.33	0.21
			WPC	**98.64**	0.12
1-6	500 (100 per class)	2000	NC	97.97	0.27
			TPL	98.09	0.09
			WPC	**99.00**	0.06

Table 5. Classification performance on each case of four-fold cross validation

Case	Methods	Accuracy	Number of Unique Words in Training Set	Time (Second)
2-1	NC	81.28	49974	8.0
	TPL	93.43	45753	4.94
	WPC	**97.92**	29540	4.23
2-2	NC	89.44	52138	6.69
	TPL	98.88	49537	3.24
	WPC	**99.04**	24289	2.23
2-3	NC	81.28	46005	6.48
	TPL	94.39	37939	2.98
	WPC	**97.44**	29502	2.29
2-4	NC	66.72	55362	6.62
	TPL	**98.24**	49550	3.2
	WPC	98.08	30040	2.36

The average classification accuracy and standard error on four-fold cross validation are for method NC (79.68, 4.07), for method TPL (96.23, 1.18) and for method WPC (98.12, 0.29). When noisy elements are removed from web pages using TPL or WPC methods, Naive Bayes classifier collects useful information on categories not affected by noise at web sites, so classification results are much better. Although TPL gets good accuracy, WPC still performs better than TPL does. On one hand, documents cleaned by TPL contain more noisy items, which decrease both classification accuracy and efficiency. On the other hand, the execution time for TPL is much longer than WPC, which can be seen from Table 3.

From results above, we can also see that WPC still gets the best classification accuracy and less standard error.

5 Conclusions and Future Work

The proposed WebPageCleaner system consists of three modules: block extraction, block importance retrieval, and cleaned files generation. The first module aims at getting the semantic content blocks from web pages. In the second module, blocks are sorted according to their contents to bring blocks with similar contents closely, and then the similarity level is computed for each neighboring pair of blocks. According to the similar level, percentage of links, and block position, the importance level for each block is calculated. Finally, a set of cleaned files are generated, which consist of up to N relevant blocks records with the highest importance levels in each page that can be fed to web content classification techniques. Although template-based approach can remove standard noisy template of a web site, it is hard to figure a site's template if one does not exist. Large sites, may have several templates for its many categories and if these are not all available in the test data set, the template approach may fail to detech duplicate blocks, while the WebPageCleaner can judge duplicate blocks from high text similarity, high text linkage percentage and others.

Future work should explore a schema that makes the Blocks table as a template datasets for a web site. Then, new web pages from that site can be mapped to the template datasets in order to clean new pages online. Such cleaned templates may also be made applicable in portable devices, such as cell phones and PDA since these devices have small browsers and only the most informative contents appropriate are displayed. More parameters like the number of images and video clips on the page blocks can also be used in judging the importance of page blocks. Work can also be extended to develop noisy templates that are easily identifiable and cleaned. Scaling technique on large web crawls of over ten million web pages may entail partitioning, cleaning and mergin of results and other methods for scalability remain open issues.

References

[Bar-Yossef & Rajagopalan, 2002] Bar-Yossef, Z. and Rajagopalan, S. 2002. Template detection via data mining and its applications. *In Proceedings of the 11th International Conference on World Wide Web, Honolulu, Hawaii, USA*, pages 580–591.

[Cai et al., 2003] Cai, D., Yu, S., Wen., J.-R. and Ma, W.-Y. 2003. Extracting content structure for web pages based on visual representation. *In Proceedings of the 5th Asia Pacific Web Conference, Xi'an, China*, pages 406–417.

[Ezeife & Ohanekwu, 2005] Ezeife, C.I. and Ohanekwu, T.E. 2005. Use of smart tokens in cleaning integrated warehouse data. *The International Journal of Data Warehousing and Mining (IJDW), Ideas Group Publishers, April–June 2005, Vol. 1, No. 2*, pages 1–22.

[Hernandez & Stolfo, 1995] Hernandez, M. and Stolfo, S. 1995. The merge/purge problem for large databases. *In Proceedings of the ACM SIGMOD, San Jose, CA, May 1995*, pages 127–138.

[Lin & Ho, 2002] Lin, S.-H. and Ho, J.-M. 2002. Discovering informative content blocks from web documents. *In Proceedings of the 8th ACM SIGKDD Knowledge Discovery and Data Mining, Edmonton, Canada* , pages 588–593.

[McCallum, 1996] McCallum, A. 1996. Bow: A toolkit for statistical language modeling, text retrieval, *http://www-2.cs.cmu.edu/ mccallum/bow/rainbow* .

[McCallum & Nigam, 1998] McCallum, A. and Nigam, K. 1998. A comparison of event models for Naive Bayes text classification. *In Proceedings of AAAI–98 Workshop on Learning for Text Categorization. AAAI Press* , pages 41–48.

[Rabin, 1981] Rabin, M.O. 1999. Fingerprinting by random polynomials. *Technical Report TR-15-81, Harvard University.*

[Shen et al., 2004] Shen, D., Chen, Z., Zeng, H.-J., Zhang, B., Yang, Q., Ma, W.-Y. and Lu, Y. 2004. Web-page classification through summarization. *In Proceedings of the 27th Annual International ACM SIGIR Conference (SIGIR'2004) on Research and Development in Information Retrieval, Sheffield, United Kingdom,* pages 242–249.

[Song et al., 2004] Song, R., Liu, H., Wen, J.-R. and Ma, W.-Y. 2004 Learning block importance models for Web pages. *In Proceedings of the 13th International Conference on World Wide Web, New York, NY, USA*, pages 203–211.

[Yi, Liu & Li, 2003] Yi, L., Liu, B. and Li, X. 2003 Eliminating noisy information in Web pages for data mining. *In Proceedings of the 9th ACM SIGKDD on Knowledge Discovery and Data Mining, Washington, D.C*, pages 296–305.

An Applied Optimization Framework for Distributed Air Transportation Environments*

Thomas Castelli, Joshua Lee, and Waseem Naqvi

Raytheon Company, Network Centric Systems
1001 Boston Post Road
Marlborough, MA 01752 USA
{Thomas_J_Castelli, leejm, Waseem_Naqvi}@raytheon.com

Abstract. In a large-scale dynamic system with multiple distributed entities, each with their own set of interests, there is a need to find a globally acceptable and optimal solution state. This solution state is, by definition, efficient to all entities with respect to their own individual goals and to the system as a whole. In these dynamic environments, this solution state can be achieved by utilizing software techniques from the field of game theory in order to make optimal decisions. We present an application built upon a generalized optimization framework that can be applied to a number of domains, such as cargo or network traffic algorithms. In this research, we used a market-based approach to air traffic flow management through a modeling and simulation environment. The aim is to allow individual aircraft a certain degree of local autonomy, much like cars on a highway. Our system is able to cope in real time with failures such as node loss and adjust system parameters accordingly to optimize results based on the goals of the involved agents. We describe tradeoffs between different agent interaction frameworks with respect to their performance in market mechanism auctions. We also discuss lessons learned while implementing this application. This research has built upon our previously reported work [20, 21] on route optimizations and airspace sector design in an air traffic control network, by adding in the goals of interested entities, e.g. airlines, aircraft, and airports, maximizing the "payoff" to each player (agent). It is intended that the results of our work will be directly used in this domain. In addition, we envision our work being leveraged for other optimization tasks such as data traffic on a network, first responder / disaster relief efforts, and other tasks where rapid solving of large-scale optimization problems is essential.

1 Introduction

We have developed a generalized optimization framework and a prototype simulation that employs this framework in the air traffic management domain. Our optimization framework, Global Optimizer and Local Strategizer (GOALS), can be applied to any number of domains where real-time optimization involving dynamic information is desired, for example, first responder communication networks, or data packet routing algorithms.

---

* Approved for public release through Raytheon Export Control, #TD-06-0017.

S. Bressan, J. Küng, and R. Wagner (Eds.): DEXA 2006, LNCS 4080, pp. 572–581, 2006.

In the air traffic management domain, the current state of modernization is focused on allowing aircraft a higher degree of autonomy. Efforts in the field are moving toward a concept of "free flight," which relaxes strict controls on routing and allows longer direct segments to be flown. In the United States, this modernization effort is evident in the Next Generation Air Transportation System (NGATS) program [15]. In Europe, the Single European Sky Air Traffic Management Research (SESAR) program [19] is working toward a less segmented air traffic management system. Given that the future of air transportation requires distributed optimization, we have investigated applying our framework in this domain with a prototype. This prototype is discussed in further detail in section 4 of this paper.

The GOALS framework consists of interested agents, which have certain local goals. A local goal is formulated by the agent without having knowledge of other agents or access to the complete state of the environment in which the agent resides. These local goals are expressed in terms of graph theory, specifically in the form of shortest path or maximum flow problems. In the future, other types of local goals may be implemented within the framework. We chose a graph representation because many of our products need the capability to solve optimization problems that can easily be represented in terms of a graph, even if the associated data changes quickly.

Each agent solves its goals locally, employing Dijkstra's algorithm for shortest path optimizations, and/or the Ford-Fulkerson method for maximum flow optimizations [4]. Once a locally optimal solution has been found, the resources needed to implement this solution are determined. The goals of some agents may be at odds with the goals of other agents. Therefore, to have each agent attempt to obtain the resources necessary for its own locally optimal solution without coordination would result in chaos. Maintaining order requires a negotiation method that allows conflicts between agents to be resolved in a manner that is beneficial to all. Rosenschein and Zlotkin [18] suggest using game theoretical methods for such negotiation, as computers are completely rational and emotionless. Our agents negotiate in the global space for a solution that may not be locally optimal for the agent, but is instead globally optimal for all agents.

The local agent attempts to obtain the needed resources in a marketplace, using methods such as market mechanism auctions [7]. If the resources necessary for a local agent's optimal solution are not available, the agent will try for the next best suboptimal solution, and so on until the necessary resources have been acquired. The resulting solution is globally optimal even if it is not locally optimal. Within a marketplace, each agent exercises its own strategies. The marketplace must allow for rapid processing in a large-scale, dynamic environment.

Our proof of concept air traffic management application uses an English auction (highest bid wins) methodology. The GOALS framework makes it easy to substitute another type of distributed market system for the English auction, and allows for parallel markets to operate simultaneously. We require market schema that operate in real time, are fault-tolerant, and can be distributed.

2 Overview of Principles

The GOALS framework is general enough to allow any type of market to be implemented and easily interfaced with our agents. Figure 1 shows a UML model of our market architecture. Any type of market inherits from the Market class. A market is effectively a forum where collector agents ("buyers") negotiate with distributor agents ("sellers") for available resources. In our application, we have modeled aircraft as collector agents, and centers (controllers) as distributor agents.

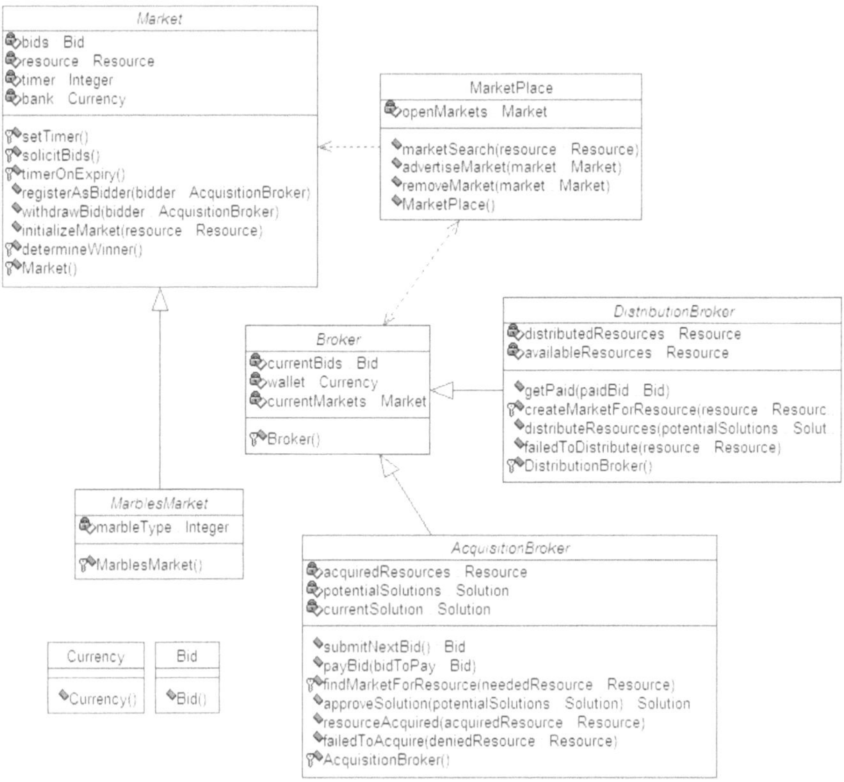

Fig. 1. UML Model of the Market package

One problem with using a standard English auction mechanism for markets is that it is possible in such a market for overly wealthy agents to starve out other agents, denying needed resources. A potential solution to this problem is the use of Vickrey-Clarke-Groves (VCG) auctions [16], which ensure fairness and honesty in the marketplace.

One implementation of VCG auction mechanisms which we considered was a Marbles system [7]. The main issue with the pure Marbles implementation is that Marbles strategies have a concept of an agent who gives up in bidding for a resource ("altruistically commit suicide by permanently withdrawing [7]") in order to serve the greater global good. For some applications of our framework, most notably in air traffic management applications, giving up is simply not an option. Our resources in this particular domain represent routes to fly. An aircraft in flight cannot give up on obtaining a path and hover in its current position. In such a case, aircraft and center agents (controllers) can negotiate amongst each other rather than each having a self-centered bidding strategy.

Each agent models its problem space as a graph. We model any airport, navigational fix, intersection, or navigational aid as a node. Airway sections can then be represented as edges between these nodes. Edge weights depend on the particular local goal desired. For example, if an aircraft's local goal is to minimize fuel usage, edge weights could represent the estimated amount of fuel used by traversing that edge.

It is anticipated that our agents will have some combination of goals, therefore a formula for edge weights must be determined which considers each goal. Either weights are determined using a single goal or by combining multiple goals, thus taking into account the importance of each local goal to the agent. Once this has been accomplished, we find the optimal solution with these weights in place. Each agent ranks the importance of its local goals. This ranking leads to a clear definition of the utility of a particular solution within the domain space. Therefore, the agent can create a function by which it determines the weights involved in its own local graph representation of the operating environment. This function will also reflect the dynamic nature of the situation; weather, for example, can affect the time in flight for an airway segment, and will change in time.

The ability to optimize multiple local goals simultaneously becomes important if an agent cannot acquire resources for an optimal solution and must fall back to a suboptimal solution. Any combination of local goals may be selected during the market phase. Weights might also be determined in relation to global efficiency so that greedy agents will find a globally optimal solution by performing their normal local optimization tasks [8]. This, however, may not be possible in a very large environment.

Within the GOALS framework, we allow parallel markets. In addition, there may be thousands of agents in the domain. It is therefore not practical nor desirable for any one agent to know everything about the state of the world. An agent representing an aircraft flying from Boston to Chicago need not know about air traffic conditions near Los Angeles, for example. However, these conditions may indirectly affect the global state and prevent a locally optimal solution from being globally optimal.

3 Types of Agents

The idea of using intelligent autonomous agents in an air traffic management system is not new. Ljungberg and Lucas [14] used Belief-Desire-Intention (BDI) agents [17] in their prior work on the OASIS air traffic management system in Australia. Two other intelligent agent approaches we considered include Partially Observable Markov Decision Processes (POMDPs) [12] and Distributed Constraint Optimization (DCO)[13]. The following subsections briefly describe these types of agent behaviors, which lend themselves well to situations in which the state of the entire domain cannot be completely known to any one agent.

3.1 BDI Agents

A BDI agent has certain "mental attitudes" guiding its behavior. These are beliefs, desires, and intentions. Beliefs represent the information that the agent has about its current environment. Desires represent the goals that an agent has, such as what would constitute an optimal solution. Intentions represent the methods by which the agent, acting based upon its beliefs about its environment, attempts to achieve its desires [17].

3.2 POMDPs

An agent using a POMDP models its environment using a Markov Decision Process (MDP). MDPs consist of a set of states of the world and a set of actions. There is a state transition function describing the state achieved from any specific state given a certain action is taken. There is also a reward function, which describes the expected immediate reward given for taking a certain action in a certain state. Actual rewards affect future decision-making activities. The agent acts in order to maximize the expected value of the long-term reward received.

"Partial Observability" refers to the fact that the agent is unable to determine its current state with complete reliability. Randomness is therefore added to the agent's behavior in order to compensate for the uncertainty of state. A POMDP consists of an MDP, a set of possible observations that the agent can make of its world, and an observation function, which yields a probability distribution of possible observations. This is further discussed in [12].

3.3 Distributed Constraint Optimization

Distributed Constraint Optimization (DCO) is similar to the approach we chose for our agents. Each agent is given a different overlapping sub problem. Agents using DCO first find a locally optimal solution to their assigned sub problem. Then, they must interact with other agents to find a globally optimal solution.

Liu and Sycara [13] used DCO to come up with solutions to the job shop-scheduling problem (which is NP-complete). The distributed optimization they propose involves agents exchanging local views with each other. Additional constraints are imposed by the local agent in an attempt to force its locally optimal solution. If the locally optimal solution cannot be accommodated, the local agent falls back to a suboptimal solution.

In our implementation, we do not exchange local views between agents, nor impose additional constraints. Our agents do not directly interact with each other. Should the required resources not be available within the marketplace, however, the local agent falls back to a locally suboptimal solution.

We chose this method for our agents because we needed an agent that would be able to learn optimal strategies in the marketplace, and to allow agents to have a level of local autonomy. The global solutions found would therefore become better with time and practice. In future work, we plan to combine DCO with BDI behaviors, so that agents would learn optimal marketplace strategies over time.

3.4 Existing Baseline Agent Frameworks

Several standard agent frameworks currently exist which would allow our GOALS framework to interoperate with other systems. The Foundation for Intelligent Physical Agents (FIPA) [6] has published a standard by which agents from different frameworks can communicate with each other. Among the agent frameworks we have investigated are IBM's Agent Building and Learning Environment (ABLE) [2], the Java Agent

Development Framework (JADE) [1], Cougaar [9], and Cybele. ABLE, JADE, and Cougaar are all available in the public domain.

Cybele is used as a basis for Raytheon's Airspace Concepts Evaluation System (ACES). We plan to interface our optimization framework and air traffic management application into ACES for further evaluation on larger data sets. GOALS is independent of the underlying agent infrastructure, hence we plan to implement agents in both ABLE and Cybele.

We selected Cybele because of its use in ACES. Additionally, we chose ABLE as a second agent type because it is FIPA-compliant, available as a Java library, and lends itself to quick implementation. JADE is also FIPA-compliant, and we may decide to implement an adapter for JADE in the future. The U.S. Defense Advanced Research Projects Agency (DARPA) has used Cougaar in the past; however, it is not FIPA-compliant, so compatibility with systems using other types of agents cannot be guaranteed. Therefore, we chose not to pursue implementation of Cougaar agents.

4 Implementation

For our prototype simulation, we address the problem of air traffic flow. Here, aircraft seek to fly enroute from airport to airport, through various categories of controlled airspace. There may be many impediments to their being granted optimal routes, such as weather, ground stops, controller jurisdiction capacities, or airline priorities (e.g. delays, connections, or fuel). These resources and interests are gamed to provide an optimal flow from coast to coast.

We have implemented a layered architecture for our GOALS system that includes the market mechanism as shown in figure 1. Both the air traffic management simulation and optimization framework are Java applications. The internal representation for GOALS is graph based. Rather than developing a graphing capability, we selected the jGraphT libraries [11], which are available in the public domain. jGraphT was selected mainly because it allowed for rapid implementation, since most graph structures we needed were already implemented, including an implementation of Dijkstra's Algorithm for shortest paths. Others, such as the Ford-Fulkerson Method for maximum flow problems, we implemented, as it was not included in the libraries.

The various actors (e.g. aircraft, sectors, airports, weather, airlines, etc) within the system are represented as agents. These agents are annotated with a goal or interest (e.g. save fuel, minimize delays, avoid ground stops, make connections, etc). Once the locally optimal solution is determined, and required resources are assessed, "bidding" on these resources within a marketplace can commence. Centers are considered distributor agents ("sellers"), which make paths available in the market. Collector agents ("buyers") represent aircraft, and bid on the resources being offered by the distributor.

Some agents can be both collectors and distributors, for example, if a resource is won by an aircraft agent that later decides the resource is not needed. This determination may come about because the need for the resource may depend on winning other resources – if an auction is not won, the aircraft may be "stuck" with a resource it does not need and have to obtain the resources for an alternate solution. Figure 2 illustrates this situation.

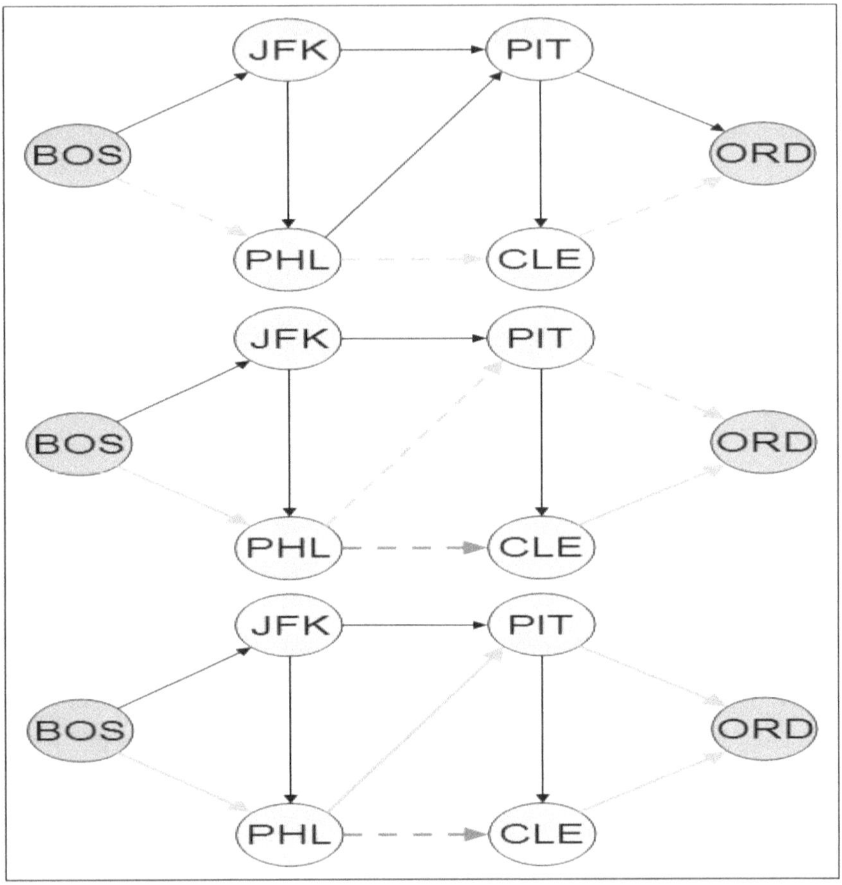

Fig. 2. An aircraft agent interacts with the market in an attempt to obtain all the resources needed for its optimal solution, but may win useless resources dependent on resources it does not win. In the upper graph, an aircraft agent flying from Boston (BOS) to Chicago (ORD) first discovers its shortest path to be through Philadelphia (PHL) and Cleveland (CLE). In the middle graph, it does not win the resource representing the path from Philadelphia (PHL) to Cleveland (CLE), so it tries for a new routing through Pittsburgh (PIT). In the bottom graph, the resource from Cleveland (CLE) to Chicago (ORD) is no longer needed, so the aircraft agent must find some way to dispense with it.

Upon completion of negotiations, the market notifies the participating agents of the results of negotiation, including what resources were transferred and at what cost. The temporal nature of resources becomes important here, both in terms of cost and resource gain. For our air traffic management application, we define a resource as the right to fly on a given segment of airway *starting at a given time*. In the situation described by Figure 2, the aircraft agent may become a distributor agent. It distributes the resource corresponding to the right to fly from Cleveland to Chicago at the designated time.

In any case, if an agent fails to acquire a resource that is needed for its optimal local solution, it becomes necessary to fall back onto a suboptimal local solution. This is accomplished simply by creating a new local goal for the agent, using the same graph but different weights, and finding the optimal solution corresponding to the new graph. Any solution in the new graph is also a feasible solution in the old graph. In fact, the optimal solutions to many local goals are determined simultaneously during the local optimization phase. This way, no additional computation time is wasted during the market phase if the agent must select a suboptimal solution.

Our prototype simulation has demonstrated that the GOALS framework is feasible for use in multi-agent distributed optimization problems where local autonomy is desired in the presence of an overarching mission goal. Individual agents attempt to obtain the most optimal solution to their local problems. The resources required to obtain this solution are governed by global, hierarchical marketplaces. In this manner, the global mission goal is satisfied, and each local agent is guaranteed the closest solution to its optimal that still satisfies the mission goal.

5 Analysis, Conclusions, and Future Work

We have developed and introduced a general framework for agent-based distributed optimization that is very flexible. The software developer can use our framework to quickly experiment with different types of markets, different types of agents and agent behaviors, and different types of agent goals. Agent goals do not have to be formulated as graph theoretic problems.

As a proof of concept for our optimization framework, we implemented a small air traffic management simulation. Nodes in the local goal graph represented either airports or transition points between center control. Aircraft agents were simulated, with goals of going from each airport to each of the other airports. Edge weights represented the physical distance between nodes (which was determined arbitrarily for this example). Each airport node was given a capacity, so that center agents could solve their maximum flow goals.

We analyzed the performance, in terms of finding the globally optimal solution, of the prototype application with several small test cases. These test cases had the desirable property of having hand-calculable solutions, but were therefore not very complicated or computing-intensive. We plan to integrate concepts from our prototype into ACES, which is a simulator capable of dealing with an entire average day's worth of air traffic in the United States. This will allow us to analyze the performance of the GOALS approach over many different criteria.

The air traffic management simulation we have developed is intended as a proof of concept only. Time and budgetary constraints did not permit us to develop this application fully. Future work will include expanding this application, and testing different agent behaviors and markets. We would also like to apply this framework to other domains, such as packet routing in a network, or the deployment of first responders in a disaster situation.

Further, we plan to add machine-learning techniques to our system, most notably in bidding strategies. Collector agents will learn what bids are optimal, and in which situations a resource is likely to be won. In addition, collectors may learn how to adjust weights in local goal graphs to arrive at feasible suboptimal solutions. This will likely include the incorporation of BDI agents and graph weighting schemes as described in prior sections. We aim to investigate agents that learn by using biologically inspired techniques such as genetic algorithms [5]. Other work in this area [3, 10, 22] indicates that machine-learning techniques can be incorporated in negotiation mechanisms.

References

1. Bellifemine, F., Caire, G., Poggi, A., and Rimassa, G. "JADE: A White Paper." In *exp*. Volume 3, No. 3. September, 2003. Pp. 6–19. http://exp.telecomitalialab.com
2. Bigus, J. P., Schlosnagle, D. A., Pilgrim, J. R., Millis, W. N. III, and Diao, Y. "ABLE: A Toolkit for Building Multiagent Autonomic Systems." In *IBM Systems Journal*, Volume 41, No. 3. September, 2002. Pp. 350–371.
3. Carmel, D. "Model-based Learning of Interaction Strategies in Multi-agent Systems." Ph.D. Thesis, Technion – Israel Institute of Technology. November 1997.
4. Cormen, T., Leiserson, C., and Rivest, R. *Introduction to Algorithms*. Cambridge, MA: MIT Press. 1998. Section VI.
5. Cliff, D. "Evolution of Market Mechanism Through a Continuous Space of Auction-Types II: Two-Sided Auction Mechanisms Evolve in Response to Market Shocks." Hewlett-Packard Techincal Report #HPL-2002-128. Bristol, England. May 8, 2002.
6. Foundation for Intelligent Physical Agents website. http://www.fipa.org
7. Frank, M., Bugacov, A., Chen, J., Dakin, G., Szekely, P., and Neches, B. "The Marbles Manifesto: A Definition and Comparison of Cooperative Negotiation Schemes for Distributed Resource Allocation." In Proceedings of the AAAI Symposium on Negotiation Methods for Autonomous Cooperative Systems, AAAI, 2001.
8. Goldberg, D., Cicirello, V., Dias, M. B., Simmons, R., Smith, S., and Stentz, A. "Market-Based Multi-Robot Planning in a Distributed Layered Architecture." In *Multi-Robot Systems: From Swarms to Intelligent Automata: Proceedings from the 2003 International Workshop on Multi-Robot Systems*, Volume 2. Kluwer Academic Publishers. 2003. Pp. 27–38.
9. Helsinger, A., Thome, M., and Wright, T. "Cougaar: A Scalable, Distributed Multi-Agent Architecture." In Proceedings of the 2004 IEEE Conference on Systems, Man, and Cybernetics. The Hague, The Netherlands. October, 2004.
10. Huang, P. and Sycara, K. "Multi-agent Learning in Extensive Games with Complete Information." In Proceedings of the Second International Joint Conference on Autonomous Agents and Multiagent Systems. Pp. 701–708. Melbourne, Australia. 2003.
11. jGraphT library. http://jgrapht.sourceforge.net
12. Kaelbling, L. P., Littman, M. L., and Cassandra, A. R. "Planning and Acting in Partially Observable Stochastic Domains." Technical Report, Brown University. January, 1997.
13. Liu, J., and Sycara, K. "Exploiting Problem Structure for Distributed Constraint Optimization." In Proceedings of the First International Conference on Multi-Agent Systems. Pp. 246–253. San Francisco, 1995.
14. Ljungberg, M. and Lucas, A. "The OASIS Air Traffic Management System." In Proceedings of the Second Pacific Rim International Conference on Artificial Intelligence. Seoul, Korea. 1992.
15. Next Generation Air Transportation System website. http://www.jpdo.aero

16. Parkes, D. C., and Shneidman, J. "Distributed Implementations of Vickrey-Clarke-Groves Mechanisms." In Proceedings of the 2004 International Conference on Autonomous Agents and Multi-Agent Systems. New York. July 2004.
17. Rao, A. S., and Georgeff, M. P. "BDI Agents: From Theory to Practice." In Proceedings of the First International Conference on Multi-Agent Systems. San Francisco. July, 1995.
18. Rosenschein, J. S., and Zlotkin, G. *Rules of Encounter*. Cambridge, MA: MIT Press. 1994.
19. Single European Air Traffic Management Research website. http://www.eurocontrol.int/sesar
20. Trott, G., Naqvi, W., and Wood, R. "Negotiating Rights of Passage." Presented at Raytheon's 3rd Systems/Software Engineering Symposium. March 2004.
21. Trott, G., and Naqvi, W. "Flow Management Resolution Advisor using Intelligent Interoperable Agents." 2003 End-Year Report for Raytheon IDEA Grant. Unpublished work.
22. Zeng, D. and Sycara, K. "Bayesian Learning in Negotiation." In *Adaptation, Coevolution and Learning in Multiagent Systems: Papers from the 1996 AAAI Spring Symposium*, pages 99–104, Menlo Park,CA, March 1996. AAAI Press. AAAI Technical Report #SS-96-01.

On the Completion of Workflows*

Tai Xin[1], Indrakshi Ray[1], Parvathi Chundi[2], and Sopak Chaichana[1]

[1] Computer Science Department
Colorado State University
Fort Collins, CO 80523-1873
{xin, iray, chaichan}@cs.colostate.edu
[2] Computer Science Department
University of Nebraska at Omaha
Omaha, NE 68182-0500
pchundi@mail.unomaha.edu

Abstract. Workflow Management Systems (WFMS) coordinate execution of logically related multiple tasks in an organization. A workflow schema is defined using a set of tasks that are coordinated using dependencies. Workflows instantiated from the same schema may differ with respect to the tasks executed. An important issue that must be addressed while designing a workflow is to decide what tasks are needed for the workflow to complete – we refer to this set as the *completion set*. Since different tasks are executed in different workflow instances, a workflow schema may be associated with multiple completion sets. Incorrect specification of completion sets may prohibit some workflow from completing. Manually generating these sets for large workflow schemas can be an error-prone and tedious process. Our goal is to automate this process. We investigate the factors that affect the completion of a workflow. Specifically, we study the impact of control-flow dependencies on completion sets and show how this knowledge can be used for automatically generating these sets. Finally, we provide an algorithm that can be used by application developers to generate the completion sets associated with a workflow schema.

1 Introduction

Workflow management systems (WFMS) recently have gained a lot of attention. They are responsible for coordinating the execution of multiple tasks performed by different entities within an organization. A group of such tasks that forms a logical unit of work constitutes a workflow. To ensure the proper coordination of these tasks, various kinds of dependencies are specified between the tasks of a workflow. The execution of a workflow must preserve the dependencies and eventually complete. Although a large body of work appears in the area of workflows [1,2,3,6,7,8,9,10,11,12,13], very few researchers have addressed the issue of workflow completion. In almost all of these works, the researchers assume that the application developer specifies what is needed for the workflow to complete. However, manually evaluating the conditions needed for workflow completion may be tedious and error-prone. In this paper, we aim to automate this process.

* This work was partially supported by NSF under Award No. IIS 0242258.

S. Bressan, J. Küng, and R. Wagner (Eds.): DEXA 2006, LNCS 4080, pp. 582–591, 2006.

A workflow is an instance of some workflow schema. A workflow schema formally specifies the tasks in a workflow and the dependencies between the tasks. Not all tasks specified in a workflow schema may be executed in a workflow instance. We refer to the set of tasks that are needed to complete a workflow instance as the completion set. The set of tasks needed to complete different workflows generated from the same schema may vary because not all instances execute the same set of tasks. Thus, a workflow schema may be associated with multiple completion sets.

Improper specification of completion sets in a workflow may result in deadlock and availability problems. If a completion set violates some dependency constraints, the states required for the workflow to complete can never be reached, and the workflow will be in the execution state infinitely. It will hold resources forever, and cause deadlock and/or unavailability problems. Let us illustrate one such problem with a simple example. Consider a workflow W_w that has a large number of tasks and dependencies. Specifically, there is an *exclusion* dependency existing between tasks T_{wm} and T_{wk}, which requires that T_{wk} must abort if T_{wm} commits. In other words, it is not possible for both these tasks to commit in the same instance. This implies that T_{wm} and T_{wk} can never be placed in the same completion set. Now, suppose an application developer, who is specifying completion sets for this workflow, overlooks this dependency and places both T_{wm} and T_{wk} in the same completion set CT_t. The consequence is that this workflow will never complete and the resource availability of the system will be compromised.

Due to the large number of tasks and dependencies that can exist in a complex workflow, correctly calculating all the completion sets manually can be a time-consuming and error-prone work. To solve this problem, we need an approach that generates all the possible completion sets automatically from a given workflow schema. In this paper, we propose one such approach. We begin by identifying the impact of dependencies on the completion set of a workflow. We then show how the knowledge of the dependencies can be exploited to generate the completion sets. Every completion set produced by our approach will satisfy the dependency constraints and it will be feasible to execute all the tasks in a given completion set. This, in turn, will ensure that the workflow completes.

The rest of the paper is organized as follows. Section 2 defines our workflow processing model and describes the different kinds of dependencies that may be associated with it. Section 3 presents the details of the algorithm and shows how to generate all the possible completion sets correctly. Section 4 concludes the paper with pointers to future directions.

2 Our Model for Workflows

We begin by giving some definitions.

Definition 1. [Workflow Schema] *A* workflow schema W_w *is a triple* $< S, D, C >$, *where, S is a set of tasks, D is the set of dependencies used to coordinate the execution of the tasks in S, and C is the set of completion sets in* W_w, *which defines the conditions for complete execution of* W_w.

Definition 2. [Task] *A* task T_{wi} *is the smallest logical unit of work in an workflow. It consists of a set of data operations (read and write) and task primitives (begin, abort and commit).*

The begin, abort and commit primitives of task T_{wi} are denoted by b_{wi}, a_{wi} and c_{wi} respectively. The execution of these primitives is often referred to as an event. Thus, we can have begin, commit or abort events.

Definition 3. [Completion Set] *Each* completion set $C_t \in C$ *is specified by* $(CT_t, \ll_t)$, *where* CT_t *is the set of tasks that must be committed and* $\ll_t$ *is the order in which they must be committed. Formally,* $CT_t \subseteq S$ *is the set of tasks which must be committed for this workflow to complete, and* $\ll_t$ *is the ordering relation that specifies the commit order of tasks in* CT_t.

In order to properly coordinate the different tasks in a workflow, control-flow dependencies are specified on the task primitives, which control the occurrence and/or ordering of the *begin, commit, and abort* events of different tasks.

Definition 4. [Control-flow Dependency] *A* control-flow dependency *specified between a pair of tasks* T_{ij} *and* T_{ik} *expresses how the execution of a primitive (begin, commit, and abort) of* T_{ij} *causes (or relates to) the execution of the primitives (begin, commit and abort) of another task* T_{ik}.

A comprehensive list of transaction dependency definitions can be found in [2,4,5]. We describe the fifteen commonly used dependencies. In the following descriptions T_{ij} and T_{ik} refer to the tasks and b_{ij}, c_{ij}, a_{ij} refer to the events of T_{ij} that are present in some history H, and the notation $e_{ij} \prec e_{ik}$ denotes that event e_{ij} precedes event e_{ik} in the history H.

- **[Commit dependency]** ($T_{ij} \rightarrow_c T_{ik}$): If both T_{ij} and T_{ik} commit then the commitment of T_{ij} precedes the commitment of T_{ik}. Formally, $c_{ij} \Rightarrow (c_{ik} \Rightarrow (c_{ij} \prec c_{ik}))$.
- **[Strong commit dependency]** ($T_{ij} \rightarrow_{sc} T_{ik}$): If T_{ij} commits then T_{ik} also commits. Formally, $c_{ij} \Rightarrow c_{ik}$.
- **[Abort dependency]** ($T_{ij} \rightarrow_a T_{ik}$): If T_{ij} aborts then T_{ik} aborts. Formally, $a_{ij} \Rightarrow a_{ik}$.
- **[Weak abort dependency]** ($T_{ij} \rightarrow_{wa} T_{ik}$): If T_{ij} aborts and T_{ik} has not been committed then T_{ik} aborts. Formally, $a_{ij} \Rightarrow (\neg (c_{ik} \prec a_{ij} \Rightarrow a_{ik})$.
- **[Termination dependency]** ($T_{ij} \rightarrow_t T_{ik}$): Task T_{ik} cannot commit or abort until T_{ij} either commits or aborts. Formally, $e_{ik} \Rightarrow e_{ij} \prec e_{ik}$, where $e_{ij} \in \{c_{ij}, a_{ij}\}$, $e_{ik} \in \{c_{ik}, a_{ik}\}$.
- **[Exclusion dependency]** ($T_{ij} \rightarrow_{ex} T_{ik}$): If T_{ij} commits and T_{ik} has begun executing, then T_{ik} aborts. Formally, $(c_{ij} \Rightarrow (b_{ik} \Rightarrow a_{ik})$.
- **[Force-commit-on-abort dependency]** ($T_{ij} \rightarrow_{fca} T_{ik}$): If T_{ij} aborts, T_{ik} commits. Formally, $a_{ij} \Rightarrow c_{ik}$.
- **[Force-begin-on-commit/abort/begin/termination dependency]** ($T_{ij} \rightarrow_{fbc/fba/fbb/fbt} T_{ik}$): Task T_{ik} must begin if T_{ij} commits(aborts/begins/terminates). Formally, c_{ij} (a_{ij} / b_{ij}/ T_{ij}) $\Rightarrow b_{ik}$.
- **[Begin dependency]** ($T_{ij} \rightarrow_b T_{ik}$): Task T_{ik} cannot begin execution until T_{ij} has begun. Formally, $b_{ik} \Rightarrow (b_{ij} \prec b_{ik})$.
- **[Serial dependency]** ($T_{ij} \rightarrow_s T_{ik}$): Task T_{ik} cannot begin execution until T_{ij} either commits or aborts. Formally, $b_{ik} \Rightarrow (e_{ij} \prec b_{ik})$ where $e_{ij} \in \{c_{ij}, a_{ij}\}$.
- **[Begin-on-commit dependency]** ($T_{ij} \rightarrow_{bc} T_{ik}$): Task T_{ik} cannot begin until T_{ij} commits. Formally, $b_{ik} \Rightarrow (c_{ij} \prec b_{ik})$.

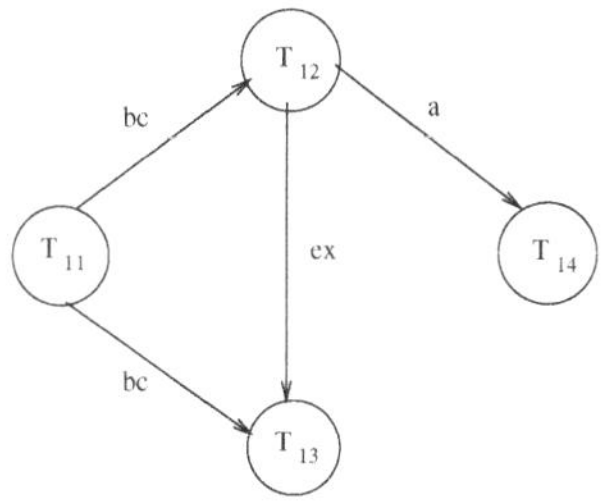

Fig. 1. Dependencies in the Example Workflow

[Begin-on-abort dependency] ($T_{ij} \rightarrow_{ba} T_{ik}$): Task T_{ik} cannot begin until T_{ij} aborts. Formally, $b_{ik} \Rightarrow (a_{ij} \prec b_{ik})$.

A workflow W_w can be represented in the form of a graph $G_w =< V, E >$ which we term as the *dependency graph*. The task $T_{w1}, T_{w2}, \ldots, T_{wn}$ defined in S correspond to the different nodes of the graph. Each dependency between transactions T_{wi} and T_{wj} is indicated by a directed edge (T_{wi}, T_{wj}) that is labeled with the name of the dependency. Let $W_1 =< S, D, C >$ be a workflow where $S = \{T_{11}, T_{12}, T_{13}, T_{14}\}$, $D = \{T_{11} \rightarrow_{bc} T_{12}, T_{11} \rightarrow_{bc} T_{13}, T_{12} \rightarrow_{ex} T_{13}, T_{12} \rightarrow_{a} T_{14}\}$, and $C = \{(\{T_{11}, T_{12}, T_{14}\}, \{T_{11} \ll T_{12}\}), (\{T_{11}, T_{13}\}, \{T_{11} \ll T_{13}\})\}$. The labels on each edge corresponds to the dependencies that exist between the tasks. $L(T_{11}, T_{12}) = \{bc\}, L(T_{11}, T_{13}) = \{bc\}, L(T_{12}, T_{13}) = \{ex\}$, $L(T_{12}, T_{14}) = \{a\}$. This transaction has two completion sets: $(\{T_{11}, T_{12}, T_{14}\}, \{T_{11} \ll T_{12}\})$ and $(\{T_{11}, T_{13}\}, \{T_{11} \ll T_{13}\})$. This transaction can be represented graphically as shown in Figure 1. A real world example of such a transaction may be a workflow associated with making travel arrangements. The tasks perform the following tasks. (i) Task T_{11} – Reserve a ticket on Airlines A, (ii) Task T_{12} – Purchase the Airlines A ticket, (iii) Task T_{13} – Cancels the reservation, and (iv) Task T_{14} – Reserves a room in Resort C. There is a *begin-on-commit* dependency between T_{11} and T_{12} and also between T_{11} and T_{13}. This means that neither T_{12} nor T_{13} can start before T_{11} has committed. This ensures that the airlines ticket cannot be purchased or canceled before a reservation has been made. The *exclusion* dependency between T_{12} and T_{13} ensures that either T_{12} can commit or T_{13} can commit but not both. In other words, either the airlines ticket must be purchased or the airlines reservation canceled, but not both. Finally, there is an *abort* dependency between T_{14} and T_{12}. This means that if T_{12} aborts then T_{14} must abort. In other words, if the resort room cannot be reserved, then the airlines ticket should not be purchased.

3 Generate the Completion Sets Automatically

Impact of Dependencies on Completion Sets: Different control-flow dependencies have different impacts on deciding the completion set. For instance, with a *begin-on-abort* dependency $T_{wi} \rightarrow_{ba} T_{wj}$, T_{wj} cannot begin and hence it cannot commit without the abort event of T_{wi} in the history. Therefore, if one wants to have T_{wj} in a completion set CT_t, T_{wi} cannot be in the same completion set – $T_{wj} \in CT_t \Rightarrow T_{wi} \notin CT_t$. The control-flow dependencies that impact a completion set CT_t are listed in Table 1.

Table 1. Impacts of Dependencies on Deciding Completion Sets

Dependency	Impact
$T_{wi} \rightarrow_{sc} T_{wj}$	$T_{wi} \in CT_t \Rightarrow T_{wj} \in CT_t$
$T_{wi} \rightarrow_{a} T_{wj}$	$T_{wj} \in CT_t \Rightarrow T_{wi} \in CT_t \wedge T_{wj} \prec T_{wi}$
$T_{wi} \rightarrow_{ex} T_{wj}$	$T_{wi} \in CT_t \Rightarrow T_{wj} \notin CT_t$
$T_{wi} \rightarrow_{fca} T_{wj}$	$T_{wi} \in CT_t \Rightarrow T_{wj} \in CT_t \wedge T_{wj} \prec T_{wi}$
$T_{wi} \rightarrow_{c} T_{wj}$	$T_{wi} \in CT_t \wedge T_{wj} \in CT_t \Rightarrow T_{wi} \prec T_{wj}$
$T_{wi} \rightarrow_{t} T_{wj}$	$T_{wi} \in CT_t \wedge T_{wj} \in CT_t \Rightarrow T_{wi} \prec T_{wj}$
$T_{wi} \rightarrow_{s} T_{wj}$	$T_{wi} \in CT_t \wedge T_{wj} \in CT_t \Rightarrow T_{wi} \prec T_{wj}$
$T_{wi} \rightarrow_{bc} T_{wj}$	$T_{wj} \in CT_t \Rightarrow T_{wi} \in CT_t \wedge T_{wi} \prec T_{wj}$
$T_{wi} \rightarrow_{ba} T_{wj}$	$T_{wj} \in CT_t \Rightarrow T_{wi} \notin CT_t$

Strategies for Generating Completion Sets: The algorithm for generating completion sets automatically will use the graph representing the workflow. The dependency graph will include both the directly given dependencies and the implicit dependencies. Implicit dependencies [11] arise because of the interaction of the given dependencies. For instance, the $T_{wi} \rightarrow_{sc} T_{wk}$ and $T_{wk} \rightarrow_{ex} T_{wm}$ dependencies will imply an implicit dependency $T_{wi} \rightarrow_{ex} T_{wm}$. An example of the dependency graph is shown in Figure 2. The steps for generating completion set for this workflow are shown in Figure 3.

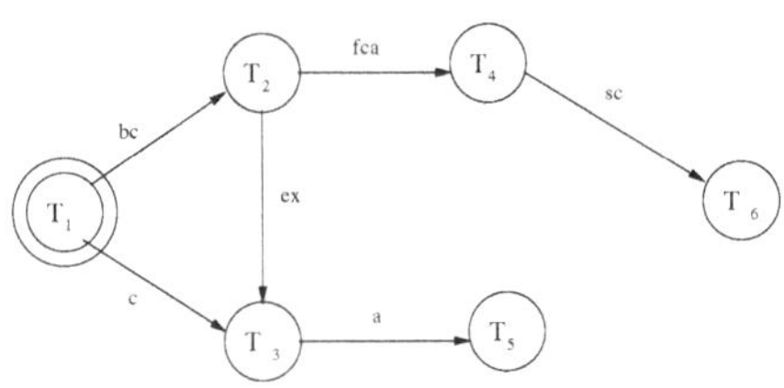

Fig. 2. An Example of Workflow and its Dependency Graph

We assume that every dependency graph has a start node which is the one that has no incoming edges. For instance, in Figure 2, the task T_1 is the start node. We assume that the start node represents the first task to be executed in a workflow and is present in all completion sets. When generating completion sets for the workflow, we construct a tree structure. Each node of this tree is associated with a set of tasks. This set represents the prefix of a completion set which we obtained by traversing the graph so far. The root of this tree contains the start node of the graph. Each leaf node represents a completion set. The strategy for computing completion sets is described below.

(i) We insert the start node into the root of the tree as shown in Figure 3.
(ii) We consider one dependency $T_{wm} \rightarrow_d T_{wn}$ at a time, and insert new child node(s) into the tree. We add the task T_{wm} or T_{wn} into the completion set of the child node(s), if it does not violate the dependency constraints. We use Table 1 for this purpose.

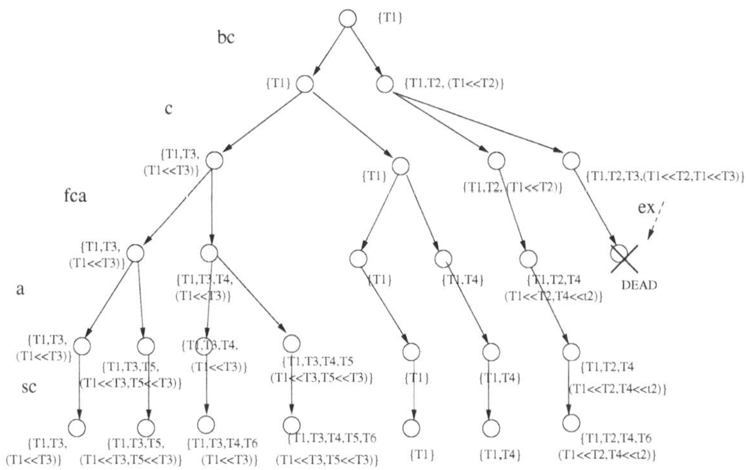

Fig. 3. Generate Completion Sets for Workflow in Figure 2

1. If it is a *strong commit* or a *force-commit-on-abort* dependency and the completion set contains T_{wm}, then we only generate one child node, where we insert T_{wn} into the existing completion set. For the force-commit-on-abort dependency, we also have to add the $T_{wn} \prec T_{wm}$ in its new completion set.
2. If it is an *exclusion* dependency and the completion set contains T_{wm}, we only generate one child since we cannot insert T_{wn}. The child node has the same completion set as the parent node. However, if we already have both T_{wm} and T_{wn} in the completion set, we have to remove this node from the tree since it now contains an incorrect completion. This is shown in the rightmost node in Figure 3.
3. For *commit, begin-on-commit, termination, serial* dependencies, if the completion set contains T_{wm}, we generate two nodes – one that contains T_{wn} and one that does not. With the child that contains T_{wn}, the ordering requirement $T_{wm} \prec T_{wn}$ is inserted into the completion set.
4. If it is an *abort* dependency, and the completion set of this node contains T_{wn}, then we only generate one child node, where T_{wm} is inserted into the completion set, and also has $T_{wn} \prec T_{wm}$ in the new completion set.
5. If it is a *begin-on-abort* dependency, and the completion set of this node contains T_{wn}, we only generate one child node since we cannot insert T_{wm} into the existing completion set. However, if we already have both T_{wm} and T_{wn} in the completion set, we have to remove this node from the tree.
6. For all other dependencies (like *force-begin-on-begin* dependency), if the completion set of this node contains T_{wm}, we will generate two child nodes. One node contains T_{mn} and one does not, because these dependencies have no impact on completion sets.

(iii) The operations in step (ii) continue until all the dependencies are considered in the dependency graph. Finally we have the complete tree where every leaf node contains one completion set.

Algorithms to Compute Completion Sets Automatically: We next give the algorithm for building all possible completion sets. The algorithm is organized in two steps - (i) build the derived dependency set and (ii) compute all possible completion sets based on the derived dependency set.

In the first step, the specification of the workflow is used to build the initial dependency set (IDS), which records every dependency $T_{wi} \rightarrow_{d_x} T_{wj}$ as an edge of the form (T_{wi}, T_{wj}, d_x), where T_{wi}, T_{wj}, and d_x represent the source node, the destination node, and the dependency respectively. Then the IDS is used to build the derived dependency set (DDS). This procedure has several rounds of iterations. In each iteration, the algorithm scans all the dependencies currently in the DDS and check whether new edges could be implied by the existing edges. The process is repeated until no more new edges can be derived.

Algorithm 1
Input: the workflow specification $AT_t = < S, D, C >$
Output: a derived dependency set (DDS) of the workflow
Procedure GenerateDDS(AT_t)
begin
  //Build the initial dependency set, according to the specification
  $IDS = \{\}$; // set of edges
  for every dependency $(T_{wi} \rightarrow_{d_x} T_{wj}) \in AT_t(D)$
    generate an edge (T_{wi}, T_{wj}, d_x); //dependency of type x from T_{wi} to T_{wj}
    $IDS = IDS + (T_{wi}, T_{wj}, d_x)$;
  // initiate the derived dependency set
  done == false;
  $DDS == IDS$;
  mark every edge in DDS as *unchecked*
  while (done = false)
  begin
    for each edge $(T_{wi}, T_{wj}, d_x) \in DDS$
    begin
      // If this dependency implies a relationship, insert the implicit edge
      if this edge is *unchecked*
        if $d_x = sc$
          generate an edge (T_{wj}, T_{wi}, c);
        else if $d_x = a$
            generate an edge (T_{wi}, T_{wj}, c);
        else if $d_x = fca$
            generate an edge (T_{wj}, T_{wi}, bc);
      // insert the implied edges based on interaction of dependencies
      for each edge $(T_{wj}, T_{wk}, d_p) \in DDS$ that is *unchecked*
        if (T_{wi}, T_{wj}, d_x) and (T_{wj}, T_{wk}, d_p) imply an implicit dependency d_t
          generate an edge (T_{wi}, T_{wk}, d_t);
      for each edge $(T_{wi}, T_{wk}, d_q) \in DDS$ that is *unchecked*
        if (T_{wi}, T_{wj}, d_x) and (T_{wi}, T_{wk}, d_q) imply an implicit dependency d_s
          generate an edge (T_{wj}, T_{wk}, d_s);

end
// mark existing edges as *checked*;
for every edge $\in DDS$
set edge as *checked*
// insert newly generated edges, make them as *unchecked*;
for every newly generated edge e_{new} in this round
set edge e_{new} as *unchecked*
$DDS = DDS + e_{new}$
if there is no new edge inserted in this round
done = true;
end
end

Following, we compute all the possible completion sets based on the DDS obtained above. A queue is used to simulate the breadth-first traversal of the tree. The queue maintains the part of completion sets we have obtained so far. We first consider the start node, generate a completion set containing only this task and insert it into the queue. Then we take one dependency at a time, and compute the new set of completion sets that can be obtained by applying this dependency with the existing completion sets in the queue. The rules for computing new set of completion sets are based on Table 1. The newly obtained set will replace all the old completion sets in the queue and the process is repeated until all the dependencies are considered.

Algorithm 2
Input: a derived dependency set (DDS) of the workflow
Output: a set containing all possible completion set for this workflow
Procedure GenerateCompletionSet
begin
create two queues, one completion sets queue, and one temp queue
generate a completion set $(CT_t, \ll_t)$ where $CT_t = \{T_{ws}\}$, $\ll_t = \{\}$, T_{ws} = start node
insert this initial completion set into the completion set queue
for every edge (T_{wi}, T_{wj}, d_x) in the DDS
/* consider this dependency with every completion set in the queue */
for every completion set CT_t in the completion set queue
if $T_{wi} \notin CT_t$ AND $T_{wj} \notin CT_t$
/* this dependency is not relevant with this completion set */
continue; /* do nothing here */
else if $T_{wi} \in CT_t$ /* this completion set contains T_{wi} */
if $d_x = sc$
$CT_t = CT_t \cup \{T_{wj}\}$
insert $(CT_t, \ll_t)$ to the temp queue
if $d_x = fca$
$CT_t = CT_t \cup \{T_{wj}\}$
$\ll_t = \ll_t \cup (\{T_{wj} \ll T_{wi})$
insert $(CT_t, \ll_t)$ to the temp queue
if $d_x = ex$

```
                if $T_{wi} \in CT_t \wedge T_{wj} \in CT_t$
                  remove $(CT_t \ll_t)$, this set is infeasible
                else   /* cannot have $T_{wj}$ in the new set */
                    insert $(CT_t, \ll_t)$ to the temp queue
              if $d_x = c$ OR $d_x = bc$ OR $d_x = t$ OR $d_x = s$
                /* generate two new sets, one contains $T_{wj}$ and one not */
                insert $(CT_t, ll_t)$ to the temp queue
                $CT_s = CT_t \cup \{T_{wj}\}$
                $\ll_s = \ll_t \cup \{T_{wi} \ll T_{wj}\}$
                insert $(CT_s, \ll_s)$ to the temp queue
              if $d_x = ba$
                if $T_{wj} \in CT_t$   /* have both $T_{wi}, T_{wj}$ */
                  remove $(CT_t, \ll_t)$, this set is infeasible
              else   /* for all other dependencies */
                  /* generate two new sets, one contains $T_{wj}$ and one not */
                  insert $(CT_t, \ll_t)$ to the temp queue
                  $CT_s = CT_t \cup \{T_{wj}\}$
                  insert $(CT_s, \ll_t)$ to the temp queue
          else if $T_{wj} \in CT_t$   /* this completion set contains $T_{wj}$ */
              if $d_x = a$
                $CT_t = CT_t \cup \{T_{wi}\}$
                $\ll_t = \ll_t \cup \{T_{wj} \ll T_{wi}\}$
                insert $(CT_t, \ll_t)$ to the temp queue
              if $d_x = ba$
             insert $(CT_t, \ll_t)$ to the temp queue /* cannot have $T_{wi}$ in the new set */
        end for
        /* let temp queue be the new completion set queue, clean up the temp queue */
        let completion set queue equals to the temp queue
        reset the temp queue to be empty
      end for
      return the completion set queue
end
```

4 Conclusion

An workflow is composed of a number of cooperating tasks that are coordinated by dependencies. The dependencies make the workflow more flexible and powerful. Completion sets are also specified in the workflow to identify complete executions. However, incorrect specification of completion sets can lead to deadlock and unavailability problems. The completion sets must conform to the dependencies in the workflows. In this paper, we looked at how the dependencies can impact the completion set, and gave an algorithm to generate all possible completion sets automatically. A lot of work remains to be done. We need to give proof of formal correctness. We also need to evaluate the complexity of the algorithm used in computing the completion sets. In future, we plan to provide more efficient algorithms.

References

1. G. Alonso, D. Agrawal, A. Abbadi, M. Kamath, R. G., and C. Mohan. Advanced Transaction Models in Workflow Contexts. In *Proceedings of the Twelfth International Conference on Data Engineering*, pages 574–581, February 1996.
2. V. Atluri, W-K. Huang, and E. Bertino. An Execution Model for Multilevel Secure Workflows. In *Proceedings of the Eleventh IFIP WG11.3 Working Conference on Database Security*, pages 151–165, August 1997.
3. P. C. Attie, M. P. Singh, A. P. Sheth, and M. Rusinkiewicz. Specifying and Enforcing Intertask Dependencies. In *Proceedings of the Nineteenth International Conference on Very Large Data Bases*, pages 134–145, Dublin, Ireland, August 1993. Morgan Kaufmann.
4. A. Biliris, S. Dar, N. Gehani, H.V. Jagadish, and K. Ramamritham. ASSET: A System for Supporting Extended Transactions. In *Proceedings of ACM SIGMOD International Conference on Management of Data*, May 1994.
5. P. Chrysanthis. ACTA, A Framework for Modeling and Reasoning about Extended Transactions Models. Ph.D. Thesis, September 1991.
6. D. Hollingsworth. Workflow Reference Model. Technical report, Workflow Management Coalition, Brussels, Belgium, 1994.
7. I. Ray, T. Xin, and Y. Zhu. Ensuring Task Dependencies During Workflow Recovery. In *Proceedings of the Fifteenth International Conference on Database and Expert Systems*, Zaragoza, Spain, August 2004.
8. M. Rusinkiewicz and A. P. Sheth. Specification and Execution of Transactional Workflows. In *Modern Database Systems*, pages 592–620, 1995.
9. M. P. Singh. Semantical Considerations on Workflows: An Algebra for Intertask Dependencies. In *Proceedings of the Fifth International Workshop on Database Programming Languages*, Electronic Workshops in Computing. Springer, 1995.
10. W.M.P. van der Aalst, K. M. van Hee, and G.J. Houben. Modelling Workflow Management Systems with High-Level Petri Nets. In *Proceedings of the Second Workshop on Computer-Supported Cooperative Work, Petri Nets and Related Formalisms*, October 1994.
11. T. Xin and I. Ray. Detecting Dependency Conflicts in Advanced Transaction Models. In *Proceedings of the Ninth International Database Applications and Engineering Symposium*, Montreal, Canada, July 2005.
12. T. Xin, Y. Zhu, and I. Ray. Reliable Scheduling of Advanced Transactions. In *Proceedings of the Nineteenth IFIP WG11.3 Working Conference on Data and Applications Security*, Storrs, Connecticut, August 2005.
13. Y. Zhu, T. Xin, and I. Ray. Recovering from Malicious Attacks in Workflow Systems. In *Proceedings of the Sixteenth International Conference on Database and Expert Systems*, Copenhagen, Denmark, August 2005.

Concurrency Management in Transactional Web Services Coordination

Adnene Guabtni[1], François Charoy[2], and Claude Godart[3]

[1] guabtni@loria.fr
[2] charoy@loria.fr
[3] godart@loria.fr
University Henri Poincaré Nancy 1
INRIA - LORIA laboratory, BP 239, F-54506
Vandouvre-lès-Nancy Cedex, France

Abstract. The Business Process Execution Language BPEL4WS has emerged to introduce process dimension in Web Services coordination. At the same time, a lot of needs related to business process management appeared. In this article we focus on transactional management in Web Services platforms. WS-Transaction specification had a big impact on usage of Web Services in critical situations such as financial services. This usage of transactions in web services coordination also introduced concurrency problems similar to those encountered in transactional databases world due to hard transactional constraints especially for isolation mechanisms. Today, WS-Transactions provide flexible atomicity in Web Services coordination (WS-BusinessActivity) but isolation flexibility is not provided. Isolation mechanisms used today are not really adapted to Service Oriented environments and we aim to make them more 'process friendly'. In this paper, we focus on this important part of concurrency problems and propose a new view of WS-Transactions based on Behavioural Spheres approach. This contribution suggests a reorganisation of the WS-Coordination framework adding WS-IsolationSphere for isolation management and the WS-Sphere coordination type for generalising any behaviour management in Web Services coordination.

1 Introduction

Companies are migrating their applications towards a Service oriented Architecture and Web Services represent an adapted way to perform interoperability between different platforms. In such environment, distributed and composed e-services were very useful and specifications like BPEL4WS [6] have been defined to build business processes in Web Services environments. Web Services Orchestration introduced workflow concepts in this context and revealed some transactional needs such as atomicity and isolation to ensure correct execution. These needs were usually performed by traditional transaction protocol such as the two phase commit (2PC). WS-Transactions were introduced to relax isolation in composed Web Services by releasing locks on transaction resources before

S. Bressan, J. Küng, and R. Wagner (Eds.): DEXA 2006, LNCS 4080, pp. 592–601, 2006.

their completion in order to permit other transactions to access them concurrently. Implementations of WS-Transaction specification are currently emerging in order to ensure this flexibility in existing platforms but problems related to undesired phenomena caused by this flexibility are not yet resolved. Suppose that a transaction T_1 uses a resource R_1 on which it specified a lock. Suppose also that, due to flexibility reasons, T_1 releases the lock on R_1 before its completion and a transaction T_2 uses the resource R_1 while T_1 has not yet finished its execution. If T_1 fails, all changes made on the resource R_1 should be cancelled (this process is called compensation). Also transactions that depend on data updated by T_1 should be aborted to ensure some coherence of the data/execution. This kind of problem may represent a strategic issue for processes that need a high level of correctness such as financial services.

In this article we propose a point of view that considers isolation as a property that concerns not only activities but also processes. Isolation will be related to sets of business activities allowing adaptation of concurrency during the business process execution. That will enhance concurrency management in Web Services coordination and make it possible to maintain a high degree of flexibility while cascade cancellation and similar undesired phenomena can be reduced considerably. This approach is inspired from sphere of control of C. T. Davies [7] and Isolation spheres that we started to define in [3] and this carries out us to introduce the concept of WS-IsolationSphere. We propose also to reorganise the WS-Coordination framework introducing WS-Sphere coordination type for generalising any behaviour management in Web Services coordination.

We start our paper by presenting what has been done in Web Service Transactions support and what are the different problems related to it. Then we propose our approach based on Isolation Spheres to ensure a process-friendly isolation. Finally we explore the implementation of such approach in the WS-Coordination framework and extensions to other behaviour.

2 Related Work: WS-Technologies

Business process specification for Web Services BPEL4WS started in the last five years with an expansion of multiple specifications (XLANG, BPML, WSFL, BPSS, WSCL, WSCI, WS-Choreography and BPEL4WS). These specifications were defined based on numerous business process challenges such as coordinating communication between services, correlating message exchanges between parties, implementing parallel processing of activities, transforming data between partner interactions, supporting long running business transaction and providing consistent exception handling.

Our research focuses on Web Services orchestration/choreography but some clarification needs to be done about the signification of the terms orchestration and choreography. We mean by a Web Services orchestration the execution of a business process under control of a single endpoint (inside organisation, commonly workflow) while choreography represents the observable public exchange of messages, rules and agreements between different business process endpoints (between organisations). Contrary to orchestration, choreography does not include concurrency management because concurrent data access is usually limited to the same endpoint.

As shown in figure 1, BPEL4WS and CDL4WS (Choreography Definition Language for Web Services) represent the Business Process management both inside and between organisations. Other protocols like WS-Reliability, WS-Security, WS-Coordination and WS-Transactions ensure the Quality of Service part of the entire Web Services Business Process environment.

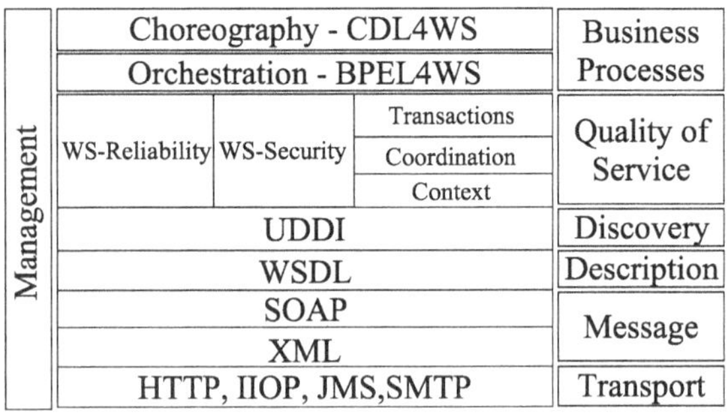

Fig. 1. Standards used with BPEL

In this article we focus on the WS-Coordination and WS-Transaction levels and this will not include WS-Choreography. The challenge of our work is to express flexible isolation requirements in business process environment. First we detail what is already done in WS-Coordination [4] and WS-Transaction specifications [5].

WS-Coordination / WS-Transactions

WS-Coordination specification provides standard mechanisms to create and register services, using separately defined protocols to coordinate the execution of distributed operations in a Web Services environment. It defines a coordination framework supporting the following services:

- Activation Service to create a new coordination activity and to specify the coordination protocols available for the activity.
- Registration Service to register participants and to select a coordination protocol for the activity.
- Coordination Service for activity completion processing using the selected coordination protocol.

WS-Coordination specification proposes customisable coordination types and protocols. WS-Transaction specification represents the specification of two WS-Coordination types that are WS-AtomicTransaction and WS-BusinessActivity as follows:

- WS-AtomicTransaction represents the coordination of activities that express the 'all or nothing' behaviour. Two protocols are possible:
  - Completion protocol: usually, the coordination initiator uses this protocol to tell the coordinator to try a commitment or a rollback.
  - Two phase commit (2PC): A participant registers to the 2PC protocol in order to initiate a two Phase Commitment with other participants that registered also to the same protocol. Two types of this protocol are available: Volatile 2PC (used for volatile resources such as cache) and Durable 2PC (used for durable resources such as database).
- WS-BusinessActivity handle long lived activities by allowing partial commitment of participants. Business activities support two coordination types
  - AtomicOutcome coordination type must direct all participants to close or all participants to compensate.
  - MixedOutcome coordination type may direct each individual participant to close or compensate.

  In both coordination types, registered participants can choose between two protocols possible with WS-BusinessActivity. These two protocols introduce the notion of completion decision maker as follows:
  - BusinessAgreementWithParticipantCompletion: When a participant registers for this protocol with its coordinator, it must know when it has completed all work for the business activity. The participant must notify its coordinator when its work is done.
  - BusinessAgreementWithCoordinatorCompletion: When a participant registers for this protocol with its coordinator, it relies on its coordinator to tell it when it has received all requests to perform work within the business activity.

3 Motivation

Transactional behaviour supported by the WS-Transaction specification ensures correct and flexible atomicity in Web Services platforms but do not provide such flexibility for isolation constraints. This is due to the fact that isolation in business processes is managed most of the time by the underlying database system and this thanks to locking strategies on data. Some of these strategies provide more flexibility like the SQL isolation levels but they are adapted only to database systems. They also do not take sufficiently into account process aspects because accesses to data are usually considered as independent accesses without particular relations between them.

In such context, we need to provide a 'process friendly' isolation strategy that provides the missing flexibility in transactional Web Services coordination. We propose isolation spheres for Web Services as a solution to the problem and we propose a perspective for similar solutions based on behaviour spheres. In the next section we expose the isolation spheres approach.

4 Isolation Spheres Approach

Isolation Spheres are inspired from the spheres of control [7]. An isolation sphere is defined by a set of activities inside a process. For these activities we want to ensure some properties regarding data accessed by the activities (Cohesion property of a sphere) and data produced by the activities (Coherence property of a sphere).

Cohesion property is based on the notion of cohesive view on data. This means that all activities of the sphere have the same view on the data they access which ensures that data values used by the sphere's participants have been set (created or updated) by:

- Activities **participant** to the sphere (any internal data manipulation performed by a participant is visible by the other participants to the sphere). We call such data values 'Sphere-Produced Values' (SPV).
- Activities **non-participant** to the sphere but their manipulation of the data has been performed before any sphere's participant started. We call such data values 'Pre-Sphere Values' (PSV).

We introduce in this paper the notions SPC and PSV to clarify the means of cohesion in such context. These two notions are applicable to data values and not data item itself. This means that a data can have a value that is PSV and after a participant update, it have a new value that is SPV. That's why SPV and PSV data values are disjoint due to the disjunction of participants and non participants to the sphere. Updates done by activities outside of the sphere during the execution of the sphere's participants need to be avoided. This cohesive view represents the basis of cohesion in a group of activities. Cohesion is expressed through different cohesion levels [3] that are Read Uncommitted, Read Committed, Repeatable Read and Serialisable.

These levels define the way the common view of the sphere on data is managed and depend on the nature of used data values. We say that a data value is an '**uncommitted**' one if it is the result of a manipulation performed by an activity not yet completed (usually such data values represent uncompleted or temporary values). If such activity is completed, the data value is called '**committed**'.

- **Read Uncommitted** level allows the participants to the sphere to use uncommitted data during their execution (both for SPV and PSV).
- **Read Committed** level allow the participants to the sphere only reading committed values during their execution (both for SPV and PSV).
- **Repeatable Read** level allows the participants to the sphere to read values of data (both for SPV and PSV) with the certainty that during their use of the data, they will not change.
- **Serialisable** level emulates an execution in series of the activities participating to the sphere. Such execution concerns only the sphere's participants and prevents concurrency inconvenience between them. The execution is similar, from data changes point of view (both for SPV and PSV), to a serial execution of activities of the sphere. External activities do not suffer of such

hard constraint except if they access to data used by the sphere's participants. In this latter case, they are constrained to be serialised with sphere's participant's activities.

Coherence of a sphere represents how activities of the sphere share their data outside of the sphere. In order to control the coherence between data used by activities of the sphere and those by the rest of the processes including concurrent isolation spheres, it is essential to define a level of coherence of the sphere. Isolation spheres ensure some cohesion inside the group and also some coherence of the activities external to the sphere using the same data. The levels of coherence are the following:

- **Cooperative coherence:** All values of data written by the activities participating to the sphere are visible outside of the sphere as soon as they are produced.
- **Activity coherence:** Only values written by the terminated activities participating to the sphere are visible outside of the sphere.
- **Sphere coherence:** The sphere acts as a transaction. The values written by activities participating to the sphere are visible at the end of the execution of all activities of the sphere (that we call also the end of the sphere).

The control of the two dimensions (cohesion + coherence) makes it possible to define in finer way isolation requirements for groups of activities. The choice of cohesion and coherence levels allows estimating the degree of divergence between activities of the sphere and those external to the sphere and the degree of data exchange flexibility between the activities of the sphere and those outside.

5 Isolation Spheres / Behavioural Spheres as Web Services Challenges

We consider Web Services platforms as very interesting area for isolation sphere application. The WS-Coordination is able to accommodate the isolation sphere approach. WS-Coordination allows grouping several Web Services that can join or leave the coordination service. This behaviour express what isolation spheres aim to perform: grouping services together over a coordination service and ensuring flexible isolation constraints on their execution.

Although isolation spheres goal concerns transactional behaviour, we think that we need to separate atomicity needs and isolation ones. We propose to include a WS-IsolationSphere specification to the WS-Coordination types family without including it to the WS-Transaction one. To make possible this separation, we propose to reorganise the existing WS-Coordination types. We propose to consider WS-Coordination types as parts of one of the multiple Behavioural Spheres (Atomicity sphere, Isolation Sphere, Compensation Sphere, Multiple Instantiation Sphere, ...).

Behaviour Spheres propose to make separation of concerns between process design and behaviour properties specification. Properties concerned by this approach were related to transactional behaviour and spheres introduced a lot of flexibility and expressiveness in this topic such as Atomicity Spheres [9][1][10] and Compensation Spheres [8]. We also identified other applications such as instantiation management with multiple instantiation [2]. In this work, we focus on the case of isolation management. Behavioural Spheres consider some properties (atomicity, isolation, compensation, security, and so on) as applied to groups of activities or sub processes. To clarify which situation is adapted to the Behavioural Sphere approach we provides three main principles to respect:

- **Principle 1:** Separation of concerns between process design and behavioural properties specification.
- **Principle 2:** Behaviour supported by a sphere and applied to the entire sphere's activities do not produce the same effects when applied to each activity of the sphere separately.
- **Principle 3:** The use of Behaviour Spheres introduces flexibility and increases expressiveness compared to non-sphere approaches.

We identified a set of Behavioural Spheres adapted to Web Services environment and we propose to use WS-Coordination to provide a framework for Behavioural Spheres specifications that we call WS-Sphere. We propose a non exhaustive family of WS-Sphere coordination types composed of WS-AtomicitySphere, WS-IsolationSphere, WS-JointCompensationSphere and WS-MultipleInstantiationSphere. These four types that we have identified are those we guess compatible with the Behavioural Sphere approach.

The existing WS-Transaction family can be considered as part of the Atomicity Sphere type. Figure 2 illustrates the global organisation of the WS-Sphere integration with WS-Coordination.

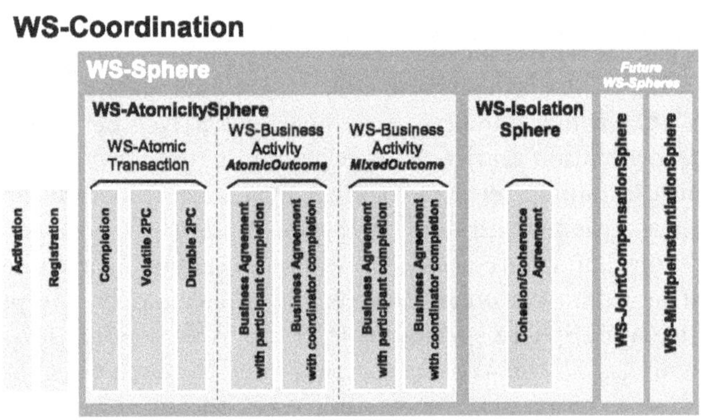

Fig. 2. WS-Sphere integration to WS-Coordination

Our main contribution aims to reorganise the WS-Transaction specification and to propose a solution to isolation management in Web Services coordination.

5.1 WS-IsolationSphere Proposal

Our approach based on isolation spheres consider two isolation dimensions: cohesion and coherence. It consists in a process-driven point of view and can also be specified over WS-Coordination and provide a new type of WS-Sphere that we call WS-IsolationSphere.

A WS-IsolationSphere represents a new type of coordination focused on isolation management. It inherits WS-Coordination properties (Activation and Registration) and it is initiated over the choice of a cohesion and a coherence level (Cohesion/Coherence Agreement) when a participant registers to a WS-IsolationSphere. The requirements ensured by the coordination framework depend on these two levels. During the registration process, the participant and the coordinator exchange the coordination context that already implements extensibility elements. We propose to use this standard way to communicate the cohesion and coherence levels to the coordinator registration service similar to the following context:

```
<?xml version="1.0" encoding="utf-8 "?>
<S:Envelope xmlns:S="http://www.w3.org/2001/12/soap-envelope"
    <S:Header>
        . . .
        <wscoor:CoordinationContext
            xmlns:wsme="http://www.w3.org/2002/06/msgext"
            xmlns:wscoor="http://www.w3.org/2002/06/Coordination"
            xmlns:myApp="http://www.w3.org/2002/06/myApp">
            <wsme:Identifier>http://www.loria.fr/Coor/123</wsme:Identifier>
            <wsme:Expires>2006-10-22T14:30:00.000-05:00</wsme:Expires>
            <wscoor:CoordinationType>
                http://xml-soap.org/2006/03/IsolationSphere
            </wscoor:CoordinationType>
            <wscoor:RegistrationService>
                <Address>
                    http://myservice.com/mycoordinationservice/registration
                </Address>
                <myApp:BetaMark> ... </myApp:BetaMark>
                <myApp:EBDCode> ... </myApp:EBDCode>
            </wscoor:RegistrationService>
            <myApp:CohesionLevel>
                 RepeatableRead
            </myApp:CohesionLevel>
            <myApp:CoherenceLevel>
                 ActivityCohrence
            </myApp:CoherenceLevel>
        </wscoor:CoordinationContext>
        . . .
    </S:Header>
```

The implementation of software capabilities in web services platforms depends on the used information system. We suggest a solution based on middlewares between the Web Service Execution Engine and the DataBase System. It is important to note that isolation management is limited to the same endpoint. Usually, different endpoints do not use the same database and are not located on a same Web Services Execution Engine compliant with WS-IsolationSpheres.

5.2 Nested Spheres and Registration/Exit Services

Contrary to WS-Transaction, the registration service for a WS-IsolationSphere is able to decide to redirect a registration to another WS-IsolationSphere. Once an isolation sphere coordinator is initiated by an initiator that determines the coordinator cohesion and coherence levels during the first registration, participants can register and select both cohesion and coherence levels. Differences between the choice of these levels and those of the coordinator can occur. Also differences from one participant to another can occur. This is a natural phenomenon due to the difference of participant requirements. We propose a procedure executed for each registration to an Isolation Sphere coordinator as follows:

```
Procedure : Register(Part,Coor,PCsL,PCrL)
Coor : the current coordinator ID
Part : the participant ID
PCsL : Participant Cohesion Level
PCrL : Participant Coherence Level
SubCoords[] : list of sub coordinators of Coor
BEGIN
IF(CCsL(Coor)==PCsL && CcrL(Coor)==PCrL) {
  ValidateRegistration(Part,Coor); }
ELSE
  FORALL(subc IN SubCoords) {
    IF(CCsL(subc)==PCsL && CcrL(subc)==PCrL) {
        ValidateRegistration(Part,Coor);
        ValidateRegistration(Part,subc); }
  }
NewCoor = create_sub_coordinator(Coor);
ValidateRegistration(Part,Coor);
ValidateRegistration(Part,NewCoor);
END;

CCsL(c) : returns the cohesion level of a given coordinator c
CCrL(c) : returns the coherence level of a given coordinator c
```

Using the isolation sphere registration procedure, nested spheres are possible. The implementation of such registration procedure enhance the flexibility of isolation management: participants are not obliged to use only coordinator levels but they can propose different levels that coexist with the coordinator's ones.

Isolation spheres can then imbricate and isolation behaviour is enriched. A Sphere can contain other sub spheres that have different isolation needs. A sub sphere defines its own levels for cohesion and coherence but can also benefit from the impact of isolation levels of the upper sphere. Such registration procedure induces an Exit procedure that redirect also to other sub spheres as follows:

```
Procedure : Exit(Part,Coor)
Coor : the current coordinator ID
Part : the participant ID
PCsL : Participant Cohesion Level
PCrL : Participant Coherence Level
SubCoords[] : list of sub coordinators of Coor
BEGIN
ValidateExit(Part,Coor);
FORALL(subc IN SubCoords) {
  IF(Participate(Part,subc))
     ValidateExit(Part,subc); }
END;

Participate(p,c) : returns true if p is a participant of coordinator c
CCsL(c) : returns the cohesion level of a given coordinator c
CCrL(c) : returns the coherence level of a given coordinator c
```

6 Conclusion

In this work, we proposed to introduce isolation sphere approach, and more generally behavioural sphere approach in WS-Coordination framework. We integrated WS-Sphere encapsulating WS-AtomicitySphere (including the existing

WS-Transaction), WS-IsolationSphere and other proposals such as WS-ComensationSphere and WS-MultipleInstantiationSphere. We focused on WS-IsolationSphere to introduce flexible isolation management in Web Services coordination using the duality cohesion/coherence levels. We provided registration procedure allowing nested spheres and redirected registration to respond to web services requirements.

More research need to be performed in the following areas. Firstly, we intend to consider compatibility of Behaviour Spheres of different nature and especially atomicity and isolation ones. Additionally we plan to investigate how such heterogeneous Behaviour Spheres can imbricate or even intersect. Finally we intend to implement a full-operational Web Service Execution Engine allowing such WS-Spheres and we aim to implement lower level capabilities to ensure cohesion and coherence levels respect.

References

1. Wijnand Derks, Juliane Dehnert, Paul Grefen, and Willem Jonker. Customized atomicity specification for transactional workflow. In *Proceedings of the Third International Symposium on Cooperative Database Systems for Advanced Applications (CODAS'01)*, pages 140–147. IEEE Computer Society, 2001.
2. Adnene Guabtni and François Charoy. Multiple instantiation in a dynamic workflow environment. In Anne Persson and Janis Stirna, editors, *Advanced Information Systems Engineering, 16th International Conference, CAiSE 2004, Riga, Lavtia*, volume 3084 of *Lectures Notes in Computer Science*, pages 175–188. Springer, Jun 2004.
3. Adnene Guabtni, François Charoy, and Claude Godart. Spheres of isolation: adaptation of isolation levels to transactional workflow. In Wil M.P. van der Aalst et al., editor, *Business Process Management, 3rd International Conference, BPM 2005, Nancy, France*, volume 3649 of *Lectures Notes in Computer Science*, pages 458–463. Springer, September 2005.
4. IBM, BEA Systems, Microsoft, Arjuna, Hitachi, IONA, ftp://www6.software.ibm.com/software/developer/library/WS-Coordination.pdf. *Web Services Coordination*, August 2005.
5. IBM, BEA Systems, Microsoft, Arjuna, Hitachi, IONA, http://www-128.ibm.com/developerworks/library/specification/ws-tx/. *Web Services Transaction*, Aug 16 2005.
6. IBM, BEA Systems, Microsoft, SAP AG, Siebel Systems, http://www-128.ibm.com/developerworks/library/specification/ws-bpel/. *Business Process Execution Language for Web Services*, version 1.1 edition, Feb 01 2005.
7. Charles T. Davies Jr. Data processing spheres of control. *IBM Systems Journal 17(2): 179-198*, 1978.
8. Frank Leymann. Supporting business transactions via partial backward recovery in workflow management systems. In *BTW*, pages 51–70, 1995.
9. Frank Leymann and Dieter Roller. *Production Workflow*, chapter Chapter 7 : Workflows and Transactions. Ed. Prentice Hall, Inc., Upper Saddle River, New Jersey, second edition edition, 2000.
10. Willem-Jan van den Heuvel and Sergei Artyshchev. Developing a three-dimensional transaction model for supporting atomicity spheres. *International Workshop on Web Services Research, Standardization, and Deployment*, 2002.

Acquisition of Process Descriptions from Surgical Interventions

Thomas Neumuth[1], Gero Strauß[1,2], Jürgen Meixensberger[1,3], Heinz U. Lemke[1,4], and Oliver Burgert[1]

[1] Innovation Center Computer Assisted Surgery (ICCAS), University of Leipzig
Philipp-Rosenthal-Str. 55, 04103 Leipzig
firstname.lastname@medizin.uni-leipzig.de
[2] Department of ENT-surgery, University Hospital Leipzig
[3] Department of Neurosurgery, University Hospital Leipzig
[4] Department of Radiology, University of Southern California

Abstract. The recording and analysis of process descriptions from running surgical interventions is a very new and promising field named *Surgical Workflows.* Surgical Workflows fulfill two major objectives: they form the base of scientific evaluation and rapid prototyping of surgical assist systems, and they pave the road for the entering of workflow management systems into the operating room for intraoperative support of the surgeon. In this paper we describe how process descriptions from surgical interventions can be obtained for Surgical Process Modelling (SPM) as a specific domain of Business Process Modelling (BPM). After the introduction into the field of Surgical Workflows and the motivation of the research efforts, we deal with theoretical considerations about surgical interventions and the identification of classifications. Based on that, we propose the extendable structure for computational data acquisition support and conclude with use cases. The presented approach was applied to more than 200 surgical interventions of 10 different intervention types from otorhinolaryngology, neurosurgery, heart surgery, eye surgery, and interventional radiology, and it represents an ongoing project.

1 Introduction

The development of *surgical assist systems* (SAS) is often driven by emerging technologies and not by the needs of the end user - the surgeons. The systems do not adopt to the surgical routine and therefore are often not accepted by the surgeons. This motivates the methodical and scientific analysis of surgical interventions [1,2] for the development of SAS which solve clinical problems in a feasible way. The analysis is based on *Surgical Workflows.* In medical engineering the term Surgical Workflows refers to the general methodological concept of the acquisition of process descriptions from surgical interventions, the clinical and technical analysis of them, and the automated processing into workflow schemes that are able to drive a workflow management system as a meta process control for the operating room of the future. To be able to use Surgical Workflows

S. Bressan, J. Küng, and R. Wagner (Eds.): DEXA 2006, LNCS 4080, pp. 602–611, 2006.

for analysis purposes or the derivation of research needs for SAS systems, one needs a technical description of the surgical intervention [3,4,5]. Today, a surgical intervention is treated more as an art rather than a well-defined activity which can be entered into a formal model, the *Surgical Process Model*. Therefore, there is a need for describing the intraoperative surgical reality. To obtain reliable data for carrying out research on process descriptions of surgical interventions, it is important to find a way to describe the surgical steps and their contents to set up a proper data acquisition process. The first step is the conceptual separation of entities participating in the intervention.

The particular features of abstraction, significance, and presentation, which characterize general model theory [6], can be applied to the field of Surgical Workflows. The Surgical Process Model is an abstraction of a surgical intervention. Only such characteristics of the original that are of interest for the model-user, e.g. the surgeon or the medical engineer, are recorded. The significance demands a limitation of the data manifold that can be acquired. It is, on the one hand, oriented towards surgical questions, e.g. "Is there a qualitative improvement or advancement in the patient outcome when a specific surgical tool is used?" On the other hand it has to be useful to build the base for technical developments. A technical question could be: "Which information is consumed or produced in which surgical work steps?"

Only a few approaches deal with the description of surgical interventions. These approaches have some limitations we want to adjust with our work. As requirements we set: vertically hierarchical decomposition and horizontal classification of entities (cf. Sect. 2), both on a sufficient level of detail; a formal or semiformal structure with an ontology or recording scheme; the application in multiple surgical disciplines and computational support for data acquisition and further processing. MacKenzie et al. [7] present a hierarchical decomposition, but no horizontal classification and further no (semi-)formal representation of their recording structure. In [8] these requirements are fulfilled, but the horizontal classification is done only implicitly and the application towards multiple surgical disciplines has not been shown. Furthermore, this work is focused on interventions with multimodal image-guidance restricting the application field. Münchenberg's approach [9], due to its focus on robot assistance, was only shown on a real specific application case. The EN 1828 [10] aims at decomposing the terminological phrases of surgical statements according to a reference concept system. It is a top-down approach and applicable to multiple surgical disciplines, but it does not deal with data acquisition. A medical approach in [11] was set up without computational support or any formalization, but it shows a proper use case. Contributions from the BPM domain such as BPMI [12] or the work of the WfMC [13] generally do not reach by their intention a sufficient level of detail for carrying out research on Surgical Workflows.

In Sect. 2 we deal with considerations about vertically hierarchical and explicitly horizontal classifications, and we propose a recording structure. In Sect. 3 we show the applicability towards intervention types of several surgical disciplines and adequate software support for data acquisition.

2 Methods

2.1 Structuring Surgical Interventions

During the recording of the surgical intervention course, the key issue is coping with information overload. A simple question such as: "Who does what and when?" can result in a massive amount of data. The first step for structuring is a classification along structural axes that have to be identified. For structuring surgeries, two general axes can be formulated: a *horizontal* axis with different kinds of entities that can be recorded and a *vertical* axis with different levels of granularity.

These granularity levels determine in which detail the process is recorded and later analyzed. To illustrate this we take an intervention whose surgical core activity is a cutting of tissue and assume that this cutting raises hemorrhage. The protruding blood has to be suctioned off simultaneously to the cutting process. This single work step can be examined on the vertical axis under various levels of granularity (see Fig. 1):

(i) a cumulative step "cutting" can be defined as the smallest possible partial work step for the surgeon, which comprises the partial work steps of cutting and suctioning,
(ii) partial work steps can be defined for "cutting" and "suctioning", which can occur independently from one another,
(iii) partial work steps can be defined which subdivide the suctioning process into actions such as "surgeon uses aspirator for suctioning" or "surgeon discontinues suctioning", e.g for some time to gain a better prospect of the surgical field, but resumes suctioning after a very short period of time.

The higher the vertical resolution, the more information can be obtained, e.g. about the used body parts of the surgeon. The granulation level in concordance with (ii) allows for a definition of body parts such as "left hand of the surgeon" and "right hand of the surgeon". If a process description requires additionally the activities of the scrub nurse and an assistant on the same level of granularity, level (ii) will result in six concurrent and simultaneous strands along the time line, which furthermore can have various causal relations.

Horizontal classifications aim at the separation of entities regarding their capacities. For the classification of abstract entities that can be framed, we applied the factual perspectives function, behaviour, organization, information, and operation [14] on Surgical Workflows [15]. One of the major advantages of this classification is its orthogonality: the several classes represent different complementary perspectives. The *organization* perspective shows which participant (e.g. surgeon, assistant, etc.) performs a work step as an organizational unit. In Fig. 1 (i) is executed by the surgeon, whereas he is seen as an abstract atomic entity, and (ii) + (iii) additionally refer to the used hands. The function perspective describes function-oriented work units that are executed. As *functional* units in intervention descriptions, the activities in conjunction with the treated structure can be recognized. The *information* perspective deals with consumed or produced data. For the acquisition of surgeries information like the completion of precedent work steps, computational data (images, signals), technical parameter, but also interparticipant communication are relevant. The *operation* perspective reflects the surgical instruments and tools that are used to execute a work unit. The *behavior* perspective focuses on the control flow elements. In a rough classification, we simply divide it into temporal, logical and causal behavior. Temporal behaviour means that work units are oriented along a timeline and therefore to each other. Logical behavior focuses on behavioral units such as AND-constructs, parallel executions of work steps as well as synchronisations and loops. Causal behavior states causal dependencies of work units on other work units.

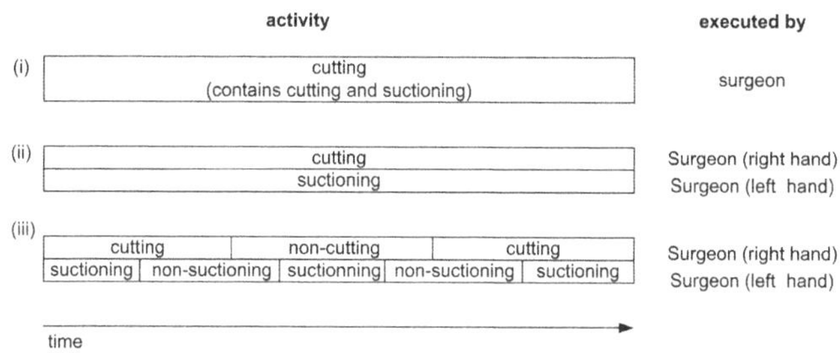

Fig. 1. Examples of Granularity Levels

2.2 A Data Structure for Surgical Process Descriptions

We defined a data structure capable of containing relevant data about surgical interventions - the recording scheme. It is presented in Fig. 2 as a simplified UML class diagram. The central object is `Rec_workflow`. It reflects the record of a Surgical Workflow of one surgical case. Generally, it consists of three categories of data: *header data*, *body data*, and *relational data*.

Header data are intended to provide a facility to consider contextual information of the recorded surgical intervention, the main classes are:

- `Patient` related information containing data such as the patients age or sex,
- the surgical `Discipline` with the child elements `Diagnosis` and `Therapy`,
- `Participant` with the elements `Position` (e.g. surgeon) and `Actor` (e.g. right hand),
- `Rec_Date`, the date of recording,
- `Rec_Location`, the place of recording for indicating institutions or specialized operating rooms,
- `Rec_by` for the recording person.

The purpose of the header data is to express on a general level where and when the intervention takes places, to whom it happens, and who is acting. The header can be extended easily for including information of the similar category, such as patient related radiological images used during the intervention or surgical experience with the intervention type.

The *body data* are subdivided into `Activity`, `Event`, and `State`. `Activity` is intended to represent a surgical work step. Each `Activity` consists of:

- `Starttime` and `Stoptime`,
- one or more `Actuator` that have the same position as stated in the `Participant` element. The actuator additionally indicates various `Usedbodyparts`, derived from `Actor`,
- `ActivityData` that specify the goal of the work step by sampling the surgical deed as `Action` in form of a verb, `UsedInstrument` for supporting the deed, and `TreatedStructure` as referential localization inside the patient's body.

The sequential occurrence of *activities* symbolizes the acquired workflow for each actuator and explains on a detailed level what is done, where, whereby, and when. Case dependent extensions are informational units, such as the generation of an image after X-Ray use as output of an activity, blood pressure check as input, or detailed spatial data, e.g. for navigation use.

The concept of `State` is used to present differentiated subsystems. As an example, the gaze direction of the surgeon is considered in the system states of "surgeons eyes on monitor", "surgeons eyes on situs" or "other direction" [7], assuming that no other gaze directions are of interest. Similarly, computational states can be included in the SPM. The temporal information related with `State` is the time when a state transition occurs. Every subsystem is considered of being in a default state at the beginning of the data acquisition and the points in time for edges between the states are acquired.

`Event` is a related concept. They are predefined to exist at a point of time. The difference to states is that `Event` is not restricted to a subsystem and can exist unbounded. Events consider dedicated aspects of the surgery, such as communication between participants, announced cognitive decisions of the participants, or the explicit capturing of computational events like error messages of mechatronic support systems etc.

The use of the proposed concepts, namely *activities*, *states* and *events* raises another question: the causal relations between them. Using only the concepts mentioned above, a process description exists, but contents are only related by temporal information. To acquire an appropriate process description, the recorded components have to be linked causally. `Relation` consists of `Input`, `Output` and `type`. `Input` and `Output` are references to instances of `Activity`, `Event`, and `State`. Types can be defined by natural language expressions, such as *consists-of*, *caused*, etc. Thereby expressions such as "message A - caused - activity B" or "activity C - belongs to - interventional phase D" can be sampled. This concept offers the opportunity to preaggregate the Surgical Procedure Model into surgical phases if the process is recorded on a detailed level of granularity and contains a lot of activities. For the example, a subsystem "phases" consisting of the states, e.g. *preparational phase* (default), *surgical core activities*, and *completion phase* is set up. By using a relation such as *belongs to*, activities can be allocated to these phases and therefore extend the already existing temporal relation by causal aspects.

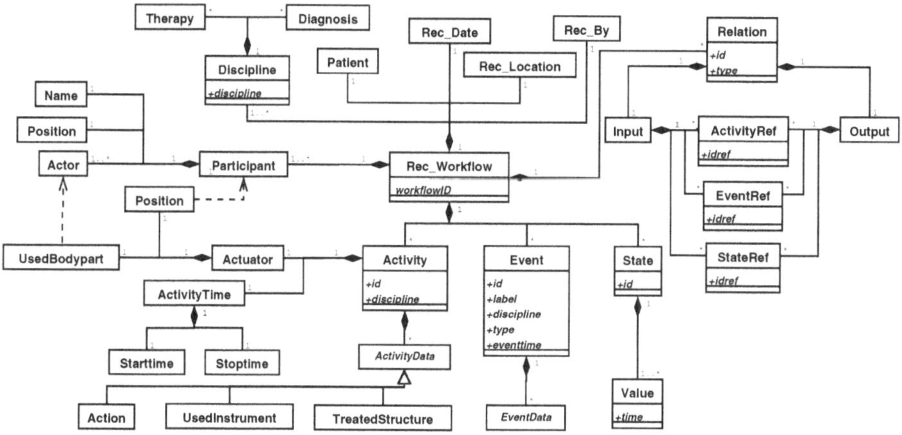

Fig. 2. Simplified Recording Scheme for Surgical Procedure Models as UML class diagram

3 Results

The approach presented an opportunity for computer supported acquisition of process instances from surgical interventions. The recording is done with computational support by trained medical students. An editor is used to facilitate the recording of the surgical work steps ergonomically and to deal with the challenges mentioned so far. The purpose of the editor is to support the person recording the data in dealing with the complex relationships and concurrencies. The values of `UsedInstrument`, `Action`, and `TreatedStructure` are loaded from register files according to `Therapy` selected in the header data. This provides several advantages:

- the contents are provided according to the intervention type, e.g. for an intervention on the vocal chords only the relevant anatomic structures on the procedure path to and around the vocal chords have to be considered. Furthermore, surgeons from different disciplines sometimes use different names for the same surgical instruments;
- by using predefined selectable contents, the recording persons are obliged to use appropriate terminology, which builds the base for a detailed comparability;
- the contents can be provided by remote server applications if a spatial separation of the editor and the register files is sensible, e.g. for multicenter studies where all centers have to use the same glossary database.

The contents of the register files containing a list of instruments or actions are provided for the editor from a glossary database. A general glossary for Surgical

Workflow recording should come from specifications like Functional Model of Anatomy[5] or GALEN[6].

The output protocol contains the recorded aspects of the surgical intervention and serves as a starting point for further processing. As output format, XML was chosen for flexibility. A direct storage of the protocol into a database was not implemented, because of the irreconcilability of backing up alterable recording schema caused by the work in progress and the relatively static character of database models.

In Fig. 3 an example result of post-processing of the resulting XML is shown. The image presents the graphical progress of a microlaryngoscopy, an intervention type from otorhinolaryngology, with detected sequential and parallel activities and one revealed loop. The graphical presentation was generated in Scalable Vector Graphics by applying some simple algorithms on the protocol. The shapes represent the activities of the surgeon and the scrub nurse; the alignment inside the surgeons' column is oriented along the used hand for execution.

Up until May 2006, the entities of the presented approach was used to record and analyze more than 200 surgical interventions from otorhinolaryngology (functional endoscopic sinus surgery, microlaryngoscopy, panendoscopy), neurosurgery (craniotomy, discectomy, hypophysisadenoma), heart surgery (mitral valve reconstruction), eye surgery (cataract interventions), and interventional radiology (nerve blocks, facet blocks). The records were taken at the University Hospital Leipzig, the Heart Center Leipzig and the Georgetown University Medical Center, Washington D.C.

4 Conclusion

The acquisition and analysis of process descriptions from running surgical interventions is a very new and promising field in medical engineering. The first results we have achieved show that the protocols can be used for the detailed description of surgical interventions for *Surgical Process Modelling*.

We identified horizontal and vertical classifications regarding orthogonal perspectives and different levels of granularity that have been considered during the data acquisition. The awareness of these granularity levels raises a number of considerations: there is an increasing complexity and amount of data along with a finer granulation, a problem of a clear definition of activities, and it is more difficult to analyze and post-process if an increasing amount of information needs to be considered. Regarding the recording scheme, our approach allows records on several levels of granularity and provides an opportunity to analyze surgical interventions in detail.

Our approach could be improved by some methodical changes: It would be useful to formalize the recorded entities with a domain specific extension of a foundational top-level ontology like the GFO framework [17], such as presented

[5] http://sig.biostr.washington.edu/projects/fm/

[6] Generalized Architecture for Languages, Encyclopedia and Nomenclatures in medicine; http://www.opengalen.org/index.html

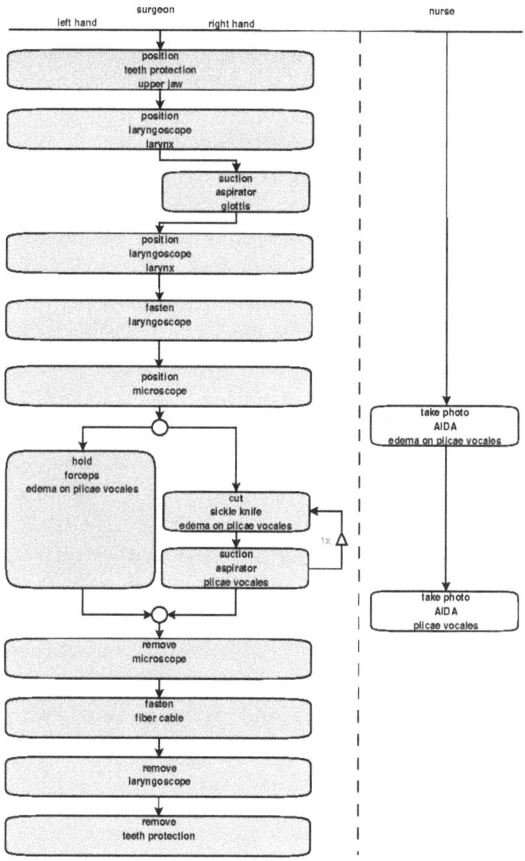

Fig. 3. Graphical Representation of a Microlaryngoscopy Case

in [18] to leave the formal model open for later enhancements or to map this formalization into technical process descriptions such as Petri nets, Event Driven Process Chains, or other established descriptions in Business Process Modelling. Furthermore, the manual capacity of human recorders has its limitations. This can be advanced in three methodical directions: At first, the records should be objectified by video support. Secondly, it would be useful to have tracking support for data acquisition because the manual recording is not feasible in the long term. As an optimal solution, a complete and automated tracking would be useful, but it is not reliable due to the present state of the general technical progress. Additionally, there is also an economic question. Finally, an online connection to ontological knowledge-modelling applications such as Protégé[7] should be established. This could decrease the recording stress or prevent erroneous recording, e.g. by suggesting surgical instruments depending on a chosen action

[7] http://protege.stanford.edu

or nearby anatomic structures depending on a spatial position. In the future, the latter enhancement can be further facilitated by reasoning support. Reversely, the recording results can contribute to the construction of self-extending domain specific surgical knowledge-frameworks.

As application domains that can profit by these approaches, MacKenzie et al. [7] named the evaluation of operating room layouts; improvements of physical, animal, augmented or virtual surgical training and simulation systems; the evaluation of surgical performance with skills levels and learning curves or customized preoperative procedure planning. Jannin et al. [8] mentioned the generation of detailed structured interventional reports; the surgical planning support; a prediction based on the query of similar cases; interdisciplinary analyses of surgical procedures and the contribution of a large world wide intervention database for quality improvement.

Moreover, many methods from the Business Process Domain such as Business Process Analysis and Optimization as well as quality management methods or risk management can be applied. In the long term, the automated derivation of workflow schemes from the models and their use for workflow management systems or process control systems for surgical support, the driving of virtual surgical training systems by what-if-scenarios or surgical education systems are enabled by these basic works.

The data acquisition methodology and tools presented in this paper form a sound basis for further work in the research field of Surgical Workflows. Based on that, the *Surgical Process Models* and *Surgical Workflow* software systems can yield to various new *Surgical Assist Systems.*

Acknowledgements

The Innovation Center Computer Assisted Surgery (ICCAS) at the Faculty of Medicine at the University of Leipzig is funded by the German Federal Ministry for Education and Research (BMBF) and the Saxon Ministry of Science and the Fine Arts (SMWK) in the scope of the initiative *Unternehmen Region* with the grant numbers 03 ZIK 031 and 03 ZIK 032.

References

1. Lemke, H.U.: Surgical Workflow and Surgical Picture Archiving and Communication Systems. Lecture at the UCLA Seminars on Imaging and Informatics, Arrowhead (2004)
2. Cleary, K., Kinsella, A., Mun, S.K.: OR2020 workshop report: operating room of the future. in Lemke, H.U., Inamura, K., Doi, K., Vannier, M.W., Farman, A.G.(eds.): Proceedings of the 19th CARS 2005, Elsevier ICS Vol. 1281, Elsevier, Amsterdam (2005) 832-838
3. Burgert, O., Neumuth, T., Fischer, M., Falk, V., Strauß, G., Trantakis, C., Jacobs, S., Dietz, A., Meixensberger, J., Mohr, F.W., Korb, W., Lemke, H.U.: Surgical Workflow Modeling. MMVR 2006

4. Burgert, O., Neumuth, T., Strauß, G., Trantakis, C., Falk, V., Lemke, H.U.: Workflow-analysis of Surgical Interventions in ENT and Neurosurgery. in Weber, S., Langlotz, F., Bier, J., Lueth, T.C. (eds.): CAS-H - 3rd International Symposium Proceedings, VDI Verlag, Düsseldorf (2005) 85 - 86
5. Neumuth, T., Durstewitz, N., Fischer, M., Strauß, G., Dietz, A., Meixensberger, J., Jannin, P., Cleary, K., Lemke, H.U., Burgert, O.: Structured Recording of Intraoperative Surgical Workflows, in Horii, S.C., Ratib, O.M. (eds.): Medical Imaging 2006 – PACS and Imaging Informatics, Progress in Biomedical Optics and Imaging Vol. 7(31), SPIE, Bellingham, WA (2006) CID 61450A
6. Stachowiak, H.: Allgemeine Modelltheorie, Springer, Wien (1973)
7. MacKenzie, C.L., Ibbotson, J.A., Cao, C.G.L., Lomax, A.J.: Hierarchical decomposition of laparoscopic surgery: a human factors approach to investigating the operating room environment. Min Invas Ther Allied Techn, 10(3), (2001) 121-127
8. Jannin, P., Raimbault, M., Morandi, X., Riffaud L., Gibaud, B.: Models of Surgical Procedures for Multimodal Image-Guided Neurosurgery. J Comp Aid Surg, 8(2), (2003) 98-106
9. Münchenberg, J.E.: Rechnergestützte Operationsplanung in der Mund-Kiefer-Gesichts-Chirurgie. PhD Thesis, University of Karlsruhe (2001)
10. CEN: Health Informatics - Categorial structure for classifications and coding systems of surgical procedures. EN 1828:2002, CEN/TC 251 (2002)
11. Fischer, M., Strauß, G., Burgert, O., Dietz, A., Trantakis, C., Meixensberger, J., Lemke, H.U.: ENT-surgical workflow as an instrument to assess the efficiency of technological developments in medicine. in Lemke, H.U., Inamura, K., Doi, K., Vannier, M.W., Farman, A.G.(eds.): Proceedings of the 19th CARS 2005, Elsevier ICS Vol. 1281, Elsevier, Amsterdam (2005) 851-855
12. Object Management Group: Business Process Modelling Notation Specification – final adopted specification. dtc/06-02-01, OMG/BPMI, Needham, MA (2006)
13. Workflow Management Coalition: Workflow Process Definition Interchange - XML Process definition Language. Document Number WfMC-TC-1025, version 1.0, WfMC, Lighthouse Point, FL (2002)
14. Jablonski, S., Bussler, C.: Workflow Management: Modeling Concepts, Architecture and Implementation. Thomson Learning, Thomson (1996)
15. Neumuth, T., Schumann, S., Strauß, G., Jannin, P., Meixensberger, J., Dietz, A., Lemke, H.U., Burgert, O.: Visualization Options for Surgical Workflows. accepted for Computer Assisted Radiology and Surgery (2006)
16. Neumuth, T., Pretschner, A., Trantakis, C., Fischer, M., Lemke, H.U., Burgert, O.: An Approach to XML-based Description of Intraoperative Surgical Workflows. Eckstein, R., Tolksdorf, R.: Tagungsband Berliner XML-Tage 2005, Humboldt University Berlin, Berlin, (2005) 147-152
17. Herre, H., Heller, B., Burek, P., Hoehndorf, R., Loebe, F., Michalek, H.: General Formal Ontology (GFO) – a foundational ontology integrating objects and processes. Onto-Med Report Nr. 8, Research Group Ontologies in Medicine (Onto-Med), University of Leipzig, Leipzig (2006)
18. Burgert, O., Neumuth, T., Lempp, F., Mudunuri, R., Meixensberger, J., StrauSS, G., Dietz, A., Jannin, P., Lemke, H.U.: Linking Top-level Ontologies and Surgical Workflows. accepted for Computer Assisted Radiology and Surgery (2006)

Adaptive Policies in Information Lifecycle Management

Rohit M. Lotlikar[1] and Mukesh Mohania[2]

[1] IBM India Research Lab-Bangalore,
IBM, EGL-D Block, Domlur Inner Ring Rd, Bangalore, 560071, India
rohitmlo@in.ibm.com
[2] IBM India Research Lab-Delhi,
Block 1, IIT, Hauz Khas, New Delhi, 110016, India
mkmukesh@in.ibm.com

Abstract. Adaptive policies contain parameters and take into consideration performance feedback to modify values of these parameters adaptively. We propose a method (applicable to the domain of Information Lifecycle Management) to automatically adapt these parameters. Design issues such as selection of sensors, desired ranges for sensors and effects of parameter sensitivity such as over-correction and under-correction are discussed.

1 Introduction

Policies are commonly used in systems to automate system behavior while reducing (preferably eliminating) the amount of human involvement/intervention needed. Policies are meant to be modifiable, so that the policy can be changed to suit changed requirements or operating conditions. A Policy has been described as [1] "a set of considerations designed to guide decisions of courses of action."

In Information Lifecycle Management, policies are used to automate various tasks such as backup, archival, restore, deletion and migration of data [2]. The typical considerations in formulating these policies include business requirements and regulations, IT infrastructure, and expected operating conditions. However, if subsequently, operating conditions diverge beyond what the policies were intended to handle, the system may not exhibit the desired behavior, and performance indicators may degrade, which is clearly undesirable. Unchecked, this may lead to violations of service level objectives (SLO's). In such a situation, the administrator needs to identify the policies which need modification and determine the proper modification for each of these policies.

Typically, the modification involves simply adjustments to policy parameter values rather than a change to the nature of the task performed by the policy, and we refer to such a modification as "tuning". If this tuning is performed automatically in response to state feedback, the policy is termed as *adaptive*. Adaptive policies have been used for, as an example, in load balancing [3] and well as for caching web pages [4]. Adapting policy parameters typically requires knowledge of the behaviour of the system and the solution techniques required are necessarily domain dependent. The contribution of our paper is a new algorithm for adapation of policy parameters applicable to the domain of Information

S. Bressan, J. Küng, and R. Wagner (Eds.): DEXA 2006, LNCS 4080, pp. 612–621, 2006.

Lifecycle Management and a study of the issues involved. This adaptation algorithm borrows ideas from control theory.

The organization of this paper proceeds as follows. In section 2, we describe related work in this area. In section 3, we describe the role that adaptive policies can play in Information Lifecycle Management and illustrate how the need for policy tuning arises. In section 4, we describe our model for automatically tuning the parameters of these adaptive policies. We perform experiments based on the scenario presented in section 3 to assess our model, these experiments and the results are described in section 5. Section 6 concludes with a discussion of the pros and cons of the proposed approach.

2 Preliminaries

2.1 Policy Structure

We use the standard ECA model in which policies consist of three components - an Event, a Condition and an Action, as explained below.

- **Event** Policies are invoked/evaluated either by an external event (such as network initialization, violations of thresholds) or by time based events (e.g. "every Sunday at 1:00 am").
- **Condition** This specifies the "if clause" under which the decision component of an invoked policy will be executed out.
- **Action** This specifies the "then clause", for example, "archive orders placed more than 365 days ago".

The condition of the policy is defined on certain *state variables* which typically are indicators of the state or health of the managed system. When the policy is invoked, the condition is evaluated, and if this condition is true, the Action part of the policy is executed. The ECA model applies to both static and adaptive policies.

2.2 Adaptive Policies

For a policy to be considered adaptive, the policy must contain one or more parameters which are automatically tuned. These parameters could be part of the event, part of the condition or part of the action. Static policies may also contain parameters, however the parameters are not automatically updated. An example of a static policy without parameters is "If temperate exceeds 85 F turn air-conditioner ON". An example of a policy with parameters is "if temperate in the room exceeds 85 F turn air-conditioner to setting X" where X is a parameter and may be OFF, LOW, MEDIUM or HIGH. If the room temperate is used to determine the value of X, then the policy is *adaptive*.

2.3 Illustrative Scenario for Policy Adaptation

We consider a database of a department store. The store consist of three departments - clothing, hardware and sports. There are 3 corresponding *orders* tables - *clothing* table, *hardware* table and the *sports* table which store information about the orders placed with each department. Each order is in the form of a record containing *orderDate* and other fields. Once an order is placed, its record will remain in the table until it is archived or deleted by a policy.

We consider the following 5 policies (the first 4 of which involve archival or deletion of data) on the managed resource. The purpose of these policies is to prevent the size of the database and individual tables from growing too large, as this causes degradation in database performance.

Of the 5 policies, $P_{clothing}$ and $P_{hardware}$ are adaptive, the other 3 are static. $P_{clothing}$ contains an adaptive parameter n_c and $P_{hardware}$ contains an adaptive parameter n_h. n_c is part of the *Action* while n_h is part of the *Event*. n_h affects the frequency of evaluation of $P_{hardware}$, for example if $n_h = 2$, then $P_{hardware}$ will be evaluated every alternate week.

- **Overall policy** $P_{overall}$ **:** Every other Sunday at 3 am, delete records corresponding to orders older than 28 days from clothing, hardware and sports tables.
- **Policy for clothing department** $P_{clothing}$ **:** Every other Monday at 3 am, if the size of the clothing orders table exceeds 2000 records, archive records corresponding to orders older than n_c days from it.
- **Policy for hardware department** $P_{hardware}$ **:** Every n_h^{th} Thursday at 3 am, if the size of the hardware orders table exceeds 2000 records, archive records corresponding to orders older than 14 days from it.
- **Policy for sports department** P_{sports} **:** Every other Wednesday at 3 am, if the size of the sports orders table exceeds 2000 records, archive records corresponding to orders older than 14 days from it.
- **DBA Alert policy** P_{alert} **:** Every Wed at 1 pm, if the size of the database exceeds 10000 records, send an alert message to the DBA.

From performance considerations, the administrator determines that performance begins to progressively degrade for table sizes in excess of table sizes in excess of 2500. Accesses are infrequent after the first 7 days of order placement, rare after 14 days and practically nil after 21 days. The appropriate value for n_c would have to lie in the range of 7 to 21,

When archival takes place, there is a large drop in the sizes of tables on which archival is performed. The table size is at a local maximum just before archival begins. Large variations in table sizes are clearly undesirable because there would be a corresponding variation in database performance as well. Hence, increasing the frequency of evaluation of $P_{hardware}$ decreases the variation in the size of the hardware table.

To understand how the proposed model is useful, we study a few scenarios (or alternatively, *use cases*) and compare the kind of feedback we would like to get (i.e ground truth) with the feedback provided by the model.

3 Model for Adaptation of Policy Parameters

In this section we describe our proposed model for adaptation of policy parameters.

3.1 Learning Policy Parameters

Our technique borrows concepts from Control theory [5], which has been found to be applicable for management of performance of IT systems [6].

Given a policy parameter to be tuned, the first step is to identify the facet of system behavior that is influenced by this parameter and associate it with a measurable quantity which we call a *sensor*. For example, the parameter n_c of $P_{clothing}$ controls the size of the clothing table at the completion of the execution of its action. In our model, each sensor is associated with a "desired range" of values. The administrator specifies two values - the *upper-bound* and *lower bound* to define the desired range. The objective is to vary (adapt) policy parameters so as to maintain the sensor values between their respective lower-bound and upper-bound.

Assumptions Made. The following are the assumptions made in our model.

- Each parameter is numeric (integral or decimal) and is allowed to take on one of 3 values - denoted as LOW, MEDIUM and HIGH (the *parameter set*).
- Other factors remaining constant, the influence of a parameter on the corresponding sensor is assumed to be monotonic, i.e. the increasing the parameter value will either always increase the sensor value or will always decrease it. This influence is represented by a sensor-parameter matrix as depicted in Figure 4. The impact column describes whether incrementing the policy parameter has either the effect of increasing (excitatory influence) or decreasing the sensor values (inhibitory influence).
- Each parameter influences one and only one sensor.

Our model does not support the association of multiple parameters with a sensor, nor does it support the association of a parameter with multiple sensors. Multiple parameters are allowed within a policy, each of these must be associated with a unique independent sensor.

Learning Rule. The deviation of the sensor value from the desired-range is discretized into 3 categories as "within desired range", "exceeds upper bound" and "below lower bound". To translate this error signal into changes to parameter values, we make use of what we call *adaptation rules.* Each parameter is associated with an adaptation rule. The adaptation rule is analogous to the "controller module" in control theory.

The Adaptation rule for a parameter is framed based on the manner in which the parameter affects the sensor. The adaptation rule is depicted in Figure 1.

sensor value	**action to take on parameter**
above upper bound	decrement if excitatory, increment if inhibitory
below lower bound	increment if excitatory, decrement if inhibitory
within desired range	no action

Fig. 1. The adaptation rule (for some one parameter)

The overall adaptation mechanism is graphically depicted in Figure 2.

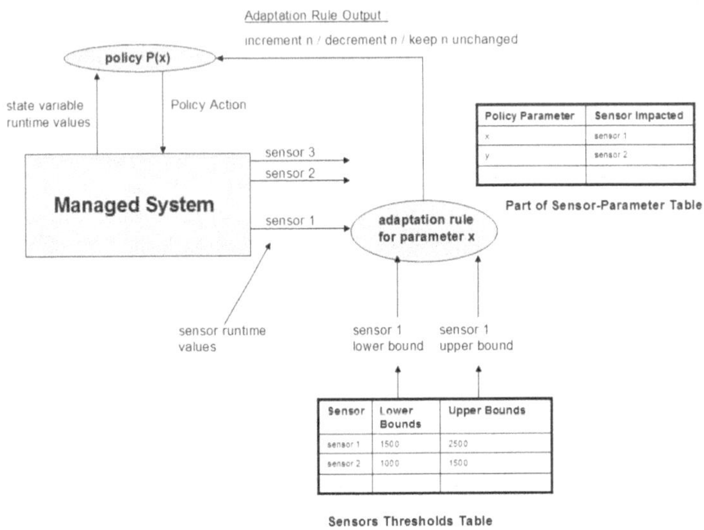

Fig. 2. Graphical Depiction of the Model for Adaptation of Policy Parameters

3.2 Design Issues

Defining Appropriate Sensors. For each parameter, the associated sensor should represent a quantity which is most directly and strongly influenced by the parameter. If this is not the case, the ability of the adaptation algorithm to maintain the sensor values within desired ranges will be undermined.

Parameter Sensitivity. Invocation of the adaptation rule and parameter update may take place anytime, however the effect of the parameter update is manifested only at the subsequent execution of the policy containing that parameter. This effect can be categorized as

- The sensor value is drawn into the desired range
- The sensor value is "over-corrects" i.e. the sensor value overshoots (transitions across) the desired range to other side of the desired range.
- The sensor value is "under-corrected" the sensor value does not transition into or across the desired range.

"Over-correction" is more likely when the sensor value is relatively sensitive to the parameter or if the desired range is relatively narrow. In this case, stability of the system is compromised, because parameter and sensor values can oscillate due to repeated updates.

"Under-correction" happens because of the relative insensitivity of a sensor value to a parameter update or because the sensor value is outside of the desired range by a large margin.

If such over-correction or under-correction takes place, the policy administrator needs to be alerted to take appropriate action, which may include adjusting the upper and lower bounds or the values corresponding to LOW, MEDIUM and HIGH of the parameter. We do not consider automatic adjustment of parameter values to handle such over-correction or under-correction because this would require making restrictive assumptions on the behavior of the system limiting its practical utility.

In our model, an oscillation is identified by a "round-tripping" of a parameter values in which the parameter value is not maintained constant for more than two evaluations. For example, if the sequence of parameter values at consecutive policy evaluations are MEDIUM-LOW-MEDIUM, or MEDIUM-LOW-LOW-MEDIUM, both these are treated as oscillations. However the sequence MEDIUM-LOW-LOW-LOW-MEDIUM is not considered as an oscillation since the parameter value remains constant at LOW for more than 2 firings.

4 Experimental Testbed and Validation

In this section we present an experimental setup to test the proposed models. We work with the example policies stated in section 2.

4.1 Experimental Setup

Orders are placed 24 × 7, at an average rate r_w that varies with the hour of the day and with the day of the week. We capture the placement of orders by inserts which occur randomly at an average rate r_w which varies with the time of the day and day of the week. For the experiment, we assume that 1 second of simulation time corresponds to 1 hour of simulated time; thus 200 days of data is being captured in 80 minutes of simulation.

The workload as well as policies are started at time $t = 0$. Initially the database is assumed to be empty (containing no data). Consequently, in the initial stages, none of the archival policies fire. After a few minutes (of simulation time), the size of the database and individual tables cross threshold sizes for which respective policy conditions evaluate to TRUE.

We test our model under a workload profile for which at intermediate time points the rate of order placement is modified to simulate changing operating

Sensor	Definition	lower bound	upper bound
s_c	Clothing table size at end of execution of $P_{clothing}$	1500	2500
s_h	Hardware table size at evaluation of $P_{hardware}$	2000	3000

Fig. 3. Sensor Design for the experimental setup

Policy	policy parameter	sensor impacted	impact	parameter set
$P_{clothing}$	n_c	s_c	inhibitory	LOW = 7, MEDIUM = 14 HIGH = 21
$P_{hardware}$	n_h	s_h	inhibitory	LOW = 1 MEDIUM = 2 HIGH = 4

Fig. 4. The sensor-parameter Table for the experimental setup

Scenario	Parameter under consideration	parameter set	observation
1	n_c	$7, 14, 21$	effect on s_c
2	n_c	$4, 14, 21$	over-correction of s_c
3	n_h	$1, 2, 4$	effect on s_h

Fig. 5. The different scenarios

conditions. At the start of week 8 (56 days), the rate of orders is suddenly doubled. At the start of week 16 (108 days) it is brought back down to its original value.

To study the effect of the adaptive learning of policy parameters, we compare the values of sensors s_c and s_h under different scenarios with and without adaptation of policy parameters. The sensors defined are shown in Figure 3. The parameter choices are shown in Figure 4. The scenarios we consider are depicted in Figure 5.

4.2 Operational Scenarios

Scenario 1 tests how our model responds to wide swings in workload. Scenario 2 illustrates how over-correction and oscillation can set in due to poor choice of the parameter value set. In Scenario's 1 and 2, the parameter n_c is adapted while Scenario 3, the parameter n_h is adapted. In all scenario's the initial values of n_c or n_h are NORMAL.

4.3 Simulation Results

- Scenario 1:
  - Without adaptation : From Figure6 (left), it is seen that when the rate of orders is doubled, the clothing table size at completion of policy execution (corresponds to the bottom of valleys of table size and is captured by sensor s_c) exceeds the upper-bound of 2500 and reaches around 3800.
  - With adaptive policies : From Figure6 (right) At $t = 72$ days, the upper bound on s_c is exceeded causing n_c of $P_{clothing}$ to be updated from

NORMAL to LOW (based on the adaptation rule). This causes s_c to reduce to around 2000 (for subsequent policy firings), which is within the desired range. At $t = 108$ days when the rate of incoming orders is brought back to normal, s_c crosses the lower bound of 1500. The value of n_c is then adapted from LOW to NORMAL, and subsequently from $t = 142$, s_c returns to the desired range.

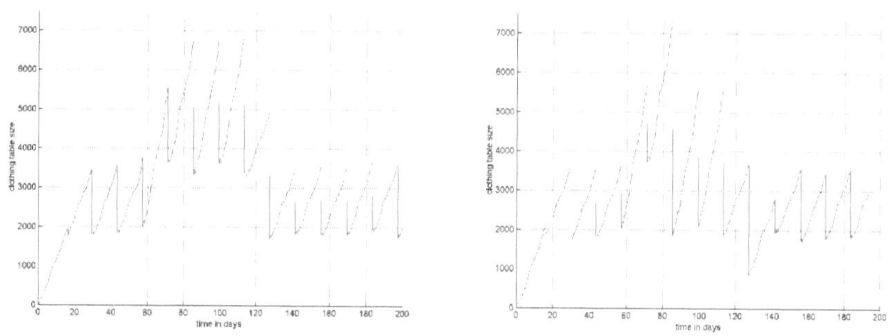

Fig. 6. Impact of adaptation of $P_{clothing}$ on clothing table size. Left: without adaptation, Right: with adaptation.

- Scenario 2 :
  - Figure 7 corresponds to Scenario 2. Doubling of the workload starting $t = 56$ results in the upper bound being exceeded at $t = 72$, and the adaptation rule updates n_c from NORMAL to LOW. In this case LOW = 4, and at the next execution of the clothing policy (at $t = 86$), all orders older than 4 days are deleted from the clothing table, and the value of the clothing table size recorded by sensor s_s at the end of policy execution is 1267 meaning that the sensor value has overshot the lower bound of 1500. Since the sensor value is now below the lower bound, the adaptation rule updates n_c from LOW to NORMAL. This is treated as an oscillation, and is caused by poor choices of values in the parameter set. Another oscillation cycle of NORMAL-LOW-NORMAL follows. These oscillations cease subsequently only because the workload returns to its initial value. Due to oscillation, the fluctuation of Table size is worse than without adaptation (compare with Figure 6 (left)).
- Scenario 3 :
  - Figure 8 corresponds to Scenario 3. Without adaptation, $P_{hardware}$ always executes every alternate week. Doubling of the workload at $t = 56$ causes s_h to exceed 3000, which is outside the desired range. With adapation, the evaluation frequency of the policy is increased to weekly after $t = 68$, and the peak value remains within the desired range. When the workload falls off to its initial value at $t = 108$, the evaluation frequency returns to every alternate week. The benefit of adapation is that the variation (max minus min) in table size has reduced.

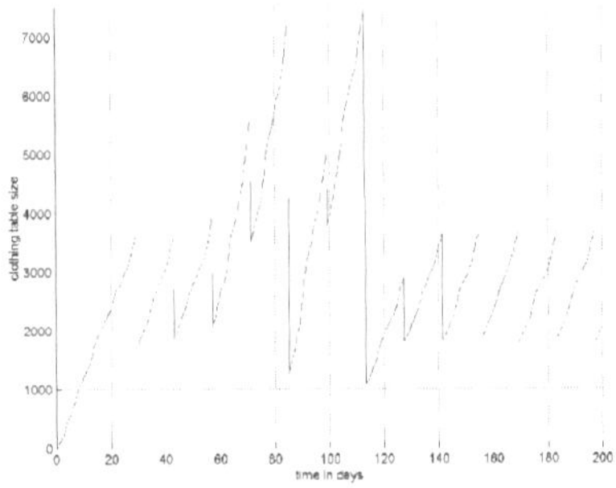

Fig. 7. Scenarios 2: Illustration of over-correction of clothing table size on account of poor choice for parameter n_c

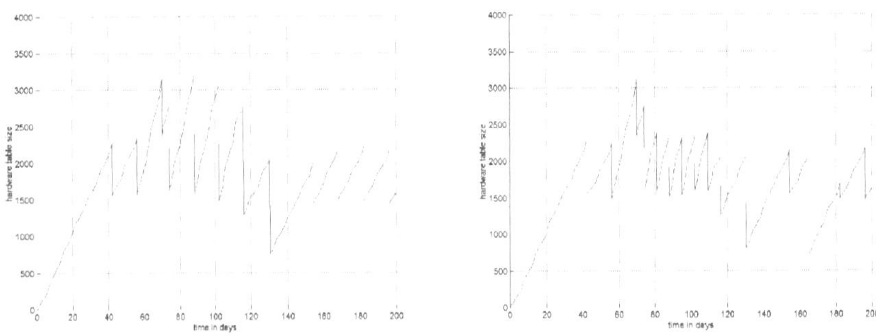

Fig. 8. Scenario 3: Note the impact of adaptation of $P_{hardware}$ (its evaluation frequency) on hardware table size. Left: without adaptation, Right: With adaptation.

5 Conclusions

The main contribution of this paper was in showing how adaptive policies can be useful for Information Lifecycle Management and presenting a method for performing the adaptation. Generally, the policy parameters which are made adaptive would influence certain operational variables (sensors) whose values we desire to control. In out framework, each parameter is associated with a sensor. The adaptation algorithm adapts these parameters so that the actual sensor values are maintained within the desired bounds.

The primary design criteria involved in using our method are selection of sensors, the selection of the desired range for each sensor and the value set for each parameter. Provided that these are properly chosen, we demonstrated that our method is robust to wide swings in operating conditions.

There undesirable consequences of improper selection of these design criteria, this includes over-correction and under-correction of sensor values. Both these conditions are easily detected when they occur, and alarms raised so the damage is limited. Automated correction of these situations is not practicable because it requires a model of system behavior.

References

1. Masullo, M.J., Calo, S.B.: Policy management: An architecture and approach. In: Proceedings of the IEEE First International Workshop on Systems Management, New York, NY, USA, ACM Press (1993) 13–26
2. Ashton, L.L., Baker, E.A., Bariska, A.J., Dawson, E.M., Ferziger, R.L., Kissinger, S.M., Menendez, T.A., Shyam, S., Strickland, J.P., Thompson, D.K., Wilcock, G.R., Wood, M.W.: Two decades of policy-based storage management for the ibm mainframe computer. IBM Syst. J. **42**(2) (2003) 302–321
3. Zhang, Y., Hakozaki, K., Kameda, H., Shimizu, K.: A performance comparison of adaptive and static load balancing in heterogeneous distributed systems. In: 28th Annual Simulation Symposium, IEEE Press (1995) 332
4. Podlipnig, S., Boszormenyi, L.: A survey of web cache replacement strategies. ACM Comput. Surv. **35**(4) (2003) 374–398
5. Ogata, K. In: Modern Control Engineering, Prentice Hall Professional Technical Reference (2001)
6. Diao, Y., Hellerstein, J., Parekh, S.: Using fuzzy control to maximize profits in service level management. IBM Syst. J. **41**(3) (2002) 403–420

Implementation and Experimentation of the Logic Language $\mathcal{NP}$ *Datalog*

S. Greco, C. Molinaro, and I. Trubitsyna

DEIS, Univ. della Calabria, 87030 Rende, Italy
{greco, cmolinaro, irina}@deis.unical.it

Abstract. This paper presents a system prototype implementing $\mathcal{NP}$ *Datalog*, a Datalog-like language for expressing $\mathcal{NP}$ search and optimization problems. $\mathcal{NP}$ *Datalog* extends $\texttt{DATALOG}^{\neg s}$ (DATALOG with stratified negation) with intuitive and efficient constructs, i.e. constraints and a restricted form of (exclusive) disjunction used to define (nondeterministically) subsets (or partitions) of relations. The system translates $\mathcal{NP}$ *Datalog* queries into OPL programs, then solves them by using the ILOG Solver [16]. Thus, it combines an easy formulation of problems, expressed by means of a declarative logic language, and an efficient execution of the ILOG Solver. Several experiments show the effectiveness of this approach.

1 Introduction

It is well-known that $\mathcal{NP}$ search and optimization problems can be formulated as $\texttt{DATALOG}^{\neg}$ (Datalog with unstratified negation) queries under nondeterministic stable model semantics so that each stable model corresponds to a possible solution [11,14,19]. Although the use of (declarative) logic languages facilitates the process of writing complex applications, the use of unstratified negation allows programs to be written which in some case are neither intuitive nor efficiently valuable. This paper presents the implementation and experimentation of the logic language $\mathcal{NP}$ *Datalog*, a restricted version of $\texttt{DATALOG}^{\neg}$ which admits only controlled forms of negation, such as stratified negation, exclusive disjunction and constraints. $\mathcal{NP}$ *Datalog* has the same expressive power as $\texttt{DATALOG}^{\neg}$, enables a simpler and intuitive formulation for search and optimization problems and can be easily translated into other formalisms. The example below shows how the *Vertex Cover* problem can be expressed in $\mathcal{NP}$ *Datalog*.

Example 1. Given an undirected graph $G = \langle N, E \rangle$, a subset of the vertexes $V \subseteq N$ is a *vertex cover* of G if every edge of G has at least one end in V. The problem can be formulated in terms of the $\mathcal{NP}$ *Datalog* query $\langle \mathcal{P}_1, \texttt{v(X)} \rangle$ with $\mathcal{P}_1$ defined as follows:

$$\texttt{v(X)} \subseteq \texttt{node(X)}$$
$$\texttt{edge(X, Y)} \Rightarrow \texttt{v(X)} \vee \texttt{v(Y)}$$

where $\subseteq$ denotes the subset relation and $\Rightarrow$ is used to define constraint. The first rule guesses a subset of node, while the latter constraint verifies the vertex

S. Bressan, J. Küng, and R. Wagner (Eds.): DEXA 2006, LNCS 4080, pp. 622–633, 2006.

cover condition. The optimization problem computing a cover with minimum cardinality can be simply expressed by means of the query $\langle \mathcal{P}_1, \texttt{min}|\texttt{v(X)}|\rangle$. □

The evaluation of logic programs with stable model semantics can be carried out by means of current ASP (Answer Set Programming) systems which compute the semantics of $\texttt{DATALOG}^{\neg}$ programs [5,24]. An alternative solution consists in reducing problems expressed by means of logic formalisms (usually extensions of Datalog) into equivalent SAT problems and evaluating the target problems by means of SAT solvers [20]. In this paper a different solution, based on the rewriting of logic programs into constraint programming, is proposed. More specifically, the paper presents a prototype of the system $\mathcal{NP}$ *Datalog*/ILOG, obtained by first translating $\mathcal{NP}$ *Datalog* queries into OPL (Optimization Programming Language) [26], a constraint language well-suited for solving both search and optimization problems, and then executing the target OPL code by means of the ILOG OPL Studio platform [16].

Example 2. The optimization query of Example 1 is translated into the OPL code:

```
var bool v[node];
minimize  sum (x in node) v[x]
subject to{
        forall (⟨x, y⟩ in edge) { 1 ⇒ (v[x] + v[y] > 0); };
};
```

where the second statement expresses the optimization condition (minimizes the cardinality of v), while the last one corresponds to the vertex cover condition. □

In order to verify the effectiveness of the system prototype, several experiments were performed. The efficiency of $\mathcal{NP}$ *Datalog*/ILOG is compared with respect to those of logic programming systems based on stable models, such as DLV, smodels and ASSAT [5,24,2] and constraint logic programming systems, such as SICStus Prolog and ECLiPSe [23,8].

The paper is organized as follows: Section 2 presents the $\mathcal{NP}$ *Datalog* language; Section 3 describes the system prototype implementation; Section 4 illustrates the performance of the system; finally, in Section 5 conclusions are drawn.

2 NP Datalog

Familiarity is assumed with disjunctive logic programs, disjunctive deductive databases, (disjunctive) stable model semantics and computational complexity [1,12,18]. In this section the language $\mathcal{NP}$ *Datalog* is presented[1]. This language restricts the use of unstratified negation of $\texttt{DATALOG}^{\neg}$ without loss of its expressive power and can be executed more efficiently or easily translated into

[1] Syntax, semantics, expressiveness and implementation of the language are presented in [30] and [15] more formally.

other formalisms. $\mathcal{NP}$ *Datalog* extends DATALOG$^{\neg_s}$ with two simple forms of unstratified negation embedded into built-in constructs: exclusive disjunction, used in partition rules, and constraint rules. A $\mathcal{NP}$ *Datalog partition rule* is a disjunctive rule of the form $p_1(\mathbf{X}) \oplus \cdots \oplus p_k(\mathbf{X}) \leftarrow Body(\mathbf{X}, \mathbf{Y})$ or of the form $p_0(\mathbf{X}, c_1) \oplus \cdots \oplus p_0(\mathbf{X}, c_k) \leftarrow Body(\mathbf{X}, \mathbf{Y})$, where (i) $p_0, p_1, ..., p_k$ are distinct IDB predicates not defined elsewhere in the program, (ii) $c_1, ..., c_k$ are distinct constants, (iii) $Body(\mathbf{X}, \mathbf{Y})$ is a conjunction of literals not depending on predicates defined by disjunctive rules, and (iv) $\mathbf{X}$ and $\mathbf{Y}$ are vectors of range restricted variables. The intuitive meaning of these rules is that the projection of the body relation on $\mathbf{X}$ is partitioned nondeterministically into k relations or k distinct sets of the same relation. A *generalized partition rule* is a (generalized) disjunctive rule of the form $\oplus_L\ p(\mathbf{X}, L) \leftarrow Body(\mathbf{X}, \mathbf{Y}), d(L)$, where d is a database domain predicate, specifying the domain of the variable L. The intuitive meaning of such a rule is that the projection of the relation defined by $Body(\mathbf{X}, \mathbf{Y})$ on $\mathbf{X}$ is partitioned into a number of subsets equals to the cardinality of the relation d. The existence of *subset rules* is also assumed, i.e. rules of the form $s(\mathbf{X}) \subseteq Body(\mathbf{X}, \mathbf{Y})$, where s is an IDB predicate symbol not defined elsewhere in the program (*subset predicate symbol*) and $Body(\mathbf{X}, \mathbf{Y})$ is a conjunction of literals not depending on predicates defined by partition or subset rules. Observe that a subset rule of the above form corresponds to the generalized partition rule with $\mathsf{d} = \{0, 1\}$; while every generalized partition rule can be rewritten into a subset rule and constraints. A *constraint (rule)* is of the form $\Leftarrow Body(\mathbf{X})$, where (i) $Body(\mathbf{X})$ is a conjunction of literals, and (ii) $\mathbf{X}$ is a vector of range restricted variables. A constraint rule of the above form is satisfied if the conjunction $Body(\mathbf{X})$ is false. We shall often write constraints using rules of the form $A_1 \vee ... \vee A_k \Leftarrow B_1, ..., B_m$ (or $B_1, ..., B_m \Rightarrow A_1 \vee ... \vee A_k$) to denote a constraint of the form $\Leftarrow B_1, ..., B_m, \neg A_1, ..., \neg A_k$ (i.e. negative literals are moved from the body to the head).

Definition 1. An $\mathcal{NP}$ *Datalog* program consists of three distinct sets of rules:

1. *partition* and *subset* rules defining *guess (IDB) predicates*,
2. standard *stratified datalog rules* defining *standard (IDB) predicates*, and
3. *constraints rules*.

where (i) every guess predicate is defined by a unique subset or partition rule and does not depend on other guess predicates; (ii) every recursive predicate does not depend on guess predicates. □

Definition 2. An $\mathcal{NP}$ *Datalog search query* over a database schema $\mathcal{DS}$ is a pair $Q = \langle \mathcal{P}, g(t) \rangle$, where $\mathcal{P}$ is a $\mathcal{NP}$ *Datalog* program and $g(t)$ is an IDB atom denoting the output relation. An $\mathcal{NP}$ *Datalog optimization query* is a pair $opt(Q) = \langle \mathcal{P}, opt|g(t)| \rangle$, where $opt \in \{min, max\}$[2]. □

$\mathcal{NP}$ *Datalog* queries, expressing the *vertex cover* search and optimization problems, were presented in Example 1. The following example shows graph coloring problems, expressed by means of $\mathcal{NP}$ *Datalog* queries.

[2] In this paper optimization queries compute the maximum or minimum cardinality of the output relation, but, in general, any polynomial function can be used.

Example 3. A *k-coloring* of a graph G is an assignment of one of k possible colors to each node of G such that no two adjacent nodes have the same color. The problem can be expressed as $\langle \mathcal{P}_3, \texttt{col(X,C)} \rangle$ where $\mathcal{P}_3$ consists of:

$$\oplus_C \; \texttt{col(X,C)} \leftarrow \texttt{node(X), color(C)}.$$
$$\Leftarrow \texttt{edge(X,Y), col(X,C), col(Y,C)}.$$

and the base relation `color` contains exactly k colors. The first rule guesses a k-coloring for the graph, while the second one is a constraints stating that two joined nodes do not have the same color. The query modelling the *Min Coloring* problem is obtained from the the k-coloring example by adding a rule storing the used colors `used_color(C)` $\leftarrow$ `col(X, C)` and replacing the query goal with `min|used_color(C)|`.

3 Implementation

Several languages for hard search and optimization problems have been designed and implemented. These include logic languages based on stable models (e.g. DLV [9], smodels [25]), constraint logic programming languages (e.g. SICStus Prolog [23], ECLiPSe [29], Mozart [28]) and constraint programming languages (e.g. ILOG OPL [26,27], Lingo [10]). The advantage of using logic languages based on stable model semantics with respect to constraint programming is their ability to express complex $\mathcal{NP}$ problems in a declarative way. On the other hand constraint programming languages are very efficient in the solution of optimization problems.

As $\mathcal{NP}$ *Datalog* is a language to express $\mathcal{NP}$ problems, the implementation of the language can be carried out by translating queries into target languages specialized in optimization problems such as constraint programming. Thus, the implementation of $\mathcal{NP}$ *Datalog* is carried out by means of a system prototype translating $\mathcal{NP}$ *Datalog* queries into OPL programs. OPL is a constraint language well-suited for solving both search and optimization problems. OPL programs are computed by means of the ILOG OPL Studio system [16].

This section informally shows how $\mathcal{NP}$ *Datalog* queries are translated into OPL programs. Without loss of generality, for the sake of simplicity of presentation, it is assumed that our programs satisfy the following conditions:

- guess predicates are defined by either generalized partition rules or subset rules;
- standard predicates are defined by a unique extended rule of the form $\texttt{A} \leftarrow \texttt{body}_1 \vee \cdots \vee \texttt{body}_m$, where $\texttt{body}_i$ is a conjunction of literals;
- constraint rules are of the form $\texttt{A} \Leftarrow \texttt{B}$, where `A` is a disjunction of atoms and `B` is a conjunction of atoms;
- constants appear only in atoms of the form $\texttt{x}\,\theta\,\texttt{y}$, $\theta \in \{>, <, \leq, \geq, =, \neq\}$.

$\mathcal{NP}$ *Datalog* programs have associated a database schema specifying the used database domains and for each base predicate the domains associated with each attribute. Starting from the database schema, the schema of every derived predicate is deducted and new domains, obtained from the database domains, are introduced. For instance, the database schema associated with the graph used in the k-coloring problem of Example 3 is DOMAINS = {node, color}; PREDICATES = {edge(node, node)}; whereas the schema associated with the derived predicate col is col(node, color).

Thus, given a database D and a query $Q = \langle \mathcal{P}, G \rangle$, an OPL program equivalent to the application of the query Q to the database D is generated. It is first shown how databases are translated and next the compilation of queries and the optimization of the target code are presented.

Database Translation. Base unary relations are translated into enumerated types. The translation of a base relation with arity greater than 1 consists of two steps: declaring a new record type and declaring a set of records of such type. For instance, the translation of the database containing the facts node(a), node(b), node(c), node(d), edge(a, b), edge(a, c), edge(b, c) and edge(c, d), consists of the following OPL declarations:

```
enum node {a, b, c, d};
struct edge_type {node s; node t;};
{ edge_type } edge = {⟨a, b⟩, ⟨a, c⟩, ⟨b, c⟩, ⟨c, d⟩};
```

Query Translation. Firstly, as IDB predicates are associated with boolean arrays, the following predefined type bool is declared: **range** bool 0..1. Then, for each IDB predicate p with arity k, a k-dimensional boolean array of variables is introduced as follows **var** bool $\mathtt{p}[\mathtt{D}_1, ..., \mathtt{D}_k]$, where $\mathtt{D}_1, ..., \mathtt{D}_k$ denote the domains on which the predicate p is defined. For instance, for the binary predicate col of Example 3 the declaration **var** bool col[node, color] is introduced. A search (resp. optimization) $\mathcal{NP}$ $\mathcal{D}atalog$ query Q is translated into an OPL search (resp. optimization) program by translating each rule of Q into corresponding OPL statements. A *subset rule* of the form $\mathtt{s}(\mathtt{X}_1, ..., \mathtt{X}_k) \subseteq \mathtt{body}(\mathtt{X}_1, ..., \mathtt{X}_k, \mathtt{Y}_1, ..., \mathtt{Y}_n)$ is translated into an OPL statement specifying that if $\mathtt{s}(\mathtt{X}_1, ..., \mathtt{X}_k)$ is true, then $\mathtt{body}(\mathtt{X}_1, ..., \mathtt{X}_k, \mathtt{Y}_1, ..., \mathtt{Y}_n)$ must be true too, for some values of $\mathtt{Y}_1, ..., \mathtt{Y}_n$. For instance, the subset rule $\mathtt{e}(\mathtt{x}, \mathtt{y}) \subseteq \mathtt{edge}(\mathtt{x}, \mathtt{y})$ is translated into the OPL following statement:

```
forall (x in node, y in node)
        { e[x, y] ⇒ ((sum(⟨x, y⟩ in edge) 1 > 0) > 0); };
```

The constraint ensures that the subset is defined on the existing edges.

A generalized partition rule $\oplus_{\mathtt{L}}\mathtt{s}(\mathtt{X}_1, ..., \mathtt{X}_k, \mathtt{L}) \leftarrow \mathtt{body}(\mathtt{X}_1, ..., \mathtt{X}_k, \mathtt{Y}_1, ..., \mathtt{Y}_n), \mathtt{d}(\mathtt{L})$, defining the guess predicate s, is translated into OPL instructions stating that (i) if the body is true, then $\mathtt{s}(\mathtt{X}_1, ..., \mathtt{X}_k, \mathtt{L})$ must be true too, for a unique value of L in the base relation d; (ii) if $\mathtt{s}(\mathtt{X}_1, ..., \mathtt{X}_k, \mathtt{L})$ is true, then the body must be true too, for some values of $\mathtt{Y}_1, ..., \mathtt{Y}_n$. For instance, the partition rule of the Example 3 is translated as follows:

```
forall (x in node)  { 1 ⇒ (sum(c in color) col[x, c] = 1); };
forall (x in node, c in color)  { col[x, c] ⇒ 1; };
```

Here the first constraint guarantees for each node x the assignment of exactly one color c; while the second one ensures that the coloring is defined on the existing nodes. Note that this code can be optimized (e.g. the second constraint can be omitted as it is always satisfied); for more details see the next paragraph.

A standard rule of the form $\mathtt{p}(\mathtt{X}_1, ..., \mathtt{X}_k) \leftarrow \mathtt{Body}_1(\mathtt{X}_1, ..., \mathtt{X}_k, \mathtt{Y}^1_1, ..., \mathtt{Y}^1_{n_1}) \vee \cdots \vee \mathtt{Body}_m(\mathtt{X}_1, ..., \mathtt{X}_k, \mathtt{Y}^m_1, ..., \mathtt{Y}^m_{n_m})$ is translated into OPL instructions stating that the rule head is true iff the rule body is true. For instance, the standard rule of the Example 3 is translated into the OPL code:

$$\textbf{forall}(\mathtt{c}\ \textbf{in}\ \mathtt{color})\ \{\ \mathtt{used\_color}[\mathtt{c}] \Leftrightarrow (\textbf{sum}(\mathtt{x}\ \textbf{in}\ \mathtt{node})\ \mathtt{col}[\mathtt{x},\mathtt{c}] > 0);\ \};$$

The above constraint guarantees that a color c is used iff there exists a node x colored with c.

A constraint of the form $\mathtt{A} \Leftarrow \mathtt{B}$ is translated into an OPL statement declaring that if B is true, then A must be true too. For instance, the constraint of the Example 3 is translated into the following statement:

$$\textbf{forall}\ (\mathtt{x}\ \textbf{in}\ \mathtt{node},\ \mathtt{y}\ \textbf{in}\ \mathtt{node},\ \mathtt{c}\ \textbf{in}\ \mathtt{color})$$
$$\{\ (((\textbf{sum}(\langle \mathtt{x},\mathtt{y}\rangle\ \textbf{in}\ \mathtt{edge})\ 1 > 0) * \mathtt{col}[\mathtt{x},\mathtt{c}] * \mathtt{col}[\mathtt{y},\mathtt{c}]) > 0) \Rightarrow 0;\ \};$$

The constraints ensures that no two joined nodes x and y are colored with the same color c.

Code Optimization. The number of (ground) constraints can be strongly reduced by applying simple optimizations to the OPL code. A very simple optimization consists in deleting the OPL constraints whose head is always true (e.g. the head consists of the constant 1) as they are always satisfied. An additional simple optimization can be performed by moving conditions defined inside an OPL constraint into the associated **forall** or **sum** instruction.

A further optimization can be carried out by reducing the size of the arrays of variables corresponding to guess predicates. In particular, given a guess predicate s with arity k defined by a generalized partition rule, instead of declaring a k-dimensional array of boolean variables, it is possible to introduce a (k-1)-dimensional array of variables of type $\overline{\mathtt{dom}}$, a domain which extends the database domain dom, associated with the generalized partition rule, with the new constant null. Clearly, to make consistent the OPL program, every instance of $\mathtt{s}[\mathtt{X}_1, ..., \mathtt{X}_{k-1}, \mathtt{C}]$ must be substituted with $(\mathtt{s}[\mathtt{X}_1, ..., \mathtt{X}_{k-1}] = \mathtt{C})$ and in each **forall** or **sum** statement the condition $\mathtt{C} <> \mathtt{null}$ must be verified.

Observe that, if the body of the partition rule only contains unary base predicates (i.e. database domains) and all head variables appear once, the head atom is true for all possible values of its variables. Therefore, it is possible to use the original domain dom and it is not necessary to introduce the additional condition stating that the value of the variable cannot be null.

Another optimization regards the deletion of unnecessary variables. Often the OPL code contains constructs of the form:

$$\textbf{forall}(\mathtt{X}_1\ \textbf{in}\ \mathtt{D}_1, ..., \mathtt{X}_n\ \textbf{in}\ \mathtt{D}_n)\ (\textbf{sum}(\langle \mathtt{X}_1, ..., \mathtt{X}_k\rangle\ \textbf{in}\ \mathtt{T})\ 1 > 0)\ [\ * \langle\mathtt{Condition}\rangle\ ]\ \langle\mathtt{Statement}\rangle$$

(the squared parentheses denote an optional component). In such a case the **sum** construct can be deleted so that the constraint can be rewritten as:

forall($\langle$X$_1$, ..., X$_k\rangle$ **in** T, X$_{k+1}$ **in** D$_{k+1}$, ..., X$_n$ **in** D$_n$) 1 [* ⟨Condition⟩] ⟨Statement⟩

The following example shows the version of the min coloring program, obtained by applying the above optimizations.

Example 4. Min Coloring (optimized version).

```
var  color col[node];  var  bool used_color[color];
minimize  sum(c in color) used_color[c]

subject to  {
    forall (c in color)
        { used_color[c] ⇔  (sum(x in node) (col[x] = c) > 0); };
    forall (⟨x, y⟩ in edge)
        { ((col[x] = col[y]) > 0) ⇒ 0; };
};
```

Architecture. A system prototype was carried out by implementing modules translating $\mathcal{NP}$ $\mathcal{D}atalog$ queries into OPL programs and using the OPL ILOG system to execute the target code. The system architecture, depicted in Fig. 1, consists of five main modules whose functionalities are next briefly discussed.

- *User Interface* – This module receives in input a pair of strings identifying the file containing the source database and the file containing the query. The module, verifies that both the database and query have been already translated and, then, asks the module *ILOG Solver* to execute the query. If the database (resp. query) has not been translated it sends to the module *Database compiler* (resp. *Query compiler*) the name of the file containing the source database (resp. query) to be translated. Moreover, this module is in charge of visualizing the answer to the input query.
- *Database compiler* – This module translates the source database into an OPL database; both the source and output databases are contained into text files.

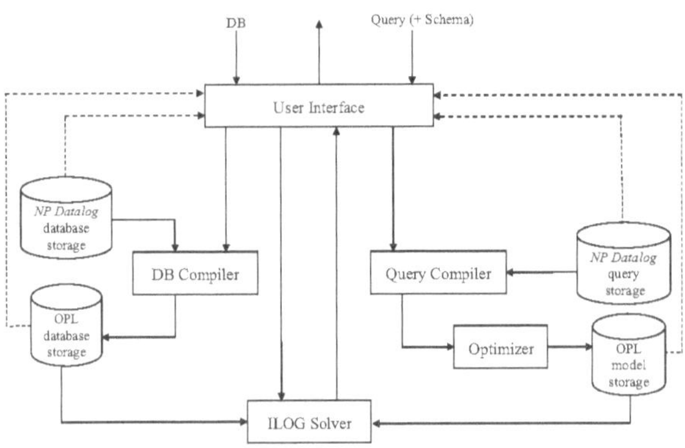

Fig. 1. System Architecture

- *Query compiler* – This module receives in input an *NP Datalog* query contained in a text file and gives in output a text containing the corresponding OPL code. In order to check the correctness of the query and to generate the target code the module uses the information on the schema of the predicates.
- *Optimizer* – This module rewrites the OPL code received from the module *Query compiler* and gives in output a file (with extension "mod") containing the target OPL code.
- *Query executor* – This module consists of the ILOG OPL Studio which executes the query, stored by the module *Optimizer* into the *OLP model storage*, over a database stored into the *OPL database storage*. The module *Query executor* interacts with the module *User Interface* by providing to it the obtained result.

4 Experiments

Several experiments comparing the performance obtained by implementing *NP Datalog* over the ILOG OPL Studio against constraint logic programming and answer-set logic languages were performed. The experiments show the advantages of combining declarative logic languages with constraint programming solvers. More specifically, *NP Datalog*/ILOG was compared with *SICStus Prolog*, *ECLiPSe*, *DLV*, *smodels* and *ASSAT* [23,8,5,24,2]. For SICStus Prolog and ECLiPSe, which are not based on stable model semantics, the problems were rewritten so that their execution by means of systems using top-down evaluation strategies proves to be efficient. All experiments were carried out on a PC with Pentium 4, 2.8 GHz, 1 GB of RAM under the operating system Linux. Performances of the different systems were evaluated by estimating the time necessary to answer the query.

Results. In order to provide a flavor of the feasibility of this approach in the following some experimental results are provided. In particular, the performance obtained for the 3-Coloring and the Min-Coloring problems will be reported. Three different sets of undirected graphs were used:

- structured graphs such as the ones depicted in Fig. 2(i) and Fig. 2(ii),
- random graphs generated by means of Culberson's graph generator [4],
- benchmarks graphs used to test other systems [3].

Considering structured graphs, instances with *base* = *height* were used. Here *base* denotes the number of nodes in the same row, *height* the number of nodes in the same column. The global number of nodes in the graph is *base* × *height*. Considering random graphs, two different sets of instances were generated. They were obtained by first generating an initial random graph with 10000 (resp. 1000) nodes and then deleting, at each step, 1000 (resp. 100) nodes, randomly selected, from the graph obtained at the previous step. Clearly, by deleting a node x, the arcs ending to or starting from x are also deleted. All graphs randomly generated are 3-colorable.

3 Coloring. The *3-Coloring* query was evaluated with different types of graphs. The results of the experiments, on structured graphs of the form in Fig. 2(i) (resp. Fig. 2(ii)), are reported in Fig. 3(i) (resp. Fig. 3(ii)) and show the execution times as the size of the graph changes. The x-axis reports the number of nodes in the same layer (i.e the value of base) while the y-axis shows the time taken to evaluate the query (in seconds). Observe that the scale of the y-axis is logarithmic, thus the improvement obtained by using $\mathcal{NP}\,\mathcal{D}atalog$/ILOG is extremely high. Concerning benchmark domains used to test other systems,

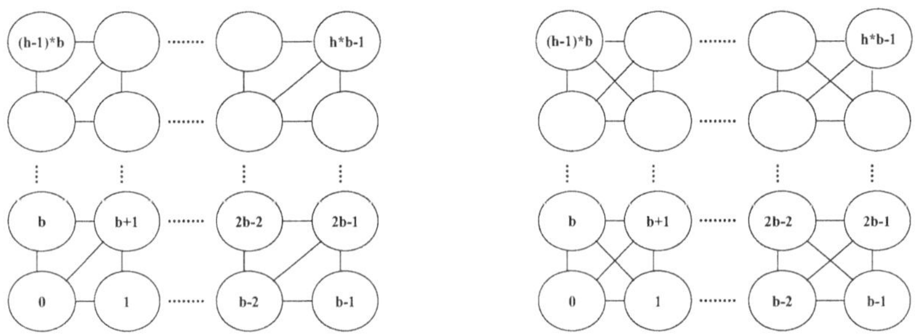

(i) (ii)

Fig. 2. Graph structures

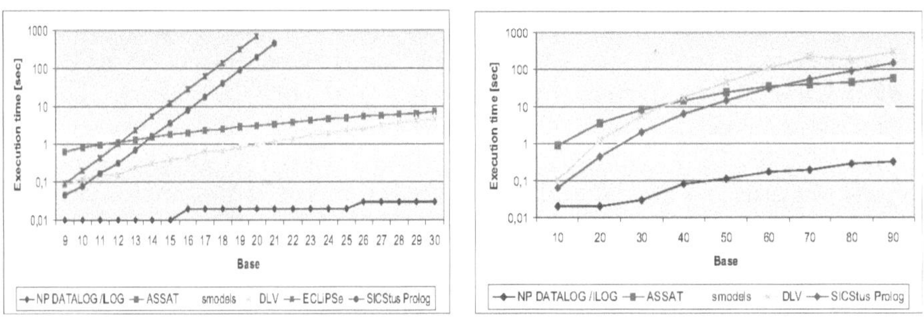

(i) (ii)

Fig. 3. Execution time for the 3-coloring problem on structured graphs

instance graphs were considered which were used by the ASSAT developers to compare its performance with smodels and DLV [3]. The results of our experiments are reported in Fig. 4. They confirm the results presented in the ASSAT's web site, where the system ASSAT is compared with DLV and smodels. The figure shows that, for large graphs, the system ASSAT is about one order of magnitude faster than smodels, while $\mathcal{NP}\,\mathcal{D}atalog$/ILOG is about one order of magnitude faster than ASSAT.

Finally, considering random graphs, for small graphs (with a few hundred nodes as in Fig. 5) smodels outperforms ASSAT, while for large graph (with

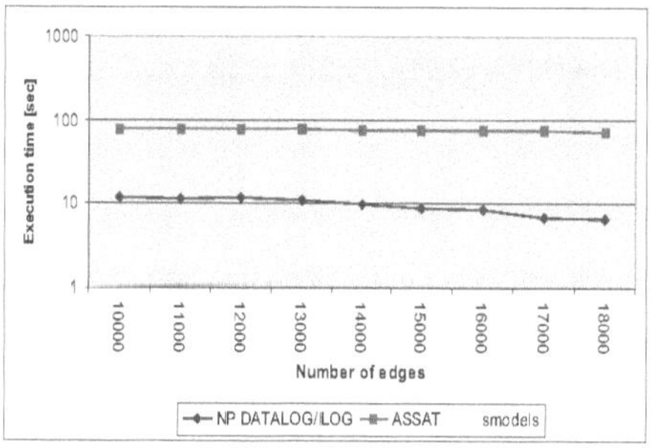

Fig. 4. 3-coloring problem on benchmarks graphs

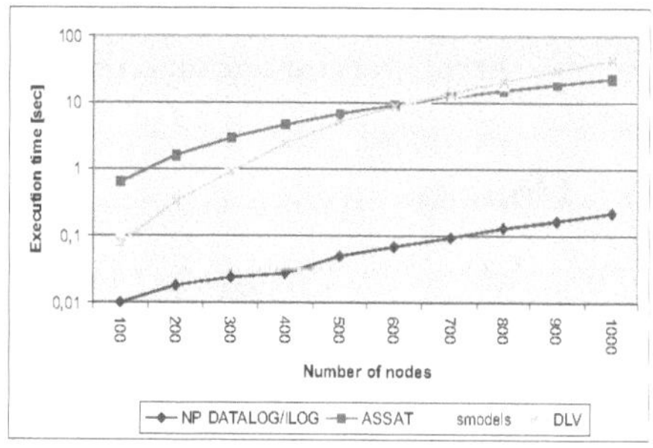

Fig. 5. 3-coloring problem on random graphs

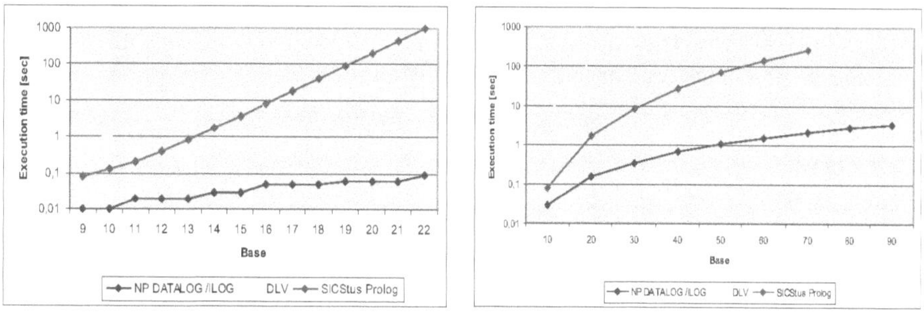

(i) (ii)

Fig. 6. Execution time for the Min-Coloring problem on structured graphs

several thousand nodes) ASSAT outperforms smodels. Also in this case, for all types of graph, the system $\mathcal{NP}$ *Datalog*/ILOG is faster than the other systems. Note that for random graphs, for each number of nodes, five different graphs were considered. Thus, the values in Fig. 5 are obtained by evaluating five times the query (over the different graphs) and computing the mean values.

Min Coloring. The last experiment, here reported, considered the min coloring optimization problem. The results in Fig. 6 were obtained by executing the query on structured graphs. Instances having the structure reported in Fig. 2(i) need at least three colors to be colored, whereas instances having the structure reported in Fig. 2(ii) need at least four colors to be colored. The number of colors available in the database was fixed for the two structures, respectively, to four and five (one color more than necessary to color the graph). It can be noted that for large, 3-colorable graphs DLV is faster than SICStus Prolog, but for small 3-colorable graphs and graphs not 3-colorable SICStus Prolog is faster than DLV. For all types of graphs $\mathcal{NP}$ *Datalog*/*ILOG* outperforms both the system here considered. For large, random, 3-colorable graphs, similar results showing that SICStus Prolog runs out of time and that $\mathcal{NP}$ *Datalog*/ILOG outperforms DLV, were obtained.

More results showing the effectiveness of $\mathcal{NP}$ $\mathcal{D}atalog$/ILOG can be found on the web site `http://wwwinfo.deis.unical.it/~irina/NPDatalog/NPDatalog.htm`.

5 Conclusions

$\mathcal{NP}$ search and optimization problems can be formulated as DATALOG$^\neg$ queries under nondeterministic stable model semantics. In order to enable a simpler and more intuitive formulation of such problems, recently, the $\mathcal{NP}$ $\mathcal{D}atalog$ language, allowing search and optimization queries to be expressed using only simple forms of unstratified negations, has been proposed. This paper has presented the implementation and experimentation of the language. In particular, the prototype was carried out by implementing a compiler translating $\mathcal{NP}$ $\mathcal{D}atalog$ queries into OPL programs, and evaluating the OPL programs by means of the ILOG OPL Studio. Several experiments comparing the computation of queries by different systems have showed the validity of this approach, which combines an easy formulation of problems and an efficient execution.

References

1. Abiteboul, S., Hull, R., and Vianu, V., *Foundations of Databases*. Addison-Wesley, 1994.
2. ASSAT. *http://assat.cs.ust.hk/*.
3. ASSAT experimental data on the Graph Coloring Domain. *http://assat.cs.ust.hk/Assat-2.0/coloring-2.0.html.*
4. Culberson's graph generator. *http://web.cs.ualberta.ca/~joe/Coloring/Generators/generate.html.*
5. DLV. *http://www.dbai.tuwien.ac.at/proj/dlv/*.
6. East, D., and Truszczynski, M., DATALOG with Constraints - An Answer-Set Programming System. *AAAI/IAAI*, 163-168, 2000.
7. East, D., and Truszczynski, M., Predicate-calculus based logics for modeling and solving search problems *ACM Transaction on Computational Logic* (to appear), 2005.
8. ECLiPSe. *http://www.clps.de/eclipse.html.*
9. Eiter, T., Leone, N., Mateis, C., Pfeifer G., and Scarcello, F., A Deductive System for Non-monotonic Reasoning. *LPNMR*, 363–374, 1997.
10. Finkel, R. A., Marek, V. W., and Truszczynski, M., Constraint Lingo: towards high-level constraint programming. *Software Practice and Experience*, 34(15), 1481-1504, 2004.
11. Gelfond, M., and Lifschitz, V., The Stable Model Semantics for Logic Programming. *Proc. 5th Int. Conf. on Logic Programming*, 1070–1080, 1988.
12. Gelfond M. and Lifschitz V. Classical negation in logic programs and disjunctive databases. *New generation Computing*, 9(3/4), pages 365–385, 1991.
13. Greco, S., Saccà, D., and Zaniolo C., Datalog with Stratified Negation and Choice: from P to D^P. *Proc. Int. Conf. on Database Theory*, 574–589, 1995.
14. Greco, S., and Saccà, D., NP-Optimization Problems in Datalog. *ILPS*, 181–195, 1997.

15. Greco, S., Molinaro, C., Trubitsyna, I., and Zumpano, E., Implementing NP Datalog. *Technical report – University of Calabria, submitted to an International Journal.*
16. ILOG OPL Development Studio. *http://www.ilog.com/products/oplstudio/.*
17. Jaffar, J., Michaylov, S., Stuckey, P.J., Yap, R., The CLP(R) Language and System. *ACM Transaction on Programming Languages and Systems* 14(3), 339-395, 1992.
18. Johnson, D. S., A Catalog of Complexity Classes. In *Handbook of Theoretical Computer Science*, Vol. 1, J. van Leewen (ed.), North-Holland, 67– 161, 1990.
19. Kolaitis, P. G., and Thakur, M. N., Logical Definability of NP Optimization Problems. *Information and Computation*, No. 115, 321–353, 1994.
20. Lin, F., and Zhao, Y., ASSAT: computing answer sets of a logic program by SAT solvers. *Artificial Intelligene* 157(1-2), 115–137, 2004.
21. Marriott, K., Stuckey, P. J., *Programming with Constraints: an Introduction*, MIT, 1998.
22. Niemela, I., Simons, P., Soininen, T., Stable Model Semantics of Weight Constraint Rules. In *Proc. Int. Conf. on Logic Progr. and Nonmon. Reas.*, 317-331, 1999.
23. SICStus Prolog. *http://www.sics.se/isl/sicstuswww/site/index.html.*
24. Smodels. *http://www.tcs.hut.fi/Software/smodels/.*
25. Syrjanen, T., and Niemela, I., The Smodels System. *LPNMR*, 434-438, 2001.
26. Van Hentenryck, P., *The OPL Optimization Programming Language*, Mit Press, 1999.
27. Van Hentenryck, P., Michel, L., Perron, L., Regin, J. C., Constraint Programming in OPL, *Proc. Int. Conf. on Principles and Practice of Decl. Progr.*, 98–116, 1999.
28. Var Roy P., Logic Programming in Oz with Mozart, *ICLP*, 38–51, 1999.
29. Wallace, M., Schimpf, J., ECLiPSe: Declarative Specification and Scaleable Implementation. *Proc. Int. Work. on Practical Aspects of Decl. Langu.*, 365-366, 1999.
30. Zumpano, E., Greco, S., Trubitsyna, I., and Veltri, P., On the semantics and expressive power of Datalog-like languages for NP search and optimization problems. *Proc. ACM Symp. on Applied Computing*, 692-697, 2004.

Converting a Naive Bayes Models with Multi-valued Domains into Sets of Rules

Bartłomiej Śnieżyński

AGH University of Science and Technology, Department of Computer Science, Krakow, Poland
sniezyn@agh.edu.pl

Abstract. Nowadays, several knowledge representation methods are being used in knowledge based systems, machine learning, and data mining. Among them are decision rules and Bayesian networks. Both methods have specific advantages and disadvantages. A conversion method would allow to exploit advantages of both techniques. In this paper an algorithm that converts Naive Bayes models with multi-valued attribute domains into sets of rules is proposed. Experimental results show that it is possible to generate rule-based classifiers, which have relatively high accuracy and are simpler than original models.

1 Introduction

Nowadays, several knowledge representation methods are popular in knowledge based systems, machine learning, and data mining. Among them are decision rules and Bayesian networks. Both methods have specific advantages and disadvantages.

Bayesian models provide very well founded uncertainty representation. If a knowledge base is created manually, Bayesian networks seem to represent uncertainty and dependency better than rules [1,2]. Tuning a set of rules takes a lot of time (see e.g. [3]). However, if a knowledge base is generated automatically from data, it is not a problem. Another issue is the accuracy of the models. Probabilistic classifiers may be better than rule based ones, but the difference is usually small.

In many application domains, such as security systems, medical diagnosis, etc. very important issue is understanding of the knowledge, especially if it is generated automatically. In such domains, before the knowledge is used, it should be verified by a human expert. It is difficult to verify a knowledge that in in a form difficult to grasp. Next, generated classifiers are often used with a supervision of a human. To verify a system's decision, the supervisor should have a possibility to check and understand the justification of the answer. What is also very important, using machine learning one can discover a new domain knowledge. This can not be done without feedback from a human expert. To make it possible, the knowledge generated has to have a form that is easy to interpret for humans. Generally, rules seem to correspond to human way of thinking very well [4], much more than probabilistic models.

S. Bressan, J. Küng, and R. Wagner (Eds.): DEXA 2006, LNCS 4080, pp. 634–643, 2006.

To exploit advantages of both knowledge representation techniques, it would be good to have tools, which are able to transform knowledge between these formalisms. In this paper a method of converting a simple probabilistic model – Naive Bayes (NB) into a set of decision rules is presented. Such a conversion can be used for a knowledge visualization purposes and also to generate knowledge bases for diagnostic systems. It can be also considered as a method of NB pruning, which decreases its complexity.

This paper is a continuation of the work published in [5], where a method for two-valued attribute domains was described and tested. In this paper multi-valued domains are considered.

In the next section the method is described, next we show preliminary experimental results, and related research. Conclusions and plans of the future research conclude the paper.

2 Conversion Algorithm

2.1 Bayesian Networks and Naive Bayes

Naive Bayes (NB) is a simple probabilistic classifier, which is a special case of a Bayesian network. Generally, a Bayesian network is a pair (G, P), where G is a structure graph, which in this case is very simple (see Fig. 1) and P is a set of local, conditional probability distributions between variables and its parents. Variables X_1, X_2, ..., X_n correspond to attributes, variable Y represents a class. A consequence of the NB structure is an assumption about conditional independence of variables X_1, X_2, ..., X_n.

Domains of the variables are denoted by $D_Y, D_{X_1}, D_{X_2}, \ldots, D_{X_n}$. In this paper we assume that all domains are discrete and finite.

For the NB inference and learning algorithms are straightforward. Probability distribution of a class variable for example $e = (X_1 = e_1, X_2 = e_2, ..., X_n = e_n)$ is calculated using the following formula:

$$P(class(e) = y_j) = \frac{P(Y = y_j)\prod_{i=1}^{n} P(X_i = e_i | Y = y_j)}{\prod_{i=1}^{n} P(X_i = e_i)} \tag{1}$$

What is surprising, in spite of unnatural assumptions about conditional independency between attributes, Naive Bayes classifiers perform very well [6].

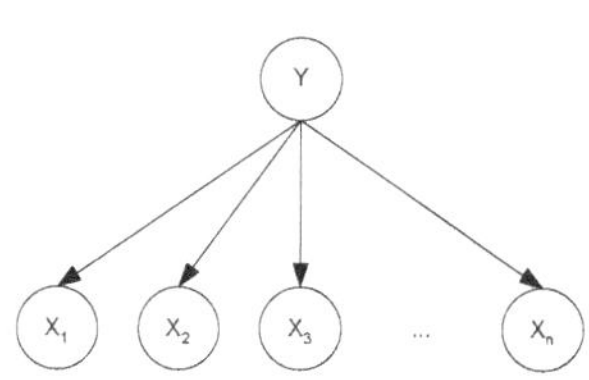

Fig. 1. Structure of naive Bayes

2.2 Simple Conversion

NB can be transformed into a set of rules by generating $|D_Y|$ rules for every value of every X_i variable. Rules would have the following form:

$$X_i = x_j^i \rightarrow Y = y_k, \quad (2)$$

where $x_j^i \in D_{X_i}, y_k \in D_Y$ are variable values. Because such rules have various strength, we need also a way to represent it. It can be done by labelling rules.

Choosing appropriate labels is very important, because it has a strong influence on the rule-based classifier performance. The choice can be formalized by defining a label algebra and a function transforming conditional probabilities into labels.

Label algebra can be defined as the following pair:

$$\mathcal{L} = (L, \star), \quad (3)$$

where L is a set of labels with linear order (to choose the highest value during classification of examples), and $\star : L^2 \rightarrow L$ is an aggregation operator, which is also used during the classification, if two (or more) rules match the example. In such a case, rules are aggregated. $\star$ should be associative and commutative to make the result of rule application independent from the order, therefore $\star$ can be extended to operate on a set of labels.

Labelled rule is a pair

$$r : l, \quad (4)$$

where r is a rule defined above, and $l \in L$. Rule labels are calculated using transformation function $f : [0, 1] \rightarrow L$. Rule $X_i = x_j^i \rightarrow Y = y_k$ has a label $l = f(P(X_i = x_j^i | Y = y_k))$

Having a set of labelled rules, which form a knowledge base KB, we can classify an example $e = (X_1 = e_1, X_2 = e_2, \ldots X_n = e_n)$:

$$class(e) = \arg\max_{y_k} \star\{l | X_i = e_i \rightarrow Y = y_k : l \in \mathrm{KB}\}. \quad (5)$$

If attribute value is missing in the example, we assume that no rule matches this attribute.

In the experiments (presented in Section 3) two label algebras are used: continuous: $([0, 1], \star)$ and discrete: $(\{0, 1\}, \star)$, where $\star$ is a classical multiplication. As a consequence, two transformation functions are defined: $f_1(p) = p$ (identity), and $f_2(p) = \mathrm{round}(p)$. The use of other algebras is also possible. One of the solutions is to rescale probability values into the range $[-1, 1]$ and apply Certainty Factors style of aggregation [7].

2.3 Pruning

The conversion described above has a serious drawback – it does not decrease model's complexity. To overcome this shortcoming, we introduce pruning to eliminate rules with low significance.

A method of pruning in the case of $|D_{X_i}| = 2$ is presented in [5]. In such a case, probabilities $P(X_i = x_j^i|Y = y_k)$ close to 0.5 have lower influence on the hypothesis than ones with value close to 1 or 0. Therefore we can create rules for these probabilities, which have distance from 0.5 greater than a given threshold.

If $|D_{X_i}| > 2$ we can use Entropy measure. It can be defined for a bunch of rules. The bunch of rules B_{ik} is a set of rules with the same variables in the premise and the same value in the consequence:

$$B_{ik} = \{X_i = x_j^i \to Y = y_k : l\}_{j=1,2,\ldots,|D_{X_i}|}. \tag{6}$$

Entropy E is defined as follows:

$$E(B_{ik}) = \sum_{j=1}^{|D_{X_i}|} -P(X_i = x_j^i|Y = y_i)\log_2 P(X_i = x_j^i|Y = y_i). \tag{7}$$

If $P(X_i = x_j^i|Y = y_i) = 0$ we assume that $P(X_i = x_j^i|Y = y_i)\log_2 P(X_i = x_j^i|Y = y_i) = 0$. To have normalized values, the normalized Entropy $En(Bik)$ is defined:

$$En(B_{ik}) = En(B_{ik})/E_{max}(|D_{X_i}|), \tag{8}$$

where $E_{max}(n)$ is a maximal Entropy for a domain of size n.

High values of the normalized Entropy mean a high disorder and low information, therefore rules that belong to a bunch with such values of En are pruned. In order to have similar meaning of the threshold value t as in [5], i.e. to represent a low pruning by values close to 0 and a strong pruning by values close to 1, rule from B_{ik} is pruned iff $En(B_{ik}) > (1 - t)$.

2.4 Defaults

The transformation defined above does not include probability distribution of a class variable Y, which is a class distribution. It can be taken into account by completing the set of rules with $|D_Y|$ default rules of the form

$$\to y_i : l_i, \tag{9}$$

where $y_i \in D_Y$, and $l_i = P(Y = y_i)$. These rules have an empty premise part and they always match examples during classification. In such a case $\star$ operator domain should be extended to cover the $[0, 1]$ range.

2.5 Full Algorithm

Full algorithm for conversion of NB models into a set rules is presented in Fig. 2. Input data consists of a NB to convert, a threshold t, which is used to eliminate rules with low significance, and a boolean value *defaults*, which is used to specify if defaults should be added. Output consists of a set of rules R.

If $f(p) = \text{round}(p)$, set of rules can be presented in a more user friendly form. Rules with the same consequent and the same label can be merged into one decision rule by connecting premises with "OR" connective (see examples in Fig. 4).

Data: $\{P(X_i = x_j^i | Y = y_k), P(Y = y_k)\}$ – NB conditional probabilities,
    t – probability threshold, *defaults* – should defaults be added
Result: R – Set of rules
begin
    $R := \emptyset$;
    foreach *Variable* X_i **do**
        foreach *Value* $y_k \in D_Y$ **do**
            if $En(B_{ik}) \leq (1 - t)$ **then**
                foreach *Value* $x_j^i \in D_{X_i}$ **do**
                    $p := P(X_i = x_j^i | Y = y_k)$;
                    $R := R \cup \{X_i = x_j^i \rightarrow Y = y_k : f(p)\}$;
                end
            end
        end
    end
    if *defaults=true* **then**
        foreach *Value* $y_k \in D_Y$ **do**
            $R := R \cup \{\rightarrow Y = y_k : P(Y = y_k)\}$;
        end
    end
    return R
end

Fig. 2. Algorithm for conversion of NB models into sets of rules

3 Experimental Results

The following data sets were used to test the conversion algorithm: Iris, Wisconsin Breast Cancer (WBC), Soybean, Audiology, and Congressional Voting Records. They were obtained from the UCI Machine Learning Repository [8]. The first one is well known data with three classes representing species of iris. Second one contains patient data with two classes representing benign and malign types of cancer. Third one contains data with 19 types of soya diseases. Fourth one (donated to UCI by Prof. Jergen, Baylor College of Medicine) contains 24 classes of audiology problems. In this data set Bser attribute was removed because it was known for four examples only. In the last data set attributes represent vote records of United States Congressmen, the class represents theirs party. Summary of these sets is presented in Tab. 1.

Table 1. Data sets

Data set	#classes	#attr.	#nominal attr.	#numeric attr.	missing val.	#instances
Iris	3	4	0	4	none	150
WBC	2	9	0	9	several	699
Soybean	19	35	35	0	several	683
Audiology	24	69	69	0	several	226
Voting	2	16	16	0	many	435

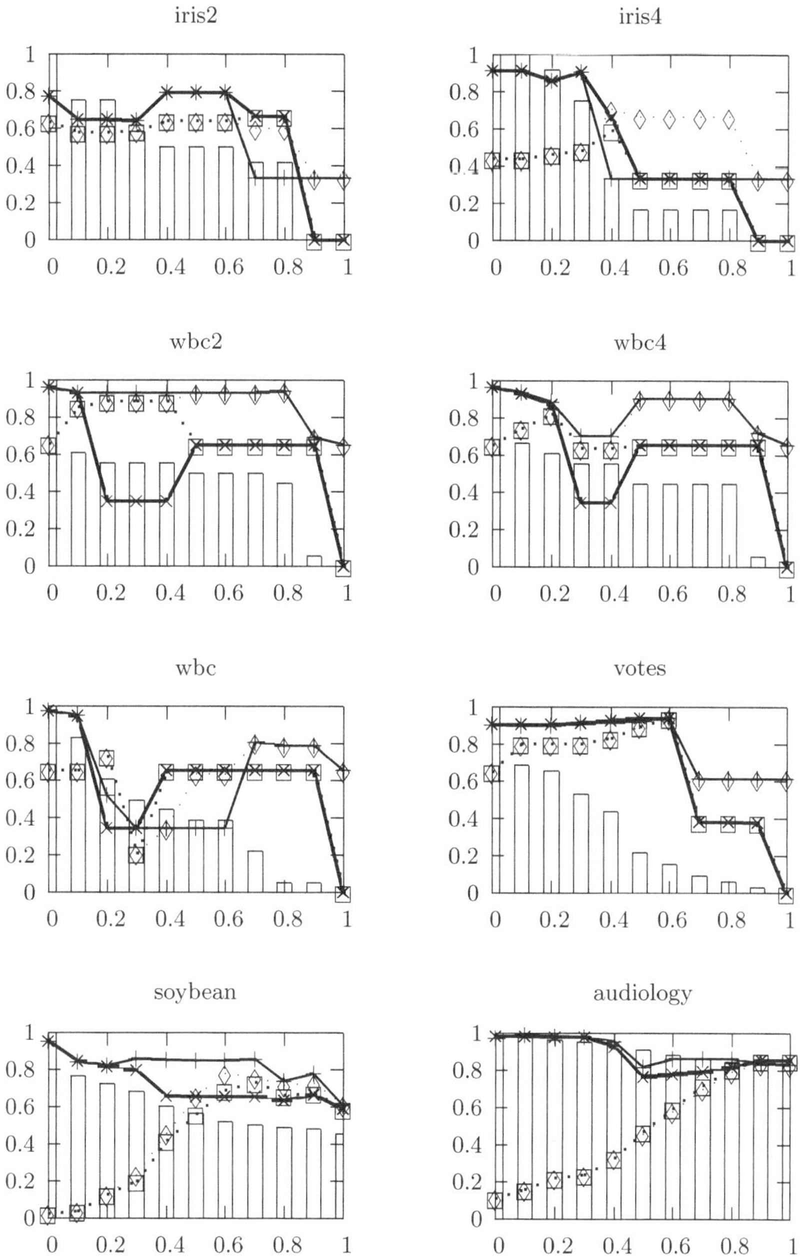

Fig. 3. Dependency of the accuracy of rule based classifiers generated form Naive Bayes models from the threshold; bars (⊓) represent the relative number of rules (number of rules after pruning divided by the original number), diamonds (◇) discrete label algebra with defaults, boxes (□) discrete without defaults, pluses (+) continuous label algebra with defaults, exes (×) continuous without defaults

Table 2. Number of rules (without defaults)

t	Iris2	Iris4	WBC2	WBC4	WBC	Votes	Soybean	Audiology
0.0	24	48	36	72	178	64	1881	3648
0.1	18	48	22	48	148	44	1439	3563
0.2	18	44	20	44	108	42	1364	3514
0.3	14	36	20	40	88	34	1286	3477
0.4	12	16	20	40	79	28	1134	3393
0.5	12	8	18	32	69	14	1066	3326
0.6	12	8	18	32	69	10	977	3225
0.7	10	8	18	32	39	6	948	3139
0.8	10	8	16	32	9	4	919	3080
0.9	0	0	2	4	9	2	907	3035
1.0	0	0	0	0	0	0	857	3018

To check how numer of attributes influences the performance, the Iris and WBC data sets were discretized using equal width method. Domains with 2 and 4 values were created. Corresponding data sets are denoted by Iris2, Iris4, WBC2, WBC4. WBC is a set without discretization.

NB classifiers were generated for this data sets using Genie tool [9]. Accuracy of generated classifiers on the training data is 78.67% for the Iris2, 91.33% for Iris4, 95.85% for the WBC2, 96.71% for WBC4, 96.13% for WBC, 90.34% for the Voting, 95.02% for Soybean, and 97.34% for Audiology.

From these classifiers rule sets were generated using threshold from 0 to 1, with continuous ($f(p) = p$)) and discrete ($f(p) = \text{round}(p)$) labels, with and without default rules. Classifiers were tested on the training data. These experiments were performed using software developed by the author.

If there are no default rules and no rule is chosen during classification, it counts as a wrong answer. Accuracy measures for generated rule sets are presented in Fig. 3. Numbers of rules for different thresholds are presented in Tab. 2.

As we can see, accuracy of the rule-based classifiers is quite high. In simple domains (Voting, WBC, Iris) it is still high even when 80% of rules are eliminated.

Increasing the number of ranges in a discretization decreases slightly the accuracy after pruning. It is easily noticeable in the WBC.

Adding defaults increases the accuracy for high threshold values, when the number of rules is decreased significantly. Stronger influence on the accuracy has the type of the label algebra (and the transformation function). Accuracy of classifiers with continuous labels decreases when more rules are pruned; however there is often a local maximum for a threshold value about 0.6. Accuracy of classifiers with discrete algebra usually increases (when nonsignificant rules with label values rounded to 0, which strongly decrease class probability, are eliminated), and accuracy of the classifier becomes higher. If too many rules are removed, accuracy drops down.

This result suggests that other aggregation methods may improve classifier's performance for low values of the threshold; however for the purpose of knowledge visualization it is not a vital issue, because performance for a reduced number of rules is more important.

Number of rules is reduced significantly in most data sets. Even in WBD data set, where attribute domains have 10 values, the number of rules was reduced to less than 10%. For sets such as Soybean and (especially) Audiology rule reduction is not so successful. It is a result of the presence of many conditional probabilities equal to 1.0 or 0.0.

To present results of the conversion, merged rules with discrete labels for threshold $t = 0.9$ for WBC and $t = 0.6$ for Voting are presented in Fig. 4. These sets of 2 and 4 rules are more easy to interpret for human beings that NB classifiers that are described by 72 (for WBC) and 64 (for Voting) conditional probabilities represented by real numbers. In Voting data set the number of rules can be decreased more, because generated rules form complementary pairs.

```
mitoses = 1 -> benign : 1

mitoses = 2 OR mitoses = 3 OR mitoses = 4 OR mitoses = 5 OR
    mitoses = 6 OR mitoses = 7 OR mitoses = 8 OR mitoses = 10
    -> benign : 0
```

(a)

```
physician_fee_freeze = n OR
    export_administration_act_south_africa = y -> democrat: 1

physician_fee_freeze = y OR
    export_administration_act_south_africa = n -> democrat: 0

physician_fee_freeze = y OR el_salvador_aid = y
    OR crime = y OR duty_free_exports = n -> republican: 1

physician_fee_freeze = n OR el_salvador_aid = n OR crime = n OR
    duty_free_exports = y -> republican: 0
```

(b)

Fig. 4. Rules (without default) generated for the WBC, $t = 0.9$ (a), and Voting, $t = 0.6$ (b) data sets; labels are discrete

4 Related Research

The most related paper to this research is [10], where possibility of using Certainty Factor model to represent Bayesian networks is analyzed. Methods for Noisy-OR, Noisy-AND, Noisy-MIN, Noisy-MAX and propagation of evidence are presented. It appears that many solutions used in practical applications of probabilistic models correspond to methods invented by Buchanan and Shortliffe.

Another interesting work is [11], where conversion of Bayesian networks into probabilistic horn abduction language is proposed. However, this formalism is more complicated than decision rules and resulting knowledge bases are not so easy to interpret.

Knowledge conversion methods in the opposite direction (from rule-based systems into probabilistic models) were investigated in a number of publications (e.g. [12,13,14]). There are also several works that aim at exploring problems that appear in probabilistic interpretation of Certainty Factor model (e.g. [1,15]).

Some transformation methods between other knowledge representation techniques are also considered in the literature. Probably the most commonly used is a conversion of decision trees into decision rules that is implemented in C4.5 [16]. A conversion in the opposite direction is also developed. AQDT method generates decision trees from sets of attributional rules [17]. Interesting transformation of a frame-based representation with uncertainty into a Bayesian model is described in [18].

5 Conclusion and Further Research

Transforming probabilistic models learned from data into decision rules can be very useful for visualization purposes. It allows to extract strong patterns appearing in a probabilistic models and present it in a user friendly way.

The idea of intended application is to use a fast Naive Bayes model learning algorithm to generate a classifier from a big data set. Such a classifier can be next converted into a set of rules. These rules can be examined by users or used for classification.

Experimental results show that rule sets generated from Naive Bayes models are clear and accuracy of such classifiers is relatively high, comparing to the accuracy of original models. However, in some domains the number of rules is too high for human interpretation.

In the near future, we would like to make more experiments on a number of problem domains. Next, we would like to test several other label algebras. We are also planning to investigate possibilities of generalizing the method for more complex Bayesian networks and to develop a complete tool for such conversion.

References

1. Heckerman, D. In: Probabilistic interpretation for MYCIN's uncertainty factors. North-Holland (1986) 167–196
2. Heckerman, D.: An empirical comparison of three inference methods. In: Proceedings of the Fourth Workshop on Uncertainty in Artificial Intelligence, Association for Uncertainty in Artificial Intelligence, Mountain View, CA (1988) 158–169
3. Lucas, P., Janssens, A.: Development and validation of hepar, an expert system for the diagnosis of disorders of the liver and biliary tract. Medical Informatics **16** (1991) 259–270

4. Newell, A., Simon, H.: Human Problem Solving. Prentice-Hall (1972)
5. Sniezynski, B.: Converting a naive bayes model into a set of rules. In Kłopotek M. et al., ed.: Intelligent Information Processing and Web Mining. Advances in Soft Computing, Springer (2006) Accepted for publication.
6. Friedman, N., Geiger, D., Goldszmidt, M.: Bayesian network classifiers. Machine Learning **29** (1997) 131–163
7. Buchanan, B., Shortliffe, H.: Rule-based expert systems: The MYCIN experiments of the Stanford heuristic programming project. Addison-Wesley (1984)
8. Newman, D., Hettich, S., Blake, C., Merz, C.: UCI repository of machine learning databases (1998)
9. Druzdzel, M.: A development environment for graphical decision-analytic models. In: Proc. of the 1999 Annual Symposium of the American Medical Informatics Association (AMIA-1999), Washington, D.C. (1999) 1206
10. Lucas, P.: Certainty-factor-like structures in bayesian belief networks. Knowl.-Based Syst **14** (2001) 327–335
11. Poole, D.: Probabilistic horn abduction and bayesian networks. Artificial Intelligence **64** (1993) 81–129
12. Korver, M., Lucas, P.: Converting a rule-based expert system into a belief network. Medical Informatics **18** (1993) 219–241
13. Shwe, M., Middleton, B., Heckerman, D.E., Henrion, M., Horvitz, E.J., Lehmann, H., Cooper, G.F.: Probabilistic diagnosis using a reformulation of the INTERNIST-1/QMR knowledge base i: Probabilistic model and inference algorithms. Methods of Information in Medicine **30** (1991) 241–255
14. Middleton, B., Shwe, M., Heckerman, E., M.H.D., Horvitz, E.J., Lehmann, H., Cooper, G.F.: Probabilistic diagnosis using a reformulation of the INTERNIST-1/QMR knowledge base ii: Evaluation of diagnostic performance. Methods of Information in Medicine **30** (1991) 256–267
15. van der Gaag, L.: Probability-based models for plausible reasoning. PhD thesis, University of Amsterdam (1990)
16. Quinlan, J.: C4.5: Programs for Machine Learning. Morgan Kaufmann (1993)
17. Michalski, R.S., Imam, I.: Learning problem-oriented decision structures from decision rules: The aqdt-2 system. In: Methodology for Intelligent Systems of the 8th International Symposium on Methodology for Intelligent Systems (ISMIS-94). Volume 869 of Lecture Notes in Artificial Intelligence., Springer (1994) 416–426
18. Koller, D., Pfeffer, A.: Probabilistic frame-based systems. In: Proc. of 15th National Conference on Artificial Intelligence AAAI-98. (1998) 580–587

Hypersphere Indexer

Navneet Panda, Edward Y. Chang, and Arun Qamra

University of California, Santa Barbara, CA

Abstract. Indexing high-dimensional data for efficient nearest-neighbor searches poses interesting research challenges. It is well known that when data dimension is high, the search time can exceed the time required for performing a linear scan on the entire dataset. To alleviate this *dimensionality curse*, indexing schemes such as *locality sensitive hashing* (LSH) and *M-trees* were proposed to perform *approximate* searches. In this paper, we propose a *hypersphere indexer*, named Hydex, to perform such searches. Hydex partitions the data space using concentric hyperspheres. By exploiting geometric properties, Hydex can perform effective pruning. Our empirical study shows that Hydex enjoys three advantages over competing schemes for achieving the same level of search accuracy. First, Hydex requires fewer seek operations. Second, Hydex can maintain sequential disk accesses most of the time. And third, it requires fewer distance computations.

1 Introduction

Nearest neighbor search has generated substantial interest because of a wide range of applications such as text, image/video, and bio-data retrieval. These applications represent objects (text documents, images, or bio-data) as *feature vectors* in very high-dimensional spaces. A user submits a query to a search engine, which returns objects that are similar to the query. The similarity between two objects is measured by some distance function (e.g., Euclidean) over their feature vectors. The search returns the objects that are *nearest* to the query object in the high-dimensional vector space.

The prohibitive nature of exact nearest-neighbor search has led to the interest in *approximate nearest-neighbor* (A-NN) search that returns instances (objects) approximately similar to the query instance [1,10]. The first justification behind approximate search is that a feature vector is often an approximate characterization of an object, so we are already dealing with approximations [13]. Second, an approximate set of answers suffices if the answers are relatively close to the query concept. Of late, two approximate indexing schemes, *locality sensitive hashing* (LSH) [11] and M-trees [8] have been popular. These approximate indexing schemes speed up similarity search significantly (over a sequential scan) by slightly lowering the bar for accuracy.

In this paper, we propose a *hypersphere indexer*, named Hydex, to perform approximate nearest-neighbor searches. First, the indexer finds a roughly central instance among a given set of instances. Next, the instances are partitioned based on their distances from the central instance. Hydex builds an *intra-partition indexer* (or local indexer) within each partition to efficiently retrieve relevant instances. It also builds an *inter-partition* indexer to help a query identify a good starting location in a neighboring partition to search for nearest neighbors. A search is conducted by first finding the

S. Bressan, J. Küng, and R. Wagner (Eds.): DEXA 2006, LNCS 4080, pp. 644–654, 2006.

partition to which the query instance belongs. Hydex then searches in this and the neighboring partitions to locate nearest neighbors of the query. Through empirical studies on two large, high-dimensional datasets, we show that Hydex significantly outperforms both LSH and M-trees in both IO and CPU time.

The rest of the paper is organized as follows. In Section 2, we discuss related work. Section 3 describes Hydex's operations. Section 4 presents experimental results. We offer our closing remarks in Section 5.

2 Related Work

Existing indexers can be divided into two categories: *coordinate-based* and *distance-based*. The coordinate-based methods work on data instances residing in a vector space by partitioning the space into *minimum bounding regions* (MBRs). A top-k nearest-neighbor query can be treated as a range query, and ideally, the best matches can be found after examining only a small number of MBRs. Examples of coordinate-based methods are the X-tree [4], the R^*-tree [3], the TV-tree [14] and the SR-tree [12], to name a few. A big disadvantage of these tree-structures is the exponential decay in performance that accompanies an increase in the dimensionality of data instances [19]. This phenomenon has been reported for the R^*-tree, the X-tree, and the SR-tree, among others. The decay in performance can be attributed to the almost exponential number of rectangular MBRs (in the cases of the X-tree and the R^*-tree) or spherical MBRs (in the cases of the SR-tree, the TV-tree, and the M-tree)[1] that must be examined for finding nearest neighbors. In contrast to these tree-structures, each partition of Hydex has only two neighboring partitions, independent of data dimension.

The distance-based methods do not require an explicit vector space, but rely only on the existence of a pairwise distance metric. The M-tree [9] is a representative scheme that uses the distances between instances to build an indexing structure. (Some other distance-based methods are the multi-vantage-point trees [5], geometric near-neighbor access trees [6], and spatial approximation trees [16].) Given a query point, it prunes out instances based on distance. The M-tree performs IOs to retrieve relevant data blocks into memory for processing; however, the disk accesses cannot be sequential since the data blocks can be randomly scattered on disks. In contrast to the M-tree, our proposed indexer, Hydex, can largely maintain contiguous layout of neighboring partitions on disks, so its IOs can be sequential and hence more efficient.

When data dimension is very high, the cost of supporting exact queries can be higher than that of a linear scan. The work of [11] proposes an approximate indexing strategy using locality sensitive hashing (LSH). This approach attempts to hash nearest-neighbor instances into the same bucket, with high probability. A top-k approximate query is supported by retrieving the bucket into which the query point has been hashed. To improve search accuracy, multiple hash functions must be used. Theoretically, the number of hash functions to be used is given by $(\frac{n}{B})^{\rho}$, where n is the number of instances in the dataset, B is the number of instances that can be accommodated in a single bucket, and

[1] To ensure retrieval of the exact set of top-k nearest neighbors, a search needs to examine all 3^d neighboring MBRs [13]. For the tree-structures using spherical MBRs, [19] reports that their performance decays almost as rapidly as the tree-structures using rectangular MBRs.

ρ a tunable parameter. As we will show in Section 4, Hydex outperforms LSH in two aspects. First, Hydex requires fewer IOs compared to LSH to achieve the same level of search accuracy. Second, when a dataset is relatively static (without a large number of insertions), Hydex can largely maintain its IOs in sequential order, whereas LSH cannot.

3 Algorithm SphereDex

Our proposed Hydex aims to improve the performance of nearest-neighbor searches using a three-pronged approach. First, we attempt to reduce the number of IOs. Second, when multiple disk blocks must be retrieved, we make the IO sequential as much as possible. Third, when data is finally staged in main memory for processing, we minimize the amount of data to be examined to obtain the top-k approximate nearest neighbors.

3.1 Create—Building the Index

The indexer is created in four steps.

- **1.** Finding the instance $\mathbf{x}_c$ that is approximately centrally located in the data space,
- **2.** Separating the instances into partitions based on their distances from $\mathbf{x}_c$,
- **3.** Constructing an *intra-partition indexer* in each partition, and
- **4.** Creating an *inter-partition* index.

Choosing the center instance
Input: *Dataset instances*: $\{\mathbf{x}_1 \cdots \mathbf{x}_n\}$. *Output*: *Approximate center instance* $\mathbf{x}_c$.

Definition 1. *The center instance is the instance at the smallest distance from the centroid of the data instances.*

This is done to ensure that the instances are "roughly" uniformly distributed in all directions around the reference point. The centroid of the available instances can be computed in O(n d) time, and finding the instance at the smallest distance from the centroid takes O(n d) time. Therefore, overall this step can be accomplished in O(n d) time and O(d) space. As reported in *http : //www.cs.ucsb.edu/ ~ panda/dexa06_long.pdf* the choice of a random instance as center instance leads to a small degradation in performance only.

Partitioning the Instances
Input :$\{\mathbf{x}_1 \cdots \mathbf{x}_n\}$, $\mathbf{x}_c$, *# of instances per partition*: g. *Output*: *# of partitions*: n_p, *Partitions*: $P[1] \cdots P[n_p]$.

Once the center instance has been determined, our next step is to partition the instances in the dataset based on their sorted distances from the center instance. This step requires O(n log n + n d) time and O(n) space. The created partitions (alongwith associated index structures developed below) are then placed on the disk. Our placement policy aims to achieve two goals. First, we would like to place adjacent partitions contiguously on the disk to achieve sequential disk accesses. Second, we need to reserve space within partitions to accomodate insertions of new data instances. Details of the insertion and placement policy may be found at *http : //www.cs.ucsb.edu/ ~ panda/dexa06_long.pdf*

Intra-partition Index

Input : $P[1] \cdots P[n_p]$, g. *Output*: *Local indices*: $S[1] \cdots S[n_p]$.

An intra-partition index (or local index) is created for each partition and stored on disk along with the instances in the partition. For each instance, this local index stores a sorted list of instances ranked according to their distances from this instance to allow the algorithm to quickly converge on the instances closest to the query. Maintaining this data structure for all pairs would take up O(g^2) space. Instead, in Section 3.2, we detail an approach storing two reduced sets of information for each instance reducing the space requirement to O(g log g) for each partition. Operations on this local index are explained in Section 3.2 when we discuss query-processing.

Inter-partition Index

Input : n_p, $P[1] \cdots P[n_p]$, g. *Output*: *Inter-partition indices*: I.

We also maintain a data structure which contains neighborhood information across adjacent partitions. This index gives Hydex a good location to search for k-NNs when a search transitions from one partition to the next. Intuitively, a good starting point to continue searching is an instance that is very close to the current set of top-k results. This index stores, for each instance in a partition, its nearest neighbor(s) in the adjacent partition(s). Building this index requires O(n g d) time. The storage required to maintain this index is of the order O(n).

3.2 Search—Querying the Index

Given a query instance, query processing begins by finding the approximate nearest neighbors of the query in the partition to which it belongs. Thereafter, adjacent partitions are retrieved and searched for better nearest neighbors. The set of nearest neighbors improves as we continue to retrieve and process adjacent partitions. Hydex terminates its search for top-k when the constituents of the top-k set do not change over the evaluation of multiple partitions, or when the query time expires.

Identification of Starting Partition

Input : *Query instance*: $\mathbf{x}_q$, $\mathbf{x}_c$, $Delim$. *Output*: Partition number: α.

First, we identify the partition to which the query instance $\mathbf{x}_q$ belongs. Instead of maintaining the distances of all the instances from the center, we keep another sorted list, $Delim$, of the distances of only the starting instance of each partition which is searched for the distance between $\mathbf{x}_q$ and $\mathbf{x}_c$. The cost of this binary search is O(log n_p) (n_p denotes the number of partitions).

Intra-Partition Search

Input : $\mathbf{x}_q$, $P[\alpha]$, $S[\alpha]$, $I[\alpha]$. *Output*: Approximate k-NNs of $\mathbf{x}_q$.

Once the starting partition $P[\alpha]$ has been identified, we retrieve the instances in that partition and the associated local index $S[\alpha]$ from the disk (if not yet cached in main memory). We then look for the nearest neighbor of $\mathbf{x}_q$ among the instances in $P[\alpha]$. From that one single nearest neighbor, we can use the intra-partition index $S[\alpha]$ to harvest the approximate k-NNs of $\mathbf{x}_q$. We start by selecting an arbitrary instance $\mathbf{x}_0$ in $P[\alpha]$, and then iteratively find instances closer to $\mathbf{x}_q$ (than $\mathbf{x}_0$).

Figure 1 depicts an example partition $P[\alpha]$. The local index of $\mathbf{x}_0$ contains nine data instances: $\mathbf{x}_0 \cdots \mathbf{x}_8$. The query instance $\mathbf{x}_q$ is located at the top of the figure. We use $\mathbf{x}_0$ as an anchor to find instances closer to $\mathbf{x}_q$. Pictorially, Figure 1 shows that a better nearest neighbor than $\mathbf{x}_0$ lies within a radius of a from $\mathbf{x}_q$. Let the distance between $\mathbf{x}_0$ and $\mathbf{x}_q$ be a. Starting at $\mathbf{x}_0$, we seek to find an instance as close to $\mathbf{x}_q$ as possible. The intra-partition index of $\mathbf{x}_0$ contains an ordered list of instances based on their distances from $\mathbf{x}_0$. For the example in Figure 1, the neighboring points of $\mathbf{x}_0$ appear in the order of $\mathbf{x}_3$, $\mathbf{x}_1$, $\mathbf{x}_4$, $\mathbf{x}_5$, $\mathbf{x}_2$, $\mathbf{x}_6$, $\mathbf{x}_7$, and $\mathbf{x}_8$ on its sorted list. To find an instance closer than $\mathbf{x}_0$ to $\mathbf{x}_q$, we search this list for instances at a distance of about a from $\mathbf{x}_0$. To do so, the instance performs a binary search for a and picks up the first instance $\mathbf{x}_n$ in its sorted list closer to $\mathbf{x}_q$ than itself (in this case, $\mathbf{x}_1$ is chosen after rejecting $\mathbf{x}_4$ and $\mathbf{x}_5$). The next iteration then commences with the new anchor $\mathbf{x}_n$.

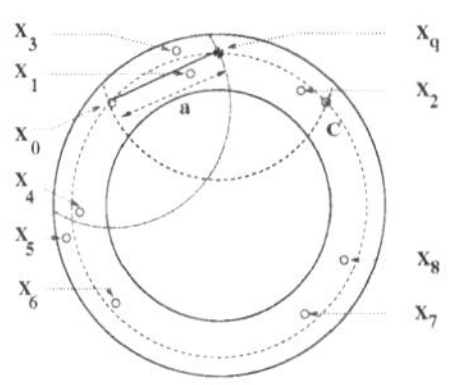

Fig. 1. Arrangement of instances

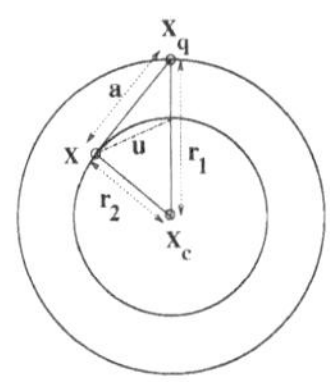

Fig. 2. Processing other partitions

The iterations continue till no nearer instance than the current anchor can be found. The approximate top-k instances nearest to $\mathbf{x}_q$ are the k nearest neighbors on the current anchor's intra-partition sorted list. To evaluate the performance of our intra-partition search algorithm, we present the number of distance computations (between instances in the dataset and $\mathbf{x}_q$) in $http://www.cs.ucsb.edu/\sim panda/dexa06\_long.pdf$.

Size of the Local Index. Instead of storing the distances of all the instances from $\mathbf{x}_i$ in the local index of $\mathbf{x}_i$, if we stored just the distances of $log\ g$ items, the probability of not finding an instance closer to the query point after evaluating all these instances would be $\frac{1}{2^{log g}}$, which is essentially $\frac{1}{g}$. In our local index for every instance we store two sets of information.

- *1. The distances of only O(log g) instances for every instance $\mathbf{x}_i$ in the partition.* Let $L = (l_1, l_2, l_3, \cdots, l_g)$ be the ordering of all instances in the partition based on their distances from $\mathbf{x}_i$. Let $L_1 = (l_1, l_2, \cdots, l_{\frac{g}{2}})$ and $L_2 = (l_{\frac{g}{2}+1}, l_{\frac{g}{2}+2}), \cdots, l_g$ be two equal halves of L. In our local index we store the distances of $4 \times log\ \frac{g}{2}$ instances with $log\ \frac{g}{2}$ distances from each end of L_1 and L_2, thus selecting

$$l_1, l_2, l_4, \cdots, l_{2^{\lfloor log \frac{g}{2} \rfloor}}, l_{\frac{g}{2}}, l_{\frac{g}{2}-1}, l_{\frac{g}{2}-3}, \cdots, l_{\frac{g}{2}-2^{\lfloor log \frac{g}{2} \rfloor}+1},$$
$$l_{\frac{g}{2}+1}, l_{\frac{g}{2}+2}, l_{\frac{g}{2}+4}, \cdots, l_{\frac{g}{2}+2^{\lfloor log \frac{g}{2} \rfloor}+1}, l_g, l_{g-1}, l_{g-3}, \cdots, l_{g-2^{\lfloor log \frac{g}{2} \rfloor}+1}.$$

The $4 \times log\ \frac{g}{2}$ instances are chosen to accommodate instances spread out over the entire spectrum of distances of instances in the partition.

- *2. The distances of the r closest instances for every* $\mathbf{x}_i$. As we get closer to the query instance, the number of instances on the list that are examined becomes small (because distance a to the query instance comes down), and the possibility of not finding an instance closer to the query instance becomes more likely. This situation is addressed by adding the instances closest to $\mathbf{x}_i$ in the partition to our index. That is, we add the distances of the instances, $l_1, l_2, \cdots, l_t$, to our index for $\mathbf{x}_i$.

Combining the above two sets, the local index of Hydex uses O($g\ log\ g\ +\ t\ g$) space per partition. With values of t close to O($log\ g$), the total space required for the local index would therefore be O($g\ log\ g$) per partition and O($n\ log\ g$) overall. Constructing this local index for all partitions requires O($n\ g\ log\ g + n\ g\ d$) time.

Our empirical studies show that a typical g is in the order of thousands, and t is about 30. For $g = 1000$, the probability of not finding an instance closer to the query instance, after evaluating all the instances in the local index of $\mathbf{x}_i$, is less than 10^{-10} ($\leq 2^{-log(\frac{g}{2})^4} = \frac{1}{(\frac{g}{2})^4}$). With $t \approx 30$, this probability, even when the anchor is close to the query instance, is given by $\frac{1}{2^{30}}$ ($\approx 10^{-9}$). Therefore, the number of distances stored in the local index of instance $\mathbf{x}_i$ is bounded by $4 \times log\frac{g}{2} + 30$. (However, since some of the chosen positions overlap, the number of instances chosen is lower than this number.) For $g = 1000$, the number of instances stored is about 60 ($\leq 4\ log(1000/2) + 30$).

Search in Adjacent Partition As the algorithm proceeds, starting from the partition to which the query instance belongs, we advance to adjacent partitions. Having identified the instance $\mathbf{x}$ in a partition close to the query instance, we use the inter-partition index to select a good starting instance in the adjacent partition. Since the inter-partition index contains the instance from the adjacent partition closest to the instance $\mathbf{x}$, there is a high probability that the inter-partition index will give an instance very close to the query instance. This has the effect of lowering the number of iterations needed to converge to the approximate best instance in the adjacent partition. Figure 2 presents the scenario when searching adjacent partitions and details of computations necessary are presented in the appendix of the online version at *http://www.cs.ucsb.edu/~panda/dexa06_long.pdf.*

4 Experiments

In this section, we present an evaluation of our indexing approach and make comparisons with existing techniques to demonstrate its effectiveness. We were interested in the following key questions:

- Using random IOs, how does Hydex compare with LSH and M-tree? (Section 4.2)
- When Hydex maintains sequential IOs, what is the additional gain? (Section 4.2)

Answers to other questions like "How do insertions affect sequential access?", "What is the maximum space reservation possible without a decay in performance?", "What is the percentage of data Hydex processes compared to competing schemes?", "What is the impact of a poor center instance?" are presented in the online version of the paper at $http://www.cs.ucsb.edu/\sim panda/dexa06\_long.pdf$ because of space limitations.

4.1 Setup

It would be impossible to compare our method with every published indexing scheme so we chose to compare Hydex with two representative schemes: LSH and the M-tree. LSH was chosen because it outperforms many traditional schemes, and it has been used in real applications [18,7]. An approximate version of the algorithm was presented in [8]. For a fair comparison, we chose the algorithm presented in [8] and used the code provided by M. Patella. The code is available on request, but it is not part of the basic download available at [17].

Datasets. We used two datasets for conducting our experiments. The first dataset [15] is the same as the largest dataset used by LSH. It contains $275,465$ feature vectors. Each of these was a 60-dimensional vector representing texture information of blocks of large aerial photographs. The second dataset contained $314,499$ feature vectors. Each of these was a 144-dimensional vector representing color and texture information for each image.

In our experiments on each dataset, we chose $2,000$ instances randomly from the dataset and created an index using the rest of the dataset. As in [11] our experiments aimed at finding the performance for a top-10 approximate NN search. The results are averaged over all the approximate 10-NN searches.

Comparison metric. The objective of our experiment was to ascertain how quickly the approximate results could be obtained using the index. Following [2] the effective error for the 1-nearest neighbor search problem is defined as

$$E = \frac{1}{|Q|} \sum_{query \mathbf{x}_q \in Q} (\frac{d_{index}}{d^*} - 1),$$

where d_{index} denotes the distance from a query point $\mathbf{x}_q$ to a point found by the indexing approach, d^* is the distance from $\mathbf{x}_q$ to the closest point, and the sum is taken over all queries. For the approximate k-nearest neighbor problem, as in [11], we measure the distance ratios between the closest point to the nearest neighbor, the 2nd closest one to the 2nd nearest neighbor and so on, finally averaging the ratios. In the case of LSH, the sum is calculated over all queries returning more than k results. Under LSH, queries returning less than k results are defined as misses.

We compare methods based on the number of *disk accesses* performed. Our measure of disk accesses takes into account both the seek time and the data transfer time as outlined below. To correctly gauge the impact of data transfer time we compute the disk transfer time in units of the seek time. The number of disk accesses is then the total number of seeks performed (both the actual seeks and the seeks to account for the data transfer). To understand the relationship between seek time and data transfer time, we look at the time the disk takes to transfer 1 MB of data. Current disk technology can maintain a sustained throughput in the range of 50-70MB/s. Therefore, transferring

1MB of data takes roughly 14-20ms. Average seek times are usually in the range of 10ms. Thus, the ratio of transfer time to seek time ranges from 1.4 to 2. Since the exact time varies from disk to disk, we use the ratio of the times in our calculations and select a higher value of the ratio (2) to allow the competing index structures the maximum benefit. Further, since the other index structures transfer only small chunks of data in each access to the disk, the time they require to transfer data has been assumed to be 0. We also present graphs with different ratios between seek and transfer time for the sake of completeness.

4.2 Performance with Disk IOs

We compared the performance of the two approaches in cases when the index needs to be accessed from the disk. In such cases, the cost of distance computations becomes insignificant when compared to the cost of disk access. We count only the total number of seeks performed by LSH. The number of seeks performed by LSH is controlled by parameter l. The space used by our indexing structure is O($log\ g$) per instance, g being the number of instances assigned to a partition. As explained in Section 3.2, when $g = 1000$, we store approximately 60 distances for each instance. If we limit ourselves to 2 bytes for each distance, we can get 4 digits of precision. Also, since there are 1000 instances in the partition, to maintain unique identifiers for them we need only 10 bits. The total space required to store the index associated with one instance is therefore $60 \times (2 + \frac{10}{8})$ bytes, which is equal to 60×3.25 bytes.

The results are presented in Figures 3,4. The x-axis represents the percentage of error, and the y-axis the number of disk accesses. The second y-axis, when used, represents the number of partitions. Many of the curves pertaining to Hydex overlap.

Performance under random access. In the case of the first dataset, LSH used $l \approx 70$ hash functions to achieve acceptable error rates. Hence the total time taken by LSH would be given by $t_{LSH} = l \times (t_{seek} + t_{rot}) = 70 \times (t_{seek} + t_{rot})$. Here, t_{seek} is the average seek time and t_{rot} is the average rotation latency. Compared to this, our method has to retrieve whole partitions. Thus, we need to compute the space required to store the partitions. In the case of the first dataset, where each instance has 60 features, each partition takes up space $g \times d + g \times \beta \times log\ g$.

But, as explained above, $\beta \times log\ g$ is equal to 60×3.25 when $g = 1000$. Hence, the total space consumed is equal to $1000 \times 60 + 1000 \times 60 \times 3.25$, where, as in LSH, each dimension can be stored in 1 byte. Therefore, the total space required to store a partition is 0.255MB. The total time consumed is therefore given by

$$r \times t_{seek} + r \times t_{rot} + r \times 0.255 \times t_{tr},$$

where, t_{tr} is the time taken to transfer 1MB of data from the disk and r is the number of partitions transferred. The rotation latency, t_{rot}, is about half the seek time, t_{seek}. Since t_{tr} takes less than twice the average seek time, the equation simplifies to $r \times t_{seek}(1 + 0.5 + 0.51)$. (We also present data for other ratios between seek time and transfer time in the graphs shown in Figure 3. In the graph legend the first value after Hydex is the average seek time in milliseconds and the second value is the data transfer rate in MB/s). Taking the ratio of the times taken by LSH and our method we get

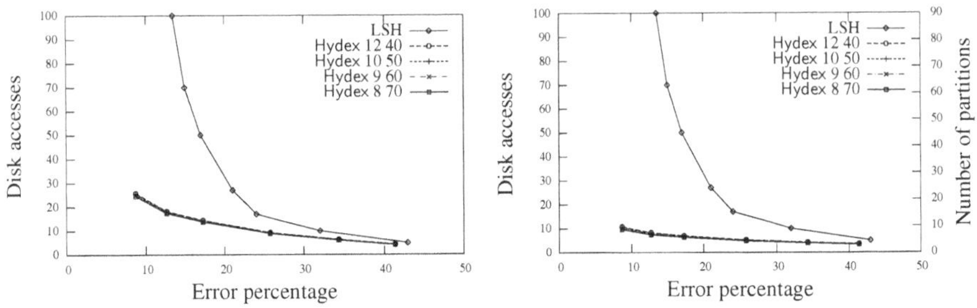

(a) *vs.* LSH: random access (b) *vs.* LSH: sequential access

Fig. 3. Hydex *vs.* LSH: first dataset

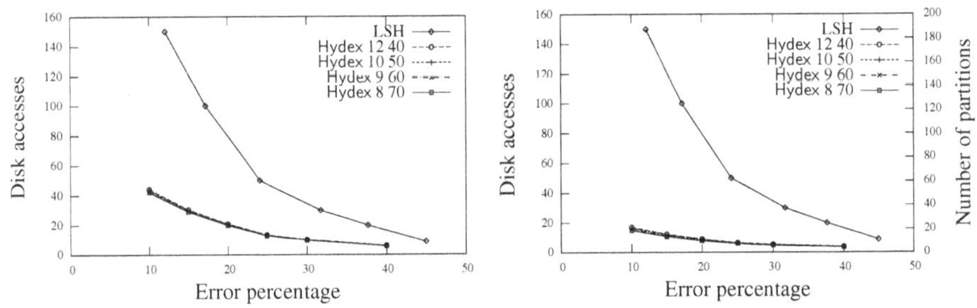

(a) *vs.* LSH: random access (b) *vs.* LSH: sequential access

Fig. 4. Hydex *vs.* LSH: second dataset

$$Speedup = \frac{70 \times (t_{seek} + 0.5 \times t_{seek})}{r \times t_{seek}(1 + 0.5 + 0.51)} = \frac{70 \times 1.5}{r \times (2.01)}.$$

Therefore, if our approach is able to retrieve the approximate set of instances in less than $\frac{70 \times 1.5}{2.01}$ partitions, then we have speedup. This value is roughly equal to 52. We found (Figure 3(c)) that the average number of partitions that had to be evaluated before achieving the same level of error was 12. The speedup is ≈ 4 times.

Similar analysis for the second dataset can be done as follows. The space required for each partition of the second dataset is given by $1000 \times (144 + 3.25 \times 60)$ bytes (0.339MB). For the second dataset, LSH required $l > 130$ to achieve 15% error rate. Therefore, $Speedup = \frac{130 \times (t_{seek} + t_{rot})}{r \times t_{seek}(1+0.5+2\times 0.339)} = \frac{130 \times 1.5}{r \times (2.178)}$. To achieve parity with the time taken by LSH we would need to evaluate $r = 89$ partitions. We show in Figure 4(c) that in this case the average value of r is 21. The speedup is approximately 4.

Performance under sequential access. In this case, we would need at most two seek operations and the rest of the time would be spent in transferring the partitions. Here, we assume that space has been reserved for another g instances in each partition to accommodate insertions. The total time consumed for the first dataset is therefore given by $2 \times t_{seek} + 2 \times t_{rot} + 2r \times 0.255 \times t_{tr}$. Since t_{tr} is less than twice the average seek time and t_{rot} is about half of the average seek time, the equation simplifies to

$2 \times t_{seek}(1.5 + 2r \times 0.255)$. (We also present data for other ratios between seek time and transfer time in the graphs shown in Figure 4. In the graph legend the first value after Hydex is the average seek time in milliseconds and the second value is the data transfer rate in MB/s). Taking the ratio of the times taken by LSH and our method,

$$Speedup = \frac{70 \times (t_{seek} + t_{rot})}{2t_{seek}(1.5 + 2r \times 0.255)} = \frac{35 \times 1.5}{1.5 + 0.51r}.$$

Therefore, if our approach can retrieve the approximate set of instances in fewer than $\frac{34 \times 1.5}{0.51}$ partitions, then we achieve speedup. This value is roughly equal to 100. Since the average number of partitions required to be evaluated before achieving the same level of error is 12, the speedup is on the order of 8 times.

Similar analysis for the second dataset can be done as follows.

$$Speedup = \frac{130 \times (t_{seek} + t_{rot})}{2t_{seek}(1.5 + 2r \times 0.339)} = \frac{65 \times 1.5}{1.5 + 0.678r}.$$

To achieve parity with the time taken by LSH we would need to evaluate $r = 141$ partitions. The average value of r is 21 for 15% error. Hence, the speedup is approximately 6.5 times. We do not present the graph in this case because of space limitations. Our experiments with M-tree show that the number of IO operations performed by the index are much higher on both the data sets. This makes using M-trees for searching prohibitively expensive.

5 Conclusion

We have presented a new approach to efficiently index high-dimensional vector spaces. This approach minimizes IOs to reduce the seek overheads. Strategies were presented to minimize the number of distance computations performed. We studied the tradeoff between sequential access using space reservation and random placement of partitions. Experimental comparison with LSH and M-tree showed the good performance of our approach.

References

1. S. Arya, D. Mount, N. Netanyahu, R. Silverman, and A. Wu. An optimal algorithm for approximate nearest neighbor searching in fixed dimensions. In *Proceedings of the 5th SODA*, pages 573–82, 1994.
2. S. Arya, D. M. Mount, N. S. Netanyahu, R. Silverman, and A. Y. Wu. An optimal algorithm for approximate nearest neighbor searching in fixed dimensions. *JACM*, 45(6), 1998.
3. N. Beckmann, H. Kriegel, R. Schneider, and B. Seeger. The R^* tree: An efficient and robust access method for points and rectangles. In *ACM SIGMOD Intl. Conf. on Mgmt. of Data*, pages 322–331, 1990.
4. S. Berchtold, D. Keim, and H. Kriegel. The X-tree: An index structure for high-dimensional data. In *22nd Conference on Very Large Databases*, pages 28–39, 1996.
5. T. Bozkaya and M. Ozsoyoglu. Indexing large metric spaces for similarity search queries. *ACM Trans. on Database Systems*, 24(3):361–404, 1999.

6. S. Brin. Near neighbor search in large metric spaces. In *The VLDB Journal*, 1995.
7. J. Buhler. Efficient large-scale sequence comparison by locality-sensitive hashing. In *Bioinformatics*, volume 17, pages 419–428, 2001.
8. P. Ciaccia and M. Patella. Pac nearest neighbor queries: Approximate and controlled search in high-dimensional and metric spaces. In *In Proceedings of International Conference on Data Engineering*, pages 244–255, 2000.
9. P. Ciaccia, M. Patella, and P. Zezula. M-tree: An efficient access method for similarity search in metric spaces. *Proc. 23rd Int. Conf. on Very Large Databases*, pages 426–435, 1997.
10. K. Clarkson. An algorithm for approximate closest-point queries. In *Proceedings of the 10th SCG*, pages 160–164, 1994.
11. A. Gionis, P. Indyk, and R. Motwani. Similarity search in high dimensions via hashing. In *The VLDB Journal*, pages 518–529, 1999.
12. N. Katayama and S. Satoh. The SR-tree: an index structure for high-dimensional nearest neighbor queries. In *ACM SIGMOD Int. Conf. on Mgmt. of Data*, pages 369–380, 1997.
13. C. Li, E. Chang, H. Garcia-Molina, and G. Wilderhold. Clindex: Approximate similarity queries in high-dimensional spaces. *IEEE Transactions on Knowledge and Data Engineering (TKDE)*, 14(4):792–808, July 2002.
14. K.-I. Lin, H. V. Jagadish, and C. Faloutsos. The TV-tree: An index structure for high-dimensional data. *VLDB Journal: Very Large Data Bases*, 3(4):517–542, 1994.
15. B. S. Manjunath. Airphoto dataset. *http://vision.ece.ucsb.edu/download.html*.
16. G. Navarro. Searching in metric spaces by spatial approximation. In *SPIRE/CRIWG*, pages 141–148, 1999.
17. M. Patella. M-tree website. *http://www-db.deis.unibo.it/Mtree/download.html*.
18. A. Qamra, Y. Meng, and E. Y. Chang. Enhanced perceptual distance functions and indexing for image replica recognition. In *IEEE Transactions on Pattern Analysis and Machine Intelligence (PAMI)*, volume 27, 2005.
19. R. Weber, H.-J. Schek, and S. Blott. A quantitative analysis and performance study for similarity-search methods in high-dimensional spaces. In *Proc. 24th Int. Conf. Very Large Data Bases, VLDB*, pages 194–205, 24–27 1998.

Distributed Continuous Range Query Processing on Moving Objects*

Haojun Wang, Roger Zimmermann, and Wei-Shinn Ku

University of Southern California, Computer Science Department,
Los Angeles, CA, USA
{haojunwa, rzimmerm, wku}@usc.edu

Abstract. Recent work on continuous queries has focused on processing queries in very large, mobile environments. In this paper, we propose a system leveraging the computing capacities of mobile devices for continuous range query processing. In our design, continuous range queries are mainly processed on the mobile device side, which is able to achieve real-time updates with minimum server load. Our work distinguish itself from previous work with several important contributions. First, we introduce a distributed server infrastructure to partition the entire service region into a set of service zones and cooperatively handle requests of continuous range queries. This feature improves the robustness and flexibility of the system by adapting to a time-varying set of servers. Second, we propose a novel query indexing structure, which records the difference of the query distribution on a grid model. This approach significantly reduce the size and complexity of the index so that in-memory indexing can be achieved on mobile objects with constrained memory size. We report on the rigorous evaluation of our design, which shows substantial improvement in the efficiency of continuous range query processing in mobile environments.

1 Introduction

With the growing popularity of GPS-enabled mobile devices and the advances in wireless technology, the efficient processing of *continuous range queries*, which is defined as retrieving the information of moving objects inside a user-defined region and continuously monitoring the change of query results in this region over a certain time period, has been of increasing interest. Continuous range query processing is very important due to its broad application base. For instance, the Department of Transportation may want to monitor the traffic change on a freeway section to develop a traffic control plan. In a natural disaster, it is highly desirable to locate all fire engines within a certain area for emergency response. Continuous range queries pose new challenges to the research community because the movement of objects causes the query results to change correspondingly. Applying a central server processing solution where moving objects periodically update their locations is obviously not scalable. On the other hand, the growing computing capabilities of mobile devices has enabled approaches such as

* This research has been funded in part by NSF grants EEC-9529152 (IMSC ERC), CMS-0219463 (ITR), IIS-0534761 and equipment gifts from the Intel Corporation, Hewlett-Packard, Sun Microsystems and Raptor Networks Technology.

S. Bressan, J. Küng, and R. Wagner (Eds.): DEXA 2006, LNCS 4080, pp. 655–665, 2006.

$MobiEyes$ [2] and MQM [1] that use mobile devices to answer continuous range queries, where a centralized server acts as a mediator. However, these solutions suffer from some limitations. First, a centralized server is not robust enough under certain situations. In the mentioned example of natural disasters, some servers might be down or only provide limited computational capacity. Therefore, it is highly desirable to have a fault resilient infrastructure. Second, the communication between the server and moving objects should be minimized in order to manage data in large mobile environments. Finally, the memory and computing capabilities of mobile devices are limited so that the implementation of in-memory processing on moving objects needs to be carefully considered.

In this paper, we address the problem of processing real-time continuous range queries by proposing a robust and scalable infrastructure. The goal is to build a system that supports a large number of moving objects with limited server and communication resources. In our design, continuous range queries are mainly processed by mobile devices. Our work distinguishes itself from previous work with two contributions. First, we propose a distributed server infrastructure. We introduce the feature of *service zones*. A service zone is a subspace being recursively binary partitioned from the entire service region. Each server controls a service zone. Our system is able to adaptively allocate and merge service zones as servers join or leave. In addition, we propose a novel *grid index* on continuous range queries. Instead of recording the distribution of queries, our design of grid index preserves the change of the query distribution and is more compact than other grid index structures. Our experimental results show that our design is very efficient to support numerous continuous range queries with a very large number of moving objects under the mobile environments.

The rest of this paper is organized as follows. The related work is described in Section 2. In Section 3 we introduce the design of service zones, grid index, and the support of continuous range query processing. The experimental validation of our design is presented in Section 4. Finally, we discuss the conclusions and future work in Section 5.

2 Related Work

A number of studies have addressed continuous spatial queries. Related work, such as presented in [10], [11], and [14], addressed the processing of continuous spatial queries on the server. For the efficient processing of a large number of continuous queries at the same time, Prabhakar et al. [7] addressed the issue of stationary continuous queries in a centralized environment. In addition, Mokbel et al. [5] proposed SINA that supports moving queries over moving objects in server-based processing. By contrast, MQM [1], and MobiEyes [2] assume a distributed environment, where the mobile hosts have the computing capability to process continuous queries. A centralized server is introduced by both approaches to work as a mediator coordinating the query processing. In MQM, the concept of *resident domain* is introduced as a subspace surrounding the moving object to process continuous queries. Continuous queries are partitioned into a set of *monitor regions*, where only the monitor regions covered by the resident domain will be sent to the moving object. However, partitioning continuous queries is inefficient because it increases the number of queries in the system.

On the issue of moving object indexing, the *TPR-Tree* [9] and its variants have been proposed to index moving objects with trajectories. However, the support of continuous queries by these methods is very inefficient. Kalashnikov et al. [4] evaluated the efficiency of indexing moving objects and concluded that using a grid approach for query indexing results in the best performance. Other methods to process continuous queries without a specific index can be found such as the usage of *validity regions* [11], *safe regions* [3], *safe periods* [5], and *No-Action regions* [13]. These approaches have in common that they return a valid time or region of the answer. Once the result becomes invalid, the client submits the query for reevaluation.

Our work distinguishes itself from the above approaches, by specifically addressing the scalability and robustness of the system. We adaptively organize servers to cooperatively work in the entire service space. Furthermore, we propose a grid index that is able to be implemented as an in-memory data structure on mobile devices. There is no restriction on the movement of objects and the system is extremely efficient to support continuous range queries with a very large number of moving objects.

3 System Design and Components

3.1 System Infrastructure and Assumptions

Figure 1 illustrates the system infrastructure of our design. We are considering mobile hosts with abundant power capacity, such as vehicles, that are equipped with a Global Positioning System (GPS) for obtaining continuous position information. We assume that the mobile host has some memory and computing capacity to store the queries and process range query operations. In our paper, we use the term moving objects to refer to these mobile hosts participated in the query processing. On the base-station side, our design has two assumptions. First, the servers and moving objects communicate via cellular-based wireless network. Moreover, protocols such as *GeoCast* [6] can be adopted for sending messages within a certain region. Second, the servers with spatial databases are connected via the wired Internet infrastructure. Each server is able to receive query requests from any user and forward them to the appropriate servers.

In our design, moving objects are represented as points and range queries are denoted as rectangular regions. Given a set of moving objects and continuous range queries, the challenge is to calculate which objects lie within which query regions at a certain time.

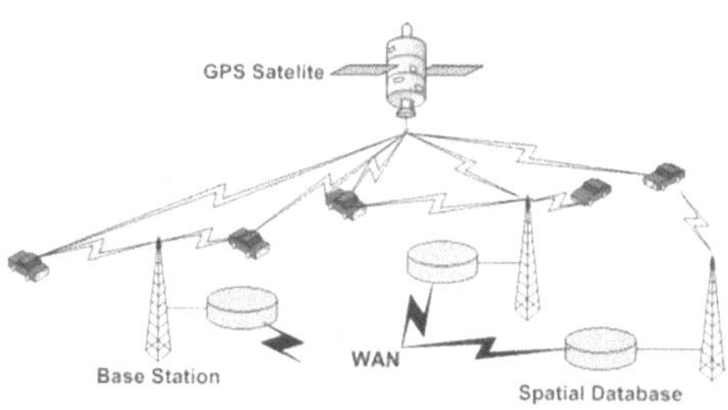

Fig. 1. The system infrastructure

In this paper, we focus on range queries, which are widely used in spatial applications and can be used as preprocessing tools for other queries, such as nearest neighbor queries. For simplicity, we use the term queries to refer to continuous range queries in the following sections.

3.2 Server Design

In this section, we describe our design of the server infrastructure. First, we describe how the system adaptively manages the service region by adapting to a time-varying set of servers through the concept of the service zone. Next, we present another important feature, the grid index. By using the grid index, our system avoids excessive query retrieval from the server and significantly reduces the communication overhead.

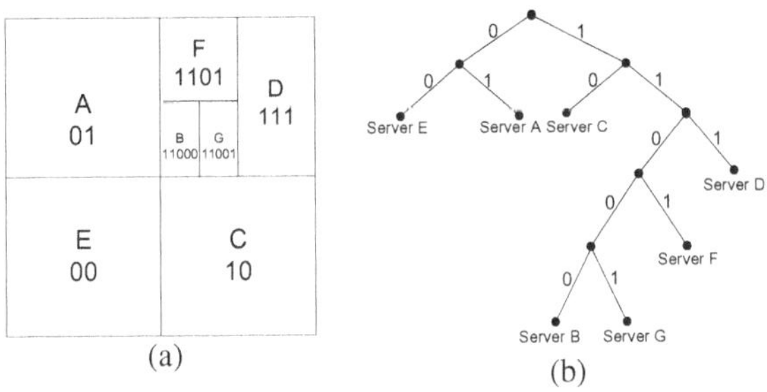

Fig. 2. An example of the system with 7 servers and their service zone identifier (SID) tree

Service Zones. We leverages the design of Content Addressable Network (CAN) [8] to dynamically partition the entire service region into a set of subspaces. Each subspace is controlled by a server. We define the term *service zone* as the subspace controlled by a server. Each service zone is addressed with a service zone identifier (SID), which is calculated from the location of the service zone. Figure 2a shows an example of the entire service region partitioned into 7 service zones. The service zone partitioning is a binary partition approach that always equally divides a larger service zone into two smaller child service zones. Hence the corresponding SID address for service zones can be represented with a binary tree structure as shown in Figure 2b. Each server maintains a routing table with tuples $\langle SID, address \rangle$ storing the routing information of its neighbor servers. By using the same routing mechanism as CAN, our system is able to allocate any service zone with complexity of $O(n\log n)$ in a system of n servers.

When a new query q is submitted, the system first forwards it to all servers covered by its query region through the M-CAN multicast algorithm from the design of CAN. When a server receives the query, it is inserted into the query repository. Consequently, the grid index on the server is updated. We will describe the details of the grid index in the next section. Finally, the server broadcasts a message $GridIndexUpdate(G_{Index})$ to all moving objects associated with it, where G_{Index} is the updated grid index.

When a query q is about to be deleted, the server searches through its repository to delete the corresponding entry. Consequently, the server updates the grid index.

When a new server joins the system, several steps must be taken to allocate a service zone for it. First, the new server must find a bootstrap server, which is already a member of the system. Second, the bootstrap server broadcasts a message that a new server is about to join the system. Other servers in the system reply back with the information of its current system load and service zone. Our goal is the balance the system load among servers. Hence the server with the highest system load (for instance, average used disk space, average memory usage, or other user identified resources) will be performed a partition to divide the corresponding service zone into halves. Next, the bootstrap server sends a message to the partitioned server to forward queries overlapping the new server's service zone. The partitioned server also broadcasts the updated service zone information to moving objects associated with it. Moving objects register with the new server if their current locations are controlled by the new server. After the new server receives queries forwarded from the partitioned server, it creates and maintains the grid index correspondingly. Finally, the neighbors of the partitioned server will be notified to update their routing tables.

When a server leaves the system, we need to ensure that the corresponding service zone is taken over by the remaining servers. The departing server explicitly hands over its repository of moving objects and queries to one of its neighbors whose service zone can be merged with the departing servers zone to produce a valid single service zone.

Grid Index. The memory capacity of moving objects is limited. On the other hand, it is highly desirable to have an index structure that helps moving objects to retrieve queries from the server only when they are very close to the queries. Therefore, the index also needs to be compact in terms of the size to be used on moving objects. Here we present a grid index structure fulfilling these requirements.

Previous work of grid-based indexing on continuous queries, such as [4] and [2], aims at random data access by recording the distribution of queries. However, objects move continuously along a trajectory in mobile environments, therefore queries in large parts of the service region can be pruned and no random access is needed. Based on this observation, our grid index preserves the difference of the query distribution that can be efficiently used for continuous query processing.

The basis of our grid index is a set of cells. Each cell is a region of space obtained by partitioning the entire service region using a uniform order. Figure 3a demonstrates a system with 7 servers. Figure 3b shows the entire service region divided into 64 grid cells. Figure 3c shows how these grid cells are distributed on the example servers. By

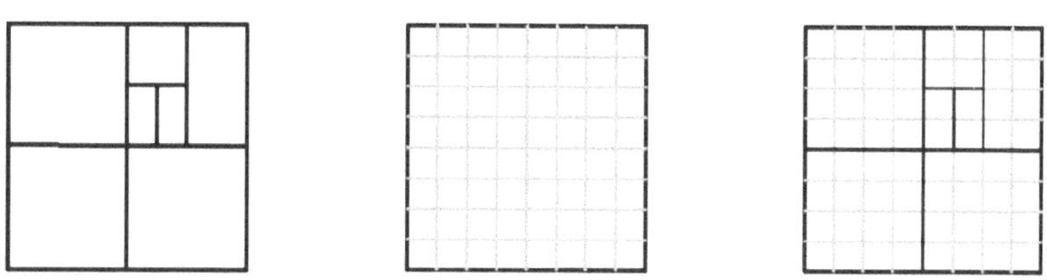

(a) A 7 service zone example (b) A 64 grid cell example (c) Service zones and grid cells overlapping

Fig. 3. Service zones and grid cells

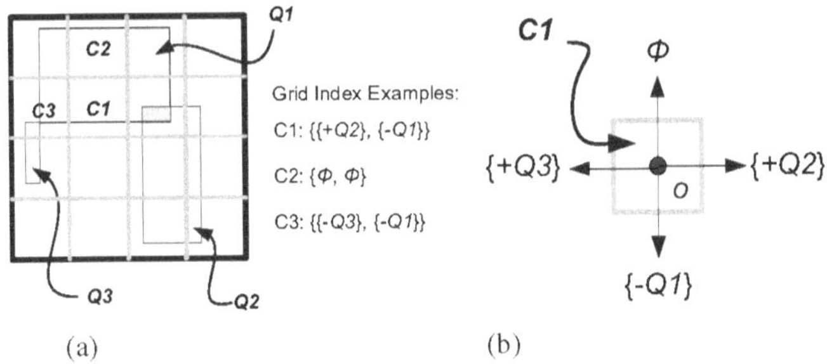

Fig. 4. The grid index

using a uniform grid order to partition the service region into grid cells, given the coordinates of an object, it is easy to calculate the cell in which the object resides.

The server maintains the grid index in its service zone. For each cell, the grid index structure consists of two lists identified as *right*, and *lower* that record the change of the query distribution from the right and lower neighbor cells, respectively. In the example shown in Figure 4a, a service zone is divided into 16 grid cells. Cell $C1$, $C2$, and $C3$ are partially covered by a query $Q1$. There are queries $Q2$ and $Q3$ covering the right and left neighbor cells of $C1$, repectively. As shown in Figure 4a, the grid index for cell $C1$, $C2$, and $C3$ is $\{\{+Q2\}, \{-Q1\}\}$, $\{\ \emptyset, \emptyset\ \}$, and $\{\{-Q3\}, \{-Q1\}\}$, respectively.

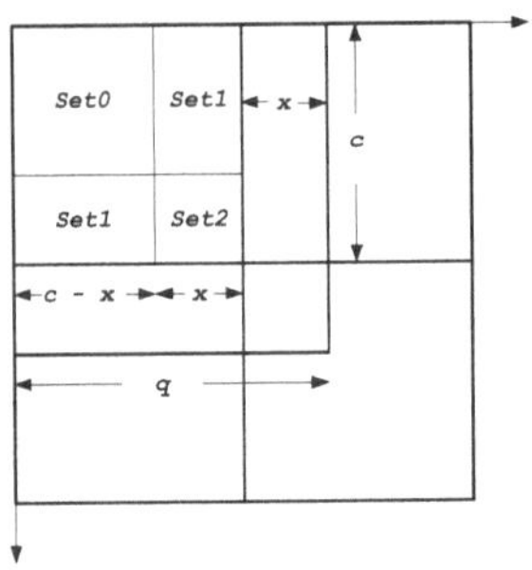

Fig. 5. Number of Grid Index Entries Analysis

Once a moving object is associated with a server, the server will forward the grid index of its service zone to the moving object. By using the grid index stored in its local memory the moving object is able to forecast the query locations with a refined granularity. As an example shown in Figure 4b, if there is a moving object o in the cell $C1$ is about to move across the right edge of $C1$, the right list of $C1$ is $\{+Q2\}$. Hence the object submits a request to retrieve the query $Q2$ from the server. If the object is about to cross the lower edge of $C1$, since the lower list of $C1$ is $\{-Q1\}$. The object could either to retain the information of query $Q1$ if there is enough memory or remove $Q1$ if more memory is needed for query processing. If the object is about to move across the upper edge of $C1$, the lower list of the upper neighbor cell will be retrieved and the values in the list will be inversed. In this example, the object retrieves the lower list of $C2$ and calculate the inverse value, which is $\emptyset$. This indicates that there is no query that needs to be retrieved from the server. When the object is about to move across the left edge of $C1$, a similar process will be performed on the right list of the left neighbor cell (i.e., $C3$). In this example, the inverse value of the list is $\{-Q3\}$. Therefore, the moving object submits a request to retrieve the query $Q3$ from the server.

To study the impact of our design on the index size, let us assume the shape of queries and grid cells are square and the length of each side of a query Q is q. Let c denote the side of each grid cell with $q > c$. Then q can be represented as $i \times c + x$, where $x \subset [0, c)$ and i is an integer. Without loss of generality let us consider the case where the top-left corner of query q is located somewhere within the top-left grid cell of the system as shown in Fig 5. It can be verified that if the top-left corner of Q is inside $Set0$ it will result in $4(i+1)$ index entries. For $Set1$ the number of index entries is $2(i+1)+2(i+2)$, and for $Set2$ it is $4(i+2)$. Assuming uniform distribution of queries, on the average Q results in $4(q+c)/c$ index entries. On the other hand, recording the distribution of queries requires $(q+c)^2/c^2$ index entries on each Q [12]. For all $q/c \geq 3$, our approach requires less index entries than recording the distribution of queries on the grid.

3.3 Query Processing on Moving Objects

In this section, we describe the functionality of the moving objects. In our design, the following information is stored in the memory of moving objects for query processing:

- OID: the unique identifier of the moving object.
- $currentPos$: the current location of the moving object.
- G_{Index}: the grid index of the current service zone covering the moving object.
- $Queries$: the list of queries received from the server.

Table 1. Message types in query processing

Notation	Definition
$RegisterObject(OID)$	The message to register a moving object on a server.
$UnregisterObject(OID)$	The message to delete a moving object on a server.
$UpdateResult(OID, QID, Flag)$	The message to update a query result.
$RequestQueries(OID, Q_{List})$	The message to retrieve a set of queries.
$GridIndexUpdate(G_{Index})$	Updating the grid index broadcasted by the server.

In order to implement the query processing mechanism on the mobile object, a set of messages is defined as shown in Table 1.

A moving object is associated with a server at all times. When a moving object turns its power on, it broadcasts a message $RegisterObject(OID)$. The server monitoring the location of the object inserts it into the object repository and replies back with a $GridIndexUpdate(G_{Index})$ message. The server also sends the set of queries covering the current grid cell of the moving object.

When a moving object is about to leave its current service zone, it sends a message $UnregisterObject(OID)$ to the server. The server deletes the moving object from its repository and sends back a set of tuples$\langle SID, address\rangle$ from its routing table identifying adjacent service zones. The moving object sends a $RegisterObject(OID)$ message to the server controlling the zone it is entering.

When a moving object is about to move into a new grid cell, it consults the grid index as described in the previous section. If there are queries in the grid index needing to be retrieved, the moving object sends a message $RequestQueries(OID, Q_{List})$ to the server, where Q_{List} is a list of queries with query identifier QID. Once the server receives the message, it will send the corresponding queries to the moving object.

At all times, the moving object checks its current location $currentPos$ against the queries in the $Queries$ list. If the object moves into or moves out of a query, it sends a message $UpdateResult(OID, QID, Flag)$ to the server, where QID is the query identifier and $Flag$ indicates whether the object resides in the query region.

Query processing on moving objects enables real time updates to the query result while reducing the cost of server processing substantially. We study the impact of our techniques in experiments and show that the results match our analytical expectation.

4 Experimental Evaluation

In this section we describe the experimental verification of our design. There are three metrics of interest extensively studied in our simulations. First, the *number of grid index entries* is measured as the average number of index entries generated on a server and forwarded to moving objects associated with it. This measure indicates the efficiency of our grid index design and whether the grid index can be used for in-memory processing on moving objects. Second, the *server communication cost* is measured as the average number of messages transmitted from servers to the moving objects. More specifically, the server communication cost consists of the registration messages, which are generated when a moving object enters or leaves a service zone, and the query retrieval messages, which are generated when a server receives a $RequestQueries$ message from a moving object. This metric implies whether the server may become a bottleneck in the system. Finally, the *mobile communication cost* is measured as the total number of messages transmitted from moving objects to servers. The mobile communication cost also consists of registration messages and query retrieval messages. Additionally, query update messages are generated by moving objects when they enter or leave a query region. This measure reflects the prime query processing cost and hence is important to demonstrate the scalability of our system.

4.1 Simulator Implementation

We implemented a prototype simulator that is structured into three main components: the *service zone generator*, the *object and query loader*, and the *performance monitor*.

The service zone generator creates a virtual square space with a 100km × 100km dimension. In the experiments, we partition the space into 64 service zones. Each service zone is identified by a SID representing a server.

In the next step, the object and query loader generates moving objects and imports continuous range queries into the system. We use the random walk model to simulate the movement of objects. Initially 10,000 objects are uniformly distributed in the space. Each of them moves with a constant velocity, which is randomly selected in the range from 10m to 20m per second, for a duration that is exponentially distributed with mean value equal to 100 seconds. We also generated two sets of rectangular regions as continuous range queries that are uniformly distributed in the space with an average area size of 1% and 10% of the plane size, respectively.

After the objects and queries are loaded into the system, the performance monitor generates the grid index for each server with 256 grid cells partitioning the entire service space. Each simulation runs for 5,000 seconds and the performance monitor reports the number of grid index entries, the server communication cost, and the mobile communication cost. Currently, our simulation is focused on the system performance in the steady state, i.e., we do not add any more queries when the objects start to move. We plan to implement a dynamic simulation environment in the future.

4.2 Simulation Results

We were first interested in the efficiency of our grid index in terms of the size. Figure 6a plots the total number of grid index entries in the system as a function of the number of queries. The results clearly show that the total number of grid index entries increases linearly with the number of queries. Additionally, our grid index structure performs more efficiently with a larger average query size. With an average query size equal to 10% of the entire space, our grid index only doubles the number of entries compared with the case when the average query size equals 1% of the space. This behavior corroborates our analytical results described in Section 3. Furthurmore, the absolute size of the grid index is very small. If we use 16 bytes to identify a query, it only takes 3.35 MB to represent 10,000 queries with an average size of 10% of the space. Figure 6b shows the benefit of using a distributed infrastructure on the server side that further reduces the size of the grid index on each server. In the case of 10,000 queries with an average size of 10% of the space, on average the size of index entries is 54 KB on each server. This substantially reduces the requirement of memory on moving objects.

Figures 7a illustrates the average communication cost on each server with the set of queries with an average area size of 10% of the plane. As a general trend, the number

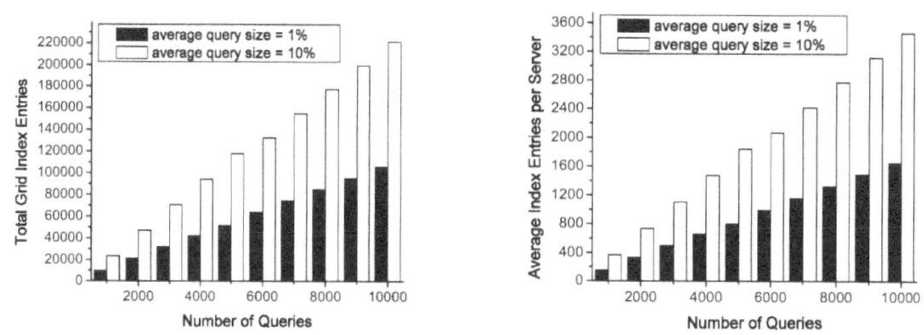

(a) The total number index entries in the system

(b) The average number of index entries on each server

Fig. 6. The number of grid index entries as a function of the number of queries

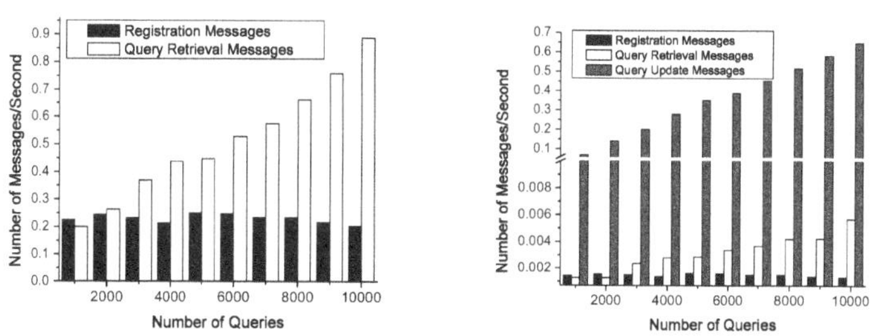

(a) The server communication cost

(b) The mobile communication cost

Fig. 7. The server and mobile communication cost as functions of the number of queries of query retrieval messages increases with the number of queries. Intuitively, with a larger number of queries, the possibility for objects to retrieve query information from the server is larger. More importantly, the server communication cost is small in our simulation results. With 10,000 queries and 10,000 objects in the system, the server communication cost is about 1 message per second, which demonstrates that our server infrastructure is very scalable and suitable for mobile environments. Figure 7b demonstrates the mobile communication cost with respect to the number of queries. It shows that the query update messages are the primary cost of mobile communication cost. However, with 10,000 queries, the object query update message count on each object is about 0.7 per second. Assuming the size of query update message is 32 byte, the average message size transmitted from each object is about 22 bytes/second. Therefore, our design on the mobile object side is very scalable.

5 Conclusions and Future Directions

Continuous range queries have generated intense interest in the research community because the advances in GPS devices is enabling new applications. We have presented a novel system that utilizes the computing capability of moving objects for continuous range query processing. Our design of service zones and a grid index is able to provide accurate real time query results for a very large number of moving objects and queries.

In the future, we intend to study the communication costs so that the size of the grid can be optimized with regard to the query distribution. Moreover, a dynamic grid index retrieval from the server with respect to the memory capacity on moving objects is worth exploring.

References

1. Y. Cai, K. Hua, and G. Cao. Processing Range-Monitoring Queries on Heterogeneous Mobile Objects. In *International Conference on Mobile Data Management*, pages 27–38, 2004.
2. B. Gedik and L. Liu. MobiEyes: Distributed Processing of Continuously Moving Queries on Moving Objects in a Mobile System. In *International Conference on Extending Database Technology*, pages 67–87, 2004.
3. H. Hu, J. Xu, and D. L. Lee. A Generic Framework for Monitoring Continuous Spatial Queries over Moving Objects. In *SIGMOD*, pages 479–490, 2005.
4. D. V. Kalashnikov, S. Prabhakar, S. E. Hambrusch, and W. G. Aref. Efficient Evaluation of Continuous Range Queries on Moving Objects. In *International Conference on Database and Expert Systems Applications*, pages 731–740, 2002.
5. M. F. Mokbel, X. Xiong, and W. G. Aref. SINA: Scalable Incremental Processing of Continuous Queries in Spatio-temporal Databases. In *SIGMOD*, pages 479–490, 2004.
6. J. C. Navas and T. Imielinski. GeoCast - Geographic Addressing and Routing. In *International Conference on Mobile Computing and Networking*, pages 66–76, 1997.
7. S. Prabhakar, Y. Xia, D. Kalashnikov, W. G. Aref, and S. Hambrusch. Query Indexing and Velocity Constrained Indexing: Scalable Techniques for Continuous Queries on Moving Objects. In *IEEE Transaction on Computers*, 2002.
8. S. Ratnasamy. A Scalable Content-Addressable Network. In *Ph.D. Dissertation University of California Berkeley*, 2002.

9. S. Saltenis, C. S. Jensen, S. T. Leutenegger, and M. A. Lopez. Indexing the Positions of Continuously Moving Objects. In *SIGMOD*, pages 331–342, 2000.
10. Z. Song and N. Roussopoulos. K-Nearest Neighbor Search for Moving Query Point. In *SSTD*, pages 79–96, 2001.
11. Y. Tao, D. Papadias, and Q. Shen. Continuous Nearest Neighbor Search. In *VLDB*, pages 287–298, 2002.
12. H. Wang, R. Zimmermann, and W.-S. Ku. ASPEN: An Adaptive Spatial Peer-to-Peer Network. In *ACM GIS*, pages 230–239, 2005.
13. X. Xiong, M. F. Mokbel, W. G. Aref, S. E. Hambrusch, and S. Prabhakar. Scalable Spatio-temporal Continuous Query Processing for Location-aware services. In *International Conference on Scientific and Statistical Database Management*, page 317, 2004.
14. J. Zhang, M. Zhu, D. Papadias, Y. Tao, and D. L. Lee. Location-based Spatial Queries. In *SIGMOD*, pages 443–454, 2003.

Optimal Route Determination Technology Based on Trajectory Querying Moving Object Database

Kyoung-Wook Min, Ju-Wan Kim, and Jong-Hyun Park

LBS Research Team, Telematics Research Group, Telematics&USN Research Division, ETRI, 161 Gajeong-dong, Yuseong-gu, Daejeon, 305-350 Korea
{kwmin92, juwan, jhp}@etri.re.kr

Abstract. Recently, the LBS (Location-based services), which make use of location information of moving objects, have obtained increasingly high attention. We can store and manage the trajectories of moving objects such as vehicles by querying moving object database management system. Therefore, it may be used to deliver better services to users by past trajectory information. In this paper, we describe a novel method that determines an optimal route by querying the trajectory of moving objects stored in moving object database system. In general, the route determination algorithms are not proper in real world because these make use of only static properties of road segments. However, our approach can determine the optimal route using dynamic attributes such as passing time and real speed of road segments extracted from the trajectories of moving objects. So we can provide more optimal route than results of conventional route determination methods without traffic information gathering devices.

1 Introduction

The characteristic of the real-world objects is that their state in space changes over time. As a computing power and technology grows, new advanced applications are entering the stage to manage space-time varying objects, such as land parcel, rivers, roads, taxis, buses and cellular phone users, etc. Recent advances in wireless networks, the location determination technology and the mobile applications have led to the emergence of the LBS [1, 2, 3]. Nowadays, the navigation system, the most popular application in LBS and telematics fields, can be expanded into integration GPS receiver and other technology to provide seamless location information in an urban area where a GPS signal is locally unavailable, such as in a tunnel, near a building, and so on [4]. Therefore we can track the location of moving object in everywhere and to provide the services efficiently, the reliable system is required that could acquire, store, and query the large number of locations. The time-evolving locations of moving objects can't be managed by existing commercial Database Management System (DBMS) as well as Geographic Information System (GIS). The reason is that there is a critical set of capabilities that are needed by moving object database applications [5], such as LBS, and are lacking in existing DBMS and GIS. So, to provide

S. Bressan, J. Küng, and R. Wagner (Eds.): DEXA 2006, LNCS 4080, pp. 666 – 675, 2006.

more reliable LBS, the Moving Object Database Management System (MODBMS) must be supported and therefore, we can retrieve space-time varying object by querying. The one of MODBMS queries, the trajectory query is retrieving data which are sequential moving point of some object in the past [6]. By this trajectory querying, we can extract the route that someone had being moved through in the past. About route determination problem, there have been so many researches. Specially, the shortest paths problem in networks has been the subject of extensive research for many years resulting in the publication of a large number of scientific papers [7, 8, 9]. But the entire route determination algorithm is dependent on the static information of road network. The route which has the minimum cost of travelling through by comparing the static properties of the road segment such the limited speed and length is chosen as a result. Therefore the estimation value of the pass time through this route is computed using values of the speed and the length properties of the road segment of which result route consists. However this estimation information is not proper in the real world because the pass time is changing dynamically.

The ultimate goal of this research is developing optimal route determination methodology by analyzing the result of trajectory querying MODBMS in order to provide more reliable route information. The rest of this paper is organized as follows. The problem on existing route determination algorithms is discussed in section 2 and the overall system architecture is introduced in section 3. In section 4, the scheme of the method of optimal route determination by trajectory querying MODBMS is presented in greater detail and finally, the summary and future work is given in section 5.

2 Problem Statement

The shortest path algorithm and the other similar route determination algorithm are dependent on static property values of road network data. For example, in Fig.1, if the function *GetRoute* is retrieving the route from S point to E point then the result can be like below.

ROUTE route = GetRoute(S, E, RoadNetwork);

The *route* consists of two segments, *S→J, J→E,* and *route.Distance* is 7 km, *route.PassTime* is 7 minutes. This result of the function *GetRoute* must be selected by taking into account the values of properties of each road segment such as the limit speed, the length and so on. In general, however, we know that speed of vehicle seems to be reduced in the curved section of the road as well as at the signal lamp of the junction. Therefore, the estimation pass time, 7 minutes, may be not probable and we can guess that liable the pass time is longer than one of result route. If we have the past trajectory of some vehicle of passing from S to E, the result information is possible to be in table 1. We can easily know that the time period of passing through the route is different as time frame is varying. If we can have the past moving time through some trajectory shown in table 1, it is much helpful to determine the route and provide more accurate information for traveling.

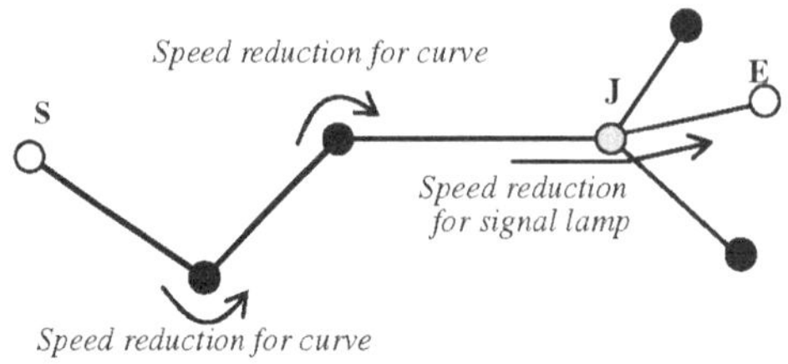

	From S To J	From J To E
Speed:	60 km/hr	30 km/hr
Distance:	6 km	1 km
Estimate Time:	6 min	1min

Fig. 1. The cost estimation of route from S to E. The route is consists of two road segments, S→J and J→E. We can estimate the pass time by computing the values of speed and distance of each road segment.

Table 1. The cost of route[S, E] in real world. The time_stamp is the time instance value when the car passes through the point.

CarID	$S_{time\ stamp}$	$E_{time\ stamp}$	Pass Time[S, E]
A001	08:00	08:15	15 min
A003	14:13	14:25	12 min
B001	15:59	16:09	10 min
C001	18:20	18:33	13 min
C002	21:09	21:18	9 min

3 System Architecture

In this section, we describe the logical system architecture to explain the contribution of our paper that can be applicable to determining the optimal route as analyzing past trajectories resulted by querying MODBMS. Overall system architecture is shown in Fig. 2. The system consists of 3 layers that are the database layer, the route analysis layer and the application layer. In the database layer, to determine route by static algorithm like shortest path algorithm, the road network data are managed in the spatial DBMS. And to retrieving the past trajectories, the moving object data are managed in the MODBMS. In the route analysis layer, the result route is selected by comparing route by deterministic algorithm with past trajectories by querying MODBMS using some special analysis factors. In the application layer, the client application requests the route information and in case of the mobile device, must report its position acquired by a GPS receiver to MODBMS.

3.1 Data Model

In the above architecture, the road network and the moving object are very important basic data which we can determine optimal route by analyzing. Some analysis factors are needed to compare the static route with trajectories and will be shown in detail in section 4.3.

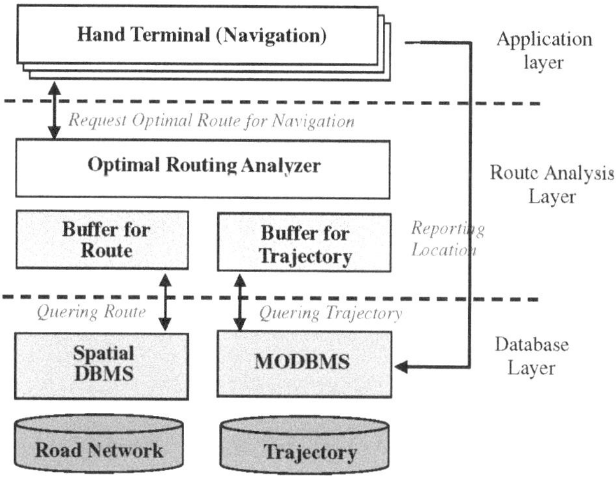

Fig. 2. The system architecture to determine optimal route by trajectory querying **MODBMS**

Road Network
The representation of a road network is given by a two-tuple *RN = (S, N),* where *S* is set of segment and *N* is a set of connection node.
Segment
We define a road segment as *(ns, ne, list of intermediate point, properties)*. More specifically, *ns* is start node, *ne* is end node, where $ns \neq ne$. The geographic information of segment is composed of *ns, ne*, and *list of intermediate point*. The *properties* are length, max speed and min speed.
Node
We define a node as *(p, prop)*. Specifically, $p = (x, y)$, *prop* is a set of connected link.
Moving Object
The representation of a moving object is given by *(p, time, velocity, and segment)*. The *p* is coordinates as position and the *time* when and *segment* on which it had been.
Trajectory
The representation of a trajectory is given by *(MBRT, list of moving object)*. The *MBRT* is minimum bounding rectangle and time period covered all list of moving object, given by *(x1, y1, x2, y2, from, to)*

3.2 The MODBMS (Moving Object Database Management System)

The MODBMS can be interfacing external client with the *MOQL* (Moving Object Query Language) [10] – SQL like format. And there are several components: query processing, buffer management, location index, storage. In this paper, we exclude detailed structure and function of moving object database. We can query trajectory that has list of consecutive moving object to MODBMS. The MODBMS supports several API by interfacing *MOQL*; the example query statements are in Fig. 3. The examples are meaning – finding some car which had been in some area and at some time; the time stamp in first, the time slice in second.

Find car which were within 1km from point (x,y) at time t.
SELECT ID FROM FLEETTABLE WHERE WITHINS(SNAPSHOT(location,t), BUFFER(MPOINT(x, y), 1000)) = TRUE;
Find car which were within 1km from point (x,y) between time t1 and t2.
SELECT ID FROM FLEETTABLE WHERE WITHINS(SLICE(location,t1,t2), BUFFER(MPOINT(x, y), 1000)) = TRUE;

Fig. 3. The Examples of moving object query statements. The first query is the snapshot query and the second query is the time slice query.

4 The Proposed Method to Determine Optimal Route

In this section, we explain the method of determining optimal route in detail. In the first place, we describe the process of acquiring position from of GPS device and reporting it in the client side and consequently, updating it to MODBMS in the server side.

4.1 The Process of Reporting and Updating Position

Client Side Process Scenario

The mobile handset client with the GPS device must be able to acquire its current position and report it to MODBMS. A series of client side process is like below.

The client side program code that is acquiring its position and reporting to server side

```
P_before ← Ø
do
    P_gps ← GetGPS()
    P_current ← CoordinateTransformation(P_gps, CoordType)
    P.segment ← GetSegment(P_current, RN)
    if P_current.segment ≠ P_before.segment then
        report(P_current)
    P_before ← P_current
while sleep()
```

The case of reporting position to server is that the acquiring position is on the new segment which the position of before time is not, like Fig. 4.

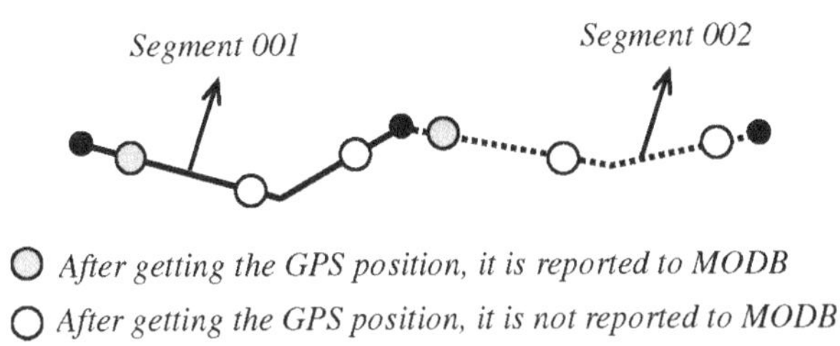

Fig. 4. The case of reporting position to the server. If the moving object is on the new segment, then reports its position to the server.

Server Side Process Scenario
After reporting the position to the server, it is stored to a MODBMS by executing following query statement:

```
INSERT INTO table (position.ID, position.x, position.y,
position.time, position.velocity, position.segment);
```

4.2 The Extract the Road Segments from the Trajectory

The real moving distance of the past trajectory cannot be computed which is the query result of MODBMS. As the trajectory consists of list of discrete moving points, that is to say, the distance of the trajectory is the Euclidean distance. In order to extract the real continuous moving distance, the road segments must be picked out which the moving object had moved on. After extracting the road segments, we can calculate the real moving distance as summing up the length values of each road segment. Fig.5. shows the trajectory distance and road segments distance.

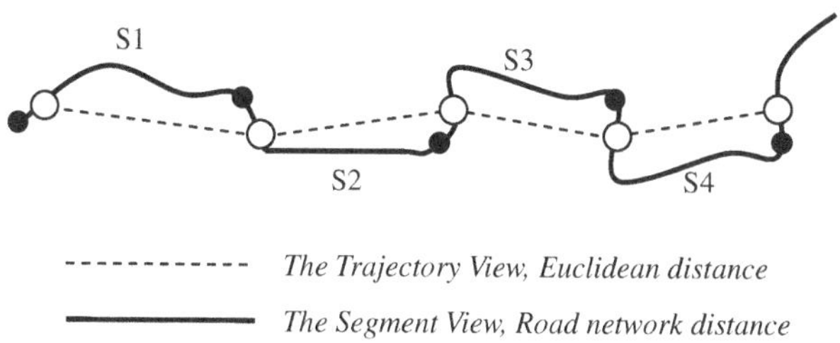

Fig. 5. The trajectory view vs segment view. We can calculate the real moving distance as extracting the road segments which trajectory was on.

We can calculate the actual moving distance and the pass time of the moving object from the trajectory like a following process:

```
distance ← Ø, passTime ← Ø
for each mo ∈ trajectory do
    segment ← GetSegment(mo.segment, RN)
    distance += segment.length
passTime.from ← trajectory.MBRT.from
passTime.to ← trajectory.MBRT.to
```

4.3 The Analysis of Determining Optimal Route

The source and destination location must be predefined to determine the route for navigation. In the static route determination algorithm, the result route consists of geometrical polyline and other information that is the total distance and the estimated pass time through the polyline. To choose more accurate route information, we select the past trajectories that are compared with static route. We can extract trajectories as querying MODBMS and these trajectories had to pass through same source and destination location of the static route. Fig. 6 Shows a trajectory query statements. In the second query statement, the time slice parameter is added to before one.

Find car which passed through from the region A to B
SELECT ID, POSITION FROM FLEETTABLE WHERE PASSES(POSITION, POLYGON(region A)) = TRUE AND PASSES(POSITION, POLYGON(region B)) = TRUE;
Find car which passed through from the region A to B between time t1 and t2
SELECT ID, POSITION FROM FLEETTABLE WHERE PASSES(POSITION, MPOLYGON(t1, t2, region A)) = TRUE AND PASSES(POSITION, MPOLYGON(t1, t2, region B)) = TRUE;

Fig. 6. The trajectory query statements. In the second statement, the time slice parameter is added to the first statement.

Table 2. The Optimal Route Determination Analysis Factor (ORDF)

Factor	Description	Weight
Distance (f_d)	road network distance	w_d
Pass Time (f_t)	pass time of consecutive segment	w_t
Time Frame (f_f)	special time frame like rush hour	w_f
Day of week (f_w)	special day of week like a festive day	w_w
Speed (f_s)	keeping speed of consecutive segment	w_s
		$\text{sum}(w_{0\sim n})=1$

The query result trajectories are the candidate routes which are compared with the static route which is the result of static algorithm such as shortest path [6]. We can consider some factors to compare the static route with the trajectories. The ORDF (Optimal Route Determination Factors) are very important element to determine realistic route. For example, the business man who was a stranger in this city is going to move from A to B and it was 08:30. He executed route determination algorithm in navigation device and the result route information were geographical, visual route, 10km distance and 10 minutes estimated time. But if he did not know it was rush hour, the incorrectness information of route messed up his plan. If he had known someone's experience going from A to B in similar time frame, he should not trust that result. Also, if he knew the other route information based on experience that takes less pass time but longer distance than before one, he had made a choice of this one unhesitatingly. If the experiential and statistical route information can be supported, these are very helpful to determine an optimal route. We can extract this assistant information by querying MODBMS and choose optimal route by analyzing with ORDF.

We can predefine the some factors to compare static route with trajectories for determining optimal route. Table 2 shows some optimal route determination factors. We define 5 factors and each factor is assigned the weight, and we can calculate route cost with mixing some factors of ORDF. The route which has minimum cost can be chosen as an optimal route. We define some variable to explain the usage of ORDF in order to determine optimal route.

The ***OR*** is an optimal Route, ***SR*** is a static route, T_i is ith trajectory resulted by querying MODBMS, and N_T is a number of trajectories, and the function $Cost(T_i)$ is a route cost of ith trajectory, $w(f_i)$ is weight of ith ORDF. Sum of weight of each factor must be 1 like (1).

$$f_{set} = \{f_0, \sim, f_n\}, \ \sum_{i=0}^{n} w(f_i) = 1, \quad f_{set} \subset ORDF \tag{1}$$

The route cost is calculated as formula (2) and we must normalize the value of each factor of trajectory chosen from ORDF for analyzing. For example, in case of distance factor f_d, ordering value of each distance of all trajectories can be considered normalized value and in case of time frame, ordering the difference value between departure time and *trajectory.from* can be also normalized value.

$$Cost(T_k) = \sum_{i=0}^{n} w_i * Normalization(T_k.f_i) \tag{2}$$

Finally, the optimal route is determined which has the minimum value of each route cost of trajectories.

$$OR = \begin{cases} \min(Cost(T_0),...,Cost(T_n)), & \text{if } N_T \neq 0 \\ SR & \end{cases} \tag{3}$$

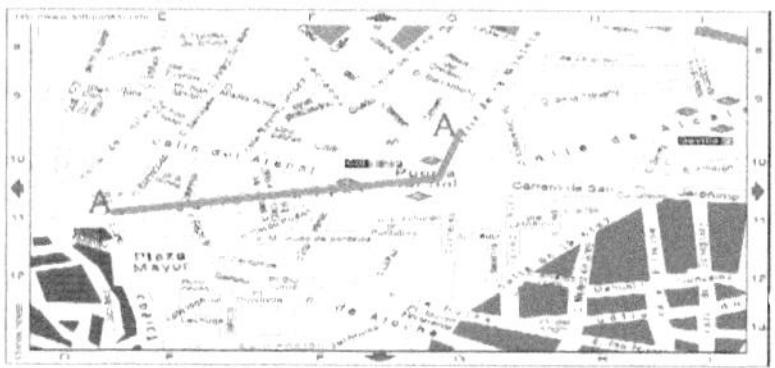

Static Algorithm Result	
Factor	Value
Distance	30 km
Pass time	30 min
Departure time	10:00

a. route of static algorithm result

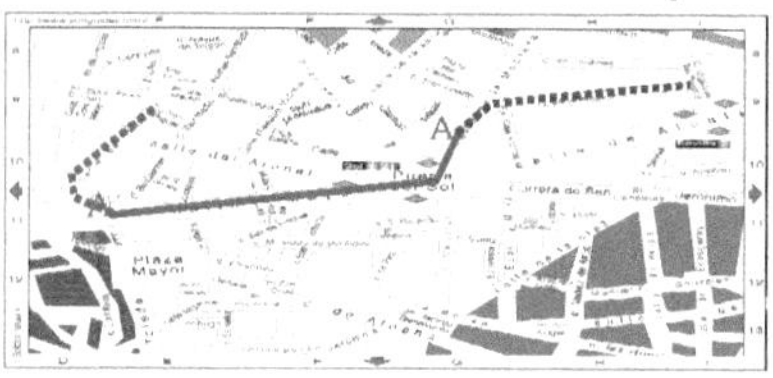

Trajectory Result 1	
Factor	Value
Distance	30 km
Pass time	45 min
Time frame	10:00

b. trajectory result 1

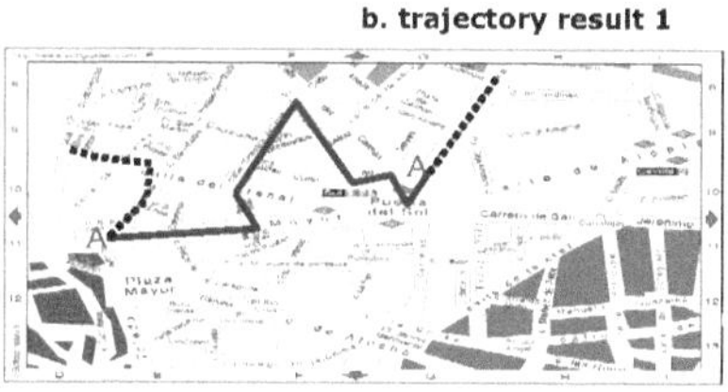

Trajectory Result 2	
Factor	Value
Distance	40 km
Pass time	25 min
Time frame	10:10

c. trajectory result 2

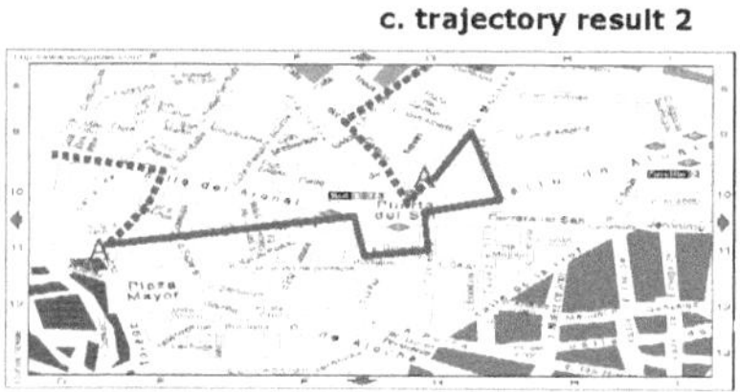

Trajectory Result 3	
Factor	Value
Distance	32 km
Pass time	29 min
Time frame	15:10

d. trajectory result 3

Fig. 7. The example of selecting optimal route. There are three trajectories resulted by querying MODBMS. The ORDF consists of f_d, f_t, f_f.

Fig. 7 shows the example of selecting optimal route as analyzing static route and three trajectories with ORDF, $\{f_d, f_t, f_f\}$

In fig.7, we define factor f_0 is distance, f_1 is pass time, f_2 is time frame and assign weight to each factor, $w(f_0) = 0.1$, $w(f_1) = 0.4$, $w(f_2) = 0.5$. In this case, we consider f_3 time frame as most important factor. The result route cost of each trajectory is $Cost(T_1)=1.8$, $Cost(T_1)=1.7$, $Cost(T_1)=6.8$ in case of defining the normalized value of each factor as ordering value of distance, pass time, difference value between departure time and time frame of trajectory. The static route and first trajectory have same distance and similar time frame but pass time is longer than 30 minutes in experiential real environment. And the time frame factor can be considered as important factor because the information of distance and pass time of route is more reliable in the similar time frame state. In this paper, we define normalized function as simply but normalized function must be more complicated in order to enhance reliability and provide more accuracy to determine optimal route.

5 Summary and Future Works

The route information from the static algorithm is not reliable frequently in real environment, since that information is dependent on static properties of road segment such as speed, length and so on. In real world, this static route information cannot guarantee the reliability and correctness of route information. In this paper, we suggest the methodology of determining optimal route using past moving information based on experience, statistics. The trajectory is the past sequential moving point of vehicles and can be retrieved by querying MODBMS. To extract more liable route information, we can use some analysis factors such as distance, pass time, time frame and so on. We define these factors as ORDF. As analyzing static route and trajectories with ORDF, we can calculate the cost of each trajectory and the trajectory which has a minimum cost can be considered as more liable route information. Next time, we will elaborate this methodology and implement system to be applicable in real telematics and LBS fields. As acquiring the large volume of historical location of real vehicles, we will estimate system performance and reliability of result route.

References

1. Erwig, M., Guiting, R. H., Schneider, M., and Vazirgiannis, M., "Spatio-Temporal Data Types: An Approach to Modeling and Querying Moving Object in Databases," GeoInfomatica, Vol.3, No.3, pp.269-296, 1999
2. Sh, S.L. and Wa, D., "Handling Disaggregate Spatiotemporal Travel Data in GIS," GeoInformatica Vol.4, No.2, pp.161-178, 2000
3. Wolfson, O., Chamberlain, B. X. S., Sistla, P., Xu, B., and Zhou, X., "DOMINO: Database fOr MovINg Objects tracking," ACM International Conference on SIGMOD, pp.547-549, 1999
4. Seong-Baek Kim, Kyung-Ho Choi, Seung-Yong Lee, Ji-Hoon Choi, Tae-Hyun Hwang, Byung-Tae Jang, and Jong-Hun Lee, "A Bimodal Approach for Land Vehicle Localization," ETRI Journal, vol. 26, no. 5, Oct. 2004, pp.497-500
5. Wolfson, O., Xu, B., Chamberlain, S., and Jiang, L., SSDBM 1998, pp. 111-122

6. Pfoser, D., Jensen, C. S. and Theodoridis, Y., "Novel Approaches to the Indexing of Moving Object Trajectories," Proc. Of the 26th Conference on VLDB, Cairo, Egypt, 2000.
7. Stefano Pallottino, Maria Grazia Scutella, "Shortest Path Algorithms in Transportation Models: Classical and Innovative Aspects," Technical Report, Univ. of Pisa, 1998.
8. Chang Wook Ahn, R. S. Ramakrishna, "A Generic Algorithm for Shortest Path Routing Problem and the Sizing of Populations," IEEE Transaction on Evolutionary Computation, pp. 566-579, Vol. 6, No. 6, 2002
9. Stephan Winter, "Weighting the Path Continuation in Route Planning," In Proceedings of 9th ACM International Symposium on Advances in Geographic information System, pp. 173-176, 2001
10. 10.Jaiho Lee, Kyoungwan An, and Jonghyun Park, "Design of Query Language for Location-Based Services," W2GIS 2005, LNCS 3833, pp.11-18, 2005.

Efficient Temporal Coalescing Query Support in Relational Database Systems

Xin Zhou[1], Fusheng Wang[2], and Carlo Zaniolo[1]

[1] Computer Science Department
University of California, Los Angeles
Los Angeles, CA 90095, USA
{xinzhou, zaniolo}@cs.ucla.edu
[2] Integrated Data Systems Department
Siemens Corporate Research
Princeton, NJ 08540, USA
fusheng.wang@siemens.com

Abstract. The interest in, and user demand for, temporal databases have only increased with time; unfortunately, DBMS vendors and standard groups have not moved aggressively to extend their systems with support for transaction-time or valid-time. This can be partially attributed to the expected major R&D costs to add temporal support to RDBMS by directly extending the database engine. The newly introduced SQL:2003 standards have actually significantly enhanced our ability to support temporal applications in commercial database systems. The long recognized problem of coalescing, which is difficult to support in the framework of SQL:1992, can now be effectively supported in RDBMS. In this paper, we investigate alternatives of temporal coalescing queries under temporal data models in RDBMS. We provide an SQL:2003-based query algorithm and a native relational user defined aggregates (UDA) approach – both approaches only require a single scan of the database. We conclude that temporal queries can be best supported by OLAP functions supported in the current SQL:2003 standards. These new findings demonstrate that the current RDBMS are mature enough to directly support efficient temporal queries, and provide a new paradigm for temporal database research and implementation.

1 Introduction

In this paper, we seek to support historical information management and temporal queries without extending current standards. Our insistence on using only current standards is inspired by the lessons learned from the very history of temporal databases, where past proposals failed to gain much acceptance in the commercial arena, in spite of great depth, breadth [1,2] and technical elegance [3,4]. An in-depth review of the technical (and often non-technical) reasons that doomed temporal extensions proposed in the past would provide an opportunity for a very interesting and possibly emotional discussion; but such a discussion is outside the scope of this paper. Here, we simply accept the fact that temporal extensions to existing standards are very difficult to sell, in spite of the growing pull by temporal applications; then, we move on from there by

S. Bressan, J. Küng, and R. Wagner (Eds.): DEXA 2006, LNCS 4080, pp. 676–686, 2006.

exploring solutions that do not require extending current standards. This low-road approach is hardly as glamorous as the "new temporal standards" approach pursued in the past, but it is not without interesting research challenges and opportunities, as we will show in this paper. In particular, with the introduction of SQL:2003, new opportunities are offered by recent developments that have taken information systems well beyond SQL:1992, and provide new approaches to support temporal query models with current DBMS engines [5].

Supporting temporal database models and temporal queries at the logical level is only one facet of the problem; the other is their efficient implementation. In particular, classical queries, such as temporal coalescing that are known to be difficult to support, provide a natural acid test for the efficiency of an implementation. Temporal coalescing is a key challenge for temporal databases, both at the logical and physical level and much research work has been motivated by this problem.

In this paper, we show how to support temporal coalescing and aggregates efficiently using SQL:2003 OLAP functions and UDAs—that are currently supported in many commercial RDBMS and require only a single scan of relations. We show that temporal queries can be nicely expressed, and efficiently supported, and conclude that RDBMS plus SQL:2003/UDA provides a promising new paradigm for temporal database research and implementation.

2 Temporal Coalescing: The Pain of Temporal Databases

Coalescing is a data restructuring operation that plays a key role in temporal databases, insofar as it can be as similar to duplicate elimination in conventional databases. Coalescing merges tuples that have identical attribute values and overlapping or adjacent timestamps [6]. For instance, consider the snapshot of a temporal relation in Table 1 that records information about employees working in a company. In this table, a new timestamped tuple is generated whenever there is a change in any of the attribute values. The well-known problem with this representation is that coalescing is needed when some of the attributes are projected out [7], and much previous research has focused on this problem. For instance, the solution proposed by TSQL2 [3] consists in assuming that coalescing is performed automatically, rather than having to be specified in the query—in analogy to duplicate elimination in relational databases.

Table 1. The table EMPLOYEE_HISTORY

EMPNO	SALARY	TITLE	DEPTNO	TSTART	TEND
1001	60000	Engineer	d01	1995-01-01	1995-05-31
1001	70000	Engineer	d01	1995-06-01	1995-09-30
1001	70000	Sr Engineer	d02	1995-10-01	1996-01-31
1001	70000	Tech Leader	d02	1996-02-01	1996-12-31

For instance,if the manager of the organization is interested in the history of the salary of employee "1001", then the following The TSQL2 statement will be used:

QUERY 1. *TSQL2's expression to query the history of the salary of employee 1001*:

```
SELECT EMPNO, SALARY
FROM EMPLOYEE_HISTORY (EMPNO, SALARY)
WHERE EMPNO = 1001
```

While this TSQL2 query contains no explicit coalescing statement, it produces the result shown in Table 2, below, where coalescing has been applied to *EMPNO* and *SALARY* attributes (*EMPNO* is the primary key of the temporal relation and *SALARY* is the time-varying attribute of the user interest). Indeed, since the timestamps of the three tuples with a salary of 70000 are adjacent, these tuples are coalesced into a single tuple as shown in Table 2. The *TSTART* value of the new timestamp is the *TSTART* value of the first tuple, where the *TEND* value is the *TEND* value of the last tuple.

Table 2. The result of Query 1

EMPNO	SALARY	TSTART	TEND
1001	60000	1995-01-01	1995-05-31
1001	70000	1995-06-01	1996-12-31

While TSQL2 [3] eliminates the need to explicitly specify coalescing, and also supports a rich set of features and predicates to manipulate temporal databases, it requires many extensions to current standards and leaves many questions about efficient implementations unanswered. Currently, TSQL2 has not implemented in commercial RDBMS, nor it has been incorporated into the SQL:2003 standards.

A second interesting approach that avoids the need to perform coalescing after projection is the point-based temporal model [8].

Bohlen et al. [6] proposed that coalescing can be achieved through (i) a SQL implementation, (ii) a main memory implementation, or (iii) a DBMS implementation. The DBMS implementation approach requires modifying the underlying DBMS internals, which is difficult and expensive. The main memory implementation approach works by loading a relation into main memory, coalescing it, and then storing it back to the database. This approach suffers from two main problems. First, in many cases, it is impossible to load the whole relation into main memory. Second, it is an expensive task to periodically move a relation from the database to the running application and then store it back to the database. The SQL implementation approach aims at expressing coalescing operation as a set of SQL commands that run on the database and generate a coalesced relation. However, the expression of such coalescing query itself is very complex. Moreover, the query often requires several database scans as well as self-join(s) on the entire temporal relation table, which can be very expensive. Alternative algorithms for implementing coalescing queries are briefly reviewed in Section 3.

In this paper, we introduce the novel idea of using SQL:2003 analytic functions to support temporal coalescing. The paper is organized as follows. After a careful review of current coalescing query support with pure SQL:1992 standard in Section 3, we introduce our novel algorithm SSC in Section 4; our algorithm only needs one scan of incoming tuples to realize coalescing. We further show that this algorithm can be well supported under SQL:2003 framework, without any external programming extension. Section 5 tackles the problem using a different approach: we employ user-defined-aggregates (UDA)—a native SQL extension that can be utilized to handle the coalescing queries. The performance study in Section 6 shows that the SQL:2003 method is much more efficient and scalable than the pure SQL:1992 approaches discussed in Section 3. Section 7 concludes our discussion.

3 Support Coalescing with Pure SQL:1992 Queries

There are several alternatives to implement coalescing queries using SQL:1992, either through SQL/PSM, cursors, or entire SQL [9]. The first two require either external programming modules or in-memory cursors, which are inefficient due to the high I/O manipulation cost. However, implementing coalescing entirely in SQL always has the problem that the coalescing query is considerably very complex and often has multiple nested "NOT EXISTS" clauses [7], as well as self-join(s). Query 2 is the pure SQL:1992 expression of the query corresponding to Query 1. Note that this query requires 6 database scans, as well as several self-joins to the entire temporal relation.

QUERY 2. *Pure SQL:1992 implementation of coalescing Query 1*:

```
WITH Temp(Salary, TSTART, END) AS
(SELECT SALARY, TSTART, END
FROM EMPLOYEE_HISTORY
WHERE EMPNO = 1001 )

SELECT DISTINCT F.Salary, F.TSTART, F.TEND
FROM Temp AS F, Temp AS L
WHERE F.TSTART < L.TEND AND F.Salary = L.Salary
AND NOT EXISTS
(SELECT * FROM Temp AS M
WHERE M.Salary = F.Salary
AND F.TSTART < M. TSTART AND M.TSTART < L.TEND
AND NOT EXISTS
(SELECT * FROM Temp AS T1
    WHERE T1.Salary = F.Salary
    AND T1. TSTART < M. TSTART AND M.TSTART <= T1.TEND)
)
AND NOT EXISTS
(SELECT * FROM Temp AS T2
WHERE T2.Salary = F.Salary
AND
    ((T2. TSTART < F. TSTART AND F.TSTART <= T2.TEND)
    OR
    (T2.TSTART < L.TEND AND L.TEND < T2.TEND))
)
```

Other alternatives to implement coalescing entirely in traditional SQL include: i) using COUNT aggregate instead of NOT EXISTS clauses [9], and ii) using recursive SQL queries [10]. Although the coalescing queries in these alternatives are relatively shorter than Query 2 and require fewer accesses to the entire temporal relation, they require heavier joins.

In summary, pure SQL:1992 support for temporal coalescing queries requires multiple table accesses as well as heavy join operations among the tables, which is far from satisfactory to support temporal database model under current SQL framework.

4 Support Coalescing with SQL:2003 OLAP Functions

SQL:2003 provides advanced support for analytics on moving windows, with new constructs such as OVER, PARTITION BY, PRECEDING, FOLLOWING, etc. Indeed, coalescing operations can be conveniently supported using SQL:2003 standards without any extension to current SQL framework. In this section, we first show a novel Single Scan Coalescing algorithm (SSC) to support coalescing with one single scan of the input tuples without join, then we propose the SQL:2003 statements to implement this algorithm.

4.1 SSC: A Single Scan Coalescing Algorithm

Without loss of generality, suppose we want to coalesce four tuples with the same time-varying attribute value and different time periods, as in Figure 1 (a).

First, we detect all distinct timestamps from the input tuples. Thus in this example, we have eight distinct timestamps, as in Figure 1 (b). Notice that timestamp t_4 appears twice.

Next, for each timestamp, we need to keep information of whether it is a *TSTART*, or an *TEND* timestamp. We maintain two values to keep the count of *TSTART* and *TEND* timestamps which have occurred respectively, with initial value (s,0)/(e,0), and update these two values upon every new timestamp, as in Figure 1 (c). For instance, for timestamp t_1, since it is a *TSTART* timestamp, we get (s,1)/(e,0). For t_2, another *TSTART* timestamp, we increase the count of *TSTART* timestamps, and get (s,2)/(e,0).

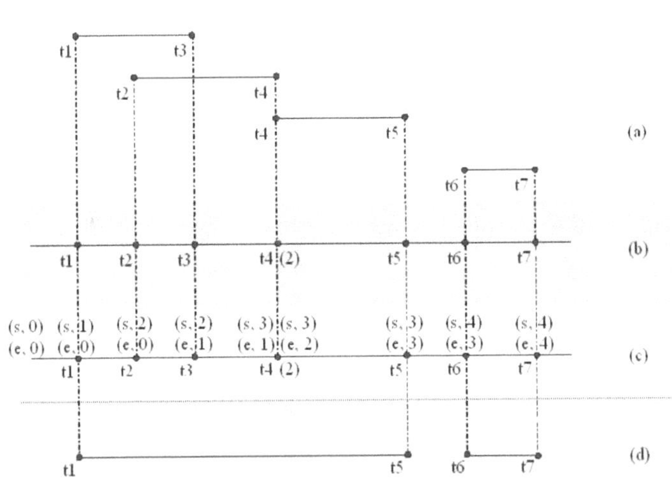

Fig. 1. SSC: Single Scan Coalescing Algorithm

At timestamp t_4 where both *TSTART* and *TEND* occurred, we increase the count by one for both the *TSTART* timestamp and the *TEND* timestamp.

Last, we can output all coalesced periods, which are from timestamp t_i to t_j, where t_{i-1} has (s,m)/(e,m), and t_j has (s,n)/(e,n). As in Figure 1 (d), there are two coalesced periods: t_1 to t_5, and t_6 to t_7. Intuitively, at timestamp t_i, all previous periods have been output as one coalesced period, and a new coalescable period begins from t_i. At time t_j, we have seen an equal number of *TSTART* and *TEND* timestamps; thus, a coalesced period ends at time t_j, and t_j is the *TEND* value of our coalesced output.

We observe that if all the timestamps are ordered in the input, we can output all the coalesced periods with a single scan of all the input tuples. And in the reality of transaction time databases, all the timestamps are indeed already ordered by the passage of transaction time, which guarantees the efficiency of SSC algorithm.

4.2 SQL:2003 Implementation of SSC

With the introduction of SQL:2003 analytic functions, the SSC algorithm can be supported directly with pure SQL, as shown in the following example.

QUERY 3. *SQL:2003 implementation of coalescing Query 1*:

```
WITH T1 (Start_ts, End_ts, ts, salary) AS (
  SELECT 1, 0, TSTART, SALARY
  FROM EMPLOYEE_HISTORY
  WHERE EMPNO = 1001
  UNION ALL
  SELECT 0, 1, TEND, SALARY
  FROM EMPLOYEE_HISTORY
  WHERE EMPNO = 1001
),

T2 (Crt_Total_ts, Prv_Total_ts, ts, Salary) AS (
  SELECT
       sum (Start_ts) - sum(End_ts)
       OVER (PARTITION BY Salary
             ORDER BY ts, End_ts ROWS UNBOUNDED PRECEDING),
       sum (Start_ts) - sum(End_ts)
       OVER (PARTITION BY Salary
             ORDER BY ts, End_ts
             ROWS BETWEEN 1 PRECEDING AND UNBOUNDED PRECEDING),
       ts,
       Salary
  FROM T1
  WHERE Crt_Total_ts = 0 OR Prv_Total_ts = 0
)

SELECT
  Salary,
  max(ts) OVER (PARTITION BY Salary ORDER BY ts ROWS 1 PRECEDING),
  ts
FROM T2 WHERE Crt_Total_ts = 0;
```

In this implementation, the first temporary table *T1* extracts all *TSTART* or *TEND* timestamps from the input tuples, where "1" in *Start_ts* (or *End_ts*) column denotes a

TSTART (or *TEND*) timestamp. For a certain timestamp value t_i, table *T2* keeps the difference between the total count of *TSTART* and the total count of *TEND* timestamps until t_i (stored as *Crt_Total_ts*). Similarly, it keeps the difference between the total count of *TSTART* and the total count of *TEND* timestamps until t_{i-1} (stored as *Prv_Total_ts*). Thus, *Crt_Total_ts*= 0 means that there are equal number of *TSTART* and *TEND* timestamps at t_i, and t_i should be a *TEND* timestamp in one of the coalesced periods. If *Prv_Total_ts* is 0, there is an equal number of *TSTART* and *TEND* timestamps before t_i, so t_i should be a *TSTART* timestamp for one of the coalesced periods. The final SELECT clause pairs all the result timestamps and output them.

Such an SQL statement can be predefined as a built-in coalescing function, which are transparent to the users. The beauty of this SQL statement is that, it only requires a single scan of the input tuples, since all the timestamps are already ordered. With this approach, we can implement all kinds of coalescing functionalities under the current relational database framework, without any complex extension for temporal applications.

4.3 Generalized SQL:2003 Implementation for Coalescing

The basic SQL:2003 implementation for salary coalescing query on employee "1001" can be very easily extended to handle all kinds of complex coalescing queries on different attributes.

- *Coalescing on a single attribute.*
  If we remove the condition *EMPNO*= 1001, the SQL:2003 query in Section 4.2 requires a single attribute (SALARY) coalescing. For another example, say that we want to return the history information with valid periods for each *DEPTNO*; then in the original query we need to (1) remove the WHERE condition in *T1*, and (2) replace *Salary* with *DEPTNO* for every sub query.
- *Coalescing on multiple attributes.*
  If we want to return the salary history for every employee, instead of a single employee "1001", the query becomes a coalescing query on the two attributes *EMPNO* and *SALARY*. In this case, we need to modify the original query by (1) removing the WHERE condition in *T1*, (2) adding *EMPNO* attribute in the return clause of *T1*, and (3) using "PARTITION BY EMPNO, SALARY" to replace "PARTITION BY SALARY" in every sub query.

5 Support Coalescing with User-Defined Aggregates

After using SQL:2003 to support temporal queries in current relational DBMS, we will now explore an alternative approach based on user defined aggregates (UDA). UDA represent a powerful DBMS extension which is efficiently supported in many commercial systems, such as Oracle [11]. UDA natively written in SQL, along with window constructs, are available in the UCLA the Stream Mill system [12], which was used to support windows, time-series queries, and data mining queries.

As a result, we can implement a single-scan algorithm to SSC, directly using SQL-compatible UDAs, and integrate it as system predefined aggregates for users to invoke. Due to space limitation, we only list the pseudo-code as in Algorithm 1.

Algorithm 1. UDA Pseudo-code for coalescing query with a single scan

```
1: Define table Temp (TSTART, TEND) to store the current coalesced period, initially empty;
2: Insert the first tuple's TSTART and TEND value into Temp;
3: for every new input tuple T do
4:    if T.TSTART <= Temp.TEND then
5:       //new tuple coalescable with current period
6:       Update Temp.TEND with T.TEND;
7:    else
8:       //current coalesced period ends, a new coalescing period begins
9:       Output the tuple in Temp, then update Temp with T.TSTART and T.TEND;
10:   end if
11: end for
12: Output the tuple in Temp;
```

Such a UDA can be correctly evaluated with the input tuples ordered by the *TSTART* values, which is realistic in transaction databases. The first (TSTART, TEND) input tuple is stored in *Temp* table (line 1-2). If the incoming tuple intersects with the current period in *Temp* table, the *TEND* value in the table will be updated to reflect the new *TEND* value (line 4-6). If the input tuple does not intersect, we get one result in the *Temp* table, which needs to be output, and deleted from *Temp* table, and the new input tuple will be stored into *Temp* table (line 7-9). We also return the final coalesced period after the last input tuple (line 12).

We will show in next section that this UDA approach beats the traditional pure SQL coalescing queries in performance, although it is not as efficient as the SQL:2003 SSC implementation. Nevertheless, UDA provides a native SQL support for many advanced queries, such as the classical temporal coalescing query, which otherwise needs external programming language to solve SQL's query limitation. Indeed, other complex temporal aggregates, for instance, "return all employees' average salaries along the history", can be efficiently supported with native UDA, which only requires one single scan of the input tuples. Due to the space limitation, we omit the details here.

6 Performance Study

We study the performance of coalescing queries with the three approaches: i) SSC approach with SQL:2003, ii) user defined aggregates approach, iii) SQL:1992 approach with "NOT EXIST" clause and iv) traditional SQL approach with recursive queries. We choose Oracle 10g Release 1 as our database server. We executed all of our queries on a personal computer equipped with an AMD Athlon XP 1500+ processor at 1.3 GHz and 512 MB of memory. The operating system we use is Fedora Core Version 3 Linux OS. The Oracle database server support SQL:2003, recursive SQL, and UDA features.

We choose a simulated employee history database as our test data. The data set models the history of employees over 17 years, and simulates the increases of salaries, changes of titles, and changes of departments. The data schema follows that in Figure 1. The total transaction database size is 120MB.

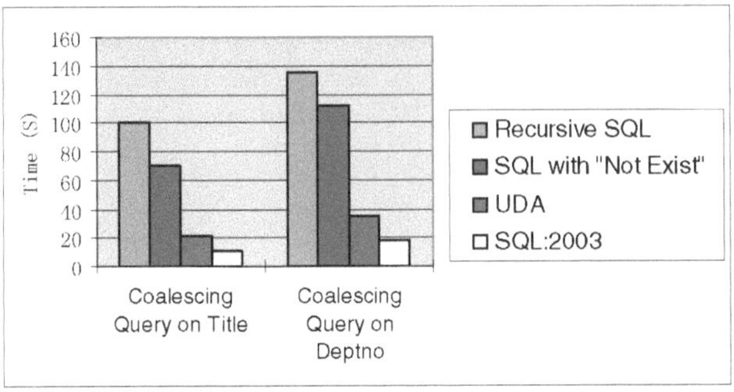

Fig. 2. Query Performance on Single Attribute

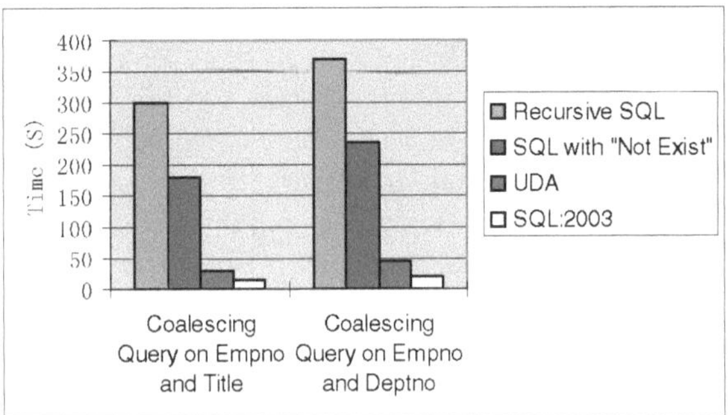

Fig. 3. Query Performance on Two Attributes

We first test the performance of single-attribute coalescing. We run two queries, coalescing on *DEPTNO* and coalescing on *TITLE*, respectively. The execution time is shown in Figure 2.

The result shows that the performance from our SSC SQL:2003 implementation beats all other approaches. The UDA approach comes close to SSC approach, with an overhead of pre-compilation and initialization time. If we run the experiments multiple times, the overhead can actually be omitted, and the UDA approach then has very close execution time with SSC approach. This proves that UDA approach is another choice for efficient coalescing. The traditional SQL:1992 implementations, using recursive SQL or SQL with "NOT EXIST", are much slower than the two we proposed.

When it comes to two-attribute coalescing, for example, coalescing on *EMPNO* and *TITLE*, or on *EMPNO* and *DEPTNO*, the traditional SQL:1992 algorithm takes extremely long time to get the result. We have to test the four queries, on one third of the original transaction database size, and the result is shown in Figure 3. The difference ratio is similar to that in Figure 2, except that every query takes longer execution time, due to more returned tuples.

Scalability of SSC Algorithm. We further test the scalability of our SSC SQL:2003 query, with two-attribute coalescing, on a faction of the original data set: 1/4, 1/2, and

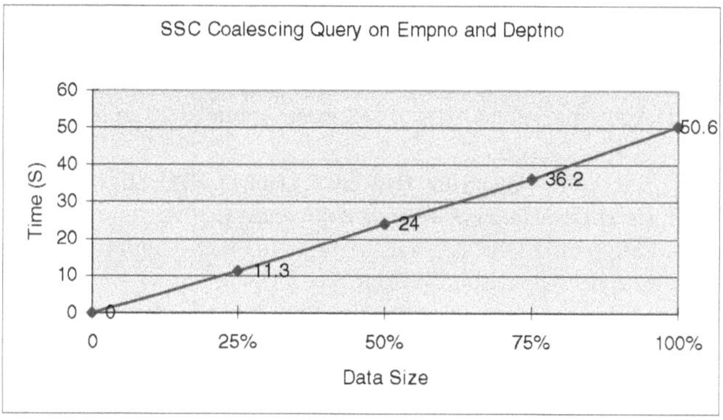

Fig. 4. Query Scalability of SQL:2003 Implementation of SSC

3/4, respectively. Figure 4 shows that our algorithm is linear scalable in term of database size, which conforms to its single scan feature.

7 Conclusion

In this paper, we aim at directly supporting efficient temporal coalescing queries within existing commercial RDBMS, without any extension to current systems. We propose two approaches: the first is based on SQL:2003 OLAP functions, and the second on user-defined aggregates. Both approaches only require a single scan of the database for the query execution and use minimal joins; this makes it possible to provide efficient temporal coalescing. The performance study shows that both the SQL:2003 OLAP approach and UDA approaches achieve good performance, and the first approach is particularly efficient. Moreover, for both approaches, their single-scan property guarantees their scalability.

The results of our study demonstrate that current commercial RDBMS can provide efficient support for complex temporal queries. This positive outcome outlines a promising direction for future developments in commercial databases, and database research.

References

1. G. Ozsoyoglu and R.T. Snodgrass. Temporal and Real-Time Databases: A Survey. *TKDE*, 7(4):513–532, 1995.
2. F. Grandi. An Annotated Bibliography on Temporal and Evolution Aspects in the World Wide Web. In *TimeCenter Technique Report*, 2003.
3. R. T. Snodgrass. *The TSQL2 Temporal Query Language*. Kluwer, 1995.
4. Richard T. Snodgrass, Michael H. Böhlen, Christian S. Jensen, and Andreas Steiner. Transitioning Temporal Support in TSQL2 to SQL3. *Lecture Notes in Computer Science*, 1399:150–194, 1998.
5. F. Wang, C. Zaniolo, and X. Zhou. Temporal XML? SQL Strikes Back! *Time*, 2005.
6. M. H. Böhlen, R. T. Snodgrass, and M. D. Soo. Coalescing in Temporal Databases. In *VLDB*, 1996.

7. C. Zaniolo, S. Ceri, C.Faloutsos, R.T. Snodgrass, V.S. Subrahmanian, and R. Zicari. *Advanced Database Systems*. Morgan Kaufmann Publishers, 1997.
8. D. Toman. Point-based Temporal Extensions of SQL. In *DOOD*, pages 103–121, 1997.
9. R. T. Snodgrass. Developing Time-Oriented Database Applications in SQL. *Morgan Kaufmann*, 1999.
10. T.Y. Leung and H. Pirahesh. Querying Historical Data in IBM DB2 C/S DBMS Using Recursive SQL. In *Recent Advances in Temporal Databases*, 1995.
11. SQL 2003 Standard Support in Oracle Database 10g, otn.oracle.com/products/database/ application_development/pdf/SQL_2003_TWP.pdf.
12. C. Zaniolo, R. Luo, H. Wang, et al. Stream Mill: Bringing Power and Generality to Data Stream Management Systems. World Wide Web, `http://wis.cs.ucla.edu/` `http://wis.cs.ucla.edu/`.

Efficient Evaluation of Partially-Dimensional Range Queries Using Adaptive R*-tree

Yaokai Feng[1] and Akifumi Makinouchi[2]

[1] Graduate School of Information Science and Electrical Engineering, Kyushu University, Japan
fengyk@is.kyushu-u.ac.jp
[2] Department of Information Network Engineering, Kurume Institute of Technology, Japan
akifumi@cc.kurume-it.ac.jp

Abstract. This paper is about how to efficiently evaluate partially-dimensional range queries, which are often used in many actual applications. If the existing multidimensional indices are employed to evaluate partially-dimensional range queries, then a great deal of information that is irrelevant to the queries also has to be read from disk. A modification of R*-tree is described in this paper to ameliorate such a situation. Discussions and experiments indicate that the proposed modification can clearly improve the performance of partially-dimensional range queries, especially for large datasets.

1 Introduction

Multidimensional range queries are necessary in many applications, including relational datasets [1,2], XML datasets [16], and GIS systems. In order to improve the search performance, multidimensional indices are very helpful[1,2,16].

Let us make clear the difference of the two terms *index dimensions* (*attributes*) and *query dimensions* (*attributes*). The dimensions (attributes) that are used to build the index are called index dimensions (attributes) and the dimensions that are used to form the query range for a range query are called query dimensions. An n-dimensional index is often used for evaluating n-dimensional queries. However in many applications using range queries, the query dimensions of each range query are likely of only part (rather than all) of the index dimensions [15,16]. Such range queries are referred to herein as partially-dimensional (PD) range queries. That is, although the index is built in an n-dimensional space, the actual range queries may only use d dimensions in the n dimensions ($d < n$). For example, the range query with d_1 and d_2 as query dimensions is a PD range query for the four-dimensional index built with d_1, d_2, d_3, and d_4 as index dimensions. Of course, the existing multidimensional indices can also be used in the cases of PD range queries. The problem is "efficiency". We will show that, if the existing multidimensional indices are used for PD range queries, a great deal of information that is irrelevant to the queries also has to be loaded from disk. This paper shows that PD range queries can be efficiently evaluated using

S. Bressan, J. Küng, and R. Wagner (Eds.): DEXA 2006, LNCS 4080, pp. 687–696, 2006.

Adaptive R*-tree (denoted herein as AR*-tree), which is based on R*-tree [3]. R*-tree is a well-known and widely-used variant of the R-tree family. R*-tree is also used in some commercial database products [8].

Since there are probably many possible combinations of attributes that are used in PD range queries, it is not always feasible in applications with large datasets for one index to be built for each possible combination of query attributes, because (1) numerous indices have to be constructed and managed, (2) many attributes are repeatedly included in different indices, which is too space-consuming for large datasets and results in a large update cost, and (3) the combinations of query attributes that can possibly be used in the user-provided PD queries are often unpredictable. Note that, there are a total of $(2^n - 1)$ possible combinations for n index attributes.

In the remainder of this paper, following the related works in Section 2 are two naive methods for PD range queries in Section 3. Then, AR*-tree is described in Section 4. AR*-tree can efficiently handle PD range queries with any combinations of query dimensions. The experimental results are presented in Section 5. Finally, Section 6 concludes this paper.

2 Related Work

Many index structures have been proposed in the recent decades. Examples include R*-tree [3], X-tree [4], and A-tree [5]. V. Gaede and O. Gunther conducted a survey on multidimensional indices [6] and a more recent survey has been presented by Y. Cui [7]. Some of these index structures (e.g., R*-tree) have been popularly used in research and several commercial database products. Multidimensional indices such as Octrees and Target Tree are also used in computer-assisted surgery (CAS), in which two-dimensional images are used to guide surgical procedures. Recently, the use of multidimensional indices has been introduced to the field of relational data [1,2]. However, all these existing multidimensional indices are directed to "all-dimensional range queries" (referred to herein as *AD range queries*, in which a query range is given in each of index dimensions). If these indices are employed to PD range queries, then the information in the irrelevant dimensions also has to be read from disk.

UB-tree is another approach to indexing multidimensional data. UB-tree uses a space-filling curve to map a multidimensional universe to one-dimensional space with the goal of sorting multidimensional data. However, the neighboring relationships that exist in the original space cannot be maintained in the mapped data. For each range query, the space-filling curve may be cut into many intervals by the query range. In order to obtain the correct results of range queries, the algorithm has to check all of the intervals included in the query ranges and the number of these intervals may be enormous in multi-dimensional spaces. In addition, the above-mentioned problems still exist when UB-tree is used for PD range queries.

In the study [12] by S. Berchtold, et al., a higher-dimensional index is divided into several lower-dimensional indices. The lower-dimensional indices are used in stead of the higher-dimensional index and their intermediate search results are intersected to obtain the final search result. They attempted to alleviate the "dimensionality curse" problem to some extent. Their approach cannot efficiently deal with PD range queries because the query dimensions and the number of query dimensions are very flexible and cannot be fixed and determined in advance.

The term of partial-record accesses was used in the paper [13], in which a buffer pool and storage management architecture is proposed that decouples the memory page layout from the non-volatile storage data organization. However, that proposal implements the partial-record accesses by a data placement strategy among the different levels of the memory hierarchy. That paper is on how to physically organize the original relational data. A multi-dimensional clustering method is also proposed [14]. However, it is also on the physical organization of the original relational data. In addition, there has been significant recent interest in column-oriented databases (or say "column-store"), in which the attributes are stored separately, such that successive values of that attribute are stored consecutively on disk. This is in contrast to most common database systems that store relations in rows ("row stores") where values of different attributes from the same record are stored consecutively. Our study is different from all of the methods mentioned here in that the present study is on multi-dimensional indexing and does not touch upon the physical organization of the original relational data. For example, unlike column-stores, we do not obtain the record-data through different "mini-pages".

3 Two Naive Methods for PD Range Queries

3.1 All-Dimensional Index

As mentioned above, the existing multidimensional indices are designed to evaluate AD queries. This is because all of the objects are clustered in the leaf nodes according to their information in all index dimensions and every node contains information of its entries in all of the index dimensions. Actually, they also can be applied to evaluate PD range queries. Using one n-dimensional index in the entire n-dimensional index space, one PD range query with d ($d < n$) query dimensions can be evaluated by simply extending the query range in each of the $(n - d)$ irrelevant index dimensions to the entire data domain.

3.2 Multi-Btree

Another approach to handling PD range queries is called *Multi-Btree* in this paper. In this approach, one B-tree (or a variant thereof) is constructed in each index dimension, using the projections of the objects (tuples for relational data). For PD range queries, the corresponding B-trees are used individually and their results are intersected to obtain the final query result. In total, n B-trees should be constructed in advance for an n-dimensional index space.

Figure 1 is an example of a two-dimensional PD range query evaluated using multi-Btree, where the two dimensions (d_1 and d_2) are used as query dimensions. In this case, the two B-trees constructed on d_1 and d_2 are used.

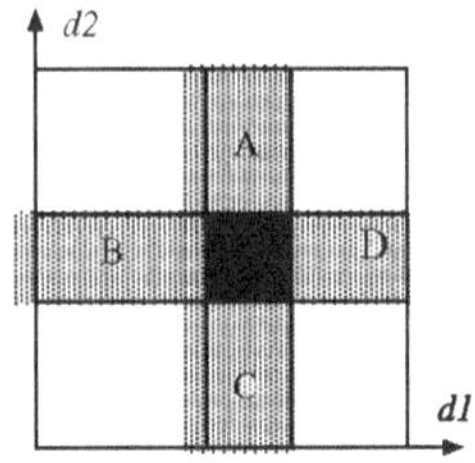

Fig. 1. An PD range query using multi-Btree

In Fig.1, the thick shadow region is the given query range. Two range queries are firstly evaluated on the two corresponding B-trees, respectively. All of the objects located in the vertical shadow region and the horizontal shadow region are reported as intermediate results, R_1 and R_2, then the final result of this PD range query is given by $R_1 \cap R_2$.

4 AR*-tree

AR*-tree is described in this section, including its structure, an search algorithm for PD range queries and a discussion on search performance.

4.1 Structure

The key concept of AR*-tree is to divide each of the n-dimensional R*-tree nodes into n one-dimensional nodes (these n one-dimensional nodes form a *node-group*), each of which holds the information in one dimension, while each node of R*-tree holds the information in all of the index dimensions. The general structure of AR*-tree is depicted in Fig.2.

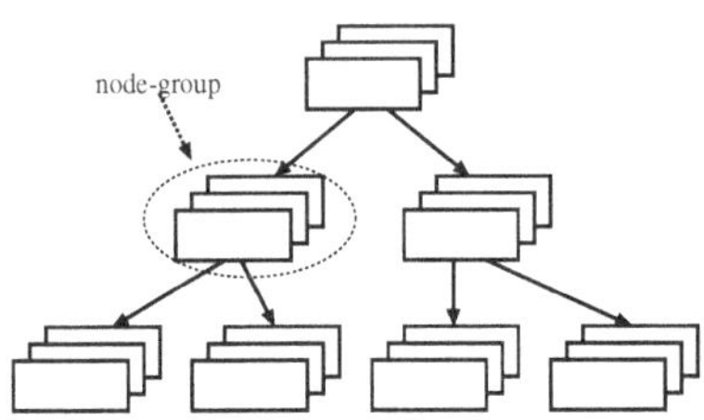

Fig. 2. General structure

Whereas every entry in R*-tree nodes includes the MBR information in all of the dimensions, each entry in the nodes of AR*-tree includes only one-dimensional information. In each node-group, each set of entries having the same index (location) and distributed in different nodes forms an *entry of node-group*, which corresponds to a complete MBR. Each entry of every node in one node-group corresponds to an edge of the MBR, while each of the entries in the index nodes of R*-tree corresponds to a complete MBR.

The question then arises as to whether the total number of nodes in AR*-tree becomes n times that in R*-tree since each node of R*-tree has been divided into n nodes. However, this is not the case because the maximum number of entries in each node of AR*-tree increases greatly, because the dimensionality of each node in AR*-tree decreases from n to 1.

The structure of AR*-tree guarantees that it can be applied to PD range queries with any combinations of query dimensions and that only the relevant one-dimensional nodes are visited.

4.2 Algorithms of AR*-tree

The insert and delete algorithms of AR*-tree is naive extensions of the counterparts of R*-tree. An algorithm for range queries is shown in Table 1.

Table 1. Algorithm for range queries on AR*-tree

```
Procedure RangeQuery (rect, node-group)
Input:    rect: query range
     node-group: initial node-group of the query
Output: result: all the tuples in rect
Begin
For each entry e *) in node-group Do
     If e INTERSECT rect in all the query dimensions **) Then
        If (node-group is not at leaf) Then
          RangeQuery (rect, e.child); //e.child means the child node-group of e
        Else result ← e
EndFor
End
```

* An entry includes all parts with the same index in the nodes of this node-group.

** In the visited node-groups, not all nodes of the query dimensions are necessary to be checked.

Staring with the root node-group, each entry of the current node-group needs to be checked as to whether its MBR intersects the query range. If its MBR intersects the query range, and the current node-group is not at the leaf level, then this algorithm is invoked recursively with the corresponding child node-group. Note that, when each entry e of the current node-group is checked, (1) not all of the nodes in this node-group have to be accessed (such irrelevant nodes are skipped), and (2) even, not all of the nodes in the relevant dimensions (query dimensions) have to be visited, because further checks are not necessary after the current entry is found not to intersect the query range in the current dimension.

4.3 Discussion on Search Performance

A disadvantage of R*-tree exists in that each node contains n-dimensional information, but only d-dimensional information is necessary for one PD range query having d ($d < n$) query dimensions. This means that a great deal of unnecessary information, i.e., the information in the irrelevant dimensions, also has to be read from disk, which certainly degrades the search performance, especially for large datasets. The main advantage of AR*-tree over R*-tree is that, for PD range queries, only the information in the relevant dimensions needs be visited.

The main advantages of AR*-tree over multi-Btree are as follows. (1) When an entry of a node-group is checked to determine whether it intersects the query range, AR*-tree can make a decision according to information in all of the query dimensions, i.e., mutual reference is possible. As a result, the regions A, B, C, and D in Fig.1 can be skipped. However, mutual reference is impossible in queries using multi-Btree because each B-tree contains only one-dimensional information and these B-trees are used independently. That is, during searching on each B-tree, the algorithm cannot realize the query ranges in the other query dimensions. Thus, many unnecessary investigations are thus performed, and a great deal of irrelevant information is read from disk. (2) In AR*-tree, only one index is needed, while multiple B-trees are necessary in multi-Btree. Both the management/update of such B-trees incur additional costs. (3) In multi-Btree, too many intermediate results may be reported and the intersection operation on the intermediate results may be very time-consuming. Considering a dataset having 1,000,000 data points uniformly distributed in a six-dimensional space. Assume that the given PD range query has four query dimensions and that the query range in each of the four query dimensions is 1/10 of the entire data domain in each respective dimension. In this case, the final result has only $10^6/10^4 = 100$. However, the query result on each B-tree has 10^5 objects! and the total number of intermediate results is 4×10^5!

Table 2. Symbols and their descriptions

n	number of index dimensions
d	number of query dimensions
S	volume of the entire index space
S_q	volume of the query range (the ranges in the irrelevant dimensions are extended to the whole data ranges)
M_r	capacity of each R*-tree leaf node
M_g	capacity of each leaf node-group in AR*-tree
N_l	number of R*-tree leaf nodes
N_g	number of AR*-tree leaf node-groups

Here is a simple mathmatical comparison between AR*-tree and R*-tree. The objects are assumed to be distributed uniformly in the index space. The necessary symbols are shown in Table 2.

For R*-tree, the average number of leaf-node accesses, R_l, can roughly be given by

$$R_l = \frac{S_q}{S} \times N_l.$$

If AR*-tree is used, then the average number of leaf node groups intersecting the query range, AR_g, can roughly be given by

$$AR_g = \frac{S_q}{S} \times N_g.$$

It is easy to understand that the maximum number of entries in each leaf node of AR*-tree is roughly n times that in each leaf node of R*-tree. We have

$$\frac{N_g}{N_l} \approx \frac{M_r}{M_g} \approx \frac{1}{n}.$$

In each accessed node-group of AR*-tree, at most d nodes (see Table 1) are visited for each d-dimensional PD range query. Thus, the number of leaf nodes (not the node-groups) that must be visited, AR_l , can be given by

$$AR_l \leq AR_g \times d \approx \frac{S_q}{S} \times N_g \times d \approx \frac{S_q}{S} \times \frac{1}{n} \times N_l \times d = \frac{d}{n} \times R_l < R_l.$$

The above equation indicates that, for PD range queries with $d < n$, the number of accessed leaf nodes in the case of AR*-tree is less than that in the case of R*-tree. If $d = n$, then the number of accessed leaf nodes may be approximately the same and it is also possible that $AR_l < R_l$. More importantly, for a fixed n, the lower the number of query dimensions, the bigger the advantage of AR*-tree compared to R*-tree.

The above equation can be explained as follows. Because the capacity of each leaf node-group in AR*-tree is roughly n times that of each leaf node in R*-tree, the number of accessed leaf node-groups in AR*-tree is approximately $1/n$ times that of the accessed leaf nodes in R*-tree. However, in each of the accessed leaf node-groups of AR*-tree, at most d nodes must be visited.

Next, let us see AR*-tree and R*-tree for AD range queries. Although all of the nodes in the visited node-groups intuitively have to be accessed for AD range queries, it is actually not true.

For one n-dimensional AD range query in an n-dimensional index space $\{d_1, d_2, ..., d_n\}$, if all the entries in the current node-group do not intersect the query range in the k-dimensional space $\{d_1, d_2, ..., d_k\}$ $(k < n)$, then the nodes of this node-group in dimensions $d_{k+1}, ..., d_n$ can be skipped. This means that, in the visited node-groups, the information in one or more dimensions possibly need not be read from secondary storage even for all-dimensional range queries. On the contrary, in R*-tree, the information corresponding to all of the dimensions in the visited nodes have to be read from disk. Thus, even for AD range queries, the AR*-tree also possibly has better search performance. Note that, for the higher-dimensional spaces, because the MBRs (entries) in each node-group become sparser, it generally becomes possible to skip more nodes in the visited node-groups. A more detailed explaination can be found in [15].

5 Experiments

A six-dimensional dataset with Zipf distribution (constant is 1.5 like [10,11]), having 200,000 objects, is used to examine the behavior of AR*-tree.

Although the size of main memory in many systems has increased greatly in recent years, indices for large datasets still tend to be stored in secondary storage, especially their leaf nodes. That is, the I/O cost is still the performance bottleneck for many systems with large datasets. In our experiment, the node size is set to be 4096 bytes. Search performance is measured in terms of the number of leaf node accesses and the number of total node accesses. Only the former is presented because of the limitation of pages and because that (1) the leaf nodes constitute the overwhelming majority of the total nodes and tend to be stored in secondary storage [9], (2) AR*-tree may be lower than R*-tree because each node-group can hold more entries than one R*-tree node. Thus, comparison in the number of leaf node accesses is fairer, and (3) no new observations for the number of all of the node accesses.

PD range queries are tested with different numbers of query dimensions, ranging from 1 to 6. B^+-tree is used in multi-Btree. Without loss of generality, the query ranges in all of the query dimensions are set to be equal. These ranges are varied from 10% to 100% in increments of 10%. The query for the range of the same size is repeated 100 times with random locations, and the averages are presented. The parameters of the indices are shown in the following table.

	Adaptive R*-tree	R*-tree	Multi-Btree
Capacity of each leaf node	340	77	340
Height	3	4	3
Total number of leaf nodes	4848 (808 groups)	4439	6777 (six B^+-trees)

The experimental results are depicted in Fig. 3 (a) ~ (f), where the X-axis represents the side length of the query range in each dimension and the Y-axis represents the number of leaf node accesses. In these figures, the number of leaf node accesses in the case of multi-Btree indicates the total number of the leaf node accesses on all of the relevant B^+-trees. The experiment result shows that

(1) For $d = 1$ (d is the number of query dimensions), the search performance of AR*-tree is slightly worse than multi-Btree, but it is far better than R*-tree.

(2) From d=2, the search performance of AR*-tree begins to outperform that on multi-Btree and remains better than that on R*-tree. In addition, as d increases, the performance advantage of AR*-tree over multi-Btree becomes larger. However, the performance advantage of AR*-tree compared to R*-tree becomes weaker as d increases.

(3) The search performance of R*-tree becomes better as d increases. This is because the search region can be limited in more dimensions.

(4) As d increases, the search performance of AR*-tree varies in an interesting way. The number of accessed node-groups decreases in the same reason as (3). However, the number of accessed nodes in each accessed node-group may increases. Under these two conflicting influences, as d increases, the search performance of the AR*-tree does not change much when the query range size is less than 40%. However, if the query range size exceeds 40%, the search performance of AR*-tree degrades clearly as d grows.

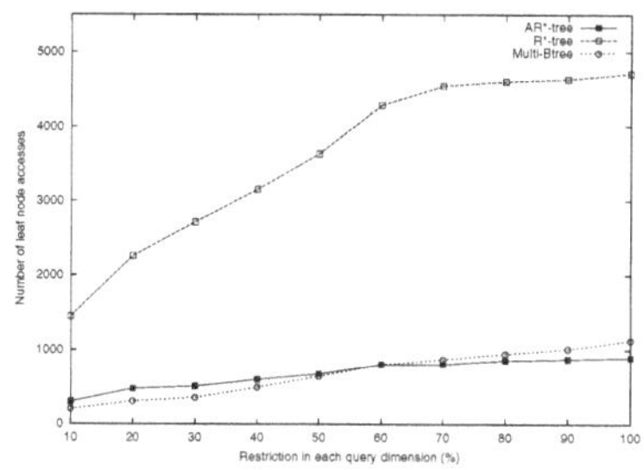

(a) Number of query dimensions is 1

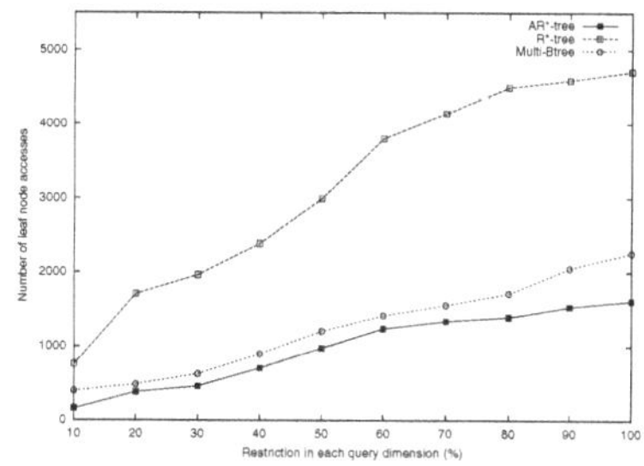

(b) Number of query dimensions is 2

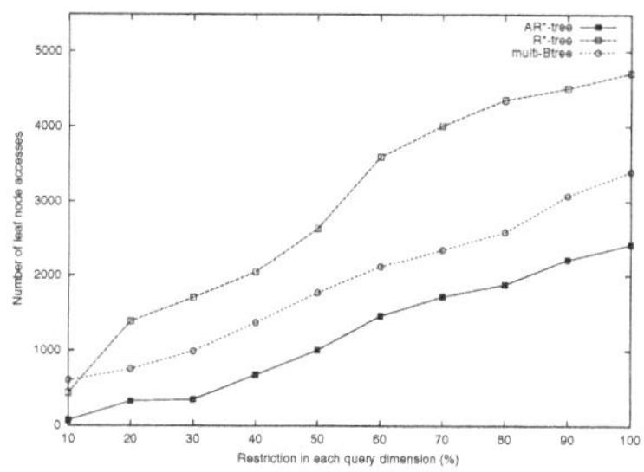

(c) Number of query dimensions is 3

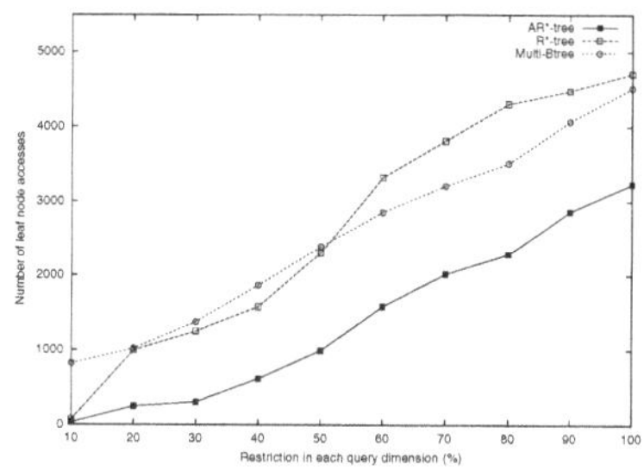

(d) Number of query dimensions is 4

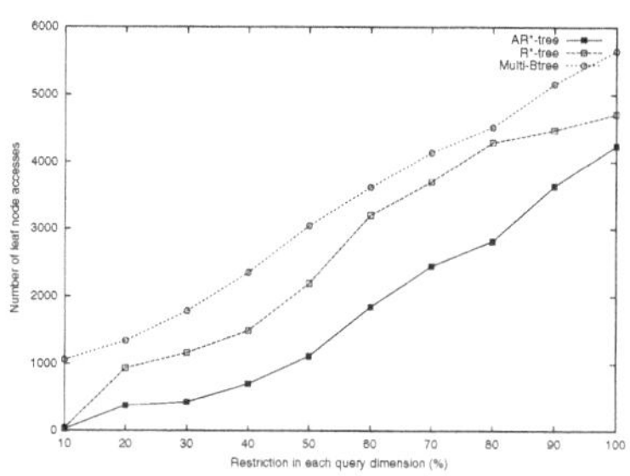

(e) Number of query dimensions is 5

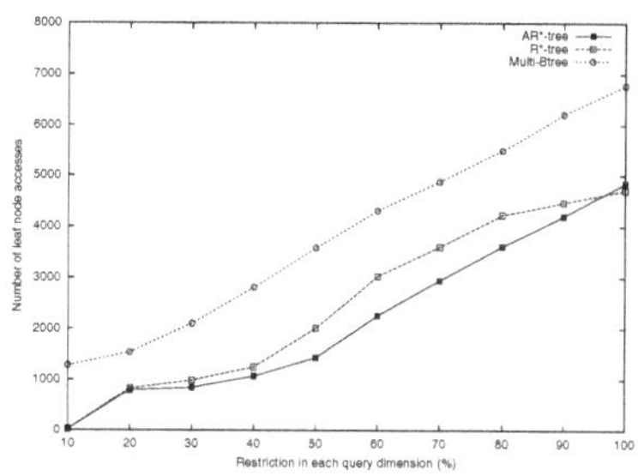

(f) Number of query dimensions is 6

Fig. 3. Experimental result for range queries

6 Conclusions

In this paper, we firstly pointed out that the existing multidimensional indices are not appropriate for partially-dimensional range queries (called PD range queries). And then, we showed that partial-dimensional range queries can be efficiently evaluated using a modification of R*-tree, called Adaptive R*-tree. The discussions and the experiments indicated that the Adaptive R'*-tree has a clearly better performance for PD range queries than the naive methods, R*-tree and multi-Btree. Although R*-tree was used in this paper, the other hierarchical MBR-based multidimensional indices can also be employed.

Acknowledgment

This research was supported in part by Japan Society for the Promotion of Science through Grants-in-Aid for Scientific Research 17650031 and 16200005.

References

1. V. Markl, M.Zirkel, and R.Bayer: Processing Operations with Restrictions in Relational Database Management Systems without External Sorting. Proc. ICDE Intl. Conf., pp. 562-571, 1999.
2. V.Markl, F.Ramsak, and R.Bayer: Improving OLAP Performance by Multidimensional Hierarchical Clustering. Proc. IDEAS Intl. Symposium, pp165-177, 1999.
3. N. Beckmann, et. al.: The R*-tree: An Efficient and Robust Access Method for Points and Rectangles. Proc. ACM SIGMOD Intl. Conf., pp.322-331, 1990.
4. S.Berchtold, D.Keim, H.P.Kriegel: The X-tree: An Index Structure for High-dimensional data. Proc. The 22nd VLDB Intl. Conf., pp.28-39, 1996.
5. Y. Sakurai, M. Yoshikawa, S. Uemura and H. Kojima: The A-tree: An Index Structure for High-Dimensional Spaces Using Relative Approximation. Proc. The 26th VLDB Intl. Conf., pp.516-526, 2000.
6. V. Gaede and O. Gunther: Multidimensional Access Methods. ACM Computing Surveys, Vol.30, No.2, pp.170-231, 1998.
7. Y. Cui: High-dimensional Indexing. Lecture Notes in Computer Science (LNCS), Vol. 2341 (Monograph), 2003.
8. Informix Spatial DataBlade Module. IBM (ww306.ibm.com/software/data/Informix/blades/spatial/rtree.html), 2004.
9. G.R.l Hjaltason and H. Samet: Distance Browsing in Spatial Database. ACM Transactions on Database Systems, Vol.24, No.2, pp. 265 318, 1999.
10. S. Hong, B. Song and S. Lee: Efficient Execution of Range-Aggregate Queries in Data Warehouse Environments. Proc. 20th international Conference on CONCEPTUAL MODELING (ER 2001), pp.299-310, 2001.
11. C. Zhang, et.al.: On Supporting Containment Queries in Relational Database Management Systems. Proc. SIGMOD Intl. Conf., pp. 425-436, 2001.
12. S. Berchtold, et.al.: Optimal Multidimensional Query Processing Using Tree Striping. Proc. 2nd intl. Conf. on Data Warehousing and Knowledge Discovery (DaWak), pp. 244-257, 2000.
13. M. Shao, et al.: Clotho: Decoupling Memory Page Layout from Storage Organization. Proc. VLDB Intl. Conf., pp. 696-707, 2004.
14. B. Bhattacharjee, et. al.: Efficient Query Processing for Multi-Dimensionally Clustered Tables in DB2. Proc. VLDB Intl. Conf. 2003.
15. Y. Feng, and A. Makinouchi: Ag-Tree: A Novel Structure for Range Queries in Data Warehouse Environments. Proc. 11th International Conference on Database Systems for Advanced Applications (Dasfaa 2006), LNCS 3882, pp. 498-512, 2006.
16. T. Grust: Accelerating XPath Location Steps. Proc. ACM SIGMOD International Conference, pages 109-120, 2002.

Parallelizing Progressive Computation for Skyline Queries in Multi-disk Environment

Yunjun Gao, Gencai Chen, Ling Chen, and Chun Chen

College of Computer Science, Zhejiang University, Hangzhou 310027, P.R. China
{gaoyj, chengc, lingchen, chenc}@cs.zju.edu.cn

Abstract. Given a set of d-dimensional points, skyline query returns the points that are not dominated by any other point on all dimensions. In this paper, we study an interesting scenario of skyline retrieval, where multi-dimensional points are distributed among multiple disks. Efficient algorithms for parallelizing progressive skyline computation are developed, using the parallel R-trees. The core of our scheme is to visit more entries from some disks simultaneously and enable effective pruning strategies with dominance checking to prune away the non-qualifying entries. Extensive experiments with synthetic data confirm that our proposed algorithms are both efficient and scalable.

1 Introduction

Skyline query is one of important operations for several applications involving multi-criteria decision making, and has received considerable attention in the database community. Given a set of d-dimensional points, the skyline comprises all the points that are not dominated by others in all dimensions. A point p dominates another p' if the coordinate of p on each dimension is smaller than or equal to that of p', and strictly smaller on at least one dimension. Consider, for instance, Figure 1(a) where $d = 2$, and each point corresponds to a hotel record. The room *price* of a hotel is represented the x-axis, and the y-axis specifies its *distance* to the beach. Clearly, hotel a dominates hotels b, d and e, since the former is closer to the beach and cheaper than the latter. Hotels a, g, i and n form the skyline, for which there is no any other hotel in $\{a, b, \ldots, m, n\}$ that is better on both dimensions.

Skyline computation has been extensively studied, and a large number of skyline processing methods have been also proposed [1, 3, 4, 5, 6, 8, 10, 11, 12, 13, 14, 15, 17, 18, 19, 20]. These approaches can be divided into two categories. Specifically, (i) non-index-structure-based schemes, which do not assume any index structure on the underlying dataset, but they compute the skyline through scanning the entire dataset at least once, leading to expensive CPU overhead; (ii) index-structure-based solutions, which significantly reduce query cost by performing the search on an appropriate index structure (e.g., R*-tree [2]). Our work in this paper belongs to the latter.

Surprisingly, in spite of the numerous bibliographies for the skyline queries, to our knowledge, there is little prior work on skyline retrieval in parallel environment (e.g., multi-disk architecture, etc.). Existing algorithms for skyline

S. Bressan, J. Küng, and R. Wagner (Eds.): DEXA 2006, LNCS 4080, pp. 697–706, 2006.

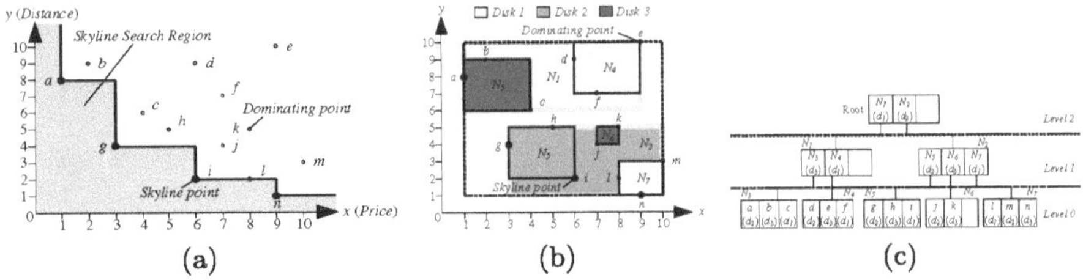

Fig. 1. Example of the skyline and the corresponding parallel R-tree

computation can efficiently execute in the serial context that uses only a single disk. However, they cannot be directly applied to the parallel setting, and their performance degrades even after modification, because they do not exploit any kind of parallelization.

Motivated by this problem, in this paper, we study an interesting scenario of skyline retrieval, where multi-dimensional points are distributed over multiple disks. On this multi-disk architecture (consisting of one processor with several disks attached to it), two efficient algorithms for parallelizing progressive skyline computation, termed Basic Parallel Skyline (BPS) and Improved Parallel Skyline (IPS) algorithms, are developed using the parallel R-trees [9]. The core of our solution is to access more entries from some disks simultaneously and enable several effective dominance checking based pruning strategies to discard non-qualifying entries. Finally, extensive experiments with synthetic data show that the proposed algorithms are both efficient and scalable.

The rest of the paper is organized as follows. Section 2 discusses related work on skyline queries. Section 3 describes BPS, providing an analysis of its efficiency. Section 4 presents IPS, together with the pruning heuristics with dominance checking and a proof of its optimality. Section 5 experimentally evaluates the efficiency and scalability of BPS and IPS under a variety of settings. Section 6 concludes the paper with some directions for future work.

2 Related Work

In this section, we survey the related work on skyline queries. Borzsonyi *et al.* [3] first introduce the skyline operator in the database context and develop two skyline query algorithms, i.e., Block Nested Loop (BNL) and Divide-and-Conquer (D&C). Chomicki *et al.* [5] present a Sort-First-Skyline (SFS) algorithm as an improved version of BNL. Tan *et al.* [17] first propose *progressive* technique that can return skyline points instantly, and develop two solutions, called Bitmap and Index, respectively. Another two progressive skyline computation methods, involving Nearest Neighbor (NN) and Branch-and-Bound Skyline (BBS), are proposed by Kossmann *et al.* [10] and Papadias *et al.* [14], respectively, using nearest neighbor search [16,7] on datasets indexed by R-trees.

Recently, Balke *et al.* [1] extend the skyline retrieval problem to the web information systems, and two algorithms including Basic Distributed Skyline

(BDS) and Improved Distributed Skyline (IDS) that compute the skyline in the distributed environment are proposed. Nevertheless, they return all skyline points at the end rather than progressively. To settle this problem, Lo *et al.* [12] devise a Progressive Distributed Skyline (PDS) algorithm. In addition, Lin *et al.* [11] and Tao *et al.* [18] independently study *continuous skyline monitoring* on data streams. Chan *et al.* [4] investigate skyline computation for partially ordered domains. Godfrey *et al.* [6] present an algorithm, termed Linear-Elimination-Sort for Skyline (LESS), which has attractive worst-case asymptotical performance. Pei *et al.* [15] and Yuan *et al.* [20] separately present the *skyline cube* consisting of the skylines in all possible subspace. More recent, Tao *et al.* [19] study skyline computation in subspace. Huang *et al.* [8] consider skyline retrieval in a mobile and distributed environment. Morse *et al.* [13] examine *continuous time-interval skyline queries*. Our work in this paper differs from the above skyline processing approaches in that we aim at computing the skyline in the multi-disk setting, as opposed to serial one.

3 Basic Parallel Skyline Algorithm

3.1 Algorithm Description

The key idea of the Basic Parallel Skyline (BPS) algorithm is to exploit sufficient parallelism to visit all relevant entries in multiple disks at the same time. BPS follows the best-first nearest neighbor search paradigm. It means that BPS always processes the entry with the minimal *mindist* at a time. Initially, BPS creates and initializes M heaps (representing $H_1, H_2, \ldots, H_M$) for M disks, suppose that the number of disks is M. Then, it inserts all the entries enclosed in the root node of parallel R-tree into respective heap sorted in ascending order of their *mindist*. Next, BPS circularly computes the skyline until all heaps become empty. Each circulation, the entry E_{min} with the smallest *mindist* in all the non-empty heaps is found firstly. If E_{min} is dominated by some skyline point discovered, then it is discarded, this circulation is done, and the algorithm proceeds to repeat the next loop. Otherwise, BPS determines whether E_{min} is a data point or not. If so, E_{min} must be a skyline point, and is en-heaped into a list S that is used to keep the skyline accordingly. If not (i.e., E_{min} is an intermediate entry), BPS expands all the first non-leaf entries among all the non-empty heaps by parallelism, after which their children that are not dominated by any skyline point in S are inserted into the corresponding heap. Figure 2 shows the pseudo-code of BPS. Note that E_{min} is checked for dominance thrice, and other entries are done the operation twice, such that all the entries that are dominated by some skyline point found do not need to be accessed. As depicted in Figure 2, the operations in lines 12 through 21 are performed in parallel.

To summarize the description of BPS algorithm, we employ an illustrative example to simulate its execution. As an example, we use the set of 2-dimensional data points of Figure 1(a), organized in the parallel R-tree [9] of Figure 1(c) with node capacity = 3. In Figure 1(c), nodes are numbered from N_1 to N_7, and the symbols d_1 through d_3 in each entry specify disk 1 to disk 3, respectively. The distances from the origin of data space are computed according to L_1 norm (i.e., *Manhattan distance*), that is, the *mindist* of a point equals the sum of its coordinates (e.g., $mindist(g) = 7$) and the *mindist* of a MBR (i.e., intermediate entry) equals the *mindist* of its bottom-left corner point (e.g., $mindist(N_5) = 5$). Figure 3 illustrates the executive steps of BPS, where *MHS* denotes the maximal heap size. Also notice that skyline points found are bold and pruned entries are shown with strikethrough fonts.

```
Algorithm BPS (parallel R-tree, M)
/* M denotes the number of disks; S specifies a list used to keep skyline points. */
1. Create and initialize M heaps (i.e., hp1, hp2, ..., hpM) for M disks;
2. S = Ø;
3. Insert all entries of the root R into respective heap;
4. While existing non-empty heap(s) in {hp1, hp2, ..., hpM} do
5.   Find the entry Emin with the minimum mindist to origin in {hp1, hp2, ..., hpM};
6.   If Emin is dominated by some point in S then
7.     Discard Emin;
8.   Else  // Emin is not dominated
9.     If Emin is a data point then
10.      Insert Emin into S;
11.    Else  // Emin is an intermediate entry
12.      For i = 1 to M parallel do
13.        If the i-th heap (i.e., hpi) is not empty then
14.          Remove top entry Ei;
15.          If Ei is dominated by some point in S then
16.            Discard Ei;
17.          Else  // Ei is not dominated
18.            If Ei is an intermediate entry then
19.              For each child ei of Ei do
20.                If ei is not dominated by some point in S then
21.                  Insert ei into corresponding heap;
22. Enddo
End BPS
```

Fig. 2. Pseudo-code of a BPS algorithm

Action	Heap 1 Contents	Heap 2 Contents	Heap 3 Contents	E_{min}	S	*MHS*
Access root	$(N_1, 7)$	$(N_2, 4)$	Ø	N_2	Ø	1
Expand N_1, N_2	$(N_7, 9)$, $(N_4, 13)$	$(N_5, 5)$	$(N_3, 7)$, $(N_6, 11)$	N_5	Ø	2
Expand N_7, N_5, N_3	**(*i*, 8)**, ~~(*e*, 10)~~, ~~(*l*, 10)~~, ~~(N_4, 13)~~	**(*g*, 7)**, **(*a*, 9)**, ~~(*m*, 13)~~	~~(*h*, 10)~~, **(*n*, 10)**, ~~(*b*, 11)~~, ~~(N_6, 11)~~	*g*	{*g*, *i*, *a*, *n*}	4

Fig. 3. Illustration of the execution of BPS

3.2 Analysis

This section analyzes the efficiency of BPS. The following lemmas ensure that BPS can correctly compute the skyline, without reporting any false hits. Note that we omit the proofs of them due to the limitation of space.

Lemma 1. *BPS visits entries (involving intermediate and data point entries) of a parallel R-tree in ascending order of their distance to the origin of the data space.*

Lemma 2. *Skyline points are progressively returned by BPS during the execution of the algorithm.*

Lemma 3. *If either an intermediate or a data point entry is not examined, then it must be dominated by some skyline point discovered.*

As shown in our experiments, the heap size of BPS can be further reduced. Continuing the running example, Figure 3 holds some redundant entries that do not contribute to the final skyline (e.g., N_4, N_6, b, h, etc.). Thus, they should not be inserted into the heaps. Based on this observation, an improved parallel algorithm for skyline computation, called IPS, is proposed in Section 4.

4 Improved Parallel Skyline Algorithm

4.1 Pruning with Dominance Checking

All non-qualifying entries do not need to be inserted into the heaps for accessing later. As we can achieve by careful dominance checking for each entry before it is en-heaped there. Next, we discuss the pruning strategy that is inspired by the analysis of the Dominance Region (DR) of per entry. For simplicity, we consider only 2-dimensional (2D) data space in the following discussion. However, similar conclusions also hold in d ($d > 2$) dimensions.

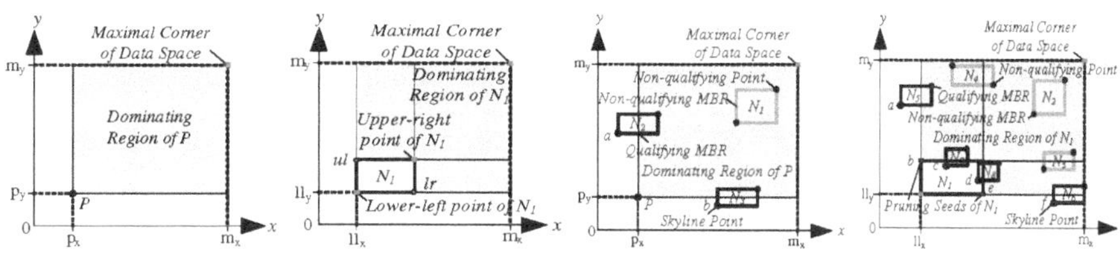

(a) DR of P (b) DR of N_1 (c) Pruning with P (d) Pruning with N_1

Fig. 4. DRs of one point, one MBR, and their pruning ability

Let the coordinates of the maximal corner of data space be (m_x, m_y), then towards a point P with coordinates (P_x, P_y), its DR is the rectangle whose diagonal is the line segment with P and the maximal corner of the data space as coordinates. Figure 4(a) shows the DR of P (indicated the shaded rectangle). Similarly, for an intermediate entry (i.e., MBR) N, the DR of N is determined by its own boundaries and the boundaries of the data space. As an example, Figure 4(b) shows this situation, and the DR of N_1 is specified by the shaded area. From the diagram, we can also see that the N_1's DR is the union of the dominating regions of ul and lr, i.e., formally, DR (N_1) = DR $(ul) \bigcup$ DR (lr), where ul and lr denote the upper-left vertex of N_1 and the lower-right vertex of N_1, respectively. Thus, it implies that the N_1's ability to dominate other entries can be done by dominance checking with ul and lr. For this reason, we call that ul and lr the *pruning seeds* of N_1. Evidently, any entry, including point and

MBR, that fully falls into the DR of point P (or MBR N) must be dominated by P (or N), and be excluded from the skyline. In contrast, the entry has to be visited further because it may potentially contain (or be) the skyline point. For ease to presentation, we also use the two 2D illustrations as demonstrated in Figures 4(c) and 4(d) in our discussion.

4.2 Algorithm Description

Like BPS, Improved Parallel Skyline (IPS) algorithm is based on best-first nearest neighbor search paradigm, but (unlike BPS) it enables effective dominance checking based pruning strategy (depicted in Section 4.1) to discard unnecessary entries for the skyline in order to greatly decrease the memory space and speed up its execution. Figure 5 shows the pseudo-code of IPS. Notice that E_{min} is checked for dominance thrice, and other entries are done the operation twice. Furthermore, IPS also implements pruning twice. Specifically, (i) line 20 filters all the entries dominated by some skyline point found in the heaps, and (ii) line 23 prunes all entries dominating each other in an auxiliary heap (e.g., hp of Figure 5). After pruning, only the entries that act on the final skyline are inserted into the heaps, such that the maximal heap size is reduced by factors, as well as the query cost is decreased accordingly. Additionally, as shown in Figure 5, the operations enclosed in lines 12 to 21 can be performed by parallelizing. As with the settings of Figure 3, Figure 6 illustrates the executive steps of IPS. As shown Figure 6, the MHS of IPS is smaller significantly than that of BPS, which is also verified by the experiments in Section 5.

```
Algorithm IPS (parallel R-tree, M)
/* M denotes the number of disks; S specifies a list used to keep skyline points; hp is a temporary
heap used to filter non-qualifying entries visited that do not contribute to the final answer. */
1. Create and initialize M + 1 heaps (i.e., hp, hp1, hp2, ..., hpM);
2. S = Ø;
3. Insert all entries of the root R into respective heap;
4. While existing non-empty heap(s) in {hp1, hp2, ..., hpM} do
5.    Find the entry Emin with the minimum mindist to origin in {hp1, hp2, ..., hpM};
6.    If Emin is dominated by some point in S then
7.       Discard Emin;
8.    Else   // Emin is not dominated
9.       If Emin is a data point then
10.         Insert Emin into S;
11.      Else   // Emin is an intermediate entry
12.         For i = 1 to M parallel do
13.            If the i-th heap (i.e., hpi) is not empty then
14.               Remove top entry Ei;
15.               If Ei is dominated by some point in S then
16.                  Discard Ei;
17.               Else   // Ei is not dominated
18.                  If Ei is an intermediate entry then
19.                     For each child ei of e do
20.                        If ei is not dominated by some point in S then
21.                           Insert Ei into the heap hp;   // hp should be further checked
            // Check whether all the entries in hp are qualifying ones or not. If not, discard them.
22.         If hp is not empty then
23.            Prune all the non-qualifying entries in hp;
24.            While hp is not empty do
25.               Remove top entry e;
26.               Insert e into corresponding heap;
27.            Enddo
28. Enddo
End IPS
```

Fig. 5. Pseudo-code of a IPS algorithm

Action	Heap 1 Contents	Heap 2 Contents	Heap 3 Contents	E_{min}	S	MHS
Access root	$(N_1, 7)$	$(N_2, 4)$	Ø	N_2	Ø	1
Expand N_1, N_2	$(N_7, 9)$	$(N_5, 5)$	$(N_3, 7)$	N_5	Ø	1
Expand N_7, N_5, N_3	**(*i*, 8)**	**(*g*, 7)**, **(*a*, 9)**	**(*n*, 10)**	g	$\{g, i, a, n\}$	2

Fig. 6. Illustration of the execution of IPS

4.3 Discussion

Similar to BPS, IPS can correctly return the entire skyline, without lose any valid one. In this section, we focus on the analysis of *Skyline Search Region* (SSR), which is the part of the data space that may contain some skyline points. Consider, for instance, Figure 1(a), the SSR is the shaded area defined by the skyline (i.e., $\{a, g, i, n\}$) and the two axes. Then, we prove that IPS is optimal in terms of I/O cost.

Lemma 4. *IPS must visit all the entries (containing intermediate and data point entries) of a parallel R-tree that fully fall into or intersect the SSR, instead of accessing those entries lying in the exterior of the SSR during the processing of skyline retrieval.*

Theorem 1. *The number of node accesses for IPS is optimal.*

Proof. The Theorem 1 trivially holds, because Lemma 4 guarantees that the heaps used by IPS store only the entries that may contain (or be) skyline points, and those entries are en-heaped at most once, according to their *mindist*. □

5 Experimental Evaluation

In this section, we experimentally evaluate the efficiency and scalability of the proposed algorithms under a variety of settings. Following the common methodology in the literature, we deployed the independent (uniform) and anti-correlated datasets with dimensionality (d for short) varied from 2 to 5 and cardinality (N for short) in the range [128k, 2M], respectively. Each dataset is indexed by a parallel R-tree [9] distributed over multiple disks that are simulated on one 80 Giga disk (whose type is "*ST380011AS*") using several identifiers of disk (specified *diskid*), and disk assignment straightforwardly follows the *Round-Robin* heuristic. The node size of the parallel R-tree is fixed to 1024 bytes.

The experiments investigated several factors, including the number of disk (*disks* for short), d, N, and *progressive* behavior, which affect the performance of the algorithms. Notice that the query cost is calculated as the sum of the CPU time and the I/O overhead computed by charging 10ms for each node access. Both algorithms (involving BPS and IPS) were coded in C++ language. All experiments were performed on a Pentium IV 3.0 GHz PC with 1024 MB RAM running Microsoft Windows XP Professional. We utilized L_1 norm to compute the *mindist* from the origin of the data space in all experiments.

The effect of the number of disk. The first set of experiments studied the influence of *disks* (varied between 2 and 10) on the performance of BPS and IPS, using the datasets with d = 3D and N = 512k. Figure 7 plots the maximal heap size (MHS for short), node accesses (NA for short), and query time (Secs) as a function of *disks*, respectively. Clearly, in Figure 7, the MHS of IPS is smaller than that of BPS, which explains that the memory consumption of BPS can be reduced further, and our proposed pruning strategy with dominance checking (discussed in Section 4.1) is efficient. As confirmed in the subsequent experiments. In addition, as *disks* increases, the NA and query cost decrease, which is caused by the growth of parallelism. However, the performance of IPS again outperforms that of BPS in all cases.

The effect of dimensionality. To examine the impact of dimensionality d, we employed the datasets with N = 512k and *disks* = 6 (which is the midvalue used in Figure 7), altering d from 2D to 5D. Figure 8 shows these experimental results. Similar to Figure 7, the efficiency of IPS is over that of BPS, especially

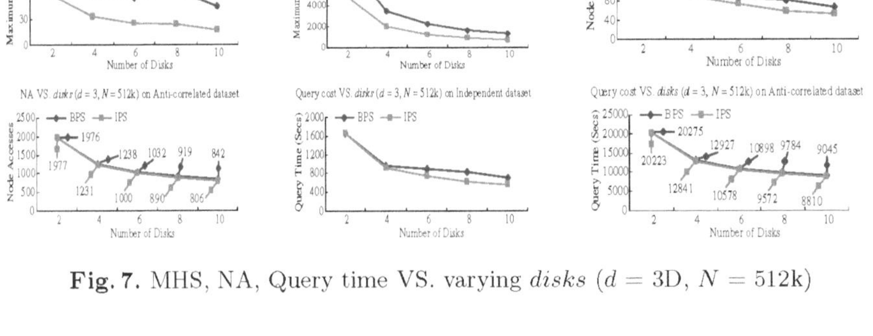

Fig. 7. MHS, NA, Query time VS. varying *disks* (d = 3D, N = 512k)

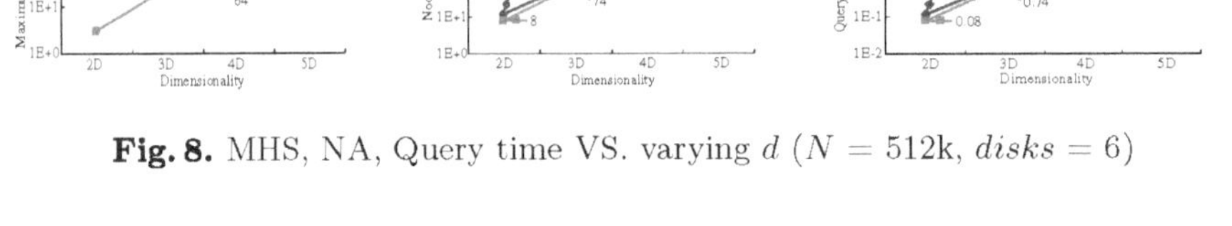

Fig. 8. MHS, NA, Query time VS. varying d (N = 512k, *disks* = 6)

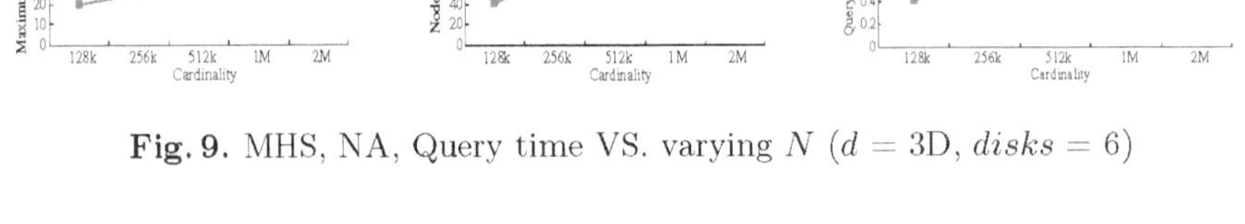

Fig. 9. MHS, NA, Query time VS. varying N (d = 3D, *disks* = 6)

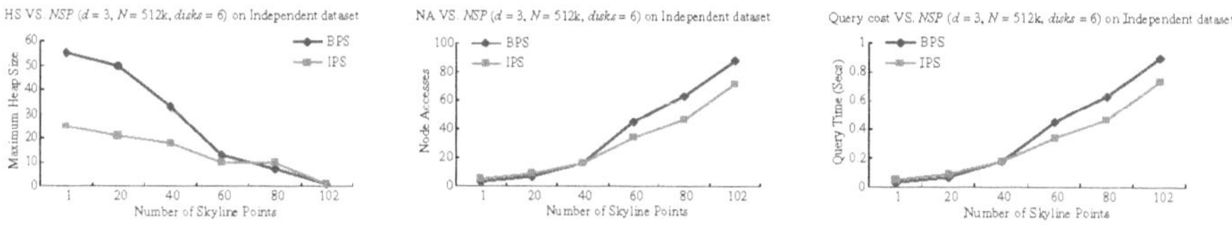

Fig. 10. MHS, NA, Query time VS. varying NSP ($d = 3\text{D}$, $N = 512\text{k}$, $disks = 6$)

in low dimensions (e.g., $d = 2$ or 3). Although the gain of IPS reduces in high dimensions (e.g., $d = 5$), it is yet less than BPS, which is also pointed out by the number at the side of each polyline in the diagrams. As expected the efficiency of both algorithms degrades due to the growth of the number of skyline points and the poor performance of parallel R-trees in high dimensions.

The effect of cardinality. Figure 9 illustrates MHS, NA, and query time versus cardinality N for 3D (the parameter $d = 3\text{D}$ is also the median value used in Figure 8) datasets with N changed in the range [128k, 2M] and *disks* = 6. Obviously, IPS consistently exceeds BPS. Specifically, the MHS of IPS is several orders of magnitude smaller than that of BPS. Towards NA, IPS is less than BPS. Also, IPS is faster than BPS for query cost.

***Progressive* behavior.** Finally, we inspected the *progressive* behavior of the algorithms for skyline computation on 3D datasets. Figure 10 compared MHS, NA, and query cost as a function of the number of skyline points (NSP for short) for datasets with $d = 3\text{D}$, $N = 512\text{k}$, and *disks* = 6. Notice that the NSP in the final skyline is 102 for independent dataset. From the diagrams, we see that IPS evidently exhibits smaller heap size than BPS (over orders of magnitude) in most cases, because the non-qualifying entries are discarded by IPS. Also notice that the heaps reach their maximal size at the beginning of both algorithms, and stepwise decrease with the growth of NSP. The reason of this case is these algorithms insert all the qualifying entries visited in the heaps (due to no any skyline point found) before they discover the first skyline point. For NA and query cost, BPS first outperforms IPS since the latter has to expend some time to prune away the non-qualifying entries. However, the difference gradually decreases as NSP increases, and then IPS is better than BPS, which is due to some redundant entries storing in the heap of BPS.

6 Conclusion

This paper studies the problem of parallelizing progressive computation for skyline queries in the multi-disk environment. We propose two efficient parallel algorithms for skyline queries, referred to as BPS and IPS, using the parallel R-tree as the underlying structure. Furthermore, IPS captures optimal I/O (i.e., the number of node accesses) and enables several effective pruning strategies to discard the non-qualifying entries during the execution of the algorithm.

Finally, considerable experiments with synthetic datasets show that the presented algorithms are efficient and scalable, as well as IPS outperforms BPS. In the future, we plan to explore the new parallel skyline computation methods in a shared-nothing environment (i.e., multi-processor architecture).

References

1. Balke, W.-T., Guntzer, U., Zheng, J.X.: Efficient Distributed Skylining for Web Information Systems. In: EDBT. (2004) 256-273
2. Beckmann, N., Kriegel, H.-P., Schneider, R., Seeger, B.: The R*-tree: An Efficient and Robust Access Method for Points and Rectangles. In: SIGMOD. (1990) 322-331
3. Borzsony, S., Kossmann, D., Stocker, K.: The Skyline Operator. In: ICDE. (2001) 421-430
4. Chan, C.-Y., Eng, P.-K., Tan. K.-L.: Stratified Computation of Skylines with Partially-Ordered Domains. In: SIGMOD. (2005) 203-214
5. Chomicki, J., Godfrey, P., Gryz, J., Liang, D.: Skyline with Presorting. In: ICDE. (2003) 717-719
6. Godfrey, P., Shipley, R., Gryz, J.: Maximal Vector Computation in Large Data Sets. In: VLDB. (2005) 229-240
7. Hjaltason, G.R., Samet, H.: Distance Browsing in Spatial Databases. ACM TODS **24** (1999) 265-318
8. Huang, Z., Jensen, C.S., Lu, H. Ooi, B.C.: Skyline Queries against Mobile Lightweight Devices in MANETs. In: ICDE. (2006) 66
9. Kamel, I., Faloutsos, C.: Parallel R-trees. In: SIGMOD. (1992) 195-204
10. Kossmann, D., Ramsak, F., Rost, S.: Shooting Stars in the Sky: An Online Algorithm for Skyline Queries. In: VLDB. (2002) 275-286
11. Lin, X., Yuan, Y., Wang, W., Lu, H.: Stabbing the Sky: Efficient Skyline Computation over Sliding Windows. In: ICDE. (2005) 502-513
12. Lo, E., Yip, K.Y., Lin, K.-I., Cheung, D.W.: Progressive Skylining over Web-Accessible Databases. DKE. (to appear)
13. Morse, M., Patel, J., Grosky, W.: Efficient Continuous Skyline Computation. In: ICDE. (2006) 108
14. Papadias, D., Tao, Y., Greg, F., Seeger, B.: Progressive Skyline Computation in Database Systems. ACM TODS **30** (2005)41-82
15. Pei, J., Jin, W., Ester, M., Tao, Y.: Catching the Best Views of Skyline: A Semantic Approach Based on Decisive Subspaces. In: VLDB. (2005) 253-264
16. Roussopoulos, N., Kelley, S., Vincent, F.: Nearest neighbor queries. In: SIGMOD. (1995) 71-79
17. Tan, K.-L., Eng, P.-K., Ooi, B.C.: Efficient Progressive Skyline Computation. In: VLDB. (2001) 301-310
18. Tao, Y., Papadias, D.: Maintaining Sliding Window Skylines on Data Streams. TKDE **18** (2006) 377-391
19. Tao, Y., Xiao, X., Pei, J.: SUBSKY: Efficient Computation of Skylines in Subspaces. In: ICDE. (2006) 65
20. Yuan, Y., Lin, X., Liu, Q., Wang, W., Yu, J.X., Zhang, Q.: Efficient Computation of the Skyline Cube. In: VLDB. (2005) 241-252

Parameterizing a Genetic Optimizer

Victor Muntés-Mulero[1], Marta Pérez-Casany[2], Josep Aguilar-Saborit[1], Calisto Zuzarte[3], and Josep-Ll. Larriba-Pey[1]

[1] Computer Architecture Dept. Universitat Politècnica de Catalunya,
[2] Applied Mathematics II Dept. Universitat Politècnica de Catalunya,
C/Jordi Girona 1-3, 08034 Barcelona, Spain
{vmuntes, jaguilar, larri}@ac.upc.edu, marta.perez@upc.edu
http://www.dama.upc.edu
[3] IBM Canada Ltd, IBM Toronto Lab., 8200 Warden Ave.,
Markham, Ontario, Canada L6G1C7
calisto@ca.ibm.com

Abstract. Genetic programming has been proposed as a possible although still intriguing approach for query optimization. There exist two main aspects which are still unclear and need further investigation, namely, the quality of the results and the speed to converge to an optimum solution. In this paper we tackle the first aspect and present and validate a statistical model that, for the first time in the literature, lets us state that the average cost of the best query execution plan (QEP) obtained by a genetic optimizer is predictable. Also, it allows us to analyze the parameters that are most important in order to obtain the best possible costed QEP. As a consequence of this analysis, we demonstrate that it is possible to extract general rules in order to parameterize a genetic optimizer independently from the random effects of the initial population.

1 Introduction

Deciding the optimal query execution plan (QEP) for very large join queries is a well-known and important NP-hard problem of query optimization in relational databases. Applications like SAP or those involving information integration often need to combine a large set of tables to reconstruct complex business objects. For instance, the SAP schema may contain more than 10,000 relations and may join more than 20 of these in a single SQL query.

Several approaches aim at solving the large join query problem. Evolutionary algorithms applied to query optimization have been presented as a possible solution [1,7,10,11]. Whether evolutionary algorithms are a competitive approach or not is still an intriguing question. One of the major obstacles for randomized techniques is the difficulty to demonstrate if they are robust and predictable, and whether it is possible to parameterize them in a sound way.

We present a statistical analysis, based on more than 72000 executions, that allows us to understand that the behavior of a genetic optimizer depends on a reduced set of parameters and that there exist configurations of these parameters that are consistently better than others. Given the complexity of this problem, it

S. Bressan, J. Küng, and R. Wagner (Eds.): DEXA 2006, LNCS 4080, pp. 707–717, 2006.

is difficult to find an appropriate statistical model because this implies to carry out a large number of executions. For this reason, a study of the whole space of possible queries is out of the scope of this paper and, thus, we focus on the specific case of star-join queries.

The rest of this paper is organized as follows. Section 2 briefly describes the genetic optimizer used for this work. Section 3 presents our statistical model. Section 4 presents a set of recommendation on how to parameterize a genetic optimizer based on the model obatained. Section 5 references some related work. Finally, Section 6 concludes this paper and proposes future work lines.

2 The Carquinyoli Genetic Optimizer

We use the Carquinyoli Genetic Optimizer (CGO) which is presented and validated for a real data workload comparing its results with a commercial optimizer in [7]. The cost model used in CGO is based on that proposed in [9]. In order to simplify the cost functions, this cost model only takes into account the I/O accesses incurred by the QEP. It does, however, consider some advanced features like the use of bit filters in the hash join operations and blocking techniques to reduce disk utilization. A detailed description of the model is presented in [6].

2.1 Genetic Optimizer Behavior and Genetic Operations

In order to create a statistical model to predict the average cost for the execution of the QEP obtained by CGO, we must determine the most influent factors related to the genetic optimizer. A *factor* is considered to be a categorical variable, i.e. a variable that gives the appropriate label of an observation after allocation to one of several possible categories or values [2], that are called *levels* in statistics.

Initially, the database and the query are fixed by the user and the system obtains a query graph. These first steps are deterministic and cannot be altered by the optimizer. CGO is based on genetic programming and it uses the same execution patterns of any evolutionary algorithm. The optimizer randomly chooses N execution plans from the search space to create a first set of members to begin with the evolution process. Although N is tunable, the process of selecting random QEPs from the search space and the creation of each population is completely random and, consequently, it cannot be controlled by the user. Since the size of the search space needed for very large join queries is enormous, the quality of the small initial sample might be of major importance to determine the effective approximation of the algorithm to a near-optimal solution. We call P the initial population created for each execution. Two kinds of operations are used to produce new members in the population: *crossover operations*, which combine properties of the existing members in the population, and *mutation operations*, which introduce new properties into the population (further information about these operations can be found in [7]). In order to keep the size of the population constant, a third operation, usually referred to as *selection*, is used to discard the worst fitted members, using the cost of the QEP. This process generates a new population, also called generation, that includes both the old and the new members that have survived to the selection operation. This is repeated iteratively until a *stop condition* ends the execution. Once the stop criterion is met, evolutionary algorithms take the best solution from the final population. In our study we fix the number of generations, denoted by G, as the stop criterion. For each generation we apply C crossover operations and M mutation operations. C and M are studied in this paper. The appropriate value of G is unknown and it is also one of the objects of our study.

There might be more parameters to take into consideration. However, as we will see in the following section, the statistical model is accepted only considering the variance produced by these parameters, namely N, G, C, M and P. This implies that the effect of other parameters can be neglected.

3 Statistical Model

In this section we study the effect of different variables on the average cost of the best QEP obtained after an execution of CGO by means of an statistical model. The technique used to find this model is the *Analysis of Variance* which is the equivalent to regression when we have categorical variables instead of continuous variables. The Analysis of Variance (from here on ANOVA) is the statistical technique that allows us to distinguish between the variability in the data due to a specific cause, controlled by the experimenter, from the variability prompted by other circumstances [5]. As a broad outline, ANOVA aims at decomposing the total variability of a sample among different parts corresponding to the factors that could potentially be the cause. Once the contribution of each level of each factor in the result is estimated, by comparing variances using a Fisher test we can decide if the differences caused by the different levels of a factor are statistically significant or not. In our case, the ANOVA allows us to estimate the contribution of each parameterizable value in the optimizer, in the cost of the best QEP obtained after the optimization process. Therefore, we will be able to see whether the contribution of each variable, alone or in combination with others, is significant or not.

If the levels of a factor are fixed a priori, they are considered constants and the factor is known as a fixed effects factor. If they have been randomly selected from all possible values, then they are considered observations of a random variable and the factor is considered a random effects factor. In order to define an appropriate model to fit a set of data, it is very important to distinguish between crossed factors and nested factors. Two factors A and B are crossed when each level of A is observed for each level of B and vice versa. Given two crossed factors it makes sense to ask for their interaction, i.e. the situation where two explanatory variables do not act independently on the response variable. More exactly, A and B interact when the effect of a given level of A depends on the level of B with which is combined. In the next section, we will see that ANOVA allows to determine which interactions are significant. We say that a factor A *is nested in* B, when the levels of A are sub-sampled in each level of B, i.e. each level of A occurs at only one level of B.

In order to accept a specific model as a good model to fit a set of data, two conditions must be met: (i) $\mathcal{R}^2$ must be close to one, where $\mathcal{R}^2$ ranges from 0 to 1 and it is defined as the proportion of the variability in the data explained by the model and (ii) the residuals, a measure of the discrepancy between the real values and the values predicted by the model, must be independent and follow a normal distribution with mean zero and constant variance. We use the Statistical Analysis System (SAS) Rel. 8.00 to create and analyze the models.

3.1 Variables in the Model

Given a star join query Q, we call R the number of relations accessed by that query and S the selectivity of the query. More exactly S represents the probability of a tuple in a base relation to qualify and to be returned as a result.

Once a query is fixed, our statistical model aims at predicting the average cost of the returned QEP depending on factors N, G, C, M and P mentioned above. As a consequence, the *average cost of the returned QEP* is the dependant variable or y variable. Factors N, G, C and M have been fixed to take just three different levels each. Thus, they can be considered as fixed effect factors. We consider the levels of C and M proportional to N and, for that reason, C and M are nested in N. As mentioned before, the quality of the first initial population P created from scratch can affect the quality of the obtained plan. As opposed to the previous factors, P is a random effects factor.

3.2 Description of the Experiments

The decisions taken in this section are based on empirical considerations from experiments done in previous ad-hoc tests, in order to use reasonable and realistic values. Table 1 summarizes the levels used for the different fixed effects factors in the experiment. Figure 1 depicts the design of our experiment. For both $R = 20$ and $R = 50$ we create 9 different queries, three for each value of S, $S = 10^{-2}$, $S = 10^{-4}$ and $S = 10^{-8}$. Given a query, we create 15 initial populations, 5 for each level of N. Once we have created the populations, we run 270 executions. This set of executions is divided into three subsets, corresponding to the three levels in G. For every level of G, we subdivide the executions into 9 subsets

Table 1. Independent factor levels studied in the experiment

Independent Variables	Studied Levels
N (Number of members)	$4R$, $8R$ and $12R$
G (Number of generations)	50, 100, and 200
C (Number of crossovers)	$\frac{N}{8}$, $\frac{N}{4}$ and $\frac{N}{2}$
M (Number of mutations)	$\frac{N}{8}$, $\frac{N}{4}$ and $\frac{N}{2}$

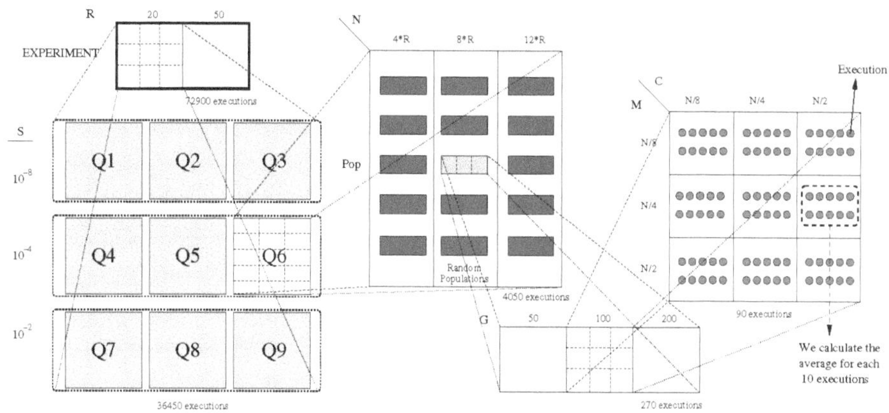

Fig. 1. Design for obtaining the results

corresponding to the crossing between C and M. Finally, for every possible configuration of the levels of each factor we run 10 executions and obtain the average best cost. The value of this average corresponds to the observations of variable y. Therefore, since we have run 72900 independent executions, the number of observations for the dependant variable is equal to 7290.

Database schema and Star Join Query Generation. We have randomly generated two databases containing 20 and 50 relations respectively. Both schemas contain a large *fact table* or *central relation* and 19 and 49 smaller *dimension tables*. The central relation contains a foreign key attribute to a primary key in each dimension relation. Most of the dimensions have a significantly lower cardinality compared to the fact table and, a smaller set of dimensions have a cardinality closer to the cardinality of this central relation, which typically corresponds to real scenarios (similar to the TPC-H database schema). We define an index for every primary key.

As explained before, once the databases are defined, we randomly define two sets of 9 star-join queries Q_{20} and Q_{50}, one for each database schema, and a separate set of 6 queries Q_{Test} (3 for each database schema). The first two sets will be used to define the statistical model. The third set has been created for testing purposes and will only be used to validate the model.

3.3 Model Definition

The process of building a model that properly predicts the behavior of a random variable in front of some factors is iterative. Following, we initially present a simple example that allows us to understand how to build a statistical model using the ANOVA technique. Let us suppose that we need to study the impact of the number of processors and the memory available on the execution time of a process. To that end, we study the case for 2, 4 and 8 processors (first factor) and 512 MB and 1 GB memory cards (second factor). For any combination of a specific number of processors and a specific amount of memory, we run the process ten times obtaining ten observations. This gives a $3 \times 2 \times 10 = 60$ total number of observations. The initial model to analyze the set of data obtained would be the following:

$$y_{ijk} = \mu + \alpha_i + \beta_j + (\alpha\beta)_{ij} + e_{ijk}$$

where, y_{ijk} is the kth observation of the response variable under the ith condition of the number of processors (i has three possible levels, i.e. it can take three possible values: $i = 1$ corresponds to 2 processors, $i = 2$ corresponds to 4 processors and $i = 3$ corresponds to 8 processors) and the jth condition of the memory available (which has two possible levels: $j = 1$ corresponds to 512 MB and $j = 2$ corresponds to 1 GB). Parameter μ indicates the expected time if the number of processors and the memory available is unknown. Its estimation corresponds to the average of all the observations. Parameter α_i is a real number that indicates the variation from μ produced by the knowledge of the number of processors corresponding to the ith level of A. Analogously β_j is a real number that indicates the variation from μ produced by the knowledge of the available memory corresponding to the jth level of factor B. It has sense to assume that $\alpha_1 + \alpha_2 + \alpha_3 = 0$ and $\beta_1 + \beta_2 = 0$. The term $(\alpha\beta)_{ij}$ corresponds to the interaction of the two factors. Its value represents the contribution in the execution time of the fact that the observation has been obtained under the ith level of the number of processors and the jth level of the available memory. This interaction will not be significant if the effect of the number of processors is the same for any amount of available memory. It has sense to assume that $\forall i \, (\alpha\beta)_{i1} + (\alpha\beta)_{i2} = 0$ and $\forall j \, (\alpha\beta)_{1j} + (\alpha\beta)_{2j} + (\alpha\beta)_{3j} = 0$. The ANOVA technique allows us to estimate the value for each of these parameters and to accept or refuse the following three hypothesis: $\alpha_1 = \alpha_2 = \alpha_3$, $\beta_1 = \beta_2$ and $\forall i_1, i_2 \in \{1, 2, 3\} \forall j_1, j_2 \in \{1, 2\} \, (\alpha\beta)_{i_1 j_1} = (\alpha\beta)_{i_2 j_2}$. If any of these equalities is accepted it means that the corresponding factor or interaction is statistically not significant and can be removed from the model in order to simplify it. For further details we refer the reader to [8].

Analogously, for our data, we depart from the model that contains all the factors and the first-order interactions and then we eliminate the terms that are not statistically significant. An important conclusion from this departure model is that the interaction between the number of crossovers and the number of mutations is not statistically significant, i.e. it does not seem to have any impact on the variability in the average cost. The final model is the following:

$$y_{ijklm} = \mu + \delta_i + \gamma_j + \alpha_{k(i)} + \lambda_{l(i)} + \phi_{m(i)} + (\delta\gamma)_{ij} + (\gamma\alpha)_{jk(i)} + (\gamma\lambda)_{jl(i)} + e_{ijklm}$$

where, y_{ijklm} is the average cost of the best fitted QEP found during the optimization process, for 10 executions under the ith, jth, kth, lth, mth levels of the corresponding factors; μ is the common expected value; δ_i, γ_j, $\alpha_{k(i)}$, $\lambda_{l(i)}$ and $\phi_{m(i)}$ correspond to the main effects of N, G, C, M and P. Interaction $(\delta\gamma)_{ij}$ corresponds to the interaction of the ith level of N with the jth level of G. Analogously, $(\gamma\alpha)_{jk(i)}$ and $(\gamma\lambda)_{jl(i)}$ correspond to the interactions of the jth

Table 2. $\mathcal{R}^2$ values classified depending on the selectivity and the number of relations

$\mathcal{R}^2$ summary									
	$S = 10^{-2}$			$S = 10^{-4}$			$S = 10^{-8}$		
	Q1	Q2	Q3	Q1	Q2	Q3	Q1	Q2	Q3
$R = 20$	0.868	0.894	0.812	0.838	0.826	0.799	0.798	0.409	0.601
$R = 50$	0.939	0.924	0.923	0.862	0.810	0.868	0.703	0.763	0.706

level of G and the lth level of M respectively with the kth level of C and are both nested in N. Note that it is only possible to consider interactions between crossed factors. Also, observe that the levels corresponding to nested factors must be always associated to the level of the factor in which they are nested, indicated by the subscript (i). e_{ijklm} corresponds to the experimental error and contains the information in the observations which is not explained by the considered factors.

Following, in order to confirm that our model is appropriate, we are going to see that conditions i) and ii) mentioned at the beginning of this section are satisfied. Table 2 wraps up the $\mathcal{R}^2$ obtained after fitting the data of each query using our model. The model explains the variability in the real data set almost perfectly for queries involving a large number of relations when the constraints in the query are not very restrictive ($S = 10^{-2}$) (it explains more than 90 % of the variability). Independently of the number of relations, if S is larger than 10^{-8} the variability explained by the model is always larger or equal than 80 %. The model is still appropriate if $S = 10^{-8}$ and $R = 50$, although the $\mathcal{R}^2$ values decrease a little bit and are around 70 %. For $S = 10^{-8}$ and $R = 20$, we have obtained two non-acceptable $\mathcal{R}^2$ values below 65%. We have studied these last two cases in detail. Our conclusions are as follows: in the case of $S = 10^{-8}$ most of the potential tuple results are discarded because the selectivity is too strict, resulting in a very low data flow cardinality in the QEP. Since the join operations can be executed in memory and do not incur extra I/O, all the implementations have a similar cost and most of the executions are likely to reach a QEP with a near-optimal cost. Occasionally, for a small number of generations, i.e. $G = 50$, the genetic optimizer does not reach a QEP with a cost similar to the rest of executions. In general, we will always reach this low cost, except for the cases where we limit the number of generations to a minimum. Therefore, the conclusions extracted from the model can be always applied, except for the scenario with $S = 10^{-8}$ and $R = 20$, where we must apply even additional simpler rules, namely, granting that $G > 50$.

In order to check condition ii) mentioned before, we work with the studentized residuals which are defined as the difference between the observed and the predicted values divided by the standard deviation of all those differences. In general, we accept normal distributions of residuals for those queries with $S = 10^{-4}$ and $S = 10^{-2}$. Figure 2 shows the distribution of the studentized residuals for a data set corresponding to a query with $R = 50$ and $S = 10^{-2}$. For queries with $S = 10^{-8}$, residuals have a larger kurtosis [2] than the corresponding normal distribution with the same mean and variance.

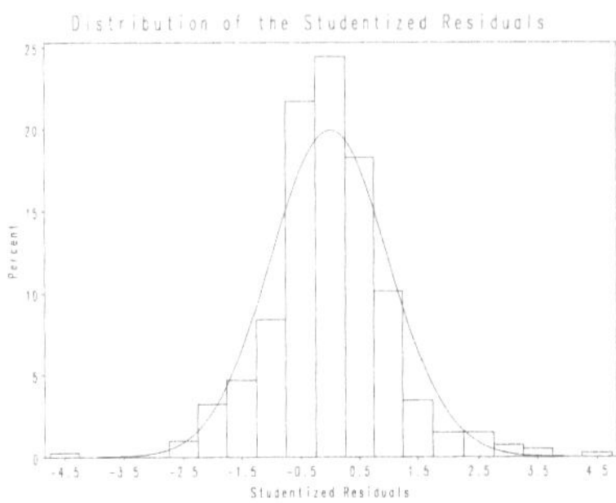

Fig. 2. Residual distribution for a query with $R = 50$ and $S = 10^{-2}$

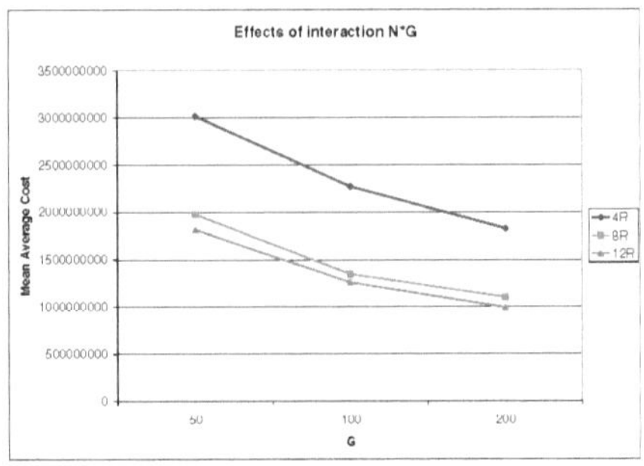

Fig. 3. Polygonal plot corresponding to the interaction between N and G for a given query

In order to test the generality of the model and to be able to state that the model is good for any query we use the 6 queries in Q_{Test}. After fitting the model to these queries, five of the $\mathcal{R}^2$ are larger than 0.86 and the remaining one is equal to 0.78.

3.4 Discussion of the Results

Our model satisfactorily predicts the real cost values. This means that we can assure that the factors used in the model are the most significant ones and, also, that they are sufficient to explain the variability of the quality of the results. More specifically:

- All the factors, N, G, C, M and P, independently, explain a significant part of the variability in the data set. From the ANOVA analysis we conclude that N and G are, in general, the factors that have a larger impact on the average cost, specifically larger than the impact of P. Although both, C and M are statistically significant and, therefore, explain part of the variability, their impact on the average cost is lower than the impact of the number of members or the number of generations. The analysis also shows that the number of crossover operations is, in general, more relevant than the number of mutation operations. Specifically, for any level of N considered, we obtain, on average, differences of over 30% in y between the cases using $N/2$ and $N/8$ crossover operations. However, these differences range from 11% to 16%, depending on N, when we vary the number of mutation operations.
- Even more important, although a genetic optimizer is subject to random variability like any other random algorithm, we can explain the variability in the data without considering the effect of the initial population on the contribution of every other factor in the model. In that sense, we can extract conclusions from the other factors, independently from the initial population, which implies that a genetic optimizer can be parameterized using fixed criteria.

- Interaction $(\delta\gamma)_{ij}$ is significant for all data sets. This means that the impact of a fixed level of G (i.e. number of generations) on the average cost depends on the level of N (i.e. number of members in the population). Figure 3 shows a graphical representation of this interaction. While the effect of the interaction is not very marked, it is significant. The plot also shows that the level of N is very important. Specifically, we can observe that the real quality improvement is found between $4R$ and $8R$, whereas the latter and $12R$ cannot be considered significantly different. This effect shows up for all the queries.
- Interaction $(\gamma\alpha)_{jk(i)}$ (corresponding to the interaction between levels of factors N and C) is considered significant in 14 out of the 16 data sets, meaning that for a fixed number of members in the population (N), the importance of the number of crossovers (C) depends on the number of generations.
- Finally, $(\gamma\lambda)_{jl(i)}$ (corresponding to the interaction between levels of factors N and M) is statistically relevant for queries with selectivity $S = 10^{-2}$ while it is not significant for queries with low values of S. This means that, for very low selectivity, the contribution on the average cost of a given number of mutations M is independent of the number of generations G.

4 Practical Recommendations to Tune a Genetic Optimizer

In this section we present a set of practical recommendations that can help, both a user or a self-tunable system, to decide appropriate values for parameterizing a genetic optimizer for star-join queries:

N (Number of Members). The number of members in the population is the most important factor. Thus, we must be very careful choosing the proper value for this factor. In general, we recommend using populations containing a number of members equal to 8 times the number of accessed relations, knowing that $12R$ is not significantly different from $8R$.

G (Number of generations). In general, the higher the number of generations, the higher the probability to achieve a near optimal plan. Nevertheless, we must distinguish between two different scenarios. On the one hand, for queries with very restrictive constraints, we must only guarantee a minimum number of generations ($G > 50$) to get a near-optimal QEP. On the other hand, for queries with light restrictions and heavy data flows, the number of generations must be as large as possible and, in general, the limit depends on the time we can afford waiting for the optimization process. However, generally speaking, 200 generations is an interesting value since, in our results, we have observed that, in a lot of cases, it was enough to guarantee the convergence of the algorithm to the cost which could well be a near-optimal taking into account the characteristics of the queries used in the experiments.

C (Number of crossover operations). The number of genetic operations executed in each generation is important, although its impact is lower than the previous factors. In general, we recommend to use $N/2$ crossover operations per generation. However, if the implementation of these operations given a specific genetic optimizer is too time-consuming, we can afford to reduce it to $N/4$, without losing much quality.

M (Number of mutation operations). Analogously to the recommendations for C, executing a large number of mutation operations is not bad. Again, we have a trade-off between quality and time. However, in this case, we can afford reducing the number of mutation operations, even more than C.

5 Previous Work

State-of-the-art query optimizers, which typically employ dynamic programming techniques [9], have difficulties handling large number of joins due to the exponential explosion of the search space and resort to heuristic approaches. Greedy algorithms, as well as any other type of heuristic algorithm [4,12,13], do not consider the entire search space and thus may overlook the optimal plan.

Several variants of randomized algorithms have been proposed in [3,10]. Randomized search techniques like Iterative Improvement or Simulated Annealing iteratively explore the search space and converge to a nearly optimal solution.

The application of genetic algorithms to query optimization was first proposed in [1]. The first genetic optimizer prototype was created for PostgreSQL, but its search domain was reduced to left-deep trees and mutation operations were deprecated, thus bounding the search to only those properties appearing in the execution plans of the initial population. Steinbrunn et al. [10] present a detailed depiction of a genetic algorithm for query optimizers and show that its performance is always among the best when compared to competing algorithms. Genetic programming was introduced in [11] proposing a methodology closer to the nature of the problem. Muntés et al. [7] present the Carquinyoli Genetic Optimizer (CGO) which is validated for a real data workload comparing its results with a commercial optimizer.

6 Conclusions and Future Work

We have presented a statistical model that allows us to understand some unknown issues in genetic optimization. Our work lets us formulate a simple set of rules to help with the parametrization of a genetic optimizer. In particular, we have studied in depth the case for star-join queries. We have also shown that the analysis method presented in this paper is a powerful tool to analyze an optimizer and could be used to study other types of queries.

We have proven that, although the random effects of the initial population in the genetic evolution has an impact on the average cost of the obtained best plan, this does not prevent us from being able to extract general rules to tune a genetic optimizer. Nevertheless, this brings us the need for exploring new possibilities of reducing the randomness of evolutionary approaches, without loosing the essentials of the genetic algorithms mechanics. The proposed set of rules brings us a step further in the field of autonomic computing, by clarifying some aspects necessary to create a self-tuning genetic optimizer.

To summarize, our study shows that the randomness in evolutionary algorithms applied to query optimization only has a partial impact on their robustness, meaning that we can predict their general behavior and reinforce further exploration around genetic approaches.

References

1. K. Bennett, M. C. Ferris, and Y. E. Ioannidis. A genetic algorithm for database query optimization. In R. Belew and L. Booker, editors, *Proceedings of the Fourth International Conference on Genetic Algorithms*, pages 400–407, San Mateo, CA, 1991. Morgan Kaufman.
2. B. S. Everitt. *The Cambridge Dictionary of Statistics.* Cambridge Univ. Press, Cambridge, UK, 1998.
3. Y. E. Ioannidis and E. Wong. Query optimization by simulated annealing. In *SIGMOD '87: Proceedings of the 1987 ACM SIGMOD international conference on Management of data*, pages 9–22, New York, NY, USA, 1987. ACM Press.
4. R. Krishnamurthy, H. Boral, and C. Zaniolo. Optimization of nonrecursive queries. In *VLDB*, pages 128–137, 1986.
5. D. Montgomery. *Design and Analysis of Experiments.* John Wiley & Sons, New York, 1991.
6. V. Muntes, J. Aguilar, C. Zuzarte, and J. L. Larriba. An io-based cost model for the carquinyoli genetic optimizer. Technical Report UPC-DAC-RR-2005-69, Dept. d'Arqu. de Comp. UPC (http://www.dama.upc.edu), 2005.
7. V. Muntés-Mulero, J. Aguilar-Saborit, C. Zuzarte, and J.-L. Larriba-Pey. Cgo: a sound genetic optimizer for cyclic query graphs. In *Proc. of ICCS 2006*, pages 156–163, Reading, UK, May 2006. Springer-Verlag.
8. H. Scheff. *The Analysis of Variance.* John Wiley & Sons, Inc., New York, NY, USA, 1959.
9. P. G. Selinger, M. M. Astrahan, D. D. Chamberlin, R. A. Lorie, and T. G. Price. Access path selection in a relational database management system. In *Proceedings of the 1979 ACM SIGMOD international conference on Management of data*, pages 23–34. ACM Press, 1979.
10. M. Steinbrunn, G. Moerkotte, and A. Kemper. Heuristic and randomized optimization for the join ordering problem. *VLDB Journal: Very Large Data Bases*, 6(3):191–208, 1997.
11. M. Stillger and M. Spiliopoulou. Genetic programming in database query optimization. In J. R. Koza, D. E. Goldberg, D. B. Fogel, and R. L. Riolo, editors, *Genetic Programming 1996: Proceedings of the First Annual Conference*, pages 388–393, Stanford University, CA, USA, 28–31 July 1996. MIT Press.
12. A. Swami. Optimization of large join queries: combining heuristics and combinatorial techniques. In *SIGMOD '89: Proceedings of the 1989 ACM SIGMOD international conference on Management of data*, pages 367–376. ACM Press, 1989.
13. Y. Tao, Q. Zhu, C. Zuzarte, and W. Lau. Optimizing large star-schema queries with snowflakes via heuristic-based query rewriting. In *CASCON '03: Proceedings of the 2003 conference of the Centre for Advanced Studies on Collaborative research*, pages 279–293. IBM Press, 2003.

Interpolating and Using Most Likely Trajectories in Moving-Objects Databases

Byunggu Yu[1] and Seon Ho Kim[2]

[1] Computer Science Department, University of Wyoming, Laramie, WY 82071, USA
yu@uwyo.edu
[2] Computer Science Department, University of Denver, Denver, CO 80208, USA
seonkim@cs.du.edu

Abstract. In recent years, many emerging database applications deal with large sets of continuously moving data objects. Since no computer system can commit continuously occurring infinitesimal changes to the database, related data management techniques view a moving object's trajectory as a sequence of discretely reported spatiotemporal points. For each pair of consecutive committed trajectory points, a spatiotemporal uncertainty region representing all possible in-between trajectory points is defined. To support trajectory queries with a non-uniform probability distribution model, the query system needs to compute (interpolate) the "most likely" trajectories in the uncertainty regions to determine the peak points of the probability distributions. This paper proposes a generalized trajectory interpolation model using parametric trajectory representations. In addition, the paper expands and investigates three practical specializations of our proposed model using a moving object with momentum, i.e., a vehicle, as the exemplar.

1 Introduction

With advances in GPS (Global Positioning System), RFID (Radio Frequency Identification) technology, and sensor technology, emerging database applications begin to deal with large sets of objects each of which can continuously move in a geographic space and frequently report its current spatiotemporal attribute values, such as position, velocity, and acceleration, to the database server. These applications include mobile communication systems, location-based services, digital battlefields, transportations, air- or ground-traffic control systems, and sensor networks, to name a few. In the future, more complex and larger applications that deal with higher dimensional attributes (e.g., moving sensors capturing multiple stimuli) will become commonplace – increasingly complex sensor devices will proliferate alongside potential applications associated therewith.

To support such *moving-objects database* (*MOD*) applications, one requires an online database server that can store, update, and retrieve large sets of moving objects. Each moving object has both spatiotemporal properties representing the trajectory and non-spatiotemporal properties such as identification, associated phone number, and

S. Bressan, J. Küng, and R. Wagner (Eds.): DEXA 2006, LNCS 4080, pp. 718 – 727, 2006.

owner's name. Conventional database technology can efficiently manage the non-spatiotemporal properties of moving objects and efficiently process queries referring to only non-spatiotemporal properties of moving objects. To support the new applications, it is important to design and implement a MOD server that can also efficiently process queries referring to the spatiotemporal trajectories.

A MOD server must be able to keep track of the trajectories of individual moving objects to process queries referring to the trajectories. Existing techniques view a trajectory as a sequence of connected segments in a 2-, 3-, or 4-dimensional space. This is due to the fact that, although objects can continuously move or change, database management systems cannot deal with continuously occurring infinitesimal changes – this would effectively require infinite computational speed and sensor resolution. Thus, each object's combined attribute values (states) spanning multiple dimensions – location as the lowest order derivative in the spatiotemporal context, and velocity and acceleration as higher order derivatives – can only be discretely updated. In turn, each segment is associated with a certain degree of uncertainty that encloses all possible unknown locations of the object for that segment.

This paper presents our study of trajectory representation models, specifically most likely trajectory representation of moving objects with momentum. Representing the trajectory of a moving object more accurately with a fewer number of reported points is an important issue in designing MOD servers because the frequency of trajectory updates is a significant factor in determining the performance of a real-time MOD server.

This paper also proposes a solution framework for the following issue: Since queries referring to moving object trajectories are processed over the uncertainty regions, each resulting object should be associated with the probability (or likelihood) that the trajectory really satisfies the query predicate with respect to the reference object. To support this, the probability distribution of all possible states must be defined for each uncertainty region. Many practical applications require a non-uniform probability model such as the skew-normal distribution. However, there is a marked lack of investigation on this problem – relevant MOD techniques define only the uncertainty boundaries. To support probabilistic trajectory query processing with a non-uniform distribution model, the query system needs to accurately estimate the "most likely" states of the objects, given a time point, in order to determine the peak points of the corresponding probability density surfaces of all possible states.

The rest of this paper is organized as follows. Section 2 presents related work and proposes a framework for processing trajectory queries. Section 3 describes conventional line-based trajectory models, and proposes a generalized parametric trajectory model. In Section 4, we quantify our discussion by comparing real trajectory gathered from a GPS device with analytical results from our trajectory models and from conventional line-based models. Conclusions and future research directions are discussed in Section 5.

2 Related Work and Proposed Application

A moving object's trajectory stored in a database is a sequence of connected segments in space-time, and each segment has two endpoints that are consecutively reported (factual) states. Only reported states are stored in the database (due to the fact that a database cannot be continuously updated) [13]. Given the theoretical possibility of an infinite number of states between two reported states, a mathematical model and computational approach is required to manage the in-between and future states. For these reasons, a number of uncertainty models have been proposed.

One of the proposed models is as follows: at any point in time, the spatial state of each object must be within a certain distance *d*, of its last reported state; if the object moves further than *d*, it reports its new state and, if necessary, changes *d* for future updates [12]. Another model, known as the network movement model [12], is a one-dimensional model assuming that, at any point in time, the object is moving along one of a set of predetermined straight lines. Another model in [5] assumes that an update occurs whenever the object's velocity (speed or direction) changes. Other models assume that the object travels with known velocity along a straight line, but can deviate from this path by a certain distance [8, 9].

A spatial model of uncertainty in the recorded trajectories is found in [4]. Assuming the maximum velocity of an object (one of the properties of the object's *dynamics*) is known, all possible states of the object during the time interval between two consecutive observations lie on a certain ellipse (called the error ellipse). With this model, any update policy can be used to optimize the database system: Several update policies (also known as the dead-reckoning policies), such as the fixed time-interval update, plain dead-reckoning, and adaptive dead-reckoning, have been separately investigated [11]. Although we can generalize this ellipse model to 3- or higher dimensional moving objects using the notion of hyper-ellipse, this model is inefficient for spatiotemporal range queries: a 3-dimensional spatiotemporal query window whose extent is 0.1 along every dimension occupies 0.1^3 in the original space-time but 0.1^2 (a much larger portion) in the projected space, resulting in an enlarged search space. A spatiotemporal uncertainty model that produces 3-dimensional cylindrical uncertainty regions representing the past uncertainties of trajectories is found in [10].

More recently developed uncertainty model reported in [14] formally defines both past and future "spatiotemporal" uncertainties of trajectories of any dimensionality. Figure 1 shows two examples of this trajectory uncertainty model, given the maximum velocity M_v. The *uncertainty region* of the object during t_i-t_j is defined to be the overlap between the two cones whose tops are, respectively, P_1 and P_2. The *snapshot* of the object at any time point t_k that is between t_i and t_j is the uncertainty region's cross section produced by the cutting plane $time = t_k$.

One can further improve this model (i.e., reduce the size of the spatiotemporal uncertainty region) by taking into account more dynamics and derivatives related to velocity, acceleration, and even higher derivatives (please contact the authors for more details).

Because of this uncertainty, each result object of a query referring to the trajectories must be associated with the probability (or likelihood) that the item really satisfies the query predicate. This is more pronounced when the uncertainty regions are very large. As an extreme case, let us suppose that the uncertainty regions are bounded only by the boundaries of the data space (i.e., $M_v = \infty$). In this case, given any query point, or region, at a point *t* in time, every object has a non-zero probability that it intersects the query point or region at *t*, except for the ones that have an exact state at *t*. Therefore, in order to properly adopt existing trajectory query processing algorithms (e.g., [2, 3]), one needs a probability distribution model that can represent the probability distribution of all possible states of each snapshot.

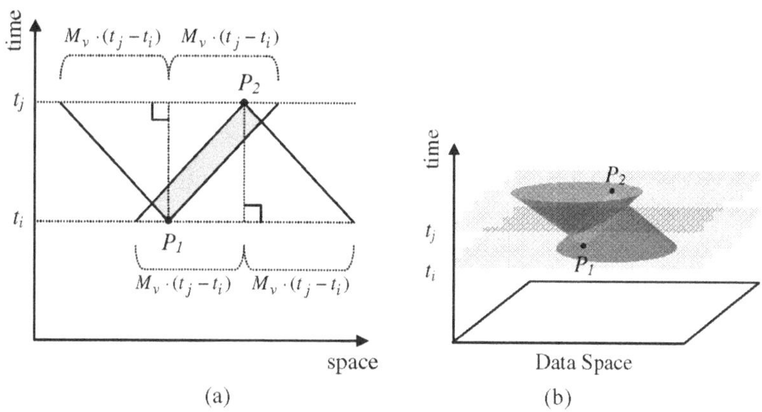

Fig. 1. Spatiotemporal uncertainty region representing a trajectory segment: (a) in a 2-dimensional space-time; (b) in a 3-dimensional space-time

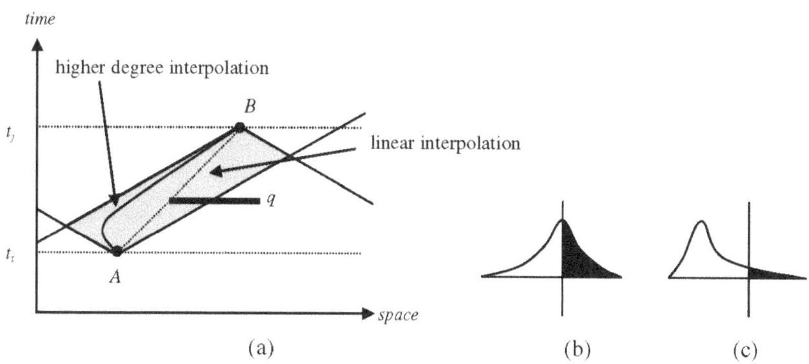

Fig. 2. (a) shows a trajectory segment that can possibly intersect q, where q is a query region; (b) and (c) show skew-normal probability distributions of a snapshot that overlaps q

As shown in Figures 2a and 2b, given a time point, the linear trajectory interpolation model can be used to determine the peak of the skew-normal probability density surface [1, 7] of all possible states. In this case, because the query range, q, reaches the peak point, the linear model reports 50 % of the probability that the actual state is covered by q (Figure 2b). However, considering a more skewed distribution of possible states (Figures 2a and 2c), the linear model reports too optimistic results because the probability becomes much lower than 50%. Our proposed "most likely" trajectory model will more accurately estimate the actual trajectory, resulting in a more accurate estimation of the probability.

3 Most Likely Trajectory: A Parametric Approach

We propose a generalized, parametric trajectory interpolation model (Definition 1) connecting any two consecutive reported states.

Definition 1. Given a pair <P_i P_j> of consecutive reported states, the most likely trajectory segment of degree $2n+1$ is defined as follows:

$P^{(0)}(u) = \sum_{k=0}^{2n+1} a_k u^k$, where $0 \leq u \leq 1$ is a free-variable parameter, $n \geq 0$ is the number of derivatives written in each reported state P and the coefficients are derived by solving the following constraints for $a_0, a_1, \ldots, a_{2n+1}$: for ($l$=0; $l \leq n$; l++) {$P^{(l)}(u=0)=P_i^{(l)}$ and $P^{(l)}(u=1)=P_j^{(l)}$}, where $P^{(l)}$ is the lth derivative of a state P.

Given any pair <P_i P_j> of consecutive reported states, most MOD techniques, as surveyed in [10, 13], uses the linear interpolation (i.e., a special case of Definition 1 with n=0) assuming that the velocity of the object is fixed during the time period of the segment. The first non-linear model investigated in [13] is a special case of Definition 1 with n=1 assuming that the acceleration changes linearly in only one direction during the period. In contrast, the 5th degree trajectory (n=2), which is possible in our model, can accommodate smoothly changing accelerations. Considering fast changing objects that are affected by momentum, not only the locations but also some higher order derivatives change without angle. Unlike fast changing objects, some slowly changing objects (e.g., animals and humans) can change velocity more abruptly. Importantly, the generalized trajectory interpolation model in Definition 1 provides a basis for investigating optimization solutions that, given a proper description of a moving-objects set, can adaptively choose the most efficient equation (i.e., $n \geq 1$).

3.1 Specialization 1

Considering a discrete sequence of reported states each of which is a location-time <X, Y, Z, T>, where X, Y, and Z are spatial coordinates and T is a time value, Definition 1 can be specialized to obtain a connected sequence of spatiotemporal linear trajectory segments that passes through the joints (reported states) <$P_0^{(0)}$ $P_1^{(0)}$ $P_2^{(0)}$ … $P_n^{(0)}$> where, for all $k = 0,..,n$, $P_k^{(0)}$ is a location-time <X_k, Y_k, Z_k, T_k> in the data space-time.

To spatiotemporally connect consecutive reported states $P_i^{(0)}$ and $P_j^{(0)}$, where i = 0,..,n-1 and $j = i+1$, we use the following parametric linear function (a special case of Definition 1 with n = 0): $P^{(0)}(u) = a_0+a_1u$. To derive the coefficients, solve the following constraints for a_0 and a_1: $P^{(0)}(u=0)= P_i^{(0)}$ and $P^{(0)}(u=1)= P_j^{(0)}$. Substituting the derived coefficients into the parametric linear function, we have the following function:

$$P^{(0)}(u) = \begin{bmatrix} 1 & u \end{bmatrix} \begin{bmatrix} 1 & 0 \\ -1 & 1 \end{bmatrix} \begin{bmatrix} P_i^{(0)} \\ P_j^{(0)} \end{bmatrix}, \quad (1)$$

where $0 \leq u \leq 1$.

3.2 Specialization 2

Considering a sequence of reported trajectory states each of which consists of a location-time <X, Y, Z, T> and a velocity <X'=ΔX/ΔT, Y'=ΔY/ΔT, Z'=ΔZ/ΔT>, one can use a parametric cubic function $P^{(0)}(u) = a_0+a_1u+a_2u^2+a_3u^3$ (a special case of Definition 1) to connect each pair of two consecutive joint-velocities <$P_i^{(0)}$ $P_i^{(1)}$> and <$P_j^{(0)}$ $P_j^{(1)}$>, where $P_i^{(0)}$ = <X_i, Y_i, Z_i, T_i>, $P_j^{(0)}$ = <X_j, Y_j, Z_j, T_j>, $P_i^{(1)}$ = <$X_i' \cdot (T_j-T_i)$, $Y_i' \cdot (T_j-T_i)$, $Z_i' \cdot (T_j-T_i)$, T_j-T_i>, and $P_j^{(1)}$ = <$X_j' \cdot (T_j-T_i)$, $Y_j' \cdot (T_j-T_i)$, $Z_j' \cdot (T_j-T_i)$, T_j-T_i>.

One can derive the coefficients of $P^{(0)}(u) = a_0+a_1u+a_2u^2+a_3u^3$ by solving the following constraints for a_0, a_1, a_2, and a_3: $P^{(0)}(u=0) = P_i^{(0)}$; $P^{(0)}(u=1) = P_j^{(0)}$; $P^{(1)}(u=0) = P_i^{(1)}$; $P^{(1)}(u=1) = P_j^{(1)}$. Substituting these coefficients into the polynomial equation, we have the following function:

$$P^{(0)}(u) = [1 \quad u \quad u^2 \quad u^3]\begin{bmatrix} 1 & 0 & 0 & 0 \\ 0 & 0 & 1 & 0 \\ -3 & 3 & -2 & -1 \\ 2 & -2 & 1 & 1 \end{bmatrix}\begin{bmatrix} P_i^{(0)} \\ P_j^{(0)} \\ P_i^{(1)} \\ P_j^{(1)} \end{bmatrix}, \tag{2}$$

where $0 \leq u \leq 1$.

3.3 Specialization 3

Considering a sequence of reported states each of which consists of a location-time <X, Y, Z, T>, a velocity <X'=ΔX/ΔT, Y'=ΔY/ΔT, Z'=ΔZ/ΔT>, and an acceleration <X''=ΔX'/ΔT, Y''=ΔY'/ΔT, Z''=ΔZ'/ΔT>, we can use a parametric function of degree 5, $P^{(0)}(u) = a_0+a_1u+a_2u^2+a_3u^3+a_4u^4+a_5u^5$ (a special case of Definition 1), to connect each pair of two consecutive joint-velocity-accelerations $<P_i^{(0)}\ P_i^{(1)}\ P_i^{(2)}>$ and $<P_j^{(0)}\ P_j^{(1)}\ P_j^{(2)}>$, where $P_i^{(0)} = <X_i, Y_i, Z_i, T_i>$; $P_j^{(0)} = <X_j, Y_j, Z_j, T_j>$; $P_i^{(1)} = <X_i'\cdot(T_j-T_i), Y_i'\cdot(T_j-T_i), Z_i'\cdot(T_j-T_i), T_j-T_i>$; $P_j^{(1)} = <X_j'\cdot(T_j-T_i), Y_j'\cdot(T_j-T_i), Z_j'\cdot(T_j-T_i), T_j-T_i>$; $P_i^{(2)} = <X_i''\cdot(T_j-T_i)^2, Y_i''\cdot(T_j-T_i)^2, Z_i''\cdot(T_j-T_i)^2, 0>$; $P_j^{(2)} = <X_j''\cdot(T_j-T_i)^2, Y_j''\cdot(T_j-T_i)^2, Z_j''\cdot(T_j-T_i)^2, 0>$.

One can derive the coefficients of $P^{(0)}(u) = a_0+a_1u+a_2u^2+a_3u^3+a_4u^4+a_5u^5$ by solving the following constraints for a_0, a_1, a_2, a_3, a_4, and a_5: $P^{(0)}(u=0) = P_i^{(0)}$; $P^{(0)}(u=1) = P_j^{(0)}$; $P^{(1)}(u=0) = P_i^{(1)}$; $P^{(1)}(u=1) = P_j^{(1)}$; $P^{(2)}(u=0) = P_i^{(2)}$; $P^{(2)}(u=1) = P_j^{(2)}$. Substituting these coefficients into the parametric function, we have the following function:

$$P^{(0)}(u) = [1 \quad u \quad u^2 \quad u^3 \quad u^4 \quad u^5]\begin{bmatrix} 1 & 0 & 0 & 0 & 0 & 0 \\ 0 & 0 & 1 & 0 & 0 & 0 \\ 0 & 0 & 0 & 0 & 0.5 & 0 \\ -10 & 10 & -6 & -4 & -1.5 & 0.5 \\ 15 & -15 & 8 & 7 & 1.5 & -1 \\ -6 & 6 & -3 & -3 & -0.5 & 0.5 \end{bmatrix}\begin{bmatrix} P_i^{(0)} \\ P_j^{(0)} \\ P_i^{(1)} \\ P_j^{(1)} \\ P_i^{(2)} \\ P_j^{(2)} \end{bmatrix}, \tag{3}$$

where $0 \leq u \leq 1$.

4 Experiment

To compare the three specialized models of the most likely trajectory, we placed a GPS device (Trimgle Navigation's ProXRS Receiver with GPS logger) in a car and drove from a location near the north boundary of Denver, Colorado, to Loveland, Colorado, USA along Interstate highway 25. Every second, we logged a spatiotemporal data from the GPS device. The acceleration vector of each logged state was calculated using the second degree approximation on the recorded velocities (for the first and the last trajectory points, the first degree approximation was used). Then, we divided the recorded trajectory states, each of which consists of a location-time

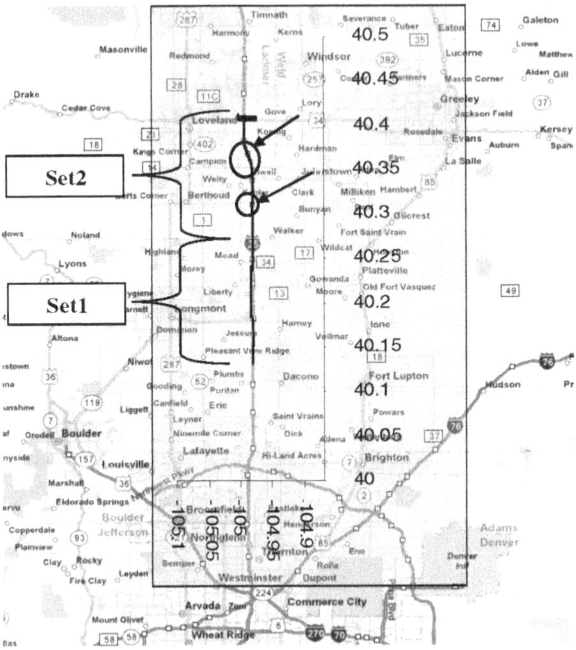

Fig. 3. A real trajectory states collected

<longitude, latitude, altitude, time>, a velocity <longitude', latitude', altitude'>, and a derived acceleration <longitude'', latitude'', altitude''>, into two subsets: Set1 consisted of 482 recorded states logged every second; Set2 consisted of 742 recorded states logged every second. Note that Set1 represents driving on a relatively straight road and Set2 represents some winding trajectory.

For each of Set1 and Set2, we randomly selected logged spatiotemporal records with various sampling ratios. The three specialized models (i.e., Equations 1, 2, and 3) were used to connect the selected samples (4-dimensional spatiotemporal trajectories were produced). Figure 4 gives a magnified view of the circled parts in Figure 3 (the sampling ratio was about 5%; for illustration sake, we projected the 4-dimensional spatiotemporal trajectories onto the XY-plane).

For each of the three specialized models, we quantified the actual deviations between the non-sampled real location-times and the corresponding estimates. In all tested cases, the higher degree models, Equations 2 and 3, produced significantly smaller average deviations (up to more than 3 times smaller, Figure 5) and standard error deviations (Figure 6) than the linear model Equation 1. For example, with 37 sampled out of 742 states in Set2, the average distance deviation of Equations 1, 2, and 3 were 19, 21, and 62 meters, respectively. Their maximum deviations in this section were 162, 231, and 683 meters, respectively. As shown in Figure 6, the standard deviations in this section were 35, 41, and 134 meters.

For all cases, we observed that the difference between the linear model and the higher degree models was significant and became greater when the actual trajectory is winding (Set2) (Figures 5 and 6). In most cases, the 5th degree model excelled the 3rd degree model.

In our experiments using a Linux machine equipped with an Intel Pentium III 800MHz and 256MB main memory space, the linear model took 0.7 – 0.8 microseconds of CPU time to interpolate a point in-between two consecutive joint states. The cubic model and the 5th degree model required 4.3 – 4.6 microseconds and 10.8 – 11.1 microseconds, respectively.

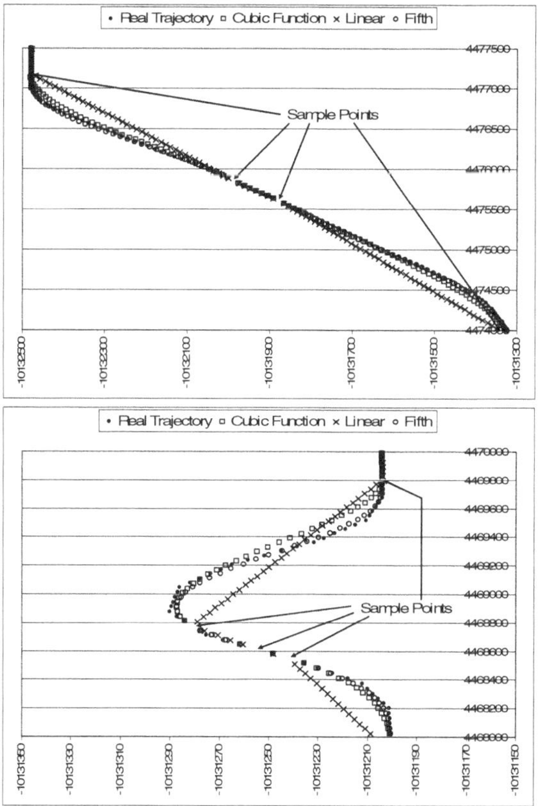

Fig. 4. Two parts of the trajectory projected onto XY-plane and elongated along X-axis for better visual comparison: the X-axis is longitude in meters; the Y-axis is latitude in meters; the sampling ratio was 37/742 (≈ 5%)

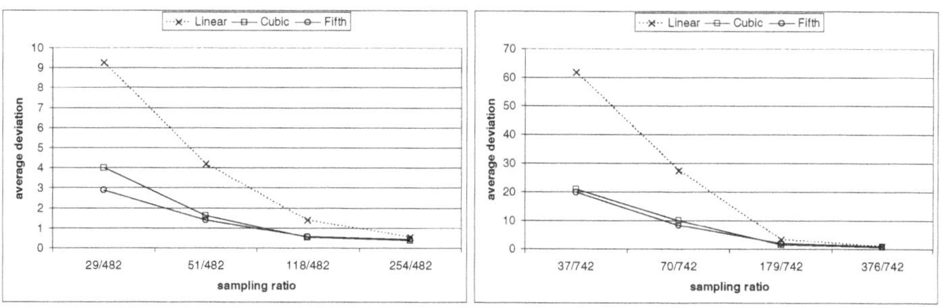

(a) (b)

Fig. 5. Average spatial deviations (in meters) with various sampling ratios on (a) Set1 and (b) Set2

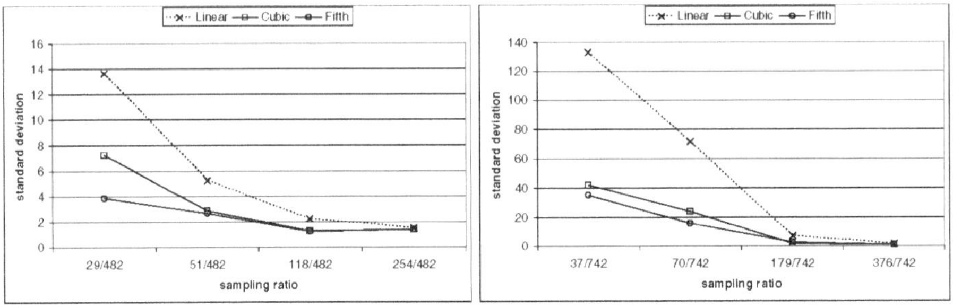

(a) (b)

Fig. 6. Standard error deviations (in meters): (a) Set1 and (b) Set2

5 Discussion

For the tested cases, both velocity and acceleration varied smoothly because of the momentum gained while moving. However, the linear model assumes that the velocity of the object is fixed during the period of each segment and the 3rd degree model assumes that the acceleration changes linearly in only one direction during the period. The 5th degree model considers both varying velocity and acceleration so it can present the most accurate trajectories with the same set of recorded states, which can be used for a better estimation of the probabilistic trajectory queries.

Moreover, the performance of MOD can be significantly enhanced as follows: 1) given a maximum allowed deviation between a point of a database trajectory and the corresponding point of the real trajectory, a smaller number of trajectory update transactions is required; 2) a reduced amount of secondary storage space is occupied by trajectories, 3) the trajectory index structure size is reduced; 4) a smaller number of disk I/Os are performed in processing trajectory update transactions and trajectory queries. For example, given a maximum deviation threshold (e.g., 62 meters) for update, the higher degree models reduce the number required updates by a factor of up to 5. In typical situations, this has more significant impacts on the system performance and scalability than the CPU overhead. However, investigating the relevant issues in developing an adaptive system that can automatically balance the CPU-I/O trade-offs using various trajectory models will be practically viable for some application systems that have a severely limited CPU power or extremely fast secondary storage.

By taking into account for how the environment may be variably constraining movement and thus variably affecting the set of possible positions of the object, one can contextualize (modify) the probability distribution as well as the most likely trajectory state of each individual snapshot. A related preliminary study, contextualizing the probability distribution of vehicle whereabouts with geographic road data sets, can be found in [6]. If the contextualization of uncertainty regions can be properly performed, the spatiotemporal regions requiring indexing can also be commensurately limited and the query results will be associated with more probable likelihoods. We reserve this as our future work.

References

1. Azzalini and A. Capitanio, "Statistical applications of the multivariate skew-normal distribution. Journal of the Royal Statistical Society," B(61): 579—602, 1999.
2. R. Cheng, D.V. Kalashnikov, and S. Prabhakar, "Evaluating Probabilistic Queries over Imprecise Data," ACM SIGMOD, 551—562, 2003.
3. R. Cheng, D.V. Kalashnikov, and S. Prabhakar, "Querying Imprecise Data in Moving Object Environments," IEEE TKDE, 16:9, 1112—1126, 2004.
4. D. Pfoser and C.S. Jensen, "Capturing the Uncertainty of Moving-Objects Representations," SSDBM 123—132, 1999.
5. D. Pfoser and C.S. Jensen, "Querying the Trajectories of On-Line Mobile Objects," ACM MobiDE, 66—73, 2001.
6. S.D. Prager, "Environmental Contextualization of Uncertainty for Moving Objects," GeoComputation, Ann Arbor, Michigan, 2005.
7. Development Core Team R: A language and environment for statistical computing, R Foundation for Statistical Computing, Vienna, Austria, 2004.
8. A.P. Sistla, O. Wolfson, S. Chamberlain, and S. Dao, "Querying the Uncertain Position of Moving Objects. Temporal Databases," Research and Practice, no. 1399, 1998.
9. G. Trajcevski, O. Wolfson, F. Zhang, and S. Chamberlain, "The Geometry of Uncertainty in Moving Object Databases," Int'l Conf. on Extending Database Technology, 2002.
10. G. Trajcevski, O. Wolfson, K. Hinrichs, and S. Chamberlain, "Managing Uncertainty in Moving Objects Databases", ACM Transactions on Database Systems, Vol. 29, No. 3, 463-507, 2004.
11. O. Wolfson, L. Jiang, A.P. Sistla, S. Chamberlain, N. Rishe, and M. Deng, "Databases for Tracking Mobile Units in Real Time," ICDT International Conference on Database Theory, Lecture Notes in Computer Science, Springer-Verlag, Berlin Heidelberg New York, 169—186, 1998.
12. O. Wolfson, A.P. Sistla, S. Chamberlain, and Y. Yesha, "Updating and Querying Databases that Track Mobile Units. Distributed and Parallel Databases," 7:3, 257—387, 1999.
13. B. Yu, S.H. Kim, T. Bailey, and R. Gamboa, "Curve-Based Representation of Moving Object Trajectories," IEEE International Database Engineering and Applications Symposium, 419—425, 2004.
14. B. Yu, S.D. Prager, and T. Bailey, "The Isosceles-Triangle Uncertainty Model: A Spatiotemporal Uncertainty Model for Continuously Changing Data," In: C. Gold (Eds.), Workshop on Dynamic & Multi-dimensional GIS, International Society for Photogrammetry and Remote Sensing, XXXVI:2/W29, ISPRS ICWG II/IV, Wales, UK, 179—183, 2005.

Relaxing Constraints on GeoPQL Operators to Improve Query Answering

Arianna D'Ulizia[1], Fernando Ferri[1], Patrizia Grifoni[1], and Maurizio Rafanelli[2]

[1] IRPPS-CNR, via Nizza 128, 00198 Roma, Italy
{arianna.dulizia, fernando.ferri, patrizia.grifoni}@irpps.cnr.it
[2] IASI-CNR, viale Manzoni 30, 00185 Roma, Italy
rafanelli@iasi.cnr.it

Abstract. In this paper the problem of matching a query with imprecise or missing data is analyzed for geographic information systems, and an approach for the relaxation query constraints is proposed. This approach, similarly with the 9-intersection matrix between two sets of points presented in [1] [2] [3], proposes the representation of two symbolic graphical objects (SGO) in terms of interior, boundary, and exterior points, applied to each of the configurations between two objects. The paper distinguishes the different configurations considering the results obtained from the 9 intersections, not only by whether results are null or not null. This approach allows a more detailed similarity graph to be defined. The aim of the proposed methodology is to relax geographical query constraints, in order to obtain meaningful answers for imprecise or missing data. In this paper the polyline-polygon case is discussed in detail.

Keywords: Geographical query languages, relaxing constraints, spatial operators.

1 Introduction

Many authors have studied how to formulate queries using pictorial configurations. This technique is particularly common when querying geographical databases. A pictorial query on a geographical database allows the user to describe the configuration of the geographical objects of interest, expressing his/her "mental model" of the query [4]. When a query search condition does not match with those in the database, users would rather receive approximate answers by relaxing some constraints than no information at all. It would therefore be useful to obtain as answers not only configurations exactly matching the sketch representing the pictorial query, but also similar configurations obtained by relaxing some of the constraints in the pictorial query. The most common approach for relaxing constraints is to measure the distance from the drawn query using criteria defined for the specific domain. Criteria for constraint selection generally involve the definition of weights assigned to the different types of constraints and, within these, to the specific constraint expressed in the query.

In the case of pictorial queries on a geographical database, constraints can be classified as three main types: spatial, structural, and semantic. In this paper spatial constraints refer to the spatial relationships existing between geographical objects, structural constraints refer to the internal characteristics of geographical objects and

S. Bressan, J. Küng, and R. Wagner (Eds.): DEXA 2006, LNCS 4080, pp. 728 – 737, 2006.

semantic constraints refer to the concepts represented by the geographical objects. These types of constraints and how to relax them have been discussed in various papers in literature.

With reference to the spatial constraints in [5], [6], in order to decide which constraints should be relaxed and which must be maintained a computational model must be defined for the similarity of the spatial relations by which to transform the pictorial query. This query, drawn by a sketch, can be represented as a semantic network of objects and the binary relations among them. Each object corresponds to one node. The oriented edges between two nodes correspond to the binary spatial relations. This paper considers five types of spatial relations: base topological binary, detailed topological binary, metric refining, base cardinal directions, and detailed cardinal directions. A weight for the possible relaxation of each relation is considered. The similarity between topological relations is described by the conceptual *similarity graph,* which links the most similar relations, defining the weight of each relaxation. The answers to queries made using a sketch are given assigning a total score calculated by the computational model.

Structural constraints can be relaxed by evaluating the similarity between geographical objects. As they are described by a set of attributes, a measure of the structural similarity of two geographical objects can be obtained by considering the similarity of their attributes, types and values [7]. This approach is frequently used to measure the concept similarity starting from the attributes, which describe the concept and similarity of XML documents, whose structure is described by a tree.

Finally, the semantic constraint can be relaxed. This means that even if a concept expressed in the pictorial query is missing in the geographical database, it can be substituted with a similar concept which is present.

In this paper we discuss the relaxation of spatial constraints. Various papers in the last few years have studied problems regarding topological relations between pairs of objects in a 2-dimensional space. Two models for binary topological relations - the 4-Intersection model and the 9-Intersection model - have been proposed [1, 2, 3] and compared [8]. Two more models of conceptual similarity among topological relations between a line and a region were then developed from this start point [9]. A further study of spatial similarity and a computational method to evaluate the similarity of spatial scenes based on the ordering of spatial relations is discussed in [10].

More recently, two papers studied spatial neighborhoods between objects [11, 12]. In [11] the authors examined topological relations between two regions, comparing two strategies to minimize topological constraints in a query expressed by a visual example, and presenting search results in terms of number and similarity values. In [12] the authors presented an idea on how results of qualitative spatial reasoning can be exploited in reasoning about action and change. They investigated how its conceptual neighborhood structure can be applied in the situation calculus for qualitative reasoning about relative positional information.

The paper is structured as follows: in Section 2 the GeoPQL operators are briefly introduced and two query examples are given, Section 3 examines a computational model for determining the most conceptually similar relations for each configuration and studies the polyline-polygon relation and finally Section 4 concludes.

2 GeoPQL Operators

The Geographical Pictorial Query Language (GeoPQL, [4] and its evolutions [13][14]) allow the user to specify queries using *symbolic graphical objects (SGO)* that have the appearance of the three classic types of shapes: point, polyline and polygon. The user can assign each SGO with a semantic linked to the different kinds of information (layers) in the geographical database. Constraints can be imposed on both the attributes of the geographical data and their topological position and the query's target information (a specified layer or a set of layers) can be specified. Queries can thus be formulated by simply drawing a spatial representation of the SGO without the need to know a complex syntax or the database's structure. The GeoPQL algebra consists of 12 operators: Geo-union, Geo-difference, Geo-disjunction, Geo-touching, Geo-inclusion, Geo-crossing, Geo-pass-through, Geo-overlapping, Geo-equality, Geo-distance, Geo-any and Geo-alias. Geo-touching is equivalent to the *meet* operator, Geo-crossing refers to the crossing of two polylines, Geo-pass-through refers to a polyline which passes through a polygon, Geo-alias allows the same SGO to be duplicated in order to express the OR operator, and, finally, Geo-any permits any relationship between a pair of SGO to be considered valid, i.e. there is no constraint between the two SGO. This operator allows an unambiguous visual query to be obtained. For example, Figure 1 shows two pictorial queries, Q1 and Q2, which represent sketches of the mental models of the user's queries:

Q1 "Find all the *Provinces* which are PASSED THROUGH by a *River*"
Q2 "Find all the *Regions* which are PASSED THROUGH by a *River* AND which OVERLAP a *Forest*".

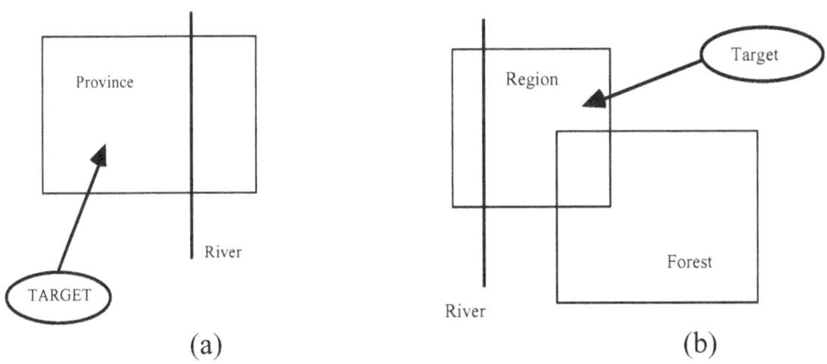

Fig. 1. Query examples in GeoPQL

3 Constraint Relaxation for Polyline-Polygon Configurations

The real world in the geographic domain can be represented as a set of features, called Symbolic Graphical Objects (SGO) [4]: *Point*, *Polyline*, and *Polygon*. This representation is used in GeoPQL to draw pictorial queries and obtain both the number of SGO, which verify the query, and the objects selected in the geographical database, which are the result of the query target.

To relax the constraints which produce a null value as the answer to a given query, we need to define the conceptual similarity graph of the possible configurations between a pair of SGO. Each configuration identifies a set of GeoPQL operators. A brief analysis of the spatial configuration between a polygon and a polyline is given below.

First, we define a polyline, which is strictly connected to the concept of topological curve, i.e. a geometrical one-dimensional and continuous object. Formally, a topological curve is defined as follows. Let I be an interval of real numbers (i.e. a non-empty connected subset of $\mathbb{R}$). Then a curve γ is a continuous mapping $\gamma : I \to X$, where X is a topological space. The curve γ is said to be simple if it is injective, i.e. if for all x, y in I, we have $\gamma(x) = \gamma(y) \to x = y$. If I is a closed bounded interval $[a, b]$, we also allow the possibility $\gamma(a) = \gamma(b)$ and we say that γ is closed. So by polyline, we mean a topological curve that can also be closed.

This study considered a large number of different configurations between a polyline and a polygon.

In [1] the authors distinguish 19 different binary topological relationships using the 9-Intersection model, which defines binary topological relations between a polyline L and a polygon P on the basis of the nine intersections of L's interior (L°), boundary (∂L) and exterior (L⁻) with the interior (P°), boundary (∂P) and exterior (P⁻) of P. The following 3x3 matrix is used to represent these criteria:

$$\begin{pmatrix} L^\circ \cap P^\circ & L^\circ \cap \partial P & L^\circ \cap P^- \\ \partial L \cap P^\circ & \partial L \cap \partial P & \partial L \cap P^- \\ L^- \cap P^\circ & L^- \cap \partial P & L^- \cap P^- \end{pmatrix}$$

The matrix values are empty (∅) or not-empty (¬∅), depending on the intersection set (empty or not-empty).

We have drawn more than 19 configurations, so we have determined the correspondence between our configurations and the 19 relations drawn in [1][2]. We found that different configurations correspond to the same 9-Intersection matrix. Figure 2 shows all the configurations we drew and their corresponding 9-Intersection matrices.

Each configuration considered in Figure 2 identifies a set of GeoPQL operators. For example, if we consider the configuration in the first row of Figure 2, we have the following association between configuration and association:

A: Geo-disjunction; B: Geo-touching; C: Geo-touching; D: Geo-touching, Geo-inclusion; E: Geo-touching, Geo-inclusion.

To distinguish configurations that correspond to the same 9-Intersection matrix, the paper considers the number of contact points (touching or crossing) between the two objects, i.e. the cardinality (number of points) of the intersection between the polyline's interior and the boundary of the polygon. For example, considering configurations with the same 9-Intersection matrix, in Figure 3a the cardinality of $(L^\circ \cap \partial P)$ is 2, while in Figure 3b the cardinality of $(L^\circ \cap \partial P)$ is 4.

These considerations led us to consider three matrices, the first to represent the point cardinality of the intersection of the polyline's interior, boundary and exterior with the interior, boundary and exterior of the polygon, the second to represent the polyline cardinality of the same intersection sets and the third to represent the polygon cardinality of the same intersection sets. These are called zero-dimensional 9-Intersection matrix M_0, one-dimensional 9-Intersection matrix M_1 and bi-dimensional 9-Intersection matrix M_2. Zero-dimensional matrix elements are represented by $|L \cap P|_P$ to indicate the point cardinality of the intersection. In the same way, one-dimensional matrix elements are represented by $|L \cap P|_L$ and bi-dimensional matrix elements by $|L \cap P|_A$.

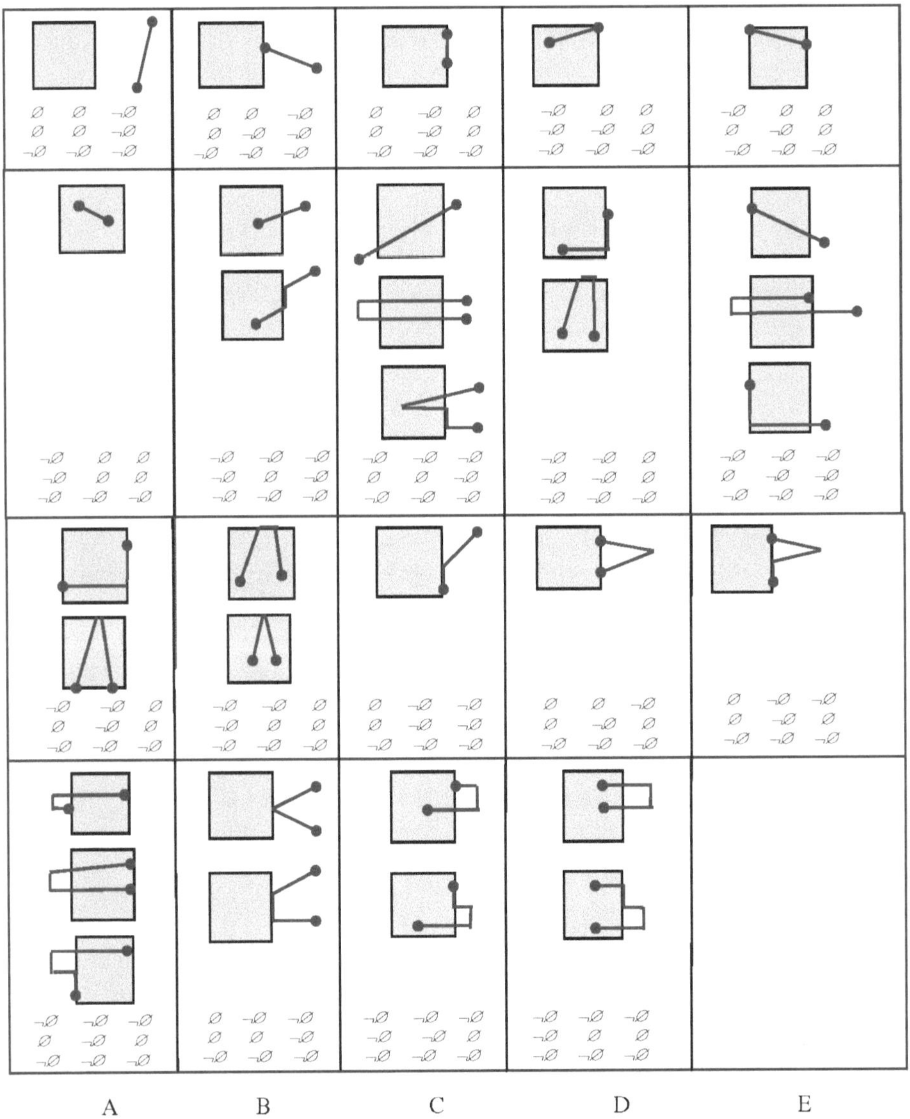

Fig. 2. Configurations between a polyline and a polygon

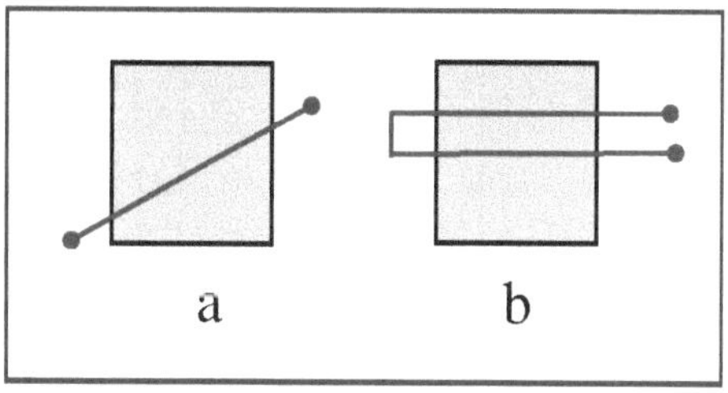

Fig. 3. Configurations with different cardinality for the intersection ($L^\circ \cap \partial P$)

$$\mathbf{M_0} = \begin{pmatrix} |L^\circ \cap P^\circ|_P & |L^\circ \cap \partial P|_P & |L^\circ \cap P^-|_P \\ |\partial L \cap P^\circ|_P & |\partial L \cap \partial P|_P & |\partial L \cap P^-|_P \\ |L^- \cap P^\circ|_P & |L^- \cap \partial P|_P & |L^- \cap P^-|_P \end{pmatrix}$$

$$\mathbf{M_1} = \begin{pmatrix} |L^\circ \cap P^\circ|_L & |L^\circ \cap \partial P|_L & |L^\circ \cap P^-|_L \\ |\partial L \cap P^\circ|_L & |\partial L \cap \partial P|_L & |\partial L \cap P^-|_L \\ |L^- \cap P^\circ|_L & |L^- \cap \partial P|_L & |L^- \cap P^-|_L \end{pmatrix}$$

$$\mathbf{M_2} = \begin{pmatrix} |L^\circ \cap P^\circ|_A & |L^\circ \cap \partial P|_A & |L^\circ \cap P^-|_A \\ |\partial L \cap P^\circ|_A & |\partial L \cap \partial P|_A & |\partial L \cap P^-|_A \\ |L^- \cap P^\circ|_A & |L^- \cap \partial P|_A & |L^- \cap P^-|_A \end{pmatrix}$$

We modified the domain of Egenhofer and Herring's 9-Intersection matrix from $\{\varnothing, \neg\varnothing\}$ to the set of natural numbers, to indicate the intersection cardinality.

We can distinguish an infinite number of configurations with this formalism. For brevity, Figure 4 gives all the configurations drawn and their corresponding zero-dimensional, one-dimensional and bi-dimensional 9-Intersection matrices.

As the aim of our work was to design a computational model to determine the most conceptually similar relations for each configuration, we introduce a similarity graph. This connects all configurations by the lowest topological distance. To calculate the distance between two configurations, c_A and c_B, we calculate the differences of the corresponding elements in each of the three matrices and then compute the sum.

$$D_{C_A,C_B} = \sum_{K=0}^{2} \sum_{i=0}^{2} \sum_{j=0}^{2} M_K^A[i,j] - M_K^B[i,j] \tag{1}$$

The following rules are used to execute the differences, to indicate the difference between an empty intersection, an intersection with a finite number of elements (points, polylines or polygons) and an intersection with an infinite number of elements:

$$\infty - n = 1 \qquad n - \infty = 1 \qquad \infty - 0 = 2 \qquad 0 - \infty = 2 \qquad \infty - \infty = 0$$

$$0 - 0 = 0 \qquad n - 0 = 1 \qquad 0 - n = 1 \qquad n - m = 0 \qquad \forall\, n, m \in N^+$$

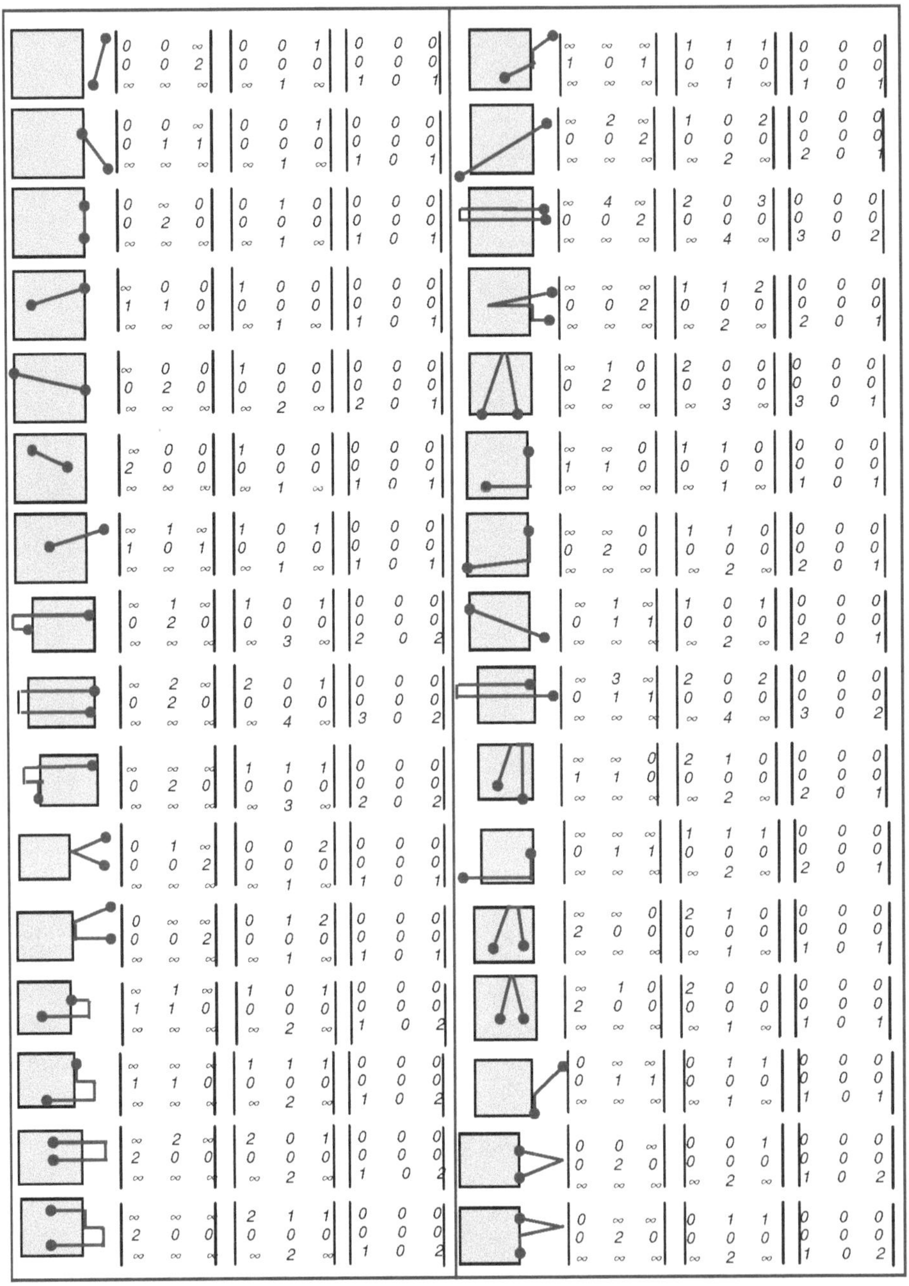

Fig. 4. Configurations between a polyline and a polygon and 9-intersection matrices

So we can develop a similarity graph in which each configuration is depicted as a node and the topological distances are the links between the nodes. A set of GeoPQL operators can be associated with each spatial configuration, as described for Figure 2.

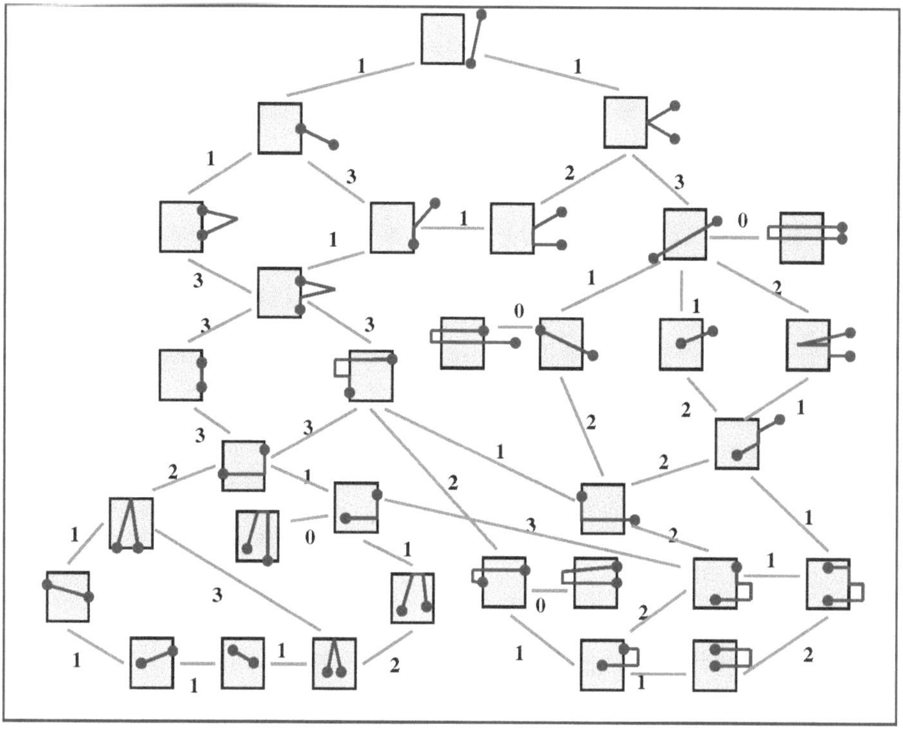

Fig. 5. The similarity graph for the considered configurations

Figure 5 shows the similarity graph for the configurations of Figure 2. Nodes are configurations and edges represent topological distances between configurations measured using the formula (1). Some configuration pairs may have 0 topological distance, however a more accurate measure of similarity can be considered and configurations with 0 topological distance can be sorted by increasing cardinality.

For example, the two configurations shown in Figure 3 and again in the top right of the graph in Figure 5 have 0 topological distance. The corresponding matrices M_0, M_1 and M_2 differ for some elements, as shown in Figure 6.

To calculate the configuration's total cardinality we sum the cardinalities of all intersections with a finite number of elements, i.e. all the elements of M_0, M_1 and M_2 that are different from 0 and ∞. In this example, configuration (a) has a total cardinality of 12, while configuration (b) has a total cardinality of 20.

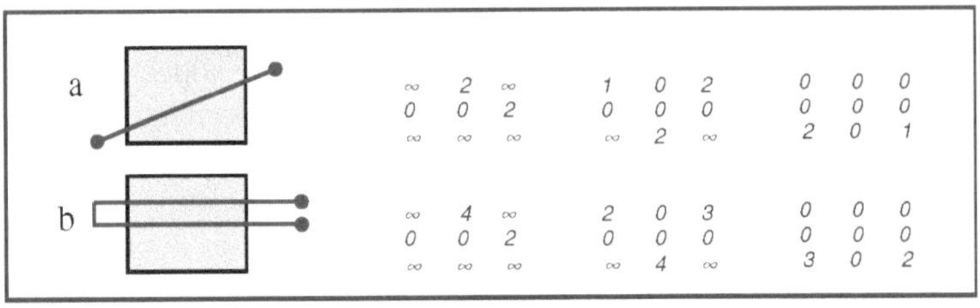

Fig. 6. Similarity of a pair of configurations with 0 topological distance

4 Discussion and Conclusion

In this paper we considered a large number of different configurations between a polyline and a polygon, more than the 19 different binary topological relationships presented in [1][2]. We determined the correspondence between our configurations and these 19 relations. To distinguish the different configurations having the same 9-Intersection matrix we considered the number of contact points (touching or crossing) between the two objects, i.e. the cardinality (number of points) of the intersection between the polyline's interior and the boundary of the polygon.

This led us to consider three matrices, the first to represent the point cardinality of the intersection of polyline's interior, boundary and exterior with those of the polygon, the second to represent the polyline cardinality of the same intersection sets and the third to represent the polygon cardinality of the same intersection sets. We modified the domain of the 9-Intersection matrix in [1][2] from $\{\emptyset, \neg\emptyset\}$ to the set of natural numbers to indicate the intersection cardinality, thus distinguishing an infinite number of configurations. In order to design a computational model to determine the most conceptually similar relations for each configuration, we introduced a similarity graph, which connects all configurations with the lowest topological distance. We calculated this distance between any two configurations and developed a similarity graph in which each configuration is depicted as a node and the topological distances are the links between the nodes.

Studies in progress are examining the configurations "polyline-polyline" and "polygon-polygon" (all configurations including a point are a sub-set of these).

References

1. M.J.Egenhofer, "Reasoning about binary topological relations" 2nd Symposium SSD'91, LNCS n. 525, pp. 143-160, August 1991
2. M.J.Egenhofer, J.Sharma "Topological relations between regions in R^2 and Z^{2}* " 3rd Intern. Symposium on Large Spatial Databases – SSD93, LNCS n. 692, pp. 316-336, 1993
3. M.J.Egenhofer, R.D.Franzosa "Point-set topological spatial relations" Intern. Journal of Geographical Information Systems, Vol.5, N.2, pp. 161-174, 1991
4. F.Ferri, M.Rafanelli "GeoPQL: a Geographical Pictorial Query Language that resolves ambiguities in query interpretation" *Journal of Data Semantics*, Springer-Verlag Publ., LNCS n. 3534, pp.50-80, 2005

5. M.A.Rodriguez, M.J.Egenhofer "Comparing Geospatial Entity Classes: an Asymmetric and Content-Dependent Similarity Measure" International Journal of Geographical Information Science 18(3), pp. 229-256, 2004
6. M.A.Rodriguez, M.J.Egenhofer "Determining Semantic Similarity among Entity Classes from Different Ontologies" IEEE Transactions on Knowledge and Data Engineering, Vol.15, n.2, pp. 442-456, 2003
7. F.Ferri, A.Formica, P.Grifoni , M.Rafanelli "Evaluating semantic similarity using GML in Geographic Information Systems" OTM'05 Workshops, Agia Napa, Cyprus, LNCS n.3762, Springer-Verlag Publ., pp. 1009-1019
8. M.J.Egenhofer, J.Sharma, D.M.Mark "A critical comparison of the 4-intersection and 9-intersection models for spatial relations: formal analysis" Autocarto 11, R.McMaster & M.Armstrong Ed.s, October 1993
9. M.J.Egenhofer, D.M.Mark "Modeling conceptual neighborhoods of topological line-region relations" Intern. Journal of Geographical Information Systems, Vol.9, N.5, pp. 555-565, 1995.
10. H.T.Bruns, M.J.Egenhofer "Similarity of spatial scenes" 7th Int. Symp. On Spatial Data Handling, pp.173-184, Delft, The Netherlands, 1996
11. M.A.Rodriguez, M.J.Egenhofer, A.D.Blaser "Query pre-processing of topological constraints: comparing a composition-based with neighborhood-based approach" SSTD'03, pp. 362-379, 2003
12. F.Dylia, R.Moratz "Exploiting qualitative spatial neighborhoods in the situation calculus" Int. Conference on Spatial Cognition, LNCS n. 3343, pp. 304-322, 2005
13. F.Ferri, P.Grifoni, M.Rafanelli "XPQL: a pictorial language for querying geographic data" 15th , DEXA '04, Zaragoza, Spagna, LNCS N. 3180, Springer-Verlag Publ., pp. 925-935, 2004
14. F.Ferri, P.Grifoni, M.Rafanelli "Querying by Sketch Geographical Databases and Ambiguities", DEXA '05, Copenhagen, Denmark, LNCS N. 3588, Springer-Verlag Publ., pp. 925-935, 2005.

High-Dimensional Similarity Search Using Data-Sensitive Space Partitioning

Sachin Kulkarni[1] and Ratko Orlandic[2]

[1] Illinois Institute of Technology, Department of Computer Science,
Chicago 60616, USA
kulksac@iit.edu
[2] University of Illinois at Springfield, Computer Science Department,
Springfield 62703, USA
rorla2@uis.edu

Abstract. Nearest neighbor search has a wide variety of applications. Unfortunately, the majority of search methods do not scale well with dimensionality. Recent efforts have been focused on finding better approximate solutions that improve the locality of data using dimensionality reduction. However, it is possible to preserve the locality of data and find exact nearest neighbors in high dimensions without dimensionality reduction. This paper introduces a novel high-performance technique to find exact *k*-nearest neighbors in both low and high dimensional spaces. It relies on a new method for data-sensitive space partitioning based on explicit data clustering, which is introduced in the paper for the first time. This organization supports effective reduction of the search space before accessing secondary storage. Costly Euclidean distance calculations are reduced through efficient processing of a lightweight memory-based filter. The algorithm outperforms sequential scan and the VA-File in high-dimensional situations. Moreover, the results with dynamic loading of data show that the technique works well on dynamic datasets as well.

1 Introduction

Many traditional access methods are ineffective in high-dimensional spaces [10, 19]. Moreover, real high-dimensional data are often correlated or clustered, and the data tends to occupy only a small fraction of the space [5]. An appropriate similarity search method must be aware of the locality of data in high dimensions. However, most methods for finding the locality of data rely on dimensionality reduction. Unless a multi-step approach is applied [16], this leads to approximate results.

The problem of similarity search can be stated as follows: Given a database with N points and a query point q in some metric space, find $k \geq 1$ points closest to q [6]. Effective solutions to this problem find applications in computational geometry, geographic information systems, multimedia databases, data mining, etc. Most of these applications deal with Euclidean multi-dimensional spaces.

In order to tackle the "curse of dimensionality", various approximate solutions based on dimensionality reduction have been proposed [2, 6, 7]. Aggarwal [2] emphasized the need to distinguish between the localities in the data and introduced a concept of locality sensitive subspace sampling. The concept of locality sensitive hashing

S. Bressan, J. Küng, and R. Wagner (Eds.): DEXA 2006, LNCS 4080, pp. 738–750, 2006.

(LSH) is developed in [7]. The emphasis in [2] and [7] is on finding the locality of the data in a way that makes the process of dimensionality reduction more "data aware". The focus here is on local rather than global distribution of data.

Significant effort in finding the exact nearest neighbors has yielded limited success. The SR-Tree [9] uses both a hyper-sphere and hyper-rectangle to represent a region and improves search efficiency over the SS-tree and R-tree. However, as reported in [4], the SR-Tree is at par with sequential scan when dimensionality is at least 20. Blott and Weber [5] proposed the VA-File, which applies a filter to the sequential scan using the concept of vector approximations. The bit-encoded approximations provide bounds to guide the elimination of points during the search. The solution is simple and tends to be efficient.

A-tree [15] and i-distance [19] are reported to work well in high dimensions. The A-tree is an index structure that stores virtual bounding rectangles, which approximate minimum bounding rectangles. i-distance uses the concept of space partitioning to separate the data into different regions. The data for each region are transformed into a single-dimensional space in which the similarity is measured.

Our quest is for a solution with an efficient and scalable search, acceptable data-loading time, and the ability to work on incremental loads of data. Despite considerable work done in the area, this formulation of the problem of exact similarity searching in high-dimensional spaces is still an intriguing one.

In this paper, we introduce a new way of arranging data on storage to facilitate efficient search. A new space partitioning method is proposed along with a new algorithm for exact similarity search in high-dimensional spaces. The basic idea is to separate clusters in the dataset and eliminate searching over the empty space, thus improving the retrieval performance. We adopt an explicit density-based clustering using the efficient $\text{GARDEN}_{\text{HD}}$ clustering technique [13], which is different than the sampling-based approach proposed in [19]. We then apply a new space partitioning technique, called DSGP (data-sensitive gamma partitioning), which operates on the compact cluster representation of data produced by $\text{GARDEN}_{\text{HD}}$.

The paper also presents the results of comprehensive experiments showing that our approach can efficiently find exact *k* nearest neighbors in high dimensions. Moreover, it can work efficiently on dynamically growing data. The algorithm is compared to the sequential scan, the VA-File, and the GammaSLK partitioning and indexing technique without explicit data clustering [12].

The rest of this paper is organized as follows. Section 2 gives the basic design principle underlying the proposed approach and our clustering and partitioning schemes. Section 3 presents the system architecture and briefly reviews the adopted Γ partitioning and $\text{GARDEN}_{\text{HD}}$ clustering. Section 4 introduces the data-sensitive space partitioning. Section 5 introduces the proposed algorithm for similarity search. Section 6 provides experimental evidence. Section 7 concludes the paper.

2 Design Principle

For generality, let us use the term *storage cluster* to denote the spatial region formed by points in a storage unit, which we assume to be an index page. Then the design principle underlying our approach can be stated as follows: *multi-dimensional data must be grouped on storage in a way that minimizes the extensions of storage clusters along all relevant dimensions and achieves high storage utilization.*

The term "relevant dimensions" refers to the fact that multi-dimensional region queries may have "affinity" for certain dimensions, consistently leaving other dimensions unrestricted. However, since exact similarity searching must restrict the search space in all dimensions, the clustering scheme used for storage organization must treat all data dimensions as equally important. Assuming a multi-dimensional space defined by relevant dimensions, the stated principle implies that the storage organization must maximize the densities of storage clusters both by increasing the number of points in the clusters and by reducing their volumes. To increase the densities of storage clusters, the organization must reduce their internal empty space. For best results, the database system should employ a genuine clustering algorithm for this purpose.

To understand the logic behind this principle, let us assume for the moment an idealized system that, for any given query, accesses only those pages on secondary storage containing data items that satisfy the query. Moreover, assume that N data items are divided into $M << N$ pages and that $K << N$ items satisfying the query are randomly distributed among the pages. Then, a well-known Cardenas expression $A = M\cdot(1-(1-1/M)^k)$ gives a good estimate of the number of accessed pages for the given query. Note that the number of pages with useful data is at most $min\{K, M\}$ and, when $K << M$, the above expression can be approximated by $A \approx M\cdot(1-(1-K/M)) = K$.

Eliminating the assumption that data items are randomly distributed among the pages, the number of accessed pages can be estimated by a more general expression, valid for any $K, M \le N$: $A = K/I$, where $I \ge 1$ is the average number of items that satisfy the query in an accessed page. Since the goal of clustering data on storage is to increase the number of useful items in any page accessed by a typical query, the parameter $H = I/C \le 1$, where C is the page capacity, is a good measure of the quality of clustering with respect to the given query. Obviously, when $C = 1$ or $H = I/C$, clustered storage organization has the same effect as the organization with randomly distributed data. However, when $C >> 1$ and H is as close to 1 as possible, the performance improvement can be significant—as much as C times fewer page accesses. For this to happen, the storage utilization must also be high.

To develop an appropriate clustering strategy, let us now consider the problem of supporting multi-dimensional region queries, which restrict the ranges of values in one or more dimensions of a D-dimensional unit space $[0,1]^D$. We use the term *storage cluster* to denote a spatial region consisting of points in a storage unit, i.e. a page.

In this context, increasing H implies increasing the probability that each storage cluster with useful data is completely covered by the query. However, since clustering must benefit not one but many different queries, the storage organization must be such that, for every storage cluster S and any query Q, it decreases the probability $P(S \cap Q)$ that S overlaps Q (which would trigger access to the corresponding page), while increasing the probability $P(S \subseteq Q)$ that it is covered by Q. Assuming that S is represented by its minimum bounding hyper-rectangle, and that all possible positions of S are equally likely, one can easily show that, for data dimensionality D:

$$P(S \cap Q) = \prod_{i=1}^{D} \min\{Q_i + S_i, 1\} \quad \text{and} \quad P(S \subseteq Q) = \prod_{i=1}^{D} \max\{\frac{Q_i - S_i}{1 - S_i}, 0\},$$

where S_i and Q_i are the extensions (lengths) of S and Q, respectively, in an axis i.

Since the extensions of any given query are fixed, the way to reduce $P(S \cap Q)$ and increase $P(S \subseteq Q)$ for an arbitrary query Q is to reduce the lengths S_i of S along all dimensions i restricted by Q (i.e., all i for which $Q_i < 1$). This and the earlier observation about storage utilization lead to the design principles stated earlier.

We refer to the process of detecting dense areas (*dense cells*) in the space with minimum amounts of empty space as *data space reduction*. In this context, *data clustering* is a process of detecting the largest areas with this property, called *data clusters*. The stated design principle can be achieved either by clustering or by data space reduction only. However, a facility to do both is an advantage.

Explicit data clustering with effective data space reduction can facilitate various kinds of retrieval, including similarity searching, by enabling a close-to-optimal assignment of data to pages and a significant reduction of the search space even before the retrieval process hits persistent storage. For effective data space reduction, the clustering method should operate directly in the given (externally defined) space without dimensionality reduction, and it should not be governed by any expectation about the number of clusters. To be useful for storage organization, it must also be very efficient. This set of requirements motivates the design of the $\text{GARDEN}_{\text{HD}}$ clustering algorithm for high-dimensional datasets introduced in [12] and the DSGP data-sensitive space partitioning technique introduced later in this paper.

3 System Architecture

Figure 1 gives the architecture of our system for efficient retrieval of data that scales well with the increasing dimensionality. The process of data clustering produces a compact cluster representation of data. Operating on this representation, the partitioning module produces a data-sensitive Γ space partition (see below). The derived space partition is maintained by a light-weight in-memory structure, called the *Γ filter*.

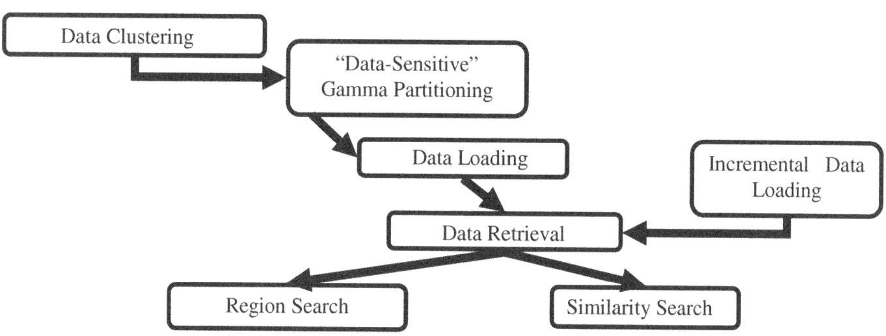

Fig. 1. Key processes of the system

In the process of data loading, this memory structure acts like a filter that channels the points of each region in the space partition into a separate KDB-tree index. Together, these indices represent clustered data storage. With the facility for incremental loading, the system can subsequently accept new data points through the existing space partition. The processes of data retrieval include both region and similarity-search queries, which undergo two levels of filtering—one in the memory-resident Γ filter and the other in the selected indices on disk.

The KDB-tree indexing technique is not necessarily optimal for this environment. The R-tree would yield faster retrieval, but at the expense of slower insertions. In environments with frequent insertions, the later cost is not insignificant.

3.1 Gamma Partitioning

Γ space partitioning was first introduced in [11]. A D-dimensional space is partitioned by several nested hyper-rectangles whose low endpoints lie in the origin of the space. The outermost hyper-rectangle is the space itself. We call these nested hyper-rectangles *partition generators*, or just *generators*. The space inside one generator and outside its immediately enclosed generator, if any, is called *Γ subspace*. Except for the innermost subspace, each Γ subspace is further divided into at most D hyper-rectangular regions, called *Γ regions*, by means of $(D-1)$-dimensional hyper-planes, each of which lies on an upper boundary of the inner generator. Beginning with the outermost generator, these Γ regions are carved out from the base region one by one (see Figure 2c below). Each coordinate of the high endpoint of a generator gives the position of the hyper-plane that separates a Γ region from the space in which the subsequent Γ regions lie. Note that, if G is the number of generators and D the number of dimensions, the total number of created regions is at most $1+(G-1)\cdot D$.

In our system, Γ space partition is compactly represented by the Γ filter. During the insertions, for each Γ region, the Γ filter dynamically maintains its *live region*, i.e. the minimum bounding hyper-rectangle enclosing the points in the Γ region.

3.2 GARDEN$_{HD}$ Clustering

GARDEN$_{HD}$ [13] is designed to provide a fast and accurate insight into data distribution in order to facilitate data mining or retrieval. This clustering method efficiently and effectively separates disjoint areas with points, which is the primary reason we selected it for this application. With an appropriately selected density threshold, which is the only input parameter, GARDEN$_{HD}$ runs in $O(N\log N)$ time [13], where N is the number of D-dimensional points in the dataset.

GARDEN$_{HD}$ is a hybrid of cell- and density-based clustering that operates in two phases. Employing a recursive space partition using a variant of Γ partitioning [13], the first phase performs an efficient data space reduction, identifying rectangular cells whose density is above the user-defined threshold. In the second phase, the adjacent dense cells are merged into larger clusters. It is the application of Γ partitioning that enables the algorithm to efficiently cluster data in high-dimensional spaces without dimensionality reduction.

4 Data Sensitive Gamma Partitioning – DSGP

The partitioning method, called *DSGP* (*Data-Sensitive Gamma Partitioning*), uses the cluster representation of data produced by GARDEN$_{HD}$ and generates a space partition in which well-separated clusters appear in different regions of the space. DSGP runs in time equivalent to $O(L^2)$ comparisons of D-dimensional points, where L is the number of clusters detected by $GARDEN_{HD}$.

Each data cluster is approximated by its minimum bounding hyper-rectangle (MBR), represented by the low and high endpoints. As in "data blind" Γ partitioning into regions of equal volume [11], DSGP produces static Γ regions, but around spatial clusters. The number of resulting regions depends on the number of clusters. The objective is to store points of each disjoint cluster into a separate KDB-tree index.

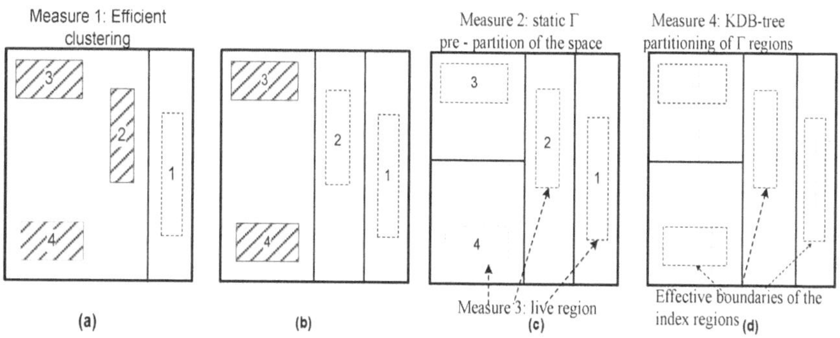

Fig. 2. Steps of the DSGP space partitioning

Figure 2 illustrates the steps of the data-sensitive space partitioning strategy. Figure 2a shows four clusters detected by $GARDEN_{HD}$. The DSGP procedure starts by sorting the clusters based on their high endpoints along each dimension. As a result, each dimension is associated with a sorted list of cluster indices. The procedure detects the gaps between clusters as follows: going from the higher to lower coordinates along each dimension, the low endpoint of each cluster is compared with the high endpoint of the next cluster until a gap is found. A partitioning hyper-plane is drawn in the middle of a detected gap, perpendicular to the dimension with the *minimum-containment region* above the gap. By the "minimum-containment region", we mean a Γ region with the smallest number of clusters. The resulting space partition is stored in the Γ filter. The live regions bounding the points of each Γ region in the Γ filter are determined dynamically during initial and incremental data loading.

In Figure 2a, Cluster 1 has been assigned to the first Γ region. Hence, it is eliminated from further consideration. The same procedure is repeated, and Cluster 2 is assigned to another partition along the same dimension (Figure 2b). In the next iteration, a gap is found along the second dimension (Figure 2c). The last cluster is assigned to the remaining Γ region. During data loading, the constructed KBD-tree indices perform implicit partitioning of the respective Γ regions into a collection of index regions, each of which bounds the points in an index page (Figure 2d). Since no point can fall outside the live region of the corresponding Γ region, the KDB-tree index regions are effectively bounded by the corresponding live regions.

If multiple clusters appear in the same Γ region, the DSGP procedure performs "slicing" of the Γ region, so that each slice of the Γ region contains only one cluster.

The current slicing procedure requires a pair-wise comparison of the given cluster MBRs. It is also possible that no gap can be found during an iteration of this algorithm or during slicing of a Γ region. In such a case, DSGP performs a "data blind" Γ partitioning [12] of the space (region) in which the overlapping cluster MBRs appear.

5 Similarity Search

Through the constructed Γ filter representing the partition produced by DSGP, data points are inserted into appropriate KDB-tree indices. As points are inserted, live regions of the Γ regions and their slices are dynamically formed. Each inserted point either grows a live region or falls inside it. For a point lying inside a live region, its distance to the geometric center of the live region is calculated. This point becomes a representative of the region if it is closer to the center of the live region than the previous representative, if any. Note that the dynamic computation of representatives takes place after the clustering and partitioning is performed on an early data sample.

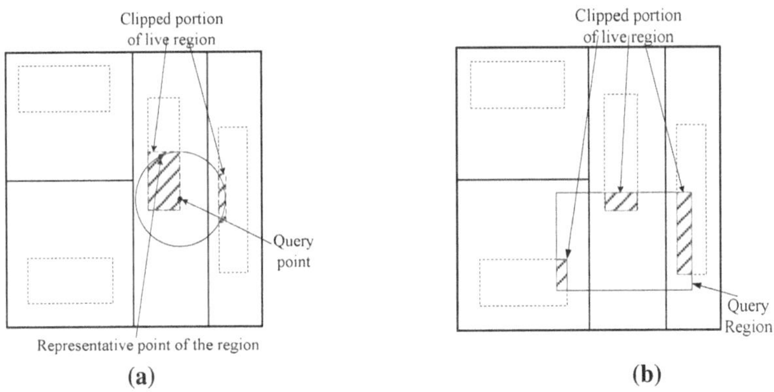

Fig. 3. *k*-nearest neighbor and region search

Figure 3 depicts the processes of nearest neighbor and region searching. The nearest neighbour search in Figure 3a uses a query hyper-sphere with the query point at the center and the distance to its closest region representative as the radius. In this example, the hyper-sphere intersects two live regions and requires the region searches only for the overlapping clipped portions of the live regions. Figure 3b is included to emphasise that region search can be performed in a similar way. Figure 4 gives the algorithm for nearest-neighbor searching, called GammaNN (the *k*-NN algorithm is a simple variant of this). A similar procedure can be used for region search as well.

Once the live regions that overlap the query hyper-sphere or query rectangle (window) are determined, they are clipped against the hyper-sphere or the query window, respectively. The KDB-tree corresponding to an overlapping live region is then queried with the appropriate clip of the query window. In the case of *k*-nearest neighbor searching, the query hyper-sphere dynamically shrinks as the new nearest neighbors are detected. The points returned by the interrogated KDB-tree indices are compared with the query point to construct the resulting list of k-nearest neighbors. For a region search, the points returned by the KDB-tree indices represent the result set.

```
Input:
    Q;                      // query point:
    NoRegions;              // number of Gamma regions
    Regions;                // list of Gamma regions
Output:
    Result.Point;           // nearest neighbor
    Result.Distance;        // distance to the nearest neighbor
Local:
    Slice;                  // a slice of a region (region can have one or more slices)
    Slice.LR;               // live region of the given slice
    TempResult;             // contains a temporary NN and the distance to it
    Distance ← ∞, Dist;     // temporary distance
    Qclip;                  // query window (clip) by which an index is searched

BEGIN GammaNN
                            // find closest representative and "construct" the sphere
 for i=1 to NoRegions do
   if sphereIntersectsGammaRegion (Q, Distance, Region[i]) then
     if Region[i].Cardinality > 0 // in a data-blind partition, region can be empty
       for j=1 to Region[i].NoSlices do
         if sphereIntersectsLiveRegion (Q, Distance, Region[i].Slice[j].LR)
           begin
           MarkSlice (Region[i].Slice[j]); // mark slice for later inspection
           if Dist ← calculateDistance (Slice[j].Repr, Q) < Distance then
             begin Slice ← Region[i].Slice[j]; Distance ←Dist; end
           end
                            // examine points in the "closest" slice
 Qclip ← constructSearchWindow (Q, Distance, Slice.LR); // construct query clip
 Result ←searchIndex (i, Qclip); // search index and return the temporary NN
 Distance ← Result.Distance;
                            // examine points in other slices, shrinking the sphere
 for each other Slice in the list of marked slices do
   if sphereIntersectsLiveRegion (Q, Distance, Slice.LR) then
     begin     // since the sphere is shrinking, we had to test for overlap again
     Qclip ← constructSearchWindow (Q, Distance, Slice.LR);
     TempResult ←searchIndex (i, Qclip);
     if TempResult.Distance < Distance then
       begin Distance ← TempResult.Distance; Result ←TempResult; end
     end
END GammaNN
```

Fig. 4. GammaNN algorithm for nearest-neighbor searching

6 Experimental Evidence

The experiments were performed on simulated and real data on a PC configuration with a 3.6 GHz CPU, 3GB RAM, and 280GB disk. In all structures, the page size was 8K bytes. We assumed a normalized D-dimensional space $[0,1]^D$. Each coordinate of a point was packed in 2 bytes. The GammaNN implementations with and without explicit clustering are referred to here as 'data aware' and 'data blind' [12] algorithms, respectively. The static Γ partitioning of the data blind GammaNN was obtained assuming 3 generators, decided based on a number of experiments. In the synthetic data of up to 100 dimensions, the points are distributed across 11 clusters—one in the center and 10 in random corners of the space. The real data is a 54-dimensional forest cover type ("covtype") set obtained from the UCI machine learning repository[1].

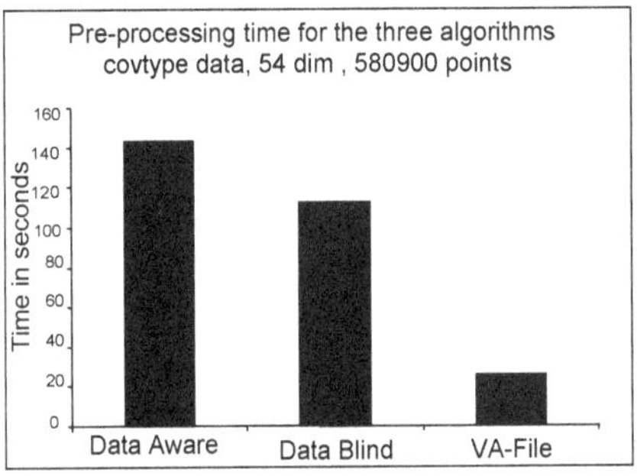

Fig. 5. Preprocessing time including the time for data loading

Figure 5 gives the pre-processing time for two versions of GammaNN and the VA-File. For the data-blind algorithm, this time includes the time of space partitioning, I/O (reading the data), and the time for data loading (i.e., the construction of indices plus insertion of data). The data-aware algorithm includes the clustering time in addition. Observe that the pre-processing time of this algorithm is heavily dominated by the construction of KDB-tree indices, whereas $\text{GARDEN}_{\text{HD}}$ clustering is fast.

For the VA-File technique, the pre-processing time includes the time to generate the VA-File. Since this time is dominated by the calculation of approximation values [17] and requires no insertion of points into any data structure, faster pre-processing for VA-File is expected. However, since the pre-processing time is usually amortized over a large number of queries, it is much less consequential than the search time.

Figure 6 shows the results on 100,000 synthetic data points as their dimensionality increases from 10 to 100. The data-aware algorithm is more than eight times faster than sequential scan and six times faster than the VA-File. The data-aware method and the VA-File incur almost the same number of page accesses to the data. However, this is because we counted only accesses to index or data pages, respectively. In other words, no page access was counted for the processing of the Γ filter or the VA-File, which favors the latter technique. If the VA-File were maintained on disk, the VA-File

[1] http://kdd.ics.uci.edu/databases/covertype/covertype.data.html.

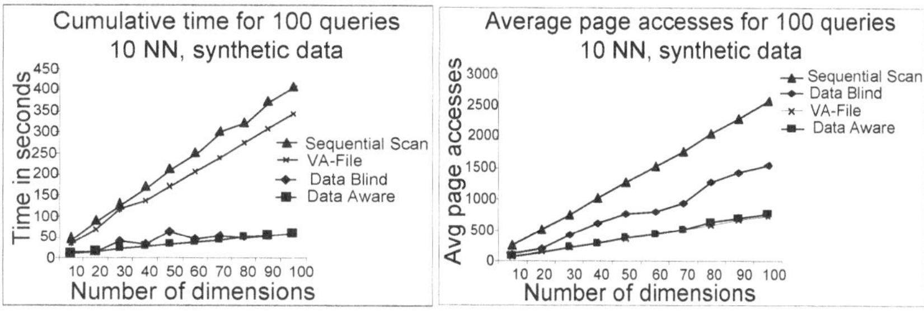

Fig. 6. Synthetic data with query distribution same as data, 10 NN

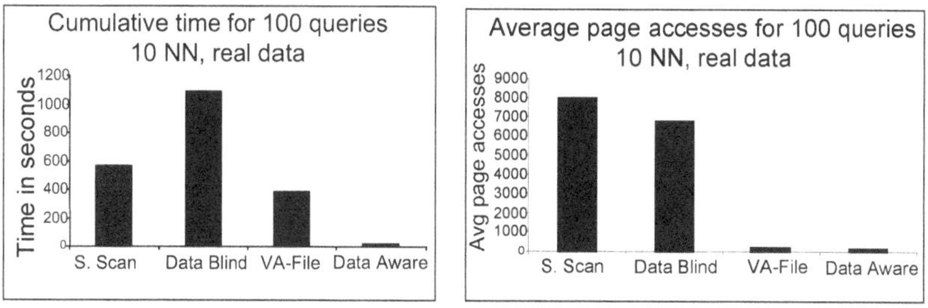

Fig. 7. Real data with 100 queries selected from the real data file, 10 NN

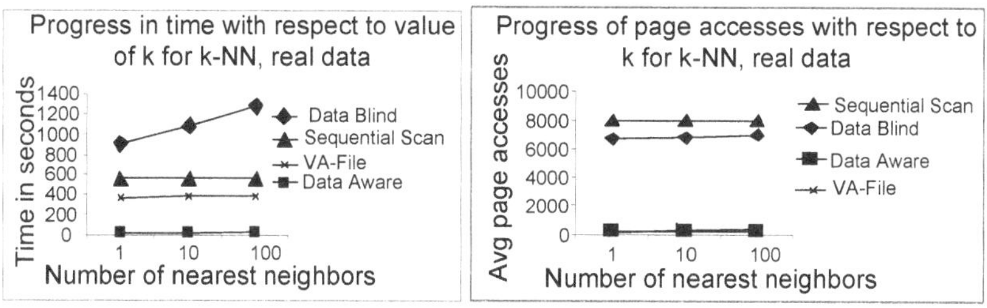

Fig. 8. Progress as the number of nearest neighbors increases on real data

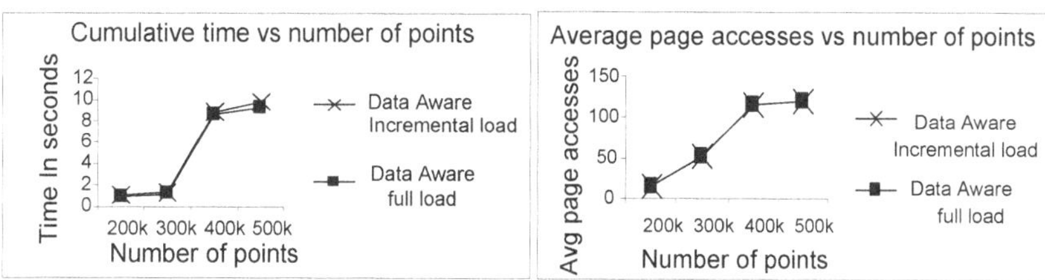

Fig. 9. Time and average page accesses for incremental load on real data

technique would incur many more page accesses, and the relative differences with respect to GammaNN variants would be closer to those observed for processing times.

Figure 7 shows that the data-aware algorithm is significantly faster than sequential scan and the VA-File. For this experiment, 580,900 points were loaded into each structure, and the remaining 100 points in the data set were used as query points. Also noteworthy is that the data-aware algorithm accesses only about 3% of all data points.

Figure 8 shows the changes in performance of different methods with respect to the increasing value of k in k-NN searching. Except for the data-blind algorithm, all methods have a stable performance as k grows up to 100.

Figure 9 shows the performance of the data-aware algorithm on incremental loading of the real data set. The clustering and space partitioning were performed on the first 100,000 points in the set, which were loaded into the structure. The results of 10-NN queries were recorded after subsequent incremental loads of 100,000 points. No re-clustering was performed after an incremental load. However, as described earlier, the live regions and their respective representatives were dynamically modified during the incremental loads. The equivalent results of the same algorithm but without incremental loading (in Figure 9, referred to as "data aware, full load"), i.e. after clustering the entire subset of the data, are used as benchmarks.

One can observe from Figure 9 that the data-aware GammaNN algorithm results in almost the same number of page accesses and the query execution times with or without incremental loading of data. This suggests that GammaNN reacts well to incremental loads. As in this case, in many practical environments, it will require no re-clustering of data even after many incremental loads. This is particularly important for scientific applications, which regularly obtain data through incremental loads.

7 Discussion and Conclusions

In this paper, we proposed a new technique for exact similarity searching in high dimensionalities, called GammaNN. The GammaNN technique employs explicit data clustering using a new density-based clustering method and a new data-sensitive space partitioning method in order to preserve the locality of data and reduce the volumes of data clusters on storage. The application of a memory-based filter with live regions further improves the performance of similarity searching.

The comparison of the data-sensitive and data-blind approach clearly highlights the importance of clustering data on storage for efficient similarity search. Our approach can support exact similarity search while accessing only a small fraction of data. The algorithm is very efficient in high dimensionalities and performs better than sequential scan and the VA-File technique. The performance remains good even after incremental loads of dynamically growing data sets without re-clustering.

The high performance of GammaNN similarity searching is mainly due to the structure's adherence to the design principle stated in Section 2. By detecting dense areas in the space, the data clustering facility determines the spatial proximity of data. The data-sensitive space partitioning enables a static pre-clustering of data on storage according to their spatial proximity. Storing the points of every region into a separate KDB-tree enables a dynamic sub-clustering of data into index pages corresponding to relatively small and dense regions in the space, as required by our design principle.

The application of the memory-resident filter is important for several reasons. It dynamically channels incoming data into appropriate indices. It dramatically reduces the number of costly distance computations. With the dynamically-maintained live regions, it also reduces the amount of searching over empty space, enabling a potentially significant reduction of search space before accessing the storage.

In our future work, we plan to incorporate R-trees into the system and provide a facility for handling data with missing values.

Acknowledgment

This material is based upon work supported by the National Science Foundation under grant no. IIS-0312266.

References

1. Aggarwal, C.C.: On the effects of dimensionality reduction on high dimensional similarity search, Proc. 20th PODS Conf., (2001) 256–266
2. Aggarwal, C.C.: Hierarchical subspace sampling: A unified framework for high dimensional data reduction, selectivity estimation and nearest neighbor search, Proc. ACM SIGMOD Conf., (2002) 452-463
3. Berchtold, S., Ertl, B., Keim, D., Kriegel, H.P., Seidl, T.: Fast nearest neighbor search in high-dimensional space, Proc. 14th ICDE Int. Conf. on Data Engineering, (1998) 209-218.
4. Beyer, K.S., Goldstein, J., Ramakrishnan, R. and Shaft, U.: When is `nearest neighbor' meaningful?, Proc. 7th Int. Conf. on Database Theory, (1999) 217-235
5. Blott, S., Weber, R., A simple Vector-Approximation file for similarity search in high-dimensional vector spaces. Technical report, Esprit Project Hermes (no. 9141), (1997)
6. Fagin, R., Kumar, R., Shivakumar, D.: Efficient similarity search and classification via rank aggregation, Proc. Proc. ACM SIGMOD Conf., (2003) 301-312
7. Gionis, A., Indyk, P., Motwani, R.: Similarity search in high dimension via hashing, Proc. 25th VLDB Conf., (1999) 518-529
8. Hinneburg, A., Aggarwal, C.C., Keim, D.A.: What is nearest neighbor in high dimensional spaces?, Proc. 26th VLDB Conf., (2000) 506-515
9. Katayama, N., Satoh, S.: The SR-tree: An index structure for high-dimensional nearest neighbor queries, SIGMOD Record 26(2): (1997) 369-380
10. MacQueen, J.: Some methods for classification and analysis of multivariate observations. In Proc. 5th Berkeley Symp. Math. Statist, Prob. 1: (1967) 281–297
11. Orlandic, R., Lukaszuk, J., Swietlik, C.: The design of a retrieval technique for high-dimensional data on tertiary storage, SIGMOD Record 31(2): (2002) 15–21
12. Orlandic, R., Lukaszuk, J.: Efficient high-dimensional indexing by superimposing space-partitioning schemes, Proc. 8th International Database Engineering & Applications Symposium IDEAS'04, (2004) 257-264
13. Orlandic, R., Lai, Y., Yee, W.G.: Clustering high-dimensional data using an efficient and effective data space reduction, Proc. ACM Conference on Information and Knowledge Management CIKM'05, (2005) 201-208
14. Robinson, J.T.: The K-D-B-Tree: A search structure for large multidimensional dynamic Indexes, Proc. ACM SIGMOD Conf., (1981) 10-18
15. Sakurai, Y., Yoshikawa, M., Uemura, S., Kojima, H.: The A-tree: An index structure for high-dimensional spaces using relative approximation, Proc. 26th VLDB Conf., (2000) 516-526

16. Seidl, T., Kriegel, H.P.: Optimal multi-Step k-nearest neighbor search. Proc. ACM SIGMOD Conf., (1998) 154-165
17. Weber, R., Schek, H.J., Blott, S.: A quantitative analysis and performance study for similarity search methods in high-dimensional spaces, Proc. 24th VLDB Conf., (1998) 194-205
18. Weber, R., Zezula, P.: The theory and practice of similarity searches in high dimensional data spaces (extended abstract), 4th DELOS Workshop, 1997
19. Yu, C., Ooi, B.C., Tan, K.L., Jagadish, H.V.: Indexing the distance: An efficient method to KNN processing, Proc. 26th VLDB Conf., (2001) 421-430

Truly Adaptive Optimization: The Basic Ideas

Giovanni Maria Sacco

Dipartimento di Informatica, Università di Torino, Corso Svizzera 185,
10149 Torino, Italy
sacco@di.unito.it

Abstract. A new approach to query optimization, truly adaptive optimization (TAO), is presented. TAO is a general optimization strategy and is composed of three elements:

1. a fast solution space search algorithm, derived from A*, which uses an informed heuristic lookahead;
2. a relaxation technique which allows to specify a tolerance on the quality of the resulting query execution plan;
3. a paradigm to prove the suboptimality of search subspaces. Non-procedural pruning rules can be used to describe specific problem knowledge, and can be easily added to the optimizer, as the specific problem becomes better understood.

The main contribution over previous research is the use of relaxation techniques and that TAO provides a unifying framework for query optimization problems, which models a complexity continuum going from fast heuristic searches to exponential optimal searches while guaranteeing a selected plan quality. In addition, problem knowledge can be exploited to speed the search up. As a preliminary example, the method is applied to query optimization for databases distributed over a broadcast network. Simulation results are reported.

1 Introduction

Non-procedural query interfaces for relational database systems provide a high degree of data independence and greatly simplify user interaction with the database. The selection of efficient strategies to solve user queries is delegated to a system component called the query optimizer. The query optimizer selects an execution plan on the basis of the estimated costs of different plans that can be used to solve the query.

Research on query optimization [2] has polarized on two different, unreconciled extremes. On the one hand, a number of works uses the exhaustive exploration of the solution space to select the plan with the minimum estimated cost among all the possible plans that can be used to solve the query. As an example, a breadth-first exhaustive search is used in the optimizer of System R [14], a centralized relational database system, and in R* [17], its distributed counterpart. More recent approaches are iterative dynamic programming [9], and the blackboard approach [8].

The main objection to this approach is that query optimization is known to be NP-hard [3], so that the enumeration of all the possible plans requires significant resources for complex queries on several relations. Another important and often overlooked

S. Bressan, J. Küng, and R. Wagner (Eds.): DEXA 2006, LNCS 4080, pp. 751 – 760, 2006.

objection is that estimates of execution costs are known to suffer from significant errors. Pushing the optimization process to a point where discrimination among plans falls inside the estimation error obviously produces no meaningful benefits.

On the other hand, many algorithms use a priori heuristics to derive efficient execution plans. Heuristic strategies require a relatively low amount of resources, depending on the refinement of the strategy, but can be seriously suboptimal. Known problems with heuristics are: a) the use of a priori strategies, usually tailored on intuitive "average" cases; b) the difficulty in optimizing weighted combinations of objective functions; c) no indication on plan quality, in terms of how far is the selected solution from the theoretical optimum; and d) "one size fits all": heuristics do not account for the relative importance of queries. Thus, the selected plan for a given query is always the same, regardless of its frequency of execution.

Alternative approaches to heuristic optimization are randomized algorithms [7], that have constant space overhead but whose running time is usually unpredictable because they are non-deterministic. Typically, randomized algorithms are slower than heuristics and dynamic programming for simple queries and faster than both for very large queries. The best known randomized algorithm for query optimization is 2PO and is a combination of applying iterative improvement and simulated annealing [7]. In many situations, 2PO produces good plans. However, there are situations in which 2PO produces plans that are orders of magnitude more expensive than an optimal plan.

The goal of our research is to provide a single, general and efficient optimization framework that can bridge the gap between exhaustive methods and heuristic solutions by allowing a tolerance on the quality of evaluation plans to be set. Such a tolerance is used to model a complexity continuum going from fast heuristic searches (infinite tolerance) to exponential optimal searches (no tolerance). Thus, as in heuristic strategies, we can speed up the search by providing approximate, suboptimal solutions. Differently from heuristics, however, we are able to guarantee that the selected solution does not exceed the admissible tolerance. In addition, the framework can exploit problem knowledge in order to speed the search up: problem knowledge is at the basis of heuristics, but is usually not exploited by exhaustive strategies.

The optimization framework proposed here is general and can be applied to any optimization problem. In order to provide examples and initial performance measures, it is applied to a simple distributed query optimization problem. The sample problem is not interesting per se, but because it is NP-hard without unnecessary complexities, and it allows the easy gathering of preliminary measures on our approach.

2 Background

Adaptive optimization [1] was the first method to apply results from Artificial Intelligence, namely the A* search algorithm [10], to query optimization and to reconcile these two antithetic approaches into a "middle-of-the-way" approach, called adaptive optimization. In adaptive optimization, the optimization problem is solved through an efficient search of the solution space, which is significantly faster than previous enumerative methods. In addition, the portion of the solution space to be searched can be controlled by a parametric pruning criterion based on the cost of the solution space node to which it is applied.

The A* method [10], a well-known graph search technique, is used in adaptive optimization. A* expands at each stage the node n (not yet expanded) having the smallest total expected cost f*(n) given by:

$$f^*(n) = g(n) + h^*(n) \tag{1}$$

where g(n) is the total cost incurred in producing the database state represented by n, and h*(n) is the estimated cost to reach a state at which the query is solved, from state n. It can be proved [10], that if h*(n)<=h(n) for all n's, where h(n) is the actual future cost to solve the query, A* is guaranteed to reach the optimum. This constraint is called the *admissibility constraint.*

In adaptive optimization, the user (or more likely, the system administrator) can choose h*(n)=0, for all n's, which satisfies the admissibility constraint but results in an inefficient breadth-first search. Alternatively, the user can use the cost of a heuristic solution from n (such as the Initial Feasible Solution in point-to-point networks [4]) as h*(n). This estimate produces a more focused search but does not generally satisfy the admissibility constraint, so that the optimum is not guaranteed. Finally, the amount of resources spent in optimization can be reduced by specifying a parametric pruning criterion, which operates on a list of successors of node n ordered by increasing total cost. Let mtc designate the minimum estimated total cost node. The user can specify that each successor node s such that f*(s)/f*(mtc)>1+T is to be pruned. That is nodes whose total cost is beyond a specified deviation from the minimum are pruned. In addition, the user can request that only the N lowest cost successors of n be retained.

This type of search allows implementing a number of strategies, from greedy searches (if only one successor is retained for each expanded node) to exhaustive searches (if no successor is pruned). The term adaptive is used to indicate that heuristic pruning only depends on the cost of active nodes, rather than on a priori heuristics. In addition, this strategy allows the user to specify tight pruning on one-shot queries (for which very efficient plans are relatively unimportant), and loose pruning or no pruning at all, for often repeated queries (for which even small savings are important in a large scale economy).

Although adaptive optimization goes a long way towards low-cost high-quality query optimization, it does have a number of problems: a) it is quite inefficient for complex queries, so that tight pruning criteria must generally be used; b) it does not give an indication of the quality of the plan unless when used to reach an optimal solution (i.e. with h*(n)=0 and no pruning); and c) it is quite difficult to understand the implications, in terms of space and time, of selected values of N and T.

3 Truly Adaptive Optimization

Truly adaptive optimization (TAO) improves over adaptive optimization in two main ways. First, it concentrates on approximate solutions, since there is little interest in reaching the theoretical optimum because of errors in cost estimates. Differently from adaptive optimization that relaxes the search in order to reduce effort, but is unable to give indications on the quality of the resulting plan, here we want to be able to guarantee that the resulting plan is within a specified tolerance from the optimal solution. At the same time, we want to reduce the search effort as the tolerance on plan quality increases.

In order to meet these goals, algorithm A* with no parametric pruning is used as a basis. Admissible h*(n) estimates are obtained by *completely reduced plans.* A completely reduced plan for n relations is a plan in which all relations are considered in their completely reduced form (i.e. containing the minimum number of tuples and attributes required to compute the result) and are processed by the least expensive actions.

When a node n is selected for expansion, a feasible plan for n, FP(n), is computed by *heuristic lookahead.* FP(n) is the result of a heuristic solution from n, obtained by expanding depth-first the successors of n with minimum f* cost. Initially, the feasible plan from the initial node I, FP(I), is computed. This feasible plan is updated whenever a better feasible plan is computed, so that the cost of FP(I) gives at each stage the minimum cost of a feasible solution, HC(I). At the same time, the estimated cost of the node n, f*(n) to be expanded gives an underestimate of the cost of an optimal solution from I that includes n. Since the node n to expanded by A* is the node with the minimum estimated cost, the search process can be stopped when

$$HC(I)/f^*(n) <= 1+T \quad (2)$$

where T (T≥0) is the tolerance specified (*relaxed search*).

In this way, the optimization process can be seen as a refinement of the best heuristic solution so far obtained. Such a refinement is only carried out as required by the specified tolerance and stops when the heuristic solution is good enough. Thus, this relaxation models a complexity continuum going from going from fast heuristic searches (infinite tolerance) to exponential optimal searches (no tolerance). As in heuristic strategies, we can speed up the search by providing approximate, suboptimal solutions. Differently from heuristics, however, we are able to guarantee that the selected solution does not exceed the admissible tolerance.

Relaxation plays a central role in TAO because it is the only mechanism used to produce approximate solutions.. First of all, the higher the tolerance is, the lower the search effort generally is. In the limit case of an infinite tolerance, the first heuristic solution computed by TAO is acceptable, and the search is immediately terminated. In this case, the complexity of a TAO search equals the complexity of a greedy heuristic strategy: the minimum complexity for a meaningful optimization strategy. As the tolerance decreases, more and more solutions will be tested. TAO can be then practically applicable even to very complex problems by specifying relatively large tolerances in order to decrease the amount of resources needed for the search. Significant tolerances are required anyway because of compound errors in result estimates.

The second improvement over adaptive optimization is a uniform way of exploiting problem knowledge. Problem knowledge is the basis of heuristic strategies. Optimal solution space search strategies do not account for it, except, as in A*, to improve estimates of future costs and consequently the penetrance of the search. Estimates of future costs are an important part of TAO and admissible estimates were discussed above. In addition, a paradigm to accommodate non-procedural problem knowledge in order to speed up the search is used.

Whereas heuristics use problem knowledge to specify which portions of the solution space are considered, the mechanism used in TAO, *pruning rules*, specifies which portions of the solution space can be proved suboptimal and can therefore be pruned without losing optimal solutions. Pruning rules are based on the following *harmless pruning paradigm*: given two nodes n and n', n' can be harmlessly pruned iff, assuming that an optimal solution is reachable from n', it can be proved that an optimal solution is also reachable from n. Pruning a node n means removing it and its successors. Storage is released so that there is a decrease in the workspace requirements. A decrease in the time complexity of the search occurs if a pruned node n would have eventually been considered for expansion.

As we will show in the following, there are a number of general pruning rules that are applicable to any optimization problem, while other rules can be derived for specific problems. Among general rules, the duplicate state rule is especially important for query optimization. This rule states that given two nodes n and n' that represent the same database state, only the node with the minimum total estimated cost needs to be retained. Due to join commutativity, the same database state can be produced by a combinatorial number of plans. Only the lowest cost plan to reach a database state needs to be preserved. This action obviously preserves the optimum, and is especially important to reduce the search effort.

In summary, truly adaptive optimization is composed of three main elements:

1. a fast search strategy based on the A* search algorithm
2. a mechanism to specify an acceptable tolerance on the quality of resulting plans
3. a mechanism to specify pruning rules: rules that account for general and problem specific knowledge and can be used to prune portions of the solution space, while retaining the optimum solution.

TAO is a general optimization framework and can be applied to any optimization problem. However, for expediency, we will refer specifically to the application of TAO to distributed query optimization in the following discussion.

4 Pruning Rules

A number of pruning rules can be applied to any optimization problem, and consequently to problems different from query optimization. In addition, rules may be defined at different levels of abstraction for query optimization in general, for distributed query optimization, and for specific problems (specific rules for distributed query optimization in point-to-point tree networks are discussed in [13]). A few general pruning rules are discussed in the following.

Higher cost rule: Any node n such that $f^*(n) \geq HC(I)$ can be pruned.

Proof: By the admissibility of h*: $f^*(n) \leq f(n)$. Consequently, $HC(I) \leq f(n)$, and if an optimal solution is reachable from n, it is also reachable using the current heuristic solution from HC(I). Therefore, nodes having an expected cost higher than the cost of the current heuristic solution can be safely pruned.

Whenever a node n with minimum f* is selected by heuristic lookahead, the heuristic can keep track of the minimum f*(n') among the siblings n' of n. We denote this quantity by F*(n); it provides the total expected cost of the cheapest alternative to the selected node. When HC(n) becomes available (i.e. when the heuristic backs up from its recursive descent), the following rule can be applied to immediately detect when the siblings of a heuristically generated node are suboptimal, and consequently to prune them before expansion:

Alternate cost rule: Let n' be the son of n for which the heuristic solution was computed. If $g^*(n) + HC(n) \leq F^*(n')$, then n need not be expanded (and no siblings of n' are consequently generated).

Proof: By contradiction. Let an optimal solution be reachable from a sibling of n', n", but not from n'. By the admissibility of h*: $f(n'') \geq F^*(n')$. Therefore, $g(n) + HC(n) \leq f(n'')$, against the hypothesis.

In most searches, a given database state can be represented by a set N of nodes. This is mainly due to join commutativity: all the sequences derived by permutation from a set of joins produce the same database state. Only the cheapest node for a given database state needs to be preserved. The following rule applies:

Duplicate state rule: Given two nodes, n and n', both representing the same database state, n can be pruned if $f^*(n) \geq f^*(n')$.

Proof: Since n and n' correspond to the same state, $h^*(n)=h^*(n')$. Consequently, $f^*(n) \geq f^*(n')$ implies that if an optimal solution is reachable from n it is also reachable from n'.

Hashing techniques can be used to efficiently detect state duplication. If a heuristic solution from n has already been computed, and $f^*(n) = f^*(n')$, then n is to be retained, and n' pruned, in order to avoid the recomputation of the heuristic. If $f^*(n) > f^*(n')$, the heuristic solution from n is absorbed by the new node n'. The duplicate state rule significantly reduces the solution space to be searched.

Assume that an action α is being applied, and that it has a minimum cost, i.e. equal to the cost in the completely reduced plan. This means that

1. action α must be performed to find a solution (otherwise its cost in the completely reduced plan would be 0), and
2. that no other action can decrease its cost.

Action α is thus a locally optimal move and should be immediately performed. Consequently, all the siblings of the node generated by α (i.e. alternate actions) need not be considered.

Process ASAP rule: Let $n_1, \ldots, n_i, \ldots, n_k$ be the set N of all the immediate successors of node n. If a node n_j exists, such that $f^*(n.) / f(n) = 1$, then all the siblings of n_j can be pruned.

Proof: If the condition is met, the action, which generates nj from n, has the same cost in the current plan and in the completely reduced plan, i.e. the minimum possible cost. Remember that only necessary actions have a non-null cost in the completely reduced plan. Consequently, no decrease in the cost of the action is obtained by postponing it, and the action is a local optimal move. This rule is especially useful to avoid exploring all the permutations of actions in a set of completely reduced relations.

5 Experimental Data

Two different distributed query optimization problems were studied [12] in order to investigate the most important properties of TAO. These problems are defined on databases distributed over a broadcast network [11]. Here we studied two different formulations: 1. only relation transmissions are considered; and 2. both relation and attribute transmissions for semijoins are considered.

The experiments were conducted on samples of random queries generated by a query synthesizer. For each random query, a random initial database state was generated by the synthesizer. Each sample consisted of 3500 queries, subdivided into 7 sets from 3- to 9-relation queries.

The first experiment was designed to investigate whether TAO searches offer a significant speedup over A* searches, and to compare plan quality and search effort of TAO vs. a heuristic strategy. These experiments were conducted on optimization experiment 1. The reference heuristic is strategy B-1 by Sacco [11], which iteratively broadcasts the smallest relation not yet transmitted. In order to characterize the search requirements, we used the total number of nodes created t, which gives a measure of time complexity. Simulated strategies are:

1. a uninformed A* search (h*(n)=0, for all n's)
2. an informed A* search with the elimination of duplicate states (h*(n) is estimated by completely reduced plans)
3. a TAO search with generally applicable rules but no relaxation
4. the B-1 heuristic algorithm

T's for the first three strategies are reported in figure 1. From these results, it can be concluded that uninformed A* searches are not practical except for problems on few variables. A case for considering informed searches and the elimination of duplicate states is provided by strategy (2), whose space and time complexity appears practical even for problems with many variables. TAO searches produce significant improvements over strategy (2) both in time and in space. In particular, for 9-relation queries, 4.9 plans were inspected and 3 plans stored, on the average. This compares favourably with heuristic B-1, which stores approximately 2 plans.

Table 1 reports the observations on plan quality for the B-1 heuristic and the first successful TAO heuristic lookahead. The heuristic used in TAO lookahead appears consistently better than B-1, with an average deviation from the optimum not exceeding 4% and a maximum observed deviation of 110%. In addition, over 63% of the plans generated by the first TAO heuristic solution are optimal. These results provide a good case for the use of *informed heuristic strategies*. However, the quality of heuristic plans depends on the specific optimization problem: in fact, the heuristic lookahead for problem 2 produced average deviations from optimum ranging from 6% to 21%, and a maximum observed deviation of 5921%. Therefore, heuristic strategies can be acceptable for ad-hoc queries, but their worst case can be quite bad for heavy, highly repeated queries, for which the slightly higher cost of a TAO search appears well justified.

The second experiment addresses relaxed searches. Since TAO searches are very efficient for problem 1, we used the more complex problem 2. Results are aggregated by number of possible actions at the start node, that more closely models actual query

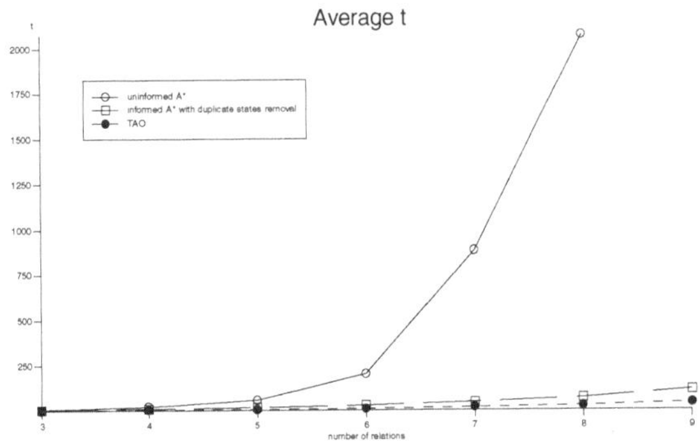

Fig. 1. Average t for problem 1

Table 1. Comparison of costs of heuristic solutions

#rel	B-1		TAO heuristic lookahead	
	Mean deviation	Max deviation	Mean deviation	Max deviation
3	0.03	0.92	0.01	0.67
4	0.05	0.92	0.02	0.94
5	0.07	0.84	0.03	0.73
6	0.08	1.35	0.03	0.53
7	0.07	1.43	0.04	0.93
8	0.10	1.47	0.04	1.10
9	0.09	1.28	0.03	1.02

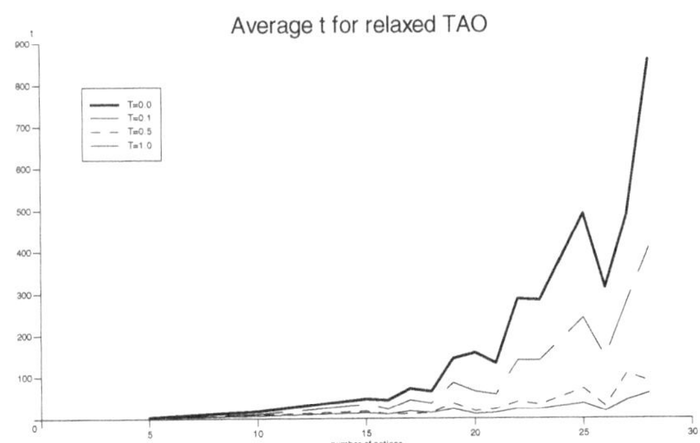

Fig. 2. Average t for optimal and relaxed TAO searches (problem 2)

complexity than the number of relations in the query. The results reported are relative to a 10%, a 50% and a 100% tolerance. Because of estimation errors, we believe that at least a 100% tolerance would be used in practice. Results are reported in figure 2, and show that even minimal tolerances produce significant benefits. Although relaxed searches guarantee that no plan deviates from the optimum more than the allowed tolerance, actual average deviations are very low and range from 1% (10% tolerance) to 15% (100% tolerance). Consequently, even large tolerance produce very good plans, on the average.

6 Conclusions

Our primary goal in the present research was to bridge the gap between exhaustive and heuristic optimization, and produce a single, general and coherent framework that can be easily adapted to any optimization problem and can be used to produce solutions whose cost is within a predefined deviation from an optimal solution. With respect to previous research, the "one size fit all" approach is finally overcome, and the required quality of execution plans can account for their frequency, criticity, and expected estimation errors. In practice, as we indicated previously, we expect relaxed searches to be the norm, with admissible deviations as large as 100% from optimal costs. The experiments conducted show that TAO searches are indeed close contenders of heuristic searches, as far as search effort and resources are concerned. Even moderate tolerances produce a significant search speedup, while selected plans are, on the average, much better than the admissible deviation. Analytic measurements for pruning rules are not reported here, but the results reported in [13] show that they can produce a significant, additional decrease in the overall complexity of the search.

This paper is primarily based on an unpublished research corpus dating back from the'80s. A number of important papers have appeared since, and new optimization strategies proposed. However, the main motivations of the present research are still valid [18]. The severe impact of estimation errors on plan optimality is now widely recognized and analysed in literature [6]. The fact that heuristic strategies produce plans whose uncontrolled quality may be abysmally low is now acknowledged [15]. There is a growing consensus on the fact that optimization costs must be reduced, or at least controlled. For instance, Ilyas et al. [5] propose a strategy to reduce optimization costs by using an acceptable upper bound on the estimated cost of optimization to stop the optimization process before completion, if required. Although there is a bound on optimization effort, there is no guarantee on the quality of the solution. In relaxed TAO searches, on the contrary, the plan generated is guaranteed within a predefined tolerance from the optimum, but no bound on the time required for optimization can be guaranteed. However, this approach can easily incorporated in TAO, with the significant benefit that an upper bound on the resulting plan quality is available, if the TAO search is prematurely terminated.

Finally, we believe the results reported by Waas and Galindo-Legaria [16] to be especially relevant here. Their work shows that with a relatively small sample from the solution space, it is possible to find plans that are pretty close to the optimum. In fact, the percentage of plans that are within twice the optimum cost is non-trivial. These results confirm our evidence of the high efficiency of TAO, even on queries on many relations.

References

1. Balbo, G., Di Leva, A., Sacco, G. M., Adaptive query optimization in point-to-point networks, in: "Distributed Data Sharing Systems", (F.A. Schreiber, ed.), North-Holland, 1984
2. Chaudhuri, S., An overview of query optimization in relational systems, Proceedings of the seventeenth ACM SIGACT-SIGMOD-SIGART symposium on Principles of database systems, 1998, 34 - 43
3. Hevner, A.R., The optimization of query processing in distributed database systems, Ph.D. Thesis, Purdue University, W.Lafayette, IN, 1979
4. Hevner, R.A., Yao, S.B., Query processing in distributed database systems, IEEE Trans. On Software Engineering, SE-5:3, 1979
5. Ilyas, I., et al. Estimating compilation time of a query optimizer, Proceedings of the 2003 ACM SIGMOD international conference on Management of data, 2003, 373 - 384
6. Ioannidis, Y. E., Christodoulakis, S., On the propagation of errors in the size of join results, Procccding of the ΛCM SIGMOD Conf., 1991
7. Ioannidis,Y.E., Kang, Y. C. Randomized algorithms for optimizing large join queries. In Proc. of the 1990 ACM SIGMOD Conf., 312–321, 1990
8. Kemper, A., et al. A blackboard architecture for query optimization in object bases. In Proceedings of the Conference on Very Large Data Bases, 1993
9. Kossmann,D., Stocker, K. Iterative dynamic programming: A new class of query optimization algorithms. ACM Transactions on Database Systems 25, 1, 2000
10. Nilsson, N.J., Principles of artificial intelligence, Tioga Publishing Company, Palo Alto, CA, 1980
11. Sacco, G.M., Distributed query evaluation in local area networks, Proceed. IEEE Conf. on Data Engineering, 1984
12. Sacco, G. M., Truly adaptive query optimization , Dept. of Computer Science, Univ. of Torino, Italy, TR 4/8/84, 1984
13. Sacco, G. M., Truly adaptive query optimization in point-to-point tree networks, Dept. of Computer Sciences, University of Torino, Italy, TR 3/21/89, 1989
14. Selinger, P.G., et al, Access path selection in a relational database management system , Proceed. ACM SIGMOD Conference, 1979
15. Steinbrunn, M., Moerkotte, B., Kemper, A., Heuristic and randomized optimization for the join ordering problem, The VLDB Journal, 6:3, 1997, 191 - 208
16. Waas, F., Galindo-Legaria, C., Counting, enumerating, and sampling of execution plans in a cost-based query optimizer, Proceedings of the 2000 ACM SIGMOD Conference, 2000, 499 - 509
17. Williams, R. et al.. R*: An Overview of the Architecture. IBM Research, RJ3325, 1981 Reprinted in: M. Stonebraker (ed.), Readings in Database Systems, Morgan Kaufmann Publishers, 1994, 515–536.
18. Winslett, M., David DeWitt speaks out, ACM SIGMOD Record, 31:2, 2002, 50 – 62.

Applying Cosine Series to XML Structural Join Size Estimation

Cheng Luo, Zhewei Jiang, Wen-Chi Hou, Qiang Zhu, and Chih-Fang Wang

[1] Computer Science Department in Southern Illinois University Carbondale, Carbondale, IL 62901, U.S.A.
{cluo, zjiang, hou, wang}@cs.siu.edu
[2] Computer and Information Science Department in University of Michigan, Dearborn, MI, 48128, U.S.A.
qzhu@umich.edu

Abstract. As XML has become the de facto standard for data presentation and exchanging on the Web, XML query optimization has emerged as an important research issue. It is widely accepted that structural joins, which evaluate the containment (ancestor-descendant) relationships between XML elements, are important to the XML query processing. Estimating structural join size accurately and quickly thus becomes crucial to the success of XML query plan selection. In this paper, we propose to apply Cosine transform to structural join size estimation. Our approach captures structural information of XML data using mathematical functions, which are then approximated by the Cosine series. We derive a simple formula to estimate the structural join size using the Cosine series. Theoretical analyses and extensive experiments have been performed. The experimental results show that, compared with state-of-the-art IM-DA-Est method, our method is several order faster, requires less memory, and yields better or comparable estimates.

1 Introduction

Extensible Markup Language (XML) has recently become the de facto standard for presenting, storing, and exchanging data on the Internet. Queries over XML data are usually specified as pattern trees [12] or path expressions [3,5].

Existing approaches that estimate the XML query selectivity follow two trends. One is to estimate the selectivity of path expressions or pattern trees [1,4,7,13]. Methods in this direction rely on some statistics to capture the structures of XML documents. The other trend is to identify the key operations performed in the query and estimate the selectivity of these operations. Since trees can be viewed as collections of paths, and paths can be further interpreted as links between pairs of XML nodes, structural joins that study the structural relationships between pairs of XML nodes have been recognized as vital operations of XML queries. A structural join between an ancestor set A and a descendant set D is to find all pairs of x, y such that $x \in A, y \in D$ and x contains y.

Due to the importance of structural join operations, a variety of methods have been proposed. While most of them concentrate on efficient execution of structural join operations[9,17,2,11], few [16,15] address the issue of structural join

S. Bressan, J. Küng, and R. Wagner (Eds.): DEXA 2006, LNCS 4080, pp. 761–770, 2006.

size estimation, which is nevertheless crucial to the query optimization because from which selectivity of the paths or trees can be derived easily.

Wu, et al. [16] proposed the PH histogram and Coverage histogram while Wang, et al. [15] proposed the adaptive PL histogram, as well as two sampling methods called IM-DA-Est and PM-Est. The PH histogram and Coverage histogram [16] represent the entire XML dataset as a two-dimensional feature space and partition this space into predefined grid cells. Each grid cell is associated with a count that indicates the number of nodes that fall in it. A structural join is then estimated according to the spatial relationships between grid cells. The PL histogram models the XML dataset as a one-dimensional feature space and a structural join is computed as the sum of the average number of descendant nodes contained in each bucket. IM-DA-Est and PM-Est [15] perform structural joins on samples and then scale up the results proportionally to estimate the structural join size. It has been shown [15] that Wang's IM-DA-Est provides the best estimation in all the methods discussed.

In this paper, we approximate the distribution of the nodes that satisfy a predicate with a small number of Cosine coefficients, and then estimates the join size by performing simple calculations on these coefficients. The experimental results show that, compared with state-of-the-art method IM-DA-Est, our method can be more than 10^5 times faster, requires much less memory space, and generates better or comparable results.

The rest of the paper is organized as follows. Section 2 briefly reviews related research in XML structural join size estimation. Section 3 models the distribution of XML nodes by mathematical functions and applies Cosine series to XML structural join size estimation. Section 4 compares our method with the sampling based method IM-DA-Est. Detailed theoretical analyses and experimental results are presented. Finally, Section 5 concludes this paper.

2 Related Work

To facilitate structural join operations, Wu, et al. [16] proposed a region coding scheme, which is similar to the one adopted in the Niagara [17] project. The coding scheme assigns a pair of values, *start* and *end*, called the region codes, to each node in the XML data tree. The region codes specify the nodes' locations and coverage. A structural join between an ancestor node a and a descendant node d is essentially to evaluate the logical expression of $a.start \leq d.start$ && $d.end \leq a.end$.

Existing techniques addressing structural join include histogram- and sampling-based algorithms [15,16]. The PH histogram [16] maps XML nodes to points in a two-dimensional space that is partitioned into predefined grid cells. The structural join size is estimated by examining the spatial relationships between the grid cells based on the assumption that XML nodes are uniformly distributed in the two-dimensional space. However, such an assumption could lead to poor estimation accuracy especially when the ancestor nodes are not self-nested. The Coverage histogram [16] is thus proposed to remedy this problem by estimating the fraction of coverage.

Wang, et al. [15] proposed the PL (Point-Line) histogram algorithm. It maps ancestors to ranges and descendants to points in a one-dimensional space. It has been shown [15] that in most situations, PL histogram generates more precise estimates than PH and Coverage histograms. However, when the descendants are sparse, PL histogram can have a very high inaccuracy in the estimates [15].

Wang, et al. [15] have also proposed two sampling-based methods, IM-DA-Est and PM-Est. Both methods estimate structural join size by first computing the structural join sizes over samples and then scaling up the results proportionally. The estimation accuracy of the sampling methods generally relies on the regularity of the structural relationships of the XML data. When the structural relationship is irregular, the estimation accuracy could be poor. IM-DA-Est was shown to yield better estimation than all other methods discussed [15]. However, compared with histogram methods that use only statistics, the sampling approaches are generally very slow. To expedite structure join size estimation, external index structures, such as XR tree [18] and T^+ tree [15], are used in IM-DA-Est and PM-Est. Nevertheless, there is still much room for improvement on the estimation speed.

3 Estimating XML Structural Join Size

This section presents the mathematical framework for applying the Cosine transform to structural join size estimation.

3.1 Assumptions and Definitions

An XML document is generally represented by an XML data tree $\mathcal{T}$. Without loss of generality, we assume that the region coding assigns a pair of *integer* values, namely (start, end), to each node in the XML data tree. The root node has the region code $(0, n)$, where n is the smallest integer number for the root node to cover all of its descendants. The region $[0, n]$ is also termed the *coding domain Dom.*

A *predicate* is a selective condition based on the values and structures of the XML data. For instance, a predicate like "tag name=student" selects tags whose names equal *student*. Evaluating a predicate against the XML data tree returns the set of nodes that satisfy the predicate. For simplicity, hereafter we shall call nodes that satisfy a predicate p the p nodes.

3.2 Modeling the Structural Join

We model the structural information of predicates by defining two types of distribution functions, one describing the coverage of the predicates and the other showing the predicates' start positions, such that the structural join size can be easily computed as their inner products. The functions are formally defined as follows.

Definition 1. *The coverage function of a predicate p at position $pos \in$ Dom, denoted as $\mathcal{C}_p(pos)$, is the number of p nodes whose region codes cover pos.*

Definition 2. *The start-position function of a predicate p at position pos* $\in$ Dom, *denoted as* $\mathcal{S}_p(pos)$, *is the number of p nodes whose start region codes equal pos.*

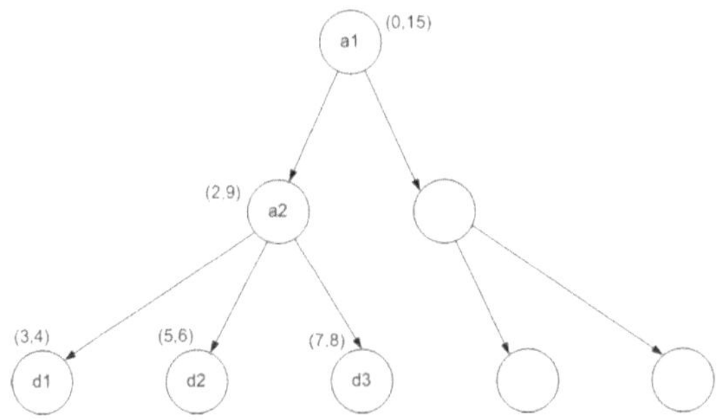

Fig. 1. An XML Data Tree

Figure 1 shows an example of an XML data tree, in which two nodes, namely $a1$ and $a2$, satisfy the predicate A, and three other nodes, namely $d1$, $d2$ and $d3$, satisfy the predicate D. Nodes that are of interest also have their region codes labelled close by. For example, node $d2$ has region codes (5, 6).

Figures 2 through 3 show the corresponding distribution functions for the two predicates. For example, $\mathcal{C}_A(6)$ equals 2 because both A nodes, namely $a1$ and $a2$, cover position 6.

The coverage function is intended for use when the predicate acts as the ancestor in a structural join and the start-position function is used when the predicate acts as the descendant. The value of $\mathcal{C}_p(pos)$ can be greater than 1 since the nodes satisfying p and covering pos might be nested; the value of $\mathcal{S}_p(pos)$ can only be either 0 or 1 because no nodes can have two identical start region codes.

Let us now illustrate the computation of the structural join size using the distribution functions. Consider the structural join between A and D, in which A is the *ancestor predicate* and D is the *descendant predicate.* Given a position pos in the coding domain Dom, $\mathcal{S}_D(pos)$ indicates whether there is a D node that starts at pos, and $\mathcal{C}_A(pos)$ is, by definition, the number of A nodes that cover pos and consequently cover the D node starting at pos according to the strictly nested property of XML data. Thus the product of $\mathcal{C}_A(pos) \times \mathcal{S}_D(pos)$ denotes the number of pairs of A node and D node that have the containment relationship at position pos. Note that each D node is only modeled once at its start-position. Consequently, the structural join size is computed as the sum of the products of $\mathcal{C}_A(pos) \times \mathcal{S}_D(pos)$ for all the positions in the coding domain Dom, which is exactly the inner product of $\mathcal{C}_A$ and $\mathcal{S}_D$, denoted as $\langle \mathcal{C}_A, \mathcal{S}_D \rangle$, over the coding domain. For example, from Figures 2 and 3, $\langle \mathcal{C}_A, \mathcal{S}_D \rangle = 6$, which is precisely the structural join size between A and D.

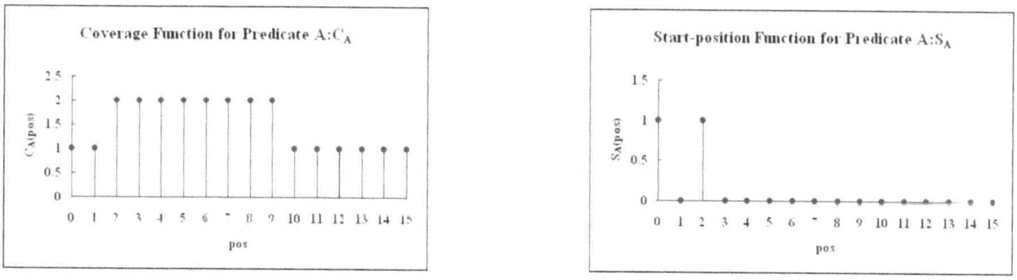

Coverage Function for A Start-position Function for A

Fig. 2. Distribution Functions for A

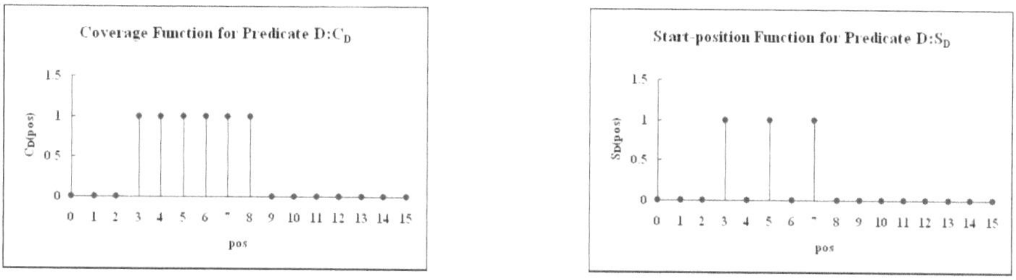

Coverage Function for D Start-position Function for D

Fig. 3. Distribution Functions for D

Lemma 1. *The structural join size between any pair of ancestor predicate A and descendant predicate D is the inner product of $\mathcal{C}_A(pos)$ and $\mathcal{S}_D(pos)$, denoted as $\langle \mathcal{C}_A, \mathcal{S}_D \rangle$, over the coding domain, namely:*

$$\sum_{pos \in \text{Dom}} \mathcal{C}_A(pos) \times \mathcal{S}_D(pos) \tag{1}$$

The above reasoning can be easily extended to multi-structural join size calculation. Theorem 1 generalizes the multi-structural join size computation.

Theorem 1. *The structural join size among any ancestor predicates A_1, A_2, $\cdots$, A_n and a descendant predicate D, is the inner product of $\mathcal{C}_{A_1}(pos)$, $\mathcal{C}_{A2}(pos)$, $\cdots$, $\mathcal{C}_{p_n}(pos)$ and $\mathcal{S}_D(pos)$, denoted as $\langle \mathcal{C}_{A_1}, \mathcal{C}_{A_2}, \cdots, \mathcal{C}_{pAn}, \mathcal{S}_D \rangle$, over the coding domain, namely: $\sum_{pos \in \text{Dom}} \mathcal{C}_{A_1}(pos) \times \cdots \times \mathcal{C}_{A_n}(pos) \times \mathcal{S}_D(pos)$.*

It is worth noting that while Wang's approach [15] uses tables and other data structures to store the structural information, ours models the information as mathematical functions. Consequently, to estimate the structural join size, their methods require intensive search over some data structures, while our method involves only computations of mathematical formulas. The distinction of how the information is represented results in completely different methods.

3.3 Structural Join Size Estimation

we use the Cosine transform to derive approximate distribution functions that need little storage space. The coding domain *Dom*, namely $[0, n]$, is mapped to the region [0, 1] and each position *pos* in *Dom* is normalized by dividing n. For example, $0^z = 0$ and $n^z = 1$, where the superscript ^{z} stands for normalized.

We denote the coverage function $\mathcal{C}_A$ on the new domain [0, 1] as $\mathcal{C}'_A$, such that $\mathcal{C}_A(pos) = \mathcal{C}'_A(pos^z)$. Likewise, the start-position function $\mathcal{S}_D$ is redefined on [0, 1] as $\mathcal{S}'_D$ and $\mathcal{S}_D(pos) = \mathcal{S}'_D(pos^z)$.

The two new distribution functions can now be expressed in Cosine series as: $\mathcal{C}'_A(pos^z) = \sum_{k=0}^{\infty} a_k \phi_k(pos^z)$ and $\mathcal{S}'_D(pos^z) = \sum_{k=0}^{\infty} b_k \phi_k(pos^z)$ respectively, where $a_k = \langle \mathcal{C}'_A, \phi_k \rangle$,$b_k = \langle \mathcal{S}'_D, \phi_k \rangle$, $\phi_k(x) = 1$ when $k = 0$; otherwise, $\phi_k(x) = \sqrt{2} \cos k\pi x$.

Now Equation 1 can be rewritten as:

$$\langle \mathcal{C}'_A, \mathcal{S}'_D \rangle \tag{2}$$

By Parseval's identity [8], the following equation holds:

$$\langle \mathcal{C}'_A, \mathcal{S}'_D \rangle = \sum_{k=0}^{\infty} a_k \times b_k \tag{3}$$

From Equations 2 and 3, the structural join size is computed as: $\sum_{k=0}^{\infty} a_k \times b_k$.

The join size can be approximated by using only the first m coefficients of each series as $\sum_{k=0}^{m-1} a_k \times b_k$.

4 Experimental Results

In this section, we report the experimental results of our Cosine Series based structural join size estimation method named CS-Est. Since Wang, et al [15], has shown that their sampling based estimation method, IM-DA-Est, outperforms other approaches such as the PH Histogram and Coverage Histogram [16], PL Histogram and PM-Est [15], here we shall only compare with the IM-DA-Est method.

We have implemented the IM-DA-Est and our CS-Est methods. We conducted experiments on a PC with a Pentium 4 processor and 256M RAM.

The datasets we used include a synthetic XML benchmark dataset XMARK [14] and a real XML database DBLP [6], which have also been used in [15,16]. For each dataset, we select pairs of predicates by the element tag name and then perform a structural join between each pair. Detailed descriptions of the datasets and selected queries can be found in the full version of this paper [10].

4.1 Storage Space

CS-Est estimates the structural join size by summing up the products of the Cosine coefficients of the coverage and start-position functions in question. Therefore, the memory space our method requires is for the storage of the Cosine coefficients.

As for the IM-DA-Est method, firstly, it needs to store the start-position table for each descendent predicate, from which samples are drawn. The table size is in the order of the number of descendent nodes in question. Secondly, it needs to check the structural relationships between the sample descendant nodes and the ancestor nodes by probing one of the external index structures, the XR-tree [18] and T-tree [15], both of which have a B^+ tree structure. An XR-tree (or a T-tree) is built for each ancestor predicate and requires a space in the order of the size of the ancestor nodes in question.

Let us use an example to illustrate the difference in memory usage. In the experiments, besides the external index structure used for examining the ancestor predicate, even the smallest table used for the descendant predicate *annotation* has $21,750$ entries, which amounts to $4 \times 21,750 = 87,000$ bytes of memory consumption for the IM-DA-Est method; while our CS-Est method consume only 200, 400 or 800 bytes memory for different settings. Even disregarding the external index structure, the memory consumption of IM-DA-Est is at least 100 times greater than ours. In short, our method requires much less memory space than IM-DA-Est.

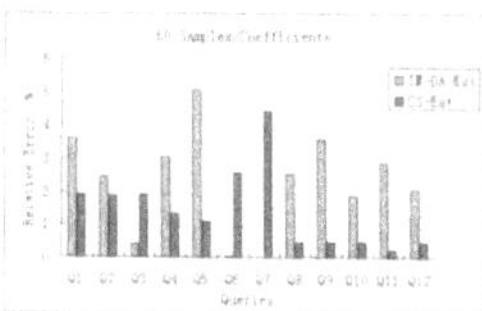

(a) Space Limit:200 Bytes

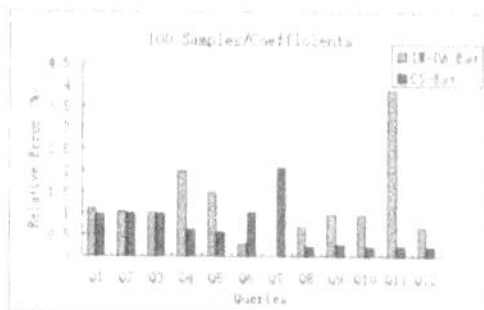

(b) Space Limit:400 Bytes

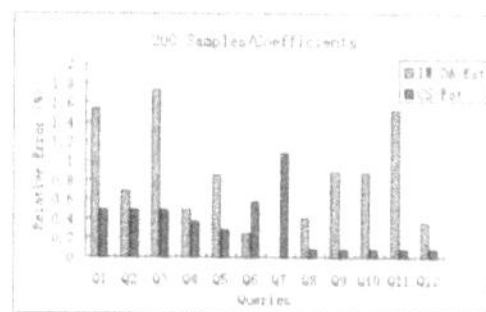

(c) Space Limit:800 Bytes

Fig. 4. Performance on XMARK

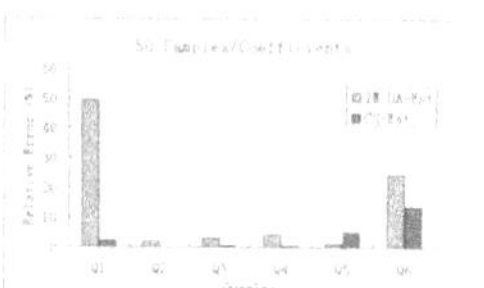

(a) Space Limit:200 Bytes

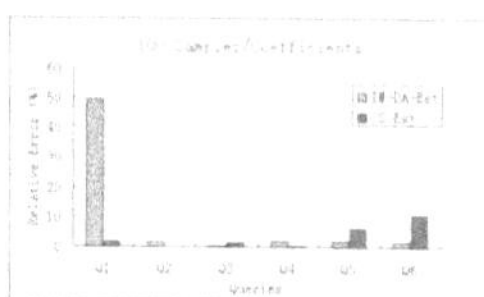

(b) Space Limit:400 Bytes

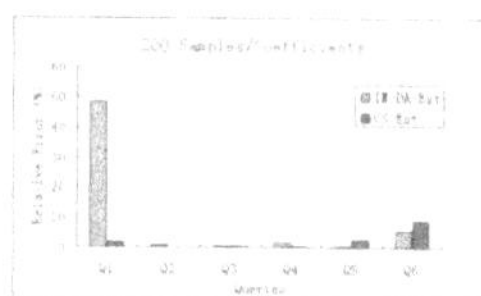

(c) Space Limit:800 Bytes

Fig. 5. Performance on DBLP

4.2 Estimation Error

The relative estimation error is used as the metric to determine the accuracy of the estimates. It is defined as $\frac{|x-\hat{x}|}{x} \times 100\%$, where x is the actual join size and $\hat{x}$ is the estimate.

The estimation accuracy depends on the number of samples drawn in the IM-DA-Est method, and the number of coefficients used in the CS-Est method. Here, we shall compare the accuracy based on the same number of samples and coefficients. Since each sample or coefficient consumes 4-byte memory space, one can alternatively use memory constraints to specify the sample or coefficient sizes, as adopted in [15]. It should be noted that the memory constraints shown in the figures are only the sizes of the samples used by the IM-DA-Est for estimation. They do not include the memory space for the external index structure and the table as mentioned above. However, these memory constraints do indicate all the memory space required by our method.

Figure 4 shows the performance on the XMARK dataset while figure 5 shows the performance on the DBLP database. Each figure has three sub-figures that correspond to the three memory space constraints respectively. The x axis denotes the queries executed and the y axis shows the absolute value of the relative estimation error. Results from the IM-DA-Est method and the CS-Est method are placed side by side for easy comparison.

The effectiveness of IM-DA-Est method relies on the regularity of the structural relationships between the ancestor and descendant nodes while the performance of the CS-Est method depends on how well the distribution functions are approximated. Figure 4 shows the performance on the XMARK dataset. Both methods perform quite well. The good performance is due to the regularity exhibited in the ancestor-descendant relationships for the IM-DA-Est method and the smoothness of the coverage functions for the CS-Est method.

Figure 5 shows the performance on the DBLP dataset. Our method yields below or near 10% errors for all queries and outperforms IM-DA-Est for most of the queries.

Figure 6 shows how the estimation accuracy of IM-DA-Est responds to the number of samples used and Figure 7 shows how CS-Est responds to the number of coefficients used. The figures show that generally the relative errors reduce with the increase of the number of samples and coefficients.

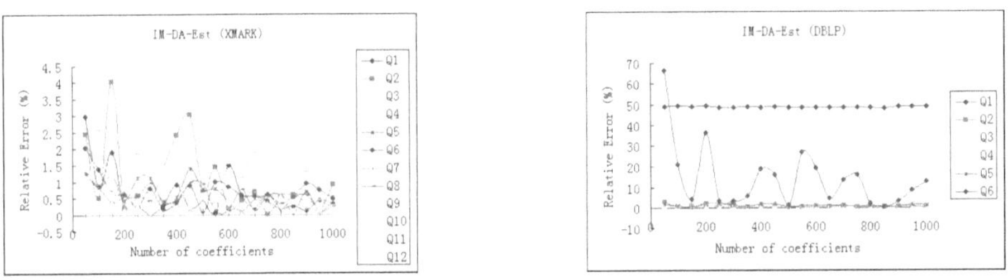

IM-DA-Est on XMARK IM-DA-Est on DBLP

Fig. 6. Estimation Accuracy versus Number of Samples

4.3 Estimation Time

Our method estimates the structural join size by summing up the products of pairs of coefficients. On average, it takes less than 0.1 μs to compute the product of a pair of coefficients. As for the IM-DA-Est method, it needs to probe an external index tree for each sample to find out the number of covering ancestor nodes, which may require several disk accesses[15]. Indeed, it may take, for example, $O(log_F N + R)$ disk accesses on an XR-tree in the worst case [18], where N is the number of indexed nodes, F is the fanout of the XR-Tree and R is the output size. The modern hard disk access time is about 4 ms. Therefore, even with only one disk access per sample, our method is still 10^5 times faster than IM-DA-Est, assuming the same number of samples and coefficients are used. As part of the query optimizer, the structural join size estimation is expected to be performed quickly and frequently. Our method certainly demonstrates its superiority also in this regard.

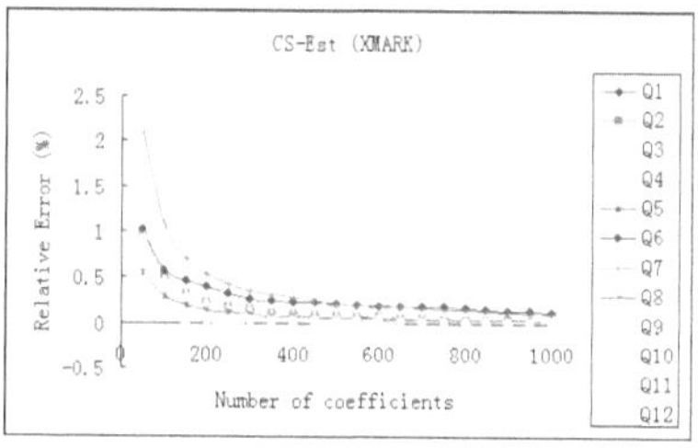

CS-Est on XMARK

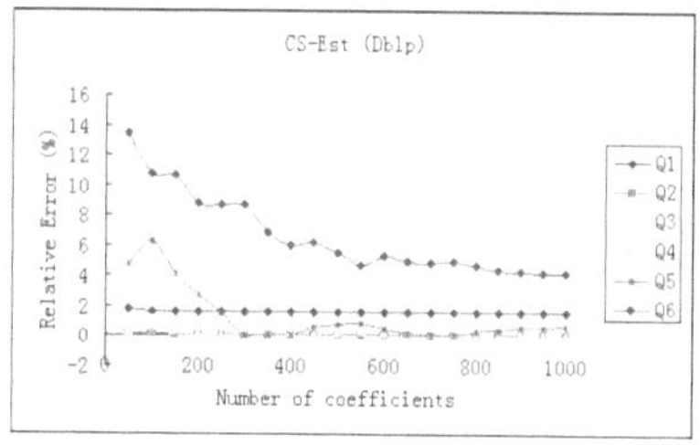

CS-Est on DBLP

Fig. 7. Estimation Accuracy versus Number of Coefficients

5 Conclusions and Future Work

In this paper, we propose to apply the Cosine transform to XML structural join size estimation. We choose to represent the structural information of XML data as functions, which opens the door for utilizing mathematical transforms to summarize the structural information. We use the Cosine transform to approximate this information and derive a simple formula for XML structural join size estimation.

Extensive theoretical analyses and experiments have been conducted. It is shown that, compared with state-of-the-art method IM-DA-Est, our method is faster, requires less space, and generates better or comparable results.

By modeling the structural information as functions, other existing well-known techniques, such as wavelet and sketch, can now be applied to XML structural join size estimation problem. In the future, we will try these techniques out and report our findings.

References

1. Ashraf Aboulnaga, Alaa R. Alameldeen, Jeffrey F. Naughton: Estimating the selectivity of XML path expressions for internet scale applications. Proceedings of 27th International Conference on Very Large Data Bases (2001) 591–600
2. Al-Khalifa, S., Jagadish, H. V., Koudas, N., Patel, J. M., Srivastava, D., Wu, Y.: Structural joins: A primitive for efficient XML query pattern matching. ICDE (2002) 141–152

3. Chamberlin, D., Florescu, D., Robie, J., Simeon, J., Stefanescu, M.: XQuery 1.0: An XML Query Language. W3C Working Draft http://www.w3.org/TR/xquery/ (2004)
4. Chen, Z., Jagadish, H. V., Korn, F., Koudas, N., Muthukrishnan, S., Ng, R. T., Srivastava, D.: Couting twig matches in a tree. Proceedings of the 17th International Conference on Data Engineering (2001) 595–604
5. Clark, J., DeRose, S.: XML Path Language (XPath). W3C Working Draft http://www.w3.org/TR/xpath (1999)
6. DBLP data set http://www.informatik.uni-trier.de/ley/db/index.html
7. Freire, J., Haritsa, J. R., Ramanath, M., Roy, P., Siméon, J.: Statix: making XML count. Proceedings of the 2002 ACM SIGMOD International Conference on Management of Data (2002) 181–191
8. Issacson, E., Keller, H. B.: Analysis of Numerical Methods Theorem 3. Dover Publications (1994) 238
9. Li Q., Moon, B.: Indexing and querying XML data for regular path expressions. VLDB (2001) 361-370
10. Luo, C., Jiang, Z., Hou, W-C., Zhu, Q., Wang, C-F.:Applying the Cosine Series to XML Structural Join Size Estimation at http://www.cs.siu.edu/c̃luo/Estimate.pdf
11. McHugh, J., Widom, J.: Optimizing branching path expressions. VLDB (1999) 315–326
12. Paparizos, S., Al-Khalifa, S., Chapman, A., Jagadish, H. V., Lakshmanan, L. V. S., Nierman, A., Patel, J. M., Srivastava, D., Wiwatwattana, N., Wu, Y., Yu, C.: TIMBER: A Native System for Querying XML. VLDB J, Vol. 11-4 (2002) 274–291
13. Polyzotis, N., Garofalakis, M. N.:Statistical synopses for graph-structured XML databases. Proceedings of the 2002 ACM SIGMOD International Conference on Management of Data (2002) 358–369
14. Schmidt, A., Waas, F., Kersten, M., Florescu, D.,Manolescu, L., Carey, M. J., Busse, R.: The XML benchmark project. Technical report CWI (2001)
15. Wang, W., Jiang, H., Lu, H., Yu, J. X.: Containment join size estimation: models and methods. Proceedings of the 2003 ACM SIGMOD International Conference on Management of Data (2003) 145–156
16. Wu, Y., Patel J. M., Jagadish, H. V.: Estimating answer sizes for xml queries. 8th International Conference on Extending Database Technology (2002) 590–608
17. Zhang, C., Naughton, J. F., DeWitt, D. J., Luo Q.,Lohman, G. M.: On supporting containment queries in relational database management systems. SIGMOD (2001)
18. Jiang, H.,Lu, H.,Wang, W.,Ooi, B.: XR-Tree: Indexing XML Data for Efficient Structural Join. Proc. of ICDE, India, (2003) 253–264

On the Query Evaluation in Document DBs*

Yangjun Chen

Department of Applied Computer Science
University of Winnipeg
Winnipeg, Manitoba, Canada R3B 2E9
ychen2@uwinnipeg.ca

Abstract. In this paper, we study the query evaluation in document databases. First, we show that a query represented in an XML language can be generally considered as a labeled tree, and the evaluation of such a query is in fact a tree embedding problem. Then, we propose a strategy to solve this problem, based on dynamic programming. For the ordered tree embedding, the proposed algorithm needs only $O(|T|\cdot|P|)$ time and $O(|T|\cdot|P|)$ space, where $|T|$ and $|P|$ stands for the numbers of the nodes in the target tree T and the pattern tree P, respectively. This computational complexity is better than any existing method on this issue. In addition, how to adapt this method to the general tree embedding is also discussed.

1 Introduction

In XML, data is represented as a tree; associated with each node of the tree is an element type from a finite alphabet Σ. The children of a node are ordered from left to right, and represent the content (i.e., list of subelements) of that element. XML queries such as XPath, XQuery, XML-QL and Quilt use tree patterns to extract relevant portions from the input database. A tree pattern query (or called a query tree) that we consider in this paper, denoted by *TPQ* from now on, is defined as follows. The nodes of a tree are labeled by element types from $\Sigma \cup \{*\}$, where * is a wild card, matching any element type. The type for a node v is denoted $\tau(v)$. There are two kinds of edges: child edges (*c*-edges) and descendant edges (*d*-edges). A *c*-edges from node v to node u is denoted by $v \to u$ in the text, and represented by a single arc; u is called a *c-child* of v. A *d*-edge is denoted $v \Rightarrow u$ in the text, and represented by a double arc; u is called a *d-child* of v.

In any DAG (*directed acyclic graph*), a node u is said to be a descendant of a node v if there exists a path (sequence of edges) from v to u. In the case of a TPQ, this path could consist of any sequence of *c*-edges and/or *d*-edges.

An embedding of a TPQ P into an XML document T is a mapping f: $P \to T$, from the nodes of P to the nodes of T, which satisfies the following conditions:

1. Preserve node type: For each $v \in P$, v and $f(v)$ are of the same type.
2. Preserve *c*/*d*-child relationships: If $v \to u$ in P, then $f(u)$ is a child of $f(v)$ in T; if $v \Rightarrow u$ in P, then $f(u)$ is a descendant of $f(v)$ in T.

Any document T, in which P can be embedded, is said to contain P and considered to be an answer.

---

* The author is supported by NSERC 239074-01 (242523) (Natural Sciences and Engineering Council of Canada).

S. Bressan, J. Küng, and R. Wagner (Eds.): DEXA 2006, LNCS 4080, pp. 771 – 780, 2006.

To handle all the possible XPath queries, we allow a node u in a TPQ P to be associated with a set of predicates. We distinguish among three different kinds of predicates: *current node related predicates* (called *current*-predicates), *child node related predicates* (called *c*-predicates), and *descendant related predicates* (called *d*-predicates). A *current*-predicate p is just a built-in predicate applied to the current node; i.e., a node v in T, which matches u, must satisfy this predicate associated with u. A *c*-predicate is a built-in predicate applied to the children of the current node. That is, for each node v in T, which matches u, each of its children (or one of its children) must satisfy this predicate. Similarly, a *d*-predicate must be satisfied by all the descendants of the node (or one of its descendants), which matches u. Without loss of generality, we assume that associated with u is a conjunctive-disjunctive normal form: $(p_{11} \vee ... \vee) \wedge ... \wedge (p_{k1} \vee ... \vee p_{ki_k})$, where each p_{ij} is a predicate.

For example, the following XPath query:

chapter[section[//paragraph[text() contains 'informatics']/following-sibling::*][position() = 3]]/*[self::section or self::chapter-notes]

can be represented by a tree shown in Fig. 1.

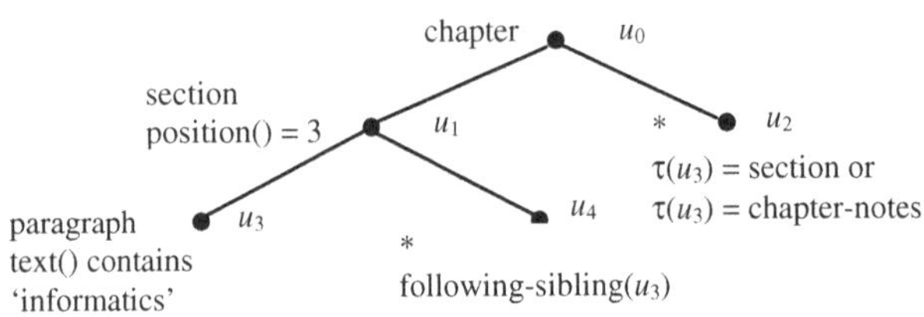

Fig. 1. A sample TPQ

In the query tree shown in Fig. 1, each node is labeled with a type or *, and may or may not be associated with a conjunctive-disjunctive normal form of predicates, which are used to describe the conditions that the node (and/or its children) has to satisfy, or the relationships of the node with some other nodes:

u_0 - $\tau(u_0)$ = chapter. It matches any node v in T if it is associated with type 'chapter'.

u_1 - $\tau(u_1)$ = section; and associated with a current predicate position() = 3. It matches any node v in T if it is a third child of its parent and associated with type 'section'.

u_2 - $\tau(u_2)$ = *; and associated with a disjunction of current-predicates: $\tau(u_2)$ = section or $\tau(u_2)$ = chapter-notes. It matches a node v in T if it is associated with type 'section' or 'chapter-notes'.

u_3 - $\tau(u_3)$ = paragraph; associated with a *c*-predicate: text() contains 'informatics'. It matches a node v in T if it is associated with type 'paragraph' and has a text child that contains word 'informatics'.

u_4 - $\tau(u_4)$ = *; associated with a current-predicate: following-sibling(v_3), which indicates that if u_4 match a node in T, that node must directly follows any node that matches u_3, i.e., any node with type 'paragraph' and having a text child node that contains word 'informatics'.

Accordingly, the embedding f of a TPQ P into a document T is modified as follows.

1. For each $v \in P$, v and $f(v)$ are of the same type; and $f(v)$ satisfies all the *current*-predicates associated with v.
2. If $v \rightarrow u$ in P, then $f(u)$ is a child of $f(v)$ in T; and $f(u)$ satisfies all the c-predicates associated with v. If $v \Rightarrow u$ in P, then $f(u)$ is a descendant of $f(v)$ in T; and $f(u)$ satisfies all the d-predicates associated with v.

Recently, much research has been conducted on the evaluation of such XML queries [1, 5, 6, 7, 8]. Here, we just mention some of them, which are very closely related to the work to be discussed. The first one is based on *Inversion on elements and words* [8], which needs $O(n^m)$ time in the worst case where n and m are the number of the nodes in T and P, respectively. The second is based on *Inversion on paths and words* [5], which improves the first one by introducing indexes on paths. The time complexity of this method is still exponential and needs $O((n \cdot h)^k)$ time in the worst case, where h is the average height of a document tree and k is the number of joins conducted. The main idea of the third method is to transform a tree embedding into a string matching problem [6, 7]. The time complexity is $O(n \cdot m \cdot h)$. This polynomial time complexity is achieved by imposing an ordering on the siblings in a query tree. That is, the method assumes that the order of siblings is significant. If the query tree is ordered differently from the documents, a tree embedding may not be found even though it exists. In this case, the query tree should be reordered and evaluated once again. Another problem of [6] is that the results may be incorrect. That is, a document tree that does not contain the query tree may be designated as one of the answers due the *ambiguity* caused by identical sibling nodes. This problem is removed by the so-called *forward prefix* checking discussed in [7]. Doing so, however, the theoretical time complexity is dramatically degraded to $O(n^2 \cdot m \cdot h)$. The last one is to represent an XPath query as a *parse tree* and evaluate such a parse tree bottom-up or top-down [1]. In [1], it is claimed that the bottom-up strategy needs only $O(n^5 \cdot m^2)$ time and $O(n^4 \cdot m^2)$ space, so does its top-down algorithm. But in another paper [2] of the same authors, the same problem is claimed to be NP-complete. It seems to be controversial. In fact, the analysis made in [1] assumes that the query tree is ordered while by the analysis conducted in [2] the query tree is considered to be unordered, leading to different analysis results.

In this paper, we present a new algorithm based on the ordered tree embedding. Its time complexity is bounded by $O(n \cdot m)$.

2 A Strategy Based on Ordered-Tree Embedding

In this section, we mainly discuss a strategy for the query evaluation based on the ordered tree embedding, by which the order between siblings is significant. The query evaluation based on the unordered tree embedding is discussed in the next section.

In general, a tree pattern query P can be considered as a labeled tree if we extend the meaning of label matching by including the predicate checking. That is, to check whether a node v in a document T matches a node u in P, we not only compare their types, but also check whether all the predicates associated with u can be satisfied. Such an abstraction enables us to focus on the *hard* part of the problem.

In the following, we first give the basic definitions over the ordered tree embedding in 2.1. Then, we propose an algorithm for solving this problem in 2.2.

2.1 Basic Concepts

Technically, it is convenient to consider a slight generalization of trees, namely forests. A forest is a finite ordered sequence of disjoint finite trees. A tree T consists of a specially designated node *root*(T) called the root of the tree, and a forest $<T_1, ..., T_k>$, where $k \geq 0$. The trees $T_1, ..., T_k$ are the subtrees of the root of T or the immediate subtrees of tree T, and k is the out-degree of the root of T. A tree with the root t and the subtrees $T_1, ..., T_k$ is denoted by $<t; T_1, ..., T_k>$. The roots of the trees $T_1, ..., T_k$ are the children of t and siblings of each other. Also, we call $T_1, ..., T_k$ the sibling trees of each other. In addition, $T_1, ..., T_{i-1}$ are called the left sibling trees of T_i, and T_{i-1} the direct left sibling tree of T_i. The root is an ancestor of all the nodes in its subtrees, and the nodes in the subtrees are descendants of the root. The set of descendants of a node v (excluding v) is denoted by *desc*(v). A leaf is a node with an empty set of descendants. The children of a node v is denoted by *chidren*(v).

Sometimes we treat a tree T as the forest $<T>$. We also denote the set of nodes in a forest F by $V(F)$. For example, if we speak of functions from a forest F to a forest G, we mean functions mapping $V(F)$ onto $V(G)$. The size of a forest F, denoted by $|F|$, is the number of the nodes in F. The restriction of a forest F to a node v with its descendants is called a subtree of F rooted at v, denoted by $F[v]$.

Let $F = <T_1, ..., T_k>$ be a forest. The preorder of a forest F is the order of the nodes visited during a preorder traversal. A preorder traversal of a forest $<T_1, ..., T_k>$ is as follows. Traverse the trees $T_1, ..., T_k$ in ascending order of the indices in preorder. To traverse a tree in preorder, first visit the root and then traverse the forest of its subtrees in preorder. The postorder is defined similarly, except that in a postorder traversal the root is visited after traversing the forest of its subtrees in postorder. We denote the preorder and postorder numbers of a node v by *pre*(v) and *post*(v), respectively.

Using preorder and postorder numbers, the ancestorship can be checked as follows.

Lemma 1. Let v and u be nodes in a forest F. Then, v is an ancestor of u if and only if $pre(v) < pre(u)$ and $post(u) < post(v)$.

Proof. See Exercise 2.3.2-2 in [4].

Similarly, we check the left-to-right ordering as follows.

Lemma 2. Let v and u be nodes in a forest F. Then, v appears on the left side of u if and only if $pre(v) < pre(u)$ and $post(v) < post(u)$.

Proof. The proof is trivial.

Now we give the definition of ordered tree embeddings. In this definition, we simply use 'label matching' to refer to both type matching and predicate checking.

Definition 1. Let P and T be rooted labeled trees. We define an ordered embedding (f, P, T) as an injective mapping f: $V(P) \rightarrow V(T)$ such that for all nodes $v, u \in V(P)$,

i) label(v) = label($f(v)$); (label preservation condition)
ii) if (v, u) is a *c*-edge, then $f(v)$ is the parent of $f(u)$; (child condition)

iii) if (v, u) is a d-edge, then $f(v)$ is an ancestor of $f(u)$; (ancestor condition)
iv) v is to the left of u iff $f(v)$ is to the left of $f(u)$. (Sibling condition)

As an example, we show an ordered tree embedding in Fig. 2.

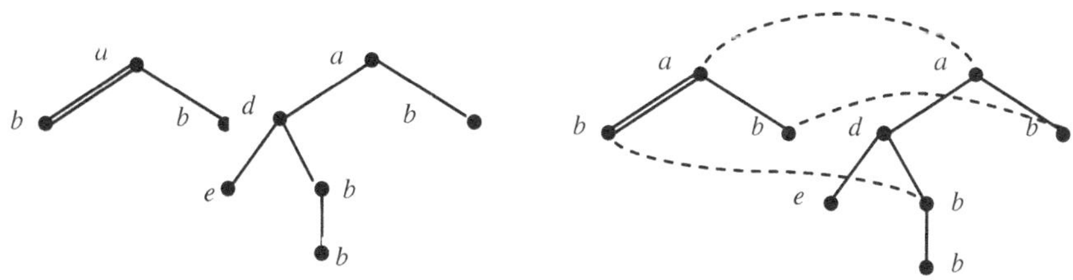

Fig. 2. An example of ordered tree embedding

In Fig. 2(a), the tree on the left can be embedded in the tree on the right because a mapping as shown in Fig. 2(b) can be recognized, which satisfies all the conditions specified in Definition 1. In addition, Fig. 2(b) shows a special kind of tree embeddings, which is very critic to the design of our algorithm and also quite useful to explain the main idea of our design.

Definition 2. Let P and T be trees. A *root-preserving* embedding of P in T is an embedding f of P in T such that $f(\text{root}(P)) = \text{root}(T)$. If there is a root-preserving embedding of P in T, we say that the root of T is an occurrence of P.

For example, the tree embedding shown in Fig. 2(b) is a root preserving embedding. Obviously, restricting to root-preserving embedding does not lose generality.

Finally, we use Lemma 2 to define an ordering of the nodes of a forest F given by $v \prec v'$ iff $post(v) < post(v')$ and $pre(v) < pre(v')$. Also, $v \preccurlyeq v'$ iff $v \preccurlyeq v'$ or $v = v'$. The *left relatives*, $\text{lr}(v)$, of a node $v \in V(F)$ is the set of nodes that are to the left of v (i.e., all those nodes that precede v both in preorder and postorder), and similarly the *right relatives*, $\text{rr}(v)$, is the set of nodes that are to the right of v (i.e., all those nodes that follow v both in preorder and postorder).

Throughout the rest of the paper, we refer to the labeled trees simply as trees since we do not discuss unlabeled trees at all.

2.2 Algorithm Description

The algorithm to be given is in fact a dynamic programming solution. During the process, two $m \times n$ ($m = |P|$, $n = |T|$) matrices are maintained and computed to discover tree embeddings. They are described as follows.

1. The nodes in both P and T are numbered in postorder, and the nodes are then referred to by their postorder numbers.
2. The first matrix is used to record subtree embeddings, in which each entry c_{ij} ($i \in \{1, ..., m\}$, $j \in \{1, ..., n\}$) has value 0 or 1. If $c_{ij} = 1$, it indicates that there is a root preserving embedding of the subtree rooted at the node indexed by i (in P) in the subtree rooted at the node indexed by j (in T). Otherwise, $c_{ij} = 0$. This matrix is denoted by $c(P, T)$.

3. In the second matrix, each entry d_{ij} ($i \in \{1, ..., m\}, j \in \{0, ..., n - 1\}$) is defined as follows:

$$d_{ij} = \min(\{x \in \mathrm{rr}(j) \mid c_{ix} = 1\} \cup \{\alpha\}),$$

where $\alpha = n + 1$. That is, d_{ij} contains the closest right relative x of node j such that $T[x]$ contains $P[i]$, or $n + 1$, indicating that there exists no right relative x of node j such that $T[x]$ contains $P[i]$. This matrix is denoted by $d(P, T)$.

In the above definitions of matrices, we should notice that the indexes of $d(P, T)$ is slightly different from those of $c(P, T)$. That is, for $d(P, T)$, $j \in \{0, ..., n - 1\}$ (instead of $\{1, ..., n\}$), and $j = 0$ is considered to be a virtual node to the left of any node in T.

The matrix $c(P, T)$ is established by running the following algorithm, called *ordered-tree-embedding* while $d(P, T)$ is employed to facilitate the computation. Initially, $c_{ij} = 0$, and $d_{ij} = 0$ for all i and j. In addition, each node v in T is associated with a quadruple $(\alpha(v), \beta(v), \chi(v), \delta(v))$, where $\alpha(v)$ is v's preorder number, $\beta(v)$ is v's postorder number, $\chi(v)$ is v's level number, and $\delta(v) = \min(desc(v))$. By the level number of v, we mean the number of ancestors of v, excluding v itself. For example, the root of T has the level number 0, its children have the level number 1, and so on. Obviously, for two nodes v_1 and v_2, associated respectively with $(\alpha_1, \beta_1, \chi_1, \delta_1)$ and $(\alpha_2, \beta_2, \chi_2, \delta_2)$, if $\chi_2 = \chi_1 + 1$, $\alpha_1 < \alpha_2$ and $\beta_1 > \beta_2$, we have $v_2 \in children(v_1)$.

In the following algorithm, we assume that for T there exists a virtual node with postorder number 0, which is to the left to any node in T. This is a modified version of the algorithm described in [3], adapted to handling of different kinds of edges (c-edges and d-edges).

```
Algorithm ordered-tree-embedding(T, P)
Input: tree T (with nodes 0, 1, ..., n) and tree P (with nodes 1, ..., m)
Output: c(P, T), which shows the tree embedding.
begin
  for u := 1, ..., m do
     {for v := 0, ..., n - 1 do {d_uv := n + 1;}
      l := 0;
      for v := 1, ..., n do
        {if label(u) = label(v) then
          let u_1, ..., u_k be the children of u;
          j := δ(v) - 1;
          i := 1;
          while i ≤ k and j < v do
          {j := d_{u_i, j};
            if (u, u_i) is a d-edge then
               {if j ∈ desc(v) then i := i + 1;}
            else /*(u, u_i) is a c-edge.*/
               {if j ∈ children(v) and j is a c-child then i := i + 1;}
            }
          if j = k then
            {c_uv := 1;
              while l ∈ lr(v) do {d_ul ; = v; l := l + 1;}
            }
        }
end
```

To know how the above algorithm works, we should first notice that both T and P are postorder-numbered. Therefore, the algorithm proceeds in a bottom-up way (see line 1 and 4). For any node u in P and any node v in T, if label(u) = label(v), the children of u will be checked one by one against some nodes in *desc*(v). The children of u is indexed by i (see line 6); and the nodes in *desc*(v) is indexed by j (see line 10). Assume that the nodes in *desc*(v), which are checked during the execution of the while-loop (see lines 9 - 15), are $j_1, ..., j_h$. Then, for each j_g ($1 \leq g \leq h$), the following conditions are satisfied (see line 10):

(i) $\delta(v) \leq j_g < v$ (i.e., $j_g \in desc(v)$),

(ii) There exists u_i such that $j_g = d_{u_i, j_{g-1}}$ with $j_0 = \delta(v) - 1$.

Therefore, for any j_a and $j_b \in \{j_1, ..., j_h\}$, they must be on different paths according to the definition of $d(P, T)$. In addition, in the while-loop, if (u, u_i) is a d-edge, the algorithm checks whether $j \in desc(v)$ (see line 12). If it is the case, u_i has a matching counterpart in *desc*(v) and i will be increased by 1. Thus, in a next step, the algorithm will check the direct right sibling of u_i against a node in the right relatives of j. If (u, u_i) is a c-edge, we will check whether $j \in children(v)$ and j is c-child (see line 14). If $i = k$ (i.e., *desc*(v) contains all subtrees $P[u_1]$, ..., $P[u_k]$), we will have a root-preserving embedding of $P[u]$ in $T[v]$. Therefore, c_{uv} is set to 1 (see line 17). Also, for any node l in the left relatives of v, d_{ul} is set to v (see line 18). It is because v must be the closest right relative of any of such nodes in T such that the subtree rooted at it (i.e, $T[v]$) root-preservingly contains $P[u]$.

Example 1. As an example, consider the trees shown in Fig. 3. The nodes in them are postorder numbered.

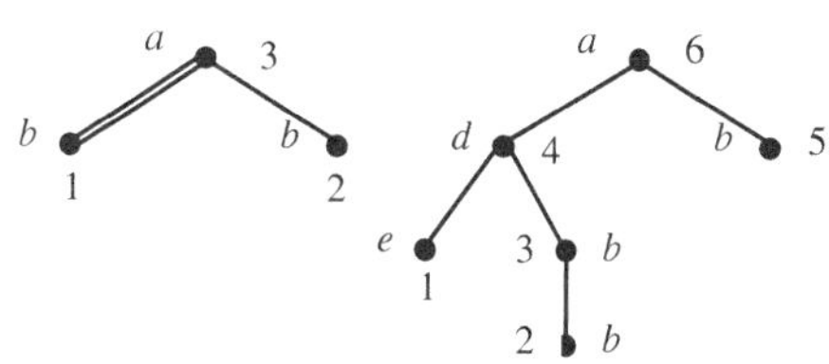

Fig. 3. Labeled trees and postorder numbering

When we apply the algorithm to these two trees, $c(P, T)$ and $d(P, T)$ will be created and changed in the way as illustrated in Fig. 4, in which each step corresponds to an execution of the outmost for-loop.

In step 1, we show the values in $c(P, T)$ and $d(P, T)$ after node 1 in P is checked against every node in T. Since node 1 in P matches node 2, 3 and 5 in T, c_{12}, c_{13}, and c_{15} are all set to 1. Furthermore, d_{10} is set to 2 since the closest right relative of node 0 in T, which matches node 1 in P, is node 2 in T. The same analysis applies to d_{11}. Since the closest right relative of node 2, 3, 4 in T, which matches node 1 in P, is node 5 in T, d_{12}, d_{13}, and d_{14} are all set to 5. Finally, we notice that d_{14} is equal to 7, which indicates that there exists no right relative of node 5 that matches node 1 in P.

step 1:

$c(P, T)$

	0	2	3	4	5	6
1	1	1	1	0	1	0
2	0	0	0	0	0	0
3	0	0	0	0	0	0

$d(P, T)$

	1	2	3	4	5	6
1	2	2	5	5	5	7
2	0	0	0	0	0	0
3	0	0	0	0	0	0

step 2:

$c(P, T)$

	1	2	3	4	5	6
1	0	1	1	0	1	0
2	0	1	1	0	1	0
3	0	0	0	0	0	0

$d(P, T)$

	3	2	3	4	5	6
1	2	2	5	5	5	7
2	2	2	5	5	5	7
3	0	0	0	0	0	0

step 3

$c(P, T)$

	4	2	3	4	5	6
1	0	1	1	0	1	0
2	0	1	1	0	1	0
3	0	0	0	0	0	1

$d(P, T)$

	2	2	3	4	5	6
1	2	2	5	5	5	7
2	2	2	5	5	5	7
3	6	7	7	7	7	7

Fig. 4. A sample trace

In step 2, the algorithm generates the matrix entries for node 2 in *P*, which is done in the same way as for node 1 in *P*.

In step 3, node 3 in *P* will be checked against every node in *T*, but matches only node 6 in *T*. Since it is an internal node (in fact, it is the root of *P*), its children will be further checked. First, to check its first child, the algorithm will examine d_{10}, which is equal to 2, showing that node 2 in *T* is the closest right relative of node 0 that matches node 1 in *P*. In a next step, the algorithm will check the second child of node 3 in *P*. To do this, d_{22} is checked. d_{22}'s value is 5, showing that the closest relative of node 2 in *T*, which matches node 2 in *P*, is node 5 in *T*. In addition, since the edge (3, 2) in *P* is a *c*-edge, the algorithm will check whether node 5 in *T* is not only a child of node 6, but also a *c*-child. Since it is the case, we have a root-preserving embedding of *P*[3] in *T*[6]. Finally, we notice that when the second child of node 3 in *P* is checked, the algorithm begins the checking from d_{22} rather than d_{20}. In this way, a lot of useless checkings is avoided.

Proposition 1. Algorithm *ordered-tree-embedding*(*T*, *P*) computes the values in $c(P, T)$ and $d(P, T)$ correctly.

Proof. The proposition can proved by by induction on the sum of the heights of *T* and *P*.

Proposition 2. Algorithm *ordered-tree-embedding*(*T*, *P*) requires $O(n \cdot m)$ time and space, where $n = |T|$ and $m = |P|$.

Proof. During the execution of the outermost for-loop, *l* may increases from 0 to *n*. Therefore, the time spent on the execution of line 18 in the whole process is bounded by $O(n)$. An execution of the while-loop from line 9 to 15 needs $O(d_u)$ time, where d_u represents the outdegree of node *u* in *P*. So the total time is bounded by

$$O(n) + O(\sum_{u=1}^{m}\sum_{v=1}^{n} d_u) = O(n) + O(\sum_{v=1}^{n}\sum_{u=1}^{m} d_u)$$

$$= O(n) + O(\sum_{v=1}^{n} m) = O(n{\cdot}m).$$

Obviously, to maintain $c(P, T)$ and $d(P, T)$, we need $O(n{\cdot}m)$ space.

3 On the Evaluation of General Tree Pattern Queries

In this section, we briefly discuss how to use the algorithm for ordered tree embedding to evaluate general tree pattern queries. For this, we need to consider the following problem:

> The ordering of siblings in a pattern (query) tree may be different from that in a target (document) tree.

In order to tackle this problem, we will change the sibling order in a query according to DTD if it is available. If the corresponding DTD does not exist, we store the document trees according to the lexicographical order of the names of the elements/attributes. Whenever a query arrives, the query tree will be constructed according to the same order. However, in the case that a branch has multiple identical child nodes, the tree isomorphism problem cannot be avoided by enforcing sibling order. For example, a query of the form: /X[Y/Z/B]/Y/A can be represented as a tree shown in Fig. 5(a) or a tree shown in Fig. 5(b).

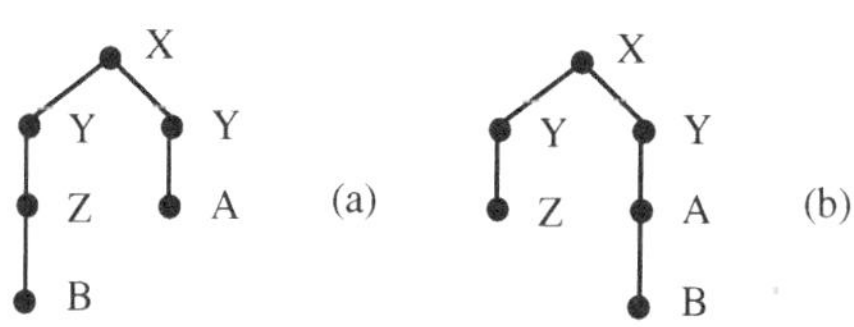

Fig. 5. Tree pattern queries

In this case, a sibling order cannot be specified lexicographically or by DTD schema. In order to find all matches, we have to check these two trees separately and unify their results.

4 Conclusion

In this paper, a new strategy for evaluating XPath queries is discussed. The main idea of the strategy is to handle an XPath query as tree embedding problem, by which the label matching includes both the type matching the predicate satisfaction. A dynamic programming method is proposed to check the ordered tree embedding, by the ordering of siblings is important. The algorithm needs only O(|*T*|·|*P*|) time and O(|*T*|·|*P*|) space, where |*T*| and |*P*| stands for the numbers of the nodes in the target tree *T* and the pattern tree *P*, respectively. Finally, how to adapt this method to the unordered tree embedding is briefly discussed.

References

[1] G. Gottlob, C. Koch, and R. Pichler, Efficient Algorithms for Processing XPath Queries, *ACM Transaction on Database Systems*, Vol. 30, No. 2, June 2005, pp. 444-491.

[2] G. Gottlob, C. Koch, and K.U. Schulz, Conjunctive Queries over Trees, in *Proc. PODS 2004*, June 2004, Paris, France, pp. 189-200.

[3] Pekka Kilpelainen and Heikki Mannila. Ordered and unordered tree inclusion. *SIAM Journal of Computing*, 24:340-356, 1995.

[4] D.E. Knuth, *The Art of Computer Programming, Vol. 1*, Addison-Wesley, Reading, MA, 1969.

[5] C. Seo, S. Lee, and H. Kim, An Efficient Index Technique for XML Documents Using RDBMS, *Information and Software Technology* 45(2003) 11-22, Elsevier Science B.V.

[6] H. Wang, S. Park, W. Fan, and P.S. Yu, ViST: A Dynamic Index Method for Querying XML Data by Tree Structures, *SIGMOD Int. Conf. on Management of Data*, San Diego, CA., June 2003.

[7] H. Wang and X. Meng, On the Sequencing of Tree Structures for XML Indexing, in *Proc. Conf. Data Engineering*, Tokyo, Japan, April, 2005, pp. 372-385.

[8] C. Zhang, J. Naughton, D. DeWitt, Q. Luo and G. Lohman, "On Supporting Containment Queries in Relational Database Management Systems, in *Proc. of ACM SIGMOD Intl. Conf. on Management of Data*, California, USA, 2001.

A Novel Incremental Maintenance Algorithm of SkyCube

Zhenhua Huang and Wei Wang

Fundan University, China
{weiwang1, 051021055}@fudan.edu.com

Abstract. Skyline query processing has recently received a lot of attention in database community. And reference [1] considers the problem of efficiently computing a SkyCube, Which consists of skylines of all possible non-empty subsets of a given set of dimensions. However, the SkyCube is can not use further as original data set is changed. In this paper, we propose a novel incremental maintenance algorithm of SkyCube, called *IMASCIR*. *IMASCIR* splits the maintenance work into two phases: identify and refresh. All the materialized SkyCube views share two tables which stores the net change to the view due to the change to the original data set. In the phase of identify, we identify and store the source changes into these shared tables. Then in the phase of refresh, each materialized view is refreshed individually by applying these two shared tables. Furthermore, our experiment demonstrated that *IMASCIR* is both efficient and effective.

1 Introduction

Recently, there has been a growing interest in so-called skyline queries[2,3]. The skyline of a set of points is defined as those points that are not dominated by any other point. A point dominates another point if it is as good or better in all dimensions and better in at least one dimension.

Numerous algorithms have been proposed for skyline retrieval. Borzsonyi et al.[2] propose the methods based on divide-and-conquer(DC) and block nested loop(BNL). Specifically, DC divides the dataset into several partitions that can fit in memory. The skylines in all partitions are computed separately using a main-memory algorithm, and then merged to produce the final skyline. BNL essentially compares each tuple in the database with all the other records, and outputs the tuple only if it is memory. The skylines in all partitions are computed separately using a main-memory algorithm, and then merged to produce the final skyline. BNL essentially compares each tuple in the database with all the other records, and outputs the tuple only if it is not dominated in any case. The sort-first-skyline(SFS)[4] sorts the input data according to a preference function, after which the skyline can be found in another pass over the sorted list. Tan et al.[3] propose a solution that deploys the highly CPU-efficient bit-operations by computing the skyline from some bitmaps capturing the original dataset. The authors also provide another method based on some clever observations on the relationships between the skyline and the minimum coordinates of individual points. Kossmann et al.[5] present an algorithm that finds the skyline with numerous nearest neighbor searches. An

S. Bressan, J. Küng, and R. Wagner (Eds.): DEXA 2006, LNCS 4080, pp. 781 – 790, 2006.

improved approach following this idea appears in[6]. Balke et al.[7] study skyline computation in web information systems, applying the "threshold" algorithm of [8].

Furthermore, we are interested in a class of new applications of skyline queries proposed in the reference [1] whose authors consider the problem of efficiently computing a SkyCube, Which consists of skylines of all possible non-empty subsets of a given set of dimensions. However, the SkyCube will expand exponentially if the data set and the number of dimensions of tuples become more enormous. And unluckily, the SkyCube is can not use further as original data set is changed. So, if usrs want to use this SkyCube again, it will return the wrong result. The most direct method to solve this problem is to try to compute the full SkyCube again. But it is impossible since it is of no effect at all.

In this paper, we propose a novel incremental maintenance algorithm of SkyCube, called *IMASCIR*(Incremental Maintenance Algorithm of SkyCube based on Identify and Refresh). *IMASCIR* splits the maintenance work into two phases: propagate and refresh. Each materialized SkyCube view has its own table which stores the net change to the view due to the change to the original data set. In the phase of propagate, we propagate the source changes to their tables. Then in the phase of refresh, each materialized SkyCube view is refreshed individually by applying its table.

2 Terminology and Notations

In this section, we give several concepts corresponding to Skyline and SkyCube.

Definition 1 (n-dominate). Let Ω is the set of n-dimensional tuples, and there are two tuples: $T(d_{1t}, d_{2t}, \ldots, d_{nt})$, $S(d_{1s}, d_{2s}, \ldots, d_{ns}) \in \Omega$. We call T *n-dominate* S(and denoted as $P \succ Q$), if they satisfy as follows($1 \le i \le d$):

1) $\forall i\ (d_{it} = d_{is} \vee d_{it} \succ d_{is})$;
2) $\exists i\ (d_{it} \succ d_{is})$.

Definition 2 (Skyline Set). The *skyline set* of Ω is denoted as $\nabla(\Omega)$, and it satisfy:

$$\nabla(\Omega)=\{ P \in \Omega | \neg\exists Q (Q \in \Omega \wedge Q \succ P)\}.$$

In order to discuss SkyCube conveniently, we must extend the domain of each dimension and two elements, i.e. "$\perp$" and "*ALL*", are added in it. "$\perp$" corresponds to empty, and the meaning of "*ALL*" is the same in the reference [9].

Definition 3 (n-dimensioanl Preference Function). Let Ω is the set of n-dimensional tuples, and $\Psi=\{O_1(d_1,d_2,\ldots,d_n), O_2(d_1,d_2,\ldots,d_n),\ldots, O_k(d_1,d_2,\ldots,d_n)\} \subseteq \Omega$. A function f^R is called a *n-dimensioanl preference function* if it satisfies as follows:

1) $f^R : d_1 \times d_2 \times \ldots \times d_n \rightarrow R^+$;
2) $\forall O_i, O_k (O_i \prec O_t \Rightarrow f^R(O_i) < f^R(O_t))$。

From definition 4, we see that a n-dimensioanl preference function makes the set of tuples which is out of order into an orderly one. For instance, given $f^R(O_1) < f^R(O_2) < \ldots < f^R(O_k)$, then the object sequence corresponding to f^R is $\Theta < O_k, O_{k-1}, \ldots, O_1 >$.

Definition 4 (∇ Filter Function). $\hbar_{\nabla}: 2^{d1 \times d2 \times \ldots \times dn} \rightarrow d_1 \times d_2 \times \ldots \times d_n$ is called ∇ *filter function* over the power set of $d_1 \times d_2 \times \ldots \times d_n$(to the set $d_1 \times d_2 \times \ldots \times d_n$) if only if there exists a function $\hbar_{\nabla}^{assist}$: $(d_1 \times d_2 \times \ldots \times d_n) \times (d_1 \times d_2 \times \ldots \times d_n) \rightarrow d_1 \times d_2 \times \ldots \times d_n$ (called ∇ filter assistant function) which satisfies:

$$\forall \Gamma \in 2^{d1 \times d2 \times \ldots \times dn}, \Gamma^2 \subseteq \Gamma, \quad \hbar_{\nabla}(\Gamma) = \hbar_{\nabla}^{assist}(\hbar_{\nabla}(\Gamma^2), \hbar_{\nabla}(\Gamma - \Gamma^2)).$$

Definition 5 (∇ AggregationFunction). ∇ *aggregation function* $\xi_{aggr} = \hbar_{\nabla} \oplus f^R$. It combine n-dimensioanl preference function f^R with ∇ filter function $\hbar_{\nabla}$. First, it filters tuples on Ω using $\hbar_{\nabla}$, then makes the remaining tuples orderly using f^R.

Definition 6 (SkyCube). A *SkyCube* is defined as a 7-tuple $<\varpi$,D,Dom,O,O_ Dom,*f*, $\xi_{aggr}>$, where

1) ϖ is an identifier of a SkyCube;
2) D={ $d_1, d_2, \ldots, d_n$}, called the set of identifiers of dimensions;
3) Dom=dom(d_1)xdom(d_2)x...xdom(d_n), called the domain over n-dimensional space;
4) O is object identifiers over n-dimensional space;
5) O_ Dom is the domain of objects over n-dimensional space;
6) f : Dom→O_ Dom is partial mapping over Dom to O_ Dom;
7) ξ_{aggr} is a ∇ aggregation function over Dom.

3 SkyCube Maintenance Algorithm

The SkyCube maintenance problem is the problem of keeping the contents of the materialized SkyCube view consistent with the contents of the original data set as the original data set is modified. Maintenance of a SkyCube view may involve several steps, one of which brings the view table up-to-date. We call this step refresh. A SkyCube view can be refreshed within the transaction that updates the original data set, or the refresh can be delayed. The former case is referred as *immediate SkyCube view maintenance*, while the latter is called *deferred SkyCube view maintenance*.

In this section, we employ the deferred mode, with the source changes received during the day applied to the SkyCube views in a nightly batch window. The work involves updating the original data set, and maintaining all the materialized SkyCube views. During that time the original data set is unavailable to users. The main aim of maintenance is to minimize the batch window.

Based on these points above, we propose a novel incremental maintenance algorithm of SkyCube, called *IMASCIR*(Incremental Maintenance Algorithm of SkyCube based on Identify and Refresh). *IMASCIR* splits the maintenance work into two phases: *identify* and *refresh*. All the materialized SkyCube views share two tables, called δ tables, which stores the net change to the view due to the change to the original data set. In the phase of identify, we identify and store the source changes into δ tables. Then in the phase of refresh, each materialized SkyCube view is refreshed individually by applying these tow δ tables. Identify phase can take place without locking the materialized SkyCube views so that the original data set can continue to be made available for querying by users. Materialized SkyCube views are not locked until the refresh phase, during which time the materialized SkyCube view is updated from the δ tables. So the identify phase can occur outside the batch window.

3.1 Phase Ⅰ: Identify

Multiple SkyCube views can be arranged into a (partial) lattice. Figure 1 shows a lattice wich corresponds to four dimensions A, B, C, D. And cube ABCD is the ancestor of all other cubes. Obviously, for a set of N-dimensional tuples, there exists at most 2^N -1 SkyCube views. Furthermore, the theorem 1 and the corollary 1 proposed in [1] show that offspring SkyCube views can be computed by ancestor SkyCube views.

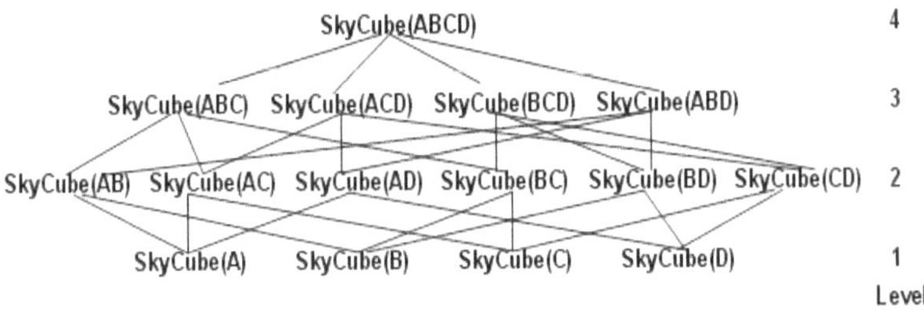

Fig. 1. Lattice Structure of a SkyCube

Theorem 1. Given a set S of data points on dimension set D, U and V are two sub dimension sets (U,V $\subseteq$ D), where U $\subset$ V. On dimension set V, each skyline point q in $SkyCube_u(S)$ is

1) either dominated by another skyline point p in $SkyCube_u(S)$;
2) or a skyline point in $SkyCube_v(S)$.

Corollary 1 (Distinct Value Condition). Given aset S of data points on dimension set D. For any two data points p and q, if $p(a_i) \neq q(a_i)$ ($\forall a_i \in$ D), then for two sub dimension sets U and V, (U, V $\subseteq$ D), where U$\subset$ V, $SkyCube_u(S) \subseteq SkyCube_v(S)$.

In this phase (i.e. identify phase), we use two tables which are shared by all the materialized SkyCube views to store the net change to the views due to the change to the original data set. One of these two tables is called insertion δ table (denoted as $\delta^{\lhd}$ table), which is used for tuples added into the original data set. Another one is called deletion δ table (denoted as $\delta^{\rhd}$ table), which is used for tuples removed from the original data set.

It is important to note that in the OLAP applications [10], in order to store the net change, each materialized DataCube view must has its own tables, that is, it needs $2\times|MV|$ tables for all the materialized views. The main reason is that in the OLAP applications, each materialized DataCube view has different net change when the original data set is changed. However, in the SKYLINE query applications, when the original data set is changed, all the materialized SkyCube views have the same net change. Hence, we only need two shared tables in this phase.

3.2 Phase II: Refresh

The phase of refresh can be processed as soon as the first phase finished.

Given a directed acyclic graph G(V,E), then there exists a sequence $v_1<v_2<\ldots<v_t$ which is topologically orderly, that is, v_i precedes v_{i+1}, where $i\in[1,t-1]$. On the other hand, it is obvious that not only SkyCube views lattice but also δ -lattice are the directed acyclic graphs. So, we can refresh offspring SkyCube views after it's ancestor SkyCube views. Our algorithm, i.e. *IMASCIR*, maintain the cube in topological order, hence, we can guarantee that ancestor SkyCube views are "clean" and can be used in the case of recomputation.

In the following part of this section, we'll discuss how to refresh a single materialized view. The procedures to refresh theoriginal data set are rather easy and will not be mentioned here.

For each materialized view, refresh procession includes two procedures as follows:

1) *Ref_Insert*: mainly modifying the SkyCube view with the $\delta^{\lhd}$ table.
2) *Ref_Delete*: mainly modifying the SkyCube view with the $\delta^{\rhd}$ table.

Ref_Insert procedure applies the changes represented in the $\delta^{\lhd}$ table to the SkyCube view. Firstly, Ref_Insert procedure compares tuples in the $\delta^{\lhd}$ table and filters those tuples which are dominated by the others which are in the $\delta^{\lhd}$ table. Secondly, Ref_Insert procedure uses the remaining tuples in the $\delta^{\lhd}$ table to filter those tuples in the SkyCube view which are dominated by the remaining tuples in the $\delta^{\lhd}$ table. Finally, Ref_Insert procedure modifies the object sequence generated by the n-dimensioanl preference function f^R of this SkyCube view. Ref_Insert procedure describes as follows.

```
Ref_Insert procedure
   Z := Skyline_Computing(δ◁ table);
   Chang from the object sequence Θ<O_k,O_k-1,…,O_1> to the set
   Φ {O_1,O_2,…,O_k} using the n-dimensioanl preference
   function f^R of the SkCube view;
   H=Skyline_Computing(Φ ∪ Z);
   Chang from the set H {O_1,O_2,…,O_h} to the new object
   sequence Θ'<O_h,O_h-1,…,O_1> using the n-dimensioanl
   preference function f^R of the SkCube view;
END
```

```
Skyline_Computing (similar to the one proposed in the
reference [4])
Input:  the set of N-dimensional tuples;
Output: the set which are not dominated by the others which
are in the input set;
```

```
Description:
list := Sort_set(Input) using the operator η = Σ_{i=1}^{N}(π_i(O));
 Z := ∅;
 t := 1;
 Z := Z∪{list[0]};
 list.delete(0);
 While(list.count>0) do
     f := false;
     For j := 1 to t do
         If (∀w∈[1,N],(π_∂w(O)≥π_∂w(list[i]))  then
              f=true;
              break;
      If (f = false) then
          Z := Z∪{list[0]};
          t := t+1;
      list.delete(0);
  Return(Z).
```

Ref_Delete procedure applies the changes represented in the $\delta^{\triangleright}$ table to all the SkyCube views. According to theorem 2, Ref_Delete recomputes the SkyCube views with the topological order, i.e. $v_1<v_2<\ldots<v_t$ (v_t is the ancestor of all SkyCube views). And it can guarantee all the SkyCube views are correct after processing Ref_Delete procedure.

Theorem 2. Let $G(V, E)$ is a directed acyclic graph, where V={all the SkyCube views} and E={all the edges which are from the parent SkyCube view to the child SkyCube view}. If a tuple is deleted from a child SkyCube view, when recomputing this SkyCube view, we only need to use the tuples which are in it's parent SkyCube view instead of the whole original data set.

For a single SkyCube view Υ, Ref_Delete procedure first compares the the $\delta^{\triangleright}$ table with the SkyCube view, and return immediately if all the tuples which are in the $\delta^{\triangleright}$ table are not in the SkyCube view. However, if a tuple O is deleted from the SkyCube view, some tuples which are dominated by the tuple O originally may become new skyline objects now. So, the part work of Ref_Delete procedure is to process these tuples in it's parent SkyCube view of Υ according to theorem 2. Note that when we compute the SkyCube view γ^{root} which is the root vertex in the SkyCube-lattice (that is, γ^{root} is the ancestor of all other SkyCube views), Ref_Delete procedure must use the original data set since γ^{root} does not have the parent SkyCube view.

Ref_Delete procedure describes as follows.

```
Ref_Delete procedure
1. Chang from the object sequence Θ<O_k,O_k-1,…,O_1> to the set
   ϕ{O_1,O_2,…,O_k} using the n-dimensioanl preference
   function f^R of the SkCube view ϒ;
2. If ϒ = γ^root then
     Φ := {the original data tuples};
```

```
3.  Else
4.   Search for the parent SkyCube view of ϒ denoted as γ^Parent ;
     /* the cardinality of γ^Parent is minimal among all the
       parent SkyCube views of ϒ */
5.   Chang from the object sequence Θ'<Pm, Pm-1,…, P1> to the
     set Φ{P1, P2,…, Pm} using the n-dimensioanl preference
     function f^R of the SkCube view γ^Parent ;
6.  For each tuple O in the δ^▷ table do
7.    If O in the SkyCube view ϕ then
8.      For each tuple T in Φ−ϕ
9.        If T is not dominated by O then
10.         add t into ϕ;
11. ϕ := ϕ- δ^▷ ;
12. Chang from the set ϕ{O1,O2,…,Oh} to the new object sequence
    Θ'<Oh,Oh-1,…,O1>  using  the  n-dimensioanl  preference
    function f^R of the SkyCube view.
```

4 Experiments

In this section, we report the results of our experimental evaluation in terms of time for maintaining the SkyCube views.

The databases used in all our experiments are generated in a similar way as described in [2]. We compare our algorithm with the naïve method which processes changes of all the SkyCube views by recomputing the original data set, and use tuples of dimensions 2, 5, 8 and 10. For the sake of simplicity, the type of all the attributes of tuples is integer. Moreover, we let the cardinality of $\delta^{\triangleleft}$ table equals to the one of $\delta^{\triangleright}$ table.

The first case: we fix the cardinality of the original data set (number of tuples=10^5), and the number of refreshing data tuples changes from 5×10^3 to 3.0×10^4. Figure 2 shows the result of the experiment of this case. From Figure 2, we see that the runtime of naïve method is much more than our algorithm, i.e. *IMASCIR*, in particular, the number of dimensions increase to 10. When the number of dimensions of tuples equals to 10, runtime of naïve method is over 13200 seconds since the naïve method processes changes of all the SkyCube views(about 2^{10}-1) by recomputing the original data set. Although the number of SkyCube views is also about 2^{10}-1 in our algorithm, recomputing of each SkyCube view only need the data set of its parent SkyCube view. So, our algorithm saves fairly much time. In Figure 2(d), runtime of *IMASCIR* does not exceed 3000 seconds, and only about 22 percent of the naïve method. Futhermore, we observe that the slope of curve produced by the naïve method equals to 0 since the naïve method always recompute the original data set whose cardinality is a constant (i.e. 10^6) and $|\delta^{\triangleleft}|=|\delta^{\triangleright}|$.

The second case: we fix the size of refreshing data (size=2×10^4), and the cardinality of the original data set changes from 0.5×10^5 to 3×10^5. Figure 3 shows the result of the experiment of this case. From Figure 3, we see that the runtime of naïve method is

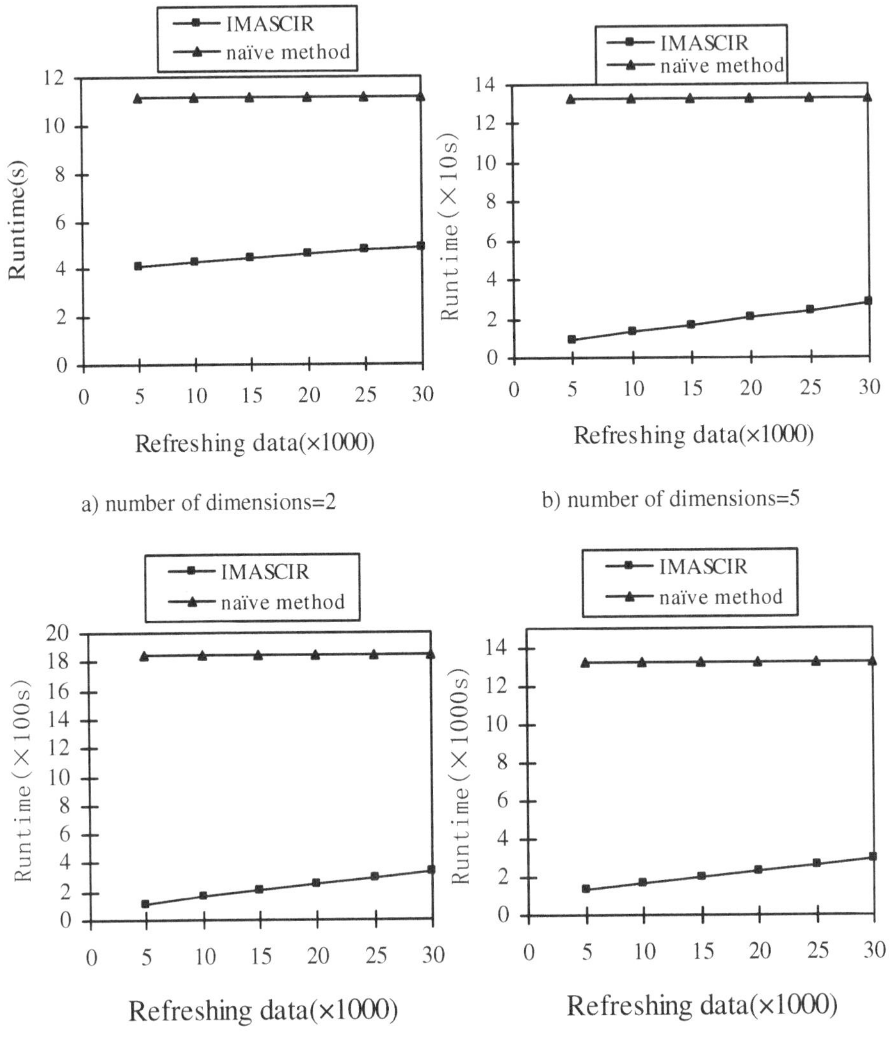

a) number of dimensions=2

b) number of dimensions=5

c) number of Dimensions=8

d) number of dimensions=10

Fig. 2. Runtime vs. the Cardinality of Refreshing Data

much more than our algorithm, i.e. IMASCIR.. And the superiority of our algorithm in comparison with the naïve one is more distinct with the increase of the cardinality of the original data set and the number of dimensions. For example, when the number of dimensions of tuples is 10 and the cardinality of original data set is 3×105, the runtime of naïve method is over 118800 seconds, however, IMASCIR does not exceed 21000 seconds, and only about 17 percent of the naïve method. Furthermore, we observe that the slope of curve of IMASCIR is fairly more small than that of the naïve method.

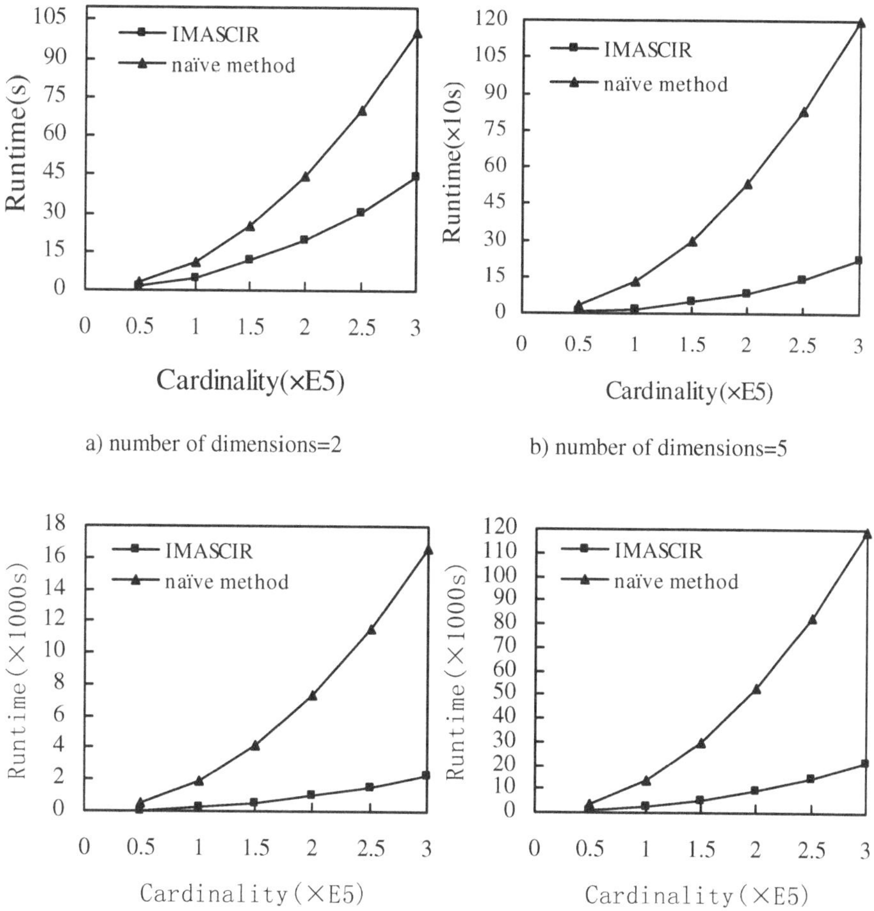

a) number of dimensions=2

b) number of dimensions=5

c) number of Dimensions=8

d) number of dimensions=10

Fig. 3. Runtime vs. the Cardinality of Original Data Set

5 Conclusions

In this paper, we are interested in a class of new applications of skyline queries, i.e. SkyCube. It is obvious that the SkyCube will expand exponentially if the data set and the number of dimensions of tuples become more enormous. And unluckily, the SkyCube is can not use further as original data set is changed. So, if usrs want to use this SkyCube again, it will return the wrong result. The most direct method to tackle this problem is to try to compute the full SkyCube again. But it is impossible since it is of no effect at all. Based on these considerations, we propose a novel incremental maintenance algorithm of SkyCube, called *IMASCIR*. *IMASCIR* splits the maintenance work into two phases: identify and refresh. All the materialized SkyCube views share two tables which store the net change to the view due to the change to the original data set. In the phase of identify, we identify and store the source changes to these two tables.

Then in the phase of refresh, each materialized SkyCube view is refreshed individually by applying these two tables. And our experiment demonstrated that *IMASCIR* is both efficient and effective.

References

[1] Yuan, Y., LIN, X., Liu, Q., Wang, W., Yu, J. X., Zhang, Q.: Efficient Computation of the Skyline Cube. *VLDB*, 2005.

[2] Borzsonyi, S., Kossmann, D., Stocker, K.: The Skyline Operator, *International Conference on Data Engineering ICDE*, 2001.

[3] Tan, K.L., Eng, P.K., Ooi, B.C.: Efficient Progressive Skyline Computation. *VLDB*, 2001.

[4] Chomicki, J., Godfrey, P., Gryz, J., Liang, D.: Skyline With Pre-sorting. *International Conference on Data Engineering ICDE*, 2003.

[5] Kossmann, D., Ramsak, F., Preparata, F. P.: Shooting Stars In The Sky : An Online Algorithm For Skyline Queries. *VLDB*, 2001.

[6] Papadias, D., Tao, Y., Fu, G., Seeger, B.: An Optimal And Progressive Algorithm For Skyline Queries. *SIGMOD*, 2003.

[7] Balke, W-T., Guntzer, U., Zheng, J.X.: Efficient Distributed Skylining For Web Information Systems, *EDBT*, 2004.

[8] Fagin, R., Lotem, A., Naor, M.: Optimal Aggregation Algorithms For Middleware. *PODS*, 2001.

[9] Gray, J., Chaudhuri, S., Bosworth, A.: Data Cube: a relational aggregation operator generalizing group-by, cross-tab, and sub-totals. *Data Mining and Knowledge Discovery*, 1997.

[10] Mumick, D.Q., Mumick, B.: Maintenance of Data Cubes and Summary Tables in a Warehouse. *International Conference on Data Engineering ICDE*, 1997.

Probabilistic Replication Based on Access Frequencies in Unstructured Peer-to-Peer Networks

Takahiro Hara, Yuki Kido, and Shojiro Nishio

Graduate School of Information Science and Tech., Osaka University
{hara, kido.yuki, nishio}@ist.osaka-u.ac.jp

Abstract. Recently, there has been increasing interest in research on data sharing through peer-to-peer networks. In this paper, assuming a data-sharing service, we propose a new replication strategy that achieves not only load balancing but also improvement of search performance. The proposed strategy creates replicas at each peer on the path along which a query is successfully forwarded, depending on the peer's rank of access frequency to the data. Moreover, we verify the effectiveness of the proposed strategy by simulation experiments.

1 Introduction

Recently, peer-to-peer (P2P) systems and applications have been becoming popular and a large number of research projects on P2P systems are ongoing. P2P systems are distributed systems in which a node communicates with other nodes and acts as both client and server in a context. Nodes in P2P systems are called *peers*.

A decentralized P2P system has no central server; instead, peers form an ad hoc network and send their queries to other peers. Some decentralized P2P systems are *structured*, whereby they have close coupling between the P2P network topology and the location of the data. Typical examples are Chord[16], Content-Addressable Network (CAN)[14], Pastry[15], Tapestry[17], and Kademlia[13]. These systems precisely determine the placement of data items based on *Distributed Hash Tables (DHTs)*. The others are *decentralized*, whereby they have neither a central server nor any precise control over the network topology or data placement. Typical examples are Gnutella[7] and JXTA[8]. The network is formed by peers based on some loose rules, and the placement of data items is not based on any knowledge of the network topology. To find a required data item, a peer issues queries to its neighbors. *Flooding* is typically used for this aim, where the query is propagated to all neighbors within a certain hopcount, which is called *TTL (Time To Live)*.

Unstructured P2P systems have an advantage of being built easily and flexibly. Because of this advantage, most P2P systems currently in service use unstructured networks for looking up data[6,7]. Thus, in this paper, we assume data sharing in an unstructured P2P system. It is commonplace in an unstructured P2P network that data items are replicated on multiple peers in the network for

S. Bressan, J. Küng, and R. Wagner (Eds.): DEXA 2006, LNCS 4080, pp. 791–800, 2006.

efficient data retrieval, improving data availability, and load balancing[3,4,5,12]. In [3], the authors discussed the optimal ratios of numbers of replicas allocated in the network. As a conclusion, the *square-root** allocation, in which the ratios of numbers of replicas are proportional to the square-root of their query rates (access frequencies), is the optimal policy in terms of query efficiency. The authors also discussed that a simple replication algorithm, called *path replication*, can nearly achieve the square-root* allocation. In path replication, when a query is successful, the target data item is replicated at all peers along the path from the query-issuing peer to the peer that responded to the query.

However, as described in Section 3, we found that replica allocation based on path replication is not close enough to the square-root* allocation and can be further improved. Therefore, in this paper, we propose a replication strategy that almost achieves the square-root* allocation. In this strategy, similar to path replication, the target data item of a query is replicated at peers along the path from the query-issuing peer to the query-responding one. In doing so, at these peers replicas are allocated with probabilities determined based on the rank of the item's query rate among all data items.

The remainder of the paper is organized as follows. In Section 2, we show our assumed system model and in Section 3 describe the results of preliminary experiments. In Section 4, we propose a replication strategy based on the experimental results. Section 5 contains the results of the performance evaluation. Finally, in Section 6 we summarize this paper.

2 System Model

The system model assumes an unstructured peer-to-peer network in which peers access and replicate data items held by others as the originals (primary copies). When a peer requests a data item, it floods the network with a query message that has a TTL. If more than one peer that holds the requested data item or its replica is found by the query flood, the query-issuing peer accesses the data item (replica) held by the peer with the shortest hopcount among them.

In [1], it is reported that real unstructured P2P networks have *power-law* degree distributions. Here, it is defined that a network follows the power-law when the degree of peer i, d_i, which is the number of i's adjacent peers in the P2P network, is expressed by $d_i \propto 1/r_i^\beta$ ($\beta \geq 0$). Here, r_i denotes the rank of peer i, which is its index in the descending order of outdegree (number of adjacent peers). Several recent works have concentrated on the properties of these power-law networks[2,9,10].

Based on the above fact, in this paper, we assume that the network follows the power-law. Specifically, the network is constructed by connecting peers at random according to the power-law, which is called a *PLRG* (*Power-law Random Graph*). For simplicity in discussion, we assume that each peer's rank is equal to the peer's identifier, i.e., $r_i = i$, without loosing generality. The degree of peer i is expressed by the following equation:

$$d_i = \lfloor \omega / i^\beta \rfloor \quad (\beta \geq 0), \tag{1}$$

where, ω denotes the maximum number of adjacent peers and β denotes the network parameter that determines the density of the network.

The access probability (query rate), q_j, to data item j in the entire network follows the Zipf distribution[18] and is expressed by the following equation:

$$q_j = \frac{j^{-\alpha}}{\sum_{m=1}^{k} m^{-\alpha}}. \tag{2}$$

Here, k denotes the total number of data items in the entire network, and α denotes the Zipf coefficient, where a larger α represents a greater skew in the query rate among data items. Equation 2 represents that data items with smaller identifiers are requested more frequently, i.e., $q_1 \geq q_2 \geq \cdots \geq q_k$. This is for simplicity in discussion but we can arbitrarily change this order without losing generality.

We assume that the system parameters, such as, β, ω, α and the rank of query rates for all data items are known. Of course, we know that this assumption is not always true in a real environment; specially in an unstructured P2P network, it is unrealistic to obtain global information on the rank of query rates for all data items. We adopted this assumption to examine the behavior and the characteristics of our proposed replication strategy. Our approach can be applied, however, in an environment without this assumption. For example, the rank of query rates can be estimated by monitoring query messages exchanged among peers. Though by this estimation each peer can obtain only the local information on query rates around the itself, this is usually sufficient because a query propagates only around the peer within a predetermined TTL. In addition, the local information obtained by this estimation is sometimes better than the global information if the locality exists in query rates of data items.

3 Preliminary Experiments

In this section, we show the results of our preliminary experiments to examine how well path replication achieves the square-root* allocation and its impact on the query success ratio. We also explain the motivation and idea of our approach.

3.1 Simulation Environment

The number of peers in the entire network is 3,000. The number of types of data items is 500 and each of them is held by a particular peer as the original. For simplicity, all data items are of the same size and not updated, i.e., their replicas do not become stale. Each peer has a memory space to replicate up to five data items. Initially, replicas are allocated in the entire network according to the square-root* allocation. Peers do not disappear from the P2P network either intentionally or by a failure.

The probability that each peer issues a query to a data item at a unit of simulation time is 0.1. For simplicity, all peers have the same access characteristics and follow the query rates shown in Equation (2). Queries are processed by flooding with TTL=10. Based on the above environment, we perform simulation experiments for 4,000 units of time.

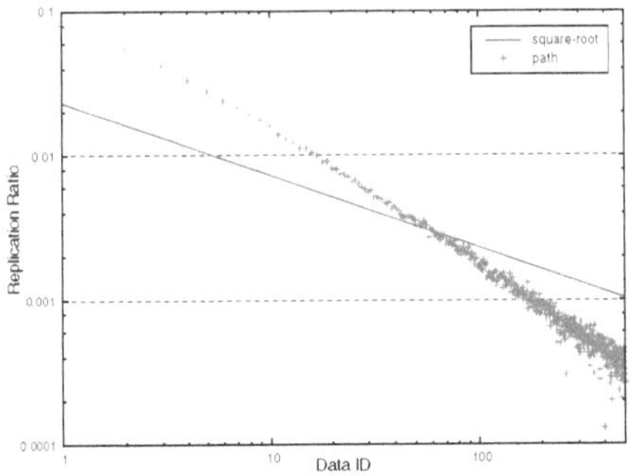

(a) Path replication

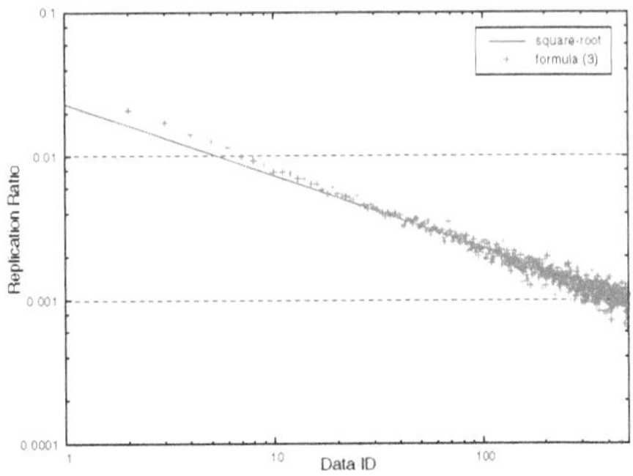

(b) Equation (3)

Fig. 1. Replica allocation by path replication

3.2 The Number of Replicas and Query Success Ratio

Figure 1(a) shows the distribution of replicas among peers when applying path replication, denoted by "path," where ω, β, and α, are set to 225, 0.8, and 1.0, respectively. The horizontal axis indicates the data identifier (i.e., the rank of query rate) and the vertical axis indicates the ratio of the number of replicas to the total number of replicas in the entire network. For comparison, the ideal distribution based on the square-root* allocation is also shown as "square-root."

From this result, path replication allocates more replicas than those in the ideal case for data items whose data identifiers are lower than 50. The smaller the identifier, i.e., the higher the query rate, the larger the difference with the ideal case. On the other hand, it allocates fewer replicas for data items with low query rates. This shows that path replication allocates too many replicas of data items with high query rates, and that replicas of data items with low query rates are usually replaced with those with high query rates.

To solve this problem and approach to the square-root allocation, replication of data items with high query rates should be restricted. Based on this fact, in our approach each data item is replicated at peers along the path from the query-issuing peer to the data holder with a certain probability determined by the rank of the query rate of the data item. Here, path replication is a special case for this approach where the probability is always set as 1.

In our approach, the key issue is how to determine the appropriate replication probability, R_j, for each data item j. To solve this problem, we conducted a large number of experiments and found that the following replication probability is nearly optimal in this simulation environment.

$$R_j = 0.05 + 0.95 \times (\frac{j}{k})^{\frac{1}{2}}. \tag{3}$$

Figure 1(b) shows the distribution of replicas among peers when applying Equation (3) to determine the replication probabilities, denoted by "Equation (3)." This result confirms that this approach is effective to almost achieve the square-root* allocation.

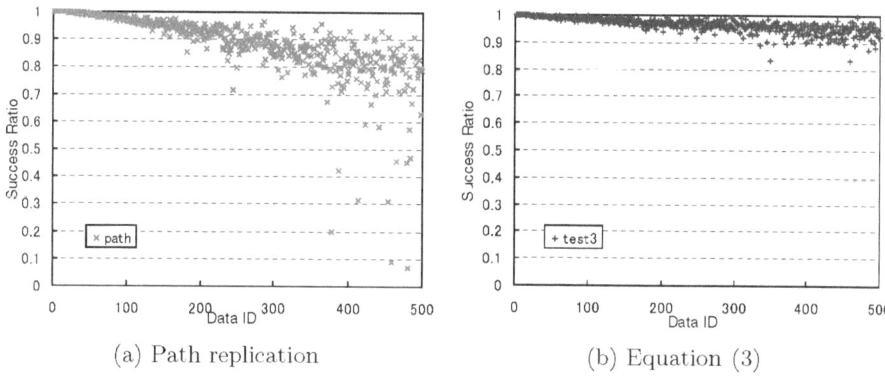

Fig. 2. Query success ratio

Figure 2 shows the query success ratios for data items when applying path replication and data replication based on Equation (3). The success ratio of each data item is defined as the ratio of successful queries to the total number of queries issued for the item during the simulation time. These results show that by approaching the square-root* allocation, the success ratios increases, especially for those for data items with low query ratios.

4 Probabilistic Replication Based on Query Rates

Though replication based on Equation (3) achieves nearly optimal replica allocation, it is specialized for the environment in the preliminary experiments in Section 3. Therefore, in this section, we provide a general and formal method that aims to achieve the square-root* allocation.

In our proposed method, similar to path replication, when a query is successful the target data item is replicated at peers along the path from the query-issuing peer to the peer that responded to the query. At each peer along the path, based on the replication probability determined by the rank of query rate of the target item, it is randomly decided whether the target item is replicated. The replication probability of data item j, i.e., j-th rank, is given by the following formula based on the results of the preliminary experiments:

$$R_j = a + (1.00 - a)(\frac{j}{k})^c. \quad (4)$$

Here, a and c are parameters varying from 0 to 1 and are used to adjust the difference in replication probabilities between data items with high query rates and those with low query rates. The optimal values for these two parameters change according to changes in the system environment, i.e., α, ω, and β.

5 Performance Evaluation

In this section, we present the results of simulation experiments to evaluate the performance of our proposed method. The simulation model is basically the same as that described in Section 3. Note that from our prior experiments, not described here, it is shown that the initial allocation of replicas at the beginning of the simulation does not affect the replica allocation in the steady state. Thus, we chose the square-root* allocation as the initial allocation.

In this paper, we define the following metric to examine how the replica allocation is close to the square-root* allocation:

$$V = \frac{1}{k}\sum_{j=1}^{k}\frac{|e_j - s_j|}{s_j}. \tag{5}$$

Here, both e_j and s_j denote the ratio of the number of replicas of data j to the total number of replicas in the entire network, e_j is the actual ratio resulting from applying a replication method, and s_j is the ideal ratio according to the square-root* allocation. The smaller V is, the closer the replica allocation is to the square-root* allocation.

5.1 Access Skew and Optimal a and c

We examine the values of a and c in Equation (4) that gives the smallest V when varying α (parameter determining the access skew) by 0.1 in the range from 0.0 to 1.2. In the simulation experiments, both a and c are varied by 0.05 in the range from 0.00 to 1.00; ω and β are fixed to 225 and 0.8, respectively. Table 1 shows the test results, and indicates that there is a correlation between α and the optimal values of a and c. When α is small, large a and small c give a replica allocation close to the square-root* allocation, and vice versa.

For comparison, Figure 3 shows the impact of α on V in path replication. In this graph, the horizontal axis indicates α and the vertical axis indicates V. The result shows that as α increases, V also grows, i.e., in path replication the replica allocation is farther from the square-root* allocation. On the contrary, our proposed method gives a much lower V independent of the value of α. This shows that appropriate settings of a and c work well to restrict the excessive replication of data items with high query rates.

5.2 Network Density and Optimal a and c

Next, we examine the values of a and c that give the smallest V when varying ω and β (parameters determining the network density). In doing so, the total number of links in the entire network is fixed to 6,000 and ω is set to a value

Table 1. Optimal a and c varying α

α	0.0	0.1	0.2	0.3	0.4	0.5	0.6	0.7	0.8	0.9	1.0	1.1	1.2
a	0.85	0.55	0.40	0.05	0.00	0.05	0.00	0.05	0.05	0.00	0.05	0.00	0.00
c	0.05	0.15	0.20	0.15	0.20	0.25	0.30	0.35	0.45	0.45	0.55	0.55	0.60
V	0.046	0.048	0.049	0.049	0.052	0.057	0.057	0.063	0.069	0.075	0.091	0.102	0.120

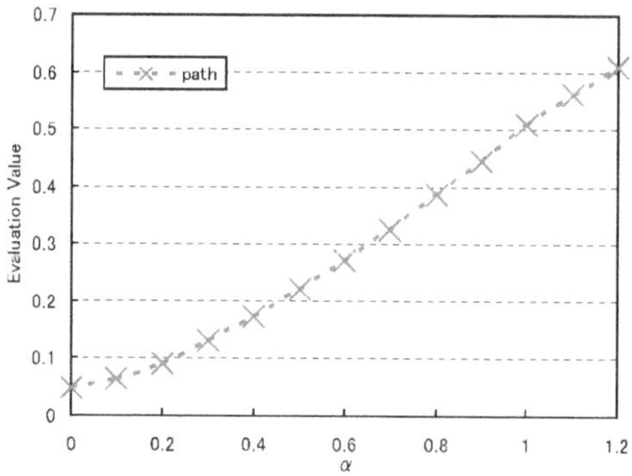

Fig. 3. V varying with α (path replication)

Table 2. Optimal a and c varying with β (TTL $= \infty$)

β	0.0	0.1	0.2	0.3	0.4	0.5	0.6	0.7	0.8	0.9	1.0
a	0.40	0.40	0.20	0.10	0.00	0.00	0.00	0.00	0.00	0.00	0.00
c	0.95	0.70	0.45	0.45	0.40	0.45	0.45	0.45	0.45	0.45	0.50
V	0.108	0.184	0.093	0.073	0.075	0.076	0.077	0.074	0.077	0.079	0.082

that gives 6,000 links when varying β. When β is small, all peers have a similar number of links (nearly random network), whereas when β is large, few peers have a large number of links and others have few links. Note that β strongly affects the query success ratio, i.e., the larger the β, the higher the query success ratio when TTL is fixed to a constant value. Thus, in this subsection we first assume that TTL is infinite so that every query succeeds. By doing so, we can examine the effect of β without considering the impact of the success ratio. Then, we set TTL as 10, similar to the above experiments, and examine the effect of β.

TTL $= \infty$: Next, we examine the optimal values of a and c when varying β by 0.1 in the range from 0.0 to 1.0. Both a and c are varied by 0.05 in the range from 0.00 to 1.00; α is fixed to 1.0 and TTL is set as infinite. Table 2 shows the results, which indicate that there is a correlation between β and the optimal values of a and c. When β is small, large a and small c give a replica allocation close to the square-root* allocation, and vice versa.

Figure 4 shows the average path lengths (hopcounts) for accessing data items where $\beta = 0.0$ and $\beta = 0.8$. From these graphs, we see that the path lengths get longer as the query rates decrease. The average path lengths vary from 40 to 800 where $\beta = 0.0$ and from 2 to 6 where $\beta = 0.8$. When β is very small, no peer has a large number of links, thus the number of peers to which a message can reach by one-hop transmission is very small. This makes the difference in path lengths between data items with high query rates and those with low rates very large. Since the path length of a data item with a low query rate becomes very long, the replication probability for this item should be set to a low value

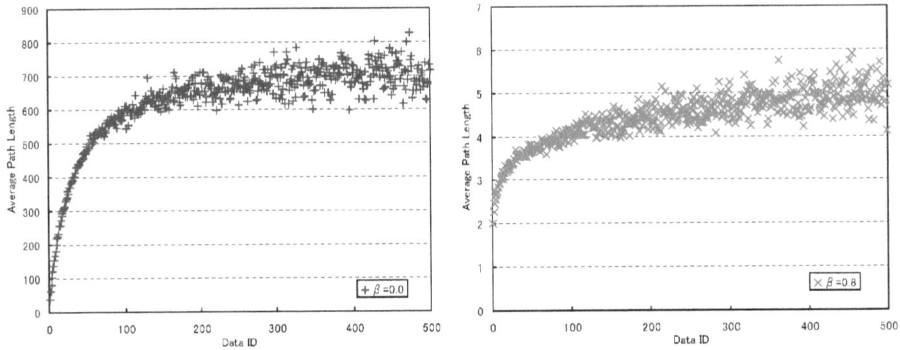

(a) $\beta = 0.0$ (b) $\beta = 0.8$

Fig. 4. Average path length

Table 3. Optimal a and c varying with β (TTL = 10)

β	0.0	0.1	0.2	0.3	0.4	0.5	0.6	0.7	0.8	0.9	1.0
a	0.00	0.00	0.00	0.00	0.00	0.00	0.05	0.05	0.05	0.00	0.00
c	1.00	1.00	1.00	0.90	0.85	0.75	0.80	0.60	0.55	0.45	0.45
V	0.280	0.272	0.270	0.265	0.257	0.233	0.146	0.098	0.091	0.080	0.080
Success ratio	0.30	0.30	0.33	0.47	0.61	0.78	0.90	0.98	0.99	1.00	1.00

in order to avoid excessive replication of this item. This is why the optimal value of a is large where β is small as shown in Table 2.

TTL = 10: Next, we examine the optimal values of a and c in the same environment as in the above experiment except that TTL is set to 10. Table 3 shows the results. "Success ratio" denotes the average query success ratio for all data items. The results show that if β is equal to or larger than 0.7, V and the optimal values of a and c are almost the same as those where TTL is infinite. However, if β is equal to or smaller than 0.4, the optimal values of a and c are about 0.0 and 1.0, respectively, and they are very different to those where TTL is infinite. This is due to the drop in the query success ratio. When β is small, the average success ratio becomes low as shown in Table 3, and this performance drop is more serious for data items with low query rates. Thus, the optimal values of a and c become those to restrict excessive replication of data items with high query rates and promote the replication of data items with low ones.

6 Conclusion

In this paper, we proposed a replication strategy that almost achieves the square-root* allocation. In this strategy, similar to path replication, the target data item of a query is replicated at peers along the path from the query-issuing peer to the query-responding peer. In doing so, at these peers replicas are allocated with probabilities determined based on the rank of the item's query rate.

We conducted simulation experiments to evaluate the performance of our proposed strategy. The results revealed that our strategy achieves data replication much closer with the square-root* allocation than does path replication. We also showed that the optimal values of a and c, which are adjustable parameters in our strategy, change according to changes in the system environment, such as in access characteristics and network density. Specifically, when the query success ratio becomes low due to low network density or TTL restriction, the optimal values of a and c are those increasing the difference in replication probabilities between data items with high query rates and those with low query rates.

Although in this paper we assumed that system parameters, such as β, ω, and α, and rank in query rates of all data items, are known, this assumption is not always true in a real environment as described in Section 2. Thus, as part of our future work, we plan to extend our proposed strategy to estimate these parameters and the query rates by monitoring query messages exchanged among peers. We also plan to extend our method to adapt to various system environments except for power-law networks and Zipf-based access characteristics.

Acknowledgments

This research was partially supported by The 21st Century Center of Excellence Program "New Information Technologies for Building a Networked Symbiotic Environment" and Grant-in-Aid for Exploratory Research (17650029), for Scientific Research on Priority Areas (18049050), and for Scientific Research (A)(17200006) of the Ministry of Education, Culture, Sports, Science and Technology, Japan.

References

1. L. A. Adamic, R. M. Lukose, A. R. Puniyani, and B. A. Huberman. Search in Power-Law Networks, *Physical Review E*, 64(4):46135-46143, 2001.
2. T. Bu and D. Towsley. On Distinguishing Between Internet Power Law Topology Generators, In *Proc. INFOCOM 2002*, 2002.
3. E. Cohen, and S. Shenker. Replication Strategies in Unstructured Peer-to-Peer Networks, In *Proc. SIGCOMM'02*, pages 177-190, 2002.
4. F. M. Cuenca-Acuna, R. P. Martin, T. D. Nguyen. Autonomous Replication for High Availability in Unstructured P2P Systems, In *Proc. SRDS 2003*, pages 99-108, 2003.
5. A. Datta, M. Hauswirth, and K. Aberer. Updates in Highly Unreliable, Replicated Peer-to-Peer Systems, In *Proc. ICDCS'03*, pages 76-85, 2003.
6. FreeNet, http://freenet.sourceforge.net.
7. Gnutella, http://www.gnutella.com.
8. JXTA, http://www.jxta.org.
9. P. Keyani, B. Larson, and M. Senthil. Peer Pressure: Distributed Recovery from Attacks in Peer-to-Peer Systems, In *Proc. Networking Workshop 2002*, pages 306-320, 2002.

10. J. Kleinberg. The Small-World Phenomenon: An Algorithm Perspective, In *Proc. STOC2000*, pages 163-170, 2000.
11. Q. Lv, P. Cao, E. Cohen, K. Li, and S. Shenker. Search and Replication in Unstructured Peer-to-Peer Networks, In *Proc. ICS'02*, pages 84-95, 2002.
12. G. On, J. Schmitt, R. Steinmetz. The Effectiveness of Realistic Replication Strategies on Quality of Availability for Peer-to-Peer Systems, In *Proc. P2P'03*, pages 57-65, 2003.
13. P. Maymounkov, and D. Mazieres. Kademlia: A Peer-to-Peer Information System Based on the Xor Metric, In *Proc. IPTPS'02*, pages 53-65, 2002.
14. S. Ratnasamy, P. Francis, M. Handley, and R. Karp. A Scalable Content-Addressable Network, In *Proc. SIGCOMM'01*, pages 161-171, 2001.
15. A. Rowstron, and P. Druschel. Pastry: Scalable, Distributed Object Location and Routing for Large-scale Peer-to-Peer Systems, In *Proc. Middleware 2001*, pages 329-350, 2001.
16. I. Stoica, R. Morris, D. Karger, M. F. Kaashoek, and H. Balakrishnan. Chord: A Scalable Peer-to-Peer Lookup Service for Internet Applications, In *Proc. SIGCOMM'01*, pages 149-160, 2001.
17. B. Zhao, J. Kubiatowicz, and A. Joseph. Tapestry: An Infrastructure for Wide-area Fault-tolerant Location and Routing, In *Proc. SIGCOMM'01*, pages 161-170, 2001.
18. G.K. Zipf: *Human Behavior and the Principle of Least Effort*, Addison-Wesley, 1949.

Role-Based Serializability for Distributed Object Systems

Youhei Tanaka[1], Tomoya Enokido[2], and Makoto Takizawa[1]

[1] Tokyo Denki University, Japan
{youhei, taki}@takilab.k.dendai.ac.jp
[2] Rissho University, Japan
eno@ris.ac.jp

Abstract. In the role-based access control model, a role is a set of access rights. A subject doing jobs is granted roles showing the jobs in an enterprise. A transaction issued by a subject is associated with a subset of roles granted to the subject, which is named *purpose*. A method with a more significant purpose is performed before another method with a less significant purpose. We discuss which purpose is more significant than another purpose. We discuss two types of role-ordering (RO) schedulers SRO and PRO where multiple conflicting transactions are serializable in the significant order of subjects and purposes, respectively. We evaluate the RO schedulers compared with the traditional two-phase locking protocol in terms of throughput.

1 Introduction

In the role-based access control (RBAC) model [4,9,11], a *role* shows a job function in an enterprise. A role is a collection of access rights (or permission) which a subject playing the role is allowed to issue for objects in an enterprise. Here, an *access right* (or *permission*) is given a pair $\langle o, op \rangle$ of an object o and a method op. Only a subject granted a role including an access right $\langle o, op \rangle$ can manipulate the object o through the method op. In the *discretionary* approach [7,10], a subject granted a role can further grant the role to another subject. A *transaction* is an atomic sequence of methods [1,5]. A collection of conflicting transactions are required to be serializable to keep objects consistent. Locking protocols [1] are based on a principle that only the first comer is a winner. In a timestamp ordering scheduler [1], each transaction is assigned timestamp showing when the transaction is initiated. Objects are manipulated by conflicting transactions in the timestamp order and no deadlock occurs.

The authors [3] discuss the role-ordering (RO) scheduler where each transaction is associated with only one role. However, each subject is rather granted multiple roles. A collection of the roles assigned to a transaction T shows the *purpose* of the subject to perform T. We discuss which purpose is more significant than another in terms of significancy of roles in the purposes. In addition, authorizers are more significant than authorizees. We define the significantly precedent relation among subjects by using the significancy of purpose and the

S. Bressan, J. Küng, and R. Wagner (Eds.): DEXA 2006, LNCS 4080, pp. 801–811, 2006.

authorization relation. A transaction issued by a more significant subject is considered to be more significant from the subject point of view. On the other hand, a transaction T with a more significant purpose is more significant than another even if T is issued by a less significant subject from the purpose point of view. We discuss two types of role-ordering (RO) schedulers, SRO and PRO based on the significancy of subject and purpose, respectively, to serialize conflicting transactions in the role-based ordering relation.

In section 2, we define dominant relations among roles. In section 3, we discuss the role-ordered serializability. In section 4, we discuss SRO and PRO schedulers. In section 5, we evaluate the RO schedulers in terms of throughput.

2 Significancy of Roles

An object is an encapsulation of data and methods [6]. A pair of methods op_1 and op_2 *conflict* if and only if (iff) the result obtained by performing the methods depends on the computation order. Otherwise, op_1 and op_2 are *compatible*. A *transaction* is an atomic sequence of methods [1]. Multiple conflicting transactions have to be *serializable* [1,5]. Let $\mathbf{T}$ be a set $\{T_1, ..., T_n\}$ of transactions. A schedule H of $\mathbf{T}$ is a sequence of methods performed. A transaction T_i *precedes* T_j in H ($T_i \rightarrow_H T_j$) iff for some pair of conflicting methods op_i from T_i and op_j from T_j, op_i is performed before op_j. H is *serializable* iff $\rightarrow_H$ is acyclic.

In access control models [1,8,9,11], a *subject* like a user issues methods to *objects* like databases. A role is a collection of *access rights* in the RBAC [4,9]. If a subject s is first granted a role R including an access right $\langle o, op \rangle$, s can invoke a method op on an object o. In an enterprise, a subject s plays some *roles* and performs a task for some *purpose* in the roles. If a pair of tasks in different jobs concurrently use an object, a more significant task should take the object. Suppose there are roles *president* and *secretary* for a *bank* object B and a pair of persons with roles *president* and *secretary* issue transactions T_1 and T_2, respectively, to check a current balance in B. Since *president* is more significant than *secretary*, T_1 should be processed prior to T_2. Next, *secretary* issues a transaction T_3 to withdraw money from B for *payment* purpose and the *president* issues T_4 to *check* a current balance. Although *president* is more significant than *secretary*, the *payment* purpose is more significant than the *check* purpose. Therefore, T_3 should be processed prior to T_4 from the *purpose* point of view. Let $Srole_s$ be a family $\{R_1, ..., R_m\}$ of roles granted to a subject s. A transaction T_i issued by a subject s is associated with a *purpose* $Prole_i$ ($\subseteq Srole_s$). Let Sub_i denote a subject which initiates a transaction T_i. Thus, there are a pair of points, subjects and purposes to be considered on the significancy of transactions.

There are *class* and *object* types of methods. Class methods are ones for *creating* and *dropping* an object. Object methods are ones for manipulating an object. Object methods are furthermore classified into *change* and *output* types. In an *output* method, data is derived from an object. In a *change* method, an object is changed. A subject usually more carefully issues *withdraw* than *deposit*. Thus, some methods are more significant than others in an application. A method op_1 *semantically dominates* op_2 on an object o ($op_1 \succeq\!\succeq op_2$) iff an application considers op_1 to be more significant than op_2. op_1 is *semantically equivalent* with op_2 ($op_1 \cong op_2$) if $op_1 \succeq\!\succeq op_2$ and $op_2 \succeq\!\succeq op_1$. op_1 is *more semantically significant* than op_2 ($op_1 \succ\!\succ op_2$) if $op_1 \succeq\!\succeq op_2$ but $op_1 \ncong op_2$. op_1 and op_2 are *semantically uncomparable* ($op_1 \parallel op_2$) iff neither $op_1 \succeq\!\succeq op_2$ nor $op_2 \succeq\!\succeq op_1$.

[Definition]. A method op_1 is *more significant* than op_2 on an object o ($op_1 \succ op_2$) iff 1) op_1 is a class type and op_2 is an object type, 2) op_1 is a *change* type and op_2 is an *output* one, or 3) op_1 and op_2 are a same object type and $op_1 \succ\!\succ op_2$. op_1 is *significantly equivalent* with op_2 ($op_1 \equiv op_2$) iff op_1 and op_2 are a same type and $op_1 \cong op_2$. op_1 *significantly dominates* op_2 ($op_1 \succeq op_2$) iff $op_1 \succ op_2$ or $op_1 \equiv op_2$. op_1 and op_2 are *significantly uncomparable* ($op_1 \parallel op_2$) iff neither $op_1 \succeq op_2$ nor $op_2 \succeq op_1$.

Suppose a *bank* object B supports methods *create*, *drop*, *withdraw*, *deposit*, and *check*. The class method *create* is more significant than *withdraw*. *withdraw* $\succ$ *deposit* since *withdraw* $\succeq\!\succeq$ *deposit*. Since *create* $\cong$ *drop*, *create* $\equiv$ *drop*. In Figure 1, $\alpha \rightarrow \beta$ shows $\alpha \prec \beta$.

An object o_1 is *more significant* than o_2 ($o_1 \succ o_2$) iff o_1 is more secure than o_2 [2]. o_1 and o_2 are *significantly equivalent* ($o_1 \equiv o_2$) iff o_1 and o_2 are classified into a same security class. o_1 *significantly dominates* o_2 ($o_1 \succeq o_2$) iff $o_1 \succ o_2$ or $o_1 \equiv o_2$. $o_1 \parallel o_2$ iff neither $o_1 \succeq o_2$ nor $o_2 \succeq o_1$.

[Definition]. Let α_1 and α_2 be access rights $\langle o_1, op_1\rangle$ and $\langle o_2, op_2\rangle$. α_1 is *more significant* than α_2 ($\alpha_1 \succ \alpha_2$) iff 1) $o_1 \succ o_2$, 2) $op_1 \succ op_2$ and $o_1 \equiv o_2$, or 3) $\alpha_1 \succ \alpha_3$ and $\alpha_3 \succ \alpha_2$ for some access right α_3. α_1 and α_2 are *significantly equivalent* ($\alpha_1 \equiv \alpha_2$) iff 1) $op_1 \equiv op_2$ and $o_1 = o_2$, or 2) $o_1 \equiv o_2$ and $o_1 \neq o_2$. α_1 *significantly dominates* α_2 ($\alpha_1 \succeq \alpha_2$) iff $\alpha_1 \succ \alpha_2$ or $\alpha_1 \equiv \alpha_2$. α_1 and α_2 are *significantly uncomparable* ($\alpha_1 \parallel \alpha_2$) iff neither $\alpha_1 \succeq \alpha_2$ nor $\alpha_2 \succeq \alpha_1$.

Let **A** be a set of access rights. An access right β is *maximally reachable* from α ($\beta \leftharpoondown \alpha$) iff $\beta \succeq \alpha$ and no access right γ such that $\gamma \succeq \beta$ in **A**.

[Definition]. A role R_1 *significantly dominates* R_2 ($R_1 \succeq R_2$) iff 1) for some role α in R_2, there is $\beta \in R_1$ - R_2 such that $\beta \leftharpoondown \alpha$ in $R_1 \cup R_2$ and 2) for every $\beta \in R_1$, there is no $\alpha \in R_2$ such that $\alpha \leftharpoondown \beta$ in $R_1 \cup R_2$.

A role R_1 is *significantly equivalent* with R_2 ($R_1 \equiv R_2$) iff $R_1 \succeq R_2$ and $R_2 \succeq R_1$. R_1 and R_2 are *significantly uncomparable* ($R_1 \parallel R_2$) iff neither $R_1 \succeq R_2$ nor $R_2 \succeq R_1$. A *least upper bound* $R_1 \sqcup R_2$ is a role R_3 such that $R_3 \succeq R_1$ and $R_3 \succeq R_2$ and no role R_4 such that $R_3 \succeq R_4 \succeq R_1$ and $R_3 \succeq R_4 \succeq R_2$. A *greatest lower bound* $R_1 \sqcap R_2$ is similarly defined. $R_1 \cup R_2$ and $R_1 \cap R_2$ show the union and intersection of R_1 and R_2. $R_1 \sqcap \cdots \sqcap R_m \preceq R_i \preceq R_1 \sqcup \cdots \sqcup R_m$ holds but $R_1 \cap \cdots \cap R_m \preceq R_i \preceq R_1 \cup \cdots \cup R_m$ may not hold.

For access rights $d = \langle B, deposit\rangle$, $w = \langle B, withdraw\rangle$, and $c = \langle B, create\rangle$, $d \prec w \prec c$ in the *bank* object B. For roles $R_1 = \{d, c\}$ and $R_2 = \{w\}$, c is *maximally reachable* from d and w in $R_1 \cup R_2$ ($c \leftharpoondown d, w$). Hence, $R_1 \succeq R_2$.

Next, we consider roles $R_1 = \{c, d\}$ and $R_2 = \{e, f\}$ in Figure 2, where a, ..., f are access rights and a directed edge $\alpha \rightarrow \beta$ shows $\alpha \preceq \beta$. $R_1 \parallel R_2$. $R_1 \cup R_2 = \{c, d, e, f\}$. $R_1 \parallel (R_1 \cup R_2)$ and $R_2 \parallel (R_1 \cup R_2)$. $R_1 \sqcap R_2 = \{d, f\}$ and $R_1 \sqcup R_2 = \{a, b\}$. $R_1 \sqcap R_2 \preceq R_1 \preceq R_1 \sqcup R_2$.

[Definition]. Let $\mathbf{R}_1$ and $\mathbf{R}_2$ be families of roles. $\mathbf{R}_1$ *significantly dominates* $\mathbf{R}_2$ ($\mathbf{R}_1 \succeq \mathbf{R}_2$) iff $\sqcap_{R \in \mathbf{R}_1} R \succeq \sqcup_{R \in \mathbf{R}_2} R$. $\mathbf{R}_1$ and $\mathbf{R}_2$ are *significantly equivalent* ($\mathbf{R}_1 \equiv \mathbf{R}_2$) iff $\mathbf{R}_1 \succeq \mathbf{R}_2$ and $\mathbf{R}_2 \succeq \mathbf{R}_1$. $\mathbf{R}_1$ and $\mathbf{R}_2$ are *significantly uncomparable* ($\mathbf{R}_1 \parallel \mathbf{R}_2$) iff neither $\mathbf{R}_1 \succeq \mathbf{R}_2$ nor $\mathbf{R}_2 \succeq \mathbf{R}_1$.

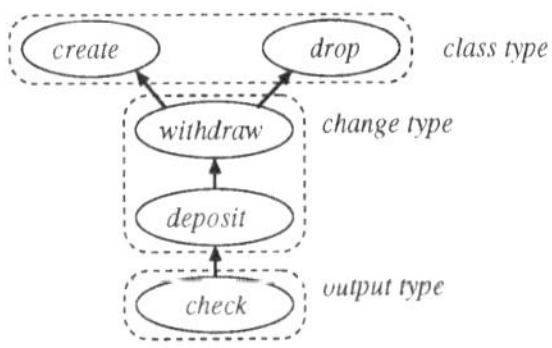

Fig. 1. Method significancy

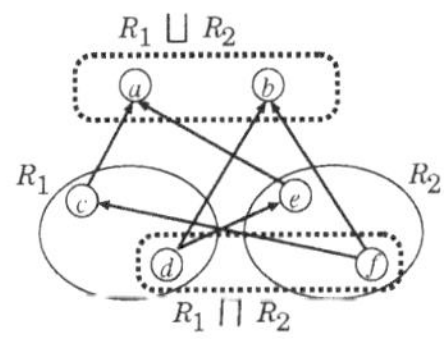

Fig. 2. Roles

3 Role-Ordered Serializability

3.1 Significancy of Transactions

[Definition]. A subject s_i *precedes* s_j on a role R ($s_i \Rightarrow_R s_j$) iff s_i grants R to s_j or $s_i \Rightarrow_R s_k \Rightarrow_R s_j$ for some subject s_k. s_i and s_j are *independent* on R ($s_i \parallel_R s_j$) iff neither $s_i \Rightarrow_R s_j$ nor $s_j \Rightarrow_R s_i$.

Suppose a subject s_1 is granted roles $Srole_1 = \{R_1, R_2, R_3\}$ and s_2 is granted $Srole_2 = \{R_2, R_3, R_4\}$. Suppose $s_1 \Rightarrow_{R_2} s_2$, $s_1 \Rightarrow_{R_3} s_2$, $s_1 \parallel_{R_1} s_2$, and $s_1 \parallel_{R_4} s_2$. Suppose $Srole_1 \succeq Srole_2$, i.e. $R_2 \sqcap R_3 \sqcap R_4 \succeq R_1 \sqcup R_2 \sqcup R_3$. However, $Srole_1$ is more significant than $Srole_2$ from the authorization point of view.

[Definition]. A subject s_i *S-dominates* s_j ($s_i \succeq^S s_j$) iff 1) $Srole_i \succeq Srole_j$ and 2) $s_i \Rightarrow_R s_j$ for some role $R \in Srole_{ij}$ and $s_j \not\Rightarrow_R s_i$ for every $R \in Srole_{ij}$ if $Srole_i \parallel Srole_j$.

In Figure 3, a directed edge $R_i \rightarrow R_j$ shows $R_i \preceq R_j$. For subjects s_1 and s_2, $Srole_1 = \{R_1, R_2, R_3\}$ and $Srole_2 = \{R_3, R_4\}$. Here, $R_1 \sqcap R_2 \sqcap R_3 = R_3$ and $R_3 \sqcup R_4 = R_3$. $s_1 \succeq^S s_2$ since $R_1 \sqcap R_2 \sqcap R_3 \succeq R_3 \sqcup R_4$, i.e. $Srole_1 \succeq Srole_2$. Next, suppose $Srole_3 = \{R_1, R_4\}$ and $Srole_4 = \{R_2, R_4\}$. Neither $R_1 \sqcup R_4 \succeq R_2 \sqcap R_4$ nor $R_2 \sqcup R_4 \succeq R_1 \sqcap R_4$, i.e. $Srole_3 \parallel Srole_4$. $Srole_3 \cap Srole_4 = \{R_4\}$. Suppose $s_3 \Rightarrow_{R_4} s_4$. Here, $s_3 \succeq^S s_4$ from the rule 2).

[Definition]. For transactions T_i and T_j issued by subjects s_i and s_j, s_i *P-dominates* s_j with respect to the purposes of T_i and T_j ($s_i \succeq^P_{ij} s_j$) iff 1) $Prole_i \succeq Prole_j$ and 2) $s_i \Rightarrow_R s_j$ for some role $R \in Prole_{ij}$ and $s_j \not\Rightarrow_R s_i$ for every role $R \in Prole_{ij}$ if $Prole_i \parallel Prole_j$.

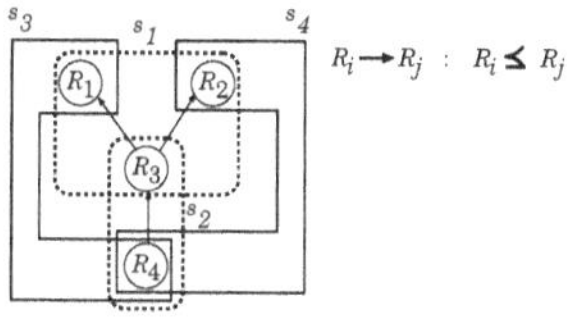

Fig. 3. Significancy of roles

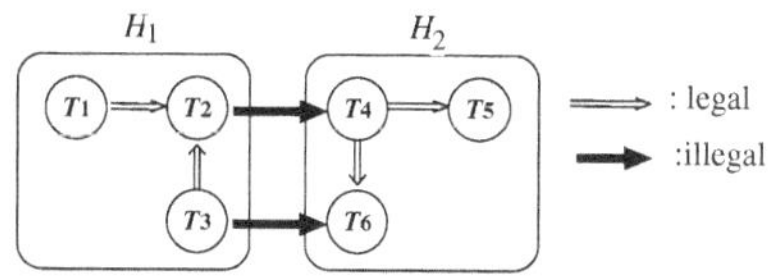

Fig. 4. Schedule H

In Figure 3, s_3 issues a transaction T_3 with a purpose $Prole_3 = \{R_4\}$ and s_4 issues T_4 with $Prole_4 = \{R_2\}$. $R_2 \succeq R_4$. Hence, $s_4 \succeq^P_{34} s_3$ although $s_3 \succeq^S s_4$.

[Definition]. For a pair of conflicting transactions T_i and T_j,

- T_i *S-dominates* T_j ($T_i \succeq^S T_j$) iff $Sub_i \succeq^S Sub_j$.
- T_i *P-dominates* T_j ($T_i \succeq^P T_j$) iff $Sub_i \succeq^P_{ij} Sub_j$.

[Definition]. Let $\succeq^\Box$ show a dominant relation of transactions for a dominant type $\Box \in \{S, P\}$. For a pair of conflicting transactions T_i and T_j, $T_i \succeq^\Box T_j$ iff $T_i \succeq^S T_j$ or $T_i \succeq^P T_j$, $T_i \equiv^\Box T_j$ iff $T_i \succeq^\Box T_j$ and $T_j \succeq^\Box T_i$, and $T_i \parallel^\Box T_j$ iff neither $T_i \succeq^\Box T_j$ nor $T_j \succeq^\Box T_i$.

$T_i \sqcup^\Box T_j$ is the least upper bound of T_i and T_j on $\succeq^\Box$. $T_i \sqcap^\Box T_j$ is the greatest lower bound of T_i and T_j on $\succeq^\Box$.

3.2 RO Partitions

A schedule H of a transaction set $\mathbf{T}$ is a partially ordered set $\langle \mathbf{T}, \rightarrow_H \rangle$. H is *serializable* iff $\rightarrow_H$ is acyclic [1]. If $T_1 \succeq^\Box T_2$, "$T_1 \rightarrow_H T_2$" is *legal* in H. A schedule $H = \langle \mathbf{T}, \rightarrow_H \rangle$ is *legal* with respect to $\succeq^\Box$ iff $T_1 \rightarrow_H T_2$ if $T_1 \succeq^\Box T_2$ for every pair of T_1 and T_2 in $\mathbf{T}$. In order to make a schedule *legal*, methods from transactions are required to be buffered until all the transactions are initiated. We introduce the *RO-partition* of the schedule to improve the performance.

[Definition]. A schedule $H = \langle \mathbf{T}, \rightarrow_H \rangle$ is *RO-partitioned* into subschedules H_1, ..., H_m where $H_i = \langle \mathbf{T}_i, \rightarrow_{H_i} \rangle$ ($i = 1, ..., m$):

1. $\mathbf{T}_i \cap \mathbf{T}_j = \phi$ for every pair of H_i and H_j and $\mathbf{T}_1 \cup \cdots \cup \mathbf{T}_n = \mathbf{T}$.
2. $T_1 \rightarrow_{H_i} T_2$ if $T_1 \succeq^\Box T_2$ for every pair of transactions T_1 and T_2 in each H_i.
3. $T_1 \rightarrow_H T_2$ if $T_1 \rightarrow_{H_i} T_2$ for every pair of transactions T_1 and T_2 in each H_i.
4. For every pair of H_i and H_j, if $T_{i1} \rightarrow_H T_{j1}$ for some pair of transactions T_{i1} in H_i and T_{j1} in H_j, there are no pair of transactions T_{i2} in H_i and T_{j2} in H_j such that $T_{j2} \rightarrow_H T_{i2}$.

In Figure 4, suppose $T_1 \succeq^\Box T_2$, $T_3 \succeq^\Box T_2$, $T_4 \succeq^\Box T_5$, $T_4 \succeq^\Box T_6$, $T_4 \succeq^\Box T_2$, and $T_6 \succeq^\Box T_3$. Here, subschedules H_1 with $\mathbf{T}_1 = \{T_1, T_2, T_3\}$ and H_2 with $\mathbf{T}_2 = \{T_4, T_5, T_6\}$ are RO partitions of H. Transactions in H_1 can be ordered in $\succeq^\Box$ without waiting for transactions in H_2. Since $T_2 \preceq^\Box T_4$ and $T_3 \preceq^\Box T_6$, T_4 and T_6 cannot be performed as long as every transaction completes in H_1.

[Definition]. A schedule H of $\mathbf{T}$ is *RO-serializable* with respect to subschedules H_1, ..., H_n iff H is RO partitioned into the subschedules H_1, ..., H_n.

[Theorem.] A history H is serializable if H is RO-serializable with respect to some *RO-partition* H_1, ..., H_n.

4 Role-Ordering (RO) Schedulers

We discuss types of *role-ordering* (RO) schedulers to make transactions RO-serializable. Suppose objects o_1, ..., o_l ($l \geq 1$) are distributed in servers and multiple transactions T_1, ..., T_m ($m \geq 1$) are on clients c_1 ..., c_n ($n \geq 1$). We assume a network is reliable. Each transaction T_t first sends a *begin* request b_t to every target object. Then, T_t issues methods and lastly either a *commit* (cm_t) or *abort* (ab_t) request to the objects.

Each client c_s manipulates a variable cf_s where initially $cf_s = 1$. c_s periodically sends a *fence* message k to make an RO-partition, which carries $k.f$ ($= cf_s$). Each time sending a *fence*, $cf_s := cf_s + 1$ in c_s. Each object o_i has a variable f_i where initially $f_i = 1$. If an object o_i receives a *fence* whose cf is f_i from every client, requests received before the *fences* are included in an RO-partition and are sorted in the relation $\succeq^{\square}$. There are a set RQ_i of local receipt queues RQ_{i1}, ..., RQ_{in}, a global receipt queue GRQ_i, and an auxiliary global receipt queue $AGRQ_i$ for each o_i ($i = 1$, ..., l). A request r issued from a transaction on a client c_s to o_i is stored in RQ_{is} ($s = 1$, ..., n). *Begin* and *fence* requests are moved to $AGRQ_i$ to make a partition. Transactions in a partition are ordered in $\succeq^{\square}$. Requests are moved to GRQ_i and are performed in $\succeq^{\square}$. The following procedures are used to manipulate a queue Q for a request r:

1. r := **top**(Q) : r is a top request in Q.
2. **enqueue**(r, Q) : r is enqueued into Q.
3. **enqueue2**(r, Q, e_1, e_2) : r is inserted between elements e_1 and e_2 in Q.
4. r := **dequeue**(Q) : r (= **top**(Q)) is dequeued from Q.
5. **ROsort**(Q, e_1, e_2) : requests between elements e_1 and e_2 in Q are sorted in the significantly dominant relation $\succeq^{\square}$ of transactions.
6. r_1 := **next**(r, Q) : r_1 is a request which directly follows r in Q.
7. **fence**(r) : **true** if r is a *fence*, else **false**.
8. k := **min_fence**(Q) : k is a *fence* where $k.f$ is minimum in Q.

RQ_i ($= \{RQ_{i1}$, ..., $RQ_{in}\}$) is manipulated by the following procedures:

1. **check_fence**(RQ_i) : **true** if every RQ_{is} includes such a fence message k_s that $k_s.f = f_i$, else **false**.
2. **top_check**(RQ_i) : **true** if the top request in every RQ_{is} is a fence message k_s where $k_s.f = f_i$ for every client c_s ($s = 1$, ..., n), else **false**.

Variables $\mathbf{E}_i$ and $\mathbf{TE}_i$ denote methods and transactions being currently performed on an object o_i, respectively.

1. **Mcompatible**(op, $\mathbf{E}_i$) : **true** if $\mathbf{E}_i = \phi$ or op does not conflict with every method in $\mathbf{E}_i$, else **false**.
2. **Tcompatible**(op, $\mathbf{TE}_i$) : **true** if $\mathbf{TE}_i = \phi$ or transactions conflicting with and preceding a transaction $Tr(op)$ in $AGRQ_i$ are completed, else **false**.
3. **check_subschedule**(k) : for every transaction T_t such that the *begin* b_t precedes a *fence* k in $AGRQ_i$, **true** if cm_t or ab_t in GRQ_i, else **false**.
4. **perform**(op) : op is performed on an object o_i.

The following conditions have to be satisfied to realize the RO-serializability:

[Role-based serializability (RBS) conditions]

1. Methods in every global receipt queue GRQ_i are sorted in the significantly dominant relation $\succeq^{\Box}$ of transactions ($i = 1, ..., l$).
2. For op_t = **top**(GRQ_i), if op_t precedes a conflicting method op_u from T_u in some GRQ_i, op'_t from T_t precedes a conflicting method op'_u in every GRQ_j.

We discuss how the RO scheduler handles requests. Here, a pair of variables **head**$_i$ and **tail**$_i$ are used to denote requests in $AGRQ_i$.
[**Receiving procedure**] On receipt of a request r from T_t on a client c_s;

```
if (T_t is initiated on c_s) { enqueue(r, RQ_is); RBS(); }
```

[**RBS()**]

```
while (check_fence(RQ_i)) {
  if top_check(RQ_i) {
    r := dequeue(RQ_i1); enqueue(r, GRQ_i); enqueue(r, AGRQ_i);
    for (j = 2; j ≤ n; j++) dequeue(RQ_ij); f_i = f_i + 1; }
  else {
    for (j = 1; j ≤ n; j++) {
      while (not fence(r := top(RQ_ij)) {
        if (r = b_t) { r := dequeue(RQ_ij); enqueue(r, AGRQ_i); }
        else { head_i := top(AGRQ_i); tail_i := top(AGRQ_i); r_1 := NULL;
              while (r_1 = NULL) {
                if (tail_i = b_Tr(r)) { r_1 := tail_i;
                  while (not fence(tail_i)) tail_i := next(tail_i, AGRQ_i);
                } else if (fence(tail_i)) {
                  head_i := tail_i; tail_i := next(tail_i, AGRQ_i);
                } else tail_i := next(tail_i, AGRQ_i); }
          r := dequeue(RQ_ij); enqueue2(r, GRQ_i, head_i, tail_i);
          ROsort(GRQ_i, head_i, tail_i); } } } }
```

[**Delivery**()] Methods in GRQ_i are delivered as follows:

{ **if** (**not fence**(r := **top**(GRQ_i)) {
  if (**check_subschedule**(**min_fence**($AGRQ_i$))) {
    if (**Mcompatible**(r, $\mathbf{E}_i$) and **Tcompatible**(r, $\mathbf{TE}_i$))
    { **if** $Tr(r) \notin \mathbf{TE}_i$, $\mathbf{TE}_i := \mathbf{TE}_i \cup \{Tr(r)\}$;
      $\mathbf{E}_i := \mathbf{E}_i \cup \{r\}$; r := **dequeue**(GRQ_i); **perform**(r);
    } **else return**;
  } **else return**;
} **else** { /* top of GRQ_i is a fence message. */
  if ($\mathbf{E}_i = \phi$) **dequeue**(GRQ_i); } **return**; }

[**Completion of a method**] On completion of a method *op*,
{ $\mathbf{E}_i := \mathbf{E}_i$ - $\{op\}$;
  if (($op = cm_t$) or ($op = ab_t$)) {
    $\mathbf{TE}_i := \mathbf{TE}_i$ - $\{T_t\}$; *begin* request b_t is removed from $AGRQ_i$; }
} **Delivery**();

Suppose transactions T_1 on a client c_1 and T_2 and T_3 on c_2 issue requests to objects o_1 and o_2 as shown in Figure 5. Suppose $T_1 \succeq^{\square} T_2$, $T_3 \succeq^{\square} T_1$, and $T_3 \succeq^{\square} T_2$. Each transaction T_t first sends a *begin* request b_t to o_1 and o_2, and then issues methods (t = 1, 2, 3). op_{lt} is a method and e_t shows a *commit* (cm_t) or *abort* (ab_t) issued by T_t. Each client c_s sends a *fence* k_s to o_1 and o_2 every τ time units (s = 1, 2). Initially, $cf_s := 1$ and $f_i := 1$. cf_s is incremented by one each time c_s sends a *fence*. o_i waits until a *fence* k_s where $k_s.f = f_i$ is received from every c_s. If received, a partition is obtained by including requests preceding k_s in each RQ_{is}. Every request r preceding k_s in each RQ_{is} is moved to $AGRQ_i$ or GRQ_i. If r is *begin* and method, r is enqueued into $AGRQ_i$ and GRQ_i, respectively. The requests in $AGRQ_i$ and GRQ_i are ordered in $\succeq^{\square}$. For example, the *begin* b_1 precedes b_2 in $AGRQ_i$ since $T_1 \succeq^{\square} T_2$ in Figure 5. If a top is a *fence* k_s where $k_s.f = f_i$ in RQ_{is} for every c_s, k_s is removed from RQ_{is} and a new *fence* k where $k.f = k_s.f$ ($= f_i$) is enqueued into $AGRQ_i$ and GRQ_i. Here, $f_i := f_i + 1$. If a method request r from T_s follows the *fence* k_s in RQ_{is}, r is enqueued into GRQ_i. Here, suppose the *begin* b_t is between a pair of *fences* k_1 and k_2 where $k_2.f = k_1.f + 1$ in $AGRQ_i$. The request r is stored in between $k_1.f$ and $k_2.f$ in GRQ_i. In Figure 5, method requests from T_2 on o_1 are stored between the top r_1 and the *fence* k in GRQ_1. Requests between r_1 and k are ordered in $\succeq^{\square}$ since b_2 is stored between the top and the *fence* k in $AGRQ_1$. In addition, method requests from T_1 on o_2 are stored between the top r_2 and the *fence* k in GRQ_2. Requests between r_2 and k are ordered in $\succeq^{\square}$. Here, b_3 from T_3 is enqueued after the *fence* k in $AGRQ_i$. In addition, a method request from T_3 is stored between the *fence* k and the bottom of GRQ_i since b_3 is stored between k and the bottom of $AGRQ_i$.

In order to improve the throughput, the schedule H is *RO-partitioned* into subschedules H_1, ..., H_m. Since *begin* requests b_1 from T_1 and b_2 from T_2 precede a fence k in $AGRQ_i$ and GRQ_i includes *commits* e_1 ($= cmt_1$) of T_1 and e_2 of

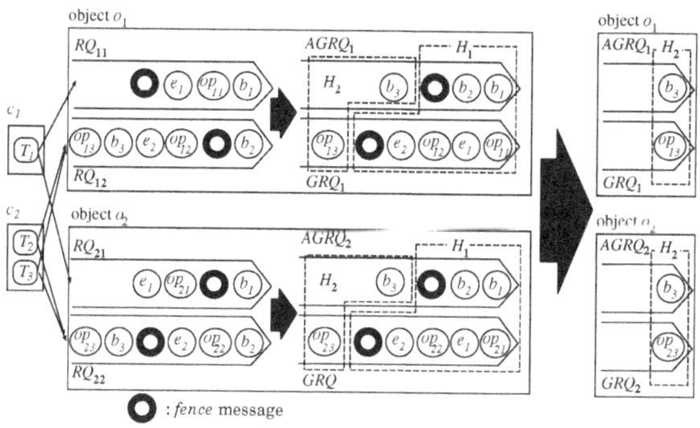

Fig. 5. State of local receipt queues

T_2, the method requests of T_1 and T_2 are dequeued from GRQ_i and performed on o_i. That is, a subschedule H_1 is started on o_i. Here, b_t of T_t is removed from $AGRQ_i$ when a *commit* or *abort* of T_t is completed on o_i. In Figure 5, b_1 and b_2 are removed from $AGRQ_i$ when e_1 and e_2 complete on o_i, respectively. If the tops of $AGRQ_i$ and GRQ_i are *fences* and all methods preceding the *fences* in GRQ_i complete on o_i, the *fences* are removed from GRQ_i and $AGRQ_i$. That is, H_1 is finished on o_i. Then, H_2 is started if cm_t or ab_t of each T_t precedes the next *fence* k' in $AGRQ_i$ in GRQ_i. In Figure 5, since there is neither a next fence k' in $AGRQ_i$ nor cm_3 and ab_3 in GRQ_i, H_2 cannot be started.

5 Evaluation

We evaluate two types of the RO schedulers, *SRO* for $\succeq^S$ and *PRO* for $\succeq^P$ in terms of computation time of each method compared with the 2PL protocol. We assume it takes a same time α to perform every method in a system. The *computation ratio* τ is $1/\alpha$. The larger τ is, the higher throughput. If all the transactions are serially performed, $\tau = 1$. $\tau = 0$ if no method is performed. If a pair of conflicting methods are concurrently issued to an object, $\tau = 2/3$ since one method has to wait until the other method completes. There are five *Bank* objects o_1, ..., o_5 and five subjects s_1, ..., s_5. Each object supports five types of methods as shown in Figure 1. $o_1 \equiv \cdots \equiv o_5$. *check* is compatible with itself. Three roles R_1, R_2, and R_3 are owned by s_1, where $R_1 \succeq R_2 \succeq R_3$. Here, $s_1 \succeq_{R_i} s_2$, $s_1 \succeq_{R_i} s_3$, $s_1 \succeq_{R_i} s_4$, $s_1 \succeq_{R_i} s_5$ for every role R_i ($i = 1, ..., 5$). $s_2 \succeq_{R_3} s_4$ and $s_3 \succeq_{R_3} s_5$. $Srole_1 = \{R_1, R_2, R_3\}$, $Srole_2 = Srole_3 = \{R_2, R_3\}$, and $Srole_4 = Srole_5 = \{R_3\}$. $Prole_1 = Prole_4 = Prole_5 = \{R_3\}$ and $Prole_2 = Prole_3 = \{R_2, R_3\}$.

We assume each subject s_i initiates a same number l of transactions on each client. Each transaction issues five methods randomly selected from 25 methods on the five objects. Figure 6 shows the computation ratio τ for the number of $5l$ transactions. For example, the computation ratio τ with *SRO* and *PRO* is 10 times larger than 2PL for 30 transactions. This means, the *SRO* and *PRO* schedulers imply higher throughput than the 2PL protocol.

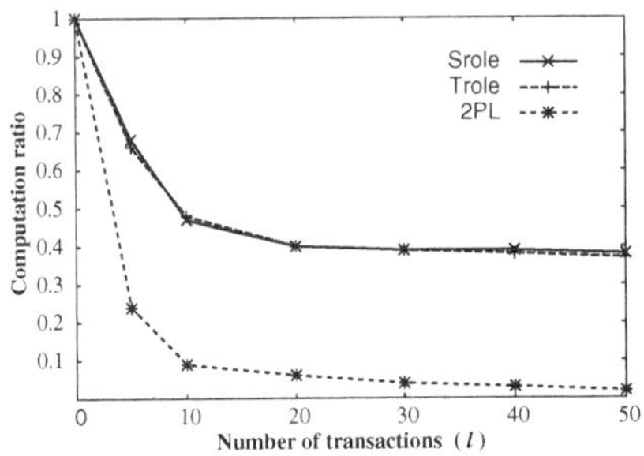

Fig. 6. Computation ratio

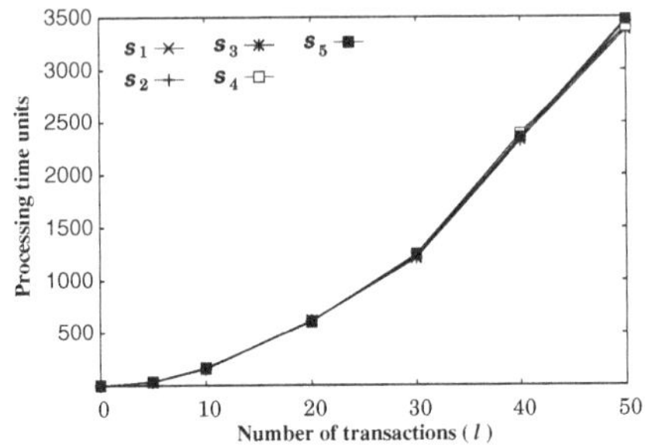

Fig. 7. 2PL protocol

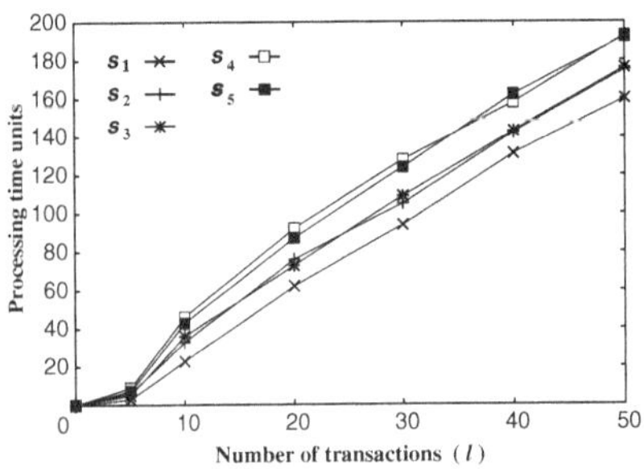

Fig. 8. SRO : processing time

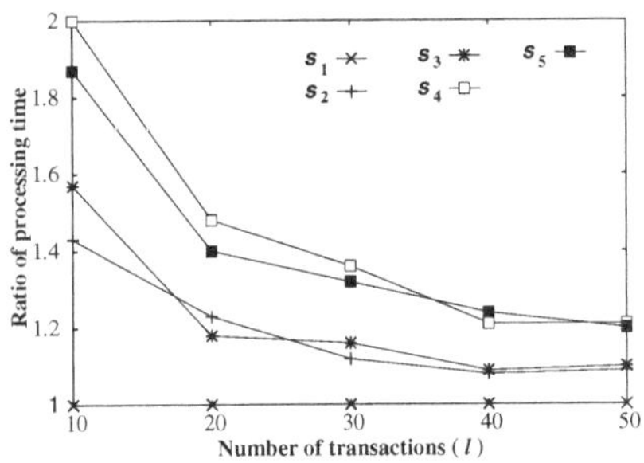

Fig. 9. SRO : ratio of processing time

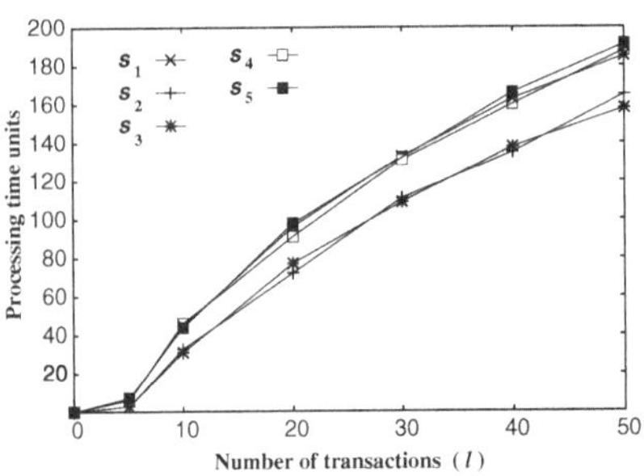

Fig. 10. PRO : processing time

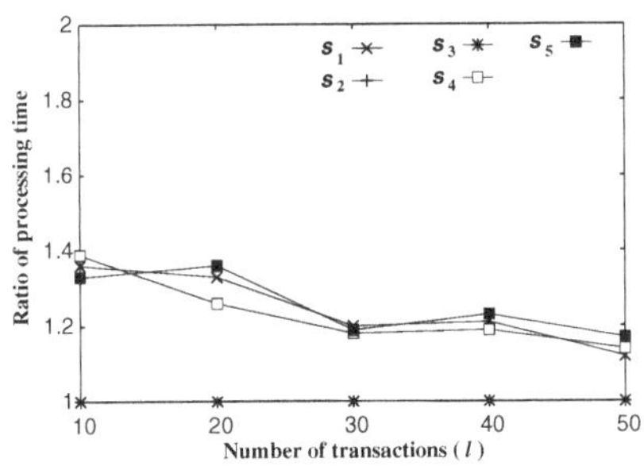

Fig. 11. PRO : ratio of processing time

Figures 7, 8, and 10 show the average processing time of each transaction for the total number l of transactions. "s_i" shows a transaction issued by a subject s_i. Figure 7 shows the processing time of each 2PL transaction. Since transactions are arbitrarily performed independently of the significancy of subjects and roles, every transaction almost implies the same processing time. In the *SRO* scheduler, the processing time of a transaction issued by s_1 is the minimum where s_1 is more significant than the other subjects. Figure 9 shows the ratio of the processing time of each transaction to s_1. For $l = 50$, the second significant transactions s_2 and s_3 take about 10% longer time than s_1 and the least significant transactions s_4 and s_5 take about 20% longer than s_1. The more significant a subject is, the shorter processing time a transaction issued by the subject implies. In the *PRO* scheduler, the transactions s_2 and s_3 are the most *P-significant* and the others s_1, s_4, and s_5 are *P-significantly equivalent* from *purpose* point of view. As shown in Figure 11, s_2 and s_3 are processed about 10% faster than the others.

6 Concluding Remarks

In this paper, a transaction with more significant roles is performed prior to another transaction with less significant roles. Multiple conflicting transactions are ordered according to the significantly dominant relation $\succeq^{\Box}$. A subject issues a transaction with *purpose*, subset of the roles of the subject. Transactions are ordered in two ways, significancy of *subjects* issuing the transactions, and *purposes* of the transactions. We discussed how to implement two types of RO schedulers, SRO and PRO on multiple objects. We evaluated SRO and PRO compared with 2PL in terms of throughput. In the RO schedulers, the more significant transactions are, the earlier performed. In addition, the higher throughput is implied than 2PL.

References

1. P. A. Bernstein, V. Hadzilacos, N. Goodman.: Concurrency Control and Recovery in Database Systems. Addison-Wesley, (1987).
2. D. E. Denning and P. J. Denning.: Cryptography and Data Security. Addison-Wesley Publishing Company, (1982).
3. T. Enokido and M. Takizawa.: Concurrency Control Based-on Significancy on Roles. Proc. of the IEEE 11th International Conference on Parallel and Distributed Systems (ICPADS2005), (2005) 196–202.
4. D. F. Ferraiolo, D. R. Kuhn, and R. Chandramouli.: Role Based Access Control. Artech House, (2005).
5. J. Gray.: Notes on Database Operating Systems. Lecture Notes in Computer Science, Vol. 60 (1978) 393–481.
6. O. M. G. Inc.: The Common Object Request Broker : Architecture and Specification. Rev. 2.1, (1997).
7. Oracle Corporation.: Oracle8i Concepts Vol. 1. Release 8.1.5., (1999).
8. R. S. Sandhu.: Lattice-Based Access Control Models. IEEE Computer, Vol. 26 No. 11 (1993) 9–19.
9. R. S. Sandhu, E. J. Coyne, H. L. Feinstein, and C. E. Youman.: Role-Based Access Control Models. IEEE Computer, Vol. 29 No. 2 (1996) 38–47.
10. Sybase.: Sybase SQL Server. http://www.sybase.com/.
11. Z. Tari and S. W. Chan.: A Role-Based Access Control for Intranet Security. IEEE Internet Computing, Vol. 1 (1997) 24–34.

MDSSF - A Federated Architecture for Product Procurement

Jaspreet Singh Pahwa[1], Pete Burnap[1], W.A. Gray[1], and John Miles[2]

[1] School of Computer Science and
[2] School of Engineering, Cardiff University, UK
{J.S.Pahwa, P.Burnap, W.A.Gray}@cs.cardiff.ac.uk, MilesJC@cardiff.ac.uk

Abstract. A new architecture of database federation called the MDSSF (Multiple Database Search Service Federation) is presented to support the procurement activities of the AEC (Architecture, Engineering and Construction) industry projects. In order to make procurement decisions, a contractor requires access to product information from several different product suppliers when constructing artefacts such as a hospital, or an office block. This product information is available from the online systems of product suppliers. However, this approach requires a contractor to visit several websites in order to find the right product which is time consuming and the product data available from different product suppliers is heterogeneous. The MDSSF architecture provides an integrated means of accessing product information from a large number of product suppliers using a single system. It brings together autonomous product suppliers to share product information with the federation users such as contractors and potential buyers using a common data model. It also creates an environment for product suppliers to compete with each other in a virtual market place based on the product information they provide to federation users. The MDSSF gives its users a Grid enabled database search mechanism for searching a large number of supplier databases in real time and protects product related sensitive data from exposure to business competitors. We describe the architecture and distinctive features of the MDSSF.

1 Introduction

Information access and its management is an important area of research for creating new models of information retrieval and sharing for meeting information needs of business organisations. Network technologies such as the Grid and Web Services together with federated database architectures provide a new means of collaboration and information exchange between the actors within a given industry. One of the features of the Grid is that it provides middleware to enable distributed computing in a particular domain to achieve high-end computational capabilities and high-throughput computing [1]. Web Services is a paradigm for enabling computing in distributed and heterogeneous environments [2] [3]. Research in the area of Engineering Federated Information Systems (EFIS) has

S. Bressan, J. Küng, and R. Wagner (Eds.): DEXA 2006, LNCS 4080, pp. 812–821, 2006.

recognised the GRID computing as an emerging area for building new models of data exchange [4].

This paper describes an architecture of a new model of database federation called the MDSSF (Multiple Database Search Service Federation) which supports members of consortia such as contractors, buyers, etc. in the AEC (Architecture, Engineering and Construction) industry. The architecture was developed to support a need to provide product information to consortia for procurement of products and supplies where such information is available from several different systems. A consortium continually needs an up-to-date product information from several different suppliers so that they can make informed decisions about which product to use in construction projects. A new approach is needed if this information is to be provided in an integrated way so that several different suppliers can come together to share their product related data with contractors and potential buyers using a common standard via a single system. The approach must protect autonomy of product suppliers, allow competing products to be searched, compared and judged on the basis of their specifications against the project requirements. It must also protect confidential information of different product suppliers.

The MDSSF data sharing architecture brings together autonomous contractors and suppliers. The architecture enables creation of a Virtual Distributed Database (VDD) of product information where product information is supplied by a large number of suppliers using a standard data representation. The VDD can be queried by contractors in order to find needed product information. The architecture of the MDSSF is created by utilising the features of federated database architectures such as distribution of data and autonomy of local database systems (DBS) and coupling them with Grid technology to provide scalability support. The federation model adopts a service oriented architecture for its flexibility in retrieving data from the databases of several suppliers and sharing it with contractors. We describe the architecture of the MDSSF through its distinctive features. The paper is organised as follows. In section 2 we provide background information on product procurement in construction industry that underpins the need for a new data sharing architecture. Section 3 identifies some of the limitations of individual online systems for information sharing. We describe the VDD of the MDSSF in section 4. The architecture of the MDSSF and its distinctive features are presented in section 5. Related projects are briefly summarised in section 6 and conclusions and further work are presented in section 7.

2 Background

In the construction industry supply chain, procurement plays a significant role. An important function of the procurement phase is searching for desired products over a wide range of available products from a large number of product suppliers. In large projects a large quantity of various kinds of construction material is required. For example a typical hospital has thousands of rooms. Each room needs light fittings, a door, floor and ceiling, floor and ceiling coverings, furniture, power sockets, some form of ventilation such as windows, walls, wall coverings, etc. Multiplying the requirements by a few thousand rooms gives us the scale of purchases needed to build a hospital. These purchases are made from a wide range of product suppliers.

Many companies/product suppliers do their business via web-based E-commerce systems [5]. E-commerce systems enable sharing of product information with contractors and potential buyers. Acquiring information from websites has become vital for contractors as more and more procurement websites are available on the internet [6]. By using an E-commerce system for construction materials, different kinds of information pertaining to materials, suppliers, manufacturers, buyers, agents, buying patters, buyer's reviews on products and services, etc. can be shared with its users [5].

From the perspective of suppliers, E-commerce systems act as a mechanism for disseminating product information to a large number of potential buyers and contractors. It is a medium for the suppliers to market their products. Suppliers constantly look for new channels which enable them to quickly disseminate product information to potential buyers as reduction in the time to market is a competitive advantage [7].

3 Limitations of Accessing Information from Individual E-commerce Systems

Procurement planning is a critical activity and is unique for each project [8]. For an efficient procurement strategy, it is important for a contractor to have the knowledge of suppliers who can meet different requirements and deliver the right products under given constraints. Since different projects have different requirements, access to a large body of product information is required. Such information is available via the E-commerce systems of several organisations. This approach however, has certain limitations. Construction materials generally have a large number of specification parameters. Entering the specifications into web-based forms of several E-commerce sites to find the best product is a time-consuming task for a contractor. A contractor has to: acquire and maintain a list of several web addresses; interpret and understand the semantics and navigation methods used in different sites; be aware of new sites coming into the market; and do a manual evaluation of all the information acquired from different websites [5]. As time plays an important role in Engineering, Procurement and Construction (EPC) projects [7], delays in procurement can have implications on the project's progress and costs.

Different E-commerce websites have their own material searching and display patterns and use different attributes for storing construction material data [5]. There is heterogeneity in the management of similar types of information by different suppliers. Two product suppliers selling the same or similar products but storing it differently using different attributes make it difficult for a contractor to identify the similarities between the two. Construction material information available in individual E-commerce systems is limited and the information systems are isolated with no interaction with each other [5]. It is difficult for a contractor to find all the information using one system and even more difficult to do a comparison of the products supplied by different suppliers based on criteria such as product specification, cost, availability and delivery time.

4 The MDSS – A Virtual Distributed Database (VDD)

Consideration of the above problems led us to design a federated database architecture which uses a VDD to federate a large number of supplier databases and allows access to them using a single system. Fig. 1 is a conceptual view of the MDSSF. The VDD does not store any product information but uses a Grid enabled Multiple Database Search Service (MDSS) which lies in the the heart of the MDSSF to search a large number of product supplier databases. By using a single system, a contractor can retrieve product information from several supplier databases without visiting different E-commerce sites.

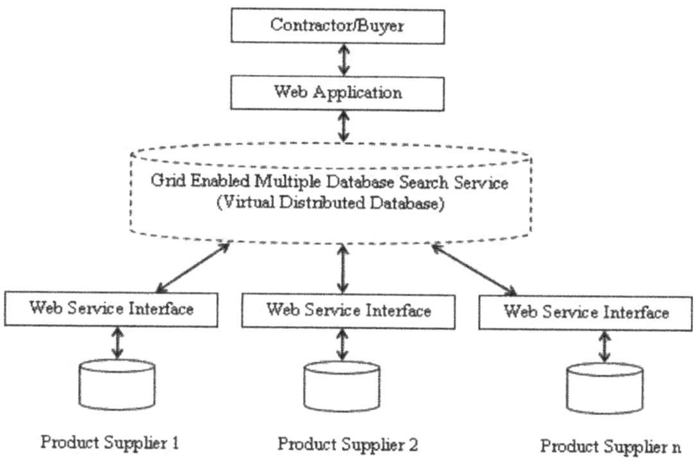

Fig. 1. Conceptual View of the MDSS Federation

The MDSS aids in searching information about products where the product information is provided by the DBS of product suppliers who participate in the federation. Bringing together product information from different sources allows it to be judged on the basis of the requirements of the project and provides contractors with a mechanism to procure products from those product suppliers that best match the project needs. In the federation a particular type of product can be supplied by more than one supplier. This gives contractors a choice of suppliers. So suppliers have to compete with each other, as it is likely that the product supplier having the most competitive price may win orders. However there can be other deciding factors also which may influence the decision of a contractor to opt for a particular supplier, for its ability to meet other project constraints such as product availability, delivery time, bulk purchase options, etc. In this respect the MDSSF allows product suppliers to compete with each other in a virtual market place.

The VDD of the MDSSF is based on the concept of a homogeneous data model so that product data available to its contractors from product suppliers can be represented using a single, agreed format. Representation of data in a standard format enables its usage in a standardised way. By using an agreed data representation format for storing similar product information supplied by different suppliers enables a buyer to gain access to the desired product information quickly and efficiently as lack of standard representation schemas is an obstacle to information sharing [5].

5 The MDSSF System Architecture

The key concepts of a federated database system (FDBS) are autonomy of components and partial and controlled sharing of data [9]. The MDSSF presents a new database federation model to support data retrieval operations from the perspective of: federation users; its model of cooperation; its subscription based approach and the use of Grid technology for performing a distributed search.

In the present paper we aim to describe the architecture of the MDSSF and its use in a business model of procurement of products in the construction industry. We believe that the architecture can also be used in other application areas where product information is required from product specifications and product data managed by several autonomous organisations. The authors in collaboration with an industrial partner (ActivePlan Solutions Ltd., `http://www.activeplan.co.uk`) have developed a prototype software system which is based on the architecture of the MDSSF. In the present paper we provide a summary of the components of the software system such as its homogeneous data model and the Grid enabled search mechanism whilst describing the architectural features of the MDSSF. We do not describe in detail these components which are beyond the scope of this paper. The software system and its components are presented in greater detail in our earlier publication [10].

5.1 Federation Users

There can be two types of users wishing to access data from a FDBS: users within an organisation but belonging to its different sections/departments and users outside the organisation. Data sharing approaches identified in [9], [11], [12], [14] cater to the first type of users who belong to an organisation and the databases that are federated also belong to the organisation itself. The Myriad System [15] also uses FDBS technology but provides enterprise-wide information integration only. As part of this research effort, we aim to create a federated architecture where product information is shared with federation users (such as contractors) who do not belong to the data sharing organisations (such as suppliers). This is a complicated issue because in the first place, the users are external to the data sharing organisations and secondly the data which is shared comes from several product suppliers. Since there are several autonomous product suppliers and contractors, the need for a federated database architecture was identified so that data sharing could take place in a coherent fashion.

5.2 The Cooperation Model of the MDSSF

A FDBS is a collection of cooperating but autonomous DBSs that provide support to global applications built over it [9], [16]. The component DBSs take part in a federation to serve data needs of federation users. Key characteristic of a FDBS is 'cooperation among independent systems' for data sharing [9]. However in the MDSSF we have adopted a different model of cooperation which enables sharing of data with federation users and not between organisations who supply product information to the federation. MDSSF does not allow cooperation between product suppliers as data sharing between them does not takes place. The product suppliers are business organisations who do not wish to disclose their product related sensitive data to their competitors who are also participating in the federation. They only cooperate with the centralised MDSS so that appropriate information about their products are supplied and sent to the contractor in a standard data structure of the VDD. Federated database architectures described in [11], [12] propose data sharing techniques between the components of the federation and therefore do not meet the architectural requirements of the MDSS Federation.

5.3 Subscription of the MDSSF Data Model by Product Suppliers

The data model of the VDD can be described as the *canonical* or *common data model* (CDM) [9] of the MDSSF. The MDSSF allows the CDM of the federation to be subscribed by participating product suppliers. We have implemented a DBS based on the CDM of the federation. The product information can be provided by a supplier to potential buyers and contractors using two different methods. In the first method, a product supplier subscribes to the DBS of the MDSSF. This requires downloading and installing the DBS by a supplier into their local system. By using database operations provided as part of the DBS, a supplier can create product descriptions and store them locally in the relations and attributes of the DBS. This approach is suitable for small and medium organisations who do not use database systems for managing product data but provide product information to buyers in text files or in document formats such as PDF. This approach however, requires a supplier to manually input all the text based product information into the subscribed DBS. By using the DBS of the federation a supplier can not only organise its product information in a structured format but also gain an opportunity to provide product information to potential buyers to retrieve from its database when a search takes place. Hence by participating in the federation, product suppliers gain the opportunity to market their products. The DBS of the MDSSF allows suppliers to create product descriptions. In order to describe products in greater detail, the DBS, via its operations allows different kinds of specifications such as length, width, height, weight, price, delivery time, etc. to be assigned to a product. The DBS also provides the facility to handle complex product attributes such as sub-specifications and allows the specifications to be represented in the form of lists, groups and tables. It provides versioning support for suppliers to list new products into their DBS with enhanced features and functionality. The DBS of the MDSSF is described in greater detail as part of our earlier publication [10].

In the second approach, suppliers can provide their data to federation users by mapping the schema of product data in their product database to the schema objects of the CDM of the MDSSF. This approach is suitable for the suppliers who already have their own database systems managing product information. Establishing mappings by a product supplier is a difficult process as it requires resolving different types of heterogeneities in order to transform queries and results between the schemas of the CDM of the federation and a legacy database application. It is a requirement of the MDSSF that all the data be provided to federation users by using the CDM of the federation. A CDM provides a mechanism to describe same or similar products supplied by different suppliers using a standard data representation. The CDM also provides a mechanism for describing data based on its semantics.

5.4 The Grid Enabled MDSS

The Grid enabled MDSS retrieves product information from a large number of autonomous supplier databases. The MDSS is implemented using the Grid middleware Globus Toolkit 3.0.2 (core) available from the Globus Alliance [13]. By using Grid technology as part of the MDSS, we provide a mechanism to access and process large scale information in a separate process which is external to the boundary of supplier databases. The MDSS searches for the desired products based on criteria submitted by a contractor. Fig. 2 shows the conceptual view of the MDSS in the MDSSF.

A search takes place in a cluster of machines in the Grid network where machines collaborate to perform the search. Important components of the MDSS system are a Master Grid Service (MGS) and Database Search Services (DSS). The search takes place in the Grid network so that a large number of product supplier databases can be searched in real time in response to a contractor's request. The MGS distributes search jobs across a number of machines running DSSs in a grid cluster which perform data retrieval operations. A DSS retrieves product data by invoking the Web Service interface of supplier databases which sends the information back in the form of XML documents. The XML documents provide product information in a format that preserves the semantics of the CDM of the federation subscribed by product suppliers via its DBS. Similar product data retrieved from the databases of several suppliers is aggregated in the Grid environment and is sent to the requesting contractor. The web application displays the results to the contractor by using its GUI features which allow the contractor to make a comparison of products which are similar and retrieved from a large number of supplier databases.

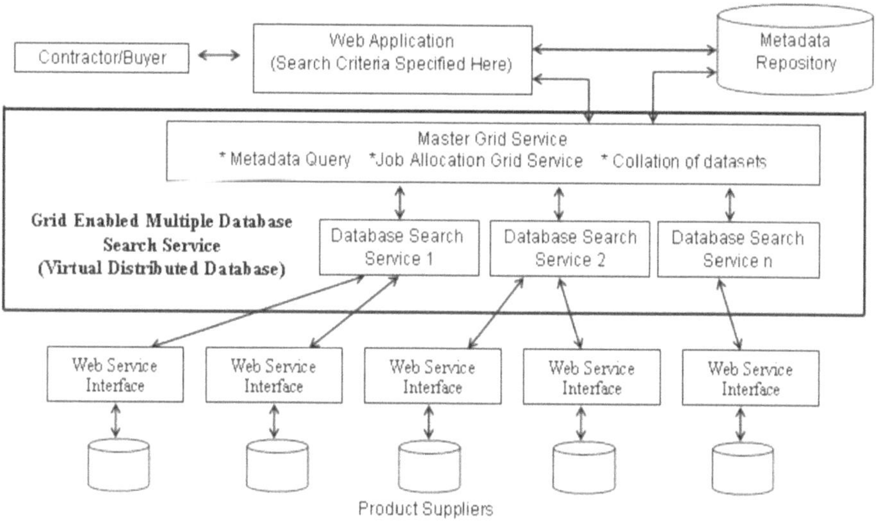

Fig. 2. The MDSS Federation

The distinguishing features of the MDSSF architecture with regards to other federation models identified in [9], [11], [12], [17], [18] is its ability to serve as a mechanism which brings together product suppliers and buyers by establishing a standard criteria for information storage and exchange and its search model which uses the Grid technology to provide a scalable support when searching large number of supplier databases.

6 Related Projects

There are numerous projects in the area of information access such as the DBMS-Aglet Framework [19], InfoSleuth [20], TSIMMIS [21], DISCO [22], COntext INterchange (COIN) [23], Information Manifold [24], Multibase [25], WebFINDIT [26], etc. which use various techniques for information retrieval from heterogeneous sources by incorporating concept such as agents, ontologies, information brokering, mediators, wrappers, web query interfaces, coalitions, service links etc. The techniques identified in these projects do not fully meet the architectural requirements of the MDSSF. Additionally, the architecture of the MDSSF has features of Federated Information Systems (FIS) but it does not fully conform to the FIS types identified in [17].

This is because of the problem we are trying to address which is: creating a federation in which more than one organisation participates by subscribing to the data model of the VDD; and for the users who do not belong to the participating organisations in order to enable data sharing between autonomous product suppliers and contractors.

7 Conclusions and Further Work

This paper described the architecture of the MDSSF which provides a novel data sharing mechanism not supported by previous federated database architectures. The MDSSF presents a database federation model for searching a large number of supplier databases in the procurement phase in AEC industry projects. It provides a mechanism for bringing together autonomous product suppliers, buyers and contractors by establishing a standard criteria for information exchange. We described how the requirement of accessing product information provided by a large number of product suppliers via a single integrated mechanism is achievable by creating a federated database architecture which uses Grid technology to provide scalability and Web Services to give flexibility in data sharing. By using a subscription based approach the problem of heterogeneity that exists because of the lack of standard mechanisms for storing product information by product suppliers can be overcome. As part of further work we aim to improve the overall design of the components of the federation and provide support for partial and controlled sharing of data - a feature of FDBS architectures [9] so that product suppliers reveal information about their products depending on the needs of contractors. We also aim to implement a security infrastructure to protect confidential information from being viewed by unauthorised party. This is particularly important as product suppliers do not wish to reveal their data to business rivals.

References

1. Foster, I., Kesselman, C.: Computational Grids, Chapter 2 of The Grid: Blueprint for a New Computing Infrastructure. Morgan-Kaufman, 1999.
2. Foster, I., Kesselman, C., et al.: The Physiology of the Grid: An Open Grid Services Architecture for Distributed Systems Integration. Open Grid Service Infrastructure WG, Global Grid Forum, 2002.
3. Graham, S., Simeonov S., et al.: Building Web Services with Java: Making sense of XML, SOAP, WSDL, and UDDI. Sams Publishing. (2002)
4. Wyss, C.M., James, A., et al.: Report on the Engineering Federated Information Systems (EFIS 2003), ACM SIGSOFT Software Engineering Notes. **29(2)** (2004)
5. Kong S.C.W., Li H., et al.: Enabling information sharing between E-commerce systems for construction material procurement. Automation in Construction. **13(2)** (2004) 261-276
6. Dzeng, R.-J., Chang, S.-Y.: Learning search keywords for construction procurement. Automation in Construction **14(1)** (2005) 45-58
7. Mahmoud-Jouini, S.B., Midleret, C., et al.: Time-to-market vs. time-to-delivery Managing speed in Engineering, Procurement and Construction projects. International Journal of Project Management. **22(5)** (2004) 359-367
8. Yeo, K.T., Ning, J.H.: Integrating supply chain and critical chain concepts in engineer-procure-construct (EPC) projects. International Journal of Project Management. **20(4)** (2002) 253-262
9. Sheth, A.P., Larson, J.A.: Federated database systems for managing distributed, heterogeneous, and autonomous databases. ACM Computing Surveys (CSUR). **22(3)** (1990) 183-236

10. Pahwa, J.S., Burnap, P., et al.: Creating a Virtual Distributed Database - Data Definition and Search Model for Collaborative Virtual Teams in the Construction Industry. Proc. 21st Annual British National Conference on Databases. **2** (2004) 3-17
11. Heimbigner, D., McLeod, D.:A federated architecture for information management. ACM Transactions on Information Systems (TOIS). **3(3)** (1985) 253-278
12. Hsiao, D.K.:Federated databases and systems: part I - a tutorial on their data sharing. The International Journal on Very Large Data Bases. **1(1)** (1992) 127-180
13. (2006) The Globus Alliance website. [Online]. Available `http://www.globus.org/`
14. Hsiao, D.K.: Federated Databases and Systems: Part II - A Tutorial on Their Resource Consolidation. The International Journal on Very Large Data Bases **1(2)** (1992) 285-310
15. Hwang, S.-Y., Lim, E.-P., et al. The MYRIAD federated database prototype. Proc. ACM SIGMOD International conference on Management of data. **23(2)** (1994)
16. Conrad, S., Eaglestone, B., et al.: Research issues in federated database systems: Report of EFDBS'97 workshop. ACM SIGMOD Record. **26(4)** (1997) 54-56
17. Busse, S., Kutsche, R.-D., et al: Federated Information Systems: concepts, terminology and architectures. Technical Report Nr. 99-9. TU Berlin. (1999)
18. Linn, C., Howarth, B.: A Proposed Globally Distributed Federated database: A Practical Performance Evaluation. Proc. Third International Conference on Parallel and Distributed Information Systems. IEEE Computer Society Press. (1994) 203-212
19. Papastavrou, S., Samaras, G., et al.: Mobile agents for World Wide Web distributed database access. IEEE Transaction on Knowledge and Data Engineering. **12(5)** (2000) 802-820
20. Bayardo Jr., R.J., Bohrer, W., et al.: Infosleuth: Agent-based semantic integration of information in open and dynamic environments. ACM Intl. Conf. on Management of Data (SIGMOD). (1997)
21. Garcia-Molina, H., Papakonstantinou, Y., et al.:The TSIMMIS Approach to Mediation: Data Models and Languages. Journal of Intelligent Information Systems. **8** (1997) 117-132
22. Tomasic, A., Raschid, L., et al.:Scaling access to heterogeneous data sources with DISCO. IEEE Transactions on Knowledge and Data Engineering **10(5)** (1998) 808-823
23. Bressan, S., Goh, C.H., et al.: The context interchange mediator prototype. Proc. ACM SIGMOD international conference on Management of data. (1997) 525-527
24. Levy, A.Y., Rajaraman, A., et al.: Querying heterogeneous information sources using source descriptions. Proc. Twenty-second International Conference on Very Large Databases. (1996) 251-262
25. Huang, J.-W., MultiBase: a heterogeneous multidatabase management system. Proc. Eighteenth Annual International Computer Software and Applications Conference. COMPSAC 94. (1994) 332-339
26. Bouguettaya, A. Benatallah, B., et al.:Supporting dynamic interactions among Web-based information sources. IEEE Transactions on Knowledge and Data Engineering. **12(5)** (2000) 779-801

Argumentation for Decision Support

Katie Atkinson[1], Trevor Bench-Capon[1], and Sanjay Modgil[2]

[1] Department of Computer Science, University of Liverpool, Liverpool, UK
{katie, tbc}@csc.liv.ac.uk
[2] Advanced Computation Lab, Cancer Research UK, Lincoln's Inn Fields, London, UK
sm@acl.icnet.uk

Abstract. In this paper we describe an application based on a general approach towards modelling practical reasoning through defeasible argumentation. The purpose of the paper is to show how the incorporation of an argumentation component can add value to a collection of existing information agents. The example application is a system for reasoning about the medical treatment of a patient. An agent, called the *Drama* agent, orchestrates a number of information sources to supply a set of arguments on the basis of which the decision regarding treatment can be taken. We describe the general approach and its instantiation for this application, and illustrate the operation of the system with a running example.

1 Introduction

We describe an application based on a general approach towards modelling practical reasoning through defeasible argumentation[1] to show how an argumentation component can add value to a collection of existing information resources. The example application is a system for reasoning about the medical treatment of a patient. We assume that a number of information sources, representing different areas of medical knowledge and facts about individuals, and different policies and perspectives relevant to the problem are available. The focus of this paper is the *Drama* (for Deliberative Reasoning with ArguMents about Actions) agent which orchestrates these contributions in argumentation terms, and comes to a decision based on an evaluation of the competing arguments. We begin by describing our general approach to such deliberative reasoning. Section 2 will give an overview of the application. Section 3 will describe how the general approach is used in the particular application using a representative example of such deliberation, and section 4 will discuss the potential advantages of the approach.

A general approach to persuasive and deliberative reasoning about action has been presented in [1]. First a presumptive justification for a course of action is found. This takes the form of an instantiation of the argument scheme AS1:

AS1 In the circumstances R
We should perform action A
Whose effects will result in state of affairs S
Which will realise a goal G
Which will promote some value V.

[1] For a comprehensive survey of logical models of argument see [3].

S. Bressan, J. Küng, and R. Wagner (Eds.): DEXA 2006, LNCS 4080, pp. 822–831, 2006.

AS1 is an enrichment of the *Sufficient Condition Scheme*, one of the presumptive argument schemes for practical reasoning proposed by Walton [9]. This enrichment allows us to additionally distinguish between: the consequences of the action (S); the *desired* consequences of the action (G); the *reason* why those consequences are desired (V).

These distinctions have been found to be crucial in some applications, including reasoning with legal cases and reasoning about political decisions [1]. The importance of making these distinctions will be further shown in the example.

Next the presumptive justification must be subjected to a critique. Associated with an argument scheme are a number of characteristic critical questions, which could lead to the justification being defeated. This critique will also identify alternative actions for consideration. In [1] sixteen critical questions associated with AS1 are identified. Two sample critical questions are: *are the current circumstances in fact R*? and *are there alternative ways to achieve the goal G*? Each critical question has associated with it preconditions for making a counter argument. Thus an agent could question the truth of the circumstances if it believed that they were other than R, or could suggest an alternative action if it believed that it would also realise G. Preconditions in terms of the beliefs and desires of an agent are given in [1]. For each critical question whose preconditions are satisfied, one or more arguments attacking the original justification can be produced. These arguments may in turn be subject to the same process of critical questioning to generate counter arguments.

When the set of arguments and counter arguments have been produced, it is necessary to consider which of them should be accepted. In order to do this the arguments $Args$ together with the binary *Attack* relation on $Args$ are organised into an *argumentation framework* $(Args, Attack)$, as introduced by Dung in [5]. In [5] an argument $A1$ is always *defeated* by an attacker $A2$, unless $A2$ can itself be defeated. This is appropriate to reasoning about beliefs, but when reasoning about actions we are, to a certain extent, free to choose what we will attempt to bring about. Thus we may choose to reject an attacker even if it cannot be defeated, provided we regard the purpose motivating the attacked argument as more important. For example, an argument $A2$ that a particular drug is expensive attacks an argument $A1$ for prescribing the drug. However, we may none the less choose to prescribe it (accept the argument $A1$) if that would serve a purpose (promote a value) we rate more highly than expense. To accommodate the notion of the value promoted by the acceptance of an argument we use an extension of Dung's framework, *value-based argumentation frameworks* [2]. The idea is that we are given an *argumentation framework*, a set of values V, a function val mapping each argument to a value $v \in V$, and a set of *audiences* a (in the sense of [6]) to which the arguments are addressed. Each audience is represented (as in [2]) by a strict partial ordering $>_a$ on the values. Then, for a given audience $>_a$, $A2$ defeats $A1$ iff $A2$ attacks $A1$ and $val(A2) \not>_a val(A1)$. Note that by this definition, if $A2$ attacks $A1$ and both promote the same value then the attacks always succeeds as a defeat.

For a given audience and defined defeat relation, we can then determine which arguments in $Args$ are acceptable by determining the preferred extension. The preferred extension is the maximal (under set inclusion) subset S of $Args$ such that no two arguments in S defeat each other, and all arguments A in S are acceptable with respect to S, i.e., for any argument A in S, if A is defeated by an argument A' that is not in S, then there exists an argument in S that defeats A'. The preferred extension thus represents the maximal consistent set of acceptable arguments with respect to the argumentation framework and a given audience or value ordering. Cycles in the same value give rise to multiple preferred extensions (e.g., $A1$ $A2$ attack each other and promote the same value). In building the framework it is necessary to resolve cycles in a single value by expressing a preference for one of the arguments in the cycle, based on considerations other than the value: for example that the action is intrinsically preferred.

It has been shown in [2] that an efficient algorithm exists for the computation of the preferred extension of such a framework for a given value ordering, once the cycles have been resolved. We may therefore compute the preferred extensions corresponding to the possible value orderings to discover the dialectical status of the arguments in the framework. When evaluated the arguments may have a unique status, or their status may be dependent on the value ordering. In this latter case the agent may either commit to a particular value ordering, or determine the value ordering in the course of its deliberation [4]. Thus the Drama agent will deliberate on a course of action by:

- obtaining a presumptive justification for some course of action,
- generating any counter arguments to the course of action by posing critical questions, where each such counter-argument is itself subject to counter-arguments (posing of critical questions),
- selecting the course of action by organising the resulting arguments into an argumentation framework, and calculating the preferred extension corresponding to its ranking of values.

In the next section we will discuss the particular application which we will use to exemplify our approach in this paper.

2 Deliberative Reasoning About Medical Treatment

Clinical guidelines promote best practice in clinical medicine by specifying the selection and sequencing of medical actions for achievement of medical goals. There is a large body of research into computational support for authoring and enactment of clinical guidelines [8]. Authoring tools support specification of a guideline in some suitable knowledge representation formalism. This specification can then be executed in a specific clinical context so as to enforce compliance with the best practice encoded in the guideline. The authored guidelines need to be specified at a level of abstraction that enables enactment in any number of contexts. It is at execution time that the context dependent choice of specific medical actions must be made.

For example, a guideline may indicate that treatment of a patient recovering from myocardial infarct (heart attack) requires realisation of the treatment goals: treat pain; treat sickness; prevent blood clotting. It is at execution time that one must take into account the specific context in order to choose which precise action should be chosen for realising each of these goals. Examples of contextual factors that influence the decision include:

- information about the specific patient being treated, e.g., administration of a particular drug for preventing blood clotting may for safety reasons be contraindicated by a patient's clinical history,

- concomitant treatments, e.g., the efficacy of a drug for preventing blood clotting may be reduced by drugs being administered for a gastrointestinal condition,
- local resource constraints, e.g., budget constraints at the local hospital may indicate a preference for one drug over another,
- local organisational policies, e.g., the local health authority may have evidence based preferences for one drug over another.

We propose that it is through deliberative argumentation of the type described in this paper that one can model how these contextual factors can be brought to bear on the decision as to what is the most appropriate treatment action in a given situation. In particular, by structuring a recommendation for action as an argument instantiating argument scheme AS1, one can effectively account for the influence of contextual factors on the decision making process; i.e., by instantiating AS1's critical questions. Furthermore, the complexity and diversity of the contextual knowledge and reasoning suggests that the information required to be considered may best be distributed across a number of information sources.

In the example below, the medical knowledge cited is for illustrative purposes only: we make no claims for it either as a model of the medical domain, or as a representation of the state of the art of medical systems. Our purpose is only to show how value can be added by the addition of an argumentation agent capable of reasoning with multiple perspectives and drawing on a range of sources.

3 Application to the Medical Domain

In our application we locate all argumentation knowledge inside the Drama agent, and the other resources are conventional knowledge and database systems. In particular these other resources are independent of values. The other resources that the Drama agent will interact with in our example are shown in Table 1. Some will contain generic medical knowledge, while others are specific to the organisation.

Table 1. Resources in the Drama System

Resource	Type	Scope
Treatment KB	Knowledge Base	Generic Medical Policy and Knowledge
Policy KB	Knowledge Base	Organisation Specific Knowledge
Safety KB	Knowledge Base	Generic Medical Knowledge
Patient DB	Database	Patient Specific Information
Cost KB	Knowledge Base	Organisation Specific Knowledge
Efficacy KB	Knowledge Base	Specific Medical Knowledge

Following the general approach, the Drama agent will use critical questions to identify the information required to generate arguments. In any particular application a characteristic set of the critical questions will be pertinent (see [1]). In this application we assume that all resources have a common vocabulary, and any information given can be accepted as true. Given these assumptions there are five critical questions pertinent to this particular application:

- CQ1: Are there alternative ways of realising the same effects?
- CQ2: Are there alternative ways of realising the same goal?
- CQ3: Are the assumptions on which the argument is based true?
- CQ4: Does performing the action have a side effect which demotes some other value?
- CQ5: Will the action have the effects described?

The Drama agent now constructs an argumentation framework by instantiating AS1 and posing these critical questions. We will illustrate the operation of the system with a running example of a patient whose health is threatened by blood clotting. The framework begins with the null option - do nothing (EA0). The purpose of this is similar to the assumption of the negation of the desired goal in refutation resolution: extensions of the resulting argument frameworks will be acceptable only if they do not contain this argument. The goal of preventing blood clotting is now issued to the *Treatment KB*.

The Treatment KB is one among a number of treatment knowledge bases, each of which is specialised for recommending treatment actions for a medical speciality. In our example, the Treatment KB is specialised to the cardiac domain. For the purposes of this example we will suppose that the Treatment KB, and the other KBs, use simple Prolog rules and are capable of solving a goal and returning a proof trace. The Treatment KB might include (P denotes the patient in question):

```
prevent_blood_clotting(P):-
  reduce_platelet_adhesion(P).
prevent_blood_clotting(P):-
  increase_blood_clot_dispersal_agents(P).
reduce_platelet_adhesion(P):-
  not contraindicated(aspirin,P),
  prescribe(aspirin,P).
reduce_platelet_adhesion(P):-
  not contraindicated(chlopidogrel,P),
  prescribe(chlopidogrel,P).
increase_blood_clot_dispersal_agents(p):-
  not contraindicated(streptokinase,P),
  prescribe(streptokinase,P).
```

It will therefore be able to return the information that blood clotting can be prevented by reducing platelet adhesion, which can, assuming aspirin is not contraindicated, be achieved by prescribing aspirin. The Drama agent can use this information to instantiate AS1, thus providing a justification for this action:

EA1. *Assuming no contradictions, we should prescribe aspirin, which will reduce platelet adhesion, preventing blood clotting, and so is an efficacious course of action.*

This argument has to be subjected to a critique to ensure that there are no better alternatives. The Drama agent will go through its repertoire of critical questions. Posing

CQ1 will ask for alternative solutions to reduce platelet adhesion from the Treatment Agent and elicit the information that chlopidogrel will also reduce platelet adhesion. Asking CQ2 will seek further solutions from the Treatment Agent for preventing blood clotting and will identify the alternative course of action of administering streptokinase, which has the same goal of preventing blood clotting, but via a different effect of increasing the blood's production of agents that disperse clots. These are formed into two arguments, EA2 and EA3:

EA2. *Assuming no contradictions, we should prescribe chlopidogrel, which will reduce platelet adhesion, preventing blood clotting, and so is an efficacious course of action.*

EA3. *Assuming no contradictions, we should prescribe streptokinase, which will increase blood clot dispersal agents, preventing blood clotting, and so is an efficacious course of action.*

These three arguments all mutually attack one another, giving rise to the argumentation framework shown in Figure 1.

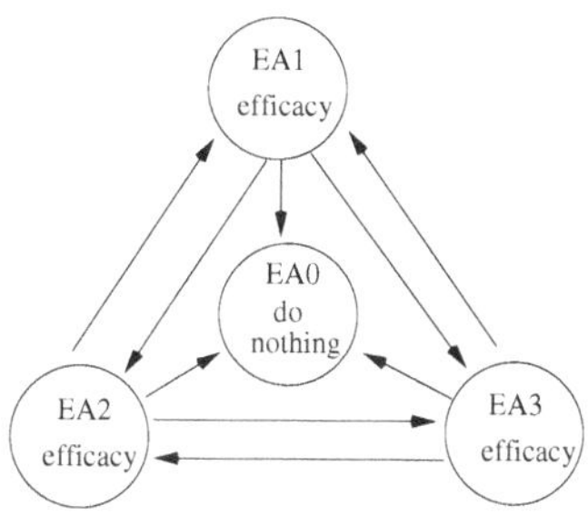

Fig. 1. Initial Argumentation Framework

Any of EA1, EA2 or EA3 would serve to defeat EA0, 'do nothing'. However, they are in mutual conflict. As they all relate to the same value (which means that the preferred extension is empty for all audiences), there is a free choice between them. They can be chosen according to intrinsic preferences regarding the goal or the actions themselves. The Drama agent therefore contacts the *Policy KB* to see what the preferences of the organisation are.

The Policy KB contains organisation specific information to determine preferences between goals, effects and actions. Any criteria could be used here. For the purposes of the example we will assume that the Policy KB prefers the effect 'reduce platelet adhesion' as a means by which the goal can be realised, since the effect of increasing blood clot dispersal agents has potentially more undesirable side-effects. Hence, the Policy KB will favour actions with the former effect over actions with the latter effect. This, however, does not discriminate between aspirin and chlopidogrel. Again many criteria are possible: it could depend on local stocks held, or a local preference for generic drugs. Here we will assume that cost is the basis for preference and that aspirin is cheaper than chlopidogrel.

We represent these preferences in our argumentation framework by removing the attacks of the unfavoured actions, so that EA1 is no longer attacked, and EA3 no longer attacks EA2 (see Figure 2, ignoring the dotted arrows indicating arguments submitted later on). Now EA1 will form the preferred extension of this framework, and so its action is currently the best candidate. There remain, however, some further critical questions that can be asked of EA1.

EA1 assumed that aspirin was not contraindicated. CQ3 instructs us to test this assumption. This is the role of the *Safety KB*. The Safety KB has knowledge of contraindications of the various drugs, and the reasons for the contraindication. The Safety KB might contain:

```
contraindicated(D,P):-
  risk_of_gastric_ulceration(D,P).
risk_of_gastric_ulceration(D,P):-
  increased_acidity(D),
  history_of_gastritis(P),
  not acid_reducing_therapy(P).
increased_acidity(aspirin).
```

When contacted by the Drama agent it will use this knowledge, together with patient specific information obtained from the *Patient DB* to inform the Drama agent that since the patient has a history of gastritis, aspirin is contraindicated because its acidity may result in gastric ulceration. The Drama agent will form this into an argument motivated by the value of safety. Note that because each of the information sources represents a particular perspective on the problem, the Drama agent may ascribe a motivating value to the argument on the basis of its source.

EA4. *Where there is a history of gastritis and no acid reducing therapy, we should not prescribe aspirin, which would cause excess acidity, which would risk ulceration, and so is unsafe.*

When EA4 is added to the argumentation framework (arrow 1 in Figure 2), EA4 attacks EA1. Assuming that safety is preferred to efficacy, EA4 defeats EA1 and so EA2 replaces EA1 in the preferred extension.

Assuming EA2 cannot be attacked by CQ3, the next critique follows from CQ4. Efficacy is not the only value: any action must be acceptable within the cost constraints of the organisation. Answering this critical question is the province of the *Cost KB*. This KB will have knowledge of the budgetary constraints on treatment, and will compare the cost of the proposed treatment with these constraints. Suppose that chlopidogrel exceeds these limits. At the minimum this is simply a query as to whether the cost of the treatment exceeds a given threshold, posed to a database of treatment costs. The Drama agent can now form the argument EA5:

EA5. *Where cost of chlopidogrel is £N, we should not prescribe chlopidogrel, which would cost £N, exceeding our budget, which demotes the value of financial prudence.*

Adding EA5 (arrow 2 in Figure 2) means that EA2 is defeated if cost is preferred to efficacy. This now means that EA3 is in the preferred extension. Since it is unchallenged there is an obligation to critique the proposal to prescribe streptokinase, by returning to CQ3 and CQ4. Suppose that streptokinase is not contraindicated, and that it falls within the cost constraints. There remains CQ5, and we must now investigate whether streptokinase will be effective for the particular individual we are treating. The *Efficacy KB* will contain specific data from clinical trials and past cases indicating the efficacy of actions with respect to treatment goals for particular patient groups. Perhaps (and this is simply an illustrative conjecture on our part) the efficacy of streptokinase has been found to depend on age. The Efficacy KB may then contain rules such as:

```
effectiveness(P, streptokinase, prevent_blood_clotting, 90):-
  age(P,A),A < 50.
effectiveness(P, streptokinase, prevent_blood_clotting, 30):-
  age(P,A),A > 49.
acceptable(P, Treatment, prevent_blood_clotting):-
  effectiveness(P, Treatment, prevent_blood_clotting, E),E > 75.
```

Together with particular patient data obtained from the Patient DB, the Efficacy KB passes this information to the Drama agent which expresses it as EA6:

EA6. *Where patient is aged 72, we should not prescribe streptokinase, as the likelihood of success is 30%, which is below the required threshold, which demotes efficacy.*

We add EA6 to the framework, as shown in Figure 2 (arrow 3). EA3 is attacked by an argument with the same value and so is defeated. If safety is preferred to efficacy then EA1 is defeated by EA4. If cost is preferred to efficacy then EA2 is defeated by EA5. This would mean that EA0 would be included in the preferred extension as all its attackers are defeated. However, as stated from the outset, this is unacceptable as the patient's health is then in jeopardy. There are two possibilities: either we must re-order our values so that efficacy is preferred to one of safety or cost (respectively making EA1 or EA2 preferred), or else we must find an argument with which to defeat the attackers of one of EA1–3 and so reinstate one of our actions.

Suppose we re-order the values so as to prefer efficacy to at least one of the other values i.e., we must choose whether we disregard safety or cost. The choice will depend on the particular circumstances: it may be that the Drama agent is allowed to exceed budget if necessary, in which case efficacy will be preferred to cost and chlopidogrel will be prescribed. But if the cost constraint is rigid, there may be no better option than to disregard the contraindications and risk using aspirin, believing the complications to be less threatening than the immediate danger.

These hard choices can, however, be avoided if we can succeed in defeating one of the attacking arguments. We therefore run through our critical questions with respect to the arguments currently in the preferred extension of the framework. CQ3 can be posed with respect to EA4, as it is predicated on an assumption that there is no acid reducing therapy prescribed to the patient. We may therefore return to another Treatment KB and attempt to find such an acid reducing therapy. This will supply the knowledge that a proton pump inhibitor (a particular type of acid reducing therapy) will have the desired effect. We can form this into EA7:

EA7. *Where there are no contraindications, prescribing a proton pump inhibitor, will prevent excess acidity, removing risk of ulceration, promoting the value of safety.*

The complete argumentation framework after the addition of EA7 is shown in Figure 2:

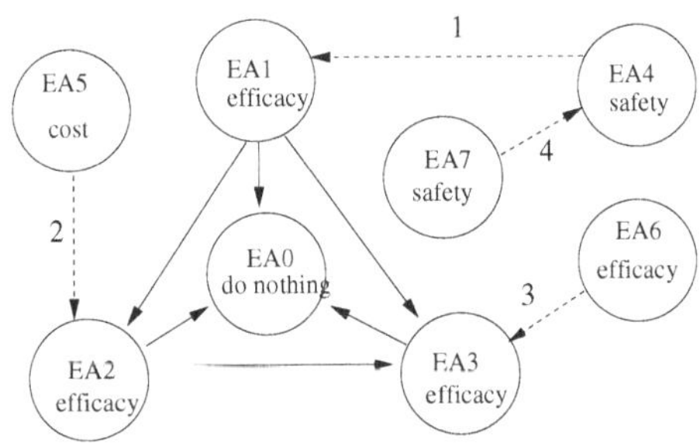

Fig. 2. Final Argumentation Framework showing all critiques

Of course, EA7 is now subject to critical questioning. Assuming, however, that there are no alternatives, that it is not contraindicated, within budget and likely to be effective, the argument gathering stops here as we have now exhausted our critical questions. We compute the preferred extension by first including the arguments with no attackers: EA5, EA6 and EA7. EA7 defeats EA4 because they are motivated by the same value. This means that EA1 can be included, as its only attacker is defeated. EA1 thus defeats EA2 and EA3, again because they are motivated by the same value, and also excludes EA0, as desired. Note that in this case we need express no value preferences: the preferred extension is the same irrespective of value order. From this we conclude that aspirin is the preferred treatment, and should be recognised as such by any audience.

4 Discussion

The system for deliberative reasoning described above has a number of worthwhile features:

- It models deliberation using a model of argument with presumptive justification subject to critique, which has been developed to capture a number of features of practical reasoning observed in the philosophical [7] and informal logic literature [9]. These include the defeasible nature of putative solutions, the importance of perspectives (values), and the potential for context dependent orderings on perspectives to accommodate different audiences.
- This model is effected inside a single agent: the other components in the system can therefore be conventional knowledge and database systems, simplifying their participation in other systems. If, however, more sophisticated resources, such as autonomous agent systems, are available, these can be used by the Drama agent without modification.

- The various perspectives which need to be considered when making a medical decision are kept separate, and it is made explicit from which perspective the various arguments derive. This means that the perspectives can be given their due weight, but discounted if necessary.
- Each of the information sources used by the Drama agent is dedicated to the provision of particular information, has no need to consider every eventuality, and plays no part in the evaluation. This simplifies their construction and facilitates their reuse in other applications.
- Distinction can be made between information sources which are generic and those which are particular to a specific organisation or individual.
- Critiques are made only as and when they can affect the dialectical status of arguments already advanced. This means that all reasoning undertaken is of potential relevance to the solution.
- Patient information is made available only as and when needed.

The combination of the use of a well motivated model of deliberation, use wherever possible of conventional and generic components, and the ability to make flexible and context dependent decisions, provides, we believe, an approach to reasoning about decisions based on several information sources (such as is the case in medicine) that has considerable potential.[2]

References

1. K. Atkinson. *What Should We Do?: Computational Representation of Persuasive Argument in Practical Reasoning*. PhD thesis, Department of Computer Science, University of Liverpool, Liverpool, UK, 2005.
2. T. Bench-Capon. Persuasion in practical argument using value based argumentation frameworks. *Journal of Logic and Computation*, 13 3:429–48, 2003.
3. C. Chesñevar, A. Maguitman, and R. Loui. Logical models of argument. *ACM Computing Surveys*, 32(4):337–383, 2000.
4. S. Doutre, T. Bench-Capon, and P. E. Dunne. Explaining preferences with argument position. In *Proceedings of the Ninteenth International Joint Conference on Artificial Intelligence (IJCAI 2005)*, pages 1560–1561, 2005.
5. P. M. Dung. On the acceptability of arguments and its fundamental role in nonmonotonic reasoning, logic programming and n-person games. *Artificial Intelligence*, 77:321–357, 1995.
6. C. Perelman and L. Olbrechts-Tyteca. *The New Rhetoric: A Treatise on Argumentation.* University of Notre Dame Press, Notre Dame, IN, USA, 1969.
7. J. R. Searle. *Rationality in Action.* MIT Press, Cambridge, MA, USA, 2001.
8. S. W. Tu and M. A. Musen. Representation formalisms and computational methods for modeling guideline-based patient care. In M. Mussen M. Stefanelli B. Heller, M. Loffler, editor, *Proceedings of First European Workshop on Computer-based Support for Clinical Guidelines and Protocols*, Leipzig, Germany, 2000. IOS Press.
9. D. N. Walton. *Argument Schemes for Presumptive Reasoning.* Lawrence Erlbaum Associates, Mahwah, NJ, USA, 1996.

[2] Trevor Bench-Capon and Sanjay Modgil acknowledge partial support received from the European Commission through Project ASPIC (IST-FP6-002307). We would like to thank the anonymous reviewers for their comments and suggestions. We are also grateful to Peter McBurney for his contributions to our work on argumentation and practical reasoning.

Personalized Detection of Fresh Content and Temporal Annotation for Improved Page Revisiting

Adam Jatowt[1], Yukiko Kawai[2], and Katsumi Tanaka[1]

[1] Kyoto University
Yoshida-Honmachi, Sakyo-ku, 606-8501
Kyoto, Japan
{adam, tanaka}@dl.kuis.kyoto-u.ac.jp
[2] Kyoto Sangyo University
Motoyama, Kamigamo, Kita-Ku, 603-8555
Kyoto, Japan
kawai@cc.kyoto-su.ac.jp

Abstract. Page revisiting is a popular browsing activity in the Web. In this paper we describe a method for improving page revisiting by detecting and highlighting the information on browsed Web pages that is fresh for a user. Content freshness is determined based on comparison with the previously viewed versions of pages. Any new content for the user is marked, enabling the user to quickly spot it. We also describe a mechanism for visually informing users about the degree of freshness of linked pages. By indicating the freshness level of content on linked pages, the system enables users to navigate the Web more effectively. Finally, we propose and demonstrate the concept of determining user-dependent, subjective age of page contents. Using this method, elements of Web pages are annotated with dates indicating the first time the elements were accessed by the user.

Keywords: page revisiting, fresh information retrieval, change detection.

1 Introduction

The Web is a very dynamic environment, with many changes occurring frequently. Several studies have confirmed this by measuring the frequency of Web changes (e.g. [2], [3] and [8]). This volatility makes the Web attractive and is one of the reasons for its great popularity. Users have access to the freshest news and information at any time. This is in contrast to traditional media like newspapers where readers have to wait certain periods of time for each new edition. Many Web users have favorite pages that they frequently revisit [4], [12]. Usually, such pages not only contain high quality content, but are also frequently changing since otherwise they would soon become uninteresting or even obsolete to users. This is because Web site administrators not only want to attract new users to their pages but also to encourage return visits. In general, the revisiting frequency is dependent on the page quality and the overlap of the page content with users' interests, but it is also related to the page-updating frequency.

S. Bressan, J. Küng, and R. Wagner (Eds.): DEXA 2006, LNCS 4080, pp. 832 – 841, 2006.

However, revisiting pages can sometimes be costly or can be a waste of time. Users coming to the page in search of new content may have problems noticing it especially if the page is large and changes are not easily visible. Often, top pages of popular Web sites (e.g. some news sites) introduce only short sentences containing links which lead to the novel content being published on separate pages. Noticing all such changes in the page may be troublesome and take time. Also, fresh information may be hidden in lower levels of a Web site's topology and thus be difficult to find. Users who wish to obtain new content have to access them one by one to check for new information. Such navigation is usually based on users' intuition and guesswork whether linked pages are worth revisiting, and may result in incurred costs and waste of time.

Sometimes users may even be misled to visit unchanged pages when expecting new content. For example, a page might have a link labeled "new," causing an average user to think that new content has been added since his last visit. The user might thus access this link only to find that the content is still old from his perspective. The "new" label is actually aimed at first time or infrequent visitors. Frequent visitors are expected to remember all the places they previously visited if they do not want to waste time viewing the same content twice. However, in contrast, some of the content on such a page may actually be new from the revisitor's perspective, but, having already visited the page, he or she may not visit it again since he or she may believe that the page content has not changed. In both cases, page viewing is ineffective, and the user can become frustrated. In the first case, the user might revisit the page too often, thereby losing time and incurring costs, while in the second case, he or she might miss content updates. One solution is a personalized, freshness-oriented browsing style due to which the user is clearly informed, without much effort, about the location and amount of fresh for him or her content on visited pages or sites.

In this paper we propose an approach to support browsing by automatically detecting the content that is fresh for the user. This user-dependent freshness determination is made possible by storing and analyzing the pages previously viewed by the user. We have built a browsing system that not only indicates the page elements that are novel for the user but also calculates the freshness of links occurring on the page and displays them in different colors based on their freshness values. The browser enables users to easily find content that is new to them and the links worth visiting. It can be especially helpful for users who have problems remembering previously seen versions of pages and who cannot easily spot changes in the page content. In addition, such browsing and navigation aid could be used for mobile browsing scenarios, where screen limitations may not enable viewing the whole page and limited bandwidth may not allow for unrestricted browsing of Web sites.

We also propose the concept of user-oriented temporal annotation of page content. Using this method, a user can know when he or she viewed certain content on a page for the first time and thus can determine how obsolete or how new it is for him or her. It is possible to recall the time when a given part of the page has been seen for the first time, hence putting a temporal constraint on it. If a part of the page content was seen by the user for the first time at a certain time point t_s, then during later visits to the page the user can be informed that the content is at least not younger than t_s. Thus the user can treat the particular content differently based on the date it was first encountered. Additionally, considering the number of page revisits since t_s, it is also possible to approximately assess how much the content is already known to the user.

In general, we provide a new kind of contextual information to users that is determined by considering their browsing histories, informing them on what they have not yet viewed and on what and when they have seen. The enhanced browsing is provided to reduce the cost and time spent revisiting pages without requiring much effort from the user. The user-oriented temporal annotation of page content enables users to obtain the information about the subjective age of page objects and allows one to better understand and orient themselves in the present content of pages. The proposed concepts are designed for users who do not have much time for browsing but frequently visit favorite pages that are highly volatile.

After first discussing related research in Section 2, we will describe in Section 3 our proposals for the user-oriented freshness detection and temporal annotation of page contents. In Section 4, we discuss their implementation. Finally, we conclude in Section 5 with a summary of the key points.

2 Related Research

Browsing Web pages is one of the most popular activities on the Internet. Users browse not only for relevant information but also, in many cases, for fresh content. However, there has been little research so far, of which we are aware, into combining change detection with browsing to facilitate fresh information retrieval. The exception is WebGuide system [7], which enables users to compare differences between pages with respect to two dates and to visualize changes in Web sites. Our approach is different in that we focus on integrating change detection with browsing. We propose a novel visualization method of fresh content on pages by utilizing link color changes and by displaying numerical values of freshness degrees of Web pages. This enhances navigation in revisited pages with minimal user interaction. The user is also informed about the overall freshness degree of the page content. Finally, we propose a new time-based annotation method with the user-oriented dates of content viewing.

Improving browsing by utilizing a user's browsing history has been already researched before (e.g. [9]). The pages that a person has visited constitute an easy to use set of data and are quite effective at measuring person's interests. However, rather than searching for content similar to previously viewed content that the user might be attracted to, we try to detect the fresh content for the user. Additionally, we utilize the browsing history for determining the user-oriented age of page objects. This differs from previous proposals of browsing history visualization in that it maps the user browsing activity directly onto the present content of the page.

So-called current awareness systems (e.g. [1], [6] and [11]) are tools for informing users about page updates. A popular one, Rich Site Summary (RSS), is a Web feed that provides summaries of the new content on Web sites. This enables users to track updates to sites. Other systems detect content changes in some pre-determined sets of resources and notify users about such changes. For example, a work by Qiang et al. [11] contains several effective approaches into detecting changes and measuring change importance in Web structures. Usually, current awareness systems require users to specify beforehand pages of interest. However, users may have trouble listing all such pages. Additionally, these systems may cause an information overload by continuously sending information about new content appearing on the specified pages, especially in cases of highly volatile pages. While the user could theoretically specify the exact types of content that he or she is interested in, in order to minimize this overload, doing so would be difficult and impractical. Content filtering cannot be done effectively as users are often interested in novel content, and which content will be interesting for them is hard to predict. Furthermore, many users are accustomed to actively viewing the Web, and they often actively revisit pages without waiting for an alert from change detection systems. In our approach, we integrate change detection with browsing, thus eliminating the burden of registration of interesting Web pages by the user. Consequently, the proposed system detects browsing-derived changes extracted between consecutive visits of pages by the user.

3 System Overview

3.1 Freshness Degree

Let us suppose that a user has a favorite page, which he or she frequently revisits. For each visit, we store a view $V(t_i)$ of the page which is a snapshot of the page, where t_i denotes the timestamp of the view. The snapshot reflects the state of the page as it was perceived by the user and contains elements j ($j \in V(t_i)$) that occur on the page view $V(t_i)$. After several revisits of the page $V(t_1),\ldots,V(t_n)$, at time points $t_1,\ldots,t_n$, three attributes $(\tau_{ins}(j), \tau_{del}(j), \omega(j))$ are assigned to each element j at each page view; $\tau_{ins}(j)$ is the time point when the user saw the particular element for the first time, $\tau_{del}(j)$ denotes the time point when the user saw it for the last time and $\omega(j)$ specifies the element's viewing frequency. Representing each element occurring in a certain view $V(t_i)$ of the page by the triple $(\tau_{ins}(j), \tau_{del}(j), \omega(j))$ enables the system to determine how obsolete or well-known the element is for the user. The perception of the page contents from the perspective of the user-oriented freshness is thus changing every time he or she accesses the page.

The freshness degree of the page is computed as the ratio of the amount of fresh content to the total amount of the page content. We represent it as a linear combination of freshness degrees of text and images:

$$\text{TotalFreshness} = \alpha * \text{TextFreshness} + (1 - \alpha) * \text{ImageFreshness}\,. \tag{1}$$

The amount of textual content is expressed as the number of words while the amount of image content is estimated by the dimensions of images on the page.

In addition, we can try to estimate the level of surprise of the user upon not seeing certain content on the page that is related to the long-term perception of the page content:

$$Surprise = \frac{\sum_{j=1}^{M} \left[size(j) * \left(t_{n-1} - \tau_{ins}(j)\right) * \omega(j)\right]}{\sum_{j=1}^{N} \left[size(j) * \left(t_{n-1} - \tau_{ins}(j)\right) * \omega(j)\right]}\,. \tag{2}$$

The surprise is related to the expectation of the user that no change will happen on the page. This can be expressed by using the time period that elapsed since the first view of the page content and the number of times it has been viewed by the user. Equation 2 is computed using the content of the current page version $V(t_n)$ and the last-visited page version $V(t_{n-1})$; $size(j)$ is the size of an element j and N is the number of distinct elements on $V(t_{n-1})$, M is the number of elements that were deleted since the last view of the page. The surprise level calculated in this way could be used to modify the total freshness degree of the page in order to represent more personalized, subjective freshness degree of the page.

A reader should note that the relevance of content is not taken into consideration in the proposed system. We assume that the content on frequently revisited or favorite pages is most likely interesting to the user. However, a relevance-aware freshness degree could be computed, for example, by considering the frequency of query words in the novel content or its overlap with the model of user interest.

3.2 Fresh Content Detection and Indication

When the user revisits a page, the present version of the page is compared with the recently visited one. Any added content is marked to draw the user's attention. For example, the background color of the text may be changed. Except for content comparison of the currently viewed Web page, there is a mechanism provided that estimates the degree of freshness for each page to which the current page has links. Then each link has assigned the degree of freshness which is shown next to the text in the anchor tag of the link. Additionally, link color is changed to indicate its freshness degree. Link-color changing has been used on the Web for some time. According to some estimate [10], 74% of Web sites use a link-color changing mechanism. Its prime aim is to inform users about the links that have been already visited by them. Hence, its main objective is to assist users with Web navigation rather than to inform them about the freshness of the content on the previously visited pages. Even if the contents of a previously visited page have been changed since the last visit, the corresponding link will still be displayed in the visited-link color. Therefore, this mechanism just informs the user about the pages he or she has visited without providing any information about changes to their contents. Thus, a user will not become aware of any changes in the content for a page already visited if he or she deems the page not worth revisiting by simply judging its freshness by the changed color of the link. Moreover, the marking process is an either/or process, meaning that only two colors are used to differentiate between visited and unvisited links. Our user-oriented freshness detection approach with link freshness visualization overcomes this problem. Below is the summary of the whole algorithm.

1. The pages viewed by the user are stored in a cache or database during browsing.
2. The current version of the accessed page is compared with the latest version viewed by the user.
3. Any added content is color-coded.
4. If any links on the current version of the accessed page have been already visited by the user then the current versions of the linked pages are compared with the latest versions viewed by the user.

5. For all linked pages that the user has viewed, the added contents are identified, and the pages' degrees of freshness are calculated. The links to these pages are shown in different colors depending on their freshness degrees. Additionally, freshness degrees and dates of their last visits may be displayed. The links for pages that have not been viewed by the user are left unchanged.

Figure 1 illustrates the steps involved in freshness-based annotating of the content and links. The links are shown in different colors depending on their corresponding degrees of freshness. Additionally, the text boxes indicating values of the freshness degrees are attached to the links. The user can spot which parts of the page are new to him or her and also see which linked pages contain large amounts of new content. The system thus facilitates the detection of fresh information in currently viewed pages and, at the same time, directs the user to fresh content on the linked pages.

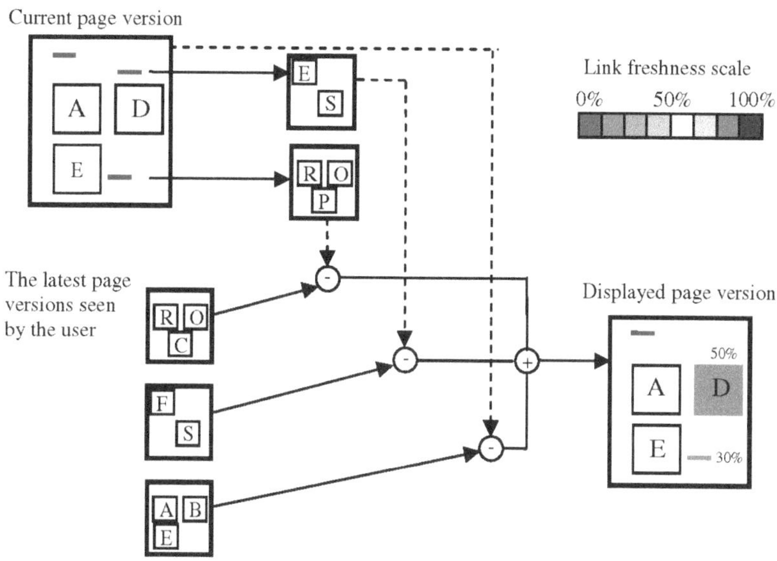

Fig. 1. Personalized, freshness-oriented annotation of page contents and links

The process can be fine tuned, for example, by setting a minimum time for considering the page content to have been viewed; similar to the process used in some mail clients, such as for example Microsoft Outlook. A scrolling-aware mechanism can also be implemented to categorize page parts into those seen and unseen by the user. In addition, page content viewed more than a certain period of time ago can be considered as new or partially new again by assigning time-dependent weights to the stored page versions. Finally, freshness degree can be propagated between pages and thus the freshness rate of larger page structures can be determined. For example, we may calculate the total freshness rate of the site or its part. In our implementation, however, we limit the change detection down to one level.

3.3 Detection and Visualization of Subjective Age of Page Content

Upon request the system visualizes the user-oriented, subjective age of different objects of page content. Elements on the current view of the page have dates $\tau_{ins}(j)$ attached denoting the timestamps of the particular page views when the user saw the elements on the page for the first time. To compute these dates the system does a search in the stored sequence of page views to find the earliest page view when particular elements first appeared. It compares the stored page views with the current version of the page for detection of overlapping content. The timestamp of the oldest page view containing a particular element is considered as the origin date, $\tau_{ins}(j)$. Two kinds of search algorithms can be used here: sequential and binary search. Sequential search is more effective for relatively short browsing histories of pages with few past page snapshots while the binary method works better for larger amounts of past data.

A special approach may be applied for processing links. Links can have two kinds of user-oriented dates: one is the date of seeing the anchor text of the link for the first time on the page while the other is the date when the linked page was actually accessed by the user.

By the user-oriented age visualization, the system makes it possible for a user to re-order chronologically page content based on its viewing history. The user can know how old the page content is from his or her point of view. Consequently, a kind of temporal context is assigned to the current page content that can shed new light on content elements.

4 System Implementation

We have built a prototype browser in C#. In addition to having all the standard components of a traditional Web browser, it has a freshness mode and age display buttons. The system stores the contents of page versions visited by the user in the local cache. The dates of the page accesses are also recorded. When the freshness mode button is on, the system takes the URL of the current page and compares it with the previously viewed version of the page. We use the diff algorithm [5] to detect textual changes as it is a commonly used and easy to implement change computation algorithm. The detection of new images is done by comparing their *src* and *alt* attributes inside image tags. The fresh content on the current page is highlighted by a different background color that can be specified by a user, and the total freshness rate of the page and the date of its last access are shown in the bottom bar of the browser. The freshness mode is automatically switched off when the page is accessed for the first time.

In addition to comparing the content between the current and previously viewed versions, the system also fetches all the URL addresses of the links present on the current page and determines whether the linked pages have been previously accessed. No action is taken for those that have not been visited. For the previously accessed one, the system compares the content of its current version with that of the one recently visited. Depending on the amount of new content, a certain color is associated to the link based on the defined color scale, and the freshness degree of the page and the date of its last access are displayed in small font to the right of the link's anchor text. We have used the color scale that to some extent resembles the currently used link-color changing style in the Web. According to this scale, a page with completely new content for the user will have a link in the standard blue color, while a page with completely known content ($V(t_{n-1}) = V(t_n)$, where t_n is the present moment) will have a dark red color. Pages with other freshness degrees will have links displayed in colors that are between blue and red depending on their amounts of new content (see Figure 1). Freshness degree was calculated using Equation 1.

If one of the links is clicked, the browser loads the requested page, indicates its new content and displays the freshness degree of the page. If the user then returns to the page from where the link was followed, the system displays the page with the same markings as before. The only change is the update of the visited link markings. The system does not re-compute the freshness of the page as the user may not have finished viewing the fresh content and links from before and would likely have forgotten which ones they were. The user likely needs more time to view all of the fresh content on the page and those on the linked pages before the page freshness is recomputed. Thus, in the current implementation, only when the user switches off and on the freshness mode button is the page freshness recomputed and the fresh content marked. When the freshness mode button is off, the system works as a traditional browser. Figure 2 shows an example of an annotated page. The parts in yellow indicate the fresh content for the user.

When the age display button is pressed then the age computation and visualization process is triggered for the currently viewed Web page content. The system compares previous views of the page with the current view to find the earliest page snapshots containing content elements. The comparison sequence depends on whether sequential or binary searches are used. The former is used when the number of stored past page snapshots is below a pre-defined threshold; otherwise the latter is utilized. The system tries to group and embrace by visual frames the neighboring parts of the page content that have the same dates. Each frame has a date added in the bottom-right corner in a small font. This is done in order to minimize the amount of additional content introduced into the page so that the original layout and outlook of the page are changed as littler as possible. Figure 3 shows an example of an annotated page using the user-oriented age determination. Upon pressing the button again the system comes back to the original outlook of the page.

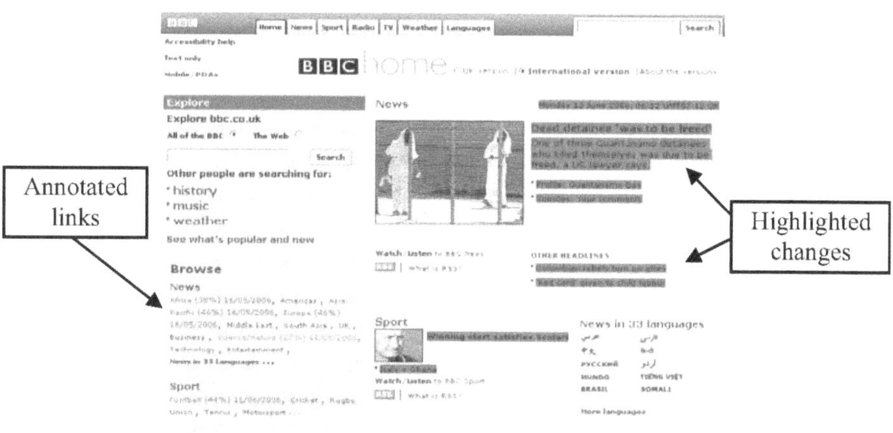

Fig. 2. Example of an annotated page with fresh content

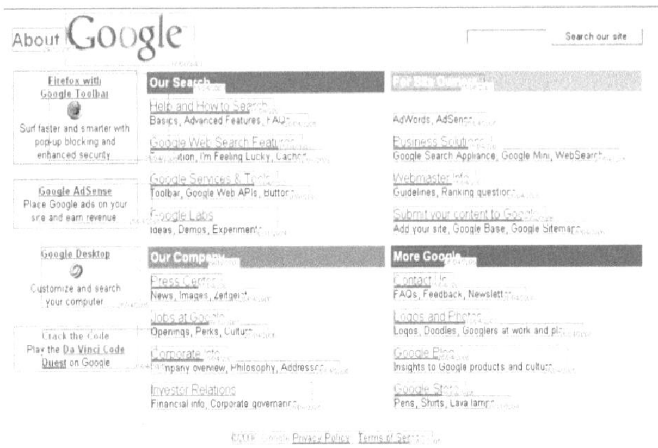

Fig. 3. Example of an annotated page with user-oriented, subjective age of the content

5 Conclusion

Incorporation of the mechanism for the personalized freshness detection into a browser enables easy identification of content that has not yet been viewed by the user. This improves the browsing experience by making the user aware of content that is fresh from his or her viewpoint. It extends the already widely accepted mechanism of link color changing to using an array of colors to indicate the degree of content freshness of linked pages. This approach is proposed to facilitate browsing and navigation by decreasing the cost and time needed to find fresh content.

In addition, the system is equipped with the mechanism for the user-oriented detection of the subjective age of page content. It displays the information about dates when the user has seen certain content on the page for the first time and hence determines the age of the page content from the point of view of the user. This may help the user to better understand the current content on the accessed pages and the distribution of added changes in time.

Acknowledgements. This research was partially supported by the Japanese Ministry of Education, Culture, Science and Technology Grant-in-Aid for Scientific Research in Priority Areas entitled: Content Fusion and Seamless Search for Information Explosion (#18049041, Representative Katsumi Tanaka), and by the Informatics Research Center for Development of Knowledge Society Infrastructure (COE program by the Japanese Ministry of Education, Culture, Sports, Science and Technology) as well as by the Japanese Ministry of Education, Culture, Science and Technology Grant-in-Aid for Young Scientists B (#18700111).

References

1. Boyapati, V., Chevrier, K., Finkel, A., Glance, N., Pierce, T., Stockton, R., Whitmer, C.: ChangeDetector™: A Site Level Monitoring Tool for WWW. In Proceedings of the 11th International WWW Conference. Honolulu, Hawaii, USA (2002) 570-579
2. Brewington, B.E., Cybenko, G.: How Dynamic is the Web? In Proceedings of the 9th International World Wide Web Conference. Amsterdam, The Netherlands (2000) 257-276

3. Cho, J., Garcia-Molina, H.: The Evolution of the Web and Implications for an Incremental Crawler. In Proceedings of the 26th International Conference on Very Large Databases (VLDB). Cairo, Egypt (2000) 200-209
4. Cockburn, A., McKenzie, B.: What Do Web Users Do? An Empirical Analysis of Web Use. International Journal of Human-Computer Studies 54(6) (2001) 903-922
5. Diff Algorithm: http://www.codeproject.com/cs/algorithms/diffengine.asp
6. Douglis, F., Ball, T., Chen, Y., Koutsofios, E.: AT&T Internet Difference Engine: Tracking and Viewing Changes on the Web. World Wide Web Journal 1(1) (1998) 27-44
7. Douglis, F., Ball, T., Chen, Y.-F., Koutsofios E.: WebGUIDE: Querying and Navigating Changes in Web Repositories. In Proceedings of the 5th International World-Wide Web Conference on Computer Networks and ISDN Systems. Amsterdam, The Netherlands (1996) 1335-1344
8. Fetterly, D., Manasse, M., Najork, M., Wiener, J.L.: A Large-scale Study of the Evolution of Web Pages. In Proceedings of the 12th International World Wide Web Conference. Budapest, Hungary (2003) 669-678
9. Lieberman, H.: Letizia: An Agent That Assists Web Browsing. In Proceedings of the International Joint Conference on Artificial Intelligence. Montreal, Canada (1995) 924-929
10. Nielsen, J.: "Change the Color of Visited Links". Jakob Nielsen's Alertbox, (2004), http://www.useit.com/alertbox/20040503.html
11. Qiang, M., Miyazaki, S., Tanaka, K.: WebSCAN: Discovering and Notifying Important Changes of Web Sites. In Mayr, H.C., Lazansky, J., Quirchmayr, G., Vogel, P. (Eds.): Proceedings of the 12th International Conference on Database and Expert Systems Applications. Lecture Notes in Computer Science, Vol. 2113. Springer-Verlag, Berlin Heidelberg New York (2001) 587-598
12. Herder, E., Weinreich, H., Obendorf, H., Mayer, M.: Much to Know about History. In Proceedings of the Adaptive Hypermedia and Adaptive Web-based Systems Conference. Dublin, Ireland (2006)

Clustering of Search Engine Keywords Using Access Logs

Shingo Otsuka and Masaru Kitsuregawa

Institute of Industrial Science, The University of Tokyo
4-6-1 Komaba, Meguro-ku, Tokyo 153-8505, Japan
{otsuka, kitsure}@tkl.iis.u-tokyo.ac.jp

Abstract. It the becomes possible that users can get kinds of information by just inputting search keyword(s) representing the topic which users are interested in. But it is not always true that users can hit upon search keyword(s) properly. In this paper, by using Web access logs (called panel logs), which are collected URL histories of Japanese users (called panels) selected without static deviation similar to the survey on TV audience rating, we study the methods of clustering search keywords. Different from the existing systems where the related search keywords are extracted based on the set of URLs viewed by the users after input of their original search keyword(s), we propose two novel methods of clustering the search words. One is based on the Web communities (set of similar web pages); the other is based on the set of nouns obtained by morphological analysis of Web pages. According to evaluation results, our proposed methods can extract more related search keywords than that based on URL.

1 Introduction

Users search information they are interested in by using search engines in cyberspace. Due to the improvement of searching accuracy with development of technologies, it becomes possible that users can get various kinds of information by just inputting keywords representing the topic which users are interested in. However, it is not always true that users can hit upon search keywords properly. In some search engines like *Google*, you can get some results and some spelling suggestion even if you misspelled its search keywords. For example, '*I want to search one bank but forgot its name.*', '*I forget the search keywords but it's related to bank.*' and so on. In this case, just submitting '*bank*' as a search keyword to search engines will not produce satisfactory results since the search keyword is too general. It is important to present some related words to hit on as search for users who are unfamiliar to search engines.

On the other hand, it is possible to extract search keywords (inputted by users) and URLs accessed after users checking the logs recorded by the search engine sites. It is hard to collect this information because they are not open to the public. Recently, similar to survey on TV audience rating, a new kind of business appeared, which collects URL histories of Japanese users (called panel)

S. Bressan, J. Küng, and R. Wagner (Eds.): DEXA 2006, LNCS 4080, pp. 842–852, 2006.

who are selected without statistic deviation. By analyzing these logs (called panel logs) which are merged from accessing history of panels, it becomes possible to collect all the web pages (URLs) accessed as well as search keywords inputted by users.

In this paper, we propose two novel methods of clustering of search engine keywords by using access logs in order to find related search keywords associated with the search keywords submitted by users. One is based on the web communities (set of similar web pages)[1]; the other is based on the set of nouns obtained by morphological analysis of web pages. According to evaluation results, our proposed methods can extract more related search keywords than previous methods that based on URLs. Experiment results also show that the methods based on web community as well as nouns have different characteristic while extracting the related search keywords.

The rest of the paper is organized as follows. Section 2 will review related works. In Section 3 we will explain technology which is necessary to understand our proposed methods. Our proposed methods of clustering search keywords using panel logs will be discussed in Section 4. Section 5 will show experimental results and evaluation, while Section 6 will give the conclusion.

2 Related Works

Until now, many works have been done based on web access logs as follows[1, 2]:

- users' behavior.[3, 4]
- the relationship between web pages.[5, 6]
- search engine sites.[7, 8, 9]
- access logs visualization.[10, 11]

Most of previous works are focused on user behavior by analyzing access logs from a certain web server. [12] uses proxy logs which are similar to the panel logs. To the best of our knowledge, we are the only research using the panel logs, detailed research is not done in others[4].

Results of works related search keywords clustering are not opened to the public because these results are directly connect to e-commerce business and it is hard to get search keywords data. [9] describes extracting related information like '*summer* and *vacation*' using search logs inputted in NTT[2] DIRECTORY. The purpose of this work is to extract synonyms based on search keywords frequency and intervals of input search keywords during a certain fixed period. Lycos and Microsoft publish search keywords research using access logs from search engine sits[7, 8]. These works classify search keywords based on the set of URLs and directories visited by the users after input of their original search keywords. Our methods use contents analysis of web pages visited by the users and community technique. Therefore these researches are also different from our methods.

---

[1] In this paper, *community* means *web community*.

[2] Nippon Telegraph and Telephone Corporation.

3 Technology for Search Keyords Clustering

In this section, we describe concepts of panel logs, web community and web pages archive, which is necessary to understand the proposed methods.

3.1 Panel Logs

We use web access logs provided by '*Video Research Interactive Inc.*' in this paper and we call these access logs '*panel logs*'. This company is one of internet rating company. Figure 1 is the outline of panel log collection.

- This company selects users based on RDD (Random Digit Dialing) and requests to become panels.
- Panels reply to some questionnaires and are requested to install the software in his (her) computer if they agree to become a panel.
- This software sends automatically panel's perusal information on web pages to the server of this company.

We do not use the questionnaire data and the panels profile data as in Figure 1 due to privacy reasons.

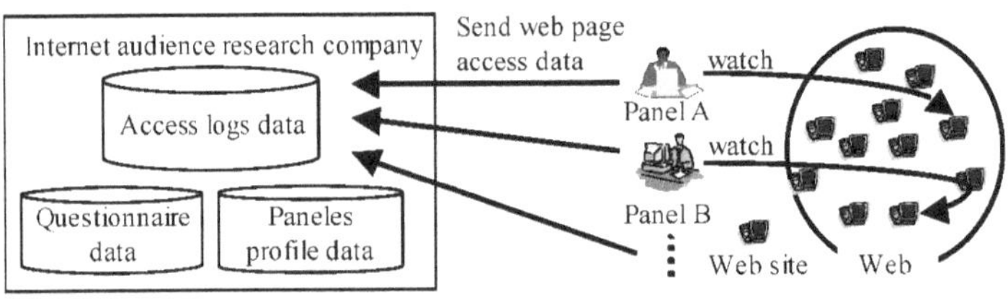

Fig. 1. Collection method of panel logs

Table 1. The details of the panel logs

An amount of data	about 10(Giga byte)
A term of collecting data	45(weeks)
A number of access	55,415,473(access)
A number of session	1,148,093(session)
A number of panels	about 10,000(persons)
A kind of URL	7,776,985(variety)
A kind of search keywords	334,232(variety)

Details of the data are shown in Table 1. The panel logs consist of *panel ID, access time of web pages, reference second of web pages, URLs of accessed web page and so on.* The data size of panel logs we used is 10GB and all used panels are in Japanese. Panel ID is a unique ID which is assigned to each panel, and it is specific to an individual panel. Notice that panel logs also include search keywords submitted to search engines.

Usually, analysis of access logs uses the concept of *session* which is a sequence of web accesses. A session is defined as a set of URLs visited by a panel during a web browsing activity. We employed a well-known 30 minutes threshold for the maximum interval[13], such that two continuous accesses within 30 minutes interval are regarded as in a same session.

3.2 Web Community

In this paper, we define a web community as '*a set of relating web pages which are connected by hyperlinks*'. Most studies on web communities can be roughly classified into two kinds. One study is extracting dense subgraphs[14] and the other is extracting complete bipartite graphs[15]. The former one determines the borderline between inside and outside of web community using the theorem of "Maximum Flow Minimum Cut" based on network theory. The latter one extracts complete bipartite graphs in web snapshot since hyperlinks between web pages which convey the message of common interest topics represented by complete bipartite graphs.

In our previous work, we created a web community chart[16] based on the complete bipartite graphs, and extracted communities automatically from a large amount of web pages.

3.3 Web Pages Archive

We periodically crawl web page written in Japanese. We crawled 4.5 million web pages during the panel logs collection period and automatically created 17 hundred thousand communities from one million selected pages. Since the time of the web page crawling for the web communities is in between the duration of panel logs collection, there are some web pages which are not covered by the crawling due to the change and deletion of pages which were accessed by the panels.

Thus we define *matching factor* as follows to examine matching ratio between the URLs belonging to web-communities and the URLs included in panel logs.

$$matching\ factor = \frac{\begin{array}{c}the\ matching\ number\ of\ URLs\ belong\ to\ communities\\ and\ included\ in\ panel\ logs\end{array}}{the\ number\ of\ URLs\ included\ in\ panel\ logs}$$

We measured the *matching factor* and the result was only about 19%. If we delete the directory (file) part in URLs, the matching factor increases about 40% and when we delete the 'subdomain part', the matching factor improves further about 8%. By modifying URLs, about 65% of the URLs included in panel logs are covered by the URLs in the web communities. The details are mentioned in [4].

Our proposed methods require analyzing web pages are visited by various panels and these pages are one million. Therefore we check our web pages archive in order to examine whether the web page at the time of panel log collection exist. As a result, about 68 hundred thousand web pages at the time of panel log collection are saved in archive.

4 Methods of Search Keywords Clustering with Panel Logs

The search results in search engine sites (e.g. Yahoo!, Google, Lycos and so on.) are usually present as the lists of URLs related with the search keywords following page titles and abstracts of the pages. The users (who inputted search keywords in search engine sites) click and view his (her) interest pages, after reading page titles and abstracts. We consider that these clicked (viewed) pages (we call *clicked page sets*) are high relevance to the search keywords. Therefore, we extract many sets of a search keywords and clicked pages in panel logs, and we cluster the search keywords using these sets.

We remove multiple search keywords [3] because most search keywords are one word in panel logs as results of our preliminary experiment. We don't discuss about the methods of using multiple search keywords in this paper.

4.1 Definition of Feature Spaces

We newly define three feature spaces as *noun space*, *community space* and *URL space* in order to cluster search keywords. The noun space is created using nouns extracted from texts of clicked page sets. The community space is created using web community technique as mentioned in Session 3.2. The URL space is using previous works as mentioned in Session 2 and we define this feature space in order to compare with the above two feature spaces.

4.2 Definition of Similarity

We define A as a universal set of all search keywords:

$$A = \{a_1, a_2, \ldots, a_x, \ldots, a_n\}$$

(a_x is any search keywords and n is the number of total search keywords.)

We also define T_x which is feature space of a_x as follows.

$$T_x = \{t_{x1}, t_{x2}, \ldots, t_{xm}\}$$

(t_x is URL if feature space is the URL space, t_x is community ID[4] if feature space is the community space and t_x is the noun if feature space is noun. And m is a number of total feature space.)

Similarity of any two search keywords a_x, a_y in A is defined as:

$$K_{xy} = \frac{|T_x \cap T_y|}{|T_x \cup T_y|}$$

[3] Actually, in our experiments, we remove multiple search keywords inputted in Japanese. Therefore, the search keywords translated from Japanese to English may become multiple search keywords. For example, a word 'exchange rate' is single word in Japanese.

[4] Consider each communities have unique ID.

Moreover, it is possible to get frequency of URLs visited by different users by clicking information in panel logs. Therefore, we define similarity considering the frequency. Let T_x and T_y be the feature space of a_x and a_y which are any words and its' intersection of set are T_z. Then we define frequency space H_z considering the frequency as

$$H_z = \{(h_{z1}, h_{z2}, \ldots, h_{zj})\}$$

(h_{z1} is the total number of frequency of T_x and T_y, and j is the number of the feature space in the intersection of sets of T_x and T_y.)

Then there is similarity $K\mathrm{f}_{xy}$ considering the frequency as follows.

$$K\mathrm{f}_{xy} = \frac{The\ total\ number\ of\ H_z}{The\ total\ number\ of\ frequency}$$

We define *high frequency elements* as URLs, communities and nouns contained in any clicked page sets. For example, high frequency elements of URLs are *Yahoo!, MSN, Google and so on*, and high frequency elements of nouns are *I, today, news and so on*. We define a similarity *Kd* as the results of calculation excluded high frequency elements from feature space of T_x and T_y and a similarity *Kfd* as the results of calculation excluded high frequency elements from frequency space of H_z. Therefore, it is possible to say that similarity *Kfd* is the concept of tf*idf taken in similarity space *K*.

5 Experiments

In this paper, we experiment for search keywords inputted 4 times or more in panel logs since the small number of times of input is inaccurate. These search keywords are 30,000 and a number of high frequency elements of noun space is 4,565 words, in case of URL space is 4 URLs and in case of community space is 9 communities.

In this paper, we used panel logs which are collected from Japanese people. Therefore, all results have been translated from Japanese vocabulary items.

5.1 Search Keywords Cluster Viewer

We calculated similarity of 30,000 search keywords and make the *search keywords cluster viewer (SKCV)* which displays search keywords related to search keywords inputted by users (we call *target keywords*). The results of using the SKCV are shown in Figure 2,3. It is possible to adjust slide bar in the lower center of Figure 2,3. An edge will be connected to two words when relevance to nodes (which is extracted related search keywords) is high. And we setup the edges to become short when relevance to nodes is high.

Nodes with high relevance are displayed near each other although it is meaningless in the position of each node. It is possible to understand results to be

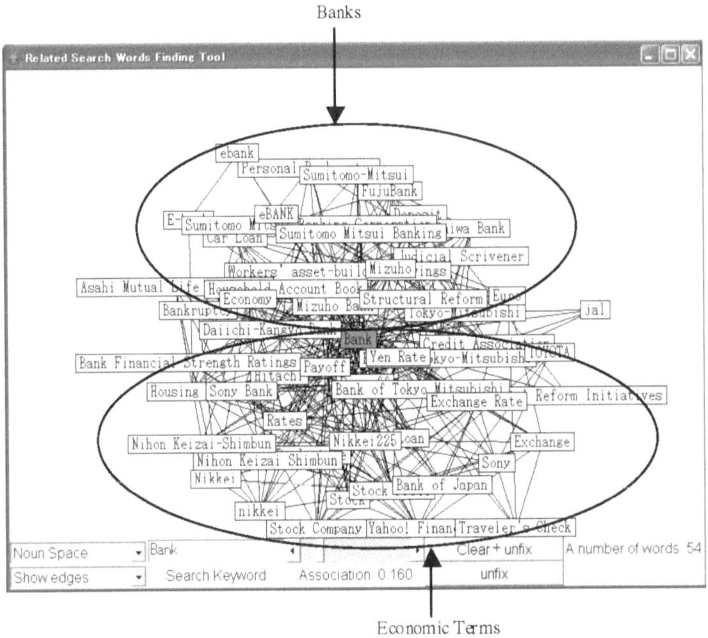

Fig. 2. An example of expression using noun space

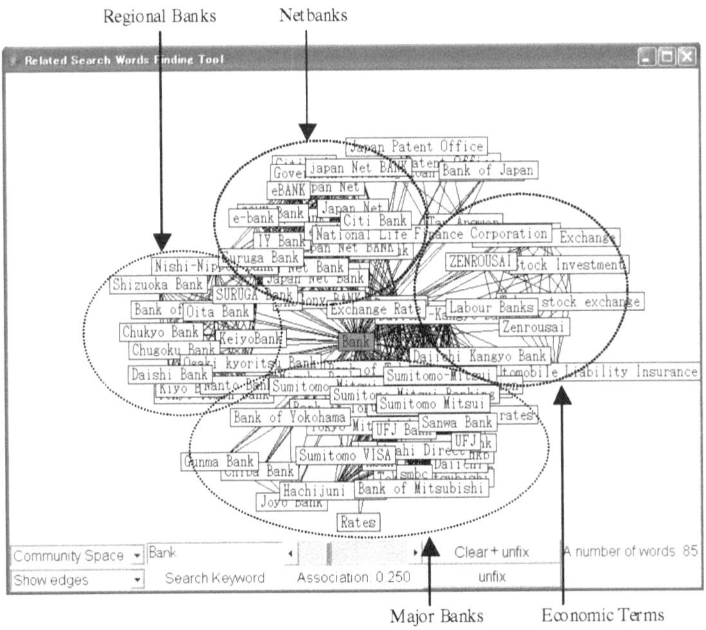

Fig. 3. An example of expression using community space

Table 2. Character of evaluated search keywords

Search keywords	A number of input frequency	Ranking of input times	A number(variety) of veiwed by the users after input search keywords		
			URL	Community	Noun
Bank	330(times) 94(sessions)	679	24(times) 20(variety)	24(times) 10(variety)	6,591(times) 1,725(variety)
University	799(times) 195(sessions)	168	31(times) 8(variety)	31(times) 5(variety)	5,255(times) 483(variety)

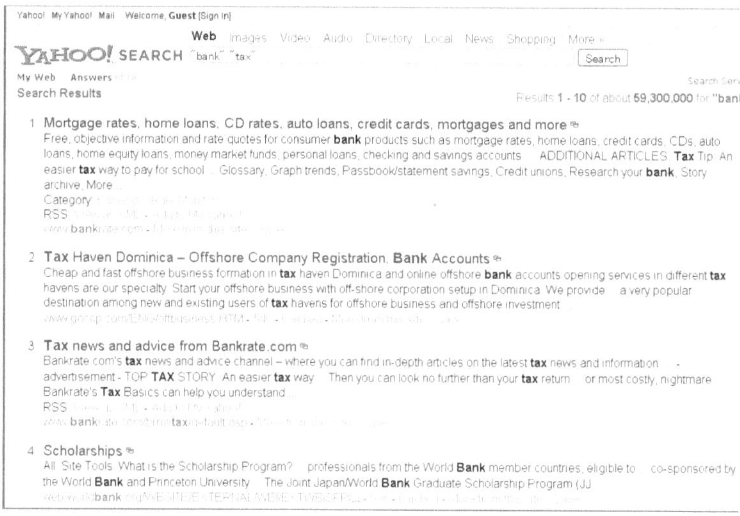

Fig. 4. An example of search keywords 'bank' and 'tax' in the Yahoo! site

divided into a group of banks and economic terms from a result of Figure 2. And in Figure 3, related search keywords are grouped as: Major banks group[5] (lower left side in the Figure 3), regional banks group (left side), internet banks (upper side), and economic terms (right side).

5.2 Evaluation

We evaluate three feature spaces and four similarities (*K, Kf, Kd and Kfd*) on three hundred thousand search keywords obtained in the experiment.

In the experiments, we test on two general words *Bank* and *University*. The details of these search keywords are shown in Table 2. We extract related search keywords related with *Bank* and *University* from three hundred thousand search keywords using three feature spaces and four similarities, and we evaluate

[5] Well known banks in Japan.

relevance of search keywords and extracting related search keywords. We define the judgment of relevance to extract related search keywords based on search keywords (Bank and University) as follows.

Category1,2. We decide *Category1* if the relation between related search keywords and search keywords is high. And we regard *Category2* if it is judged that there was a certain relation although the relationship is not higher than *Category1*.

Yahoo! judgment. In Yahoo! site, we can see the results with page titles and brief abstracts as Figure 4 when users do search. We consider that the relevance between target keywords and displayed keywords (in SKCV) is high if both keywords exist simultaneously in the results of page titles or brief abstracts. We judge true when page titles include target keywords and displayed keywords simultaneously. Generally, brief abstracts consists of sentences in various places in a web page and each sentence is divided with '... '. We judge true in case of existing target keywords and displayed keywords appear in the same single sentence as two or more topics on one page may be treated. For example, we show a result search keywords 'bank' and 'tax' at the same time in the Yahoo! sites in Figure 4. We judge true because the page title or brief abstracts of the second result in Figure 4 includes 'bank' and 'tax' simultaneously. we judge false in the case of the first result in Figure 4 because the title does not include both keywords and they don't appear simultaneously in any of the single sentence of the brief abstract. We also judge false in the case of the third and the fourth result in Figure 4 because these titles and brief abstracts include only one side of keywords. Although Category1,2 are subjective because of our judgment, Yahoo! judgment is more objective than Category1,2.

5.3 Similarity and Feature Spaces

First, we show the results in Figure 5 when the target keyword is *Bank* and the number of displayed keywords is 10 and 100 . We define precision as *'the number of displayed keywords judged as Category1 or 2 divided by a total number.'* in case of Category1,2 and as *'a number of displayed keywords Yahoo! judgment divided by a total number.'* in case Yahoo! judgment, respectively. The noun space tends to extract Category2 more than other feature spaces. And we can get good precisions using similarity *Kfd* regardless of feature space and a number of extracted search keywords.

Next, we examine search keywords *University* and show the results in Figure 6[6]. The similarity *Kfd* is as good as the results of *Bank*. Similarity *Kfd* is the best precision unless the result of community space in case of target keywords 'bank'. And our proposed feature spaces (noun space and community space) are better precision than existing feature space (URL space) in almost all the cases.

[6] We omit a result of Category1,2 because their results show the same tendency as Yahoo! judgment.

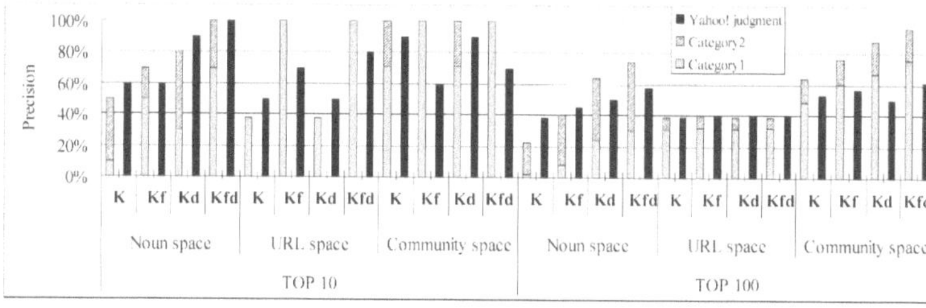

Fig. 5. Precision of 'bank'

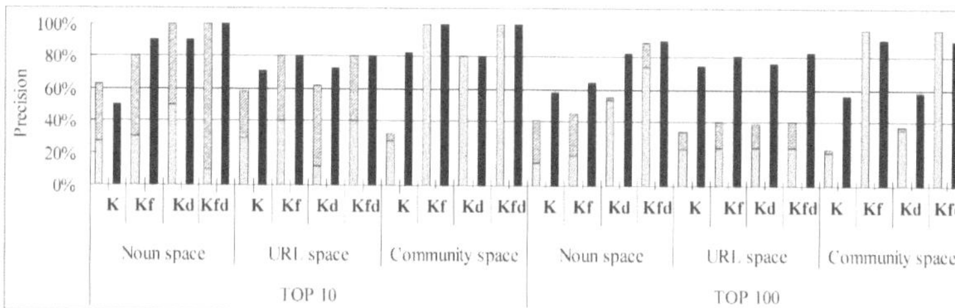

Fig. 6. Precision of 'university'

6 Conclusion

In this paper we proposed two novel feature spaces and the method of similarity to cluster search keywords using panel logs based on web community and noun. We also show our tool for viewing search keywords cluster and evaluate our proposed methods.

As an application of this tool, it is possible to indicate related search keywords like *payoff* and *Workers' asset-building savings* using related search keywords extracting with noun space when the users do not remember search keywords related to bank.

Acknowledgment

We would like to thank Jun Hirai from Systems Integration Technology Center, Toshiba Solutions Corporation. And we also wish to thank Video Research Interactive, Inc. for providing the panel logs.

References

[1] Eirinaki, M., Vazirgiannis, M.: Web mining for web personalization. ACM Transactions on Internet Technology (ACM TIT) **3**(1) (2003) 1–27

[2] Cooley, R., Mobasher, B., Srivastava, J.: Web mining: Information and pattern discovery on the world wide web. Proceedings of the 9th IEEE International Conference on Tools with Artificial Intelligence (ICTAI'97) (1997)

[3] Ungar, L., Foster, D.: Clustering methods for collaborative filtering. AAAI Workshop on Recommendation Systems (1998)
[4] Otsuka, S., Toyoda, M., Hirai, J., Kitsuregawa, M.: Extracting user behavior by web communities technology on global web logs. Proc. of 15th International Conference on Database and Expert Systems Applications (DEXA'2004) (2004) 957–968
[5] Su, Z., Yang, Q., Zhang, H., Xu, X., Hu, Y.: Correlation-based document clustering using web logs. 34th Hawaii International Conference on System Sciences (HICSS-34) (2001)
[6] Tan, P., Kumar, V.: Mining association patterns in web usage data. International Conference on Advances in Infrastructure for e-Business, e-Education, e-Science, and e-Medicine on the Internet (2002)
[7] Beeferman, D., Berger, A.: Agglomerative clustering of s earch engine query log. The 6th ACM SIGKDD International Conference on Knowledge Discovery and Data Mining (KDD2000) (2000)
[8] Wen, J., Nie, J., Zhang, H.: Query clustering using user logs. ACM Transactions on Information Systems (ACM TOIS) **20**(1) (2002) 59–81
[9] Ohkubo, M., Sugizaki, M., Inoue, T., Tanaka, K.: Extracting information demand by analyzing a www search log. IPSJ Journal **39**(7) (1998) 2250–2258
[10] Koutsoupias, N.: Exploring web access logs with correspondence analysis. Methods and Applications of Artificial Intelligence, Second Hellenic (2002)
[11] Prasetyo, B., Pramudiono, I., Takahashi, K., Kitsuregawa, M.: Naviz: Website navigational behavior visualizer. Advances in Knowledge Discovery and Data Mining 6th Pacific-Asia Conference (PAKDD2002) (2002)
[12] Zeng, H., Chen, Z., Ma, W.: A unified framework for clustering heterogeneous web objects. The Third International Conference on Web Information Systems Engineering (WISE2002) (2002)
[13] Catledge, L., Pitkow, J.: Characterizing browsing behaviors on the world-wide web. Computer Networks and ISDN Systems (27(6)) (1995)
[14] Flake, G., Lawrence, S., Giles, C.L., Coetzee, F.: Self-organization and identification of web communities. IEEE Computer **35**(3) (2002) 66–71
[15] Kumar, R., Raghavan, P., Rajagopalan, S., Tomkins, A.: Trawling the web for emerging cyber-communities. Proc. of the 8th WWW conference (1999) 403–416
[16] Toyoda, M., Kitsuregawa, M.: Creating a web community chart for navigating related communities. In: Conference Proceedings of Hypertext 2001. (2001) 103–112

Non-metric Similarity Ranking for Image Retrieval*

Guang-Ho Cha

Department of Computer Engineering, Seoul National University of Technology
Seoul 139-743, South Korea
ghcha@snut.ac.kr

Abstract. Over many years, almost all research work in the content-based image retrieval has used Minkowski distance (or L_p-norm) to measure similarity between images. However such functions cannot adequately capture the aspects of the characteristics of the human visual system. In this paper, we present a new similarity measure reflecting the nonlinearity of human perception. Based on this measure, we develop a similarity ranking algorithm for effective image retrieval. This algorithm exploits the inherent cluster structure revealed by an image dataset. Our method yields encouraging experimental results on a real image database and demonstrates its effectiveness.

1 Introduction

Similarity search is essential to media information retrieval systems. Users usually choose an image to query k most similar images in query-by-example paradigm. To facilitate content-based image retrieval, many heuristics were developed to faithfully represent image contents in search engine designs. The central problems regarding the retrieval task are concerned with interpreting the contents of the images in a collection and ranking them according to the degree of relevance to the user query. Knowing how to extract this information is not the only difficulty; another is knowing how to use it to decide *relevance*. The decision of relevance characterizing user information need is a complex problem. To be effective in satisfying user information need, a retrieval system must view the retrieval problem on "human side" rather than on "computational side".

As a step towards perceptual retrieval on human side, many researchers have proposed the use of relevance feedback to improve the retrieval effectiveness [3, 4, 6, 7, 8, 12, 15]. In relevance feedback, the user is given an opportunity to provide feedback to the system regarding the set of retrievals computed. This feedback is used to compute a next set of retrievals that better match the user's expectation. Although relevance feedback is an approach to improve the retrieval effectiveness, the power of relevance feedback is still restricted by the similarity measure and the ranking method employed by the retrieval system. Another problem with relevance feedback is that after every round of user interaction, usually the top-k results with respect to the query have to be recomputed using a modified similarity measure. This is time-consuming and user must have patience to proceed multi-round feedback.

* This work was supported by grant No. B1220-0501-0233 from the University Fundamental Research Program of the Ministry of Information & Communication in Republic of Korea.

S. Bressan, J. Küng, and R. Wagner (Eds.): DEXA 2006, LNCS 4080, pp. 853 – 862, 2006.

In order to measure perceptual similarity, recently, DynDex [1] proposed a non-metric distance function, dynamic partial function (DPF) and proved its closer match with the perceptual similarity than Minkowski metric. However, it is difficult to determine the number of relevant features in DPF.

Therefore, we attempt to address the aforementioned problem by using a *nonlinear* approach to simulate human perception. We adopt a *Gaussian* function as our basic similarity model to nonlinearly transform traditional distances into a similarity in a feature space. Compared to the Minkowski-like distance functions, this approach offers a more accurate modeling of the notion of similarity from the user's viewpoint.

Based on this similarity model, we propose a new similarity measure and a ranking algorithm that exploit the inherent cluster structure of a dataset. Our similarity measure is consistent with the *cluster assumption* [16] that the points on the same cluster structure are more similar to each other than to points outside the structure. This similarity measure is the basis of our similarity ranking algorithm. In other words, we consider the ranking problem as the cluster identification problem.

2 General Framework

2.1 Motivating Examples

Example 1. The user wants to select two images via query-by-example in the hand-written digit image database. Fig. 1(a) is a query image and Figs. 1(b) and 1(c) may be the query result if a human selects two images, and those are the actual result from our similarity search experiment. When we use Minkowski distance metric, on the other hand, Figs. 2(b) and 2(c) are the actual result of the traditional similarity search experiment. This means that there may exist a discrepancy between human perception and the Minkowski-like distance functions. Therefore, in content-based image retrieval, it is necessary to establish the link that bridges the gap between human perception and distance calculation.

(a) (b) (c)

Fig. 1. Human perception based retrieval: (a) a query image; (b) and (c) similarity search results

(a) (b) (c)

Fig. 2. Euclidean distance based retrieval: (a) a query image; (b) and (c) the similarity search results

Example 2. Fig. 3 shows another example to explain our motivation. Assume that we are given a set of points constructed with two clusters. A query point is represented by + and we want six points nearest to the query point +. If we search six nearest neighbors (NNs) to the query by pairwise Euclidean distance metric, the six NNs resulting from the search are the points within the circle whose center is the query point + (see Fig. 3(a)). However, as described in Example 1, when we consider the distribution of the given dataset, as shown in Fig. 3(b), the six points in cluster A may be more relevant to the query point than the points in cluster B even though some of them have longer Euclidean distance than some points in cluster B.

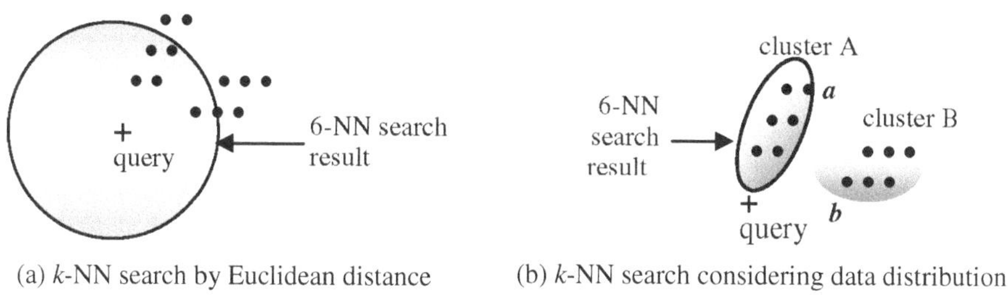

Fig. 3. k-NN search results based on two different models

From these motivating examples, we can assume that in image similarity ranking it may be desirable that closer points have more similar rankings than the points far away even though they are behind with respect to Euclidean distance based ranking. If we base similarity ranking on this concept, in Fig. 3(b), the right-most point a in cluster A should be ranked to be more relevant to the query point than the point b in the left-most in cluster B. This agrees with the consistency assumption [16]: (1) points in the same local high density region are more similar to each other than to points outside this region (local consistency); (2) points in the same global structure are more similar to each other than to points outside this structure (global consistency).

2.2 Nonlinear Similarity Model

Constructing an effective content-based image retrieval system requires accurate characterization of visual information. Conventional models based on Minkowski distance functions do not adequately capture all the aspects of the characteristics of the human visual system. The visual section of the human brain is known to use a *nonlinear* processing system for tasks such as pattern recognition and classification [2]. We refer to the systems that evaluate the degree of similarity between two images linearly proportionally to the magnitude of their distances as the *linear* model-based retrieval methods.

In order to simulate human perception for similarity evaluation between images, we first establish a *nonlinear* model. The assumption for the nonlinear approach is that the same lengths of the distances do not always give the same degrees of similarity when judged by humans [13]. In other words, the linear model is not competent for the nonlinear nature of human perception and cannot cope with the complex decision boundary. We therefore propose to use a nonlinear criterion in performing similarity comparison.

The nonlinear model is constructed by a mapping function $f(x)$ that uses feature values of input image x to evaluate the degree of similarity to a given query [4]. In its most common form, the input-output mapping function should be *smooth* in the sense that similar inputs correspond to similar outputs. We adopt a *Gaussian* function as our basic similarity model for the input-output mapping function:

$$G(x_i, x_j) = \exp(-d(x_i, x_j)^2 / \sigma^2) \quad (1)$$

The activity of function G is to perform a Gaussian transformation of the distance $d(x_i, x_j)$, which describes the degree of similarity between x_i and x_j. The scaling parameter σ^2 controls the smoothness of the distance between x_i and x_j and it is specified by a user. Gaussian function possesses an excellent nonlinear approximation capability [2, 10], and we utilize the Gaussian function to simulate the human perception. The space containing the original data is called the *input space*. The Gaussian function creates a new space called the *feature space* that is a nonlinear transformation of the input space. Throughout our work, we conduct the similarity comparison in the induced feature space.

2.3 Similarity Measure

In order to apply the nonlinear similarity concept and the consistency assumption to the content-based image retrieval, we consider the intrinsic structure and the distribution revealed by the dataset when we compute the similarity value of data objects. For this purpose, we introduce the concept of *similarity distribution*. Our experimental evaluation shows that improved results are obtained when similarity comparison is done not by the computation of pairwise object distances but based on the distribution of similarities that occur in a dataset.

Assume a set of points $X = \{x_1, x_2, \ldots, x_m\}$, with each point $x_i \in R^n$. Let x_q, $q \notin \{1, 2, \ldots, m\}$, be the query point, and the set X contains the points we would like to rank according to their relevance to the query point x_q. We define a vector $s_i = [s_{iq}, s_{i1}, s_{i2}, \ldots, s_{im}]^T$, where s_{ij} is the similarity value between two objects x_i and x_j. The similarity value s_{ij} is computed by the Gaussian nonlinear similarity model defined by Eq. (1), i.e., $s_{ij} = \exp(-d(x_i, x_j)^2 / \sigma^2)$. We consider the vector s_i as the *distribution of similarities* between the point x_i and all other points in a given dataset including the query point. The vector $s_q = [s_{qq}, s_{q1}, s_{q2}, \ldots, s_{qm}]^T$ represents the distribution of similarities between the query point x_q and all other points including the query point itself. According to Eq. (1), s_{qq} is defined to be 1.0.

We define the *similarity value* of a point x_i to the query point x_q by the *dot product* of the similarity distribution for x_i and that for x_q. A dot product is a similarity measure that is of particular mathematical appeal. The geometric interpretation of the dot product is that it computes the cosine of the angle between two vectors, provided they are normalized to length 1. Moreover, the distance between two vectors is computed as the length of the difference vector. To summarize, our similarity measure is defined by the dot product of two similarity distribution vectors in Gaussian feature space. The similarity value s_{iq} of point x_i to the query point x_q is computed by

$$s_{iq} = s_i^T \cdot s_q = s_{iq} s_{qq} + \sum_{j=1}^{m} s_{ij} \cdot s_{qj} = s_{iq} + \sum_{j=1}^{m} s_{ij} \cdot s_{qj} \tag{2}$$

In the above Eq. (2), s_i and s_q are the similarity distribution vectors for points x_i and x_q, respectively, and the similarity values s_{ij} and s_{qj} are computed by Eq. (1). The similarity measure given by Eq. (2) denotes the actual similarity value between the query point and point x_i plus the linear combination of the similarity values between point x_i and its neighbors, weighted by its neighbors' similarity values to the query point. Therefore, the similarity value of a point affects its neighbors' similarity values, and if two points are close, they are more influenced by each other because their respective similarity values to query point are weighted by the similarity value between two points. With this similarity metric based on the similarity distribution, the points clustered near the query point are favored in similarity ranking.

Notice that the similarity measure given by Eq. (2) is recursively defined. The initial similarity value s_{iq} is computed by Eq. (1). In order to recursively accumulate the propagation effect of the similarity values through the dataset, we continuously replenish s_{iq} with the newly computed s_{iq} (s_{iq} is equal to s_{qi} for all i) until it reaches a stable value. This procedure is similar to the concept of the label propagation in semi-supervised learning [16, 17] and the work on spreading activation networks [11]. In summary, the similarity score of x_i is iteratively computed at time t until it has a stable value as follows:

$$s_{iq}(t+1) = s_i^T \cdot s_q([t), t = 1, 2, \ldots, l \tag{3}$$

Therefore, a point tends to have a high similarity value if its near neighbors have high similarity values, and this effect increases gradually by the continuous replenishment of its neighbors' newly computed similarity values.

2.4 Similarity Ranking Algorithm

We provide a similarity ranking algorithm **MultiRank** for multipoint k-NN queries based on our similarity measure.

Algorithm MultiRank

[Input] A set of points $X = \{x_1, \ldots, x_q, x_{q+1}, \ldots, x_m\} \subset R^n$, where $x_1, \ldots, x_q$ are query points and the rest $x_{q+1}, \ldots, x_m$ are the data points we would like to rank according to their relevance to q query points

[Output] The ranked list of data points

1. Construct a similarity matrix $K \in R^{m \times m}$ defined by
   $K_{ij} = \exp(-d(x_i, x_j)/\sigma^2)$ if $i \neq j$, and $K_{ii} = 0$
2. Construct a diagonal matrix D defined by
   $$D_{ii} = \sum_{j=1}^{m} K_{ij}$$
3. Form a normalized similarity matrix $K' = D^{-1}K$.
4. Create the initial similarity values $s_{ij}(0)$ between a point x_i and the query point x_j, $1 \leq j \leq q$, $q+1 \leq i \leq m$.

$$s_{ij}(0) = \begin{cases} 1 & \text{for } 1 \le i \le q, \text{ i.e., both } x_i \text{ and } x_j \text{ are query points.} \\ \exp(-d(x_i, x_j)/\sigma^2) & \text{for } q+1 \le i \le m. \end{cases}$$

5. **for** $t = 1, 2, 3, \ldots$ **do** // iteration to achieve stable similarity values
6. **for** $i = q+1$ to m **do** // for each data point
7. **for** $j = 1$ to q **do** // for each query point
8. $s_{ij}(t) = K'_{ij} + \sum_{k=q+1}^{m} K'_{ik} s_{kj}(t-1)$
9. **end for**
10. **end for**
11. Normalize s_{ij} by dividing it by $\max_{q+1 \le i \le m} \{s_{ij}\}$.
12. **until** $s_{ij}(t)$ is stable ($t = 10 \sim 20$ is actually sufficient)
13. Let s_{ij}^* be the limit of the sequence $\{s_{ij}(t)\}$. Compute the similarity score s_i^* of x_i to q query points by $s_i^* = \max_{1 \le j \le q} \{s_{ij}^*\}$.
14. Sort the set $S = \{s_{q+1}^*, s_{q+2}^*, \ldots, s_m^*\}$ in nonincreasing order and return the top k points as the result.

At first sight, this algorithm seems complex, but it has a simple explanation. The algorithm is inspired by the work from spectral clustering [5], spreading activation network [11], and more specifically semi-supervised learning of Zhu et al. [17] and Zhou et al. [16].

In step 1, we construct the matrix K composed of object-object similarities, i.e., K_{ij}, $i \ne j$, gives a similarity value between two points x_i and x_j. K_{ii} is zero to avoid reinforcement of self-similarity value. Actually, this similarity matrix K is precomputed before the search, and therefore it is not a burden during the search. Steps 2–3 and 11 provides a suitable normalization necessary for convergence of the algorithm. In step 11, we normalize the similarity values among query points by dividing the similarity values by the maximum value for each query. Zhu et al. [17] proved that this kind of label propagation algorithm converges to a simple solution. For most queries in our experiments, in fact, the algorithm almost converges to a fixed point by around 10 iterations, and therefore $t = 10$ is sufficient for most cases. During steps 6 – 10, the similarity value of each point to the query point is propagated to its neighbors until a final stable state is obtained. By propagating similarity values through data regions, the consistency assumption used in semi-supervised learning [17] is attained. It means that the algorithm tends to rank data points with respect to the intrinsic cluster structure.

Example 3. To illustrate the effect of our algorithm, let us consider a toy dataset. We use a dataset containing 74 2-dimensional points shown in Fig. 4. The dataset has two cluster structures. Every point should be similar to the points in its neighborhood, and furthermore, points in one cluster should be more similar to each other than to points in the other cluster. The similarity ranking results are given in Figs. 4 and 5. Fig. 4 shows the ranking result when a single query point + is used, and Fig. 5 shows the result for two query points + and ×. The number beside each point denotes the ranking assigned to that point. As shown in Figs. 4 and 5, it is demonstrated that our ranking algorithm exploits the global cluster structure of the dataset. These results are obtained with the number $t = 10$ of iterations. We believe that for many real world applications including image searches this kind of retrieval based on the global cluster

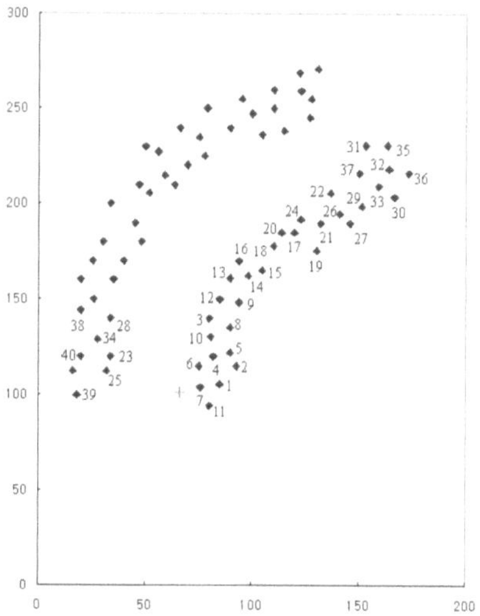

Fig. 4. Ranking on single query point +

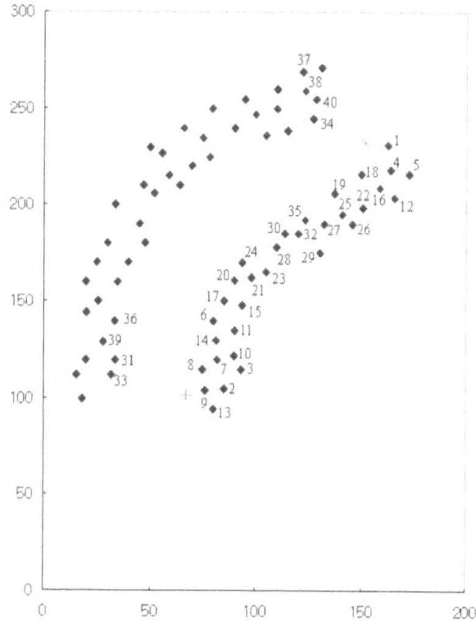

Fig. 5. Ranking on two query points × and +

structure is superior to the local methods that rank data by pairwise Euclidean distance as we illustrated in Examples 1 and 2.

3 Experiments

For experimental evaluation of our methods, we use the MNIST database that contains 28 × 28 120,000 handwritten digit images. The MNIST database is the currently used classifier benchmark in the AT&T and Bell Labs and many methods have been tested with this database. The feature of each image is represented by a 784-dimensional vector. In our experiments, we use only the first 6,000 images from the MNIST database and perform a similarity search to return the k most similar images for the given query images.

To obtain an objective measure of performance, we assume that a query concept is an image category, i.e., one of the labels '0', '1', …, '9' given to each digit category.

We evaluate *precision* for k-NN queries, where k is 10 – 100, and precision is computed by the fraction of the returned k images that belong to the query image category.

We perform 100 k-NN queries and average their performance. The query images are randomly selected from the MNIST database. In order to provide the intuition for our method, we show the k-NN search results in Figs. 6 – 9. Figs. 6 and 7 are the results using single query image. The top-left image is the query image. Note that there are many digits other than '9' in Euclidean distance based ranking in Fig. 7. Figs. 8 and 9 show the results when two images are used as a query. The top-left two images are query images. The first query uses as the query images the images with two similar digits '4'. The second query uses as query images the very different two image for digits '0' and '6'. For multi-point (or disjunctive) queries, we use the aggregate dissimilarity measure of Falcon [15] with the constant $\alpha = -3$. As shown in Figs. 8 and 9, there are many digits other than the query images when we use Falcon's aggregate dissimilarity measure. On the other hand, our method generates the uniform result. This experimental result provides indirect proof of superiority of our method.

Fig. 10 compares the precision performance for k-NN queries among our search method, Euclidean distance based method, and the SVM_{Active} method [12]. In [12] SVM_{Active} shows better performance compared with other three query refinement methods: (1) query reweighting methods such as MARS [7] (2) the query point movement methods such as MARS [8, 6], MindReader [3], (3) the query expansion methods such as Falcon [15]. Therefore, we compare our method with SVM_{Active}. SVM_{Active} is a relevance feedback method based on active learning with support vector machines (SVM) [14]. It retrieves top-k images after a few relevance feedback rounds. In each round of relevance feedback, SVM_{Active} determines the images as "relevant" if they have the same label as the query image's. In the experiment of SVM_{Active}, we conduct four relevance feedback rounds and use 100 training images per round. Fig. 14 shows the average top-k precision for three different methods. SVM_{Active} shows the worst performance. The poor performance of SVM_{Active} is caused by the size and complexity of the 784-dimensional MNIST database. Our method achieves at least 90% precision on the top-k results, whereas the Euclidean distance based method cannot achieve our performance.

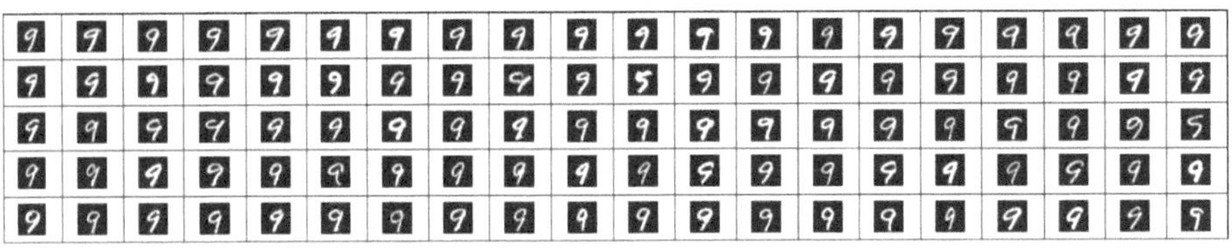

Fig. 6. Top 100 images by our similarity ranking, where the top-left image is the query image

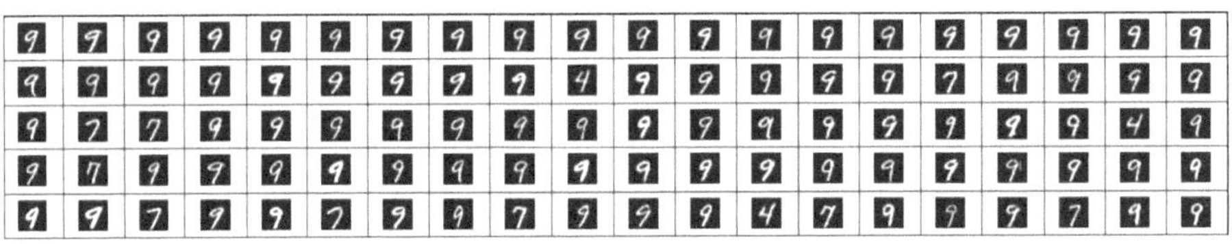

Fig. 7. Top 100 images by Euclidean distance based ranking

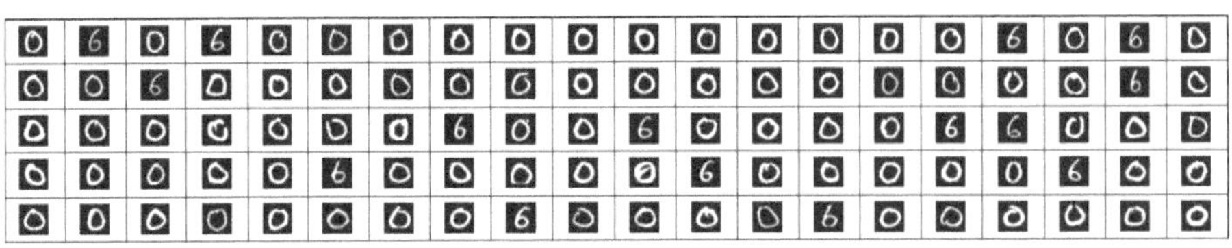

Fig. 8. Top 100 images by our similarity ranking, where the top-left 2 images are the query images

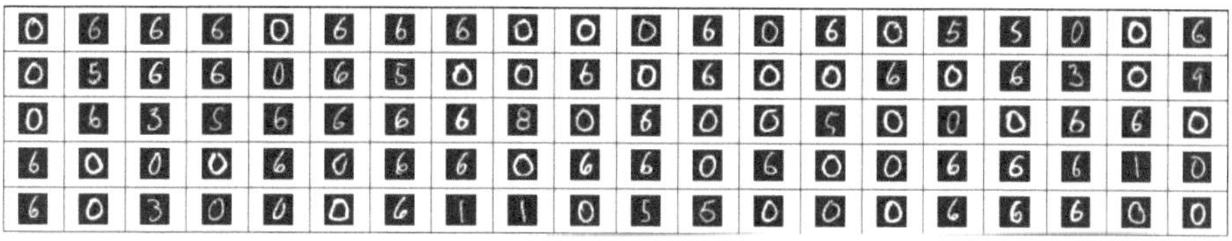

Fig. 9. Top 100 images computed by Falcon's aggregate similarity metric

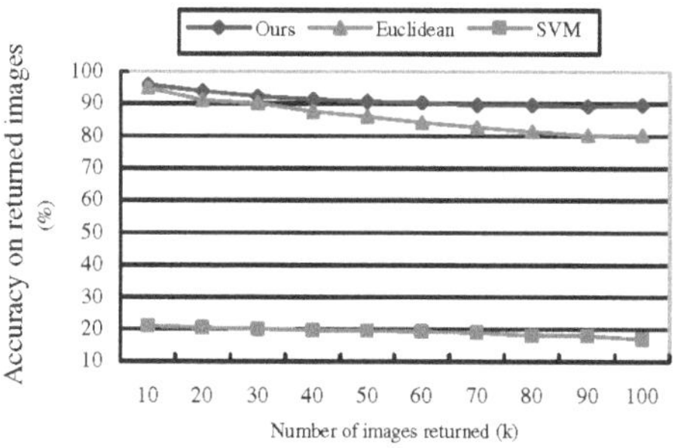

Fig. 10. Single-point queries: average top-k precision

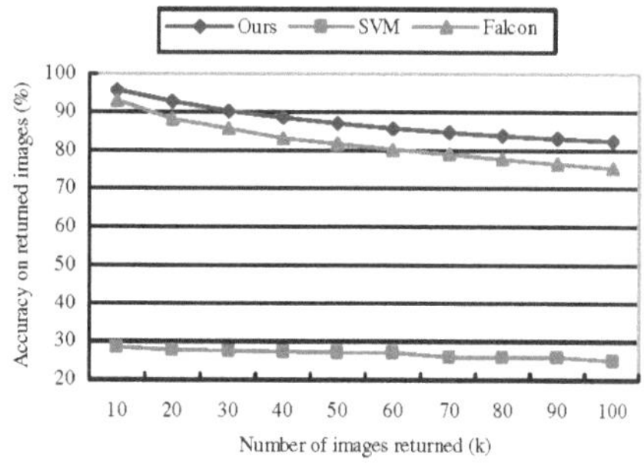

Fig. 11. Multi-point queries: average top-k precision

Fig. 11 shows the precision result for multi-point k-NN searches. Our method achieves over than 80% precision in any cases, whereas SVM_{Active} and Falcon cannot achieve this performance.

4 Conclusions

We have presented a new similarity measure and ranking algorithm based on a nonlinear similarity model for effective image retrieval. This similarity measure and the ranking algorithm consider the intrinsic structure and the distribution revealed by the dataset. Our ranking algorithm supports relevance feedback effectively since it can easily support the multi-point similarity query. Our content-based image search scheme has demonstrated its effectiveness and outperformed the existing image retrieval methods such as SVM_{Active}, Falcon, and Euclidean distance based method. Our scheme takes advantage of the intuition that the same portions of the distances given by Minkowski function do not always give the same degrees of similarity when judged by humans.

References

1. K.-S. Goh, B. Li, and E. Chang, "DynDex: A Dynamic and Non-metric Space Indexer," *Proc. ACM Multimedia*, 2002, 466-475.
2. S. Haykin, *Neural Networks: A Comprehensive Foundation*, NY: Maxmillan, 1994.

3. Y. Ishikawa, R. Subramanya and C. Faloutsos, "MindReader: Querying databases through multiple examples, *Proc. VLDB Conf.*, 1998, 218-227.
4. P. Muneesawang and L. Guan, "An Interactive Approach for CBIR Using a Network of Radial Basis Functions, *IEEE Trans. on Multimedia*, 6(5):703-716, 2004.
5. A.Y. Ng, M.I. Jordan, and Y. Weiss, "On Spectral Clustering: Analysis and Algorithm," *Advances in Neural Information Processing Systems*, 14, Cambridge, Mass., 2002, MIT Press.
6. K. Porkaew and K. Chakrabarti, "Query refinement for multimedia similarity retrieval in MARS," *Proc. ACM Multimedia*, 1999, 235-238.
7. Y. Rui et al., "Relevance feedback: A Power tool for interactive content-based image retrieval," *IEEE Trans. Circuits and Video Technology*, 8(5), 1998, 644-644.
8. Y. Rui, T. Huang, and S. Mehrotra, "Content-based image retrieval with relevance feedback in MARS," *Proc. Int'l Conf. on Image Processing*, 1997.
9. B. Schölkopf, A. Smola, and K. Müller, "Nonlinear Component Analysis as a Kernel Eigenvalue Problem," *Neural Computation*, Vol. 10, pp. 1299-1319, 1998.
10. B. Schölkopf et al., "Comparing Support Vector Machines with Gaussian Kernels to Radial Basis Function Classifiers," *IEEE Trans. on Signal Processing*, Vol. 45 (1997) 2758-2765
11. J. Shrager, T. Hogg and B.A. Huberman, "Observation of phase transitions in spreading activation networks," *Science*, 236, 1987, 1092-1094.
12. S. Tong and E. Chang, "Support Vector Machine Active Learning for Image Retrieval," *Proc. ACM Multimedia Conf.*, 2001, 107-118.
13. R.L.De Valois and K.K.De Valois, *Spatial Vision*, Oxford Science Publications, 1988.
14. V.N. Vapnik, *Statistical Learning Theory*, Wiley, NY, 1998
15. L. Wu, C. Faloutsos, K. Sycara and T.R. Payne, "FALCON: Feedback Adaptive Loop for Content-Based Retrieval, *Proc. of VLDB Conf.*, pp. 297-306, 2000.
16. D. Zhou et al., "Learning with Local and Global Consistency," *Advances in Neural Information Processing Systems*, 16, Cambridge, Mass., 2004, MIT Press.
17. X. Zhu and Z. Ghahramani, "Learning from labeled and unlabeled data with label propagation," Technical report CMU-CALD-02-107, CMU, 2002

An Effective Method for Approximating the Euclidean Distance in High-Dimensional Space

Seungdo Jeong[1], Sang-Wook Kim[2], Kidong Kim[3], and Byung-Uk Choi[2]

[1] Department of Electrical and Computer Engineering, Hanyang University
17 Haengdang-dong, Sungdong-gu, Seoul, 133-791 Korea
sdjeong@mlab.hanyang.ac.kr

[2] College of Information and Communications, Hanyang University
17 Haengdang-dong, Sungdong-gu, Seoul, 133-791 Korea
{wook, buchoi}@hanyang.ac.kr

[3] Department of Industrial Engineering, Kangwon National University
192-1 Hyoja2-Dong, Chunchon, Kangwon-Do, 200-701 Korea
kdkim@kangwon.ac.kr

Abstract. It is crucial to compute the *Euclidean distance* between two vectors efficiently in high-dimensional space for multimedia information retrieval. We propose an effective method for approximating the Euclidean distance between two high-dimensional vectors. For this approximation, a previous method, which simply employs *norms* of two vectors, has been proposed. This method, however, ignores the *angle* between two vectors in approximation, and thus suffers from large approximation errors. Our method introduces an additional vector called a *reference vector* for estimating the angle between the two vectors, and approximates the Euclidean distance accurately by using the estimated angle. This makes the approximation errors reduced significantly compared with the previous method. Also, we formally prove that the value approximated by our method is always smaller than the actual Euclidean distance. This implies that our method does not incur any *false dismissal* in multimedia information retrieval. Finally, we verify the superiority of the proposed method via performance evaluation with extensive experiments.

1 Introduction

Recently, multimedia data has been increasing rapidly owing to the popularization of information superhighway. One of the important research issues in the multimedia area is to offer effective information retrieval that searches for data, in which users are interested, accurately and efficiently.

In most previous studies on multimedia applications, a multimedia object is represented as a feature vector, and accordingly a multimedia database is deemed as a set of feature vectors in multi-dimensional space. Multimedia information retrieval is defined as searching for such feature vectors matched to a given query vector in multi-dimensional space. For effective multimedia information retrieval, we should extract a large number of features from each object. Thus, feature vectors are normally high-dimensional: i.e., from several tens to a few hundreds of dimensions [3,6,7,8].

S. Bressan, J. Küng, and R. Wagner (Eds.): DEXA 2006, LNCS 4080, pp. 863–872, 2006.

User queries can be classified into two types: range queries and k-nearest neighbor(k-NN) queries. The *range query* is to retrieve feature vectors whose dissimilarity to a query vector is within a tolerance ϵ. The *k-NN* query is to retrieve k feature vectors that are most similar to a query vector [2,3,5]. Previous studies used the *Euclidean distance* as a measure for computing similarity between two vectors [1,3,6].

In high-dimensional space, however, the time of computing the Euclidean distance between two vectors occupies a quite large part of the total retrieval time. If we can identify data vectors that do not belong to the final result, without computing their actual Euclidean distance to a query vector, we can reduce the total retrieval time significantly. For this reason, most previous methods perform multimedia information retrieval in two steps: pre-processing step and post-processing step. The former is to form a set of candidate vectors that have high possibility to belong to a final result. The latter is to validate every candidate vector [1]. We call this the *two step searching.* On the other hand, it is also possible to examine every data vector by computing its actual Euclidean distance to a query vector. We call this the *exhaustive searching.*

To find a set of all the correct answers in the two step searching, we have to form a candidate set including *all* the correct answers in the pre-processing step. A *false dismissal* is a data vector that is a correct answer, but is not included in the final result set because of being excluded in the candidate set. A *false alarm* is a data vector that is not a correct answer, but requires post-processing needlessly because of being included in the candidate set [1]. Though a false alarm is resolved through the post-processing, it makes the overall processing time increase. For correctness and efficiency in multimedia information retrieval, *our goal is to guarantee no false dismissal and also to minimize the number of false alarms.*

In this paper, we address approximating the Euclidean distance effectively. The Euclidean distance can be computed by using the norms of two vectors and the *angle* between them. However, previous studies ignore the angle and thus incur large approximation errors [4,5]. We propose a novel method that reduces the number of false alarms significantly by taking the angle information into account in approximating the Euclidean distance. Thus, our method reduces the post-processing time considerably. Also, it guarantees no false dismissal since the approximation function lower-bounds the Euclidean distance.

2 Related Work

2.1 Approximation by Using the Cauchy-Schwartz Inequality

$$< X, Y > = \sum_{i=1}^{n} x_i \cdot y_i \leq \|X\| \|Y\| \tag{1}$$

$$D(X, Y) = \sqrt{\sum_{i=1}^{n} (x_i - y_i)^2} = \sqrt{\|X\|^2 + \|Y\|^2 - 2 < X, Y >} \tag{2}$$

$$D_{cs}(X,Y) = \sqrt{\|X\|^2 + \|Y\|^2 - 2\|X\|\|Y\|} \leq D(X,Y) \tag{3}$$

Equation (1) is the Cauchy-Schwartz inequality that represents a relationship between the inner product and norms of two vectors. It defines the upper bound of their inner product. The Euclidean distance between two vectors, $D(X,Y)$, is defined as equation (2) by using the norms and the inner product of two vectors. By substituting the inner product term by a multiplication of norms in equation (1), we can define the lower bound of the Euclidean distance, $D_{cs}(X,Y)$, as in equation (3).

Applying this result to the multimedia information retrieval, we save norms of all data vectors as *abstract information*. When a query vector is given, we approximate the Euclidean distance by using the norm of the query vector and the saved norm of every data vector, like the mid term of equation (3). In this pre-processing step, data vectors having their approximated distance to a query vector smaller than a given tolerance ϵ are included in a candidate set. Because the mid term of equation (3) always returns the lower bound of the Euclidean distance, the approximated distance is always less than or equal to the actual Euclidean distance, thus the method does not incur false dismissal. Besides, the computation time can be reduced remarkably compared with that for computing the actual Euclidean distance because only norms instead of all the dimension values are considered.

However, the method suffers from large errors because the approximation is based on only one norm value. Especially, as the dimensionality of vectors increases, the errors also increase, and thus make the number of false alarms increased greatly. Consequently, this delays the post-processing time.

2.2 Magnitude Approximation

Magnitude approximation is a method proposed to overcome the large errors in the method using the Cauchy-Schwartz inequality [4]. In this method, the inner product is approximated by equation (4).

$$< X, Y >^k \approx b_1\psi_1(X)\psi_1(Y) + b_2\psi_2(X)\psi_2(Y) + \cdots + b_k\psi_k(X)\psi_k(Y) \tag{4}$$

$$\psi_k(X) = x_1^k + x_2^k + \ldots + x_n^k \tag{5}$$

In equation (4), ψ_k means the k squares of the k-th norm as equation (5), b_i is the optimal coefficient for each term in the approximation function. The optimal coefficient is calculated by using the *least square method* [4]. The Euclidean distance is estimated by substituting the approximation function for the inner product in equation (2). The optimal coefficient, however, varies according to data distribution and the value of k. Furthermore, the approximation function is not guaranteed to be the lower bound of the Euclidean distance [4]. Thus, it has a serious drawback of incurring false dismissal, and thus is applied to only a very limited range of applications that allow false dismissal.

2.3 Shape Approximation

Equation (5) has a property of symmetry. In other words, all vectors with different combinations of dimension values show the same k-th norm. This is the primary cause to incur approximation errors. *Shape approximation* is a method proposed to reduce these errors [5]. By dividing one vector into several disjoint subgroups and calculating their individual k-th norms, the shape information of a vector is partially captured. This reduces the number of false alarms successfully. However, shape approximation also suffers from false dismissal because its approximation function does not always produce the lower bound of the Euclidean distance.

3 Proposed Method

3.1 Basic Concept

Computing of the Euclidean distance can be reformulated as in equation (6). The approximation function using the Cauchy-Schwartz inequality does not consider the *cosine component* between two vectors. We note that this is the main cause of large approximation errors.

$$\begin{aligned} D(X,Y) &= \sqrt{\|X\|^2 + \|Y\|^2 - 2 < X,Y >} \\ &= \sqrt{\|X\|^2 + \|Y\|^2 - 2\|X\|\|Y\|cos\theta} \end{aligned} \quad (6)$$

In this paper, we propose a novel method for approximating the Euclidean distance between two vectors more accurately by reflecting the cosine component between two vectors. The Euclidean distance between given two vectors is computed by using their norms and the cosine component between two vectors as in equation (6). However, we cannot be aware of the angle θ between a query vector and every data vector that is necessary to compute the cosine component until a query vector is given. Of course, it is possible that we can compute the angle between a query vector and every data vector in query processing. In this case, however, the pre-processing step takes long time due to this costly computation. The key idea of our method does reduce this time by storing some abstract information to approximate the angle at the time of database construction.

Figure 1 shows the concept of angle approximation proposed in this paper. If we know the angle θ_{RX_i} between a *reference vector* R and the i-th data vector

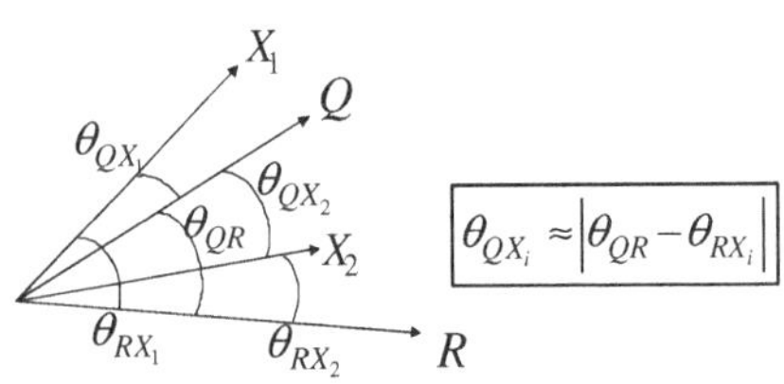

Fig. 1. Angle approximation using a reference vector

X_i, by merely computing the angle θ_{QR} between a query vector and a reference vector, we can approximate the angle θ_{QX_i} between a query vector and the i-th data vector by a simple calculation given in equation (7). Thus, we select a reference vector, then save angles between the reference vector and every data vector as abstract information. These angles can be computed by using vector norms and an inner product as in equation (8). We can compute the angle for every vector without a query vector given because equation (8) has nothing to do with a query vector. The function, which approximates the distance to be compared with a tolerance in pre-processing, is given in equation (9).

$$\bar{\theta}_{QX_i} = |\theta_{QR} - \theta_{RX_i}| \tag{7}$$

$$\theta_{RX_i} = cos^{-1}\left(\frac{< X_i, R >}{\|X_i\|\|R\|}\right) \tag{8}$$

$$\bar{D}(Q, X_i) = \sqrt{\|X_i\|^2 + \|Q\|^2 - 2\|X_i\|\|Q\|cos\bar{\theta}_{QX_i}} \tag{9}$$

3.2 Construction of Abstract Information

In constructing abstract information, we compute and save the information used for approximation in query processing, from n-dimensional feature vectors of multimedia data. First, we choose a reference vector. To minimize Euclidean distance between data vectors and reference vector, we use first principal component of PCA as a reference vector. We omit the details due to space limitations.

Then, we compute the norm and the angle for every n-dimensional data vector. The abstract information saved in a database consists of a set of entries, each of which is composed of $< \|X_i\|, \theta_{RX_i} >$ per data vector, and a reference vector.

3.3 Query Processing

Query processing finds out a set of correct answers whose distance to a query vector is actually smaller than a tolerance given by a user. We can improve efficiency by using the abstract information prepared in advance.

When a query vector is given, we first compute norms of a query vector and a reference vector. Next, we calculate the angle θ_{QR} between a query vector and a reference vector using equation (8). Then, we approximate the angle between a query vector and every data vector using the abstract information. It is noted that this approximation requires only a simple subtraction as shown in equation (7), rather than a costly inner product operation. Then, we approximate the Euclidean distance by using equation (9) with the approximated angle $\bar{\theta}_{QX_i}$. A data vector is regarded as a candidate, if its approximated distance to a query vector is less than a tolerance. In post-processing, we find correct answers from a candidate set by computing their actual Euclidean distance to a query vector.

3.4 Discussions

This section shows that the proposed method guarantees no false dismissal and also reduces the number of false alarms significantly compared with the previous method.

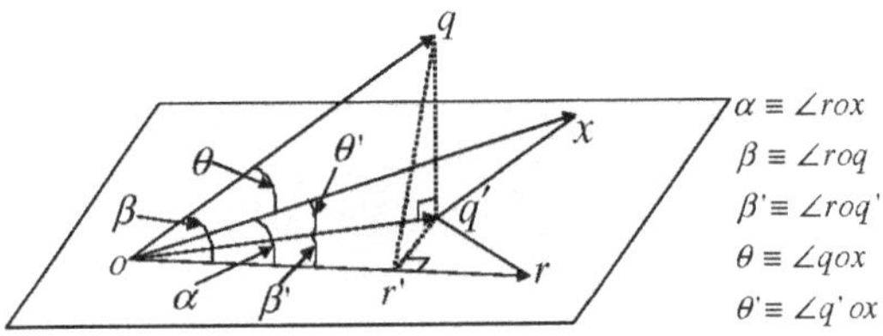

Fig. 2. The relationship among a reference vector R, a query vector Q, and a data vector X

Theorem 1. *In Fig. 2, α is the angle between $\overrightarrow{or}$ and $\overrightarrow{ox}$. β is the angle between $\overrightarrow{or}$ and $\overrightarrow{oq}$. θ is the angle between $\overrightarrow{oq}$ and $\overrightarrow{ox}$. The sum of any two angles among α, β, θ is always greater than or equal to the other angle.*

Proof. Omitted due to space limitations. Refer to [10].

Corollary 1. *The approximated angle between a query vector and a data vector by equation (7) is always less than or equal to the original angle. That is, $\theta \geq |\alpha - \beta|$.*

Proof. Omitted due to space limitations. Refer to [10].

Corollary 2. *The approximated distance obtained by the approximated angle is always less than or equal to the actual Euclidean distance.*

$$< X, Y >= \|X\|\|Y\|cos\theta \leq \|X\|\|Y\|cos\theta' \quad (10)$$

Proof. Omitted due to space limitations. Refer to [10].

Corollary 2 is to show the proposed approximation function lower-bounds the Euclidean distance, and thus implies our method does not incur false dismissal in multimedia information retrieval.

The relationship among the actual Euclidean distance function D, the proposed approximation function $\bar{D}$, and the approximation function using the Cauchy-Schwartz inequality D_{cs} is shown in equation (11).

$$\begin{array}{rl} & D(X,Y) \geq \bar{D}(X,Y) \geq D_{cs}(X,Y) \\ where, & D(X,Y) = \sqrt{\|X\|^2 + \|Y\|^2 - 2\|X\|\|Y\|cos\theta} \\ & \bar{D}(X,Y) = \sqrt{\|X\|^2 + \|Y\|^2 - 2\|X\|\|Y\|cos\bar{\theta}} \\ & D_{cs}(X,Y) = \sqrt{\|X\|^2 + \|Y\|^2 - 2\|X\|\|Y\|} \end{array} \quad (11)$$

We observe that the proposed approximation function lower-bounds the Euclidean distance function, and also upper-bounds the approximation function using the Cauchy-Schwartz inequality. Therefore, our method not only reduces the number of candidates, but also guarantees no false dismissal. In the worst case, our method forms a set of candidates same as those from the method using the Cauchy-Schwartz inequality. On the other hand, in the best case, our method forms a set of candidates including only correct answers.

4 Performance Evaluation

4.1 Environment for Experiments

We used synthetic and real-life data sets for experiments. A synthetic data set is composed of 10,000 data vectors and their values for each dimension are in the range of [0, 1]. A data set consists of a number of clusters over multi-dimensional space, each of which contains up to 100 data vectors. The real-life Corel image data set consists of 68,040 images [9]. The feature vector extracted from each image is a co-occurrence texture in 4 directions: horizontal, vertical, and two diagonal directions. Co-occurrence is composed of the second angular moment, contrast, inverse difference moment, and entropy for each direction. So, each vector has 16 dimensions.

We compared our method with the one using the Cauchy-Schwartz inequality. We excluded magnitude approximation and shape approximation mentioned in Section 2 because they cause false dismissal. First, we compared the average number of candidates obtained after the pre-processing step for 100 random queries. This experiment runs repeatedly with a varying number of dimensions of the feature vectors.

The number of candidates indicates the load of the post-processing step: i.e., the time spent in post-processing is proportional to the number of candidates. However, the total retrieval time is also related to the time spent in the pre-processing step. Thus, we also measured the overall query processing time, which contains both the pre-processing time and the post-processing time. We summated total processing times for processing 100 random queries. In this experiment, we stored all data vectors and the abstract information in main memory. The hardware platform for the experiments is the PC equipped with 2.8G Pentium IV CPU and 512 MB RAM. The software platform is MS Windows 2000 and Visual C++ 6.0.

4.2 Experimental Results

Figure 3 shows the number of candidates obtained from pre-processing of two methods: our method and the one using the Cauchy-Schwartz inequality for k-NN queries.

The approximation function using the Cauchy-Schwartz inequality lower-bounds the actual Euclidean distance, but incurs a lot of false alarms since it ignores the cosine component between a query vector and a data vector. The proposed method uses the angle component additionally in approximation, thus, reduces the number of false alarms significantly. In our experiment, the number

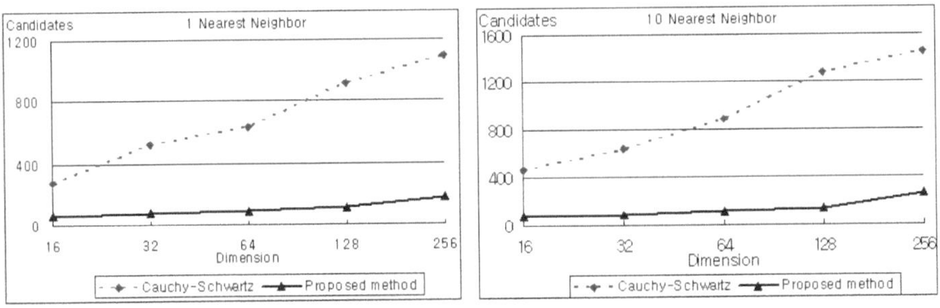

(a) 1-NN (b) 10-NN

Fig. 3. The number of candidates according to varying numbers of dimensions

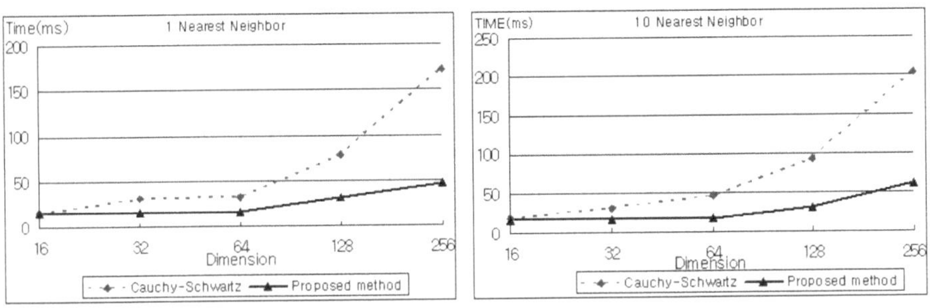

(a) 1-NN (b) 10-NN

Fig. 4. The query processing time according to varying numbers of dimensions

of candidates is smallest in 16 dimensions and 1-NN queries. In this case, those data vectors, whose actual distances to a query vector have been computed, were only 0.62% of total data vectors. Even in the case of 256 dimensions and 10-NN queries, those were only 2.6%. We see that the method removes 80~90% candidates, which are false alarms, compared with that using the Cauchy-Schwartz inequality according to the number of dimensions. Furthermore, our method maintains a similar level in terms of the number of candidates even though the number of dimensions increases. On the contrary, in the method using the Cauchy-Schwartz inequality, the number of candidates increases rapidly as the number of dimensions increases.

Figure 4 shows the query processing time for processing 100 random queries with different numbers of dimensions. Here, we only display the result for 1-NN and 10-NN queries in Fig. 4. However, we note that others are shown to have similar tendencies in our experiments. In the case of the method using the Cauchy-Schwartz inequality, the number of candidates increases rapidly as the number of dimensions increases. This causes the heavy load in the post-processing step. As a result, the total processing time gets larger. In our method, though more time was spent in the pre-processing step because the approximation using the angle is complex and thus requires a little more time, the post-processing time

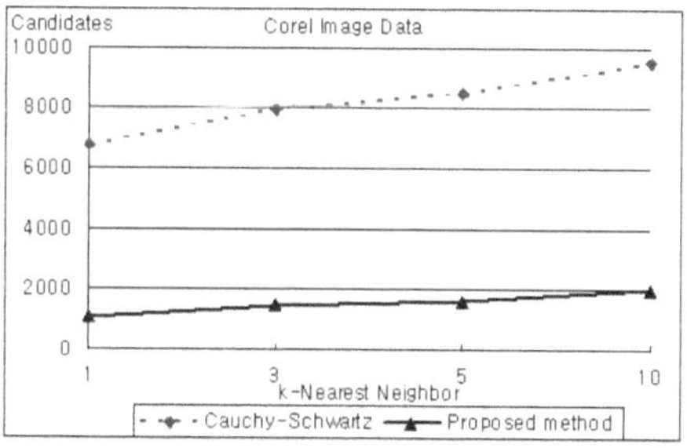

Fig. 5. The number of candidates according to varying numbers of final results

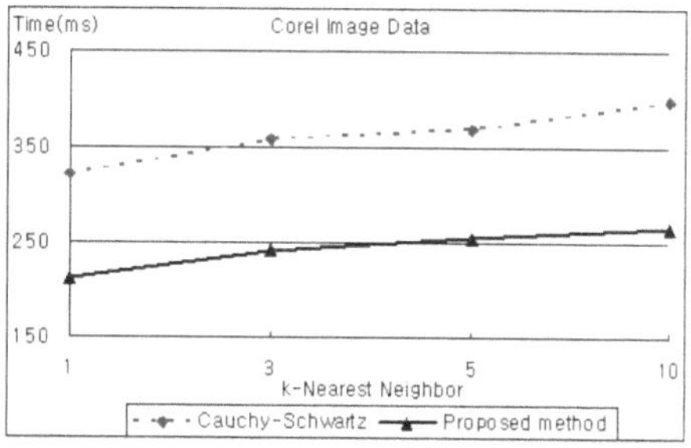

Fig. 6. The query processing time according to varying numbers of final results

reduces significantly because the number of candidates decreases remarkably. As a result, the effect of the performance improvement of our method gets higher as the number of dimensions increases.

Figure 5 and Fig. 6 show the experimental results for the real-life data set containing the Corel images. Those show the number of candidates and the query processing time with a changing tolerance, respectively. The experimental results reveal the tendency similar to that of a synthetic data set. In the case of 1-NN queries, only 1.56% of total data vectors are selected as candidates in our method. However, the number of candidates becomes larger as a tolerance gets larger. The result of the query processing time is also quite similar to that of a synthetic data set. Also, we see that Fig. 5 and Fig. 6 show tendencies very similar to each other in the result. Therefore, we confirmed that the number of candidates is a dominant performance factor in query processing.

5 Conclusions

In multimedia information retrieval, the Euclidean distance is widely used as a similarity measure. The time of computing the Euclidean distance between query and data vectors occupies a large part of the total retrieval time in high-dimensional space. Therefore, we can reduce the total query processing time significantly by shortening the computation time of the Euclidean distance.

In this paper, we have proposed an effective method for approximating the Euclidean distance between two high-dimensional vectors. Our method introduces an additional vector called a reference vector for estimating the angle between the two vectors, and approximates the Euclidean distance accurately by reflecting the estimated angle. This makes the approximation errors reduced significantly compared with the previous method. Also, we have formally proved that the distance approximated by our method is always smaller than the actual Euclidean distance. This implies that our method does not incur any false dismissals in multimedia information retrieval. Finally, we have verified the superiority of the proposed method via performance evaluation with extensive experiments. The results show that the proposed method 4.5 to 6.5 times outperforms the previous method. Moreover, our method is shown to get more effective as the number of dimensions increases and a tolerance gets smaller. This property is quite desirable when we take the characteristics of real environment for multimedia information retrieval into account.

Acknowledgement

This research was supported by the KRF(Korea Research Foundation) Grant funded by the Korean Government (MOEHRD) (KRF-2004-041-D00566) and also by the MIC(Ministry of Information and Communication) of Korea under the ITRC(Information Technology Research Center) support program supervised by the IITA(Institute of Information Technology Assessment) (IITA-2005-C1090-0502-0009).

References

1. R. Agrawal, C. Faloutsos, and A. Swami: Efficient Similarity Search in Sequence Database. In Proc. of the 4th Int'l Conf. on Foundations of Data Organization and Algorithms. (1993) 69–84
2. K. S. Beyer, J. Goldstein, R. Ramakrishnan, and U. Shaft: When Is Nearest Neighbor Meaningful? In Proc. of the 7th Int'l Conf. on Database Theory. (1999) 217–235
3. C. Bohm, S. Berchtold, and D. A. Keim: Searching in High-Dimensional Spaces-Index Structures for Improving the Performance of Multimedia Databases. ACM Computing Surveys. Vol. 33, Issue 3 (2001) 322–373
4. O. Egecioglu and H. Ferhatosmanoglu: Dimensionality Reduction and Similarity Computation by Inner Product Approximations. In Proc. of the 9th ACM Int'l Conf. on Information and Knowledge Management. (2000) 219–226
5. U. Y. Ogras and H. Ferhatosmanoglu: Dimensionality Reduction Using Magnitude and Shape Approximations. In Proc. of the 12th Int'l Conf. on Information and Knowledge Management. (2003) 99–107
6. C. Faloutsos, R. Barber, M. Flickner, W. Niblack, D. Petkovic, and W. Equitz: Efficient and Effective Querying By Image Content. In Journal of Intelligent Information Systems. Vol. 3 No. 3/4 (1994) 231–262
7. T. Seidl and H.-P. Kriegel: Efficient User-Adaptable Similarity Search in Large Multimedia Databases. In Proc. of 23rd Int'l Conf. on Very Large Data Bases. (1997) 506–515
8. R. Weber, H. J. Schek, and S. Blott: A Quantitative Analysis and Performance Study for Similarity-Search Methods in High-Dimensional Spaces. In Proc. of 24th Int'l Conf. on Very Large Data Bases. (1998) 194–205
9. http://kdd.ics.uci.edu/databases/CorelFeatures/CorelFeatures.html
10. S. Jeong, S.-W. Kim, K. Kim, and B.-U. Choi: An Effective Method for Approximating the Euclidean Distance in High-Dimensional Space. (Unpublished manuscript)

Dynamic Method Materialization: A Framework for Optimizing Data Access Via Methods

Robert Wrembel, Mariusz Masewicz, and Krzysztof Jankiewicz

Poznań University of Technology, Institute of Computing Science
Poznań, Poland
{rwrembel, mmasewicz, kjankiewicz}@cs.put.poznan.pl

Abstract. This paper addresses the problem of selecting right methods for materialization. In our approach, the selection of methods is based on method execution statistics that are constantly gathered in our prototype system. Based on the statistics, the prototype selects methods whose materialization is profitable. The proposed mechanism was extensively evaluated by experiments whose results are shown in this paper.

1 Introduction

Optimizing access to data returned by methods is an important research and technological issue in various object systems, e.g. CAD, CAM, CASE, GIS, object and object-relational databases, object-relational data warehouses (with materialized object views), multimedia data warehouses, spatial data warehouses, as well as in distributed object environments. The fact that methods are expressed in an object language, taking advantage of inheritance, overloading, and late binding makes the optimization of method executions challenging. A promising technique applied in this area is called method materialization (also known as precomputation or caching).

Basically, method materialization consists in computing the result of a method and storing it persistently on a disk. Then, every subsequent invocation of the same method can be handled by reading the already materialized value. A drawback of this technique is that values of materialized methods become invalid when objects used for computing them change. As a consequence, materialized results have to be invalidated and recomputed.

While applying method materialization one has to address the two following issues, namely (1) *how to materialize methods and how to maintain materialized results*, as well as (2) *which methods to materialize*. The first problem was addressed in several research publications e.g., [1,2,9,15]. The second problem is similar to materialized view selection that was extensively investigated in the research literature, e.g. [4,16,17]. In our opinion, materialized method selection is more difficult to handle than materialized view selection since method codes and dependencies between them are much complex than dependencies between materialized views. Materialized method selection, to the best of our knowledge, has not been addressed so far. Moreover, a common limitation of the approaches

S. Bressan, J. Küng, and R. Wagner (Eds.): DEXA 2006, LNCS 4080, pp. 873–882, 2006.

to method materialization is that they do not consider dependencies between methods where one method calls another one.

In our approach, further called the *hierarchical materialization*, we address the two materialization issues mentioned above. The *hierarchical materialization* takes into account chains of method invocations and materializes method results hierarchically, cf. Section 3. Materializing hierarchically method m_i causes that values of intermediate methods called from m_i are also materialized. These intermediate results are used for recomputing m_i quicker after its invalidation.

In this paper we contribute the solution to the materialized method selection problem. The selection of methods for materialization is supported in our approach by the so called *dynamic materialization*, cf. Section 4. In the *dynamic materialization*, only these methods are materialized whose computation is costly and whose materialized results can be maintained at low costs. To this end, method execution statistics (method execution time, the number of method calls, the number of method invalidations) are collected by the system. Based on the statistics, the system automatically selects appropriate methods for materialization. When the number of updates invalidating a materialized result increases beyond a threshold, the system automatically dematerializes a given method. The *hierarchical* and the *dynamic materialization* were implemented in a prototype system and were evaluated experimentally. The experimental results, discussed in this paper (cf. Section 5), show that an overall system's performance increases while using our materialization techniques. We observe the system's performance improvement for various method call graphs, as well as for different method access patterns containing interchanged method reads and updates (method invalidations).

2 Related Work

Several approaches to method materialization have been proposed in the literature. They can be characterized as persistent approaches, e.g. [1,8,9,12] and temporal approaches, e.g. [2,15].

The analytical framework for estimating costs of caching complex objects was presented in [8]. A procedural and an object identity based representations were analyzed. In this approach, the maintenance of cached (materialized) values was not taken into consideration. In the approach presented in [1], results of materialized methods are stored in a B-tree based method-index. The application of method materialization is limited to methods that: (1) do not have input arguments, (2) compute values based on only atomic types, and (3) do not modify values of objects. Otherwise, a method is left as a non-materialized one. The concept presented in [9] allows to materialize methods that use input arguments. Materialized results are persistently stored in a dedicated data structure. For the purpose of method invalidations, the system maintains information about attributes whose values are used for the materialization. Moreover, every object has appended the set of those method identifiers that used it. In this approach a system's designer has to explicitly define in advance (during a system's design phase) data structures for storing materialized results for all methods, even if the materialization may not be used at all.

A common limitation of these three approaches is that they do not take into account dependencies between methods, where one method calls others.

In [12] the authors proposed to decompose complex methods into the graph of component methods. The semantics of complex and component methods is then analyzed in order to figure out which results to cache. The approach requires huge secondary storage as method results are cached extensively. Moreover, the maintenance of cached results is not supported. In the work presented in [2,15] method results are cached in memory. When a program or query using a method ends, cached results are removed. In [15] only methods with constant input values are cached.

Two loosely coupled related concepts to method materialization concern a cost model for method executions [3] and indexing methods along an inheritance hierarchy [11]. The cost model developed in [3] includes the number of O/I operations and CPU time, but it does not consider method materialization. In [11], the authors proposed and evaluated R-tree based indexes for the optimization of searching methods. This approach focuses on indexing metadata on methods, rather than method values.

3 Hierarchical Method Materialization

This section outlines the *hierarchical materialization*, originally presented in [6], and overviews storage structures.

Concept

Materializing hierarchically method m_i results in storing persistently the result of m_i as well as the results of other, intermediate, methods called from m_i. When object o_i, used for the materialization of m_i, is updated or deleted, then the value of m_i has to be invalidated and recomputed. This recomputation can use unaffected intermediate materialized results, thus reducing the recomputation time overhead.

The *hierarchical materialization* differs from the approaches presented in [1,8,9] as it supports also materialization of intermediate methods. It differs from the caching technique proposed in [12] as in the *hierarchical materialization* cached results are kept up to date.

The hierarchical materialization can be used among others in: (1) object distributed environments (e.g. Corba) for synchronizing replica objects; (2) multimedia databases and data warehouses [14] for computing parameters of images; (3) object-relational data warehouses [5] as a technique for materializing views.

Storage Structures

The hierarchical materialization is supported by several data structures, cf. [6]. The most important ones include: the *Materialized Method Results Structure* (*MMRS*), the *Graph of Method Calls* (*GMC*), and the *Inverse References Index* (*IRI*).

The *MMRS* stores all materialized results of all methods, i.e.: (1) materialized values of methods, (2) identifiers of objects used for computing the values, and (3) arrays of input argument values passed to a materialized method. Calling method m_i for a given object and with a given array of input argument values results in searching the *MMRS*. If the result is found, it is returned. Otherwise, the result is computed, stored in the *MMRS*, and returned to a user. When a base object of m_i is updated or deleted, then a materialized value becomes invalid and is removed from the *MMRS*.

A given value v_i of materialized method m_i executed with a given set of input argument values $\{a_1, a_2, ..., a_n\}$ for object o_i can be shared by multiple methods calling m_i. The first method that calls m_i materializes its result. Any other method calling m_i with $\{a_1, a_2, ..., a_n\}$ for object o_i accesses the already materialized value in the *MMRS*.

The hierarchical materialization analyzes and maintains dependencies between methods where one method calls another one. These dependencies are stored in the *GMC*. Its content is used by the procedure that stores and invalidates materialized results.

In order to invalidate values of dependent materialized methods, the system must also be able to traverse a composition hierarchy in an inverse direction. To this end, we use the so called *inverse references*. An inverse reference for object o_j is the reference from o_j to other objects that are referencing o_j. The references are maintained in the *IRI*.

Method Code Modification

In order to support the hierarchical materialization, the code of materialized method m_i has to be extended with a section that verifies whether the value of m_i invoked for object o_i with a given set of input values has already been stored in the *MMRS*. Codes of methods are automatically augmented by our prototype system. An augmented code is inserted between tags that have to be explicitly placed in a method by a programmer.

4 Dynamic Method Materialization

Finding the right set of methods for materialization is difficult as for each method m_i one has to take into account: (1) its execution/response time, (2) the number of reads of materialized m_i, and (3) the number of invalidations of m_i, i.e. the number of updates of its base objects. Finding appropriate methods for materialization is supported in our approach by the *dynamic materialization*. It is designed for optimizing a system's performance for a set of operations, including method m_i reads and its base object updates. Such a set will further be called a *workload*.

The *dynamic materialization* has two following features.

1. It allows to find the set M of methods whose materialization improves system's performance for a given workload. When the workload changes, then the materialization of previously selected methods in M may no longer be

profitable. In this case the materialization is automatically turned off for some or all methods in M.
2. It allows to change automatically the moment of rematerializing invalidated results of methods. Method m_i can be recomputed either (1) just before reading its value (so called *late* or *lazy rematerialization*) or (2) immediately after its base object was updated (so called *early* or *immediate rematerialization*) [10].

The *dynamic materialization* is managed by a software module, called *access optimizer* that is responsible for selecting appropriate methods for materialization. To this end, the module monitors methods access patterns and gathers methods execution statistics. The statistics include CPU time and the number of disk accesses for: (1) methods' executions, (2) methods' invalidations and recomputations, and (3) reads of materialized values. The statistics also include counters of base objects updates.

The materialization of method m_i will reduce access time to data returned by m_i if the following rule holds for every reading operation in the workload, cf. [13]: an overall time spent on reading materialized value v of m_i requested by the number r of reading operations plus an overall time spent on rematerializing the value of m_i caused by the number of u update operations is lower than an overall time spent on computing the result of non-materialized m_i.

5 Performance Evaluation

The described *dynamic materialization* combined with *hierarchical materialization* was evaluated by experiments on a PC with Pentium III (1.13GHz) and 256 MB of RAM, under Windows 2000. The goal of the experiments (making the main paper contribution) was to measure an overall system's response time by applying the dynamic materialization technique, for a given workload. The system's response time was measured for: (1) different shapes of the *GMC*s (cf. Section 3) that methods formed; (2) different number of base objects being updated, causing invalidations and rematerializations of different number of previously materialized results.

Three different shapes of the *GMC*s were evaluated that differed with respect to: the number of levels and the number of nodes in each level. These two parameters had impact on the size of our test database. A generic, parameterized shape of our test *GMC* is shown in Figure 1. Root method m_0 at level 0 calls j methods at level 1. Each of these methods further calls j methods at a lower level. The parameters of our test GMCs are presented in Table 1.

The experiments tested overall system's response time for a given workload including 1000 operations. The number of read (r) and update (u) operations in the workload was parameterized from 0 to 1000, so that $r + u$ remained constant. Moreover, the number of intermediate results of methods invalidated by base object updates was also parameterized and ranged from 20% to 80% of total materialised results, i.e. from 20% to 80% of the *GMC* branches were

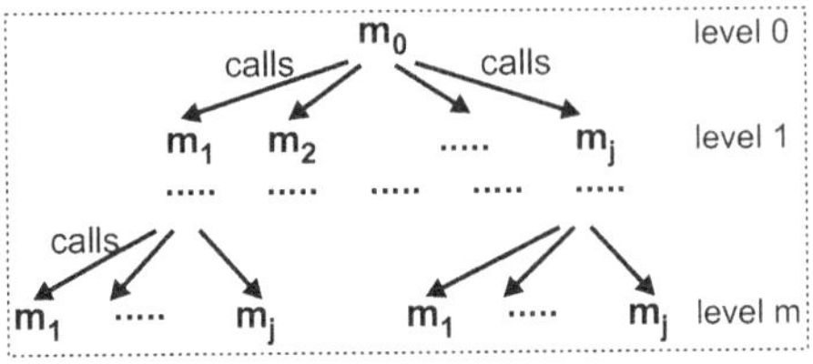

Fig. 1. A generic shape of the test *GMC*

Table 1. Parameters of the test *GMC*s

	Number of levels	Number of methods in each level (where level number>0)	Database size
GMC_1	7	10	105GB
GMC_2	5	20	15GB
GMC_3	3	100	980MB

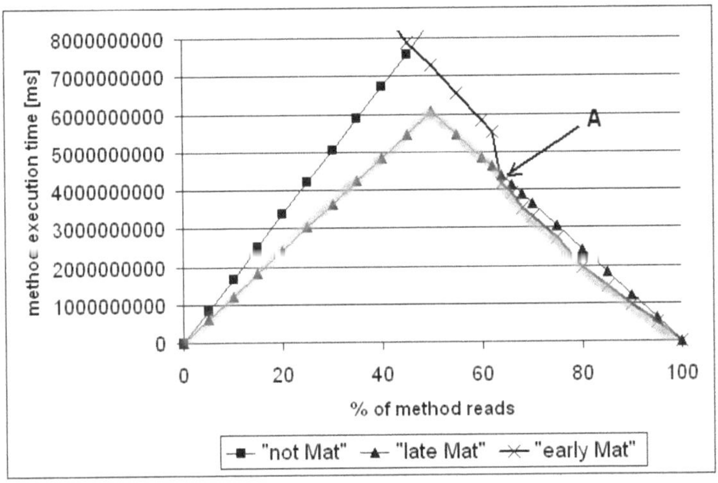

Fig. 2. System response times for: non-materialized method m_0, hierarchical materialization of m_0 for early and late rematerialization strategies (GMC_1; 60% of invalidated intermediate materialised results)

invalidated. The obtained overall system's response times were measured for root method m_0 (cf. Figure 1).

Figure 2 presents overall system's response times for executing method m_0 parameterized by the number of calls of m_0. The percent of reading operations to base objects updating operations in the workload was changing from 0% (only updates) to 100% (only reads). The results were obtained for GMC_1 and 60% of invalidated intermediate materialized results. The *"not Mat"* curve represents the execution time of a non-materialized method. In this case, the system's response time drastically increases when the number of method reads increases. The *"late Mat"* curve represents the execution time of m_0 after applying the

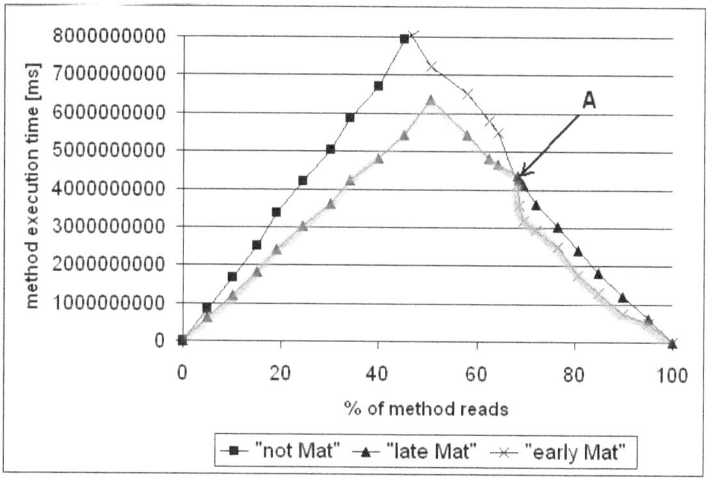

Fig. 3. System response times for: non-materialized method m_0, hierarchical materialization of m_0 for early and late rematerialization strategies (GMC_2; 60% of invalidated intermediate materialised results)

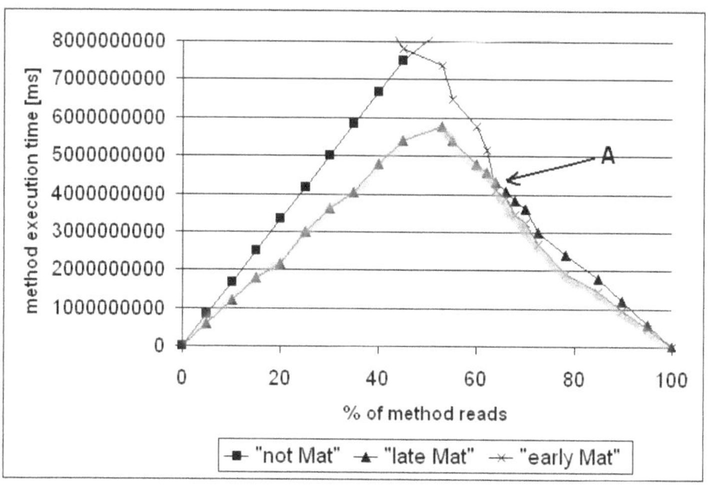

Fig. 4. System response times for: non-materialized method m_0, hierarchical materialization of m_0 for early and late rematerialization strategies (GMC_3; 60% of invalidated intermediate materialised results)

hierarchical materialization and when method rematerialization was done just *before* the method value was requested and read. *"early Mat"* represents the execution time when the rematerialization of m_0 was done immediately *after* invalidating its result, i.e. immediately after its base object update occured. An overall system's response time after applying the *dynamic materialization* is marked in the figures as the gray-bold-semitransparent curve.

As we can observe from Figure 2, the late rematerialization substantially outperforms the early rematerialization when the percent of method reads in the workload is lower that about 65%, cf. point A in the chart. After that point, the early rematerialization gives slightly better performance than the late one. For this reason, the access optimizer module automatically switches between the late and early rematerialization strategies (cf. point A) depending on the percent of m_0 reads in the workload. Thus, it guarantees that the most efficient strategy is used at a given moment and for a given workload.

Figures 3 and 4 present overall system's response times for executing method m_0 in a function of the percent of reads of m_0 in the test workload, for 60% of invalidated branches, for GMC_2 and and GMC_3, respectively. The efficiency characteristics show that also for other shapes of the GMCs the *dynamic materialization* improves a system's performance (cf. the gray-bold-semitransparent curve). For these two tested graphs our access optimizer module switches from the late to the early rematerialization strategy when the number of read operations in the workload exceeds 60% (cf. threshold point A).

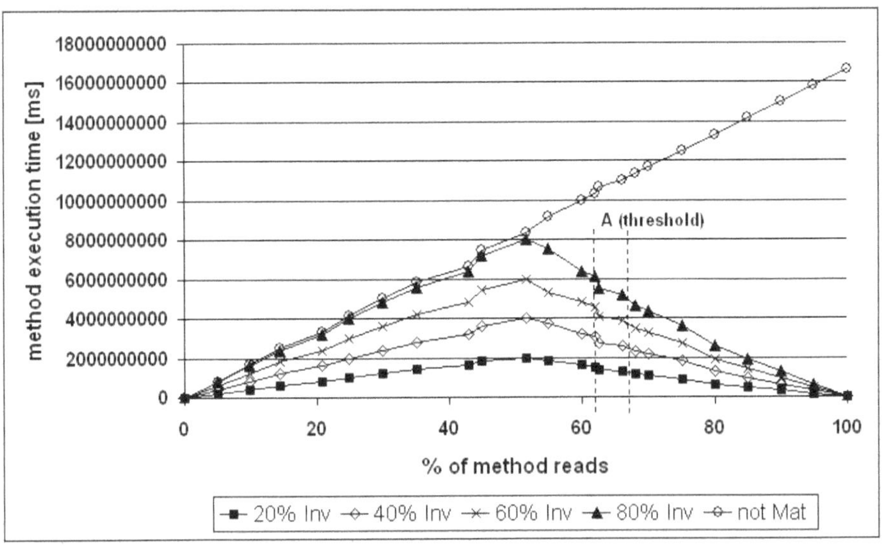

Fig. 5. Comparison of overall system response times for: (1) non-materialized method m_0 and (2) dynamically materialized m_0 (GMC_3; 20%, 40%, 60%, and 80% of invalidated intermediate materialised results)

Figure 5 summarizes overall system's execution times for: (1) non-materialized method m_0 (the *"not Mat"* curve) and (2) dynamically materialized m_0. These characteristics were measured for GMC_3 for 20% (marked as *"20% Inv"* on the chart), 40% (*"40% Inv"*), 60% (*"60% Inv"*), and 80% (*"80% Inv"*) of invalidated intermediate materialised results. As we can observe from the chart, methods with fewer invalidated results perform better than those with a greater number of invalidated results. Moreover, even when 80% of intermediate mateiralized results is invalidated, the system still performs slightly better than without materialization applied, within the range between 0% and 55% of method reads.

As our further experiments show, when the number of invalidated intermediate materialized results exceeds 80% of total materialized results for a given method m_i, then the system performance deteriorates. In this case, the access optimizer module automatically swithches off the materialization of this method (m_0 in our test environment). As a consequence, all materialized results of the method are removed from the *MMRS* and the method is executed from scratch every time it is called (cf. the *"not Mat"* curve).

We conducted several other experiments with different GMCs and different percents of branches invalidated (not discussed here due to space limit). The experiments show that our prototype system behaves in all those scenarios similarly to the scenarios presented in this paper, i.e. we obtained an increase in the system's performance.

6 Summary

In this paper we addressed two important issues concerning method materialization, namely materialization technique and method selection for materialization. We tackle the first issue by applying hierarchical materialization since it was proved to be a promising and efficient technique for some types of systems (cf. [6,7]), whereas the selection of methods for materialization and methods recomputation moment is based on the *dynamic materialization*. To the best of our knowledge, it is the first approach to automatic optimization of method executions. The dynamic materialization can be applicable to every system that uses methods.

As our experiments show, by using the *dynamic materialization* combined with the hierarchical materialization, an overall system's performance can be improved: (1) even when the number of invalidated intermediate materialized results is great (up to 80% in our experiment); (2) regardless the shape of the *Graph of Method Calls*; (3) for workloads composed of various numbers of method reads and base object updates.

In future, we plan to analyze patterns of sequences of method reads and its base object updates in workloads for the purpose of discovering frequent patterns. Based on these frequent patterns, we plan to predict forthcoming patterns for the purpose of selecting the most appropriate strategy of rematerializing methods.

References

1. Bertino E.: Method precomputation in object-oriented databases. SIGOS Bulletin, 12(2,3), 1991
2. Eder J., Frank H., Liebhart W.: Optimization of Object-Oriented Queries by Inverse Methods. Proc. of East/West Database Workshop, 1994
3. Gardarin G., Sha F., Tang Z. H.: Calibrating the Query Optimizer Cost Model of IRO-DB, an Object-Oriented Federated Database System. Proc. of VLDB, 1996
4. Gupta A., Mumick I.S. (eds.): Materialized Views: Techniques, Implementations, and Applications. MIT Press, 1999
5. Huynh T.N., Mangisengi O., Tjoa A.M.: Metadata for Object-Relational Data Warehouse. Proc. of DMDW, 2000
6. Jezierski J., Masewicz M., Wrembel R., Czejdo B.: Designing Storage Structures for Management of Materialised Methods in Object-Oriented Databases. Proc. of OOIS, 2003, LNCS 2817
7. Jezierski J., Masewicz M., Wrembel R.: On Optimising Data Access via Materialised Methods in Object-Oriented Systems. Proc. of ADVIS, 2004, LNCS 3261
8. Jhingran A.: Precomputation in a Complex Object Environment. Proc. of ICDE, 1991
9. Kemper A., Kilger C., Moerkotte G.: Function Materialization in Object Bases: Design, Realization, and Evaluation. IEEE TKDE, 6(4), 1994
10. Kemper A., Moerkotte G.: Object-Oriented Database Management: Applications in Engineering and Computer Science. Prentice Hall, 2004
11. Kratky M., Stolfa S., Snasel V., Vondrak I.: Efficient Searching in Large Inheritance Hierarchies. Proc. of DEXA, 2005, LNCS 3588
12. Liu Y. A., Stoller S. D., Teitelbaum T.: Static Caching for Incremental Computation. ACM Trans. on Programing Languages and Systems, 20(3), 1998
13. Masewicz M., Wrembel R., Jezierski J.: Optimising Performance of Object-Oriented and Object-Relational Systems by Dynamic Method Materialisation. Proc. of ADBIS (short papers), 2005
14. Ben Messaoud R., O. Boussaid O., Rabaséda S.: A New OLAP Aggregation Based on the AHC Technique. Proc. of ACM DOLAP, 2004
15. Pugh W., Teitelbaum T.: Incremental Computation via Function Caching. Proc. of ACM POPL, 1989
16. de Sousa M. F., Sampaio M. C.: Efficient Materialization and Use of Views in Data Warehouses. SIGMOD Record, 28(1), 1999
17. Theodoratos D., Xu W.: Constructing Search Space for Materialized View Selection. Proc. of ACM DOLAP, 2004

Towards an Anti-inference (K, ℓ)-Anonymity Model with Value Association Rules

Zude Li, Guoqiang Zhan, and Xiaojun Ye

Institute of Information System and Engineering
School of Software, Tsinghua University, Beijing, 100084, China
{li-zd04, zhan-gq03}@mails.tsinghua.edu.cn, yexj@tsinghua.edu.cn

Abstract. As a privacy-preserving microdata publication model, K-Anonymity has some application limits, such as (1) it cannot satisfy the individual-defined k mechanism requirement, and (2) it is attached with a certain extent potential privacy disclosure risk on published microdata, i.e. existing high-probability inference violations under some prior knowledge on k-anonymized microdata that can surely result in personal private information disclosure. We propose the (k, ℓ)-*anonymity* model with data generalization approach to support more flexible and anti-inference k-anonymization on a tabular microdata, where k indicates the anonymization level of an identifying attribute cluster and ℓ refers to the diversity level of a sensitive attribute cluster on a record. Within the model, k and ℓ are designed on each record and they can be defined subjectively by the corresponding individual. Beside, the model can prevent two kinds of inference attacks for microdata publication, (1) inferring identifying attributes values when their value domains are known; (2) inferring sensitive attributes values with respect to some value associations in the microdata. Further, we propose an algorithm to describe the k-anonymization process in the model. Finally, we take a scenario to illustrate its feasibility, flexibility, and generality.

1 Introduction

An individual represented as a record in a database might be re-identified by joining the released data with another public database. To reduce the risk of this attack type, *k-anonymity* is proposed as a privacy-preserving microdata publication model against individual re-identification on published microdata [15,19]. Many instances illustrating such attacks are listed in literature such as [15,19,12,8,9,2,13], which are the motivations for most *k-anonymity* models introduced in the past several years. In general, *k-anonymity* means that one can only be certain that a value is associated with one of at least k values, or in a dataset, each record is indistinguishable from at least *k-1* other records on identifying attributes [19,12].

For current *k-anonymity* models on microdata with relational table schema consisting of identifying attributes and sensitive attributes, the k value is statically predefined before anonymization, and it is *table-level* as it is used to

S. Bressan, J. Küng, and R. Wagner (Eds.): DEXA 2006, LNCS 4080, pp. 883–893, 2006.

anonymize all tuples of identifying attributes in the table to achieve the *k-anonymity* objective: for any tuple of identifying attributes, there are at least *k-1* other tuples same to it. But such a statically predefined table-level k value mechanism is not always suitable for some microdata publication applications.

Example 1. In a public Job-Hunting database, individual data are handled with current *k-anonymity* technologies before publication for preventing individual re-identification. As the application required, it is more reasonable for individuals to define the re-identification levels (i.e. the k values) on their data. Lets take Table 1 (the original microdata) as an instance. Suppose $< BirthDate, Sex, Zipcode >$ is the identifying attribute set and *Disease* is the sensitive attribute indicating individual disease history. Ideally, an individual with index 2 may set k to 1 since she is always healthy (i.e. her *Disease* value is "No") and she hopes anybody know it, while another with index 7 may define k as large as possible since he has AIDS history and he thinks it can influence his obtaining employment. Unfortunately, current *k-anonymity* models cannot satisfy this requirement of setting different k values as individuals required.

Table 1. A table of health data in the Job-Hunting database

	BirthDate	Sex	Zipcode	Disease
1	11-12-39	F	13068	Flu
2	11-02-39	F	13068	No
3	08-24-57	F	14092	B. Cancer
4	08-02-57	M	13053	Stoke
5	08-02-42	M	13053	Stoke
6	11-22-42	M	13053	Flu
7	07-25-42	M	13053	AIDS

Table 2. The derived *2-anonymous*, *2-diverse* table of Table 1

	BirthDate	Sex	Zipcode	Disease
1	11-*-39	F	13068	Flu
2	11-*-39	F	13068	No
3	08-*-57	*	1****	B.Cancer
4	08-*-57	*	1****	Stoke
5	*-*-42	M	13053	Stoke
6	*-*-42	M	13053	Flu
7	*-*-42	M	13053	AIDS

Furthermore, privacy attacks may exist in a *k-anonymized* dataset when there is little diversity for those sensitive attribute clusters [12], such as an extreme situation, k tuples of same identifying attributes values map to a sensitive attribute cluster with just one value element, which indicates an individual who satisfies the identifying attributes values can be guessed mapping to the exact sensitive attribute value with 100% probability by attackers. The *ℓ-diversity* mechanism is proposed as an extended mechanism of *k-anonymity* to prevent such a situation through explicitly requiring each sensitive attribute cluster (i.e. q^**-block* in [12]) contains at least ℓ well-represented value elements [12]. Whether a cluster is *ℓ-diverse* is judged as whether its entropy is enough large. The entropy on a cluster just describes the difference degree of elements inside, but unable to reflect the factual high-probability risk of inferring a value element in a cluster caused by existed attribute or value associations in the table.

Example 2. By using *2-diversity* on Table 1 while k is 2, we can get the derived table for publication (Table 2). In the table, each tuple of <BirthDate,

Sex, Zipcode> maps to at least 2 *Disease* values. For instance, <08-*-57, *, 1****> maps to the 2-size cluster {B.Cancer, Stoke} (here * denotes a suppression value). Since it is well-known that the probability of Breast Cancer (B.Cancer) on female is much higher than that on male, which can be seen as a value association between Sex and Disease, it can be inferred from Table 2 with factual high probability that a female (male, respcctively) born in August of 1957 (i.e. satisfying 08-*-57) had B.Cancer (Stoke, respectively).

Beside, in Table 2, if the value domain of BirthDate is known to the attacker, the probability of inferring the exact value from 08-*-57 is increased to $\frac{1}{2}$ but not $\frac{1}{30}$, since there are just 2 values in the domain satisfying 08-*-57. As it is unreasonable to suppose the attacker has no such prior knowledge, the problem that how to prevent this kind of inference attacks is still open in current *k-anonymity* research.

We propose the *(k, ℓ)-anonymity* model to support the individual-defined (*k*, ℓ) mechanism for more flexible individual data anonymization, where *k* indicates the anonymization level of an identifying attribute tuple and ℓ indicates the diversity level of a sensitive attribute cluster. As later observed, this model can prevent the above inference violations caused by some prior knowledge.

Its main advantages include, (1) individual has rights to define the *k* and ℓ values for his/her personal data, i.e. for the ith record in the derived microdata, there are k_i tuples of same anonymized identifying attributes values mapping to the sensitive attribute value cluster of ℓ_i size ($\ell_i \leq k_i$); (2) value associations are modelled in the anonymization process to remove the factual high-probability inference violations; (3) the value domains of identifying attributes are supposed known publicly, which make the inference prevention more robust than most current models. Overall, the main contribution of this paper is the *(k, ℓ)-anonymity* model, together with the algorithm that describes the detail process of applying the model on an original microdata to derive the anonymized microdata for publication.

The rest of this paper is organized as follows: Section 2 defines some concepts and notations for discussion convenience later on. Section 3 and Section 4 propose our *(k, ℓ)-anonymity* model and its implementation algorithm. Section 5 gives an application scenario describing how to take the algorithm on a table for publishing without individual re-identification violations. Section 6 discusses some related work on this topic. Finally, Section 7 gives a short conclusion for the paper and proposes the focuses of our future work.

2 Concepts and Notations

Suppose individual data are recorded in a relational table with m attributes and n records stored in database, mainly including identifying attributes and sensitive attributes (here we ignore the unique identity attributes and others). The schema of such a table in database refers to m-tuple $<A_1, A_2, \cdots, A_m>$, where A_i ($1 \leq i \leq m$) is an attribute, and the value domain of A_i is denoted as D_i including the values that may appear on A_i. An attribute is named as a *sensitive* attribute whose value for any particular individual must be kept secret from others. We take $\mathcal{SI}$ to denote the sensitive attribute set in the table. Beside, a record in a table is a set of m-tuple $<a_1, a_2, \cdots, a_m>$, where $a_i \in D_i$. We assume that each record refers to an individual, and a table instance is a set of records and just a subset of a larger population Ω. For convenience, we use table to stand for table instance in the paper.

Attribute association, $A_i, A_{i+1}, \cdots \rightarrow A_j, A_{j+1}, \cdots [p]$, indicates that any value of attribute tuple $<A_j, A_{j+1}, \cdots>$ can be correctly inferred with probability p by the value of attribute tuple $<A_i, A_{i+1}, \cdots>$. For example, the following attribute association holds: BirthDate → Age [100%], since for anybody, the age can be sure inferred when the birthdate (month-day-year) is known. Similar to attribute association, *value association* indicates that some special values of $<A_j, A_{j+1}, \cdots>$ can be correctly inferred with p by some values of $<A_i, A_{i+1}, \cdots>$. For example, the value association, Sex = M → Disease = B.Cancer [0%], indicates a male has very small probability (about 0%) to have B.Cancer. In this paper, we suppose attribute associations can be easily removed before anonymizing a table (through normalization). For instance, if BirthDate and Age coexist in a table, we simply remove the Age attribute without any information loss in effect, since it can be fully inferred by the BirthDate attribute.

Quasi-Identifier Attribute Set: In a table, a set of identifying attributes is called a *Quasi-Identifier attribute set* ($\mathcal{QI}$), if they can be joined with external information to uniquely re-identify at least one individual in Ω (with sufficiently high probability) [15,9,8].

Definition 1 (K-Anonymity). A table $\mathcal{T}$ satisfies k-anonymity if for every record t ($t \in \mathcal{T}$), there exist $k-1$ other records $ti_1, \cdots, ti_{k-1} \in \mathcal{T}$, such that $t[\mathcal{QI}_i] = ti_1[\mathcal{QI}_i] = \cdots = ti_{k-1}[\mathcal{QI}_i]$, where $t[\mathcal{QI}_i]$ denotes the projection of t onto the attributes in $\mathcal{QI}_i$, $\mathcal{QI}_i \in \mathcal{QI}$ (similar for $ti_j[\mathcal{QI}_i]$, $1 \leq j \leq k-1$).

The above k is predefined on the scale of the whole table. As we analyzed above, it is not always suitable for some applications. So we define the notion of k on a record for the individual-defined anonymization feature on $\mathcal{QI}$.

Definition 2 (K on Record). The k_i value on the ith record in a table refers to the size of the anonymized $\mathcal{QI}$ cluster mapping to the ith $\mathcal{SI}$ tuple.

Definition 3 (ℓ-Diversity). A table satisfies ℓ-diversity if any $\mathcal{SI}$ cluster mapping to a $\mathcal{QI}$ tuple includes at least ℓ completely different elements on $\mathcal{SI}$.

In this paper, we suppose $\mathcal{SI}$ in a table includes just one sensitive attribute. With it, the above definition is same to that in [12]. Similarly, we can define the notion of ℓ on a record for the individual-defined diversity feature on $\mathcal{SI}$.

Definition 4 (ℓ on Record). The ℓ_i value on the ith record in a table refers to the amount of different elements in the $\mathcal{SI}$ cluster mapping to the ith $\mathcal{QI}$ tuple.

For discussion convenience, we take $\mathcal{K}$Cluster and $\mathcal{L}$Cluster to denote the $\mathcal{QI}$ tuple cluster mapping to a $\mathcal{SI}$ tuple and the $\mathcal{SI}$ tuple cluster mapping to a $\mathcal{QI}$

tuple in an anonymized table. They on the ith record are denoted as $\mathcal{K}Cluster_i$ and $\mathcal{L}Cluster_i$, respectively. For example, in Table 2, $\mathcal{L}Cluster_1$ = {Flu, No}, $\mathcal{K}Cluster_1$ = {<11-*-39, F, 13068>}.

In this paper, we take data generalization approach to implement the *k-anonymization* process on an initial table, take $*$ to denote a suppression on the data for hiding some specific information. As above discussed, each attribute in a table has a value domain containing all values appeared in the table. Given a domain, it is possible to construct a more "general" domain in a variety of ways, such as the way in [15,18]. We use $<$ to denote *domain generalization relation*. For instance, on attribute Sex, the following domain generalization relation holds: $\{F, M\} <_\nu \{*\}$. Further, we use $<_\nu$ and $<_\nu^+$ to denote *direct* (explicit) and *indirect* (implicit) *value generalization relation*. The latter indicates a sequence of several direct generalization relations. For examples, 11-02-39 $<_\nu$ 11-*-39 refers to that 11-*-39 is a direct generalization of 11-02-39; An indirect relation 11-02-39 $<_\nu^+$ *-*-39 indicates 11-02-39 $<_\nu$ 11-*-39 and 11-*-39 $<_\nu$ *-*-39.

We endow the attacker with considerable power, even suppose the attacker can compute the value domain of each attribute and the corresponding value generalization hierarchies. Under this assumption, some inference problems may potentially exist. For example, it is meaningless to generalize 13053 to 1305* for Zipcode, since there is just one value in the domain on Table 1 satisfying 1305*. An attacker can infer 13053 from 1305* if the value domain is known. In another word, there is no specific information loss to the attacker on the above generalization relation. It is different from most anonymization cost metrics, since in them, generalization from 13053 to 1305* indicates the probability of inferring 13053 from 1305* is $\frac{1}{10}$ but not $\frac{1}{1}$ under our assumption. Formally, we define the notion of *anonymization degree* to express this idea.

Definition 5 (Anonymization Degree). Anonymization degree (AD) on a value generalization relation ($v_i <_\nu v_j$) in value domain D (i.e. $v_i \in D$) refers to the amount of values in D satisfying v_j, denoted as $AD(v_i <_\nu v_j)$.

For instances, on Zipcode of Table 1, $AD(13053 <_\nu 1305*) = 1$, $AD(13053 <_\nu^+ 130{*}{*}) = AD(13053 <_\nu^+ 13{*}{*}{*}) = 2$, $AD(13053 <_\nu^+ 1{*}{*}{*}{*}) = 3$. The anonymization degree of a $\mathcal{K}Cluster$ is the amount of $\mathcal{QI}$ tuples in the table satisfying the cluster. For example, the AD value on $\mathcal{K}Cluster$ {<08-*-57, *, 1****>} (in Table 2) is 2, since there are just 2 $\mathcal{QI}$ tuples in the Table 1 satisfying it: <08-24-57, F, 14092> and <08-02-57, M, 13053>.

With this definition, it is easy to ascertain the exact inference probability on a value generalization relation. For example, the exact probability of inferring 13053 from 1305* is $\frac{1}{1}$ but not $\frac{1}{10}$. Formally, we take $Pr(v_i <_\nu v_j)$ to denote the probability of correctly inferring v_i from v_j, the following holds:

$$Pr(v_i <_\nu v_j) = \frac{1}{AD(v_i <_\nu v_j)}. \tag{1}$$

Definition 6 (Diversity Degree). Diversity degree (DD) on a cluster is the amount of different elements in the cluster.

AD and *DD* are defined as the base for the *k-anonymous* and the *ℓ-diverse* feature on the $\mathcal{K}$*Cluster* and the $\mathcal{L}$*Cluster* on a record for implementing the following improved *k-anonymity* model, (*k*, *ℓ*)*-anonymity*.

3 (K, ℓ)-Anonymity Model

We propose (*k*, *ℓ*)*-anonymity* to support the individual-defined (*k*, *ℓ*) mechanism for more flexible individual data publication, as well as to achieve the more robust anti-inference ability on anonymized microdata.

In this model, (*k*, *ℓ*) is designed on the record level, in which k is defined by the individual as the anonymization level on $\mathcal{QI}$ of the record, ℓ is defined by the individual as the diversity level on $\mathcal{SI}$ of the record.

Definition 7. A table with n records satisfies (*k*, *ℓ*)*-anonymity*, *iff* $\forall i, (1 \leq i \leq n), k_i \times 2 - 1 \geq AD_i \geq k_i$ and $DD_i \geq \ell_i$ hold, where AD_i is the anonymization degree on $\mathcal{K}Cluster_i$, DD_i is the diversity degree on $\mathcal{L}Cluster_i$;

From the definition, it is obvious that the model is more flexible and has more strong expression ability. It can work as general *k-anonymity* models when setting all k_i to a constant k and all ℓ_i to 1; It can work as *ℓ-diversity* when setting all ℓ_i and k_i to a constant ℓ.

As a standard for the optimal or the most-approximate-optimal anonymization solution, a reasonable anonymization cost metric is indispensable. General anonymization cost metrics are based on either the amount of suppression cells or the generalization height or height ratio, such as the metrics in [1,13,18,2]. The former kind of metrics cannot really represent the precise anonymization loss. For instance, with it, there is no difference between 08-02-57 $<_\nu$ 08-∗-57 on *BirthDate* and F $<_\nu$ ∗ on *Sex*. In fact, the specific information loss on the latter relation is more severe than that on the former, since all values in *Sex* domain satisfy ∗ and just 2 *BirthDate* values satisfy 08-∗-57 in Table 1. Metrics on generalization height or height ratio need generalization hierarchy structures on $\mathcal{QI}$, which cannot be satisfied for some attributes, such as attributes for partition illustrated in [11,7,8]. In our model, the anonymization cost metric is based on the notion of *anonymization coverage ratio*.

Definition 8 (Anonymization Coverage Ratio). Anonymization coverage ratio (*ACR*) on a value generalization relation $v_i <_\nu v_j$ in value domain D is the ratio of its anonymization degree to the size of D, denoted as below:

$$ACR(v_i <_\nu v_j) = \frac{AD(v_i <_\nu v_j)}{|D|}. \tag{2}$$

The anonymization cost metric (*Cost*) on an anonymized table with n records is the sum of that on each record ($Cost(i)$), which is computed as below:

$$Cost = \sum_{i=1}^{n} Cost(i) = \sum_{i=1}^{n} \sum_{j=1}^{|\mathcal{QI}|} ACR_{ij} \times c_j, \quad ACR_{ij} = \frac{AD_{ij}}{|D_j|}, \tag{3}$$

where AD_{ij} indicates the anonymization degree on the jth attribute in $\mathcal{QI}$ of the ith record, D_j is the value domain of the jth attribute in $\mathcal{QI}$, c_j is a factor indicating a weighted value on the jth attribute in $\mathcal{QI}$.

Comparing to other metrics, *Cost* and $Cost(i)$ (on the ith record) have two advantages: (1) They represent the real anonymization loss even if the value domains of $\mathcal{QI}$ are known; (2) They can express some anonymization biases with the factor c on each attribute in $\mathcal{QI}$, which is useable in special situations.

4 (K, ℓ)-Anonymity Algorithm

To implement the *(k, ℓ)-anonymity* model on an original table with the above *Cost* metric, we propose the *(k, ℓ)-anonymity* algorithm with graph representation. Firstly, we define some prerequisites for the algorithm as below (for the ith record in the original table $\mathcal{T}$ with n records):

$$\sum_{j=1}^{n} Count(j) \geq k_i \geq \ell_i > 1; \ |D'_{\mathcal{SI}}| \geq \ell_i. \tag{4}$$

Where $Count(j) = 1$, iff $k_j > 1$, or $Count(j) = 0$; $D'_{\mathcal{SI}}$ is the set of $\mathcal{SI}$ tuples satisfying $k_j > 1$ $(1 \leq j \leq n)$; $k_i = 1$ indicates the record should not be anonymized when publishing. $\ell_i = 1$ is meaningless except when $k_i = 1$, since it results in an obvious inference attack.

The algorithm takes graph representation to compute *Cost* when anonymizing table $\mathcal{T}$ and achieve the optimal or the most-approximate-optimal derived table $\mathcal{T}'$. The core handling process of the algorithm is described as follows:

(1) **Creating clusters**: For the ith record, build a minimal-cost k_i-size $\mathcal{K}Cluster_i$ with the *Cost* metric satisfying that the corresponding $\mathcal{L}Cluster_i$ is ℓ_i*-diverse*;
(2) **Combining clusters**: If exist a record is included in two or more $\mathcal{K}Clusters$, combine them as a unified one;
(3) **Decomposing clusters**: Decompose a $\mathcal{K}Cluster$ into two minimal-cost clusters with the *Cost* metric if at least one of the following conditions holds:
- exist the ith and j^{th} $\mathcal{QI}$ tuples in $\mathcal{K}Cluster$ satisfy $k_i \geq k_j \times 2$;
- exist the ith $\mathcal{QI}$ tuple in $\mathcal{K}Cluster$ satisfies $k_i \times 2 \leq |\mathcal{K}Cluster|$.

In detail, for the first phase, $\mathcal{K}Cluster_i$ should be k_i-size, which infers to the anonymization degree on the ith record is at lease k_i and the diversity degree on the ith record is at least ℓ_i, which is the necessary condition for *(k, ℓ)-anonymity* on the ith record. Beside, to compute the anonymization degree and diversity degree on a record should consider the influence by relative value associations since the inference violations caused by them should be removed when publication.

Another, $\mathcal{L}Cluster_i$ contains at least ℓ_i different elements, which equals to satisfying the simple kind of ℓ*-diversity* requirement for the anonymization on the record. Even, such a requirement can be replaced by the entropy ℓ*-diversity* requirement in [12] for more reasonable diversity measurement on $\mathcal{L}Clusters$.

The above algorithm is sound and complete for microdata publication on a relational table. As the above analysis, the *(k, ℓ)-anonymity* requirement can be satisfied through the three phases. Furthermore, if there are n' clusters created by Phase (1), then Phase (2) will be finished in at most n' times of combining these clusters, and create n'' new clusters. Finally Phase (3) will be ended within at most $n'' \times log_2(\frac{n}{n''})$ times of decomposing these clusters.

Beside, its time complexity is $\mathcal{O}(n^2)$, mainly on the first phase for computing *Cost* among records and creating the minimal-cost $\mathcal{K}$*Cluster* for each record.

5 Application Scenario

As an illustration, we take the above algorithm to anonymize Table 1. Suppose the k and ℓ values for each record in Table 1 are predefined as below:

Record	1	2	3	4	5	6	7
k	2	1	3	2	2	2	3
ℓ	2	1	2	2	3	2	3

Suppose the factor c for all attributes in $\mathcal{QI}$ are same to 1. We take the *Cost* metric to create the initial clusters as presented in Phase (1) below. Based on it, we execute the combining cluster procedure and get the temporary result in Phase (2) below. Then we can achieve the result listed in Phase (3) below through decomposing some clusters. Finally, the anonymized table (Table 3) for publishing derived from Table 1 can be achieved as below.

Graph 1. The phases' results by the algorithm on Table 1

	Cluster	k	ℓ
1	{1,4}	2	2
2	{2}	1	1
3	{1,3,4}	3	3
4	{4,6}	2	2
5	{5,6,7}	3	3
6	{5,6}	2	2
7	{5,6,7}	3	3

Phase (1)

$\Longrightarrow$

Cluster	k	ℓ
{1,3,4,5,6,7}	6	4
{2}	1	1

Phase (2)

$\Longrightarrow$

Cluster	k	ℓ
{1,3,4}	3	3(2)
{2}	1	1
{5,6,7}	3	3

Phase (3)

Table 3. The derived table with our (k, ℓ)-anonymity model

	BirthDate	Sex	Zipcode	Disease
1	*-*-*	*	1****	Flu
2	11-02-39	F	13068	No
3	*-*-*	*	1****	B.Cancer
4	*-*-*	*	1****	Stoke
5	*-*-42	M	13053	Stoke
6	*-*-42	M	13053	Flu
7	*-*-42	M	13053	AIDS

The *Cost* on Table 3 is approximately computed as 14. It should be noted that ℓ value on cluster $\{1, 3, 4\}$ in Phase 3 is 2 but not 3 because of the value association relation: Sex = M $\rightarrow$ Disease = B.Cancer [0%].

6 Related Work

As well as data suppression [15] and data swapping [3,4], data generalization is a data preprocess approach for microdata publication, which involves replacing (or recording) a value with a less specific but semantically consistent value [15]. Comparing to other technologies, it can release data while ensure individual privacy information and maintaining data integrity to the extent [2].

K-anonymity is proposed as a privacy-preserving microdata publication model, in which data generalization technology is used to anonymize data for supporting more usage convenience as well as preventing privacy disclosure instead of simple data suppression [15,18]. It is proved that to make a table satisfy *k-anonymity* is a $\mathcal{NP}$-*hard* problem even when the attribute values are ternary [13,2]. As an alternative approach, some approximation algorithms are proposed, such as an algorithm in [2] can achieve $\mathcal{O}(k)$-*approximation*. It is based on graph representation, consisting of two procedures: (1) producing a forest with trees of size at least k, and (2) decomposing large components in the forest into smaller ones. Both two procedures need the time complexity $\mathcal{O}(kn^2)$.

Beside, anonymization cost metric mechanisms in current *k-anonymity* models can be classified into four types [10]: (a) on generalization hierarchy height or height ratio; (b) on the amount of suppression cells or distance among tuples; (c) on partition, and (d) on entropy. In detail, Sweeney's *Prec* calculation [18] and Aggarwal's *Cost* computation [2] are in type (a), which need generalization hierarchy on each attribute in $\mathcal{QI}$. Aggarwal's *Hamming distance* computation [1] and Meyerson's *Diameter* calculation [13] are in type (b). Lyengar's *CM* formula [11], Bayardo's *DM, CM* formulas [7], and Lefevre's C_{AVG} formula [8] are in type (c). Sweeney's *Anonymity level* with *bin* size [17], Machanavajjhala's *Entropy* calculation [12], and Fung's *Entropy* formula [5] are in type (d).

Furthermore, to allow individual to define the protection level on the data is a feature for many privacy protection models, including Fine-Grained Access Control (FGAC) [14], Multi-Level Relational Data Model (MLR) [6,16], Purpose-Based Access Control [21], etc. The Micro-View mechanism is to take data generalization to balance the confidentiality and availability of privacy data w.r.t. the predefined type and privacy level on them [20]. One common problem for these mechanisms is the high cost for managing such record-level or element-level privacy labels.

7 Conclusion

In conclusion, we propose the requirement for individual-defined (k, ℓ) mechanism for more general and flexible *k-anonymity* application, and analyze some privacy inference violations existed in current *k-anonymity* models. Motivated by them, we define the (k, ℓ)-anonymity model, which is an improved *k-anonymity* model supporting the individual-defined (k, ℓ) mechanism and preventing some inference violations in the derived table caused by attribute or value associations and the prior knowledge on value domains of identifying attributes. In future, we will fully study the inference violations among multiple derived tables. Another, we will continue focusing on anti-inference k-anonymity modelling.

References

1. Gagan Aggarwal, Tomas Feder, and etc. Anonymizing tables for privacy protection. *Available: http://theory.standford.edu/ rajeev/privacy.html*, 2004.
2. Gagan Aggarwal, Tomas Feder, and etc. Approximation algorithms for k-anonymity. *Journal of Privacy Technology*, Nov. 2005.
3. Tore Dalenius and Steven Reiss. Data swapping: A technique for disclosure control. *Journal of Statistical Planning and Inference*, 6, 1982.
4. G.T. Duncan and S.E.Feinberg. Obtaining information while preserving privacy: A markov perturbation method for tabular data. *Joint Statistical Meetings*, 1997.
5. Benjamin C.M. Fung, Ke Wang, and Philip S.Yu. Top-down specialization for information and privacy protection. *In Proc. of ICDE'06*, 2006.
6. Sushil Jajodia and Ravi S. Sandhu. Toward a multilevel secure relational data model. *In Proc. of SIGMOD'91*, pages 50–59, 1991.
7. Reberto J.Bayardo and Rakesh Agrawal. Data privacy through optimal k-anonymization. *In Proc. of ICDE'05*, 2005.
8. Kristen LeFevre, David J.DeWitt, and Raghu Ramakrishnan. Multidimensional k-anonymity. *Technical Report, Available: www.cs.wisc.edu/techreports/2005/*.
9. Kristen Lefevre, David J.DeWitt, and Raghu Ramakrishnan. Incognito: Efficient full-domain k-anonymity. *In Proc. of SIGMOD'05*, 2005.
10. Zude Li, Guoqiang Zhan, and Xiaojun Ye. Towards a more reasonable generalization cost metric. *In Proc. of BNCOD'06*, 2006.
11. Vijay S. Lyengar. Transforming data to satisfying privacy constraints. *In Proc. of SIGKDD'02*, 2002.
12. Ashwin Machanavajjhala, Johannes Gehrke, and Daniel Kifer. ℓ-diversity: Privacy beyond k-anonymity. *In Proc. of ICDE'06*, 2006.
13. Adam Meyerson and Ryan Williams. On the complexity of optimal k-anonymity. *In Proc. of PODS'04, France*, 2004.
14. Shariq Rizvi, Alberto Mendelzon, S.Sudarshan, and Prasan Roy. Extending query rewriting techniques for fine-grained access control. *SIDMOD'04, Jun.*, 2004.
15. Pierangela Samarati and Latanya Sweeney. Protecting privacy when disclosing information: K-anonymity and its enforcement through generalization and suppression. *Technical Report, SRI Computer Science Lab.*, 1998.
16. Ravi Sandhu and Fang Chen. The multilevel relational (mlr) data model. *ACM Transactions on Information and System Security*, 1(1):93–132, 1998.
17. Latanya Sweeney. Guaranteeing anonymity when sharing medical data, the datafly system. *Journal of the American Medical Informatics Association*, 1997.
18. Latanya Sweeney. Achieving k-anonymity privacy protection using generalization and suppression. *In International Journal on Uncertainty, Fuzziness and Knowledge-based Systems*, 10(5):571–588, 2002.

19. Latanya Sweeney. K-anonymity: A model for protecting privacy. *International Journal on Uncertainty, Fuzziness and Knowledge-based Systems*, 10(5):557–570, 2002.
20. Ji won Byun and Elisa Bertino. Vison paper: Micro-views, or how to protect privacy while enhancing data usability. *SIGMOD Record, March*, 2005.
21. Ji won Byun, Elisa Bertino, and Ninghui Li. Purpose-based access control of complex data for privacy protection. *In Proc. of SACMAT'05, Stockholm, Sweden*, Jun. 2005.

Analysis of the Power Consumption of Secure Communication in Wireless Networks

Kihong Kim[1], Jinkeun Hong[2], and Jongin Lim[3]

[1] National Security Research Institute,
161, Gajeong-dong, Yuseong-ku, Daejeon, 305-350, South Korea
hong0612@hanmir.com

[2] Division of Information & Communication Engineering, Baekseok University,
115, Anseo-dong, Cheonan-si, Chungnam, 330-740, South Korea
jkhong@bu.ac.kr

[3] Graduate School of Information Security /
Center for Information Security Technologies, Korea University,
1, 5-ka, Anam-dong, Sungbuk-ku, Seoul, 136-701, South Korea
jilim@korea.ac.kr

Abstract. With the growth of the Internet, communication and network security have been the focus of much attention. In addition, deployment of resource intensive security protocols in battery-powered mobile devices has raised power consumption to a significant design basis of network design. In this paper, we propose a power-efficient secure communication restart mechanism for a wireless network and analyze the power consumed while restarting a secure communication. An experimental test bed was developed to inspect the proposed mechanism and to evaluate it in terms of power consumption relative to that of conventional secure communication restart mechanisms. Using our enhanced mechanism, we were able to reduce the power consumed during a secure communication restart by up to 60% compared with conventional restart mechanisms.

1 Introduction

Secure communication over public wired and wireless networks demands end-to-end secure connections to ensure data confidentiality, integrity, and authentication. That is, secure communication is achieved by employing security mechanisms at various layers of the network protocol such as a secure socket layer (SSL) [1], Internet security protocol (IPSec) [2], transport layer security (TLS) [3], and wireless transport layer security (WTLS) [4]. Security mechanisms used to provide secure communication employ handshaking schemes for establishing secure communication and secure data transfer schemes for secure data transmission/reception.

Such security mechanisms consume power while establishing and performing the secure communication. Power consumed by secure communication on battery-powered mobile devices is very important. In addition, deployment of resource intensive security mechanisms in mobile computing and communication

S. Bressan, J. Küng, and R. Wagner (Eds.): DEXA 2006, LNCS 4080, pp. 894–903, 2006.

devices has raised power consumption characteristics to a significant design basis of network design. There are two main sources of power consumption during a secure communication: cryptographic loads and data transmission/reception. The former is the cryptographic computations used to establish the secure communication and to support encryption and authentication during secure communication, while the latter is the handshaking message exchange during secure communication establishment and secure data transfer during secure communication [5].

There have been several important studies in the field of secure wired and wireless communication power consumption. A framework for analyzing the power consumption of cryptographic and security protocols was set forth by N. R. Potlapally et al. [6]. The study in [7] analyzed the various sources of power consumption for WTLS and IPSec and proposed techniques to minimize the power consumption. Meanwhile, mutual authentication protocols for a low-power network environment were proposed in [8] [9]. Power management techniques for mobile communication have been devised by R. Kravets and P. Krishnan [10]. H. Woesner et al. presented power saving mechanisms in emerging standards for wireless LAN [11]. S. Singh and C. S. Raghavendra proposed a power aware multi-access protocol with signaling for ad-hoc networks [12].

In terms of efficiency, the performance considerations for a secure wireless environment, such as mobility, bandwidth, and bit error rate (BER), are very significant. Of particular significance for a secure connection point is the power efficiency of the secure communication restart for fast restart of secure communication. In this paper, a power-efficient secure communication restart mechanism for application in a secure wireless network is presented and its power consumption while restarting a secure communication is analyzed. Our work differs from previous works in that it concentrates on power consumption characteristics of a secure communication restart. An experimental test bed was developed to inspect the proposed restart mechanism and to evaluate it against the power consumption of conventional restart mechanisms. Using our enhanced mechanism, we were able to reduce the power consumed during a secure communication restart by up to 60% compared with conventional restart mechanisms.

The remainder of this paper is organized as follows. Section 2 describes the handshaking process to establish secure communication using WTLS. Section 3 provides details of the conventional and proposed secure communication restart mechanisms. Section 4 describes the experimental test bed used in this paper to analyze power consumption while restarting a secure communication and presents the results of power consumption according to each restart mechanism. Finally, section 5 summarizes the results of this paper.

2 Handshaking Process Using WTLS

The wireless application protocol (WAP) shown in Fig. 1 is a protocol suite created for mobile devices such as mobile phones and other mobile terminals [4]. The WTLS protocol is the security layer of the WAP. It provides privacy, authentication, and integrity in the WAP.

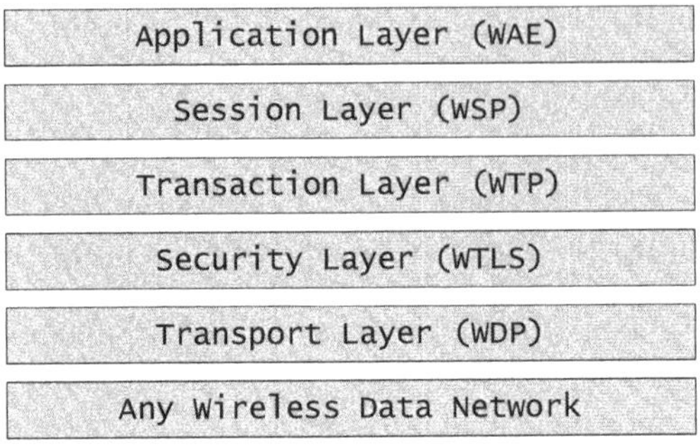

Fig. 1. WAP architecture

The WTLS determines the session key handshaking mechanism for secure services and transactions in secure wireless networks, and consists of the following phases: the handshaking phase, the change cipher spec phase, and the record protocol phase (RP) [13] [14]. In the handshaking phase, all the key techniques and security parameters, such as protocol version, cryptographic algorithms, and method of authentication, are established between the client and the server. That is, the handshaking phase is used to negotiate the security parameters between the client and the server. After the key handshaking phase is complete, the change cipher spec phase is initiated. The change cipher spec phase handles the changing of the cipher. Through the change cipher spec phase, both the client and the server send the finished message, which is protected by a RP data unit that is applied by the negotiated security suites [15] [16]. The RP phase is a layer protocol phase that accepts raw data to be transmitted from the upper layer protocols. The RP compresses and encrypts the data to ensure data integrity and authentication. It is also responsible for decrypting and decompressing data it receives and verifying that the data has not been altered. Fig. 2 summarizes the handshaking process used by the WTLS for secure communication establishment.

3 Secure Communication Restart Mechanisms

3.1 Conventional Mechanisms to Restart Secure Communication

After completion of the handshaking process shown in Fig. 2, a secure communication between the client and server is established. However, data frame loss occurs because of bit slips, channel loss, reflection, and diffraction in the communication channel. If a data frame is lost, the output of the decryptor will be unintelligible for the receiver and restart of lost connections will be required. In order to restart secure communication after data frame loss in the communication channel is detected, a restart mechanism is used. For the sake of performance, the restart mechanism should be as fast as possible. The aim of the secure communication restart is to ensure that the encryptor and decryptor

Fig. 2. Handshaking message exchange during secure communication establishment

have the same new internal state at a certain time. An internal state that is different from all previous communications has to be chosen so as to prevent the reuse of session keys or IVs [17, 18, 19, 20].

In order to overcome the problems caused by these data frame losses, restart mechanisms for secure communication have been suggested. Such mechanisms are based on one of two methods: 1) premaster secret regeneration and retransmission, which results in a new master secret and new key blocks; or 2) random value regeneration and retransmission, in which random value is only used to change the key block in each secure communication restart.

Fig. 3 shows a restart mechanism using premaster secret regeneration and retransmission. In this mechanism, a new premaster secret is generated and sent in each secure communication restart, and thus it results in the generation of a new master secret and new key block. Therefore, new session keys and new IVs are generated for every communication restart. However, since a new premaster secret is generated and sent in each secure communication restart, this mechanism has disadvantages such as a large cryptographic computation load and a considerable time delay including channel delay.

This mechanism is based on the following procedure. First, secure communication between the client and server is performed for a certain time Δt, and then data frame loss occurs. After the server realizes the data frame loss, it requests a new premaster secret for a secure communication restart. The client generates a new premaster secret and sends $E_{KUS}[Premaster\ Secret]$ encrypted with the server's public key to the server. The client then generates a new master secret

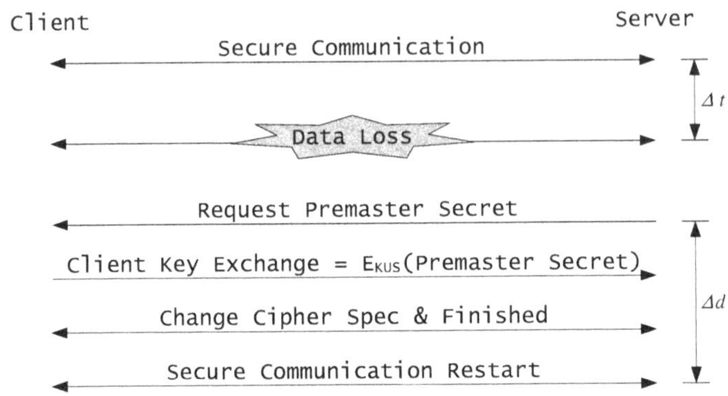

Fig. 3. Message exchange during restart mechanism using premaster secret

using the new premaster secret and the original random value cached in the initial hello message stage, and generates a new key block using the new master secret and original random value. The generated key block is hashed into a sequence of secure bytes, which are assigned to the message authentication code (MAC) keys, session keys, and IVs. Thus, new session keys and IVs are generated.

$$New\ MS = PRF(New\ PS, "MS", Original\ CR + Original\ SR) \quad (1)$$

$$New\ KB = PRF(New\ MS, "KE", Original\ CR + Original\ SR) \quad (2)$$

Here, MS is the master secret, KB is the key block, PS is the premaster secret, CR is the client random value, SR is the server random value, PRF is the pseudo random function, and KE is the key expansion. The client then sends the finished message to the server. The server generates a new master secret and a new key block, and also sends the finished message to the client. After the session restart time Δd, secure communication is restarted.

The restart mechanism using a random value is shown in Fig. 4. In this mechanism, a new random value is generated and sent in each communication restart, which results in the generation of a new key block in each communication restart. As with premaster secret regeneration and retransmission, this mechanism also suffers from large cryptographic load and time delay.

Secure communication is performed for a certain time Δt, and then data frame loss occurs. After realizing the data frame loss, the server requests a new random value for communication restart. The client generates a new random value and includes it in a hello message. After the server receives the hello message, it sends its own hello message that includes its new random value. The server also generates a new key block using the new random value and cached original master secret, and then generates new session keys and new IVs. Thus, a restarted secure communication will use the same master secret as the previous one. Note that, although the same master secret is used, new random values

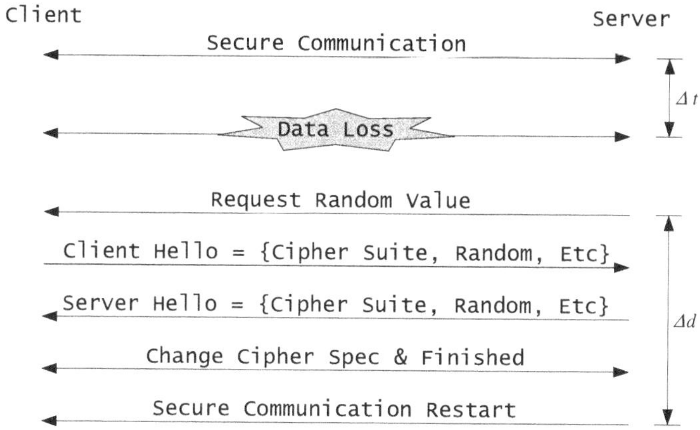

Fig. 4. Message exchange during restart mechanism using random value

are exchanged in the secure communication restart. These new random values are taken into account in the new key block generation, which means that each secure connection starts up with different key materials: new session keys and new IVs.

$$New\ KB = PRF(Original\ MS, "KE", New\ CR + New\ SR) \quad (3)$$

Finally, the server sends the finished message to the client. The server generates a new key block, resulting in new session keys and new IVs, and it also sends the finished message to the client. After the session restart time Δd, secure communication is restarted.

3.2 Proposed Mechanism to Restart Secure Communication

In order to solve the problems inherent in conventional restart mechanisms and to reinitiate secure communication such that it is much faster than in the conventional mechanisms, we propose a power-efficient secure communication restart mechanism that uses an IV count value.

Fig. 5 shows the proposed restart mechanism, in which a count value of IV is sent to generate the new IVs in each each secure communication. After detecting the data frame loss during secure communication, the server requests a new count value of IV for communication restart. The client sends a new count value IV and generates new IVs using the count value. That is, the count value is used to generate new message protection materials, which means that each secure communication starts up with different IVs. Therefore, a restarted communication will use the same session keys as the previous secure communication. Note that, although the same session keys are used, new IVs are used in the secure communication restart. The client sends the change cipher spec and finished message to the server. The server generates new IVs using the received count

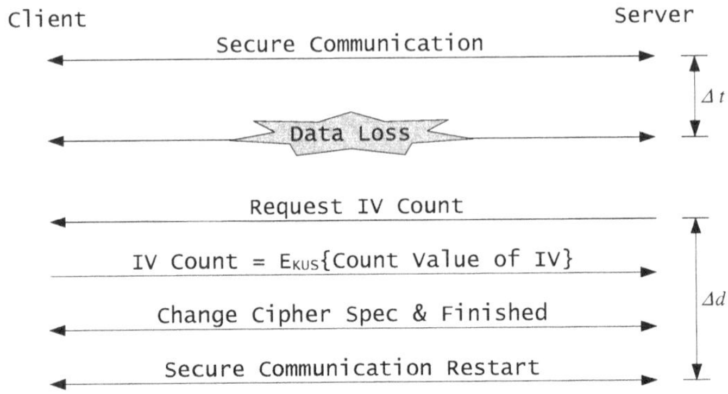

Fig. 5. Message exchange during restart mechanism using IV count

value, and then sends the change cipher spec and finished message to the client. The client and server finally have the new IVs after communication restart time Δd, as represented by Eq. (4).

$$IV_C = IV_0 + \nu, \quad 1 \leq \nu \leq 2^{IV\ Size} - 1 \tag{4}$$

Here, IV_C is the value of IV in each communication and IV_0 represents the value of the original IV. ν is a count value in each communication restart and is increased by a value of one for every communication restart.

4 Performance Analysis

In this paper, in order to verify the performance of the proposed mechanism, we compared and analyzed the power consumption by our proposed mechanism with that of conventional mechanisms.

We computed the total power consumed during a secure communication restart by each mechanism. The test bed system consists of a 32bits 80MHz MPC860 microprocessor with a 16kbyte instruction cache and an 8kbyte data cache, 4Mbyte flash ROM, 32Mbyte SDRAM, and 2Mbyte SRAM. We measure the current drawn by the restart process executing on the test bed using a Tektronix current probe and a Tektronix oscilloscope. Voltage was held constant at 3.3V, the nominal operating voltage of the test bed system. In order to ensure consistency and accuracy of our results, we averaged each of the results over several iterations for each mechanism. We assume that data transmission/reception rates are identical at 14.4kbps. The power consumption values correspond to the client.

Table 1 shows a comparison of the power consumption according to each mechanism for secure communication restart. Here, T1 is the transmission bits at each 1 iteration, TC1 is the transmission bits at each 1 iteration with 50% redundancy channel coding, and TC3 is the transmission bits at 3 iterations with 50% redundancy channel coding. When measuring the power consumption

Table 1. Power consumption to restart secure communication at 14.4kbps

Mechanism		Power Consumption (mW)
Premaster Secret	T1	41mW
	TC1	84mW
	TC3	252mW
Random Value	T1	78mW
	TC1	157mW
	TC3	462mW
Proposed	T1	30mW
	TC1	50mW
	TC3	186mW

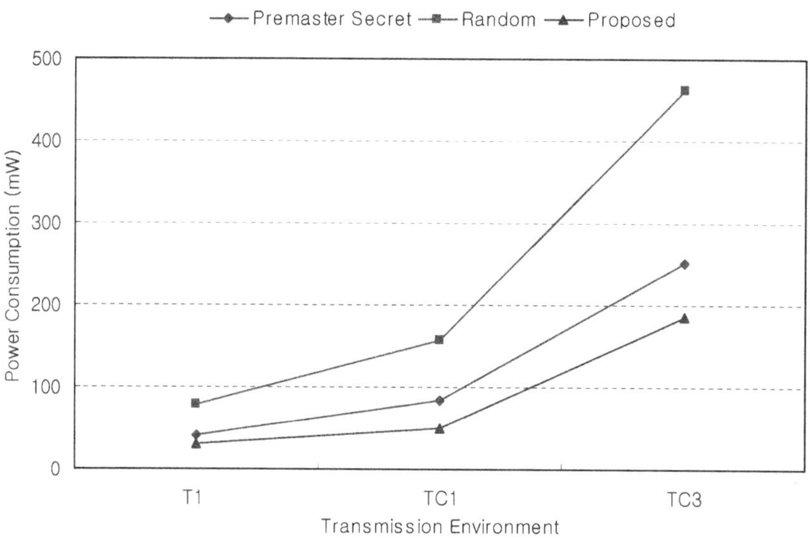

Fig. 6. Power consumption according to the transmission environment

in the TC3 environment, the power consumption in each mechanism is provided: 252mW in the mechanism using a premaster secret, 462mW in the mechanism using a random value, and 186mW in the proposed mechanism. Thus, the proposed mechanism reduces power consumption by more than 26% in comparison with the mechanism using a premaster secret, and by about 60% when compared with the mechanism using a random value.

Fig. 6 illustrates the power consumption outline in Table 1, demonstrating that the power consumption from the proposed mechanism is smaller than that from the conventional mechanisms.

5 Conclusions

Wireless networks are inherently unreliable and discontinuous, resulting in frequent data frame losses. If a data frame is lost, the output of the decryptor will be unintelligible for the receiver and restart of lost connections will be required. In order to restart secure communication after data frame loss in a communication channel is detected, a restart mechanism is used. Therefore, secure communication restart and transfer recovery, together with fast secret materials generation, are critical with respect to power efficiency of mobile devices.

In this paper, we presented a power-efficient secure communication restart mechanism for application in a secure wireless network and evaluated it against the power consumption of conventional restart mechanisms. An experimental test bed was developed to inspect the conventional and proposed restart mechanisms and to analyze the power consumption required to restart a secure communication for each mechanism. Using our enhanced mechanism, we were able to reduce the power consumed during a secure communication restart by up to 60% compared with conventional restart mechanisms. Therefore, the proposed mechanism provides a power-efficient restart of secure communication, while reducing the consumed power in a WTLS protocol environment. This work can be extended to many wired and wireless network protocols including TLS, SSL, and an aeronautical mobile environment.

References

1. SSL 3.0 Specification. http://home.netscape.com/eng/ssl3/3-spec.htm.
2. IPSec Working Gruop. http://www.ietf.org/html.charters/ipsec-charter.html.
3. TLS Working Group. http://www.ietf.org/html.charters/tls-charter.html.
4. WAP Froum. Wireless Transport Layer Security Spec. http://www.wapforum.org.
5. R. Karri and P. Mishra. Optimizing the Energy Consumed by Secure Wireless Sessions - Wireless Transport Layer Security. *Mobile Networks and Applications*, Kluwer Academic Publishers, pp.177-185, 2003.
6. N. R. Potlapally, S. Ravi, A. Raghunathan, and N. K. Jha. A Study of the Energy Consumption Characteristics of Cryptographic Algorithms and Security Protocols. *IEEE Transaction on Mobile Computing*, Vol. 5, No. 2, pp.128-143, 2005.
7. R. Karri and P. Mishra. Minimizing Energy Consumption of Secure Wireless Session with QoS Constraints. *ICC'02*, pp.2053-2057, 2002.
8. M. Jakobsson and D. Pointcheval. Mutual Authentication for Low-Powered Mobile Devices. *Financial Cryptogaphy*, pp.178-195, 2001.
9. D. S. Wong and A. H. Chan. Mutual Authentication and Key Exchange for Low Power Wireless Communications. *MILCOM'02*, pp.39-43, 2002.
10. R. Kravets and R. Krishnan. Power Management Techniques for Mobile Communication. *MobiCom'99*, 1999.
11. H. Woesner, J. P. Ebert, M. Schlager, and A. Wolisz. Power Saving Mechanisms in Emerging Standards for Wireless LANs: The MAC-Level Prospective. *IEEE Personal Communication System*, pp.40-48, 1998.
12. S. Singh and C. S. Raghavendra. PAMAS-Power Aware Multi-Access Protocol with Signaling for Ad-hoc Networks. *Computer Communications Review*, 1998.

13. P. Mikal. WTLS : The Good and Bad of WAP Security. http://www.advisor.com/Articles.nsf/aid/MIKP0001, 2001.
14. M. J. Saarinen. Attacks against the WAP WTLS Protocols. http://www.freeprotocols.org/harmOfWap/wtls.pdf, 1999.
15. Mohmad Badra et al.. A New Secure Session Exchange Key Protocol for Wireless Communication. *IEEE PIMRC'03*, 2003.
16. Mohammad Ghulam Rahman and Hideki Imai. Security in Wireless Communications. *Wireless Personal Communications*, No. 22, Kluwer Academic Publishers, 2002.
17. J. Daemen, R. Govaerts, and J. Vandewalle. Resynchronization Weakness in Synchronous Stream Ciphers. *EUROCRYPT'93*, 1993.
18. R. K. Nichols and P. C. Lekks. *Wireless Security - Models, Threats, and Solutions*, McGraw-Hill Telecom, 2002.
19. E. Amoroso. *Fundamentals of Computer Security Technology*, PTR Prentice Hall, Englewood Cliffs, New Jersey, 1993.
20. F. Armknecht, J. Lano, and B. Preneel. Extending the Resynchronization Attack. *SAC'04*, 2004.

Implementing Authorization Delegations Using Graph

Chun Ruan[1] and Vijay Varadharajan[1,2]

[1] School of Computing and Information Technology
University of Western Sydney, Penrith South DC, NSW 1797 Australia
{chun, vijay}@cit.uws.edu.au
[2] Department of Computing
Macquarie University, North Ryde, NSW 2109 Australia
vijay@ics.mq.edu.au

Abstract. Graph-based approach to access control models have been studied by researchers due to its visualization, flexible representation and precise semantics. In this paper, we present a detailed graph-based algorithm to evaluate authorization delegations and resolve conflicts based on the shorter weighted path-take-precedence method. The approach makes it possible for administrators to control their granting of authorizations in a very flexible way. The correctness proof and time complexity of the algorithm are provided. We then consider how the authorization state can be changed, since in a dynamic environment an authorization state is not static. The detailed algorithm of state transformation and its correctness proof are also given.

Keywords: authorization delegation, access control, weighted graph.

1 Introduction

The use of the graph-based framework to specify and evaluate the authorizations has several advantages. Firstly, it provides the intuition through visualizing a system's access control policies. In a graph-based approach, nodes are usually used to denote entities and edges to denote different relations between entities. An administrator can see the subjects (roles, users), objects(files, records), access rights granted to subjects over the objects, and possible constraints. It is also possible to provide different subgraphs to different administrators based on their special interests and privileges. Secondly, it provides the formal basis for the precise semantics of the access control policies. Authorization states are represented through graphs and the state changes upon the graph transformations. Thirdly, the existing graph theory results and approaches provide great potential for their applications to the domain of authorization. The connection between graphs and information security is increasingly recognized. Rich and flexible graph representations and well-developed graph techniques can help to achieve flexible access control models.

Different graph-based models have been proposed over the years [7]. The take-grant model [3] is among the earliest applications of graph theory to access control.

S. Bressan, J. Küng, and R. Wagner (Eds.): DEXA 2006, LNCS 4080, pp. 904–913, 2006.

It uses nodes to represent the subjects and objects, and the labelled arcs the authorization. an arc labelled with one or more rights indicates that the source vertex is authorized to perform the rights on the destination vertex. Two special rights take and grant are introduced to transfer the rights from one subject to another which are implemented through graph transformation. More recently, Jaeger and Tidswell have used graphs to model constraints [1]. Nyanchama and Osborn have discussed the conflict of interest policies in their role-graph model [4]. Also Koch et al have used graph to specify the administration of RBAC systems [2].

Different from their work, we focus on using graph approach to representing the positive and negative authorizations, tracing the administrative privilege delegations, and solving conflicts caused by the multiple administrators of access rights. We have presented a weighted graph based model (WGBM) [6] which allows the grantors to assign a weight to their granting of authorizations. The weight is a non-negative number, with a smaller number representing a higher priority. A conflict resolution method based on the shorter weighted path-take-precedence is proposed. The approach makes it possible for administrators to control their granting of authorizations in a very flexible way. In fact, different conflict resolution policies can be achieved through different weights assigned to the authorizations. For example, if all the weights are 0, then all the grantors have the same priority with respect to their granting of authorizations. On the other hand, when all the weights are positive and equal, the predecessors will have higher priority than the successors along the delegation paths. In this paper, we present a detailed algorithm to implement the conflict resolution method. The correctness proof and time complexity of the algorithm are also provided. We further consider how the weighted authorization state can be changed, since in a dynamic environment an authorization state is not static. The detailed algorithm of state transformation and its correctness proof are also given.

The remainder of the paper is organized as follows. Section 2 gives a brief review of WGBM. Section 3 presents the algorithm for evaluating the stable graph, its correctness proof and time complexity. Section 4 describes how to transform the graph when updating the authorization state. Section 5 concludes the paper.

2 A Brief Review of WGBM

In this section we give a brief review of the weighted graph based model for authorization and delegation. Please see [6] for the detailed description.

An *Authorization* is of the form $(s, o, t, r, g) : w$, where s,o,t,r,g denote subject, object, grant type, access right and grantor, respectively. w is a non-negative integer denoting the weight of the authorization. Intuitively, an authorization $(s, o, t, r, g) : w$ states that grantor g has granted subject s the access right r of type t on object o with the weight w. Lesser the weight, the higher priority it denotes. We consider three grant types: *delegable*, *positive* and *negative*, which are denoted by $*$, $+$ and $-$ respectively. $*$ means that the subject has been granted the right to grant r on o as well as r on o. $+$ means that the subject has been granted r on o, while $-$ means that the subject has been denied r on o. An *authorization state*, denoted by $\mathcal{A}$, is the set of all authorizations at a given time.

A weighted digraph is used to represent an authorization state. For every object o and access right r, let $G_{o,r}$ represents all the authorizations on o and r such that for each weighted authorization $(s, o, t, r, g) : w$, there is an arc of type t from g to s in $G_{o,r}$ labelled with w. We use a solid arc to denote $*$, dotted arc to $+$, and an arc with a number of small vertical lines to $-$.

We say that an authorization state $\mathcal{A}$ is *delegation correct*, if a subject s can grant r on o to other subjects if and only if s is the owner; or s has been granted r of delegatable type $*$ on o. Two authorizations $(s, o, t, r, g) : w$ and $(s', o', t', r', g') : w'$ are *contradictory* if $s = s', o = o', r = r', g = g', but\, t \neq t'$. It means that a grantor gives the same subject two different types of authorizations over the same object and access right. An authorization state $\mathcal{A}$ is *not contradictory* if for any a and a' in $\mathcal{A}$, a and a' are not contradictory. An authorization state is **consistent** if it is delegation correct and not contradictory.

Due to the existence of multiple grantors, conflicts may occur in a consistent state where a subject receives two different types of access right from different grantors. More formally, two authorizations $(s, o, t, r, g) : w$ and $(s', o', t', r', g') : w'$ are *conflicting* if $s = s'$, $o = o'$, $r = r'$, $t \neq t'$ and $g \neq g'$. Conflicts must be resolved properly in a decentralized authorization model. In our model, we try to find a shortest path from the root to a subject in $G_{o,r}$ which is able to keep the resulting state delegation correct, since lower weight denotes higher priority. A *useful path* is defined for this purpose. A *useful path* to any vertex s in $G_{o,r}$ is a path: $s_o, s_1, ..., s_k, s\ (k \geq 0)$, where s_o, s_1,...,s_k is a delegation path as well as a shortest path to s_k when $k > 0$. To solve the conflicts, only the arcs on useful paths can compete with each other, and the arc in the shortest useful path will override the others. An authorization $(s, o, t, r, g) : w$ is *active* if the corresponding arc (g, s) in $G_{o,r}$ is in a shortest useful path to s (therefore will not be overridden). Otherwise it is inactive. Please note that, an active path to a vertex s is not necessarily the shortest path from s_o to s, but is definitely the shortest useful path from s_o to s. Let $\mathcal{A}$ be a consistent authorization state, then the subset of all of its active authorizations forms its **effective authorization state**, denoted by $Eff(\mathcal{A})$.

There may exist multiple active paths to a vertex s if they have the same shortest length, as is the case of *Sam* in Figure 1. Therefore conflicts may still exist in an effective state. In this case, we say the conflicts are *incomparable*. Incomparable conflicts can be resolved based on the types of authorizations, such as $- > + > *$ which favors security, or the other way around in favor of accessibility. If an authorization state $\mathcal{A}$ is consistent, then the maximal consistent and conflict-free subset of $Eff(\mathcal{A})$ forms a **stable authorization state** of $\mathcal{A}$, denoted as $stable(\mathcal{A})$.

Example 1. Suppose a Patient Bob delegates the Read right on his health file (F) to his two doctors Alice and Tom with the same weight 1. Bob also denies

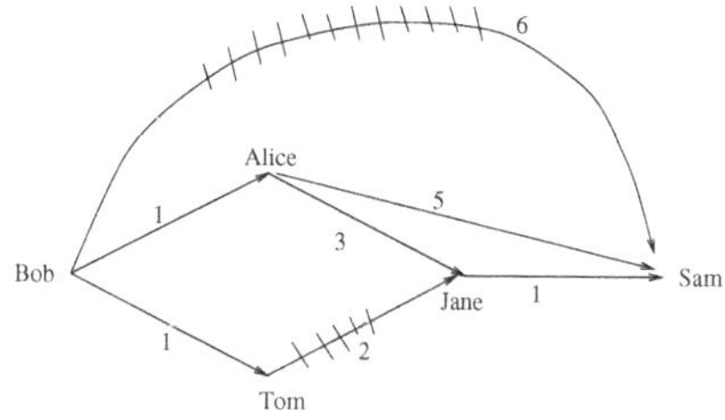

Fig. 1. $G_{F,R}$

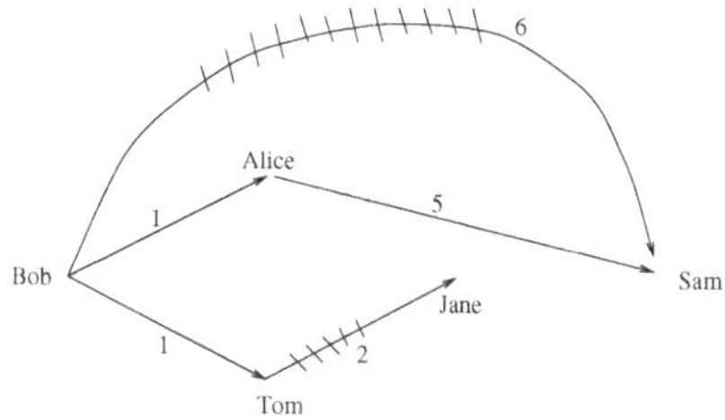

Fig. 2. $\text{Eff}(G_{F,R})$

the health researcher Sam to access his record with weight 6. Jane is a health consultant. Alice further delegates the Read right to Jane with weight 3, but Tom denies Jane to read with weight 2. Both Alice and Jane delegate the Read right to Sam with weight 5 and 1 respectively. Thus we have following authorizations: $(Alice, F, *, R, Bob) : 1$, $(Tom, F, *, R, Bob) : 1$, $(Jane, F, -, R, Tom) : 2$, $(Jane, F, *, R, Alice) : 3$, $(Sam, F, *, R, Jane) : 1$, $(Sam, F, -, R, Bob) : 6$, $(Sam, F, *, R, Alice) : 5$. The corresponding $G_{F,R}$ is shown in Figure 1.

The effective authorization state of Figure 1 is shown in Figure 2. As you can see, there are two active paths to Sam: $(Bob, Alice, Sam)$ and (Bob, Sam). Neither of them is the shortest path from Bob to Sam. In fact, $(Bob, Tom, Jane, Sam)$ is the shortest path but not a useful path to Sam since $(Tom, Jane)$ is not a delegation arc. $(Bob, Alice, Jane, Sam)$ is also shorter but not a useful path to Sam as well since $(Alice, Jane)$ is overridden by $(Tom, Jane)$.

There are two stable authorization states of Figure 2, with one removing (Bob, Sam), and the other removing $(Alice, Sam)$ from Figure 2. The former favors accessibility, while the latter favors security.

3 Algorithm

Now we present the algorithm to compute the stable authorization state. A weight function w matches each arc in $G_{o,r}$ to its weight. That is, $w((g, s)) = w$. An arc type function t matches each arc to its type. That is, $t((g, s)) = t$. The algorithm is based on Dijkstra's distance algorithm [5].

Algorithm 1. *Evaluate_Stable_Graph*$(G_{o,r})$
Input: $G_{o,r} = (V, E, s_o, P, t, w)$ for some object o and access right r, with root s_o, incomparable conflict resolution policy P, arc type function t, and weight function w. $G_{o,r}$ is consistent.
Output: $Stable(G_{o,r}) = G' = (V', E', t', w')$
Method: Label each vertex v with $l(v)$, which is the length of a shortest useful path from s_o to v that has been found at that instant.

```
begin
    l(s_o) = 0;
    for all v ≠ s_o set l(s_o) = ∞;
    T = V; V' = ∅; E' = ∅;
    while T ≠ ∅
    begin
        Find v ∈ T with finite minimum label l(v);
        if such a v does not exist then exit;
        V' = V' ∪ {v};
        if v ≠ s_o then
            For every v' ∈ p(v)
            begin
                E' = E' ∪ {(v', v)};
                t'((v', v)) = t((v', v));
                w'((v', v)) = w((v', v));
            end
        if v = s_o or there exists v' ∈ p(v) such that t((v', v)) = * then
            begin
                For every e = (v, x)
                    if l(x) > l(v) + w(e) then
                    begin
                        l(x) = l(v) + w(e);
                        p(x) = {v};
                    end
                    else
                        if l(x) = l(v) + w(e) then
                            if t(e) = t((y, x)), where y is in p(x)
                                then p(x) = p(x) ∪ {v}
                                else
                                    begin
                                     select one between v and y according to P;
                                     if v is selected then p(x) = {v};
                                    end
            end
        T = T − {v};
    end
end
```

Example 2. We now apply the algorithm to the digraph of Figure 1, finding its $Stable(G_{F,R})$. Suppose P is defined as: $- > + > *$. The major steps performed and the actions taken are as follows:

1-3. $l(Bob) = 0$, and $l(v) = \infty$ for all other vertices, $T = \{Bob, Alice, Tom, Jane, Sam\}, V' = \emptyset, E' = \emptyset$.
4. Since T is not empty, we continue.
6. Select Bob, since it has minimum label.
8. $V' = \{Bob\}$
16-33. We examine the arcs out of Bob and set $l(Alice) = 1, l(Tom) = 1, l(Sam) = 6, p(Alice) = p(Tom) = p(Sam) = \{Bob\}$
34. $T = \{Alice, Tom, Jane, Sam\}$
6. Select $Alice$(or Tom), since it has minimum label.
8. $V' = \{Bob, Alice\}$
12. $E' = \{(Bob, Alice)\}$
16-33. We examine the arcs out of $Alice$ and set $l(Jane) = 4, p(Jane) = \{Alice\}, p(Sam) = \{Bob\}$. Note that $Alice$ cannot be added to $p(Sam)$ according to the incomparable conflict resolution policy P ($- > + > *$) at step 30.
34. $T = \{Tom, Jane, Sam\}$
6. Select Tom, since it has minimum label.
8. $V' = \{Bob, Alice, Tom\}$
12. $E' = \{(Bob, Alice), (Bob, Tom)\}$
16-33. We examine the arcs out of Tom and set $l(Jane) = 3, p(Jane) = \{Tom\}$
34. $T = \{Jane, Sam\}$
6. Select $Jane$, since it has minimum label.
8. $V' = \{Bob, Alice, Tom, Jane\}$
12. $E' = \{(Bob, Alice), (Bob, Tom), (Tom, Jane)\}$
16-33. Since there exists no $v' \in p(Jane)$ such that $t((v', Jane)) = *(p(Jane) = \{Tom\}, t((Tom, Jane)) = -)$, nothing changes.
34. $T = \{Sam\}$
6. Select Sam, since it has minimum label.
8. $V' = \{Bob, Alice, Tom, Jane, Sam\}$
12. $E' = \{(Bob, Alice), (Bob, Tom), (Tom, Jane), (Bob, Sam)\}$
16-33. We examine the arcs out of Sam and nothing changes.
34. $T = \emptyset$, and the algorithm stops.

Theorem 1. *Algorithm Evaluate_Stable_Graph*$(G_{o,r})$ *is correct, and Stable* $(G_{o,r})$ *can be computed by Evaluate_Stable_Graph*$(G_{o,r})$ *in* $O(N^2)$ *time, where* N *is the number of vertices in* $G_{o,r}$.

Proof. We prove by induction on the order in which vertices are deleted from T and entered V'. Take as the induction hypothesis the following assertion: At the kth iteration (1) the label of a vertex v in V' is the length of the shortest useful path from s_o to this vertex, and (2) the label of a vertex not in V' is the length of the shortest useful path from s_o to this vertex that contains only (besides the vertex itself) vertices in V'.

When $k = 0$, $V' = \{s_o\}$, so the length of the shortest useful path from s_o to itself is 0 (here we are allowing a path to have no arcs in it), and the length of the shortest useful path from s_o to a vertex other than s_o is ∞.

Assume that the inductive hypothesis holds for the kth iteration. Let v be the vertex added to V' at the $(k+1)$st iteration so that v is a vertex not in V' at the end of the kth iteration with the smallest label (in case of ties, any vertex with smallest label may be used). From the inductive hypothesis we see that vertices in V' before the $(k+1)$st iteration are labelled with the length of the shortest useful path from s_o. Also v must be labelled with the length of the shortest useful path to it from s_o. If this were not the case, at the end of the kth iteration there would be a useful path of length less than $l_k(v)$ containing a vertex not in V' (because $l_k(v)$ is the length of the shortest useful path from s_o to v containing only vertices in V' after the kth iteration). Let u be the first vertex not in V' in such a useful path. There is a useful path with length less than $l_k(v)$ from s_o to u containing only vertices of V'. This contradicts the choice of v. Hence (1) holds at the end of the $(k+1)$st iteration.

Let u be a vertex not in V' after $k+1$ iterations. A shortest useful path from s_o to u containing only elements of V' either contains v or it does not. If it does not contain v, then by the inductive hypothesis its length is $l_k(u)$. If it does contain v, then it must be made up of a useful path from s_o to v of shortest possible length containing elements of V' other than v, where the in-arc of v is of type $*$ when the length is greater than 0, followed by the arc from v to u. In this case its length would be $l_k(v) + w(v,u)$. This shows that (2) is true, since $l_{k+1} = min\{l_k(u), l_k(v) + w(v,u)\}$.

For each vertex v, it is not difficult to see that we have used $p(v)$ to record all parents of v that make its label $l(v)$ (when $l(v)$ is finite) and have highest priority according to policy P if incomparable conflicts exist on v. We have entered the corresponding in-arcs to E' when v is selected. Thus we have entered all the useful paths that make $l(v)$ to E' which are not overridden under policy P for each vertex v, and this concludes the proof of the first part of the theorem.

We now determine the time complexity of the algorithm. Note that in line 6 the minimum label of T must be found. This can certainly be done through $|T| - 1$ comparisons. Initially, $T = V$, and line 34 reduces T one vertex at a time. Thus the process is repeated N times. The time required in line 6 is then on the order of $\sum_{i=1}^{N} i$ and therefore is $\mathcal{O}(N^2)$. in Line 10, $p(v)$ has at most N elements. So the for loop requires at most $\mathcal{O}(N^2)$. Line 18 uses each arc once at most, so it requires at most $\mathcal{O}(|E|) = \mathcal{O}(N^2)$. The entire algorithm thus has time complexity $\mathcal{O}(N^2)$.

Suppose an access request (s, o, r) means that subject s wants to exercise access right r on object o. The procedure of evaluating the request can be outlined as follows:

1. If s is the root of $G_{o,r}$, return *yes*;
2. Compute $stable(G_{o,r})$.
3. If s is not in V', return *undecided*;
4. Let (g, s) be the in-arc of s in E', if $t'((g,s)) = *$ or $+$ return *yes* else return *no*.

4 Authorization State Transformation

4.1 Authorization Update

As mentioned earlier, in a dynamic environment, an authorization state is not static since users may need to add, update, or revoke certain authorizations. In this section, we consider how the authorization state can be changed.

Here we only consider addition and revocation, since update can be realized through them. We need to guarantee that the state remain consistent after the update. Recall that a state is consistent if it is not contradictory (a grantor cannot grant the same subject two different types of the same access right) and delegation correct (A grantor should have the right to grant).

In the case of addition, suppose U is a set of authorizations to be added to the current state S. Then, obviously, U should not be contradictory as this will cause the new state contradictory. A contradictory can still happen between a new authorization in U and an old authorization in S. In this case, use the new one to replace the old one. Although S is delegation correct, after U is added, the delegation correctness may not hold any more. So we need to compute its maximum delegation correct sub-state. Algorithm 2 is designed for this. The procedure of processing addition of a set of authorizations can be outlined as follows:

1. Check authorizations to be added. If there exists a contradictory, then remove them from the set.
2. Add authorizations to the corresponding $G_{o,r}$. If this results two arcs between two vertices, remove the old arc. The resulting state is then not contradictory.
3. Use Algorithm 2 to compute the maximum delegation correct sub-state. The output will be the new consistent authorization state.

For revocation, on the other hand, it will not affect the property of 'not contradictory' of the current state. However, it may cause the resulting state delegation incorrect. So we also need to use Algorithm 2 to calculate the maximum delegation correct sub-state after the deletion. Further more, we need to check if the requester of an authorization revocation is the grantor of it. That is, an authorization $a = (s, o, t, r, g) : w$ can be revoked only when the requester is g. The procedure of processing revocation of a set of authorizations can be outlined as follows:

1. Check authorizations to be revoked. If the requester is not the grantor of an authorization, then remove them from the set.
2. Remove the authorizations from the corresponding $G_{o,r}$.
3. Use Algorithm 2 to compute the maximum delegation correct sub-state. The output will be the new consistent authorization state.

4.2 Algorithm

Now we present the algorithm to compute the maximum delegation correct subset of a set of authorizations. Obviously we only need to guarantee that $G_{o,r}$ is delegation correct for any object o and access right r. Let $DeleCorrect(G_{o,r})$ denote its maximum delegation correct subset.

Algorithm 2. *Evaluate_DeleCorrect_Graph*$(G_{o,r})$
Input: $G_{o,r} = (V, E, s_o, t, w)$ for some object o and access right r, with root s_o, arc type function t, and weight function w. $G_{o,r}$ is consistent.
Output: $DeleCorrect(G_{o,r}) = G' = (V', E', t', w')$

begin
  $l(s_o) = t$;
  for all $v \neq s_o$ set $l(v) = f$;
  $T = V; V' = \emptyset; E' = \emptyset$;
  while T $\neq \emptyset$
  begin
    Find $v \in T$ with label $l(v) = t$;
    if such a v does not exist **then exit**;
      begin
        $V' = V' \cup \{v\}$;
        for all v' such that $(v, v') \in E$;
          begin
            $E' = E' \cup \{(v, v')\}$;
            $V' = V' \cup \{v\}$;
            $t'((v, v')) = t((v, v'))$;
            $w'((v, v')) = w((v, v'))$;
            if t((v,v'))=$*$ **then** $l(v')$=t
          end
      end
    $T = T - \{v\}$;
  end
end

Theorem 2. *Algorithm Evaluate_DeleCorrect_Graph is correct, and* $DeleCorrect(G_{o,r})$ *can be computed by Evaluate_DeleCorrect_Graph*$(G_{o,r})$ *in* $\mathcal{O}(N^2)$ *time, where* N *is the number of vertices in* $G_{o,r}$.

Proof. For the correctness, we need to prove two sides. On the side of delegation correctness, we need to prove that for each arc (v, v') in the output $G' = (V', E', t', w')$, there exists a delegation path (every arc on the path is of $*$ type) from s_o to v; On the side of the maximum delegation set, we need to prove that for each arc (w, w') in $G_{o,r}$, if there exists a delegation path from s_o to w, then (w, w') should also be in G'.

If (v, v') is in G', then based on the algorithm, $l(v) = t$, which means that either $v = s_o$ or there exist an arc (v'', v) of type $*$ such that $l(v'') = t$. This means that there exists an delegation path from s_o to v.

On the other hand, suppose (w, w') is in $G_{o,r}$ and there exists a delegation path from s_o to w. To prove (w, w') is also in G', we only need to show $l(w) = t$ at some time. Suppose the delegation path is $s_o, w_1, w_2, ...w_n, w$. We prove by induction on the length of the path. When $n = 0$, it is obviously true. Assume that the inductive hypothesis holds when $n = k$, which means $l(w_k) = t$. Since arc (w_k, w_{k+1}) is of $*$ type, $l(w_{k+1})$ will be set to t when w_k is selected from T. Since T is a finite set, and the selected element whose label is t will be removed from T, w_k will eventually be selected.

For the time complexity, it is not difficult to see that it is $\mathcal{O}(N^2)$, since the algorithm only visits each arc in $G_{o,r}$ at most once to move it to the new graph.

5 Conclusion

Authorization delegation and negative authorizations are two significant issues in a decentralized authorization model. In [6] we have proposed a weighted authorization model to handle authorization delegation and conflict resolution. In this paper, we developed the detailed algorithm to implement the model. The correctness proof and complexity of the algorithm are also provided. Since in a dynamic environment an authorization state is not static, we also considered how an authorization state can be changed and developed the algorithm to deal with the authorization state transformation.

References

1. T. Jaeger and J. E. Tidswell. Practical safety in flexible access control models. *ACM Trans. on Info. and System Security*, 4(2):158-190, 2001.
2. M. Koch, L. V. Mancini and F. Parisi-Presicce. Administratice Scope in the Graph-Based Framework. *Proceedings of the ninth ACM Symposium on Access control Models and Technologies*, pp 97-104, 2004.
3. R.J. Lipton and L. Snyder. A Linear Time Algorithm for Deciding Subject Security. *Journal of the ACM*, 24(3):455-464, 1977.
4. M. Nyanchama and S.L Osborn. The Role Graph Model and Conflict of Interest. *ACM Trans. on Info. and System Security*, 1(2):3-33, 1999.
5. K.H. Rosen, Discrete mathematics and its applications, McGraw-Hill Inc. Publishing Company, 1991.
6. C. Ruan and V. Varadharajan, A weighted graph approach to authorization delegation and conflict resolution. em Proceedings of the 9th Australasian Conference on Information Security and Privacy, pp 402-413, 2004.
7. R. Sandhu, A perspective on graphs and access control models. ICGT pp 2-12, 2004.

Modeling and Inferring on Role-Based Access Control Policies Using Data Dependencies

Romuald Thion and Stéphane Coulondre

LIRIS: Lyon Research Center for Images and Intelligent Information Systems, Bâtiment Blaise Pascal, 20 av. Albert Einstein, 69621 Villeurbanne Cedex, France
firstname.surname@liris.cnrs.fr

Abstract. Role-Based Access Control (RBAC) models are becoming a de facto standard, greatly simplifying management and administration tasks. Organizational constraints were introduced (e.g.: mutually exclusive roles, cardinality, prerequisite roles) to reflect peculiarities of organizations. Thus, the number of rules is increasing and policies are becoming more and more complex: understanding and analyzing large policies in which several security officers are involved can be a tough job. There is a serious need for administration tools allowing analysis and inference on access control policies. Such tools should help security officers to avoid defining conflicting constraints and inconsistent policies.

This paper shows that theoretical tools from relational databases are suitable for expressing and inferring on RBAC policies and their related constraints. We focused on using Constrained Tuple-Generating Dependencies (CTGDs), a class of dependencies which includes traditional other ones. We show that their great expressive power is suitable for all practical relevant aspects of RBAC. Moreover, proof procedures have been developed for CTGDs: they permit to reason on policies. For example, to check their consistency, to verify a new rule is not already implied or to check satisfaction of security properties. A prototype of RBAC policies management tool has been implemented, using CTGDs dedicated proof procedures as the underlying inference engine.

1 Introduction

DataBases Management Systems (DBMS) are cornerstones of Information Systems (ISs): they provide mechanisms to store, modify, retrieve and query information of an organization. In order to enhance security of data, Access Control (AC) mechanisms have been developed to manage users' rights over data stored in the DBMS. In its broader sense, AC, denotes the fact of determining whether a *subject* (process, computer ...) is able to perform an *operation* (read, write ...) on an *object* (a tuple, a table, ...). An operation right on an object is called *permission*. AC policies define the subjects' permissions.

Applications developed using DBMS can contain large amount of data with highly differentiated access for different users, depending upon their function or role within the organization [1]. Role-Based Access Control (RBAC) received considerable attention as an alternative to traditional mandatory and discretionary AC policies in databases.

S. Bressan, J. Küng, and R. Wagner (Eds.): DEXA 2006, LNCS 4080, pp. 914–923, 2006.

The RBAC models constitute a family in which permissions are associated with roles. A role is a job function or job title within the organization. Users are made members of appropriate roles. Permissions are not directly assigned to users (roles can be seen as collections of permissions) [2]. RBAC provides a powerful mechanism for reducing the complexity, cost, and potential for error in assigning permissions to users within the organization. RBAC was found to be among the most attractive solutions for providing AC in e-commerce, e-government or e-health [1,3].

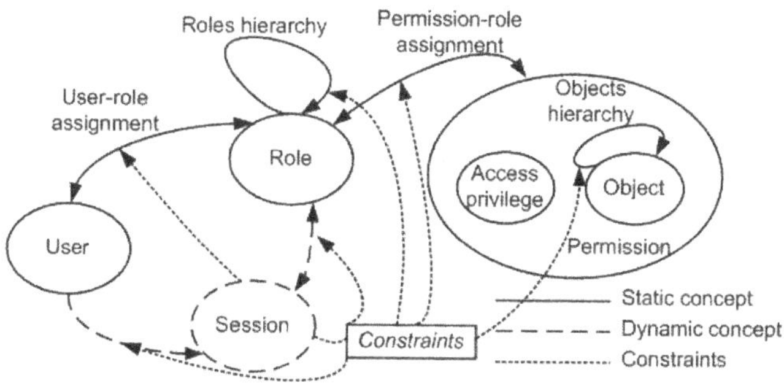

Fig. 1. RBAC Model

Nevertheless the number of users in RBAC policies is increasing and rules are more and more complex: diverse constraint[1] types have been introduced to reflect peculiarities of organizations. RBAC constraints specify conditions that cannot be violated by the components of the system.

Policies engineering is considered to be of high practical importance [4]: a large part of flaws in ISs are due to administration mistakes or security misconceptions. There is a need for tools facilitating design and maintenance of RBAC policies. According to the authors of [5], such tools need to be able to capture AC model mechanisms and peculiarities (e.g. RBAC constraints). These tools need to be able to check consistency of policies and to answer queries for particular permissions or relation holdings in the policies. Last requirement is a comprehensible inference mechanism, even by non-logicians. Our goal is to provide a formal framework satisfying these requirements.

Thus our contribution is twofold:

- identification of a theoretical tool from the databases field suitable for homogenous modeling of RBAC principles and its related constraints right into the relational model,

[1] *Constraint* may be a confusing word in this paper: it may either designate relations between variables (e.g., $X \leq Y, X \geq 2 \times Z + 1, 3 = T, 2 \neq 3$, etc.), restrictions on RBAC model's concepts (e.g. nobody is allowed to assume simultaneously roles r_1 and r_2) and even data dependencies (integrity constraints). In this paper we do not use the term *integrity constraints*, *constraints* refers to semantic relations between variables and *RBAC constraints* or *organizational constraints* refers to restriction among elements in RBAC policies.

- use tools built (e.g. proof procedures) on top of the underlying theoretical model to provide a set of tools facilitating design and management of RBAC policies in order to detect and correct administration mistakes or misconceptions.

The class of dependencies we focused on is Constrained Tuple-Generating Dependencies (CTGDs). CTGDs is among the widest class of dependencies [6]. We will show that a this framework is an appropriate formal tool for representing and checking RBAC policies.

In the next section we will introduce CTGDs and proof procedure related in. Section 3 will show how CTGDs can be used to model RBAC concepts, constraints and assignments, of which implements will be shown in section 4. Section 5 will summarize some papers related to this work. Finally, last section will discuss our work and presents perspectives using databases dependencies for security purposes.

2 Background

2.1 Constrained Tuple-Generating Dependencies

The authors of [6] expose a kind of data dependencies upon the most expressive existing: CTGDs, generalizing traditional dependencies such as FDs, MVDs or EGDs. CTGDs extend Tuple-Generating Dependencies (TGDs, which are also known as *Generalized Dependencies* [7,8]) with a constraint domain (e.g. linear arithmetic over integers, rationals or real). Constraints are quite interesting when used jointly with existential quantifiers because they permit a more precise definition of such *partially known* facts. CTGDs are interesting for DBMS storing complex data such as spatial, audio, image, video or temporal data. CTGDs can be represented formally in First-Order Logic (FOL) by formulae of the form [7]:

$$\forall X\ p_1(X_1) \wedge \ldots \wedge p_i(X_i) \wedge c(X) \rightarrow \exists Y\ q_1(X \cup Y_1) \wedge \ldots \wedge p_j(X \cup Y_j) \wedge c'(X \cup Y)$$

where p_i and q_j are predicates symbols, $X = X_1 \cup \ldots \cup X_i$ is the set of all terms (no functions symbols) in the left hand side. Terms of X are universally quantified. $Y = Y_1 \cup \ldots \cup Y_j$ does not designate all terms in the right hand side, but only those that are not bound by the universal quantifier on the left hand side. Terms of Y are existentially quantified. Finally, c and c' are conjunctions of linear constraints $(<, >, \leq, \geq, \neq, =)$ over terms (terms of X for c and terms of $X \cup Y$ for c').

For example, the following dependency from [6] expresses that cpath(source, destination, cost), which contains the cheapest path between any two points in a directed graph with edge weights, is a transitive closed relation obeying the triangle inequality: $\forall S_1, D_1, C_1, D_2, C_2\ cpath(S_1, D_1, C_1) \wedge cpath(D_1, D_2, C_2) \rightarrow \exists C_3\ cpath(S_1, D_2, C_3) \wedge C_3 \leq C_1 + C_2$.

2.2 Dedicated Proof Procedures for CTGDs

The authors of [6] propose two bottom-up chase over CTGDs. Their paper addresses the implication problem, that is, given a collection of CTGDs F, and a single CTGD g, determine whether in every database state where F is satisfied, it is also the case that g is satisfied. The chase proves if F logically implies g, stated briefly as $F \models g$.

The operational nature of these proof procedures is based on the concept of tuple (a grounded atom, with no variables). Basic outline of such procedures is based on [9] with the adjunction of constraints: hypothesize the existence of some tuples in the relations such that the antecedent l of g is satisfied, treat F as defining a closure operator generating tuples $F(l)$. On each computation step of $F(l)$, the following condition is tested:

- if $F(l)$ contains a copy of r, infer $F \models g$,
- if $F(l)$ contains an inconsistency produced by constraints, infer $F \models g$ vacuously,
- if $F(l)$ does not contain a copy of r, infer $F \not\models g$.

The CTGDs implication problem is semi-decidable: the procedures may run forever. As each basic step is producing new facts through implication, we can practically bound up the number of successively applied CTGDs (e.g. to avoid circular generating facts leading to infinite loop), but it is unsound and must be reserved for implementation purpose. However, there exist decidability results for specific subclasses of CTGDs. For example, the chase is decidable for Full-TGDs, TGDs without existentially quantified variable [9].

3 A Framework for Expressing and Checking RBAC Policies

According to the authors of [10] we use the following predicates to model core concepts of RBAC policies:

- $ura(User, Role)$, to define User Role Assignments,
- $pra(Access, Object, Role)$, to define Permission Role Assignment
- $permitted(User, Access, Object)$, to specify that user $User$ is granted $Access$ access privilege on object $Object$.

3.1 Capturing Axiomatic Definition of RBAC Model

Once basic elements of the policies are defined, we need to model the "axiomatic of RBAC": the core of the AC model which settles how an access is granted to a user through role assignment and how is defined hierarchy. We model an RBAC axiomatic based on [10]. $dSenior(SeniorRole, JuniorRole)$ to define direct inheritance between roles and $senior(SeniorRole, JuniorRole)$ to define role hierarchy (the transitive closure of $seniorDirect$).

- role inheritance is transitive: $senior(X, Y), dSenior(Y, Z) \rightarrow senior(X, Z)$,
- role inheritance is irreflexive: $senior(X, X) \rightarrow \bot$,
- a user is access granted to an object if he is assigned to a role which is assigned to this permission: $ura(U, R), pra(A, O, R) \rightarrow permitted(U, A, O)$,
- eventually through inheritance $ura(U, R1), senior(R1, R2), pra(A, O, R2) \rightarrow permitted(U, A, O)$.

3.2 Capturing Organizational Constraints

Constraints are an important aspect of RBAC and are a powerful mechanism for laying out higher-level organizational policy [2]. The best known RBAC constraints are:

Mutually exclusive roles constraints settle that no user can be assigned two roles which are in conflict with each other. In other words, it means that conflicting roles cannot have common users. $ssd(Role1, Role2)$, specificy that $Role1$ and $Role2$ are in Static Separation of Duties (SSD): they are mutually exclusive. Mutually exclusive roles can produce inconsistency. The authors of [11] describe a set of properties that must hold in any RBAC policy. These properties are described in the example of section 4.

Cardinality constraints settle that a number of assignments is limited. Cardinality constraints of n maximum users assigned to role r can be expressed in CTGDs by $\wedge_{i=1}^{n+1} ura(U, N_i)\ \{\forall i \in [1..n], \forall j \in [i+1..n+1]\, N_i \neq N_j\} \rightarrow \bot$. Mutually exclusion and cardinality constraints are not limited to role and can be used on any element of the policy model (for example with access: no role can be granted both read access and write access on an object o). Our approach can be generalized for maximum number of roles assigned to users or to permissions.

More generally, Nullity Generating Dependencies of the form $p_i(X) \wedge c \rightarrow \bot$ can be used to model RBAC constraints: an RBAC constraint define that if a certain state (the left hand side of the CTGD) is reached, then the policy is inconsistent (right hand side is $\bot$).

Prerequisite constraints settle that if a particular relation holds, another holds too. Variables appearing only within the terms of the tail in CTGDs are existentially quantified. Intuitively that does mean *at least one element such as ... exists.* This semantic is used to take into account prerequisite RBAC constraints. E.g. role r_2 is required by role r_1: *for any user assigned to role r_1, at least one another user must be assigned to role r_2*, $ura(U_1, r_1) \rightarrow ura(U_2, r_2)\ U_1 \neq U_2$. Other prerequisite constraints can be expressed using CTGDs, according to administrator's need. CTGDs can model other forms of prerequisite constraints on any RBAC concept.

3.3 Inference on Policies

Depending on which stage of the RBAC specification one is working on, different needs of verification may exist:

- during the stage of modeling axiomatic (the core policy model), we are likely to check the expected behavior of the model and rules redundancies. E.g. how authorizations are derived from user-role and permission-role assignment,
- during the stage of defining the role hierarchy, we are likely to check a set of properties. E.g. there is no cycle in the hierarchy, or no role inherits the administrator role,
- during the stage of defining user-role and permission-role assignment we are likely query the policy and to check a set of properties. E.g there is no two roles which have exactly the same permissions,

Table 1. Reduction of security administration needs into CTGDs-dedicated tools

Security requirements	Reduction into CTGDs
Security property that must hold in all RBAC policy instances. *no role can be senior to itself*	Model the property to verify by a single CTGD and use proof procedure to check implication from axiomatic of RBAC and organizational constraints
Check if a policy is consistent	Try to derive $\perp$ from the policy by proof procedure
Security property that must hold in a policy instance. *no role inherits the administrator role*	Model the property to verify by a single CTGD and verify if it is satisfied by the database instance
Policy management capabilities: queries and data manipulation *which users are assigned to role student?*	Process query over the database

- during the stage of defining constraints it is interesting to check whether the policy is consistent, in other words if we settled facts violating constraints.

The second termination case (vacuously) of algorithms from [6] is very useful while checking AC policies, it denotes that the policies are inconsistent. This semantic is interesting for security administrators when dealing with constrained AC policies: if there are facts violating constraints, the policy is inconsistent.

4 Experimental Validation

This section illustrates how a RBAC policy can be modeled into CTGDs. The sample code is separated into four parts: the first one models the core mechanisms of the RBAC model and settles a set of properties that must holds in any RBAC policy [11]. The second part is a sample role hierarchy used in a virtual organization. Unfortunately we are limited to toy sample or randomly generated policies, because organizations are not likely to share such sensitive information. Next is a sample definition of User-Role Assignments and Permission-Role Assignments. The last part defines a set of specific organizational constraints that must hold in this particular policy.

```
%axiomatic definition of RBAC policies and generic constraints
%------------------------------------------------------------
%senior is the transitive closure of dSenior
dSenior(SeniorRole,JuniorRole)->senior(SeniorRole,JuniorRole).
senior(SeniorRole,InterRole), dSenior(InterRole,JuniorRole)-> senior(SeniorRole,JuniorRole).
senior(Role,Role)->false.

%granting access to user through role assignments
ura(User,Role),pra(Access,Object,Role)->permitted(User,Access,Object).
ura(User,SeniorRole),senior(SeniorRole,JuniorRole),
pra(Access,Object,JuniorRole)->permitted(User,Access,Object).

%Property P1: any two roles assigned for a same user are not in separation of duties
ura(User,Role1),ura(User,Role2),ssd(Role1,Role2)->false.
```

```
%Property P2: no role is mutually exclusive with itself
ssd(Role,Role)-> false.

%Property P3: mutual exclusion is symetric
ssd(Role1,Role2)->ssd(Role2,Role1).

%Property P4: any two roles in ssd do not inherits one another
senior(Role1,Role2),ssd(Role1,Role2)->false.

%Property P5: there is no role inheriting to roles in ssd
ssd(Role1,Role2),senior(SeniorRole,Role1),senior(SeniorRole,Role2)->false.

%Property P6: If a role inherits another role and
%that role is in SSD with a third one, then the inheriting
%role is in SSD with the third one.
ssd(Role1,Role2),senior(SeniorRole,Role1)->ssd(SeniorRole,Role2).

%definition of role hierarchy
%---------------------------
%roles and hierarchy (with directly senior predicate) modeling
->role(student),role(researcher),role(teacher),role(phDStudent).
->role(postPhD),role(lecturer),role(seniorLecturer),role(professor).
->dSenior(phDStudent,student), dSenior(phDStudent,researcher).
->dSenior(postPhD,phDStudent), dSenior(postPhD,teacher).
->dSenior(lecturer,teacher), dSenior(lecturer,researcher).
->dSenior(professor,seniorLecturer), dSenior(seniorLecturer,lecturer).

%definition of assignments
%-------------------------
%Permission-Role Assignments
->pra(read,test,student),pra(write,test,teacher),pra(read,finalTest,professor).
->pra(read,smallPaper,lecturer),pra(write,bigPaper,professor).

%User-Role Assignments
->ura(alice,student),ura(bob,phDStudent),ura(charly,professor).

%definition of organizational constraints
%----------------------------------------
%prerequisite on permissions: if one can read and object, another one can write
pra(read,Object,Role1) -> pra(write,Object,Role2) {Role1=\=Role2}.

%uniqueness constraint on manager
ura(User1,manager),ura(User2, manager){User1=\=User2}->false.

%mutually exclusives roles: student and professor
->ssd(student,lecturer).
```

We have described chase procedures as algorithms proving that a set of CTGDs F implies a single CTGD g: $F \models g$. The above ruleset is such an F collection, and g is the security property to check. The table 1 describes how tools dedicated to CTGDs can be used by administrators to design, verify and manage their policies. Six properties ($P1$ to $P6$) are settled in the sample policy, the authors of [11] have manually demonstrated the following theorem: $P2 \wedge P3 \wedge P6 \Rightarrow P4 \wedge P5$.

Our first example illustrates how chase procedures for CTGDs can be used to automatically proove the same theorem:

- let F be the collection of CTGDs modeling properties $P2$, $P3$ and $P6$,
- let be g_1 the CTGD modeling properties $P4$,
- let be g_2 the CTGD modeling properties $P5$.

The chase procedure prove that $F \models g_1$ and $F \models g_2$, we can conclude the properties $P4$ and $P6$ are redundant. Such functionalities are very interesting for security administrators: they can check that security properties ($P4$ and $P6$ in this example) hold in all RBAC policy instances (that satisfy $P2$, $P3$ and $P6$ in the example).

Another example is $g \equiv ura(joe, student), ura(joe, seniorLecturer) \rightarrow$: "is the policy consistent if *joe* is assigned to both *student* and *seniorLecturer*?". Clearly, with such assignments to user *joe*, the policy is inconsistent: roles *student* and *lecturer* are in SSD, *student* and *seniorLecturer* are in SSD too according to property $P6$. thus the policy is inconsistent using property $P1$. It is very interesting for administrators to conduct such verifications *before* any assignment: they can ensure the consistency of their policy in the presence of updates.

We have implemented a toolkit, "TGDToolBox", written in C++ to provide a set of functions to deal with data dependencies (e.g. syntatic analysis, unification of atoms, variables renaming). We implemented the chase procedures described in [6] using this library to run examples from this section. Actually, the prototype is able to handle hundreds of CTGDs and to answer in interactive time. We are currently using the toolkit to develop new proof procedures for dependencies [8,12]. Using the proof procedures as an inference engine, we have built a proof of concept Microsoft Visio 2003 Template dedicated to RBAC policies design. This template provides an iconic interface for RBAC policy management. It is able to determine if a permission is granted to a user through his role assignment, it can check if the set of policies is consistent and can answer queries about the relations holding in the RBAC policy.

5 Related Works

Our work has been influenced by [10] which express RBAC models with Constraint Logic Programming and [13] which describes the "Flexible Authorization Framework", that can be analyzed using a variant of Datalog (typically either safe stratified Datalog or Datalog with constraints).

The three main arguments we focused on are providing a framework which:

- is able to capture all relevant concepts of RBAC models,
- can benefit researches (e.g. evolutions, theoritical results, implementations) from a well established community,
- can be easily linked with other components of ISs (e.g. databases).

The authors of [10] describe AC programs able to deal with RBAC models. This very complete work addresses many problems arising with the use of closed policies (access denied as a default action, authorizations are only ever positive), open policies (access granted as a default action) or hybrid policies (authorizations and denial can be explicitly defined). However, logical programs are not intuitive for non-specialits and the logic used do not integrate existential quantifiers. Moreover, RBAC policy are already widespread, a framework base on databases makes integration of administration tools and security data easier.

The autors of [4] argue"'... extensive research activity has resulted in the definition of a variety of AC ... Thus, the need arises for developing tools for reasoning about the characteristics of these models. These tools should support users in the tasks of model specification, analysis of model properties, and authorization management". Their logical framework is based on the C-Datalog language, whereas our is based on CTGDs, which is a able to deal with a wider class of rules thanks to existential quantifiers and constraints within both head and tail of dependencies.

The authors of [14] describe a fragment of FOL which tractable and sufficiently expressive to capture policies for many applications. This work is really interesting and points out tractability and complexity results on their logic. Constraints in policies are necessary to capture peculiarities of organizations, but modeling such restrictions is not develop in [14]. We do agree the authors statement about the use of logic programming by non-logicians, but we disagree that a "filling the blank on English sentences interface is sufficient for security administrators. We think that administrators must have a computer-aided software engineering (CASE) interface to design and check policies and such a CASE should provide a comprehensible trace of reasoning.

6 Conclusions and Further Work

We are confident that CTGDs can be used to express other AC models such as Task-BAC, Workflow-BAC, Mandatory-AC or Organization-BAC. Our fragment of FOL is really closed to the ones used in [10] or [4], which are able to deal with temporal aspects and at least mandatory and discretionary AC models.

For sake of clarity the example exposed in section 4 does not include sessions. According to [10] sessions and dynamic constraints can be captured easily with CLP. We are investigating the interest of chase procedure to check RBAC policies involving sessions. For example, using chase procedure we might answer queries like *Are the policies consistent for all possible sessions?*. Moreover, incorporating the model for administration of roles exposed in [15] is promising for distributed policies verification purposes.

Integrating of temporal aspects in RBAC models has been investigated in [16]. The authors of [10] use the Constraint Logic Programming framework. We can use the same approach to model Temporal-RBAC models, and according to [17] we extend the inequalities to geographical trigerring of assignments. Integrating temporal or geographical concerns into CTGDs, is mainly related to the choice of a right *constraint domain* [6]. For example, to define that a role is assigned to a user only on [t1, t2] shift, (between the times t1 and t2): $time(H)\{t1 \leq H \leq t2\} \rightarrow ura(user, role)$.

A promising opening to the use of CTGDs for AC modeling purpose is the result exposed by the authors of [12]. They propose a new kind of dependencies subsumming CTGDs : Disjunctive-CTGDs. Their enhanced expressivity can be used to model new kinds of organizational constraints involving disjunctions, classes of constraints which have not been studied in the AC literature yet.

References

1. Ramaswamy, C., Sandhu, R.: Role-based access control features in commercial database management systems. In: Proc. 21st NIST-NCSC National Information Systems Security Conference. (1998) 503–511
2. Sandhu, R.S., Coyne, E.J., Feinstein, H.L., Youman, C.E.: Role-based access control models. IEEE Computer **29**(2) (1996) 38–47
3. CERT/CC, U.S.S., magazine, C.: E-crimewatch survey. Technical report, http://www.cert.org/archive/pdf/ecrimesummary05.pdf (2005)
4. Bertino, E., Catania, B., Ferrari, E., Perlasca, P.: A logical framework for reasoning about access control models. ACM Trans. Inf. Syst. Secur. **6**(1) (2003) 71–127
5. Bonatti, P.A., Samarati, P.: Logics for authorization and security. In Chomicki, J., van der Meyden, R., Saake, G., eds.: Logics for Emerging Applications of Databases, Springer (2003) 277–323
6. Maher, M.J., Srivastava, D.: Chasing constrained tuple-generating dependencies. In: PODS, ACM Press (1996) 128–138
7. Abiteboul, S., Hull, R., Vianu, V.: Foundations of Databases. Addison-Wesley (1995)
8. Coulondre, S.: A top-down proof procedure for generalized data dependencies. Acta Inf. **39**(1) (2003) 1–29
9. Beeri, C., Vardi, M.Y.: A proof procedure for data dependencies. J. ACM **31**(4) (1984) 718–741
10. Barker, S., Stuckey, P.J.: Flexible access control policy specification with constraint logic programming. ACM Trans. Inf. Syst. Secur. **6**(4) (2003) 501–546
11. Gavrila, S.I., Barkley, J.F.: Formal specification for role based access control user/role and role/role relationship management. In: ACM Workshop on Role-Based Access Control. (1998) 81–90
12. Wang, J., Topor, R., Maher, M.: Reasoning with disjunctive constrained tuple-generating dependencies. Lecture Notes in Computer Science **2113** (2001) 963–973
13. Jajodia, S., Samarati, P., Sapino, M.L., Subrahmanian, V.S.: Flexible support for multiple access control policies. ACM Trans. Database Syst. **26**(2) (2001) 214–260
14. Halpern, J.Y., Weissman, V.: Using first-order logic to reason about policies. In: CSFW, IEEE Computer Society (2003) 187–201
15. Sandhu, R.S., Munawer, Q.: The arbac99 model for administration of roles. In: ACSAC, IEEE Computer Society (1999) 229–240
16. Bertino, E., Bonatti, P.A., Ferrari, E.: Trbac: A temporal role-based access control model. ACM Trans. Inf. Syst. Secur. **4**(3) (2001) 191–233
17. Grumbach, S., Rigaux, P., Segoufin, L.: Spatio-temporal data handling with constraints. GeoInformatica **5**(1) (2001) 95–115

Multi-dimensional Dynamic Bucket Index Based on Mobile Agent System Architecture

Marcin Gorawski and Adam Dyga

Silesian University of Technology
Institute of Computer Science
Akademicka 16, 44-100 Gliwice, Poland
M.Gorawski@polsl.pl, A.Dyga@polsl.pl

Abstract. This paper describes the idea of a bucket index employed for processing of intensive reading streams coming from huge telemetry networks. This data structure answers approximate spatio-temporal range queries concerning utility usage in user selected region and time. The index structure continuously adjusts to data distribution changes and, as opposed to traditional indexing methods, is capable of processing of the updates on the fly. A stochastic prediction model is also used to estimate utility usage in the near future. The presented indexing technique is implemented in a distributed system based on mobile agents. The mobile architecture is used to control the workload of network hosts.

1 Introduction

In recent years there has been an increase in the popularity of *telemetry networks* which are very flexible and allow clients – water, gas and electricity consumers – to freely choose a provider. Immense telemetric systems consisting of large number of meters that report their states at short intervals are sources of data streams which require efficient processing.

A *telemetry system* consists of a central server, data collection nodes and meters. The meters periodically send their states to the collection nodes which in turn transmit the data to the central server using GPRS/GSM protocol.

The main purpose of the system is to provide the user with information regarding utility usage within selected region and time. Such knowledge can be used for example by a utility provider (e. g. power plant) to estimate and adjust the future production rate to expected demand.

The problem of indexing of spatio-temporal telemetric data has been previously described in [2] and [3]. The indexing technique utilized there is based on the aR-Tree, which is built using data written by an ETL process in the data warehouse with a cascaded star model. This work has the same purpose but the update operations are processed continuously on the fly, passing by the data warehouse. Bucket index presented in this paper is based on the idea of adaptive multi-dimensional histogram (AMH) proposed in [4] – a structure used for approximate processing of spatio-temporal aggregate queries.

S. Bressan, J. Küng, and R. Wagner (Eds.): DEXA 2006, LNCS 4080, pp. 924–934, 2006.

The main contribution of this work is the modification of AMH that facilitates processing of regularly reported meter values and its application in a distributed mobile agent system. The detailed description of the modified AMH has been presented in [1], but in this paper, due to lack of space, it is presented in a shortened form. The original (centralized) histogram ([4]) was used to index moving object positions. The approach presented there assumed that every object (e.g. a car on the road) periodically issues updates concerning its position. That approach, however, is unrealistic in the real world. The more likely situation is when the traffic rate is measured by a static meter and reported to the central server at regular intervals. This paper presents a practical method of processing and storing of report streams coming from a large number of meters.

The data structure presented in [4] can't be applied directly to meter reading processing due to a different nature of the information. The work of [4] indexes the current number of cars within cell area and the buckets are created by grouping the square-shaped cells with similar number of objects. Every location update contains old and new position of a moving object. When an object issues an update, the number of objects in the cell covering the old (new) location is decreased (increased). This way every cell contains current number of objects within its extent. Meter readings have very different nature. A meter is a static object that periodically reports a value that is continuously increased (e.g. energy usage meter state). Such updates consist of two timestamps (times of collection of previous and current meter state) and the amount of used utility during this period. The value that needs to be indexed is not simply a current attribute of a cell, but information that also spans an undetermined time interval in the past. Processing of this kind of information requires a special approach.

2 Bucket Index

2.1 Adaptive Multi-dimensional Histogram

Problem Definition. AMH (*adaptive multi-dimensional histogram*) covers a two-dimensional space containing utility meters and a central server gathering information (readings) coming from the telemetry system. Each reading contains the current meter state, timestamp and identification number of the source meter. All meters report their states periodically. The two-dimensional data space is partitioned into a regular cell grid. The square-shaped cells track utility usage within their borders (see below).

A spatio-temporal range query $q(q_R, q_T)$ retrieves the amount of utility used (e.g. electricity, water, gas) within a rectangular region q_R in the time span defined by $q_T = (t_s, t_e)$. If the query region covers a large number of meters, exhaustive examination of all data sources or cells may be very costly. AMH (*adaptive multi-dimensional histogram*) mitigates this problem by grouping neighboring cells with similar usage into rectangular buckets. The bucket information is updated upon arrival of new updates and the bucket regions (cell groups) continuously adapt to data distribution changes. The adaptation process (reorganization) is performed incrementally when the CPU is idle, i.e. there are no updates or queries to process.

Approximate Usage Tracking Based on Stepping Time Window Algorithm. A cell of the grid can cover several meters reporting their states in an unsynchronized manner. To group a number of cells together, we need to compare the average utility usage in their extents during similar time periods (equal in length).

Each cell tracks the utility usage during a fixed-length time period called the *time window*. As new updates arrive, the time window is shifted in such a way that its end is always aligned with the collection time of the most recent collected reading and the approximate value is altered. Consider a cell containing four electricity meters L1 – L4, which send subsequent readings separated by undetermined time intervals (Fig. 1). A reading from meter L1 comes in the first step. It reports that 10 kWh was used between timestamp 1 and 6. This is the first update therefore the time window (whose length equals 6 time units) is set to (0, 6). The time span of the reading is entirely enclosed by the window W_1, thus the whole usage associated with the reading is stored in the cell (U_1=10). In the next step, meter L2 sends its reading. This reading was collected later than the first one therefore the time window is shifted to the right to position W_2=(1, 7). The window W_2 covers the previous window in 5/6 thus such portion of U_1 is transferred to W_2. Moreover, the usage associated with the reading L2 (12 kWh) is also added to W_2 and, as a result, the approximate usage is calculated as $U_2 = \frac{5}{6} * 10 + 12 = 20\frac{1}{3}$. Similar computations are performed for the subsequent readings.

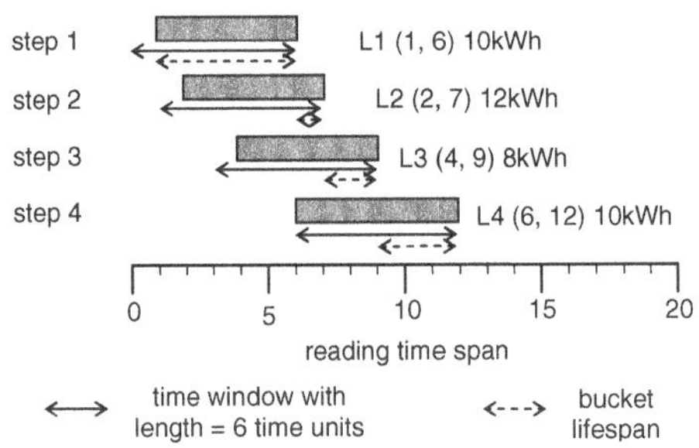

Fig. 1. Cell and bucket update

Note that the stepping window size should be tuned to the expected state reporting period (which is usually known). If the window size is too large, the approximate usage U_i will follow the actual value very slowly. On the other hand, if the window is too small, U_i will strongly depend only on the most recent received reading.

Structure. Given a cell grid, AMH generates $n \le B$ rectangular buckets, where B is a maximum allowed number of buckets. For each bucket b_k ($1 \le k \le n$) we denote (i) as n_k the number of cells it covers, (ii) as f_k the average usage computed based on cell contents ($f_k = (1/n_k)\Sigma_{\forall \text{ cell in } b_k} U_C$, where U_C is the usage associated with cell c (see previous section)) and (iii) as v_k the variance $v_k = (1/n_k)\Sigma_{\forall \text{ cell in } b_k} (U_C - f_k)^2$. The main aim of AMH is to minimize the *weighted variance sum* (*WVS*) of all buckets, formally (after [4]): $WVS = \sum_{i=1}^{n} (n_i \cdot v_i)$.

Each bucket stores the following information: R – coordinates of rectangular extent, $L=(l_s, l_e)$ – the lifespan and U_L – the lifespan usage (amount of a utility used in the lifespan L and region R). AMH maintains a *binary partition tree* (BPT), which speeds up bucket search operations during processing of updates or queries. The tree leaf corresponds to an existing bucket and intermediate node is associated with the rectangular extent that encloses the extents of its children. Initially, there is only one leaf node in the BPT which covers the entire data space. Subsequent buckets are created through bucket splits but their number never exceeds system parameter B.

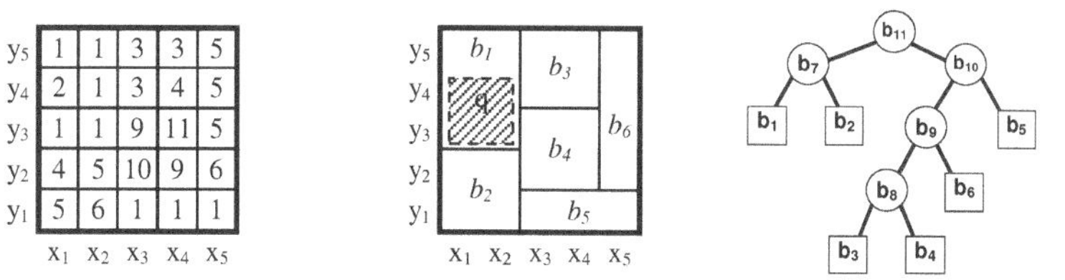

(a) Usage in cells (b) Bucket extents (c) Binary partition tree

Fig. 2. AMH [4]

Fig. 2a illustrates an example of a grid consisting of 25 cells. Figures 2b and c show generated buckets and corresponding BPT. For instance, intermediate node b_8 covers the buckets b_3 and b_4. This means that those buckets were created by splitting b_8.

Information Update. Each update is processed in two steps. First, the cell that contains the source meter coordinates is updated according to the stepping time window algorithm. Second, the bucket covering the source meter is located using BPT and its information is updated. If the reading time span intersects the lifespan of the bucket, U_L is increased by the usage u that corresponds to the processed reading proportionally to intersection ratio of the reading time span to the bucket lifespan.

Consider a sequence of updates as in Fig. 1, but this time processed in a bucket. In the first step, the meter L1 sends its reading. This is the first reading therefore the bucket b_1 is created with lifespan (1, 6) which is equal to the reading time span. Next, the meter L2 sends a reading with time span (2, 7). The time intervals (1, 6) and (2, 7) intersect, so the usage in bucket b_1 needs to be altered. As a result of the modification, the usage U_{L_1} is increased by $\frac{(2,7)}{(1,6)} * 12[\text{kWh}] = \frac{4}{5} * 12 = 9\frac{3}{5}[\text{kWh}]$. Then the bucket b_1 is removed and stored in a past index and a new bucket b_2 is spawned with the same extent but with altered lifespan L_2=(6, 7) and lifespan usage $U_{L_2} = \frac{1}{5} * 12 = 2\frac{2}{5}$.

Bucket Split. Buckets splits are performed in regions where the variance is large and has a negative effect on the accuracy of AMH. Bucket split improves the accuracy by (i) reducing variance and (ii) decreasing the bucket extent. Towards this, the algorithm selects a bucket with the *highest split benefit* (*SBen*) and splits it at the "best position". Split benefit is computed as the difference between values of *WVS* before and after the split. To find the highest split benefit of a bucket the algorithm examines all possible split positions.

Bucket Merge. A merge is performed when the number of buckets reaches the maximum value *B*. In such a case, the algorithm searches BPT for the bucket with the smallest *merge penalty* (*MPen*). *MPen* is defined as the increase of *WVS* being a consequence of merging the bucket with its sibling. For instance, merging b_3 with b_4 (Fig. 2c) increases *WVS* by $n_8 v_8 - (n_3 v_3 + n_4 v_4)$, removes the buckets from BPT and makes b_8 a leaf. Fig. 3 presents a pseudo-code of the bucket merge algorithm.

```
Initial assumption: minMPen = ∞ .
if (bucket is a leaf)
      compute its f_b and v_b using cell contents
else
      invoke Bucket-merge for the left child
      invoke Bucket-merge for the right child
      compute f_b and Mpen_b based on children information
      if (MPen_b < minMPen)
            minMPen = MPen_b
end if
```

Fig. 3. Bucket merge algorithm

Normally, when the index is not being reorganized, the buckets do not store information about the average usage or variance of covered cells. Because of this, these values need to be computed before each merge. To find the bucket with the smallest merge penalty, the algorithm processes all nodes of BPT using a single post-order traversal, i.e. the children are processed before the parent.

Query Processing. A query result is found by processing all buckets whose extents intersect the query region q_R. Fig. 2b illustrates an example query *q*. The query processing algorithm traverses the nodes b_{11}, b_7 and reaches leaf b_1. The query result is computed as bucket lifespan usage U_L multiplied by (i) coverage ratio of query region to bucket extent and (ii) intersection ratio of query time span to bucket lifespan. Formally, the query answer is computed as $q_{result} = c_R * c_T * U_L$, where $c_R = \frac{q_R}{R}$ and $c_T = \frac{q_T}{L}$ where factors c_R and c_T have values in range [0.0; 1.0].

2.2 Past Index

The past index stores dead buckets, i.e. buckets removed from AMH. A bucket in AMH dies when its extent changes due to split or merge or its information is updated. In each case, the following information is stored in the past index: bucket lifespan *L*, enclosed region *R* and lifespan usage U_L recorded in the bucket. The implementation is based on a packed B-Tree, in which each intermediate entry of the tree stores a lifespan that encloses lifespan of its all children and leaf nodes store information about the buckets.

2.3 Prediction Model

The prediction model forecasts a utility usage in the next time step based on previous steps. This estimation is done using *exponential smoothing* – a well-known method in time series analysis. According to this method, the value S'$_1$ in the next time step is computed as $S'_1 = \alpha S_0 + \alpha(1-\alpha)S_{-1} + \alpha(1-\alpha)^2 S_{-2} + ... + (1-\alpha)^n S_{-n}$, where S_0 is the actual value at the current timestamp, S_{-i} is the actual value at the past time step i, α is the *smoothing parameter* in the range (0,1) and n is the number of steps (history depth). In our case a time step corresponds to a fixed-length time interval, e.g. if meters report their states approximately every 20 minutes, then a 30-minute interval can be assumed as a time step.

3 Mobile Agent Based Distributed System

3.1 System Overview

In order to implement the presented indexing technique, we have created a distributed system based on mobile agents. *Mobile agent* is a software entity consisting of code and state that can move from one location (node) to another where it resumes its execution. The nodes in our system are stationary components called *platforms*. Fig. 4 illustrates the system architecture we have developed and implemented in Java 1.5 environment using CORBA as a middleware technology.

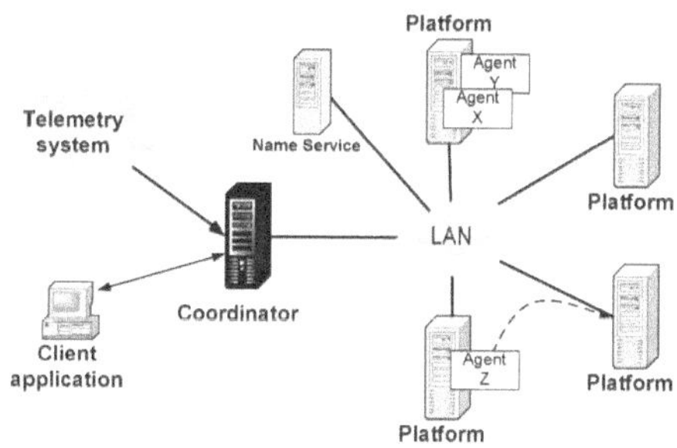

Fig. 4. Distributed system architecture

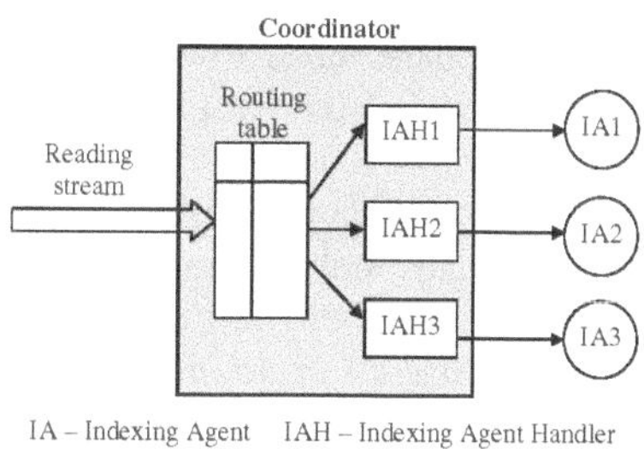

Fig. 5. Coordinator structure

The meter readings come from the telemetry system and are passed to the *coordinator* that is a stationary component which separates the external world from the distributed mobile system and its internal complexity. For security reasons the mobile system is not be accessible from the outside world. To ensure rapid agent migrations, the platforms are connected through a fast internal LAN network. The coordinator is responsible for authentication and authorization of external requests, meter reading forwarding and coordination of distributed index operations (e.g. forwarding of queries and merging partial results). It also has the capability of buffering of index updates which is required at the time when an indexing agent migrates from one platform to another, because during this period the agent is not able to process any data. Simplified coordinator structure is demonstrated in Fig. 5. The incoming readings are routed through routing table that maps meter IDs to indexing agent handlers (IAH).

The agent handlers work as separate threads that queue received readings and send them to associated indexing agents.

The platforms provide basic functions for execution and migration of mobile agents. There are two types of agents running in the system. The *indexing agents* make up the distributed bucket index and store the telemetry data. The data partitioning is done on the level of single meters, i.e. upon registration each meter is assigned exactly to one indexing agent (according to round-robin algorithm). Another type of agent is the *meta-agent* that is responsible for workload balancing of network hosts (see section 3.3). Finally, the *Name Service* (part of CORBA middleware) maintains a hierarchical structure which stores remote references of objects working in the system. The *client application* is a front-end GUI application that allows querying the information stored in the index and presenting it in graphical form.

3.2 Agent Migrations

One of the key operations in the system is the migration process of the indexing agent. The agent, in order to migrate to another platform, has to move both its code and state (data). When such a process is started (e.g. externally by the meta-agent – see 3.3), the agent must perform the following steps: 1) block all external update operations, 2) serialize all data either to the main memory (if available) or to the disk, 3) invoke a remote method call to copy the code and the data to the destination platform 4) start up a new copy of the agent on the remote platform, 5) if previous steps succeed inform all external invokers (e.g. the coordinator) of blocked update operations that the updates need to be send again but this time to the new agent copy and 6) shutdown and remove itself from the source platform. The blocking in the first step is required to prevent data modification attempts during steps two and three when the updates cannot be processed. The whole system is implemented in Java, so the agent code is usually small and is send as a JAR archive. Agent data, however, can be much larger (even tens of MB), so the data transfer in step three is based on a remote iterator that is passed in the method invocation to the remote platform and used to fetch agent data iteratively in portions (e.g. 64kB). Such an approach does not require that all agent data on the source platform is serialized to the memory and allows to avoid creation of large buffers in the underlying CORBA middleware during the remote method invocation. Due to this temporary agent unavailability, the coordinator must be capable of buffering of the updates during the migration process.

3.3 Workload Balancing Algorithm

The meta-agent (whose idea is taken from [5]) uses an algorithm that periodically checks the workload of all platforms (see Fig. 6). It computes the *scaled variability factor* $V' = \frac{s}{\bar{x}} * v_r$, where s is the standard deviance and $\bar{x}$ is the average available computing power in the mobile system (each platform tracks the CPU usage according to the moving average algorithm). If the V' is larger than a preset threshold V'_T (a system parameter), the meta-agent decides to perform an agent migration in order to improve the workload distribution. The coefficient $v_r = \sqrt[3]{\frac{\bar{x}}{\overline{x_{max}}}}$ (where $\overline{x_{max}}$ is the average of maximum computing powers of all hosts) has been introduced to reduce the *V'* value and prevent unnecessary agent migrations when the average workload of all hosts is very high (note that $\frac{\bar{x}}{x_{max}}$ is a value in range [0; 1]).

To perform a migration, all platforms are sorted in descending order of currently available computing power. Then, the least active agent from the last platform on the list is moved to the platform at the beginning of the list. If the destination platform's free memory capacity doesn't allow to upload the agent, the algorithm tries to move it to the next platform from the list. The same approach applies to source platforms – if the source platform for some reason cannot release an agent (e.g. due to error or no agents present) then the previous platform is selected from the list. What is important, the algorithm must obey one rule: the available computing power of the source (destination) platform candidate has to be lower (higher) than the average available power $\bar{x}$. If this requirement cannot be fulfilled the migration does not take place.

```
Initial assumption: n – number of platforms
for each platform
        retrieve its available and maximum computing power
compute x̄ and V'
if (V' > V'_T)
        create a list L of all platforms sorted in ascending order of available computing powers
        source := L[0], dest := L[n-1]
        loop
                try to move the least active agent from platform source to platform dest
                if (migration succeeded)
                        return SUCCESS
                if (migration failed due to source platform)
                        source:= source + 1
                if (migration failed due to dest platform)
                        dest := dest -1
                if (L[source] > x̄ or L[dest] < x̄)
                        return FAILURE
        end loop
```

Fig. 6. Workload balancing algorithm

4 Experimental Evaluation

To evaluate the accuracy and performance of the distributed bucket index we have conducted several experiments. The summary of parameters of the index we used in our experiments is given in Table 1.

The platforms and the coordinator (along with a reading generator) run on 3GHz Pentium 4 class machines connected via 100Mbit/s network.

4.1 Approximation and Prediction Accuracy

The approximation accuracy has been measured using a single (one agent version) index built on readings generated for 20 000 meters randomly distributed over the area of interest. In order to simulate fluctuation of the average utility usage over time, randomly chosen values, by which the meter states are increased, are additionally multiplied by the *amplifier factor* whose value is a function of simulation time.

Table 1. Index and Simulation Parameters

Parameter	Symbol	Value
Cell grid resolution	w x h	100 x 100
Stepping time window size	W	30 min
Past index node capacity	N_c	1000
Number of meters		20 000
Usage between two subsequent meter readings		Random in range 0.0 – 20.0
Time gap between two subsequent meter readings		Random in range 10 – 20 min
Interval between index reorganizations	R_T	500 or 5000 updates
Simulation time		0:00 – 23.49
Prediction model time step length		30 min
Number of prediction model steps	n	6
Smoothing factor	α	0.3
Query region side length	q_L	Random in range 1–10% or 2-20% of region side length

The index is reorganized every 500 or 5000 processed updates (depending on the experiment). This approach simulates a real world situation where the reorganization process modifies the index occasionally only when the CPU is not busy processing the updates or queries. Each reorganization is associated with several bucket splits and at most one bucket merge.

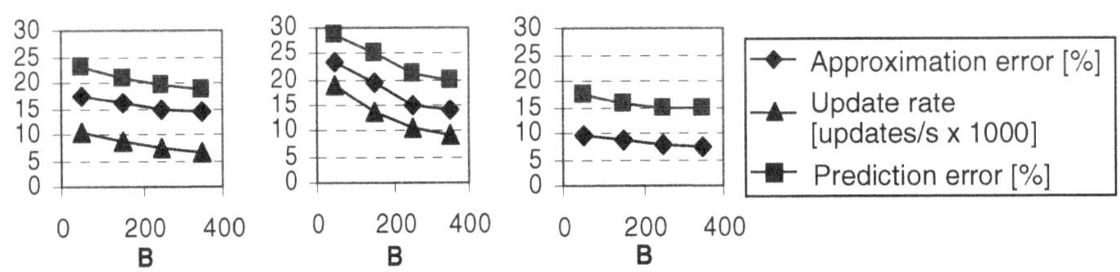

(a) R_T=500 q_L=1..10% (b) R_T=5000 q_L=1..10% (c) R_T=5000 q_L=2..20%

Fig. 7. Approximation and prediction error vs. *B*

Having built the index based on the whole day readings (0:00–23:49) we measure the error rate of the index caused by the approximation (i.e. grouping of cells) by comparing the results of random historical queries uniformly distributed over the area of interest with the actual usage generated by the generator. To perform the comparison we send 200 random forecasting queries concerning 30 minute time intervals between 3:00 (to ensure the prediction model can use at least 6 previous steps) and 23:30 (to be able to compare the actual value with the predicted one in the period 23:30 – 24:00).The results are demonstrated in Fig. 7.

The error rate slightly decreases with *B* because the data distribution in the cell grid is better modeled for larger values of *B*. The prediction error is always higher because of the error caused by the prediction model. Fig. 7 also shows that the update rate drops with *B* because for larger values of *B* the BPT is higher and the update algorithm needs to traverse longer path from the root to the leaf every time an update is received.

Fig. 7a and b show the results for different values of R_T. As expected, if AMH is being reorganized more often (Fig. 7a) the bucket index achieves better accuracy; however, frequent reorganizations require more computing power. Interesting observation is that for high values of *B* the error rate is similar both for R_T=500 and 5000. This shows that for high values of *B* the index accuracy is less influenced by the input stream rate.

Comparison of figures 7b and c shows that the query region size has also impact on the error rate what is explained by the fact, that larger query regions do not require high data granularity.

4.2 Speed-Up of the Distributed Version

The advantage of the distributed mobile version is measured in a system configuration consisting of four platforms, one coordinator host and one host running a reading generator. The simulation described in the previous section is repeated for a various number of agents placed on platforms according to the round-robin algorithm.

For settings with one to four indexing agents the speed-up is almost linear (Fig. 8). For larger number of agents the maximum update rate increases only slightly. This is explained by the fact that the CPUs of platforms were almost fully loaded already at the configuration with four agents, so adding more agents does not increase the maximum processing speed significantly. However the mobile agents, along with the meta-agent watching over the system, can help to balance the workload of the platforms what is demonstrated in the next section.

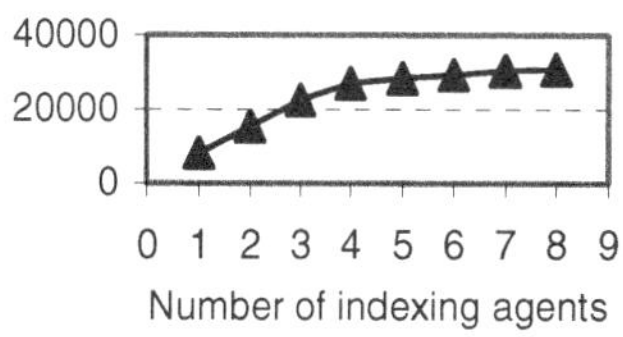

Fig. 8. Update rate (updates/s) as a function of number of agents

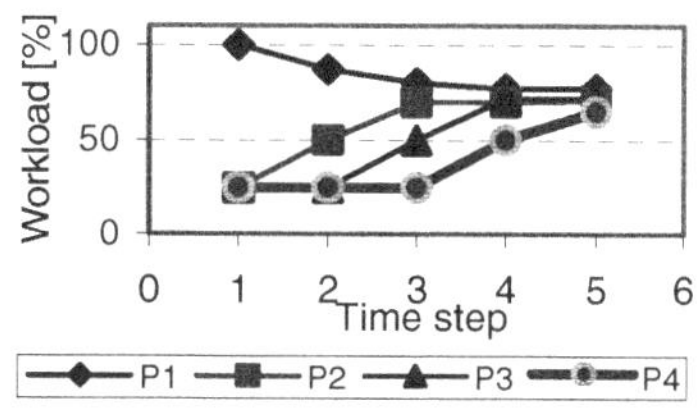

Fig. 9. Workload balancing

4.3 Workload Balancing

To evaluate the proposed workload balancing algorithm we test a configuration with one meta-agent and eight indexing agents. Five of them are initially placed on one of the platforms while the remaining six are evenly placed on the other three. Then we start the simulation at the maximal possible update rate and observe the CPU usage of the platforms (Fig. 9). At the beginning, the workload of the platform P1 (which hosts five indexing agents) is almost 100% and the other platforms, hosting 2 agents each, is about 25%. At the second time step the meta-agent decides to migrate an agent from platform P1 to P2. After the migration the workload of P2 increases gradually (the increase is not instant due to the moving average algorithm used to measure the CPU usage). In the third step the meta-agent moves an agent from P1 to P3 whose workload increases as well. Eventually, the workloads of all the platforms happen to be similar. Note that the workloads of platforms do not reach the 100% level, because for such amount of agents and platforms the coordinator host and the network become the bottleneck on the data transfer path.

5 Conclusions

In this paper we have presented the idea of the adaptive multi-dimensional histogram designed to index telemetric readings and applied in a mobile agent system. We have shown that the cell grouping technique allows to process and store large amount of data without using many system resources or storage space. Excellent index accuracy is ensured by partial reorganizations performed during "idle CPU states." This approach is different as opposed to traditional static index structures whose rebuild process is very costly and always must be performed from the beginning.

Historic data stored in the index is used to forecast utility usage in the near future according to exponential smoothing method. In our case, this method proved to be effective because the achieved prediction accuracy is satisfactory.

The idea of bucket index has been implemented in a distributed mobile agent system based on mobile agents. A set of experiments proved that the mobile architecture significantly improves the processing performance and helps to control the workload.

References

1. Gorawski M., Dyga A. *Indexing of Spatio -Temporal Telemetric Data based on Distributed Mobile Bucket Index*. Parallel and Distributed Computing and Networks (PDCN), February 14-16, 2006, Innsbruck, Austria.
2. Gorawski, M., Malczok, R., *Distributed Spatial Data Warehouse Indexed with Virtual Memory Aggregation Tree*. 5th Workshop on Spatial-Temporal DataBase Management (STDBM_VLDB'04), Toronto, Canada 2004.
3. Gorawski, M., Malczok, R. *On Efficient Storing and Processing of Long Aggregate Lists*. Proceedings of the 7th International Conference Data Warehousing and Knowledge Discovery (DaWak2005, LNCS 3589), Copenhagen, Denmark 2005.
4. Sun, J., Papadias, D., Tao, Y., Liu, B. *Querying about the Past, the Present and the Future in Spatio-Temporal Databases*. Proceedings of the 20th IEEE International Conference on Data Engineering (ICDE), Boston, MA, 2004.
5. Dimarzo, G., Romanovsky, A. *Designing Fault-Tolerant Mobile Systems*. Revised Papers from the International Workshop on Scientific Engineering for Distributed Java Applications (LNCS 2604), London, UK, 2002.

An Incremental Refining Spatial Join Algorithm for Estimating Query Results in GIS

Wan D. Bae, Shayma Alkobaisi, and Scott T. Leutenegger

Department of Computer Science, University of Denver
2360 South Gaylord Street, Denver, CO 80206, U.S.A.
{wbae, salkobai, leut}@cs.du.edu

Abstract. Geographic information systems (GIS) must support large georeferenced data sets. Due to the size of these data sets finding exact answers to spatial queries can be very time consuming. We present an incremental refining spatial join algorithm that can be used to report query result estimates while simultaneously provide incrementally refined confidence intervals for these estimates. Our approach allows for more interactive data exploration. While similar work has been done in relational databases, to the best of our knowledge this is the first work using this approach in GIS. We investigate different sampling methodologies and evaluate them through extensive experimental performance comparisons. Experiments on real and synthetic data show an order of magnitude response time improvement relative to the exact answer obtained when using the R-tree join.

1 Introduction

Geographic Information Systems (GIS) are used in many fields and applications for exploring large data sets in order to obtain intuition and insight into the stored information. GIS queries often compute exact numerical query answers. However, computing the exact answers to queries in large databases can be time consuming. Often an approximate answer is sufficient and can prevent wasted computation time, thus allowing a more interactive exploration of the data. Our goal is to speed up the exploratory process of GIS data while providing a statistical confidence of preliminary results through an incremental refining process. For example, instead of waiting a long time for an exact answer, we compute an approximate answer, say bounded by 5% of the exact answer with 95% probability (confidence level), in $\frac{1}{20}$ of the time needed for an exact answer. To make the system more interactive, the user is given the ability to stop queries whenever the answer is "good enough". This approach allows the user to quickly obtain an idea of whether or not the query is useful and can therefore modify it or stop it accordingly. While GIS and spatial databases offer many sophisticated algorithms for computing exact query answers for spatial data, many of these techniques are time prohibitive for the exploration of large spatial data sets. Thus, many GIS applications can benefit from our approximate and fast approach.

S. Bressan, J. Küng, and R. Wagner (Eds.): DEXA 2006, LNCS 4080, pp. 935–944, 2006.

In this paper we present the *Incremental Refining Spatial Join (IRSJ)* algorithm. The *IRSJ* algorithm provides an order of magnitude improvement in response time relative to a full R-tree join. The algorithm achieves its reduced execution time by providing query estimates obtained from a subset of the full join directed by random sampling. We experimentally compare two versions of the *IRSJ* algorithm against each other as well as against the time needed to obtain an exact answer using a full R-tree join algorithm.

2 Background

2.1 Overview of GIS and Motivation

GIS data are used to describe the geometry and location of various types of geographic phenomena [12]. Geographic or spatial queries are performed on a spatially indexed database in order to obtain answers that depend on spatial relationships between data items [13]. Examples of spatial relationships include intersection, containment, and adjacency. While our approach can be used for any of these, in this paper we focus on finding an estimate of the number of intersections. An example where our method would be useful is "How many mineral plants intersect radiometric aged areas in the US?", where this query returns the number of areas that can be of interest to geologists to estimate the earth's age. Such a query would likely take a long time to find the exact number of intersections. Our approach allows the time to be dramatically reduced if the user is willing to accept an estimated value within a bounded confidence interval.

2.2 Related Work

Our work follows the lead of online query processing work done at the University of California-Berkeley [1,3,4]. The authors proposed an interface for online relational aggregation to provide the user with the ability to control the query execution process. The goal was to minimize time by obtaining an approximate query answer instead of computing the exact answer. They proposed the "ripple join" as part of this paradigm. We follow their general framework but devise a new approximate sampling based join algorithm to work for spatial data.

Spatial relations are usually indexed using R-trees [8]. An R-tree is a height balanced tree structure adapted from the B-tree to support spatial data. An R-tree stores the minimum bounding rectangles (MBRs) of objects. When performing a query, all rectangles that intersect the query region are retrieved. This is done in a recursive way starting from the root and following the paths down to the leaf level. A spatial join computes the pairwise intersection of all data objects in two spatial data sets. Many spatial join algorithms based on R-trees have been proposed with perhaps two of the most common being found in [9,10]. Our algorithm follows a similar approach to that found in [10]. A data item from one data set is joined with the other data set by executing a window query. For example, if we join "cities" and "rivers", then the MBR of a city provides the query MBR to be executed against the river data set. Our work differs from the past work in that we only execute intersection queries for a subset of the "outer" data set through sampling. We incrementally refine the query answer until we get the desired confidence interval accuracy.

Another approach for obtaining join selectivity estimates is to use histogram-based methods [11]. Such methods offer the promise of even faster query estimates than our method, but still have disadvantages. Although the experimental results in [11] show low error, the method is not bounded whereas our method provides error confidence intervals and the ability to incrementally tighten the intervals. Also the histogram methods provide an estimate of the number of joins, but they do not provide actual join results. Our method can be used to produce a subset of the actual join results rather than just an estimate of the number of tuples that will join.

3 The Incremental Refining Spatial Join in GIS

Our incremental refining spatial join algorithm consists of three steps: sampling, spatial joining, and refining the estimation of the query result.

3.1 Random Data Sampling

Sampling chooses a subset of the data to obtain query estimates. Chosen samples should accurately represent the entire data set, and a confidence interval is used to reflect the accuracy of the estimated value [14,15]. We consider two common database sampling methods: tuple-level and page-level [5]. In tuple-level sampling, a number of tuples are chosen as samples, each with the same probability. Tuple-level sampling obtains random samples regardless of data clustering, however, its performance is poor if no index is available. If an index is available, then performance is improved since the sampling predicate is applied inside the index of leaf pages. In page-level sampling, pages are chosen as samples instead of tuples. If a page is chosen at random, all tuples in that page are processed to calculate the number of intersections for that page. Page-level sampling has better performance than tuple-level in terms of I/Os [5]. However, aggregate estimate accuracy can be worse when using page-level sampling due to the correlation of data within a page. The query estimations and the confidence intervals are statistically meaningful only if samples are retrieved in random order. [6] presented techniques for random sampling from various indices to produce meaningful confidence intervals.

In our experiments we used one of the weighted random sampling methods, *Acceptance/Rejection* in [6,7], in which the inclusion probability is proportional to some parameter of the item sampled. We investigated tuple-level and page-level sampling with varying data sets and buffer sizes. We do sampling incrementally without replacement.

Algorithm 1. $IRSJ_t(R, S, C_f, n)$

```
C ← 0; C_I ← 0 { count, confidence interval}
repeat
    for i = 0 to k do
        L ← Choose leaf from R at random
        M ← MBR of a randomly chosen tuple within L
        I ← number of intersections of a Window Query(M, S)
        C ← C + I
    end for
    C_I ← Compute confidence interval using C
    EV ← Compute estimated value using C
until The desired confidence interval C_f is attained
```

3.2 The Incremental Refining Spatial Join Algorithm (*IRSJ*)

We have developed and compared two *IRSJ* versions: $IRSJ_t$ and $IRSJ_p$ for tuple-based and page-based sampling, respectively. Assume we have two data sets, denoted R and S, that we wish to join. Let R be the outer data set and S be the inner data set. We assume R and S are both indexed by R-trees.

In $IRSJ_t$ we select a page of R at random and choose one tuple within this page at random. We use the MBR of this tuple as the MBR of an intersection query to query data set S using its R-tree. The number of intersections is reported and used in calculating a running estimated value and a confidence interval. Algorithm 1 describes $IRSJ_t$, where C_f is the desired confidence interval and k (updating rate) is the number of tuples in each sampling step. A tradeoff exists between the rate at which the confidence intervals are updated and the time to which the interval length decreases at each update. In our experiments we used $k = 30$. Since pages may contain a different number of tuples, especially if R is indexed by an R-tree, it is necessary to choose pages with a probability relative to the number of tuples within the page.

In $IRSJ_p$ we sample a page of R at random for each update. The difference between $IRSJ_t$ and $IRSJ_p$ is that in $IRSJ_p$ we compute an intersection query for each tuple within a sampled page, then use the obtained average as a single sample. Due to likely correlation of tuples within a page, it is necessary to treat the average of the page as a single value when calculating the confidence interval.

4 Confidence Interval Calculation

To provide bounds on the accuracy of our incremental result, we concurrently calculate and return to the user the current estimated value and confidence interval. We give an overview of the statistical method used in *IRSJ* and present the confidence interval of a population proportion based on the Central Limit Theorem (CLT) [2,14,15]. CLT states that the sampling distribution of the sample mean approximates a normal distribution for a specified number of samples from any population. The approximation improves with more samples. For the confidence interval we use the binomial probability distribution. The outcome of each trial (join) is either "intersect" or "does not intersect". The binomial distribution is determined by the number of trials n and the probability p of success in a single trial. The probability of a success remains the same from one trial to the next. We assume that the normal curve is a good approximation to the binomial distribution. Empirical studies have shown that these methods are quite good when both $np > 5$ and $nq > 5$, where $q = 1 - p$ [15].

We describe the way to obtain the confidence intervals of a population proportion. Let r be the number of successes out of n trials in a binomial experiment. We take the sample proportion of successes $\hat{p} = r/n$ as our point estimate for p, the population proportion of successes, and point estimate for q is $\hat{q} = 1-\hat{p}$. The difference between the actual value of p and the estimate $\hat{p}$ is called the error estimate for using $\hat{p}$ as a point estimate for p. For large samples the distribution of $\hat{p}$ is well approximated by a normal curve with mean $\mu = p$ and standard error $\sigma = \sqrt{\frac{pq}{n}}$. Since the distribution of $\hat{p}$ is approximately normal, we use features of the standard normal distribution to find the difference $\hat{p}-p$. An interval that estimates a population parameter within a range of possible values at a specified probability is called confidence level c. Let z_c be the number such that an area equal to c under the standard normal curve falls between $-z_c$ and z_c. Then we have $P(-z_c\sqrt{\frac{pq}{n}} < \hat{p} - p < z_c\sqrt{\frac{pq}{n}}) = c$.

We call E the maximal error tolerance of the error of estimate $|\hat{p} - p|$ for a confidence level. To find the confidence interval for p, we have $P(\hat{p}-E < p < \hat{p}+E) = c$. The difficulty is that we may not know the actual values of p or q in most situations, so we use our point estimates $p \approx \hat{p}$ and $q = 1-p \approx 1-\hat{p}$ to estimate E. These estimates are safe for most practical purposes since we are dealing with large-sample theory. Then the confidence interval for p is $\hat{p} - E < p < \hat{p} + E$, where $\hat{p} = \frac{r}{n}$: we have $E = z_c\sqrt{\frac{\hat{p}(1-\hat{p})}{n}} = z_c\sqrt{\frac{\hat{p}\hat{q}}{n}}$, where z_c= critical value for confidence level c taken from a normal distribution.

In $IRSJ_t$, $n = n_t$, the number of tuples processed and in $IRSJ_p$, $n = n_p$, the number of pages processed. Note that $n_p \leq n_t$. Different sampling methods generalize the standard CLT of confidence interval formulas [14]. We use the following formula for the confidence interval of $IRSJ_t$:

$$E = z_c\sqrt{\frac{\hat{p}(1-\hat{p})}{n-1} \cdot \frac{N-n}{N}}$$

5 Experiments

In this section we present experimental results of the $IRSJ_t$ and $IRSJ_p$ algorithms on both synthetic and real GIS data sets. We compare the algorithms to each other as well as to obtain an exact answer using a full R-tree join algorithm [9]. We show the estimated values and the corresponding confidence intervals returned to the user with a 95% confidence level. We present the number of I/Os with varied buffer sizes as well as the number of node (page) accesses. All code is implemented in Java.

5.1 Datasets and Experimental Methodology

We consider both synthetic and real data sets in our studies. Our synthetic data sets consist of (i) uniform (random) and (ii) skewed (hyper-exponential) distributions. For the uniform data set, (x,y) locations are distributed uniformly and independently between 0 and 1. The (x,y) locations for the skewed data sets are independently drawn from a hyper-exponential distribution with mean 0.3 and variance 0.25. Let U and S denote uniform and skewed distributed data sets, respectively. We considered all join combinations: $S \bowtie S$, $U \bowtie S$, $S \bowtie U$, $U \bowtie U$. We vary the number of tuples of each data set between 100,000 and 600,000 tuples. We only present the most illustrative subset of our results due to space limitations. Results not shown also resulted in up to an order of magnitude improvement in performance. Our real data sets are from the U.S. Geological Survey in 2001 and 2005 [16]: (i) Mineral Resources in the US (outer relation R): U.S. Geological Survey, 2005. (ii) Geochemistry of unconsolidated sediments in the US (inner relation S): U.S. Geological Survey, 2001. The two data sets have 300,434 and 199,850 tuples (MBRs), respectively.

Our experiments are conducted using the following parameters: R-tree page size of 4Kbytes with fan-out size of 100 for leaf and non-leaf nodes and minimum capacity of 40. Since R-trees are disk-based index structures, the natural performance metric is the number of page I/Os required for a given buffer size. We assume an LRU buffer and vary buffer size between 300 and 1800 pages resulting in the buffer holding between 3% and 60% of the inner R-tree.

5.2 Synthetic Data Results

We first present results for the synthetic data sets. In Figure 1 (a) and (c) we plot the running estimated query result versus the numbers of tuples processed. The smoother line is for $IRSJ_t$ while the jagged line is for $IRSJ_p$. In Figure 1 (a) the outer data set is uniform while the inner data set is skewed, and in Figure 1 (c) the outer data set is skewed while the inner data set is uniform. In Figure 1 (b) and (d) we plot the confidence interval versus time measured as the number of buffer misses. Figure (b) corresponds to (a) and figure (d) to (c). The time to process a page of tuples in $IRSJ_p$ is greater than the time to process a tuple in $IRSJ_t$, thus, the most fair comparison is time which is directly proportional to the number of buffer misses. The top curve is for $IRSJ_p$ and the lower curve is for $IRSJ_t$. The vertical line on the right is the execution time needed for a full R-tree join algorithm. The estimate accuracy is significantly worse under $IRSJ_p$ than $IRSJ_t$. Put another way, the $IRSJ_t$ algorithm takes less time to obtain the same accuracy as $IRSJ_p$. Note that the time to obtain an exact answer is more than an order of magnitude greater than that needed to get an accuracy within 5% using $IRSJ_t$.

In Figure 2 we show experimental results when we vary the size of the data sets and also vary buffer size to keep the buffer size fixed at 10% of the inner R-tree size. As can be seen, the full R-tree join requires 4-16 times more disk access

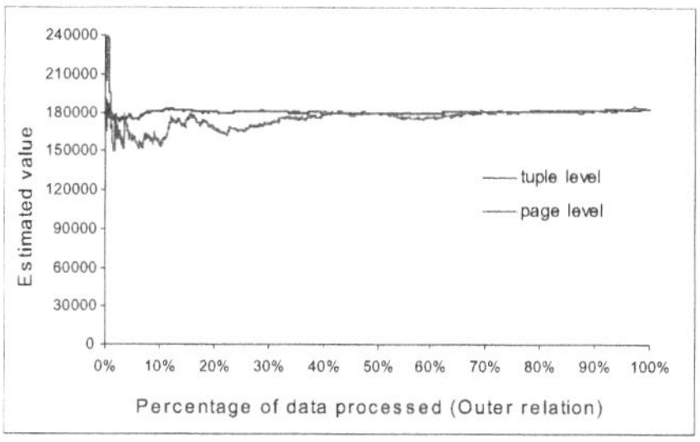

(a) Estimated Value: U-600K ⋈ S-400K

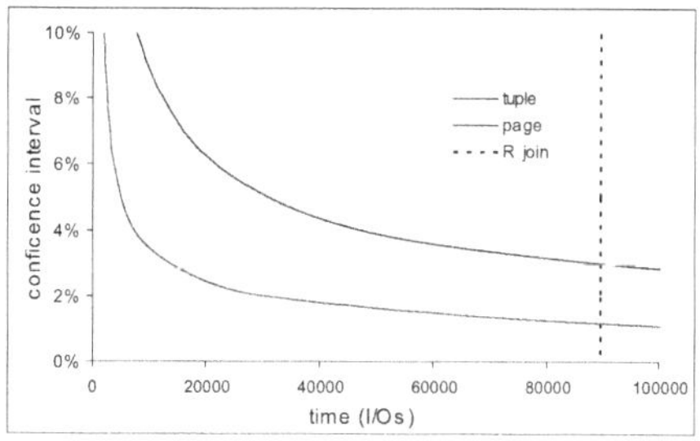

(b) Confidence Interval: U-600K ⋈ S-400K

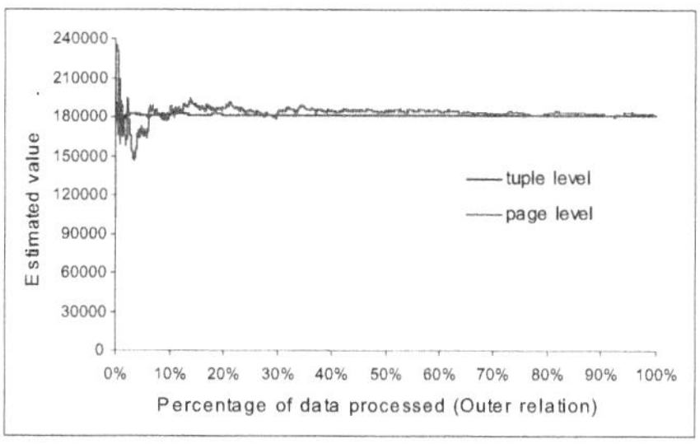

(c) Estimated Value: S-600K ⋈ U-400K

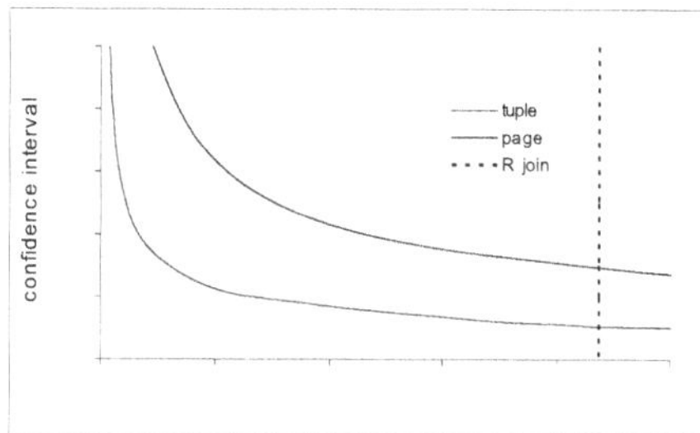

(d) Confidence Interval: S-600K ⋈ U-400K

Fig. 1. Estimated Value and Confidence Interval for synthetic datasets 600K ⋈ 400K

than $IRSJ_t$ with a 5% half confidence interval. As the data set size increases the advantage of $IRSJ_t$ over the full R-tree join increases. Thus, for larger data sets, as expected in a real GIS, the benefit of our proposed approach will be even greater. Figure 3 shows the results for an experiment where the size of data sets is varied while buffer size is fixed at 1200 pages. Experiment results show that $IRSJ_t$ provides an I/O performance improvement of more than an order of magnitude relative to the R-tree join.

5.3 GIS Real Data Result

We now present results for the U.S.G.S. data sets. Our query is to join mineral resources with geochemical unconsolidated sediments in the US. The query returns the number of intersections of mineral resources and geochemical unconsolidated sediments. In Figure 4 we plot the accuracy and confidence intervals for $IRSJ_t$ and $IRSJ_p$. Again, the smoother line is for $IRSJ_t$ while the jagged line is for $IRSJ_p$. As can be seen, $IRSJ_t$ takes less I/Os to get the same accuracy as $IRSJ_p$. In Table 1 on page 943 we present the number of I/Os and the number of node accesses with buffer size 5% and 10% of the inner R-tree. For a buffer size of 10%, the R-tree join requires 74 times more I/Os than the $IRSJ_t$ with a 5% half confidence interval. In Figure 5 we present results of our experiments when we vary buffer size from 300 to 1800 pages. The experiment results again show that $IRSJ_t$ provides a good estimation in very early query processing stages.

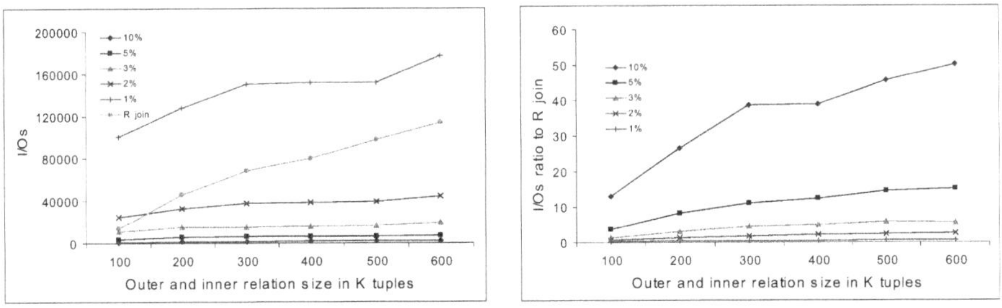

(a) I/Os with 10% buffer (b) I/O Ratio to R-tree join

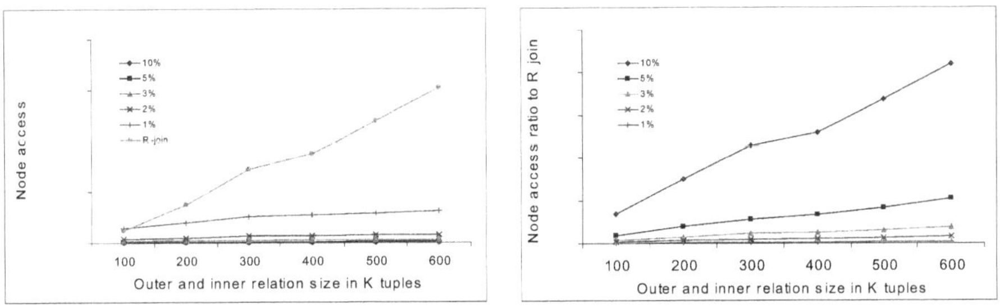

(c) Node Accesses with 10% buffer (d) Node Access Ratio to R-tree join

Fig. 2. I/Os and Node Accesses of $IRSJ_t$ for varying size of synthetic datasets with 10% buffer size and Ratio to a full R-tree join: $R(\text{uniform}) \bowtie S(\text{skewed})$

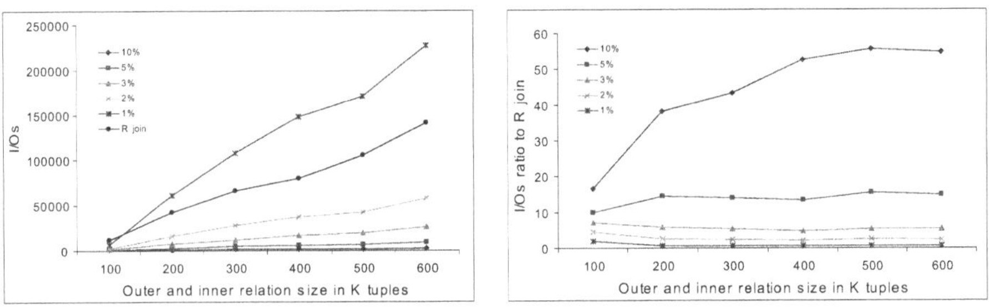

(a) I/Os (b) I/O Ratio to R-tree join

Fig. 3. I/Os and Ratio of $IRSJ_t$ to a full R-tree join for varying size of synthetic datasets with a fixed buffer size 1200

6 Conclusions

In this paper we proposed the Incremental Refining Spatial Join ($IRSJ$) algorithm to efficiently estimate the results to spatial queries. We implemented two versions of $IRSJ$: one based on tuple-level sampling ($IRSJ_t$) and the other based on page-level sampling ($IRSJ_p$). Our experiments show that the time

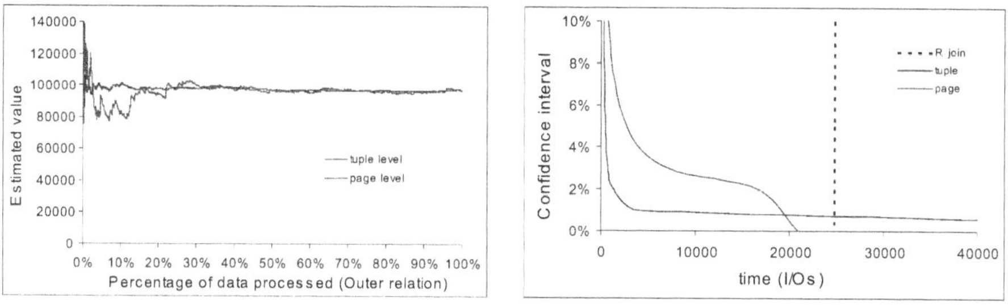

(a) Estimated Value (b) Confidence Interval

Fig. 4. Estimated Value and Confidence Interval for the real datasets

Table 1. I/Os and Node Accesses of $IRSJ_t$ and a full R-tree join for the real datasets: H.C.I.=Half Confidence Interval, Buffer size=Percent of relation size

	Buffer Size	H.C.I.=10	H.C.I.=5	H.C.I.=3	H.C.I.=2	H.C.I.=1	R-join
I/Os	5%	233	403	770	1896	8159	27756
	10%	182	333	752	1164	3795	24756
Node Accesses	5%	780	2591	6933	18299	87233	262200
	10%	668	2136	9028	19671	85822	262200

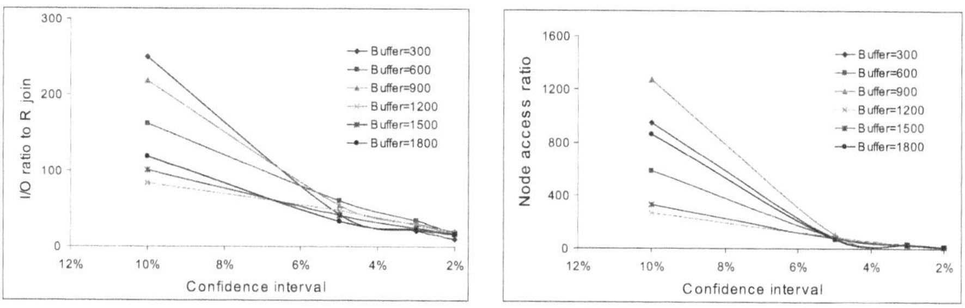

(a) I/O ratio to R-tree join (b) Node Access ratio to R-tree join

Fig. 5. I/Os and Node Access Ratio to a full R-tree join for the real datasets

(I/Os) required to obtain a reasonably accurate estimate was order of magnitude smaller than the time needed for an exact answer obtained using a full R-tree join algorithm using both real and synthetic data sets. We also observed that as the size of data sets increases, the improvement of $IRSJ_t$ over the full R-tree join also increases. Thus, the benefit of our approach will be even greater for larger GIS data sets. Perhaps surprisingly, our tuple-level sampling algorithm performed better than our page-level sampling algorithm. This is a result of only being able to use one datum in confidence interval calculation due to data set clustering which violates the needed independence. In our future work we plan to investigate different sampling methods to improve the performance of *IRSJ* and develop a mathematical model to determine the optimal sampling strategy. Further, we plan to explore the utility of *IRSJ* for answering multiway joins.

Acknowledgments

The following people provided helpful suggestions during early stages of this work: Mario Lopez, Sada Narayanappa, Brandon Haenlein, and Mohammed Albow. Help in statistics was graciously provided by Prof. Ray Boersema and Prof. Tom Obremski.

References

1. Hellerstein, J. M., Hass, P. J., Wang, H. J.: Online aggregation. In Proc. ACM SIGMOD. (1997) 171–182
2. Hass, P. J.: Large-sample and deterministic confidence intervals for online aggregation. In Proc. SSDM. (1997) 51–63
3. Hass, P. J., Hellerstein, J. M.: Ripple Joins for Online Aggregation. In Proc. ACM SIGMOD. (1999) 287–298
4. Hellerstein, J. M., Avnur, R., Raman, V.: Informix under CONTROL: Online Query Processing. Data Mining and Knowledge Discovery. Vol.12 (2000) 281–314
5. Seshadri, S.: Probabilistic methods in Query Processing. Ph.D. Dissertation. University of Wisconsin. (1992)
6. Olken, F.: Random Sampling from Databases. Ph.D. Dissertation. University of California, Berkeley. (1993)
7. Rubinstein, R. Y.: Simulation and the Monte Carlo Method, John Wiley and Sons, Inc. (1981)
8. Guttman, A.: R-trees: a Dynamic Index Structure for Spatial Searching. In Proc. ACM SIGMOD. (1984) 45–57
9. Brinkhoff, T., Kriegel, H., Seeger, B.: Efficient Processing of Spatial Joins Using R-trees. In Proc. ACM SIGMOD. (1993) 237–246
10. Papadias, D., Mamoulis, N., Theodoridis, Y.: Processing and Optimization of Multiway Spatial Joins Using R-trees. In Proc. ACM PODS. (1999) 44–55
11. An, N., Yang, Z., Sivasubramaniam, A.: Selectivity estimation for spatial joins. In Proc. ICDE. (2001) 368–375
12. Medeiros, C. B., Pires, F.: Databases for GIS. ACM SIDMOD Record. Vol.23, No.1 (1994) 107–115
13. Larson, R. R.: Geographic Information Retrieval and Spatial Browsing. GIS and Libraries. University of Illinois. (1996) 81–127
14. Scheaffer, R. L., Mendenhall, W., Ott, R.L.: Elementary Survey Sampling. 5th edn. New York. Duxbury Press. (1995)
15. Serfling, R. J.: Basic Statistics for Business and Economics. McGraw-Hill. 4th edn. New York. (2002)
16. USGS Mineral Resources On-Line Spatial Data : http://tin.er.usgs.gov/. (2001, 2005)

Extensions to Stream Processing Architecture for Supporting Event Processing*

Vihang Garg, Raman Adaikkalavan, and Sharma Chakravarthy

IT Laboratory & Department of Computer Science and Engineering
The University of Texas at Arlington, Arlington, TX 76019
{adaikkal, sharma}@cse.uta.edu

Abstract. Both event and stream data processing models have been researched independently and are utilized in diverse application domains. Although they complement each other in terms of their functionality, there is a critical need for their synergistic integration to serve newer class of pervasive and sensor-based monitoring applications. For instance, many advanced applications generate interesting simple events as a result of stream processing that need to be further composed and detected for triggering appropriate actions. In this paper, we present EStream, an approach for integrating event and stream processing for monitoring changes on stream computations and for expressing and processing complex events on continuous queries (CQs). We introduce masks for reducing uninteresting events and for detecting events correctly and efficiently. We discuss stream modifiers, a special class of stream operators for computing changes over stream data. We also briefly discuss architecture and functional modules of EStream.

1 Introduction

Recently, *Data Stream Management Systems* (DSMSs) have received considerable attention. A number of issues have been addressed ranging from architecture [1,2] to scheduling strategies [3,4] to Quality of Service(QoS) [5,6]. Similarly, *event processing* [7,8,9,10,11] has received a lot of attention in the last decade. Different computational models for event processing such as Petri nets [8], extended automata and event graphs [7,9] have been proposed and implemented. Although both of these areas have been developed independently and are useful for a variety of applications, neither of them is individually adequate for a number of real-world applications. By integrating an expressive event processing system with a stream processing system synergistically, the scope of events can be expanded to arbitrary continuous queries which is not the case currently. Hence the integration of the event and stream processing will provide an end-to-end solution for a large class of applications.

In this paper, we briefly describe *MavStream* [12,13,14] and *LED* [10,11] as examples of home-grown stream and event processing architectures, respectively.

* This research was supported in part by NSF Grants IIS-0326505, and EIA-0216500, MRI 0421282, and IIS 0534611.

S. Bressan, J. Küng, and R. Wagner (Eds.): DEXA 2006, LNCS 4080, pp. 945–955, 2006.

We have extended both the event and stream processing systems[1]. We propose an integrated model and discuss its various stages. We introduce stream modifiers, a class of stream operators for computing changes over stream data. We introduce masks for reducing uninteresting events generated from continuous queries and for detecting events correctly and efficiently. Finally, we present the functional modules of the integrated system and experiments demonstrating the effectiveness of masks.

2 Background: MavStream and Local Event Detector

MavStream: [12,13,14] has been developed for processing continuous queries (CQs) over streams and is modeled as a client-server architecture. Each CQ from the user is converted into a plan object and is sent to the server. *MavStream server* is responsible for converting the plan object into a query tree and processing it to give the desired output. The *instantiator* traverses the plan object in a bottom-up fashion and populates the operator instances with the predicates (conditions) defined in the query plan object. The *scheduler* is responsible for scheduling the operators of a CQ using a determined strategy. It schedules operators of a query based on its state and priority. The QoS optimization depends upon the scheduling strategy selected by the scheduler. The scheduling strategies [4,14] supported are: Round-Robin, Weighted round-robin, Path capacity scheduling (for minimizing tuple latency), Segment scheduling and Simplified segment scheduling (both for balancing memory usage and tuple latency).

Local Event Detector (LED): [10,11] is based on the event-condition-action (or ECA) paradigm. ECA rules consist of events (occurrence of interest), conditions (simple or a complex query) and actions (operations to be performed when conditions evaluate to true). Simple events are predefined domain specific events. *Event Operators* are used to construct composite events. Some of the event operators supported are: OR, AND, Sequence, NOT, Aperiodic, Periodic, Plus, and Cumulative Aperiodic and Periodic. When a simple event is detected/raised, an event object is created and is placed in a notify buffer. They are then propagated to other composite events who subscribe to it in the Event Detection Graph (EDG). LED supports four *event consumption modes* (recent, chronicle, continuous and cumulative) for capturing meaningful application semantics and to reduce the space and computation overhead for the detection of composite events. *Rule Priority* can be assigned to each rule. Rules can be specified either in the immediate or the deferred coupling mode.

3 Integrated Model

Four stage integrated model is shown in Figure 1. Each stage is briefly explained below.

[1] Due to space constraints we will explain some of the extensions to stream processing. For more details refer [15,16].

Continuous Query Processing Stage: This stage represents the MavStream stream processing system that accepts stream data as input and produces stream data as output. CQs output data streams in the form of tuples. MavStream, in addition to those discussed in Section 2, has a number of stream operators: Select, Project, Join, Aggregates (sum, count, max, min, and average) and Group By. Output from a CQ is propagated to the event processing stage through the event generation and stream modifiers stage.

Event Processing Stage: This stage represents the LED event processing architecture, where simple and composite events are defined and event detection graphs corresponding to those events are constructed. LED consumes detected simple events from the notify buffer via the LED thread and propagates it to the composite event nodes (parent node) in the event graph. In the integrated model simple events are raised by the event generation and stream modifiers stage.

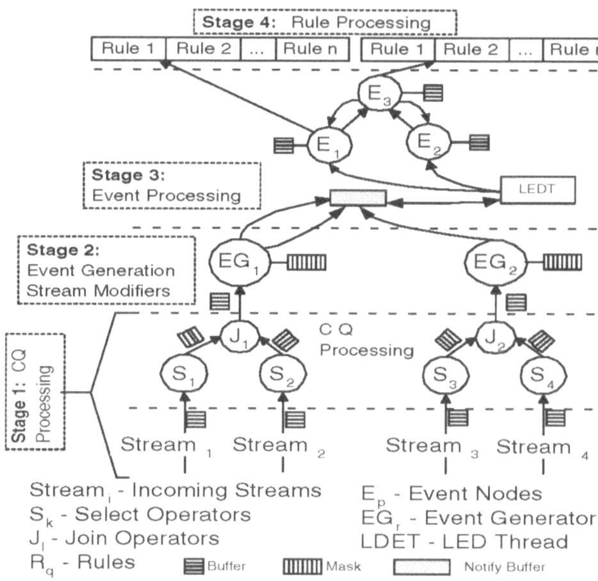

Fig. 1. Four Stage Integrated Model

Rule Processing Stage: Rule processing is also a part of LED and it processes rules that are associated with simple and composite events. When events are detected, conditions (specified as methods) are evaluated and when they return TRUE corresponding actions are performed. Rules can also be added at runtime.

Coupling Event and Stream Processing: This represents the stage 2 with event generation and stream modifiers. In addition to the conceptual extensions to both the models, *stage 2* has been added to facilitate seamless integration of the two systems. The seamless nature of our integrated model is due to the compatibility of the chosen event processing model (i.e., data flow computation using an event detection graph) with the model used for stream processing (data flow computation using a network of queues).

Users can define simple events on named CQs with optional masks. Once defined, there should be a mechanism for converting stream tuples into event tuples. Several designs for generating events were considered and analyzed before settling on the one described in this paper [15]. *Event Generator Operator (EG)* is designed as the root node of a CQ. EG converts stream tuples from CQ output into event objects, populates event attribute values and inserts event objects into the notify buffer. In addition, EG node can also pass the output directly to applications. In order to facilitate the conversion, EG contains the mapping of events that need to be generated for CQs.

Masks are defined for simple events and they provide a mechanism for filtering events based on one or more event attribute values. Mask processing, described later, has been introduced to filter simple events using arbitrary conditions on the attributes of the event. As event objects are generated from the CQs, masks are pushed into the EG operator node and are evaluated. The event generator operator can take any number of masks and for each mask, a different event tuple/object is created and sent to the notify buffer. Masks reduce the load on the event processor as unlike stream processing there are no queues to hold events in the event processing stage. Masks can be added/modified dynamically at runtime.

For the stream-side, we have introduced a new class of operators called *Stream Modifiers* for computing the change in the values of attributes between two tuples of the data stream. Stream modifiers are supported both in windowed and non-windowed modes. The extensions identified and implemented in the form of stream modifiers enable one to convert stream output into interesting changes that are used as events for further monitoring.

Thus, when an event is defined on a CQ , an EG operator node is created. In addition, stream modifiers can also be a part of the CQ before sending the output to the EG node. When a stream tuple is output from the stream modifier or from any other CQ node, it is propagated to the EG node. Since a conventional stream processing system is likely to output a large number of tuples/events, both *stream modifiers* and *masks* facilitate filtering of uninteresting events.

4 Stream-Side Extensions

4.1 Stream Modifiers

Operators currently supported in MavStream were derived from relational operators. In many scenarios, these operators are not adequate as it is necessary to compute various changes on the output of stream processing as events. *Stream Modifiers* are used to detect changes in the output to determine whether it is of interest as an event or not.

A *tuple* is represented as: $(A_1, A_2, \cdots, A_n)$, where n is the total number of attributes in the stream schema (e.g., $(CarId, Speed, Direction, Lane) =$

$\{1, 45, East, 3\}$). Let *SubTuple* T_i $(A_1, \cdots, A_m)$ represent the values of attributes $A_1, \cdots, A_m$ for the ith state/tuple of data stream. If `m = n` then T_i represents the complete stream tuple. For example, T_1(CarId, Speed) for the data stream can be represented as $\{1, 45\}$, assuming the tuple defined above is the first tuple of the stream. Let State function $S_i(A_j)$ represent the value of the jth attribute in i^{th} tuple of the stream.

In the following definition, [ ] indicates optional parameters. *A stream modifier is defined as a function to compute changes (i.e., relative change of an attribute) between a two tuples/states (not necessarily consecutive) of its input stream.* It is denoted by $M(< A_1, A_2, \cdots, A_m > [, P < pseudo >][, O|N])$, where M is called modifier function that computes a particular kind of change. $< A_1, A_2, \cdots, A_m >$ are the parameters required by the modifier function M on which the change is to be computed, and $\mathtt{m} \leq \mathtt{n}$. In the following $P < pseudo >$, the parameter P defines a pseudo value for M function in order to prevent runtime exceptions (i.e., underflow, division by zero). The $O|N$ part is called modifier profile, which determines whether the oldest values or the latest values of the SubTuple shall be given as output. If O is specified, the oldest values are output or the latest values are output if N is specified. The modifier profile is optional and the default is O. Currently, we have implemented various stream modifiers[15]; Adiff(), RDiff() and ASlope() with both modifier profiles and in both windowed and non-windowed versions. Below we explain the Adiff() with O modifier profile.

ADiff() is used to detect absolute changes over two states. It returns absolute change of the values of attributes $(A_1, A_2, \cdots, A_m)$, and SubTuple for the rest of the attributes based on the modifier $O|N$ profile. It is formally defined for case O as follows:

$$ADiff((A_1, A_2, \cdots, A_m >)[O])$$
$$= (\tfrac{s_{i+1}(A_1) - s_i(A_1)}{s_i(A_1)} \cdots \tfrac{s_{i+1}(A_m) - s_i(A_m)}{s_i(A_m)}) + T_i(A_{m+1}, A_{m+2}, \cdots, A_n)$$

Windowed and Non-Windowed Stream Modifiers: Windowed stream modifiers compute the changes between the first and the last tuple of the window. It is denoted by $M(< A_1, A_2, \cdots, A_m > [, P < pseudo >][, O|N], windowSpecs)$, where the $windowSpecs$ define the begin and the end time of the window. The design also supports overlapped windows and hence maintain a three tuple synopsis, given by:

- First tuple synopsis: stores the first tuple of the current window.
- Last tuple synopsis: stores the last tuple of the current window.
- Overlap first tuple synopsis: stores the first tuple of the overlap window.

The algorithm for windowed stream modifiers based on the three tuple synopsis is shown in Algorithm 1. *Non-Windowed modifiers* do not support intervals and directly produce the change between two consecutive tuples and are active till the time events need to be generated. Synopsis of a single tuple is kept, which is incrementally updated whenever an output is produced.

Algorithm 1. Windowed Stream modifier

```
while current tuple timestamp < end time of event generation do
  if tuple timestamp is within current window bounds then
    if first tuple then
      update first tuple synopsis with current tuple
      continue while loop
    end if
    update the last tuple synopsis with current tuple
    if current tuple timestamp is greater than next begin window time then
      update Overlap first tuple synopsis with current tuple
    end if
  else
    compute change for current window using first tuple synopsis and last tuple
    synopsis
    update first tuple synopsis with Overlap first tuple synopsis
  end if
end while
stop modifier
```

4.2 Handling Masks

This operation is incorporated into the event generator operator node. It can evaluate any complex condition (as a *mask*) on the attributes of the event. Mask is applied after stream modifiers are applied and before converting the resulting tuples into an event object. The input to this operator is an attribute-based condition (mask) and the list of attributes that need to be output. Mask condition is defined on the attributes of an event. Masks provide a mechanism by which attribute-based constraints can be applied to the generation of events from the output of CQs for reducing uninteresting events and for reducing load for event and rule processing. In EStream, as events are generated by a CQ, it is possible to apply a mask that filters a generic event into different types of events. Processing masks uses the FESI Ecma Condition Evaluator for evaluation of the complex conditions. Mask processor maps the attributes over which the condition is defined, to the position in input stream and evaluates complex conditions on it. The tuple is output or filtered depending on whether the condition evaluator evaluates tuple attributes to TRUE or not, based on the condition.

5 Functional Modules of EStream

EStream, as shown in Figure 2, is implemented by integrating the *LED* into the *MavStream* server. Both systems are homegrown and are implemented in Java. One of the design decisions was to put both into the same address space as other alternatives would involve inter-process communication and additional switching overhead. EStream server consists of an input processor (to accept the continuous event query or CEQ), CQ instantiator (create operator nodes corresponding to

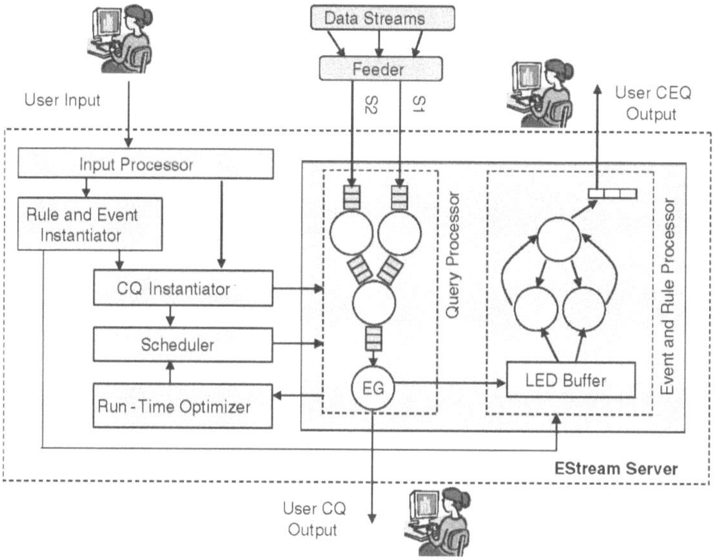

Fig. 2. EStream Architecture

CQs and the EG interface), a rule and event instantiator (create the events and rules of a CEQ), a scheduler (that schedules CQs at the operator level), a runtime optimizer, a stream query processor, an event generator interface, and an event and rule processor,

Input Processor accepts the CEQs from the user. *CEQ* consists of CQs, stream modifiers, events, masks and rules. The CEQ is parsed to separate the information pertaining to CQs, events, and rules. Below shown is a CEQ, but in a separated form with CQ, event and rule definition. The CEQ named AUTOMATEDMONITOR is to monitor the speed of cars with CarId > 100 to be within the speed limit in the residential area. If the speed of the car is above 30 mph then a ticket should be generated and mailed to the owner.

```
CREATE CEQ AUTOMATEDMONITOR AS
  CREATE CQ CARIDGT100
    SELECT * from CarLocStr
    WHERE carId > 100
  CREATE EVENT "ResidentialSpeedingTicket" on CARIDGT100
    MASK (CARIDGT100.speed > 30 AND CARIDGT100.area = "Residential")
  CREATE RULE "SpeedingTicket"
    ON "ResidentialSpeedingTicket"
    CONDITION TRUE
    ACTION "GenerateTicket"
```

In the above, CARIDGT100 is a CQ with SELECT operator for monitoring cars that have CarId > 100. Once the CQ generates the output, events are generated if the specified MASK is satisfied. Once the event is generated, associated rule SpeedingTicket is raised and tickets are generated. This query is kept simple for illustration purposes and hence does not include stream modifiers.

Although a CEQ consists of a one or more CQs, events, and rules, they have to be processed and instantiated in a specific order. Events cannot be created before stream queries, and rules cannot be associated unless event nodes are in place. The ECA part of CEQ is given to the rule and event instantiator which generates the event detection graph for the events. Event container temporarily stores the information regarding events and rules until they can be created. Once events are created, rules are defined on the event nodes specified in the CEQ. Since both LED and MavStream are in the same address space, the APIs of LED can be called for the creation of event nodes and associating rules on the event nodes created. Rule and event processor is responsible for detecting events and triggering appropriate actions when rule conditions evaluate to TRUE.

The CQ part of CEQ is given to the CQ instantiator, that generates a query plan using the query plan generator and instantiates the operator nodes. Each operator definition is populated in a data structure called *operatorData* which is wrapped in an *operatorNode* that has references to the parent and child operators. The query scheduler schedules the query and is executed by the query processor. Query processor has the implementation of all operators including stream modifiers and the EG interface.

Stream modifiers are supported along the lines of aggregate operators (as unary operators) beyond (typically) the aggregate operators. The event generation for each CQ is done by the event generator operator attached as the root operator of each query after it is instantiated. Stream tuples are fed to the event generator operator where they are filtered against available masks and then converted into event objects. The mask filtering is combined with the event generator node which takes several arbitrary conditions (select-like) and generates different event types based on the definition associated with an event specification. Attributes of the stream tuples are inserted as event attributes and event objects are inserted into the notify buffer. This is implemented by making extensions to the query processor and the instantiator by implementing the event generator operator and associating it before every query is scheduled. At runtime the event generator is responsible for raising events which are enqueued in the notify buffer as event objects. The checking of masks before event generation significantly reduces the number of events generated, thus reducing the load on the event processing. If the selectivity of a mask is low (on a scale of 0 to 1), it filters more events. Event objects are consumed from the LED buffer and are propagated to the event detection graphs. For each detected event, associated rules are triggered which in turn checks the associated condition and execute the action if the condition evaluates to TRUE. The runtime optimizer monitors the QoS of the CQ output and if the user defined performance metric is not met, then it dynamically changes the scheduling strategy associated with the stream computational model.

5.1 Experiments

The experiment and the results shown below demonstrates the effect of masks in the EG interface. The query we have used is the CEQ AUTOMATEDMONITOR defined previously. This experiment was run on a machine with a single Xeon processor (2.4GHz, 1GB RAM) running Red Hat Linux 8.0 operating system. The data set for performance evaluation is a modified version of the data set used by the Stanford Stream project [17,18]. The scheduling strategy used is the path capacity scheduling [4,14]. This experiment was completely executed in main memory.

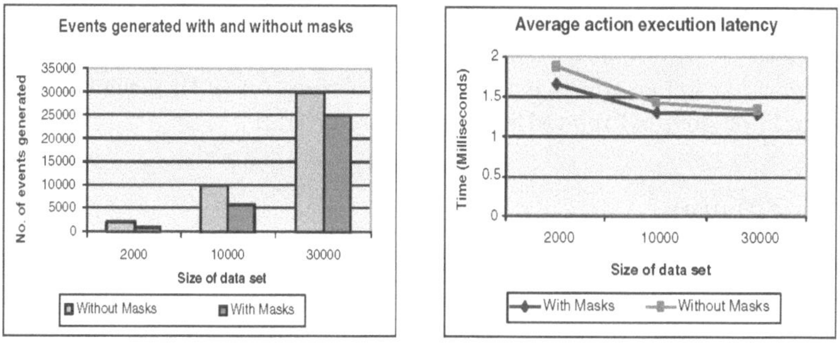

(a) Events Generated With and Without Masks

(b) Average Action Execution Latency

Fig. 3. Query Experiments With and Without Masks

From Figure 3(a) and Figure 3(b), it is evident that with the application of masks, the number of events generated is significantly reduced, thus reducing the traffic in the notify buffer and the event and rule processor. If masks are not used, then we have to filter the speed and residential area constraints in the condition portion of the rule i.e., *after* the event is detected and propagated. This will add a significant computational overhead to the system. With the application of masks in event generator node, only those events whose conditions evaluate to true are generated. This results in a significant decrease of the average event execution latency for various data sets and can be seen from the Figure 3(b).

6 Related Work

Our work is closely related to the two threads of work, event processing [7,9,8,11] and stream processing [1,2,3,4,5,6,12]. To the best of our knowledge there is no system that has integrated the two. Most of the stream processing systems (Aurora, STREAMS, Telegraph, etc.) use the data flow model. The event processing systems, on the other hand have different computational models such as the Event Detection Graph (EDG), Petri Nets and Finite Automaton.

HiFi generates simple events out of receptor data at its Edges [19] and provides the functionality of complex event processing on these Edges. It addresses the issue of generating simple events by virtual devices that interact with the heterogeneous sensors to produce application level simple events. Although this system is a step in the right direction for the detection of events over sensor data, it does not define and detect events over stream queries. The events detected at Edges are simple events and cannot be defined over the result of the data preprocessed by a Continuous Query. *Tiny DB* has Event Based Queries [20,21], which is processing of events over stream queries. The events are initiated by low-level lying operating system events.

Our work is a comprehensive one which examines the general purpose stream and event processing systems for integration. We have taken an initial step in combining the two systems with extensions that are critical for their effectiveness. Further work is being addressed on broader issues on both stream and event processing. For detailed related work please refer [15].

7 Conclusion

In this paper, we have given a summary of the *design and implementation* of EStream, a system that addresses the need of advanced applications that require not only stream processing but also event processing. We have given an integrated model that combines stream processing and event processing systems that support: i) Events on arbitrary continuous queries, ii) Stream modifiers to capture complicated changes over windows, and iii) Filtering of uninteresting event generation using user-defined masks.

Future work includes attribute-based semantics for events, extending current window concept to a more expressive semantic window, scheduling and QoS aspects for event processing.

References

1. S. Madden and M. J. Franklin, "Fjording the Stream: An Architecture for Queries over Streaming Sensor Data," in *Proc. of ICDE*, 2002.
2. J. Chen *et al.*, "NiagaraCQ: A Scalable Continuous Query System for Internet Databases," in *Proc. of SIGMOD*, 2000.
3. B. Babcok *et al.*, "Operator scheduling in data stream systems," *The VLDB J.*, vol. 13, pp. 333–353, 2004.
4. Q. Jiang and S. Chakravarthy, "Scheduling Strategies for Processing Continuous Queries over Streams," in *Proc. of BNCOD*, Jul. 2004.
5. B. Babcock, M. Datar, and R. Motwani, "Load Shedding for Aggregation Queries over Data Streams," in *Proc. of ICDE*, Mar. 2004.
6. N. Tatbul *et al.*, "Load Shedding in a Data Stream Manager," in *Proc. of VLDB*, Sep. 2003.
7. A. P. Buchmann *et al.*, *Rules in an Open System: The REACH Rule System.* Rules in Database Systems, 1993.
8. S. Gatziu and K. R. Dittrich, "Events in an Object-Oriented Database System," in *Proceedings of Rules in Database Systems*, Sep. 1993.

9. S. Chakravarthy and D. Mishra, "Snoop: An Expressive Event Specification Language for Active Databases," *Data and Knowledge Engineering*, vol. 14, no. 10, pp. 1–26, Oct. 1994.
10. S. Chakravarthy *et al.*, "Design of Sentinel: An Object-Oriented DBMS with Event-Based Rules," *Information and Software Technology*, vol. 36, no. 9, pp. 559–568, 1994.
11. R. Adaikkalavan and S. Chakravarthy, "SnoopIB: Interval-Based Event Specification and Detection for Active Databases (in press)," 2005. [Online]. Available: http://dx.doi.org/10.1016/j.datak.2005.07.009
12. Q. Jiang and S. Chakravarthy, "Data Stream Management System for MavHome," in *Proc. of ACM SAC*, Mar. 2004.
13. A. Gilani, S. Sonune, B. Kendai, and S. Chakravarthy, "The Anatomy of a Stream Processing System," in *Proc. of BNCOD*, Jul. 2006.
14. S. Chakravarthy and V. K. Pajjuri, "Scheduling Strategies and Their Evaluation in a Data Stream Management System," in *Proc. of BNCOD*, Jul. 2006.
15. V. Garg, "Estream: An integration of event and stream processing," Master's thesis, The Univ. of Texas at Arlington, 2005. [Online]. Available: http://itlab.uta.edu/ITLABWEB/Students/sharma/theses/Gar05MS.pdf
16. Q. Jiang, R. Adaikkalavan, and S. Chakravarthy, "Towards an Integrated Model for Event and Stream Processing," *TR CSE-2004-10, CSE Dept., Univ. of Texas at Arlington*, 2004.
17. A. Arasu *et al.*, "Linear Road: A Stream Data Management Benchmark," in *Proc. of VLDB*, Sep. 2004.
18. R. Motwani *et al.*, "Query Processing, Resource Management, and Approximation in a Data Stream Management System," in *Proc. of CIDR*, Jan. 2003.
19. S. Rizvi *et al.*, "Events on the edge (demo)," in *Proc. of SIGMOD*, 2005.
20. S. R. Madden *et al.*, "The Design of an Acquisitional Query Processor for Sensor Networks," in *Proc. of SIGMOD*, 2003.
21. S. R. Madden *et al.*, "TAG: a Tiny AGgregation Service for Ad-Hoc Sensor Networks," *In Proc. of OSDI*, Dec. 2002.

Author Index

Lecture Notes in Computer Science

For information about Vols. 1–4040

please contact your bookseller or Springer

Vol. 4180: M. Kohlhase, OMDoc – An Open Markup Format for Mathematical Documents [version 1.2]. XIX, 428 pages. 2006. (Sublibrary LNAI).

Vol. 4163: H. Bersini, J. Carneiro (Eds.), Artificial Immune Systems. XII, 460 pages. 2006.

Vol. 4162: R. Královič, P. Urzyczyn (Eds.), Mathematical Foundations of Computer Science 2006. XV, 814 pages. 2006.

Vol. 4153: N. Zheng, X. Jiang, X. Lan (Eds.), Advances in Machine Vision, Image Processing, and Pattern Analysis. XIII, 506 pages. 2006.

Vol. 4151: A. Iglesias, N. Takayama (Eds.), Mathematical Software - ICMS 2006. XVII, 452 pages. 2006.

Vol. 4146: J.C. Rajapakse, L. Wong, R. Acharya (Eds.), Pattern Recognition in Bioinformatics. XIV, 186 pages. 2006. (Sublibrary LNBI).

Vol. 4144: T. Ball, R.B. Jones (Eds.), Computer Aided Verification. XV, 564 pages. 2006.

Vol. 4139: T. Salakoski, F. Ginter, S. Pyysalo, T. Pahikkala, Advances in Natural Language Processing. XVI, 771 pages. 2006. (Sublibrary LNAI).

Vol. 4138: X. Cheng, W. Li, T. Znati (Eds.), Wireless Algorithms, Systems, and Applications. XVI, 709 pages. 2006.

Vol. 4137: C. Baier, H. Hermanns (Eds.), CONCUR 2006 – Concurrency Theory. XIII, 525 pages. 2006.

Vol. 4134: K. Yi (Ed.), Static Analysis. XI, 443 pages. 2006.

Vol. 4133: J. Gratch, M. Young, R. Aylett, D. Ballin, P. Olivier (Eds.), Intelligent Virtual Agents. XIV, 472 pages. 2006. (Sublibrary LNAI).

Vol. 4130: U. Furbach, N. Shankar (Eds.), Automated Reasoning. XV, 680 pages. 2006. (Sublibrary LNAI).

Vol. 4129: D. McGookin, S. Brewster (Eds.), Haptic and Audio Interaction Design. XII, 167 pages. 2006.

Vol. 4128: W.E. Nagel, W.V. Walter, W. Lehner (Eds.), Euro-Par 2006 Parallel Processing. XXXIII, 1221 pages. 2006.

Vol. 4127: E. Damiani, P. Liu (Eds.), Data and Applications Security XX. X, 319 pages. 2006.

Vol. 4124: H. de Meer, J.P. G. Sterbenz (Eds.), Self-Organising Systems. XIV, 261 pages. 2006.

Vol. 4121: A. Biere, C.P. Gomes (Eds.), Theory and Applications of Satisfiability Testing - SAT 2006. XII, 438 pages. 2006.

Vol. 4119: C. Dony, J.L. Knudsen, A. Romanovsky, A. Tripathi (Eds.), Advanced Topics in Exception Handling Components. X, 302 pages. 2006.

Vol. 4117: C. Dwork (Ed.), Advances in Cryptology - Crypto 2006. XIII, 621 pages. 2006.

Vol. 4116: R. De Prisco, M. Yung (Eds.), Security and Cryptography for Networks. XI, 366 pages. 2006.

Vol. 4115: D.-S. Huang, K. Li, G.W. Irwin (Eds.), Computational Intelligence and Bioinformatics, Part III. XXI, 803 pages. 2006. (Sublibrary LNBI).

Vol. 4114: D.-S. Huang, K. Li, G.W. Irwin (Eds.), Computational Intelligence, Part II. XXVII, 1337 pages. 2006. (Sublibrary LNAI).

Vol. 4113: D.-S. Huang, K. Li, G.W. Irwin (Eds.), Intelligent Computing, Part I. XXVII, 1331 pages. 2006.

Vol. 4112: D.Z. Chen, D. T. Lee (Eds.), Computing and Combinatorics. XIV, 528 pages. 2006.

Vol. 4111: F.S. de Boer, M.M. Bonsangue, S. Graf, W.-P. de Roever (Eds.), Formal Methods for Components and Objects. VIII, 447 pages. 2006.

Vol. 4109: D.-Y. Yeung, J.T. Kwok, A. Fred, F. Roli, D. de Ridder (Eds.), Structural, Syntactic, and Statistical Pattern Recognition. XXI, 939 pages. 2006.

Vol. 4108: J.M. Borwein, W.M. Farmer (Eds.), Mathematical Knowledge Management. VIII, 295 pages. 2006. (Sublibrary LNAI).

Vol. 4106: T.R. Roth-Berghofer, M.H. Göker, H. A. Güvenir (Eds.), Advances in Case-Based Reasoning. XIV, 566 pages. 2006. (Sublibrary LNAI).

Vol. 4104: T. Kunz, S.S. Ravi (Eds.), Ad-Hoc, Mobile, and Wireless Networks. XII, 474 pages. 2006.

Vol. 4099: Q. Yang, G. Webb (Eds.), PRICAI 2006: Trends in Artificial Intelligence. XXVIII, 1263 pages. 2006. (Sublibrary LNAI).

Vol. 4098: F. Pfenning (Ed.), Term Rewriting and Applications. XIII, 415 pages. 2006.

Vol. 4097: X. Zhou, O. Sokolsky, L. Yan, E.-S. Jung, Z. Shao, Y. Mu, D.C. Lee, D. Kim, Y.-S. Jeong, C.-Z. Xu (Eds.), Emerging Directions in Embedded and Ubiquitous Computing. XXVII, 1034 pages. 2006.

Vol. 4096: E. Sha, S.-K. Han, C.-Z. Xu, M.H. Kim, L.T. Yang, B. Xiao (Eds.), Embedded and Ubiquitous Computing. XXIV, 1170 pages. 2006.

Vol. 4094: O. H. Ibarra, H.-C. Yen (Eds.), Implementation and Application of Automata. XIII, 291 pages. 2006.

Vol. 4093: X. Li, O.R. Zaïane, Z. Li (Eds.), Advanced Data Mining and Applications. XXI, 1110 pages. 2006. (Sublibrary LNAI).

Vol. 4092: J. Lang, F. Lin, J. Wang (Eds.), Knowledge Science, Engineering and Management. XV, 664 pages. 2006. (Sublibrary LNAI).

Vol. 4091: G.-Z. Yang, T. Jiang, D. Shen, L. Gu, J. Yang (Eds.), Medical Imaging and Augmented Reality. XIII, 399 pages. 2006.

Vol. 4090: S. Spaccapietra, K. Aberer, P. Cudré-Mauroux (Eds.), Journal on Data Semantics VI. XI, 211 pages. 2006.

Vol. 4089: W. Löwe, M. Südholt (Eds.), Software Composition. X, 339 pages. 2006.

Vol. 4088: Z.-Z. Shi, R. Sadananda (Eds.), Agent Computing and Multi-Agent Systems. XVII, 827 pages. 2006. (Sublibrary LNAI).

Vol. 4085: J. Misra, T. Nipkow, E. Sekerinski (Eds.), FM 2006: Formal Methods. XV, 620 pages. 2006.

Vol. 4082: K. Bauknecht, B. Pröll, H. Werthner (Eds.), E-Commerce and Web Technologies. XIII, 243 pages. 2006.

Vol. 4081: A. M. Tjoa, J. Trujillo (Eds.), Data Warehousing and Knowledge Discovery. XVII, 578 pages. 2006.

Vol. 4080: S. Bressan, J. Küng, R. Wagner (Eds.), Database and Expert Systems Applications. XXI, 959 pages. 2006.

Vol. 4079: S. Etalle, M. Truszczyński (Eds.), Logic Programming. XIV, 474 pages. 2006.

Vol. 4077: M.-S. Kim, K. Shimada (Eds.), Geometric Modeling and Processing - GMP 2006. XVI, 696 pages. 2006.

Vol. 4076: F. Hess, S. Pauli, M. Pohst (Eds.), Algorithmic Number Theory. X, 599 pages. 2006.

Vol. 4075: U. Leser, F. Naumann, B. Eckman (Eds.), Data Integration in the Life Sciences. XI, 298 pages. 2006. (Sublibrary LNBI).

Vol. 4074: M. Burmester, A. Yasinsac (Eds.), Secure Mobile Ad-hoc Networks and Sensors. X, 193 pages. 2006.

Vol. 4073: A. Butz, B. Fisher, A. Krüger, P. Olivier (Eds.), Smart Graphics. XI, 263 pages. 2006.

Vol. 4072: M. Harders, G. Székely (Eds.), Biomedical Simulation. XI, 216 pages. 2006.

Vol. 4071: H. Sundaram, M. Naphade, J.R. Smith, Y. Rui (Eds.), Image and Video Retrieval. XII, 547 pages. 2006.

Vol. 4070: C. Priami, X. Hu, Y. Pan, T.Y. Lin (Eds.), Transactions on Computational Systems Biology V. IX, 129 pages. 2006. (Sublibrary LNBI).

Vol. 4069: F.J. Perales, R.B. Fisher (Eds.), Articulated Motion and Deformable Objects. XV, 526 pages. 2006.

Vol. 4068: H. Schärfe, P. Hitzler, P. Øhrstrøm (Eds.), Conceptual Structures: Inspiration and Application. XI, 455 pages. 2006. (Sublibrary LNAI).

Vol. 4067: D. Thomas (Ed.), ECOOP 2006 – Object-Oriented Programming. XIV, 527 pages. 2006.

Vol. 4066: A. Rensink, J. Warmer (Eds.), Model Driven Architecture – Foundations and Applications. XII, 392 pages. 2006.

Vol. 4065: P. Perner (Ed.), Advances in Data Mining. XI, 592 pages. 2006. (Sublibrary LNAI).

Vol. 4064: R. Büschkes, P. Laskov (Eds.), Detection of Intrusions and Malware & Vulnerability Assessment. X, 195 pages. 2006.

Vol. 4063: I. Gorton, G.T. Heineman, I. Crnkovic, H.W. Schmidt, J.A. Stafford, C.A. Szyperski, K. Wallnau (Eds.), Component-Based Software Engineering. XI, 394 pages. 2006.

Vol. 4062: G. Wang, J.F. Peters, A. Skowron, Y. Yao (Eds.), Rough Sets and Knowledge Technology. XX, 810 pages. 2006. (Sublibrary LNAI).

Vol. 4061: K. Miesenberger, J. Klaus, W. Zagler, A.I. Karshmer (Eds.), Computers Helping People with Special Needs. XXIX, 1356 pages. 2006.

Vol. 4060: K. Futatsugi, J.-P. Jouannaud, J. Meseguer (Eds.), Algebra, Meaning, and Computation. XXXVIII, 643 pages. 2006.

Vol. 4059: L. Arge, R. Freivalds (Eds.), Algorithm Theory – SWAT 2006. XII, 436 pages. 2006.

Vol. 4058: L.M. Batten, R. Safavi-Naini (Eds.), Information Security and Privacy. XII, 446 pages. 2006.

Vol. 4057: J.P.W. Pluim, B. Likar, F.A. Gerritsen (Eds.), Biomedical Image Registration. XII, 324 pages. 2006.

Vol. 4056: P. Flocchini, L. Gąsieniec (Eds.), Structural Information and Communication Complexity. X, 357 pages. 2006.

Vol. 4055: J. Lee, J. Shim, S.-g. Lee, C. Bussler, S. Shim (Eds.), Data Engineering Issues in E-Commerce and Services. IX, 290 pages. 2006.

Vol. 4054: A. Horváth, M. Telek (Eds.), Formal Methods and Stochastic Models for Performance Evaluation. VIII, 239 pages. 2006.

Vol. 4053: M. Ikeda, K.D. Ashley, T.-W. Chan (Eds.), Intelligent Tutoring Systems. XXVI, 821 pages. 2006.

Vol. 4052: M. Bugliesi, B. Preneel, V. Sassone, I. Wegener (Eds.), Automata, Languages and Programming, Part II. XXIV, 603 pages. 2006.

Vol. 4051: M. Bugliesi, B. Preneel, V. Sassone, I. Wegener (Eds.), Automata, Languages and Programming, Part I. XXIII, 729 pages. 2006.

Vol. 4049: S. Parsons, N. Maudet, P. Moraitis, I. Rahwan (Eds.), Argumentation in Multi-Agent Systems. XIV, 313 pages. 2006. (Sublibrary LNAI).

Vol. 4048: L. Goble, J.-J.C.. Meyer (Eds.), Deontic Logic and Artificial Normative Systems. X, 273 pages. 2006. (Sublibrary LNAI).

Vol. 4047: M. Robshaw (Ed.), Fast Software Encryption. XI, 434 pages. 2006.

Vol. 4046: S.M. Astley, M. Brady, C. Rose, R. Zwiggelaar (Eds.), Digital Mammography. XVI, 654 pages. 2006.

Vol. 4045: D. Barker-Plummer, R. Cox, N. Swoboda (Eds.), Diagrammatic Representation and Inference. XII, 301 pages. 2006. (Sublibrary LNAI).

Vol. 4044: P. Abrahamsson, M. Marchesi, G. Succi (Eds.), Extreme Programming and Agile Processes in Software Engineering. XII, 230 pages. 2006.

Vol. 4043: A.S. Atzeni, A. Lioy (Eds.), Public Key Infrastructure. XI, 261 pages. 2006.

Vol. 4042: D. Bell, J. Hong (Eds.), Flexible and Efficient Information Handling. XVI, 296 pages. 2006.

Vol. 4041: S.-W. Cheng, C.K. Poon (Eds.), Algorithmic Aspects in Information and Management. XI, 395 pages. 2006.

Kolibri 360 GmbH
Ferdinand-Jühlke-Straße 7
99095 Erfurt, Deutschland
produktsicherheit@kolibri360.de